AN INTEGRATED APPROACH TO COMMUNICATION THEORY AND RESEARCH

This volume provides an integrated overview of communication study for the student. In preparing to teach introductory graduate courses, the authors could not find a single text that provided both theoretical coverage of the broad scope of communication study, as well as a text that integrated the theory with the research. This book puts theory into research and explains how research operates within theory. To explicate the integration process, the chapter contributors—experts in their respective areas—offer samples in the form of hypothetical studies, published studies, or unpublished research, showing how theory and research are integrated in their particular fields.

The book is different from other texts available for the graduate student or faculty member who wants a good overview of not only the field, but also sample research stemming from its various component parts. The material presented is designed to further understanding among scholars and students regarding the mass/human communication divide, as well as different approaches to integrating theory and research in different areas of communication. The editors hope that this volume will pique scholarly interest, and challenge theorists and researchers to look at the broader scope of communication study, and begin to work together in formulating a truly grounded communication approach to communication theory and research.

Don W. Stacks (Ph.D., University of Florida, 1978) is Professor of Communication and Director of the Public Relations Program at the School of Communication, University of Miami. He is the author of six books on communication topics, a member of the Arthur W. Page Society, and serves as a Trustee or Board member for the Institute for Public Relations, Association for Education in Journalism & Mass Communication, and International Public Relations Association. He has received numerous awards and was recently voted as a Research Fellow by the Eastern Communication Association, as well as the Jackson, Jackson & Wagner Behavioral Science Prize winner and named as a winner of the Provost's Award for Scholarly Activity.

Michael B. Salwen (Ph.D., Michigan State University, 1985) was professor of communication at the University of Miami, Coral Gables, FL. His research focused on the social effects of mass communication and international communication. He'd worked as a reporter for several local newspapers in New Jersey and Pennsylvania. He developed a keen interest in the third-person effect and sought to identify and predict the underlying factors of this perceptual process with different mass media issues. He was a prolific scholar, authoring and editing several books, and was an associate editor for *Journalism and Mass Communication Quarterly*.

COMMUNICATION SERIES
Jennings Bryant/Dolf Zillman, General Editors

Selected titles in Communication Theory and Methodology subseries (Jennings Bryant, series advisor) include:

PLANNING STRATEGIC INTERACTION
Attaining Goals Through Communicative Action
Berger

MEDIA EFFECTS: ADVANCES IN THEORY AND RESEARCH
Third Edition
Bryant/Oliver

AMERICAN COMMUNICATION RESEARCH
The Remembered History
Dennis/Wartella

CRAFTING SOCIETY
Ethnicity, Class, and Communication Theory
Ellis

MESSAGE PRODUCTION
Advances in Communication Theory
Greene

HUMAN COMMUNICATION THEORY AND RESEARCH
Concepts, Contexts, and Challenges, Second Edition
Heath/Bryant

HOLLYWOOD PLANET
Global Media and the Competitive Advantage of Narrative Transparency
Olsson
AMERICAN PRAGMATISM AND COMMUNICATION RESEARCH
Perry

ANALYZING MEDIA MESSAGES
Using Quantitative Content Analysis in Research
Riffe/Lacy/Fico

AN INTEGRATED APPROACH TO COMMUNICATION THEORY AND RESEARCH

Second Edition

Edited by
Don W. Stacks
Michael B. Salwen

Routledge
Taylor & Francis Group

NEW YORK AND LONDON

First published 1996 by LEA
This second edition published 2009
by Routledge
270 Madison Ave, New York, NY 10016

Simultaneously published in the UK
by Routledge
2 Park Square, Milton Park, Abingdon, Oxon OX14 4RN

Routledge is an imprint of the Taylor & Francis Group, an informa business

© 1996 LEA, 2009 Taylor & Francis

Typeset in Goudy by EvS Communication Networx, Inc.
Printed and bound in the United States of America on acid-free paper by Edwards Brothers, Inc.

Library of Congress Cataloging in Publication Data
An integrared approach to communication theory and reserach / edited by Don W. Stacks and Michael B. Salwen. — 2nd ed.
p. cm.
1. Communication—Methodology. 2. Mass media—Methodology. I. Stacks, Don W. II. Salwen, Michael Brian.
P91.I558 2008
302.201—dc22
2008016359

ISBN 10: 0-8058-6381-8 (hbk)
ISBN 10: 0-8058-6382-6 (pbk)
ISBN 10: 0-203-88701-8 (ebk)

ISBN 13: 978-0-8058-6381-9 (hbk)
ISBN 13: 978-0-8058-6382-6 (pbk)
ISBN 13: 978-0-203-88701-1 (ebk)

CONTENTS

Preface to the 1996 Edition   ix
Preface to Second Edition   xiii

PART I
Studying "Theory"—Doing "Research"   1

1   Integrating Theory and Research: Starting with Questions   3
     DON W. STACKS AND MICHAEL B. SALWEN

2   Thinking about Theory   13
     STEVEN H. CHAFFEE

3   Thinking Quantitatively   30
     MICHAEL J. BEATTY

4   Thinking Qualitatively: Hermeneutics in Science   40
     JAMES A. ANDERSON

PART II
Mass Communication: Approaches and Concerns   59

5   Mass Communication Theory and Research: Concepts and Models   61
     BRADLEY S. GREENBERG AND MICHAEL B. SALWEN

6   Media Gatekeeping   75
     PAMELA J. SHOEMAKER AND TIM P. VOS

7   The Agenda-Setting Role of the News Media   90
     SEBASTIÁN VALENZUELA AND MAXWELL MCCOMBS

8   Cultivation Analysis: Research and Practice   106
NANCY SIGNORIELLI AND MICHAEL MORGAN

9   Theories and Methods in Knowledge Gap Research   122
CECILIE GAZIANO AND EMANUEL GAZIANO

10   Uses and Gratifications   137
ZIZI PAPACHARISSI

11   Spiral of Silence: Communication and Public Opinion as Social Control   153
CHARLES T. SALMON AND CARROLL J. GLYNN

12   International Communication   169
ROBERT L. STEVENSON

13   Violence and Sex in the Media   181
JENNINGS BRYANT AND R. GLENN CUMMINS

14   Social Science Theories of Traditional and Internet Advertising   198
SHELLY RODGERS, ESTHER THORSON, AND YUN JIN

PART III
Human Communication Approaches and Concerns   221

15   Human Communication Theory and Research: Traditions and Models   223
VIRGINIA P. RICHMOND AND JAMES C. MCCROSKEY

16   The Rhetorical Perspective: Doing, Being, Shaping, and Seeing   232
J. DAVID CISNEROS, KRISTEN L. MCCAULIFF, AND VANESSA B. BEASELY

17   Persuasion   245
MICHAEL D. MILLER AND TIMOTHY R. LEVINE

18   Interpersonal Communication   260
CHARLES R. BERGER

19   Modeling Cultures: Toward Grounded Paradigms in Organizations and Mass Culture   280
MARK Y. HICKSON III, JEAN BODON, AND THERESA BODON

20 Intercultural Communication   299
THOMAS M. STEINFATT AND DIANE M. MILLETTE

21 Intrapersonal Communication and Imagined Interactions   323
JAMES M. HONEYCUTT, CHRISTOPHER M. MAPP, KHALED A. KNASSER, AND JOYCEIA M. BANNER

22 Nonverbal Communication   336
AMY S. EBESU HUBBARD AND JUDEE K. BURGOON

23 Small Group Communication   348
JOSEPH A. BONITO, GWEN M. WITTENBAUM, AND RANDY Y. HIROKAWA

24 Watch Your Neighbor Watching You: Applying Concertive Control in Changing
Organizational Environments   370
PHILLIP K. TOMPKINS, YVONNE J. MONTOYA, AND CAREY B. CANDRIAN

PART IV
Integrated Approaches to Communication   387

25 Internet Communication   389
MARCUS MESSNER AND BRUCE GARRISON

26 Organizational Legitimacy: Lessons Learned from Financial Scandals   406
MARCIA W. DISTASO AND TERRI A. SCANDURA

27 Diffusion of Innovations   418
EVERETT M. ROGERS, ARVIND SINGHAL, AND MARGARET M. QUINLAN

28 Credibility   435
CHARLES C. SELF

29 Political Communication   457
LYNDA LEE KAID

30 Public Relations and Integrated Communication   473
DOUG NEWSOM

31 Health Communication   489
CHARLES ATKIN AND KAMI SILK

CONTENTS

32 Feminist Theory and Research   504
   KATHARINE SARIKAKIS, RAMONA R. RUSH, AUTUMN GRUBB-SWETNAM, AND CHRISTINA LANE

33 Communication Ethics   523
   DONALD K. WRIGHT

PART V
Future of Theory and Research in Communication   **539**

34 Communication Theory and Research: The Quest for Increased Credibility
   in the Social Sciences   541
   TONY ATWATER

35 The Future of Communication Theory and Research   546
   HARTMUT B. MOKROS AND GUSTAV W. FRIEDRICH

   Contributors   553
   Index   561

PREFACE TO THE 1996 EDITION
The Integrative Process

This volume focuses on *integrating* theory and research in communication study. The terms "theory" and "research" are often linked together, like bread and butter, bagel and cream cheese, or speech communication and mass communication. It is stating the obvious to say that theory and research should be similarly linked together. Despite the obviousness of this statement, it comments on our field that a volume such as this that links communication theory and research in the same chapters is needed.

Our purpose in editing this volume is to provide both seasoned scholars and beginning students unfamiliar with the state of theory and research in various areas of communication study to provide a taste, a sampler if you will, of current theory *and* research in communication. To explicate the integration process, the chapter contributors, experts in their respective areas, offer sample studies in the form of hypothetical studies, published studies, or unpublished research, showing how theory and research are integrated in their particular areas.

The idea for this book grew out of a series of informal discussions between the coeditors by the water cooler, in the photocopy room, in the hallway, by the coffee machine, and outside faculty mailboxes. In these discussions, we complained about the difficulty of teaching communication students communication theory and research. As with many programs, theory and research are taught in the University of Miami's School of Communication as separate courses. This clean curricular separation, however, bears no resemblance to how the courses are actually taught. Faculty who teach communication theory often digress into a discussion on research methods to make sense of exemplar studies. This is no small matter; sometimes an entire theory class is devoted to discussions of research methods. Likewise, faculty who teach research methods have—out of necessity—had to bring discussion of theory into their courses. It was clear that the teachers were not to blame for this situation; the curriculum was at fault. In attempting to alleviate the problem of linking theory and research in communication study, we were astounded to find that no single volume attacked the problem of linking theory and research in communication studies. Some volumes examine the human and speech communication areas, whereas others focus on the mass communication areas—but none could be found that combine both areas under the rubric *communication*.

We do not claim that this book will resolve the difficulties regarding the distinction between theory and research in general, and communication theory and research in particular. We are not arguing for a wholesale revamping in communication curriculum to integrate theory and research, for we realize how easy it is to advocate curricular change but how difficult it is to exercise change in practice. The purpose is simply to explicitly recognize that theory and research are related and must be addressed together even in courses that involve largely theory or largely research.

While the book was in progress, we extended the integration process to address issues regarding the integration of mass and speech communication, what we call human communication. To do otherwise would have defied our purpose of leaving the reader with an appreciation of current theory and research in the various areas of communication study. It is important that all communication scholars, no matter what their areas, have some familiarity with the broader field. The state of communication study is such that most researchers are trained in either mass or human communication and, as a result, have a certain way of approaching communication or are more familiar with one area than the other.

In editing the book we wrestled with the best way of organizing the various theoretical approaches to communication. We originally opted for the traditional bifurcation of *communication* into mass communication and human communication, and, to some extent, we have followed this course. Part I examines general questions related to theory and research methodology. Part II examines important theoretical approaches to mass communication. Part III does the same with human communication approaches.

As we quickly learned, this bifurcation does not lend itself well to communication study. As we enter the 21st century, with new media technologies that do not fit neatly into either mass communication or human categories, the bifurcation promises to raise more problems. Therefore, while we were editing the book, we invited Kathleen Reardon and Emmeline G. de Pillis to write a lead chapter for an additional section, Part IV, to cover chapters that we were having particular difficulty classifying into sections, those that crossed the traditional divide between mass and human communication.

Even in the sections in which we classified chapters as mass or human communication, we recognize that others might have classified them differently. Our decisions were admittedly subjective, but not arbitrary. The decisions were based partly on how the contributors approached their chapters. In this regard, we might have placed the chapters in different sections had they been written in different ways. For example, it might seem traditional to place advertising and public relations back to back (the two are often grouped together, like theory and research); but we decided that the advertising chapter took a more traditional mass communication approach, while the public relations chapter addressed issues involving organizational communication, and therefore we placed it in Part IV, *Integrated Approaches*. Likewise, persuasive communication is an area of interest in both mass and human communication, but the chapter contributors took more of what we regarded as a human communication approach. Similarly, as the contributors of the chapter on the spiral of silence themselves noted, the model involves the interaction of both human communication as well as mass communication. But because of the chapter's emphasis on mass communication, it was placed in the mass communication section. The political communication chapter also took a largely mass communication approach.

Our point here—by noting our difficulties in classifying the chapters—is to emphasize the *artificiality* of the bifurcation. As editors, we treated the bifurcation as a convenient means of organizing a book, for a book must have organization. And practically speaking, despite the noted occasional problems, most chapters fit the bifurcation fairly well. Further, the bifurcation reflects a reality of communication study today which we would have been foolish to ignore. Still, our decision to bifurcate mass and human communication should not blind us to the similarities shared by all the areas of communication study.

In keeping with the difficulty in distinguishing mass and human communication, we invited Tony Atwater and Gustav W. Friedrich, former heads of leading mass (Association for Education in Journalism and Mass Communication) and human (Speech Communication Association) communication associations, respectively, to offer their thoughts in the final section, Part V, on where communication theory and research is going.

We are not so naive as to believe that this book will lead to a unified field of *communication* study, or even the utopian goal of a discipline of communication, and perhaps these goals are not even desirable. If the book succeeds in furthering understanding among scholars and students regarding the mass—human communication divide and different approaches to integrating theory and research in different areas of communication, that will be a small triumph. We also realize, after working and arguing this project between ourselves, that to become a discipline we need more cross-communication, more dialogue with our brothers and sisters who examine different areas of a larger area. To this end, we hope that some of the material presented piques scholarly interest, challenges theorists and researchers to look at the broader scope of communication study (which, based on many of the chapters, has taken the first steps toward integrating the many areas of communication presented), and begin to work together in formulating a truly grounded *communication* approach to *communication* theory and research.

Don W. Stacks
Michael B. Salwen

PREFACE TO THE SECOND EDITION
Further Thoughts on the Integrative Process and Communication

There is a saying that "the more things change, the more they remain the same." While rere-cruiting authors and working with the "updates" to 33 of the 35 chapters contained in the volume that refrain kept going through my head. As you read through this volume, you will find that we as a discipline have dug our holes deeper and, as the communication practitioner often puts it, continued to exist in theory and research silos. As Harmut Mokros and Gus Friedrich lament in chapter 35, we are no closer to integrating mass and human communication than we were 12 years ago.

There has been change. In the years between the first and second editions we (meaning the authors who contributed to that first edition) have lost four contributors to death and a couple more simply never responded to the invitation to update and revise their contributions. The field of communication has lost some giants, and lost them early in their careers. Michael Salwen, Steven Chaffee, Robert Stevenson, and Everett Rogers all passed away in the intervening years. We miss them for not only what they have contributed, but for what they didn't have the chance to contribute. Michael Salwen's untimely death hit me particularly hard—Mike was a friend and a colleague, good thinker and researcher, and someone who would passionately argue for or against a point. It was during one of our arguments years ago that the concept which drove what became known as "Big Blue" was operationalized and brought to life with the contributions of some of the field's greatest thinkers.

Since the 1996 edition of *An Integrated Approach to Communication Theory and Research* there have been a number of other books that have attempted to put communication theory and research together, but their approaches were limited in scope and took the writers' perspec-tives of the field. In the Second edition, we have once again let the chapter authors define their areas—something that sometimes may seem redundant. This redundancy is, however, good—it establishes that there is a foundational theoretical base in the field—whether that field be on the human, mass, or a combination (integration) of fields. Regardless, the basics are the same: an understanding of theory and research methods that drive our descriptions, understanding, and predictions of communication.

This edition asked contributors to do the same thing: Write their chapter as if a student had asked them what their area was about and how they would conduct research in that area—possibly to demonstrate through a sample research project. In addition, as we did in the 1st edition, all main contributors were asked to co-author if they wanted to with a colleague or graduate student, thus getting a second perspective on the material. For the Second edition we asked authors to provide a list of suggested readings on the topic with the idea that these readings would provide more depth to the area if the reader were to delve further into it.

I would like to thank a number of people without whom this edition would have been difficult to produce. First, University of Miami School of Communication graduate students Devonie

Nicholas and Koichi Yamamura reviewed all chapters, double checked references, and did a final check for grammar and spelling and formatting problems. Their diligent work helped make this edition better. Second, Linda Bathgate at Routledge/Lawrence Erlbaum Associates and her staff, Kerry Breen and Sarah Stone ensured that the final product would be worthy of its authors. And, finally, a thank you to Glen Broom of San Diego State University for providing the suggested readings for Steven Chaffee's chapter and Yorgo Pasadeos of the University of Alabama for the suggested readings for Robert Stevenson's chapter.

Most of what we wrote in the First edition's preface remains true today. Who knows what we might write in the Third edition.

Don W. Stacks
Coral Gables, FL

Part I

STUDYING "THEORY"—
DOING "RESEARCH"

1

INTEGRATING THEORY AND RESEARCH
Starting with Questions

Don W. Stacks and Michael B. Salwen

Toward the end of their academic careers, most graduate students are required to demonstrate their ability to integrate theory and research methodology in their field of study by completing a project, thesis, or dissertation. Students of communication, particularly those concentrating on mass communication, have been so inculcated with the practice and application of their field that they often find this task daunting—and sometimes irrelevant.

This is a perhaps understandable reaction to theory (the rationale we extend to understand the world around us) and research (ways to test or make sense of that rationale from either quantitative or qualitative approaches) from those whose lifetimes involved a certain respect for "common sense." But as Albert Einstein (1960) warned against a blind reliance on common sense:

> Conclusions obtained by purely rational processes are, so far as reality is concerned, entirely empty. It is because he recognized this, and especially because he impressed it upon the scientific world, that Galileo became the father of modern physics and in fact of the whole modern natural science.... (p. 81)

The thesis or dissertation process might seem intimidating, especially as critics harp on such seemingly trivial matters as measuring tools, study designs, statistical or interpretative procedures, tests for reliability and validity, units of analysis, metaphor, meaning, and historical significance. But theory and research, despite the fact that their qualities seem mystical to the initiate, are by no means extraneous to understanding the communication process—whether it be an understanding of the theoretical or applied aspects of communication. The purpose of the thesis or dissertation exercise is to master a skill that has its own commonsense standards that differ from traditional standards.

The purpose of the thesis or dissertation is more than simply to master the content. It involves learning via a mode of conceiving and conceptualizing in which hypotheses or research questions are derived from theory. The hypotheses or research questions are then tested in a manner that adheres to agreed-upon standards for gathering evidence, be they quantitative or qualitative in nature.

Mastering narrow and perhaps esoteric bodies of research and conducting research based on the literature has, admittedly, little value for students unless they plan to continue in that area. But mastering theoretically based research skills are immensely valuable to the student, scholar, or practitioner who plans to generate or consume primary or secondary research in the future.

Where No One Has Gone Before

Theory organizes and refines our ideas, like a map for exploring unexplored territories. Imagine exploring new lands without at least examining the maps and writings of past explorers to see what rivers and lands they traversed. Although we do not put complete faith in old adventurers' maps and writings, we would be foolish to ignore what others have done.

The novice researcher or the seasoned scholar, excited by a new idea while in the bath, almost always emerges from the bathroom proclaiming that "no one has ever thought of this before." That researcher is like the explorer who believes no one has ever gone, or tried to go, where he or she plans to go. Even cursory investigation, however, usually reveals that others have gone—or tried to go—where the novice researcher plans to go. Theoretically driven research involves building and testing on the knowledge of previous explorers.

In this opening chapter, we examine the link between theory and research methodology, and integrate these two primal aspects of academic study in communication. Our approach is simple: The research process itself is integrated. One cannot conduct good research without theory and good theory development requires good verification.

The Communication Process

The research process in communication begins with a good question, perhaps later developed into a hypothesis, tested in the most rigorous and appropriate way. Research, then, advances the theory behind the question/hypothesis, leading to refinements in the ways in which theory and research are conducted.

Few explorers discovered new lands or routes without some knowledge of those who went before them. Each explorer makes new headway for the next. But metaphors are never perfect, and the communication process studied by communication researchers is not exactly like finding a new land. So far as the communication process is concerned, there is no final "place" to be discovered, where a theoretical "flag" can be planted. Yet there is something to be gained by acquiring knowledge about a process that may never be completely understood.

The integration of theory and research methodology and the communication process are similar processes. Each begins with information gleaned from some source, and integrates that information into a message of some form (e.g., verbal or nonverbal) or some medium (e.g., interpersonal or mass mediated) that conveys meaning. Information takes on different forms at different times in both processes; sometimes it merely exists, much like background noise or something noted in the environment; sometimes it consists of symbols and signs, such as the words on this page, only written in a language you may not understand (French, Greek, Latin). Either way, there is no intent, it is just there. To some, to be considered communication, the information must be intentionally sent and intentionally received (Burgoon & Ruffner, 1978). Dittman (1972) pointed out that a message may be subliminal—not consciously received—and yet still impact our thoughts, attitudes, and behaviors. Burgoon and Ruffner (1978) argued that communication has not occurred unless both source and receiver perceive a message to be intentional. Others (Hickson & Stacks, 1993; Malandro, Barker, & Barker, 1989) considered communication to occur if either sender or receiver perceives intent. Either way, information often leads to communication, depending on how the researcher has defined communication.[1]

Perhaps the phrase human communication is all too often used to describe all communication. This is not feasible when it is necessary to distinguish mass mediated communication from nonmediated communication. The research process begins when the researcher reviews the literature relevant to the question or hypothesis of interest, yielding the literature review. Previous theory and research form the basis for a new approach, model, or theory that interprets communication differently. Thus, information is basic to both the communication and the theory–research process; it begins the process by pointing to something new, either in the environment (such as Newton's apple leading us to gravity) or in a specific literature (such as theories of how the brain operates coming from neurophysiological studies).

We all are familiar with the cliché that "knowledge is power." But what does this really mean? Knowledge about the communication processes has very practical applications for a variety of purposes—persuading other people to do what you want, for good or evil purposes; teaching elementary students; launching an information campaign to reduce AIDS risk behaviors; selling soap; educating the public about some important issue; brainwashing the people; aggrandizing all power and becoming an absolute dictator; and so forth.

Thanks to our explorer-researchers, we have refined many of our ideas about human and mass communication processes. With some historical perspectives, we see that the communication process was once guided by naive theories, some as simple as those used to understand language acquisition. Language was once conceived as arising from physical exertion (yo-he-ho), from imitation of nature sounds (onomatopoeic, e.g., bow-wow), or when the mouth and vocal organs tried to pantomime body gestures (Gray & Wise, 1959). The mass communication process was once guided by a simplistic notion of a direct and universal "hypodermic-needle" effects model on a malleable and passive audience (Severin & Tankard, 1992, pp. 90–108). This model, too, is now in disrepute.

Today we can look back on the earlier generation of communication researchers who gave us various language acquisition and hypodermic-needle models of communication and wonder how they could have ever been so naive. Perhaps future generations will see us in much the same way.

The Research Process

We begin our journey by fleshing out the relationship between theory and research. In exploring this relationship we focus on the asking of "good" research questions that lead to important hypotheses. We then examine how the question dictates the methodology used to test the theoretical relationships. Finally, we examine the research process as a whole, coming full circle to understanding and predicting communication.

The research process begins by asking research questions. Research questions are drawn from the systematic study of an area of communication interest. Whereas a systematic study of the literature is necessary, "good" questions are also derived from old-fashioned common sense.

Questions can be derived either deductively or inductively. The scientific method gives more credence to the inductive process, or hypothetico-deductive logic, in which questions are induced from general principles. That is, they take a law-like approach, much like that found in Berger and Calebrese's (1975) interpersonal communication model of uncertainty reduction. Deduction, on the other hand, arrives at truth and questions from rationale observation (Westley, 1958). Deduction can be as simple and elegant as the syllogism, "All humans are mortal; Judy is a human; therefore, Judy is mortal" or as complex as the rule-based, practical syllogism, "Jim wants good grades; to get good grades he must study; therefore Jim must study to get good grades." The two examples differ in their range of generality (cf., Stacks, Hickson, & Hill, 1991). The former has low generalizability, it is simple logic in a law-like manner; the latter is midrange and more practical, and it requires a mediating factor.

Deduction is the way of everyday common sense and rationalism. But induction has its own logic. The logic of induction serves to restrain the dangers of total reliance on common sense that Albert Einstein warned against.

At one time, it seemed eminently sensible to thinkers that the earth was the center of the universe. After all, common wisdom told us that God placed humankind above all others, and by simply looking up at the skies it appeared that the heavens surrounded the Earth. From this observation, we deduced that humans must be in the center.

Induction forces us to challenge our notions of common sense. Long ago we learned that the Earth is not the center of our universe and that the Earth is round. The danger with a total reliance on induction is that it assumes that the theory and research methodology and not the researcher—who after all is a rational human being—can apply his or her reason to understanding the communication process (cf., Stacks & Hocking, 1992). This sometimes leads to a belief that the observations (data) are real—a philosophical stance sometimes called logical positivism, which some critics brand as blind empiricism.

In reality, most researchers maintain a dialectic between induction and deduction, drawing on each as needed. The researcher is a human being, not a machine, involved in the theory development process and does not shy away from making cautious "creative leaps" (Tichenor & McLeod, 1989, p. 16). Diehard logical positivists fear that without total reliance on hypothetico-deductive logic, researchers will draw back to a simple rationalism of their forbearers, who believed that the Earth was the center of the universe. On the other hand, we do not want to bend over backwards too far in the other direction and abandon blind empiricism for blind humanism.

While contemporary social science has been influenced by logical positivism, few social scientists today adhere to the strict logical positivism espoused by Wittgenstein and the Vienna Circle of Scientists of the 1920s (Bergman, 1967). They posited a rigid and uncompromising form of empiricism that only recognized truths validated through specified procedures of observation. Questions that cannot meet these rigid standards are rejected as inappropriate for scientific study. Whereas critics often attack logical positivism as if they were attacking modern social science, their criticisms are aimed at a largely "dead horse" philosophy that few contemporary social science researchers adhere to (Hanfling, 1981, p. 171).[2]

Asking Questions

The question-asking process in theory and research is more complex than simply generating the research question or questions guiding a particular study. Communication researchers ask questions in each step of the theory and research process.

An early stage in the theory–research process is concerned with defining the variables being studied. This stage is concerned with asking questions of definition that establish the phenomenon under study. This involves *questions of fact*. For example, what is *mass communication*? How does it differ from *human (speech) communication*? Are there differences in persuasibility in mass and speech communication? Are there similarities?

After researchers establish what is being studied, questions then focus on the relationships that communication variables have with the phenomenon under study. These are *questions of variable relations*; in answering them we seek to establish if two or more variables are related to each other in observable ways; and, if so, how.

Some questions are not factually oriented; instead they relate to considerations that focus more on the goodness or value of the variables being studied and the study as a whole. These are questions of value that examine the aesthetic or normative features of communication. These questions examine how appropriate or inappropriate communication is, its value, or its beauty. Questions of value are related to the next category of question—questions of policy.

Questions of policy focus on how the communication phenomena under study affect how communication should be practiced (Stacks & Hocking, 1992). Questions of policy are especially important to media practitioners. They wrestle with ethical concerns as to whether, in their quest for profits, they are doing the right thing. In this regard, applied communication researchers should heed the warnings of "critical scholars" who fear that communication research is often used merely to sell communication goods like commodities without regard for the social good (Bottomore, 1984).

We turn now to a more in-depth examination of each of these types of questions asked by researchers in the theory and research process.

Questions of Definition

All research, once the basic theoretical framework is established, begins with some form of definition, of elaborating the primitive terms in theory. Theory attempts to define the phenomena under study using terms and phrases, often loosely, to communicate meaning. At a gut level, most communicators believe they know what they mean by the symbols (words) they use; most message receivers also believe they know what was meant in the communicator's selection of symbols. But once we finish describing our theoretical frameworks, and roll up our sleeves for the nitty-gritty research work, we often find arguments between communicators and message receivers over what our seemingly obvious terms mean.

Of importance to theory and research is the ability to take an abstract concept and define it in such a way as to be testable. Until a concept has been defined in a certain agreed-on manner that meets criteria of reliability (it is consistent) and validity (it measures what we think it measures), the concept is nothing more than a primitive term (it is so basic that it could take on multiple meanings, such as love, aggressiveness, or power) with imprecise meaning. We now have to define our concepts in terms that are precise, measurable, reproducible, and demonstrate that our measures of the variables really represent what we tried to theoretically explain.

Some questions of definition in the physical sciences, such as of the quark (the smallest unit in the physical universe), were once only potentially definable. Until recently there was no method with which to test for their existence. Quarks were always theoretically defined in such a way as to be potentially observable (definable). Quarks were finally observed, but not until the equipment necessary to measure their existence was finally invented. The same is true in communication. Concepts such as attitudes, beliefs, and values are all abstractions requiring theoretical definitions that allow for potential observation and measurement.

Questions of definition also stipulate how a phenomenon is to be measured. This is called an operational definition. Operational definitions bridge the gap between theory and method by constructing a variable (something that can be observed, measured) from a theoretical abstraction. Suppose we have a theory that predicts that media violence is related to aggression. Media violence could take on many forms: channels, such as MTV, news coverage, or prime time shows, on the one hand, or messages, such as depictions of physical abuse or harsh language on the other. The operational definition defines the concept in such a way that the researcher can test for the presence or absence (dichotomous measure) or degree (continuous measure) of media violence. Likewise, our theory must operationally define aggression.

The question of definition is found in all research, qualitative or quantitative. Some definitions obtained from previous research are called reportative; they have a conventional meaning, one well understood by others researching in the area. Other definitions are stipulative; they are unique to the particular theoretical approach being tested. Whenever we use stipulative definitions, we must be sure that they are clearly and usefully defined in ways that make them operable (cf., Hocking, Stacks, & McDermott, 2003, p. 9). Similar to the observation of the quark, recent physics theory has been advanced by the observation of the black hole, which was long ago hypothesized to exist; only with the advent of the Hubble Telescope, however, were astronomers able to actually see it.

Questions of Variable Relations

Questions of variable relations stem from questions of definition. Once the theoretical phenomenon has been demonstrated to be potentially observable (i.e., operationally defined), we now move to examine the relations between and among variables. Questions of variable relations assume that for every action there is a potential reaction. That is, based upon theory, changes in one variable have some hypothesized change with other variable(s).[3]

Questions of variable relations might ask how a change—whether manipulated or natural in one variable—might have some predictable change in another variable; or what happens when one variable is combined with another; or how an array of variables changes when one or many other variables change. How can we even speculate on variable relations? Speculations do not come out of thin air. Researchers examine a good deal of research by others and come to believe—based on theory development—that such variable relations exist.

Questions of variable relations are the building blocks of research that help us discover objective ways of understanding the world. In communication research predicting relationships often takes methodological form in experiments (which provide the only way to establish causal relationships between variables), survey research, and manifest content analysis (the actual content being analyzed). Experiments are most amenable to quantitative analysis, which usually examines how a number of people are affected by the concepts under study. Some questions are tested by qualitative methods, such as latent content analysis (ideas or themes related to or underlying the content being analyzed) or in-depth interview methodology.

Questions of variable relations serve an important role in communication research. They establish whether theoretical concepts can be verified across a diverse population. They also provide researchers a way of objectively measuring whether predicted differences or relationships occur. Does watching violent television produce violence in viewers? Is there a difference between the ways in which countries use satellite technology? Do superiors communicate differently with subordinates? Do quality circles yield increased worker morale and productivity? Each of these questions has terms or concepts that have been defined. Each concept is potentially testable and can be verified or refuted according to some criteria.

As will be discussed in later chapters, an empirical observation of variable relations does not necessarily mean that one variable causes the other. For example, during the 19th century an Italian prison physician, Cesare Lombroso, claimed that he had discovered a biological cause for crime. He even produced empirical evidence for his theory. Through correlational research, Lombroso found that Italian criminals tended to have dark skins, sloping foreheads, jutting chins, and long arms. This was a potentially remarkable discovery. On closer inspection, however, it was found that the physical traits of criminals described by Lombroso were actually descriptions of those of people from the poor, southern region of Italy, especially Sicily. Sociologists took Lombroso's same data and applied a more plausible theoretical interpretation—that poverty and the ills associated with poverty, not physical traits, are associated with crime (Pick, 1986).

Questions of Value

Questions of value ask about subjective evaluations on such matters as goodness, beauty, rightfulness, or appropriateness. Although questions of value could be operationally defined to be empirically tested, for the most part their answers lie within the individual and generally accepted ethical norms.

Much research in rhetorical criticism, media content, interpersonal relations, international mass communications, journalism ethics, and feminist theory address questions of value.

Although all theoretically driven research involves questions of value to varying degrees, some communication researchers working in areas such as feminism, cultural studies, critical theory, and so forth, are often explicit about the values underlying their research.

Questions of value lead the researcher to reexamine the original questions of fact or conceive and devise important steps in theory construction and validation. Even Paul F. Lazarsfeld, whom some critics wrongly describe and deride as a diehard logical positivist, was concerned about values (Pasanella, 1994). His landmark mass communication studies focused on ways to study voting and increase voter turnout—an important issue of value in a democratic society. Similarly, the landmark experimental research on attitude change by Carl Hovland and his colleagues at Yale University were motivated by a desire to counter Nazi propaganda and motivate American soldiers to fight for their country during World War II (Hovland, Janis, & Kelly, 1953).

Much international and intercultural communication research has been guided by questions of value. Underlying the study of cross-national and cross-cultural communication is the belief that if we could only use communication effectively to break down the cultural and national barriers that separate people we could achieve peace and understanding. This optimistic, and perhaps naive, view reached its pinnacle during the 1960s, when, according to some interpretations, Canadian scholar Marshall McLuhan espoused the centrality of electronic media as a means to better the world. McLuhan predicted that the new electronic communication would turn the world into a "global village" breaking down all barriers of misunderstanding.[4]

The science fiction-humor writer Douglas Adams addressed the issue of a universe in which all races could communicate with each other in his *Hitchhiker's Guide to the Galaxy* (a four-part trilogy!). Unlike many science fiction writers, Adams addressed how alien races could communicate with each other. Thanks to a remarkable little fish called the babel fish, which you stick in your ear, you can understand all languages. The result of the babel fish was enhanced social communication throughout the Galaxy. The outcome, however, was far from the peace-through-communication model that some communication researchers might expect:

> The practical upshot of all this is that if you stick a babel fish in your ear you can instantly understand anything said to you in any form of language. The speech patterns you actually hear decode the brain wave matrix which has been fed into your mind by your babel fish.... [T]he poor babel fish, by effectively removing all barriers to communication between different races and cultures, has caused more and bloodier wars than anything else in the history of creation. (Adams, 1979, pp. 59–61)

Questions of Policy

Policy questions ask whether some action or policy should be implemented. Most researchers do not have the political power to implement policy, so questions of policy often concern researchers as advocates for or against certain causes. For example, based upon research and commonsense judgments of right or wrong, researchers might advocate that the U.S. government continue or refrain from broadcasting propaganda messages to Cuba through Radio Martí.

When researchers pose questions of policy, they typically have answered, or at least addressed, questions of definition, fact, and value—all of which impact on the final policy decision. But they also bring to the policy debate appeals to reason based on right and wrong. For example, in addition to empirical research findings, advocates for the continuation of Radio Martí will point to political oppression in Cuba and argue that messages over Radio Martí will provide what they believe is truthful information to Cubans. They might also use empirical data to support their views, such as the results of surveys of recent Cuban emigres. On the other hand, critics of Radio Martí will point to data that show that Radio Martí is ineffective—either because it is not being heard or is not believed—and appeal to the moral incorrectness of intrusion in other cultures as well as ascribing questionable or bad motives to the U.S. government.

Mass communication researchers have especially been interested in policy concerning such matters as media violence, journalism ethics, and so forth. According to the tenets of traditional democratic theory, the raison d'étre of mass communication is to create an informed public for a functioning democracy (Berelson, 1952; Sabine, 1952). The economic goals of mass media in most capitalist systems, however, mean that mass media industries are usually motivated by profit. This profit motive was not unforeseen or regarded as uniformly bad, according to some liberal thinkers, so long as there are sufficient checks to ensure that mass media provide some acceptable level of information for an enlightened public while the media industries also earn reasonable profits. The only problem is that often the profit goal supersedes the enlightenment goal, resulting in a dearth of useful information. As the social critic and rock star Bruce Spring-steen (1992) observed in his song "57 Channels (and Nothin' On)" about the information revolution in cable television:

> Man came by to hook up my cable TV
> We settled in for the night my baby and me
> We switch 'round and 'round 'til half-past dawn
> There was fifty-seven channels and nothin' on.

Human communication researchers are generally less concerned with policy questions; they tend to focus more on questions of variable relations and value (especially when in rhetorical research which focuses on the value of a speech or rhetorical campaign). However, research in freedom of speech tends to look at policy and the law that inhibits or enhances our expressions.

Questions of policy do not fall into "basic" theory or research. Rather, they are asked when we feel we have tested the theories sufficiently to recommend a course of action to lawmakers and other policy-making institutions. Most communication policy questions have dealt with the media, although more are coming to be asked in organizational communication research.

"Good Questions"

Defining what research questions are is quite simple. In so doing we have relied on the reporta-tive definition of questions used by Hocking, Stacks, and McDermott (2003), who in turn relied on Miller and Nicholson's (1976) approach to communication theory and research methodology. To varying degrees, each of the questions posed can be verified in the literature, assessed for its value, and even establish a research policy. Determining when a "good" question has been asked is not as simple. Just because a question is of interest to the researcher does not mean that it is good. It could be trivial (it affects no one). It could be useless (others have already asked similar questions and found no clear response). It could be irrelevant (it doesn't deal with communica-tion). It could be impossible to test. Or, it could be significant and extend our knowledge of how and why we communicate. A good research question stems from a well-conceived theoretical approach to how humans communicate. Further, a good research question almost always dictates the method most appropriate to answer that question.

As with good theory, a good research question will lead to other significant questions. The relationship between theory and research methodology is more than a two-sided sword where one side proposes a view of the world and the other tests that view. Theory and research work hand-in-hand. Sometimes it is the research methodology that alters the way the question is posed and tested which, in turn, produces new theory. In this regard specific research methods are as heuristic as theory. Theory and research methodology involve a single integral process by which we attempt to better understand how and why people communicate or fail to communicate.

The Rest of the Book

In the rest of the book, the reader should keep in mind the questions each approach asks. Look closely at how they are answered, how they are tested. What stage of theoretical development do they reflect? How significant are the questions asked? What methods are required to answer them? How sophisticated are they? These questions may not yield answers until later. However, we believe that a basic understanding of the major questions being asked by communication researchers should provide the impetus to better understand where the communication discipline is and where it may be going. It should also provide the information necessary to formulate and state good research questions based on an understanding of communication research.

Notes

1. The distinction between human communication and mass communication is somewhat arbitrary yet historical. Throughout this book we will use the term human communication when focusing on those approaches and theories that have emerged from the speech communication and interpersonal communication approaches. Mass communication is used to describe approaches and theories that focus on mediated messages and channels of communication (e.g., newspaper, radio, television). Obviously, the two areas overlap in a variety of areas as seen in Part IV, which examines areas that have extended beyond this traditional dichotomy.
2. Social science today reflects an epistemological view that can be more properly described as logical empiricism than logical positivism (Carnap, 1953). Logical positivism has its intellectual roots in the physical sciences, where universal laws underlie theory; social science involves recurring regularities that are more rule-based (Stacks et al., 1991). Rather than being grounded in universal laws, logical empiricism puts forth law-like statements that do not have to be universally true (Miller & Berger, 1978). The arguments of the 1970s regarding which philosophical approach is best have been supplanted by a growing movement toward triangulation, or theory and research that employs a combination of approaches.
3. This is what Stacks (2002) and Hocking, Stacks, and McDermott have labeled a "question of fact."
4. For critical analyses of the myth of globalization, see Ferguson (1992) and Curtin (1993).

References

Adams, D. (1979). *The hitchhiker's guide to the galaxy.* New York: Pocket Books.

Berelson, B. (1952). Democratic theory and public opinion. *Public Opinion Quarterly, 16,* 313–330.

Berger, C. R., & Calabrese, R. J. (1975). Some explanations in initial interaction and beyond: Toward a developmental theory of interpersonal communication. *Human Communication Research, 1,* 99–112.

Bergman, G. (1967). *The metaphysics of logical positivism.* Madison: University of Wisconsin Press.

Bottomore, T. (1982). *The Frankfurt school.* Chichester, Sussex: E. Harwood.

Burgoon, M., & Ruffner, M. (1978). *Human Communication.* New York: Holt, Rinehart & Winston.

Carnap, R. (1953). Testability and meaning. In H. Feigl & M. Brodbeck (Eds.), *Readings in the philosophy of science* (pp. 47–52). New York: Appleton-Century-Crofts.

Curtin, M (1993). Beyond the vast wasteland: The policy discourse of global television and the politics of American empire. *Journal of Broadcasting & Electronic Media, 37,* 127–145.

Dittman, A. T. (1972). *Interpersonal messages of emotion.* New York: Springer.

Einstein, A. (1960). The method of science. In E.H. Madden (Ed.), *The structure of scientific thought* (pp. 80–93). Boston: Houghton-Mifflin. (Original work published 1933)

Ferguson, M. (1992). The mythology about globalization. *Journal of Communication, 7,* 69–93.

Gray, G. W., & Wise, J. M. (1959). *The bases of speech*. New York: Harper & Row.

Hanfling, O. (1981). *Logical positivism*. New York: Columbia University Press.

Hickson, M. L., & Stacks, D. W. (1993). *NVC: Nonverbal communication studies and applications* (3rd ed.). Dubuque, IA: William Brown.

Hocking, J. E., Stacks, D. W., & McDermott, S. T. (2003). *Communication research* (3rd ed.). Boston: Allyn & Bacon.

Hovland, C. I., Janis, I. L., & Kelley, H. H. (1953). *Communication and persuasion*. New Haven, CT: Yale University Press.

Malandro, L., Barker, L. L., & Barker, D. (1989). *Nonverbal communication* (2nd ed.). Reading, MA: Addison-Wesley.

Miller, G. R., & Berger, C. R. (1978). On keeping the faith in matters scientific. *Western Journal of Speech Communication, 42*, 44–57.

Miller, G. R., & Nicholson, H. (1976). *Communication inquiry: A perspective on a process*. Reading, MA: Addison-Wesley.

Pasanella, A. K. (1994). *The mind traveller: A guide to Paul F. Lazerfeld's research papers*. New York: Freedom Forum Media Studies Center.

Pick, D. (1986). The faces of anarchy: Lombroso and the politics of criminal science in post-unification Italy. *History Workshop, 21*, 60–86.

Sabine, G. (1952). The two democratic traditions. *Philosophical Review, 61*, 451–474.

Severin, W. J., & Tankard, J. W., Jr. (1992). *Communication theories: Origins, methods, and uses in the mass media* (2nd ed.). New York: Longman.

Stacks, D. (2002). *Primer of public relations research*. New York: Guilford.

Stacks, D. W., Hickson, M. L., & Hill, S. R. (1991). *An introduction to communication theory*. Dallas, TX: Holt, Rinehart & Winston.

Springsteen, B. (1992). 57 channels (and nothin' on). *On human touch* [compact disk]. New York: Columbia.

Tichenor, P. J., & McLeod, D. M. (1989). The logic of social and behavioral science. In G. H. Stempel, III, & B. H. Westley (Eds.), *Research methods in mass communication* (pp. 19–29). New York: Prentice-Hall.

Westley, B. H. (1958). Journalism research and scientific method: II. *Journalism Quarterly, 35*, 307–316.

Suggested Readings

Chaffee, S. H. (1991). *Communication concepts 1: Explication*. Newbury Park, CA: Sage.

Hymes, D. (1974). *Foundations of sociolinguistics: An ethnographic approach*. Philadelphia: University of Pennsylvania Press.

Kerlinger, F. N., & Lee, H. B. (2000). *Foundations of behavioral research* (4th ed.). New York: Holt, Rinehart & Winston.

Osgood, C. E., Suci, G. J., & Tannenbaum, P. H. (1957). *The measurement of meaning*. Urbana: University of Illinois Press.

Popper, K. R. (1968). *The logic of scientific discovery* (2nd ed.). New York: Harper Torchbooks.

2

THINKING ABOUT THEORY

Steven H. Chaffee[1]

Theorizing about human communication is a very common human activity. We could not live effective lives if we did not formulate, and act upon, general suppositions about why people say what they say, for example, or how what we say affects other people. Indeed, understanding communication has such obvious survival value that one might imagine theorizing to be a genetically inherited propensity throughout our species.

Research on human communication, on the other hand, is a rare activity, one that requires a number of intellectual skills that are developed only through academic discipline. Basic to almost all of these skills is the decidedly uncommon activity of theorizing for research. That is the subject of this chapter; to a great extent it is the purpose of this entire book.

Most readers will be familiar with two meanings of theory: theory as abstract ideas and theory as predictable findings. Neither of these quite describes the underlying process of theorizing as it will be described here. This chapter will emphasize a third meaning, one built around concept explication—a kind of thinking that connects the other two notions of theory to one another. These three interconnected ideas are diagrammed in Figure 2.1. The terms in boxes represent the elements of one's theory, and the terms outside the boxes (in italics) represent one's theorizing.

Theory as Abstract Ideas

The most popular meaning of "theory" in this field is an abstract scheme of thought about communication. The ancient tradition of rhetorical theory provides many examples. Media criticism, based on abstract suppositions about how communication ought to serve society, provides more. Professional "rules of thumb" about how best to design a newspaper, to concoct a TV commercial, or to tell a joke, are also theories in this sense. In each of these examples, theorizing involves imagined events; observing these events is not as a rule deemed necessary. Observation is, though, the main business of empirical research, and it takes us to the second meaning of "theory."

Theory as Predictable Findings

In the academic field of communication research, the term "theory" is sometimes applied to a consistent research result. This is a positivist view of knowledge, favored by cataloguers of findings such as Berelson and Steiner (1964). For example, studies indicate reliably different patterns of communication behavior in relation to knowledge among people located in different socioeconomic strata. Individuals who do not know much about an issue are unlikely to seek information about it, for instance, but when an argument reaches them they may be more readily persuaded than are those with a stronger backlog of knowledge. Researchers use replicated

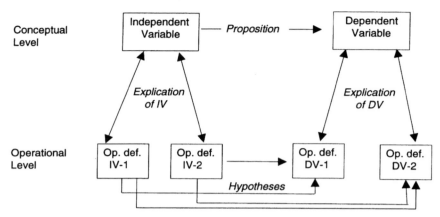

Figure 2.1 A schematic view of theorizing.

findings like these to predict what to expect in a new study and professional communicators use them in planning how to communicate with different publics.

Concept explication comes into play at this point, where predictable findings from past studies are compared with the abstract terms of a general theory. Are the two related? This kind of question requires us to theorize. The answers determine where our research will lead in the long run.

To connect predictable results to abstract notions requires some assumptions, the most basic of which is that both kinds of theory should relate to the same phenomena. We assume not only that generalizable principles about communication exist, but that they can be studied directly and expressed in a common language if we work hard enough to achieve it.[2] The ongoing linkage between the intellectual world of abstract theory and the observable world of replicable findings is called empirical theory.

Within the framework of empirical theory, there are both horizontal and vertical connections (represented by arrows in Figure 2.1). Each of these entails a different kind of thinking. The horizontal connection—the proposition—refers to thinking at the conceptual level. It involves both abstract concepts and a relationship between them. For example, John Milton and Thomas Jefferson, in arguing for freedom of expression, asserted in somewhat different terms that "truth will [win] out" (Milton, 1644/1949) if opposing beliefs are allowed to contest freely in "the marketplace of ideas." Translating this into the language of research, a policy of constraint versus freedom to express contrasting viewpoints is an independent variable (it is manipulated as either constraint or freedom), and the emergence of truth is a dependent variable (it is observed or measured for the effect of that policy on it). The mental arrow connecting the two is a causal (albeit rather hazy) one. The argument, though, is almost purely rhetorical, not intended to be tested in a scientific sense.[3]

At the bottom of Figure 2.1 is a second set of horizontal lines representing the parallel proposition but at the operational level. Here, replicable findings enter the picture; a theory should presumably produce a reliable result in the real world, or we should not have much use for it. In mainstream communication research, however, mere findings are not considered theories in themselves. Rather they are physical operations (either observations or manipulations), designed to indicate variation in the more abstract ideas postulated at the conceptual level. That is, the observable phenomena at the operational level are only part of one's theorizing and then only to the extent that they are connected to abstract concepts. Predicted relationships between operational definitions are called hypotheses. When a hypothesis has been deduced from a larger proposition, research to test the hypothesis can be interpreted as a test of the larger proposition as well. A major purpose of theorizing, then, is to foster hypothesis-testing research; communication scientists try to design studies that bear upon questions that go beyond the literal limits of their evidence.

These assumptions about concepts, their operational definitions, and the parallel propositions and hypotheses in a complex theoretical scheme, are generally accepted among empirical scientists who study communication processes.[4] The outlines of Figure 2.1 should be discernible to the reader throughout this book, although the terms and empirical content of concepts and hypotheses will vary from chapter to chapter.

Figure 2.1 also calls attention to the vertical arrows, which represent explication of the concepts and their operational definitions. The diagram is drawn in causal form, with arrows indicating which idea leads to which. Horizontally, theory-building and theory-testing both lead logically from the independent (causal) variable on the left, to the dependent (criterion) variable on the right. Vertically, the arrows lead in both directions because—over time—that is how explication works for the researcher. While later chapters are concerned mainly with causal propositions and hypotheses, this chapter concentrates more on the ongoing dialectic between a communication variable's conceptual and operational manifestations.

When an empirical scholar theorizes about communication, thinking can run upward or downward. Often one begins by reading about and discussing an idea and then thinks downward toward operational definitions. After some research on these measures, the scholar may rethink the conceptual meaning in light of new findings. In writing these ideas into a research report, it is common to reinterpret the research literature, seeing matters with sharpened eyes. Research, then, is not so much the production of a single study as it is an engagement of the researcher in a long-term commitment to imagine, and then try to find out, what is going on when humans communicate with one another. The reciprocating arrows running up and down in Figure 2.1 represent this continuing activity.

An Example: Video Games and Violence

To make things more concrete, let's use Figure 2.1 as an outline to theorize and study a communication process. Consider the possible effects of violence in video games, a topic of current public concern. Most people come to this topic by observing disturbing amounts of violence—in both video games and daily life. The idea of doing research, and thereby doing some good as well, has occurred to quite a few communication researchers. How to proceed?

Organized thinking usually begins at the conceptual level. A first step (as indicated by the first downward arrow) might be to analyze what is meant by "violence" and "video games," and then to look for operational definitions. The beginning of a definition might, for example, emerge from an inventory of current video games on the market, grouping games into different types and noting the extent to which each involves violence. Surveys of manufacturers, of game stores or arcades, or of young people who play a lot of video games, could provide a starting point. This early empirical work should, in turn, lead back up to a clarified conceptual definition of the independent variable. Now that we have examined a fair amount of the violence in video games, just what does it mean?

We probably cannot observe the "content" of a video game without playing it— without experiencing the game directly. (Indeed, an attempt to classify video game content might lead to the conclusion that video games do not themselves "contain" violence, but they do bring violent experiences into their players' lives.) From our experience, and from discussing similar experiences with other players, an intuitive sense of some possible effects of violent video games might emerge. After playing such a game for a time, a person may feel different: perhaps a bit energized, perhaps tired, perhaps hostile, perhaps happy or relieved of cares, and so forth. Grounded in players' reports of these self-observations (at the operational level), as the investigators, we might begin to conceptualize one or more possible effects of interest, as represented by Figure 2.1's right-side upward arrows.

Next comes some reading of a relevant literature, such as child psychology, on postulated effects. Prior studies have tested such theorized processes as arousal, social learning, catharsis, and disinhibition, in relation to television and film violence. What have they found? We might next design an experiment to test a proposition about the arousing, or modeling, or cathartic, or disinhibiting, effect of playing violent video games as compared with nonviolent alternatives. Laboratory procedures contrived to observe these effects would represent added downward arrows on the right-hand side of Figure 2.1 which by now can be regarded as outlining the dynamic general process of theorizing and not just the video game-aggressiveness cycle.

Research is of course much more complicated than this. Indeed, the example here, of effects of violent video games, has been successfully pursued by only a few investigators to date. This chapter aims to ease the process of research, by breaking down the steps represented by the vertical arrows in Figure 2.1.

Another Example: Gender and Family Interaction

To explore how concept explication proceeds, let's consider a more universal example. Most of us as we grow up become conscious of interacting differently with our mothers and our fathers. As we reflect upon this difference, we begin to theorize, trying to generalize our family experience to the world beyond the home. We may decide that our interaction patterns are due to age differences, or role relationships, or gender. Each conception refers to a different interpretation outside one's own family—that is, it implies a different kind of theory.

As we begin the process of research, each theory points us in a distinct direction for study. We are no longer considering the totality of our own communication with our parents, but the specific concept of, say, gender effects on interaction *as it applies to everyone*. The researcher who selects gender interaction as a domain of inquiry will soon discover a large number of prior studies, a number of competing conceptualizations, and some conflicting or anomalous (i.e., nonreplicated) findings. (Once we focus on a limited domain, this wealth of viewpoints stimulates theorizing, although at first it may be disconcerting.) Another researcher, looking instead at age as the critical concept for theorizing about parent–child interaction patterns, would read a different set of results and theoretical explanations, and conduct a different kind of study. As we move beyond our own parents and personal experience, the naive theorist is succeeded by the disciplined investigator.

At home watching television, we may notice *varieties of interaction*. The television set in the living room displays more instances of communication between parents and children, which could also be ascribed to gender (or to age). The whole household may share in watching a popular situation comedy that features families and their problems, an experience that could provide inspiration for several different studies. We might examine sex-role differentiation in television, and compare it to real life. Does television portray family interaction patterns accurately? This question could lead to a separate survey of how people typically interact at home, for comparison. Or we might study whether homes where a particular situation comedy is often watched conform more closely to the television norm than do households where there is less exposure to this television model. Another research direction might be to interview people regarding the extent to which they see television families as the norm. Do they take television as reality, or as fiction? (A likely answer: "some of both.") Next, research could attempt to relate these perceptions to expectations within each family, regarding the behavior of different members.

What is going on in these sketchy (and sometimes fanciful) examples is an ongoing interplay between ideas and real-world studies. This entire process, including the seminal idea, the literature review, the research, and the hypotheses, constitutes theorizing. Let's look at this process more carefully, considering how a single concept evolves.

Concept Explication

Most students new to research would like to work toward completing a project, such as a thesis or research report. In theorizing, though, one does not simply begin at a clearly marked starting point, proceed through a series of discrete steps, and eventually finish. Self-contained reports, such as theses and journal articles, flow from one's research; but in a rich program of study, the background work of theorizing is never finished, and each stage impinges on others. Nonetheless, it is possible to describe some definable phases in thinking through one's plan for a study, a process usually called *concept explication*.[5] The following sequence orients the beginner whose immediate goal is to get some results worth reporting.

Preliminary Identification

Before we can do much with an idea, it needs a name. Most often, of course, the chosen concept already has a name (or several) in the literature. Sometimes, though, current usage proves inadequate, and a new or modified name is needed. Results of communication research are presented mostly via words, and the ideas a word represents should remain consistent throughout a program of study.[6] Disciplined use of words encourages other scholars to employ the same terminology so that a growing body of research can be cumulative. Identification of a concept by giving it a preliminary name is a key starting point.

McCombs and Shaw (1972), for example, launched a major subfield of mass communication research when they coined the term "agenda setting." The same idea had been broached as "status conferral" by Lazarsfeld and Merton (1948), who lumped together effects on the "status of an issue" with the more commonplace idea of the social "status of an individual." As a result the theory that media coverage can elevate the political importance of an *issue* escaped most students of media effects, until McCombs and Shaw revived it under a new name. It is important, when choosing the label for a new idea, to school yourself in the way people use the terms under consideration.

New ideas are often identified by novel usages of terms already in common use within the field. There is no rule of thumb, except to devise a working title that you can easily use to explain what you have in mind and how it differs from other, more familiar concepts. Sometimes this is best accomplished by resurrecting an obscure or archaic term, such as "heterophily" (Rogers, 1983). Sometimes acronyms, which use the first letter of each word in a technical phrase to create a memorable abbreviated "word," can be devised—often with a touch of whimsy. An example is the method called signaled stopping technique (SST), introduced by researchers at the University of Washington (Carter, Ruggels, Jackson, & Heffner, 1973) about the time a Seattle aircraft plant lost a huge contract to build a supersonic transport (also SST).

An oxymoron (a combination of words that are mutually contradictory) can stimulate thought about relationships between its constituent terms. Examples include such phrases as "public opinion" and "mass communication," which juxtapose macroscopic and microscopic referents. Oxymorons do not lend themselves to clear explication, which would expose their inherent ambiguities. But an oxymoron can provide a distinctive rubric to describe a subfield of research. For example, "attitude change" mixes the idea of change with the term "attitude," normally defined as a stable motivational trait, to emphasize the difficulty of bringing about this kind of change. The analogous term "opinion change" does not evoke the same sense of persuasive power, because opinions are imagined as less deep-rooted, fixed, and emotional than attitudes (Hovland, Janis, & Kelley, 1953).

Another approach is to accept a popular term in the communication industry, but to explicate it from a new perspective. Steuer (1992), for example, showed that the oxymoron "virtual reality" can direct a coherent program of research if it is conceptualized as a perception of the person rather than a technological device.

Occasionally in science a concept comes to be known by the name of its discoverer or inventor. This eponymic honor is usually bestowed by usage among colleagues, not by oneself. Osgood (1952) may have missed his chance at immortality by giving his data collection tool the unique (and somehow euphonious) name, the "semantic differential." Likert (1932), less elegantly, entitled his rather similar procedure "sum-mated ratings"—and it is known to practically everyone today as a "Likert scale."

The point is that a good deal of care should go into choosing a name for one's concept, devising a label that is both distinctive and memorable. A considerable number of poor choices have been made over the years; the ideas involved have often been lost along with their names. The first task of concept naming, however, is not salesmanship but focusing attention on the essential features of the idea as you develop it into a tool for your own research. Tichenor, Olien, and Donohue's (1970) term "knowledge gap," which refers to effects of communication on variance (rather than central tendency) in a social system, is not just a felicitous catch-phrase. It pithily calls attention to a potential societal dysfunction, and has been used to organize dozens of innovative studies (Rogers, 1976).

Preliminary Definition

Explication involves more than simply looking up a term in a dictionary, or tracing its etymology, although those are useful early steps.[7] For research, we need to study the ways other researchers have been using the concept—what they mean by it, and how it is represented in their studies. At this point we are leaving the world of common language, and joining a discipline of scholars who make distinctions that are not required in everyday usage.

Because a communication concept is likely to be rich in meanings, explication itself involves hypotheses. That is, an empirical definition is itself a kind of proposition, one that is tested at an early stage in a research program. The everyday phrase "attention to television," for example, is represented by very different operational definitions in experiments on psychophysiological responses (Reeves, Thorson, & Schleuder, 1986) and field surveys on cumulative learning (Chaffee & Schleuder, 1986). In a laboratory experiment, *a participant's attention elicited by a televised stimulus* is largely reflexive and automatic, dictated by the immediate situation. Survey researchers, on the other hand, ask how much *a respondent pays attention while watching television* habitually over time. Entirely different research procedures are used when investigators are studying these different conceptions of attention in television viewing, and the theories in question are if anything even more different. The fact that "attention" or "watching television" might be indistinguishable verbally does not mean that they refer to the same kinds of human events in the two research traditions. Nonetheless, the survey questioning method is useful to validate the laboratory manipulation (Reeves et al., 1986).

Communication research makes special demands on our conceptual tools because much of what we mean by "communication" is not observed directly; it is imagined. In the last example, for instance, the difference between the attention one voluntarily pays to television, and that which is elicited even from an unmotivated viewer, is not directly observable; it is inferred based upon distinct theories and supportive evidence.

Some components of the communication process can, however, be experienced directly. We can, for example, keep track of the words we say or read, and of the reactions we and others have to them. These real-life experiences are *percepts*, meaning that we perceive them in ourselves and others. They provide the raw data for our theorizing about communication in broader ways. If we had no concrete percepts, it would be hard to imagine doing communication research at all. Concepts connect percepts, which everyone has, to theories, which communication scientists build and test.

Observation

Like everyone else, students of communication spend a great deal of time observing human activity. But we would never learn much new about communication by simply observing what goes on naturally around us. Communication scholars go to extraordinary efforts to gather evidence that would not otherwise enter their lives. I have at times noted my colleagues and students engaged in these kinds of activities; although they do not seem bizarre to me, they might to a visitor not used to communication research work:

- Reading through very old newspapers, keeping a careful record of statements of a certain kind.
- Hiding behind a one-way mirror, observing children watching television.
- Editing a video presentation that incorporates material from several different sources, to be shown to college students in an experimental laboratory.
- Calling randomly selected telephone numbers, and asking the adult who has had the most recent birthday what she thinks about a current news issue.
- Sitting in the corner of a meeting room, making tallies of who says what to whom, in a group brought together to work on a contrived problem.

The reader should by this point recognize these procedures as *operational definitions*, or, more exactly, as operations whose purpose is to satisfy requirements set forth in a definition. Each has been painstakingly arranged because the investigator thinks of it as representing some more general concept, not because the evidence being gathered would be terribly important in and of itself. Communication researchers spend much of their workdays defining their concepts operationally. Digging through archives, coding messages, running participants through an experiment, and interviewing respondents in a survey, are all time consuming. But a thousand hours spent categorizing utterances of husbands on TV, or measuring the pulse rates of sophomores who are being shown an erotic film, or asking people how they decided which way to vote, may be pointless if the resultant data do not serve a conceptual purpose. Explication can save many wasted hours. Theorizing, although it may be challenging, is certainly more pleasant work than most data collection activities.

Primitive and Derived Terms

Conceptualization is built of words, and we must find the best place to start building. At some point in the explication process, it is useful to consider which terms are *primitive*, words that we take as commonly understood, or as givens (Hempel, 1952). The existence and acceptability of these few concepts are assumed, which means they are not questioned within the program of research that is built upon them.[8]

Primitive terms differ at various levels of analysis. Commonly, one essential given is the individual. To get on with our work, we usually assume that we know what a person is when we see one.[9] Some branches of communication research also assume the existence of supra-individual entities, such as families or communities or organizations or societies. These terms are often *derived* from the primitive term "person." That is, some researchers define an organization, say, as a combination of persons with specific boundary conditions added.[10] Similarly, the term "word" is often treated as a primitive term, and concepts like "sentence" or "message" are then derived from it.

Time and space are also common primitive terms. We conventionally define people in relation to one another in these terms, such as saying that *two people together* constitutes a "couple." The term "together" here refers to juxtaposition in time and space; two people must be together in one place for a reasonably long time before we consider them a couple. Time and space are conveniences, and we would be foolish to expend a lot of time and effort on their definition. They would then cease to be convenient.[11] Explication includes stating the assumptions made about primitive terms and the terms derived from them for our convenience.

Validity

Validity is the most general criterion of communication research. When we operationalize a concept, we try to evaluate its validity in terms of our explication. That is, does the operational definition represent the concept as we have defined it? Are we measuring what we intend to measure?

The same question applies to theory testing. When we test a hypothesis (a particular statement relating two operational definitions) to what extent does it represent a valid test of the more general proposition relating the two concepts? Explication relating each concept to its operational definition is central to this evaluation of a theory via hypothesis testing.[12]

The distinction between internal and external validity (Campbell & Stanley, 1966) can be applied to both the measurement of a single concept and the testing of a theory involving two or more concepts. Internal validity refers to what is done, what is found, and what is inferred within a single study. Has each concept been operationalized in a way that is reliable and appropriate to its explication? Has the hypothesis been tested so that alternative explanations for the findings have been ruled out?

External validity refers to the generalizability of a particular study to other settings, times, or units of study (e.g., persons). Is each operationalization consistent with the larger universe of measures that might represent the concept in question? Are inferences from a study applicable to conditions other than those which obtain in it? In theorizing such questions are considered in connection with research evidence from each study.

Reliability

Reliability is a statistical criterion for evaluating the usefulness of an operational procedure. It refers to the replicability of a result across a series of observations or studies. Whereas validity refers to the relationship between the conceptual definition and its operational definition, reliability has to do with operational definitions. In practice, research procedures to maximize reliability sometimes do so at some expense to validity; this is a matter of balance: Some degree of reliability is necessary to validity.

For example, consider the problem of measuring people's use of radio news. One possible question wording is, "Did you listen to news on the radio yesterday?" This is likely to produce fairly reliable reports, because most people can remember yesterday clearly. But that reliable item might not be especially valid as an indicator of a given person's habits; yesterday might have been an unusual day, either for the person or in the news. On the other hand, many people listen to radio news only when commuting to work; if they happen to be interviewed on a Sunday about listening "yesterday" they will report not listening, even though they may do so five days a week. If radio-listening habits are the focus of one's research interest, a more valid question might be, "How many days a week do you typically listen to news on the radio?" The person may not have the long-term recall and mathematical skills to give a precisely correct (i.e., highly reliable) answer, yet the vaguer measure might be more useful for the researcher.

Validity is evaluated in terms of one's explication, whereas reliability can be estimated for any operational procedure whether it represents a larger concept or not. The explication of a concept, in turn, is located within the larger theoretical structure outlined in Figure 2.1. What this means in the example of radio news listening is that the choice between a highly specific question ("yesterday") and a more general question ("typically") depends on how the measure is to be employed. If the study's purpose is a descriptive survey, the "yesterday" question is probably preferable, because across a large number of responses random effects such as days of the week and other specific circumstances tend to average out. That is, the aggregate data yield the best (most reliable) estimate of what typically occurs. If the purpose is to test hypotheses about other variables that might predict radio listening, or about possible effects of radio news on individuals, then the more general measure that estimates most validly the typical radio use of each individual may be preferable.

Unit of Analysis

A basic question that can be surprisingly tricky is, "For what class of entities does this concept vary?" Is it an attribute of individual persons, of aggregates such as communities or nations, of messsages, of events, or of some other unit? Units of analysis should be the ones talked about in your theorizing and the ones that are observed and described in empirical work. Inconsistency in the unit of analysis is a common error in communication research. On the one hand, it is risky to draw psychological inferences about individuals from observing patterns in aggregates, a practice often called the "ecological fallacy." Conversely, there are pitfalls in treating aggregated individual observations as if they represent some higher-order entity, as is done in polling when a large number of personal interviews are combined to say something about "the public's" opinion.

Study of media audiences is plagued by shifting units of analysis. A newspaper is almost always read by one person at a time, but television sets tend to be viewed by several people at once; it is very difficult to calibrate the two activities on a common scale. Newspaper or magazine circulation is usually calculated by the number of copies that are sold; as a rule the number that are read is lower, and the total number of readers is higher. Television ratings are calculated by household, and include such attributes as "woman aged 18–49" without much evidence that the woman so described watches television, or the specific program in question. Advertising is planned at the level of the market, which may be a local newspaper's circulation zone, a radio station's signal range, or a television network's specific segment of the national market.

These shifts in units of analysis cause few problems for the media marketing industry, which is mainly interested in reliable descriptive data. So long as numbers are compiled in the same way from place to place and from month to month, they can be compared across space or time. One can determine, for example, if newspaper reading is declining, or if more people watch television on weeknights than on weekends. But shifting units of analysis create difficulties in theorizing, when a researcher tries to match audience figures to some motivation or media effect. A common unit for television viewing is time spent with the medium, for example, but if that metric were applied to the newspaper a slow reader might be ranked above someone who has actually processed more words but in a shorter time. Using words as the unit of analysis for television, on the other hand, misses much of what TV, a rich audiovisual medium, provides. Comparing the relative impact of these different media is similarly difficult. For example, if we ask whether the newspaper or television has greater impact on voters, should this be tested using time spent, or words processed, or some other method of assessing the independent variable? When the unit of analysis changes from one concept to another in the same theoretical structure, theory testing becomes very slippery business.

Relationship to Time

Another basic query in theorizing concerns time. If a concept is an attribute of individuals, does it vary across persons at a given point in time (cross-sectional variance), or across times for a given person (process variance)? "Attitude," for example, is a cross-sectional concept whereas "attitude change" is a process concept. Many social attitudes do not seem to change within the same individual, so they are of limited applicability for theorizing and research on communication processes. Fear of crime is cross-sectionally correlated with heavy television use, for instance, but that does not guarantee that depriving a person of television would allay his fear of being a crime victim. In theorizing, it is essential to keep the many cross-sectional findings separate from the rarer studies in which process variance (change) has actually been observed. Experimental tests are generally preferred for effects hypotheses because time is controlled by the experimenter, and differences can be unambiguously attributed to processes set in motion by the communication intervention.

Many concepts are attributes of a social aggregate, rather than individual units of analysis. Examples that are sometimes related to communication factors include presidential popularity, crime rates, and fashions. These may vary across time either because individual members of the aggregate are changing ("process variance"), or because they are being replaced by new members who are different ("invasion and succession") even though no individual has changed. In the latter situation, causal theorizing may not be applicable. Newspaper reading, for example, has gradually declined in the United States as new generations reared on television have entered adulthood; the change in the aggregate has not been much due to any tendency for individuals to abandon their newspaper habits, but rather to a disinclination among young people to start reading. Hence, attempts to explain "why people are dropping the newspaper" miss the mark; very few individuals are doing that, so there are no reasons why. It is also instructive that, while newspaper reading is positively correlated cross-sectionally with people's education levels, the historical decline in readership has occurred even while the median level of education among American adults has increased by nearly two years. To account for the decline, then, requires more than a set of individual-level predictor variables.

Literature Review

One of the most ominous terms one encounters upon entering a field of research is *review of the literature*. In the long run, literature search does involve a good deal of work—searching out relevant studies, reading them, and synthesizing them into a coherent whole. But it is better characterized as a number of episodes of literature-searching; not all of this is done at any one time, and certainly not all of it is completed before we begin theorizing in anticipation of our own study.[13] While many good research ideas occur when we are reading other people's research, theorizing usually begins before much effort is put into a broad-scale search for related studies. Explication can help to bound a search on a concept, by sorting out those few writings that deal with the idea being developed.

Once a concept is defined preliminarily, reading studies related to it becomes a surprisingly pleasant and rewarding phase of research. The trick is to skim quickly past articles that involve the term being used but not the same meaning, at the same time looking for research involving the concept even though the name is not the same. Occasionally a very rich review of a literature closely related to the concept of interest is found. The bibliography of a well-crafted research article or book chapter can provide an excellent start.

Failure to find prior syntheses of research literature may be either a good sign or a bad one. If the reason that no one has previously analyzed research on a concept is that it is a novel idea that can be heartening. It suggests that you may be on to something new and different—a scholar's ideal. But the absence of prior research may instead mean that the concept has not been very fruitful for other investigators; if so, you could be heading into a blind alley. In any event, it is helpful in constructing an analysis of the literature to know what, if anything has been done on the subject by others with an idea that is similar to your own.

Meaning Analysis

It is neither necessary nor possible to track down every existing study. But a literature review will be more productive if you find examples of the full *variety* of meanings of your concept that communication scholars use. A good exercise at this stage in theorizing is to sort out the various meanings and terms into groups. Some usages may be discarded early on, but sometimes the category system itself can be a theoretical analysis. Linz and Malamuth (1993), for example, were able to organize an immense variety of studies by keying on three terms that at first blush might seem to refer to the same kind of messages: *obscenity*, *pornography*, and *erotica*.

They found that each of these terms tends to be favored within one of three distinct intellectual traditions, which they called conservative-moralist, feminist, and liberal, respectively. This meaning analysis enabled them to compare the three traditions and to identify more subtle distinctions in theorizing and research generated from each viewpoint. It also served to pinpoint the distinctly feminist context of their own experiments on effects of pornography.

Operational Contingencies

A literature review can organize studies alongside one another and explore differences among them. This becomes more possible as the literature review proceeds and focuses on details of those findings most relevant to your theorizing. This is done through attention to operational contingencies.

Each study in the published literature has been conducted under specific conditions, such as its historical time, place, and research method. These are necessary contingencies for doing the study at all; they constrain the operational definition of a concept in each instance. Theorizing ordinarily extends well beyond a specific measure in a particular context. For example, an investigation of the capacity of television to inform people finds very different operational measures of information in studies of politics versus health practices, and different results with children versus adults. Sorting out the literature in terms of these operational contingencies helps you comprehend the potential range of measures, and to adjudicate conflicting findings. Television news exposure is, for example, consistently found to be a strong correlate of political knowledge in studies of children and adolescents (Atkin, 1981), but only rarely in surveys of adults (McLeod & McDonald, 1985). Information encountered in a political campaign is less likely to be accepted than is information from a public health campaign. These study differences can become an important part of theorizing about the more general phenomenon.

Operational contingencies vary between studies, but they are usually not variables within a given study. To take advantage of them, organize the literature review according to those operational features that seem to make a difference in results. This kind of literature review can produce hypotheses based on between-studies variables. For example, Martin, McNelly, and Izcaray (1976) examined more than a dozen surveys of mass media use in western hemisphere nations. They found some studies reporting high correlations between use of various mass media and the person's education and income. In a second group of studies, education and income were neither correlated with film attendance nor with radio nor TV use. When the literature was divided in this way the first set of studies turned out to be almost entirely rural surveys, and the second group all urban. This led to an empirical analysis comparing urban dwellers who had recently moved to the city versus those who had always lived there; the results for these two subsamples paralleled those in the two groups of prior studies, which in turn helped them to clarify the meaning of the entire literature on the subject of socioeconomic status (SES) and media use.

Identification of operational contingencies that affect relationships between concepts is a product of synthesis, not just of reading and abstracting each study. Simply to paraphrase an unorganized string of studies one at a time, or even to group research reports in terms of their general conclusions, will not help identify operational contingencies that divide a literature.

Synthesis

A literature review often becomes a study in itself. Some of the most useful advances in communication research have been analytic literature reviews. Rogers's monumental volume *Diffusion of Innovations* (1964, 1983), for example, began as the literature review section of his doctoral dissertation. By organizing and synthesizing thousands of studies of diffusion around a set of conceptual distinctions and empirical generalizations, Rogers founded an entire subdiscipline within communication research. His literature analysis became the main product of his theorizing, which enabled other scholars to locate their specific diffusion studies in a larger theoretical context.

Empirical Definition

The continuing process of theorizing is a kind of working understanding with oneself that both guides the literature review and prevents it from going on indefinitely. In practice the scholar begins by reading a few studies, then moves to explication, refines the preliminary definition, and returns to the literature search with a sharper definition. To read in advance the entire body of work loosely connected to a topic is usually much too time consuming to be practical. Explication helps to restrict efforts to those studies relevant to the concept being formulated—and only those studies.

Empirical definition is accomplished by gradually developing *rules of inclusion and exclusion*. That is, abstract meanings become translated, through empirical research, into statements of the conditions required by the explicated concept. Festinger (1957), for example, experimented for a number of years on the concept of cognitive dissonance. He viewed dissonance as conceptually similar to the overlapping concept called cognitive conflict, but the two conditions led to different theoretical predictions for communication behavior. Eventually he concluded that the boundary between the two was the making of a decision; specifically, conflict became defined as predecisional and dissonance as postdecisional (Festinger, 1964). This helped him to adjudicate the literature and focus his students on either dissonance or conflict without confusing the two streams of research.

Empirical Study

There is no clear-cut demarcation between literature analysis and empirical study. Conceptual ideas continue to change throughout a program of research; surprising results should generate a revised interpretation of the prior literature. New theorizing is as important to this process as are new findings.

Once a scholar has collected a set of data, there is a tendency to become exclusively operational in one's thinking. If you do so, bear in mind that the larger goal is to use your data to advance your theorizing. Given the centrality of concept explication to this process, it makes sense to begin by considering each variable in its own right.

Univariate Analysis

Presuming one has in hand a synthesis of the research literature on one's concept, the first empirical step is univariate analysis. In content analysis and survey research, and no less for dependent variables in controlled experiments, descriptive statistics such as the mean, variance, skewness, and reliability of each measure deserve careful examination. Even here we are in a sense testing hypotheses by comparing what we find to what others have found with similar measures in prior studies. Are the estimates of communication activity higher, or lower, than expected? Is the distribution of values normal, so that you can safely use the variable in correlational analyses? Does the range seem more restricted than you expected based on prior studies? How does the measure vary across time, and how might this affect the kinds of theories you should relate it to?

These operational questions are more closely related to theorizing than they might appear. Communication process theories are often couched in extensive terms that assume that every variable covers a wide range of possible values across units of analysis, and for the same unit over time. For example, the hypothesis, "Increased exposure to television violence heightens tendencies toward aggressive behavior," assumes that a person's television violence exposure and her aggressiveness can both increase. The companion formulation, "Decreased exposure reduces aggressive tendencies" assumes that both can go down. But do they? Very few studies empirically examine individuals whose habitual exposure to televised violence changes significantly, up or down; television use is a habit that is constrained by lifestyle, by preferences of others watching television in the same household, and by what is available to watch. These constraints in turn limit theorizing, or at least force the theorist to be more specific as to precisely what proposition is at stake and how much to expect of evidence bearing on an ambitious hypothesis.

Bivariate Analysis

The next step in data analysis, and hence in theorizing, is to look for variables that are associated empirically with each measure of interest. This should be arranged in parallel with a literature review section on the same correlates. Prior research can indicate two kinds of correlates: within each study and across studies. Correlations within studies are usually reported as such, whereas only the person reviewing the literature is in a position to note patterns across studies.

One common bivariate question is whether indicators of SES correlate in a consistent way with a particular form of communication. Many media use studies, for example, report correlations with education, income, or occupational status. New data can be evaluated in this context: Have you found roughly the same patterns of correlations as in prior studies? Most present U.S. surveys find SES negatively correlated with time spent watching television. But in some developing countries the reverse is true—the television set is a luxury only the well-to-do can afford; indeed, that was also the case in the United States in the early 1950s. Even though theorizing about television's effects may not involve consideration of the person's SES, it is important to know how the two measures correlate to compare the tests to others' findings. Thus, we should keep SES factors in mind when theorizing about the specific process of interest if testing hypotheses with contemporary U.S. data. Empirical measures are affected by the social structure in which the data are collected; such contextual factors may need to be controlled in statistical analysis.

The seemingly inconsistent pattern of SES-television correlations across the history of empirical studies can be described by considering bivariate and univariate relationships together. When television use is very low (i.e., few people in the society have access to television reception), the SES-television correlation should be positive. As the mean level rises (i.e., as television use diffuses throughout the society), the correlation gradually flattens and then reverses. When almost everyone can watch television, it tends to be used most heavily by those in the lower socioeconomic brackets. The same historical pattern would probably be found for almost any major technological innovation, from the sewing machine to the typewriter to the word processor. Initially these "new toys" are prized possessions of the elite few, in homes of the rich and offices of supervisors. Eventually, though, they become work stations, often symbolic of the low estate of women in the work force. Evidence on such a general proposition regarding the social meaning of technological innovations is very unlikely to be shown within any single study. It is offered here more as conjecture than as an established finding, to remind the reader that theorizing persists long after even a great deal of research has seemingly been completed.

Construct Validation

Ultimately one asks not just that an operational definition work in a loose pragmatic sense, but that it work the way one's theorizing has predicted. This is a question that arises rather late in a program of research. Successful theory testing is, however, far from the end of one's efforts. If a suspect measure "works" for your purposes better than a measure you felt passed all interim tests (e.g., reliability) better, you still have empirical work to do. You need to figure out what the "successful" operationalization contains that is missing from the other measure, and begin to build upon that. The term "construct" is used to refer to a concept that has acquired both empirical and theoretical meaning through a coherent program of study. Construct validation refers to consistency throughout a theoretical structure, conceptual and operational, including the linking explications.[14] This pursuit may send you back to even the earliest stages in this outline.

Conclusion

This chapter outlines the steps that lie ahead for those undertaking a commitment to study some facet of human communication. The discussion has constantly shifted between theory and method, and between the conceptual and the operational levels of thinking, because that is how theorizing is done.[15] The agenda of activities may seem imposing, and certainly one implication here is that communication research is an extensive, long-run, and demanding activity.

Balanced against the sheer volume of work that one undertakes in entering this field is the framework for organizing one's research and thinking that has been outlined here. Reading prior literature, explicating central concepts, collecting and analyzing data, and writing research conclusions, are activities that occupy the scholar's time at different points in the research process. Theorizing provides a sense of the relationship of these parts to one another, and to the whole, that can make the work of communication research both intellectually productive and enjoyable.

Notes

1. The author is indebted to Richard F. Carter, Jack M. McLeod, and Byron Reeves for many of the ideas underlying this chapter. Among those who commented helpfully on an earlier draft are Ben

Detember, Glenn Leshner, Dennis Kinsey, Jim Coyl, Bob Meeds, Andrew Mendelsohn, Ekaterina Ognianova, Jane B. Singer, and Charlie Wood.

2. This is not always so. For some aspects of communication, there may be no general principles to discover, or they may be so abstract as to elude observation or verbal expression. An assumption is not a fact, just an untested premise that we accept for the time being; it enables us to proceed in a line of inquiry. If research based on one assumption produces no consistent results, and hence no generalization, it is sensible to discard it and start anew. Kuhn (1970) has noted that anomalous results in a program of research lead to a shift from one scientific paradigm to an alternative set of assumptions.

3. President Thomas Jefferson, who considered himself a scientific thinker, claimed to have empirical evidence that supported the theory. In his Second Inaugural address (1805/1984) he praised the American people for "the discernment they have manifested between truth and falsehood." The public, he asserted, "may safely be trusted to hear everything true and false, and to form a correct judgment between them."

4. These assumptions are not shared throughout the entire academic field of communication. Some empiricists stay very close to their data, and trust only replicable findings, not more general theories. More commonly, many theorists do not intend their writings to be subjected to empirical testing. Indeed, many scholars do not accept the premise that communication phenomena follow lawful patterns at all. Because they make radically different starting assumptions, they conduct research that is markedly distinct in nature from what is described in this chapter.

5. For a philosophical analysis of explication primarily in the physical sciences, consult Hempel (1952). Regarding its applicability to communication research, see Chaffee (1991).

6. Research is often presented with numerical entries in tables, but a number is of little interest outside the confines of a specific study unless it is connected to a concept.

7. A dictionary tells what the term means in popular usage. An unabridged dictionary gives its specialized meanings in some esoteric contexts. An etymology indicates the purposes the word served when people invented it, and when others adapted it to new meanings.

8. In other words, the primitive terms of an established tradition may very well be challenged. Kuhn's (1970) concept of a paradigm shift to a new scientific tradition could be described as a rejection of one set of primitive terms, and their replacement with a new set.

9. The conceptual and operational definition of "human being" can be quite controversial in some fields, such as zoology or medical ethics. Scientists attempting to define the beginning or end of life, or the distinctions among higher primates, use a different set of primitive terms from those employed in communication research.

10. In other studies, though, an organization may simply be treated as a primitive term without saying exactly who or what comprises it.

11. In some sciences, including some areas of communication science, considerable effort is given over to explication of time or space (e.g., Kline, 1978).

12. "Validity" does not mean "truth," and truth is not a criterion for communication research. We usually intend our propositions to be true, but only after surviving many tests might a scientific statement come to be accepted as lawful. Very few communication theories ever reach this status. Truth is not so hard to abandon in explication as it is in other aspects of theorizing, however. Most of us can accept the assumption that there is no *true* definition for a concept, no one operationalization that *truly* represents the abstract concept. The best assumption is that there is no *true* definition for a concept, no one operationalization that *truly* represents the abstract concept best.

13. Published research articles and unpublished dissertations are organized to be read in a logical sequence, and hence give the impression that the work they describe was performed in the same sequence. This is almost never the case. The origination point of most communication research, if it could be located in the final published report, would be typically found 30% to 40% of the way into the text.

14. Cook and Campbell (1979) take the position that construct validity relates primarily to explication, but most methods texts emphasize instead that constructs are validated to the extent that they enter into relationships with other constructs as predicted by the overall theory.

15. A succinct summary of this chapter might be: "Theorizing is never done."

References

Atkin, C. K. (1981). Communication and political socialization. In D. D. Nimmo & K. R. Sanders (Eds.), *Handbook of political communication* (pp. 299–328). Beverly Hills, CA: Sage.

Berelson, B., & Steiner, G. (1964). *Human behavior: An inventory of scientific findings.* New York: Harcourt, Brace & World.

Campbell, D. T., & Stanley, J. C. (1966). *Experimental and quasi-experimental designs for research on teaching.* Chicago: Rand McNally.

Carter, F., Ruggels, W. L., Jackson, K. M., & Heffner, M. B. (1973). Application of signaled stopping technique to communication research. In P. Clarke (Ed.), *New models for mass communication research.* 15–43). Beverly Hills, CA: Sage.

Chaffee, S. H. (1991). *Communication concepts 1: Explication.* Newbury Park, CA: Sage.

Chaffee, S. H., & Schleuder, J. (1986). Measurement and effects of attention to media news. *Human Communication Research, 13,* 76–107.

Cook, T. D., & Campbell, D. T. (1979). *Quasi-experimentation: Design and analysis issues for field settings.* Chicago: Rand McNally.

Festinger, L. (1957). *A theory of cognitive dissonance.* Stanford, CA: Stanford University Press.

Festinger, L. (1964). *Conflict, decision and dissonance.* Stanford, CA: Stanford University Press.

Hempel, C. G. (1952). *Fundamentals of concept formation in empirical science.* Chicago: University of Chicago Press.

Hovland, C. I., Janis, I. L., & Kelley, H. H. (1953). *Communication and persuasion: Psychological studies of opinion change.* New Haven, CT: Yale University Press.

Jefferson, T. (1984). Letter to Judge John Tyler. In M. D. Patterson (Ed.), *Thomas Jefferson: Writings.* New York: Library of America. (Original work published)

Kline, F. G. (1978). Time in communication research. In P. M. Hirsch, P. V. Miller, & F. G. Kline (Eds.), *Strategies for communication research* (pp. 187–204). Beverly Hills, CA: Sage.

Kuhn, T. S. (1970). *The structure of scientific revolutions* (2nd ed.). Chicago: University of Chicago Press.

Lazarsfeld, P. F., & Merton, R. K. (1948). Mass communication popular taste, and organized social action. In L. Bryson (Ed.), *The communication of ideas* (pp. 95–118). New York: Harper & Brothers.

Likert, R. (1932). A technique for the measurement of attitudes. *Archives of Psychology, 22,* 5–55.

Linz, D., & Malamuth, N. (1993). *Communication concepts 5: Pornography.* Newbury Park, CA: Sage.

Martin, R. R., McNelly, J. T., & Izcaray, F. (1976). Is media exposure unidimensional? A socioeconomic approach. *Journalism Quarterly, 53,* 619–625.

McCombs, M. E., & Shaw, D. E. (1972). The agenda setting function of mass media. *Public Opinion Quarterly, 36,* 176–187.

McLeod, J. M., & McDonald, D. (1985). Beyond simple exposure: Media orientations and their impact on political processes. *Communication Research, 10,* 155–174.

Milton, J. (1949). *Areopagitica* (J. W. Hales, Ed.). London: Oxford University Press. (Original work published 1644)

Osgood, C. E. (1952). The nature and measurement of meaning. *Psychological Bulletin, 49,* 197–237.

Reeves, B., Thorson, E., & Schleuder, J. (1986). Attention to television: Psychological theories and chronometric measures. In J. Bryant & D. Zillmann (Eds.), *Perspectives on media effects* (pp. 251–279). Hillsdale, NJ: Erlbaum.

Rogers, E. M. (1964). *Diffusion of innovations.* New York: Free Press.

Rogers, E. M. (1976). Communication and development: The passing of the dominant paradigm. *Communication Research, 3,* 213–240.

Rogers, E. M. (1983). *Diffusion of innovations* (3rd ed.). New York: Free Press.

Steuer, J. (1992). Defining virtual reality: Dimensions determining telepresence. *Journal of Communication, 42,* 73–93.

Tichenor, P. J., Donohue, G. A., & Olien, C. N. (1970). Mass media and differential growth in knowledge. *Public Opinion Quarterly, 34,* 158–170.

Suggested Readings

Bryant, J., & Zillman, D. (2002). *Media effects: Advances in theory and research.* Mahwah, NJ: Erlbaum.

Chaffee, S. H. (1991). *Communication concepts 1: Explication.* Newbury Park, CA: Sage.

Hempel, C. G. (1952). *Fundamentals of concept formation in empirical science.* Chicago: University of Chicago Press.

Shoemaker, P. J., Tankard, J. W., Jr., & Lasorsa D. L. (2004). *How to build social science theories.* Thousand Oaks, CA: Sage.

Stinchcombe, A. L. (1968). *Constructing social theories.* New York: Harcourt, Brace & World.

3

THINKING QUANTITATIVELY

Michael J. Beatty

What are the components of competent interpersonal communication? What factors contribute to perceptions of political candidates' credibility? What vocal characteristics are associated with confidence? Communication scholars seek to answer or uncover clues pertaining to these and a myriad of other questions about communication. Sometimes research is conducted for the purpose of testing existing theories, or to produce data to construct new ones. At other times, research is designed to answer immediate, practical questions or to provide information critical to problem solving.

Underlying any research project, regardless of its intended purpose, are assumptions about what constitutes knowledge. These assumptions, known as **epistemological assumptions,** are foundational in the development of criteria for assessing the value or worth of data generated by research. Since the late 1960s, many communication scholars have embraced epistemological assumptions consistent with a scientific approach to the study of communication. Adopting a scientific perspective inevitably leads to the subject matter of this chapter, thinking quantitatively.

This chapter explores how quantitatively oriented communication scholars think—and why they think as they do. Earlier chapters focused on establishing a theoretical base for communication study; this chapter and the next explore how scholars test their theories. Perhaps quantitative thinking within a scientific paradigm can best be appreciated against the backdrop of alternative ways of answering questions about communication. As a starting point, let us examine nonscientific alternatives along with the reasons why they are rejected by scholars working from a scientific perspective.

Unscientific Sources of Knowledge about Communication

The alternatives to scientific knowledge acquisition are intuition, tradition, common sense, personal experience, authority, and rationalism (Kerlinger, 1986). Scientists do not assert that these widespread sources of opinion are without value. At times, each provides reasonably accurate and informative perspectives to questions. Knowledge sources must be evaluated more rigorously than by casually observing that they are sometimes accurate; a stopped watch displays time accurately twice in a 24-hour period—but it is nevertheless stopped. Scientists consider the **potential** for being misled when assessing the merits of any method for gaining knowledge, looking for logical weaknesses, as well as dependence on subjective human judgments. Mindful of these criteria for evaluating knowledge sources, we will examine each unscientific approach.

Intuition

Intuition commonly functions as a source of unscientific information about communication. By **intuition,** we mean vague feelings, sometimes referred to as **gut reactions.** When we distrust a person without reason, enter into a contract because we "have a good feeling about it," or feel that the media are too liberal, we are using intuition.

One problem with intuition as a knowledge source is that our intuitions are often wrong. To illustrate, when we ask college students what they would do if they learned that their spouse was having an affair, almost all report that they would terminate the marriage. However, research shows that in most instances the relationships do not end after infidelity is discovered, and in the cases that do, it is the unfaithful spouse who usually initiates divorce proceedings. Complicating matters, our memories are often highly selective; we conveniently forget when we are wrong, thereby leading to a false confidence in intuition.

A second problem arises because intuitions are feeling-based. Mood—and a host of other psychological and physiological factors—influence intuition. For example, ample evidence shows that we tend to evaluate opposite sex strangers more positively when our first encounter takes place in an aesthetically pleasing, comfortable room than when initial meetings occur in an ugly, uncomfortable space (Maslow & Mintz, 1956). Research also shows that most people are unaware of contextual effects on intuition. Finally, ask five people to make predictions based on intuition and we are likely to receive five different answers. We simply cannot place enough confidence in intuition to accept it as a source of information about communication.

Tenacity

A second source of information, known as **tradition** or **tenacity**, includes unquestioned belief in superstitions, truisms, and myths. These forms of knowledge are often passed from generation to generation through cultural mechanisms such as family, media, and religious and educational institutions. As an information source, tenacity is pervasive. Like intuition, however, many tenaciously held beliefs are inaccurate. For instance, at one time everyone held tenaciously to the beliefs that the Earth was flat; that the sun revolved around the earth; that applying leeches to the ill was good medical practice; and that Salem, Massachusetts was plagued with witches. Scientific breakthroughs in medicine, physics, and genetics, to name a few disciplines, continually expose the erroneous nature of previously held beliefs. Moreover, across and within cultures there is considerable variance in perspectives: What seems obvious to one social group is often rejected as ludicrous by another. Tenacity, like intuition, is an unacceptable way to answer communication questions.

Common Sense

Common sense, a third unscientific way of knowing, consists of generating what appear to be obvious answers to communication questions. Appeals to this source of knowledge are accompanied by prefacing or supporting remarks such as "it's obvious that…," "everybody knows…," "any halfway intelligent person can see that…," or "it's just common sense." Common sense, however, is often wrong; people often disagree about what constitutes the commonsense thing to do in a particular situation. Furthermore, communication problems abound for which common sense provides no insight. This is particularly true for complex problems. For example, although some children raised by verbally abusive parents become verbally abusive parents as adults, many do not. What factors inhibit or encourage intergenerational transfer of parenting behaviors? There exist no commonsense answers to such questions.

Personal Experience

Personal experience is often used as a knowledge source. We possess a wealth of personal experiences and—while experience is an extremely valuable resource—there are three reasons to be cautious about deriving knowledge claims about communication based on experiences. First, personal experience is both subjective and uncontrolled, leaving us susceptible to misperception and misinterpretation of events. While we are limited in the amount of information we can process, the quantity of stimuli in any given situation is virtually unlimited. As noted earlier, we often attend to events and stimuli selectively: We simply do not, and we cannot pay attention to every sound; we don't notice everything there is to see; some things go undetected. Rather, we attend to some stimuli and block out others, some of what we do hear, we hear incorrectly, yielding an experience that is necessarily incomplete and often inaccurate as well.

Second, we selectively remember characteristics of experience. Anyone who has ever studied for a college examination realizes that some of the subject matter, although we read it and perhaps even hear it in lecture, was somehow inaccessible on exam day. Thus, our memories of events are incomplete and often inaccurate. Problematic also is that selectivity is often driven by strong preconceptions. That is, we often attend, perceive, accept, and recall data that confirm our beliefs and attitudes whereas we tend to ignore, distort, discount, and forget data which disconfirm our beliefs and attitudes.

Finally, even if we could hone our perceptual skills so that all stimuli could be processed accurately, and fully retrieved on demand, our conclusions would not necessarily be consistent with the experiences of others. Factors such as communication competence level, physical attractiveness, vocal characteristics, social status, media use, and so forth might lead to different outcomes, even if we said and did everything identically. Overall, personal experience falls short of the mark as a knowledge source.

Authority

A fifth unscientific source of knowledge, **authority**, consists of appealing to experts for answers to our questions. We are surrounded by experts and authorities: professors, physicians, attorneys, journalists, economic advisors, stockbrokers, marriage counselors, automobile mechanics, and news anchors, to name but a few. Although experts frequently provide valuable service, there is often disagreement among them, and, of course, they can be wrong. A more important issue for our discussion, however, concerns how the experts gained their knowledge in the first place. If their knowledge was acquired through intuition, tenacity, or experience, it is subject to many of the caveats already mentioned. Assuming that an expert's knowledge is the product of scientific inquiry, it is the scientific inquiry—not the expert—that is the source of the knowledge. Well informed experts can disseminate knowledge but they are not acceptable as progenitors of it.

Rationalism

A final unscientific way of deriving answers is through rationalism, or logic, usually in the form of deduction. Accordingly, knowledge takes the form of conclusions, which are deduced from premises. For example, suppose that (1) supportive messages usually produce positive emotions in receivers, and that (2) positive emotional experiences usually produce interpersonal attraction. Applying logic we would conclude, therefore, that supportive messages usually produce interpersonal attraction.

Two major problems are associated with rationalism as a source of knowledge. First, we must consider how the truth of the premises was determined. Logic cannot produce premises, and without valid premises, sound conclusions cannot be deduced. Second, if we apply logic in this form to syllogisms consisting of premises that are not absolutely true, erroneous conclusions can be deduced even when strictly adhering to the rules of deduction. Reconsider our example. For convenience suppose that by usually, we mean 70 percent of the time. Thus, the probability of supportive statements resulting in positive receiver affect is .70, and the probability of positive emotions leading to interpersonal attraction is also .70. What then is the probability that supportive messages lead receivers to be attracted to the source of those messages? The correct answer is calculated by multiplying the probabilities for the two separate premises (i.e., $.70 \times .70 = .49$). To say that one of two events is more likely to occur than the other requires a probability greater than .50. In contrast to the logically drawn conclusion, our calculation indicates that if we had to predict whether supportive statements produce interpersonal attraction, the more accurate prediction would be that, more often than not, supportive messages do not produce interpersonal attraction.

Logicians have devised methods under the rubric of quantifiable logic for syllogisms in which premises vary in the degree to which they hold true. However, logic itself does not provide those crucial probability estimates; nor does it produce the premises. While logic is an essential tool used by scientists, it alone is insufficient as a knowledge source because its use requires existing knowledge in the form of premises.

Thinking Quantitatively in a Scientific Perspective

As hinted throughout this brief review of the unscientific sources of knowledge, we need a more precise and objective approach to generating knowledge. This leads us to consideration of the scientific perspective to knowledge acquisition and the role of quantitative thinking within that perspective.

Regardless of field of study, the activities of scholars committed to a scientific approach to generating answers to questions, whether theoretical or practical in nature, can almost always be described in terms of a five-step process known as the **scientific method.** It is, therefore, instructive to briefly review the steps with special focus on how they differ from unscientific ways of gaining knowledge and how quantitative thinking is central to performing those steps. The scientific method consists of the following five steps: (1) observe a phenomenon that needs to be explained; (2) construct provisional explanations or pose hypotheses; (3) design an adequate test of the hypotheses; (4) execute the test; and (5) accept, reject, or modify our hypotheses based on the outcome of our test.

Curiosity

The first step describes a basic characteristic of scientific thinking, **curiosity**. We notice that some people enjoy public speaking whereas others experience considerable apprehension and dread at the mere prospect of it. We notice, for instance, that some people seem to imitate what they see in the media, while others do not. We notice that some achieve more popularity in social situations than do others. When we focus on such observations and feel compelled to explain them, we have engaged in the first step of the scientific method. As noted in chapter 2, at this point, scholars engage in an exhaustive survey of existing research seeking an existing explanation. If one cannot be found, they move to the next step.

Conceptualizing

It is at the second step, **conceptualizing** (constructing provisional explanations), that we begin to differentiate scientific from unscientific thinking. Not having found an explanation for a phenomenon, scholars look for clues in existing research. Under a scientific framework, input from intuition, tradition, experience, common sense, experts, and logic might be incorporated during the construction of provisional explanations, but we do not, at this point, accept the validity of those explanations. Suppose that we felt compelled to explain why people differ regarding fear of public speaking. Assume that a review of the research literature provides no insight whatsoever. When we think about the times we made presentations to an audience, it seems that we were most nervous when we were unprepared. Our provisional explanations begin to take shape. We suspect that preparation underlies confidence. This explanation squares with conclusions drawn from other unscientific sources. Based on our personal experiences we propose a tentative hypothesis: Speakers who are prepared will experience less fear while delivering a speech than speakers who are unprepared.

Operationalizing

Upon constructing a hypothesis, the scientist moves to the third step, **operationalizing**; constructing an adequate test of it. This phase further differentiates scientific and unscientific thinking and, furthermore, the role of quantitative thinking becomes profoundly evident.

In the simplest sense, quantitative thinking means attaching numerical values to concepts. Actually, we think quantitatively every day. When we request an estimate for automobile repair, ask about salary on a job interview, or inquire about delivery time for a new purchase, we expect quantitative answers. Responses such as "the cost will be reasonable," "the salary is good," and "it won't take too long" are usually unsatisfactory; they are vague responses and do not facilitate our decision making. We want the answers regarding costs to be quantified in terms of dollars and those concerning time to be quantified in terms of days or hours. Clearly, such estimates will be somewhat inaccurate. We understand that quantified answers are only estimates and we expect them to be imperfect. Obviously, precise estimates are ideal. However, we know that reasonably accurate estimates are more useful in our decision making and planning than no estimate at all.

Returning to our speaking example, an adequate test of the hypothesis involves comparing the fear levels of prepared and unprepared speakers. However, several practical questions arise with respect to designing our test. Exactly how much preparation is required to achieve a "prepared" state? Do we mean an hour, a day, a week? Should we include groups of speakers engaged in various amounts of preparation? How many prepared and unprepared speakers should we sample to provide a fair test? How should we determine speakers' levels of nervousness? Do we think that people are either nervous or calm (a dichotomous measure) or do we think there are degrees of nervousness (a continuous measure)? When we ask people to report their degree of nervousness, should we use a scale from 1 to 10 (a self-report measure), or should we monitor some physiological responses during speeches (a direct observation measure)? How long should the presentations be; how large the audience?

The preceding questions are but a few examples of the types of decisions requiring quantitative thinking. While methods for dealing with these types of design questions are the subject matter of entire series of books and sequences of courses, our focus is only on the significance of quantitative approaches to making these important choices.

Characteristic of scientific endeavor are detailed and specific definitions of crucial variables. These definitions are termed **operational definitions.** Carefully describing the type and duration of preparation and the other variables in our study provides a clear picture of our experiment for others. In this way, other researchers interested in the phenomenon we investigated can comprehend exactly what we meant by **preparation, audience,** and so forth. Furthermore, clear operational definitions permit others to replicate our study. That is, they can conduct it for themselves, checking our results or making small modifications in the design to fit their interpretations of our results.

In addition to being specific, scholars operating under a scientific perspective are obligated to provide evidence for the **validity** and **reliability** of operational definitions. Therefore, in our public speaking study, we would be obligated to show that the questionnaire we used to measure nervousness does in fact measure nervousness (is valid) and does so consistently time after time (is reliable). We would be obligated to show that the speakers in our study actually prepared for the duration we assert. Likewise, we would be obligated to show that the audience size and speaking task were representative of what we normally expect in public speaking situations. (Would we accept as a "typical public speaking situation" a person sitting at a desk, speaking for one minute about the weather to one other person?) There are bound to be numerous reasonable and, therefore, valid ways to operationalize variables. Clearly, no single study will include all possible ways to define variables. Key, however, to scientific inquiry is the researcher's acceptance of the responsibility for providing clear, valid, operational definitions. This is not to say that we must agree with researchers' decisions. We are free to define the same variables in other ways, provided that we can present valid evidence for our definitions. Of importance is the public nature of those definitions, the clarity of which is greatly enhanced when expressed in quantitative terms (e.g., "The audience consisted of 24 undergraduate college students, 12 males and 12 females").

Designing and Executing the Test

Another feature of the scientific method is the testing of hypotheses that take care to control the influences of other, extraneous variables. Within a scientific paradigm, the researcher accepts the responsibility for ensuring that the observed effects are not due to some other variable. Suppose that in our public speaking study the unprepared speakers all happen to have clinical neuroses, whereas the prepared group was emotionally stable. In such a case we could never be completely sure whether preparation really was the cause of nervousness during public speaking. That is, neurotic individuals might always experience fear whether they are prepared or not. Conversely, unprepared emotionally stable individuals might not experience nervousness during a speech although their performance might suffer. Therefore, scientists must rule out **all** competing explanations.

If we suspected that individuals' neuroses might **confound** our findings we could control for its effects through matching, covariance, randomization, or experimental control. For example, we could administer a "neuroses test" to all speakers and make sure that stable people and people with neuroses were equally represented in both prepared and unprepared conditions.[1] If we were able to place speakers in the prepared and unprepared speech situations so that the set of neuroses scores in one speech situation was the same as that in the other, we would be using a *matched design* for the study.

A second way to control for neuroticism effects would be to employ a statistical technique called *covariance analysis*. A comprehensive explanation of this technique is beyond the scope of this chapter.[2] Briefly, however, it permits researchers to estimate the effects of one variable (such as preparedness) on another (such as nervousness during speaking) over and beyond any effect to a variable that needs to be controlled (such as existence of neuroses).

Although the preceding methods of controlling variables are widely used in the behavioral sciences, they are restricted in some significant ways. Specifically, researchers must suspect that a particular variable will contaminate the results (through a review of existing literature) and that a limited number of variables can be controlled through matching or covariance analysis. The most powerful form of controlling differences among people in a sample is *randomization*. If we select a sufficiently large sample (e.g., 200 speakers) and randomly assign them to either the prepared or unprepared condition, we will have distributed the extraneous variables so that they are equally represented in both speaking conditions. In other words, rather than actively controlling for extraneous variables, we randomly assign participants to the different conditions on the assumption that the effects of all extraneous variables (both known and unknown) are equally distributed among participants in different groups.

Another way to neutralize extraneous variables is through *experimental control*, holding certain factors constant. For instance, in our study, we might make sure that all speeches were delivered in the same room, under similar conditions (e.g., lectern versus no lectern, audience size and feedback, etc.). An appropriate test of the effects of any variable requires testing under comparable conditions. If the unprepared group, in fact, performs in a cold room, without a lectern, to an inattentive, unresponsive audience but the prepared group speaks from behind a lectern, in a comfortable room, to a receptive audience, the effects of preparation have not been fairly and adequately tested. Indeed, the different conditions, singularly or in combination, cannot be ruled out and therefore remain as competing explanations for the speakers' levels of nervousness.

Scientific scholars, thinking about tentative explanations quantitatively, provide clear definitions of variables, offer evidence for their validity, and exert control over as many extraneous factors as possible. They attempt to provide fair and adequate tests of their hypotheses. Once accomplished, they execute the study.

Analysis and Interpreting Data

The final stage of the scientific process calls for the rejection, acceptance, or modification of the explanation based on an analysis of the data. During this step the role of quantitative thinking is paramount because the analyses of the data are based on statistical procedures.

The Concept of Variance

To understand why statistical analyses are essential to a scientific approach to communication research, consider the alternative to our nervousness/public speaking study. We have strong validity evidence for our variables and we accomplished control through randomization in our study's design. Furthermore, the study was conducted without fault. Therefore, we examine the nervousness scores, which we will assume ranged from 0 to 100, for prepared and unprepared speakers, and we observe that, although the average score for the prepared group is lower than that of the unprepared group, there is considerable dispersion, termed *variance,* among nervousness scores within each group. That is, we note that some prepared speakers report nervousness scores as low as 0 but others report scores as high as 52. Similarly, the scores reported by unprepared speakers range from 50 to 100. Furthermore, as our inspection of the data shows, a few prepared speakers were *more* nervous than some of the unprepared speakers. What should we conclude about the test of our hypothesis that preparation determines speakers' nervousness?

Before a scientific interpretation of the data can be offered, we must be attentive to possible sources of the variance in scores within prepared and unprepared groups of speakers. The categories that follow apply to all sorts of studies. However, it would be instructive to relate each to our sample study. Part of the variance in scores is attributable to *sampling error*. Despite our efforts to assign speakers to prepared and unprepared groups on a random basis, some differences between comparison groups are bound to happen in any study due to chance. Part of the variance is attributable to *measurement error*. No matter how rigorously we measure variables, our estimates of them are inherently imperfect. Our questionnaires, for example, might include words or phrases that are interpreted by some respondents in a manner different than we intended. Part of the variance is attributable to *design error*. Although substantial effort is expended to collect data under conditions that approximate the contexts and situations of interest, data collection environments are always imperfect. Perhaps the speaking task was too short to stimulate fear in some of the participants. Finally, some of the variance could represent *real error*. If preparation is not a determinant or is only one of the determinants of nervousness, our hypothesis is at least partially in error.

Statistical Significance and Magnitude of Effects

In light of the aforementioned set of issues, how can the test of the hypothesis be interpreted in an objective and adequate manner? Statistical analyses provide systematic procedures for accounting for the sources of variance or error in data. The various statistical tests permit researchers to separate the effect of the explanatory variable or variables (preparedness in our example) from the effects of the error sources.

Through statistical analyses we are able to estimate the probability that our findings are due to chance, instead of the explanatory variable or variables. These probability estimates are known as *significance* levels—frequently reported in the form, p < .05, which means that the probability of the findings being due to chance is less than 5 in 100 (or 1 in 20). This particular level, referred to as the .05 level of statistical significance, has traditionally served as the standard for accepting data as evidence for the hypothesis in most social science disciplines. When scholars refer to their findings as statistically significant, they mean the probability that their observed pattern of results is due to chance is no more than 5 in 100.

There are two basic mistakes, however, that researchers can make when interpreting statistical tests. They can claim a hypothesized difference exists when it truly does not (called *Type I error*) or they can claim a hypothesized difference does not exist when it actually does (called *Type II error*). Researchers try to avoid each by first ensuring that they have enough observations (participants) to adequately have sampled the population they are observing and examining by statistical means the *power* of their tests (which indicates whether or not a nonsupported hypothesis failed to be supported because there were no actual differences or because there were insufficient participants to adequately test whatever relationship was hypothesized). In general, the larger the sample size, the more powerful the statistical tests.

Furthermore, we can estimate the portion of the effect that is specifically attributable to the explanatory variable(s). When scholars report "variance explained" (or "accounted for"), the square of correlation coefficients (r^2), eta (η) or omega square (ω^2), or the d statistic, they are informing us about the relative magnitude of the explanatory variable(s)' impact. That is, how much the variables explain—or do not explain (i.e., $1 - r^2$ = variance unexplained)—the changes in the variables of interest.

In sum, the linchpin of quantitative thinking is statistical analysis. Although the example used throughout this chapter depicts an admittedly simplistic conceptualization of a complex communication problem, it served only to illustrate a process. In reality, statistical analyses have been designed to handle multiple explanatory and outcome variables, as well as complex relationships between and among variables.[3]

Depending on the outcome of our statistical analysis, we are positioned to interpret the results of our test and evaluate our hypothesis. Perhaps we found that the difference in nervousness scores was statistically significant, and that virtually all of the difference between the average nervousness scores for the two groups was attributable to whether the speakers were prepared. In other words, there is strong support for the hypotheses, indicating evidence for our explanation. Perhaps the differences were statistically significant but the variance explained in nervousness scores due to preparation was small. Assuming we were attentive to sources of error discussed above, we might modify our hypothesis by suggesting that preparation affects nervousness, but additional variables must be studied to better explain why some people are nervous and others are confident during public speaking. Perhaps we found that our results were not significant: The differences between prepared and unprepared speakers large enough to reject chance as a plausible explanation. Because there are numerous criteria regarding research design and statistical analysis that must be satisfied before it can be concluded that a variable or set of variables has no effect on another, scholars usually conclude that they failed to support the hypothesis in such cases. Thinking quantitatively about the analyses of hypotheses makes it possible to clearly articulate the bases for evaluations of hypotheses and the theoretical speculation from which they emerged.

Concluding Remarks

At the outset of this chapter, the point was made that the aim of research was to answer questions about communication. Research conducted from a scientific point of view is well-rooted in the field of communication and has been a rich source of information about a broad range of subject matter. Although numerous processes contribute to the formation of ideas, questions, and hypotheses about communication, scientific endeavor is required to verify or validate those hypotheses. Regardless of how intriguing a particular notion about communication might be, untestable hypotheses are of little use to scholars building theories of communication from a scientific perspective.

Adopting a scientific perspective commits scholars to thinking quantitatively in several ways. It requires us to think quantitatively when defining and measuring concepts, describing relationships between variables in precise mathematical terms, and assessing the merit of hypotheses.

This chapter should not be construed as suggesting that a quantitative approach to communication inquiry is easily accomplished or is somehow objective, straightforward, and always accurate in its conclusions. Without question, the history of social science, communication included, is replete with findings that were later amended or substantially qualified in some way. On the contrary, quantifying communication concepts is a messy business often rewarded by criticism and controversy. However, scientific progress is inevitably incremental, requiring programs of research which refine and extend prior work. Rarely, if ever, are single studies sufficient as sources of scientifically derived knowledge. Instead, hypotheses are retested employing different samples, operational definitions, and research designs. As mentioned, many times findings do not hold up across studies.

Indeed, the vast majority of scholars who are committed to a scientific perspective are painfully aware that quantitative methods are often imperfect. However, we also recognize that quantitative analysis is an indispensable tool in the study of human communication and, as with any tool, its ultimate value depends on the motivations and competence of its user. From a scientific perspective, deeper and more comprehensive understanding of human communication will follow deeper and more comprehensive understanding and application of all aspects of scientific methodology.

Notes

1. There are a variety of tests available for measuring variables. See, for example, Miller (1983) or Rubin, Palmgreen, and Sypher (1994).
2. See Kerlinger (1986); Hocking, Stacks, and McDermott (2003); and Wimmer and Dominic (1994) for more comprehensive treatments.
3. For an excellent overview, see Williams and Monge (2003).

References

Hocking, J. E., Stacks, D. W., & McDermott, S. T. (2003). *Essentials of communication* research (3rd ed.). New York: Allyn & Bacon.

Kerlinger, F. N. (1986). *Foundations of behavioral research* (3rd ed). New York: Holt, Rinehart & Winston.

Maslow, A. H., & Mintz, N. L. (1956). Effects of esthetic surroundings: I. Initial effects of three esthetic conditions upon perceiving "energy" and "well-being" in faces. *Journal of Psychology, 41,* 247–254.

Miller, D. C. (1983). *Handbook of research design and social measurement.* New York: Longman.

Rubin, R. B., Palmgreen, P., & Sypher, H. E. (Eds.). (1994). *Communication research measures.* New York: Guilford.

Williams, F. N., & Monge, P. G. (2003). *Reasoning with statistics* (5th ed.). New York: Holt, Rinehart & Winston.

Wimmer, R. D., & Dominick, J. R. (1994). *Mass media research: An introduction* (4th ed.). Belmont, CA: Wadsworth.

Suggested Readings

Bickman, L. (Ed.) (2000). *Research design: Donald Campbell's legacy.* Thousand Oaks, CA:Sage.

Hayes, A. F. (2005). *Statistical methods for communication science.* Mahwah, NJ: Erlbaum.

Kerlinger, F. N., & Lee, H. B. (2000). *Foundations of behavioral research* (4th ed.). Orlando, FL: Harcourt.

Kirk, R. E. (1995). *Experimental design: Procedures for the behavioral sciences* (3rd ed.). Pacific Grove, CA:Brooks/Cole.

4

THINKING QUALITATIVELY

Hermeneutics in Science

James A. Anderson

Qualitative research is a most lively signifier. It is used to indicate a set of text-based or observational methods that are themselves used as companions to quantitative methods (Wilk, 2001). It is used to point to an independent set of methodologies that can be used with or without quantitative methods, but remain within the same epistemological framework (e.g., Chick, 2000). Finally it is used to designate an entirely different paradigm of science that is not only independent of quantitative methods but also of its epistemological foundation (Denzin & Lincoln, 1994).

The term "qualitative" itself is more than a little ambiguous. Let's clear it up a bit. "Qualia" is the term cognitivists and philosophers alike use to refer to the products of consciousness—the distinctions, connections, modulations, intentionalities by which we make sense of the world (Sturgeon, 1994). On the other side, there are qualities. The qualities assigned to qualitative research appear to be characteristics that do not have material, objective boundaries, and whose identity and identification requires some judgment to be applied—what philosophers have long called "secondary qualities" (Walcott, 1926).[1] A quality of this sort appears in the interaction between an object and a mind—quality and qualia. A quality is necessarily subjective; it requires a judgment to appear. It is, however, not idiosyncratic—it is not dependent on a particular individual's judgment.

In the first two uses of the term "qualitative research," we regularly turn qualities into quantities (units of things) through coding. Coding is the assignment of a value to a textual segment as in content analysis, to a pictorial element in a visual analysis, to an interaction as in interaction analysis, to a conversational fragment in a narrative analysis, to an action routine in an episodic analysis, and the like. When the coding is done by multiple coders (and there is sufficient agreement among them) the assigned values take on objective characteristics and conventional quantitative analyses can be applied. The analysis is conducted over the codes and the original, foundational texts of words, conversations, discourses, pictures, video, interactions, and so forth, recede from the analysis. One can say that the subjective is conventionalized through the rules and procedures of the coding.

If one looks at it carefully within these first two uses of the term, qualitative, the only difference between qualitative and quantitative methods is that quantification occurs at different stages and by different personnel in the research process. In quantitative measurements—the typical scales of these methods—quantification is produced in the data collection by the respondent as governed by the scalar forms developed by the researcher. In qualitative measurements, quantification is conducted after data collection through the coding process and is done by the research staff according to the rules developed by the researcher. Researchers can talk about using quantitative and qualitative methods to triangulate to a common concept or to use multiple methods to address a common research question because the epistemological framework that supports these methodologies is the same.

Paradigmatic Qualitative Research

This is all good stuff but it has little to do with paradigmatic qualitative research. The qualitative research that I want to write about is not some set of methods like case studies or long-form interviews whose applications are either companionable or consistent with quantitative research, but rather a particular paradigm in the scientific study of human action. This chapter, then, will be primarily concerned with the characteristics and boundaries of the paradigm variously known as qualitative research, naturalistic inquiry, the interpretive turn, or hermeneutic empiricism. It will redraw the science of human inquiry in the image of this old but now reinvigorated paradigm that provided the science of Charles Sanders Peirce, Max Weber, George Herbert Mead, John Dewey, and Talcott Parsons and the researchers in the Chicago School.[2]

Communication scholars employing a hermeneutic science approach seek to test their theories in light of daily events, in commonly placed situations, framed by the interaction of their participants. This approach focuses on the "accounts of everyday life" (Stacks, Hickson, & Hill, 1991, p. 306). Hermeneutics is the method through which theorists seek to discover the "conscious experience of communication."

Philosophical Assumptions

To understand qualitative thinking we must first examine its general philosophical approach and the phenomenological assumptions under girding hermeneutic research. Let me start by dividing the real into two parts: one that is constructed of material conditions and the other that is constructed of social practices. In this division gravity is a material condition, but the law of gravity, which is the publicly agreed upon explanation for gravity, is the product of social practices. Gravity will not change under our current material conditions, but the law of gravity would immediately change if the collective of science decided on what it considered to be a better explanation. Qualitative research starts with the assumption that its proper object is that portion of the reality in which we live that is socially constructed.

One of the characteristics of the socially constructed real is that it is produced through material, social, semiotic practices and continues to be real only as long as those practices persist. In the United States, we drive on the right side of the road. We do that not because of some material requirement of motion but because of socially enacted traffic law, custom, and practice. For example, in the city, we build thoroughfares that are wide enough to have a right and left side. If you live in the wilds of the country, there are roads too narrow to have sides. Urban realities no longer apply. You will make a life-threatening mistake if you think you have the right-of-way when local practice dictates that you don't.

Socially constructed realities create two levels of analysis. Not only does the analyst want to know the characteristics of the real (the rules of the road in our example) but also the material practices by which the real is produced and sustained. Consider in our example, the millions of dollars and huge effort expended in driver training, licensing, lane striping, traffic signs, law enforcement, adjudication, and so forth. Consequently if one makes a claim of what something is (an ontological claim), one must also be prepared to explain how it comes into existence (a praxeological claim). The claims of what something is and how it comes to be produces the explanation of why it works the way it does (the ultimate epistemological claim).

Social constructions also shift the location of the explanation. In metric[3] empiricism (my term for quantitative research), explanation must be located in the individual (an epistemological requirement known as methodological individualism). What this means is that everything needed to explain some activity of the individual must be found within the boundaries of the individual. This requirement for good explanation is why such theoretical structures as attitudes, scripts, and schemata have developed because they are contained within the mind of the individual and not yet through direct social practices.

In hermeneutic empiricism (let me use these two forms—metric empiricism (ME) and hermeneutic empiricism (HE)—to underscore the paradigmatic nature of our discussion) the location for good explanation is in social practices (an epistemological requirement known as methodological holism). So what difference does it make? In the typical cognitive theory that is the engine for most of ME, I drive on the right side of the road because I have an embedded script (from all that driver training) that tells me to drive on the right side of the road. In HE, I drive on the right side of the road because *you* drive on the right side of the road. There is nothing like headlights coming at you to enforce behavior.[4]

There are two other distinctions that have to be made between ME and HE. Both of these differences have to do with the characteristic explanation that is produced by each form. Metric empiricism works from a metric logic of quantities and rates, similarities and differences, dependence and independence, operations and results. It depends on "things." "Things" (it's a technical term) have clear boundaries (thing and not thing) and mutually exclusive characteristics (thing 1 not thing 2). One can count things, measure their boundaries, figure their proportion among other things, and so on to create all the sorts of information that we find in the ME explanation.

Socially constructed things have an uncertain existence; they depend on social practices for their ontology—for their "beingness." What is an act of violence? What is a virgin? What is a commercial? What is a subordinate? Certainly we can provide definitions for each of these; the point is that we have to provide definitions for each. Their "thingness" is socially constructed and exists only as long as others agree. Race was once a biological certainty, now it is a self-designation, but in both cases it is the product of the material practices of distinction. Race disappears when it no longer matters. The question for HE, then, is "How do we make it matter?" What is the narrative line in action and discourse that sustains the existence of socially constructed concepts such as race?[5]

Hermeneutic empiricism, then, works from a narrative logic of routines and actions, critical instances and episodes, conversation and discourse, text and practice. Narrative logic depends on the quality of the story that can be told. Stories have agents that both generate the action and represent some cultural understanding. They have recognizable action that has a beginning, middle, and end. They have motive, intentionality, and consequence. The hermeneutic empiricist both tells the story and interprets it.

The last of these scene-setting distinctions has to do with the goal of the paradigmatic science. The epistemological foundation for metric empiricism invokes a process of increasing precision of description of some independent, objective condition. The goal is to arrive at the final statement about something. We want a transcendental law that holds for all conditions within the scope of the law. That still leaves us with a lot of wiggle room for new work but ultimately a topic can become settled. There is no need to do additional work (and it won't be accepted in the public record anyway). The narrative work of hermeneutic empiricism is built on a different epistemological foundation—one that holds that knowledge is itself socially constructed, universally expanding, and limited only by our interest and enthusiasm for achieving a new narrative on the topic. There is no final answer, only an increasing density of narrative.

That density of narrative itself is a player in the socially constructed reality that it intends to explain. It is one of the practical resources that bring that reality into existence. As a participant in the social construction, it bears some of the responsibility for the consequences of the reality so constructed. It is a co-conspirator if you will. The claim that science is a player in the reality it studies thrusts new responsibilities on the scientific endeavor. For the past 350 years or so since the writings of David Hume, the Scottish empirical philosopher, science has been given a free pass to say whatever it thought to be true without entailing any responsibility for the consequences of the claim.

The principle of social construction changes everything, because it introduces the constituting action of science. And here we clearly leave the look-see-write domain of objectivist ethnography. Because science participates in the social processes by which something else comes into existence, which in turn is the object of scientific study, science helps to create the very set of conditions that it sets out to study. For example, if we develop a test for communication competency (the test being a practice of the scientific study of competency) and it is accepted by the communication discipline (the acceptance being the social process of reality construction) communication competency is the test that we developed. If our test systematically privileges certain cultural characteristics (such as intelligence tests are claimed to do), we are to be held responsible for damage done. It can't be our fault, however, if there is no constituting action—if the terms of our test are determined by the objective reality of competence. So, indeed social construction changes everything.

This newfound responsibility for the consequences of what is claimed to be true also introduces the critical into science. The critical in the study of human action is determined to pursue social justice. Consequently science is not only held responsible for the bad that might intentionally or unintentionally accrue to its findings, it is also responsible for pursuing the good. For many this is an unacceptable formulation of science. It would appear to return us to the pre-Enlightenment days when science was in the service of a dominant religio-political ideology. The answer to that objection is that science has always been in the service of the dominant ideology (where did you think the money came from). What has saved science and what will allow this formulation of science has not been some unique connection to the true, but the twin principles of public presentation and critical review. What Karl Popper (1959) calls "critical rationalism" and what might now be called public (rather than self) reflexivity (Kobayashi, 2003). A publicly reflexive science (one that looks back on itself as an object of study) accepts its constituting action and enters the public struggle to attain the good (Erickson & Gutierrez, 2002).

Theory in Hermeneutic Empiricism

We have been redrawing the fundamental character of the study of human action to open up the space for a different kind of science—one that is constituting, and reflexive (rather than deterministic and objective). That kind of science in turn requires us to rethink the theories that we use to formulate research. Very simply, the typical cognitivist theories of ME just won't do. Theories appropriate to HE will have the following seven characteristics.

Multiple Domains of Experience

Human engagement of the phenomenal world occurs across multiple domains (Roth, 1987). We are first of all material entities in a physical world. We are also living organisms giving expression to the principles of animation. But, we inhabit yet another domain—the domain of the sign. It is within this semiotic domain that we make sense of ourselves, our world, and our manner of being in it (Peirce, 1931, 1932, 1958; Popper & Eccles, 1977).

A Grant of Understanding

Hermeneutic theories generally hold that human behavior is organized in action signs which are understandable as indicative of what is being done. Human behavior is always a symbolic expression, never simply an objective fact (Alvesson, 2003; Benwell, 2005; Parsons, 1937; Schutz, 1965; Weber, 1974).

The Centrality of Communication

The peculiar human character arises within the semiotic domain through the practices of communication. It is managed through the iconic, discursive, and performative practices which are the resources for our communicative efforts. A study of human behavior, then, is a study of communication (Bakhtin, 1986; Bellah, Madsen, Sullivan, Swindler, & Tipton, 1985; Habermas, 1981/1984; Saville-Troike, 2002).

A Focus on Relationships Rather than Separate Entities

"Sum of the parts" arguments and methods in which individual characteristics are examined and then "added up" to make the whole are not appropriate. Human behavior is understood as dialogic emerging in the interaction between self and other (Goffman, 1959; Miller, 1982).

The Acceptance of Agency

Hermeneutic theories, while emphasizing the collective and the relational, acknowledge the contribution of the particular individual as an active, performing initiator, albeit one who is also an agent of collective understanding. Evidence and claim must preserve the individual's contribution (Newell, 1986).

An Emphasis on Historic Performances

Historic here does not mean "of the past"; it refers to the study of actual performances of identified, contributing actors. It is the researcher's job to detail the performance, the circumstances of its presentation, all that constitutes the historical frame. The researcher, then, is often directed toward the participant–observation method of ethnography (Anderson, 1991; Anderson & Goodall, 1994). There is no requirement, however, to employ those methods.

The Subjectivity of Analysis

The scientific study of the human condition is itself an expression of that condition (Bohman, 1991). Hermeneutic science would hold that truth is a human accomplishment within the semiotic domain. This truth construction accommodates the characteristics of the phenomenal world but is not determined by them (Schutz, 1965; Weber, 1974). Hermeneutic theories then—as with all theories—must be empirically adequate. From the qualitative approach, we are true to ourselves in the human truths expressed in local performances by social agents— here nominated as scientists—making politically significant and ethically accountable choices (Anderson, 1992; Barab, Thomas, Dodge, Squire, & Newell, 2004; Harding, 1986; Slembrouck, 2004).

The Conduct of Hermeneutic Empiricist Research

How does all of this come together as actual research? Studies within the domain of qualitative research often begin with interests in how something is done, the social value of an activity or symbolic resource, the meaning of an action or text, or the requirements of some consequential accomplishment. It is assumed that these interests are best explored in the everyday contexts of the actions, texts, and accomplishments. There is a resistance to—if not an outright rejection of—formal, decontextualized, or recontextualized approaches. The place of analysis is the "life-world"; and the first task is to enter the researcher into the meaning of production sites of interest. At this stage of the research we are concerned with the strategies and tactics of field methods (e.g., Buroway, 2003; Erlandson, Harris, Skipper, & Allen, 1993; Lofland, 1975).

For the past three years, I have been working to learn about the homeless, to understand the narrative of homelessness, the narratives of the homeless, and the narratives that surround and situate the homeless.[6] These are three different constructions. The first is directed toward developing an understanding of what it means to be homeless. The second is concerned with how the life (or lives as it turns out) of homelessness is lived. And the third focuses on the narratives that are external to the homeless. They break two ways: The surrounding narratives look at the way the homeless are described and understood by those of us who cross the threshold of a home each day, and the situating narratives look at the justifications for individual and institutional actions that affect the homeless.

These interests mark off several different groups of people and types of texts for engagement. To get to the meaning of homelessness and the lives that are led in it, I needed to be with the homeless. To get to the surrounding narratives of the domesticated, I needed to talk with them and examine how homelessness is dealt with in the press and popular media. And finally, to get to the situating narratives, I needed to talk with agencies, social workers, police, legislators, and the like and to investigate legislation, policies, rules, and regulations that would govern the actions of the homeless.

These represent the major methodologies of qualitative research: Participant observation will be the method of entering the life-world of the homeless, the conversational or long form interview to capture the narratives of the domesticated and the agency, and close reading strategies to work with the texts of the press, legislation, and policy.

Participant Observation

I think I finally get it. I am watching James sitting on the floor in the foyer of the women's shelter. The foyer is the space between the double set of entrance doors, just wide enough for one door to close before the next door is opened. James's "girl friend" died in the shelter yesterday, and the staff has cleared out her bunk and locker. They delivered five black garbage bags to James to sort though and dispose. As a male, James is not allowed in the waiting room, and it is bitter cold outside. (Of course, Bob and I are both males, standing behind the reception desk, but James by definition is not the same male as we.)

James looks old to me, though he may be in his 40s; he is toothless and weathered (HUD statistics tell me that less than 2 percent of the homeless are over 62). He has been someone I wanted to know, but he has always been distant and never accepted my offers of conversation. He is well known in the community of the homeless. I've watched him work the courtyard on a number of occasions. He dispenses advice, counsel, and wisdom. Knows the system, the people, and the best places. He is cordial and witty with the staff; focused and serious with the community members. He has a history that others whisper.

Today, James sits where you and I would never think of sitting, sorting through the effects of a woman called a girl friend. Five garbage bags: when my mother closed up her house we filled a 30-foot dumpster with her effects once the agencies refused to accept any more donations. What does a man without a place do with even five garbage bags of stuff?

Homelessness is both a condition and way of being in the world. Many of us have been or will be technically homeless (without a mailing address) as we hunt for an apartment or travel to a new job. Most people resolve their homelessness quickly and the episode simply becomes an (or another) interesting moment of personal history of how they slept in their car for three days when they first came to town. That sort of homelessness rarely reaches the agency level, is not counted in homelessness statistics, but can be a regular feature of transient workers.

About 700,000 people each day in the United States do reach agency recognition as homeless. These are folks, both sheltered and unsheltered (terms for being in agency facilities or not) who have made use of some agency facilities or services (beds, meals, outreach, travel services). A fairly sizeable segment of them will need extended help to get off the streets. They need shelter while they find a job or retrain into a new one. Ultimately they pass back over to the domesticated side, though many stay at risk for a repeat episode as a member of the "precariously housed."

The last group is James's group, whom the agencies call the chronically homeless. They are predominantly single, adult males. Many more of them are unsheltered than sheltered, and the two groups are very different. The estimates for Salt Lake City float between 1,000 and 5,000 chronically homeless.

As a communication scholar, I am not authorized to solve the homeless problem. But homelessness as a target for social concern and political action is indeed a communication problem. The discourse that surrounds homelessness in its various forms provides the basis for our response to and actions toward the homeless. It is my goal to complexify that discourse to make the simple narratives that support comfortable solutions untenable. I do it by having real stories—stories that were gained by being there as they unfolded in action (for more on this notion of stories and practical action see Goodall, 2004).

Entering the Scene

To gain those stories the researcher has to enter the scene. The scene of the homeless is varied and dispersed, but it has its concentrations, the camps on the river, the central city, and the agencies. I enter the scene at the agencies as a volunteer in a role that is recognizable by all and unremarkable as well.[7] The volunteer is a marginal position neither staff nor client. Turnover is high, few last more than a month. Little is expected of the volunteer, but one can go anywhere and talk to anyone. Ignorant questions are expected. It's a catbird seat.

Reading and Writing

Once the scene has been entered, the researcher works back and forth between reading and writing the scene. Reading involves the processes of making the scene sensible as a more or less coherent unity of action. Let's examine the three (reading, constructing, and action) in reverse order.

Unity of Action

The assumption of a (more or less) coherent unity exemplifies qualitative research's top-down character. This character sees human actions as more than opportunistic behaviorism or deterministic cognitivism; they are meaningful acts intentionally orientated in a larger action. The great challenge in the homeless study has been to come to understand a very alien life-world that gives meaning to the daily actions of surviving and succeeding as a member of the community of the homeless. It took a year of weekly site visitations before I was able to write field notes that cohered. It took another year before I could recognize both the community of the homeless and the possibility of success within it.

Constructing the Scene

Making the scene sensible involves the conjoint intentionalities of the agent(s) of the scene and the agent(s) of the research. When we read the sentences on this page we make sense of the textual resources provided in accordance with the local characteristics of personal identity, as well as the cultural characteristics of the subjectivity of engagement. In that intersection of resource and engagement, the text is made sensible (we might say that it is activated toward some end). In the same way, when the researcher reads the scene, her or his identity and subjectivity is present in the reading. She or he is the instrument of the work of interpretation.

Probably no other characteristic of qualitative research evokes so much controversy and confusion as the recognition that we are implicated in the explanations we provide. For the radical hermeneuticist (Caputo, 1987; Pollock, 2006), this recognition is a four square stance against even the possibility of objectivity. For the much less reconstructed grounded theorist (Glaser & Strauss, 1967, the classic reference; Strauss & Corbin, 1990 and Glaser, 1998 are the more controversial), this amounts to a recognition that, of course, someone has to do it.

Methods of Reading

Finally—and first—there is some process, some method of reading which the researcher put in place. Qualitative research of the empirical sort[8]—a distinction which separates it from cultural analysis or critical studies (Blaikie, 1993; Nakayama & Krizek, 1995; see also chapter 3, this volume)—organizes those processes hierarchically according to the directness of the researcher's experience in the action under analysis.

Remembering, then, that the experience of interest is in the meaning of things, participation is a method of reading, but participation as a member is the privileged form. Conversations, often called long-form interviews, and walking one through (sometimes called protocol analysis) are types of interactive reading that occupy the middle rungs of the hierarchy. One-way observation or the analysis of tapes is lower yet. Collecting artifacts, member-made photographs, maps, and written materials are forms of noninteractive reading that are perhaps the furthest removed from direct participation.

Concurrent with, but also extending beyond reading, are the multiple processes of writing. These processes can be further divided as "writing down" and "writing up."[9] Taking photographs, making maps, recordings, transcriptions, site notes, and field notes are forms of writing down the scene. This writing down archives the scene and creates the specimens—what Lanigan (1992) called the *capta*—for analysis.

These twin processes of reading and writing down produce the research text archived in experience, in collection, and in discursive products of various sorts. This text is read, in some method of intimacy in a process of meaning attribution and written *up* in the interpretations of representational description, referential analysis, and critique. We will spend a moment with each of those elements in the example that follows. The text that follows alternates between an exemplar product of qualitative research and a discussion of the methods which led to its production.

Ray is a staffer who loves to talk of his days in retail. He finds the great lessons of life in those experiences. Bob became a drunk, got into drunken trouble, lost his job, and was spiraling down to a permanent life on the streets. But he caught himself, sobered up, and turned his life into the service of those he almost joined. Bob and I have shared the reception desk at the family shelter, the women's shelter, and now that most off-limits location for volunteers, the men's shelter. Three staffers and I check in 218 men each evening starting at 5 p.m. Each man must be recorded as in-residence and be matched with his ID number. In the old days (yesterday), they showed you their ID card and you checked their name off the list. Today it is done by computer, to provide instant access to all the staff. But the network is excruciatingly slow and it takes minutes to clear each man. At this rate it will take three hours to get everyone housed.

The men are restless. They have been dodging the hot summer sun since 7 a.m. when the shelter puts them back on the streets. They carry what they need and what they treasure. If it is not on their back, they won't have it until the end of the day, and it might just be gone at that. At this point all they want to do is get the pack off their back and their back on the bed. Their grumbling gets a bit loud as they shift their weight waiting their turn. Bob responds in a low, level voice that carries remarkably well. "Come on guys, we don't like this either. We just have to do it." At the time I thought it was just a very effective tactic. Later I came to see it as a reflection on the command and control management of the agency.

As they pass the computer station, they line up for a bag search and to check in any tools, weapons, or implements that they carry and that could be used by them or against them. Two hundred and eighteen tired and hungry men in double bunks arranged in lines head to toe, locker storage underneath. Altercations were amazingly rare (average age was mid-forties), but they did and could happen. Bag search was my job.

It was a necessary practicality to ensure that contraband such as drugs or alcohol and dangerous items such as knives and ice picks did not make their way into the shelter. Some saw it that way, but many realized that it was just one more reminder that they were without control, anything they had was at risk of confiscation, they were not trustworthy.

The rules were that everything had to be unpacked: personal papers, books, magazines, tapes, CDs, players, cell phones, computers, snacks, toiletries, medicines, dirty clothes, clean clothes, mementos, junk that might be useful, condoms, personal lubricant, hand cleaner, lotion, sun block, lip balm, gloves, jackets, raingear, extra shoes. A self-contained life to be laid out on the inspection table. If you didn't want it examined, you couldn't have it.

A few weeks later, Ray and I are at the family desk. Ray is excited. He has gotten a promotion that will have him managing another part of the operation. He will have an office, a raise, a regular job. He has passed the tests of public and client contact on the frontlines of the reception desks. His line, "we just have to do it," comes back to me. This is just like retail.

Method of Intimacy

The primary claims advanced by qualitative methods have to do with the structures and boundaries of meaningfulness in semiotically organized systems of performance and discourse. That meaningfulness, although it is locally produced by historical agents, is neither private nor personal but is under the governance of collective effort.

Let me parse those sentences for you. "Semiotically organized systems of performance and discourse" refers to qualitative research's assumption that human action and discourse[10] are intentionally,[11] rather than randomly, produced. Watching television news, therefore, is a meaningful activity for those who produce it. It has an internal organization and boundaries of where it ends or intersects with something else.

The meaningful character of performance and discourse is the sign of what is being done; its semiotic disposition. As a sign (words, symbols, and icons are also signs) it can be used in conjunction with other signs. For example, when I write to reveal myself as the author as I did in note 10 and here, I put one discursive sign in play with another.

For something that you do to be meaningful to me takes only my intention to accomplish its meaningfulness. For something you do to stand on a common ground of meaning between us requires our *joint* discipline of sign usage—yours in its performance and mine in its interpretation.[12] We cannot accomplish this discipline without collective resources of significance, or the mechanisms, by which we can coordinate our efforts.

What a researcher observes in any particular performance or discursive product is one, local, improvised expression within a system of performance or discourse. The researcher's explanatory responsibility is not only what was done in the particular, but also how it was a meaningful expression within a system of significant action.

The interpretive task, then, is to get to the expression, and consequently some part of the system of significance, through an intimate knowledge of the details of performance. Unfortunately, qualitative procedures produce prodigious amounts of textual materials. Ethnographic studies will produce site notes, field notes, and episodes; a single 30-minute interview takes 10 to 12 pages to transcribe and the protocol analysis of a single informant will triple that amount. Add to this any collected items and the scope of the problem begins to emerge.

The methods of intimacy, despite their soft-sounding name, represent as much hard work as the field methods that precede them. They require close readings, extensive indexing, a critical illumination of the allusions and figures in discourse and performance, a sensitivity to similarities and differences as well as a deep cultural understanding to contextualize the materials.

Interpretive Representation

With the procedures of interpretive representation, we move into the domain of analytic methods to answer the initial questions of "what, how, and why" of the field. Traditional and contemporary ethnographies, just as traditional and contemporary criticism or journalism, split on the issue of representation. For the traditionalist in any of these fields it is possible to represent "the other" in objective, value free description. Contemporary theorists, however, are ardent in their rejection, pointing out that objective writing is simply a practiced means of deception which deliberately masks the political efforts advanced.

In every field experience, nonetheless, there are facts which are uncontested: this person was present or not; this conversation was held; these words were spoken in an interview. Such facts, alas, are banal. They have no meaning for the agents of their creation and the service in which they will be engaged in the ethnographic argument. The moment facts become useful, they are politicized; but they are still facts.

The result is that we talk about a "constructive empiricism" (van Fraassen, 1980), which is, first of all, responsible for preserving the facts of the case, even when those facts are intractable to the interpretation the researcher wishes to advance. But constructive empiricism also acknowledges that for those facts to be meaningful, some interpretation (as opposed to their or the interpretation) must be fashioned. The explicit recognition of the constructive accomplishments of interpretation is the reflexive mark of contemporary qualitative research.

The Conversational Interview

Conversational interviews are preplanned, tactical conversations that intend to open up a topic of concern to the researcher. There are many ways to conduct them. My preference is to conduct them on-site in the process of doing something related to the scene. In that manner, the respondent can use particular cues and examples, places and people to enliven the response.

Izzy: (Hi, my name is Isabella Bloom, everybody calls me Izzy) and I are driving out in the outreach van. ["Outreach" is the term used for services provided to the unsheltered. It has been a brutal weekend. It rained Friday and then turned ice cold over Saturday and Sunday. Izzy expresses her concern that several of her clients might be in real trouble.] All of their clothes get wet. They have nothing dry to wear. They have to sleep in wet clothes and that gets their bedding wet. It all freezes to the ground. [This is my opening to turn the conversation to the topic of how staffers manage the emotional toll of service.]

J: How do you do this every week? I mean I go home after these few hours and I am emotionally exhausted. You are out there everyday.

I: It is hard. But you have to learn to manage it. If you don't, you can't help at all. [She laughs.] We went clubbing Saturday night. At the club, you know, we're doing our thing. We step out in the cold and the first thing I think is John, or Red Eagle, or one of the other guys. How is he doing tonight? Did he make it? Is he safe? And then it's into the next club and we're back doing our thing. It's some kind of switch.

J: How 'bout the frustration? The detox cycle? [In the detox cycle clients are admitted to the detox center for two weeks. Under the supportive systems of the center they get themselves cleaned up, their health and nutrition attended to, and generally on a hopeful road. Government funding cuts, however, mean that at the end of two weeks they are back on the streets with no further support. Most cycle back.]

I: I don't make them drink. At some point they have to take responsibility for their own actions. They could make it, but they choose not to.

J: [silently to himself] Wow, where do I go with this. Isn't alcoholism a disease?

The conversation continues.

About 10:30, we pull into one of the homeless service centers. One of the men has been reported sleeping on the porch a violation of the rules. "It's Bill," Izzy says, "he's a mouthwash drinker. You'll notice a particular smell." Izzy calls dispatch for a response team. In a few minutes two very large fire trucks show up. "They always send two trucks. I tell 'em just send one, but they always send two." Today they need all the men on both trucks because Bill is frozen to the wet concrete. His body temperature is so low that a solid bond of ice has formed. The EMTs have to pry him off inch by inch. Izzy deals with everything; where Bill is to be taken; how the billing is to be handled; all of the reporting. I'm stunned into silence, but for Izzy it's just another problem to be solved.

The interview and incident tell me that I have to reach a better understanding of alcohol. Later that month a press report on the high costs of arrests for public drunkenness will quote a police officer as saying, "I don't pour the alcohol down their throats. They do that to themselves."

*****

[Interviewing the domesticated at a neighborhood picnic]

Woman social worker: So, I understand you are working with the homeless.
J: Yes, do you work with the homeless in your shop?
WSW: No, we work with a different group of people.
J: So, what do you think about the homeless problem?
WSW: Well, I know you're not supposed to give them any money when they approach you on the streets [*an echo of the then current downtown alliance campaign*].

Referential Analysis

Qualitative research is *not* a descriptive method. It is not prior to something else. Qualitative research arguments can certainly end in claims which are primarily descriptive—what philosophers of science would call claims of existence or "ontological" claims, but that is not the only direction such arguments can take. They are equally adept at making claims of how things happen ("praxeological claims") or why they happen ("epistemological claims").

All such claims rise out of the methods of referential analysis. Referential analysis itself refers to the characteristic of qualitative research to be referenced to two intersecting domains: the domain of mundane practice—which provides the research site—and the domain of theory and argument—from which claims can be advanced. There are no positivist boundaries to these domains: The researcher becomes suffused in each and in the argument; information passes seamlessly between them.

There is, however, a shifting priority. In the conversational interview with Izzy, for example, obviously professionals who have to deal with the costs and consequences of alcohol addiction have a much different take on the human practices of the addiction than liberal-leaning social drinkers such as myself. There is a very different theory of alcohol in play here and one about which I will have to become sophisticated.

The shift in priorities can be seen fairly clearly in this effort. In the field stage, the priority was to provide as broad an opportunity for comment as I was able. There were no prepared questions. The strategy was simply to keep the conversation going by using active listening and passive prompting. In this analytical stage, how the practical theory of alcohol works in the strategy of managing engagement with difficult situations—that combination of matter-of-factness, nearly maternal concern, yet apparent push-back, professional execution, and social disconnection that Izzy describes—becomes a goal that cannot be met in the field. Izzy's words have to be appropriated into the work of theory building. In that moment of appropriation, what was said is taken from its priority as a sentence in a conversation and moved to its priority as a textual warrant.[13] And, of course, all of the questions about the legitimacy of that appropriation come along with it.

The neighborhood picnic conversation encapsulates what such conversations have demonstrated time and again. Most people—even those in social services—know little about the homeless beyond the uncomfortable contact in the soliciting moment. The lack of direct experience means that their narratives are particularly open to be filled by the voice of authority and of the media, which leads us to textual analysis.

Textual Analysis

In any issue of public concern, there are a variety of voices that enter the public forum. In this capital city—and the largest city of the state—we hear from homeless advocates, service agencies, governmental agencies, the downtown business alliance, state legislators, the governor and we hear from newspaper columnists. The one voice we do not hear from is that of the homeless themselves. The result is a deep segregation between the homeless and the domesticated. The homeless are truly "The Other." No homeless person can succeed in the terms of the domesticated and still be homeless. One succeeds by being restored to the domesticated life. We can see this division in a column by Rebecca Walsh in the *Salt Lake Tribune* (2007):

> Five friends with heavy backpacks and two or three plastic grocery sacks each hover by the glass doors, waiting for the security guard to open. When he does, they scatter—some heading directly for the first-floor restrooms, others for the elevators. Within minutes, they take posts at work tables, leather armchairs and computers throughout the library. The men fade from notice as they mingle with college students, teens on spring break and retirees. But for these men—and most are men—the library serves a different purpose: refuge. Many of them have nowhere else to go. The shelters are closed for the day. Jobs are a memory. Families are absent or unaware.

We learn that five homeless men are in the library for refuge, we learn that no college students, teens, or retirees are there for refuge ("different purpose"), and we learn that whatever the purposes that college students, teens, and retirees have for being in the library, the homeless do not share those purposes. In my observations of the homeless in the library, they read, surf the web, take notes, follow a line of inquiry. They seem to do it for the same reasons you and I do—to be knowledgeable and to have something to say in some venue. But their work is not our work according to Walsh. How could it be? They do not have a home to justify it.

Walsh writes further:

> Salt Lake City public libraries director Nancy Tessman acknowledges stressed librarians struggle to take care of the homeless. But Tessman tries—repeatedly—to consider them in a broader context of everyone the library serves. Each day, 5,000 people cross the library's threshold. Of those, she guesses maybe 40 are homeless—less than 1 percent. Library staff wake dozing patrons, interrupt sponge-bathing in the restrooms and are "extra vigilant" in the children's area, the library director says. Some are belligerent. But so are people angry about their overdue book fines. Some lose control of their bowels. But so did the woman who took her pre-colonoscopy drink before browsing at the library. Some parents use the library as a babysitter. The homeless use the library for shelter. And Tessman is OK with that.

In this segment the work of division continues: homeless are contrasted with "people," "parents," and a "woman." Each does discomfiting things, but the people, parents, and the woman all have reasons attached to their misbehavior. The homeless do not. The silence here is very expressive—*only* shelter is purposeful for the homeless.

At the closed of the article the library director is quoted saying, "Everybody should be in the library when they want to be and need to be." Walsh concludes her column with a different take:

> "Winter season" at the library is waning. The numbers of homeless seeking warmth and diversion in the building will dwindle. But they will be back with the first cold front. Until someone else steps up, the cycle will repeat.

The closing line states that the homeless will keep coming into the library until someone else does something about it. You can break that down into: The homeless coming into the library is a problem. The homeless come into library for shelter. Someone needs to provide them shelter someplace else. Then the problem of the homeless in the library will be resolved.

It is quite possible that Walsh sees herself as writing a column of tolerance but the angle is the problem of the homeless in the library. She makes no effort to connect with any of the five men she introduces as "five friends with heavy backpacks." Had she made that effort, we might have learned how friendship is managed in uncertainty, the work that these five actually do, and the justification they find in it. Instead we learned that the homeless are poaching shelter when others are doing "real" work, albeit with occasional missteps.

Content versus Critical Analysis

Klaus Krippendorff (2003) defines content analysis as a "research technique for making replicable and valid inferences from texts (or other meaningful matter) to the contexts of their use" (p. 18). In short, the effects texts have in different contexts. Raymie McKerrow (1989) defines critical analysis as a process that "seeks to unmask or demystify the discourse of power" (p. 91). In short, the method intentionally reveals power and its practice. The differences are substantial. In content analysis, the text is analyzed for its capacity as an agent in a context of result. In critical analysis, the text necessarily encodes the dominant interests of social power. It is the analyst's job to reveal that encoding to show the service of the text in support of those interests.

In content analysis, we typically retain the author or at least authorship, as one of the points is to be able to purposefully construct texts based on the "valid inferences" of content analysis. In critical analysis, the author and authorship both recede. The author is simply the agent of the dominant. That is not to say that Walsh is a co-conspirator. It is to say that if she is to write a competent column that will pass editorial muster, it must represent how things are (homeless in the library) and how they are meant to be (homeless someplace else).

Should someone in Salt Lake City come along and open a day shelter for the homeless with thousands of books, periodicals, sound and video recordings, high speed Internet connections, a couple of delicatessens, and a coffee shop, we could point to the effectiveness (ala Krippendorff) of the Walsh article. The fact that the suggestion is ludicrous points to the McKerrowesque power that inhabits the text.

In my interpretation of Walsh, I am unabashedly pursuing a particular interpretation. I want you to see how the article participates in the constitution of The Other (Madison, 2006). That interpretation arises out of the resources that Walsh supplies and it rings true to those resources, but it is not the only interpretation that could be produced. That is the interface between the empirical, the hermeneutic, and the critical. The empirical presents the surface text—the iceberg that floats above; the hermeneutic dives deep for the major portion. When the hermeneutic is disciplined by the critical, the major portion is the explication of power.

Ethics

Professional research employing human subjects starts with an inherent tension. Good—in the terms of commissions, salary, promotion, tenure (in the academic system)—returns to the researcher through the competent practice of research regardless of what happens to the respondents who make the research possible. In most social science research, the cost to the respondent is a minor inconvenience, an exploitation of time and talent in return for some vague promise of a contribution to the archive of public knowledge.

When science is recognized as a player in the social construction of the reality in which we live, the ante is upped considerably. For example, a story on parenting and television appeared on the front page of the May 8, 2007, *Salt Lake Tribune* with a local byline. It also appeared in the *Malaysia Star* (http://thestar.com.my/news/story.asp?file=/2007/5/8/ apworld/ 20070508113134&sec=apworld) in what seems to be a press release picked up by the Associated Press. The ostensible topic of the story is a survey of 1009 parents of children aged 2 to 24 months about their children's viewing practices. In both versions, the researchers—Fred Zimmerman, Ph.D. and Dimitri Christakis, M.D.—are soundly critical of "baby-TV," programs and DVDs that are presumably designed to up baby's IQ.

In this argument, the researchers, who also do podcasts on the topic, are well beyond the evidence provided by the survey. Their intent is clearly to influence parenting practices even though there has been no empirical test of the efficacy or lack thereof of baby-TV. This is no quiet contribution to the archive, but rather an aggressive and extensive effort to effect change. So what are the ethical implications for Zimmerman and Christakis as they receive international recognition and the acclaim of their colleagues while parents are presented with only more uncertainty? Do they know enough to justify this consequence on others?

While Zimmerman and Christakis are metric types, methodology is an unimportant part of this ethical question. It does become somewhat thickened for the hermeneutic empiricist, however. It is likely that a telephone survey of parents of babies and toddlers lasted no longer than 20 minutes. In the premier hermeneutic methods, respondent contact can be days and even years in length. There is a necessarily built up level of trust and confidence unprecedented in metric research.

Consider James, Ray, and Izzy in my examples. James and I recognize but do not know one another. Nonetheless what are the consequences for James should he read or be presented with the story? I think mine would be outrage at the exploitation of a very difficult personal moment that was public only because of the circumstances of homelessness. Am I as the researcher justified in this exploitation, because of the power of the story to show the degradation we the domesticated impose for the rights of shelter?

The fact is that I benefit from his distress in having the story to tell. As I write this paragraph I am questioning myself as to why I did not bring out one of the small tables and a folding chair. Some gesture of kindness would have been automatic in any other circumstance. But here I am a staffer, enforcing institutional rules.

And what of Ray, who would certainly recognize himself in spite of my extensive efforts to disguise him from others. He and I have known and worked together for over a year. And yes, he was told that I was a researcher studying the homeless. But, of course, one aspect of the extended contact is that my research status disappears and no special effort on his part to guard against it remains. This is the necessary assumption of all qualitative research that one's respondents are not acting in any sort of nonnormal, careful, controlled way. If they behave toward me as if they were going to appear in a book, their value is lessened.

And then, there is Izzy a late 20-something woman who enjoys the social pleasures of her age. Clubbing in Salt Lake City does not necessarily involve alcohol, but it could be expected in this example. And clubbing itself is replete with alcoholic excess. What is the difference between Jell-O shots at the bar and the brown bag circle in the parking lot? How do we blind ourselves to our own practices to judge those of The Other? Much of middle America is a paycheck or two or a nasty divorce away from homelessness.

Ray and Izzy inform us of the tensions and contradictions that exist in the life of the agency staffer. They perform on one side of a very crossable divide. They struggle for organizational success and promotion. They struggle to have some fun without the specter of what might be. The justification for telling their stories is in those insights. Is it justification enough for the increased risks that this writing poses?

One practice of amelioration is to take the story back to the person and ask for permission. It is not my practice. I believe that practice violates the contract I have with the reader that I am offering you the insights of my years of study supported by the best exemplars my field notes can provide. It is a principle that privileges you over them.

Finally there is the writing of this chapter itself. It represents a deliberate choice to highlight the homeless study to reach an audience that might otherwise have no reason to engage such a study. In the structure of the writing I am declaring that is just as important to know about the homeless as it is to know about qualitative research. I am taking advantage of you being here for one reason that I might impose another. It is the ethical problem of critical arrogance. On what basis do I know better?

Critique

The place of the critical in qualitative research is both controversial and unconventional (Carbaugh, 1989–1990; Conquergood, 1991; Cushman, 1989–1990; Goodall, 1991). Most discussions of science, at this level, follow the age of enlightenment assumption separating what is true and what is good. This is the notion of value-free science—a notion almost always marked as "not really possible" but then acted upon as if it were. Much of the practice of science would not see the section that immediately preceded this analysis as "scientific."

It is, however, the rejection of meaning realism and the acceptance of the subjectivity of analysis which opens the door to the critical in science (Taylor, 1987; Warren, 2006). When we abandon a belief in "brute sense data" and base our claims instead on the accomplishments of interpretation, we intermix what is right with what is true. This intermixing denies the scientist his or her innocence from the political outcomes of the practices of knowledge production (Jackson, 1989). Explanation and knowledge are no longer transcendental and propositional, but rather rhetorical and actional. Our knowledge claims are platforms for action; our work to advance them pushes a program of action whether we acknowledge it or not.

The strong hermeneutic position in qualitative research (Rosaldo, 1993) holds researchers responsible for both the intended and unintended consequences of their research. Something is true because we create the conditions by which it can be held to be true. Each of us, therefore, is responsible for the claims we make both for the harm they might cause and the good they should accomplish.

Paradigmatic qualitative researchers are beginning to engage this twinned responsibility in earnest. In approaches called "action research (Reason, 2004), "critical ethnography (Madison, 2006), and "performance ethnography" (Denzin, 2003) qualitative researchers are engaging in "emancipatory," "collaborative" science that acts as a "change agent" in the pursuit of social justice (Barab et al., 2004). (At this point we are about as far from traditional quantitative research as one can get.) While the rhetoric is brave, the performance of the academic researcher has been considerably less. I think it will remain so until the real outcomes in social justice are the practical outcomes for the researcher.

Notes

1. Primary qualities (mass, weight, extension) are said to belong to the object. When science limits itself to primary qualities, it is said to be objective.

2. An excellent introduction into the varieties of issues in qualitative research is in Denzin and Lincoln's *Handbook of Qualitative Research*; A comparison of their 1994 and 2005 editions will give the reader a very good idea of the movement within the field. Anderson (1986) and Lindlof and Taylor (2002) are two methods books, albeit of quite different shadings that also provide insight into differences. They provide useful guides to other literature as well.

3. Metrics are quantitative means of assessing a process such as communication.

4. It is important to note that while both paradigms make all encompassing claims, some things can be better explained in one form than in the other. Whether we ordinarily practice ME or HE, we want to avoid knee-jerk empiricism.

5. One way we do that is to continue to ask the question on survey forms.

6. Notice that I did not say that I study the homeless. For me, that creates them as an object and separates me, the scientist, from that object of study. Of course, I am not separate from the homeless as I participate in the allocation of resources—actively or passively—that create the conditions that permit homelessness to occur.

7. And was seen as a "bad boy" for the first time in my life as most thought I was on some court-order service requirement.

8. Empiricism is the philosophical position that the phenomenal world is most validly contacted through experience (as opposed to, say, formal analysis). It has many forms. Naive empiricism holds that we have an unmediated contact with the phenomenal world. Direct experience, therefore, is wholly trustworthy. Constructive empiricism (van Fraassen, 1980) holds that experience is mediated by belief, language, and so on, but there is an underlying substrata which always remains trustworthy. Hermeneutic empiricism holds that the phenomenal world appears in collectively constructed frameworks of understanding.

9. The difference between *writing down* and *writing up* is useful for understanding the different writing tasks: Writing down privileges experience, writing up privileges interpretation; my thanks to Tom Lindlof for pointing out these terms.

10. Discourse is generally defined as any extended language use, so this writing is an example of academic discourse of the textbook genre and its production, as good or bad as it may be, intends that end. It is not the discourse I would use on the mountain trail nor am I permitted to use it unmarked at home. But the discourse of home and trail is equally intentional and produced as discourse, domestic and exploring.

11. The concept of intentionality here does not suggest a causal linkage between some prior mental state and behavior produced, although that link may be present. It refers to the way things are meaningful as intentional objects of consciousness. Although I am in grave danger of this note's escaping from me, this intentionality deals with the manner in which meaning is accomplished.

12. It is this requirement for a joint discipline which privileges participant forms of observation. I can certainly watch a video tape of some action and create an analysis of it. I have no basis, however, for any claim as to the meaningfulness of the action for the performers other than an appeal to common usage.

13. Similarly, a check mark on a page is appropriated as an answer to an item in a questionnaire.

REFERENCES

Alvesson, M. (2003). Methodology for close up studies: Struggling with closeness and closure. *Higher Education, 46*(2), 169–193.

Anderson, J. A. (1987). *Communication research: Issues and methods.* New York: McGraw-Hill.

Anderson, J. A. (1991). The social action of organizing: Knowledge, practice and morality. *Australian Journal of Communication, 18,* 1–18.

Anderson, J. A. (1992). On the ethics of research in a socially constructed reality. *Journal of Broadcasting and Electronic Media, 36,* 353–357.

Anderson, J. A. (1996). *Communication theory: Epistemological foundations.* New York: Guilford.

Anderson, J. A., & Goodall, H. L., Jr. (1994). Probing the body ethnographic: From an anatomy of inquiry to a poetics of expression. In F. L. Casmir (Ed.), *Building communication theories* (pp. 87–129). Hillsdale, NJ: Erlbaum.

Bakhtin, M. M. (1986). *Speech genres and other late essays* (V. M. McGee, Trans.). Austin: University of Texas Press.

Barab, S. A., Thomas, M. K., Dodge, T., Squire, K., & Newell, M. (2004). Critical design ethnography: designing for change. *Anthropology and Education Quarterly, 35*(2), 254–268.

Bellah, R., Madsen, R., Sullivan, W., Swindler, A., & Tipton, S. M. (1985). *Habits of the heart: Individualism and commitment in American life.* Berkeley: University of California Press.

Benwell, B. (2005). "Lucky this is anonymous." Ethnographies of reception in men's magazines: A "textual culture" approach. *Discourse & Society, 16*(2), 147–172.

Blaikie, N. W. H. (1993). *Approaches to social inquiry.* Cambridge, MA: Policy Press.

Bohman, J. (1991). *New philosophy of social science.* Cambridge, MA: MIT Press.

Burowoy, M. (2003). Revisits" An outline of a theory of reflexive ethnography. *American Sociological Review 68*, 645–679.

Caputo, J. D. (1987). *Radical hermeneutics: Repetition, deconstruction and the hermeneutic project.* Bloomington: Indiana University Press.

Carbaugh, D. (1989–1990). The critical voice in ethnography of communication research. *Research on Language and Social Interaction, 23*, 261–282.

Chick, G. (2000). Writing culture reliably: The analysis of high-concordance codes. *Ethnology, 39*(4), 365–393.

Conquergood, D. (1991). Rethinking ethnography: Towards a critical cultural politics. *Communication Monographs, 58*, 179–194.

Cushman, D. P. (1989–1990). The role of critique in the ethnographic study of human communication practices. *Research on Language and Social Interaction, 23*, 243–250.

Denzin, N. K. (2003). *Performance ethnography: Critical pedagogy and the politics of culture.* Thousand Oaks, CA: Sage.

Denzin, N. K., & Lincoln, Y. S. (1994). Introduction: Entering the field of qualitative research. In N. K. Denzin & Y. S. Lincoln (Eds.), *Handbook of qualitative research* (pp. 1–17). Newbury Park, CA: Sage.

Denzin, N. K., & Lincoln, Y. S. (2005). *Handbook of qualitative research.* Newbury Park, CA: Sage. (Original work published 1994)

Erickson, F., $ Gutierrez, K. (2002). Comment: Culture, rigor and science in educational research. *Educational Researcher, 31*(8), 21–31.

Erlandson, D. S., Harris, E. L., Skipper, B. L., & Allen, S. D. (1993). *Doing naturalistic inquiry: A guide to methods.* Newbury Park, CA: Sage.

Glaser, B. G. (1998). *Doing grounded theory: Issues and discussions.* Mill Valley, CA: Sociology Press.

Glaser, B. G., & Strauss, A. (1967). *The discovery of grounded theory.* Chicago: Aldine.

Goffman, E. (1959). *The presentation of self in everyday life.* Garden City, NY: Doubleday.

Goodall, H. L., Jr. (1989). *Casing a promised land: The autobiography of an organizational detective as cultural ethnographer.* Carbondale: Southern Illinois University Press.

Goodall, H. L., Jr. (1991). Turning within the interpretive turn: Radical empiricism and a case for post-ethnography. *Text and Performance Quarterly, 11*, 153–169.

Goodall, H. L., Jr. (2004). Narrative ethnography as applied communication research. *Journal of Applied Communication Research, 32*(3), 185–194.

Habermas, J. (1984). *The theory of communicative action* (T. McCarthy, Trans.). Boston, MA: Beacon Press. (Original work published 1981)

Harding, S. (1986). *The science question in feminism.* Ithaca, NY: Cornell University Press.

Jackson, M. (1989). *Paths toward a clearing: Radical empiricism and ethnographic inquiry.* Bloomington: Indiana University Press.

Krippendorff, K. (2003). *Content analysis: An introduction to its methodology.* Thousand Oaks, CA: Sage.

Lanigan, R. L. (1992). *The human science of communicology.* Pittsburgh, PA: Duquesne University Press.

Lindlof, T. R., & Taylor, B. C. (2002). *Qualitative communication research methods* (2nd ed.). Thousand Oaks, CA: Sage.

Lofland, J. (1975). *Doing social life.* New York: Wiley.

Madison, D. S. (2005). *Critical ethnography: Methods, ethics and performance.* Thousand Oaks, CA: Sage.

Madison, D. S. (2006). The dialogic performative in critical ethnography. *Text and Performance Quarterly, 26*(4), 320–324.

Madison, G. B. (1990). *The hermeneutics of postmodernity.* Bloomington: Indiana University Press.

McKerrow, R. E. (1980). Critical rhetoric: Theory and praxis. *Communication Monographs, 56*, 96–111.

Miller, D. L. (Ed.). (1982). *The individual and the social self: Unpublished work of George Herbert Mead.* Chicago: University of Chicago Press.

Nakayama, T. K., & Krizek, R. L. (1995). Whiteness: A strategic rhetoric. *Quarterly Journal of Speech, 81,* 291–309.

Newell, R. W. (1986). *Objectivity, empiricism and truth.* London: Routledge & Kegan Paul.

Parsons, T. (1937). *The structure of social action.* New York: McGraw-Hill.

Peirce, C. S. (1931). *Collected papers* (Vol. 1). Cambridge, MA: Harvard University Press.

Peirce, C. S. (1932). *Collected papers* (Vol. 2). Cambridge, MA: Harvard University Press.

Peirce, C. S. (1958). *Collected papers* (Vol. 8). Cambridge, MA: Harvard University Press.

Pollock, D. (2006). Marking new directions in performance ethnography. *Text and Performance Quarterly, 26*(4), 325–329.

Popper, K. R. (1959). *The logic of scientific discovery.* New York: Harper & Row.

Popper, K. R., & Eccles, J. C. (1977). *The self and its brain.* Berlin: Springer-Verlag.

Reason, P. (2004). Critical design ethnography as action research. *Anthropology and Education Quarterly, 35*(2), 269–276.

Rosaldo, R. (1993). *Culture and truth.* Boston: Beacon Press.

Rose, D. (1990). *Living the ethnographic life.* Newbury Park, CA: Sage.

Roth, P. A. (1987). *Meaning and method in the social sciences: A case for methodological pluralism.* Ithaca, NY: Cornell University Press.

Saville-Troike, M. (2002). *The ethnography of communication.* Oxford: Blackwell.

Schutz, A. (1965). The social world and the theory of social action. In D. Braybrooke (Ed.), *Philosophical problems of the social sciences* (pp. 53–67). New York: Macmillan.

Slembrouck, S. (2004). Reflexivity and the research interview: Habitus and social class in parents' accounts of children in public care. *Critical Discourse Studies, 1*(1), 91–112.

Stacks, D. W., Hickson, M. L., & Hill, S. R. (1991). *Introduction to communication theory.* Fort Worth, TX: Holt, Rinehart & Winston.

Strauss, A., & Corbin, J. (1990). *Basics of qualitative research: Grounded theory procedures and techniques.* Thousand Oaks, CA: Sage.

Sturgeon, S. (1994). The epistemic view of subjectivity. *The Journal of Philosophy, 91*(5), 221–235.

Taylor, C. (1987). Interpretation and the sciences of man. In P. Rabinow & W. M. Sullivan (Eds.), *Interpretive social science: A second look* (pp. 33–81). Berkeley: University of California Press.

van Fraassen, B. C. (1980). *The scientific image.* Oxford: Clarendon Press.

Wagner, R. (1981). *The invention of culture.* Chicago: University of Chicago Press.

Walcott, G. D. (1926). Primary and secondary qualities. *The Philosophical Review, 35*(5), 465–472.

Walsh, R.(2007). *Salt Lake Tribune* retrieved April 26, 2007, from http://www.sltrib.com/search/ci_5620728.

Warren, J. T. (2006). Introduction: Performance ethnography: A *TPQ* symposium. *Text and Performance Quarterly, 26*(4), 317–319.

Weber, M. (1974). Subjectivity and determinism. In A. Giddens (Ed.), *Positivism and sociology* (pp. 23–31). London: Heinemann.

Wilk, R. R. (2001). The impossibility and necessity of re-inquiry: Finding middle ground in social science, the *Journal of Consumer Research, 28*(2), 308–312.

Suggested Readings

Denzin, N. K. (2003). Performance ethnography: Critical pedagogy and the politics of culture. Thousand Oaks, CA: Sage.

Denzin, N. K., & Lincoln, Y. (2005). *Handbook of qualitative research.* Thousand Oaks, CA: Sage.

Lindlof, T. R., & Taylor, B. C. (2002). *Qualitative communication research methods* (2nd ed.). Thousand Oaks, CA: Sage.

Madison, D. S. (2005). *Critical ethnography: Methods, ethics and performance.* Thousand Oaks, CA: Sage.

Part II

MASS COMMUNICATION
Approaches and Concerns

MASS COMMUNICATION THEORY AND RESEARCH

Concepts and Models

Bradley S. Greenberg and Michael B. Salwen

Medieval Europeans knew, spoke, and thought about a universe within their immediate observation—a slice of land carved from the forests encompassing their villages. Few ever ventured beyond the timberland. They knew from occasional travelers that there were other villages beyond the woods. But, so little did they know of the other villages that the other villages might have well been distant planets.

The development of the printing press changed the medieval view of the world. The social consequences of the printing press were demonstrated in 1517 when Martin Luther published his 95 criticisms against the Church in Rome. He was not the first person to criticize the church. But, because his seditious writings were mass circulated, within months Europe was talking about Luther's defiant act. The Church, in kind, responded with its own attacks. Luther's criticisms ushered in the Protestant Reformation and "the first propaganda war" (Burke, 1985, p. 118).

The far-reaching and often unintended effects of Luther's mass communicated messages demonstrate the multifarious nature of mass communication. Suddenly, people know and think about a world beyond their observation. Although tempting, comparing the contemporary Third World village with the medieval village before the age of printing is unwarranted. As a result of the mass media—of radio and group television viewing—today's villagers "see" a pseudo-world beyond the forests. Some Third World leaders today view Western mass media in their countries as agents of media imperialism. Not only blatant propaganda, but even entertainment programs (e.g., "I Love Lucy") are thought to have the potential for undermining traditional cultures (Salwen, 1991). Indonesian President Sukarno, a 1960s Third World spokesperson, declared: "You may not think of a refrigerator as a revolutionary weapon. But if a peasant woman sees one on TV in her village square and realizes what it could do for her and her family, the germ of revolt is planted" (quoted in Manchester, 1993, p. 9).

This chapter reviews the development of theory and research in mass communication. The chapter concludes by proposing a scheme—a model of models—to help readers organize mass communication models. The chapter's main premise is that theory and research are inseparable. Without theory to guide the interpretation of data, research activity is mere data collection in a helter-skelter fashion. When such atheoretical data are quantitatively summarized, they are open to criticism as mere "number crunching." Likewise, empty theorizing and subjective interpretations without procedures to gather data open the researcher to what critics call "naval gazing," "mere speculation," or "armchair philosophy."

Establishing a Base: Methods and Theories

Only in the 20th century did researchers formalize broad "theories" about mass communication. The rise of daily newspapers with more than one million circulation and the introduction of electronic media fostered an interest in the effects of mass communication messages. Certain attributes appeared to distinguish mass communication from other modes of human communication: the diffusion of messages from a seemingly powerful, single source to a large, heterogeneous audience; the public nature of the messages; and the lack of (or delayed) feedback from receivers to the mass communication source.

Theoretical Development

After World War I, it appeared to some observers that clever politicians and governments had manipulated communication symbols in mass communication messages to bring the world to war. A crude "theory" of "propaganda" emerged in which mass media were seen as having a "hypodermic-needle" (or "bullet theory" or "theory of uniform effects") effect of direct, universal, and massive influences on malleable and impressionable audiences.

This notion of all-encompassing effects would have two primary limitations. First, wartime propaganda—whether during World War I or our more contemporary Gulf Wars—represents a relatively unique situation with few, if any, competing messages. Antiwar propaganda is not common in the mass media of dictatorial nations or democracies; even in democracies those who oppose patriotic efforts are largely ignored by the mainstream media (Kellner, 1993). So the development of a model based on the lack of competitive messages cannot be generalized to more common situations.

A second assumption is that the receiving target (readers, listeners) is homogenous in composition and response. Yet there is no compelling evidence that audiences can be herded into a single media corral; indeed, contrary evidence suggests audiences are resistant to media messages.

Some media scholars argue that the hypodermic-needle "theory" never received serious scholarly attention; it was formulated years later for political and pedagogical reasons (Chaffee & Hochheimer, 1985; Sproule, 1989, 1990). Even if there were no hypodermic-needle theory, the mass media would be—and still are—viewed by many as powerful instruments for communicators to convey persuasive messages to audiences. The assumption of massive and unmitigated media effects certainly influenced empirical mass communication research in the "effects" tradition. Lasswell (1927), for example, described how symbols could be manipulated through the mass media:

> A new and subtler instrument...weld[s] thousands and even millions of human beings into one amalgamated mass of hate and will and hope.... The name of this new hammer and anvil of social solidarity is propaganda.... All the apparatus of diffused erudition popularizes the symbols and forms of pseudo-rational appeal; the wolf of propaganda does not hesitate to masquerade in the sheepskin. All the voluble men of the day—writers, reporters, editors, preachers, lecturers, teachers, politicians—are drawn into the service of propaganda to simplify a master voice. (p. 220)

Methodological Development

Starting in the 1920s, several modes of inquiry for studying mass communication were refined. One involved content analysis of media, defined by Berelson (1952) as "a research technique for the objective, systematic, and quantitative description of manifest content of communication"

(p. 18). A popular form, "propaganda analysis," was pioneered by Lasswell (Rogers, 1994, pp. 203–243). The Chicago School of sociology, caught up in the progressive spirit of the era, did not shy away from advocating social causes and "do-goodism." Early Chicago School research displayed a methodological eclecticism that was "empirical but not very quantitative" (Rogers, 1994, p. 152). Chicago School researchers took advantage of their inner-city environs to conduct ethnographic studies of urban problems (Vidich & Lyman, 1993), while in Europe the Frankfurt Institute of Social Research applied neo-Marxist theory to critically analyze communication and culture (Bottomore, 1984).

Despite promising qualitative research developments, by the mid-1930s mass communication research in the United States was distinguished by "an aggressively empirical spirit" (Czitrom, 1982, p. 122). A confluence of factors accounted for quantitative empirical research's popularity. Among the factors was the development of measurement tools, such as the Likert scale and the formulation of systematic methods for gathering data.

In addition, statistical techniques for analyzing large sets of data were introduced into the behavioral sciences. British mathematician Karl Pearson, for example, introduced the product-moment coefficient. Pearson, who was aware of the import of his discovery, declared that the product-moment coefficient "had the potential of introducing a major paradigm shift and revolutionizing the biological and social sciences" (cited in Tankard, 1984, p. 66).[1] Another statistical pioneer fascinated by quantitative analysis, Francis Galton, devised statistical measures of beauty, prayer, and boredom. Galton, however, serves to warn against the misuse of statistics; he applied statistical techniques to support the Eurocentric racial theories of the late 19th and early 20th centuries (Gould, 1981). Paralleling statistical advancements were technological improvements in computers that allowed researchers to analyze massive data sets (Lowery & DeFleur, 1988, p. 20; Nash, 1990). Meanwhile, within the media professions, the use of quantitative data became increasingly important for mass media "market research" (Hurwitz, 1988).

Newspapers relied on studies to learn about their readers. Developments in radio led to audience studies based on telephone coincidental calls (e.g., "What are you listening to right now?"). This technique was later adapted into the first generation of television ratings. The financial resources of media industries to fund studies, and thereby have some say over the academic research agenda, encouraged investigation in the empirical tradition. Industry influence on the academic study of mass communication was evident in advertising (Hess, 1931; Link, 1938). As Scott (1921) noted: "[I]t can be stated, without fear of contradiction, that *no advertisement that defies the established laws of psychology can hope to be successful*" (italics added, p. 2).

Despite research advances, empirical research faced a nagging problem. Conducting empirical research was expensive. Some researchers demonstrated an ability to obtain industry and government funding. But, many critics asked, at what price? Even Paul F. Lazarsfeld, who obtained substantial industry funding and was sometimes accused by critics for selling out to industry (Gitlin, 1978), was not oblivious to such dangers (Pasanella, 1994), and he warned: "[W]e academic people always have a certain sense of tightrope walking: at what point will the commercial partners find some necessary conclusion too hard to take and at what point will they shut us off from the indispensable sources of funding and data?" (Lazarsfeld, 1948, p. 116).

Mass Communication Goes Its Own Way

Many mass communication (and interpersonal communication as well) "founders" of the 1930s and 1940s were housed in sociology and psychology programs and did not call themselves communication scholars (Rogers, 1994). Lazarsfeld (1948), for example, was a sociologist who considered himself "a student of the mass media" (p. 115).

What mass communication needed was someone to champion its cause. This advocate was

Wilbur Schramm (Dennis & Wartella, 1996; Rogers, 1994; Wartella, 1994), who sought to establish communication as a legitimate academic field with a firm grounding in the behavioral sciences. In a series of edited volumes from 1948 to 1972, Schramm brought together researchers from journalism, the behavioral sciences, and the mass communications industries. These volumes (especially Schramm, 1948, 1954) trained future mass communication scholars, providing a firm research grounding for the emerging field. Although Schramm planted the seeds for a legitimate and independent field of study, it was many years before researchers viewed themselves as mass communication scholars setting an agenda for mass communication research.

Schramm did not originally distinguish mass communication from human communication. He hoped for a unified field of communication. But this contemporary separation was an inevitable result of parochial academic barriers (Reardon & Rogers, 1988). Rogers (1994, pp. 449–450) traces the human and mass communication dichotomy to 1950, when Schramm became dean of the Division of Communication, University of Illinois, in charge "of every activity at the University of Illinois that was to be even remotely connected with communication" (p. 449). However, the rhetorically oriented Department of Speech decided not to join the division.

Academic Emergence

University journalism programs would have been the most logical place in academia for the emergence of the study of mass communication. But most journalism programs emphasized vocational training. Many were dominated by former journalists who held an antipathy for behavioral research. Even in the late 1950s, now prominent researchers (e.g., Westley, 1958a, 1958b) were able to publish articles in the flagship scholarly journal in journalism that portrayed the behavioral sciences as a novel approach. Most journalism faculty saw the social scientific study of mass communication "to have no practical value whatever, in part because few effects researchers bothered to expound on the implications of their studies for journalists, and also because many such researchers wrote the results of their studies in barely comprehensible language" (Weaver & Gray, 1980, p. 142).

This is not to say that applied journalism researchers, or those in advertising and public relations, did not contribute to mass communication theory during this formative era. Journalism professionals complained (and sometimes still complain) that journalism research is not geared to industry. Meanwhile, scholars from other academic disciplines claimed (and sometimes still complain) that journalism research is atheoretical and inappropriate for the academy. To deal with these two-pronged attacks, Sloan (1990) argued that journalism programs have become a mish-mash curriculum of skills training and scholarship:

> The result has been one of the most evident, peculiar features of journalism education. One might say it is schizophrenic. It is not known which way to go: Should it become primarily professional, or should it be a traditional academic discipline? Possessing a sense of inferiority to both professional journalism and academia, it has tried to prove itself to both. One inferiority complex is difficult enough to overcome, but two create a severe problem. (p. 4)

Perhaps as a result of journalism education's confused identity and unwillingness to be at the vanguard of mass communication theory and research during the 1940s, 1950s, and much of the 1960s, when the systematic study of mass communication blossomed, sociologists and other behavioral science researchers set the agenda for mass communication theory and research (Berelson, Lazarsfeld, & McPhee, 1954; Hovland, Lumsdaime, & Sheffield, 1949; Katz & Lazarsfeld, 1954; Lazarsfeld, Berelson, & Gaudet, 1944). Their "grand studies," guided by broad research questions, yielded unanticipated findings for the development of later models (e.g., the sleeper effect, two-step flow, opinion leaders, selective perception, reinforcement).[2] Much of this early research might appear unsophisticated today; the studies were based largely on breakdowns of media use and preferences by various demographic (i.e., socioeconomic status) groups. But their impact was enormous (Katz, 1987).

Not until the 1970s, when mass communication was an established area of study, did journalism researchers Maxwell McCombs and Donald Shaw (1972) offer the agenda-setting model. McCombs and Shaw's model hypothesized that the news media prioritized, or set the agenda for public issue concerns. Agenda-setting was widely embraced by journalism scholars, and even entered common parlance among media professionals. Although the agenda-setting model was thoughtfully conceived, explicated, and provided valuable insights about the mass communication process, there were other reasons why the model was well-received. Agenda-setting was important because it was the first popular "home-grown" mass communication model from self-declared journalism researchers (Tankard, 1990).

The quantitative tradition in mass communication has become dominant in the United States today, although there has been a renewed interest in qualitative research and the macro-level social effects (Potter, 1996). In 1983, a special issue of the *Journal of Communication* devoted to the "Ferment in the Field" brought together internationally prominent scholars to comment on the alleged upheaval in communication study. A number of critical scholars, who trace their roots to the Frankfurt Institute of Social Research, contributed to the "Ferment" issue. Many neo-Marxist, critical scholars attacked behavioral researchers, sometimes savagely, for failing to criticize mass communication industries.

Critical scholarship also has had an impact on mass communication thinking. It has stimulated interest in expanding inquiry beyond media effects on audiences—traditionally the main focus of mass communication—and looking at media production processes as well. Most behavioral researchers have not, however, responded to the critical scholars' harshest criticisms. Ithiel de Sola Pool (1983) was one of the few behavioral researchers in the "Ferment" issue to directly confront the charges from his critical colleagues. His criticisms were directed at a lack of coherent methods in critical research and, from his perspective, a reliance on speculation and academic clichés:

> So where is the ferment? There is, of course, a large and dull literature that claims to have overthrown empirical behavioral research. It condemns quantification and controlled observation as arid, naive, banal, and even reactionary and immoral. I chose not to digress into a debate about the morality of acquiring knowledge. The important point here is that, if knowledge of the world is a good thing to have, there is no other way of acquiring it except by carefully and with well-designed controls.... But the scores of methodological and ideological essays about new approaches to the study of communications can hardly be honored by the term "ferment." There is a simple recipe for these essays: avoid measurement, add moral commitment, and throw in some of the following words: social system, capitalism, dependency, positivism, idealism, ideology, autonomy, paradigm, commercialism, consciousness, emancipation, cooption, critical, instrumental, technocratic, legitimation, praxiology, repressive, dialogue, hegemony, contradiction, problematic. (p. 260)

The Age of Models

A good deal of mass communication research has been guided by so-called *models*, such as agenda-setting, spiral of silence, cultivation analysis, knowledge gap, and others discussed in part

II of this book. A good deal of mass communication research also consists of bodies of research such as violence, media ethics and so forth, as the other chapters attest. Westley (1958b) noted the trend toward "conceptual models" in mass communication as an effort to "stake out significant concepts in the field, to codify scattered findings of the past and weave them into a single conceptual framework which will help give direction and focus future work" (p. 313).

Models are shorthand attempts to capture the essence of a conceptual issue or question of interest. A model "seeks to show the main elements of any structure or process and the relationships between [and among] these elements" (McQuail & Windahl, 1993, p. 2). For example, Lasswell's (1948) cryptic model: "Who Says What in Which Channel to Whom with What Effect?" This simple model directs research attention to the source, the message, the channel, the receiver, and the outcome or consequences.

Although Lasswell's model draws attention to several key elements in the mass communication process, it does no more than describe general areas of study. It does not link elements together with any specificity, and there is no notion of an active "process." Still, it generated great interest. A dozen years after Lasswell, Berlo (1960) elaborated his own source–message–channel–receiver paradigm that became a standard for the analysis of human communication processes for a decade.

According to Berlo, models are useful to the extent they:

1. specify relationships among concepts/variables. A useful model will generate conceptual hypotheses, indicating the nature and direction of linkages among the components;
2. are relatively simple to express verbally or visually;
3. characterize an active process;
4. stimulate research; and
5. are responsive to change and revision from research outcomes.

The hypodermic-needle model dominated until the 1940s. As discussed earlier, there is some question whether such a model influenced scholarly research, but anyone reading pre-World War II popular literature will see that it underlay much popular thinking about the mass media and their consequences. One medical writer noted: "The story of mass media in America reads much like the case history of a public health menace" (Starker, 1989, p. 5).

In the war and postwar period, the introduction of quantitative, empirically based research findings challenged the earlier exaggerated claims of unmitigated media effects. Only after Klapper (1960) summarized the newly accumulated research into an alternative model, resulting in the so-called limited-effects (or minimal-effects) model, was the hypodermic-needle model rejected.

Klapper shifted attention from media messages to the role of audiences in the mass communication process. This was an important development, but one diminished by researchers who became overly enthused about the power of an "active" and even "obstinate" audience able to overcome media messages (Bauer, 1964). A failing of limited-effects research is found in a reliance on short-term experiments and surveys; it largely neglected how difficult it is to measure the effects of cumulative messages. Another limitation was a concern with affective and behavioral effects, rather than cognitive effects.

From the beginning, researchers were uncomfortable with the limited-effects notion that the mass media were relatively minor contributors to media effects. The limited-effects model contends that a variety of sociological and psychological factors mediate and reduce the effects of any mass communication message. Klapper argued that the major impact of the mass media was to reinforce existing opinions, rather than modify old ones—a position as extreme as the hypodermic-needle's had been in the opposite direction. Its influence was evident in research during this period. For example, a survey on *The American Voter* (Campbell, Converse, Miller, & Stokes, 1960) noted:

> [I]t is seldom wise to rely on even the most rigorous study of mass media for indications of the public's familiarity with any specific issue. In general, public officials and people involved in public relations tend to overestimate the impact that contemporary issues have on the public. They find it difficult to believe that the reams of newspaper copy and hours of television and radio time could be ignored by any normal person within the reach of these media. The fact seems to be, however, that human perceptions are highly selective, and unless it happens to be tuned to a particular wavelength, the message transmitted will be received only as noise. (p. 99)

The limited media effects model, like the bullet theory, is no longer popular. Today, the dominant general view is moderate media effects. Still, aspects of the limited-effects model endure. McGuire (1986) chided popular commentators and empirical scholars for adhering to the "myth of massive media impact," despite what he contended was substantial empirical evidence to the contrary:

> First, we are not arguing that no media effects have been found, but only that the demonstrated effects are not large. A formidable proportion of the published studies (and presumably an even higher proportion of the unpublished studies) have failed to show overall effects sizable enough to reach the conventionally accepted .05 level of statistical significance. Some respectable studies in several of the dozen impact areas reviewed below do have impacts significant at the .05 level, but even these tend to have very small effect sizes, accounting for no more than 2 or 3% of the variance in the dependent variables such as consumer purchases, voting behavior, and viewer aggression. (p. 177)

Such overarching, grand models as the hypodermic-needle theory and limited-effects are of little value to empirical researchers interested in designing specific studies. The 1960 to 1980 period produced a variety of small-scale models which specified subprocesses of social effects within mass communication (McQuail & Windahl, 1993). The small-scale models examined small slices of mass communication processes that led researchers to appreciate both the power and limitations of the mass media. If there is any dominant grand model today, however, it is a model of moderate media effects.

Popular models of moderate effects—such as agenda setting, knowledge gap, or gatekeeping—pointed to regularities in mass communication effects and processes. These and other models are discussed at length in this section of the book. Advocates of moderate effects models accept the general processes of empirically supported mass communication models, but also understand that they are by no means universal. They call for researchers to delineate the contingent conditions, locate the intervening variables, and specify the social contexts.

A Model of Models

Several popular contemporary mass communication models receive in-depth treatments in succeeding chapters. Here we propose a scheme—a model of models—to help organize existing models and research. The scheme is useful for suggesting modified research paths. Our model is a broad classification-type model in the Lasswellian tradition for summarizing the plethora of mass communication models. It does not refer to any dynamic process.

Selection
Creation
Dissemination
Reception

Figure 5.1 Model processes.

Process-based research on mass communication phenomena can begin with a fairly linear collection of processes. After the processes are established, we can then speak of recursive or nonlinear features. The concepts are arrayed in a linear fashion in which they are likely to occur but, even here, we can graphically capture their potential for nonlinear or overlapping evolution as well. In trying to keep models relatively parsimonious, we limit our set of processes to four; each process, however, may constitute a separate model (see Figure 5.1).

Processes of Selection

Of all the stimuli available to be reported, of all that is in gatekeepers' heads to be created, of all the entertainment story ideas that exist, how are a relatively small number of stimuli chosen for development? Typical gatekeeping studies begin in editorial offices, comparing material selected from the larger quantity that goes unused. Gatekeeping research in the selection process would encompass editorial and entertainment norms and decisions about what should be covered before any actual selection or rejection decision is made.

Determining the predilections, predispositions, interests, and biases of media decision makers is crucial in understanding decision making at the initial stage, before possible alternatives exist, and how ideas or events are developed into mass communication messages. This approach raises numerous questions: Do the decision makers have personal agendas? If so, do their personal agendas influence the selection process? Are they aware of the selection processes of other relevant media decision makers? If so, how does this awareness influence their selection process? How do they decode their environment? What are their reference points? Criteria? Standards?

One can also pose questions here regarding access. It has been said that reporters are only as good as their sources. Access to sources of information, events themselves, and ideas all become variables in the selection process. This approach provokes researchers to ask important questions: Whom do you know? Whom do you trust?

The 1990 Gulf War provided another generation of war correspondents with limited access to military sites, targets, and information sources (Greenberg & Gantz, 1993). The result was a media picture of the war that was carefully constructed by the military. Media decision makers can make their selections only from those issues, events, and ideas which are accessible.

Inherent in the selection process is the entity of the media system or institution. The institution consists of individuals in various work roles with professional and social norms. It is foolhardy to think that a single omnipotent gatekeeper makes these decisions. In some cases, there are layers of people who filter the offerings; story ideas go to editors who share them with senior editors, or producers, and so on. In other contexts, selection is a group process (e.g., the designated creative advertising team for a new car will pool its impressions of the car's best features during the initial step in the advertising campaign proposal). And of course there are the mixes of individuals (the client) and groups (the ad team) and so forth.

In summary, then, the selection process links media institutions and systems with the world from which events, ideas, information, and other issues will be extracted for possible inclusion in that system's message pool.

Processes of Creation

Now the linkage shifts to encompass those media system components responsible for translating the events and ideas obtained from the selection process into sets of signs and symbols to be disseminated to receiving groups. That which has been decoded must now be encoded.

The composition of the creating unit is of interest. Is it an individual or a team? What are their respective abilities? How do they merge their talents and their disparate ideas about the event or story? To what extent are they compatible with each other? In other words, we have the same set of concerns about characteristics and predispositions of the communicators as we did when specifying their operating rules in the selection process. Here the questions apply to their encoding capabilities.

The creation process needs to identify the intentions of the communicating sources as well. If sources intend to inform rather than persuade, alternative message strategies will likely be chosen. Paralleling this should be an understanding of the motives which drive such individuals in their creative enterprises. One set of motivations relates to their understanding of the reward system accessible to them. For example, if two reporters assigned to the same story use different reference points, wherein one anticipates how her peers will respond to the story, and the second anchors her material in how the audience will respond, a basis emerges for anticipating content differences in each message.

Content differences, examined through content analysis research, have long been the subject of mass communication research. These studies lie within the creation process as its end product, although many tend to be static investigations of available content. These studies sometimes infer motives and intentions rather than directly assess them. To avoid static, descriptive outcomes, researchers can consider trend analysis (if the content has been analyzed previously) and comparative analysis (looking across different media for the same kinds of content). Both approaches permit hypothesis testing.

Content analysis is perhaps the most common research method in mass communication. The substance of these analyses normally examines content for *topics, themes,* and *styles.*

Topical analyses provide the subsequent basis for agenda-setting research. Here, content analysis is a means to understanding one component of media influence on the public. The purpose is to study how emphasized topics in the mass media encroach on the public's agenda. Media coverage of issues or individuals confers status (fame and infamy alike). Topics which are absent or less emphasized in the media are considered of less important to the public, although this conclusion is more often assumed than demonstrated.

Thematic analyses seek objective markers of how women and minorities are portrayed, how often violence is used to resolve conflict, or whether Middle Eastern combatants are given equal photo display. While topical analyses emphasize the presence and frequency of media content, thematic analyses focus on the directionality of that content.

Stylistic analyses, not as common as topical and thematic analyses, evolve from the grammar and structure of mass media messages. In the 1940s, readability research was plentiful (Flesch, 1943, 1948). Readability studies determine the comprehensibility of written passages based on measures of verbal complexity, assessed with simple tools (e.g., sentence length and syllable counts). It is unfortunate that counterpart measures of "listenability" and "viewability" have not been developed. Today, formal features in television (e.g., zooming, panning) are examined for their potential and actual impact on viewers' enjoyment and understanding (Watt & Welch, 1983) and comprise a language referred to as *media literacy.* More structural assessments (e.g., order of presentation of information or arguments, the emphasis and placement of counter-information) also fit within this creative process segment.

Topics, themes, and styles are the result of creative decisions made by individuals and small groups. They are dependent, in part, on the medium for which the messages are created. To this point, we have ignored media differences because the creative processes described are generic across all media. Their outputs, however, are media specific. So, creative process models are likely to require elements that account for media differences.

The context in which message creation processes occur also yields research considerations. For example, media creators often do their work in stressful contexts (e.g., the stress of deadlines and competitive pressure). How does stress impact on their product? Are there more errors? Does it take longer to encode? Is some amount of stress a positive motivator, while too much impedes the message creation process?

Processes of Dissemination

In practice, the concept of a dissemination process is not wholly separable from the process associated with receiving a message. It is also erroneous to assume that receivers will necessarily decode the messages as the senders intended. This separation of message dissemination and reception is an artificial and temporary separation that highlights approaches to the systematic and scientific study of mass communication. If not already apparent, all such separations are artificial, perhaps arbitrary; they are a convenient way to convey conceptions of a particular idea being studied at that time.

Dissemination processes link message producers and creators to their receivers via their messages. Gatekeepers then select from the flood of messages available to them; this is the traditional gatekeeping approach for determining how decisions are made and on what bases. As noted, this traditional gatekeeping model occurs after messages have already been created.

In part, dissemination is dependent on the media play given to any event or idea. The two most popular dissemination models have dealt with the diffusion of news, almost entirely a media system configuration, and with the diffusion of innovations, in which the media have a central, but not exclusive, role. The former is interested in how rapidly breaking news disseminates among segments of the public, whereas the latter focuses on how rapidly new products, ideas, or services disseminate.

Diffusion of news research could begin in the newsroom with the decision-making process that determines how a story will be reported, when it will be released, and what sort of play it will be given. Diffusion of innovations' interest in the mass media focuses on the media's role in providing information about the innovation, in contrast with or in juxtaposition with the role of a source. Again, decisions about which media to use for disseminating, for how long, and with what anticipated effects are difficult to assess and have not received research attention.

Content analysis in the dissemination process focuses on what media play is given to a story, event, or idea. In a specific time frame, how frequently does it appear? How prominently is it featured? The diffusion of news research tradition often has chosen to examine crisis or catastrophic news events, in which almost all the major news media interrupt their normal routine and focus most of their resources on examining the happening, such as the unexpected death of a major figure. Given the unstable nature of crisis news events, it is also fair to examine the misinformation the media provide as the raw breaking news takes form and errors subsequently are corrected.

Processes of Reception

Linking the message to the receiver begins with selectivity processes. Of all the messages available to media audiences, with which ones are they familiar or even aware? Awareness certainly precedes a certain amount of exposure. One may begin by acknowledging that there is a large business in making receivers familiar with messages. That business consists of making receivers aware that a media event will be available to attend. Whether the promotions are advertisements on ABC announcing new fall programs, or the stories and matrices in *TV Guide*, or the newspaper index at the bottom of the front page, they are designed to increase audience awareness as the first step toward increasing exposure. Their purpose is to cut into the selection process and cry out, "Try Me!"

Media use, or the time and energy spent on the mass media, is often measured by *exposure*. The issue of comparative time allocated to different media remains an enduring research concern. Is it fair to compare an hour of book reading with equal time spent watching television or reading a newspaper? Underlying the measure of media exposure is a concern with reception; it is assumed that media exposure and reception are positively correlated. While sheer time spent with media might be an operationally reliable measure, it is not a sufficient indicator of reception.

The process of selective exposure is receiving new scrutiny. Thanks to new media technologies, the public has more choices available than ever before. Rather than a half dozen off-air television stations, there are 60 to 100 cable television channels, plus another dozen offering pay-per-view, and a likely two dozen radio stations from which to select, if an Ipod isn't plugged into one's ears. A computer with a modem provides access to several information data banks (is this mass communication?) and offers hundreds of information sources. What is the process of media choice-making, within available disposable time, which leads an individual to watch this, read that, or listen to something different? The range of strategies being used by receivers to cope with an overwhelming array of media options is a fertile, but largely uncultivated, area for research.

Exposure itself has often been mapped against what are called media *gratifications*—those needs and uses which prod individuals to choose a particular media activity, usually over others that are available at the same time. These motivating tendencies have been mapped for a wide variety of content—entertainment, news, talk shows—to identify both underlying and content specific gratifications. Seeking gratifications from media experiences then can be linked to obtaining them; if what is sought is not fulfilled, what is the likelihood that one will return to that medium or that specific content for a second effort? Do some gratifications emanate from specific content and others from specific media, regardless of content offering? How much of our media exposure is gratifying in some way, or merely habitual?

Given selectivity in awareness and exposure, this phase can also include assessments of selectivity in interpretation and recall. These follow logically from exposure. They also reinforce the need to acknowledge that audiences may interpret the media systems' output in terms of their own predispositions. Furthermore, audiences are likely to recall only that which is particularly outstanding and of special utility for them. This suggests that the relationship between what was initially identified in the selection process as a candidate for subsequent media creation and dissemination may bear little resemblance to the resultant message. This assertion cuts across the modular processes described

At some point, model-making must cease and researchers commence to test the model and its components. One criterion for halting is when the model becomes overly complex. For that reason we end this effort by summarizing the elements to examine in the selection–creation–dissemination–reception criteria in the model of models in Table 5.1.

Researchers should examine much more in analyzing and critiquing mass communication models. Were we to continue our model of models, we might extend the reception process by discussing alternative potential effects one might highlight from mass media; alternatives to reinforcement effects might be one such effort. Because specification of such effects is likely to be contained within the hypotheses that link elements or concepts in each of these phases, we urge readers to continue with such speculation.

Table 5.1 Selection–Creation–Dissemination–Reception Criteria

Selection	Creation	Dissemination	Reception
Decoding	Encoding	Gatekeeping	Decoding
Accessibility	Agenda-setting	Media emphasis	Gratifications
Selective choices	Channel choices	Institutional analysis	Selective responses
Gatekeeping	Motivations	News diffusion	Choice-making
Personal agendas	Message–content analysis	Cultivation analysis	Information-seeking
Biases and interests	Content manipulations		Effects analyses
Criteria and norms	Intentions		

Summary

In summary, contemporary study of mass communication is guided by popular models, often, but not exclusively, in the effects tradition. Given the time it takes for a model to produce a coherent body of research, it is difficult to predict whether major new widely-accepted models are on the horizon. This is not entirely a bad thing; a field that willy-nilly introduces and tosses out models the way that Detroit used to introduce new car models is a field unsure of its place.

Other models are on the horizon: The third-person effect, people's attributional beliefs that mass media messages affect other people but not themselves (Davison, 1983), is gaining credence as a popular model generating a paradigmatic body of empirical research (Gunther & Mundy, 1993; Perloff, 1993). Another, the drench hypothesis, focuses on whether television effects on viewers is the result of a relatively short-term intensive impact (drench) or incremental effects attributable to the repetition of messages and images over time (Greenberg, 1988; Reep & Dambrot, 1989).

In addition to an age of models, the field is to some extent in an age of normal, fundamental research. Researchers are specifying the contingencies associated with popular models. In short, the field of mass communication has wound down from an era of rapid growth and excitement during the 1940s to 1970s and established itself as a legitimate field of study forging new paths in understanding and delineating the mass communication processes.

Notes

1. See Tankard (1984) for an account of the contributions of leading statisticians.
2. The sleeper effect posits (Hovland et al., 1949; Hovland & Weiss, 1951) that over time receivers remember parts of the messages after forgetting the source. Two-step flow and the related concept of opinion leaders come from studies (Berelson et al., 1954; Katz & Lazarsfeld, 1954; Lazarsfeld et al., 1944) in which leaders in their areas of expertise gained mass media information that they filtered to others. Selective perception and reinforcement were implicit in this research. Selective perception maintains that people actively attend to and select messages that fit preconceptions. Reinforcement is conceived as an explanation for why people seek out messages that fit preconceptions.

References

Bauer, R. A. (1964). The obstinate audience: The influence process from the point of view of social communication. *American Psychologist, 19*, 319–328.

Berelson, B. (1952). *Content analysis in communication research.* New York: Free Press.

Berelson, B. R., Lazarsfeld, P. F., & McPhee, W. N. (1954). *Voting: A study of opinion formation in a presidential campaign*. Chicago: University of Chicago Press.

Berlo, D. K. (1960). *The process of communication*. New York: Holt, Rinehart & Winston.

Bottomore, T. (1984). *The Frankfurt school*. Chichester, Sussex: E. Horwood.

Burke, J. (1985). *The day the universe changed*. Boston: Little, Brown.

Campbell, A., Converse, P. E., Miller, W., & Stokes, D. (1960). *The American voter*. New York: Wiley.

Chaffee, S. H., & Hochheimer, J. L. (1985). The beginnings of political communication research in the United States: Origins of the "limited effects" model. In E. M. Rogers & F. Balle (Eds.), *The media revolution in America and Western Europe* (pp. 267–296). Norwood, NJ: Ablex.

Czitrom, D. J. (1982). *Media and the American mind: From Morse to McLuhan*. Chapel Hill, NC: University of North Carolina Press.

Davison, W. P. (1983). The third-person effect in communication. *Public Opinion Quarterly, 47*, 1–15.

Dennis, E., & Wartella, E. (Eds.). (1996). *American communication research: The remembered history*. Mahwah, NJ: Erlbaum.

Flesch, R. (1943). *Marks of a readable style: A study in adult education*. New York: Teachers College, Columbia University.

Flesch, R. (1948). A new readability yardstick. *Journal of Applied Psychology, 32*, 221–233.

Gitlin, T (1978). Media sociology: The dominant paradigm. *Theory and Society, 6*, 205–253.

Gould, S. J. (1981). *The mismeasure of man*. New York: Norton.

Greenberg, B. S. (1988). Some uncommon television images and the drench hypothesis. In S. Oskamp (Ed.), *Television as a social issue* (pp. 88–102). Newbury Park, CA: Sage.

Greenberg, B. S., & Gantz, W. (Eds.). (1993). *Desert Storm and the mass media*. Cresskill, NJ: Hampton Press.

Gunther, A., & Mundy, P. (1993). Biased optimism and the third-person effect. *Journalism Quarterly, 70*, 355–372.

Hess, H. W. (1931). *Advertising: Its economics, philosophy and technique*. Philadelphia: Lippincott.

Hovland, C. I., Lumsdaime, A., & Sheffield, F. (1949). *Experiments in mass communication*. Princeton, NJ: Princeton University Press.

Hovland, C. I., & Weiss, W. (1951). The influence of source credibility on communication effectiveness. *Public Opinion Quarterly, 15*, 635–650.

Hurwitz, D. (1988). Market research and the study of the U.S. radio audience. *Communication, 10*(2), 223–242.

Katz, E. (1987). Communication research since Lazarsfeld. *Public Opinion Quarterly, 51*, S25–S45.

Katz, E., & Lazarsfeld, P. F. (1954). *Personal influence*. Glencoe, IL: The Free Press.

Kellner, D. (1993). The crisis in the Gulf and the lack of critical media discourse. In B. S. Greenberg & W. Gantz (Eds.), *Desert Storm and the mass media* (pp. 37–47). Cresskill, NJ: Hampton Press.

Klapper, J. (1960). *The effects of mass communication*. New York: The Free Press.

Lasswell, H. D. (1927). *Propaganda technique in the World War*. New York: Knopf.

Lasswell, H. D. (1948). The structure and function of communication in society. In L. Bryson (Ed.), *The communication of ideas* (pp. 117–130). Urbana: University of Illinois Press.

Lazarsfeld, P. F. (1948). The role of criticism in the management of mass media. *Journalism Quarterly, 25*, 115–126.

Lazarsfeld, P. F., Berelson, B., & Gaudet, H. (1944). *The people's choice: How the voter makes up his mind in a presidential campaign*. New York: Columbia University Press.

Link, H. C. (1938). *The new psychology of selling and advertising*. New York: Macmillan.

Lowery, S. A., & DeFleur, M. L. (1988). *Milestones in mass communication research* (2nd ed.). New York: Longman.

Manchester, W. (1993, October 25). A world lit only by change. *US News & World Report, 115*, 6–9.

McCombs, M. E., & Shaw, D. L. (1972). The agenda-setting function of the mass media. *Public Opinion Quarterly, 36*, 176–185.

McGuire, W. J. (1986): The myth of massive media impact: Savagings and salvagings. In G. Comstock (Ed.), *Public communication and behavior* (Vol. 1, pp. 175–257). San Diego, CA: Academic Press.

McQuail, D., & Windahl, S. (1993). *Communication models for the study of mass communication* (2nd ed.). London and New York: Longman.

Nash, S. G. (Ed.). (1990). *A history of scientific computing.* New York: ACM Press.

Pasanella, A. K. (1994). *The mind traveller: A guide to Paul F. Lazarsfeld's research papers.* New York: The Freedom Forum Media Studies Center.

Perloff, R. M. (1993). Third-person effect research 1983–1992: A review and synthesis. *International Journal of Public Opinion Research, 5,* 167–184.

Pool, I. de Sola (1983). What ferment? A challenge for empirical research. *Journal of Communication, 33,* 258–261.

Potter, W. J. (1996). *An analysis of thinking and research about qualitative methods.* Mahwah, NJ: Erlbaum.

Reardon, K. K., & Rogers, E. M. (1988). Interpersonal versus mass communication: A false dichotomy? *Human Communication Research, 15,* 284–303.

Reep, D. C., & Dambrot, F. H. (1989). Effects of frequent television viewing on stereotypes: "Drip drip" or "drench." *Journalism Quarterly, 66,* 542–550, 556.

Rogers, E. M. (1994). *A history of communication study: A biographical approach.* New York: The Free Press.

Salwen, M. B. (1991). Cultural imperialism: A media effects approach. *Critical Studies in Mass Communication, 8,* 29–30.

Schramm, W. L. (Ed.). (1948). *Communications in modern society.* Urbana: University of Illinois Press.

Schramm, W. L. (Ed.). (1954). *The process and effects of mass communication.* Urbana: University of Illinois Press.

Scott, W. D. (1921). *The psychology of advertising.* New York: Dodd, Meady.

Sloan, W. D. (1990). In search of itself: A history of journalism education. In W. D. Sloan (Ed.), *Makers of the media mind: Journalism educators and their ideas* (pp. 3–22). Hillsdale, NJ: Erlbaum.

Sproule, J. M. (1989). Progressive propaganda critics and the magic bullet myth. *Critical Studies in Mass Communication, 6,* 225–246.

Sproule, J. M. (1990). Propaganda and American ideological critique. In J. A. Anderson (Ed.), *Communication yearbook* (Vol. 14, pp. 211–238). Newbury Park, CA: Sage.

Starker, S. (1989). *Evil influences: Crusades against the mass media.* New Brunswick, NJ: Transaction.

Tankard, J. W., Jr. (1984). *The statistical pioneers.* Cambridge, MA: Schenkman.

Tankard, J. W., Jr. (1990). The theorists. In W. D. Sloan (Ed.), *Makers of the media mind: Journalism educators and their ideas* (pp. 229–286). Hillsdale, NJ: Erlbaum.

Vidich, A., & Lyman, S. M. (1993). Qualitative methods: Their history in sociology and anthropology. In N. K. Denzin & Y. S. Lincoln (Eds.), *Handbook of qualitative research* (pp. 23–59). Thousand Oaks, CA: Sage.

Wartella, E. (1994). Challenge to the profession. *Communication Education, 43,* 54–62.

Watt, J. H., & Welch, A. J. (1983). Effects of static and dynamic complexity on children's attention and recall of televised instruction. In J. Bryant & D. R. Anderson (Eds.), *Children's understanding of television* (pp. 69–102). New York: Academic Press.

Weaver, D. H., & Gray, R. G. (1980). Journalism and mass communication research in the United States: Past, present and future. In G. C. Wilhoit & H. de Bock (Eds.), *Mass communication review yearbook* (Vol. 1, pp. 124–155). Beverly Hills, CA: Sage.

Westley, B. H. (1958a). Journalism research and the scientific method: I. *Journalism Quarterly, 35,* 161–169.

Westley, B. H. (1958b). Journalism research and the scientific method: II. *Journalism Quarterly, 35,* 307–316.

Suggested Readings

Katz, E. (1987). Communication research since Lazarsfeld. *Public Opinion Quarterly, 51,* S25–S45.

McGuire, W. J. (1986): The myth of massive media impact: Savagings and salvagings. In G. Comstock (Ed.), *Public communication and behavior* (Vol. 1, pp. 175–257). San Diego, CA: Academic Press.

McQuail, D., & Windahl, S. (1993). *Communication models for the study of mass communication* (2nd ed.). London and New York: Longman.

Rogers, E. M. (1994). *A history of communication study: A biographical approach.* New York: The Free Press.

Salwen, M. B. (1991). Cultural imperialism: A media effects approach. *Critical Studies in Mass Communication, 8,* 29–30.

6

MEDIA GATEKEEPING

Pamela J. Shoemaker and Tim P. Vos

One of the most enduring areas of research in media sociology is media gatekeeping—the process by which countless occurrences and ideas are reduced to the few messages we are offered in our news media. News work—the process of newsgathering, news writing, and dissemination—has come under scrutiny in no small part because people's sense of reality is influenced by what gets into the news and what gets left out. Virtually all of news work involves gatekeeping. What will we write about? What will we include or leave out? How will the topic be shaped? But gatekeeping involves more than decisions about what to write or which images to capture. It begins when events, ideas, or people[1] first come to the attention of a news worker. From the news organization's standpoint, gatekeeping ends with selecting events, shaping news items, and disseminating them. An entirely new gatekeeping process begins when audience members make their own decisions about which news items, if any, to view, listen to, or read. This chapter, however, confines itself to the gatekeeping process that ends with the transmission of the news items. Yet this is no small task. For one event to become a news item requires a series of activities—observations, decisions, serendipity, creativity, constraints and facilitators, and a good share of luck. This might seem to result in a diverse set of events covered by the news media. Yet, we know that the news from one day is similar to that of another (Shoemaker & Cohen, 2006), and so we assume that gatekeeping is not a random process. Rather, it involves a complex series of operations that extend throughout the news production and dissemination process. Gatekeeeping can be studied on many levels of analysis, with many different research methods.

Origin of the Concept

A basic premise of gatekeeping is selection—some things are chosen and others rejected. We cannot eat every food item on the menu or buy every tomato in the grocery store. Therefore we select some items from the population of items before us. If a newspaper has space for only 5000 column inches of news, then many selection decisions must be made. First we must select from among the many events in the world those that will become news items and then decide which news items will be published. A bucket can hold only so many walnuts—which are put in the bucket and which are left on the ground? If all walnuts are the same, selection is of little importance. But if some walnuts taste better than others or some are more attractive, then selection becomes more important. So it is with news—events and news items vary according to numerous criteria.

It was in thinking about ways to change social norms that Kurt Lewin first coined the word *gatekeeping* (Shoemaker, 1991). The first pairing of the terms *gatekeeping* and *communication* came in Lewin's unfinished manuscript (published posthumously in 1947), "Frontiers in Group Dynamics: II. Channels of Group Life; Social Planning and Action Research," in the journal

Human Relations. Lewin's "theory of channels and gate keepers" was elaborated in 1951 in *Field Theory in Social Science,* an edited collection of Lewin's work. He used the concept of "gatekeeper" to illustrate how widespread social changes could be achieved in a community; he was primarily interested in how one could change a population's food habits. Lewin concluded that not everyone is equally important in making food selection choices, and he showed how influencing the person who orders or shops for food could change the food habits of the entire family.

Food, wrote Lewin, reaches the family table through *channels.* One channel begins at the grocery store, and another might begin in the family garden. Figure 6.1 illustrates how Lewin thought food passed from these two channels to the dinner table. For example, in the grocery channel, food is discovered at the grocery store, purchased or not, and, if purchased, transported to the home. These *sections* are multiple decision points. In the garden channel, decisions are made about what to plant, prune, and harvest, each a section in the channel. As fruits and vegetables grow, some will be picked from the garden by hungry children, some consumed by insects or disease, and others may die for lack of rain. Therefore, of the fruits and vegetables that could have been available to the household, only a subset is ultimately harvested and brought into the kitchen.

At this point, food from the grocery and garden channels merge; they create a combined channel with its own series of sections and gates for which new decisions are required. Should the food be refrigerated or put in the pantry? The cook must consider that food may rot in the refrigerator or languish in the deep recesses of the pantry. From among the usable food, the cook decides what to select for a given day—some items will be selected because they will "go bad" if not eaten immediately. The cook also decides how to prepare and present the food on the family's table. At every stage, a food item may be selected or rejected: Even if a potato is selected to be baked, it may be thrown away at the table if rot is exposed when it is cut open. And at each stage, the food is shaped (for example, French fried potatoes rather than mashed potatoes) and the cook decides when the food will be served and whether leftovers will become part of tomorrow's dinner.

Lewin called the entrance to each channel or section of a channel a *gate.* Movement from one channel section to another is determined by applying either a set of rules or by a *gatekeeper* making "in" or "out" decisions (Lewin, 1951, p. 186). An important part of Lewin's theory was his assertion that positive and negative forces surround the gates. For example, if an expensive cut of meat is seen in the grocery store, the meat's cost exerts a negative force against buying it—*it's so expensive, how can I afford it?* If the meat is purchased, however, its expense changes from a negative to a positive force—*it was so expensive, I must take care to transport, store, and prepare it carefully.* Because the forces surrounding a gate may differ, whether the item passes through it depends on the valence (positive or negative) and intensity of these forces. Since one channel may have multiple gates, there are many forces and many opportunities for an item to be selected or rejected.

In Figure 6.1, arrows show how forces facilitate or constrain the passage of items within a section and on both sides of a gate. Forces are designated in italics; for example, fP,EF represents the positive force associated with the attractiveness of food within the section "buying." A positive force should facilitate the food's passage past the next gate and into the "food on way to home" section.

Lewin believed that this theoretical framework could be generalized beyond the selection of food items. "This situation holds not only for food channels but also for the traveling of a news item through certain communication channels in a group, for movement of goods, and the social locomotion of individuals in many organizations" (Lewin, 1951, p. 187). Gatekeeping has proven to be a portable concept, used not only in communication but in a variety of disciplines. For

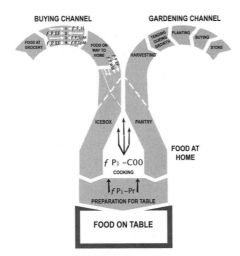

Figure 6.1 Kurt Lewin's model of how food passes through channels on its way to the table. From *Field Theory in Social Science: Selected Theoretical Papers* (p. 175), by K. Lewin, 1951, New York: Harper. Copyright 1951 by Miriam Lewin. Reprinted with permission.

example, primary care physicians are sometimes called gatekeepers for their role in controlling access to specialized physical and mental health care (Roberts & Greene, 2002).

Although Lewin's terms *channel, section, force,* and *gate* imply physical structures, they are metaphors for a process through which items may or may not pass, step by step, from discovery to use. A *channel* is a social artifact or organization that determines the hurdles an item must pass over. The news media are themselves channels, with newspapers, television and radio news programs all considering what should become news. On a smaller scale, assigning a reporter to cover education rather than crime creates a channel within which that reporter interprets the world. *Sections* correspond to ways in which the channel is organized. *Gates* are decision points, not only involving the selection of an event, but also whether it will be treated as hard or soft news, how long it will be, what sorts of visuals will be used, its prominence within the newscast or newspaper, and whether it will be followed up the next day. *Forces* are cultural norms that work for or against selection, length, and so on. *Gatekeepers* are generally people who make these decisions, but they also may be policies that people carry out.

As a social psychologist Lewin was well aware that individuals, or individual gatekeepers, acted within a social context. Lewin developed *field theory* to account for that context. He understood gatekeeping to be the outcome of a web of interconnected gates and forces within a social field, and not simply as one person making decisions. In addition, he assumed that individual decisions are grounded within the social field. In other words, they are "the product of the interaction between the person and his environment" (Schellenberg, 1978, p. 70).

Early Studies and Models

Although gatekeeping research originated in Lewin's scholarship, one of his research assistants is credited with applying gatekeeping theory to the study of news. David Manning White, from the University of Iowa, is responsible for the initial development of the research agenda for media gatekeeping. White was the first scholar to apply Lewin's channels and gatekeeper theory to a communication research project (White, 1950). White said he "thought that the complex series of 'gates' a newspaper story went through from the actual criterion event to the finished story in a newspaper would make an interesting study" (Reese & Ballinger, 2001, p. 646). His idea was to ask a small-city daily newspaper wire editor—whom he called "Mr. Gates"—to keep all copy that came into his office from three wire services during a one-week period in 1949. Mr. Gates also agreed to provide an explanation for why rejected stories (90 percent of the total received) were not used.

White (1950, p. 386) concluded that the selection decisions were "highly subjective." About one-third of the articles coming across the wires were rejected because of Mr. Gates' personal evaluation of the stories, particularly whether he believed them to be true. Other stories were rejected because of a lack of space or because similar stories had already run. White's focus on the subjective decisions of an isolated individual did little to test the broader implications of Lewin's field theory, but his study encouraged many communication researchers to look at selection decisions in news.

Subsequent gatekeeping studies questioned White's conclusion that personal decisions were very influential. Gieber (1956) said that the 16 newspaper telegraph editors he studied made decisions not based on their personal likes and dislikes, but rather because of a "straitjacket of mechanical details," such as deadlines, production requirements, and the number of competing news items (Gieber, 1964, p. 175). The importance of these impersonal factors led Gieber to interpret the wire editor's job as being passive, primarily applying the organization's policies. McNelly (1959) noted that the actions of a single gatekeeper could be exaggerated if attention was not paid to the fact that multiple actors, such as correspondents and editors, were involved in the gatekeeping process. Gieber (1960) explored how sources, bearing the values of their reference group, played a role in the construction of news. Without explicit reference to Lewin's field theory, Lewin's ideas nevertheless were finding support. In fact, Chibnall (1977) saw an interaction between the gatekeeper and his or her environment—since reporters were so dependent upon sources for access to key information, reporters often had to play by the rules sources dictated. While attempts would eventually be made to enrich and expand the theory of gatekeeping, for example, Donohew's (1967) examination of the forces at the gates, these early studies largely neglected ties not only to Lewin's field theory, but also to theories in general.

At about the same time, however, a more theoretical model of news item transmission was proposed by Westley and MacLean (1957), based on Newcomb's (1953) ABX co-orientation model. Newcomb proposed the idea of *co-orientation* as a way to study communication acts between two people (designated A and B) simultaneously orienting toward each other and toward an object (designated X)—Figure 6.2 shows how Westley and MacLean added the mass media (designated C) between the sender and the receiver. In this model, there are multiple events (Xs), some of which are discovered by sender A (in this model, a source) and then travel through the mass

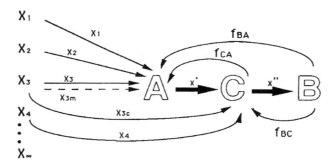

Figure 6.2 Westley and MacLean's model of mass communication process, showing C as the gatekeeper. Reprinted by permission of the Association for Education in Journalism and Mass Communication from *Journalism Quarterly, 34,* 31–38. Westley, B. H., MacLean, M. S., Jr. (1957).

media (C) to the receiver (B). Other events go directly to the media, bypassing sources. The introduction of the mass media C into Newcomb's model shows that not all messages that the sender is aware of are transmitted to the receiver.

Westley and MacLean's model views the gatekeeping process differently from that described by White. White focused on the decisions of one person, emphasizing personal and subjective aspects of the decision-making process. The Westley and MacLean model, however, emphasized the gatekeeping aspect Lewin said was governed by "impartial rules" (1951, p. 186). They saw the journalist's job as carrying out policies prescribed by an organization or social system, more or less uniformly.

This shows that gatekeeping can be studied on at least two levels of analysis—the individual and the routine practices of news work. Lewin saw gatekeeping as occurring on multiple levels of analysis. His examples include at least three levels. An *individual* can make personal decisions about what to buy at the market or cook on a given day, there are family *routines or habits* to take into account, and there are also *societal and cultural forces* at play. For example, certain foods are culturally unavailable within a given social system—insects are rarely eaten in some cultures but are prized as delicacies in others. Even if insects are culturally available as food, a particular family's eating habits may exclude insects from the shopping list. Or the individual shopper may make selections based on a personal preference that insects will be eaten only once a month.

Lewin's field theory proposed that individuals interact with their environments—what he termed "psychological ecology" (1951, p. 170). Lewin's theory later was elaborated by psychologists both as ecological systems theory and human ecology theory. Individuals must be understood within the context of four systems: a microsystem (immediate context), mesosystem (nexus of immediate contexts), exosystem (external institutions), and macrosystem (culture) (Bronfenbrenner, 1979).

The realization that gatekeeping can be studied on multiple levels of analysis makes it much more interesting. As shown by Shoemaker (1991; Shoemaker & Reese, 1996), gatekeeping in a communication context can be studied on at least five levels—individuals, the routine practices of communication work, communication organizations, social institutions, and societies. On the individual level, selection decisions are personal—*What do I like or dislike?* If not personal, selection decisions can still be driven by individual factors such as the gender, sexual orientation, education, class, or religion of an individual gatekeeper (Cohen, 1963; Johnstone, Slawski, & Bowman, 1976; Weaver, Beam, Brownlee, Voakes, & Wilhoit, 2007; Weaver & Wilhoit, 1986, 1996).

On the routine practices level, gatekeeping decisions are made according to a preestablished and generalized set of practices about how the work is to be done. Gatekeeping is "mediated by practical concerns: how to report a world of activities within the constraints of publication deadlines and news space limitations, how to determine the factual character of accounts, how to formulate events into a story, and so on" (Fishman, 1980, p. 14). *Is this newsworthy enough to be included in the day's television news program?* Such decisions cross media lines to the extent that media and communication workers share basic definitions of newsworthiness (Peterson, 1979; Tuchman, 1974). The rules are not necessarily written down nor consciously acknowledged by the gatekeeper. "The rules governing newswork are not simply given and available, but actually constructed, interpreted, and elaborated upon in the actual settings of newswork" (Lester, 1980, p. 993).

Media organizations can have different goals and structures that constrain the influences of individual gatekeepers. The profit maximizing goals of news organizations may set limits on what reporters do (Bagdikian, 2004). For example, a reporter may want to investigate suspected wrongdoing in local government but be handicapped by limited resources, such as unwillingness by editors to spend money on an investigation that may fail to yield definitive results, limited training or ability to engage in sophisticated computer-assisted reporting, or misgivings from an overly cautious legal department. Given the hierarchical organizational structure of most news organizations, individuals ultimately have to yield to decisions made elsewhere in the organization. Thus, we could also look at the gatekeeper's position within the organization as influencing the power that he or she has in making final selection decisions. Gatekeepers such as newspaper publishers and television station managers tend to have considerable power to develop policies that greatly influence selection decisions (Donohew, 1967; Hickey, 1966, 1968).

Communication organizations exist within an environment of social institutions that also affect the gatekeeping process. There are many potential influences outside of the media organization, such as sources, audiences and advertisers, markets and economic forces, government, interest groups, public relations agencies, and other media. Sources are often frontline gatekeepers, deciding to pass along some bits of information and not others (Gieber & Johnson, 1961; Soley, 1992). Perceived source accuracy is also a factor in whether a reporter will use the source. Advertisers, in their quest for the most appropriate target audiences, exert direct and indirect influence on the mass media (Soley, 2002). Some newspapers, for example, have sought information about audience likes and dislikes to produce content that is attractive to the target audience, attracting more advertising dollars (Turow, 1997). Similarly, the success of a television program has long rested on its ratings—a measure of the number and type (through demographics and psychographics) of people watching the show: Shows with poor ratings are canceled. Advertiser influence can also be indirect. Women's magazines, for example, traditionally have not run many stories about the harmful effects of smoking, presumably because the tobacco companies spend a lot of money on cigarette ads and ads for other companies that the tobacco conglomerates own (Kessler, 1989).

On the social system level of analysis, just as Lewin determined that some foods are not culturally available, events vary to the degree that they are culturally available as news items. Rape, for example, was rarely covered in newspapers a generation or two ago but today is regular fare for mainstream news media (Thomason & LaRocque, 1995). Culture—as well as other indicators of social significance, including political, military, and economic ties—also influences selection decisions, affecting the extent to which different parts of the world are covered and how they are covered (Nossek, 2004). Media in the United States tend to give more coverage to international events that relate to American national interests (Chang & Lee, 1992).

Methodology

White's (1950) study used a content analysis research design that permitted him to compare stories included in the newspaper with those rejected. This remains a preferred gatekeeping method today; studying what does not become news is perhaps more revealing of the decision-making process than is studying only the news product. If we study only what is included in a television newscast, it is difficult to know what influences the "in" and "out" decisions. For example, in her study of newspaper reporter sources, Seo (1988) found that individual source information is used in about the proportion that it is available. This puts a different light on the common finding (e.g., Gans, 1979; Sigal, 1973) that "official" sources are quoted far more than are individuals. It appears that there may be a lot more official sources available than there are individual sources, but to the extent that individual sources are available, they may be used.

Scott and Gobetz (1990) did a content analysis of the amount of "soft news" coverage on the ABC, CBS, and NBC networks. They found that the amount of soft news increased between 1972 and 1987, but why?—were there more soft news events to cover? Or did journalists select an increasing percentage of soft news items? If journalists did select a greater proportion of soft news items, why should this be so? Was it because the journalists wanted more soft news? Or did journalists perceive that audiences wanted more soft news? Or were there other influences at work, such as a change over time in organizational routines? Such questions are vital in the study of gatekeeping. It is not sufficient to show changes over time, or that one type of news item is covered more at one time point. To more fully understand the gatekeeping process, the study should consider the theoretical context of the total news environment.

This is best accomplished by combining content analysis with other research methods, such as surveys, focus groups, interviews, observation, and experiments. For example, journalists are part of the total news environment, and surveying them yields information about their backgrounds, personal values, personal characteristics, and other variables that could influence the news stories they produce. Shoemaker, Eichholz, Kim, and Wrigley (2001) surveyed both reporters and their editors in a study that compared the characteristics of news items (from a content analysis) with data from two surveys. The first went to reporters who wrote stories about U.S. congressional bills and measured their various opinions and characteristics. The second went to their editors, and asked them to assess the newsworthiness of the bills. Data from these two surveys were combined with that from the content analysis to assess the relative influence of reporters' characteristics and the newsworthiness of events on how prominently the events were covered.

Surveys can inform us about psychological determinants of gatekeeping (Chang & Lee, 1992), such as preferences for one type of content over another or role conceptions. They can measure respondents' perceptions of forces working on the selection decision (e.g., space, time, directions from superiors). These perceptions, however, may vary in reliability and validity. Survey respondents report what they know (or think they know) about their attitudes and preferences, speculate about what they would do under specified scenarios, and tell what they know about their colleagues and about how their organizations work. Such information may or may not provide valid measures of these forces and how they affect the gatekeeping process. The expression of an attitude does not always lead to attitude-consistent behavior. Still, although content analysis data can tell us what becomes news, surveys can help us understand why news items exist. Survey data do provide insight into journalists' thought processes—processes that are invisible to the content analyst.

In-depth interviews with gatekeepers yield even more information about the influences of the news environment on content. For example, Berkowitz (1990) combined four weeks of observation of television news gatekeepers with interviews of 30 to more than 60 minutes in length about why specific decisions had been made. An unstructured interview format has the advantage of allowing respondents to take the discussion wherever they wish. This can be particularly helpful when interviewing gatekeepers about why they made specific selection decisions; the interview can be personally tailored to each gatekeeper. Personalization is also a disadvantage, however, because personalized interviews are generally not comparable; by definition there are no standardized questionnaires, thus lowering the study's external validity. Internal validity may be higher than in standardized surveys, however, because the causal chain between the selection decision and its antecedents can be traced in specific and detailed ways.

Gatekeeping studies using observational methods may suffer from the usual problem of reactivity, but this is generally lessened if the observational period is longer than a few days. In Berkowitz's study of television news gatekeepers, he devoted two weeks at the beginning of the study to "familiarization with the newsroom and the station's news process" (1990, p. 57). Following this initial period, four weeks were spent observing gatekeepers at work, followed by one week devoted to personal interviews. This seven-week-long field period helped reduce the threat to internal validity due to reactivity, but it points to one of the disadvantages of observational research—it takes time to do it right: The longer the field period, the greater the external validity. The advantage of observation in studying gatekeeping is that the researcher sees decisions being made in a real newsroom under realistic conditions and can observe some of the influences affecting the decisions, thus increasing external validity. Not all influences are observable, however, such as unwritten policies or socialization to newsroom routines. Combining observational data with interviews, however, can help the researcher more fully understand the gatekeeping process.

Experimental research in gatekeeping is unusual, but a field study by Hudson (1992) looked at how television news gatekeepers rated six staged versions of a murder story in which the violence levels were manipulated. The versions ranged from a story read by an anchor with no video to a version entailing a complete video of the murder occurring, subsequent shots of the body, pools of blood, and a close-up of the victim's face. All participants viewed six versions of the story and gave each a perceived acceptability level (PAL) of the violent material. Hudson then evaluated whether PAL scores varied for "participant" and "neutral" journalists, as measured by Johnstone et al. (1976). Are there any other experiments that can be cited?

The decision as to whether to use content analysis, surveys, personal interviews, observation, or experimental methods to study gatekeeping depends on the hypotheses being tested. It is clear, however, that the fullest understanding of gatekeeping will come from a multiple-method strategy that gathers data about the total news environment.

Changes in Gatekeeping Research

If Lewin was the father of gatekeeping research, his grandchildren are now exploring the implications of field theory for gatekeeping. Scholars recognize that individual gatekeepers have the power to pass some items through gates and reject others, but studies have also shown that gatekeepers' actions must be understood within the context of their environment. The expansion of gatekeeping studies to multiple levels of analysis opens the door for the study of the most interesting of Lewin's concepts—the forces surrounding each gate. Most gatekeeping research routinely investigates the power that one or more forces have on whether a news item is permitted to pass through a gate. We are beginning to identify the forces that have the most impact on the selection of news items and whether the forces are positive or negative.

Studies on the individual level of analysis show that characteristics of individual journalists may have some influence on news. Chang and Lee's (1992) study looked at American newspaper editors' attitudes toward selecting foreign news items and on the individual forces that affect gatekeeping. They found that these editor-gatekeepers preferred international stories that had some significant impact on American security and national interests. A key individual-level force affecting the decision was that editors with an "international perspective"—"liberal with foreign news interest and foreign language training" (p. 561)—were more likely to prefer stories about world events. The more professional journalism experience editors had, the less likely they were to select international stories. In this study the important forces around the gates were the characteristics of the gatekeepers themselves. We would expect that newspaper editors have a disproportionate say about what news makes it into the newspaper and hence these individual level factors likely explain some variation in news content. But this reinforces the importance of the gatekeeper's place within an organization in explaining news content and reinforces the need for an ecological understanding of gatekeepers.

Some individual level influences may be more appropriately understood as routine factors. For example, Berkowitz's television gatekeepers claimed to make selection decisions based on their "instincts" about what makes a good news program (1990, p. 66). Berkowitz also found that "news judgment" or "news values" influence gatekeeping (1991, p. 246). It is debatable whether this outcome is best understood as influences from individual characteristics or as the result of routine definitions of newsworthiness. Clearly, there are standard criteria for newsworthiness that are common across news organizations; however, the application of newsworthiness criteria may vary within individual gatekeepers.

Combining of survey research and content analysis to study newspaper coverage of major Congressional legislation, Shoemaker et al. (2001) set gatekeepers' decisions within their ecological setting or field. The study looked at the impact of forces on two levels of analysis, the individual reporter and the assessment of newsworthiness at the routine level of the newsgathering process. The study found that individual level factors such as gender and political ideology failed to predict coverage. However, the routine of determining newsworthiness did shape the news. The authors concluded "that routine forces are more successful in winning the competition to determine what becomes news than are individual forces" (p. 242).

Other routine-level forces include how much effort a news item requires to be transformed into a story, whether selection decisions are routinely made by individuals or groups of people (Berkowitz, 1990), and the desire for a "balanced" mix of stories (Riffe, Ellis, Rogers, Van Ommeren, & Woodman, 1986; Stempel, 1985). McCombs and Becker (1979) suggest that whether a gatekeeper is assigned the work role of news manager (e.g., producer, assignment editor, news director) or information gatherer (e.g., reporter and anchor) is important in studying the gatekeeping process because people in the two types of jobs face different pressures (or *forces*). In using this role differentiation in a study of television gatekeepers, however, Berkowitz (1993) found that these work roles were not closely associated with selection of news items.

Research at the organizational level has shown that what might first appear to be individual differences can better be explained by the organizational level. For example, Kim's (2002) Q analysis of journalists found differences among broadcast journalists in their assessment of the value of international news. Kim argues, "The American television journalist is an organizational creature who subscribes to business objectives; his or her mindset operates in tandem with organizational structures and goals" (p. 449). Organizational-level research has included whether a radio station has a group affiliation (Riffe & Shaw, 1990); the number of gates a news item must pass through within the organization (Berkowitz, 1990); and resource constraints, such as number of staff, level of funding, and equipment availability (McManus, 1990). This includes the availability and capabilities of new technologies and the availability and quality of information subsidies, such as video releases (Berkowitz, 1991).

Looking at the social institution level of analysis, McManus concludes that powerful interests within government, large corporations, and the wealthy have a disproportionate capacity to provide information subsidies. "By reducing the cost of discovery of events and views flattering to themselves, these special interests can take advantage of cost-conscious media to influence what the public learns" (McManus, 1990, p. 682). Meanwhile, Riffe and Shaw (1990) found that the size of the market positively influenced the amount of news that radio stations can carry. Kim (2002) also found market size a factor in gatekeepers choosing whether to print international news.

At the social system level of analysis, studies have explored the role of cultural values or social structure on gatekeeping. For example, Ravi (2005) shows how coverage of war and conflict varies from one country to another based upon the cultural values, beliefs, and practices of those countries. "Newspaper coverage seems to reflect notions, values, and ideas that resonate within particular societies" (Ravi, 2005, p. 59). A study by Donahue, Olien, and Tichenor (1989) shows a relationship between a community's degree of pluralism and news and advertising content. Similarly, Humphreys draws a distinction between media content in "'consensual' and 'majoritarian' democracies" (1996, p. 11). The difference in state structure leads to a difference in media structure and ultimately to a difference in news content—consensual democracies afford greater pluralism of media voices (see also Hallin & Mancini, 2004). Chang, Wang, and Chen (1998) show how different social structures in China and the United States shape notions of newsworthiness in different ways, ultimately producing different television news content.

A Brief Study Proposal

To illustrate how this can be applied in a real study, we take up the topic of public relations' influence on television news. We use the concept *force* to study why events that are covered by public relations practitioners as video news releases may (or may not) become news stories.

Introduction

In gatekeeping studies, the emphasis is on whether an event makes it through a news gate. But what influences whether the event goes through the gate? Chang and Lee (1992) showed that editor-gatekeepers' personal interest in national security and national interests positively affected the extent to which they selected foreign news items. Conversely, the more professional experience editors had, the less likely they were to select international stories. Berkowitz (1990) showed that the extent to which an event fits the generally conceived concept of newsworthiness is positively related to its selection. McCombs and Becker (1979) also found that job roles could be influential in gatekeeping—news managers select different stories than do information gatherers. Whether a radio station has a group affiliation or is independent has been found to impact selection (Riffe & Shaw, 1990). Berkowitz (1991) found that the resources of the organization (e.g., number of staff) influenced news item selection.

Although these studies look at influences on news selection, they do not tie them to an important consideration in gatekeeping theory. We can use Lewin's (1951) concept *force* to predict whether an event becomes news. The idea of forces is pivotal in gatekeeping theory. This study considers the success of the video news release (VNR) as a public relations tool. VNRs carry both positive and negative forces. Their positive forces include quality and cost, whereas the public relations' goal of persuading is a negative force.

Theory

A *force* is a characteristic of an event that influences how it will move through a channel. The identification of forces that influence whether an event is the topic of a VNR, and an assessment of their relative strengths and directions, is important for the theory's growth. Positive forces tend to push items through gates, whereas negative forces push them away. What would happen if both positive and negative forces are attached to a news item? Positive forces push information about events through the channel quickly, whereas negative forces may move slowly or stop altogether.

Gates occur at various locations in the channel, and positive forces will help an event move through the gate. An event with a negative force is less likely to move through the gate. In addition to *polarity* (positive to negative), an event's forces have *strength*, varying from weak to strong. Therefore a strong positive force will move the event more quickly through the channel than will a weak positive force.

Characteristics of Forces

Public relations practitioners produce video news releases, and these VNRs have many characteristics that the gatekeeper must consider, such as the timeliness of the information and its accessibility through other means. VNRs with these characteristics might be more likely to make it on television news: VNRs are generally well done, follow the journalistic conventions of news stories, and are free of cost to the television news organization. On the other hand, the gatekeeper must also consider the fact that some hold public relations in disdain and believe that they can produce higher quality news stories (Machill, Beiler, & Schmutz, 2006). As the gate-keeper considers the VNR's many characteristics, which will be most important?

All of the forces in this example exist in time in front of the news gate; that is, the forces are known by the gatekeeper before she or he decides whether to allow the video news release to pass through the gate. However, Lewin also recognized that forces can lie behind the gate, after the decision is made to bring the VNR into the pool of stories that may be transmitted. For example, once past the gate, the previous negative force associated with public relations could dissipate—the VNR being judged more on regular journalistic news values than on this stereotype.

Media Relations

Public relations activities come from outside of the media organization and are often held in distain by reporters (Turow, 1989) who may perceive them as prejudiced sources for news items. Such attitudes create negative forces in front of news gates. Journalists are suspicious of public relations' products and prefer to create their own stories. Still, there is evidence that the news media do sometimes have use for public relations' news releases; this ranges from giving the journalist an idea for a story to using the news release in its entirety (Cameron & Blount, 1996).

The video news release imitates a news story from a television news operation, and the public relations practitioner sends it to the television station in the hope that it will help push its topic or event through the news gate and appear in the news show. In other words, the public relations practitioner's hope is that the video news release will have a strong, positive force in front of the news gate. Positive forces include the professionalism and high quality of the video news release and the fact that it is free to the television station.

This study looks at situations in which the positive or negative forces attached to the video news release triumph, resulting in the event being pushed through or away from the gate. We test the following hypothesis:

> Journalists use the text and video in video news releases about a topic to the extent that they have knowledge about the topic.

The independent variable is the amount of knowledge a journalist holds about the topic. The dependent variable is the extent to which the video news release appears in or was the impetus for a news item. Journalists who know nothing about the topic are likely to use the video news release in full, whereas those with moderate knowledge may use parts of it. Journalists who are expert in the subject/issue covered in the VNRs are least likely to use any part of the video news releases.

Although some reporters may be physicians or have expert medical knowledge, most know less, especially when they are confronted with medical advances. Medical VNRs are more likely to be used completely when the television news reporters are not scientific experts, because reporters and their producers are afraid to get the story wrong. Journalists rarely have scientific training.

Methods

To control for topics having different characteristics, in this study we looked only at events in which medical breakthroughs were announced, such as press conferences. The unit of analysis in this study is the journalist. Events eligible for inclusion in the study are medical events covered in 50 local television news programs, randomly sampled from a list of all television news markets. The study includes data from both a content analysis and a survey.

Identifying the Event

All news items about medical breakthroughs were studied during the period of 2007. *Medical breakthroughs* are events that announce a new medicine, apparatus, or procedure. They were identified by having medical students code stories in the *Journal of the American Medical Association* on a 10-point scale, according to whether the story is about an ordinary event (1) or one that is new (10). The event with the highest mean rating was identified as the study's medical breakthrough event; however, when the corporate owner of the breakthrough was contacted, it failed to provide a copy of all VNRs produced about the event. Therefore, the second-highest scoring event was used. It was about measuring brain chemistry to evaluate a person's level of depression.

Content Analysis

Next, coders contacted the 50 television stations and requested a copy of the primary news program on the day on which the medical breakthrough event was announced. All 50 news stations provided stories about the medical event. Coders then identified the names of the reporters and producers who worked on the story. If this information was not available from the video, then phone calls were made to the station. Information was available from all 50 stations, yielding 60 reporters and 50 producers.

Coders then compared the VNRs to the television news stories about this topic. The following dependent variables were coded, and intercoder reliability was assessed for each:

- number of stories about the new medical procedure
- number of stories about the disease generally
- number of (in seconds) visuals from VNR appeared in news program
- number of (in seconds) words from VNR appeared in news program
- number of (in seconds) material (visual and words) from VNR appeared in news program
- was the VNR used in its entirety?
- number of (in seconds) material (visual and words) in news program that did not come from VNR

Survey Procedures

Telephone calls were made to all 110 individuals. The questionnaire included these independent variables:

- age
- gender
- number of years experience in television news as (1) producer, (2) reporter
- number of college courses taken in (1) chemistry, (2) biology, (3) healthcare, and (4) medical topic
- number of continuing education presentations attended in these areas, also including medicine
- number of medical publications read regularly
- familiarity with medical topics in general, Likert scale
- familiarity with depression in particular, Likert scale
- personal experience with depression for (1) self, (2) close family member, (3) close friend, (4) co-worker—number of people known to have depression, in each category

Results

The data would be then be entered into a statistical computer program such as SPSS and analyzed. Familiarity would be the dependent variable and the other variables would be independent variables in the test of the hypothesis. Analysis would be by Analysis of Variance or multiple regression.

Summary

Now that gatekeeping scholarship is more than 50 years old, we need to think about elaborating the theory to address the world of the 21st century. Certainly, more research on the forces around gates needs to be done, and looking at gatekeeping as a concept on multiple levels of analysis is fruitful. But we should also operationalize aspects of gatekeeping other than mere selection. The way in which stories are shaped, timed, and presented is also part of the gatekeeping process, and such variables deserve to be included with selection in our arsenal of dependent variables. In addition, we should consider the ways in which these dependent variables may themselves interact to produce the final media content product.

Note

1. Although the piece of the world that first comes to the attention of journalists can be a person, an idea, or an event, in fact the vast majority of news is about events. Therefore, we will use the term *event* here to represent them all.

References

Bagdikian, B. H. (2004). *The new media monopoly*. Boston: Beacon Press.

Berkowitz, D. (1990). Refining the gatekeeping metaphor for local television news. *Journal of Broadcasting & Electronic Media, 34*(1), 55–68.

Berkowitz, D. (1991). Assessing forces in the selection of local television news. *Journal of Broadcasting & Electronic Media, 35*(2), 245–251.

Berkowitz, D. (1993). Work roles and news selection in local TV: Examining the business–journalism dialectic. *Journal of Broadcasting & Electronic Media, 37*(1), 67–83.

Bronfenbrenner, U. (1979). *The ecology of human development: Experiments by nature and design*. Cambridge, MA: Harvard University Press.

Cameron, G. T., & Blount, D. (1996). VNRs and air checks: A content analysis of the use of video news releases in television newscasts. *Journalism & Mass Communication Quarterly, 73*(4), 890–904.

Chang, T.-K., & Lee, J.-W. (1992). Factors affecting gatekeepers' selection of foreign news: A national survey of newspaper editors. *Journalism and Mass Communication Quarterly, 69*(3), 554–561.

Chang, T.-K., Wang, J., & Chen, C.-H. (1998). The social construction of international imagery in the post-Cold War era: A comparative analysis of U.S. and Chinese national TV news. *Journal of Broadcasting and Electronic Media, 42*(3), 277–297.

Chibnall, S. (1977). *Law-and-order news: An analysis of crime reporting in the British press*. London: Tavistock.

Cohen, B. C. (1963). *The press and foreign policy*. Westport, CT: Greenwood.

Donahue, G. A., Olien, C. N., & Tichenor, P. J. (1989). Structure and constraints on community newspaper gatekeepers. *Journalism Quarterly, 66*(4), 807–845.

Donohew, L. (1967). Newspaper gatekeepers and forces in the news channel. *Public Opinion Quarterly, 31*, 61–68.

Fishman, M. (1980). *Manufacturing the news*. Austin: University of Texas Press.

Gans, H. J. (1979). *Deciding what's news*. New York: Pantheon.

Gieber, W. (1956). Across the desk: A study of 16 telegraph editors. *Journalism Quarterly, 33*, 423–432.

Gieber, W. (1960). How the "gatekeepers" view local civil liberties news. *Journalism Quarterly, 37*, 199–205.

Gieber, W. (1964). News is what newspapermen make it. In L. A. Dexter & D. M. White (Eds.), *People, society and mass communication.* New York: Free Press.

Gieber, W., & Johnson, W. (1961). The city hall "beat": A study of reporter and source roles. *Journalism Quarterly, 38*, 289–297.

Hallin, D. C., & Mancini, P. (2004). *Comparing media systems: Three models of media and politics.* New York: Cambridge University Press.

Hickey, J. R. (1966). *The effects of information control on perceptions of centrality.* Unpublished Dissertation, University of Wisconsin, Madison.

Hickey, J. R. (1968). The effects of information control on perceptions of centrality. *Journalism Quarterly, 45*, 49–54.

Hudson, T. J. (1992). Consonance in depiction of violent material in television news. *Journal of Broadcasting & Electronic Media, 36*, 411–425.

Humphreys, P. (1996). *Mass media and media policy in Western Europe.* New York: Manchester University Press.

Johnstone, J., Slawski, E., & Bowman, W. (1976). *The news people: A sociological portrait of American journalists and their work.* Urbana: University of Illinois Press.

Kessler, L. (1989). Women's magazines' coverage of smoking related health hazards. *Journalism Quarterly, 66*, 316–322, 445.

Kim, H. S. (2002). Gatekeeping international news: An attitudinal profile of U.S. television journalists. *Journal of Broadcasting & Electronic Media, 46*(3), 431–453.

Lester, M. (1980). Generating newsworthiness: The interpretive construction of public events. *American Sociological Review, 45*(6), 984–994.

Lewin, K. (1951). *Field theory in social science: Selected theoretical papers.* New York: Harper.

Machill, M., Beiler, M., & Schmutz, J. (2006). The influence of video news releases on the topics reported in science journalism. *Journalism Studies, 7*(6), 869–888.

McCombs, M. E., & Becker, L. B. (1979). *Using mass communication theory.* Englewood Cliffs, NJ: Prentice-Hall.

McManus, J. H. (1990). How local television learns what is news. *Journalism Quarterly, 67*(4), 672–683.

McNelly, J. T. (1959). Intermediary communicators in the international flow of news. *Journalism Quarterly, 36*, 23–26.

Newcomb, T. M. (1953). An approach to the study of communicative acts. *Psychological Review, 60*, 393–404.

Nossek, H. (2004). Our news and their news: The role of national identity in the coverage of foreign news. *Journalism, 5*(3), 343–368.

Peterson, S. (1979). Foreign news gatekeepers and criteria of newsworthiness. *Journalism Quarterly, 56*(1), 116–125.

Ravi, N. (2005). Looking beyond flawed journalism: How national interests, patriotism, and cultural values shaped the coverage of the Iraq War. *Harvard International Journal of Press/Politics, 10*(1), 45–62.

Reese, S. D., & Ballinger, J. (2001). The roots of a sociology of news: Remembering Mr. Gates and social control in the newsroom. *Journalism & Mass Communication Quarterly, 78*(4), 641–658.

Riffe, D., Ellis, B., Rogers, M. K., Van Ommeren, R. L., & Woodman, K. A. (1986). Gatekeeping and the network news mix. *Journalism Quarterly, 63*(2), 315–321.

Riffe, D., & Shaw, E. F. (1990). Ownership, operating, staffing and content characteristics of "news radio" stations. *Journalism Quarterly, 67*(4), 684–691.

Roberts, A. R., & Greene, G. J. (2002). *Social workers' desk reference.* New York: Oxford University Press.

Schellenberg, J. A. (1978). *Masters of social psychology: Freud, Mead, Lewin, and Skinner.* New York: Oxford University Press.

Scott, D. K., & Gobetz, R. H. (1990). *Ownership, operating, staffing and content characteristics of "news radio" stations.* Paper presented at the Central States Communication Association.

Seo, S. K. (1988). *Source-press relationship: Major characteristics of sources which influence selection of sources in news coverage.* Paper presented at the Association for Education in Journalism and Mass Communication.

Shoemaker, P. J. (1991). *Gatekeeping.* Newbury Park, CA: Sage.

Shoemaker, P. J., & Cohen, A. A. (2006). *News around the world: Content, practitioners, and the public.* New York: Routledge.

Shoemaker, P. J., Eichholz, M., Kim, E., & Wrigley, B. (2001). Individual and routine forces in gatekeeping. *Journalism and Mass Communication Quarterly, 78*(2), 233–246.

Shoemaker, P. J., & Reese, S. D. (1996). *Mediating the message: Theories of influences on mass media content* (2nd ed.). White Plains, NY: Longman.

Sigal, L. V. (1973). *Reporters and officials: The organization and politics of newsmaking* Lexington, MA: D.C. Heath.

Soley, L. C. (1992). *The news shapers: The sources who explain the news.* New York: Praeger.

Soley, L. C. (2002). *Censorship, Inc.: The corporate threat to free speech in the United States.* New York: Monthly Review Press.

Stempel, G. H., III. (1985). Gatekeeping: The mix of topics and the selection of stories. *Journalism Quarterly, 62*(4), 791–796, 815.

Thomason, T., & LaRocque, P. (1995). Editors still reluctant to name rape victims. *Newspaper Research Journal, 16*(3), 42–51.

Tuchman, G. (1974). Making news by doing work: Routinizing the unexpected. *American Journal of Sociology, 79,* 110–131.

Turow, J. (1989). Public relations and newswork: A neglected relationship. *American Behavioral Scientist, 33*(2), 206–212.

Turow, J. (1997). *Breaking up America: Advertisers and the new media world.* Chicago: University of Chicago Press.

Weaver, D. H., Beam, R. A., Brownlee, B. J., Voakes, P. S., & Wilhoit, G. C. (2007). *The American journalist in the 21st century: U.S. news people at the dawn of a new millennium.* Mahwah, NJ: Erlbaum.

Weaver, D. H., & Wilhoit, G. C. (1986). *The American journalist: A portrait of U.S. news people and their work.* Bloomington: Indiana University Press.

Weaver, D. H., & Wilhoit, G. C. (1996). *The American journalist in the 1990s: U.S. news people at the end of an era.* Mahwah, NJ: Erlbaum.

Westley, B. H., & MacLean, M. S., Jr. (1957). A conceptual model for communications research. *Journalism Quarterly, 34,* 31–38.

White, D. M. (1950). The "gate keeper": A case study in the selection of news. *Journalism Quarterly, 27,* 383–390.

Suggested Readings

Benson, R., & Neveu, E. (2005). *Bourdieu and the journalistic field.* Malden, MA: Polity.

Berkowitz, D. (1997). *The social meanings of news: A text-reader.* Thousand Oaks, CA: Sage.

Schudson, M. (2003). *The sociology of news.* New York: Norton.

Shoemaker, P. J., & Reese, S. D. (1996). *Mediating the message: Theories of influences on mass media content* (2nd ed.). White Plains, NY: Longman.

Shoemaker, P. J., & Vos, T. P. (in press). *Gatekeeping theory.* New York: Routledge.

7

THE AGENDA-SETTING ROLE OF THE NEWS MEDIA

Sebastián Valenzuela and Maxwell McCombs

To learn about the world beyond our reach, we rely on the mass media. Newspapers, television networks, radio stations, and news websites employ hundreds of people to observe and report events that most of us cannot personally attend. What we know about wars, scientific discoveries, and political campaigns is largely based on what these news professionals decide to tell us. As Walter Lippmann long ago noted in his seminal book *Public Opinion* (1922, p. 29), "The world that we have to deal with politically is out of reach, out of sight, out of mind." When connecting to the world outside our family, neighborhood, and workplace, we deal with a second-hand reality created by journalists and media organizations.

However, due to time and organizational constraints, news outlets can provide information about only a limited number of events and issues. Because every day journalists must select, process, and filter the news, there is no guarantee that the reality portrayed in the media accurately depicts our world. The mass media focus attention on a few key priorities, those that are deemed newsworthy. Over time, those aspects of public affairs that are prominent in the media usually become prominent in public opinion, that is, the media's priorities often become the priorities of the public and policymakers; hence, the concept of setting agendas through the media, agenda setting.

This ability to influence which issues, persons, and topics are perceived as the most important of the day has come to be called the agenda-setting role of the mass media. This area of research now encompasses five distinct aspects: basic agenda-setting effects, contingent conditions for those effects, attribute agenda setting, origins of the media agenda, and consequences of the agenda-setting process for people's opinions, attitudes, and behavior.

Origins of the Agenda-Setting Idea

The idea of an agenda-setting role of the press has its origins in Walter Lippmann's *Public Opinion* (1922), which begins with a chapter titled "The World Outside and the Pictures in Our Heads." Lippmann, an American journalist and social commentator, argued that the news media determine our mental image of the larger world of public affairs that we never directly experience. We do not respond to the real world, he asserted, but to the limited pictures of the world constructed by the news media. Oftentimes, these images are incomplete and distorted. Yet, we come to regard them as true reflections of the real environment.

Not until 1968 was the idea that the press constitutes the bridge between the "world outside and the pictures in our heads" put to empirical test. At that time, Maxwell McCombs and Donald Shaw, professors at the University of North Carolina at Chapel Hill, wondered whether the issues selected and emphasized by the news media had a direct influence on our perceptions of the world beyond our comprehension. Their seminal Chapel Hill study, which gave birth to a new mass communication theory, agenda setting, used the 1968 U.S. presidential election as a case study to find out if there was a relationship between the priority issues of the mass media and the priority issues of the public (McCombs & Shaw, 1972). Is the public's view of the important issues of the campaign in direct proportion to the emphasis placed on those same issues by the mass media?

The dependent variable in the Chapel Hill study was the public agenda of issues and the independent variable was the media agenda of issues. In both cases, the term *agenda* is strictly descriptive, meaning a prioritized list of items, and should not be taken in the pejorative sense of "having an agenda" that is pursued as a premeditated goal.

To measure the public agenda, McCombs and Shaw relied on survey research. Specifically, they focused on the public's perception of the most important problem (MIP). Typically posed as an open-ended question, "What do you think is the most important problem facing this country today?" it was developed by the Gallup Poll in the 1930s and has been asked regularly since 1946. The version of the MIP question that McCombs and Shaw asked was, "What are you *most* concerned about these days? That is, regardless of what politicians say, what are the two or three *main* things which you think the government *should* concentrate on doing something about?" (1972, p. 178, original italics). The percentage of Chapel Hill voters who nominated each issue provided a succinct summary of the public agenda because the issues could be ranked according to these percentages.

The media agenda was measured by a systematic content analysis of the various issues displayed in nine major news sources used by Chapel Hill voters. The sources included network television news, elite and local newspapers, and news magazines. Because the MIP question identified five major issues of concern to Chapel Hill voters—foreign policy, law and order, fiscal policy, public welfare, and civil rights—the content analysis used the same five categories in its examination of the news coverage during the fall presidential campaign. Specifically, McCombs and Shaw measured the position and space (or time, in the case of television) devoted to each issue across the sample of news content. Just as the public agenda of issues had been rank-ordered according to the percentage of voters naming an issue, these same issues were rank-ordered on the news agenda according to the percentage of news coverage on the issues falling into each category. To measure the strength of association between the two sets of rankings, the researchers used Spearman's rho statistic, which varies from −1 (a perfect negative correlation) to +1 (a perfect positive correlation). The Chapel Hill study yielded a nearly perfect correspondence, +.967, which meant that the degree of importance accorded the five issues by voters closely paralleled their degree of prominence in the news during the previous month. This finding supported the notion that those aspects of public affairs that are prominent in the news become prominent among the public, that is, there is a transfer of salience from the media agenda to the public agenda.

The Chapel Hill study focused on a sample of undecided voters because the prevailing view at the time was that media had very limited effects on voters. Major studies in the 1940s and 1950s (Berelson, Lazarsfeld, & McPhee, 1954; Lazarsfeld, Berelson, & Gaudet, 1948) indicated that voters relied mostly on social groups and ideological predispositions to guide their voting behavior, and that the mass media basically reinforced voters' political preferences. As Joseph Klapper (1960, p. 8) had concluded eight years before the McCombs and Shaw study, "mass communication ordinarily does not serve as a necessary and sufficient cause of audience effects, but rather functions among and through a nexus of mediating functions and influences." McCombs and Shaw (1972) challenged this minimal-consequences perspective and thought the media could have strong effects, especially among undecided voters, persons interested in the presidential election but not yet committed to a candidate.

Although insightful, the Chapel Hill study provided only limited evidence of causality between the media agenda and the public agenda because it employed a one-shot research design.

To further substantiate agenda setting, the next two presidential elections were examined using panel studies to provide more powerful evidence of causality. During the summer and fall of 1972, three waves of interviewing measured the public agenda among a representative sample of voters in Charlotte, North Carolina. Having observations at different points in time allowed Shaw and McCombs (1977) to simultaneously compare the agenda-setting hypothesis with the rival hypothesis that the public agenda influenced the media agenda. The Charlotte evidence supported the agenda-setting hypothesis; that is, the influence of the news agenda at time one on the public agenda at time two was stronger than the influence of the public agenda at time one on the news agenda at time two.

During the 1976 U.S. presidential election, panels of voters were interviewed nine times from February to December in three very different communities: Lebanon, New Hampshire, a small town in the state where the first presidential primary to select the Democrat and Republican candidate for president is held each election year; Indianapolis, Indiana, a typical mid-sized U.S. city; and Evanston, Illinois, a largely upscale suburb of Chicago. Simultaneously, the election coverage of the three national television networks and the local newspapers was content analyzed. In all three settings, David Weaver and his colleagues (1981) found that the influence of both television and newspapers was greatest during the spring primaries, when voters were just beginning to tune in to the presidential campaign. The correlation between the national television agenda and the subsequent voter agenda in this period was a strong +.63, while the correlation between the agendas of the three newspapers read by these voters and their agenda of public issues was a moderate +.34. In stark contrast, the correlation between the public agenda and the subsequent television agenda—the rival hypothesis—was only +.22, and for the newspapers this rival correlation was even lower, −.08.

Since these initial election studies, the agenda-setting role of the mass media has been widely documented in more than 400 published empirical investigations, both in election and nonelection settings, for a broad range of public issues, and beyond the United States, across Asia, Latin America, Europe, and Oceania. In most studies, the methodology employed is very similar to that of the Chapel Hill study: researchers conduct a quantitative content analysis to examine the media agenda and compare their results with public opinion polls. Other methods, such as laboratory experiments, also have been employed.

This vast array of evidence documents a decisive media effect on an initial step in the formation of public opinion, the focus of public attention. The influence is on the salience of issues and other news topics, an influence on whether any significant number of people really regards it as worthwhile to hold an opinion about those issues. It is not a direct influence on attitudes and opinions, which was the main focus of media-effects research in the 1940s and 1950s. As Bernard Cohen (1963, p. 13) wrote, "the press may not be successful much of the time in telling people what to think, but it is stunningly successful in telling its readers what to think about." The emphasis is on the transfer of salience from the media agenda to the public agenda. However, as we shall see, the core idea in agenda setting has significant implications for attitudes and opinions.

Understanding How Agenda Setting Works

The repetition of messages about public issues in the news day after day, along with the pervasiveness of the mass media in our daily lives, constitutes a major source of journalism's influence on the audience. The redundancy of the press agenda allows the public to learn about issues and other news objects with little deliberate effort on their part. The incidental nature of this learning, in turn, helps issues to move rather quickly from the media agenda to the public agenda. For instance, an examination of public opinion and the *New York Times* coverage of the issue of civil rights across a 23-year period by James Winter and Chaim Eyal (1981) found agenda-setting effects within four to six weeks. Another longitudinal analysis conducted by Michael Salwen (1988) found that for the issue of the environment, the public agenda reflected the network television agenda after five to seven weeks of news coverage.

Although the benchmark for agenda-setting effects is one to two months (Wanta & Yu-wei, 1994), there are, of course, variations among individuals and across issues. Under conditions of high personal involvement, the timeframe for measurable effects may be very short. During the 1996 U.S. presidential election, Marilyn Roberts and her colleagues (2002) found that the salience of immigration, health care, and taxes on electronic bulletin boards reflected the press coverage of these issues within one to seven days.

However, the media are not the only influence that determines the public's issue priorities. The spectacular failure of the U.S. media in setting the agenda and causing a sway in public opinion during the Clinton-Lewinsky sex scandal, despite intensive news coverage that has been described as "All Monica, all the time," speaks in a loud voice about the limits of media influence. As Spiro Kiousis (2003) noted, the media may have influenced Bill Clinton's perceived favorability but not his job approval ratings. Simply put, the majority of Americans perceived the sexual scandal as irrelevant to Clinton's role as president. This should not come as a surprise because agenda setting does not overturn or nullify the basic assumption of democracy that the people at large have sufficient wisdom to determine the course of their nation, their state, and their local communities.

Individual differences in responses to the media agenda are grounded in the psychological concept of need for orientation, the idea that we have an innate curiosity about the world around us and a desire to become familiar with that world. Recall, for example, your initial feeling upon visiting a foreign city. For a wide variety of public affairs, such as evaluating a new presidential candidate or judging different public policy outcomes, the news media provide us with this orientation. Thus, the higher our need for orientation, the more we tend to search for information, rely on the media, and become predisposed to agenda-setting effects.

An individual's need for orientation in regard to public affairs is defined by two components: relevance and uncertainty (Weaver, 1980). Relevance is the initial defining condition that determines the level of need for orientation for each individual. If a topic is perceived as irrelevant, then the need for orientation is low. Individuals in this situation pay little or no attention to news reports and, at most, demonstrate weak agenda-setting effects. For individuals among whom the relevance of a topic is high, their degree of uncertainty about the topic determines the level of need for orientation. If this uncertainty is low, that is, they feel that they basically understand the topic, the need for orientation is moderate. These individuals will monitor the media for new developments and perhaps occasionally dip into additional background information, but they are not likely to be avid consumers of news about the topic. Finally, among individuals for whom both relevance and their uncertainty about a situation are high, their need for orientation is high. These individuals typically are avid consumers of the news, and strong agenda-setting effects are found among them.

Researchers have measured the concept of need for orientation in a number of different ways. In electoral settings (Weaver, 1980), relevance has been measured as the degree of interest in the political campaign, and uncertainty as the degree of confidence of the respondent's voting intention. If the individual already knows for whom to vote, he or she has a low degree of uncertainty, while those who have not yet decided have a high degree of uncertainty. More recently, Jörg Matthes (2006) has expanded the measurement of need for orientation beyond the basic agenda of issues to take into account citizens' interest in the details of those issues and journalists' perspectives on those issues.

The media, of course, are not our only source of orientation to public affairs. Personal experience, which includes communication with our family, friends, and coworkers, also informs us about many issues. The dominant source of influence will vary from issue to issue. For instance, we do not need the media to alert us about significant inflation in the economy; rather, routine purchases will reveal its presence. However, to learn about abstract economic topics such as budget deficits, our main source of information, if not the only one, is the news media. In this case, personal experience is greatly limited and, most probably, nonexistent. In theoretical terms, some issues are obtrusive, that is, they obtrude into our daily lives and are directly experienced, while other issues are unobtrusive, and we encounter them only in the news (Zucker, 1978). Consequently, the less obtrusive an issue is, the more individuals will rely on the news media for information about it and the stronger the agenda-setting effects can be. Presenting empirical evidence for the obtrusiveness hypothesis, Jian Hua Zhu and his colleagues (1993) found that the news media had a stronger influence than social interaction on the public's issue priorities in regard to international issues, while the opposite was true in the case of domestic issues.

Another constraint on the power of the news media to set the public agenda is the very limited capacity of that agenda. At any particular moment, there are dozens of issues contending for public attention, but no society and its institutions can attend to more than a few issues at a time. The public agenda typically consists of no more than three to five issues at any given time. For each year between 1999 and 2004, with a single exception, when the Gallup Poll asked a national sample the MIP question, only three issues had a constituency of 10% or more, the level which has been identified as the threshold for significant public attention (Neuman, 1990). The exception was 2002, when each poll conducted that year yielded four issues above the 10% mark. This tight constraint on the size of the public agenda is explained by the limits of the public's resources, limits that include both time and psychological capacity.

Attribute Agenda-Setting Effects

The agenda-setting role of the news media is not limited to focusing public attention on a particular set of issues, but also operates at a wider scope, influencing our understanding and perspective on the topics in the news. This becomes very clear when we think about the concept of agenda in abstract terms. Theoretically, the items that define an agenda are "objects." In most agenda-setting research, these objects are public issues, but they also could be public figures, organizations, countries, or anything else that is the focus of attention. In turn, each of these objects has numerous "attributes," those characteristics and traits that describe and define the object. While some attributes are emphasized, others are given less attention, and many receive no attention at all. Just as objects vary in salience, so do the attributes of each object. Thus, for each object there also is an agenda of attributes, which constitutes an important part of what journalists, and subsequently members of the public have in mind when they think and talk about news objects.

The influence of the news agenda of attributes on the public is the second level of agenda setting. The first level, of course, is the transmission of object salience. The second level, then, is the transmission of attribute salience. To borrow Walter Lippmann's phrase "the pictures in our heads," the agenda of issues or other objects presented by the mass media influences what the pictures in our heads are about. The agenda of attributes presented for each of these issues, public figures, or other objects literally influences the pictures themselves that we hold in mind.

The difference between first- and second-level agenda setting becomes especially clear in an electoral campaign. Candidates vying for political office are, theoretically, a set of objects whose salience among the public can be influenced by news coverage and by political advertising. Campaign managers seek to build the salience, the prominence, of their candidates among voters (first-level agenda setting). They also strive to build an image of their candidates in which specific attributes become particularly salient (second-level agenda setting).

Evidence of attribute-agenda setting dates from the 1970s: Lee Becker and Maxwell McCombs (1978) compared New York Democrats' descriptions of the eleven contenders for their party's 1976 presidential nomination with the agenda of attributes presented in *Newsweek* magazine during the first three months of the year and found significant evidence of media influence. Moreover, the correlation between the news agenda of attributes and the voter agenda of attributes increased from +.64 in mid-February to +.83 in late March. Voters not only learned the media's agenda, but with additional exposure over the weeks of the primaries they learned it even better.

In the 1990s researchers developed a more detailed picture of attribute agenda-setting. During the 1996 general election in Spain, McCombs and his colleagues (2000) conducted a stringent test of this second level of media influence by comparing the descriptions by voters in Pamplona of the three major party leaders after the elections with the presentation of these men before the elections in seven major news sources, including local newspapers, national dailies, national television networks, and televised political advertising. Two sets of candidate attributes were examined: substantive—which included issue positions and political ideology, biographical information, perceived qualifications, personality, and integrity—and affective—the positive, negative, or neutral tone of the substantive attributes. Just as in first-level agenda-setting studies, the media agenda of candidate attributes was measured by a systematic content analysis. To find out the public agenda of attributes, a survey was conducted among voters that asked an open-ended question about each of the three political leaders: "Imagine that you have a friend who didn't know anything about the candidates. What would you tell your friend about… (the name of a candidate)." This study found a high degree of correspondence between the voters' descriptions and the way the media described the candidates. Overall, the median correlation between the public agenda and the media agenda of attributes was +.72, revealing a strong second-level agenda-setting influence.

Traditionally, attribute agenda-setting studies examine the verbal content of the media agenda, even when television news is content analyzed, with coders coding the stories' text transcripts rather than their visual images. Renita Coleman and Stephen Banning (2006) challenged this approach and developed a new coding scheme for nonverbal communication, content analyzing the positive and negative facial expressions, posture, and gestures of the 2000 U.S. presidential candidates George Bush and Al Gore. Their secondary analysis of a National Election Study survey revealed a significant correlation between the candidates' nonverbal behavior in television news stories and the public agenda of affective attributes, supporting the idea that second-level agenda-setting effects can occur through visual information.

Second-level effects can also be extended to public issues, the traditional domain of agenda-setting research. Which aspects of an issue are covered in the news, and the relative emphasis on these various aspects of an issue, makes a considerable difference in how people view that issue. To rephrase Bernard Cohen's assertion, the media not only are successful in telling us *what* to think about, but they also can tell us *how* to think about some objects.

The economy, a recurring major topic on the public agenda, demonstrates strong attribute agenda-setting effects. One set of attributes associated with this general topic consists of the specific problems of the moment, their perceived causes, and the proposed solutions to these problems. Another, more narrow set of attributes consists of the pro and con arguments for the proposed solutions to economic problems. For both sets of attributes, Marc Benton and Jean Frazier (1976) found an agenda-setting influence among the general public in Minneapolis for local newspapers, but not for television news. For the specific problems, causes, and proposed solutions associated with the economy, the correlation between the newspaper agenda and the public agenda was particularly high, +.81. The degree of correspondence for the pro and con arguments for economic solutions was less, but still substantial: +.68.

Just as there is a transfer of salience from the media agenda to the public agenda of prominent news objects, there is a transfer of salience for those news objects' attributes. These two levels of influence are the core of the agenda-setting role of the news media.

Agenda Setting and Framing

The agenda-setting role of the mass media converges with many other paradigms in the communication field, including framing, priming, gatekeeping, cultivation, and the spiral of silence. The similarities and differences between agenda setting and framing are currently one of the most discussed of these theoretical connections. However, the existence of multiple definitions of framing and the lack of consensus among scholars of what aspects of perceived reality are properly designated as frames makes any comparison between agenda setting and framing a rather difficult task.

One approach sees framing as a paradigm that explores the way events and issues are presented in the media, and the subsequent influence on audience members. A frequently cited definition of framing that embodies this perspective states that a media frame is a "central organizing idea for news content that supplies a context and suggests what the issue is through the use of selection, emphasis, exclusion and elaboration" (Tankard, Hendrickson, Silberman, Bliss, & Ghanem, 1991, p. 3). This definition of framing converges with attribute agenda setting because in both cases the focus is on the salient characteristics and traits in which a topic or other news object is portrayed in the mass media. In particular, the emphasis here on "a central organizing idea" is parallel to the concept of "compelling argument" in which a particular attribute of an object on the agenda is dominant in the public mind (Ghanem, 1997). Just as the second level of agenda setting examines the attributes of news objects, this version of framing studies the frames employed to describe issues and public figures. The difference, in this case, resides in the "excluded" content, which agenda setting does not examine because it relies solely on the manifest content of news stories.

Theoretical efforts to demarcate the boundary between agenda setting and framing (Price & Tewksbury, 1997; Scheufele, 2000) on the basis of the two aspects of knowledge activation (Higgins, 1996)—the concepts of accessibility (linked to agenda setting) and applicability (linked to framing)—have found limited success. Focusing specifically on the accessibility of issue attributes, Kim, Scheufele, and Shanahan (2002) found that accessibility increased with greater newspaper use, but that the resulting attribute agendas among the public bore no resemblance to the attribute agenda presented in the news and did not replicate previous attribute agenda-setting effects found by studies over the past four decades (McCombs, 2004, Ch. 5). What emerged was a different version of media effects in which the relative amount of increased salience for the attributes among newspaper readers when compared to persons unaware of the issue largely paralleled the media agenda. Nelson, Clawson, and Oxley's (1997) experiment, which empirically distinguished accessibility and applicability, found significant effects for applicability, but not accessibility. Calling to mind the concept of need for orientation in agenda-setting theory, Nelson, Clawson, and Oxley (1997, p. 578) concluded: "Our results contribute to the growing body of evidence questioning mere accessibility models of political judgment and opinion…. Our results point to a more deliberative integration process, whereby participants consider the importance and relevance of each accessible idea."

Another approach to framing looks at the creation of media frames and how the public uses these frames to interpret social reality: "Frames are organizing principles that are socially shared and persistent over time, that work symbolically to meaningfully structure the social word"

(Reese, 2001, p. 11). This approach considers the power conflicts that lead journalists to use certain frames over other frames and to the factors associated with the audience's active interpretation of the texts that embody frames (Gamson, 2001). This version of framing involves a broader range of processes than the previous approach and diverges widely from agenda setting.

The similarities and differences between framing and agenda setting also are illustrated by Matthew Nisbet and Mike Huge's (2006) study of the framing of the plant biotechnology debate in the mass media that examined both "technical frames" (e.g., scientific discoveries) and "dramatic frames," such as ethical consequences. While the technical aspects of an issue could be thought of as attributes—and, therefore, fit with agenda setting—ethical consequences involve deeper phenomena than attributes (Weaver, McCombs, & Shaw, 2004).

In conclusion, attribute agenda-setting converges with framing when the latter is defined in terms of the characteristics in which a news object is portrayed in the media or by the public, but the two concepts diverge when framing involves more abstract, all-encompassing processes. Attribute agenda setting primarily focuses on the impact of the news media on public perceptions and offers a sound methodology to measure the paths of influence. Framing studies, on the other hand, focus on the production of different frames and the role of frames in organizing reality, employing a variety of methods and operational definitions.

Who Sets the Media Agenda?

By the 1980s, the accumulated evidence that the news media can set the public agenda was strong enough for scholars to begin exploring new venues of the agenda-setting process, particularly the origins of media coverage. If the traditional question was "Who sets the public agenda?" the new question was "Who sets the press agenda?"

The pattern of news coverage that defines the media's agenda results from three key elements: exchanges with sources that provide information for news stories, the daily interactions among news organizations themselves, and journalism's norms and traditions. The latter is at the core of the three factors of influence because the press itself is the final arbiter of what goes on the news agenda, of which events and issues will be reported and how they will be reported. The predilection of journalists for conflict and "negative" news, for instance, limits the scope and variety of the press agenda. At the same time, the press agenda is expanded when investigative reporters raise public concern about issues such as corruption in state agencies and accounting frauds in private corporations.

Prominent among the external sources of the media agenda are public officials, particularly the president, who arguably is the nation's number one agenda setter. Virtually everything that a president does, from signing international agreements to reading children's books to elementary school kids, is considered newsworthy. Being at the center of media attention provides significant opportunities for the president to set the media's agenda of issues. However, the relationship between the press and the presidential agenda is more complex than it appears to be at first.

One way of exploring this relationship is by examining the effect of the State of the Union address—essentially a shopping list of issues that the president wants the Congress to address—on the subsequent agenda of the national press. Comprehensive analysis of different U.S. presidents' official speeches to Congress, including Richard Nixon, Jimmy Carter and Ronald Reagan, revealed that in two of four instances, the media seem to have influenced, rather than followed, the president's agenda (Wanta, Stephenson, Turk, & McCombs, 1989). Only in one case—Richard Nixon's 1970 State of the Union address—did the president's agenda of issues correlate more highly with postaddress news coverage than with preaddress coverage in the *New York Times*, the *Washington Post*, and the evening news broadcasts of the three national television networks. The relationship between the news media and the White House is multidirectional and is shaped among other factors by the nature of the issues involved, the president's rhetorical ability, how much emphasis he places on the specific issues, and real-world events that may draw attention to or away from issues (Johnson, Wanta, & Boudreau, 2004).

Exploring the link between the president and the press converges with another area of agenda-setting research, that of policy agenda setting—the process by which governments make decisions about which social issues will be the focus of their attention and actions. Examples of the role that the news media play in the shaping of public policy include a seminal article on child abuse in a medical journal that stimulated considerable media attention and subsequent actions by the U.S. Congress and many state legislatures (Nelson, 1984); two series of investigative reports by a Chicago television station that led to policy changes in the city's police and fire departments (Protess et al., 1991); the influence of newspaper and television coverage of global warming on the attention to this issue by the U.S. Congress in the late 1980s (Trumbo, 1995); the coverage of Canadian newspapers on environmental topics, which predicted increased government action in this area (Soroka, 2002); the leading role of the *New York Times* in focusing the political agenda of the executive and the legislative branches in the North American Free Trade Agreement (Bartels, 1996); and prosecutors in Milwaukee who were more likely to plea bargain homicide cases that did not receive much newspaper coverage compared with those that got prominent coverage (Pritchard, 1986). Yet, because in many instances the relationship between news coverage and the evolution of public policy over time is extremely circular, the available evidence is often contradictory in regard to who influences whom. In an effort to clarify under what circumstances the mass media are able to focus political attention, Stefaan Walgrave and Peter Van Aelst (2006) presented an integrated model encompassing eight variables: issue type, media outlet, coverage type, electoral or nonelectoral context, existing institutional rules, internal decision-making practices of political actors, the government–opposition configuration, and the personal traits of political actors.

Another key influence on the news agenda is the vast network of public relations practitioners, both in the private and public sector. These communication professionals "subsidize" (Gandy, 1982) the efforts of news organizations to cover the news by providing substantial amounts of organized information, frequently in the form of press and video news releases, news conferences, planned events, and background briefings. Over a twenty-year period, Leon Sigal (1973) found that nearly half of the front-page stories in the *New York Times* and *Washington Post* were based on information provided by organized public relations efforts. Nevertheless, journalists remain the final arbiters of what is covered because they select those topics deemed most newsworthy from the vast array of material presented to them. Judy VanSlyke Turk (1986) studied the influence of public information officers of six state government agencies on Louisiana's eight major dailies and found that 82% of the time, newsworthiness was the most important consideration used by the newspapers when deciding whether to use or reject information provided in the state agencies' press releases.

Political campaigns are a special case of public relations activities. In presidential elections, candidates spend vast amounts of money on political advertising in an effort to set the voters' agenda. Major efforts are also exerted to influence the agenda of the news media because these messages are less obviously self-serving and therefore more credible to the public. At the national level, these campaign efforts enjoy considerable success in setting the media agenda during the early months of the election year. However, this influence diminishes as the campaign moves toward Election Day and garners more and more attention from journalists. This was evident during the 2004 U.S. presidential election, when cross-lagged correlations between the press releases of the Democrat candidate John Kerry and the election coverage of the *New York Times*, *Washington Post*, and *Los Angeles Times* during the last two months of the campaign revealed a strong influence of the media on the Kerry agenda (Tedesco, 2005). On the other hand, in state and local elections—settings where fewer journalistic resources are brought to bear—the candidates' influence on the press agenda is more consistent and tends to be stronger. A classic example is the 1990 Texas gubernatorial election (Roberts & McCombs, 1994), where the Republican and Democrat campaign agendas—measured as paid political advertising in Austin—exerted considerable influence on both the local newspaper (+.64) and the three local television stations (+.52).

Part of the explanation for the greater independence of the press in national elections is the influence that news media have on each other. Journalists routinely look over their shoulders to validate their sense of news by observing the work of their colleagues, especially the work of elite members of the press, such as the *New York Times*, *Wall Street Journal*, the Associated Press, and national television networks. The outcome of these continuous observations and the resulting intermedia influence is a highly redundant news agenda, a national media agenda.

This redundancy across media is not limited to election periods. In the United States, this role is played by the *New York Times*, and it is so institutionalized that the Associated Press alerts its members each day to the agenda of stories scheduled for the next morning's front page of the *Times*. It is the appearance on the front page of this newspaper that frequently legitimates a topic as newsworthy, not any response to external reality. This was evident when the *New York Times* "discovered" the cocaine problem in late 1985, which resulted in heavy coverage during 1986 in major newspapers across the country and on national television news, a pattern that peaked with two national television specials in September of that year (Reese & Danielian, 1989). A similar trend has been found for the coverage of foreign affairs, where the *Times*' news agenda influenced the news agenda of the three national networks' evening news broadcasts (Golan, 2006).

Consequences of Agenda Setting for Attitudes and Behavior

Three distinct consequences of agenda-setting effects have been identified: forming opinions, priming opinions through an emphasis on particular issues, and shaping an opinion through an emphasis on particular attributes. These consequences, in turn, have significant effects on observable behavior.

In forming an opinion, there is a fundamental link between media attention to a news object and the existence of an opinion about it. During an election, for instance, the media focus their attention on the major candidates, which, in turn, leads to more people forming opinions about them (Kiousis & McCombs, 2004). Conversely, when the press pays low attention to an election, a higher proportion of the public have no opinion about the candidates.

Also at the first level of agenda-setting, the influence of the media on the prominence of issues can influence the standards by which individuals evaluate governments and public figures, a process called priming. When asked their opinions about political topics such as performance of the president, most citizens do not engage in comprehensive analysis of their total store of information. Rather, individuals use information shortcuts and draw upon those considerations that are particularly salient (Zaller, 1992). In other words, audience members rely upon their agenda of salient objects, an agenda that is set to a considerable degree by the mass media. This agenda determines the criteria—sometimes the single criterion—on which an opinion is based.

Media priming effects were demonstrated by Shanto Iyengar and Donald Kinder (1987) in a series of experiments that compared two groups: persons who saw no television news stories on a particular issue during the week with persons who did see television news stories on that issue during the week. Among subjects exposed to major news coverage on one or more of five different issues, their ratings of presidential performance on these issues influenced their overall opinion about the president's performance far more than among those for whom these issues were not particularly salient.

Another consequence of agenda-setting effects involves the way that an issue or a political figure is presented in the media, namely, the attribute agenda. The pictures in people's minds, which include both substantive attributes and the affective tone of these attributes, are correlated with their opinions about news objects. For example, for the issue of the economy, a content analysis describing four years of news coverage was combined in time-series analyses with two indicators of consumer economic evaluations and three measures of real economic conditions (Hester & Gibson, 2003). Economic news was framed negatively more often than positively, and this negative news coverage was a significant predictor of consumer expectations about the future of the economy.

There also are significant attribute agenda-setting effects on political opinions. Hans Mathias Kepplinger and his team (1989) found that positive and negative coverage in German news magazines and newspapers explained to a great extent changes in Chancellor Helmut Kohl's job approval ratings. In the United States, Daron Shaw (1999) examined on a day-by-day basis the last three months of the 1992 and 1996 presidential campaigns and found that the interaction between the favorability of news media coverage, especially the tone of TV newscasts describing campaign events, drove much of the change in voters' preferences in the polls.

Both the first and second levels of the agenda-setting process can predict opinions and behavioral intentions. Son and Weaver (2006) examined news coverage across the 2000 presidential election and found that both the candidate's salience and favorable presentation in the mass media significantly predicted levels of aggregate public support in the 20 public opinion polls conducted by Gallup during that time. The analysis was replicated for the controversial 2006 Mexican presidential election in which national television coverage of the campaign subsequently influenced the candidates' poll standings (Valenzuela & McCombs, 2007).

Behavioral consequences of the media's agenda-setting role go beyond the political arena. The pessimistic tone of "Abreast of the Market," a column published by the *Wall Street Journal* that describes the prior day's stock market activity, foreshadows an average fall of 0.081 percentage points in the Dow Jones index on the next trading day (Tetlock, 2007). A time-series analysis of *New York Times* headlines from 1980 to 1993 found that rising numbers of negative economic headlines had a strong adverse effect on subsequent leading economic indicators, such as average weekly hours for manufacturing, average weekly initial claims for unemployment, new orders of consumer goods and materials, contracts and orders for plant and equipment, and building permits (Blood & Phillips, 1997). A study about news coverage of airplane crashes and skyjackings found that when the media focused its attention on the risks of flying, ticket sales decreased and flight insurance sales increased (Bloj, as cited in McCombs, 2004).

From the pattern of news coverage, the public learns what journalists consider the important issues and the prominent public figures of the day to be. From the details of this coverage—the agenda of attributes presented by the news media—the public forms its images and perspective about these issues and public figures. Influencing the focus of public attention is a powerful role, but, arguably, influencing the agenda of attributes, opinions, and attitudes, even observable behavior, regarding issues and political figures is the apogee of media effects.

How to Conduct Agenda-Setting Research

In the decades since the original Chapel Hill study, researchers in the agenda-setting tradition have employed a wide variety of methods and research designs. Complementing the extensive field research, the causal link between the media agenda and the public agenda has been demonstrated in controlled laboratory experiments. These field studies range from one-shot designs that rely on a single public opinion poll, to longitudinal designs, such as panel studies, where the same group of respondents is interviewed at different points in time, and trend studies, which track different samples of citizens over a period of time.

Each research design allows for different statistical analyses. In cross-sectional designs, the media agenda and the public agenda are compared by means of correlations, such as Spearman's rho and Pearson's r. In panel studies, cross-lagged correlations test the agenda-setting hypothesis as well as its rival hypothesis (i.e., the public sets the media agenda). More complex time-series analyses such as ARIMA modeling and Granger causality are employed in trend studies when there are many observations of the dependent and independent variables.

There is a four-part typology that describes the different operationalizations of the comparison between the media agenda with the public agenda. Referred to as the Acapulco typology because it was initially presented in Acapulco, Mexico (McCombs, 2004), this typology is defined by two dimensions. The first dimension distinguishes between two ways of looking at agendas. The focus of attention can either be on the entire set of items—and their respective attributes—that define the agenda or be narrowed to a single, particular item on the agenda. The second dimension distinguishes between two ways of measuring the public salience of items and items' attributes on the agenda: aggregate measures describing an entire population versus measures that describe individual responses. The combination of these two dimensions describes four distinct perspectives on agenda setting:

- Type I (competition perspective) compares the coverage for a set of major news items to the aggregate public agenda. The original Chapel Hill study took this perspective.
- Type II (automaton perspective) also examines the entire media agenda but shifts the focus to the agenda of each individual. For instance, the rank-order of an agenda of issues is determined for each individual (e.g., McLeod, Becker, & Byrnes, 1974).
- Type III (natural history perspective) narrows the focus to a single issue on the agenda, but like Type I uses aggregate measures to establish the salience of this item on the public agenda over a period of time (e.g., Brosius & Kepplinger, 1990).
- Type IV (cognitive portrait) examines the match between media coverage of a single item and the corresponding salience of that item on an individual agenda (e.g., Iyengar & Kinder, 1987).

New Arenas for Research

The agenda-setting role of the news media concerns more than the transfer of issue salience from the media agenda to the public. Although the vast majority of studies have examined issue agendas, this is only one possible operational definition of the agenda. For many, this is agenda setting because that is where this research tradition began, and it has remained the dominant focus for decades. But recall that in our review of the five stages through which agenda-setting theory has evolved, the basic proposition was restated more broadly as elements that are prominent on the media agenda over time become prominent on the public agenda. And the discussion of attribute agenda setting explicitly introduced the conceptual language of objects and attributes, which can be operationalized in many ways other than public issues.

There are many agendas in contemporary society, and in recent years, innovative scholars have applied the core idea of agenda-setting theory, the transfer of salience from one agenda to another, to a wide variety of new arenas as diverse as professional sports (Fortunato, 2001) and classroom teaching (Rodríguez Díaz, 2004). Some involve specialized versions of the media agenda. Others involve the agendas of other social institutions. In turn, the scope of the publics range from the general public to highly limited publics.

One rapidly expanding research area is the business news agenda and its impact on corporate reputations and economic outcomes ranging from profits to stock prices (Carroll & McCombs, 2003). As independent variables, the reputations of a corporation and its chief executive officer (CEO) influence financial performance. As a dependent variable, a growing body of research grounded in agenda-setting theory documents the influence of the news media, both the specialized business press and the business coverage of general news media, on corporate reputations. There are both first-level agenda-setting effects, the influence of media coverage on awareness and prominence of a company or its CEO, and attribute agenda-setting effects, influence on the images of a corporation and its CEO. These agenda-setting effects can also extend to behavior. During a three-year period when the Standard & Poor 500 stock market index increased 2.3%, the stocks of fifty-four companies featured in *Fortune* magazine increased 3.6%. Companies receiving favorable coverage increased the most, 4.7%, but any increased salience of these companies resulted in some increase, 1.9% with negative coverage and 1.7% with neutral coverage (Kieffer, cited in McCombs, 2004).

Across both the traditional and new domains of agenda setting, the Internet is a major research frontier. For some observers, the availability of many channels and the opportunity for users to seek their own personal agendas challenges a basic tenet of agenda setting that the media tend to share the same set of news priorities. Consequently, the argument goes, the power of the mass media to set the public agenda may be on the wane. However, the evidence to date shows that the distribution of public attention is far from rectangular. While the five largest American newspapers account for 21.5% of the circulation among the top 100 daily newspapers, the top five newspaper websites account for 41.4% of the total links found on the Internet to the top 100 newspapers (Hamilton, 2004). Attention on the web, it seems, is even more concentrated than in the print world. Nevertheless, researchers must continue to map the evolving agendas in this new media environment.

Agenda-setting theory continues to expand our understanding of the connections between the world outside and the pictures in our heads. Since the seminal Chapel Hill study of 1968, this connection has expanded into five different facets. Looking to the future, creative scholars will refine the core ideas of agenda setting, expand the theory in new arenas, and produce new knowledge regarding the media's role in society.

References

Bartels, L. M. (1996, September). *Politicians and the press: Who leads, who follows?* Paper presented at the annual conference of the American Political Science Association, San Francisco, CA.

Becker, L., & McCombs, M. (1978). The role of the press in determining voter reactions to presidential primaries. *Human Communication Research, 4,* 301–307.

Benton, M., & Frazier, J. P. (1976). The agenda-setting function of the mass media at three levels of "information holding." *Communication Research, 3,* 261–274.

Berelson, B., Lazarsfeld, P. F., & McPhee, W. N. (1954). *Voting: A study of opinion formation in a presidential campaign.* Chicago: University of Chicago Press.

Blood, D. J., & Phillips, P. C. B. (1997). Economic headline news on the agenda: New approaches to understanding causes and effects. In M. McCombs, D. L. Shaw, & D. Weaver (Eds.), *Communication and democracy: Exploring the intellectual frontiers in agenda-setting theory* (pp. 97–114). Mahwah, NJ: Erlbaum.

Brosius, H.-B., & Kepplinger, H. M. (1990). The agenda-setting function of television news: Static and dynamic views. *Communication Research, 17,* 183–211.

Carroll, C. E., & McCombs, M. (2003). Agenda-setting effects of business news on the public's images and opinions about major corporations. *Corporate Reputation Review, 6*(1), 36–46.

Cohen, B. (1963). *The press and foreign policy.* Princeton, NJ: Princeton University Press.

Coleman, R., & Banning, S. (2006). Network TV news' affective framing of the presidential candidates: Evidence for a second-level agenda-setting effect through visual framing. *Journalism & Mass Communication Quarterly, 83,* 313–328.

Fortunato, J. (2001). *The ultimate assist: The relationship and broadcasting strategies of the NBA and television networks.* Cresskill, NJ: Hampton Press.

Gamson, W. A. (2001). Foreword. In S. D. Reese, O. H. Gandy, Jr., & A. E. Grant (Eds.), *Framing public life: Perspectives on media and our understanding of the social world* (pp. ix–xi). Mahwah, NJ: Erlbaum.

Gandy, O. H., Jr. (1982). *Beyond agenda-setting: Information subsidies and public policy.* Norwood, NJ: Ablex.

Ghanem, S. (1997). Filling in the tapestry: The second level of agenda setting. In M. McCombs, D. L. Shaw, & D. Weaver (Eds.), *Communication and democracy: Exploring the intellectual frontiers in agenda-setting theory* (pp. 3–14). Mahwah, NJ: Erlbaum.

Golan, G. (2006). Inter-media agenda setting and global news coverage: Assessing the influence of the *New York Times* on three network television evening news programs. *Journalism Studies, 7,* 323–333.

Hamilton, J. T. (2004). *All the news that's fit to sell: How the market transforms information into news.* Princeton, NJ: Princeton University Press.

Hester, J. B., & Gibson, R. (2003). The economy and second-level agenda setting: A time-series analysis of economic news and public opinion about the economy. *Journalism & Mass Communication Quarterly, 80,* 73–90.

Higgins, E. T. (1996). Knowledge activation: Accessibility, applicability, and salience. In E. T. Higgins & A. W. Kruglanski (Eds.), *Social psychology: Handbook of basic principles* (pp. 133–168). New York: Guilford.

Iyengar, S., & Kinder, D. R. (1987). *News that matters: Television and American opinion.* Chicago: University of Chicago Press.

Johnson, T. J., Wanta, W., & Boudreau, T. (2004). Drug peddlers: How four presidents attempted to influence media and public concern on the drug issue. *Atlantic Journal of Communication, 12*(4), 177–199.

Kepplinger, H. M., Donsbach, W., Brosius, H.-B., & Staab, J. F. (1989). Media tone and public opinion: A longitudinal study of media coverage and public opinion on Chancellor Kohl. *International Journal of Public Opinion Research, 1,* 326–342.

Kim, S., Scheufele, D., & Shanahan, J. (2002). Think about it this way: Attribute agenda-setting function of the press and the public's evaluation of a local issue. *Journalism & Mass Communication Quarterly, 79,* 7–25.

Kiousis, S. (2003). Job approval and favorability: The impact of media attention to the Monica Lewinsky scandal on public opinion of President Bill Clinton. *Mass Communication & Society, 6*(4), 435–451.

Kiousis, S., & McCombs, M. (2004). Agenda-setting effects and attitude strength: Political figures during the 1996 presidential election. *Communication Research, 31*(1), 36–57.

Klapper, J. H. (1960). *The effects of mass communication.* New York: Free Press.

Lazarsfeld, P., Berelson, B., & Gaudet, H. (1948). *The people's choice* (2nd ed.). New York: Columbia University Press.

Lippmann, W. (1922). *Public opinion.* New York: Macmillan.

Matthes, J. (2006). The need for orientation towards news media: Revisiting and validating a classic concept. *International Journal of Public Opinion Research, 18,* 422–444.

McCombs, M. (2004). *Setting the agenda: The mass media and public opinion.* Cambridge, UK: Polity Press.

McCombs, M., López-Escobar, E., & Llamas, J. P. (2000). Setting the agenda of attributes in the 1996 Spanish general election. *Journal of Communication, 50*(2), 77–92.

McCombs, M., & Shaw, D. L. (1972). The agenda-setting function of mass media. *Public Opinion Quarterly, 36*(2), 176–187.

McLeod, J., Becker, L., & Byrnes, J. E. (1974). Another look at the agenda-setting function of the press. *Communication Research, 1,* 131–166.

Nelson, B. (1984). *Making an issue of child abuse: Political agenda setting for social problems.* Chicago: University of Chicago Press.

Nelson, T. E., Clawson, R. A., & Oxley, Z. M. (1997). Media framing of a civil liberties conflict and its effect on tolerance. *American Political Science Review, 91,* 567–583.

Neuman, W. R. (1990). Threshold of public attention. *Public Opinion Quarterly, 54,* 159–176.

Nisbet, M. C., & Huge, M. (2006). Attention cycles and frames in the plant biotechnology debate: Managing power and participation through the press/policy connection. *The Harvard International Journal of Press/Politics, 11*(2), 3–40.

Price, V., & Tewksbury, D. (1997). News values and public opinion: A theoretical account of media priming and framing. In G. A. Barnett & F. J. Boster (Eds.), *Progress in communication sciences: Advances in persuasion* (pp. 173–212). Greenwich, CT: Ablex.

Pritchard, D. (1986). Homicide and bargained justice: The agenda-setting effect of crime news on prosecutors. *Public Opinion Quarterly, 50*(2), 143–159.

Protess, D. L., Cook, F. L., Doppelt, J. C., Ettema, J. S., Gordon, M. T., Leff, D. R., & Miller, P. (1991). *The journalism of outrage: Investigative reporting and agenda building in America*. New York: Guilford.

Reese, S. D. (2001). Prologue—framing public life: A bridging model for media research. In S. D. Reese, O. H. Gandy, Jr., & A. E. Grant (Eds.), *Framing public life: Perspectives on media and our understanding of the social world* (pp. 7–31). Mahwah, NJ: Erlbaum.

Reese, S. D., & Danielian, L. H. (1989). Intermedia influence and the drug issue. In P. J. Shoemaker (Ed.), *Communication campaigns about drugs: Government, media, and the public* (pp. 29–46). Hillsdale, NJ: Erlbaum.

Roberts, M. S., & McCombs, M. (1994). Agenda setting and political advertising: Origins of the news agenda. *Political Communication, 11*, 249–262.

Roberts, M. S., Wanta, W., & Dzwo, T.-H. D. (2002). Agenda setting and issue salience online. *Communication Research, 29*, 452–465.

Rodríguez Díaz, R. (2004). *Teoría de la agenda-setting: Aplicación a la enseñanza universitaria* [Agenda-setting theory: Application in higher education]. Madrid: OBETS.

Salwen, M. B. (1988). Effect of accumulation of coverage on issue salience in agenda setting. *Journalism Quarterly, 65*, 100–130.

Scheufele, D. A. (2000). Agenda-setting, priming and framing revisited: Another look at cognitive effects of political communication. *Mass Communication & Society, 3*, 297–316.

Shaw, D. L., & McCombs, M. (1977). *The emergence of American political issues*. St. Paul, MN: West.

Shaw, D. R. (1999). The impact of news media favorability and candidate events in presidential campaigns. *Political Communication, 16*(2), 183–202.

Sigal, L. V. (1973). *Reporters and officials: The organization and politics of newsmaking*. Lexington, MA: D.C. Heath.

Son, Y. J., & Weaver, D. H. (2006). Another look at what moves public opinion: Media agenda setting and polls in the 2000 U.S. election. *International Journal of Public Opinion Research, 18*, 174–197.

Soroka, S. N. (2002). *Agenda-setting dynamics in Canada*. Vancouver: UBC Press.

Tankard, J. W., Hendrickson, L., Silberman, J., Bliss, K., & Ghanem, S. (1991, August). *Media frames: Approaches to conceptualization and measurement*. Paper presented at the annual convention of the Association for Education in Journalism and Mass Communication, Boston, MA.

Tedesco, J. C. (2005). Issue and strategy agenda setting in the 2004 presidential election: Exploring the candidate–journalist relationship. *Journalism Studies, 6*, 187–201.

Tetlock, P. C. (2007). Giving content to investor sentiment: The role of media in the stock market. *Journal of Finance, 62*, 1139–1168.

Trumbo, C. (1995). Longitudinal modeling of public issues: An application of the agenda-setting process to the issue of global warming. *Journalism & Mass Communication Monographs, 152*, 1–57.

Turk, J. V. (1986). Public relations' influence on the news. *Newspaper Research Journal, 7*(4), 15–27.

Valenzuela, S., & McCombs, M. (2007, May). *Agenda-setting effects on vote choice: Evidence from the 2006 Mexican election*. Paper presented at the annual conference of the International Communication Association, San Francisco, CA.

Walgrave, S., & Van Aelst, P. (2006). The contingency of the mass media's political agenda setting power: Toward a preliminary theory. *Journal of Communication, 56*, 88–109.

Wanta, W., Stephenson, M. A., Turk, J. V., & McCombs, M. E. (1989). How presidents' State of Union talk influenced news media agendas. *Journalism Quarterly, 66*, 537–541.

Wanta, W., & Yu-wei, H. (1994). Time-lag differences in the agenda-setting process: An examination of five news media. *International Journal of Public Opinion Research, 6*(3), 225–240.

Weaver, D. (1980). Audience need for orientation and media effects. *Communication Research, 3,* 361–376.

Weaver, D., Graber, D., McCombs, M., & Eyal, C. (1981). *Media agenda setting in a presidential election: Issues, images and interest.* Westport, CT: Greenwood.

Weaver, D., McCombs, M., & Shaw, D. L. (2004). Agenda-setting research: Issues, attributes, and influences. In L. L. Kaid (Ed.), *Handbook of political communication research* (pp. 257–282). Mahwah, NJ: Erlbaum.

Winter, J. P., & Eyal, C. H. (1981). Agenda setting for the civil rights issue. *Public Opinion Quarterly, 45,* 376–383.

Zaller, J. (1992). *The nature and origins of mass opinion.* New York: Cambridge University Press.

Zhu, J. H., Watt, J. H., Snyder, L. B., Yan, J., & Jiang, Y. (1993). Public issue priority formation: Media agenda-setting and social interaction. *Journal of Communication, 43*(1), 8–29.

Zucker, H. G. (1978). The variable nature of news media influence. *Communication Yearbook, 2,* 225–240.

Suggested Readings

Gross, K., & Aday, S. (2003). The scary world in your living room and neighborhood: Using local broadcast news, neighborhood crime rates, and personal experience to test agenda-setting and cultivation. *Journal of Communication, 53,* 411–426.

Lippmann, W. (1922). *Public opinion.* New York: Macmillan.

McCombs, M. (2004). *Setting the agenda: The mass media and public opinion.* Cambridge, UK: Polity Press.

McCombs, M., López-Escobar, E., & Llamas, J. P. (2000). Setting the agenda of attributes in the 1996 Spanish general election. *Journal of Communication, 50*(2), 77–92.

McCombs M., Shaw, D. L., & Weaver, D. (Eds.), *Communication and democracy: Exploring the intellectual frontiers in agenda-setting theory* (pp. 3–14). Mahwah, NJ: Erlbaum.

Meijer, M.-M., & Kleinnijenhuis, J. (2006). The effects of issue news on corporate reputation: Applying the theories of agenda setting and issue ownership in the field of business communication. *Journal of Communication, 56*(3), 543–559.

Miller, J. M. (2007). Examining the mediators of agenda setting: A new experimental paradigm reveals the role of emotions. *Political Psychology, 28*(6), 689–717.

Soroka, S. N. (2002). *Agenda-setting dynamics in Canada.* Vancouver: UBC Press.

Takeshita, T. (2006). Current critical problems in agenda-setting research. *International Journal of Public Opinion Research, 18*(3), 275–296.

Wanta, W. (1997).*The public and the national agenda: How people learn about important issues.* Mahwah, NJ: Erlbaum.

8

CULTIVATION ANALYSIS
Research and Practice

Nancy Signorielli and Michael Morgan

People around the world have been fascinated by television but concerned about its effects almost since the first show was broadcast. In this country, the popular press and politicians keep asking, "What is television doing to us?" "Is television somehow responsible for all the violence in our society?" Parents and teachers wonder whether television makes children more aggressive, or whether television helps or hinders learning. Critics of all political stripes complain about how television portrays men and women, the family, politics, war, nutrition, sexuality, consumption, minorities, substance abuse, and a host of other issues, as well as the massive number of hours we spend watching. Even as amazing new media technologies emerge that allow us to watch whatever we want, whenever we want, and wherever we are, the amount of time we spend watching television still continues to rise year after year. Given its pervasive presence in our lives, students in both high school and college want to study the effects of the mass media but often look for simple, straightforward answers to their questions. Yet, as is true in so many areas of life and social research, the questions are complex and the answers are neither simple nor straightforward.

This chapter describes one particular approach to studying the role of television in society, through a set of theoretical assumptions and methodological practices collectively known as Cultivation Analysis, part of the Cultural Indicators project, founded by George Gerbner. This project is designed to provide a broad-based, empirical approach to answering some of the questions posed above and to understanding the social consequences of growing up and living with television. The Cultural Indicators paradigm involves a three-pronged research strategy (Gerbner, 1973). The first, called *institutional process analysis*, investigates how the flow of media messages is produced, managed, and distributed. The second, *message system analysis*, has been used since 1967 to track the most stable, pervasive, and recurrent images in media content, in terms of the portrayal of violence, minorities, gender-roles, occupations, and so on. The third, the focus of this chapter, is *cultivation analysis*, which is the study of how exposure to the world of television contributes to viewers' conceptions about the real world.

Cultivation analysis is not concerned with the "impact" of any particular television program, genre, or episode. It is not concerned with formal aesthetic categories, style, artistic quality, issues of high versus low culture, or specific, selective "readings" or interpretations of media messages. Rather, cultivation researchers approach television as a *system* of messages, made up of aggregate and repetitive patterns of images and representations to which entire communities are exposed—and which they absorb—over long periods of time. All television is not the same—*American Idol* is a far cry from *The Sopranos*, which in turn bears little resemblance to *Grey's Anatomy* or to *South Park*. But there are persistent cultural themes, images, lessons, and values that cut across many genres and that emerge within many programs that seem on the surface to have little in common. In the aggregate, these interlocking and complementary patterns constitute the system of messages on which cultivation focuses.

The concept of "storytelling" is central to the theory of cultivation. Gerbner contends that the basic difference between human beings and other species is that we live in a world that is created by the stories we tell (Gerbner, 1967). All living organisms exchange energy with their environments, and many creatures exchange information and change their behavior as a result of learning. But only humans *communicate* by the manipulation of complex symbol systems. Humans therefore uniquely live in a world experienced and constructed largely through many forms and modes of storytelling. We have neither personally nor directly experienced great portions of what we know or think we know; we "know" about many things based on the stories we hear and the stories we tell.

Television has transformed the cultural process of storytelling into a centralized, standardized, market-driven, advertiser-sponsored system. In earlier times, the stories of a culture were told face-to-face by members of a community, parents, teachers, or the clergy. Today television tells most of the stories to most of the people, most of the time. Therefore, the cultural process of storytelling is now in the hands of global commercial interests who have something to sell, and who in effect operate outside the reach of democratic decision making.

Background and Scope

Like many landmark efforts in the history of communication research, the Cultural Indicators Project was launched as an independently funded enterprise in an applied context (Gerbner, 1969). The research began during the late 1960s—a time of national turmoil—after the assassinations of Martin Luther King and Bobby Kennedy and increased concern about the country's involvement in Vietnam. In 1968, The National Commission on the Causes and Prevention of Violence was formed to examine violence in society, including violence on television (Baker & Ball, 1969). Their charge was to examine the existing research relating to television's effects. The commission also funded one new study—a content analysis of violence in prime time programming under the direction of George Gerbner at the Annenberg School for Communication. This earliest research of what was to become the Cultural Indicators Project documented the extent to which violence dominated dramatic television programming, described the nature of television violence, and established a baseline for long-term monitoring of the world of television (Gerbner, 1969).

Nationwide unrest continued, as did concerns about television's impact upon Americans. In 1969, even before the report of the National Commission on the Causes and Prevention of Violence was released, Congress appropriated $1 million (a lot more money back then) and set up the Surgeon General's Scientific Advisory Committee on Television and Social Behavior to continue research about television violence. All together, 23 projects, including Cultural Indicators, were funded. Cultural Indicators research focused primarily upon the content of prime-time and weekend-daytime network dramatic programming (Gerbner, 1972).

The cultivation analysis phase of the Cultural Indicators research paradigm was first implemented with a national probability survey of adults during the early 1970s in a study funded by the National Institute of Mental Health (NIMH; Gerbner & Gross, 1976). Since then, cultivation research has continued to develop and expand in studies directed by the original investigators (with funding from numerous sources including NIMH, the American Medical Association, the Office of Telecommunications Policy, the Administration on Aging, the National Science Foundation, the Ad Hoc Committee on Religious Television Research, and other agencies), as well as studies undertaken by many other independent investigators in the United States and around the world. Over the years, the theoretical assumptions and methodological techniques of cultivation analysis have emerged as one of the most influential—and controversial—paradigms in all of communication research.

Although the earliest efforts (and many published reports) focused primarily on the nature and functions of television violence, the Cultural Indicators project was broadly conceived from the outset. Violence was studied as a demonstration of the distribution of power in the world of television, with serious implications for the confirmation and perpetuation of minority status in the real world (Gerbner, Gross, Signorielli, Morgan, & Jackson-Beeck, 1979; Morgan, 1983). For more than 30 years, cultivation research has explored an increasingly wide range of topics, issues, and concerns. Cultivation researchers have investigated, for example, the extent to which television viewing contributes to audience conceptions and actions in such realms as gender roles, age-role stereotypes, health, work, science, the family, educational achievement and aspirations, politics, and many other issues.

Cultivation research has been prominent and prolific. As of 2003, our bibliography of studies relating to Cultural Indicators listed over 150 studies published by the principal investigators (Gerbner, Gross, Morgan, & Signorielli) and their associates, along with over 250 updates, extensions, replications, reviews, and critiques by independent researchers not associated with the original research team. Since then, the number of cultivation-based studied has continued to grow, and replications have been carried out in Argentina, Australia, Brazil, England, Germany, Israel, Russia, South Korea, Sweden, and many other countries. Clearly, such a large body of work cannot be exhaustively reviewed here; in this chapter, we discuss the general theoretical assumptions underlying the idea of cultivation, and describe the methodological procedures involved in the analysis (for a more extensive discussion of the cultivation literature, see Shanahan & Morgan, 1999).

Television in Society: The Theoretical Underpinnings of Cultivation

We are a mass mediated society. The mass media, especially television, play important roles in our daily lives. Television is the source of the most broadly shared images and messages in history, both in the United States and around the world. As the number of people who have always lived with television continues to grow, the medium is increasingly taken for granted as an appliance, a piece of furniture, a storyteller, a member of the family. Few can remember, or care to remember, what life was like before television.

Television sets, which used to be placed exclusively in prominent positions in our homes, are now found in nearly every room of the house. For the most "favored" central set, furniture is arranged to provide the best sight lines to the TV, not to foster conversation. The average number of television sets per household (2.8) now exceeds the average number of people (2.5; Nielsen, 2007); as a result, viewing is increasingly more likely to separate people than to draw them together. For most viewers, expanded delivery systems such as cable, satellite, DVDs, video-on-demand, and DVRs signal even further penetration and integration of established viewing patterns into everyday life. The average household now receives over 100 channels, and the arrival of digital broadcasting has boosted this even further.

Television has thus become our nation's (and increasingly the world's) most common and constant learning environment. It both mirrors and leads society. It serves, however, first and foremost as our storyteller; it has become the wholesale distributor of images which form the mainstream of our popular culture. The world of television shows and tells us about life—people, places, striving, power, and fate. It presents the good and bad, the happy and sad, the powerful and the weak, and lets us know who or what is a success or a failure.

As with the functions of culture in general, the substance of the consciousness cultivated by television is broad, underlying global assumptions about the "facts" of life rather than specific attitudes and opinions. Moreover, television is only one of the many things that explain the world to us and our children. Television, however, is special because its socially constructed version of reality bombards all classes, groups, and ages with common perspectives at the same time. More importantly, these images are presented primarily in the guise of entertainment, whether in sitcoms, drama, action-adventures, "reality shows," or news or information programs (as the lines between these formats continue to erode).

The views of the world embedded in television drama do not differ appreciably from images presented in other media, and its rules of the social hierarchy are not easily distinguishable from those imparted by other powerful agents of socialization. What makes television unique, however, is its ability to standardize, streamline, amplify, and share with virtually all members of society these common cultural norms.

Although television has a great deal in common with other media, it is different in some important ways. People spend far more time with television than with other media; more time is spent watching television than doing any other activity except working and sleeping. Most people under 55 began watching television before they could read or probably even speak. Unlike print media (and often, the Internet), television does not require literacy; unlike theatrical movies, television runs almost continuously and can be watched without leaving one's home; unlike radio, television can show as well as tell. Each of these characteristics is significant in and of itself; their combined force is unprecedented and overwhelming.

Television is different from other media in its centralized mass production and ritualistic use of a coherent set of images and messages produced to appeal to the entire population. Therefore, exposure to all television viewing rather than only specific genres or programs is what accounts for the historically new and distinct consequences of living with television—the cultivation of shared conceptions of reality among otherwise diverse publics.

Cultivation Analysis Basics

The methods and assumptions behind cultivation analysis are different from those traditionally employed in mass communication research. For many years, research and debate on the impact of mass communication usually focused on individual messages, programs, episodes, series, or genres and their ability to produce immediate change in audience attitudes and behaviors. Cultivation analysis, in contrast, is concerned with the more general and pervasive consequences of cumulative exposure to cultural media. Although its underlying theoretical framework could be applied to any dominant form of communication, most cultivation analyses have focused on television because of the medium's uniquely repetitive and pervasive message characteristics and its dominance among other media.

In its simplest form, cultivation analysis tries to ascertain if those who spend more time watching television are more likely to perceive the real world in ways that reflect the most common and repetitive messages and lessons of the television world, compared to people who watch less television but are otherwise comparable in terms of important demographic characteristics.

People who regularly watch a great deal of television differ from those who watch less television in many ways. Although all social groups include both heavy and light viewers (relative to the group as a whole), there are overall differences between heavy and light viewers according to sex, income, education, occupation, race, time use, social isolation-integration, and a host of other demographic and social variables. But there are also differences in terms of the extent to which television dominates their sources of consciousness. Cultivation theory assumes that light viewers tend to be exposed to more varied and diverse information sources (both mediated and interpersonal), while heavy viewers, by definition, tend to rely more on television for their information.

The goal of cultivation analysis is to determine whether differences in the attitudes, beliefs, and actions of light and heavy viewers reflect differences in their viewing patterns and habits, independent of (or in interaction with) the social, cultural, and personal factors that differentiate light and heavy viewers. Thus, cultivation analysis attempts to document and analyze the independent contributions of television viewing to viewers' conceptions of social reality. The existing research reveals that we have come a long way towards this goal; at the same time, the more work that is done, the more complex the questions (and the answers) become (Shanahan & Morgan, 1999; Signorielli & Morgan, 1990).

The Myths of Selectivity, Diversity, and Choice

The cultivation perspective does not deny or minimize the importance of specific programs, selective attention and perception, specifically targeted communications, individual and group differences, and research on effects defined in terms of short-run and individual attitude and behavior change. It just sees these as separate problems, generally irrelevant to the cultivation process. The point is that exclusive concentration on those aspects and terms of traditional effects research risks losing sight of what is most fundamental and significant about television as the common storyteller of our age.

When most people watch television, the number and variety of viewing choices is limited by the fact that many programs designed for the same broad audience tend to be similar in their basic makeup and appeal, and are often broadcast during the same time slots (Signorielli, 1986). Most programs are, by commercial necessity, designed to be watched by nearly everyone, even if they are targeted in particular to those audiences that advertisers will generally pay the most to reach (that is, viewers between 18 and 49 years old). Amount of viewing typically follows the lifestyle of the viewer and is relatively insensitive to specific programs. The audience is always the group available at a certain time of the day, the week, and the season, regardless of the programs. Most viewers watch by the clock and follow established routines rather than choose each program as they would choose a book, a movie, or a magazine. Moreover, those who start by watching a specifically selected program often continue watching once their program is over. Series and fads come and go, yet despite increasing competition from everything from video games to podcasting, amount of daily viewing continues to increase in all age groups (http://www.mediainfocenter.org/television/tv_aud/time_persons.asp).

Thus, while new technologies make viewing more convenient, the more people watch the less selective they can be. Most regular and heavy viewers watch more of everything. As the number of available channels increases, the percentage of those channels actually watched declines (Nielsen, 2007). Researchers who attribute their findings to news viewing or preference for action programs, and so on, overlook the fact that people who watch more news or action programs typically watch more of all types of programs, and that, in any case, different genres of programs tend to manifest many of the same basic features of content and storytelling. Moreover, stated preference for a specific genre does not necessarily mean that this is the only type of program watched, or that this genre will be selected every time it is available for viewing.

Of course, cable, the Internet, VCRs, DVD players, DVRs and other new devices have obviously and dramatically changed the home media environment. The family without a VCR or DVD is now the exception, especially when children are present. All these alternatives have contributed to the drop in audience share (and revenue) among the major broadcasting networks

(Lawrence, 1989), and have profoundly altered the marketing and distribution of films formerly found only in movie theaters. Likewise, cable's increased channel capacities, particularly movie channels, video-on-demand, and "pay-per-view" also appear to have changed the nature of home viewing, making movie viewing less selective and less dependent upon the current daily offerings of HBO and other premium movie channels. In addition, services such as Netflix and downloading websites such as Movielink.com (among many others) give viewers home delivery of movies, thus eliminating the need to travel to the local video store to "rent" movies.

On the surface, accessories such as the VCR and more recently TiVo have undeniably changed the way television is perceived and used by the typical viewer. Through the VCR's time-shifting capabilities and TiVo's capability to select programs that meet specific profiles, viewers can watch broadcast and cable programming whenever and as often as they like. Moreover, through renting or purchasing DVDs, or downloading programs and films to a computer, cell phone, or iPod, viewers may now believe they have an unprecedented range of choice in what they select to watch.

It may appear that these technologies strongly challenge or even negate some assumptions of cultivation theory. Armed with a DVD player, a broadband Internet connection, or a DVR such as TiVo, the viewer may be more selective than ever. Instead of being limited to whatever happens to be on the air, viewers can pick and choose what they want to see from a vast range of alternatives. This scenario, however, assumes that the specific content seen by those who use these technologies (especially those who spend considerable time with media) presents alternative world views, values, and stereotypes from most network-type programs. This assumption seems unlikely, especially because available evidence suggests that these media serve mainly to intensify rather than undercut cultivation; most regular and heavy viewers use them to watch more of the most popular fare, and research has found that cultivation patterns are even more pronounced among those who use "new" delivery systems more often (Morgan & Rothschild, 1983; Morgan & Shanahan, 1991; Morgan, Shanahan, & Harris, 1990).

This should not be too surprising. Given the increasing concentration among the dominant corporations involved in the production and distribution of media content, and the fact that all these sources are trying to attract the most appealing and profitable audiences, the most popular program materials will tend to present consistent and complementary messages. For example, in regard to violence, the comparison of cable and broadcast dramatic programming (Gerbner, 1993) shows similar levels of violence overall. Specifically, although cable's children's programming had slightly lower levels of violence than children's programming on broadcast television, general cable programming was somewhat more violent than similar programs on broadcast television.

From an economic standpoint, the industry's programming practices are geared to reproduce what has already proven to be profitable (Gitlin, 1983). Hence, there is a reliance on spin-offs, formulaic script writing, and the endless recycling of recently syndicated programs or classic TV programs on cable and the Internet. In short, what is most popular, by definition, tends to reflect—and cultivate—dominant cultural ideologies. Certainly, the newer technologies allow selective viewers to seek out specialized, often "fringe" material (Dobrow, 1990), but for most average to heavy viewers, most of the time, new technologies are likely to be used to consume more of what they already watch.

Therefore, from the point of view of the cultivation of relatively stable and common images, what counts is the total pattern of programming to which entire communities are regularly exposed over long periods of time. The pattern of settings, casting, social typing, actions, and related outcomes cuts across most program types and viewing modes and defines the world of television—a world in which many viewers live so much of their lives that they cannot avoid absorbing or dealing with its recurrent patterns.

Variations in Cultivation

Cultivation is not a unidirectional flow of influence from television to audience, but part of a continual, dynamic, ongoing process of interaction among messages and contexts. In some cases, those who watch more television (the heavy viewers) are more likely—in all or most subgroups—to see the world as it is portrayed on television (i.e., to give what we call the "television answers" to survey questions about social reality). But, in many cases the patterns are more complex. Television viewing usually relates in different ways to different groups' life situations and world views.

Cultivation is both dependent on and a manifestation of the extent to which television's imagery dominates viewers' sources of information. For example, personal interaction makes a difference. Parental coviewing patterns and orientations toward television can either increase (Gross & Morgan, 1985) or decrease (Rothschild & Morgan, 1987) cultivation among adolescents; also, children who are more integrated into cohesive peer or family groups are less likely to be influenced by television (Rothschild, 1984).

Direct experience also plays a role. The relationship between amount of viewing and fear of crime is strongest among those who live in high crime urban areas (a phenomenon called *resonance*, in which everyday reality and television provide a double dose of messages that resonate and amplify cultivation). Further, relationships between amount of viewing and the tendency to hold exaggerated perceptions of violence are more pronounced within those real-world demographic subgroups (minorities) whose fictional counterparts are more frequently victimized on television (Morgan, 1983).

There are a variety of factors and processes that produce systematic and theoretically meaningful variations in cultivation patterns. One process, however, stands out, both as an indicator of differential vulnerability and as a general, consistent pattern representing one of the most profound consequences of living with television: mainstreaming.

Mainstreaming

American culture consists of many diverse currents, some weak, some strong. Some flow in the same general directions, some are crosscurrents. Yet there is a "dominant" set of cultural beliefs, values, and practices, in some ways at the core of all the other currents, and in some ways surrounding them. This dominant current is not simply the sum of all the crosscurrents and subcurrents; rather, it is the most general and stable (though not static) mainstream, representing the broadest and most common dimensions of shared meanings and assumptions. It is that which ultimately defines all the other crosscurrents and subcurrents. Because of its unique role in our society, we see television as the primary manifestation of our culture's mainstream.

The "mainstream" can thus be thought of as a relative commonality of outlooks and values that heavy exposure to the features and dynamics of the television world tends to cultivate. *Mainstreaming* means that heavy viewing may absorb or override differences in perspectives and behavior which ordinarily stem from other factors and influences. In other words, differences found in the responses of different groups of viewers, differences that usually are associated with the varied cultural, social, and political characteristics of these groups, are diminished or even absent from the responses of heavy viewers in these same groups.

As a process, mainstreaming represents the theoretical elaboration and empirical verification of the assertion that television cultivates common perspectives. It represents a relative homogenization, an absorption of divergent views, and a convergence of disparate viewers. Former and traditional distinctions (which flourished, in part, through the diversity provided by print culture) become blurred as successive generations and groups become enculturated into television's version of the world. Mainstreaming means that television viewing may reduce or override differences in perspectives and behavior which stem from other social, cultural, and demographic influences. (The notion of mainstreaming implies some special analytical strategies beyond those of "standard" cultivation analysis; these are described in the methodology.)

Criticisms of Cultivation Theory and Research

Of all the theoretical perspectives relating to mass communication, those deriving from Cultural Indicators research have probably been among the most heavily criticized. In the early 1970s the methodology and findings of the content (message system) analysis, particularly the examination of television violence, were the focus of a number of colloquies. Most of these stemmed from critiques by industry researchers and involved differences over definitions (What is violence? What is a violent act? How is violence unitized? and so on). They also addressed concerns over sample size, reliability, validity, and numerous related issues (Coffin & Tuchman, 1972–1973a, 1972–1973b; Eleey, Gerbner, & Signorielli, 1972–1973a, 1972–1973b; Blank, 1977a, 1977b; Gerbner et al., 1977a; Gerbner et al., 1977b).

Soon after the first cultivation results were published (Gerbner & Gross, 1976), cultivation analysis became the focal point of the Cultural Indicators project. Although message system analysis continued to be conducted and reported each year, the industry's critiques abated until recently, when again public concern about the level of violence on television increased. The end of the 1970s, however, brought a period of intense debate over cultivation theory and research. It is not possible or appropriate to review all the arguments and counter-arguments here. For a relatively complete account, preferably in the following order, see Doob and Macdonald (1979), Hughes (1980), Gerbner, Gross, Signorielli, and Morgan (1980a, 1980b), Hirsch (1980a), Gerbner, Gross, Signorielli, and Morgan (1981c), Hirsch (1980b, 1981a), Gerbner, Gross, Signorielli, and Morgan (1981a, 1981b), Hirsch (1981b).

Other criticisms (i.e., Potter, 1993) have been voiced about the justifications for television world answers, television viewing measures, selective viewing, small effect sizes, and again concern about the nature of the relationship. This chapter is designed to explain and describe the nature of cultivation theory and how it relates to ongoing research, so we do not address these criticisms in specific detail here. Rather, throughout this chapter is a discussion of each of these issues in relation to the theoretical underpinning of cultivation or how the studies are conducted (for detailed discussions of numerous criticisms of cultivation research, and responses to those criticisms, see Shanahan & Morgan, 1999.)

Procedures Used in Cultivation Analysis

Cultivation analysis generally begins with identifying and assessing the most recurrent and stable patterns in television content, emphasizing the consistent images, portrayals, and values that cut across most program genres. This is accomplished either by conducting a content (message system) analysis or by examining existing content studies. This phase is extremely important in the research because hypotheses concerning television's contribution to viewers' conceptions about social reality cannot be formulated without reliable information on the most stable and repetitive images and portrayals presented.

There are many critical discrepancies between "the world" and "the world as portrayed on television." The shape and contours of the television world rarely match "objective reality" (although they often do match dominant ideologies and values). Findings from systematic analyses of television's content are used to formulate questions about people's conceptions of social reality. Some of the questions are semi-projective, some use a forced-error format, and others simply measure beliefs, opinions, attitudes, or behaviors. The questions juxtapose answers reflecting the television world (developed from the findings of the content studies) with those more in line with reality. The questionnaires typically include questions relating to social reality as well as measures of television viewing and demographic variables such as age, gender, race, education, occupation, social class, and political orientation.

Using standard techniques of survey methodology, the questions are posed to samples (national probability, regional, convenience) of children, adolescents, or adults. Secondary analysis of large-scale national surveys (for example, the National Opinion Research Center's General Social Surveys; GSS) has often been used when they include questions that relate to identifiable aspects of the television world and also include measures of television viewing.

For example, one of the most examined aspects of television content is sex or gender role stereotyping. Study after study has found that women are underrepresented and that most television characters are extremely gender-typed (Signorielli, 1985), and numerous cultivation studies have explored television's contributions to gender stereotypes. Two of these examined children's responses to two sets of questions dealing with gender role attitudes and behaviors (Morgan, 1987; Signorielli & Lears, 1992a). The questions relating to gender role attitudes asked if certain chores (wash or dry the dishes, mow the lawn, take out the garbage, help with the cooking, clean the house, help with small repairs around the house, and make the bed) should be done by *boys only, girls only,* or *either girls or boys.* Responses to these questions were analyzed to indicate whether or not the answer reflected traditional gender role divisions of labor. The children's gender role behaviors were ascertained by asking which of these seven chores they did. In these studies the "television answer" was responding that only girls should do "girl chores" (wash or dry the dishes, help with the cooking, clean the house, make the bed) and that only boys should do the "boy chores" (mow the lawn, take out the garbage, help with small repairs around the house). In regard to the children's own behaviors, the "television answer" was indicating that they did those chores that were consistent with their gender.

Another study (Signorielli & Lears, 1992b) examined the relationship between television viewing and children's conceptions about nutrition. Content studies have consistently revealed that the world of television is very unhealthy (Gerbner, Gross, Morgan, & Signorielli, 1981), particularly in relation to eating habits. The children in this study were asked five questions relating to poor eating habits:

1. How often do you eat sugared cereal for breakfast?
2. How often each week do you eat at a fast food restaurant (e.g., McDonald's, Wendy's, Burger King, etc.)?
3. How often do you eat a snack each day?
4. How likely are you to eat chips, cookies, candy, cupcakes, or fruit candied snacks for snacks?
5. During the day, how likely are you to drink sugared fruit drinks, fruit punch, or soda when you are thirsty?

The "television answer" in this study was to respond that these behaviors occurred more frequently. Consistent with the study's hypotheses, heavy viewing children were more likely to have poor eating habits and to have unhealthy conceptions about food, even under controls.

Both of these studies (and many others) used questionnaires designed specifically to test cultivation-related hypotheses. Secondary analysis of existing data sets provides yet another very useful way to conduct cultivation analyses. Secondary analysis, however, is often limited by the types of questions, particularly the measures of television viewing, included in the original questionnaire. On the other hand, secondary analysis enables researchers who may be short on research funds to examine data from national probability samples or to look at the same set of questions over a longer period of time.

For example, a number of cultivation analyses focusing on the "Mean World Syndrome" have used data from the National Opinion Research Corporation's General Social Survey (GSS; see Signorielli, 1990). The GSS is a very well-respected, personal interview that has been conducted on a national probability sample since 1972. Many of the questions in the interview schedule are asked each time the survey is conducted while others are rotated and asked every other year, every couple of years or are asked of a subset of the sample each year. Television viewing was added to the GSS in 1976 and is now gathered on a subset of the sample or the entire sample each year. The questions relating to the Mean World Syndrome have been included in just about every GSS. These questions (TV answer italicized) include the following:

1. Would you say that most of the time people try to be helpful, or that they are mostly just looking out *for themselves?*
2. Do you think that most people would try *to take advantage of you* if they got a chance, or would they try to be fair?
3. Generally speaking, would you say that most people can be trusted or that *you can't be too careful* in dealing with people?

As another example, many of television's families do not fit the "traditional nuclear" model, and single-parent families are over-represented. Morgan, Leggett, and Shanahan (1999) wanted to see how those images influenced viewers' beliefs about single-parenthood and out-of-wedlock childbirth. Using GSS data, they analyzed questions in which respondents indicated their level of agreement or disagreement (using a 5-point Likert-type scale) with the statements, "People who want to have children ought to get married" and "One parent can bring up a child as well as two parents together." They found that heavy viewers were indeed more likely to accept the (idealized) image of single-parenthood presented on television.

Numerous cultivation analyses have also been conducted using other existing data sets. For example, Signorielli (1993) examined high school seniors' conceptions about work using questions included in the Monitoring the Future Survey, conducted annually by the Survey Research Center at the University of Michigan.

To simplify and facilitate the data analysis, many cultivation studies combine responses to questions about similar topics into additive indices, which are then tested for internal consistency using Cronbach's α. For example, the questions comprising the mean world syndrome are combined into an additive index (Signorielli, 1990). Similarly, Signorielli and Lears (1992a) combined the answers to questions about eating habits into the "poor eating habits" index. The higher the score on this index, the poorer the child's eating habits and the more reflective of eating habits in the television world.

Television viewing is usually assessed by asking how much time the respondent watches television on an average day. The best measures provide estimates of the number of hours the respondent watches each day. These data may be used in their original form (a ratio scale) or may be reduced to relative viewing categories (light, medium, and heavy viewing). Viewing, when so categorized, is seen in relative terms and the determination of what constitutes light, medium, and heavy viewing is decided on a sample-by-sample basis, using as close to a three-way split of hours of self-reported daily television viewing as possible. Although the more specific measures of hours of viewing each day facilitate some data analysis procedures, from a conceptual standpoint, what is important is that there are basic differences in viewing levels, not the actual or specific amount of viewing.

The substantive questions posed to respondents do not mention television, and the respondents' awareness of the source of their information is seen as irrelevant. The resulting relationships, if any, between amount of viewing and the tendency to respond to these questions in the terms of the dominant and repetitive facts, values, and ideologies of the world of television (again, other things held constant) illuminates television's contribution to viewers' conceptions of social reality.

Data analysis techniques consist of both simple and more complex procedures. The standard analysis may begin with simple cross-tabulations between television viewing (using a three-way split of light, medium, and heavy viewing) and the answers to the substantive questions (categorized by the TV and non-TV answers). The difference between heavy and light viewers is reported as the cultivation differential (CD), whereas the strength and direction of the relationship is indicated by gamma.

Typically, correlational techniques are used to look at the relationship between television viewing and responses to the substantive question. Partial correlation techniques, in particular, examine the relationship between viewing and the substantive question while controlling for pertinent demographic data. Partial correlation coefficients help to isolate what may be spurious relationships. For example, Signorielli and Lears (1992b) calculated zero-, first-, and fifth-order partial correlations coefficients, controlling for gender, race, reading level, parents' educational level, and parents' occupational status. Similarly, multiple regression analysis has been used to try to isolate the relationship between viewing and views about the world, and to explore the persistence of independent effects and interactions under multiple controls.

Mainstreaming hypotheses are tested by conducting standard cultivation analysis involving the comparison of responses given by light, medium, and heavy viewers within specific demographic subgroups, usually defined by gender, age, race, education, social class, political orientation, religiosity, and so on. Usually, some subgroups show significant associations between amount of viewing and the attitude or belief at hand while others do not. In many cases, the overall pattern of differential subgroup associations fits the mainstreaming model; that is, the subgroups showing no association tend to give the "television answer" regardless of amount of viewing (i.e., they are "already in" the mainstream), while their counterparts only give this answer if they are heavy viewers.

In these cases, the light viewers of counterpart subgroups (e.g., younger versus older; respondents, or those of lower versus higher social class, or liberals versus conservative) tend to give sharply different responses, but the heavy viewers in these subgroups converge towards the mainstream (television) view. This suggests that background, demographic factors exert a strong (and predictable) influence on attitudes, but only among lighter viewers, and the impact of these factors is markedly reduced among heavy viewers. Therefore, many studies also use regression analyses and analyses of variance to examine statistical interactions between amount of viewing and demographic characteristics. These provide stringent tests of the extent to which apparent mainstreaming patterns reflect significant interactions of television viewing with other viewer characteristics. Also, a number of cultivation studies have employed structural equation models and path analyses, especially with longitudinal panel data, where the same respondents are studied at more than one point in time; recent developments in statistical software have made these sorts of analyses more accessible and much easier to implement.

New Directions and Challenges

This chapter has focused mainly on the conceptual assumptions and analytical procedures of cultivation research, rather than its findings (but see Gerbner, Gross, Morgan, Signorielli, & Shanahan, 2002 or Shanahan & Morgan, 1999, for more results from specific cultivation studies).

The theoretical questions raised by cultivation analysis—and the methodological implications of those questions—have been continually evolving in a wide variety of new directions. A large body of work, for example, has looked inward in order to illuminate the cognitive processes by which exposure to television cultivates specific beliefs about the world. In an extensive series of experiments, Shrum (e.g., 1995, 1999) has demonstrated that heavy exposure to television's images makes those images more readily available, so that heavy viewers are more likely to rely on them when making mental judgments, in a kind of cognitive shortcut. Heavy viewers give *faster* responses to questions about social reality, in directions consistent with what cultivation predicts. A speedy response to a question implies that an answer is more readily accessible, that the general issue is more salient, and that the respondent does not have to dig very deeply to come up with an answer.

Violence and fear of crime continue to be a major focus of cultivation analysis. Although cultivation theory emphasizes overall exposure, more and more researchers are looking at specific genres of programming. For example, Weitzer and Kubrin (2004) compared the role of local and national news media and varying real world conditions in cultivating fear of crime. Holbert, Shah, and Kwak (2004) investigated the relationship of exposure to crime-related programs with attitudes about capital punishment and gun ownership. Goidel, Freeman, and Procopio (2006) examined how both TV news and reality crime shows cultivate the perception belief that juvenile crime is increasing, and the belief that imprisonment is more effective than rehabilitation. The decision to focus on specific program types is understandable in today's universe of multiple channels and fragmented audiences, but for the theoretical reasons outlined in this chapter, we encourage cultivation researchers to continue to emphasize the contribution of overall exposure.

The range of topics examined and angles explored also continues to challenge and extend the limits of cultivation research. Bilandzic (2006) offers a theoretical integration of cultivation with narrative concepts of "transportation," in which perceived social distance mediates how television content is processed, stored, and integrated into existing beliefs and attitudes. Williams (2006) conducted a longitudinal, controlled experiment to connect cultivation to the virtual world of online games. Schroeder (2005) used the Elaboration Likelihood Model to try to reconcile and synthesize conflicting arguments as to whether cultivation reflects an active, learning model or a passive, availability model.

Other recent studies have examined the psychosocial health implications of heavy viewing (Hammermeister, Brock, Winterstein, & Page, 2005), and public perceptions of biotechnology (Bauer, 2005; Besley & Shanahan, 2005). Hetsroni and Tukachinsky (2006) offer a new conceptual scheme for comparing television-world and real-world estimates. Van den Bulck (2004) contends that cultivation offers a better explanation for the relationship between television viewing and fear of crime than either mood management or withdrawal hypotheses. Shrum (2007) examines how different modes of survey data collection (telephone vs. mail) can affect cultivation relationships, in ways that shed more light on underlying cognitive processes. These are just a few examples of the way cultivation research is continually being expanded and refined.

Conclusion

As in most studies of media effects, the observable empirical evidence of cultivation is generally modest in terms of its absolute size. Even light viewers may be watching up to seven hours of television a week or more; in most national surveys we find that a trivial, and demographically eclectic, handful (about 4% or less) say they do not watch at all. But, if we argue that the messages are stable, that the medium is virtually ubiquitous, and that it is accumulated exposure that counts, then it seems reasonable that almost everyone should be affected, regardless of how much they watch. Even light viewers may watch a substantial amount of television per week and in any case live in the same cultural environment as heavy viewers; what they do not get through the tube can be acquired indirectly from others who do watch more television. It is clear, then, that the cards are stacked against finding evidence of cultivation. Therefore, the discovery of a systematic pattern of even small but pervasive differences between light and heavy viewers may indicate far-reaching consequences.

Extensive and systematic re-examination of hundreds of cultivation findings carried out over a period of more than 20 years (using the statistical techniques of meta-analysis; Shanahan & Morgan, 1999) shows that cultivation relationships typically manifest a strength of about .09 using a common metric, the Pearson correlation coefficient. While this is not a statistically massive effect, it is important to recall that "small" effects may have profound consequences over a period of time. For example, a slight but pervasive (e.g., generational) shift in the cultivation of common perspectives may alter the cultural climate and upset the balance of social and political decision making without necessarily changing observable behavior. A single percentage point difference in ratings is worth many millions of dollars in advertising revenue and, thus, may signal the success or demise of a program. It takes but a few degrees shift in the average global temperature to have an ice age or global warming. A range of 3% to 15% margins (typical of most differences between light and heavy viewers) in a large and otherwise stable field often signals a landslide, a market takeover, or an epidemic, and it certainly tips the scale of any closely balanced choice or decision.

In summary, the theory of cultivation is an attempt to understand and explain the dynamics of television as a distinctive feature of our age. It is not a substitute for, but a complement to, traditional approaches to media effects research concerned with processes more applicable to other media. Designed primarily for television and focusing on its pervasive and recurrent patterns of representation and viewing, cultivation analysis concentrates on the enduring and common consequences of growing up and living with television: the cultivation of stable, resistant, and widely shared assumptions, images, and conceptions reflecting the institutional characteristics and interests of the medium itself and the larger society. Even as our attention shifts to the latest hit show, or as we become distracted by the hottest technological advance in program delivery, television remains our common symbolic environment that interacts with most of the things we think and do. Therefore, understanding its dynamics is necessary to develop and maintain a sense of alternatives and independence essential for self-direction and self-governance in the television age.

References

Baker, R. K., & Ball, S. J. (Ed.). (1969). *Violence in the media*. Staff report to the National Commission on the Causes and Prevention of Violence. Washington, D.C.: U.S. Government Printing Office.

Bauer, M. W. (2005). Distinguishing red and green biotechnology: Cultivation effects of the elite press. *International Journal of Public Opinion Research, 17*(1), 63–89.

Besley, J. C., & Shanahan, J. (2005). Media attention and exposure in relation to support for agricultural biotechnology. *Science Communication, 26*(4), 347–367.

Bilandzic, H. (2006). The perception of distance in the cultivation process: A theoretical consideration of the relationship between television content, processing experience, and perceived distance. *Communication Theory, 16*(3), 333–355.

Blank, D. M. (1977a). Final comments on the violence profile. *Journal of Broadcasting, 21*(3), 287–296.

Blank, D. M. (1977b). The Gerbner violence profile. *Journal of Broadcasting, 21*(3), 273–279.

Coffin, T. E., & Tuchman, S. (1972–1973b). Rating television programs for violence: A comparison of five surveys. *Journal of Broadcasting, 17*(1), 3–20.

Dobrow, J. A. (1990). Patterns of viewing and VCR use: Implications for cultivation analysis. In N. Signo-rielli & M. Morgan (Eds.), *Cultivation analysis: New directions in media effects research* (pp. 71–84). Newbury Park, CA: Sage.

Doob, A. N., & Macdonald, G. E. (1979). Television viewing and fear of victimization: Is the relationship causal? *Journal of Personality and Social Psychology, 37*(2), 170–179.

Eleey, M., Gerbner, G., & Signorielli (Tedesco), N. (1972–1973a). Apples, oranges, and the kitchen sink: An analysis and guide to the comparison of "violence ratings," *Journal of Broadcasting, 21*(1), 21–31.

Eleey, M., Gerbner, G., & Signorielli (Tedesco), N. (1972–1973b). Validity indeed! *Journal of Broadcasting, 17*(1), 34–35.

Gerbner, G. (1967). Mass media and human communication theory. In F. E. X. Dance (Ed.), *Human communication theory: Original essays* (pp. 40–60). New York: Holt, Rinehart & Winston.

Gerbner, G. (1969). Dimensions of violence in television drama. In R. K. Baker & S. J. Ball (Eds.), *Violence in the media* (pp. 311–340). Staff report to the National Commission on the Causes and Prevention of Violence. Washington, D.C.: U.S. Government Printing Office.

Gerbner, G. (1972). Violence and television drama: Trends and symbolic functions. In G. A. Comstock & E. Rubinstein (Eds.), *Television and social behavior: Vol. 1. Content and control* (pp. 28–187). Washington, D.C.: U.S. Government Printing Office.

Gerbner, G. (1973). Cultural indicators: The third voice. In G. Gerbner, L. Gross, & W. H. Melody (Eds.), *Communications, technology and social policy* (pp. 555–573). New York: Wiley.

Gerbner, G. (1993). *Violence in cable-originated television programs.* Unpublished manuscript, University of Pennsylvania.

Gerbner, G., & Gross, L. (1976). Living with television: The violence profile. *Journal of Communication, 26*(2), 173–199.

Gerbner, G., Gross, L., Eleey, M., Jackson-Beeck, M., Jeffries-Fox, S., & Signorielli, N. (1977a). The Gerbner violence profile: An analysis of the CBS report. *Journal of Broadcasting, 21*(3), 280–286.

Gerbner, G., Gross, L., Eleey, M., Jackson-Beeck, M., Jeffries-Fox, S., & Signorielli, N. (1977b). One more time: An analysis of the CBS "Final comments of the violence profile." *Journal of Broadcasting, 21*(3), 297–2303.

Gerbner, G., Gross, L., Morgan, M., & Signorielli, N. (1981). Health and medicine on television. *New England Journal of Medicine, 305,* 901–904.

Gerbner, G., Gross, L., Morgan, M., Signorielli, N., & Shanahan, J. (2002). Growing up with television: Cultivation processes. In J. Bryant & D. Zillmann (Eds.), *Media effects: Advances in theory and research* (pp. 43–68). Hillsdale, NJ: Erlbaum.

Gerbner, G., Gross, L., Signorielli, N., & Morgan, M. (1980a). The "mainstreaming" of America: Violence profile no. 11. *Journal of Communication, 39*(3), 10–29.

Gerbner, G., Gross, L., Signorielli, N., & Morgan, M. (1980b). Some additional comments on cultivation analysis. *Public Opinion Quarterly, 44*(3), 408–410.

Gerbner, G., Gross, L., Signorielli, N., & Morgan, M. (1981a). A curious journey into the scary world of Paul Hirsch. *Communication Research, 8*(1), 39–72).

Gerbner, G., Gross, L., Signorielli, N., & Morgan, M. (1981b). Final reply to Hirsch. *Communication Research, 8*(3), 259–280.

Gerbner, G., Gross, L., Signorielli, N., & Morgan, M. (1981c). On the limits of "the limits of advocacy research": Response to Hirsch. *Public Opinion Quarterly, 45*(1), 116–118.

Gerbner, G., Gross, L., Signorielli, N., Morgan, M., & Jackson-Beeck, M. (1979). The demonstration of power: Violence profile No. 10. *Journal of Communication, 29*(3), 177–196.

Gerbner, G., & Signorielli, N. (1979). *Women and minorities in television drama, 1969–1978.* Philadelphia: The Annenberg School of Communications, University of Pennsylvania.

Gitlin, T. (1983). *Inside prime time.* New York: Pantheon.

Goidel, R., Freeman, C., & Procopio, S. (2006). The impact of television on perceptions of juvenile crime. *Journal of Broadcasting and Electronic Media, 50*(1), 119–139.

Gross, L., & Morgan, M. (1985). Television and enculturation. In J. Dominick & J. Fletcher (Ed.), *Broadcasting research methods* (pp. 221–234). Boston: Allyn & Bacon.

Hammermeister, J., Brock, B., Winterstein, D., & Page, R. (2005). Life without TV? Cultivation theory and psychosocial health characteristics of television-free individuals and their television-viewing counterparts. *Health Communication, 17*(3), 253–264.

Hetsroni, A., & Tukachinsky, R. H. (2006). Television-world estimates, real-world estimates, and television viewing: A new scheme for cultivation. *Journal of Communication, 56*(1), 133–156.

Hirsch, P. (1980a). On Hughes' contribution: The limits of advocacy research. *Public Opinion Quarterly, 44*(3), 411–413.

Hirsch, P. (1980b). The "scary world" of the nonviewer and other anomalies: A reanalysis of Gerbner et al.'s findings of cultivation analysis. *Communication Research, 7*(4), 403–456.

Hirsch, P. (1981a). On not learning from one's own mistakes: A reanalysis of Gerbner et al.'s findings on cultivation analysis, part II. *Communication Research, 8*(1), 3–37.

Hirsch, P. (1981b). Distinguishing good speculation from bad theory: Rejoinder to Gerbner et al. *Communication Research, 8*(1), 73–95.

Holbert, L., Shah, D., & Kwak, N. (2004). Fear, authority, and justice: Crime-related TV viewing and endorsements of capital punishment and gun ownership. *Journalism and Mass Communication Quarterly, 81*(2), 343–363.

Hughes, M. (1980). The fruits of cultivation analysis: A re-examination of the effects of television watching on fear of victimization, alienation, and the approval of violence. *Public Opinion Quarterly, 44*(3), 287–302.

Lawrence, R. (1989). Television: The battle for attention. *Marketing and Media Decisions, 24*(2), 80–82.

Morgan, M. (1983). Symbolic victimization and real world fear. *Human Communication Research, 9,* 146–157.

Morgan, M. (1987). Television, sex role attitudes, and sex role behavior. *Journal of Early Adolescence, 7*(3), 269–282.

Morgan, M., Leggett, S., & Shanahan, J. (1999). Television and "family values": Was Dan Quayle right? *Mass Communication and Society, 2*(1/2), 47–63.

Morgan, M., & Rothschild, N. (1983). Impact of the new television technology: Cable TV, peers, and sex-role cultivation in the electronic environment. *Youth and Society, 15,* 33–50.

Morgan, M., & Shanahan, J. (1991). Do VCRs change the TV picture? VCRs and the cultivation process. *American Behavioral Scientist, 35*(2), 122–135.

Morgan, M., Shanahan, J., & Harris, C. (1990). VCRs and the effects of television: New diversity of more of the same? In J. Dobrow (Ed.), *Social and cultural aspects of VCR use* (pp. 107–123). Hillsdale, NJ: Lawrence Erlbaum.

Nielsen. (2007, March 19). Average U.S. home now receives a record 104.2 TV channels, according to Nielsen. http://www.nielsen.com/media/pr_070319_download.pdf

Potter, W. J. (1993). Cultivation theory and research: A conceptual critique. *Human Communication Research, 19*(4), 564–601.

Rothschild, N. (1984). Small group affiliation as a mediating factor in the cultivation process. In G. Melischek, K. E. Rosengren, & J. Stappers (Eds.), *Cultural indicators: An international symposium* (pp. 377–387). Vienna: Verlag der Osterreichischen Akademie der Wissenschaften.

Rothschild, N., & Morgan, M. (1987). Cohesion and control: Adolescents' relationships with parents as mediators of television. *Journal of Early Adolescence, 7*(3), 299–314.

Schroeder, L. M. (2005). Cultivation and the elaboration likelihood model: A test of the learning and construction and availability heuristic models. *Communication Studies, 56*(3), 227–242.

Shanahan, J., & Morgan, M. (1999). *Television and its viewers: Cultivation theory and research.* Cambridge, UK: Cambridge University Press.

Shrum, L. J. (1995). Assessing the social influence of television: A social cognition perspective on cultivation effects. *Communication Research, 22*(4), 402–429.

Shrum, L. J. (1999). The relationship of television viewing with attitude strength and extremity: Implications for the cultivation effect. *Media Psychology, 1,* 3–25.

Shrum, L. J. (2007). The implications of survey method for measuring cultivation effects. *Human Communication Research, 33*(1), 64–80.

Signorielli, N. (1985). *Role portrayals and stereotyping on television: An annotated bibliography*. Westport, CT: Greenwood Press.

Signorielli, N. (1986). Selective television viewing: A limited possibility. *Journal of Communication, 36*(3), 64–75.

Signorielli, N. (1990). Television's mean and dangerous world: A continuation of the Cultural Indicators perspective. In N. Signorielli & M. Morgan (Eds.), *Cultivation analysis: New directions in media effects research* (pp. 85–106). Newbury Park, CA: Sage.

Signorielli, N. (1993). Television and adolescents' perceptions about work. *Youth & Society, 24*(3), 314–341.

Signorielli, N., & Lears, M. (1992a). Children, television and conceptions about chores: Attitudes and behaviors. *Sex Roles, 27*(3/4), 157–172.

Signorielli, N., & Lears, M. (1992b). Television and children's conceptions of nutrition: Unhealthy messages. *Health Communication, 4*(4), 245–257.

Signorielli, N., & Morgan, M. (Eds.). (1990). *Cultivation analysis: New directions in media effects research.* Newbury Park, CA: Sage.

Van Den Bulck, J. (2004). The relationship between television fiction and fear of crime: An empirical comparison of three causal explanations. *European Journal of Communication, 19*(2), 239–248.

Weitzer, R., & Kubrin, C.E. (2004). Breaking news: How local TV news and real-world conditions affect fear of crime. *Justice Quarterly, 21*(3), 497–520.

Williams, D. (2006). Virtual cultivation: Online worlds, offline perceptions. *Journal of Communication, 56*(1), 69–87.

Suggested Readings

Gerbner, G. (1973). Cultural indicators: The third voice. In G. Gerbner, L. Gross, & W. H. Melody (Eds.), *Communications, technology and social policy* (pp. 555–573). New York: Wiley.

Gerbner, G., & Gross, L. (1976). Living with television: The violence profile. *Journal of Communication, 26*(2), 173–199.

Morgan, M., Shanahan, J., & Signorielli, N. (in press). Growing up with television: Cultivation processes. In J. Bryant & M. B. Oliver (Eds.), *Media effects: Advances in theory and research* (3rd ed.). New York: Routledge.

Shanahan, J., & Morgan M. (1999). *Television and its viewers: Cultivation theory and research.* Cambridge, UK: Cambridge University Press.

Signorielli, N., & Morgan, M. (Eds.). (1990). *Cultivation analysis: New directions in media effects research.* Newbury Park, CA: Sage.

9

THEORIES AND METHODS IN KNOWLEDGE GAP RESEARCH

Cecilie Gaziano and Emanuel Gaziano

In 1970, Tichenor, Donohue, and Olien published a programmatic study of the social structure of public affairs and science knowledge entitled "Mass Media Flow and Differential Growth in Knowledge." By that time more than 20 years of mass communication effects research had implicitly demonstrated "the apparent failure of mass publicity to inform the public at large," with the particular finding that media campaigns tend to reach precisely those "least in need of it... [whereas] those missed were the ones the plan tried to reach" (1970, p. 161). They argued, however, that this outcome was no mere "failure" of an information campaign, but rather the product of the social structure of mass communication. Terming this effect the *knowledge gap*, they formulated a hypothesis, a set of assumptions, explanatory factors, and a pair of testable statements that could explain—and perhaps even help alleviate—this relative deprivation of knowledge between social strata.

Since then, a proliferation of contending positions regarding the knowledge gap has ranged from the research program of Tichenor, Donohue, and Olien (also known as the Minnesota Team), and their students,[1] modifying the original hypothesis, to proposals for alternate perspectives defined in opposition to the 1970 hypothesis (including some who question the idea of "gaps" altogether) and a wealth of empirical results both confirming and disconfirming the validity and usefulness of the knowledge gap hypothesis.

This chapter describes this theoretical diversity and examines the principal methods employed in knowledge gap research,[2] according to a basic typology of theoretical perspectives and conceptual models. Three competing conceptions of knowledge gap phenomena combine, in varying proportions, to comprise its theoretical dimension. A *social structural perspective* locates differential knowledge acquisition within the collectivity. A broad *symbolic interactionist perspective* accounts for the knowledge gap in terms of the situational needs and motivations of individual actors. And a *cybernetic model* conceives of knowledge deprivation in terms of the design and functioning of information delivery systems, focusing on information intake at the individual level. This typology of theories aids in the comprehension of disparate methods and empirical results.

Our intention is not to resolve differences, nor to provide synthesis, but rather to recognize and account for differing approaches that may clarify terms and facilitate conversation among researchers. Toward that end, we also hope to provide a usable vocabulary for discussing the theories and data of knowledge gap research, as well as an indication of those areas where fresh research efforts would be most profitable.

The Knowledge Gap as Societal Naturalism

The knowledge gap hypothesis was conceived against the backdrop of practical and progressive social change—in fact, a normative or ethical dimension permeates research efforts oriented toward closing knowledge gaps. As formulated by the Minnesota Team, the knowledge gap hypothesis rests upon a cumulative change model of social structure. This pragmatic model holds that an increase in knowledge leads to an "increased rate of acceptance of a pattern of behavior, a belief, a value or an element of technology in a social system" (1970, p. 159). Further, this tends to occur within certain subsystems possessing patterns of behavior and values that closely correspond to those of the intended social change. People holding different values tend to accept such innovations at a relatively reduced rate. That diverse strata acquire knowledge at different rates due to varying values and behaviors is not problematic for collective perspectives that posit relatively differentiated, specialized, and interdependent aspects of society. In other words, the existence of specialized knowledge held by certain classes and not others—for example, a knowledge of automotive repair—does not indicate a knowledge gap of societal level significance. Gaps are particularly poignant, however, when certain types of knowledge are supposed to have universal value but are not universally held. In the American context, these values include democratic participation in public affairs (cf., Schudson, 1983), as well as science knowledge or health care promotion. This normative view is also closely related to the modernization and development perspective in diffusion research (cf., Rogers, 2003).

The concept of normativity is one of a complex of themes expressed in the original hypothesis that may be summarized as *societal naturalism* (sometimes rendered *social realism*).[3] In essence, a societal naturalist perspective conceives of society as a naturally occurring supraindividual collective entity whose organizational qualities cannot be reduced to its individual parts (Levine, 1995). Such a view is well expressed in the original knowledge gap hypothesis: "As the infusion of mass media information into a social system increases, segments of the population with higher socioeconomic status tend to acquire this information at a faster rate than the lower status segments, so that the gap in knowledge between these segments tends to increase rather than decrease" (Tichenor et al., 1970, pp. 159–160).

The knowledge gap concerns systemic social relationships—that is, the relative differences in knowledge acquisition among strata—as well as the linkages among "the source, channel, and audience components of the communication subsystem" (Olien, Donohue, & Tichenor, 1983, p. 455). They draw heavily from structural functionalism, stratification theory, community studies, and conflict theory to cast knowledge gap phenomena into these properly collective terms.

The Minnesota Team refined their hypothesis with a set of assumptions: (1) education validly indicates socioeconomic status (SES); (2) information flow may be characterized by irreversible linear or curvilinear trends; (3) no upper limit of information has been reached; and (4) public affairs and science news have a "more or less general appeal" and value (1970, p. 160). Of these, the first three are explicitly designed to facilitate operationalizing the hypothesis, while the fourth is a generalization based upon the expectations of democratic and egalitarian ideology.

Although each assumption has profound consequences for the character of knowledge gap research, the definition and measurement of knowledge deserves special consideration. Throughout their studies the Minnesota Team employs the terms *knowledge* and *information* interchangeably. Yet close analysis shows that each carries a different meaning. On the one hand, knowledge denotes certain socially structured collective representations, including beliefs and values (regarding, for instance, prospects for the future, the well-being of the community), that constitute the worldviews of different strata (Tichenor, Rodenkirchen, Olien, & Donohue, 1973, pp. 60–63; Tichenor et al., 1970, p. 162). On the other hand, they conceive of information as the qualitatively undifferentiated data of the "information delivery system" (Tichenor, Donohue, & Olien, 1980, p. 180), the product of its "feedback" and "distribution-control" (Olien et al., 1983, p. 457). This homogenized and rather mechanistic view of information constitutes a muted cybernetic dimension to the original knowledge gap hypothesis.[4] A cybernetic view of information within knowledge gap research has definite advantages, not the least of which is the way it can be unproblematically measured in survey research. Furthermore, information delivery and reception provide a way of specifying the mechanisms and details of knowledge gap phenomena.

A social realist perspective locates cause within system organization itself. Social structures are conceived "to operate in such a way as to maintain themselves in some stable state" (Udy, 1968, p. 493), through self-regulatory adaptation and integration that tend to maintain equilibrium. In particular, structural functionalist views assume that a "social pattern is explained by the effects on consequences of the pattern" and excludes all explanations relying on psychological, historical, hereditary, and nonhuman environmental factors (Cancian, 1968, p. 30). The Minnesota Team specifically argued that the creation of "greater differentials in knowledge across society is itself a profound social effect" (1970, p. 170). They also noted that knowledge gaps may be considered structurally functional from two points of view: first, insofar as more highly educated persons really are at the vanguard of progressive social change and, second, in the sense that knowledge gaps serve to maintain power differentials of super- and subordination through information control (Tichenor et al., 1973).[5] In the course of maintaining existing elites, however, knowledge gaps may also increase tension within the social system, leading to further social problems (Tichenor et al., 1970). They maintain throughout their work that "social power is the basic issue in the knowledge gap phenomenon" (Olien et al., 1983, p. 458).

While arguing that gaps are structurally functional, the original hypothesis also accounts for the social roles of individuals and the mass media. The mass media function similarly to other social institutions, namely, by reinforcing or increasing existing inequalities (Tichenor et al., 1970). In particular, mass media are oriented toward the more educated and more powerful groups in society (Tichenor et al., 1980), and "systematically project definitions of issues that are conducive to the interest of established power groups" (Olien et al., 1983, p. 459). The forms and functions of the mass media are determined by social structural needs, not the needs of the media subsystem itself (p. 457). By the same token, people also play social roles. An individual's structural location increases or reduces "the likelihood that details or interpretations will ever reach [that individual] and make sense in his [or her] frame of reference" (Tichenor et al., 1980, p. 181). This is not a point about individual personalities. Although roles are played by individuals, they are structurally defined and are not the product of the "idiosyncratic behavior of persons playing roles at any given point in time" (p. 182). Nor, in this perspective, are knowledge gaps due merely to people's interests, because interest itself is a socially structured "collective concern" (Olien et al., 1983, p. 458). Finally, the specific knowledge or message content does not determine gap phenomena; the structure within which it and its interpretations are located does (Tichenor et al., 1980).

Beginning in 1973, the Minnesota Team shifted their focus from an abstract notion of social systems to a concrete, geographically grounded, idea of the community.[6] This approach allowed for a much greater specification of the relative significance of issues, community conflict levels, community characteristics such as pluralism and homogeneity, and greater attention to specific patterns of media coverage in a particular locale (Donohue, Tichenor, & Olien, 1975). Indeed, they found that knowledge gaps decrease for local issues under conditions of high significance, high community conflict, and homogeneity of population (Donohue, Tichenor, & Olien, 1975; Tichenor, Donohue et al., 1980; Tichenor, Rodenkirchen et al., 1973). In these cases, high arousal and salience induce interpersonal rather than mass communication which, in a homogenous community requiring less selective self-exposure, causes knowledge gaps to narrow. The reverse situation obtains when salience and conflict are low (in, for instance, nonlocal issues) and when a community is more complex, differentiated, and pluralistic. The original knowledge gap hypothesis calls for collective-level explanations common to a social realist perspective— whether the analytic frame is the community, the social system, or the public.

The Knowledge Gap as Individual Voluntarism

In 1977, Ettema and Kline challenged the original knowledge gap hypothesis. Citing mixed empirical results, they argued that the original hypothesis "requires a fuller understanding of the causal forces acting to widen and narrow the gap," making it necessary to specify the "contingent conditions" of gap phenomena (pp. 180–181). In the course of doing so, they shifted the underlying perspective from societal naturalism to individual voluntarism by refocusing on an individual-level account of subjectivity and agency, rather than a structural level account. They adopted a voluntarist or constructivist view of social reality, rather than a naturalist one.

In accordance with this shift, Ettema and Kline employed the concepts of symbolic interaction (although they did not use this term).[7] Broadly, *symbolic interaction* "refers to the process by which individuals relate to their own minds or the minds of others" in a way that takes account of "their own or their fellows' motives, needs, desires, means and ends, knowledge, and the like" (Swanson, 1968, p. 441). Symbolic interaction represents the instrumental activities of actors—attitudes, beliefs, motivation, perception, thought, and choice—relative to the conditions and resources of the *situation*. This view conceives of the individual as a minded entity, a self that employs signs and symbols to construct identity and take on roles within a role system. Since symbolic interaction was formulated, in part as a response to social, structural, or cultural determinism (Swanson, 1968), it is a particularly apt choice for Ettema and Kline's challenge to the Minnesota Team's work.

After dismissing structural explanations as inadequate and tautological, Ettema and Kline (1977) concluded that gap phenomena causal factors are of two types: audience-related factors such as communication skills, motivation, and media self-exposure, and message-related "ceiling effects."[8] Within the category of audience-related causes they further discern what they termed transsituational "deficit" explanations and "situation-specific" difference explanations. Ettema and Kline characterized the work of the Minnesota Team as a deficit interpretation of knowledge gap phenomena.[9] In particular, they focused on communication skills, the first contributory factor in the original formulation of the hypothesis, arguing that if communication skills deficits always obtain among persons of lower SES, then knowledge gaps will always widen and never close—thereby contradicting empirical evidence (p. 188).

As a viable alternative, Ettema and Kline (1977) offered a different interpretation of knowledge gap phenomena. This interpretation maintains that "persons from different social strata or cultures manifest their abilities in different circumstances" (Cole & Bruner, 1971, cited in Ettema & Kline, 1977, p. 187). Specifically, these circumstances occur when individuals are motivated to exercise their abilities or it is functional for individuals to do so. (Although they employ the same term, individual-level and collective-level functionalisms need to be sharply distinguished.) These situation-specific differences imply that gaps will widen when lower SES persons are less motivated to acquire knowledge, and will narrow or fail to manifest themselves when motivation or personal need for such knowledge is high. Consequently, Ettema and Kline indicated that knowledge itself is not stratified, but that differences in personal motivation produce this effect—a "situation gap." Or, put another way, they portrayed the link between specific audiences (composed of aggregated individuals, not collectivities) and specific knowledges as the relevant phenomenon (cf., p. 189).

This hypothesis reformulation allows Ettema and Kline to recast factors such as salience and conflict in terms of individual-level motivation and needs. They further reinterpret factors such as selective self-exposure and retention of information, and interpersonal communication, as intervening variables linking motivation and personal functionality to the rate of knowledge acquisition (p. 191). An equally important modification of the original hypothesis is their constructivist view of knowledge itself. Where the Minnesota Team saw one homogenous type of knowledge—public affairs data, news facts—Ettema and Kline recognized the possibility of qualitatively different types of knowledge when they wrote that "higher and lower SES persons… may well see the world in somewhat different ways" (p. 189). In other words, people may employ different cognitive schemata to interpret incoming information.

The Knowledge Gap as Atomic Naturalism (*Cum Voluntarism*)

Another perspective on knowledge gap phenomena amplifies aspects of each of the previous two, but combines them to produce something wholly different. In her work on sense-making and communication gaps, Dervin (1980, 1989) fused a cybernetic model of information delivery systems with certain insights from phenomenology to produce a mechanistic and ultra-individualist—yet situationally relative—account of gap phenomena. Heavily influenced by a library science model of information collection, storage, and retrieval, Dervin's perspective conflated all such systems together: libraries, catalogs, databases, and mass media are undifferentiated (Dervin, 1989; Dervin & Nilan, 1986).[10] These information sources, or "machines," are accessible through hardware such as telephones, televisions, radios, newspapers, and computers (p. 229), which constitute the interface for the human user. Ultimately, Dervin sought a broad reconceptualization of communication, which privileges the user and provides design principles for humanizing information delivery systems. Dervin argued for an alternative reconceptualization in terms of categories derived from user-experience because, she claimed, traditional conceptions of knowledge gaps and information inequality are wholly illusory products of observer categories.

The central opposition in Dervin's work is found between traditional and alternative approaches to communication. In her account, all traditional models of mass communication subscribe to the deficit interpretation of gap phenomena. In this source–receiver model, gaps occur "because some people are less willing and able to take in information than others" (Dervin, 1980, p. 77). The focus of this research, she claimed, is on source–goals and objective information, both of which establish information standards for which, if they are not met, "receivers are blamed when they fail to get the message" (p. 85). "Those receivers who do not catch the message are then labeled as being in gap or inequity" (p. 93). However, Dervin argued that research since the mid-1970s suggests that the knowledge gap "is more idea than reality" (p. 79), and is really merely an artifact of traditional source–receiver model assumptions. Therefore, "any data available on the presence of inequities and gaps is nothing more than numeric myths created by the use of inappropriate assumptions about the nature of information seeking and use" (p. 81).

By contrast, Dervin (1989) sought to modify the "mechanistic, transmission-oriented, objectivity-oriented" traditional model in terms of "the inner worlds of users, where most of the important acts of communicating…are performed" (p. 217). Such a view, also termed the *sense-making approach*, begins from the assumption that all individuals creatively construct meaning unique to their circumstances, within the bounds of "time, space, change, and physiology" (Dervin, 1980, pp. 92, 102; 1989, p. 223). This position entails an ultra-individualistic relativism in the sense that all "persons subjectively perceive their world" differently from other persons (Stewart, 1978, cited in Dervin, 1980, p. 89). Society itself is merely the "product of past and present cognitive/behavioral events" in aggregated form (Dervin, 1989, p. 226). Therefore, she redefined information "as the answers respondents create…to their questions in situations they personally face" (Dervin, 1980, p. 95), or more generally, as "any stimulus that alters the cognitive structure of a receiver" (Paisley, 1980, quoted in Dervin & Nilan, 1986, p. 17). In this view, collective-level gaps disappear and are replaced by "the 'gaps' seen by receivers between the pictures they have in their heads and the sense they require to design movements for their lives" (Dervin, 1980, p. 105). As in Ettema and Kline's perspective, individuals will inform themselves at the point of need, when their circumstances call for information and provide motivation (Dervin, 1980, p. 103).

Consequently, information that is sent by sources that construct meaning differently from their receivers is less useful and relevant—hence the gaps that traditional researchers find (p. 94).[11] The solution to these sense-making gaps is to train information professionals—from librarians to journalists—to "empathize systematically" (Dervin, 1989, p. 224).

The following sections of this chapter briefly review support for the original knowledge gap hypothesis and provide a research example illustrating how a knowledge gap study in a collective realist perspective incorporated theory into its methods.

Research Support for Gaps and Issues for Further Study

The problem of education-based knowledge disparities emerged early in social science research (Hyman & Sheatsley, 1947; Star & Hughes, 1950). Although knowledge differentials do not always develop, the majority of the many studies with knowledge gap data support the hypothesis (Bennett, 1989; C. Gaziano, 1983, 1997; Viswanath & Finnegan, 1996).

Under certain conditions gaps decrease or do not occur, however, and these conditions deserve closer scrutiny. Gaps may decline because topics are local or controversial, both of which tend to heighten public attention. In general, the more distant a topic is from respondents in geography and personal experience, and the more that knowledge depends on access to high-status channels and characteristics, the greater the likelihood that knowledge inequities will occur.

The role of variations in mass media attention in fostering knowledge inequalities is much less clear, however. Not all studies vary media publicity; therefore, this issue requires much more research attention. Media publicity can contribute both to increased knowledge *levels* and increased knowledge *gaps* (C. Gaziano, 1997; Kleinnijenhuis, 1991). Further, both low and high media coverage paradoxically can contribute to reduced knowledge gaps (Tichenor, Roden-kirchen et al., 1973). High media attention, especially to controversial issues, tends to bring public discussion to a boil, dispersing information throughout a community system, equalizing knowledge gaps in some cases (Tichenor et al., 1980), and broadening them in others (C. Gaziano, 1984). It is not unusual, however, to observe an awareness knowledge gap closing at the same time depth knowledge gaps are widening (C. Gaziano, 1983, 1997; Viswanath, Finnegan, Hannan, & Luepker, 1991). Depending upon the topic, greater media attention can help to narrow gaps, while moderate media coverage or lack of coverage can widen them (Viswanath, Breen et al., 2006). On the other hand, decreasing levels of media publicity can lead to narrowed knowledge differentials because of declining public interest in issues (Griffin, 1990). Decreasing levels of knowledge can be the result of forgetting previously learned information (Miyo, 1983). The activities of organized groups on issues influence the amount of media attention to many topics (C. Gaziano, 1984; Tichenor, Donohue et al., 1980), and the role of such groups deserves further study.

Differential Roles of Print and Broadcast

Television, often touted as a potential knowledge gap leveler, can contribute to increased knowledge differentials as well (Grabe, Lang, Zhou, & Bolls, 2000; Miyo, 1983; Viswanath, Breen et al., 2006), and it can contribute to knowledge gain among the less advantaged without narrowing knowledge gaps (Lemert, 1993; J. M. McLeod, Bybee, & Durall, 1979; Pan, Ostman, Moy, & Reynolds, 1994). Use of television and, to a lesser extent, newspapers contributed to smaller knowledge gaps when campaign interest and key demographics were controlled in an analysis of a presidential election (Eveland & Scheufele, 2000). See Liu and Eveland (2005) and Kwak (1999) for similar results for television. Results for newspapers in election settings are mixed (Eveland & Scheufele, 2000; Kwak, 1999; Liu & Eveland, 2005).

Motivation and Interest

Findings are not consistent for interest, motivation, involvement, or related variables. One reason is that widely varying operational definitions have been employed. Another is that levels of analysis have varied, and level of analysis should be kept in mind when comparing studies. Refining measures and clarifying findings also remain a challenge. Some authors to consult on these issues include: Griffin (1990), Kwak (1999), Salmon, Wooten, Gentry, Cole, and Kroger (1996), and Viswanath, Finnegan et al. (1991).

Factors Reinforcing Gaps

Tichenor et al. (1970) described some reasons for reinforcement of knowledge inequalities. These included: (1) communication skills; (2) amount of stored prior knowledge of pertinent topics; (3) relevant social contact (activities, reference groups, interpersonal discussion); (4) selective exposure, acceptance, and retention of information (which often are correlated with education); and (5) the nature of the mass media information-delivery subsystems. For examples of research on some of the first four issues, see D. M. McLeod and Perse (1994) and Kleinnijenhuis (1991). For work concerning the fifth, see Olien et al. (1983), and Tichenor, Olien, and Donohue (1987). For social trends that contribute to knowledge gaps, see C. Gaziano (1989, 1997, 2001).

Community structural variations have been studied by few researchers besides the Minnesota Team. Pearson (1993) studied rural, small urban, and large urban respondents in Alaska. Education increased with size and urban status of the communities and was related to media access and knowledge disparities. The Minnesota Heart Health Program (MHHP) studies showed that knowledge gaps were more likely to close in smaller, more homogeneous communities, as the Minnesota Team predicted (Viswanath, Finnegan et al., 1991). Over time, knowledge gaps ebbed and flowed, and continual introduction of new knowledge into communities impeded development of ceiling effects. For an application of knowledge gap analysis on the collective level of nations, see Bonfadelli (2005).

Cultural Context

The culture of the research setting influences results. This little researched area should be explored further. The three categories of previous research discussed under Societal Naturalism, Individual Voluntarism, and Atomic Naturalism can be considered three cells in a four-celled typology of social theories, based on unit of analysis and social ontology. A fourth cell is Collective Voluntarism, concerned with differential knowledge acquisition rates between groups with culture as an antecedent. It is elaborated further in E. Gaziano and C. Gaziano (1999). Scholars interested in such an approach would do well to refer to the work of Alcalay and Bell (1996), Rucinski (2004), and Viswanath, Breen et al. (2006).[12]

Focus on Families

One example is school-based curriculum interventions to increase citizen knowledge and participation that engaged families in the political process through their children (McDevitt & Chaffee, 2000). Another framework describes differences in the social distribution of family childrearing patterns as a primary component in development of differentials in knowledge and political participation (Gaziano, 2001). Austin argues that the relative lack of research on children and adolescents in areas pertinent to knowledge and participation gaps is a major shortcoming of communication research.[13]

Level of Analysis

Aspiring knowledge gap researchers first have the task of choosing a major theoretical perspective from which to set the level of analysis. Be aware of the theoretical assumptions of each area; the underlying dissimilarities among the three main perspectives partly account for inconsistent findings. Researchers studying knowledge gap phenomena often have borrowed concepts and variables from each of the dominant perspectives without realizing how each varies from the others in level of analysis (i.e., in terms of individuals, a community, a society). Even if hypotheses are stated in the collective terms of the classic knowledge gap hypothesis, research on knowledge disparities has tended to be on an individual level rather than on a collective level.

Research Design

Internal and external threats to validity are important considerations when designing knowledge gap research. One-shot case study designs allow little or no control over such threats (Campbell & Stanley, 1963). Among the best designs is the Solomon four-group design, combining both panel and cross-sectional samples over time, as used by Griffin (1990) and the MHHP studies, although only data from cross-sections have been published from the MHHP so far (e.g., Viswanath, Finnegan et al., 1991). For more on threats to validity regarding communication campaigns, see Chaffee, Roser, and Flora (1989). Holbrook (2002) illustrated changes in gaps across six U.S. elections, as influenced by presidential candidate debates.

Elements of a Complete Research Report

The minimum items to report in any research include: dates of research, location, sample size, completion rate and how it was calculated, interview method, population, research design, biases, operational definitions of all variables, including knowledge gaps, and statistical tests used. Some reports are unclear on some of these elements or omit some altogether—leaving the reader without a complete means of evaluation or replication.

How Theory Translates Into Research

The first step in the transition to research is specifying the independent and dependent variables. Variation in mass media publicity is the independent variable (the presumed cause) in much knowledge gap research. If alterations in media coverage are not studied, at least media use or a similar variable will provide a proxy for publicity. Knowledge gap (the SES-knowledge relation) is the dependent variable (the presumed effect). SES, derived from the subsystem of social stratification, is part of that variable (Figure 9.1). Frequently, education has been used as an indicator of SES, but components such as income or occupation are sometimes substituted or combined with other SES variables to form an index. How the SES indicator was measured should always be reported specifically. Also, education sometimes has been measured as categorical but treated statistically as continuous, the results of which can be misleading (e.g., Hewes, 1978).

Figure 9.1 Primary relationships of variables in knowledge gap research.

Abstract	
Concept:	Knowledge gap (dependent variable)
↓	
Theoretical	Magnitude of differential among education groups on
Definition:	knowledge of some issue
↓	
Operational	From Frazier (1986): Differences in knowledge scores among high,
Definition	medium and low educational groups, by one-way analysis of variance

Figure 9.2 Incorporating an abstract theoretical concept into research. (Based on Hage, 1972).

After the dependent variable is chosen, the next step is a theoretical definition of the concept, such as a dictionary definition. This is followed by an operational definition of the concept (e.g., the way it will be measured in a questionnaire). Hage (1972) provided a fuller description of these concepts in an excellent book on theory construction. Here, *knowledge gap* is the abstract concept, and its theoretical definition is the degree of relationship between education and knowledge. Figure 9.2 shows how Frazier (1986) operationalized *knowledge gap*.

Usually, education has been measured as a nominal (categorical) variable or a continuous variable. As a nominal variable, it is usually divided into either two or three categories. When three categories are used, typical groups are those without high school diplomas (low education), high school graduates (medium education), and those with some college or more (high education). If there are only two groups, the break is usually less than college (low) and some college or more (high). When continuous measurement is desired, record the exact grade number. Higher numbers would capture years of work toward advanced degrees (e.g., 17, 18, and so forth). Similarly, knowledge has been measured as two or three categories from low to high (nominal variable) or as a score (continuous variable).

The choice of measurement will depend upon the statistical test researchers wish to use for their hypotheses. Researchers will be less limited if they measure variables originally as continuous. Variables can be grouped later. Operational definitions in the literature have included the following: Pearson product–moment correlations between education and knowledge (both measured as continuous); analysis of variance results (education as a nominal variable and knowledge as a continuous variable); regression results (knowledge as a continuous variable and education as either a nominal or continuous variable); and chi-square results with both knowledge and education as nominal variables and the relationship expressed by Cramer's V statistic (Gaziano, 1997; Viswanath & Finnegan, 1996). Others have proposed study of statistical interactions between education and news media use in hierarchical multiple regression analyses of cross-sectional data (Eveland & Scheufele, 2000; Kwak, 1999; J. M. McLeod et al., 1979). Following the Minnesota Team's research on a collective level, communities varying in structural characteristics have been compared (Frazier, 1986; Pearson, 1993; Viswanath, Finnegan et al., 1991). If measuring at more than one time, compare the size of the knowledge–education relationship at each time to determine whether or not the differential is increasing, decreasing, or unchanging as media publicity changes.

Building upon Robert E. Park's (1940) distinction between *knowledge of* and *knowledge about*, which correspond roughly to awareness and depth of knowledge, respectively, researchers usually have measured *awareness* of topics as any relevant item mentioned and *depth of knowledge* as a score summing correct answers to a number of questions. Good research carefully notes how knowledge gap hypotheses are stated and how others have stated them, because deviations can inhibit comparability of findings across studies.

An Example

The progression from theory to methods can be demonstrated by a study embodying social realism elements conducted by Frazier (1986). She was concerned with the structure of public opinion within communities—relationships among social action, opinions, and knowledge, and their distribution within four communities along SES lines. Media dissemination of information was relevant in stirring up conflict and public discussion.

This process varied by community and by issue, especially in one community where the fluoridation topic was more controversial than in the others. The other topic, public policy on requiring seat belts, was not controversial in any of these communities. As the Minnesota Team showed, conflict can be a central element in reducing knowledge gaps when talk about issues permeates most or all social strata. Frazier's issues are especially of interest because they were of community-wide importance and defined in both health and public affairs terms (technical knowledge and issue knowledge).

Table 9.1 shows Frazier's theoretical and operational definitions of knowledge. Her complex measures provided a lot of information about the role of issue type in knowledge disparities. Statistical tests of her hypothesis were for differentials in knowledge scores among high, medium, and low education groups. Frazier's data showed that knowledge gaps can be curvilinear, rather than linear. Further, medium education and high education groups can be more similar than are medium and low education groups (Gaziano, 1984, Gaziano & Horowitz, 2001).

The knowledge gap hypothesis was supported for issue knowledge but not technical knowledge with regard to fluoridation, the high-conflict topic (Figure 9.3). Significant fluoridation issue knowledge differentials occurred in three communities, but an issue knowledge gap was smaller and nonsignificant in the community (Brainerd, Minnesota) in which fluoridation was the most controversial. Further, all the communities had fluoridation misinformation gaps based on education, of which Brainerd's was the most pronounced. Lower education correlated with inaccurate knowledge. Small knowledge gaps developed for technical and issue knowledge of the seat belt issue, which was less publicized and less controversial, but communities did not show appreciable differences.

Table 9.1 Theoretical and Operational Definitions of Knowledge

Theoretical definition of *technical knowledge:* "Level of knowledge of the effectiveness of fluorides and fluoridation for prevention of tooth decay and of the effectiveness of seat belts for preventing serious injuries in car accidents" (p. 115).

> Operational definition of *fluoridation technical knowledge:* Score 0 to 19 across 18 items of fluorides and fluoridation with one item weighted twice as much (concerning the one most effective way to prevent tooth decay).

> Operational definition of *technical knowledge of seat belt effectiveness:* Score 0 to 5 on four knowledge items on seat belt effectiveness (most effective way to prevent serious injuries in car accidents weighted more).

Theoretical definition of *issue knowledge:* "Level of knowledge of decision-making processes and sociopolitical issues associated with state laws requiring community water fluoridation and seat belt use" (p. 116).

> Operational definition of *fluoridation issue knowledge:* 0 to 32 across 14 items on fluoridation issue (certain items weighted more).

> Operational definition of *seat belt issue knowledge:* 0 to 19 across 9 items on seat belt issue (the one most effective way weighted twice as much).

Note: From *Community Conflict and the Structure and Social Distribution of Public Opinion,* by P. J. Frazier (1986), unpublished doctoral dissertation, University of Minnesota. Copyright P. J. Frazier. Reprinted with permission.

Hypothesis: "When an issue is controversial in a community, it is less likely that knowledge differentials will be observed according to age, education and social class levels" (p. 96). Partially supported; only education is discussed here.

Predicted relationships:

Under conditions of high controversy in a community:

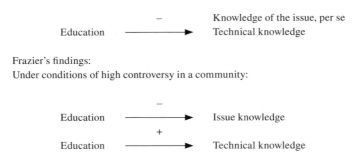

Figure 9.3 Hypothesis and findings. (Frazier, 1986)

Future Research Strategies

This chapter has examined several theoretical orientations and other research decisions that can help scholars study knowledge differentials. Based on this examination, we propose three considerations for future research. First, it is important to identify and develop a coherent theoretical perspective—or set of perspectives—on the knowledge gap. The major dimensions of such identification include the location of subjectivity (and hence agency) either at the individual or collective levels, and the conceptualization of phenomena as either "naturally occurring" or "socially constructed." Clear theory reveals those places where additional work is required. Researchers should be clear about which they are using and why, compared with other perspectives. Differences in theoretical orientation, frequently related to levels of analysis, partly account for incongruent knowledge gap research results among some studies.

Second, theory must be translated into appropriate methods. Ideally, studies would be carried out at more points in time, utilizing combinations of panel and cross-sectional designs. Those researchers interested in the construction of knowledge and the value of information should strongly consider such qualitative methods as clinical interviews, careful textual or semiotic analysis, and for an as yet undeveloped collective voluntarist approach, ethnographic methods.

Third, practical goals of knowledge gap research need to be carefully matched with underlying theory and methods. New variables are needed to increase the explanatory power of theories of knowledge inequalities. New variables could include values or behavior with respect to identifying potential change agents. Examples of work incorporating both knowledge gap and behavior gap variables are Cho and D. M. McLeod (2007), Eveland and Scheufele (2000), Frazier (1986), C. Gaziano and Horowitz (2001), Kwak (1999), D. W. Moore (1987), and Viswanath, Breen et al. (2006). Frazier also examined SES-based opinion gaps.

Finally, much discussion is needed on the issue of policy implications of knowledge differentials. Some knowledge gaps do not have serious consequences, but others, on such topics as AIDS and other health issues, do. Many hard-to-eradicate knowledge differentials have long-term implications for social stability and ever-increasing social costs of differentials in general, to say nothing of the costs to the individuals and the social segments lacking knowledge. If knowledge disparity reduction is a goal, focusing on the larger context in which differentials occur may be more fruitful than concentration on increasing information levels.

Notes

1. Because one purpose of this chapter is to identify influences in knowledge gap research, note that the first author is a former student of Phillip J. Tichenor. Both authors contributed equally to this chapter.

2. The increasing application of knowledge gap research outside of the United States and in cross-cultural settings opens up a series of important issues that we will not treat here, although the topic deserves careful scrutiny.

3. These terms and their parallels (individual voluntarism, atomic naturalism, collective voluntarism) form a framework for analyzing social theories developed by Levine (1995).

4. *Cybernetics* is a term introduced in the 1940s by Norbert Wiener (1961) who defined it as "the entire field of control and communication theory, whether in the machine or the animal" (quoted in Maron, 1968, p. 4). The cybernetic view is intellectually related to economic and maximization theories (game theory, rational choice theory, information theory) and stimulus–response behaviorism in general, and forms a variant of atomic naturalism (see Levine, 1995).

5. This latter explanation was prefigured in W. E. Moore and Tumin's (1949) functionalist account of ignorance.

6. This orientation is closely related to the work of classical human ecologists such as Robert Park and his colleagues who were also interested in the role of the mass media and the functions of community conflict (e.g., Park, 1938/1972).

7. An interactionist perspective is collective, but it is often recast in individual terms, as Ettema and Kline (1977) did.

8. We ignore the issue of ceiling effects here because they are of less interest in a general theoretical account and because the original hypothesis specifically excludes such effects from its scope.

9. There is absolutely no warrant in the work of Tichenor et al. to argue or assume that they impute deficits in basic cognitive capacity to members of low SES groups (*contra* Dervin, 1980, p. 77; Ettema & Kline, 1977, p. 190). A deficit explanation is not a logically possible cause of gap phenomena within a social realist perspective, unless one conceives of deficits as somehow socially structured. In this latter case, such deficits would have the explanatory status of a contributory factor, but not the essential cause of gap phenomena. The individualist perspective of Ettema and Kline, Dervin, and others has hindered recognition of this important point: They have committed what Lieberson calls "the fallacy of nonequivalence" (1984, p. 114).

10. Consequently, Dervin's arguments ranged throughout the "communication and information science fields" (1980, p. 74). However, we restrict our concern to those issues relevant to mass communication and knowledge gap phenomena in particular.

11. Neither Dervin's nor Ettema and Kline's perspective recognizes the possibility of structural patterns that may be reproduced without the knowledge or consent of constituent actors. Such an exclusion becomes both theoretically and practically problematic in situations where individual actors may not be aware of very real information needs; for example, among members of a population at high risk for HIV infection (Freimuth, 1990).

12. Studies of farmers in developing countries are not directly comparable to studies in industrialized nations. The media or informal communication systems and social organization are often too different to make valid comparisons. Such considerations also should be kept in mind when comparing with "control" communities.

13. Erica Weintraub Austin, professor, Edward R. Murrow School of Communication, Washington State University, on "CTM: New Topic for Discussion—The Neglected Audience," Communication Theory and Methods division e-mail discussion group, Association for Education in Journalism and Mass Communication, February 5, 2003 (ctm-discussion@journalism.wisc.edu).

References

Alcalay, R., & Bell, R. A. (1996). Ethnicity and health knowledge gaps: Impact of the California Wellness Guide on poor African American, Hispanic, and non-Hispanic White women. *Health Communication, 8*, 303–329.

Bennett, S. E. (1989). Trends in Americans' political information, 1967–1987. *American Politics Quarterly, 17*, 422–435.

Bonfadelli, H. (2005). Mass media and biotechnology: Knowledge gaps within and between European countries. *International Journal of Public Opinion Research, 17*, 42–62.

Campbell, D. T., & Stanley, J. C. (1963). *Experimental and quasi-experimental designs for research.* Chicago: Rand McNally.

Cancian, F. M. (1968). Varieties of functional analysis. In D. L. Sills (Ed.), *International encyclopedia of the social sciences* (Vol. 6, pp. 29–43). New York: Macmillan.

Chaffee, S. H., Roser, C., & Flora, J. (1989). Estimating the magnitude of threats to validity of information campaign effects. In C. T. Salmon (Ed.), *Information campaigns: Balancing social values and social change* (pp. 285–301). Newbury Park, CA: Sage.

Cho, J., & McLeod, D. M. (2007). Structural antecedents to knowledge and participation: Extending the knowledge gap concept to participation. *Journal of Communication, 57*, 205–228.

Cole, M., & Bruner, J. S. (1971). Cultural differences and influences about psychological process. *American Psychologist, 26*, 867–876.

Dervin, B. (1980). Communication gaps and inequities: Moving toward a reconceptualization. In B. Dervin & M. J. Voigt (Eds.), *Progress in communication sciences* (Vol. 2, pp. 73–112). Norwood, NJ: Ablex.

Dervin, B. (1989). Users as research inventions: How research categories perpetuate inequities. *Journal of Communication, 39*, 216–232.

Dervin, B., & Nilan, M. (1986). Information needs and uses. *Annual Review of Information Science and Technology, 21*, 3–33.

Donohue, G. A., Tichenor, P. J., & Olien, C. N. (1975). Mass media and the knowledge gap: A hypothesis reconsidered. *Communication Research, 2*, 3–23.

Ettema, J. S., & Kline, F. G. (1977). Deficits, differences, and ceilings: Contingent conditions for understanding the knowledge gap. *Communication Research, 4*, 179–202.

Eveland, W. P., Jr., & Scheufele, D. A. (2000). Connecting news media use with gaps in knowledge and participation. *Political Communication, 17*, 215–237.

Frazier, P. J. (1986). *Community conflict and the structure and social distribution of public opinion.* Unpublished doctoral dissertation, University of Minnesota, St. Paul.

Freimuth, V. S. (1990). The chronically uninformed: Closing the knowledge gap in health. In E. B. Ray & L. Donohew (Eds.), *Communication and health: Systems and applications* (pp. 171–186). Hillsdale, NJ: Erlbaum.

Gaziano, C. (1983). The knowledge gap: An analytical review of media effects. *Communication Research, 10*, 447–486.

Gaziano, C. (1984). Neighborhood newspapers, citizen groups and public affairs knowledge gaps. *Journalism Quarterly, 61*, 556–566, 599.

Gaziano, C. (1989). Mass communication and class communication. *Mass Comm Review, 16*, 29–38.

Gaziano, C. (1997). Forecast 2000: Widening knowledge gaps. *Journalism & Mass Communication Quarterly, 74*, 237–264.

Gaziano, C. (2001). Toward a conceptual framework for research on social stratification, childrearing patterns, and media effects. *Mass Communication & Society, 4*, 219–244.

Gaziano, C., & Horowitz, A. M. (2001). Knowledge gap on cervical, colorectal cancer exists among U.S. women. *Newspaper Research Journal, 22*, 12–27.

Gaziano, E., & Gaziano, C. (1999). Social control, social change, and the knowledge gap hypothesis. In D. Demers & K. Viswanath (Eds.), *Mass media, social control, and social change: A macrosocial perspective* (pp. 117–136). Ames, IA: Iowa State University Press.

Grabe, M. E., Lang, A., Zhou, S., & Bolls, P. D. (2000). Cognitive access to negatively arousing news: An experimental investigation of the knowledge gap. *Communication Research, 27*, 3–26.

Griffin, R. J. (1990). Energy in the eighties: Education, communication, and the knowledge gap. *Journalism Quarterly, 67*, 554–566.

Hage, J. (1972). *Techniques and problems of theory construction in sociology.* New York: Wiley.

Hewes, D. (1978). "Levels of measurement" problem in communication research: A review, critique, and partial solution. *Communication Research, 5*, 87–127.

Holbrook, T. M. (2002). Presidential campaigns and the knowledge gap. *Political Communication, 19*, 437–454.

Hyman, H. H., & Sheatsley, P. B. (1947). Some reasons why information campaigns fail. *Public Opinion Quarterly, 11*, 412–423.

Kleinnijenhuis, J. (1991). Newspaper complexity and the knowledge gap. *European Journal of Communication, 6*, 499–522.

Kwak, N. (1999). Revisiting the knowledge gap hypothesis: Education, motivation, and media use. *Communication Research, 26*, 385–413.

Lemert, J. B. (1993). Do televised presidential debates help inform voters? *Journal of Broadcasting & Electronic Media, 37*, 83–94.

Levine, D. N. (1995). *Visions of the sociological tradition*. Chicago: University of Chicago Press.

Lieberson, S. (1984). *Making it count: The improvement of social research and theory*. Berkeley: University of California Press.

Liu, Y.-I., & Eveland, W. P., Jr. (2005). Education, need for cognition, and campaign interest as moderators of news effects on political knowledge: An analysis of the knowledge gap. *Journalism & Mass Communication Quarterly, 82*, 910–929.

Maron, M. E. (1968). Cybernetics. In D. L. Sills (Ed.), *International encyclopedia of the social sciences*, (Vol. 4, pp. 3–6). New York: Macmillan.

McDevitt, M., & Chaffee, S. (2000). Closing gaps in political communication and knowledge: Effects of a school intervention. *Communication Research, 27*, 259–292.

McLeod, D. M., & Perse, E. M. (1994). Direct and indirect effects of socioeconomic status on public affairs knowledge. *Journalism Quarterly, 71*, 433–442.

McLeod, J. M., Bybee, C. R., & Durall, J. A. (1979). Equivalence of informed political participation: The 1976 presidential debates as a source of influence. *Communication Research, 6*, 463–487.

Miyo, Y. (1983). The knowledge-gap hypothesis and media dependency. In R. N. Bostrom (Ed.), *Communication yearbook* (Vol. 7, pp. 626–650). Beverly Hills, CA: Sage.

Moore, D. W. (1987). Political campaigns and the knowledge gap hypothesis. *Public Opinion Quarterly, 51*, 186–200.

Moore, W. E., & Tumin, M. M. (1949). Some social functions of ignorance. *American Sociological Review 14*, 787–795.

Olien, C. N., Donohue, G. A., & Tichenor, P. J. (1983). Structure, communication and social power: Evolution of the knowledge gap hypothesis. In E. Wartella, D. C. Whitney, & S. Windahl (Eds.), *Mass communication review yearbook* (pp. 455–461). Beverly Hills, CA: Sage.

Paisley, W. (1980). Information and work. In B. Dervin & M. J. Voigt (Eds.), *Progress in communication sciences* (Vol. 2, pp. 113–165). Norwood, NJ: Ablex.

Pan, Z., Ostman, R. E., Moy, P., & Reynolds, P. (1994). News media exposure and its learning effects during the Persian Gulf War. *Journalism Quarterly, 71*, 7–19.

Park, R. E. (1940). News as a form of knowledge: A chapter in the sociology of knowledge. *American Journal of Sociology, 45*, 669–686.

Park, R. E. (1972). Reflections on communication and culture. In H. Elsner, Jr. (Ed.), *The crowd and the public and other essays* (pp. 98–116). Chicago: University of Chicago Press. (Originally published in 1938)

Pearson, L. (1993). Desert Storm and the Tundra Telegraph: Information diffusion in a media-poor environment. In B. S. Greenberg & W. Gantz (Eds.), *Desert storm and the mass media* (pp. 182–196). Cresskill, NJ: Hampton Press.

Rogers, E. M. (2003). *Diffusion of innovations* (5th ed.). New York: Free Press.

Rucinski, D. (2004). Community boundedness, personal relevance, and the knowledge gap. *Communication Research, 31*, 472–495.

Salmon, C. T., Wooten, K., Gentry, E., Cole, G. E., & Kroger, F. (1996). AIDS knowledge gaps: Results from the first decade of the epidemic and implications for future public information efforts. *Journal of Health Communication, 1*, 141–155.

Schudson, M. (1983). *The news media and the democratic process, a Wye Resource Paper*. New York: Aspen Institute for Humanistic Studies.

Star, S. A., & Hughes, H. M. (1950). Report on an educational campaign: The Cincinnati plan for the United Nations. *American Journal of Sociology, 55,* 389–400.

Stewart, J. (1978). Foundations of dialogic communication. *Quarterly Journal of Speech, 64,* 183–201.

Swanson, G. E. (1968). Symbolic interaction. In D. L. Sills (Ed.), *International encyclopedia of the social sciences* (Vol. 7, pp. 441–445). New York: Macmillan.

Tichenor, P. J., Donohue, G. A., & Olien, C. N. (1970). Mass media flow and differential growth in knowledge. *Public Opinion Quarterly, 34,* 159–170.

Tichenor, P. J., Donohue, G. A., & Olien, C. N. (1980). Conflict and the knowledge gap. In *Community conflict and the press* (pp. 175–203). Beverly Hills, CA: Sage.

Tichenor, P. J., Olien, C. N., & Donohue, G. A. (1987). Effect of use of metro dailies on knowledge gap in small towns. *Journalism Quarterly, 64,* 329–336.

Tichenor, P. J., Rodenkirchen, J. M., Olien, C. N., & Donohue, G. A. (1973). Community issues, conflict, and public affairs knowledge. In P. Clarke (Ed.), *New models for mass communication research* (pp. 45–79). Beverly Hills, CA: Sage.

Udy, S. H., Jr. (1968). Social structural analysis. In D. L. Sills (Ed.). *International encyclopedia of the social sciences* (Vol. 14, pp. 489–495). New York: Macmillan.

Viswanath, K., Breen, N., Meissner, H., Moser, R. P., Hesse, B., Steele, W. R. et al. (2006). Cancer knowledge and disparities in the information age. *Journal of Health Communication, 11*(Suppl. 1), 1–17.

Viswanath, K., & Finnegan, J. R., Jr. (1996). The knowledge gap hypothesis: Twenty-five years later. In B. R. Burleson (Ed.), *Communication Yearbook 19* (pp. 187–227). Thousand Oaks, CA: Sage.

Viswanath, K., Finnegan, J. R., Jr., Hannan, P. J., & Luepker, R. V. (1991). Health and knowledge gaps: Some lessons from the Minnesota Heart Health Program. *American Behavioral Scientist, 34,* 712–726.

Wiener, N. (1961). *Cybernetics, or control and communication in the animal and the machine* (2nd ed.). Cambridge, MA: MIT Press.

Suggested Readings

Cho, J., & McLeod, D. M. (2007). Structural antecedents to knowledge and participation: Extending the knowledge gap concept to participation. *Journal of Communication, 57,* 205–228.

Dervin, B. (1980). Communication gaps and inequities: Moving toward a reconceptualization. In B. Dervin & M. J. Voigt (Eds.), *Progress in communication sciences* (Vol. 2, pp. 73–112). Norwood, NJ: Ablex.

Donohue, G. A., Tichenor, P. J., & Olien, C. N. (1975). Mass media and the knowledge gap: A hypothesis reconsidered. *Communication Research, 2,* 3–23.

Ettema, J. S., & Kline, F. G. (1977). Deficits, differences, and ceilings: Contingent conditions for understanding the knowledge gap. *Communication Research, 4,* 179–202.

Eveland, W. P., Jr., & Scheufele, D. A. (2000). Connecting news media use with gaps in knowledge and participation. *Political Communication, 17,* 215–237.

Gaziano, C. (1997). Forecast 2000: Widening knowledge gaps. *Journalism & Mass Communication Quarterly, 74,* 237–264.

Gaziano, E., & Gaziano, C. (1999). Social control, social change, and the knowledge gap hypothesis. In D. Demers & K. Viswanath (Eds.), *Mass media, social control, and social change: A macrosocial perspective* (pp. 117–136). Ames, IA: Iowa State University Press.

Kwak, N. (1999). Revisiting the knowledge gap hypothesis: Education, motivation, and media use. *Communication Research, 26,* 385–413.

Liu, Y.-I., & Eveland, W. P., Jr. (2005). Education, need for cognition, and campaign interest as moderators of news effects on political knowledge: An analysis of the knowledge gap. *Journalism & Mass Communication Quarterly, 82,* 910–929.

Olien, C. N., Donohue, G. A., & Tichenor, P. J. (1983). Structure, communication and social power: Evolution of the knowledge gap hypothesis. In E. Wartella, D. C. Whitney, & S. Windahl (Eds.), *Mass communication review yearbook* (pp. 455–461). Beverly Hills, CA: Sage.

Tichenor, P. J., Donohue, G. A., & Olien, C. N. (1970). Mass media flow and differential growth in knowledge. *Public Opinion Quarterly, 34,* 159–170.

Viswanath, K., & Finnegan, J. R., Jr. (1996). The knowledge gap hypothesis: Twenty-five years later. In B. R. Burleson (Ed.), *Communication Yearbook* (Vol. 19, pp. 187–227). Thousand Oaks, CA: Sage.

10

USES AND GRATIFICATIONS

Zizi Papacharissi

In his seminal work *The Effects of Mass Communication*, Klapper (1960) reviewed decades of research on mass communication to conclude that first, the mass media appear to have less power than the average citizen, second, that media effects are of a minor nature, and third, that the actual process of media effects is far more complex and a function of many factors. Klapper's conclusions were not dismissive of all media effects. Rather, they were directed toward effects of an indirect, long term, and complex texture, which could vary based on a combination of psychological and social factors. The work marked a departure from hypodermic effect assumptions, World War II propaganda research, and short term effect studies that had considered direct and immediate media effects. Uses and gratifications emerged as an alternative perspective that could study and understand media effects as a result of more complex processes.

Uses and gratifications (U&G) is a psychological communication perspective that examines how individuals use mass media. An audience based theoretical framework, it is grounded on the assumption that individuals select media and content to fulfill felt needs or wants. These needs are expressed as motives for adopting particular medium use, and are connected to the social and psychological makeup of the individual. Based on perceived needs, social and psychological characteristics, and media attributes, individuals use media and experience related gratifications. The perspective can be used to understand a variety of media uses and consequences. It assumes a relatively active audience, which consciously selects content and media to satisfy specific needs or desires. For example, a family may opt to watch a family-friendly reality TV show, like *American Idol*, for entertainment, or relaxation, or to simply spend some time together. Some may choose to browse newspaper content online to fulfill information needs. Or, an individual may author a blog to fulfill needs for self-expression. The U&G perspective emphasizes that motives, attitudes, and behaviors related to media consumption will vary by individual or group.

This chapter traces the development of uses and gratifications, beginning with the historical origins of the perspective, tracking progress of U&G and response to criticism, covering the current state of the perspective, and identifying operative research trends and directions. The chapter concludes with a focus on the limitations of the perspective, future research directions, and an example study.

Evolution of U&G

Uses and gratifications examines the nature of audience involvement and gratification obtained from viewing television, with an emphasis on motives for medium, psychological, and social traits that influence this use, and behaviors or attitudes that develop as a result of the combined influence of motives and traits. The origins of uses and gratifications can be traced back to Lasswell's (1948) model of who uses which media, how, and with what effect. Lasswell's identified three primary functions of the mass media: surveillance of the environment, correlation of events, and transmission of social heritage, which served as the basis for formulating media needs and expectations within the uses and gratifications model. Wright's (1960) addition of entertainment concluded the list of functions, which are reflected in motive categories and gratifications measured by U&G researchers.

Early U&G studies date back to the 1940s, with work that examined reasons why people listened to radio formats, including quiz shows and soap operas (see Herzog, 1940, 1944; Lazarsfeld, 1940). These studies pointed out that the media can help fulfill several everyday needs, and led to an examination of media processes and effects from a functional perspective (Blumler & Katz, 1974). Similar studies followed in the late 40s and 50s, in response to the appearance of television as a mass medium and eventually branched off to studies of media and politics (Blumler & McQuail, 1969). The volume and state of U&G research was at that point organized and reviewed by Katz, Blumler, and Gurevitch (1974), who defined the theoretical foundation of the perspective as resting upon:

> the social and psychological origins of (2) needs, which generate (3) expectations of (4) the mass media or other sources, which lead to (5) differential patterns of media exposure (or engagement in other activities), resulting in (6) need gratifications and (7) other consequences, perhaps mostly unintended ones. (p. 20)

Rosengren (1974) also sketched a model of the U&G paradigm that clarified several of the above components and links among them. According to the model, basic needs interact with individual characteristics (psychological setup, social position, and life history) and society (including media structure) to produce perceived problems and perceived solutions to them. The problems and expected solutions are molded into motives for communication, and lead to media and other behavior.

At the same time, critics began to point out that U&G presents a rather general approach to understanding media uses and consequences, and proposes key concepts and links to societal processes that are inadequately defined (Lometti, Reeves, & Bybee, 1977; McQuail, 1979; Swanson, 1977). For example, Swanson (1977) criticized the lack of clarity in key terms of the paradigm. McQuail (1979) argued that the approach was too individualistic, thus making it difficult to link personal media use to societal structures. Lometti, Reeves, and Bybee (1977) looked into the assumptions of uses and gratifications research and concluded that the exact relationship between gratifications sought and actual gratifications obtained remained undefined. Gitlin (1981), in a critique of limited effects empirical models, added the absence of any consideration micro or macro effects associated with power, media ownership, and ideology. Similarly, others argue that the perspective is too individualistic, making it difficult to focus on the impact media have on society and culture (Carey & Kreiling, 1974; Elliot, 1974).

Subsequent work attempted to address criticism and further refine the conceptual foundation of U&G. Specifically, Palmgreen, Wenner, and Rayburn (1980) synthesized previous literature and developed the Gratifications Sought and Obtained (GS-GO) approach, as a way of applying the expectancy-value theory to media gratifications. Palmgreen and Rayburn (1982) further explored the conceptual connections between gratifications sought and media exposure, within an expectancy values model. In the same vein, Babrow and Swanson (1988) investigated connections between antecedents and different levels of audience exposure, by relying on expectancy-value analyses of television news. Lichtenstein and Rosenfeld (1983) further undertook research that investigated the link between media choices and gratifications or functions expected, finding that gratifications are not medium specific.

Such work placed media uses and consequences within the larger context of individual everyday social habits and routines, and suggested ways in which motivations and traits lead to consumption of the media over other avenues, for the fulfillment of individual needs, thus leading to the development of the Uses and Dependency Model (A. M. Rubin & Windahl, 1986). This model clarifies the interrelationships among societal systems and media audiences, and considers the relationship between media dependency and functional alternatives, thus suggesting that people who possess a wide variety of communication channels, and are willing to use them, should be less dependent on a particular channel. This relationship indicates an interface between personal and mediated communication, as these channels overlap, complement, and substitute each other for the fulfillment of individual needs and wants (e.g., A. M. Rubin & Rubin, 1985, 2001). Within this interface, several concepts, including loneliness, intervene and lead to particular media uses, attitudes, and behaviors.

Given these theoretical and conceptual adjustments, contemporary U&G is grounded in the following five assumptions: (1) "communication behavior, including media selection and use, is goal-directed, purposive, and motivated"; (2) "people take the initiative in selecting and using communication vehicles to satisfy felt needs or desires"; (3) "a host of social and psychological factors mediate people's communication behavior"; (4) "media compete with other forms of communication (i.e., functional alternatives) for selection, attention, and use to gratify our needs or wants"; and (5) "people are typically more influential than the media in the relationship, but not always" (A. M. Rubin, 1994, p. 420).

Palmgreen (1984), summarized uses and gratifications research in six main areas that specifically relate to the scope of U&G research: (1) gratifications and media consumption; (2) social and psychological origins of gratifications; (3) gratifications and media effects; (4) gratifications sought and obtained; (5) expectancy-value approaches to uses and gratifications; and (6) audience activity. This classification still covers most work completed within U&G, which is diverse and prolific. U&G has been employed to understand various media uses and consequences, covering for instance soap operas (e.g., Alexander, 1985; Babrow, 1987; Perse, 1986; A. Rubin & Perse; 1987a; A. M. Rubin, 1985); news programs (e.g., Palmgreen, Wenner, & Rayburn, 1980; A. Rubin & Perse, 1987b; A. M. Rubin, 1981b); using the VCR (e.g., Levy, 1981, 1983, 1987; A. Rubin & Bantz, 1989; A. M. Rubin & Rubin, 1989); listening to talk radio (e.g., Armstrong & A. Rubin, 1989; Surlin, 1986; Turow, 1974); watching cable TV (e.g., Becker, Dunwoody, & Rafaell, 1983; Jeffres, 1978); channel surfing (e.g., Ferguson, 1992; Walker & Bellamy, 1991); magazine reading (Payne, Severn, & Dozier, 1988; Towers, 1987), tabloid reading (Salwen & Anderson, 1984), the Internet (e.g., Papacharissi & Rubin, 2000); reality TV (e.g., Papacharissi & Mendelson, 2007) and religious television (Abelman, 1987; Korpi & Kim, 1986; Pettersson, 1986). These particular areas of interest are examined in greater detail below.

The U&G Framework of Analysis

The strength of the U&G perspective lies in its applicability to a variety of media contexts. Despite the diversity of context and interests, U&G studies tend to share a common frame of analysis that focuses on motives, social and psychological antecedents, and cognitive, attitudinal, or behavioral outcomes. A typical U&G study will focus on a particular medium or compare uses and gratifications across media. In doing so, scholars will examine *motives*, a combination of relevant *social* and *psychological antecedents*, and consider *consequences* or *effects* associated with the given medium consumption. The following sections examine concepts typically encountered within U&G research and research methods implemented in study design.

Motives present general dispositions that influence people's actions taken for the fulfillment of a need or want and behavior. Most U&G studies investigate motives as way of understanding media consumption. For example, researchers have investigated motives for watching soap operas (e.g., Alexander, 1985; Babrow, 1987; Perse, 1986; A. Rubin & Perse, 1987a; A. M. Rubin, 1985); watching news programs (e.g., Palmgreen, Wenner, & Rayburn, 1980; Perse, 1992; A. Rubin & Perse, 1987b; A. M. Rubin, 1981b; Vincent & Basil, 1997); using the VCR (e.g., Levy, 1981, 1983, 1987; A. Rubin & Bantz, 1989; A. M. Rubin & Rubin, 1989); listening to talk radio (e.g., Armstrong & A. Rubin, 1989; Turow, 1974), watching cable TV (e.g., Becker, Dunwoody, & Rafaell, 1983; Jeffres, 1978) or reruns (Fumo-Lamude & Anderson, 1992); using the telephone (Dimmick, Sikand, & Patterson, 1994; O'Keefe & Sulanowski, 1995); watching horror movies (Johnson, 1995); for viewer archetypes (Abelman, Atkin, & Rand, 1997); using cellular phones (Leung & Wei, 2000); using the Internet (Garramone, Harris, & Anderson, 1986; Papacharissi & Rubin, 2000; Perse & Courtright, 1993; Perse & Dunn-Greenberg, 1998; Perse & Ferguson, 1994; Stafford, Kline & Dimmick, 1999; Valkenburg & Soeters, 2001); online service adoption (Lin, 2001; Lo, Li, Shih & Yang, 2005); and even online fortune telling (Kuo, 2005). Specifically pertaining to media motives, Greenberg's (1974) work was pivotal in establishing an early scale that assessed British children's TV viewing motives. A. M. Rubin (1977, 1979, 1981a) adapted the scale to American children and adults. Versions of this scale have been adapted to varying contexts to measure media motives. A. M. Rubin (1983) identified nine recurring television use motives: relaxation, companionship, entertainment, social interaction, information, habit, pass time, arousal, and escape. Researchers have come up with some additional motives, such as para-social interaction for news watching (Palmgreen et al., 1980) and surveillance and voyeurism for certain program types (Bantz, 1982).

U&G research has shown that media frequently are employed to fulfill both mediated and interpersonal needs, so both interpersonal and mediated communication motives are incorporated in studies of media consumption. Schutz (1966) argued that the following three interpersonal needs influence all aspects of communication: inclusion, affection, and control. A. Rubin, Perse, and Barbato (1988), drew upon previous research and verified six prominent motives for interpersonal communication: pleasure, affection, inclusion, escape, relaxation, and control and constructed the interpersonal communication motives scale (ICM). Affection, inclusion, and control are more interpersonally oriented needs, whereas pleasure, relaxation, and escape have also been developed within U&G theory, and used to study media use. Most contemporary U&G studies employ a combination of interpersonal and media motives to capture the unique abilities of each medium.

Social and psychological antecedents typically present mediating concepts that influence the selection of medium content, amount, and motivation of medium use, and possible outcomes of the media experience. Antecedents are preceding variables that influence media-related decisions, attitudes and behaviors.

In addition to demographic variables that may influence media uses, U&G research has linked several socio-psychological characteristics to patterns of media consumption. For example, *contextual age*, a general life-position index of aging, has been reported to influence both mass mediated and interpersonal communication (Palmgreen, 1984; R. B. Rubin & Rubin, 1992). The Contextual Age Scale (R. B. Rubin & Rubin, 1982) includes the following dimensions: physical health, interpersonal interaction, mobility, life satisfaction, social activity, and economic security. Depending on how people score on each of the dimensions and the entire scale, they may choose media use as functional alternatives, complementing or substituting for how needs are met within their contextual environments. For instance, those low on economic security or mobility are more likely to employ affordable media for entertainment or social communication not otherwise available to them (e.g., Papacharissi & Rubin, 2000; A. M. Rubin & Rubin, 1982a).

Similarly, *locus of control, a* concept that measures how people differ in the amount of responsibility for their own lives they attribute to internal or external factors, is also connected to media consumption and motives. People with high internal locus of control perceive that they are steering their own life-course, while those with high external locus of control perceive that factors outside themselves steer their life (Lefcourt, 1979; Trice, 1985) Locus of control has been shown to impact communication satisfaction (A. M. Rubin, 1993) and perceptions of fear cultivation for heavy television viewers (Wober & Gunter, 1982). Locus of control has also been shown to influence third person effect perceptual bias, in a U&G study of third person effects in the aftermath of terrorism (Haridakis & A. M. Rubin, 2005).

Affinity with certain media, and especially television, has also been linked to many motives, such as arousal, habit, pass time, escape, entertainment, companionship, and information seeking (A. M. Rubin, 1981a). A. M. Rubin (1985) found that felt affinity toward soap operas was related to entertainment and relaxation needs. Perse (1986) added that motives of information, escape, and voyeurism were related to affinity for the same genre. *Perceived realism* refers to how true-to-life viewers understand reality depictions to be, and has been used to understand how different individuals react to TV messages based on motivation (e.g., Greenberg, 1974; Rubin, 1979), or specific content like TV news (Perse, 1990; A. Rubin, Perse, & Powell, 1985; A. M. Rubin, 1981b) and soap operas (Perse, 1986; Rubin & Perse, 1987a).

Unwillingness to communicate, a psychological construct that represents "a chronic tendency to avoid and/or devalue oral communication" (Burgoon, 1976), has been connected to talk radio and Internet use. Talk radio callers, for instance, as compared to non-callers, were less willing to communicate in face-to-face interaction and found face-to-face communication to be less rewarding (Armstrong & A. Rubin, 1989). Similarly, Internet users who find face-to-face communication less rewarding are more likely to use the Internet for social communication (Papacharissi & A. Rubin, 2000; Papacharissi, 2002a, 2002b).

Additional attributes linked to media consumption include loneliness (Perse & A. M. Rubin, 1990); parasocial interaction, anxiety, creativity, and sensation seeking (Conway & A. M. Rubin, 1991). Specifically related to audience activity and involvement, Hawkins et al. (2001) found that mood and content preference were strong predictors of selective viewing and thinking while viewing.

In the same vein, Sherry (2001) found that temperament was a strong predictor of television viewing motives, and made the case for incorporating bio-behavioral tendencies into conceptualizations of U&G research. Recently, individual attitudes toward the media were connected to flow of programming and media enjoyment (Sherry, 2004).

Studies of the psychological and social origins of media consumption confirm that individuals typically employ the mass media as functional alternatives, that is, to complement or substitute for aspects of their environment they are not satisfied with (A. M. Rubin & Windahl, 1986). This pattern is evident also in outcomes generated within the uses and gratifications model.

Consequences or *effects* of media use, as examined through U&G, focus on the core concept of audience activity and employ the term "effects" with care. Uses and gratifications researchers recognize that audiences are not universally active, and frequently study level of audience activity as function of orientation toward the media. Media orientation is typically measured through motives for media use, attitudes toward the media, and psycho-social origins of media consumption. Levy and Windahl (1984) produced a typology of audience activity which identified three levels of audience activity: selectivity, involvement, and use, across three periods of activity: before, during, or after exposure. Research indicated that activity relates to medium type and gratifications sought and obtained by the media (Katz, Blumler, & Gurevitch, 1973; Lometti et al., 1977; McLeod & Becker, 1981; Palmgreen, Wenner, & Rayburn, 1981; Rayburn, Palmgreen, & Acker, 1984; A. M. Rubin, 1981a, 1981b, 1983). In a synthesis of previous research, A. M. Rubin (1994) distinguished between instrumental and ritualized orientations toward the media, arguing that these lead to different levels of audience activity and involvement with the media. Ritualized use is primarily diversionary in nature, and involves habitual use of a medium to pass the time, and relates to greater use of and affinity with the medium. Instrumental use is utilitarian and selective in nature, and connects to purposive and informational uses of the medium. Instrumental use suggests greater involvement and intentionality of use (A. M. Rubin, 1994). Ritualized and instrumental orientations lead to different types of cognitive, attitudinal and behavioral effects associated with media use.

One particular outcome of media use that has received considerable attention by U&G scholars is media dependency. Media dependency refers to the tendency to rely to heavily on a particular communication medium for the fulfillment of needs or wants. The construct is associated with patterns of media use and has frequently been operationalized as the extent to which an individual would miss a particular medium if it were not available (i.e., Ball-Rokeach & DeFleur, 1976; Greenberg, 1974; Lindlof, 1986; A. M. Rubin, 1983, 1986; A. M. Rubin & R. Rubin, 1982a; A. M. Rubin & Windahl, 1986). Dependency on a medium implies the absence of functional alternatives (Rosengren & Windahl, 1972). The Uses and Dependency Model (A. M. Rubin & Windahl, 1986) proposes a model of understanding media uses and effects, by centering on media consumptions and studying relevant concepts. Dependency is affected by social and psychological attributes, because it is these attributes that influence the availability of communication alternatives. Some research has indicated, for instance, a connection between low self-reliance and greater dependency on television (A. M. Rubin & R. B. Rubin, 1982b). In general, dependency on a particular medium augments the effects that a particular medium could produce (Miller & Reese, 1982; A. M. Rubin, 1994). Dependency also illustrates how uses and gratifications can interface mediated, personal, and political communication. The presence of functional alternatives demonstrates the multitude and diversity of communication channels individuals may use to fulfill certain needs and lessens dependency effects. Additional research in this area could connect dependency to more recent media content and phenomena, including virtual gaming, and public cynicism/decline of civic engagement to understand how reliance on a particular medium leads to certain cognitive, attitudinal, or behavioral consequences. Such research would serve to align and connect U&G with parallel theoretical perspectives that examine framing and the generation of social capital.

Another approach to media effects involves expectancy-value models integrated with gratifications sought and obtained research. Gratifications obtained are an obvious outcome of gratifications sought, but scholars have criticized the lack of conceptual distinction between the two categories. Since gratification seeking involves expectations from media consumption, expectancy theory has been employed to reinforce the theoretical foundation of U&G and understand connections between gratifications sought and obtained. The most notable effort to connect Fishbein and Ajzen's (1975) expectancy-value theory with U&G was conducted by Palmgreen and Rayburn (1982). Expectancy value theory distinguishes between informational beliefs and inferential beliefs, and considers intentions, attitudes, and behaviors as functions of the perceived likelihood (belief or expectancy) that a behavior will lead to a particular consequence. The combined model proposed by Palmgreen and Rayburn has been used primarily to measure and predict gratifications sought and obtained in new program use (e.g., Al-Amoudi, Heald, & Rayburn, 1993; Palmgreen & Rayburn, 1982). Another model, proposed by Rubin and Perse (1987a), sought to connect gratification seeking to audience activity, and specifically involvement. This particular synthesis proposed that media use progresses from expectations about the media, to gratifications sought, to behavioral intention, exposure to the media, to attention and involvement with media content. Recently, researchers have combined the expectancy value approach to understand online media adoption behaviors (Lo, Li, Shih, & Yang, 2005), and combined it with diffusion of innovations to look and consider individual differences in gaming adoption (Chang, Lee, & Kim, 2006).

Contemporary Studies

Contemporary studies explore dominant trends in uses and gratifications research and apply the framework for the study of newer media and genres. Uses and gratifications researchers routinely apply the framework to focus contemporary social phenomena and problems. For instance, in the aftermath of the Columbine and other similar violent incidents in high schools, several scholars have (re)turned their attention to the effects of viewing aggressive content. Haridakis (2002) investigated the links between viewer characteristics and exposure to television violence and aggression, and found that viewer characteristics, such as disinhibition and previous experience with crime were stronger predictors of aggression than televised violence. Similarly, Rubin, Haridakis, and Eyal (2003) investigated viewer aggression and preferences of talk shows. They found that those with higher levels of aggression were drawn to content that featured displays of anger and shock, had negative attitudes toward women, enjoyed watching others being belittled or harmed, and used the shows as a vehicle for social interaction with others. Haridakis (2006) further examined how these relationships differed by gender. In the same vein, Slater (2003) found that gender, sensation seeking, aggression, and frequency of Internet use were connected to violent media consumption, including website use, while alienation from school and family also mediated these effects. Finally, Krcmar and Kean (2005) found that neuroticism was positively related to watching violent media, with extraverts not drawn to general TV watching, but demonstrating a preference for violent content. Greene and Krcmar (2005) added that sensation seeking, verbal aggressiveness, argumentativeness, and instrumental androgyny were positively associated with exposure to violent films and horror movies, without necessarily predicting liking of those genres. These results demonstrate the utility of uses and gratifications in differentiating among several factors, including but not limited to the media, contributing to aggressive behavior. Moreover, recent studies extend the scope of U&G by adding antecedent social and psychological variables not previously explored.

In response to the present political environment, researchers have also looked at how individuals employed the media in the aftermath of the 9/11 terrorist attacks. In support of the functional alternatives hypothesis, Dutta-Bergman (2004) found evidence of complementary channel use in the aftermath of the 9/11 terrorist attacks. Boyle, Schmierbach et al. (2004) added that negative emotional response was a strong predictor of motivation for information seeking and reducing uncertainty in the aftermath of 9/11. Haridakis and Rubin (2005) investigated third person effects within the U&G framework and found internal locus of control to be a predictor of information seeking to be negatively connected to third person perceptions.

Considerable attention has also been devoted to the informational and social uses of newer media, like the Internet. Hardy and Scheufele (2005) combined research on computer-mediated communication and uses and gratifications to understand how exposure to hard news, combined with interpersonal communication could lead to greater participation in public affairs.

Uses and gratifications assumptions were also employed to understand how users select and what they expect of online news vs. traditional news media (De Waal, Schoenbach, & Lauf, 2006; Schoenbach, de Waal, & Lauf, 2005)

A similar approach was employed to understand differential exposure to online news during the conflict with Iraq, finding that those most opposed to the Bush administration were more likely to supplement their use of domestic news with an online foreign news source (Best, Chmielewski, & Krueger, 2005).

The distinction between online and offline news content presents a primary research interest. Althaus and Tewksbury (2000) found that use of online news sources is connected to newspaper reading but not to TV viewing. Along the same lines, Dimmick, Chen, and Li (2004) detected overlap between the niches of offline and online media, and a pronounced tendency for the

Internet to displace traditional news sources, like television and the print media. Kaye and Johnson (2002) identified guidance, surveillance, entertainment, and social utility as the four primary motivation of political uses of the web, connected to amount of use, trust in government, feelings of efficacy, political interest, and likelihood to vote. Finally, Chyi (2005) employed the uses and gratifications framework to understand user willingness to pay for online news content.

Finally, social connectivity enabled by newer media has also drawn attention from U&G researchers. Perse and Ferguson (2000) found learning to be the most salient motive for surfing, followed by information and entertainment. Papacharissi and Rubin (2000) examined ritualized and instrumental uses of the Internet, and found the medium to be a functional alternative for people with diminished mobility, economic security, and social interaction offline, and also for people who found face-to-face communication less rewarding. In another study of chronic loneliness and online behavior, Leung (2001) found connections between instrumental use of the media for the non-lonely, but no support for ritualized uses and the lonely group. Papacharissi further researched the uses and gratifications of personal web page authoring (2002a, 2002b) and blogging (2007), to understand how they facilitate social environments and identity expression. Hiller and Franz (2004) used U&G assumptions to trace patterns of interpersonal communication online for pre-migrants, settled, and post-migrants, and to study how the Internet helps sustain diasporic identity.

Future Directions

A principal strength of the Uses and Gratifications approach is its inherent ability to interface interpersonal and mediated communication (A. M. Rubin & Rubin, 1985, 2001). In the contemporary converging environment of traditional and newer digital technologies, media are selected by users for their availability to sustain multiple and diverse channels of communication and to fulfill needs that are both interpersonal and mediated. For instance, a blog fulfills expressive needs for some bloggers, social communication needs for others, and information seeking and surveillance needs for yet other bloggers. Reality shows like the popular *American Idol* fulfill pass time, to social connectivity to entertainment needs on variety of interactive plateaus, from television to online to mobile telephone content. With a range of functions that cover the gamut of media history, contemporary media cater to individual needs via media environments that are convergent: overlapping and complementary. With its developed repertoire of interpersonal and mediated motives, as well as social and psychological antecedents and possible communication outcomes, U&G is an ideal framework for the study of newer and convergent medium use.

To this point, the assumption of functional alternatives, essential to the contemporary articulation of U&G and related to the uses and dependency model (A. M. Rubin & Windahl, 1986), is central to the use of convergent media. As individuals select among media, old and new, that allow them to be engaged as viewers, or users, or even media content producers, it is clear how the functional alternatives illuminate individual choices, behaviors, and consequences. Medium use takes place in an environment that not only enables, but also encourages that communication channels be used simultaneously, in a complementary or substitute fashion. In a convergent media environment, all media potentially present functional alternatives to each other, based on individual needs or wants. U&G thus allows the study of this convergent media environment, without limiting researchers to specific medium use. From this point, collaboration or integration with social network perspectives could broaden the interrogative scope of U&G, by allowing it to examine not only overlapping networks of media, but also overlapping networks of media users and producers.

Integration with other perspectives could also broaden the way in which U&G handles media effects. Media effects are routinely critiqued as an underdeveloped area for U&G researchers (e.g., Blumler, 1979). Moreover, U&G has been critiqued, since its inception, for a neglect of long term social and cultural effects (Gitlin, 1981). One obvious defense is that U&G presents a psychological perspective. However, media uses often challenge the traditional divisions between society, culture, and individual psychology, and uses and gratifications, with its model of individual needs, antecedent social and psychological characteristics and wide range of consequences, contains the flexibility to incorporate the study of broader outcome variables, including power and identity (Ball-Rokeach, 1998; Jewkes, 2002) and the generation of social capital (Scheufele, 2002). In this manner, particular uses of the media could be connected to greater generation of social capital or civic engagement, or expressive use of media could be connected to the negotiation of identity and power.

Such collaboration with other perspectives could also enable U&G researchers to refine and expand their methodology, criticized by some as too reliant on self-report data produced via large population surveys (Gitlin, 1981). The convergent media environment assists social psychologists, in that it facilitates communication with participants. For instance, the online records of personal thoughts media users produce in blogs and personal homepages can serve as a promising supplement to survey instruments, or can be analyzed via content analysis to compare gratifications obtained to gratifications sought. Similarly, flexible as they may be, uses and gratifications terms may become modernized through a process of mutual integration with neighboring perspectives. The following example illustrates how the perspective can be put to use, to understand uses and consequences of newer media.

A Typical U&G Study

The advent of new media technologies, and specifically personalized publishing, has provided communication researchers with the opportunity to examine media audiences not just as consumers, but also as producers of mass media. Blogs present one iteration of personalized publishing, which allows authors to display thoughts on a web page that consists of regular or daily posts, arranged in reverse chronological order and archived (e.g., Herring, Kouper, Scheidt, & Wright, 2004). For U&G researchers, this is an opportunity to examine the audience member under a new light and in a different role. Within this particular context, U&G would be employed to understand a medium use that is purposive and relatively instrumental, in that bloggers have to make the active choice to construct and maintain a blog.

A typical U&G study of blogging, therefore, would be focused on understanding how blogs are put to use, which factors mediate that use, and what types of consequences follow this use. Therefore, the study would seek to identify motives for blogging, specify social and psychological dispositions that influence these motives, and understand how motives and dispositions combined connect to patterns of use and other behaviors, attitudes, or cognitions. Because online media have the capacity to fulfill both interpersonal needs of expression, inclusion, and social interaction and mediated needs of surveillance and information seeking, entertainment, and pass time or habit, a combination of motives should be employed to understand what needs blogging caters to. Moreover, there are aspects of blogging that are unique and different from other media, yet drive its adoption. For instance, curiosity or need to experiment with a new technology could be a possible motivator. Similarly, the desire to imitate friends with similar hobbies or to jump the cultural bandwagon of a popular trend could be another reason. Finally, blogs allow a degree of introspection and self-absorption that render them unique from other media and close to diaries—the need to make private thoughts publicly available could be further investigated.

Having compiled a list of interpersonal, mediated, and blog specific motives, the researcher could then consider possible social and psychological characteristics that lead to interest in blogging. For instance, previous research has connected the convenience and anonymity of online communication to uses of the Internet as a functional alternative for people who do not find face-to-face communication rewarding (e.g., Papacharissi & A. Rubin, 2000). Similarly, lack of mobility, diminished economic insecurity, or lack of channels for interpersonal communication has been associated with increased use of online communication channels as functional alternatives. In this sense, blogging could provide a functional alternative for individuals who do not feel comfortable, for whatever reason, expressing opinions or feelings in a face-to-face setting. Moreover, for individuals with little access to other channels of personal expression, blogging could present a meaningful outlet. Unwillingness to communicate (Burgoon, 1976) and contextual age (A. M. Rubin & Rubin, 1982b) present two dispositions that, based on previous research, could play a part in shaping motives. Scales measuring both motives and these constructs have been developed in previous research and could be adapted to the blogging context and reused in this study. A survey of bloggers, conducted via e-mail, a website or over the phone, would then combine items measuring these concepts.

More importantly, however, not all bloggers use this tool in the same manner or with the same frequency. Patterns of blogging use also need to be identified because they could naturally connect with motives and dispositions influencing blogging use. Therefore, bloggers could be surveyed about the frequency with which they blog and the type of content they prefer to feature. General media and online use should also be measured and compared to blogging. However, with blogs, researchers have an additional invaluable research resource at hand that can be used to inform their study: the content of the blog itself. Through textual or content analysis, blog content can be coded to understand (1) how the blogger puts the medium to use, in terms of post frequency and content categories; (2) strategies for communication and self-presentation the blogger adopts, and how they relate to motives and personal dispositions; and (3) how well needs are met by the medium (i.e., if needs reported in the survey match the uses expressed in the content, an argument could be made for gratifications sought matching the gratifications obtained). The combination of survey and content analysis would thus expand the methodological scope of U&G. The use of the blog text would provide a promising way of assessing consequences of medium use, besides those self-reported because bloggers frequently express satisfaction with the medium, affinity with it, and other communication outcomes via this online forum.

Conclusion

Uses and gratifications presents a strong theoretical perspective, with a history that spans more than a half century, in a field that is relatively young. The strength of the perspective lies in its ability to describe, explain, and expect media uses and consequences. The flexibility of the theoretical model it proposes progresses from motives and individual dispositions to patterns use and possible cognitive, attitudinal, and behavioral effects. Timeless assumptions the perspective contains about individual preference and interchangeability of communication channels allow its explanatory power in a traditional and convergent media environment.

References

Abelman, R. (1987). Religious television uses and gratifications. *Journal of Broadcasting & Electronic Media, 31*, 293–307.

Abelman, R., Atkin, R., & Rand, M. (1997). What viewers watch when they watch TV: Affiliation change as case study. *Journal of Broadcasting and Electronic Media, 41*(3), 360–379.

Al-Amoudi, K., Heald, G., & Rayburn, J. (1993, May). *Combining expectancy-value and uses and gratifications theory to predict Saudi Arabian television viewing and newspaper readership patterns: An exploratory analysis.* Paper presented at the meeting of the International Communication Association, Washington, D.C.

Alexander, A. (1985). Adolescents' soap opera viewing and relational perceptions. *Journal of Broadcasting & Electronic Media, 29,* 295–308.

Althaus, S., & Tewksbury, D. (2000). Patterns of Internet and traditional news media use in a networked community. *Political Communication, 17*(1), 21–45.

Armstrong, C., & Rubin, A. (1989). Talk radio as interpersonal communication. *Journal of Communication, 39,* 84–94.

Babrow, A. S. (1987). Student motives for watching soap operas. *Journal of Broadcasting and Electronic Media, 31*(3), 309–321.

Babrow, A. S., & Swanson, D. L. (1988). Disentangling antecedents of audience exposure levels: Extending expectancy-value analyses of gratifications sought from television news. *Communication Monographs, 55,* 1–21.

Ball-Rokeach, S. (1998). A theory of media power and a theory of media use: Different stories, questions, and ways of thinking. *Mass Communication and Society, 1,* 5–40.

Ball-Rokeach, S. J., & DeFleur, M. L. (1976). A dependency model of mass media effects. *Communication Research, 64,* 359–372.

Bantz, C. (1982). Exploring uses and gratifications: A comparison of reported uses of television and reported uses of favorite program type. *Communication Research 9*(3), 352–379.

Becker, L., Dunwoody, S., & Rafaell, S. (1983). Cable's impact on use of other news media. *Journal of Broadcasting, 27,* 127–142.

Best, S., Chmielewski, B., & Krueger, B. (2005). Selective exposure to online foreign news during the conflict with Iraq. *Harvard International Journal of Press Politics, 10*(4), 52–70.

Blumler, J. G. (1979). The role of theory in uses and gratifications studies. *Communication Research, 6,* 9–36.

Blumler, J. G., & Katz, E. (1974). Foreword. In J. G. Blumler & E. Katz (Eds.), *The uses of mass communications: Current perspectives on gratifications research* (pp. 13–16). Beverly Hills, CA: Sage.

Blumler, J. G., & McQuail, D. (1969). *Television in politics.* Chicago: University of Chicago Press.

Boyle, M., Schmierbach, M., Armstrong, C., McLeod, D., Shah, D., & Pan, Z. (2004). Information seeking and emotional reactions to the September 11 terrorist attacks. *Journalism and Mass Communication Quarterly, 81*(1), 155–167.

Burgoon, J. K. (1976). The unwillingness to communicate scale: Development and validation. *Communication Monographs, 43,* 60–69.

Carey, J. W., & A. L. Kreiling (1974). Popular culture and uses and gratifications: Notes toward an accommodation. In J. G. Blumler & E. Katz (Eds.), *The uses of mass communications: Current perspectives on gratifications research* (pp. 225–248). Beverly Hills, CA: Sage.

Chang, B., Lee, S., & Kim, B. (2006). Exploring factors affecting the adoption and continuance of online games among college students in South Korea: Integrating uses and gratification and diffusion of innovation approaches. *New Media & Society, 8*(2), 295–319.

Chyi, H. (2005). Willingness to pay for online news: An empirical study on the viability of the subscription model. *Journal of Media Economics, 18*(2), 131–142.

Conway, J. C., & Rubin, A. M. (1991). Psychological predictors of television viewing motivation. *Communication Research, 18,* 443–464.

De Waal, E., Schonebach, K., & Lauf, E. (2006). Online newspapers: A substitute or complement for print newspapers and other information channels? *Communications: The European Journal of Communication Research, 30*(1), 55.

Dimmick, J., Chen, Y., & Li, Z. (2004). Competition between the Internet and traditional news media: The gratification-opportunities niche dimension. *Journal of Media Economics, 17*(1), 19–33.

Dimmick, J., Sikand, J., & Patterson, S. (1994). The gratifications of the household telephone: Sociability, instrumentality, and reassurance. *Communication Research, 21*(5), 643–663.

Dutta-Bergman, M. (2004). Interpersonal communication after 9/11 via telephone and Internet: A theory of channel complementarity. *New Media & Society, 6*(5), 659–673.

Elliott, P. (1974). Uses and gratifications research: A critique and a sociological alternative. In J. G. Blumler & E. Katz (Eds.), *The uses of mass communications: Current perspectives on gratifications research* (pp. 249–268). Beverly Hills, CA: Sage.

Ferguson, D. A. (1992). Channel repertoire in the presence of remote control devices, VCRs and cable television. *Journal of Broadcasting & Electronic Media, 36*, 83–91.

Fishbein, M., & Ajzen, I. (1975). *Belief, attitude, intention, and behavior.* Reading, MA: Addison-Wesley.

Furno-Lamude, D., & Anderson, J. (1992), The uses and gratifications of rerun viewing. *Journalism Quarterly, 69*, 362–373.

Garramone, G. M., Harris, A. C., & Anderson, R. (1986). Uses of political computer bulletin boards. *Journal of Broadcasting & Electronic Media, 30*, 325–339.

Gitlin, T. (1981). *The whole world is watching: Mass media in the making of the new left.* Berkeley: University of California Press.

Greenberg, B. S. (1974). Gratifications of television viewing and their correlates for British children. In J. G. Blumler & E. Katz (Eds.), *The uses of mass communications: Current perspectives on gratifications research* (pp. 71–92). Beverly Hills, CA: Sage.

Greene, K., & Krcmar, M. (2005). Predicting exposure to and liking of media violence: A uses and gratifications approach. *Communication Studies, 56*(1), 71–93.

Hardy, B., & Scheufele, D. (2005). Examining differential gains from Internet use: Comparing the moderating role of talk and online interactions. *Journal of Communication, 55*(1), 71–84.

Haridakis, P. (2002). Viewer characteristics, exposure to television violence, and aggression. *Media Psychology, 4*(4), 323–352.

Haridakis, P. (2006). Men, women, and televised violence: Predicting viewer aggression in male and female television viewers. *Communication Quarterly, 54*(2), 227–255.

Haridakis, P., & Rubin, A. M. (2005). Third-person effects in the aftermath of terrorism. *Mass Communication and Society, 8*(1), 39–59.

Hawkins, R. P., Pingree, S., Hitchon, J., Gorham, B. W., Kannaovakun, P., Kahlor, L., et al. (2001). Predicting selection and activity in television genre viewing. *Media Psychology, 3*(3), 237–263.

Herring, S. C., Kouper, I., Scheidt, L. A., & Wright, E. (2004). Women and children last: The discursive construction of weblogs. In L. Gurak, S. Antonijevic, L. Johnson, C. Ratliff, & J. Reyman (Eds.), *Into the blogosphere: Rhetoric, community, and culture of weblogs.* Minneapolis: University of Minnesota. Retrieved June 2008, from http://blog.lib.umn.edu/blogosphere

Herzog, H. (1940). Professor quiz: A gratification study. In P. F. Lazarsfeld (Ed.), *Ratio and the printed page* (pp. 64–93). New York: Duell, Sloan & Pearce.

Herzog, H. (1944). What do we really know about daytime serial listeners? In P. F. Lazarsfeld & F. N. Stanton (Eds.), *Radio research 1942–1943* (pp. 3–33). New York: Duell, Sloan & Pearce.

Hiller, H., & Franz, T. (2004). New ties, old ties and lost ties: The use of the Internet in diaspora. *New Media & Society, 6*(6), 731–752.

Jeffres, L.W. (1978). Cable TV and interest maximization. *Journalism Quarterly, 55*, 149–154.

Jewkes, Y. (2002). The use of media in constructing identities in the masculine environment of men's prisons. *European Journal of Communication, 17*(2), 205–225.

Johnson, D. (1995). Adolescents' motivations for viewing graphic horror. *Human Communication Research, 21*(4), 522–552.

Katz, E., Blumler, J. G., & Gurevitch, M. (1973, May). *Utilization of mass communication by the individual.* Paper presented at the Conference on Directions in Mass Communication Research, Arden House, New York.

Katz, E., Blumler, J. G., & Gurevitch, M. (1974). Utilization of mass communication by the individual. In J. G. Blumler & E. Katz (Eds.), *The uses of mass communications: Current perspectives on gratifications research* (pp. 19–32). Beverly Hills, CA: Sage.

Kaye, B., & Johnson, T. (2002). Online and in the know: Uses and gratifications of the Web for political information. *Journal of Broadcasting and Electronic Media, 46*(1), 54–71.

Klapper, J. T. (1960). *The effects of mass communication.* New York: Free Press.

Korpi, M., & Kim, K. (1986). The uses and effects of televangelism: A factorial model of support and contribution. *Journal for the Scientific Study of Religion, 25*, 410–423.

Krcmar, M., & Kean, L. (2005). Uses and gratifications of media violence: Personality correlates of viewing and liking violent genres. *Media Psychology, 7*(4), 399–420.

Kuo, C. (2005). Searching for the factors and motives that influence online fortune-telling behavior. *Mass Communication Research, 85*(1), 141–182.

Lasswell, H. (1948). The structure and function of communications in society. In L. Bryson (Ed.), *The communication of ideas* (pp. 37–51) New York: Harper & Row.

Lazarsfeld, P. F. (1940). *Radio and the printed page.* New York: Duell, Sloan & Pearce.

Lefcourt, H. M. (1979). Recent developments in the study of locus of control. In B. A. Maher (Ed.), *Progress in experimental personality research* (pp. 1–39). New York: Academic Press.

Leung, L. (2001). Gratifications, chronic loneliness and Internet use. *Asian Journal of Communication, 11*(1), 96–119.

Leung, L., & Wei, R. (2000). More than just talk on the move: Uses and gratifications of the cellular phone. *Journalism and Mass Communication Quarterly, 77*(2), 308–320.

Levy, M. R. (1981). Home video recorders and time shifting. *Journalism Quarterly, 58,* 401–405.

Levy, M. R. (1983). The time-shifting use of home video recorders. *Journal of Broadcasting, 27,* 263–268.

Levy, M. R. (1987). VCR use and the concept of audience activity. *Communication Quarterly, 35,* 267–275.

Levy, M. R., & Windahl, S. (1984). Audience activity and gratifications: A conceptual clarification and exploration. *Communication Research, 11,* 51–78.

Lichtenstein, A., & Rosenfeld, L. B. (1983). Uses and misuses of gratifications research: An explication of media functions. *Communication Research, 10,* 97–109.

Lin, C. (2001). Audience attributes, media supplementation, and likely online service adoption. *Mass Communication & Society, 4*(1), 19–38.

Lindlof, T. (1986). Social and structural constraints on media use in incarceration. *Journal of Broadcasting & Electronic Media, 30,* 341–355.

Lo, V., Li, Y., Shih, Y., & Yang, S. (2005). Internet adoption, uses, and gratifications obtained. *Mass Communication Research, 83*(1), 127–165.

Lometti, G. E., Reeves, B., & Bybee, C. R. (1977). Investigating the assumptions of uses and gratifications research. *Communication Research, 7,* 319–334.

McLeod, J. M., & Becker, L. B. (1981). The uses and gratifications approach. In D. D. Nimmo & K. R. Sanders (Eds.), *Handbook of political communication* (pp. 97–99). Beverly Hills, CA: Sage.

McQuail, D. (1979). The uses and gratification approach: Past, troubles, and future. *Massacommunicatie, 2,* 73–89.

Miller, M., & Reese, S. (1982). Media dependency as interaction: Effects of exposure and reliance on political activity and efficacy. *Communication Research, 9,* 227–248.

O'Keefe, G., & Sulanowski, B. (1995). More than just talk: Uses, gratifications, and the telephone. *Journalism and Mass Communication Quarterly, 72,* 922–933.

Palmgreen, P. C. (1984). Uses and gratifications: A theoretical perspective. In R. N. Bostrom (Ed.), *Communication yearbook* (Vol. 8, pp. 20–55). Beverly Hills, CA: Sage.

Palmgreen, P. C., & Rayburn, J. D. (1982). Gratifications sought and media exposure: An expectancy-value model. *Communication Research, 9,* 561–580.

Palmgreen, P. C., Wenner, L. A., & Rayburn, J. D. (1980). Relations between gratifications sought and obtained: A study of television news. *Communication Research, 7,* 161–192.

Palmgreen, P. C., Wenner, L. A., & Rayburn, J. D. (1981). Gratification discrepancies and news program choice. *Communication Research, 8,* 451–478.

Papacharissi, Z. (2002a). The self online: The utility of personal home pages. *Journal of Broadcasting & Electronic Media, 46*(3), 346–368.

Papacharissi, Z. (2002b). The presentation of self in virtual life: Characteristics of personal home pages. *Journalism and Mass Communication Quarterly 79*(3), 643–660.

Papacharissi, Z. (2007). The blogger revolution? Audiences as media producers. In M. Tremayne (Ed.), *Blogging, citizenship, and the future of media* (pp. 21–38). New York: Routledge.

Papacharissi, Z., & Mendelson, A. (in press). The reality appeal: Uses and gratifications of reality shows. *Journal of Broadcasting and Electronic Media.*

Papacharissi, Z., & Rubin, A. (2000). Predictors of Internet use. *Journal of Broadcasting and Electronic Media, 44*(2), 175–196.

Payne, G., Severn, J., & Dozier, D. (1988). Uses and gratifications motives as indicators of magazine, readership. *Journalism Quarterly, 65,* 909–915.

Perse, E. (1986). Soap opera viewing patters of college students and cultivation. *Journal of Broadcasting & Electronic Media, 30,* 175–193.

Perse, E. (1990). Involvement with local television news: Cognitive and emotional dimensions. *Human Communication Research, 16,* 556–581.

Perse, E. (1992). Predicting attention to local television news: Need for cognition and motives for viewing. *Communication Reports, 5*(1), 40–49.

Perse, E., & Courtright, J. (1993). Normative images of communication media: Mass and interpersonal channels in the new media environment. *Human Communication Research, 19,* 485–503.

Perse, E. M., & Dunn-Greenberg, D. G. (1998). The utility of home computers and media use: Implications of multimedia and connectivity. *Journal of Broadcasting & Electronic Media, 42,* 435–456.

Perse, E., & Ferguson, D. (1994). The impact of the newer television technologies on television satisfaction. *Journalism Quarterly, 70*(4), 843–853.

Perse, E., & Ferguson, D. (2000). The benefits and costs of Web surfing. *Communication Quarterly, 48*(4), 343–359.

Perse, E., & Rubin, A. M. (1990). Chronic loneliness and television use. *Journal of Broadcasting & Electronic Media, 44,* 37–53.

Pettersson, T. (1986). The audiences' uses and gratifications of TV worship services. *Journal for the Scientific Study of Religion, 25,* 391–409.

Rayburn, J., Palmgreen, P., & Acker, T. (1984). Media gratifications and choosing a morning news program. *Journalism Quarterly, 61,* 149–156.

Rosengren, K. E. (1974). Uses and gratifications: A paradigm outlined. In J. G. Blumer & E. Katz (Eds.), *The uses of mass communications: Current perspectives on gratifications research* (pp. 269–286). Beverly Hill, CA: Sage.

Rosengren, K. E., & Windahl, S. (1972). Mass media consumption as a functional alternative. In D. McQuail (Ed.), *Sociology of mass communication* (pp. 166–194). Harmondsworth, UK: Penguin.

Rubin, A., & Bantz, C. (1989). Uses and gratifications of videocassette recorders. In J. Salvaggio & J. Bryant (Eds.), *Media use in the information age: Emerging patterns of adoption and consumer use* (pp. 181–195). Hillsdale, NJ: Erlbaum.

Rubin, A, Haridakis, P., & Eyal, K. (2003). Viewer aggression and attraction to television talk shows. *Media Psychology, 5* (4), 331–362.

Rubin, A., & Perse, E. (1987a). Audience activity and soap opera involvement: A uses and effects investigation. *Human Communication Research, 14,* 246–268.

Rubin, A., & Perse, E. (1987b). Audience activity and television news gratifications. *Communication Research, 14,* 58–84.

Rubin, A., Perse, E., & Barbato, C. (1988). Conceptualization and measurement of interpersonal communication motives. *Human Communication Research, 14* (4), 602–628.

Rubin, A., Perse, E., & Powell, R. (1985). Loneliness, parasocial interaction, and local television news viewing. *Human Communication Research, 12,* 155–180.

Rubin, A. M. (1977). Television usage, attitudes and viewing behavior of children and adolescents. *Journal of Broadcasting, 21*(3), 355–369.

Rubin, A. M. (1979). Television use by children and adolescents. *Human Communication Research, 5,* 109–120.

Rubin, A. M. (1981a). An examination of television viewing motivations. *Communication Research, 8,* 141–165.

Rubin, A. M. (1981b). A multivariate analysis of "60 Minutes" viewing motivations. *Journalism Quarterly, 58,* 529–534.

Rubin, A. M. (1983). Television uses and gratifications: The interaction of viewing patterns and motivations. *Journal of Broadcasting, 27,* 37–51.

Rubin, A. M. (1985). Uses of daytime television soap opera by college students. *Journal of Broadcasting & Electronic Media, 29,* 241–258.

Rubin, A. M. (1986). Television, aging and information seeking. *Language & Communication, 6*, 125–137.

Rubin, A. M. (1993). The effect of locus of control on communication motivation, anxiety, and satisfaction. *Communication Quarterly, 41*, 161–172.

Rubin, A. M. (1994). Media uses and effects: A uses-and-gratifications perspective. In J. Zillmann & D. Bryant (Eds.), *Media effects: Advances in theory and research* (pp. 571–601). London: Erlbaum.

Rubin, A. M., & Rubin, R. B. (1982a). Contextual age and television use. *Human Communication Research, 8*, 228–244.

Rubin, A. M., & Rubin, R. B. (1982b). Older persons' TV viewing patterns and motivations. *Communication Research, 9*, 287–313.

Rubin, A. M., & Rubin, R. B. (1985). Interface of personal and mediated communication: A research agenda. *Critical Studies in Mass Communication, 2*, 36–53.

Rubin, A. M., & Rubin, R. B. (1989). Social and psychological antecedents of VCR use. In M. R. Levy (Ed.), *The VCR age: Home video and mass communication* (pp. 92–111). Newbury Park, CA: Sage.

Rubin, A. M., & Rubin, R. B. (2001). Interface of personal and mediated communication: Fifteen years later. *Electronic Journal of Communication, 11*(1).

Rubin, A. M., & Windahl, S. (1986). The uses and dependency model of mass communication. *Critical Studies in Mass Communication, 3*, 184–199.

Rubin, R. B., & Rubin, A. M. (1982). Contextual age and television use: Reexamining a life-position indicator. *Communication Yearbook, 6*, 583–604.

Rubin, R. B., & Rubin, A. M. (1992). Antecedents of interpersonal communication motivation. *Communication Quarterly, 40*, 305–317.

Salwen, M. B., & Anderson, R. A. (1984). *The uses and gratifications of supermarket tabloid reading by different demographic groups*. East Lansing, MI: National Center for Research on Teacher Learning.

Scheufele, D. A. (2002). Examining differential gains from mass media and their implications for participatory behavior. *Communication Research, 29*(1), 46–65.

Schoenbach, K., de Waal, E., & Lauf, E. (2005). Online and print newspapers: Their impact on the extent of the perceived public agenda. *European Journal of communication, 20* (2), 245–258.

Schutz, W. C. (1966). The interpersonal underworld. *Palo Alto, CA*: Science and Behavior Books.

Sherry, J. L. (2001). Toward an etiology of media use motivations: The role of temperament in media use. *Communication Monographs, 68*(3), 274–288.

Sherry, J. L. (2004). Flow and media enjoyment. *Communication Theory, 14*(4), 328–347.

Slater, M. (2003). Alienation, aggression, and sensation seeking as predictors of adolescent use of violent film, computer, and website content. *Journal of Communication, 53*(1), 105–121.

Stafford, L., Kline, S., & Dimmick, J. (1999). Home e-mail: Relational maintenance and gratification opportunities. *Journal of Broadcasting and Electronic Media, 43*(4), 659–669.

Surlin, S. (1986). Jamaican call-in radio: A uses and gratifications analysis. *Journal of Broadcasting & Electronic Media, 30*, 459–466.

Swanson, D. L. (1977). The uses and misuses of uses and gratification. *Human Communication Research, 3*, 214–221.

Towers, W. (1987). *Adult readership of magazines and why they read*. ERIC: ED 284 282.

Trice, A. D. (1985). An academic locus of control scale for college students. *Perceptual and Motor Skills, 61*, 1043–1046.

Turow, J. (1974). Talk-show radio as interpersonal communication. *Journal of Broadcasting, 18*, 171–179.

Valkenburg, P., & Soeters, K.(2001). Children's positive and negative experience with the Internet: An exploratory survey. *Communication Research, 28*(5), 652–675.

Vincent, R., & Basil, M. (1997). College students' news gratifications, media use, and current events knowledge. *Journal of Broadcasting and Electronic Media, 41*(3), 380–392.

Walker, J. R., & Bellamy, R. V., Jr. (1991). Gratifications of grazing: An exploratory study of remote control use. *Journalism Quarterly, 68*, 422–431.

Wober, M., & Gunter, B. (1982). Television and personal threat: Fact or artifact? A British survey. *British Journal of Social Psychology, 21*, 239–247.

Wright, C. (1960). Functional analysis and mass communication. *Public Opinion Quarterly, 24*, 605–620.

Suggested Readings

Blumler, J. G., & Katz, E. (Eds.). (1974). *The uses of mass communications.* Beverly Hills, CA: Sage.

LaRose, R., Mastro, D., & Eastin, M. S. (2001). Understanding Internet usage: A social-cognitive approach to uses and gratifications. *Social Science Computer Review, 19*(4), 395–413.

Rubin, A. M. (1994). Media uses and effects: A uses-and-gratifications perspective. In J. Zillmann, & D. Bryant (Eds.), *Media effects: Advances in theory and research.* London: Erlbaum.

Rubin, A. M., & Rubin, R. B. (2001). Interface of personal and mediated communication: Fifteen years later. *Electronic Journal of Communication, 11*(1).

Ruggiero, T. E., (2001). Uses and gratifications theory in the 21st century. *Mass Communication & Society, 3*(1), 3–37.

11

SPIRAL OF SILENCE

Communication and Public Opinion as Social Control

Charles T. Salmon and Carroll J. Glynn

Conceiving public opinion as unwritten law, or as an informal mechanism of social control, is hardly new; indeed, one scholar (Noelle-Neumann, 1995) traced the notion back to antiquity and the writings of Pericles and the Old Testament. It can be found in the treatises of philosophers and scholars of many different eras and nations as well, including John Locke, James Bryce, Floyd Allport, Alexis de Tocqueville, Jacques Ellul, and others. For example, James Madison (1788/1961), writing in Federalist Paper No. 49, implicitly adopted this conceptualization:

> The strength of opinion in each individual, and its practical influence on his conduct, depends much on the number which he supposes to have entertained the same opinion. The reason of man, like man himself, is timid and cautious when left alone, and acquires firmness and confidence in proportion to the number with which it is associated. (p. 340)

In this century, sociologist W. Philips Davison (1958) drew on the notion of social control in his classic description of the public opinion process:

> Therefore, [people] are likely to speak or act in one way if they anticipate approbation and to remain silent or act in another way if they anticipate hostility or indifference.... People who do not share the opinions expressed by the crowd's leaders are likely to remain silent, fearing the disapproval of those around them. This very silence isolates others who may be opposed, since they conclude that, with the exception of themselves, all those present share the same attitude. (p. 101)

The most elaborate development of this approach to public opinion, however, is found in the work of Elisabeth Noelle-Neumann, founder and director of the Public Opinion Research Center in Allensbach, Germany, and professor of communication research at the University of Mainz. To her, *public opinion* refers to "opinions on controversial issues that one can express in public without isolating oneself" (Noelle-Neumann, 1984, pp. 62–63), a conceptualization in which communication processes and effects figure prominently. Since publication of her work in English in the early 1970s, her model of the spiral of silence has attracted considerable scholarly attention, some in the form of attempts at social scientific tests and replication, others in the form of sometimes scathing criticism and commentary. The story of the scholarly evolution of the spiral of silence model is one of science inextricably intertwined with politics, personalities, and the long shadows of history.

The present chapter has three major goals.[2] First, it draws on several of Noelle-Neumann's important works (1973, 1974, 1977, 1979, 1980, 1984, 1985, 1991) to describe the model's components in terms of three major groupings of concepts and research. Second, it traces the early development of the model from its philosophical and historical origins in German society and outlines some of its contemporary applications. Third, it reviews major conceptual and methodological conundrums which have characterized the model throughout its brief existence and offers some avenues for future applications of the model.

The Spiral of Silence Model

Noelle-Neumann's model and resulting research branches may be summarized in terms of three categories: mass media and mass communication, the individual and interpersonal communication; and implications for public opinion, including contemporary applications.

Mass Media and Mass Communication

Noelle-Neumann ascribed a particular importance to the mass media's position in contemporary society. The media are, in her words, "ubiquitous" and "consonant." Indeed, it is difficult to conceive of a day without exposure to mass media in one form or another, ranging from listening to a morning radio program or podcast, through reading newspapers, websites, and blogs, to viewing television or a film in the evening. The inescapability of the media is potentially problematic, she argued, because media content tends to be remarkably consonant. That is, there is uncanny similarity of news and other media content that belies the liberal democratic ideal of diversity. The combination of a ubiquitous and consonant media system results in a largely monolithic "climate" that envelops most individuals in society, providing in the process a largely homogeneous depiction of social reality.

In large measure, our view of social reality is distorted because of the underlying ideology of the progenitors of media content. Producers of media content and journalists in particular, Noelle-Neumann (1973, 1980) argued, tend to be more liberal than the rest of society. In part, this liberalness is a function of shared journalistic norms and values that serve to reinforce the role of journalist as critic, as a foil to government and the powerful. Reflecting this underlying liberal orientation, she continued, media content tends to be liberal, as well. The product is a media environment, forged by liberal newsmakers, enveloping the individual in society, and exposing him or her to a predominantly liberal depiction of society and the social good.[3] One of the most important functions of the media, to Noelle-Neumann, is their role as the predominant sources of cues regarding majority culture. Immersed in a ubiquitous and consonant media environment, individuals rely heavily on the media as a source of information about social roles, customs, and practices.

Noelle-Neumann claimed that this immersion in—and dependency on—the media environment induces powerful effects on individuals and that these effects occur as the result of an endless repetition of reinforcing messages and images. As a result, she argued, media effects cannot be studied validly under sterile, artificial laboratory conditions because such studies will necessarily underestimate the impact of a prolonged diet of monolithic media output emanating from a multiplicity of media sources (1973). Furthermore, in response to those who argued against her assertion of strong social control at the hands of powerful mass media, Noelle-Neumann (1998) asserted that even when media effects are difficult to measure, they may still exist, even beyond the awareness of the impacted public.

The Individual in a Social Setting

The second major strain of thought in the spiral of silence model deals with the linkage between macro- and microsocial levels of analysis. Drawing on the small-group conformity research of Solomon Asch and others (1970), Noelle-Neumann contended that individuals have an inborn fear of social isolation. To be alone, apart from, or at odds with "the crowd" is more than most individuals can endure. To wear an unpopular fashion or to express an idea that many consider old-fashioned or, worse, socially unacceptable is to risk incurring the wrath of others, a prospect that most find too unattractive to risk. As a result of this concern, individuals must constantly monitor the environment, searching for cues regarding which sentiments, ideas, knowledge, or fashions are shared by many or only by a few. Because of this fear, individuals draw on their "quasi-statistical organ" (in her later work, a quasi-statistical "sense," perhaps implying a shift from a biological to a social explanation; compare Noelle-Neumann, 1974, 1991) to gauge the nuances of culture and its dynamism. As noted, the mass media are seen as providing the bulk of the cues that serve to structure options for an individual's behavior.

An unstated assumption of this model, like most models of public opinion, is that individuals have opinions that they can and wish to articulate, a seemingly basic assumption that itself is contested (e.g., Bourdieu, 1979). Assuming this is the case, the individual is often confronted with a situation in which he or she must articulate that opinion in some social context; that is, private sentiment must become public. In this sense, Noelle-Neumann's use of the term *public* in *public opinion* is an adjective rather than a noun; it refers to an opinion that can be expressed publicly without fear of censure rather than the more typically American usage (as a noun) in which it refers to a group of individuals (Salmon & Kline, 1985).

Implications for Public Opinion

Given these presuppositions, there are two distinct implications for public opinion, one static and the other a dynamic process.

Static Version

In the case of the static outcome, if the individual perceives that his or her personal convictions are shared by the majority, he or she will be willing to express an opinion in public. On the other hand, if the perception is that the opinion represents a minority viewpoint, he or she will be reluctant to express the opinion publicly. There are thought to be two general exceptions to this outcome. First, if an individual perceives himself or herself to be in the minority but believes that his or her opinion is gaining ground—that it is viable, that it will be shared by the majority at some future point—the individual will be willing to express the opinion in public. Second, a few individuals who are apparently immune to social censure appear perennially willing to express unpopular opinions. These individuals, labeled *hardcores*, are thought to represent a relative small segment of the population (Noelle-Neumann, 1984, estimates about 15%).

Dynamic Version

Unlike the static version, which can be tested with cross-sectional data, the dynamic version incorporates the element of time into the model and must be tested using longitudinal data. If relatively few people are willing to express an unpopular viewpoint, according to this version, it will slowly slip from the public consciousness because it has no vocal proponents. Over time, the majority faction will become increasingly confident and its view increasingly pervasive. The disproportionate frequencies of expression will eventually result in a silencing of the proponents of the minority viewpoint, and their sentiment will follow the paths of other unpopular, obsolete, or dated notions. Policy makers, who themselves monitor the information environment to gauge trends in opinion climates either out of a sense of obligation to constituents or as a matter of political survival, observe that one opinion frequently is expressed and another is not (Protess et al., 1991). This social perception becomes translated into policy because only expressed opinion influences social change; silence is thought to have no impact.

Historical and Theoretical Origins

As suggested earlier, many of the constituent elements of the spiral of silence model were not newly conceived, but have been available in one form or another for centuries. Noelle-Neumann's creative contribution was to link notions of social control with mass media and interpersonal communication processes. When and how she originally did this is, like most aspects of the model, a matter of some controversy. Leo Bogart (1991), a media and public opinion scholar, contended that the spiral of silence is "more of a footnote to the history of Nazism than to the study of public opinion" (p. 49) because the model is rooted in the horrors of the World War II and, in particular, in Noelle-Neumann's first-hand experiences while a "propagandist for Nazism" writing for *Das Reich*.[4] Without question, the political conditions in Nazi Germany during the Holocaust provided an unusually vivid example of the dangers of publicly expressing opposition to a predominant political viewpoint. Indeed, in a totalitarian regime characterized by Gestapo ruthlessness and concentration camps, fear—of physical torture and death as well as milder forms of disapproval—undoubtedly was a prime motivator of social conduct, and silence a plausible means of defense.

As an ardent student of public opinion in the late 1930s, and as a journalist during the war who herself felt censured by the Nazi Party, Noelle-Neumann was certainly in a position to witness the process through which a minority faction is systematically intimidated into silence and concomitant political impotence. Nevertheless, Noelle-Neumann claimed that it was the 1965 election in the Federal Republic of Germany, rather than her first-hand experiences in Nazi Germany, which provided the inspiration for her elaborate model of communication and public opinion processes.

In that year, she found through her polling that, although the two competing political parties (the Christian Democrats and the Social Democrats) had equivalent levels of support over a 6-month period, expectations of who would win were far more dynamic, changing by some 18 percentage points over the same time period. As Noelle-Neumann (1984) wrote, "it was as though the measurements of how the electorate intended to vote and which party they expected to win had been taken on different planets" (p. 3).

Eventually the Christian Democrats won the election, leaving Noelle-Neumann (1984) with the challenge of interpreting these significant swings in voters' perceptions and preferences. Her explanation of this, under the "power" and "pressure" of public opinion was that "hundreds of thousands—no, actually millions of voters—had taken part in what was later called a 'last minute swing.' At the last minute, they had gone along with the crowd" (p. 2).

Differentiating this shift from the familiar bandwagon phenomenon, Noelle-Neumann turned to the writings of the German sociologist Ferdinand Tönnies, who is perhaps best known for his notions of *gemeinschaft* and *gesellschaft* in his discussions of traditional and modern societies, respectively. To Tönnies (1922), public opinion represented a social force, an informal mechanism of social control: "Public opinion always claims to be authoritative. It demands consent or at least compels silence, or abstention from contradiction" (p. 138). Drawing on this conceptualization, Noelle-Neumann reasoned that "social conventions, customs and norms have always been included in the domain of public opinion. Public opinion imposes sanctions on individuals who offend against convention—a process of 'social control'" (Noelle-Neumann, 1973, p. 88; see also: Noelle-Neumann, 1995). It was the empirical observation of a changing electoral mood or political climate, and reliance on a conceptualization of public opinion as a form of social control, that served as the point of departure for what would turn out to be an ambitious and influential program of research.

Contemporary Applications of the Spiral of Silence Model

As a pollster and advisor to political parties in Germany, Noelle-Neumann counseled Christian Democrats' supporters to speak up in their everyday lives—to create and reinforce the impression that they are not afraid of expressing their views, thereby presumably implying to others that their viewpoint is winning.

Proponents of numerous social causes make similar use of the spiral of silence's principles in attempts to influence public opinion and public policy. The organization of rallies, demonstrations, and marches is a common strategy employed by groups attempting to both demonstrate the magnitude of support for their issue position and to attract media coverage, the combination of which gives the appearance of confidence and burgeoning strength. Bumper stickers, political buttons, banners, and other small media are integral components of such efforts; they legitimize—and thereby foster—the public expression of a particular viewpoint. The task for a group whose opinion is shared by a majority of citizens is clear: Engage in ongoing public communication in an attempt to reinforce the perception of confidence (i.e., that its opinion is—and will remain—the dominant one). Conversely, the task for a group whose opinion is not shared by the majority is equally clear: Use public communication in an attempt to give the impression that its (minority) opinion is either the dominant one or the one with substantial momentum, or to imply that the opposing opinion (i.e., the actual majority opinion) is not widely and confidently expressed in public (Salmon & Oshagan, 1990). In this sense, public expression of opinion constructs a psychological community of heretofore isolated individuals who now know that they are not alone in their opinion. Especially within the political realm, media users—Internet users in particular—have recently seen an explosion of highly customized, targeted messages delivered through newly available communication channels, such as e-mail distribution lists, blogs, and video sharing sites, such as YouTube. Instead of casting a wide net in hopes of attracting large amounts of supporters, many candidates for political office now specialize in constructing numerous messages for different segments of the population.

That the media play a crucial role in this struggle for control of perceptions should be readily apparent. An interesting illustration of this can be found in coverage of a 1989 pro-choice rally by two student newspapers at the University of Wisconsin-Madison. *The Daily Cardinal*, which had at the time the reputation of being the more liberal of the two papers, had as its front-page headlines, "We are the Majority" and "600,000 rally in Washington, D.C." The story began:

> In a massive show of support for abortion and reproductive rights, as many as 600,000 people gathered in the nation's capital Sunday at a march sponsored by the National Organization for Women.
>
> Confirmation for the numbers cited by organizers and the city police proved difficult, as local news stations conservatively estimated the attendance at one quarter of a million people.

The Badger Herald had the reputation of being the more conservative of the two papers. On the very same day, it had as its headline on a page 3 story, "85,000 Pro-Choice Activists March in D.C." The story (Associated Press, 1989) noted that: "U.S. Park Police estimated the early crowd at 65,000 but said 20,000 other pro-abortion demonstrators were en route from nearby Robert F. Kennedy Stadium."

The interpretation is clear in both cases. The presentation of information in the liberal newspaper gave the impression of an historic gathering, a "massive show of support" for an issue position held by a "majority" of citizens. The presentation of information in the conservative newspaper, on the other hand, implicitly minimized the import of the event through its reporting of a significantly smaller crowd size, its relegation of the story to an interior page, and its marginalization of participants as "activists" and "pro-abortion demonstrators."

The social control aspects of public opinion can be observed in a variety of other situations, perhaps less dramatic but no less potent. For example, as recently as the late 1970s, cigarette smokers confidently smoked in public places and assemblages, with little fear of censure from others. Indeed, it was more likely the case that an offended nonsmoker would feel qualms about speaking out in public to ask the smoker to refrain from engaging in his or her behavior. Today, the climate of opinion has shifted dramatically. Beyond numerous statewide smoking bans in public places, smokers constantly are subjected to majority pressure to conform. What political philosopher John Locke (1824/1985) spoke of as the "law of public opinion" actually has become codified as such: Public opinion, the informal mechanism of social control has, through a burgeoning social consensus, a virtually monolithic opinion climate and the concomitant inculcation of a dominant opinion, spiraled into regulation and law, the formal mechanisms of social control.

These examples imply that the spiral of silence process is not merely an artifact of totalitarian regimes, but potentially a condition of "free" societies as well.

Conceptual and Methodological Conundrums

Though the model is intuitively seductive in its ability to explain situations such as those described above, it has not been as consistently verifiable through traditional scientific hypothesis testing. In a meta-analysis conducted by Glynn, Hayes, and Shanahan (1997), mixed results from 17 different survey studies produced a statistically significant—but quite small—relationship between individuals' perceptions that their opinion is in the majority and their subsequent willingness to express that opinion in public. Still, this synthesis of results from over 9,500 respondents and six countries focused on only the perceptual component of the model as it related to one's willingness to express an opinion. Glynn et al. further suggested that more realistic opinion expression situations would produce more interesting results, as the hypothetical situations typical of early spiral of silence research are somewhat lacking from an external validity standpoint. It perhaps suffices to say that the entire spiral of silence model itself has never been subjected to a comprehensive empirical test, even by Noelle-Neumann herself, probably because it would be far too time consuming (perhaps spanning several decades) and expensive to undertake. Instead, researchers have tended to reduce the model into discrete, manageable fragments and tested hypotheses within those fragments.

Issues in Conceptualization

With few exceptions, scholars outside of Germany generally have not found much in the way of consistent empirical support for several of the model's pivotal assumptions and claims. Researchers, however, have found what might be characterized as a modest degree of reluctance, rather than a consuming fear, about publicly expressing a minority opinion on most issues. Furthermore, what Noelle-Neumann originally posited as the "fear of isolation" may be more accurately conceived as a positive elicitation rather than a negative suppression. In other words, those who remain silent may be placing the social "face" of others above their own in an effort to maintain collective harmony (Huang, 2005; Wyatt, Katz, Levinsohn, & Al-Haj, 1996)

Indeed, it is very often the case that a plurality of those holding (or believing that they hold) the minority position are still willing to speak out, far more than the few hardcores that the model would predict. Partly as a result of such controversial empirical support for the model's contentions, there is no shortage of critiques, counter critiques, recommendations, and prescriptions (e.g., Csikszentmihalyi, 1991; Donsbach, 1988; Donsbach & Stevenson, 1984; Glynn & McLeod, 1985; Kennamer, 1990; McLeod, 1985; Merten, 1985; Moscovici, 1991; Noelle-Neumann, 1985, 1991; Price & Allen, 1990; Rusciano, 1989; Salmon & Kline, 1985; Scheufele & Moy, 2000). In this section, we review the more enduring points of contention.

Crossing International Boundaries

The spiral of silence model had its origins in Germany, and took more than a decade before scholars in the United States began investigating its merits and weaknesses. Schulz and Schoenbach (1984) noted that the first direct data-based challenge to the model "…was offered by an American graduate student at the International Communication Association (ICA) conference in Boston," and asked "Why must we allow theories that dominate our discussion of media and politics to be tested by students in other cultures?" (p. 715). According to Schulz and Schoenbach (1984), the difference in research approaches between the two countries could be characterized as, on one side of the Atlantic, a rich lode of small-scale studies probing various aspects of the theory, and on the other side, "…either one large, multi-method study for a million marks or nothing at all" (p. 715).

This difference in research approaches, though interesting in and of itself, speaks to a larger question of whether the silencing phenomenon can be adequately observed and studied in cultures other than Germany. The issue of the model's ability to "cross national boundaries," especially the issue of collectivist versus individualist cultures (e.g., Scheufele & Moy, 2000) has been debated in several essays, including those by Glynn and McLeod (1985) and Noelle-Neumann (1984, 1991), and remains one of its most problematic conceptual aspects.

As Glynn and McLeod (1985) note, Noelle-Neumann argues that certain aspects of German culture, such as differences in political campaigns or communication patterns, preclude absolute replication in other cultures. She adds that "the reality of the media in the Federal Republic of Germany and in English-speaking countries may be very different" (Noelle-Neumann, 1984, p. 68). The question remains, however, regarding what to do with the theory when it is applied in varied social settings. One approach is to consider these differences on an *ad hoc* basis and to adjust the theory for each new application. Thus, if media use is different between Germany and the United States, Noelle-Neumann (1984) suggests that "media effects should only be treated secondarily" (p. 68). A second approach, however, would be to take differences between cultures into account when developing the theory so the rationale that "this country is an exception" does not need to be invoked. This suggests that what is needed is a broader treatment of the spiral of silence where varied groups and cultures are treated as part of, rather than deviations from, the process.

We are quickly approaching the point at which such a broad integration may be possible, given that the model has been tested in such countries as Germany, the United States, Great Britain, Mexico, the Philippines, Taiwan, South Korea, China, and Japan (Salmon & Moh, 1992). The next step is to integrate results of these small-scale studies with more macro considerations of the nations, such as the degree of population homogeneity, government control of media, and conformity expected and tolerated in citizens, to truly make the spiral of silence an international model of communication and public opinion. One notion which in particular merits this type of analysis is that of *consonance* (i.e., that the media depict a relatively monolithic opinion environment), often a liberal one. Clearly, the degree of consonance achievable in a society is a function of economic and political controls on its media system, as well as various situational factors (Salmon & Moh, 1992). Further, consonance can occur at different levels of abstraction, ranging from explicit agreement on essential facts of a news story to implicit recognition of shared social norms and values.

Conformity as a Theoretical Base

A second major conceptual issue which needs elaboration involves its grounding in the literature on conformity in small-group settings. Price and Allen (1990) claimed, for example, that Noelle-Neumann overstated the ubiquity of conformity and majority influence, adding that a majority of subjects in typical Asch-type group pressure experiments (about two thirds) in fact do not conform, even to a unanimous majority. Glynn and McLeod (1985) suggested that the Asch research is pertinent to the spiral of silence as a sort of "rough analogue" (p. 47).

There are some key differences between the Asch situation and the process described by Noelle-Neumann. First, the stimuli judged by the subjects in Asch's experiments were unambiguous, and subjects made definite judgments of their own prior to being subjected to group pressures. In the case of the spiral of silence, persons may have only weakly developed views or even had no prior opinions when confronted with the opportunity or need to express an opinion. Recent work on "opinion quality" reveals that opinions, if they exist at all, may exist along a continuum of development or sophistication (see Price & Neijens, 1997). Second, in Asch's experiments, there was no interpersonal communication beyond the recording of majority opinion. In the spiral of silence, interpersonal communication plays a critical role because individuals are not subject to the confines of a laboratory situation. They may discuss the issue with friends and members of their family, and they may seek social reinforcement to anchor their opinion. Third, Asch's stimuli were generally administered at one time and effects studied soon thereafter. Noelle-Neumann, on the other hand, "gives considerable attention to the cumulative effects of opinion expressed (or not expressed) over relatively long periods of time" (Glynn & McLeod, 1985, p. 48). Fourth, Noelle-Neumann drew on Asch's work to justify her notion of fear of isolation, and yet holders of minority opinions may not be "isolated" whatsoever; indeed, in a nation of 300 million persons, a minority faction could include literally millions of people and, more importantly, members of primary and secondary groups who serve to reinforce the holding of that opinion (Salmon & Kline, 1985). Research has shown that smaller reference groups (i.e., meso-level groups) are sometimes more important than macro-level groups (Moy, Domke, & Stamm, 2001), such as a nation or state, which is composed of millions of strangers. To further complicate matters, research shows that members of minority groups may be more willing to speak out when they perceive that support for their viewpoint is declining (Price & Allen, 1990).

It would appear that there are enough differences between the spiral of silence model and conformity theory to beg consideration of an alternative theoretical base. However, aside from retentions of a better fit with the research of Muzafer Sherif (cf. Glynn & McLeod, 1985), social identification and group conflict (cf. Price, 1989; Glynn, 1997), group attractiveness (Glynn & McLeod, 1985; Salmon & Kline, 1985), or with social influence theory (Price & Allen, 1990), little has been done to advance such theory development in this area. In fact, the predominant approach has been for researchers (ourselves included) to mention weaknesses of the theory and then proceed to test hypotheses based on the theory's original premises.

Issue Differences

Although originally derived from the study of election campaigns, the spiral of silence model has been tested across a variety of issues, ranging from abortion (e.g., Bergen, 1986; Donsbach & Stevenson, 1984; Salmon & Neuwirth, 1990) to support for Radio Martí (Matera & Salwen, 1992), to English as the official language (Salwen, Lin, & Matera, 1994), to more recent examinations of the O. J. Simpson trial (Jeffres, Neuendorf, & Atkin, 1999) and public support for biotechnology (Priest, 2006). Little systematic attention, however, has been paid to how the nature of the issue influences the dynamics of the spiral of silence process (Salmon & Kline, 1985). For example, Yeric and Todd (1989) offered a typology involving three major classes of issues. The first, *enduring*, remain in the public eye over a long period of time. Examples include defense spending, health, and gun control. The second, *emerging*, are relatively new to the public, but show potential for remaining in the public consciousness and hence becoming enduring. The third, *transitory*, do not remain in the public consciousness for very long, though they may emerge and re-emerge from time to time. Though a few studies have manipulated issue types in an attempt to study the influence of issues on opinion expression (e.g., Noelle-Neumann's research program across 20 years; Salmon & Oshagan, 1990), typologies such as the one described above could provide a useful conceptual foundation for augmenting the model's explanatory power. In such an undertaking, it would be important to add another dimension, that of opinion distribution. It is highly likely, for example, that an issue for which there is nearly equal support and opposition for some policy option might behave quite differently from one for which the levels of support and opposition are quite unequal. As Scheufele and Moy (2000) noted, the spiral of silence model suggests that as the apparent majority increases in size relative to the corresponding minority, the pressure to withhold a minority viewpoint should increase.

Methodological Considerations

One of the singular strengths of the spiral of silence model is its use of highly innovative approaches to public opinion. To her credit, Noelle-Neumann provided a specified research methodology. Rather than offer a hypothetical study, it is worth examining Noelle-Neumann's own research to see how she integrated theory and research.

Designing the Classic Study

As is the case for conventional approaches to public opinion research practiced in the United States by commercial pollsters, an interviewer will ask a respondent his or her opinion about some topic (e.g., raising children). In surveys conducted by Noelle-Neumann's Allensbach Institute, women were asked whether spanking children was basically wrong or a necessary part of bringing up children. However, rather than an end, this question was merely the beginning in spiral of silence measurement, and was followed up by what has become regarded as the classic measure of public opinion for this approach:

> Suppose you are faced with a five-hour train ride, and there is a person sitting in your compartment who thinks...
>
> The ending of the question depended upon each respondent's personal opinion; that is, women...were confronted with a fellow traveler who represented a point of view diametrically opposed to their own. The question was closed in uniform fashion with "Would you like to talk with this woman so as to get to know her point of view better, or wouldn't you think that worth your while? (Noelle-Neumann, 1984, pp. 17–18)

Following the measurement phase, the analytic strategy involves comparing the willingness of supporters of spanking with that of opponents to enter into the dialogue with the fellow traveler. Hypothesis tests emanate directly from the central proposition of the spiral of silence model, namely that holders of the minority opinion will be less inclined to express their opinion in public than will holders of the majority opinion. Which faction is more confident, more willing to express a personal conviction, and hence more likely to subsequently have an influence on others' perceptions of the climate of opinion? These are the crucial research questions to be addressed in the spiral of silence approach, not merely the distribution of opposing opinions per se.

Adapting Measurement Approaches

The approach described in the previous section may be modified in any number of creative ways. For example, an interviewer may show respondents (in-person interviews) a picture of an automobile with a flat tire and then ask:

> Here is a picture of an automobile which has had its tire slashed. On the right rear window there is a sticker for a political party, but you can no longer read which party was on the sticker. But what is your guess: with which party's stickers do people run the greatest risk of having a tire slashed? (Noelle-Neumann, 1984, p. 54)

Or, an interviewer may use the following approach such as the following:

> I would like to tell you about an incident which recently took place at a large public meeting on nuclear energy. There were two main speakers: One spoke in favor of nuclear energy and the other opposed it. One of the speakers was booed by the audience. Which one do you think was booed: the speaker supporting nuclear energy or the speaker opposing it?

Implicit in these measurement approaches seems to be the notion that opinion climates potentially engender quite nasty experiences (e.g., lengthy, uncomfortable train rides, slashed tires, hostile confrontations). Several of these measurement approaches also are peculiar to the setting in which they were first conceived; for example, discussions during five-hour train rides are far more common in Europe than in the United States if only because of the greater reliance on the train system in the former. As a result, spiral of silence tests in the United States have resorted to alternative measures to assess respondents' willingness to express their opinion publicly. These include willingness to participate in a demonstration; wear a pin or button in support of some cause; or be interviewed by a TV reporter with camera and microphone for airing on the TV newscast. As Salmon and Oshagan (1990, p. 163), noted, various measures of opinion expression are distinguishable in terms of the degree to which each form of expression is public; and the degree to which feedback will be immediate and perhaps unpleasant. For example, engaging in a discussion in a train compartment involves a limited public setting—two or three other people may hear your opinion—with immediate and direct feedback. In contrast, agreeing to express an opinion to a TV reporter involves a much greater public setting—an entire community or nation—but with delayed and perhaps indirect feedback. In an attempt to assess the "public-ness" of research settings, Scheufele, Shanahan, and Lee (2001) manipulated the experimental communication target, and found that respondents who were told that their opinions would be expressed in a focus group were less willing to express opinions than those who were asked about expressing their opinions in a hypothetical social situation. For those in the focus group condition, their willingness to express their opinion was more highly related to perceptions of others' opinions.

In a meta-analysis of spiral of silence research, Glynn, Hayes, and Shanahan (1997) tested the possibility that several moderating variables, including whether the target was a media reporter, impacted respondents' willingness to express their opinions. A marginally significant difference was found between talking to a member of the media versus a non-media target, where results indicated a stronger correlation between the opinion climate and willingness to express one's opinion when talking to a non-media target. However, this relationship vanished when controlling for possible confounding factors, such as whether the communication target was a stranger and whether the target agreed or disagreed with the respondent.

Analyzing Actual and Perceived Minority Status

Although Noelle-Neumann hypothesized that holders of the minority opinion are less likely than holders of the majority opinion to engage in the conversation, some attention should be paid to the distinction between actual versus perceived minority status (Salmon & Kline, 1985). That is, we know from the literature on pluralistic ignorance (e.g., Allport, 1924; Fields & Schuman, 1976; Miller & McFarland, 1987) as well as the more generalized idea of imputing one's knowledge to others (Nickerson, 1999) that some individuals who are in the minority on some issue incorrectly believe themselves to be in the majority and vice versa. In her own research, Noelle-Neumann typically failed to analyze this distinction (an exception being Noelle-Neumann, 1973, p. 106); instead she merely compared the willingness to express an opinion among those actually in the majority and minority. At the same time, she recommended that researchers ask respondents "What do most people think" (about the issue) and "Which side is winning?" (Noelle-Neumann, 1989), as a way of gauging the respondents' perceptions of social environment dynamics. This is an area in particular in which spiral of silence analysis could greatly benefit from the infusion of ideas from other approaches to the study of individuals' perceptions of the social environment, such as pluralistic ignorance, false consensus, looking glass perception, perspective taking, impersonal impact, and the third-person effect (see Glynn et al., 1995, for a review, as well as recent studies by Petric & Pinter, 2002; Shamir, 1997).

In addition to the recent studies mentioned above, several researchers have discovered that respondents may invoke different groups at different societal levels when considering whether they are a member of a majority or minority group. Though Noelle-Neumann's original conceptualization posits that respondents use their "quasi-statistical sense" to determine the macro-level, society-wide opinion climate for a given issue, investigations of smaller, micro- or meso-level groups as key referents have yielded interesting results.

A Caveat: The Suitability of Survey Research

Attention to such matters as question wording and analytic strategies inherently assumes the legitimacy of polling and survey research itself as a means of researching public opinion, an assumption which has been contested in several insightful and scathing critiques (e.g., Blumer, 1948; Bourdieu, 1979; Pollock, 1976). Certainly, the assumption that measuring public opinion can be done in the same manner as measuring intentions to vote or purchase toothpaste is conceptually naive. And the assumption that in a public opinion poll all opinions ought to be counted the same (i.e., have the same weight) is clearly rooted in some contrived, idealized notion of democracy rather than in democracy as it actually exists in its empirical form (see Salmon & Glasser, 1995, for an extended discussion of these issues). Though all survey approaches to the study of public opinion are inherently vulnerable to such criticisms, the spiral of silence is especially vulnerable for different reasons.

At the heart of the spiral of silence phenomenon is the idea that individuals holding a minority opinion will become reluctant to express that opinion publicly. As noted (Salmon & Moh, 1992), the survey interview is itself a communication setting in which a person is asked to express an opinion to a stranger. To the extent that the respondent is influenced by the perceived climate of opinion, he or she may be unwilling to participate in a survey on that topic much as the person on the train may be unwilling to participate in the discussion in the train compartment. At the very least, this may result in different response rates for holders of different opinions and thereby threaten the validity of the conclusions. The dynamics of the two situations are different in some important ways. On the train, the fellow traveler clearly expresses his or her opinion; in the research situation, the interviewer has been trained not to reveal his or her opinion on the issue in the hopes of minimizing social pressure on the respondent. Further, the respondent is treated as anonymous, and his or her opinions confidential in the hopes of maximizing the integrity of his or her response, something which may or may not happen on the train ride but is certainly not explicitly stated as such. Nevertheless, the intriguing possibility exists that the survey approach may be inherently unsuitable for studying the very phenomenon it was designed to study.

Related to this, there are issues and topics which simply cannot be studied in certain societies and within certain population subgroups. Certain topics are "taboo' and off limits in any group, but particularly within groups characterized by deeply rooted fundamentalist values and traditions. Studies in these contexts therefore need to focus on issues that are not taboo and which can be discussed. In such settings, conclusions that the spiral of silence phenomenon does not exist are essentially missing the forest in analyzing individual trees. The fact that topics are taboo and cannot even be discussed within certain religious and ethnic groups is prima facie evidence that powerful opinion climates do indeed exist even if—or make that especially because—survey researchers cannot even ask the very questions that would be needed to empirically document the presence of some oppressive climate of opinion.

These potential *paradoxa* suggest the need for alternative and complementary methodologies to study the spiral of silence. In particular, experiments (Kennamer, 1990) and observational studies might provide important insights into the silencing process, as well as the opportunity to provide triangulation in an assessment of the validity of the survey approach. Two other methods—content analysis and interviews with journalists—have been employed to help in the interpretation of survey data on the silencing phenomenon (e.g., Noelle-Neumann, 1984), but only rarely and even then in a cursory fashion.

In an attempt to address the possibility that individual differences may lead to differential effects within the spiral of silence model, Hayes, Glynn, and Shanahan (2005a, 2005b) developed a measurement tool for assessing individual's propensity for "withholding…one's true opinion from an audience perceived to disagree with that opinion" (2005a, p. 298). Reasoning that different people may internalize and act upon social pressures in different ways, the "willingness to self-censor" scale attempts to quantify the likelihood that a person will withhold a minority opinion.

Conclusion

In its lifespan to date, the spiral of silence model has engendered a rich legacy of research and commentary and infused the fields of public opinion and communication research with some needed conceptual and methodological vitality. If only by virtue of being one of the very few communication models which explicitly links mass and interpersonal communication processes, the spiral of silence has assumed an important place in the literature on communication processes and effects. Mass communication—along with secondary effects of communication with important reference groups—is seen as forging opinion climates, the perceptions of which in turn are said to influence individuals' willingness to engage in interpersonal communication about some topic. Less developed in the model is the mechanism of reverse causality, namely the manner in which individuals' willingness to engage in interpersonal communication exerts influence on mass media portrayals of the opinion climate. By using the metaphor of the downward spiral, which implies unidirectionality, Noelle-Neumann perhaps underestimated the power of minority factions to effect social change, to overcome majority sentiment, and reverse the spiraling process through judicious use of interpersonal and small-group communication processes. Or perhaps she overestimates the power of opinion climates in pluralistic societies. While the empirical evidence shows that some individuals are reluctant to express minority viewpoints in some settings on some topics with some people, the magnitude of the phenomenon is not nearly as pronounced as is implied in the Noelle-Neumann's claims and generalizations.

Nevertheless, the model clearly remains an interesting and controversial one, obviously for what it implies about the nature and vast powers of the mass media system, but perhaps more tellingly for its preoccupation with the potentially ominous consequences of commonplace conversations and expressions of opinion. Rather than a tool for crafting compromise and mutually acceptable resolutions to social conflicts, communication is depicted as a weapon capable of progressively bludgeoning weak opinion into obscurity. This dark side aspect of the spiral of silence cannot be understated. It is a central aspect of the controversy regarding the theory. To be sure, like all current models, the spiral of silence can be criticized on theoretical and methodological grounds. But much of the criticism focuses on what the theory suggests about human nature, with human beings portrayed as weak and intimidated into silence, rather than vocal contributors to the democratic process and the marketplace of ideas.

Notes

1. The authors would like to thank Michael Huge for his assistance in preparing the revised version of this chapter.
2. Sections of this essay are drawn from previously published works by Salmon and Moh (1992), especially pages 146–152, which review the generic spiral of silence process, and from Glynn, Ostman, and McDonald (1995).
3. As Salmon and Moh (1992, p. 156) noted, Noelle-Neumann's analysis of the consonant information environment forged by a liberal media is one of the most paradoxical aspects of the model. That is, if stripped of its criticism of media liberalism, the model is surprisingly compatible with the conclusions of critical theorists such as Edward Herman and Noam Chomsky (1988) and Todd Gitlin (1980), all of whom see the media environment as essentially ubiquitous and powerful, but forged by a conservative rather than liberal media.
4. It is a matter of record that Noelle-Neumann studied and wrote several provocative articles on the topic of media and public opinion for *Das Reich* and the Frankfurter *Zeitung* during the war; however, she claims that she was ultimately fired from her jobs—effectively silenced as it were—for being anti-Nazi. Further, it is also the case that her dissertation contained what she described as "propaganda pieces," including passages explaining how this method could be useful to the Nazis. Her dissertation also used the term *Jew* regarding the writings of the American Walter Lippmann. Noelle-Neumann contended that these references were included only to appease the dictatorial censors and to conform to the prevailing regulations, both of which were essential if she was to be granted the opportunity to express her ideas publicly in a totalitarian state (Noelle-Neumann, 1992, p. 10).

References

Allport, F. H. (1924). *Social psychology*. Boston: Houghton Mifflin.

Asch, S. E. (1970). Effects of group pressure upon the modification and distortion of judgments. In J. H. Campbell & H. Hepler (Eds.), *Dimensions in communication: Readings* (pp. 170–183). Belmont, CA: Wadsworth.

Associated Press. (1989, April 10). 85,000 pro-choice activists march in D.C. *The Badger Herald* (Madison, WI), p. 3.

Bergen, L. (1986, May). *Testing the spiral of silence with opinions on abortion*. Paper presented at the annual meeting of the International Communication Association, Chicago, IL.

Blumer, H. (1948). Public opinion and public opinion polling. *American Sociological Review, 13*, 542–552.

Bogart, L. (1991). The pollster and the Nazis. *Commentary, 92*, 47–49.

Bourdieu, P. (1979). Public opinion does not exist. In A. Mattelart & S. Siegelaub (Eds.), *Communication and class struggle* (pp. 124–130). New York: International General.

Csikszentmihalyi, M. (1991). Reflections on the "spiral of silence." In J. A. Anderson (Ed.), *Communication yearbook 14* (pp. 288–297). Newbury Park, CA: Sage.

Davison, W. P. (1958). The public opinion process. *Public Opinion Quarterly, 65*, 299–306.

Donsbach, W. (1988). The challenge of the spiral-of-silence theory. *Communicare, 8*, 5–16.

Donsbach, W., & Stevenson, R. L. (1984, May). *Challenges problems and empirical evidence of the theory of the spiral of silence*. Paper presented at the annual meeting of the International Communication Association, San Francisco.

Fields, J., & Schuman, H. (1976). Public beliefs about the beliefs of the public. *Public Opinion Quarterly, 40*, 427–448.

Gitlin, T. (1980). *The whole world is watching: Mass media in the making and unmaking of the New Left*. Berkeley: University of California Press.

Glynn, C. J. (1997). Public opinion as a normative opinion process. *Communication Yearbook 20* (pp. 157–183). Thousand Oaks, CA: Sage.

Glynn, C. J., Hayes, A. F., & Shanahan, J. (1997). Perceived support for one's opinions and willingness to speak out—A meta-analysis of survey studies on the 'spiral of silence.' *Public Opinion Quarterly, 61*(3), 452–463.

Glynn, C. J., & McLeod, J. M. (1985). Implications of the spiral of silence for communication and public opinion research. In K. R. Sanders, L. L. Kaid, & D. Nimmo (Eds.), *Political communication yearbook 1984* (pp. 43–65). Carbondale: Southern Illinois University Press.

Glynn, C. J., Ostman, R. E., & McDonald, D. G. (1995). Opinions, perceptions, and social reality. In T. L. Glasser & C. T. Salmon (Eds.), *Public opinion and the communication of consent* (pp. 249–277). New York: Guilford.

Hayes, A. F., Glynn, C. G., & Shanahan, J. (2005a). Willingness to self-censor: A construct and measurement tool for public opinion research. *International Journal of Public Opinion Research, 17*, 298–323.

Hayes, A. F., Glynn, C. G., & Shanahan, J. (2005b). Validating the willingness to self-censor scale: Individual differences in the effect of the climate of opinion on opinion expression. *International Journal of Public Opinion Research, 17*, 443–455.

Herman, E. S., & Chomsky, N. (1988). *Manufacturing consent: The political economy of the mass media*. New York: Pantheon Books.

Huang, H. P. (2005). A cross-cultural test of the spiral of silence. *International Journal of Public Opinion Research, 17*(3), 324–345.

Jeffres, L. W., Neuendorf, K. A., & Atkin, D. (1999). Spirals of silence: Expressing opinions when the climate of opinion is unambiguous. *Political Communication, 16*(2), 115–131.

Kennamer, J. D. (1990). Self-serving bias in perceiving the opinions of others. *Communication Research, 17*, 393–404.

Locke, J. (1985). *The works of John Locke* (12th ed.). Frederic Ives Carpenter Memorial Collection. Westport, CT: Greenwood. (Original work published 1824)

Madison, J. (1961). The Federalist No. 49. In J. E. Cooke (Ed.), *The Federalist* (pp. 338–347). Middletown, CT: Wesleyan University Press. (Original work published 1788)

Matera, F., & Salwen, M. B. (1992). Support for Radio Martí among Miami's Cubans and non-Cubans. *International Journal of Intercultural Relations, 16,* 135–144.

McLeod, J. M. (1985). An essay: Public opinion—Our social skin. *Journalism Quarterly, 62,* 649–653.

Merten, K. (1985). Some silence in the spiral of silence. In K. Sanders, L. L. Kaid, & D. Nimmo (Eds.), *Political communication yearbook 1984* (pp. 31–42). Carbondale: Southern Illinois University Press.

Miller, D. T., & McFarland, C. (1987). Pluralistic ignorance: When similarity is interpreted as dissimilarity. *Journal of Personality and Social Psychology, 53,* 298–305.

Moscovici, S. (1991). Silent majorities and loud minorities. In J. A. Anderson (Ed.), *Communication yearbook* (Vol. 14, pp. 298–308). Newbury Park, CA: Sage.

Moy, P., Domke, D., & Stamm, K. (2001). The spiral of silence and public opinion on affirmative action. *Journalism & Mass Communication Quarterly, 78*(1), 7–25.

Nickerson, R. S., (1999). How we know—and sometimes misjudge—what others know: Imputing one's own knowledge to others. *Psychological Bulletin, 125,* 737–759.

Noelle-Neumann, E. (1973). Return to the concept of powerful mass media. *Studies of Broadcasting, 9,* 67–112.

Noelle-Neumann, E. (1974). The spiral of silence: A theory of public opinion. *Journal of Communication, 24,* 43–51.

Noelle-Neumann, E. (1977). Turbulences in the climate of opinion: Methodological applications of the spiral of silence theory. *Public Opinion Quarterly, 41,* 143–158.

Noelle-Neumann, E. (1979). Public opinion and the classical tradition: A re-evaluation. *Public Opinion Quarterly, 43,* 143–156.

Noelle-Neumann, E. (1980). The public opinion research correspondent. *Public Opinion Quarterly, 44,* 585–597.

Noelle-Neumann, E. (1984) *The spiral of silence: Public opinion—Our social skin.* Chicago: University of Chicago Press.

Noelle-Neumann, E. (1985). The spiral of silence: A response. In D. Nimmo, L. L. Kaid, & K. Sanders (Eds.), *Political communication yearbook 1984* (pp. 66–94). Carbondale: Southern Illinois University Press.

Noelle-Neumann, E. (1989). Advances in spiral of silence research. *KEIO Communication Review, 10,* 3–34.

Noelle-Neumann, E. (1991). The theory of public opinion: The concept of the spiral of silence. In J. A. Anderson (Ed.), *Communication yearbook* (Vol. 14, pp. 256–287). Newbury Park, CA: Sage.

Noelle-Neumann, E. (1992). Letter to the editor in response to Leo Bogart's "The pollster and the Nazis." *Commentary, 93,* 9–15.

Noelle-Neumann, E. (1995). Public opinion and rationality. In T. L. Glasser & C. T. Salmon (Eds.), *Public opinion and the communication of consent* (pp. 33–54). New York: Guilford.

Noelle-Neumann, E. (1998). The effect of mass media on opinion formation. In D. David & K. Viswanath (Eds.), *Mass Media, Social Control, and Social Change: A Macrosocial Perspective.* Ames, IA: Iowa State University Press.

Petric, G., & Pinter, A. (2002). From social perception to public expression of opinion: A structural equation modeling approach to the spiral of silence. *International Journal of Public Opinion Research, 14*(1), 37–53

Pollock, F. (1976). Empirical research into public opinion. In P. Connerton (Ed.), *Critical sociology* (pp. 225–236). New York: Penguin.

Price, V. (1989). Social identification and public opinion: Effects of communicating group conflict. *Public Opinion Quarterly, 53,* 197–224.

Price, V., & Allen, S. (1990). Opinion spirals, silent and otherwise: Applying small-group research to public opinion phenomena. *Communication Research 17,* 369–392.

Price, V. & Neijens, P. (1997). Opinion quality in public opinion research. *International Journal of Public Opinion Research, 9*(4), 336–360.

Priest, S. H. (2006). Public discourse and scientific controversy—A spiral-of-silence analysis of biotechnology opinion in the United States. *Science Communication, 28*(2), 195–215.

Protess, D. L., Cook, F. L., Doppelt, J. C., Ettema, J. S., Gordon, M. T., Leff, D. R., et al. (1991). *The journalism of outrage: Investigative reporting and agenda building in America*. New York: Guilford.

Rusciano, R. L. (1989). *Isolation and paradox: Defining "the public" in modern political analysis*. New York: Greenwood Press.

Salmon, C. T., & Glasser, T. L. (1995). The politics of polling and the limits of consent. In T. L. Glasser & C. T. Salmon (Eds.), *Public opinion and the communication of consent* (pp. 437–458). New York: Guilford.

Salmon, C. T., & Kline, F. G. (1985). The spiral of silence ten years later: An examination and evaluation. In K. Sanders, L. L. Kaid, & D. Nimmo (Eds.), *Political communication yearbook 1984* (pp. 3–29). Carbondale: Southern Illinois University Press.

Salmon, C. T., & Moh, C. Y. (1992). The spiral of silence: Linking individual and society through communication. In J. D. Kennamer (Ed.), *Public opinion, the press, and public policy* (pp. 145–161). Westport, CT: Praeger.

Salmon, C. T., & Neuwirth, K. (1990). Perceptions of opinion "climates" and willingness to discuss the issue of abortion. *Journalism Quarterly, 67*, 567–577.

Salmon, C. T., & Oshagan, H. (1990). Community size, perceptions of majority opinion and opinion expression. *Public Relations Research Annual, 2*, 157–171.

Salwen, M. B., Lin, C., & Matera, F. R. (1994). Willingness to discuss "official English:" A test of three communities. *Journalism Quarterly, 71*, 282–290.

Scheufele, D. A., & Moy, P. (2000). Twenty-five years of the spiral of silence: A conceptual review and empirical outlook. *International Journal of Public Opinion Research, 12*(1), 3–28.

Scheufele, D. A., Shanahan, J., & Lee, E. (2001). Real talk—Manipulating the dependent variable in spiral of silence research. *Communication Research, 28*(3), 304–324.

Schulz, W., & Schoenbach, K. (1984). Book review of "Masenmedien und Wahlen" [Mass media and elections]. *Journalism Quarterly, 62*, 715.

Shamir, J. (1997). Speaking up and silencing out in face of a changing climate of opinion. *Journalism & Mass Communication Quarterly, 74*(3), 602–614.

Tönnies, F. (1922). *Kritik der offentlicher meinung* [Critique of public opinion]. Berlin: Springer.

Wyatt, R. O., Katz, E., Levinsohn, H., & Al-Haj, M. (1996). The dimensions of expression inhibition: Perceptions of obstacles to free speech in three cultures. *International Journal of Public Opinion Research, 8*(3), 229–247.

Yeric, J. L., & Todd, J. R. (1989). *Public opinion, the visible politics* (2nd ed.). Itasca, IL: F. E. Peacock.

Suggested Readings

Glynn, C. J., Hayes, A. F., & Shanahan, J. (1997). Spiral of silence: A meta-analysis. *Public Opinion Quarterly, 61*, 452–463.

Noelle-Neumann, E. (1993). *The spiral of silence*. Chicago: The University of Chicago Press.

Price, C., & Allen, S. (1990). Opinion spirals, silence and otherwise: Applying small-group research to public opinion phenomena. *Communication Research, 17*, 369–392.

Salmon, C. T., & Kline, F. G. (1985). The spiral of silence ten years later: An examination and evaluation. In K. R. Sanders, L. L. Kaid, & D. Nimmo (Eds.), *Political communication yearbook 1984* (pp. 3–30). Carbondale: Southern Illinois University Press.

Scheufele, D. A., & Moy, P. (2000). Twenty-five years of the spiral of silence: A conceptual review and empirical outlook. *International Journal of Public Opinion Research, 12*(1), 3–28.

12

INTERNATIONAL COMMUNICATION

Robert L. Stevenson

As an area of study, international communication has no identifiable substance, body of theory, or specific research methods, only geography (Stevenson, 1992). This area of communication, perhaps more than others, is diverse and unorganized. Besides embracing anything "foreign," it includes all of the combinations of *cross*, *inter*, and *comparative* linked to *cultural*, *national*, and even *global* that surface in books, journal articles, and conference papers. The result is a set of confusing, ill-defined terms that do little to organize the area or guide its development. Is there anything that distinguishes international communication—other than geography?

Definitional Matrix

A simple, three-dimensional definitional matrix serves a good starting point for international communication. Some years ago, William Paisley (1984) proposed a two-dimensional matrix locating communication as a field of study within the behavioral sciences. He defined communication as one of the elementary behavior-defined disciplines, such as cybernetics and systems analysis, which served as elements of more general fields of study such as education (learning), economics (value), and political science (power). Communication was both one of the basic disciplines, incorporating cybernetics (self-regulating feedback) and systems analysis, as well as an element of the more general disciplines of education, political science, and economics.

Paisley's second dimension comprised disciplines defined by their units of analysis, ranging from atom and molecule (natural sciences), through cell and living subsystem (biological sciences), to individual, group, and culture (social sciences). A final category of particular interest to international communication could be the globe as a single unit. By combining the two, you define a specific behavior (such as communication) at a specific level (such as the individual). As a field, communication is studied mostly at the individual or small-group level in the United States, while in many other nations it is often studied at the economic and political levels.

At this point, communication is a behavior that incorporates some more basic behaviors (such as feedback and systems maintenance) and is itself part of more general behaviors (such as learning, value, and power). It is studied at levels ranging from the entire planet as a single system, to individual molecules or atoms. As a social science, communication studies have focused on the individual and group with some outward exploration toward the single global system, as well as inward toward biological systems. At the broader levels, social science has produced few new ideas since Marxism, now discredited both as a theory of history and a basis of social organization. Some dramatic progress can be documented at the boundary between social and biological science. This is reflected in the growth of cognitive science, which seeks to understand the brain as a biological organ as a prelude to understanding the mind, and is consistent with the tradition in Western science of reducing disciplines to lower-order components.

To separate international communication from the more general field, a third dimension is needed that includes four distinct categories: foreign, comparative, international or intercultural,[1] and global. Foreign studies are single-country or single-culture studies, usually heavy on description and light on explanation. Comparison with other countries is usually implicit, if attempted at all. Comparative studies contrast the communication behavior of individuals or institutions within one culture or nation with equivalent behavior in another, usually with some national or cultural element to explain differences. International and intercultural studies examine the flow of information and influences from one nation or culture to another. Global studies consider the planet as a single, unified system.

The three dimensions form a cube whose sides define international communication in terms of (1) a focal variable that is some aspect of communication; (2) a unit of analysis that can range from the individual to the entire globe; and (3) the delineation of national or cultural boundaries that, in most studies, provide the basis of comparison or explanation.

Methods

Is it possible to identify some areas of communication we can reasonably single out as *international* communication, although specific theories or even fragments of theory are in short supply? International communication is more an area of interest than an area rich in theory, and one that, like other areas of interest, overlaps other disciplines. Our examination begins, however, with whether there are unusual or even unique research methods appropriate for its study. Does the international communication researcher need special tools—beyond sensitivity to other cultures—appropriate to any foreign expedition?

On the whole, no: The standards and methods of scholarly research do not stop at national borders. Despite occasional references to a different reality of non-Western cultures, the rules of probability and statistical logic are the same in every country. Within every facet of the field and every discipline, the researcher's bag of tools is the same: validity (am I measuring what I'm claiming to measure?), reliability (am I describing my methods so thoroughly that others can replicate them?), and adequacy of evidence (have I considered everything?). While associated with quantitative social science where these concerns are addressed explicitly, they also underlie claims to knowledge in all disciplines.

There is, however, a special question of research method that permeates much of the international communication literature. It is the difference between *research* and *polemic*. In the 1990s, polemic is closely linked to a mixture of scholarship and ideology called *critical research*.

Critical Research

The phrase *critical research* is identified with the phrase *Frankfurt School* (Bottomore, 1984). The School, technically the Institute of Social Research, was founded in Germany in 1923. Its focus was the dark side of industrial society and, while not always Marxist as understood now, research emphasized the themes found in Marx's critique of capitalism and exported them to sociology. Modern life was contrasted with both Marx's Utopian vision of communism and with a romanticized landscape of the pre-industrial past.

Before World War II, many Frankfurt School researchers fled to the United States, where the Frankfurt School in exile met the Vienna School in exile (Delia, 1987). The two names most associated with the Vienna School were Paul Lazarsfeld and Karl Popper. Lazarsfeld, a sociologist, was to influence the development of communication research as an empirical field both in academia and the corporate world. Popper, who remained in Britain, is closely identified with positivism, a style of social science research modeled on the natural sciences, whose key elements are quantification, explicit attention to validity, reliability, and weight of evidence (significance testing), and the "scientific" method (see chapters 1 and 5, this volume). Popper is identified with the idea that a statement can never be proven true because there are always possible alternative causes; a statement can only be proven false. This research approach goes back to Descartes: Build carefully from the simplest concepts, test everything and take nothing for granted. In practice, critical research relies more on deduction and definition, reflecting its roots in Hegelian philosophy. The key elements of positivism that are contrasted to critical research are an avoidance of anything that cannot be established empirically and an indirect testing of hypotheses by falsifying the reverse null hypothesis. The former excludes value judgments, the latter excludes many of the important questions of social and global media influence.

In the debate between the Frankfurt and Vienna schools after World War II, the question of the appropriate method for communication research—even a minimally adequate method—was confused. Lazarsfeld (1941) contrasted an aloof, admittedly soft critical research that probed the crucial links between the mass media and the power structure of society with what he called administrative research. Although claiming to be sympathetic to critical research, he presented it as mere speculation. *Administrative research* was the cautious conservatism of empirical positivism, an approach greeted enthusiastically by the media and derivative industries to advance commercial and political interests.

The differences Lazarsfeld described have been exaggerated to separate communication research, especially international communication research, into two hostile camps (Blumler, 1985; Rogers, 1985). On one side is critical research, often identified as the European approach, focusing on the use of communication to maintain political and economic power systems at the national or global level and disdainful of empirical data and the scholar's traditional aloofness from political activism. On the other, the American school focused on individuals, reliant on sophisticated (and sometimes inappropriate) data analysis to generate fragments of middle-range theories, unconcerned with broader issues of distribution of wealth and power.[2]

This has changed; the poles have reversed. Other countries have improved their access to computers and data-collection methods. In the United States, communication research is often caught up in the politics and rhetoric of social protest claiming oppression, suppression, and victimization. A good deal of current domestic academic rhetoric is imported from critical research's long-standing vocabulary. The literature of international communication now debates issues with terms such as *dependency, hegemony,* and *sovereignty,* as well as the more general trendy concepts associated with postmodern scholarship. Traditional research is out, critics claim; critical research is in, with all of its vocabulary, assumptions, and ideology ("Ferment in the Field," 1983; Levy & Gurevitch, 1993/1994).

Research versus Polemic

Critics of international communication research often posit a dichotomy of critical versus administrative—or sometimes quantitative versus qualitative—methods. Within the area generally and certainly within the United States, the traditional methods, usually quantitative and almost always aloof and dispassionate, are in disrepute. To replace them, a style of committed research is proposed that rejects both traditions of impartiality and of caution in mixing scholarly research and partisan politics. This false dichotomy points toward a growing problem in communication research, and a specific problem of most international communication research. The problem is the growth of *polemic* (i.e., beginning with a conclusion and assembling data to support it, without regard to questions of reliability, validity, or adequacy of the evidence) in the guise of research.

Research *begins* with a question or hypothesis; it is the outcome of research that is in doubt, although researchers often put forward logically derived hypotheses of their expectations. The evidence may be inadequate to support any conclusion, or it may contradict the expected outcome. There are circumstances when polemic is appropriate. Political campaigning, advertising, and one's defense in a criminal trial come to mind immediately. In these circumstances, we expect the best possible case to be made. There is also an academic school—stronger in continental Europe than in the Anglo-American tradition—that values argument and rhetoric over evidence. A British observer described the 1970s international debate over "cultural imperialism" as a passage of the center of the field from "communication schools on the right bank of the Ohio River to the cafes on the left bank of the Seine" (Tunstall, 1982, p. 141). In similar fashion, the rise of critical research and its rhetoric in the United States reflects an embracing of the assumptions and vocabulary long a part of international communication.

A great deal of criticism of international communication research in the United States since 1970 is based on the assertion that it supports the existing order while claiming to be independent and value-free. However, the power of Western science in general is a product of the weight of evidence and logic that accompany claims of knowledge derived from it. The middle-range theories that communication can muster still rise or fall on the traditional criterion of empirical verification. The particular problem of international communication is that almost no research considers the variables assumed to account for the phenomenon in question. Part of the problem is a failure to develop appropriate hypotheses; part is a casual and sometimes deliberate disregard for the protections of reliability, validity, and adequacy of evidence.

Consider a hypothetical but typical international communication study submitted to a conference or journal. Its underlying premise is that media around the world support the status quo. A content analysis could be used to show that (1) coverage in *The New York Times* was more critical of the Tiananmen Square massacre than coverage in *The People's Daily* (because both papers reflect their governments' positions), or (2) coverage of Tiananmen Square was more negative than coverage of the abortive coup against President Gorbachev (because the United States opposed the Chinese government but supported Gorbachev); or (3) coverage of the coup against Gorbachev was greater than coverage of the coup against Jean-Bertrand Aristide in Haiti (because Gorbachev is White and European and Aristide is Black and from a developing country).

What is wrong with the study lies in several specifics and a couple of general problems unique to international communication. For one thing, if the hypothesis is that media systems universally maintain political hegemony, then the key variable is a constant, and no analysis is possible because there is no variance. Or the null hypothesis is predicted if the hypothesis assumes no difference between the two newspapers, which cannot be done logically. This is an assumption in the first example. However, if the study's purpose is to explain something about different media systems and the varied economic and political systems in which they function, then the basis of explanation of the difference is difficult at best and often dubious. The second example assumes that both events are equivalent, and that differences in coverage derive only from journalistic practice and political policies. The third example assumes that news coverage is determined by factors over which journalists have no control, some *-ism*, such as capitalism, imperialism, or racism. In each case, the assumption is less than persuasive at best, foolish at worst. In this hypothetical study and in most real studies, the explanatory variable is not explicit, not subjected to any real test, and not restrained by considerations of reliability, validity, or adequacy of evidence.

We learn to develop and test hypotheses in a manner such that A→B, or "if A, then B." If we can establish the presence of B, we conclude that it derives from A. This works only in a classical experiment, where the presence and absence of A is manipulated in controlled circumstances where alternatives to A are excluded. If there are multiple causes of B, then A may be sufficient but not necessary to cause B.[3]

In the real world, where at best we can choose examples or circumstances that approximate experimental conditions—virtually the only kind of research possible in international communication where we cannot manipulate or otherwise control crucial factors—research is not so clearly cut. We need to be explicit about the explanation and at a minimum treat it as a hypothesis, not a given: "A→B because of C." The full hypothesis is: "If (A→B because of C), then D." The testable hypothesis is D, and the first derivative should be the first basis of comparison: in the absence of C, A will not lead to B.

Looking at our three examples, where the explanation—implicit or explicit—is some economic or political aspect of the media system or the nation or culture in which it operates, the first test of the hypothesis is to compare media content with equivalent content in a country with a different media system. That may have been behind the intent in the first example above; in general, however, journalistic comparative studies fail to find the kinds of differences the hypotheses require and none that point to non-Western media systems that have overcome the difficulties that are the focus of most media criticism in the West.

In short, Western journalism has something in common with Churchill's definition of democracy: It is the worst in the world—except for all the others. Or, put another way, most of the failures, weaknesses, and excesses of Western mass media exist in other media systems—and are usually worse. Advanced capitalism, the universal explanation of critical analysis, fails as a general explanation of the state of global media and is not very useful as an explanation of the issues that occupy the center ground of international communication.

Critical studies should be in disrepute along with cultural studies, with which it shares roots in Marxism, since Marx failed both as a historian and prophet. But both continue to flourish in academia, perhaps even becoming bolder as the few reality-checks of communism disappear. Among scholars who built their theories on Marxist polemic, only the historian Eugene D. Genovese (1994) questioned the link between theory and practice:

> Now, as everyone knows, in a noble effort to liberate the human race from violence and oppression we [communists] broke all records for mass slaughter, piling up tens of millions of corpses in less than three-quarters of a century. When the Asian figures are properly calculated, the aggregate to our credit may reach the seemingly incredible numbers widely claimed. Those who are big on multiculturalism might note that the great majority of our victims were nonwhite. (p. 371)

In the 21st century, polemic derived from Marxist critical analysis ought not to figure heavily in international communication, but it does. An overview of several substantive issues can highlight where research and polemic overlap and possibly separate real issues from rhetoric.

Issues

The international communication section of any relevant journal or conference program embraces an extraordinarily diverse set of substantive interests as well as research methods and ideological assumptions. The area is large enough that no single book offers a concise history of its past or road map to its future. However, three broad issues are now at its center and promise to stay there well into the 21st century.

National Development and Social Change

The assumption that mass media do have—or can have—direct mass effects is a temptation for those who are committed to rapid social change. The ranks of that group range from Lenin to the federal agricultural extension service in the United States. For five decades, the two represented opposite poles of a global effort to promote economic and social change in the Third World. The promise of communication as a magic multiplier of social change is now focused on the countries emerging from the wreckage of communism (Stevenson, 1988).

The main assumption of the traditional semitheory of communication in development, which is widely known as the *dominant paradigm*, derives mostly from the work of three international communication pioneers, with long-time influence from a fourth. One was W. Walt Rostow (1960), whose study of the rise of the industrial West emphasized the importance of the creation of a critical mass of resources (people, capital, information) to spark a curve of self-sustaining, accelerating growth. The second was Daniel Lerner (1958), whose research in the Middle East after World War II seemed to put mass media—particularly radio—at the center of a rapid movement toward modern (democratic) government. The third was Wilbur Schramm (1964), whose elegant synthesis of research around the world became a guide for a generation of Western and Third World scholars and development practitioners. A good candidate for expansion of this troika is Everett M. Rogers (1962), whose early work showed how the S-curve of adoption of innovations applied to Third World development.

Rogers later recanted his support for the dominant paradigm but, like many academics of the time, embraced an alternative approach that turned out to be worse (Rogers, 1976). While accepting that the Potemkin Village facade China showed to the outside world—"a miracle of modernization...a public health and family planning system that was envied by the richest nations...increasing equality...an enviable status for women" (pp. 129–130)—Rogers overlooked the darker side of a regime that was responsible, according to estimates in 1994, for the deaths of 40 to 80 million of its own citizens (Southerland, 1994a, 1994b). The other two examples of alternative development, Tanzania and Cuba, were less bloody but produced little more than bankrupt dictatorships dependent on Scandinavian foreign aid and—in the case of Cuba—a permanent exodus to southern Florida.

The failure of the dominant paradigm to lead the Third World to political stability and economic growth in the 1960s and 1970s was ascribed to several factors, ranging from the lack of fit between a Western theory and non-Western societies to the rigidity of many Third World governments that turned a revolution of rising expectations into a revolution of rising frustrations. The critical research explanation was a global theory of neoimperialism using communication and culture to maintain the West at the center of a global system and the Third World at the periphery in a state of dependence reminiscent of 19th century colonialism. The latter led to a call for a redistribution of global information resources known as the New World Information and Communication Order (NWICO) derived from a New World Economic Order (NWEO) and "authentic" Third World development based on disengagement from the global information system.

When the fury of the NWICO debate subsided about 1980, a new interest in communication and Third World development (or more broadly after the collapse of communism) emerged with a focus on telecommunication. The current debate is improved by a lower level of rhetoric but still hampered by a lack of empirical data and perhaps by the lack of any general pattern or theory applicable to the 200-plus countries claiming United Nations seats. If anything, the focus of comparison is between the old communist nations of Europe where the hope is that *glasnost* (political democracy) will lead to *perestroika* (economic growth) and the tigers of Asia that have emphasized economic growth while maintaining authoritarian control over the mass media. The question of how, or whether, communication can be mobilized to support economic, political, and social change is one of the puzzles to be sorted out in the 21st century.

Western Dominance

The competition between Asia and central Europe shares attention with another broad issue: Western dominance of all aspects of global communication, including news, popular culture, English as the global language, and communication technology (Hachten, 1992; Merrill, 1995). Western dominance spawned the global NWICO debate, giving birth to the phrase *cultural imperialism*, which became so debased by indiscriminate use that it now can mean virtually anything or nothing at all. Western dominance shows no sign of slowing—witness the invasion of fast food and other icons of pop culture in Eastern Europe—and is still the source of irritation and conflict. Concern in Canada and France over the United States' dominance of pop culture is evidence that the issue is more than anti-Western rhetoric.

Anglo-American dominance can be explained in part by a succession of successful British colonialism and unique postwar American global influence that paved the way for a self-sustaining global culture. Other factors include the size of the English-speaking market and its competitive, commercial base as well as the intrinsic appeal of an open culture promising life, liberty, and the pursuit of happiness and the possibility of fame and fortune.

The emergence of a global culture shaped and dominated by the West in general and especially the great English-speaking arc stretching from Sydney to London and on to New York and Hollywood spawned a research agenda that will remain at the center of the field well into the next century. In addition to obvious questions of cause and effect, related issues include the role of Western media in the revolutions of 1989, the growing influence of journalism in international relations, and the still-unanswered questions of the role of communication in social change. One central and emotional question is the flow of news around a world more and more tightly bound into an Anglo-American global news system.

News Flow

Only the casual traveler from the United States—and to a lesser extent, other parts of the English-speaking world—can be unaware of the extraordinary circumstance he or she encounters in even the most remote parts of the world: newspapers, news magazines, radio and television news from home. The careful observer will also note familiar logos and credits in local media as well as a heavy dose of American coverage. People from no other region can travel the globe so surrounded by their own media environment.

As in other areas of modern communication, Anglo-American dominance of global news flow seems to grow simultaneously with a decline in traditional areas of international influence. The growth of global news systems, which communication technology makes possible, strengthens the Anglo-American imprint on the news. Even a partial listing of the major players in global news—CNN, BBC, AP, Reuters, Murdoch, Turner—reinforces the tourist's experience that news around the world is essentially Anglo-American (Negrine & Papathanassopoulos, 1990).

The trend toward globalization raises new and important questions for communication research. Beyond the obvious ones of dominance and Western or Anglo-American influence, there are new issues related to the rise of global media moguls, new definitions of wealth and sovereignty, and new problems for governments that want to control their national media.

A curious and often ignored element in the globalization issue is how much of it is non-American, even though it exudes a "Made in U.S.A." feel. For the United States, an important issue is the speed with which its popular culture industry is being sold to foreigners: Three of the "big five" Hollywood studios are owned by foreign corporations, the largest book publisher in the

United States is Germany's Bertelsmann, and magazines are now a top prize for foreign investors. The rapid development of new multimedia technology, and the surprising appearance of a fully digital high-definition television standard, may return some of the leadership in communication hardware back to the United States just as its dominance in software is diffused to a new generation of entrepreneurs outside the country.

The trend toward multinational corporate production of news and entertainment material is reflected in the rise of regional (if not truly global) organizations in most parts of the world (Tunstall & Palmer, 1991). Some are relatively well known: Televisa in Mexico, Rede Globo in Brazil, Hachette and Hersant in France, Bertelsmann and Kirch in Germany, Rupert Murdoch's media empire in Britain. In a few countries (e.g., Brazil and Italy) modern media moguls have used their visibility and money to become important political figures. Together, with their mostly Anglo-American global partners and competitors, they are shaping a new global culture that promises to change the nature and distribution of power as surely as Gutenberg's printing press did a half millennium ago.

Studying Foreign Images

Although there are plenty of studies that could be conducted in international communication, examining a major research project already conducted provides a better example of the problems and promises of international communication research. A large-scale study of foreign news in the late 1970s, possibly the most ambitious collaborative research undertaking in international communication, illustrates both the value of international cooperation in research and the pitfalls of working without agreement on even the most basic elements of theory and method. One of the original designers dismissed the final project as "a textbook example of how social science can be misused for political purposes," whereas another major participant, originally skeptical, concluded that "this study helps clear the air of the pseudo debate" (Nordenstreng, 1984, p. 137) about NWICO assertions that "probably never were true and are certainly no longer true" (p. 141).

At the UNESCO General Conference in Nairobi in 1976—the flash point of the NWICO debate—the Nordic countries introduced a resolution calling for a study of "the image of foreign countries representing different social systems and developmental stages as portrayed by mass-circulated press in respective countries." The chairman of the Section for Communication of the Finnish National Commission for UNESCO, which originated the proposal, was Kaarle Nordenstreng, long-time president of the left-leaning International Organization of Journalists (IOJ) and activist professor of journalism at the University of Tampere. The proposal was approved and passed to the International Association for Mass Communication Research (IAMCR), an academic organization then located in Britain with status as a UNESCO nongovernmental organization. A simple, conventional content analysis project was designed at the University of Leicester where IAMCR's president, James D. Halloran, was head of the Center for Mass Communication Research. After some collaboration on the design from continental colleagues, Halloran invited IAMCR members to sign on. Richard Cole, of the University of North Carolina, volunteered to represent the United States but soon became dean of the School of Journalism and passed major responsibility to Robert Stevenson, who enlisted cooperation from Donald L. Shaw.

As the project took shape, several curiosities and weaknesses were noted. The design itself was cumbersome and unimaginative, exactly the narrow quantitative American approach that Europeans, including Halloran, had frequently criticized. Each foreign story, for example, was to be coded onto four 80-column computer cards and included, among a long list of descriptive variables, a complicated measure of standardized column-centimeters. The format was redesigned to fit on one card with several added variables. Only the main news section of newspapers was to be included, and the sample weeks excluded Sundays; the effect was to eliminate most of the information critics claimed Western media failed to report.

It was clear that the world the project examined was almost entirely Western with a handful of other countries with a Western research tradition, such as Malaysia, Lebanon, and India. Africa was represented only by Nigeria, the Communist "Second World" omitted the Soviet Union and China, and Latin America was missing completely. The project was then expanded in several directions. Indiana University researchers offered to examine files of the major Western news agencies; the United States Information Agency (USIA) agreed to collect media samples from a number of missing countries and to underwrite the cost of coding. The sample was expanded to include Sundays and the entire newspaper. As a result, data were supplied on the global news agencies and media of 17 countries; 12 national teams contributed their own data.

At a meeting of participants in Paris after the data were collected, a committee was appointed to write a final report from sets of tables supplied by each team (Sreberny-Mohammadi, Nordenstreng, Stevenson, & Ugboajah, 1985). Meanwhile, the wide-ranging data were subjected to various analyses and collected in a book (Stevenson & Shaw, 1984). Data were also passed on to other researchers for further analysis, first on tape and later on personal computer disks.

The UNESCO report was mildly controversial from the beginning. Because they were not "official," Nordenstreng, the instigator of the project and member of the writing committee, wanted to exclude all non-U.S. data from the report. As a compromise, the UNESCO monograph contained all the data, but not a qualitative summary of these countries. Nordenstreng also objected when the World Press Freedom Committee, organized to defend Western media in the NWICO/NWICO debate, and Freedom House cited early conference papers. The debate was carried to the *Journal of Communication*, which published a summary of the results and two opposing interpretations of them.

For Nordenstreng (1984), it was the familiar "hijacking" of critical research:

> [the original] idea called for the use of a delicate methodological instrument that would get at the qualitative sphere of image building, instead of just employing conventional categories of content analysis such as topic/types of news, countries/regions, etc. The final project was dominated by "vulgar" categories that capture ad hoc aspects of the media content, rather than a comprehensive image carried by the content. (p. 139)

Further, "perhaps the greatest contribution of this enterprise has been through a negative case—by demonstrating the scientific inadequacy and political risks involved in one-sided quantitative consideration of mass media content" (pp. 141–142).

On the other hand, Stevenson concluded that the project demonstrated that the NWICO's ideological rhetoric was misplaced: "First, many of the charges against the Western media and news services are without evidence to support them. Second, the lack of difference among media of very different political systems argues against the theory of cultural imperialism. And third, much of the rhetoric addresses outdated questions" (Stevenson, 1984, p. 137). Results clearly did not support Nordenstreng's critical theory conclusions, a factor in his effort to disown his own creation.

By the time the UNESCO monograph appeared, the United States, Britain, and Singapore were leaving UNESCO, and the NWICO debate had largely burned itself out. If anything, however, the collapse of communism, rather than producing Hegel's "end of history" instead produced an increasingly complex and uncharted world in which communication played a more central role. There is plenty of work and opportunities for both independent and collaborative researchers in international communication.

Summary

Even without clear theoretical or methodological boundaries, and even with the confusion of politics and academics, international communication is a growing area. Researchers looking for new theoretical understanding, as well as those concerned with offering useful guidance to policy-makers, have a rich and largely unexplored terrain to explore. The world offers a fascinating and increasingly diverse array of cultures to serve as a laboratory for research in which individual and social differences are explained by national and cultural differences. In that quest, the same kinds of questions that have guided research and separated scholarship from polemic for generations are still useful.

What? Good descriptive research is still needed, and the world offers more and more examples of interesting cultures and media systems. Of special interest are the "off-diagonal" systems that vary from the general pattern: small countries that sustain a vibrant indigenous culture, developing nations with independent media, successful marriage of Western influence and tradition. Of course, the researcher's traditional protections of reliability and validity of observation and adequacy of evidence are especially important when venturing outside of one's own environment.

Why? Implicit in even descriptive research is some hint of explanation. If anything is needed in American academic research, it is a willingness to offer explanation of interesting or important phenomena and to subject hypotheses or conjectures to the glare of critical test. Anything in the definition of *international communication* offered above requires the researcher to address the question of *why* and assumes, in almost all cases, that the true definition lies somewhere in culture or nation.

So What? Not all explanations are equal in value to practitioners or theory builders, and not all research questions carry implications that justify the drudgery that research entails. Some of the implications in the examples offered here and many of the implications of the published literature are vulnerable to the "so what question?" Although harsh, it is better asked before one begins a research project than at the end.

Why bother? Too much international communication research fails both the *"why?"* and *"so what?"* questions, but even if a study can provide both explanation and implication, it may not address a very important question or add a very useful data point to the body of knowledge. The question of importance can be theoretical or pragmatic. Replicating an agenda-setting study or documenting American media influence in one more country is not likely to add to theory or offer useful guidance to policy makers.

Researchers can avoid the awkward silences that often follow these questions by thinking about them in advance. What will the presentation of results look like? If results are contrary to expectations, will it make any difference? Will the "suggestions for further research" be anything more than a summary of what I should have done in the first place?—and, of course, *"so what?"* And, why even bother to conduct this research?

The clarity of hindsight is nearly perfect, but some of its revelations can be avoided with good advance planning. Any research project consumes enough time and energy and resources that we ought not to depend on serendipity and clever data analysis to avoid the awkward silences that often follow these four questions. Good ideas are rare in international communication research, but the area is important enough that the innovative and thoughtful researcher can find a productive research career and a guarantee of encounters with interesting people, places, and ideas.

Notes

1. The difference between nation and culture is easy to define, but often difficult to deal with in practice. A nation is an independent political entity, usually identified by a flag, airline, and seat at the United Nations. A culture is a group of people who share values and behaviors derived from a common history.
2. Middle-range theories are more restricted than high generality theories, which are more general and cultural in nature and low generality, which are more restricted in nature (see Stacks, Hickson, & Hill, 1991).
3. A necessary condition is one that is required for change to occur. A sufficient condition is one that may or may not cause change.

References

Blumler, J. (1985). European-American differences in communication research. In E. M. Rogers & F. Balle (Eds.), *The media revolution in America and Western Europe* (pp. 185–199). Norwood, NJ: Ablex.

Bottomore, T. (1984). *The Frankfurt school*. London: Tavistock.

Delia, J. G. (1987). Communication research: A history. In C. R. Berger & S. H. Chaffee (Eds.), *Handbook of communication science* (pp. 2–98). Beverly Hills, CA: Sage.

Ferment in the Field. (1983). [Special section]. *Journal of Communication, 33*.

Genovese, E. D. (1994). The crimes of communism: What did you know and when did you know it? *Dissent, 41*, 371–376.

Hachten, W. (1992). *The world news prism: Changing media, clashing ideologies* (3rd ed.). Ames, IA: Iowa State University Press.

Lazarsfeld, P. F. (1941). Remarks on administrative and critical research. *Studies in Philosophy and Social Science, 9*, 2–16.

Lerner, D. (1958). *The passing of traditional society: Modernizing the Middle East*. Glencoe, IL: Free Press.

Levy, M. R., & M. Gurevitch. (Eds.). (1994). *Defining media studies: Reflections on the future of the field*. New York: Oxford University Press. (Original work published 1993)

Merrill, J. C. (Ed.). (1995). *Global journalism: Survey of international communication* (3rd ed.). New York: Longman.

Negrine, R., & Papathanassopoulos, S. (1990). *The internationalization of television*. London: Pinter.

Nordenstreng, K. (1984). Bitter lessons. *Journal of Communication, 34*, 138–142.

Paisley, W. (1984). Communication in the communication sciences. In B. Dervin & M. J. Voigt (Eds.), *Progress in the communication sciences*, (Vol. 5, pp. 1–43). Norwood, NJ: Ablex.

Rogers, E. M. (1962). *Diffusion of innovations*. New York: Free Press.

Rogers, E. M. (1976). Communication and development: The passing of the dominant paradigm. In E. M. Rogers (Ed.), *Communication and development: Critical perspectives*. Beverly Hills, CA: Sage.

Rogers, E. M. (1985). The empirical and critical schools of communication research. In E. M. Rogers & F. Balle (Eds.), *The media revolution in America and Western Europe* (pp. 219–235). Norwood, NJ: Ablex.

Rostow, W. W. (1960). *The stages of economic growth*. Cambridge, UK: Cambridge University Press.

Schramm, W. (1964). *Mass media and national development: The rule of information in developing countries*. Stanford, CA: Stanford University Press.

Southerland, D. (1993a, July 17). Uncounted millions: Mass death in Mao's China. *The Washington Post*, pp. A1, A22.

Southerland, D. (1993b, July 18). Uncounted millions: Mass death in Mao's China. *The Washington Post*, pp. Al, A13.

Sreberny-Mohammadi, A., with Nordenstreng, K., Stevenson, R., & Ugboajah, F. (1985). *Foreign news in the media: International reporting in 29 countries*. Reports and Papers on Mass Communication No. 93. Paris: UNESCO.

Stevenson, R. L. (1984). Pseudo debate. *Journal of Communication, 34*, 134–138.

Stevenson, R. L. (1988). *Communication, development, and the third world: The global politics of information*. New York: Longman.

Stevenson, R. L. (1992). Defining international communication as a field. *Journalism Quarterly*, 69, 543–553.

Stevenson, R. L., & Shaw, D. L. (Eds.). (1984). *Foreign news and the new world information order.* Ames, IA: Iowa State University Press.

Tunstall, J. (1982). The media are still American: Anglo-American media in the world after the UNESCO MacBride report. In L. E. Atwood, S. J. Bullion, & S. M. Murphy (Eds.), *International perspectives on news* (pp. 133–145). Carbondale: Southern Illinois University Press.

Tunstall, J., & Palmer, M. (1991). *Media moguls.* London: Routledge.

Suggested Readings

Anokwa, K., Lin, C. A., & Salwen, M. B. (2003). *International communication: Concepts and cases.* Belmont, CA: Thomson Wadsworth.

de Beer, A. S., & Merrill, J. C. (2005). *Global journalism: Topical issues and media systems* (4th ed.). Boston: Allyn & Bacon.

Hachten, W., & Scotton, J. (2006). *The world news prism: Global information in a satellite age* (7th ed.). Malden, MA: Blackwell.

Kamalipour, Y. R., (2007). *Global communication* (2nd ed.). Belmont, CA: Thomson Wadsworth.

McQuail, D. (2005). *Global communication: Theories, stakeholders and trends* (2nd ed.). Malden, MA: Blackwell.

Stevenson, R. L. (1994). *Global communication in the 21st century.* New York: Longman.

13

VIOLENCE AND SEX IN THE MEDIA

Jennings Bryant and R. Glenn Cummins

Perhaps no area of mass communication research has greater social implications than that on how violence and sex are portrayed in the media. This chapter examines both media violence and sexually explicit media fare as they affect the viewer. The chapter begins by looking at the role of violence in the media, reasons for that role, and the effect of violent media fare on individuals and on society. We then focus on the effects of sexually explicit media. The methods employed in conducting research in media sex and violence are then explored, and a sample study is provided.

Media Violence

In the first edition of this volume, published in the late 1990s, we noted that concerns over media violence reappeared "whenever a new entertainment or communications medium that appeals to the masses appears on the scene. Strong reactions were recorded on the appearance of popular romantic and adventure novels in the 19th century and were observed again in response to the growing popularity of motion pictures in the early part of the present century" (Gunter, 1994, p. 163). With that in mind, it has certainly been no surprise to witness the simultaneous growth of video games as a form of popular entertainment along with the growth of critics assailing video games as a causal force in numerous school shootings and other violent crimes (cf., Weber, Ritterfeld, & Kostygina, 2006). As one critic lamented soon after the fatal school shootings at Columbine High School, "Ours is a culture that glorifies violence, profits from it, sells it with the most advanced technology known to mankind. Violence bounces off satellites in outer space and beams into every American home, every hour of every day, every month of every year" (Ellis, 1999, p. A26). As such, studies investigating the effects of televised violence have continued to dominate the media effects research agenda.

What is Violence?

Perhaps the first question that should be addressed is, "What is violence?" Common definitions of *violence* per se are:

> any overt depiction of a credible threat of physical force or the actual use of such force intended to physically harm an animate being or group of beings. Violence also includes certain depictions of physically harmful consequences against an animate being or group that occurs as a result of unseen violent means. (Wilson et al., 1997, p. 53)

intentional physical harm to another individual. Excluded from this definition are accidental injury, so-called "psychological" violence, and vandalism of property. (Harris, 1994, p. 186)

the overt expression of physical force (with or without a weapon, against self or other) compelling action against one's will on pain of being hurt and/or killed or threatened to be so victimized as part of the plot. (Gerbner, Gross, Morgan, & Signorielli, 1980, p. 11)

Obviously *media violence* is this kind of behavior depicted or presented in or on media.

Why Do Media Feature Violence?

Media programming includes a great deal of violence for several reasons. Violence embodies conflict, and conflict is the heart and soul of drama. Moreover, violence is a quick and easy way to solve problems; it is a convenient short-cut to more complex forms of conflict resolution. However, by far the most compelling reason for including violence is that producers, directors, writers, and editors believe that many audience members will not choose to watch, listen to, or read the media messages they offer if these messages do not contain fist fights, shootings, car crashes, and assorted other mayhem. Time after time, media message creators and providers rationalize heavy doses of gratuitous violence by saying, "we're only giving people what they want," or "they'll go elsewhere for entertainment if we don't stick in some violence" (e.g., Easton, 1993).

Despite numerous claims for the appeal of violence, empirical evidence to support such claims is quite sparse. In one direct empirical test of this claim, Sparks, Sherry, and Lubsen (2005) exposed research participants to two versions of a theatrically released film—one containing scenes of violence or another with those scenes removed. Their results found that deleting depictions of violence from the film failed to diminish viewers' enjoyment of the movie. Those results substantiated past research suggesting that viewers either exhibit no preferences or slight preferences for violent content when choosing media fare (e.g., Diener & DeFour, 1978; Diener & Woody, 1981; Wober, 1997). On the other hand, Bryant and Musburger (1989) reported that child viewers rated a violent version of an animated television program significantly higher in enjoyment than humorous, action-packed, or control versions of the same program. Hoffner and Levine (2007) also provided meta-analytic evidence demonstrating the appeal of violence, but they added that "violence is enjoyed more by aggressively inclined individuals" (p. 236). Taken together, these investigations provide some limited evidence to substantiate the creative community's claims that the public likes media violence. But, in general, the appeal of violence does not seem to be nearly as strong as writers, producers, and editors would have us believe.

What Theories Help Explain the Effects of Media Violence?

To answer this question thoroughly, several categories of effects of media violence on individuals should be considered: behavioral, cognitive, and emotional.

Behavioral Theories

Potential behavioral effects of media violence include: catharsis, disinhibition, imitation, and desensitization. *Catharsis* holds that vicariously participating in others' fictionalized hostility or aggression enables drama watchers, readers, or listeners to be purged of their anger and hostility and thereby become less aggressive. Although much of the general public and the media creative community believe strongly in the therapeutic benefits of catharsis, scientific evidence tends not to support this popular truism (e.g., Feshback, 1955, 1961; cf., Wells, 1973). Moreover, the few studies that would appear to support cathartic effects of media violence have been severely criticized on technical grounds (Berkowitz, 1993).

The idea of *disinhibition* is that watching, reading, or listening to media violence may serve to undermine learned social sanctions against using violence that usually inhibit aggressive behavior. This reduced inhibition from watching media violence enables people to legitimize using violence in real life, so they become more aggressive. At least a dozen experimental investigations have explored potential disinhibition effects of media violence, and all provided some support for this hypothesis (e.g., Berkowitz, 1964, 1965; Donnerstein, 1980; Malamuth, 1984). In general, disinhibition effects have been more pronounced when viewers of violence were already angry while they viewed or read violent media fare (Berkowitz, 1974).

Discussions of *imitation* of media violence typically are explained in terms of social learning or social cognitive theory, which proposes that humans "have evolved an advanced capacity for observational learning that enables them to expand their knowledge and skills rapidly through information conveyed by a rich variety of models" (Bandura, 2002, p. 126). Bandura notes that because the electronic media play such a large role in many young people's lives, much of their observational learning is based on models witnessed via the mass media. Moreover, because the fictional characters of novels, television, motion pictures, and video games so often use violence to solve their problems, young viewers may learn that violent behavior is a useful and appropriate way of handling tough situations. A great number of investigations offered support for imitation effects.

In its most basic form, social learning theory explains how observers match the performances of models. For social learning of media violence to occur, four things must happen: (1) The violent behavior of the actor must be seen, read, or listened to (attentional process); (2) cognitive representations of the violent behavior must be retained (retention processes); (3) the learner must have the potential to replicate the action (production processes); and (4) the learner must have sufficient desire or will to perform the violent behavior that was witnessed (motivational processes; Bandura, 1979). The best-known early empirical examination of the modeling of violence were Bandura's Bobo doll studies (e.g., Bandura, 1965; Bandura, Ross, & Ross, 1963; Bandura & Walters, 1963). In a typical Bobo doll study, young children watched someone (either live or on film) behave aggressively toward a large inflatable doll designed to serve as a punching bag. The children were later placed in a playroom with a Bobo doll, and their behavior was observed. It was found that children frequently imitated violent behaviors of this type, whether the aggressive model was live or on film.

One additional response to depictions of media violence is a *desensitization* effect. The desensitization hypothesis argues that repeated exposure to media violence causes a reduction in emotional responsiveness (i.e., disinhibition) to violence in fiction, news, and reality fare, which, in turn, leads to an increased acceptance of violence in real life. This notion has been widely touted to explain, for example, why onlookers failed to come to the aid of mugging victims—not even making an anonymous phone call to the police from the privacy of their homes. Few studies have sought to assess disinhibition effects directly. The limited research evidence available supports disinhibition effects (Gunter, 1994).

Cognitive Theories

The study of media violence from a cognitive effects perspective refers to changes in people's beliefs, values, and attitudes that result from consuming violent media fare. In modern society, media increasingly provide vital information about life that may corroborate, contradict, or supplement learning that takes place from first-hand experience or information provided second-hand through interpersonal sources, including teachers. One area in which media appear to play an important role is in the public's perceptions about crime, especially violent crime. One theoretical perspective on media effects, *cultivation* was utilized extensively to examine cognitive effects of heavy viewing of television's crime-laden action drama. Gerbner and associates (e.g., Gerbner, Gross, Morgan, Signorielli, & Shanahan, 2002) provided evidence that heavy exposure to television drama's overly violent world cultivates exaggerated perceptions of violence in viewers' own social reality.

Priming is another example of cognitive effects of television violence. " [Priming] essentially holds that when people witness, read, or hear of an event via the mass media, ideas having a similar meaning are activated in them for a short time afterwards, and…these thoughts in turn can activate other semantically related ideas and action tendencies" (Jo & Berkowitz, 1994, p. 45). Priming has been used to explain a number of cognitive effects from witnessing violence in the mass media, including the priming of aggressive thoughts that can cause alterations in the way people interpret the actions of others, changes in beliefs about the justification of the aggressive behaviors of others, and reductions in inhibitions about participating in aggressive behavior.

One additional area of study regarding the effects of the mass media on viewers' beliefs and perceptions is the so-called *third-person effect*. The third-person hypothesis holds that "individuals will perceive media messages to have greater effects on other people than on themselves" (Salwen & Dupagne, 1999, p. 523). Although the hypothesis has been tested in a variety of contexts, much of the research in this area has focused on viewers' support for efforts to restrict media content in a variety of channels including television and violent video games (e.g.,; Hoffner et al., 2001; Hoffner & Buchanan, 2002; Rohas, Shah, & Faber, 1996).

Emotional Theories

Not all emotional effects of media violence are necessarily negative; in fact, many short-term emotional effects are essential to the enjoyment of drama, and their absence frequently leaves our entertainment experience flat. To make entertainment maximally enjoyable, we must laugh with the comic, suffer anxiety as the villain stalks the victim, experience elevated excitation at the suspense peak of the action drama, and "root, root, root for the home team" on the sportscast (e.g., Raney, 2003, 2006). All of these emotional effects are part of what we seek from entertainment, and many of them are precipitated by violence.

Because autonomic arousal in response to media depictions is largely nonspecific to particular emotions, however, it may have some unwanted behavioral consequences. *Excitation transfer theory* projects that, because of the comparatively slow decay of autonomic arousal (owing to humeral processes involved) and the individual's capacity to recognize stimulus changes and to select an appropriate response quasi-instantaneously (owing to speedy neural transmission), residues of excitation from a preceding affective reaction will combine with excitation produced by subsequent affective stimulation and thereby cause an overly intense affective reaction to the subsequent stimulus (Zillmann, 1991, p. 116).

It should be noted that the "residues of excitation" do not have to come from arousal to media violence (they can come from physical exertion, sexual arousal, feelings of annoyance, or a variety of other arousing sources), nor does excitation favor hostile, aggressive, or violent reactions (if prosocial responses are motivated, these responses are likely to be energized). However, if aggressive behavior has been instigated in the viewers and aggressive dispositions exist, residual arousal from media violence has been found to intensify motivated asocial feelings and destructive actions (e.g., Zillmann, 1971; cf. Zillmann, 1991).

A robust line of research conducted by Cantor (2002) and associates has explored an additional emotional byproduct of media violence: *fright reactions* in children. This program of research has examined many aspects of children's fright reactions, including what type of media violence frightens children, developmental differences in fright reactions, and strategies for preventing or reducing unwanted fear reactions. Their emphasis has been on *"immediate emotional response[s]* [italics added] that [are] typically of relatively short duration, but that may endure, on occasion, for several hours or days, or even longer" (Cantor, 2002, p. 288). This research takes on added importance because of recent trends in media programming for children that incorporate scary and horrific depictions, and because of the increased access of children to what has traditionally been considered programming for adults. Several interesting findings have been advanced by this research tradition, especially with regard to developmental differences in children's fear:

> pre-school children…are more likely to be frightened by something that looks scary but is actually harmless than by something that looks attractive but is actually harmful; for older elementary school children…appearance carries much less weight, relative to the behavior or destructive potential of a character, animal, or object. (Cantor, 2002, pp. 296)

> as children mature, they become more responsive to realistic, and less responsive to fantastic dangers depicted in the media. (Cantor, 2002, p. 297)

> as children mature, they become frightened by media depictions involving increasingly abstract concepts. (Cantor, 2002, p. 298)

We have briefly reviewed some of the behavioral, cognitive, and emotional effects of media violence. We would be remiss, however, if we failed to note that most of the impact of media violence is a product of cognitive, emotional, and behavioral elements combined. This very complexity is one circumstance that makes the effects of media violence so difficult to determine.

What Are the Effects of Media Violence?

Perhaps the most reliable answer to this critical question comes from the results of macroanalyses of research on the effects of media violence, including (1) syntheses of longitudinal investigations of the effects of media violence, and (2) meta-analyses, which offer a method for integrating the results of different studies on the same topic so as to get a better understanding of the "big picture." Regarding the studies examining cumulative effects, Huesmann and Miller (1994) concluded: "The data available from longitudinal studies provide additional support for the hypothesis that television violence viewing leads to the development of aggressive behavior" (p. 181).

Andison (1977) conducted a meta-analysis of 31 laboratory experiments in media violence and concluded that, overall, viewing violence led to greater aggression than viewing control materials. Much later, Wood, Wong, and Chachere (1991) conducted a meta-analysis of 28 separate experiments in which the participants were free to display "natural aggression." The authors noted that media violence did tend to heighten the likelihood of aggressive behavior and added that "the mean effect of exposure to violent media on unconstrained aggression is in the small to moderate range, typical of social psychological predictors" (p. 379). These results were later reaffirmed in subsequent meta-analysis (Christensen & Wood, 2007). Comstock and Paik (1991; Paik & Comstock, 1994) macroanalyzed more than 185 different media violence investigations and concluded that the association between exposure to television violence and aggression is quite robust: "The data of the past decade and a half strengthens [sic] rather than weakens [sic] the case that television violence increases aggressive and anti-social behavior" (p. 54).

Finally, Centerwall (1989, 1992) conducted epidemiological and population intervention studies of television violence, comparing homicide rates over a 30-year period (1945–1975) in the United States, Canada, and South Africa. The intervention on homicide rates was television set ownership. The results of this investigation were instrumental in the American Academy of Pediatrics' development of a policy statement urging parents to restrict their children's use of television to no more than two hours per day and to omit violent fare from their children's TV diet. Centerwall (1992) has not been timid in his condemnation of television violence. For example, his findings and recommendations published in *The Journal of the American Medical Association* categorically stated:

> the epidemiological evidence indicates that if, hypothetically, television technology had never been developed, there would be 10,000 fewer homicides each year in the United States, 70,000 fewer rapes, and 700,000 fewer injurious assaults. (p. 3059)

And elsewhere:

> Children's exposure to television and television violence should become part of the public health agenda, along with safety seats, bicycle helmets, immunizations and good nutrition. (p. 3063)

As stated earlier, scholars have begun to devote considerable attention in recent years to the effects of violent video game content. Anderson and Bushman's (2001) meta-analysis of 35 studies utilizing more than 4,200 research participants supported the argument that exposure to video game violence is associated with increased aggression. In his update of that meta-analysis, Anderson (2004) issued the damning conclusion: "exposure to violent video games is significantly linked to increases in aggressive behaviour, aggressive cognition, aggressive affect, and cardiovascular arousal, and to decreases in helping behaviour" (p. 113). However, Sherry's (2001, 2007) meta-analytic examination of 25 empirical studies yielded a more tentative conclusion regarding the effects of violent video game play. His results suggest, "There is a small, but significant, overall effect of video game play on aggression, but the effect is smaller than the effect of violent television on aggression" (2007, p. 250). The importance of developing further insights into the effects of video games on aggression will likely lead to continued empirical examination of their effects as they continue to grow in popularity.

Sexually Explicit Media Fare

Whereas the issue of media violence has received more *systematic research* than any other area of media effects inquiry, Kinsey, Pomeroy, and Martin (1948) noted that human sexuality has received more *thought, discussion, and treatment* than any other aspect of human behavior. Additionally, a variety of neuroendocrine and physiological connections are known to exist between sexual desire, arousal, and behavior, on the one hand, and aggressive actions, on the other (Zillmann, 1984). Sexual arousal is capable of enhancing aggression and, likewise, aggression-linked arousal is capable of intensifying sexual experience. This connection between sex and aggression gives added significance to the analysis of the effects of sexual material in the media.

It is little wonder then that numerous scholars have examined the effects of sexually explicit materials on readers, listeners, viewers, and users. It should be noted at the outset that sexually explicit communication is nothing new: Statuary featuring enlarged sexual organs dates back to 30,000 BC; human sexual intercourse was depicted in sandstone engravings from 7,000 BC; and explicit scenes of hetero- and homosexual activity were common in ancient Greece. So the explosion of XXX websites, online message boards, adult DVD's, on-demand adult videos, and specialized magazines for those with exotic sexual fetishes are but modern adaptations of a centuries-old tradition of sexually explicit material.

Then what is all the fuss about? Other than violations of moral sensibilities, which undoubtedly have accompanied the presentation of sexual material in every generation, the modern-day uproar about sexual content in media has to do with easy access: "The principal reason for the apparent revival of concerns about unregulated pornography is simply the new technology" (Zillmann & Bryant, 1989, p. xii). This concern has not waned. If anything, the increasingly ubiquitous reach of all manner of sexually explicit content via the World Wide Web has only intensified public concerns over the effects of sexually explicit content. Sexually explicit fare has gone public. It has become an affordable and readily available form of entertainment for all—children and adults alike. This has precipitated a revitalized interest in the impact of sexually explicit media content (e.g., Gunter, 2001).

Whenever sex in media is discussed, definitions are almost mandatory. Terms such as *sexually explicit, erotic,* and *pornographic* have very different meanings for different people. In the 1986 *Final Report of the Surgeon General's Commission on Pornography,* five classes of pornographic materials were identified:

1. Sexually violent materials portray rape and other instances of physical harm to persons in a sexual context.
2. Nonviolent materials depicting degradation, domination, subordination, or humiliation constitute the largest class of commercially available materials. These generally portray women as "masochistic, subservient, and overresponsive to the male interest."
3. Nonviolent and nondegrading materials typically depict a couple having vaginal or oral intercourse with no indication of violence or coercion.
4. Nudity shows the naked human body with no obvious sexual behavior or intent.
5. Child pornography involves minors and, though illegal to produce in the United States, still circulates widely through foreign magazines and personal distribution. (Harris, 1994, p. 248)

What Are the Effects of Viewing Sexually Explicit Materials?

The first effect is neither anti- or prosocial per se—it is sexual arousal. Viewing, reading, or listening to sexually explicit material causes elevated arousal in most people, whether the arousal is measured in self-reports, physiologically, or in direct genital measures, such as penile tumescence or vaginal engorgement. Contrary to what might be expected, the level of arousal is not accurately predicted by the degree of explicitness of the sexual materials. In fact, there are major individual differences in what arouses people sexually (e.g., Bancroft & Mathews, 1971).

Viewing or reading certain types of sexual materials has also been associated with cognitive effects—changes in perceptions, attitudes, and values, for example. One dimension of this is the cognitive component of disinhibition; that is, people's attitudes toward sex become less restricted after prolonged exposure to sexual fare. Evidence exists for other changes in attitudes and values after exposure to sexually explicit media as well. For example, prolonged exposure to sexually explicit messages was found to produce changes in sexual callousness, rape proclivity, moral values, family values, perception of normalcy in sexual behavior, attitudes toward censorship, general attitudes toward women, and many other cognitive effects (e.g., Zillmann, Bryant, & Huston, 1994).

With the advent of the World Wide Web, scholars have also begun to assess the cognitive impact of sexually explicit content consumed online. A number of studies have examined potential attitudinal effects of exposure to sexually explicit content on the Internet, including increased acceptance of sexual permissiveness and increased recreational attitudes about sex (Lo & Wei, 2005; Peter & Valkenburg, 2006a). In addition, scholars have found evidence supporting the third-person hypothesis concerning the effects of online sexual content (Byoungkwan & Tamborini, 2005; Lo & Ran, 2002; Lo & Wei, 2002).

A wide range of behavioral effects of using sexually explicit materials has been examined, including imitation, disinhibition, and criminal sexual behavior. In general, the evidence for imitation is anecdotal, because scientists are not willing—and often not permitted by university research regulations—to risk showing immature children sexually explicit materials to see if they can and will model the behavior they see. The *Final Report* and several other sources present a number of such anecdotes, ranging from an accidental suicide by hanging while reading and apparently imitating a "recipe" for autoerotic asphyxiation in *Hustler*, to reports of the forced bondage, rape, murder, and mutilation of an 8-year-old girl after the perpetrators read about and viewed photographs of bondage in *Penthouse*. Just how widespread such instances are has yet to be evaluated systematically (Harris, 1994).

As is the case with violence, disinhibition of sexual behavior is an issue with sexually explicit materials. This is especially critical because so many of the behaviors depicted in such materials are contrary to the prevalent norms about sexual behavior. Consider the case of rape. There is evidence that witnessing the brutal coercion of women into sexual intercourse enhanced college men's reporting that they might commit a rape if they were sure they would not get caught (Check & Guloien, 1989).

One of the behavioral effects areas where definitive research is likely never to be conducted involves sex crimes. Ethical and procedural constraints prohibit experimental research in this area. Scientists thus have resorted to procedures such as interviewing and developing clinical case studies of convicted sex criminals to determine the role of sexual materials in the etiology of such crimes. One particularly telling meta-analysis of such research revealed some interesting connections between pornography consumption and criminal offenders. Allen, D'Alessio, and Emmers-Sommer (1999) examined 45 quantitative studies that utilized sexual offenders as research participants. Dependent measures examined in the various studies included the overall use of sexually explicit content, age of first exposure, resultant physiological arousal, and the use of such content prior to some form of sexual behavior. Their results suggested, "simple frequency of use of sexual material and age at first exposure do not differentiate sexual criminal consumers from noncriminal consumers of sexual material" (p. 156). However, they add that "sexual material functions differently...for sexual offenders compared with nonoffenders" (p. 157). In short, their data suggest that sexual offenders were more likely to use such content prior to engaging in sexual behavior, and that arousal in response to such content was greater when the sexual content depicted matched the crime committed.

Other studies have explored archival evidence to determine the degree of association or correlation between changes in the availability of sexually explicit materials in a society and court records of crimes such as rape, exhibitionism, and child molestation. These results are more confusing than informative, and they may have generated more heat than light. For example, in Denmark and Japan, increases in the availability of sexually explicit materials were associated with decreases in the reporting of sex crimes. In Australia, the United States, and many other Western nations, the opposite pattern of association was found (*Final Report of the Surgeon General's Commission on Pornography*, 1986). At present, no firm conclusion can be drawn from this evidence. It would appear that cultural values, attitudes toward sex in a society, individual variables such as aggressiveness, and many other conditions operate in concert in mediating the effects of sexual materials on sex crimes.

A large body of research has presented evidence for the effects of the consumption of sexual materials on aggression. Many of the complex arguments associated with this issue are beyond the scope of this chapter. Suffice it to report that several studies have demonstrated that prolonged use of nonviolent sexual materials is capable of facilitating aggression (e.g., Baron, 1979; cf., Zillmann, Bryant, Comisky, & Medoff, 1981). Other studies have yielded evidence that was interpreted as supporting the thesis that aggression increases only when material featuring sexual violence (e.g., rape scenes, or slasher films) is consumed (e.g., Linz, Donnerstein, & Adams, 1989; Linz, Donnerstein, & Penrod, 1984). Other research seems to suggest that the effects on aggression are more pronounced for consumption of sexual violence but exist to a lesser extent for nonviolent, sexually explicit fare (e.g., *Final Report of the Surgeon General's Commission on Pornography*, 1986; Lyons, Anderson, & Larson, 1994; Mundorf, D'Alessio, Allen, & Emmers-Sommer, 2007). Still other scholars argue that the keys to explaining these apparently conflicting findings are whether women or men depicted in the films, books, magazines, or videos are demeaned or dehumanized, whether the viewer becomes disgusted or sexually excited by what he or she sees or reads, and many other elements associated with media message features and individual differences in users (e.g., Malamuth, Check, & Briere, 1986; Sapolsky & Zillman, 1981; White, 1979). How and if these issues will ever be resolved satisfactorily remains unclear. In the interim, during which time we hope that clarifying research will be conducted, evidence from (1) a meta-analysis of 81 studies on the effects on aggression and other behavioral effects of viewing sexually explicit materials, and (2) a meta-analysis of 24 articles examining the effects of exposure to pornography on acceptance of rape myths urges user caution: *Caveat emptor*—using sexually explicit materials may be harmful to your psychological well-being and to that of others in society (Allen, Emmers, Gebhardt, & Giery, 1995; Lyons et al., 1994; Mundorf et al., 2007).

Methods Used In Media Violence and Sex Research

Scholars concerned with the effects of media sex and violence have asked such a range of research questions that it has been necessary to exploit the full repertoire of extant communication research methodologies to provide adequate answers. In fact, research into the effects of media sex and violence has produced several classic communication studies.

Content Analyses

The most comprehensive systematic analysis of violence on television has been conducted by Gerbner and his associates (e.g., Gerbner et al., 2002). Since 1967, their Cultural Indicators project has performed a number of influential content analyses of media violence (among other variables of interest to their Cultural Indicators research program). Their "message system" analysis studies have tracked the nature and functions of television violence for portions of four decades, thereby providing invaluable longitudinal indicators of various aspects of the evolution of television violence. More recently, the *National Television Violence Study* (Wilson et al., 1997) provided a deeper understanding of the context of portrayals of violence by examining a variety of factors surrounding the violence, such as the nature of the perpetrator, consequences of the violence, and the realism of the portrayal. No comparable longitudinal content analytic research tradition has been established for media sex; however, a review of content trends in media sex by Greenberg (1994) identified a dozen systematic content analyses of sex in media. Moreover, scholars have utilized content analysis in recent examinations of both video game violence (e.g., Lachlan, Smith, & Tamborini, 2005) and sexually explicit content distributed via the World Wide Web (e.g., Gossett & Byrne, 2002).

Laboratory Experiments

If research into the effect of media violence would be assigned an archetype methodology, it would be the laboratory experiment. According to Geen (1994), there have been a vast number of laboratory experiments on the effects of televised violence on aggression. The most generally accepted conclusion from these investigations is that "observation of violence is often followed by increases in both physical and verbal aggression. This effect is most likely to occur when the viewer has been provoked in some way and is therefore relatively likely to aggress" (p. 152). Numerous designs and a wide range of experimental materials have been employed by researchers in investigating the effects of media violence. Although the designs and materials have varied dramatically, most have included violent media message versus nonviolent media message treatment conditions.

Similarly, Lyons et al. (1994) included 81 experiments in their meta-analysis of the effects of sexually explicit fare; the majority of these studies were laboratory experiments. They concluded: "Although there are a number of methodological shortcomings in this literature, most are likely to lead to an underestimation of the causal effects of exposure to pornography. Despite this, the vast majority of studies demonstrates consistent short-term effects" (p. 305). Obviously lab studies have been central to our understanding of the effects of pornography as well as of media violence.

Whenever laboratory experiments are employed to help us better understand human communication behavior, criticisms are apt to be voiced. These criticisms include claims that laboratory environments are (1) artificial, resulting in weak ecological validity; (2) that the sort of dependent measures that can be employed in the lab are pale analogs of real-world antisocial manifestations of sex and violence (e.g., murder, rape); (3) that most research participants in laboratory research tend to be college freshmen and sophomores selected by convenience sampling; and (4) that demand characteristics and experimenter expectations create invalid results; and the like. In truth, all of these criticisms are valid in some instances and do create undue limitations for some laboratory research. Nonetheless, a number of noteworthy lab studies have investigated the effects of media sex and violence, and when issues of media cause and effect are concerned, the alternatives typically are less credible, especially to policymakers. That is why laboratory experiments have proven to be so valuable in these research arenas.

Psychophysiological Studies

Technological developments in recent years have resulted in the increased use of an assortment of psychophysiological research methods in examining the effects of media sex and violence. For example, recent experimental studies exploring the effects of violent video games have examined a number of cardiovascular responses including heart rate and blood pressure (Ballard, Hamby, Panee, & Nivens, 2006; Panee & Ballard, 2002). Studies have also utilized functional Magnetic Resonance Imaging (fMRI) to visualize brain activity in response to violent media content (Murray et al., 2006; Weber, Ritterfeld, & Mathiak, 2006). Scholars have likewise gauged viewer arousal in response to both violent and sexual media content via skin conductance measurements (e.g., Reeves, Lang, Kim, & Tatar, 2001). The burgeoning of these methods is particularly noteworthy because it gives scholars a way of bypassing traditional self-report measures in favor of direct measures of physiological response. Moreover, it introduces an increased level of sophistication and precision as research examining the effects of media sex and violence matures.

Field Experiments

In recent years, researchers have attempted to employ the rigors of experimental methodology while leaving the confines of the laboratory to conduct "field experiments." Regarding media violence: "these studies yielded consistent findings of a positive relationship between observation of televised violence and aggression" (Geen, 1994, p. 152). Similar findings of antisocial influences have been found from field experiments testing the effects of pornography (e.g., Zillmann & Bryant, 1989).

Longitudinal Studies

With the growing realization that many media effects occur only after cumulative exposure to media messages, frequently over extended periods of time, longitudinal studies into the effects of media sex and violence have been conducted. In the area of television violence, programmatic research spanning a 15-year period by Eron, Huesmann, and their associates (e.g., Eron, Walder, & Lefkowitz, 1971; Huesmann & Eron, 1986; Huesmann, Moise-Titus, Podolski, & Eron, 2003; Huesmann & Taylor, 2006; Lefkowitz, Eron, Walder, & Huesmann, 1977) revealed "a positive relationship between childhood television viewing and subsequent aggressiveness" (Geen, 1994, p. 153). Correspondingly, regarding prolonged consumption of pornography, longitudinal research by Zillmann and Bryant (e.g., 1982, 1986, 1988a, 1988b), Check (1985), Linz (1985), Weaver (1987), and others revealed social and psychological harm from exposure to pornography.

Surveys

Because surveys often do not have the power to demonstrate the causal relationships afforded by true experiments, scientific surveys have not played as major a role in examining the effects of media sex and violence as they have in, say, attitude research. Nonetheless, surveys have been utilized productively in these areas. For example, Gerbner's cultivation analysis research has consistently used national surveys to determine public perceptions, anxiety, fear, and the like (e.g., Gerbner et al., 2002). Or, to cite just one example of such methodology applied to pornography research, an exemplary survey reported by the 1970 Presidential Commission on Obscenity and Pornography and conducted by Davis and Braught (1970) concluded, "One finds exposure to pornography is the strongest predictor of sexual deviance among the early age of exposure subjects" (p. 205). Scholars have likewise found survey research useful in examining exposure to sexually explicit content online (e.g., Peter & Valkenburg, 2006b).

Meta-Analyses

The use of meta-analysis in communication research has begun to flourish in the literature (e.g., Preiss, Gayle, Burrell, Allen, & Bryant, 2007). Numerous meta-analytic examinations of both media violence and sex have helped provide a clearer picture of the size and nature of the effects of such content, as well as a host of mediating variables in the process. In fact, in prior sections of this chapter entitled "What Are the Effects of Media Violence?" and "What Are the Effects of Viewing Sexually Explicit Materials?" meta-analyses were utilized to help define "the bottom line." The burgeoning of this method serves as evidence demonstrating a new level of maturity in media effects research, and no doubt scholars will continue to mine extant data in the research literature to generate more refined profiles of the effects of media content.

Sample Study

We said that laboratory experiments are the archetype of investigations into the effects of explicitly sexual and explicitly violent media fare; therefore, our sample study should be a lab experiment. Let's be ambitious and tackle a complex media effects question: Which facilitates interpersonal aggression most dramatically: (1) explicitly sexual but nonviolent media fare; (2) explicitly violent but nonsexual media content; or (3) explicitly sexual *and* explicitly violent media programming?

If you review the earlier sections of this chapter, you will find that both sex and violence have been found to facilitate aggression. If we have reason to believe that the effects on aggressive behavior of viewing explicit sex and explicit violence are additive, we would hypothesize the consuming media presentations featuring both sex and violence would produce the most intense levels of interpersonal aggression.

If we choose to test this admittedly oversimplified hypothesis, we would be wise to include a control communication condition that features neither sexual nor violent content. This inclusion yields a communication condition independent variable with four treatment levels (sex, violence, sex plus violence, no sex/no violence control).

Based on prior research, we also anticipate that previously provoked research participants will be more likely to engage in aggressive behavior than their unprovoked peers, so we decide to include a second independent variable of motivation to aggress (provoked, unprovoked) and test a second hypothesis, that provoked individuals will be more aggressive than unprovoked ones.

The most efficient design we can use in our laboratory experiment is a 4 (treatment level) × 2 (motivation to aggress) factorial design. This design features four levels of the communication condition and two of motivation to aggress.

Our dependent measure of aggression is the level of intensity of noxious noise research participants choose to deliver to their opponent's ear (actually a confederate's ear) in the course of playing an electronic battleship game. In this game, the confederate's performance is a constant.

One of the keys to success in this investigation is the quality of the experimental materials employed for the communication variable. Because we are communication researchers who have unlimited access to the latest in digital multimedia production and editing facilities (dreaming is cheap!), we have created a 30-minute dramatic video presentation that varies only in a three-minute provocation segment. In the explicit violent version, the villain brutally batters a female hero-protagonist; in the explicit sex version, he seduces her to achieve his dastardly ends; in the explicit sex plus violence version, a brutal rape is employed to achieve the same ends; and in the control condition, the villain uses his brain and rhetorical prowess to momentarily outwit the hero. After the provocation sequence has ended, the hero regains control and brings the villain to justice.

At the end of the video, the research participant—who has either been provoked or unprovoked prior to viewing, according to the assigned motivation-to-aggress condition—participates in the battleship game. On six occasions during the game, the opponent misses the battleship by a prescribed distance. The cumulative intensity of noxious noise the research participant delivers as feedback to the opponent is the dependent measure of aggression.

The data will be analyzed by analysis of variance utilizing packaged statistical programs (e.g., SPSS, SAS). If research participants who see the televised rape (sex plus violence) use a significantly higher level of noxious noise than research participants in the other communication conditions, the first hypothesis will be supported. If those research participants who are provoked prior to viewing utilize higher levels of noxious noise than the unprovoked research participants, the second hypothesis will be supported. We will also pay considerable attention to potential interactions between communication condition and motivation to aggress, but such considerations are beyond the scope of the present investigation.

Summary

This chapter examined the place of violence and sex in modern media presentations. It also considered the unintended social and psychological consequences these sensational elements can have. For both sex and violence, undesirable effects can occur for media consumers under some conditions. Some of the research methods that are typically utilized to examine the uses and effects of sex and violence and media were reviewed; and a sample hypothetical study that could be used to investigate the effects of sex and violence in media was presented. This brief treatment should lead you to want to learn more about this important area of media effects inquiry.

References

Allen, M., D'Allesio, D., & Emmers-Sommer, T. M. (1999). Reactions of criminal sexual offenders to pornography: A meta-analytic summary. In M. Roloff (Ed.), *Communication yearbook* (Vol. 22, pp. 139–169). Mahwah, NJ: Erlbaum.

Allen, M., Emmers, T., Gebhardt, L., & Giery, M. A. (1995). Exposure to pornography and acceptance of rape myths. *Journal of Communication, 45,* 5–26.

Anderson, C. A. (2004). An update on the effects of playing violent video games. *Journal of Adolescence, 27,* 113–122.

Anderson, C. A., & Bushman, B. J. (2001). Effects of violent video games on aggressive behavior, aggressive cognition, aggressive affect, physiological arousal, and prosocial behavior: A meta-analytic review of the scientific literature. *Psychological Science, 12,* 353–359.

Andison, F. (1977). TV violence and viewer aggression: A cumulation of study results, 1956–1976. *Public Opinion Quarterly, 41,* 314–331.

Ballard, M. E., Hamby, R. H., Panee, C. D., & Nivens, E. E. (2006). Repeated exposure to video game play results in decreased blood pressure responding. *Media Psychology, 8,* 323–341.

Bancroft, L., & Mathews, A. (1971). Autonomic correlates of penile erection. *Journal of Psychosomatic Research, 15,* 159–167.

Bandura, A. (1965). Influence of models' reinforcement contingencies on the acquisition of imitative responses. *Journal of Personality and Social Psychology, 1,* 585–595.

Bandura, A. (1979). Psychological mechanisms of aggression. In M. von Cranach, K. Foppa, W. Lepeies, & D. Ploog (Eds.), *Human ethology: Claims and limits of a new discipline* (pp. 316–379). Cambridge, UK: Cambridge University Press.

Bandura, A. (2002). Social cognitive theory of mass communication. In J. Bryant & D. Zillmann (Eds.), *Media effects: Advances in theory and research* (2nd ed., pp. 121–153). Mahwah, NJ: Erlbaum.

Bandura, A., Ross, D., & Ross, S. A. (1963). Imitation of film-mediated aggressive models. *Journal of Abnormal and Social Psychology, 66,* 3–11.

Bandura, A., & Walters, R. H. (1963). *Social learning and personality development.* New York: Holt, Rinehart & Winston.

Baron, R. A. (1979). Heightened sexual arousal and physical aggression. *Journal of Research in Personality, 13,* 91–102.

Berkowitz, L. (1964). The effects of observing violence. *Scientific American, 210,* 35–41.

Berkowitz, L. (1965). Some aspects of observed aggression. *Journal of Personality and Social Psychology, 2,* 359–369.

Berkowitz, L. (1974). Some determinants of impulsive aggression: Role of mediated associations with reinforcements for aggression. *Psychological Review, 81,* 165–176.

Berkowitz, L. (1993). *Aggression: Its causes, consequences, and control.* Philadelphia: Temple University Press.

Bryant, J., & Musburger, R. (1989, April). *Children's enjoyment of action, violence, and humor in animated television programs.* Paper presented at the Annual Convention of the Broadcast Education Association, Las Vegas, NV.

Byoungkwan, L., & Tamborini, R. (2005). Third-person effect and internet pornography: The influence of collectivism and internet self-efficacy. *Journal of Communication, 55,* 292–310.

Cantor, J. R. (2002). Fright reactions to mass media. In J. Bryant & D. Zillmann (Eds.), *Media effects: Advances in theory and research* (2nd ed., pp. 287–306). Mahwah, NJ: Erlbaum.

Centerwall, B. S. (1989). Exposure to television as a cause of violence. In G. A. Comstock (Ed.), *Public communication and behavior* (Vol. 2, pp. 1–53). Orlando, FL: Academic Press.

Centerwall, B. S. (1992). Television and violence: The scale of the problem and where to go from here. *Journal of the American Medical Association, 267,* 3059–3063.

Check, J. V. P. (1985). *The effects of violent and nonviolent pornography.* Ottawa: Department of Justice for Canada.

Check, J. V. P., & Guloien, T. H. (1989). Reported proclivity for coercive sex following repeated exposure to sexually violent pornography, nonviolent dehumanizing pornography, and erotica. In D. Zillmann & J. Bryant (Eds.), *Pornography: Research advances and policy considerations* (pp. 159–184). Hillsdale, NJ: Erlbaum.

Christensen, P. N., & Wood, W. (2007). Effects of media violence on viewers' aggression in unconstrained social interactions. In R. W. Preiss, B. M. Gayle, N. Burrell, M. Allen, & J. Bryant (Eds.), *Mass media effects research: Advances through meta-analysis* (pp. 145–168). Mahwah, NJ: Erlbaum.

Comstock, G. A., & Paik, H. (1991). The effects of television violence on aggressive behavior: A meta-analysis. In A. J. Reiss & J. A. Roth (Eds.), *A preliminary report to the National Research Council on the understanding and control of violent behavior* (pp. 41–54). Washington, D.C.: National Research Council.

Davis, K. E., & Braught, G. N. (1970). Exposure to pornography, character, and sexual deviance: A retrospective survey. *Technical report of the Commission on Obscenity and Pornography* (Vol. 7, pp. 173–244). Washington, D.C.: U.S. Government Printing Office.

Diener, E., & DeFour, D. (1978). Does television violence enhance program popularity? *Journal of Research in Social Psychology, 36,* 334–341.

Diener, E., & Woody, W. (1981). TV violence and viewer liking. *Communication Research, 8,* 281–306.

Donnerstein, E. (1980). Aggressive erotica and violence against women. *Journal of Personality and Social Psychology, 39,* 269–277.

Easton, N. J. (1993, February 7). America's mean streak: It's cool to be cool. *Los Angeles Times Magazine,* 16–20, 43–44.

Ellis, J. (1999, April 22). Colorado's carnage is inevitable in our culture of violence. *The Boston Globe,* p. A25. Retrieved March 16, 2007, from LexisNexis Academic database.

Eron, L. D., Walder, L. O., & Lefkowitz, M. M. (1971). *Learning of aggression in children.* Boston: Little, Brown.

Feshback, S. (1955). The drive-reducing function of fantasy behavior. *Journal of Abnormal and Social Psychology, 50,* 3–11.

Feshback, S. (1961). The stimulating versus cathartic effects of vicarious aggressive activity. *Journal of Abnormal and Social Psychology, 63,* 381–385.

Final Report of the Surgeon General's Commission on Pornography. (1986). Nashville, TN: Rutledge Hill Press.

Geen, R. G. (1994). Television and aggression: Recent developments in research and theory. In D. Zillmann, J. Bryant, & A. C. Huston (Eds.), *Media, children, and the family: Social scientific, psychodynamic, and clinical perspectives* (pp. 151–162). Hillsdale, NJ: Erlbaum.

Gerbner, G., Gross, L., Morgan, M., & Signorielli, N. (1980). The "mainstreaming" of America: Violence Profile No. 11. *Journal of Communication, 30,* 10–29.

Gerbner, G., Gross, L., Morgan, M., Signorielli, N., & Shanahan, J. (2002). Growing up with television: Cultivation processes. In J. Bryant & D. Zillmann (Eds.), *Media effects: Advances in theory and research* (2nd ed., pp. 43–67). Mahwah, NJ: Erlbaum.

Gossett, J. L., & Byrne, S. (2002). "CLICK HERE": A content analysis of internet rape sites. *Gender & Society, 16,* 689–709.

Greenberg, B. S. (1994). Content trends in media sex. In D. Zillmann, J. Bryant, & A. C. Huston (Eds.), *Media, children, and the family: Social scientific, psychodynamic, and clinical perspectives* (pp. 165–182). Hillsdale, NJ: Erlbaum.

Gunter, B. (1994). The question of media violence. In J. Bryant & D. Zillmann (Eds.), *Media effects: Advances in theory and research* (pp. 163–211). Hillsdale, NJ: Erlbaum.

Gunter, B. (2001). *Media sex: What are the issues?* Mahwah, NJ: Erlbaum.

Harris, R. J. (1994). The impact of sexually explicit media. In J. Bryant & D. Zillmann (Eds.), *Media effects: Advances in theory and research* (pp. 247–272). Hillsdale, NJ: Erlbaum.

Hoffner, C., & Buchanan, M. (2002). Parents' responses to television violence: The third-person perception, parental mediation, and support for censorship. *Media Psychology, 4,* 231–252.

Hoffner, C. A., & Levine, K. J. (2007). Enjoyment of mediated fright and violence: A meta-analysis. In R. W. Preiss, B. M. Gayle, N. Burrell, M. Allen, & J. Bryant (Eds.), *Mass media effects research: Advances through meta-analysis* (pp. 215–244). Mahwah, NJ: Erlbaum.

Hoffner, C., Plotkin, R. S., Buchanan, M., Anderson, J. D., Kamigaki, S. K., Hubbs, L. A., et al. (2001). The third-person effect in perceptions of the influence of television violence. *Journal of Communication, 51,* 283–299.

Huesmann, L. R., & Eron, L. D. (1986). *Television and the aggressive child: A cross-national comparison.* Hillsdale, NJ: Erlbaum.

Huesmann, L. R., & Miller, L. S. (1994). Long-term effects of repeated exposure to media violence in childhood. In L. R. Huesmann (Ed.), *Aggressive behavior: Current perspectives* (pp. 153–186). New York: Plenum.

Huesman, L. R., Moise-Titus, J., Podolski, C. L, & Eron, L. D. (2003). Longitudinal relations between children's exposure to TV violence and their aggressive and violent behavior in young adulthood: 1977–1992. *Developmental Psychology, 39,* 201–222.

Huesmann, L. R., & Taylor, L. D. (2006). The role of media violence in violent behavior. *Annual Review of Public Health, 27,* 393–415.

Jo, E., & Berkowitz, L. (1994). A priming effect analysis of media influences: An update. In J. Bryant & D. Zillmann (Eds.), *Media effects: Advances in theory and research* (pp. 43–60). Hillsdale, NJ: Erlbaum.

Kinsey, A. C., Pomeroy, W. B., & Martin, C. E. (1948). *Sexual behavior in the human male.* Philadelphia: W. B. Saunders.

Lachlan, K. A., Smith, S. L., & Tamborini, R. (2005). Models for aggressive behavior: The attributes of violent characters in popular video games. *Communication Studies, 56,* 313–329.

Lefkowitz, M. M., Eron, L. D., Walder, L. O., & Huesmann, L. R. (1977). *Growing up to be violent.* New York: Pergamon.

Linz, D. (1985). *Sexual violence in the media: Effects on male viewers and implications for society.* Unpublished doctoral dissertation, University of Wisconsin, Madison.

Linz, D., Donnerstein, E., & Adams, S. M. (1989). Physiological desensitization and judgments about female victims of violence. *Human Communication Research, 75,* 509–522.

Linz, D., Donnerstein, E., & Penrod, S. (1984). The effects of multiple exposures to filmed violence against women. *Journal of Communication, 34,* 130–147.

Lo, V-h, & Ran, W. (2002). Third-person effect, gender, and pornography on the Internet. *Journal of Broadcasting Electronic Media, 46,* 13–33.

Lo, V., & Wei, R. (2002). Third-person effect, gender, and pornography on the internet. *Journal of Broadcasting & Electronic Media, 46,* 13–34.

Lo, V., & Wei, R. (2005). Exposure to internet pornography and Taiwanese adolescents' sexual attitudes and behavior. *Journal of Broadcasting & Electronic Media, 49,* 221–237.

Lyons, J. S., Anderson, R. L., & Larson, D. B. (1994). A systematic review of the effects of aggressive and nonaggressive pornography. In D. Zillmann, J. Bryant, & A. C. Huston (Eds.), *Media, children, and the family: Social scientific, psychodynamic, and clinical perspectives* (pp. 271–310). Hillsdale, NJ: Erlbaum.

Malamuth, N. M. (1984). Aggression against women: Cultural and individual causes. In N. M. Malamuth & E. Donnerstein (Eds.), *Pornography and sexual aggression* (pp. 19–52). Orlando, FL: Academic Press.

Malamuth, N. M., Check, J. V. P., & Briere, J. (1986). Sexual arousal in response to aggression: Ideological, aggressive, and sexual correlates. *Journal of Personality and Social Psychology, 50,* 330–340.

Mundorf, N., D'Alessio, D., Allen, M., & Emmers-Sommer, T. M. (2007). Effects of sexually explicit media. In R. W. Preiss, B. M. Gayle, N. Burrell, M. Allen, & J. Bryant (Eds.), *Mass media effects research: Advances through meta-analysis* (pp. 181–198). Mahwah, NJ: Erlbaum.

Murray, J. P., Liotti, M., Ingmundson, P. T., Mayberg, H. S., Pu, Y., Zamarripa, R., et al. (2006). Children's brain activations while viewing televised violence revealed by fMRI. *Media Psychology, 8*, 25–37.

Paik, H., & Comstock, G. (1994).The effects of television violence on antisocial behavior: A meta-analysis. *Communication Research, 21*, 516–547.

Panee, C. D., & Ballard, M. E. (2002). High versus low aggressive priming during video-game training: Effects on violent action during game play, hostility, heart rate, and blood pressure. *Journal of Applied Social Psychology, 32*, 2458–2474.

Peter, J., & Valkenburg, P. M. (2006a). Adolescents' exposure to sexually explicit online material and recreational attitudes toward sex. *Journal of Communication, 56*, 639–660.

Peter, J., & Valkenburg, P. M. (2006b). Adolescents' exposure to sexually explicit material on the internet. *Communication Research, 33*, 178–204.

Preiss, R. W., Gayle, B. M., Burrell, N., Allen, M., & Bryant, J. (Eds.). (2007). *Mass media effects research: Advances through meta-analysis*. Mahwah, NJ: Erlbaum.

Raney, A. A. (2003). Disposition-based theories of enjoyment. In J. Bryant, D. R. Roskos-Ewoldsen, & J. Cantor (Eds.), *Communication and emotion: Essays in honor of Dolf Zillmann* (pp. 61–84). Mahwah, NJ: Erlbaum.

Raney A. A. (2006). The psychology of disposition-based theories of media enjoyment. In J. Bryant & P. Vorderer (Eds.), *The psychology of entertainment* (pp. 137–150). Mahwah, NJ: Erlbaum.

Reeves, B., Lang, A., Kim, E. Y., & Tatar, D. (2001). The effects of screen size and message content on attention and arousal. *Media Psychology, 1*, 49–67.

Rohas, H., Shah, D. V., & Faber, R. J. (1996). For the good of others: Censorship and the third-person effect. *International Journal of Public Opinion, 8*, 163–186.

Salwen, M. B., & Dupagne, M. (1999). The third person effect. *Communication Research, 26*, 523–549.

Sapolsky, B. S. & Zillmann, D. (1981). The effect of soft-core and hard-core erotica on provoked and unprovoked hostile behavior. *Journal of Sex Research, 17*, 319–343.

Sherry, J. L. (2001). The effect of violent video games on aggression: A meta-analysis. *Human Communication Research, 27*, 409–431.

Sherry, J. L. (2007). Violent video games and aggression: Why can't we find effects? In R. W. Preiss, B. M. Gayle, N. Burrell, M. Allen, & J. Bryant (Eds.), *Mass media effects research: Advances through meta-analysis* (pp. 245–262). Mahwah, NJ: Erlbaum.

Sparks, G. G., Sherry, J., & Lubsen, G. (2005). The appeal of media violence in a full-length motion picture: An experimental investigation. *Communication Reports, 18*, 21–30.

Weaver, J. B. (1987). *Effects of portrayals of female sexuality and violence against women on perceptions of women*. Unpublished doctoral dissertation, Indiana University, Bloomington.

Weber, R., Ritterfeld, U., & Kostygina, A. (2006). Aggression and violence as effects of playing violent video games. In P. Vorderer & J. Bryant (Eds.), *Playing video games: Motives, responses, and consequences* (pp. 347–361). Mahwah, NJ: Erlbaum.

Weber, R., Ritterfeld, U., & Mathiak, K. (2006). Does playing violent video games induce aggression? Empirical evidence of a functional magnetic resonance imaging study. *Media Psychology, 8*, 39–60.

Wells, W. D. (1973). *Television and aggression: Replication of an experimental field study*. Unpublished manuscript, University of Chicago.

White, L. A. (1979). Erotica and aggression: The influence of sexual arousal, positive affect, and negative affect on aggressive behavior. *Journal of Personality and Social Psychology, 37*, 591–601.

Wilson, B. J ., Kunkel, D., Linz, D., Potter, J., Donnerstein, E., Smith, S. L., Blumenthal, E., & Gray, T. (1997). *National television violence study* (Vol. 1). Newbury Park, CA: Sage.

Wober, J. M. (1997). Violence or other routes to appreciation: TV program makers' options. *Journal of Broadcasting & Electronic Media, 41*, 190–203.

Wood, W., Wong, F. Y., & Chachere, G. (1991). Effects of media violence on viewers' aggression in unconstrained social interaction. *Psychological Bulletin, 109*, 371–383.

Zillmann, D. (1971). Excitation transfer in communication-mediated aggressive behavior. *Journal of Experimental Social Psychology, 7,* 419–434.

Zillmann, D. (1984). *Connections between sex and aggression.* Hillsdale, NJ: Erlbaum.

Zillmann, D. (1991). Television viewing and physiological arousal. In J. Bryant & D. Zillmann (Eds.), *Responding to the screen: Reception and reaction processes* (pp. 103–133). Hillsdale, NJ: Erlbaum.

Zillmann, D., & Bryant, J. (1982). Pornography, sexual callousness, and the trivialization of rape. *Journal of Communication, 32,* 10–21.

Zillmann, D., & Bryant, J. (1986). Shifting preferences in pornography consumption. *Communication Research, 13,* 560–578.

Zillmann, D., & Bryant, J. (1988a). Effects of prolonged consumption of pornography on family values. *Journal of Family Issues, 9,* 518–544.

Zillmann, D., & Bryant, J. (1988b). Pornography's impact on sexual satisfaction. *Journal of Applied Social Psychology, 18,* 438–453.

Zillmann, D., & Bryant, J. (Eds.). (1989). *Pornography: Research advances and policy considerations.* Hillsdale, NJ: Erlbaum.

Zillmann, D., Bryant, J., Comisky, P. W, & Medoff, N. J. (1981). Excitation and hedonic valence in the effect of erotica on motivated intermale aggression. *European Journal of Social Psychology, 11,* 233–252.

Zillmann, D., Bryant, J., & Huston, A. C. (1994). *Media, children, and the family: Social scientific, psychodynamic, and clinical perspectives.* Hillsdale, NJ: Erlbaum.

Suggested Readings

Bandura, A. (2002). Social cognitive theory of mass communication. In J. Bryant & D. Zillmann (Eds.), *Media effects: Advances in theory and research* (2nd ed., 121–153). Mahwah, NJ: Erlbaum.

Bryant, J., & Miron, D. (2003). Excitation-transfer theory three-and factor theory of emotion. In J. Bryant, D. Roskos-Ewoldesen, & J. Cantor (Eds.), *Communication and emotion: Essays in honor of Dolf Zillmann* (pp. 31–60). Mahwah, NJ: Erlbaum.

Christensen, P. N., & Wood, W. (2007). Effects of media violence on viewers' aggression in unconstrained social interactions. In R. W. Preiss, B. M. Gayle, N. Burrell, M. Allen, & J. Bryant (Eds.), *Mass media effects research: Advances through meta-analysis* (pp. 145–168). Mahwah, NJ: Erlbaum.

Gerbner, G., Gross, L., Morgan, M., Signorielli, N., & Shanahan, J. (2002). Growing up with television: Cultivation processes. In J. Bryant & D. Zillmann (Eds.), *Media effects: Advances in theory and research* (2nd ed., pp. 43–67). Mahwah, NJ: Erlbaum.

Harris, R. J., & Scott, C. L. (2002). Effects of sex in the media. In J. Bryant & D. Zillmann (Eds.), *Media effects: Advances in theory and research* (2nd ed., pp. 307–332). Mahwah, NJ: Erlbaum.

Mundorf, N., Allen, M., & D'Alessio, D. (2007). Effects of sexually explicit media. In R. W. Preiss, B. M. Gayle, N. Burrell, M. Allen, & J. Bryant (Eds.), *Mass media effects research: Advances through meta-analysis* (pp. 181–198). Mahwah, NJ: Erlbaum.

Paul, B., Salwen, M. B., & Dupange, M. (2007). The third-person effect: A meta-analysis of the perceptual hypothesis. In R. W. Preiss, B. M. Gayle, N. Burrell, M. Allen, & J. Bryant (Eds.), *Mass media effects research: Advances through meta-analysis* (pp. 81–102). Mahwah, NJ: Erlbaum.

Roskos-Ewoldsen, D., Klinger, M. R., & Roskos-Ewoldesen, B. (2007). Media priming: A meta-analysis. In R.W. Preiss, B.M. Gayle, N. Burrell, M. Allen, & J. Bryant (Eds.), *Mass media effects research: Advances through meta-analysis* (pp. 53–80). Mahwah, NJ: Erlbaum.

Sherry, J. (2007). Violent video games and aggression: Why can't we find effects? In R. W. Preiss, B. M. Gayle, N. Burrell, M. Allen, & J. Bryant (Eds.), *Mass media effects research: Advances through meta-analysis* (pp. 245–262). Mahwah, NJ: Erlbaum.

Shrum, L. J. (2002). Media consumption and perceptions of social reality: Effects and underlying processes. In J. Bryant & D. Zillmann (Eds.), *Media effects: Advances in theory and research* (2nd ed., pp. 69–96). Mahwah, NJ: Erlbaum.

Sparks, G. G., & Sparks, C. W. (2002). Effects of media violence. In J. Bryant & D. Zillmann (Eds.), *Media effects: Advances in theory and research* (2nd ed., pp. 269–286). Mahwah, NJ: Erlbaum.

14

SOCIAL SCIENCE THEORIES OF TRADITIONAL AND INTERNET ADVERTISING

Shelly Rodgers, Esther Thorson, and Yun Jin

From its beginnings as social science theory in the late 19th century through today, advertising theory has taken two basic forms and sometimes a blend of the two: The first type is managerial and the second is psychological. Many of the main advertising theories are managerial, although admittedly they involve psychological variables. These theories include the hierarchy models, multi-attribute theory, means–end models, and many variations and combinations of these. These are "big picture" approaches in the sense that they provide the manager with basic stages that a consumer might go through between exposure to an advertisement and buying the product. These theories include stages that have psychological names: attention, involvement, memory, attitudes, desire, intention to purchase, beliefs, and behavior. But the theories do not focus on understanding micro-level psychological processes.

In contrast, there are also "theories" of advertising that are about the intricacies of psychological processing. In these approaches there are, for example, depth examinations of the different kinds of memory: recall, aided recall, recognition, episodic and semantic, implicit and explicit memory, and the psychological and even the physiological substrates of these types of memory. Perception, memory (and cognition), affect, attention, and involvement are some of the main psychological processes that have proven critical to understanding how advertising works. It can be argued that scientific theorizing about advertising will eventually connect the managerial models with the more basic psychological analyses and some examples of this will be seen in this review. Our guess is that both types of theory are crucial for managing advertising. Determining what to say about a brand, how to say it, what media to use, and optimal reach and frequency are questions that must be guided by a managerial model. But figuring out how to test the ways in which the resulting advertising works can be significantly aided by psychological theories.

In addition to the complexity of the question of "how does advertising work?" the Internet has brought with it a vast upheaval in how companies advertise, and even how they think about what an "ad" is, and what "media" must carry it. Do the new kinds of advertising "work" in the same way as traditional advertising? Are either the old managerial or psychological theories relevant, and if so when?

To deal with the current state of flux in the meaning of advertising and the media channels that carry it, this chapter will do the following. First, it will provide classic and Internet-updated definitions of advertising. Second, it will update the review of managerial and psychological models of traditional advertising. Third, it will introduce some theoretical approaches to Internet advertising, and again note that there are both managerial level and psychological approaches. We then end our chapter by commenting on the state of existing theoretically based advertising research and provide a few ideas about possible next steps. We also suggest a prototypic experiment that would be useful to those who wish to study advertising from a scholarly viewpoint. Because of the challenge of space, we will often identify important review articles of aid to those just beginning the adventure of learning advertising theory.

The Concept(s) of Advertising: Traditional and Internet-Based

"Advertising" refers to mediated information or persuasive messages in which the sponsor is identified. The messages are usually paid for by the sponsor, although "public service announcements" are paid for by donations (Wells, Burnett, & Moriarty, 2003, p. 10). Indeed, with the development of the Internet and the proliferation of digital delivery devices like PDAs, RSS feeds, and iPods, advertising, like every other mediated function, is changing drastically (Schumann & Thorson, 2007). Advertising is fundamentally in a state of flux, and as a result, the taxonomy of advertising introduced in the first edition of this book is now notably out of date.

That taxonomy included: product and service commercials, public service commercials, issue advertising, corporate advertising, and political advertising (Thorson, 1996, p. 212). To this taxonomy we add and briefly describe a number of advertising types that have emerged since the 1990s largely as a function of the digital revolution. These include: relationship advertising, permission advertising, experiential advertising, advertainment advertising, and consumer-generated advertising. *Relationship advertising*, which originated from customer relationship marketing (CRM), treats every message as a call to action that attempts to draw the consumer closer to the brand by meeting the specific needs of the consumer. *Permission advertising*, sometimes called permission marketing, is centered on gaining the consumer's consent before ad exposure (Godin, 1999). Examples of permission advertising include search engine optimization (SEO) and sponsor-select ads in which consumers search/select which brands, products and services they want to receive more information about. With its roots in emotional advertising, *experiential advertising* refers to advertisements that evoke a strong sensory response, as in the case of Blockbuster's 2007 Super Bowl commercial featuring a talking rabbit and gerbil, and Kleenex's "let it out" campaign that enables consumers to share tearful stories both in the form of TV commercials and posted on the Kleenex.com website. *Advertainment advertising* or simply "advertainments" are similar to experiential advertising in that their goal is to create an emotional experience with consumers but they differ in that their sole purpose is to entertain, as in the case of Burger King's subservient chicken (http://www.subservientchicken.com), which promotes BK's well-known "Have It Your Way" motto. *Consumer-generated advertising* (also known as user-generated content or UGC) is perhaps the newest form of advertising and refers to various kinds of content created by consumers in the form of online testimonials, product reviews, user-generated commercials, etc.

A common theme among these new forms of advertising is that the consumer is in control and, subsequently, must initiate contact with the advertiser. This "pull" model of advertising differs from the traditional "push" models, which are often intrusive and may not provide information that is relevant to the consumer's specific needs, as in the case of the 30-second TV commercial (e.g., see the theory of Schumann & Thorson, 2007, which explained consumer response to commercials as a function of the interruptive role they played).

The introduction of new categories of advertising is not meant to suggest that the newer forms of advertising are superior to traditional forms of advertising but suggests a new set of challenges including how to define and measure psychological concepts like interactivity and managerial concepts like personalization, and the age-old question of how to determine effectiveness of these forms of advertising. We refer back to these and other issues throughout the remainder of this chapter.

Update on Classic Theories

Here, we overview three highly influential managerial theories about how advertising works and psychological approaches on how advertising works. These managerial theories of advertising focus on hierarchy of effects, multi-attribute theory, and means–end theories.

Classic Theoretical Approaches to Advertising

Hierarchy of Effects

Although hierarchy models go back to the late 19th century (Preston, 1982), modern versions began with Lavidge and Steiner (1961). They suggested that the information consumers select from commercials travels through an ordered series of processing stages, focusing on processes such as attention, comprehension, evaluation, intention to act, and acting. McGuire (1969) suggested that the effects hierarchy should include attention, comprehension, yielding to the conclusion, retention of the new information, and behavior (purchase). Although there are variations in the assumptions of the various hierarchy models (e.g., Palda, 1996; Preston, 1982; Preston & Thorson, 1984), most assume that failure at any of the steps of the hierarchy dictates no response to the advertising. Furthermore, hierarchy models rest on the assumption that attitudes and behaviors in response to advertising are developed consciously and rationally. The emphasis on rational, conscious responses to advertising developed early in advertising's history, and remained dominant well into the 1970s (e.g., Sandage, 1973; Shimp & Gresham, 1983).

Although it seems unlikely that in the brief seconds that consumers encounter an ad they would not experience anything like the elaborate set of responses articulated by the hierarchy of effects model (see this issue and others discussed in Barry, 2002; Weilbacher, 2001), hierarchy models are particularly useful in suggesting to managers which psychological stages different kinds of advertising should be indexed with (e.g., Barry, 2002). For example, in a new campaign, the process of "awareness" is crucial. Can the ads break through surrounding clutter to register with consumers? On the other hand, an ad that attempts to explain why a new facial moisturizer is superior should be evaluated in terms of "comprehension" of the argument. It should be noted that hierarchy models have been applied to web-based advertising. For example, Korgaonkar and Wolin (1999) showed that those who held positive cognitions about the value of the Internet developed more positive views of brands, and were more likely to purchase them.

Multi-Attribute Theory

As noted above, in the 1970s, the dominant view of advertising focused on its impact on rational (rather than emotional) processes. The development of attitude structures in memory was a central unifying theme. Specifically, attitudes were conceived as reason-based valenced orientations toward some object. Underlying most research during this time was the assumption that advertising persuaded people by offering them good, logical reasons to like an object or an idea and to respond positively to it.

One of the most influential models of commercial processing of this period was the Fishbein–Ajzen Multi-Attribute Model (Fishbein & Ajzen, 1975). This attitude-based model suggested that a consumer's attitude toward any brand (or service) is determined by summing the consumer's evaluative response toward each individual product attribute (e_i), multiplied by a subjective estimate of the probability that the brand in question actually possesses attribute i (b_i). This relationship is represented by the equation:

$$A_o = b_i e_i$$

where A_o is the attitude toward the object (the brand).

According to the model, an ad changes brand attitude either by changing a person's perception of the probability that a brand has some attribute, or by changing a person's evaluative beliefs about the attribute. In applications of the model, people were assumed to process ads by continually updating their attitudes toward brands. Although any information a consumer considers relevant can be included as a product attribute according to this model, researchers generally have limited their consideration to product attributes of a rational and intrinsic nature (e.g., price, performance, and availability). While there is clear evidence that applying the Multi-Attribute Model to advertising yields useful predictions about how ads will fare (e.g., Bettman, Capon, & Lutz, 1975) and certainly that it can be applied to ask what features of a brand should be emphasized, there has been less application of the model in recent scholarly literature.

Means–End Theories

Gutman (1983) introduced what is basically a hierarchy model but one that emphasized the function of connecting brands with personal values (Olson & Reynolds, 1983). When people encounter an advertisement, they identify the benefits of the brand and then connect these benefits with higher-level personal values. If there is a match, the advertising is more effective. The model has proved useful for a variety of management questions like what market segments to address, how to handle brand image, and even sales force management (see Homer, 2006). In a recent application of means–end theory, Homer (2006) showed that affect, both positive and negative, played a role in how well brand attributes connected with personal values.

Psychologically Based Theories of Advertising

Involvement and Attention

These two psychological variables were also influential in shifting advertising theory toward the less "rational-psychology" approach. The intellectual seed for this different conception was planted in the 1960s, when Krugman (1965) introduced the critical concept of *involvement*. For Krugman, involvement referred to how many cognitive connections a person made while processing media messages. The concept of involvement, however, quickly morphed into a variety of different concepts. For example, some researchers characterize involvement as central rather than peripheral processing (Petty & Cacioppo, 1979), systematic rather than heuristic processing (Chaiken, 1980), or brand rather than non-brand processing (Gardner, Mitchell, & Russo, 1985).

Emotion

Beginning in the 1980s there was a marked shift in assumptions about how advertising worked. One of the most influential findings was that attitude toward the advertising itself (A_{ad}) was important (Mitchell, 1986). Of course, this is not a particularly rational way to think about brands. Although Multi-Attribute Theory could and was applied to understanding A_{ad}, it became clear that emotion was a crucial psychological variable in A_{ad}-mediated effects of advertising.

The initial advertising researchers that examined emotion concentrated on what "emotions" were relevant and what their impacts were (see review in Thorson, 1996, and a variety of sample approaches in Agres, Edell, & Dubitsky, 1990). Dozens of taxonomies of advertising-related emotion have been suggested. Batra and Holbrook (1987) tested Plutchik's (1980) eight emotional categories: joy, acceptance, fear, surprise, sadness, disgust, anger, and anticipation. Mehrabian and Russell (1974) employed a three-dimensional emotional system introduced by Osgood, Suci, and Tannenbaum (1957) that included the dimensions of pleasure-displeasure, arousal-non-arousal, and domination-non-domination. Batra and Holbrook (1987) showed that all three of these emotional dimensions predicted people's liking for ads and advertised brands. Edell and Burke (1987) employed three feelings scales, including upbeat, negative, and warm. They found that all three kinds of feelings that people experienced in response to ads were predictive of how they evaluated ads, how much they liked ads, beliefs they had about the brands, and their attitudes toward the brands.

The recent work with emotion has taken two general approaches. One is to weigh the importance of "cognition" versus emotion in determining the impact of advertising. For example, Leigh, Zinkhan, and Swarmingathan (2006) showed that cognitive processes were associated with free recall but that affective processes influenced recognition. The other approach is to look more in-depth at how psychological dimensions of affect like valence and arousal operate, and what this means for advertising. For example, Shapiro, MacInnis, and Park (2002) showed that people induced to be in a negatively valenced mood were better able to distinguish brand attributes related to main themes of commercials than those in positive moods. In contrast, high arousal led people to be less able to remember what brand attributes had even been presented.

Lang (2006) has developed psychophysiological theory of processing media messages, and this theory, although articulated at a micro-level, shows signs of connecting quite directly with work such as that of Shapiro and colleagues. For example, in a recent application of her approach to health messages about cancer, Lang (2006) demonstrated the usefulness of three simultaneous and ongoing physiological processes: encoding, storage, and retrieval. Her research shows that people have limited capacity to handle all three of them and when that capacity is taxed, performance is adversely affected. Depending on their content and structure, media messages may stimulate an appetitive (positively valenced) or an aversive (negatively valenced) motivation and, because the two system are independent of each other, a combination of the two. Indeed, when the operation of this physiological system is described, it predicts Shapiro et al.'s results exactly. That is, under high arousal processing, capacity is exceeded and people are less able to distinguish brand features from each other. Under mild aversive conditions like a negative mood induction, processing resources are taken away from encoding and transferred to retrieval, which leads to enhanced memory performance. The striking linkage between psychologically based and psychophysiologically based theory suggests that in the near future the two areas will be directly linked in a way that extends our understanding of exactly how commercials are processed.

Memory

Memory's role in the processing of advertisements has been a central psychological question throughout the social scientific approach to how advertising works. Clearly, some residue from an advertisement must remain with people in order for an advertisement to motivate purchase. Overviews of theories on memory applied to advertising (e.g., Thorson, 1990a, 1990b) certainly reflect memory's role in managerial models, but the predominant approach has been psychological. Some of the many psychologically based conceptualizations applied to advertising include retrieval versus computational memory (Srull, 1983, 1989); episodic and semantic memory (Thorson & Friestad, 1989; Tulving, 1972); visual versus verbal memory (Mitchell & Olson, 1981; Rossiter & Percy, 1978); and recall versus recognition measures of memory (Lynch & Srull, 1982; Singh & Rothschild, 1983).

The proliferation of psychologically-based studies of the role of memory in advertising continues. Braun-LaTour and LaTour (2004) compared long and short term memory interactions for commercials that used the same trade characters. Shapiro and Krishnan (2001) compared explicit and implicit memory processes. Till and Baack (2005) showed that highly creative commercials produced more impact on brand and executional unaided recall than more mundane commercials, but that there were no differences for other indicators of memory.

In short, research on classic theories in traditional advertising continues to show advancement since the first edition of this text in 1996 and, in some cases, new theories are being developed to explain how individuals perceive and process advertising messages. These same theories and a few new theories are also being tested and examined in the context of Internet advertising, the subject of this next section.

Internet Advertising

Since the first commercial browser was introduced and the first banner ads were sold in early 1994, the global Internet population as well as Internet advertising has been growing at an exponential speed. Seventy-five percent of the U.S. population has Internet access at home, according to Nielsen//NetRatings (2007). Internet advertising spending has also witnessed dramatic growth, from $310 million in 1996 to more than $12.5 billion in 2005 with projected revenues of $14 billion in 2007 (IAB, 2006), making the Internet the fourth largest advertising communications medium (Jupiter Communications Report, 2003). Since the commercialization of the Internet, a great deal of research has examined the advertising potential of this new medium and is the focus of this next section. Before we begin, let's take a look at what Internet advertising is.

Internet Advertising Defined: How Is It Different from Traditional Advertising?

Numerous articles and book chapters have focused on definitions of Internet advertising, which includes distinguishing between features of traditional versus Internet advertising (e.g., McMillan, 2007). Given space constraints, we will limit our review to some of the most prominent characteristics of Internet advertising and refer the reader to several recent articles for more in-depth discussion on this topic (e.g., see Johnson, Bruner, & Kumar, 2006; McMillan, 2005, 2007; Thorson, Duffy, & Schumann, 2007). Although there is no consensus on a definition of Internet advertising, six characteristics commonly discussed in the literature include: interactivity, multimedia, rich content, direct marketing capabilities, targeting, and ease of data collection.

The Internet has transformed the traditional source-oriented advertising model and *interactivity* is at the core of this change (Leckenby, 2005). As the most distinctive feature of Internet advertising (Hoffman & Novak, 1996), interactivity has been approached from a variety of perspectives including interpersonal (Rafaeli, 1988), mechanical (Steuer, 1992), and functional (Ha & James, 1998). McMillan (2002) synthesized 20 years of research on interactivity around three primary research traditions: human-to-human, human-to-document, and human-to-system interactions. Building on this conceptualization, interactivity has been characterized along several dimensions including user control, reciprocal and simultaneous communication, and addressability. *User control* means that instead of being passive targets as in the case of traditional media, Internet users actively choose, search, process, and respond to Internet advertising at will (Ghose & Dou, 1998; Liu & Shrum, 2002). Users also control timing and placement of exposure to Internet ads, and in some cases can manipulate and disseminate ad content (Gallagher, Foster, & Parsons, 2001). Unlike traditional, one-way models that emphasize the flow of information from advertiser to consumer, the Internet enables *reciprocal and simultaneous communication* between advertisers and consumers (Hoffman & Novak, 1996), which is critical for building customer relationships as well as making efficient adjustments in the course of a campaign. *Addressability* refers to the ability to remember and react to the response of a consumer (Gong & Maddox, 2003), which facilitates one-to-one marketing and product/service personalization (Newell, 1997) including global capabilities of the Internet (LaFerle, 2007). This ability has created debate over notions of mass market and geographic bounds, both of which are inherent aspects of traditional advertising (Thorson, 1996).

Multi-media presentation of ads, our second category, includes several different features that have been examined including text, image, animation, audio, video, and 3D presentation, as well as combinations of these and other characteristics. Research in this area has generally shown that multi-media increases online advertising effectiveness by synergistically delivering different aspects of a message to the target (Appiah, 2006) resulting in more favorable brand perceptions (Choi, Miracle, & Biocca, 2001).

The third characteristic, *information richness*, refers to an unlimited flow of information from unlimited sources making the Internet a superior vehicle for conveying details about the advertised brand. Relatively low information search costs also empower the consumer to make more informed purchase decisions (Leong, Huang, & Stanners, 1998).

The Internet has also been touted for its ability to offer a *direct marketing* channel in which hypertext links can be integrated into an Internet ad to connect a user directly from the advertisement to the advertiser's website (Chandon, Chtourou, & Fortin, 2003). This has created greater efficiency and more options for e-marketers and advertisers who wish to sell their products/services directly to online consumers (Liu & Shrum, 2002) as well as other commercial and non-profit companies that want to target an audience of one. In comparison to other media, the Internet also has greater *targeting* potential and offers not only demographic but also behavioral targeting using keyword searches and transaction history (Rodgers, Cannon, & Moore, 2007) to increase the relevance between the advertising and prospective consumer (Yoon & Kim, 2001).

The final characteristic of the Internet is data collection. Users leave "footprints" while roaming the Internet. IP addresses, log files, cookies, and other solutions enable websites to count hits, impressions, clicks and transactions, as well as to analyze users' browsing patterns with great ease and efficiency, thereby increasing accountability of the medium (Danaher & Mullarkey, 2003). We refer the reader to several good reviews on measurement that include techniques that are both similar to traditional advertising (such as attitude toward the ad) and different from traditional advertising (such as click-through rates) (e.g., Bhat, Bevans, & Sengupta, 2002; Pavlou & Stewart, 2000).

Each of these characteristics that define Internet advertising—interactivity, multi-media, rich content, direct marketing capabilities, targeting, and data collection—has been examined to one degree or another and other aspects of the Internet have been examined as well. Research in this area has shown that people use different information processing approaches online depending on certain contextual, personal, and structural characteristics (McMillan, Hwang, & Lee, 2003), suggesting that a single factor type does not adequately explain or account for effects resulting from Internet advertisements. Given this, we present a framework that borrows from the Interactive Advertising Model (IAM; Rodgers & Thorson, 2000) to help organize the vast and ever-increasing research on Internet advertising based on four categories—consumer-related, advertising-related, product-related, and context-related factors.

Organizing Framework

This section includes psychological factors such as user motives, attitudes, and level of involvement. It also includes management factors such as exposure, prior experiences, and skills. Additionally, there are product- and context-related factors that affect advertising.

Consumer-Related Psychological Approaches

Motives/Goals

Individual goals and motivations can affect how consumers process and evaluate Internet advertising (Rodgers & Thorson, 2000). Initial studies addressed the "what" question that consisted of identifying various types of Internet motives, and several typologies resulted out of this line of research (e.g., Sheehan, 2002). Although more than 100 Internet motives have been identified (Rodgers & Sheldon, 2002), the two most common motives (also sometimes called "modes") include information seeking and experiential surfing or browsing (see Li & Bukovac, 1999). With few exceptions, this research has shown that information seekers who tend to be goal-oriented allocate less mental effort to processing Internet ads than individuals who are in an exploratory surfing mode, which results in lower ad recall for information-seekers (Danaher & Mullarkey, 2003) and more negative attitudes toward Internet advertising (Hupfer & Grey, 2005), particularly for intrusive Internet ads such as pop-ups (Edwards, Li, & Lee, 2002). Research is now moving away from identifying Internet motives to creating valid and reliable scales that can be used to better understand information processing of ads (see Edwards, 2007; Rodgers, 2002) across cultures (Ko, Roberts, & Cho, 2006), including a four-factor scale by Rodgers and Sheldon (2002) and several "Uses and Gratifications" scales created or adapted for the Internet (e.g., Korgaonkar & Wolin, 1999; Papacharissi & Rubin, 2000).

User Involvement

Closely related to motive, user involvement has been found to play a pivotal role in determining the route of information processing. As we saw in the review of traditional advertising approaches, Elaboration Likelihood Model (Petty & Cacioppo, 1986) posits that consumers in high-involvement situations tend to use a central route to process information while those in low-involvement situations are more likely to attend to peripheral cues. This has been found true for Internet advertising as well, where consumers in high-involvement situations are more likely to click on banner ads than those in low-involvement situations (Cho, 2003) and consumers with a higher level of product involvement pay more attention to banner ads (Yoo, Kim, & Stout 2004) and remember more about the ads (Gong & Maddox, 2003). Additionally, highly involved consumers tend to perceive greater "presence" during their interaction with an Internet ad and hold more favorable attitudes toward the ad (Nicovich, 2005), and studies show that consumers of varied involvement levels are susceptible to different advertising characteristics such as animation and size of banner ads (Cho, 1999), suggesting that perhaps new managerial and psychological variables are needed to understand the effects of Internet (versus traditional) ads.

Consumer-Related Managerial Approaches

Exposure

Although many factors determine user exposure to an Internet ad, exposure itself is a significant predictor of Internet ad effectiveness. The number of times and length of exposure to an Internet ad can affect consumer responses. Briggs and Hollis (1997) found that even without a click-through, just one exposure to Internet advertising produced a sizable effect to increase brand loyalty, purchase intention, brand recognition, and elicited positive perceptions of the brands' personality. In a study conducted on Chinese consumers, Gong and Maddox (2003) found that one additional exposure to a banner ad led to better ad memory, higher brand recall, more positive brand perceptions, and greater purchase intentions. However, these findings have not always been replicated (see Dahlen, 2001; Danaher & Mullarkey, 2003).

Individual Differences

The study of individual differences assumes that cognitive processes to advertising can be aggregated across subjects (Stern, Zinkhan, & Holbrook, 2005). Although research in this general area is understudied (Leigh, 2000), a number of individual differences variables online have included visually versus verbally oriented consumers (Bezjian, Calder, & Iacobucci, 1998); need for cognition (Jee & Lee, 2002; Sicilia, Ruiz, & Munuera, 2005); and shopping styles (i.e., experiential vs. utilitarian; Jeandrain, 2001). Generally speaking, individual differences factors influence consumers' evaluation of Internet advertising and help to explain discrepant findings. For instance, Need for Cognition (NFC), or an individual's tendency to exert effort in cognitive processing, was found to affect the individual's evaluation of online advertising where consumers with high NFC perceived the site to be more interactive than low NFC consumers (Jee & Lee, 2002). Recent studies have turned attention to other individual differences variables including personality (e.g., Amiel & Sargent, 2004) and Internet dependency and addiction (Patwardhan & Yang, 2003).

Prior Experience, Attitudes and Skills

Also under-studied online is the effect of prior experience, attitudes, and Internet skills on audience processing of Internet ads. Consumers' previous Internet experience has been found to affect processing of Internet advertising, although the findings are inconclusive (Bruner & Kumar, 2000). For example, Dahlen (2001) found that inexperienced Internet users (with less than six months' experience) were more vulnerable to Internet ads than experienced users. In contrast, Chaney, Lin, and Chaney (2004) in their study of billboards in video games, found that online gamers' experience level did not affect his or her ad memory.

In addition to Internet experience, a consumer's experience with the advertised product/brand also plays a role in determining persuasive outcomes (Griffith & Chen, 2004). Additional factors that have been examined include pre-existing attitudes toward Internet advertising or Internet advertising in general (Nelson, Keum, & Yaros, 2004) as well as website schema, or the set of beliefs that a consumer forms through his or her Internet experience about how certain types of information are located on a website and how to get to specific information via hyperlinks (Bellman & Rossiter, 2004).

Advertising-Related Factors

Virtually all of the research in this area is based on managerial theory. Rodgers and Thorson (2000) conceptualized three categories for advertiser-controlled stimuli—ad type (a general structure and content type of the ad), ad format (the physical manner in which the ad appears), and ad feature (more specific characteristics within ad format). Since the IAM was published in 2000, more ad types have emerged for this category, as noted at the beginning of this chapter including advergames, mobile advertising, computer agents, and, most recently, user-generated content (UGC). Sub-categories have evolved *within* these ad types, for example, electronic word-of-mouth (eWOM) is a type of UGC. Subcategories have also emerged *across* ad types including message-related features, design-related features, forced exposure level, and interactivity level, a discussion of which follows.

Advertising Types

Since the first Internet ad came into being, the family of Internet advertising has continued to expand, from two-dimensional to three-dimensional execution, from static banners to animated banners to Web commercials, from pop-ups to pop-unders, from banners to sponsorship to product placement in video games, and recently, user-generated content (UGC). Different types of Internet advertising have been found to yield different outcomes (Li & Leckenby, 2007). For example, sponsored content was found to generate more positive company attitudes, beliefs, and greater purchase intention than banner ads (Becker-Olsen, 2003). Three-dimensional (3D) ads, due to their distinctiveness and vividness, have been found to enhance telepresence, which subsequently translates into greater product knowledge and more favorable brand attitudes than 2D ads of the same content (Grigorovici & Constantin, 2004; Ha, 2005; Li, Daugherty, & Biocca, 2002). Recent studies are attempting to determine the effects of "questionable" forms of Internet advertising such as e-mail marketing (Rodgers & Chen, 2007) and other potentially intrusive forms of Internet advertising. New areas of study are devoted to understanding types of online health advertising (Stout, Ball, & Villegas, 2007), online political advertising (Thorson & Watson, 2007; Trammell, Williams, Postelnicu, & Landreville, 2006), viral advertising (Porter & Golan, 2006), mobile advertising (Perlado & Barwise, 2005), advergames (Youn & Lee, 2005), and anthromorphic agents (Nan, Anghelcev, Myers, Sar, & Faber, 2006). Questions addressed by these studies range from defining newer forms of advertising to measuring the effects of these forms of advertising including whether new or different theories are needed to examine these effects (see Cho, 1999).

Design-Related Factors

Banner size, presence of image, and animation are among the most tested design-related variables in Internet ad research. A general conclusion could be drawn from existing literature that, larger size, presence of image, and animation all contribute to enhancing ad effectiveness in terms of quicker click response, higher perceived interactivity, higher immediate brand recall, and more favorable A_{ad}. However, even within animation, there are many variations due to ad size, shape, color, and speed. One study (Sundar & Kalyanaraman, 2004) examined animation speed and found that faster animation elicited greater physiological arousal (measured by skin conductance level) than slower animations speeds. Additional design factors that have been examined include webpage background (Stevenson, Bruner, & Kumar, 2000), homepage complexity (Geissler, Zinkhan, & Watson, 2006), customization (Kalyanaraman & Sundar, 2006), Flash (Day, Shyi, & Wang, 2006), and banner-site congruity and color (Moore, Stammerjohan, & Coulter, 2005), to name a few.

Message-Related Factors

Several message-related factors have been examined including missing information and its effect on curiosity (Menon & Soman, 2002), calls to action such as an incentive to click (Lohtia, Donthu, & Hershberger, 2003), informativeness and interestingness (Edwards, Li, & Lee, 2002), and usefulness of information (Martin, Durme, Raulas, & Merisavo, 2003). Each of these factors has been examined in the context of many different ad types including email, pop-ups, banners, etc., so it is difficult to draw conclusions given that different ad types generate different consumer responses, as noted earlier. However, it is interesting to note that the presence of these message features sometimes enhances and sometimes hurts persuasion—even within a single ad type. For example, useful information in an email ad made recipients *less* likely to visit the advertised site but *increased* the likelihood of a visit to the brick-and-mortar store advertised in the email (Martin et al., 2003). This finding highlights the complexities of Internet advertising and the need to account for the effects of message-related versus design-related factors that may exert different influences on consumer attitudes and behaviors.

Forced Exposure

In contrast to traditional media that are based on a push model of exposure, online media can exert different levels of exposure. Sophisticated ad delivery techniques enable advertisers to insert pop-ups or pop-unders in/after/between web pages, eliciting involuntary attention from the user. This distinctive feature has attracted much research examining how forced exposure levels influence ad effectiveness. Contrary to industry wisdom, research has shown that pop-up ads, which usually offend users and cause negative reactions, can also create positive associations for the advertiser (Cho, Lee, & Tharp, 2001). In contrast, pop-up ads inserted at higher levels of user cognition intensity (i.e., ads that interrupt content pages) produced greater advertising intrusiveness, which subsequently translated into greater irritation and ad avoidance by users (Edwards, Li, & Lee, 2002).

Interactivity

Arguably, the most distinctive trait of the Internet is interactivity. As noted earlier, interactivity is a multidimensional construct that is perceived, defined, and operationalized in various ways, which leads to inconclusive and oftentimes contradictory findings. Ghose and Dou (1998) found that greater degrees of interactivity led to higher quality rankings of corporate website. Coyle and Thorson (2001) operationalized interactivity along two dimensions: mapping (how similar the controls and manipulation were to their counterparts in the real world) and the range of ways in which content can be manipulated. They found that highly interactive websites enhanced telepresence but they did not find a significant relation between degree of interactivity and attitude toward the advertising. In contrast, Macias (2003) operationalized interactivity in terms of the number of choices provided by the site, presence of machine interactions, hypertext links, and reciprocal communication. Her study documented a positive and direct influence of interactivity on both users' comprehension of the ad and persuasive outcomes of the ad. Similarly, Wu (2005) found that the presence of interactive elements, such as an email hot-link, online chat-room, mouse-over effects, produced higher perceived interactivity, which subsequently led to more positive attitudes toward the website. Rather than study the effects of the entire website, Sundar and Kim (2005) investigated the effects of interactivity of individual online advertisements specifically. They operationalized interactivity as the number of hierarchically hyperlinked layers in the ad where larger numbers meant greater interactivity. Their findings indicated that interactivity influenced perceived interactivity, and increased attitudes toward the ad and product. It is interesting to note that interactivity interacts with design-related features noted earlier, for example, animation and the shape of the ad, and results suggest that interactivity may not always benefit the advertiser (Liu & Shrum, 2005).

Product-Related Factors

In recent years, more attention has been devoted to examining product type and its function on advertising effectiveness and almost all of the studies in this area have a managerial focus. Studies suggest that product attributes (high-involvement vs. low-involvement product, functional vs. expressive) play an important role in predicting how consumers process online advertising in terms of the attention given to the ad, memory retention, attitude formation, and behavioral change (Dahlen, Rasch, & Rosengren, 2003). Product attributes also interact with other factor types, for example, consumer-related attributes, and play a moderating role in some cases (Shamdasani, Stanaland, & Tan, 2001). Products also vary by the degree to which they can be digitized where music and movies can be easily transformed into digital files but apparel and food cannot.

Research has shown that products with higher digitizability generate lower perceived risk and greater purchase intention than low digitizable products (Griffith & Chen, 2004). However, the authors found no significant difference in product evaluation and likeability for high versus low digitizable products.

Context-Related Factors

Research in traditional media has shown that, for the same advertising content, different media vehicles or ad contexts can generate different effects for the same audience (Aaker & Brown, 1972). Context effects have also been found in Internet settings and represent our final category. Initial studies attempted to determine and evaluate the value of the Internet as a potential context for advertising (Ducoffe, 1996). As time continued, research areas have broadened to include design/layout of the webpage, website reputation and credibility, and congruence of the ad/web page content. Studies on *background complexity* (i.e., more items, colors, and animation) have shown that users are not distracted by complex backgrounds *but* there is a negative relationship between highly complex backgrounds and psychological responses to that background, although this effect was not replicated in subsequent experiments (Bruner & Kumar, 2000; Danaher & Mullarkey, 2003). *Congruence/relevance* between an ad and its context has been studied quite extensively in traditional advertising contexts and is beginning to be addressed by Internet advertising researchers (Rodgers, 2005). Most of these studies have yielded the consistent result that greater relevance between the ad and its context yields more positive psychological consumer responses (Choi & Rifon, 2002). Looking at ad type (i.e., sponsorships), Rodgers (2003) found that highly relevant ad/contexts yielded greater persuasion for the sponsors *and* the website in which the sponsors were housed. In fact, consumer evaluation of the host website, such as attitude toward the site and perceived site credibility, trust and reputation, has been found to affect advertising effectiveness in many cases (Chen, Griffith, & Shen, 2005; Stevenson, Bruner, & Kumar, 2000) again highlighting the importance of context selection. Context-related studies also have addressed the long-standing issue of ad placement, that is, whether the Internet is more/less effective than traditional media (Rodgers, 2005) and whether any synergistic effects can be gained in combining the Internet with other media such as TV (Chang & Thorson, 2004). Recent work is now shifting focus to understand which components of the Internet influence users' perception of the site's personality and the effects of these perceptions on information processing of those ads (Chen & Rodgers, 2006).

Practical Applications

The Impact of Corporate Responsibility Campaigns: Effects of Online Context and the Fit between Corporate Sponsors and Associated Nonprofits

Consistent with our framework, we outline an experiment that integrates psychological and management approaches. The central question is whether representation of a corporation's sponsorship of a non-profit is differentially successful depending on whether it appears in (1) an online news story, (2) an online paid advertisement in an online newspaper, or in (3) an online press release on the corporation's website. We call this variable "online message context." To make the study richer, we also ask whether message context interacts with how well the non-profit "fits" with the sponsoring corporation. The management approach here is obvious and concerns how public relations-generated messages (i.e., the news story) compare in effectiveness to advertising messages. At the same time, however, the hypotheses about how message context and corporation/non-profit fit are generated from psychological theory. Space constraints prevent complete explication of the relevant theories here, but we give a brief overview of central theoretical concepts.

Advertising research has long examined the question of "context" but most of this research occurred prior to the arrival of the Internet (e.g., Moorman, Neijens, & Smith, 2002; Schumann & Thorson, 1990). We posit here that the primary mediator of contextual impact online is "credibility" (Rodgers & Bae, 2007). Research suggests that the credibility of "news" increases the belief that the information is not tainted by selling motives, but rather is more factual and, therefore more credible (Hallahan, 1999). It may also be that just having an advertisement appear in a news site also increases the transfer of credibility from the online context to the corporation claims (Rodgers, 2007). However, a press release in a corporate website should share none of the context credibility of either of the other conditions. A number of approaches, including attribution theory (Bem, 1972) and persuasion knowledge theory (Friestad & Wright, 1994) also suggest that perceived motivations of corporations are made more positive by the context of being "news" or even being associated with news (Rodgers, 2007).

Our second variable is "fit," the relationship between the semantic network that defines the sponsored non-profit and the sponsoring corporation. A close relationship would occur when a highly salient feature of each semantic network matches. For example, the Goodrich tire company sponsors a program that refurbishes donated cars for the poor (cars-tires). A distant (or low fit) relationship would occur when low-salient features of each semantic networks match (Goodrich sponsors a 5-K run raising money for breast cancer research). Research has shown that in high fit situations as compared to low fit situations, the brand is more likely to reap positive effects on attitude toward the brand and purchase intentions (Rifon, Choi, Trimble, & Li, 2004; Rodgers, 2003, 2007).

A main theory used to explain the effect of fit relates to the psychological impact of congruency (Cornwell, Weeks, & Roy, 2005). Congruent stimuli are thought to create unique memory traces making it easier to locate congruent versus incongruent stimuli in memory (Fiske, 1982). Additionally, congruent stimuli are thought to conform to individuals' expectations and attitude change occurs in the direction of increased congruity within the individual's cognitive schema thereby leading to a favorable response (Mandler, 1981).

Sponsorship studies have demonstrated a number of positive psychological effects for congruous sponsorship links. For instance, memory and purchase intentions are higher and attitudes are more favorable for congruous versus incongruous sponsorships (Rodgers, 2007). However, a congruity effect has not always been found in sponsorship studies. For example, several studies have shown that incongruous sponsors are more advantageous than congruous sponsors in some circumstances (Jagre, Watson, & Watson, 2001). To explain this, incongruity theory suggests that objects that are seen as moderately discrepant from expectations are preferred to either extremely congruent or incongruent alternatives. We refer the reader to additional readings that help to explain the more complex aspects of congruity theory (e.g., see Cornwell & Maignan, 1998; Menon & Kahn, 2003; Szykman, Bloom, & Blazing, 2004).

Based on these areas of theory, we posit the following hypotheses:

H_1: High fit sponsor/non-profit conditions will produce more positive responses to the goals of the non-profit, to the sponsoring corporation, mediated by higher perceptions of sponsor/non-profit congruity.

H_2: More positive responses to the non-profit and the sponsoring corporation will occur to the greatest degree in the news context, second in the paid advertisement in an online newspaper, and lowest in the online press release on the corporation's website.

H_3: The high-fit advantage will be greatest in the low-credibility context (online press release) and lowest in the news context.

The last hypothesis is derived from positing that the cognitive advantages provided by congruency are not as necessary to success when the strength of the contextual credibility is high.

Conclusion

From this review, it is clear that Internet advertising represents a unique and growing subset of advertising research. Of the four areas examined, advertising related-factors have been examined the most and the least examined area is consumer-related factors. There are dozens of studies on banner ads and pop-ups, and although research has begun to examine some of the newer forms of Internet advertising such as advergames and electronic word-of-mouth, there is still a lot of work to be done in the study of other ad types outlined here. Few studies have examined the role of individual differences—a variable that has proven to be an important explanatory factor in the traditional advertising literature—and the role of emotion is seldom addressed online. We are beginning to see crossover among the four areas identified here; for example, the examination of psychological effects of interactivity (a design feature) and perceived interactivity (an individual differences variable) in a blog (an ad type/context) (Thorson & Rodgers, 2006). In general, however, most research in this area continues to be managerial-focused. Indeed, the Interactive Advertising Model (Rodgers & Thorson, 2000), which guided the organization of this section, is predominantly managerial. It appears important to begin any "new" area of advertising with these kinds of managerial approaches; only later, do the more basic studies of psychological processing become common. As the Internet continues to grow in sophistication, we expect to see even greater sophistication in Internet advertising studies that draw on one or more variables from each of the areas outlined here, as well as new variables, probably primarily psychological in nature that will arise as time goes on. Clearly, there are lots of research opportunities here.

Final Note

Our review has attempted to update the reader on advertising research since the first edition of this book and provide a new section on Internet advertising. With so few pages, it is difficult to do justice to the general area of advertising much less new and emerging areas such as Internet advertising. But we hope that the research and theory reported here offers some ideas about where to go to look for advertising research of interest. It may also help to introduce the student of communication to new ideas and concepts that can be used to better understand and test the effects of advertising and Internet advertising.

References

Aaker, D. A., & Brown, P. K. (1972). Evaluating vehicle source effects. *Journal of Advertising Research*, *12*(4), 11–16.

Agres, S. J., Edell, J. A., & Dubitsky, T. M. (1990). *Emotion in advertising: Theoretical and practical explorations*. New York: Quorum Books.

Amiel, T., & Sargent, S. L. (2004). Individual differences in Internet usage motives. *Computers in Human Behavior*, *20*(6), 711–726.

Appiah, O. (2006). Rich media, poor media: The impact of audio/video vs. text/picture testimonial ads on browsers' evaluations of commercial web sites and online products. *Journal of Current Issues & Research in Advertising*, *28*(1), 73–86.

Barry, T. E. (2002). In defense of the Hierarchy of Effects: A rejoinder to Weilbacher. *Journal of Advertising Research*, *42*(3), 44–47.

Batra, R., & Holbrook, M. B. (1987). Development of a set of scales to measure affective responses to advertising. *Journal of Consumer Research, 14,* 404–420.

Becker-Olsen, K. L. (2003). And now, a word from our sponsor. *Journal of Advertising, 32*(2), 17–32.

Bellman, S., & Rossiter, J. R. (2004). The website schema. *Journal of Interactive Advertising, 4*(2), online at http://jiad.org/vol4/no2/bellman/index.htm.

Bem, D. (1972). Self-perception theory. In L. Berkowitz (Ed.), *Advances in Experimental Social Psychology* (Vol. 6). New York: Academic Press.

Bettman, J. R., Capon, N., & Lutz, R. J. (1975). Multiattribute measurement models and multiattribute attitude theory: A test of construct validity. *Journal of Consumer Research, 1* (4), 1–19.

Bezjian, A., Calder, B., & Iacobucci, D. (1998). New media interactive advertising versus traditional advertising. *Journal of Advertising Research, 38*(4), 23–32.

Bhat, S., Bevans, M., & Sengupta, S. (2002). Measuring users' web activity to evaluate and enhance advertising effectiveness. *Journal of Advertising, 31*(3), 97–106.

Braun-LaTour, K. A., & LaTour, M. S. (2004). Assessing the long-term impact of a consistent advertising campaign on consumer memory. *Journal of Advertising, 33*(2), 49–62.

Briggs, R., & Hollis, N. (1997). Advertising on the web: Is there a response before click-through? *Journal of Advertising Research, 37*(2), 33–45.

Bruner II, G. C., & Kumar, A. (2000). Web commercials and advertising hierarchy-of-effects. *Journal of Advertising Research, 40*(1/2), 35–42.

Chaiken, S. (1980). Heuristic versus systematic information processing and the use of source versus message cues in persuasion. *Journal of Personality and Social Psychology, 39,* 752–756.

Chandon, J. L., Chtourou, M. S., & Fortin, D. R. (2003). Effects of configuration and exposure levels on responses to web advertisements. *Journal of Advertising Research, 43*(2), 217–229.

Chaney, I. M., Lin, K. H., & Chaney, J. (2004). The effect of billboards within the gaming environment. *Journal of Interactive Advertising, 5*(1), retrieved October 17, 2007, from http://jiad.org/vol5/no1/chaney/index.htm.

Chang, Y., & Thorson, E. (2004). Television and web advertising synergies. *Journal of Advertising, 33*(2), 75–84.

Chen, Q., Griffith, D. A., & Shen, F. (2005). The effects of interactivity on cross-channel communication effectiveness. *Journal of Interactive Advertising, 5*(2), online at http://jiad.org/vol5/no2/chen/index.htm.

Chen, Q., & Rodgers, S. (2006). Development of an instrument to measure web site personality. *Journal of Interactive Advertising, 7*(1), retrieved October 17, 2007, from http://jiad.org/vol7/no1/chen/index.htm.

Cho, C. H. (1999). How advertising works on the www: Modified elaboration likelihood. *Journal of Current Issues and Research in Advertising, 21*(1), 33–50.

Cho, C. H. (2003). The effectiveness of banner advertisements: Involvement and click-through. *Journalism and Mass Communications Quarterly, 80*(3), 623–645.

Cho, C. H., Lee, J. G., & Tharp, M. (2001). Different forced-exposure levels to banner advertisements. *Journal of Advertising Research, 41*(4), 45–56.

Choi, K. K., Miracle, G. E., & Biocca, F. (2001). The effects of anthropomorphic agents on advertising effectiveness and the mediating role of presence. *Journal of Interactive Advertising, 2*(1), online at http://jiad.org/vol2/no1/choi/index.htm.

Choi, S. M., & Rifon, N. J. (2002). Antecedents and consequences of web advertising credibility: A study of consumer response to banner ads. *Journal of Interactive Advertising, 3*(1), online at http://jiad.org/vol3/no1/choi/index.htm.

Cornwell, B. T., & Maignan, I. (1998, Spring). An international review of sponsorship research. *Journal of Advertising, 27,* 1–21.

Cornwell, B. T., Weeks, C. S., & Roy, D. P. (2005). Sponsorship-linked marketing: Opening the black box. *Journal of Advertising, 34*(2), 21–42.

Coyle, J., & Thorson, E. (2001). The effects of progressive levels of interactivity and vividness in web marketing sites. *Journal of Advertising, 30*(3), 65–77.

Dahlen, M. (2001). Banner ads through a new lens. *Journal of Advertising Research, 41*(4), 23–30.

Dahlen, M., Rasch, A., & Rosengren, S. (2003). Love at first site? A study of website advertising effectiveness. *Journal of Advertising Research, 43*(1), 25–33.

Danaher, P. J., & Mullarkey, G. W. (2003). Factors affecting online advertising recall: A study of students. *Journal of Advertising Research, 43*(3), 252–265.

Day, R. F., Shyi, G. C. W., & Wang, J. C. (2006). The effect of Flash banners on multiattribute decision making: Distractor or source of arousal? *Psychology & Marketing, 23*(5), 369–382.

Ducoffe, R. (1996). Advertising value and advertising on the web. *Journal of Advertising Research, 36*(5), 21–35.

Edell, J. A., & Burke, M. C. (1987). The power of feelings in understanding advertising effects. *Journal of Consumer Research, 14*, 421–433.

Edwards, S. M. (2007). Motivations for using the Internet and its implications for Internet advertising. In D. W. Schumann & E. Thorson (Eds.), *Internet advertising: Theory and research* (pp. 91–119). Mahwah, NJ: Erlbaum.

Edwards, S. M., Li, H., & Lee, J. H. (2002). Forced exposure and psychological reactance: Antecedents and consequences of the perceived intrusiveness of pop-up ads. *Journal of Advertising, 31*(3), 83–95.

Edwards, S. M., Li, H., & Lee, J. H. (2005). Forced exposure and psychological reactance: Antecedents and consequences of the perceived intrusiveness and pop-up ads. In M. R. Stafford & R. J. Faber (Eds.), *Advertising, promotion, and new media* (pp. 215–236). Armonk, NY: M. E. Sharpe.

Fishbein, M., & Ajzen, I. (1975). *Belief, attitude, intention and behavior: An introduction to theory and research.* Reading, MA: Addison Wesley.

Fiske, S. T. (1982). Schema-triggered affect: Applications to social perception. In M. S. Clark & S. T. Fiske (Eds), *Affect and Cognition: The 17th Annual Carnegie Symposium on Cognition* (pp. 55–78). Hillsdale, NJ: Erlbaum.

Friestad, M., & Wright, P. (1994, June). The persuasion knowledge model: How people cope with persuasion attempts. *Journal of Consumer Research, 21*, 1–31.

Gallagher, K. K., Foster, D., & Jeffrey Parsons, J. (2001). The medium is not the message: Advertising effectiveness and content evaluation in print and on the web. *Journal of Advertising Research, 41*(4), 57–70.

Gardner, M., Mitchell, A., & Russo, J. E. (1985). Low involvement strategies for processing advertisements. *Journal of Advertising, 14*(2), 4–12.

Geissler, G. L., Zinkhan, G., & Watson, R. (2006). The influence of homepage complexity on consumer attention, attitude and purchase intent. *Journal of Advertising, 35*(2), 69–80.

Ghose, S., & Dou, W. (1998). Interactive functions and their impacts on the appeal of Internet presence sites. *Journal of Advertising Research, 38*(2), 29–43.

Godin, S. (1999). *Permission marketing: Turning strangers into friends, and friends into customers.* New York: Simon & Schuster.

Gong, W., & Maddox, L. M. (2003). Measuring web advertising effectiveness in China. *Journal of Advertising Research, 43*(1), 34–49.

Griffith, D. A.., & Chen, Q. (2004). The influence of virtual direct experience (VDE) on on-line ad message effectiveness. *Journal of Advertising, 33*(1), 55–68.

Grigorovici, D. M., & Constantin, C. D. (2004). Experiencing interactive advertising beyond rich media: Impacts of ad type and presence on brand effectiveness in 3D gaming immersive virtual environments. *Journal of Interactive Advertising, 5*(1), retrieved October 17, 2007, from http://jiad.org/vol5/no1/grigorovici/index.htm.

Gutman, J. (1983, Spring). A means–end chain model based on consumer categorization processes. *Journal of Marketing, 46*, 60–73.

Ha, H. Y. (2005). The relationships between 3-D advertising and risk perceptions on the web: The role of brand and emotion. *Journal of Current Issues & Research in Advertising, 27*(2), 55–65.

Ha, L., & James, E. L. (1998). Interactivity reexamined: A baseline analysis of early business web sites. *Journal of Broadcasting & Electronic Media, 42*, 457–474.

Hallahan, K. (1999). Content class as a contextual cue in the cognitive processing of publicity versus advertising. *Journal of Public Relations Research, 11*(4), 293–320.

Hoffman, D., & Novak, T. (1996). Marketing in hypermedia computer-mediated environments: Conceptual foundations. *Journal of Marketing, 60*(3), 50–68.

Homer, P. M. (2006). Relationships among ad-induced affect, beliefs, and attitudes. *Journal of Advertising, 35*(1), 35–51.

Hupfer, M. E., & Grey, A. (2005). Getting something for nothing: The impact of a sample offer and user mode on banner ad response. *Journal of Interactive Advertising*, 6(1), online at http://jiad.org/vol6/no1/hupfer/index.htm.

Interactive Advertising Bureau. (2006). Internet advertising revenues continue to accelerate at an unprecedented rate with a 36% increase for first half of '06. IAB press release, retrieved September 9, 2007, from http://www.iab.net/news/pr_2006_09_25.asp.

Jagre, E., Watson, J. J., & Watson, J. G. (2001). Sponsorship and congruity theory: A theoretical framework for explaining consumer attitude and recall of event sponsorship. *Advances in Consumer Research*, 28, 439–445.

Jeandrain, A. C. (2001). Consumer reactions in a realistic virtual shop: Influence on buying style. *Journal of Interactive Advertising*, 2(1), retrieved November 11, 2007, from http://jiad.org/vol2/no1/jeandrain/index.htm

Jee, J., & Lee, W. N. (2002). Antecedents and consequences of perceived interactivity: An exploratory study. *Journal of Interactive Advertising*, 3(1), retrieved November 11, 2007, from http://jiad.org/vol3/no1/jee/index.htm

Johnson, G., Bruner, G., II, & Kumar, A. (2006). Interactivity and its facets revisited. *Journal of Advertising*, 35(4), 35–52.

Jupiter Communications Report (2003). Jupiter Research forecasts paid content will reach $2.0 billion in 2003. Press release online at http://www.jupitermedia.com/corporate/releases/03.03.24-paidcontent.html.

Kalyanaraman, S., & Sundar, S. (2006). The psychological appeal of personalized content in web portals: Does customization affect attitudes and behavior? *Journal of Communication*, 56(1), 110–132.

Ko, H., Roberts, M., & Cho, C. (2006). Cross-cultural differences in motivations and perceived interactivity: A comparative study of American and Korean Internet users. *Journal of Current Issues & Research in Advertising*, 28(2), 93–104.

Korgaonkar, P. K., & Wolin, L. D. (1999, March). A multivariate analysis of web usage. *Journal of Advertising Research*, 39, 53–68.

Krugman, H. E. (1965). The impact of television advertising: Learning without involvement. *Public Opinion Quarterly*, 29, 349–356.

LaFerle, C. (2007). Global issues in online advertising. In D. W. Schumann & E. Thorson (Eds.), *Internet advertising: Theory and research* (pp. 287–311). Mahwah, NJ: Erlbaum.

Lang, A. (2006). Using the limited capacity model of motivated mediated message processing to design effective cancer communication messages. *Journal of Communication*, 56 (Suppl. 1), S57–S80.

Lavidge, R. J., & Steiner, G. A. (1961). A model for predictive measurement of advertising effectiveness. *Journal of Marketing*, 25, 59–62.

Leckenby, J. (2005). The interaction of traditional and new media. In M. R. Stafford & R. J. Faber (Eds.), *Advertising, promotion, and new media* (pp. 3–29). Armonk, NY: M. E. Sharpe.

Leigh, J. H. (2000). An informal, qualitative analysis of shortages and abundances in academic advertising research. In G. Zinkhan (Ed.), *Advertising research: The Internet, consumer behavior, and strategy* (pp. 75–81). Chicago: American Marketing Association.

Leigh, J. H., Zinkhan, G. M., & Swaminathan, V. (2006). Dimensional relationships of recall and recognition measures with selected cognitive and affective aspects of print ads. *Journal of Advertising*, 35(1), 105–122.

Leong, E. K. F., Huang, X., & Stanners, P. J. (1998). Comparing the effectiveness of the web site with traditional media. *Journal of Advertising Research*, 38(5), 44–51.

Li, H., & Bukovac, J. L. (1999). Cognitive impact of banner ad characteristics: An experimental study. *Journalism and Mass Communications Quarterly*, 76(2), 341–353.

Li, H., Daugherty, T., & Biocca, F. (2002). Impact of 3-D advertising on product knowledge, brand attitude, and purchase intention: The mediating role of presence. *Journal of Advertising*, 31(3), 43–57.

Li, H., & Leckenby, J. D. (2007). Examining the effectiveness of Internet advertising formats. In D. W. Schumann & E. Thorson (Eds.), *Internet advertising: Theory and research* (pp. 203–224). Mahwah, NJ: Erlbaum.

Liu, Y., & Shrum, L. J. (2002). What is interactivity and is it always such a good thing? Implications of definition, person, and situation for the influence of interactivity on advertising effectiveness. *Journal of Advertising, 31*(4), 53–64.

Liu, Y., & Shrum, L. J. (2005). Rethinking interactivity: What it means and why it may not always be beneficial. In M. R. Stafford & R. J. Faber (Eds.), *Advertising, promotion, and new media* (pp. 103–124). Armonk, NY: M. E. Sharpe.

Lohtia, R., Donthu, N., & Hershberger, E. K. (2003). The impact of content and design elements on banner advertising click-through rates. *Journal of Advertising Research, 43*(3), 410–418.

Lynch, J. G., Jr., & Srull, T. K. (1982). Memory and attentional factors in consumer choice: Concepts and research methods. *Journal of Consumer Research, 9*, 18–37.

Macias, W. (2003). A preliminary structural equation model of comprehension and persuasion of interactive advertising brand Web sites. *Journal of Interactive Advertising, 3*(2), retrieved September 9, 2007, from http://jiad.org/vol3/no2/macias/index.htm.

Mandler, G. (1981). The structure of value: Accounting for taste. In M. S. Clark & S. T. Fiske (Eds.), *Affect and cognition: The 17th Annual Carnegie Symposium* (pp. 3–36). Hillsdale, NJ: Erlbaum.

Martin, B. A. S., Durme, J. V., Raulas, M., & Merisavo, M. (2003). Email advertising: Exploratory insights from Finland. *Journal of Advertising Research, 43*(3), 293–300.

McGuire, W. J. (1969). An information-processing model of advertising effectiveness. In H. L. Davis & A. J. Silk (Eds.), *Behavioral and management science in marketing* (pp. 156–180). New York: Ronald Press.

McMillan, S. J. (2002). Exploring models of interactivity from multiple research traditions: Users, documents, and systems. In L. A. Lievrouw & S. Livingstone (Eds.), *Handbook of new media: Social shaping and consequences of ICTs* (pp. 163–182). London: Sage.

McMillan, S. (2005). The researchers and the concept: Moving beyond a blind examination of interactivity. *Journal of Interactive Advertising, 5*(2), retrieved September 9, 2007, from http://jiad.org/vol5/no2/mcmillan/index.htm.

McMillan, S. (2007). Internet advertising: One face or many? In D. W. Schumann & E. Thorson (Eds.), *Internet advertising: Theory and research* (pp. 15–35). Mahwah, NJ: Erlbaum.

McMillan, S. J., Hwang, J. S., & Lee, G. (2003). Effects of structural and perceptual factors on attitudes toward the website. *Journal of Advertising Research, 43*(4), 400–409.

Mehrabian, A., & Russell, J. A. (1974). *An approach to environmental psychology.* Cambridge, MA: MIT Press.

Menon, S., & Kahn, B. E. (2003). Corporate sponsorships of philanthropic activities: When do they impact perception of sponsor brand? *Journal of Consumer Psychology, 3*(3), 316–327.

Menon, S., & Soman, D. (2002). Managing the power of curiosity for effective web advertising strategies. *Journal of Advertising, 31*(3), 1–14.

Mitchell, A. A. (1986, June). The effects of visual and visual components of advertisements on brand attitudes and attitudes toward the advertisement. *Journal of Consumer Research, 13*, 12–24.

Mitchell, A. A., & Olson, J. C. (1981). Are product attribute beliefs the only mediator of advertising effects on brand attitudes? *Journal of Marketing Research, 18*, 318–332.

Moore, R., Stammerjohan, C., & Coulter, R. (2005). Banner advertiser-web site context congruity and color effects on attention and attitudes. *Journal of Advertising, 34*(2), 71–84.

Moorman, M., Neijens, P. D., & Smith, E. G. (2002). The effects of magazine-induced psychological responses and thematic congruence on memory and attitude toward the ad in a real-life setting. *Journal of Advertising, 31*(4), 27–40.

Nan, X., Anghelcev, G., Myers, J. R., Sar, S., & Faber, R. (2006). What if a web site can talk? Exploring the persuasive effects of web-based anthropomorphic agents. *Journalism & Mass Communication Quarterly, 83*(3), 615–631.

Nelson, M., R., Keum, H., & Yaros R. A. (2004). Advertainment or adcreep: Game players' attitudes toward advertising and product placements in computer games.*Journal of Interactive Advertising, 5*(1), retrieved November 11, 2007, from http://jiad.org/vol5/no1/nelson/index.htm.

Newell, F. (1997). *The new rules of marketing: How to use one-to-one relationship marketing to be the leader in your industry.* New York: McGraw-Hill.

Nicovich, S. G. (2005). The effect of involvement on ad judgment in a video game environment: The mediating role of presence. *Journal of Interactive Advertising, 6*(1), retrieved November 17, 2007, from http://jiad.org/vol6/no1/nicovich/index.htm.

Nielsen//NetRatings (2007). United States: Average webs usage, month of March 2007, home panel (graphic), retrieved January 10, 2008, from http://www.nielsen-netratings.com/resources.

Olson, J. C., & Reynolds, T. J. (1983). Understanding consumers' cognitive structures: Implications for advertising strategy. In L. Percy & A. Woodside (Eds.), *Advances in consumer psychology* (pp. 77–90). Lexington, MA: Lexington Books.

Osgood, C. E., Suci, G. J., & Tannenbaum, P. H. (1957). *The measurement of meaning.* Urbana: University of Illinois Press.

Palda, K. S. (1996). The hypothesis of a Hierarchy of Effects: A partial evaluation. *Journal of Marketing Research, 3*(1), 13–24.

Papacharissi, Z., & Rubin, A. M. (2000). Predictors of Internet use. *Journal of Broadcasting & Electronic Media, 44*(2), 175–196.

Patwardhan, P., & Yang, J. (2003). Internet dependency relations and online consumer behavior: A media system dependency theory perspective on why people shop, chat and read news online. *Journal of Interactive Advertising, 3*(2), retrieved November 17, 2007, from http://jiad.org/vol3/no2/patwardhan/index.htm.

Pavlou, P. A., & Stewart, D. W. (2000). Measuring the effects and effectiveness of interactive advertising: A research agenda. *Journal of Interactive Advertising, 1*(1), retrieved November 17, 2007, from http://jiad.org/vol1/no1/pavlou/index.htm.

Perlado, V. R., & Barwise, P. (2005). Mobile advertising: A research agenda. In M. R. Stafford & R. J. Faber (Eds.), *Advertising, promotion, and new media* (pp. 216–277). Armonk, NY: M. E. Sharpe.

Petty, R. E., & Cacioppo, J. T. (1979). Issue involvement can increase or decrease persuasion by enhancing message-relevant cognitive responses. *Journal of Personality and Social Psychology, 37,* 1915–1926.

Petty, R. E., & Cacioppo, J. T. (1986). *The elaboration likelihood model of persuasion.* Mahwah, NJ: Erlbaum.

Plutchik, R. (1980). *Emotion: A psychoevolutionary synthesis.* New York: Harper & Row.

Porter, L., & Golan, G. J. (2006). From subservient chickens to brawny men: A comparison of viral advertising to television advertising. *Journal of Interactive Advertising, 6*(2), retrieved November 17, 2007, from http://jiad.org/vol6/no2/porter/index.htm.

Preston, I. (1982). The association model of the advertising communication process. *Journal of Advertising, 11,* 3–15.

Preston, I., & Thorson, E. (1984). The expanded association model: Keeping the hierarchy concept alive. *Journal of Advertising Research, 24,* 59–66.

Rafaeli, S. (1988). Interactivity: From new media to communication. In R. P. Hawkins, J. M. Wiemann, & S. Pingree (Eds.), *Advancing communication science: Merging mass and interpersonal process* (pp. 110–134). Newbury Park, CA: Sage.

Rifon, N. J., Choi, S. J., Trimble, C. S., & Li, H. (2004, Spring). Congruence effects in sponsorship: The mediating role of sponsor credibility and consumer attributions of sponsor motive. *Journal of Advertising, 33,* 29–42.

Rodgers, S. (2002). The interactive advertising model tested: The role of Internet motives in ad processing. *Journal of Interactive Advertising, 2*(2), online athttp://jiad.org/vol2/no2/rodgers/index.htm.

Rodgers, S. (2003). The effects of sponsor relevance on consumer reactions to Internet sponsorships. *Journal of Advertising, 32*(4), 67–76.

Rodgers, S. (2005). Intermedia effects for appropriate/inappropriate print and Internet stimuli. In M. R. Stafford & R. J. Faber (Eds.), *Advertising, promotion, and new media* (pp. 51–67). Armonk, NY: M. E. Sharpe.

Rodgers, S. (2007). Effects of sponsorship congruity on e-sponsors and e-newspapers. *Journalism & Mass Communication Quarterly, 84*(1), 24–39.

Rodgers, S., & Bae, J. (2007). Stigmatizing effects of prosocial alcohol and tobacco sponsorships. *Social Marketing Quarterly, 13*(1), 1–17.

Rodgers, S., Cannon, H. M., & Moore, J. (2007). Segmenting Internet markets. In D. W. Schumann, & E. Thorson (Eds.), *Internet advertising: Theory and research* (pp. 149–183). Mahwah, NJ: Erlbaum.

Rodgers, S., & Chen, Q. (2007). The interactive advertising model: Additional insights into response to spamming. In D. W. Schumann, & E. Thorson (Eds.), *Internet advertising: Theory and research* (pp. 259–283). Mahwah, NJ: Erlbaum.

Rodgers, S., & Sheldon, K. M. (2002). An improved way to characterize Internet users. *Journal of Advertising Research, 42*(5), 85–94.

Rodgers, S., & Thorson, E. (2000). The interactive advertising model: How users perceive and process online ads. *Journal of Interactive Advertising, 1*(1). retrieved June 15, 2007, from http://jiad.org/vol1/no1/rodgers/index.htm.

Rossiter, J. R., & Percy, L. (1978). Visual imaging ability as a mediator of advertising response. *Advances in Consumer Research, 5,* 621–629. Ann Arbor, MI: Association for Consumer Research.

Sandage, C. (1973). Some institutional aspects of advertising. *Journal of Advertising, 1,* 9–14.

Schumann, D., & Thorson, E. (1990). The influence of viewing content on commercial effectiveness: A selection-processing model. *Current Issues and Research in Advertising, 12*(1), 1–24.

Schumann, D., & Thorson, E. (2007). *Internet advertising: Theory and research.* Mahwah, NJ: Erlbaum.

Shamdasani, P. N., Stanaland, A. J. S., & Tan, J. (2001). Location, location, location: Insights for advertising placement on the web. *Journal of Advertising Research, 41*(4), 7–21.

Shapiro, W., & Krishnan, H. S. (2001). Memory-based measures for assessing advertising effects: A comparison of explicit and implicit memory effects. *Journal of Advertising, 30*(3), 1–14.

Shapiro, W., MacInnis, D. J., & Park, C. W. (2002). Understanding program-induced mood effects: Decoupling arousal from valence. *Journal of Advertising, 31*(4), 15–26.

Sheehan, K. B. (2002). Of surfing, searching, and newshounds: A typology of Internet users' online sessions. *Journal of Advertising Research, 42*(5), 62–71.

Shimp, T. A., & Gresham, L. G. (1983). A perspective on advertising literature. In J. H. Leigh & C. R. Martin, Jr. (Eds.), *Current issues and research in advertising* (pp. 39–76). Ann Arbor: Graduate School of Business Administration, University of Michigan.

Sicilia, M., Ruiz, S., & Munuera, J. L. (2005). Effects of interactivity in a Web site: The moderating effect of need for cognition. *Journal of Advertising, 34*(3), 31–45.

Singh, S. N., & Rothschild, M. L. (1983, August). Recognition as a measure of learning from television commercials. *Journal of Marketing Research, 20,* 235–248.

Srull, T. K. (1983). Affect and memory: The impact of affective reactions in advertising on the representation of product information in memory. In R. P. Bagozzi & A. M. Tybout (Eds.), *Advances in Consumer Research* (Vol. 10, pp. 244–263). Ann Arbor, MI: Association for Consumer Research.

Srull, T. K. (1989). Advertising product evaluation: The relation between consumer memory and judgment. In P. Cafferata & A. Tybout (Eds.), *Cognitive and affective responses to advertising* (pp. 121–134). Lexington, MA: Lexington Books.

Stern, B. B., Zinkhan, G. M., & Holbrook, M. B. (2005). The netvertising image: Netvertising image communication model (NICM) and construct definition. In M. R. Stafford & R. J. Faber (Eds.), *Advertising, promotion, and new media* (pp. 30–50). Armonk, NY: M. E. Sharpe.

Steuer, J. (1992). Defining virtual reality: Dimensions determining telepresence. *Journal of Communication, 42,* 73–93.

Stevenson, J. S., Bruner II, G. C., & Kumar, A. (2000). Webpage background and viewer attitudes. *Journal of Advertising Research, 40*(1/2), 29–34.

Stout, P. A., Ball, J. G., & Villegas, J. (2007). Health marketing and the Internet. In D. W. Schumann, & E. Thorson (Eds.), *Internet advertising: Theory and research* (pp. 363–395). Mahwah, NJ: Erlbaum.

Sundar, S. S., & Kalyanaraman, S. (2004). Arousal, memory, and impression-formation effects of animation speed in web advertising. *Journal of Advertising, 33*(1), 7–17.

Sundar, S. S., & Kim, J. (2005). Interactivity and persuasion: Influencing attitudes with information and involvement. *Journal of Interactive Advertising, 5*(2), retrieved November 17, 2007, from http://jiad.org.

Szykman, L. R., Bloom, P. S., & Blazing, J. (2004). Does corporate sponsorship of a socially-oriented message make a difference? An investigation of the effects of sponsorship identity on responses to an anti-drinking and driving message. *Journal of Consumer Psychology, 14*(1/2), 13–20.

Thorson, E. (1990a). Television commercials as mass media messages. In J. J. Bradac (Ed.), *Messages in communication science: Contemporary approaches to the study of effects* (pp. 195–230). Newbury Park, CA: Sage.

Thorson, E. (1990b). Consumer processing of advertising. In J. H. Leigh & C. R. Martin, Jr. (Eds.), *Current Issues and Research in Advertising* (pp. 197–230). Ann Arbor, MI: Division of Research, Graduate School of Business Administration, University of Michigan.

Thorson, E. (1996). Advertising. In M. B. Salwen & D. W. Stacks (Eds.), *An integrated approach to communication theory and research* (pp. 211–230). Mahwah, NJ: Erlbaum.

Thorson, E., Duffy, M., & Schumann, D. W. (2007). The Internet waits for no one. In D. W. Schumann, & E. Thorson (Eds.), *Internet advertising: Theory and research* (pp. 3–13). Mahwah, NJ: Erlbaum.

Thorson, E., & Friestad, M. (1989). The effects of emotion on episodic memory for TV commercials. In P. Cafferata & A. Tybout (Eds.), *Advertising and consumer psychology.* Lexington, MA: Lexington Press.

Thorson, K., & Rodgers, S. (2006). Relationships between blogs and eWOM and interactivity, perceived interactivity, and parasocial interaction. *Journal of Interactive Advertising, 6*(2), retrieved November 20, 2007, from http://jiad.org/vol6/no2/thorson/index.htm.

Thorson, K., & Watson, B. (2007). The new online campaign: Translating information into action. In D. W. Schumann, & E. Thorson (Eds.), *Internet advertising: Theory and research* (pp. 323–342). Mahwah, NJ: Erlbaum.

Till, B. D., & Baack, D. W. (2005). Recall and persuasion: Does creative advertising matter? *Journal of Advertising, 34*(3), 47–58.

Trammell, K. D., Williams, A. P., Postelnicu, M., & Landreville, K. D. (2006). Evolution of online campaigning: Increasing interactivity in candidate Web sites and blogs through text and technical features. *Mass Communication & Society, 9*(1), 21–44.

Tulving, E. (1972). Episodic and semantic memory. In E. Tulving & W. Donaldson (Eds.), *Organization of memory* (pp. 381–403). New York: Academic Press.

Weilbacher, W. M. (2001). Point of view: Does advertising cause a hierarchy-of-effects? *Journal of Advertising Research, 41*(6), 19–26.

Wells, W., Burnett, J., & Moriarty, S. (2003). *Advertising principles and practice.* Upper Saddle River, NJ: Prentice-Hall.

Wu, G. (2005). The mediating role of perceived interactivity in the effect of actual interactivity on attitude toward the website. *Journal of Interactive Advertising, 5*(2), retrieved November 20, 2007, from http://jiad. org/vol5/no2/wu/index.htm.

Yoo, C. H., Kim, K., & Stout, P. A. (2004). Assessing the effects of animation in online banner advertising: Hierarchy of effects model. *Journal of Interactive Advertising, 4*(2), retrieved November 20, 2007, from http://www.jiad.org/vol4/no2/yoo/index.htm.

Yoon, S. J., & Kim, J. H. (2001). Is the Internet more effective than traditional media? Factors affecting the choice of media. *Journal of Advertising Research, 41*(6), 53–60.

Youn, S., & Lee, M. (2005). Advergaming playing motivations and effectiveness: A 'Uses and Gratifications' perspective. In M. R. Stafford & R. J. Faber (Eds.), *Advertising, promotion, and new media* (pp. 320–347). Armonk, NY: M. E. Sharpe.

Suggested Readings

Batra, R., & Holbrook, M. B. (1987). Development of a set of scales to measure affective responses to advertising. *Journal of Consumer Research, 14*, 404–420.

Birnbaum, M. H. (2000). *Psychological experiments on the Internet.* Orlando, FL: Academic Press.

Edell, J. A., & Burke, M. C. (1987). The power of feelings in understanding advertising effects. *Journal of Consumer Research, 14*, 421–433.

Hoffman, D., & Novak, T. (1996). Marketing in hypermedia computer-mediated environments: Conceptual foundations. *Journal of Marketing, 60*(3), 50–68.

MacKenzie, S. B., & Lutz, R. J. (1989). An empirical examination of the structural antecedents of attitude toward the ad in an advertising pretesting context. *Journal of Marketing, 53*(2), 48–65.

McMillan, S. J. (2002). Exploring models of interactivity from multiple research traditions: Users, documents, and systems. In L. Liverow & S. Livingstone (Eds.), *Handbook of New Media*. London: Sage.

Mitchell, A. A., & Olson, J. C. (1981). Are product attribute beliefs the only mediator of advertising effects on brand attitudes? *Journal of Marketing Research, 18*, 318–332.

Rodgers, S., & Thorson, E. (2000). The interactive advertising model: How users perceive and process online ads. *Journal of Interactive Advertising, 1*(1), online at http://jiad.org/vol1/no1/rodgers/index.htm.

Schumann, D. W., & Thorson, E. (1999). *Advertising and the World Wide Web*. Mahwah, NJ: Erlbaum.

Schumann, D. W., & Thorson, E. (2007). *Internet advertising: Theory and research*. Mahwah, NJ: Erlbaum.

Stafford, M. R., & Faber, R. J. (2005). *Advertising, promotion, and new media*. Armonk, NY: M. E. Sharpe.

Part III

HUMAN COMMUNICATION APPROACHES AND CONCERNS

15

HUMAN COMMUNICATION THEORY AND RESEARCH
Traditions and Models

Virginia P. Richmond and James C. McCroskey

The study of human communication has a long and distinguished history. We can safely say that, since humankind first acquired the ability to communicate through verbal and nonverbal symbols and norms, people have "studied" communication. Indeed, one advantage we hold over other animals is the ability to communicate abstractions such as time, place, and space as though each was a concrete object. Thus, since the beginning of our time, we have studied human communication—albeit unscientifically at first, but through more formal systems as we came to better understand both the role of communication in society and its role in daily activity. The importance of the study of human communication is found in its inclusion in educational programs since the first formal schooling systems were developed over 5,000 years ago.

In order to understand how human communication is studied today, it is important to appreciate how we got to where we are now. We will not, however, attempt to provide a complete discussion of the history communication scholarship here. Rather, we will focus on the more important developments and time periods which have impacted on the contemporary study of human communication. Our goal is to foster an understanding of how what was done in the past influences what we do today, and most likely will influence what we do in the future.

The importance of communication in human society has been recognized for thousands of years, far longer than we can demonstrate through recorded history. The oldest essay ever discovered, written about 3,000 BC, consists of advice on how to speak effectively. This essay was inscribed on a fragment of parchment addressed to Kagemni, the eldest son of the Pharaoh Huni. Similarly, the oldest extant book is a treatise on effective communication. The *Precepts* was composed in Egypt about 2,675 BC by Ptah-Hotep and written for the guidance of the Pharaoh's son. While these works are significant because they establish that the study of human communication is older than any other area of current academic interest, the actual contribution to current communication theory was minimal.

The study of human communication today can be divided into two major classifications—rhetorical and relational (Shepherd, 1992). The rhetorical communication approach focuses primarily on the study of influence. The function of rhetorical communication is to get others to do what you want or need them to do or think the way you want or need them to think—to persuade them. The relational approach, on the other hand, examines communication from a transactional or coorientational perspective. That is, two (or more) people coordinate their communication to reach a shared perspective satisfactory to all. Of paramount concern is the relationship between the two people and the perceived well-being of the "other."

These two divergent orientations represent the dominant orientations of Western (individualistic) and Eastern (collectivistic) cultures. At their extremes, the Western (rhetorical) orientation would sacrifice relationships to accomplish influence and the Eastern (relational) orientation would sacrifice the achievement of influence to protect relationships. It is not pragmatic, however, to conceive of these two approaches to the study of human communication as polar opposites. Rather, they represent differences in emphasis. Both are interested in accomplishing objectives and maintaining good relationships through communication. Each, however, emphasizes one objective over the other.

We will examine the influence of both of these orientations toward the study of human communication. The impact of the rhetorical tradition has been the strongest and longest (McCroskey, 1968, 2006), so we will consider it first.

The Rhetorical Tradition

The rhetorical tradition begins some 2,500 years after Kagemni's early writing, during the 5th century BC, at Syracuse, in Sicily. When a democratic regime was established in Syracuse after the overthrow of the tyrant Thrasybulus, its citizens flooded the courts to recover property that had been confiscated during his reign. The "art of rhetoric" that Corax developed was intended to help ordinary people prove their claims in court. Corax and his student, Tisias, are also generally credited with the authorship of a manual on public speaking, but the work is no longer extant. Although we are not certain of its contents, scholars suggest that it included two items significant to the development of rhetorical theory. The first was a theory of how arguments should be developed from probabilities, a theory more thoroughly developed by Aristotle a century later. Corax and Tisias are also credited with first developing the concept of message organization, what we today call an introduction, a body, and a conclusion.

In Athens, during the 5th century BC, there was a large group of itinerant teachers, known as *sophists,* who established small schools and charged students for attending their lectures on rhetoric, literature, science, and philosophy. Many of these teachers became quite wealthy through their efforts. Protagoras of Abdara, sometimes called the "Father of Debate," was one of the first and most important sophists. His teachings contended that there were two sides to every proposition (a *dialectic)* and that speakers should be able to argue either side of the proposition equally well. This view, commonly accepted by today's teachers of argumentation and debate, provides the foundation in the United States for communication in today's legal and legislative systems, the very basis of democratic government itself.

Aristotle's Rhetoric

Aristotle, in the 3rd century BC, is generally considered the foremost theorist in the history of the study of human communication from the rhetorical perspective. His *Rhetoric,* written in about 330 BC, is the most influential work on the topic. It consists of three books, one primarily concerned with the speaker, another concerned with the audience, and the third with the speech itself.

Book 1 discusses the distinction between rhetorical communication and dialectical communication (the process of inquiry). Aristotle criticized his contemporaries for dwelling upon irrelevant matters in their rhetorical theories rather than concentrating on proofs—particularly enthymemes—or arguments from probabilities. He defined *rhetoric* as "the faculty of discovering in a particular case what are the available means of persuasion." To Aristotle, the means of persuasion were primarily *ethos* (the nature of the source), *pathos* (the emotions of the audience), and *logos* (the nature of the message presented by the source). He focused his concern on three types of speaking: deliberative (speaking in the legislature), forensic (speaking in the law court), and epideictic (speaking in a ceremonial situation). He was concerned with formal public speaking settings and did not address what we would call today "everyday" or "interpersonal" communication.

Within his overall theory of rhetoric, Aristotle included three critical elements. The first was that effective rhetoric is based on argumentation, and that all arguments must be based on *probabilities*. Aristotle held that absolute, verifiable truth is unobtainable in most instances. Therefore, persuasion must be based on what an audience believes to be true. Whereas his teacher, Plato, found this to be a defect in rhetoric and condemned it, Aristotle perceived it simply as a fact, and not a moral issue.

The second essential element in his approach was a conception of the rhetorical communicator's basic task was to *adapt to the audience*. Aristotle believed that you could not persuade a person unless you knew what was likely to persuade that individual. That is, he believed that a knowledge of what we now call "psychology" was essential to effective communication.

These two elements, probability and psychology, led to the third important element in his theory: rhetoric's basic "amorality." Aristotle viewed rhetoric as a tool, one which could be used by anyone—by a good person or a bad one, by a person seeking worthy ends or by one seeking unworthy ends. At the same time, he argued that rhetoric was a self-regulating art. By that he meant the person who is unethical, or who advocates evil, is less likely to be successful than the moral person advocating something good. As justification, he claimed that good and right, by their very nature, are more powerful persuasive tools than their opposites. While acknowledging that evil might win out in the short-run, Aristotle believed that evil would ultimately fail unless people arguing on behalf of good were incompetent rhetorical communicators.

During the Roman period, the 1st century AD, Aristotle's work was known and writers such as Cicero and Quintillion (often called the "greatest orator" and "greatest teacher," respectively) wrote works within the general perspective of his work, although they were not always in agreement Aristotle's ideas. In general, the Roman period applied the rhetorical theory of the ancient Greeks, and helped to spread its use across the ancient world. There was not a great amount of writing on rhetoric in the Middle Ages. During the Renaissance, however, more attention was directed toward rhetoric, and although Aristotle's works were known to the scholars of the time, most of their writings centered on matters of style rather than the concerns Aristotle had advanced.

During the 18th century writers such as George Campbell and Richard Whately in England resurrected the Aristotelian perspective toward communication and advanced it with their own theories. In the United States, Professor John Quincy Adams (the same John Quincy Adams later to become President of the United States), who held the chair of rhetoric at Harvard University, presented a series of lectures which set forth for the first time in America a thoroughly classical view of rhetoric. This view was extended in the early 20th century by the early writers, such as James Winans, in what became the field of "Speech."

American Rhetorical Study

The first professional organization of people concerned with the study of human communication, now known as the Eastern Communication Association, was formed in 1909 by a group of teachers of public speaking housed mainly in departments of English at Eastern colleges and universities. Five years later, many of these same people joined with people from other parts of the United States to form what is now known as the National Communication Association, a national professional association that was then primarily composed of teachers of public speaking.

The people in these associations were primarily concerned (then and now) with developing greater understanding of how human communication works and how people can be taught to be more effective communicators. Because the political and social systems in American society in the first half of this century were very similar to those of Greece in the time of Aristotle, the Aristotelian rhetorical tradition was an excellent fit to the needs of the scholars of that era. The Aristotelian tradition soon became solidly entrenched as the dominant paradigm for the study of human communication.

During the first half of the 20th century the study of human communication expanded rapidly into what has come to be known as the "Speech" tradition. Academic departments of speech were founded in most major colleges and universities across the United States, particularly in the large Midwestern institutions. The primary emphasis in these programs was the teaching of public speaking and the study of human communication in the Aristotelian rhetorical tradition. Most programs sponsored debating teams, á la Protagoras, and attempts to generate new knowledge about effective rhetoric were centered primarily on rhetorical *criticism* of the addresses of effective, or usually at least famous, public orators.

Although the rhetorical tradition held sway for the most part, departments of speech expanded their attention to include many other aspects of oral communication. Theater and oral reading, voice and diction, speech pathology and audiology, radio and television broadcasting, and film classes all become common. By the middle of the 20th century many of these new offerings had grown into full-blown programs. Many of these speciality areas began leaving the speech departments and forming academic units of their own. Theater and oral reading often joined other fine arts programs. Speech pathology and audiology, often accompanied by voice and diction, usually formed their own unit or joined other allied health programs. Broadcasting frequently joined with journalism, and print-oriented programs in public relations and advertising, to form mass communication programs. Sometimes film studies joined this group as well.

In many cases, departments which began with their focus on public speaking and the rhetorical tradition diversified extensively and split into several academic units. They then came full circle back to the study of public speaking and the rhetorical tradition. These programs continue to have a strong focus on public presentations, argumentation, and persuasion. Whereas, as we discuss more fully later, most of these programs made major changes in their curricula (and their names) in the last half of the 20th century, most continue to include a strong emphasis on work that follows the rhetorical tradition.

Perspectives on the Rhetorical Tradition

In order to understand the nature of the rhetorical approach to the study of human communication, it is useful to gain perspective on the culture in which it originated and where it still thrives. From today's perspective the cultures of ancient Greece and Rome had many positive and many negative characteristics. Despite their interest in philosophy, religion, and the arts and their commitment to a form of democracy, they were harsh cultures. Life expectancies were short, and life was very hard for most people.

These were slave-owning societies in which slaves could be killed or severely punished for even slight offenses against their masters. There was one dominant culture and the rulers of that culture were highly ethnocentric. People of other races and cultures were seen as inferior beings whose lives and well-being were of little value. Women were considered men's property and often treated only slightly better than the slaves. The men of the dominant race and ethnic group totally ruled society. The society was both racist and sexist, and these views were seldom challenged. For all, master and slave, that was just the way it was. From most people's perspectives, these were *not* the good old days.

The legislative and legal systems of these societies were devoted to the maintenance of the ruling class. It was important that the members of that class could resolve disputes and engage in coordinated action to maintain their power and control over the society. Understanding how to communicate effectively within this small ruling group was critical to one who wished to protect one's own interests or attain higher leadership status. Communication, then, was seen as a strategic tool—one to be used by those in power. The perspective was source-oriented—how a speaker could get an audience to do what he wanted them to do. Communication in the courts and in the legislature was primarily concerned with public speaking, and the effective orator was a much respected and powerful person.

Although we sometimes do not like to acknowledge it, this description of ancient Greece and Rome can be applied to earlier periods of Western culture, including the United States and many other societies of the 17th through 19th centuries. Like many other societies, we were a slave-owning society, one in which women, too, were seen as possessions of men. Our legislative and legal systems were modeled on Greco-Roman, Judea-Christian, Anglo-European tradition. The rhetorical orientation of the Speech Tradition was tailor-made for this society.

The mass communication tradition, like the speech tradition, sprouted from roots in the rhetorical orientation. The predecessors of many of the people working in mass communication today were in departments of journalism and advertising, as well as in speech. Since the beginnings of the study of mass communication focused on public presentation and mass influence, the rhetorical orientation also fit the needs of these early scholars.

The Relational Tradition

The relational tradition is at least as old, and possibly older, than the rhetorical tradition. However, no serious attention was devoted to this orientation in the United States until the latter half of the 20th century. The foundations of the relational orientation stem from ancient Confucian philosophy. Hence, this orientation is most commonly associated with Eastern thought.

While individualism, competition, and straightforward communication are highly valued in most Western societies, Eastern societies have higher values for congeniality, cooperation, and indirect communication which will protect the "face" of the people interacting. Maintaining valued relationships is generally seen as more important than exerting influence and control over others.

The existence of approaches to communication other than the rhetorical approach was recognized by some scholars in the United States prior the mid-20th century. However, serious attention to the relational orientation did not begin until the 1950s and 1960s. Influential writers such as Robert Oliver (1962) attempted to get the field to pay more attention to the role of culture in communication and how different cultures viewed communication in other parts of the world.

Transitioning to the Relational

A new professional association for communication scholars was founded in 1950, the National Society for the Study of Communication, now known as the International Communication Association. This group was comprised of individuals disillusioned with studying communication exclusively from the rhetorical perspective. Some were general semanticists, others were primarily concerned with communication in organizations, and others in yet more applied communication settings. In the 1960s and 1970s this association attracted many scholars who were interested in interpersonal communication or the effects of mass media, particularly those who wished to study communication employing quantitative or experimental research methodologies.

The social–scientific movement was very important for the development of the study of human communication as it currently exists. Prior to the onset of this movement, most scholarship in this area employed critical or rationalistic approaches. These approaches were seen as appropriate for the study of essentially monological, one-way communication. Their focus was on the message and context as objects of study. As this one-way, hypodermic-needle approach to understanding communication came under increasing criticism both the target of research and the methodologies for research came into question.

The social scientific approach to studying human communication had been employed by some since early in the 20th century. However, it was not until the post-World War II era that the scientific method became the method of choice for a substantial number of communication scholars. It was natural that a different scholarly method would be applied to the same kinds of questions previously asked (how to persuade effectively) and to new questions. This, indeed, was the case. In the 1960s much of the social scientific research focused on the effects of sources and messages in producing persuasive effects. So much so that, when the early books on interpersonal communication were written, there was very little social scientific research which could be cited in them. By the mid-1970s, however, it was possible to base a book on human communication almost entirely on the social scientific research (McCroskey & Wheeless, 1976).

By the time NSSC became ICA and reached its 25th anniversary, sizeable groups of scholars had formed scholarly interest areas representing organizational communication, interpersonal communication, information systems, mass communication, intercultural communication, instructional communication, health communication, and political communication. Most of these groups also included people from both the rhetorical and the relational traditions.

The quarter-century between 1950 and 1975 represented revolutionary change both in the culture of the United States and in the way people chose to study human communication. The post-World War II and Korean War eras saw dramatic increases in the enrollments of women and members of ethnic and racial minorities in American colleges and universities. Higher education no longer was the domain only of the elite, male, White ruling class.

The civil rights movement of the early 1960s was followed by the women's rights movement of the later 1960s and 1970s. The way people saw themselves relating to others began to change. There were enormous enrollment increases in colleges and universities when the "baby boomers" reached college age, which was exacerbated by rapid acceptance of the goals of the civil rights and women's rights movements.

These new students had different needs and arrived with different perspectives from those of their predecessors. Because colleges were no longer solely focused on educating "tomorrow's leaders," people began to question the extreme emphasis on teaching public speaking over other types of communication. Classes in small-group communication, and research in this area, greatly increased.

A Truly Relational Perspective

A call for more practical and realistic communication courses was heard. The response by the early 1970s was the initiation of new courses with the term "interpersonal" in their titles. Because little research from a relational perspective had been done by that time, the early courses tended to focus on rhetorical and psychological approaches to interpersonal communication. The early texts tended to focus on either humanistic (Giffin & Patton, 1971) or social scientific (McCroskey, Larson, & Knapp, 1971) orientations. A true relational perspective did not appear until later (Knapp, 1984).

Because *speech* was a term used to identify the traditional rhetorical orientation of the people who studied human communication, and the field was changing, people sought ways to change the identity of their field. While public speaking was no longer the sole, or even most important, focus of the field, people outside the field were generally unaware of this fact. At first, it seemed sufficient to simply add "communication" to the names of departments and associations. Soon it became clear that this change was not enough to make outsiders aware that a major change had been made. Thus, by the mid-1990s the term *speech* had been dropped from the names of almost all scholarly journals in the field, from the names of all the regional and many of the state professional associations, and from the names of most of the departments at major universities. The names generally were changed to "Communication" or "Communication Studies," but some were renamed "Human Communication," "Interpersonal Communication," or "Communication Sciences," although the latter could be confused with some names used by groups concerned with speech pathology and audiology.

Human Communication Today

The study of human communication today is more diversified than ever before in its history. This diversity is reflected in both what is studied and the way that one goes about studying it.

Both the rhetorical and the relational traditions are alive and well and reflected in the chapters that follow. Each chapter outlines current thinking in either what could pass for a subfield (persuasion, intercultural communication, organizational communication), or a topic area (credibility, nonverbal communication), which has been and continues to be a focus of attention for numerous scholars, or an approach that some prefer to take in their study of human communication (cultural, feminist).

Because these chapters speak to the way these subfields, areas, or approaches are examined today, there is no need to go into detail here. Within the limitations of a book this size, it is not possible to fully introduce all of the areas within the human communication side of the field. Thus, we simply mention a few that are important but for which no chapter is included here.

The individual differences approach is one which has been employed by some scholars for the past half century and continues to draw major attention today. This approach looks at how people consistently differ from one another in their communication orientations and behaviors. Sometimes this approach is referred to as the personality approach (McCroskey & Daly, 1987).

Scholars studying human communication from this approach investigate how different people have different traits or orientations which result in them communicating differently from other people and responding to others' communication differently as well. Two of the major topics within this area are concerns with people's general willingness to communicate with others and the fear or anxiety that people experience when confronted with communication (Daly & McCroskey, 1984).

With the rapid advances in social biology which indicate that personality has a firm genetic base, this area is one in which we can expect major advances in the next two decades. The possibility exists that through genetic engineering we will even be able to alter individuals' patterns of communication behavior that are found dysfunctional in society. Whether we will want to do this, however, is another question.

From the beginning of professional associations in the communication field, a significant number of the members have had a major concern with teaching. Originally that interest was centered on how to teach people to be better communicators. In recent years, this interest in instruction has expanded to a concern with the role of communication in the instructional process generally, not just in teaching communication (McCroskey, 1992). Considerable research in this area (Richmond & McCroskey, 1992) has pointed toward a central position for the study of communication to improve instruction in all disciplines.

Another applied area of communication study is an expansion of the basic interpersonal area.

It is the study of communication within the family (Pearson, 1989). Recent research has been able to track the impact of communication between parents and children into the relationships that the younger generation have years later with their significant others. It would appear that understanding the communicative relationships within the family may be key to understanding other relationships people have.

An area which has received considerable attention in recent years is the role of gender in communication (Pearson, 1985). Although research focusing on the impact of biological sex differences on communication has generally found little impact, research on culturally based gender roles has indicated a very large impact. This is an area in which cross-cultural study is particularly useful, for we have learned that gender communication roles are so socialized into people that they are unlikely to recognize they are behaving according to a norm unless they see that there are different norms in other cultures.

A comparatively new approach to the study of communication is the developmental approach (Nussbaum, 1989). This approach examines how communication orientations and behaviors are likely to change during the individual's life span. Of particular interest has been the impact of aging on communication (Nussbaum, Thompson, & Robinson, 1989).

The most recent advance in the study of human communication is the introduction of the new paradigm named "communibiology" (Beatty & McCroskey, 1997, 2001; Beatty, McCroskey, & Heisel, 1998). For the previous history of the study of communication, most scholars assumed that most if not all communication behaviors were learned. Most research relating to the causes of communication behaviors was dominated by this learning paradigm. Near the end of the 20th century, scholars in communication became suspicious of this paradigm. The results of most of the research being reported at that time indicated that learning accounted for very little variance in their data analyses. The question then, was that if learning is not the primary cause of communication orientations or behaviors, what is the real cause(s)? Beatty and McCroskey speculated that some communication behavior may be a manifestation of biological factors. The results of their research supported that view. Genetics was the first biological area that was determined to have a powerful impact on communication orientations and behavior. In particular, genetically based brain systems known to drive human temperament have also been found to predict substantial variance in orientations and behaviors associated with the communication traits of verbal aggression and communication apprehension. More recent research is uncovering other biological factors with similar impact on communication orientations and behaviors, some of which are genetically based and some not.

Summary

Although steeped in tradition, the general trend of scholarship in the human communication side of the field of communication is toward more sophisticated theoretical development. It continues to develop more diverse subareas within each larger area of the field, while grounding itself in research methodologies useful for the specific concerns in the study of communication (rather than borrowing from other fields). Its approach is also increasingly concerned with applied communication research. The study of human communication today is undertaken in a vibrant and forward looking environment, building on firm traditions but diversifying to confront newly learned realities.

References

Beatty, M. J., & McCroskey, J. C. (1997). It's in our nature: Verbal aggressiveness as temperamental expression. *Communication Quarterly, 45,* 446–460.

Beatty, M. J., & McCroskey, J. C. (2001). *The biology of communication: A communibiological perspective.* Cresskill, NJ: Hampton Press.

Beatty, M. J., McCroskey, J. C., & Heisel, A. D. (1998). Communication apprehension as temperamental expression: A communibiological paradigm. *Communication Monographs, 65,* 197–219.

Daly, J. A., & McCroskey, J. C. (1984). *Avoiding communication: Shyness, reticence, and communication apprehension.* Beverly Hills, CA: Sage.

Giffin, K., & Patton, B. R. (1971). *Fundamentals of interpersonal communication.* New York: Harper & Row.

Knapp, M. L. (1984). *Interpersonal communication and human relationships.* Boston, MA: Allyn & Bacon.

McCroskey, J. C. (1968). *An introduction to rhetorical communication.* Englewood Cliffs, NJ: Prentice-Hall.

McCroskey, J. C. (1992). *An introduction to communication in the classroom.* Edina, MN: Burgess International.

McCroskey, J. C. (2006). *An introduction to rhetorical communication* (9th ed.). Boston: Allyn & Bacon.

McCroskey, J. C., & Daly, J. A. (1987). *Personality and interpersonal communication.* Newbury Park, CA: Sage.

McCroskey, J. C., Larson, C. E., & Knapp, M. L. (1971). *An introduction to interpersonal communication.* Englewood Cliffs, NJ: Prentice-Hall.

McCroskey, J. C., & Wheeless, L. R. (1976). *Introduction to human communication.* Boston, MA: Allyn & Bacon.

Nussbaum, J. F. (1989). *Life-span communication: Normative processes.* Hillsdale, NJ: Erlbaum.

Nussbaum, J. F., Thompson, T., & Robinson, J. D. (1989). *Communication and aging.* New York: Harper & Row.

Oliver, R. T. (1962). *Culture and communication: The problem of penetrating national boundaries.* Springfield, IL: National Textbook.

Pearson, J. C. (1985). *Gender and communication.* Dubuque, IA: William C. Brown.

Pearson, J. C. (1989). *Communication in the family: Seeking satisfaction in changing times.* New York: Harper & Row.

Richmond, V. P., & McCroskey, J. C. (1992). *Power in the classroom: Communication, control and concern.* Hillsdale, NJ: Erlbaum.

Shepherd, G. J. (1992). Communication as influence: Definitional exclusion. *Communication Studies, 43,* 203–219.

Suggested Readings

Beatty, M. J., & McCroskey, J. C. (2001). *The biology of communication: A communibiological perspective.* Cresskill, NJ: Hampton Press.

Daly, J. A., & McCroskey, J. C. (1984). *Avoiding communication: Shyness, reticence, and communication apprehension.* Beverly Hills, CA: Sage.

McCroskey, J. C. (2006). *An introduction to rhetorical communication* (9th ed.). Boston: Allyn & Bacon.

McCroskey, J. C., & Daly, J. A. (1987). *Personality and interpersonal communication.* Newbury Park, CA: Sage.

McCroskey, J. C., & Wheeless, L. R. (1976). *Introduction to human communication.* Boston, MA: Allyn & Bacon.

Richmond, V. P., & McCroskey, J. C. (1992). *Power in the classroom: Communication, control and concern.* Hillsdale, NJ: Erlbaum.

16

THE RHETORICAL PERSPECTIVE
Doing, Being, Shaping, and Seeing

J. David Cisneros, Kristen L. McCauliff, and Vanessa B. Beasley

In a previous edition of this volume, Walter Fisher and Stephen O'Leary (1996) asked, "How does the rhetorical theorist theorize or philosophize?" If theory "consists of constructs that purport to explain or account for phenomena" (p. 243), it would follow that rhetorical theory is the business of explaining what rhetoric is as well as accounting for how and why it functions. Indeed, Fisher and O'Leary answered their own question by stating that the rhetorician's goal is to "identify, and occasionally help to reformulate, the rational decision rules that guide communication in the groups, cultures, and societies that we study" (p. 258). In short, studying rhetoric involves studying the rules of decision making and the ways in which we can see these rules at work within public communication, even at times when it may seem that there are no rules at all.

In this chapter we accept and extend their notions about these basic goals of rhetorical theory. To our minds, rhetorical theorists have always been interested in formulating rules and reconstructing reason in an effort to understand the relationship between public discourse and *doxa,* or situated, shared public knowledge. In other words, what we know and how we act as a society are always articulated through rhetoric. Additionally, we seek to highlight some conceptual developments that have been especially evident within rhetorical theory over the last few decades. Some rhetorical scholarship embraces a more traditional paradigm of rhetoric, one which might be classified as instrumental, in which rhetoric is viewed primarily as a strategic means to a particular suasory end. Meanwhile, other scholars have increasingly been furthering a second paradigm that seeks to explore two interrelated functions of rhetoric: its broader symbolic and constitutive impact(s). This second impulse enables theorists and critics to ask how rhetoric may impact one's sense of self as well as larger social realities and one's place within them. In addition, we discuss a third impulse in rhetorical scholarship too, one that asks questions about how ideological structures—such as those that maintain distinctions based on class, gender, and ethnicity, for example—are shaped by popular discourse. Finally, while some rhetorical scholarship seeks to outline how rhetoric works or what rhetoric does, other scholars have begun to expand our definitions of rhetoric beyond written or spoken words to include visual images, physical acts, and other types of symbolic activity.

Most contemporary theory is informed by at least one of these four different theoretical senses of what rhetoric is and what it does. While these senses are not necessarily mutually exclusive, the choice to emphasize one of them more than the others is usually an important one within case-driven rhetorical research. In other words, such theoretical commitments can have fateful implications for rhetoricians, especially to the extent that they can predispose both critics and theorists to study some questions, texts, and contexts while paying less attention to others. Before we discuss such choices and the traditions they illuminate, we first turn to an explanation of the more general and historic context for the development of rhetorical theory.

The Rhetorical Perspective: Ancient Roots, Persistent Themes

The questions rhetorical scholars ask and answer have their roots in classical Greek philosophy. Rather than arising in a post-Enlightenment age in which empiricism and positivism were prized over other ways of knowing, rhetoricians have long been interested in a more interpretive approach. Rhetorical scholars may work from different epistemological assumptions than other scholars. For instance, Fisher and O'Leary (1996) explained that one of the defining characteristics of rhetoricians is that instead of seeking "explanations entailing linear causation" as is customary in, for example, scientific research, they "are more than willing to accept explanations that assume teleological causation, reasoning from a comprehensive construct to an interpretation of particular acts, deeds, or events" (p. 244). Therefore the rhetorician is constantly seeking "better explanations" (p. 245), in Fisher and O'Leary's words, for how and why suasory communication works rather than seeking to establish new laws or patterns of its causes or effects. Rule formation is a key goal of rhetorical theory, but it is important to note at the outset that rhetoricians tend to be interested in particular kinds of rules, rules that privilege deep explanation over broad predictive utility.

This tendency is arguably a result of one of rhetoric's basic properties: contingency. As we will discuss in greater detail shortly, the ancient Greeks understood rhetoric to be a pragmatic art, situated in the immediate needs, real and imagined, of a speaker, audience members, and the larger social environment within which they found themselves. In fact, contemporary rhetorical critics are sometimes drawn to studying specific instances of rhetoric because these texts appear to be especially fitting responses to emergent or otherwise pressing exigencies. We tend to think of these texts as examples of the right thing said at exactly the right time, such as Abraham Lincoln's Gettysburg Address or Martin Luther King, Jr.'s "I Have a Dream" speech (see, for example, Black, 1994; Browne, 2002; Calloway-Thomas & Lucaites, 1993; Goodnight, 1986; Houck, 2002). Increasingly, however, there are other forms of rhetorical discourse that scholars want to understand, from less artful political speeches, to annoying infomercials on television, to inflammatory posts on personal blogs, to controversial comments on radio talk shows. Even if we might suppose that these texts, too, were crafted to meet a persuasive goal within a specific situation, the stunning breadth of what counts as rhetoric can beg questions about how something this vast can be examined critically or theorized. What does it mean, exactly, to take a rhetorical perspective on a text? What conceptual commitments are assumed to be part of such a stance? Many of the basic answers to these questions can also be found in the classical roots of rhetorical theory.

First, to take a rhetorical perspective means to assume that rhetoric itself is not inherently good or bad, but instead is a vehicle that can be used for either (or both) of these purposes. For someone new to the study of rhetoric, it can be surprising to learn that "rhetoric" is not, in fact, a pejorative term. It is true, of course, that people have long associated rhetoric with deceit, emptiness, and trickery; the ancient Greek philosopher Plato argued exactly these points in the Socratic dialogue *The Gorgias*. Plato defined rhetoric as mere "flattery" and "personal adornment," nothing more than "a habitude or knack" (Plato, 1967, 463a-b). Interestingly, we can trace the modern antipathy towards rhetoric to Plato's distrust of it in *The Gorgias*. Plato's intellectual influence on modern Western society is immeasurable, and this distinction he made between truth and "mere words" continues to inform the disparaging way many of us think about language in contemporary society. Yet most contemporary scholars of rhetoric tend to avoid definitions that carry any such presupposed normative leanings. Thus, many scholars think of rhetoric as both the study of what is persuasive and the purposive use of messages to invite assent. In short, rhetoric is the craft of producing reason-giving discourse that is grounded in social truths (Campbell & Huxman, 2003). Fisher and O'Leary (1996) stated: "rhetoric pertains to all pragmatic, persuasive discourse, honest and dishonest" (pp. 246–247). The larger point is that rhetoric is more encompassing, as a classification of discourse, than merely those expressions which one may think of as being empty, false, or misleading. Most rhetoricians would reject the phrase "mere rhetoric." "As a genre," Fisher and O'Leary write, "rhetoric names that form of communication which is argumentative or persuasive" (p. 247). "One may condemn rhetoric," they note, "but one cannot escape it" (p. 246).

If rhetoric is ubiquitous, why is it so frequently feared? It is feared because it is powerful. This is the second premise of a rhetorical perspective: that discourse, language, and persuasive symbols are influential tools within a society. In short, rhetoric matters. From studies of Hitler's propaganda efforts during World War II (Burke, 1974), to more contemporary investigations of messages about gender within popular culture (Dow, 2001; Dow & Tonn, 1993; Parry-Giles & Blair, 2002; Zaeske, 2002), rhetorical scholars agree that public discourse is influential. For this reason, rhetorical competence is an important goal for scholars interested in empowering students and thus citizens.

From Greek times onward, teachers of rhetoric have tried to provide students with descriptive and conceptual tools for understanding and, indeed, decoding rhetoric as best they can. Despite Plato's condemnation of rhetoric, the ancient Greeks saw the art of persuasive speaking as a necessary cornerstone of their inaugural democracy. Rhetoric was the ultimate skill for the ancient Greeks, useful in the assembly to sway other citizens just as it was necessary in the courts of justice to make one's case before a jury. Because of rhetoric's power and importance in their society, the Sophists—ancient Greek speech teachers—valued rhetoric above most other scholarly pursuits. Aristotle, a student of Plato and an important ancient philosopher and scientist in his own right, developed the first systematic theory of rhetoric. While for the Sophists rhetoric was a skill one could learn to do through practice, Aristotle (1954) created a *theory* of rhetoric that informed practical speaking while also providing guidelines for rhetorical analysis. For Aristotle, rhetoric had a place at the intellectual table along with philosophy and science.

Like contemporary rhetoricians, Aristotle and the Sophists saw rhetoric as pragmatic and powerful. These are properties of rhetoric that continue to fascinate rhetorical scholars today. As this brief survey makes clear, ancient tensions in the study of rhetoric literally defined the evolution of the study of rhetoric in Western civilizations and still animate research in rhetoric today. In fact, the third assumption of a rhetorical perspective starts with this simple proposition—that rhetoric can and should be carefully studied. This presumption, however, can often spur some debates. How should rhetoric be studied? To what end? Even if we are to criticize rhetoric, must we theorize it (Darsey, 1994)? Likewise, where is rhetoric located? What are the boundaries of rhetoric? These central questions continue to fuel the research of rhetorical scholars. And, just as in Ancient Greece, different scholars answer these questions distinctly, leading to a host of diverse perspectives. In the remainder of this chapter, we review some of these different answers.

The Rhetorical Perspective: Enduring Themes, Contemporary Choices

All scholars make choices regarding the focus of their study. Many recent rhetorical scholars choose to study particular examples of rhetoric as a way to learn about rhetoric as a whole. Rhetoricians study oratory for a window into the political or historic world. Others focus on how public discourse constructs peoples' identities. Still others expand the purview of rhetoric into other realms like visual arguments and mass media. Rhetoric can even serve, for some thinkers, as an avenue for political and intellectual struggle. In choosing their areas of research, rhetorical critics make choices along at least two broad levels.

At the first level, rhetoricians choose what social scientists might call a unit of analysis. That is, they decide which instances of rhetoric or messages they will study. Rhetoricians often call their units of analysis "texts" because of the traditional focus on speech texts, yet as the study of rhetoric has grown, rhetoricians have looked to other, diverse types of messages such as pamphlets, newspapers, or even television and radio messages. Likewise, non-verbal communication is also increasingly of interest to rhetoricians. What can scholars make of visual images, for example, and the persuasive impacts they may have?

At a second level, rhetorical scholars must also reflect upon the goal(s) of their research. Simply put, what is at stake in their scholarship? What is the purpose of their rhetorical analysis? Some scholars study rhetorical texts to learn more about the texts themselves or about the processes of persuasion, while others seek to understand more broadly the possible role(s) rhetoric can play within society and politics. Just like Aristotle, Plato, and the Sophists before them, rhetorical scholars tend to answer these questions differently, opening the door to a host of other questions that drive their research and study.

As we now turn to a more specific discussion of some of these different research trajectories, it is important to restate that each approach stems from a common concern with persuasion and social influence. Despite their different answers to the many historically rooted questions about rhetoric, rhetoricians are collectively concerned with interpreting texts and understanding the ways that language is used to motivate people to beliefs or actions. Yet even within this framework, we will see that a distinction between instrumental and constitutive approaches becomes more apparent. In the more established instrumental paradigm, for instance, a rhetor's language might be studied for strategies used to meet persuasive goals; in the constitutive approach, however, scholars might be more concerned with messages that a rhetor gives individuals about who they are (or whom it would like for them to be). The "rhetorical perspective" is large enough to contain both of these concerns. To begin, let's examine an approach that is more instrumental and closer to the pragmatic and persuasive classical traditions of rhetoric.

Rhetoric as Doing: Instrumental Approaches to Rhetoric

One important type of research rhetoricians do examines culturally or historically important speeches to explain both how they were designed *and* how they were strategically responsive to their circumstances. This tradition, often known as "public address" within the communication discipline, associates the value of rhetoric, generally speaking, with the pragmatic maintenance of democratic culture. Some of the questions that drive this research are: (1) what makes rhetoric worthy of note; (2) how does noteworthy rhetoric proceed internally; and (3) how does this rhetoric respond to its external context(s).

Since the units of analysis for these classical approaches are usually speeches and other persuasive texts (including political tracts, editorials, or books), "close reading" is a fitting name for the central methodological approach within this tradition. Close reading of texts seeks to note and explain their internal workings by attending to intrinsic rhetorical features such as language, tone, metaphor, and types of evidence. Michael C. Leff's scholarship exemplifies this "close reading" approach. Leff (1988) studied how a speech is constructed out of component parts that work together to form "an artistic whole" (p. 26). In his rhetorical analysis of Abraham Lincoln's address at Cooper Union, Leff (Leff & Mohrmann, 1974) immersed himself in Lincoln's rhetoric, every detail, every turn of language, and every change in tone, to "illuminate the speech as a speech" (p. 346).

This close reading approach recognizes that speeches are "carefully-crafted piece[s]" (Medhurst, 1987, p. 204) of rhetoric that demand close scrutiny. Scholars in this close reading tradition focus on descriptive study of the text and its component parts. This close reading approach may seem to closely resemble some literary analysis, but what makes this rhetorical perspective unique is that it focuses on texts that are assumed to have been created as persuasive messages intended to sway audiences. Therefore, critics in this tradition are concerned with studying texts for their own sakes as well as for how they were meant to have impact on audiences' decision making.

As the ancient Greeks knew, however, rhetoric is about more than effective speaking in the abstract; it is also a practical, situated art. Thus this neo-classical trajectory can also carefully situate great rhetoric within the complex historical and cultural context in which it occurred. Rhetoricians in this vein emphasize that rhetoric is purposive public communication meant to respond to a specific time, place, and audience. Stephen Browne (1988), for instance, continued the strategy of "close and detailed reading of the text" in his analysis of the rhetoric of political figures such as Edmund Burke (p. 215). Browne, however, recognized that the texts he analyzed (whether speeches or writings) do not exist in a vacuum, so he analyzed them in and through the political and intellectual developments of their time periods. David Zarefsky (1986, 1990) worked on the presidential rhetoric of Abraham Lincoln and Lyndon B. Johnson, among others. His goal was to explain their speeches as a way to illuminate the historical periods in which these presidents served. Working from the instrumental tradition of rhetoric, the goal here is to understand how great and important rhetoric emerged out of a specific moment in history and thus functioned to promote a message to particular audiences. In a sense, scholars in this tradition build on the Aristotelian legacy through their continual dance between rhetoric as a practically grounded art and as a theoretical program of study. That is, they make arguments about why one case (or one text) is worthy of our attention, even as they are also making arguments about how much, if anything, we can extrapolate to our understanding of other cases or times. Public address scholars typically study rhetoric as an instrument of social influence and persuasion connected to pragmatic social and political goals. Springboarding from this perspective on rhetoric, other scholars have expanded the study of the functions and purposes of rhetoric beyond explicit instances of persuasion and motivation. These new definitions posit rhetoric as more than an instrument of beliefs or actions, but as a social force that creates group identities and social relations.

Rhetoric as Being: Symbolic and Constitutive Approaches

Much of the traditional history of rhetoric has emphasized its instrumentality. That is, the study of rhetoric has often been meant to enhance our knowledge of great speeches and our understanding of persuasive speaking as a craft. Yet recognizing the power of rhetoric, like the Sophists did, leads us to the conclusion that rhetoric operates on more than just an intentional, intellectual level. Scholars have expanded the understanding of rhetoric by arguing that it has the power to create identities and motivate certain types of action. Listening to a great speech can do more than change our minds about a particular topic; it can change who we are, how we think about the world, and what our values are. Symbolic and constitutive approaches to rhetoric expand our definitions of rhetoric beyond the instrumental paradigm. Perhaps the most famous scholar to theorize this larger, societal role of language is Kenneth Burke.

Rather than focusing primarily on individual texts, Burke was interested in developing a theory of language. Burke's writings, which drew from philosophy, psychology, and literature, concerned what language is and what language does. Through his definition of "man" as the "symbol-using (symbol-making, symbol-misusing) animal," Burke (1966, p. 16) situated rhetoric at the core of what makes us human. Humanity's uniqueness, he argued, lies in its inherent symbolicity. Yet, for Burke, language was more than expression—language was a type of "symbolic action." Beyond persuasion, Burke situated identification and division as rhetoric's key functions. Language works to unite people around shared common identities or to divide people based on key constructed differences. As such, rhetoric creates attitudes, beliefs, relationships, and actions.

Burke's paradigmatic example of the symbolic power of language was the rhetoric of Adolf Hitler. Through his language, Hitler was able to create a unified German identity by scapegoating Jewish people. This identification and division fueled immense hatred and unmatched atrocities (Burke, 1974, pp. 191–220). Burke's dramatistic theory of rhetoric revolved around a pentad of terms that could be used to understand any rhetorical situation.

Ultimately, the different theoretical components Burke developed work together to enrich our notions of language; they help us recognize the power of rhetoric to create attitudes and actions. Burke's voluminous writings on rhetoric belie a simple and brief explanation, but his perspectives continue to influence rhetoricians in myriad ways. Rhetorical research stemming from Burke's work on language abounds (Dow, 1994; Ling, 1969; Ott & Aoki, 2002). Burke's work is significant because it expands our focus from what rhetoric explicitly does to the ways it defines realities, creates identities, and induces attitudes or actions.

Symbolic and constitutive approaches to rhetoric also consider the power rhetoric has to create individual and group identities. Traditionally, the speaker and the audience have been considered by most rhetoricians, including the ancient Greeks, as static and distinct identities. We assume that the speaker is speaking to an already-assembled group of people, whether large or small, in person or over the airwaves. Yet if rhetoric is symbolic action, can it act to define an audience as well as the identity of the speaker? The "constitutive" approach to rhetoric posits that audiences and speakers are never preexistent to the speaking situation but are created through the rhetorical act. Concurrently, rhetoric not only interpellates, or calls into being, its audience, but it also draws boundaries on the audience and excludes other people from this group. Your professor constitutes you as the class of students and him- or herself as the instructor. This relationship is built through your professor's rhetoric on the first day, including the way you and your classmates are addressed and the material that is covered. If your professor started the first day of class by addressing you colloquially as a friend would talk to you on a Friday night, this would constitute an entirely different set of identities and relationships.

Maurice Charland (1987) explained this constitutive perspective. He argued that the audience is not extra-rhetorical, or prior to the rhetorical act, but is constructed through the text. Michael McGee (1975) provided a concrete example of this constitutive function of rhetoric through his discussion of the common notion of "the people." He noted that the makeup of "the people" is constructed as a mythical reality based on who speaks and to whom the discourse is addressed. The notion of "Americans" can include or exclude certain groups of people depending on who is speaking and who is being addressed. According to this approach, recognizing the power of rhetoric to create identities means that critics should not only attend to the immediate audience of a text, as public address approaches tend to do, but to the ways that rhetoric calls into being an audience's identity outside of this immediate context.

The constitutive and symbolic perspectives are merely two approaches out of many that have complicated our traditional notions of rhetoric as intentional persuasive appeal. Burkean dramatism and the constitutive approach are two popular and promising theoretical approaches that illuminate the role of rhetoric in creating beliefs, attitudes, identities, and actions. These diverse theories of language thicken our understanding of what rhetoric is and what it does. Yet rhetoricians have continued to push the boundaries of rhetoric into new areas, testing what we consider purposeful, persuasive, and pragmatic discourse and what we understand this discourse to do.

Once we recognize the constitutive and symbolic power of rhetoric to motivate actions and identities, the natural question to ask is: from where do these constructions stem and whom do they serve. The symbolic and the constitutive approaches set the stage for what has been called the ideological turn in rhetorical studies. According to this perspective, rhetoric is not only persuasive and symbolic but also ideological, which is to say rhetoric creates beliefs and social relationships that serve particular interests and reinforce the power of certain powerful groups.

Critics within this strand of research often take the theoretical functions of rhetoric for granted and instead search for "powerful vested interests benefiting from and consistently urging" (Wander, 1983, p. 18) popular rhetorical constructions. What are the ideas and identities being circulated in our world through rhetoric? Whom do these rhetorical constructions benefit, and whom do they disadvantage? It is this ideological perspective to which we turn in the next section.

Rhetoric as Shaping: Ideological Approaches

The idea that rhetoric is ideological encapsulates a different and unique vision of what rhetoric is and does. Those rhetorical scholars who operate within this approach use theory in order to criticize and expose the ways rhetoric shapes systems of privilege and domination. Ideological rhetorical scholarship is a way to understand the clashing of identities. More than merely expressing competing political opinions, the ideological perspective treats rhetoric as the purveyor of ideology. While the some thinkers understand ideology as a dogmatic, negative political idea, rhetorical critics understand ideology to mean the real implications of power relationships. As such, scholars like Phillip Wander (1983) advocate a different type of rhetorical theory—one that does not just deconstruct the world, but rather analyzes the material interests at work in the world. For this type of criticism, researchers investigate how rhetoric is both created and constrained by powerful interests throughout society. In short, criticism evolves out of political action and cannot be separated from it. Therefore, this view of both rhetoric and rhetorical scholarship is very pragmatic. Since domination and power are implicated in the texts under analysis, this ideological view of rhetoric encourages action by the critic. Critics can reshape discourses of power through exposing their inner workings. The subjective feelings of the critic are involved in the writing process. Therefore, this type of scholarship involves choices that are explicitly political and opinionated in a way that other forms of criticism may not involve.

A critic concerned with an ideological approach seeks to discover whose interest rhetoric serves. In ideological approaches, criticism is a way to look at new patterns of control and power. As such, critics examine multiple texts, structures of thought, and bodies of literature. For example, Michael McGee (1980) illustrated the power of ideographs, or morally and emotionally charged terms such as "freedom" or "equality," through an analysis of diverse types of cultural discourses. Importantly, McGee stressed that ideographs could be everywhere—in many types of discourses. Invoking these terms could influence society's attitudes and consciousness to serve certain viewpoints or interests. In this type of ideological work, critics are not expected to objectively remove their interests from the analysis. Instead, for Phillip Wander, McGee, and others, criticism is informed talk about matters of social importance. Because this research is firmly rooted in societal issues, we see a variety of theoretical approaches, including Marxist and post-structuralist approaches.

The ideological approach to rhetoric stresses different systems of power. For example, Jim Aune (1990) and Dana Cloud (1996) emphasize class as a primary unit of analysis throughout much of their work. Their rhetorical scholarship examined how public discourse contributed to systems of class oppression. However, Celeste Condit (1997) urged critics to take a more practical and wide-reaching approach to power. She argued that class cannot be one's main unit of analysis because ideology reaches beyond class to include race and gender interests. Regardless of the role of class in a scholar's work, ideological critics are concerned with the historical and cultural thought exercised by the dominant culture. These critics analyze power as a dynamic process through which a body of discourse speaks to the ideological workings of society.

Ideological criticism also supports the notion that all cultural productions are infused with questions of gender and race. Feminist criticism shares similar goals with critical, ideological criticism. Like the work of scholars on social and economic class, the goal of feminist criticism is both emancipation and enlightenment. As such, feminist scholars are typically interested in unearthing texts by women rhetors and studying the ways rhetorics constitute women in good and bad ways.

Early feminist scholarship examined the ways scholarly and societal institutions worked against women. These scholars argued that the traditional ways rhetoric was studied did not lend themselves to an inclusion of female texts. In short, the standards of effective rhetoric (such as presidential inaugurals and keynotes) were not types of discourse in which women were able to participate. Therefore, feminist critics argued that the standards for speech evaluation must be rethought in order to include a more diverse range of voices. Feminist and gender critics attempted to break down the status quo of the academy and include diverse perspectives. An important starting point for this line of research came from Karlyn Kohrs Campbell (1989) who coined the term "feminine style." Campbell argued that women rhetors developed a "feminine style" of public speaking, and through this style, early women rhetors were able to bridge the tension between norms of femininity and expectations of the rhetor's role. Campbell's exploration of female rhetors provided the groundwork for feminist scholarship in communication studies. As Dow and Tonn (1993) noted, Campbell offered an "alternative critical orientation with which to understand the source, form, and function of female communicative strategies and their effectiveness in feminist movements" (p. 286). Significantly, many feminist scholars drew on Campbell's work in order to examine women's rights advocates and more contemporary women rhetors.

Celeste Condit (1997) expanded upon this traditional feminist rhetorical scholarship and argued that there are too many genders and biological identities to simplify scholarship in terms of feminine and masculine style. Instead of studying female rhetors for the ways they performed a particular "feminine style," Condit looked to the functions of rhetoric to empower and subordinate gender identities. Many media critics have embraced Condit's ideas and examined how media representations reinforce gender binaries and the idea that gender is a stable construct. Connecting with the constitutive perspective, Bonnie Dow's (2001) influential work on the television show *Ellen* exemplifies this combination of ideological and gender criticism. She argued that systems of control constrain how gender is portrayed in the mainstream media. Other scholars, such as John Sloop (2004) and Charles E. Morris (2002), examined culture's attempts to stabilize gender and sexual identities. These examples of rhetorical scholarship also compliment both traditional feminist scholarship and ideological criticism, which examine multiple discourses and broad power structures in order to construct thematic representations through a variety of texts. Therefore, as we argued in the introduction of this chapter, these types of critics choose to analyze the gender implications of discourse.

Race criticism has similar goals as both feminist scholarship and ideological studies. Also comparable are the types of research done by race theorists. Race studies typically follow one of two paths. First, many race scholars are concerned with unearthing texts from black rhetors. As such, race studies examine rhetoric and rhetorical strategies from a variety of rhetors not represented in more traditional rhetorical scholarship. Critics like Malinda Snow (1985) conformed to more instrumental types of scholarship. Snow examined Martin Luther King's "Letter from Birmingham Jail" and argued that King relied on some traditional rhetorical strategies (such as metaphors and allusions) but also invented some of his own. Likewise, Kirt Wilson (2005) studied King's Montgomery Bus Boycott address and argued that critics must not only see the address as a significant historical development but a powerful rhetorical text as well. Like feminist and gender scholars, race scholars are concerned not only with studying texts by African-American rhetors but with how discourse shapes racial identity. For example, Eric King Watts (2001) explored the rhetorical performance of W.E.B. DuBois during the Harlem Renaissance. He argued that black intellectuals face specific rhetorical problems that DuBois had to overcome.

Besides work on African-American rhetoric, there are scholars beginning work on Latino, Asian, and Muslim cultures (Enck-Wanzer, 2006; Ono, 2005; Ono & Sloop, 2002). Additionally, some scholars have begun to study the rhetorical power of white identity (Nakayama & Krizek, 1995).

Not only have rhetoricians, using theories of rhetoric centering on ideology, begun to challenge traditional ideas about what rhetoric does, rhetoricians are also beginning to expand our understandings of what rhetoric is. When we began, we introduced two questions that rhetoricians continue to wrestle with in the tradition of their ancient Greek ancestors: What is rhetoric and what is at stake in rhetoric? Much of the work we have reviewed thus far has been concerned with the latter question. Whether classical approaches that focus on rhetoric as instrumental persuasion, or ideological perspectives that examine rhetoric's role in upholding power and domination, these strands of research attempt to outline the myriad ways rhetoric works and the many effects it has. Yet, while rhetoricians have expanded the functions of rhetoric since its birth in ancient Greece, the boundaries of rhetoric are also continually pushed by the work of rhetorical scholars. In the face of monumental changes in society and culture, the natural question to ask is how the bounds of rhetoric and the limits of the text expanded in the age of the television and the Internet. We will conclude our tour of rhetorical studies by examining some perspectives on the rhetoric of the video and the image.

Rhetoric as Seeing: The Visual Turn in Rhetorical Studies

In the preceding sections we have noted how the purview of rhetorical studies has expanded as scholars complicate notions of rhetoric beyond explicitly persuasive or instrumentalist approaches to consider rhetoric's symbolic, constitutive, and ideological functions. Along with this theorization of the role of rhetoric, scholars have also expanded what is considered a rhetorical "text." Rhetoricians are turning to other forms of persuasive messages beyond public speeches, books, pamphlets, and newspapers to consider the role of visual images and videos as forms of rhetoric. This "visual turn" in rhetorical studies recognizes that images and video have become important components of our society. If images, whether on television, the silver screen, or on the web, increasingly usurp public speeches and other traditional forms of rhetoric, how does the visual operate rhetorically, and how does the advent of the visual mark monumental changes in modern culture?

The first concerns, then, that this "visual turn" has brought to the attention of rhetorical studies is how to conceptualize images, photos, and videos as suasory messages. One way to answer this question stems from the "classical" approach that studies the text within its immediate context. Operating in this close reading tradition, some visual scholars examine an image closely for how it works to persuade audiences through its format and content. Lester C. Olson (1987, 1990), for example, analyzed drawings and icons produced and published by Benjamin Franklin to determine their significance as visual arguments in the revolutionary climate of the American colonies. Robert Hariman and John Louis Lucaites (2001), on the other hand, hearkened to the constitutive approach in their study of the iconic photograph of Marines planting the American flag after their victory at Iwo Jima. Hariman and Lucaites argued that the image embodied a history of civic identity and nationalism in its visual depiction. Thus, some visual scholars expand rhetorical studies to consider the persuasive power and constitutive force of images.

Another way to answer the question of "how does an image work as rhetoric" is to consider the unique properties of images that distinguish them from traditional texts. Our modern "visual culture," some theorists argue, demands we look at images as a distinct form of rhetoric. Kathleen Hall Jamieson (1988) noted that today, "in the age of television, dramatic, digestive, visual moments are replacing memorable words" (p. x). As such, Jamieson argued that this shift from a verbal to a visual culture necessitates dramatic changes in how we think about rhetoric as a process of social influence and symbolic action. Following this call, much work on visual rhetoric centers on filling in the space of the visual in rhetorical theory. Studying images on their own terms carries with it a demand to create a "vocabulary" for images to explain their functions and effects without understanding them merely as illustrated versions of traditional, verbal texts.

One possible answer to this search for the unique role of the visual in rhetoric comes in the notion of the "image event," an exclusively visual form of rhetoric in which groups stage visual spectacles like protests meant for media dissemination (DeLuca, 1999). Another perspective rejects the separation between images and words, and studies images for how they cooperate with textual or verbal messages to create a verbal-visual "imagetext" (Finnegan, 2005). Both of these perspectives aim to develop ways of studying images as rhetoric that differentiate them from other types of verbal and textual rhetoric.

The extension of rhetoric into the visual realm provides new avenues for scholars to examine social influence, persuasion, and identity formation. Recognizing the power of images and videos, rhetoricians have begun to incorporate the visual into many already-existing scholarly perspectives on rhetoric. We can study images for what they say, what they did in their particular contexts, or the identities they constitute. Yet the "visual turn," like other movements in the study of rhetoric, has also challenged some of the fundamental tenets of rhetorical studies by positing the unique rhetoricity of images. Both of these approaches to images thicken our understandings of the functions and forms of rhetoric; in doing so, they expand the study of rhetoric into new and exciting horizons. Rhetorical theorists continue to deepen understandings of rhetoric and broaden the limits of the discipline. More recently, scholars are expanding the purview of rhetoric into the way that material objects like the Vietnam Memorial or the AIDS quilt operate rhetorically (Blair, 1999). This continuing creativity points to the perpetual promise of rhetorical studies.

Conclusion

This chapter has addressed two central questions—what is rhetoric and what is at stake in rhetoric? We traced classical approaches rooted in the Greek tradition that conceptualize rhetoric as instrumental persuasion meant for political, pragmatic ends. Other critics are concerned with how rhetoric works to unite people around shared common identities or to divide people based on key constructed differences. As such, constitutive approaches view rhetoric as symbolic and identity-producing. An ideological perspective examines rhetoric as a key tool in upholding societal power and domination. Additional strands of research attempt to outline ways rhetoric works within and across gender and race identities. We concluded this tour of rhetorical studies by examining some perspectives on the rhetoric of the visual and the image.

If nothing else, this chapter has shown that rhetorical scholarship can take many different trajectories. Perhaps it is ironic, then, that while the core of rhetorical studies involves examining the rules of decision making, it may seem there are no rules at work in the myriad ways in which rhetoricians define their task. It is true that there is much diversity in how rhetorical scholars answer these two questions: what is rhetoric, and what is at stake in studying rhetoric. At the heart of all rhetorical scholarship, are the age old questions about the role of rhetoric.

Despite the many answers rhetorical scholars develop to these questions, we all have common concerns that unite our study into a discipline. These three defining elements of the rhetorical perspective we discussed at the beginning of the chapter. Despite which texts we study or the reasons we study those texts, rhetoricians believe that rhetoric is pragmatic, powerful, and worth studying. Rhetoricians are all concerned with the study of reason-giving public discourse and the way it creates social truths and collective actions. While this chapter has only skimmed the surface of the field of rhetorical studies, it does provide us with a window into the workings of the rhetorical perspective. As new rhetorical scholars begin to ask questions and push the limits of our ideas about rhetoric, only time will tell what the rhetorical perspective has yet to uncover.

References

Aristotle. (1954). *The rhetoric and poetics of Aristotle* (W. R. Roberts & I. Bywater, Trans.). New York: Random House.

Aune, J. J. (1990). Marxism and rhetorical theory. *Communication, 11,* 265–276.

Black, E. (1994). Gettysburg and silence. *Quarterly Journal of Speech, 80,* 21–36.

Blair, C. (1999). Contemporary U.S. memorial sites as exemplars of rhetoric's materiality. In J. Selzer & S. Crowley (Eds.), *Rhetorical bodies* (pp. 16–57). Madison: University of Wisconsin Press.

Browne, S. H. (1988). Edmund Burke's "Letter to a Noble Lord": A textual study in political philosophy and rhetorical action. *Communication Monographs, 55,* 215–229.

Browne, S. H. (2002). "The Circle of Our Felicities": Thomas Jefferson's first inaugural address and the rhetoric of nationhood. *Rhetoric and Public Affairs, 5,* 409–438.

Burke, K. (1966). *Language as symbolic action: Essays on life, literature, and method.* Berkeley: University of California Press.

Burke, K. (1974). *The philosophy of literary form: Studies in symbolic action.* Berkeley: University of California Press.

Calloway-Thomas, C., & Lucaites, J. L. (Eds.). (1993). *Martin Luther King, Jr., and the sermonic power of public discourse.* Tuscaloosa, AL: University of Alabama Press.

Campbell, K. K. (1989). *Man cannot speak for her: A critical study of early feminist rhetoric* (Vol. 1). New York: Praeger.

Campbell, K. K., & Huxman, S. S. (2003). *The rhetorical act: Thinking, speaking, and writing critically* (3rd ed.). Belmont, CA: Thomson Wadsworth.

Charland, M. (1987). Constitutive rhetoric: The case of the peuple Québécois. *Quarterly Journal of Speech, 73,* 133–150.

Cloud, D. (1996). Hegemony or concordance? The rhetoric of tokenism in Oprah Winfrey's rags-to-riches biography. *Critical Studies in Mass Communication, 13,* 115–137.

Condit, C. M. (1997). In praise of eloquent diversity: Gender and rhetoric as public persuasion. *Women's Studies in Communication, 20,* 91–116.

Darsey, J. (1994). Must we all be rhetorical theorists? An anti-democratic inquiry. *Western Journal of Communication, 58,* 164–181.

DeLuca, K. M. (1999). *Image politics: The new rhetoric of environmental activism.* New York: Guilford.

Dow, B. J. (1994). AIDS, perspective by incongruity, and gay identity in Larry Kramer's "1112 and Counting." *Communication Studies, 45,* 225–240.

Dow, B. J. (2001). Ellen, television, and the politics of gay and lesbian visibility. *Critical Studies in Media Communication, 18,* 123–140.

Dow, B. J., & Tonn, M. B. (1993). "Feminine style" and political judgment in the rhetoric of Ann Richards. *Quarterly Journal of Speech, 79,* 286–303.

Enck-Wanzer, D. (2006). Trashing the system: Social movement, intersectional rhetoric, and collective agency in the Young Lords organization's garbage offensive. *Quarterly Journal of Speech, 92,* 174–201.

Finnegan, C. A. (2005). Recognizing Lincoln: Image vernaculars in nineteenth-century visual culture. *Rhetoric & Public Affairs, 8,* 31–58.

Fisher, W. R., & O'Leary, S. D. (1996). The rhetorician's quest. In M. B. Salwen & D. W. Stacks (Eds.), *An integrated approach to communication theory and research* (1st ed., pp. 243–260). Mahwah, NJ: Erlbaum.

Goodnight, G. T. (1986). Ronald Reagan's re-formulation of the rhetoric of war: Analysis of the "Zero Option," "Evil Empire," and "Star Wars" addresses. *Quarterly Journal of Speech, 72,* 390–414.

Hariman, R., & Lucaites, J. L. (2001). Performing civic identity: The iconic photograph of the flag raising on Iwo Jima. *Quarterly Journal of Speech, 88,* 363–392.

Houck, D. W. (2002). *F. D. R. and fear itself: The first inaugural address.* College Station, TX: Texas A&M University Press.

Jamieson, K. H. (1988). *Eloquence in an electronic age: The transformation of political speechmaking.* New York: Oxford University Press.

Leff, M. C. (1988). Dimensions of temporality in Lincoln's second inaugural. *Communication Reports, 1,* 26–31.

Leff, M. C., & Mohrmann, G. P. (1974). Lincoln at Cooper Union: A rhetorical analysis of the text. *Quarterly Journal of Speech, 60,* 346–358.

Ling, D. A. (1969). A pentadic analysis of Senator Edward Kennedy's address to the people of Massachusetts, July 25, 1969. *Central States Speech Journal, 21,* 81–86.

McGee, M. C. (1975). In search of "the people": A rhetorical alternative. *Quarterly Journal of Speech, 61,* 235–249.

McGee, M. C. (1980). The "ideograph": A link between rhetoric and ideology. *Quarterly Journal of Speech, 66,* 1–17.

Medhurst, M. J. (1987). Eisenhower's "Atoms for Peace" speech: A case study in the strategic use of language. *Communication Monographs, 54,* 204–220.

Morris, C. (2002). Pink herring and the fourth persona: J. Edgar Hoover's sex crime panic. *Quarterly Journal of Speech, 88,* 228–244.

Nakayama, T. K., & Krizek, R. L. (1995). Whiteness: A strategic rhetoric. *Quarterly Journal of Speech, 81,* 291–309.

Olson, L. C. (1987). Benjamin Franklin's pictorial representations of the British colonies in America: A study in rhetorical iconology. *Quarterly Journal of Speech, 73,* 18–42.

Olson, L. C. (1990). Benjamin Franklin's commemorative medal, "Libertas Americana": A study in rhetorical iconology. *Quarterly Journal of Speech, 76,* 23–45.

Ono, K. (2005). (Ed.) *Asian American studies after critical mass.* Malden, MA: Blackwell.

Ono, K., & Sloop, J. (2002). *Shifting borders: Rhetoric, immigration and California's "Proposition 187."* Philadelphia: Temple University Press.

Ott, B. L., & Aoki, E. (2002). The politics of negotiating public tragedy: Media framing of the Matthew Shepard murder. *Rhetoric & Public Affairs, 5,* 483–505.

Parry-Giles, S., & Blair, D. M. (2002). The rise of the rhetorical first lady: Politics, gender ideology, and women's voice, 1789–2002. *Rhetoric & Public Affairs, 5,* 565–600.

Plato. (1967). Gorgias (W. R. Lamb, Trans.). In *Plato in twelve volumes* (Vol. 3, pp. 447a–527e). Cambridge, MA: Harvard University Press.

Sloop, J. (2004). *Disciplining gender: Rhetorics of sex identity in contemporary U.S. culture.* Amherst: University of Massachusetts Press.

Snow, M. (1985). Martin Luther King's "Letter from Birmingham Jail" as Pauline epistle. *Quarterly Journal of Speech, 71,* 318–334.

Wander, P. (1983). The ideological turn in modern criticism. *Central States Speech Journal, 34,* 1–18.

Watts, E. K. (2001). Cultivating a black public voice: W.E.B. DuBois and the "Criteria for Negro Art." *Rhetoric and Public Affairs, 4,* 181–201.

Wilson, K. (2005). Interpreting the discursive field of the Montgomery Bus Boycott: Martin Luther King Jr.'s Holt Street address. *Rhetoric & Public Affairs, 8,* 299–326.

Zaeske, S. (2002). Signatures of citizenship: The rhetoric of women's antislavery petitions. *Quarterly Journal of Speech, 88,* 147–168.

Zarefsky, D. (1986). *President Johnson's war on poverty: Rhetoric and history.* Tuscaloosa, AL: University of Alabama Press.

Zarefsky, D. (1990). *Lincoln, Douglas, and slavery: In the crucible of public debate.* Chicago: University of Chicago Press.

Suggested Readings

History of Rhetoric

Bizzell, P., & Herzberg, B. (Eds.). (1990). *The rhetorical tradition: Readings from classical times to the present.* Boston: St. Martin's Press.

Instrumental Approach

Browne, S. H. (1996). Encountering Angelina Grimke: Violence, identity, and the creation of radical community. *Quarterly Journal of Speech, 82,* 38–54.

Jasinski, J. (1997). Instrumentalism, contextualism, and interpretation in rhetorical criticism. In A. G. Gross & W. M. Keith (Eds.), *Rhetorical hermeneutics: Invention and interpretation in the age of science* (pp. 195–224). Albany: State University of New York Press.

Symbolic and Constitutive Approaches

Black, E. (1970). The second persona. *Quarterly Journal of Speech, 56,* 109–119.

Christiansen, A. E., & Hanson, J. J. (1996). Comedy as cure for tragedy: Act Up and the rhetoric of AIDS. *Quarterly Journal of Speech, 82,* 157–172.

Ideological Approach

Lucaites, J., & Condit, C. (1990). Reconstructing <equality>: culturetypal and counter-cultural rhetorics in the martyred black vision. *Communication Monographs, 57,* 5–24.

Wander, P. (1984). The third persona: An ideological turn in rhetorical theory. *Communication Studies, 35,* 197–216.

Visual Approach

Blair, C. (2001). Reflections on criticism and bodies: Parables from public places. *Western Journal of Communication, 65,* 271–294.

DeLuca, K. M., & Peeples, J. (2002). From public sphere to public screen: Democracy, activism, and the lessons of Seattle. *Critical Studies in Mass Communication, 19,* 125–151.

Finnegan, C. A. (2003). Picturing *poverty: Print culture and FSA photographs.* Washington, D.C.: Smithsonian Books.

17

PERSUASION

Michael D. Miller and Timothy R. Levine

Implicitly or explicitly, persuasion underlies much of mass and human communication theory and research. Persuasion is a special case of the larger study of social influence. Social influence may be defined as creating, changing, or reinforcing the cognitions, affective states, or overt behaviors of another person. Persuasion involves an intentional communicative act that excludes force (i.e., coercion) and achieves private acceptance. At a minimum, a successful persuasive attempt generates some type of cognitive, affective, or behavioral modification in the target. In the following discussion we begin by defining several important terms and types of persuasion research, examine different research paradigms, explore the variables that influence persuasive strategies, and offer a sample study.

Definitional Issues

The concepts of *attitude, belief,* and *behavior* are inextricably linked to persuasion. *Attitudes* are evaluative tendencies regarding some feature of the environment and can typically be phrased in terms of like and dislike or favor and disfavor (Eagly & Chaiken, 1993). *Beliefs* are assessments that something is or is not the case. Thus, beliefs are expressed as true-false or exist-does-not-exist. For example, "I like the Miami Dolphins" expresses my attitude toward the team, while "I think the Dolphins will go to the playoffs next year" expresses a belief. *Behavior* refers to observable actions. If I bet on the Dolphins making the playoffs, I engage in a behavior.

The extent to which attitudes predict behaviors has long been controversial, and many have claimed that attitudes are, at best, only modest predictors of behaviors (LaPiere, 1934; Wicker, 1969). A meta-analysis by Kim and Hunter (1993), however, demonstrates that so long as the attitude is relevant to the behavior observed, attitudes are highly correlated with behaviors ($r = .86$) when taking measurement problems into account. A more recent meta-analysis (Cooke & Sheeran 2004) found that attitude–behavior consistency certainly exists, and is moderated by a number of indicators of attitudinal strength. Crano and Prislin (2006), however, note that behavioral manifestations of attitudes may not occur if performance of the behavior would violate the norm of self-interest (c.f., Lehman & Crano 2002).

Types of Persuasion Research

Research on persuasion can be divided into at least three categories. First, research has focused on the pragmatic issue of isolating those factors that enhance or inhibit persuasion. The second category involves explaining *why* persuasive messages are persuasive. Several theories of persuasion attempt to address this issue. Finally, researchers have investigated the selection or generation of persuasive messages. Much of this final type of research has been done under the label of compliance-gaining.

Factors Affecting Persuasion

The effectiveness of persuasive attempts can be influenced by a vast array of variables. We will focus on three broad groups that have attracted the bulk of research on persuasive efficacy: Source effects, message effects, and recipient characteristics.

Source effects refer to perceptions of sources that make them more or less influential. Aristotle's *ethos*, now more commonly referred to as source credibility, refers to perceived believability. The persuasive advantage held by credible sources has long been recognized (e.g., Hovland & Weiss, 1951). Perceived competence (or expertise) and trustworthiness are commonly recognized as contributing to perceptions of source credibility, although others have argued for additional dimensions of source credibility (e.g., Berlo, Lemert, & Mertz, 1969; McCroskey & Young, 1981; Self, chapter 28, this volume).

Other source effects include social power (e.g., French & Raven, 1959), authority (e.g., Milgram, 1974), attractiveness (e.g., Chaiken, 1979), liking (e.g., Ragan, 1971), demographic (e.g., Cantor, Alfonso, & Zillmann, 1976), and attitudinal similarity (e.g., Woodside & Davenport, 1974). Generally speaking, we are more likely to be persuaded by sources we perceive to be powerful, in authority, attractive, likable, or similar to us than by sources we perceive as not possessing these traits.

Characteristics of messages such as discrepancy, language intensity, message sidedness, and the quality and quantity of evidence provided also influence persuasiveness. *Discrepancy* refers to the distance between a target's existing attitude and the position advocated by a message (Aronson, Turner, & Carlsmith, 1963). *Language intensity* refers to the degree to which the language used deviates from neutrality. Language intensity can be manipulated through the use of adverbial qualifiers ("That is a pretty good/good/excellent idea") or through the use of metaphors, especially those that have violent or sexual content ("Current policies are raping the poor and middle-class while providing welfare for the rich"). As is the case with many message variables, language intensity interacts with other variables (such as prior attitude toward the topic, characteristics of the source, and receiver expectations) in persuasive situations (c.f., Burgoon, Jones, & Stewart, 1975; M. D. Miller & Burgoon, 1979).

Message sidedness refers to whether one side or both sides of an issue are presented. Research indicates that two-sided messages are more persuasive, so long as the opposing side is explicitly refuted (O'Keefe, 1999). Providing evidence is most effective when the targets are involved in the issue (Stiff, 1986; see also Reinard, 1988; Reynolds & Burgoon, 1983, for reviews of this literature), although some recent findings suggest strong arguments with evidence are consistently more effective regardless of audience involvement (Park, Levine, Kingsley, Orfgen, & Foregger, 2007).

Research has also examined the effectiveness of specific *message types and persuasive strategies*, especially fear appeals (e.g., Boster & Mongeau, 1984; Witte, 1992). Other examples of specific strategies which have been investigated include altercasting (Weinstein & Deutchberger, 1963), foot-in-the-door (Freedman & Fraser, 1966), door-in-the-face (Cialdini et al., 1975), low-ball (Cialdini, Cacioppo, Bassett, & Miller, 1978), moral obligations (Schmitt, 1964), and that's-not-all (Burger, 1986).

Often the intent of the persuader is to *prevent* the message recipients from changing their attitudes if they are subsequently exposed to a persuasive message. When prevention of message acceptance is the goal, refutational message strategies were found to be effective under certain conditions (e.g., Pfau, Kenski, Nitz, & Sorenson, 1990; Pfau, Van Bockern, & Kang, 1992).

The persuasive impact of messages also depends upon characteristics of the *recipient* of the message. A wide array of individual difference variables have been found to be related to persuasive impact. Mere exposure to (Zajonc, 1968; see Bornstein, 1989, for review) or mere thought

(Tesser, 1978) about issues or things can produce attitude change. Also, the recipient's gender (Eagly, 1983), intelligence (Rhodes & Wood, 1992), and personality traits, including self-esteem (Rhodes & Wood, 1992) and argumentativeness (Levine & Badger, 1993), appear to influence persuasion. Dillard and Nabi (2006) discuss how individual differences in emotional reactivity to cancer messages influence receptivity to persuasive and counterpersuasive messages in cancer prevention and detection. Johnson and Eagly (1989) and Cho and Boster (2005) distinguish between outcome-relevant involvement, value-relevant involvement, and impression-relevant involvement, and how each of these functions differently in affecting persuasion.

Theories of Persuasion

A number of theories have been advanced to explain how, when, and why people are persuaded. Although no one theory can entirely explain persuasion, each is useful in understanding some aspect of persuasion.

Behavioristic learning theories represent one approach to explaining persuasion. Applications of classical, operant, and vicarious conditioning may result in persuasion (e.g., Eagly & Chaiken, 1993; Miller, Burgoon, & Burgoon, 1984; Staats & Staats, 1958).

Other theories argue people are motivated to maintain consistency. Heider's (1946) balance theory and Festinger's (1957) theory of cognitive dissonance are examples of consistency theories. Dissonance theory is noteworthy for a number of reasons, including placing an emphasis on counterattitudinal advocacy. In the traditional persuasion paradigm, the persuader is the primary source of persuasive messages (G. R. Miller & Burgoon, 1973). The persuader generates and transmits a persuasive message to the persuasive target. In counterattitudinal situations, the persuasive target is induced to become the primary symbolizing agent (G. R. Miller & Burgoon, 1973). That is, the persuasive target generates a message advocating a position different from the one he or she privately holds. Under certain conditions, this active encoding approach has been found to be an extremely effective persuasive strategy.

Dissonance theory is also noteworthy for generating a tremendous amount of research and theory development. The theory generated many important lines of research, several alternative interpretations of the theory, and a number of theoretical alternatives to dissonance theory.

Self-perception (Bem, 1967) was originally advanced as an alternative to dissonance theory. Bem argued that under certain conditions people infer their attitudes from observing their own behaviors. Thus, we "discover" our own attitudes in much the same way we would make attributions about the attitudes of another person—we make inferences based on observed behavior. Research suggests that self-perception best explains proattitudinal effects, while dissonance theory explains counterattitudinal effects (Fazio, Zanna, & Cooper, 1977).

Another theory originally advanced as an alternative to dissonance is self-presentation. Self-presentation comes from the symbolic interactionist perspective. Although this approach has received more attention in psychology than in the communication discipline, it offers intriguing explanations and hypotheses concerning persuasion and a variety of interpersonal outcomes (c.f., Leary, 2007; Leary & Kowalski, 1990). Interestingly, after 50 years of reinterpretations, alternatives and critiques of the theory, some psychologists have recently argued for a return to original interpretations of dissonance (c.f., Joule & Azdia, 2003).

Social judgment theory (Sherif, Sherif, & Nebergall, 1965; see Granberg, 1982, for review) assumes that people perceive persuasive messages in much the same way they make judgments about physical stimuli. This theory predicts a nonlinear relationship between discrepancy and attitude change, where the optimal degree of discrepancy is a function of the target's ego involvement with the topic.

The cognitive response approach (Petty, Ostrom, & Brock, 1981) and the theory of planned behavior (Ajzen & Fishbein, 2000, 2005) assume that targets of persuasive messages actively evaluate those messages, whereas research on heuristics (Cialdini, 1993; Tversky & Kahneman, 1974) assumes that persuasion is a result of mindless decision rules. The elaboration likelihood model (ELM; Petty & Cacioppo, 1986) attempts to integrate these approaches by arguing that all persuasion can be viewed along a continuum defined by cognitive effort. The ELM, however, has proven controversial on several grounds, including its controversial conceptualization of argument quality and failure to specify which of several "peripheral" routes to persuasion might be used (e.g., Eagly & Chaiken, 1993; Park et al., 2007; Stiff, 1986). The systematic–heuristic model has been advanced as an alternative to ELM (Chaiken, 1987).

Of these approaches, the theory of planned behavior has generated an especially large number of studies applying the theory to a wide number of situations. In part, the theory argues that attitudes, along with subjective norms and subjective notions of behavioral control predict behavioral intentions. Intentions, along with perceived and actual behavioral control, predict behavior. Tests of the model have repeatedly shown intentions to be a significant predictor of subsequent behavior. See, for example, Sheeran's (2002) meta-analysis of other meta-analyses. In addition, other elements of the model have been shown to predict intentions (Armitage & Conner, 2001).

Message Selection and Generation

Most traditional persuasion research is based on the experimental manipulation of an experimenter's preestablished and pretested message on an audience. However, a program of research arose based not on persuasive exposure, but instead on the selection or generation of message strategies used in influencing others. Based on Marwell and Schmitt's (1967) classic study of the typology of compliance-gaining message strategies, Miller, Boster, Roloff, and Seibold's (1977) research on compliance-gaining message selection has stimulated a good deal of research. Most compliance-gaining research has sought to either identify and classify the types of messages individuals use to influence others (e.g., Cody, McLaughlin, & Jordan, 1980; Kearney, Plax, Richmond, & McCroskey, 1985) or determine the situational (e.g., Dillard & Burgoon, 1985; G. R. Miller et al., 1977; M. D. Miller, 1982) and individual difference variables (e.g., Boster & Levine, 1988) that influence compliance-gaining message selection or generation. Reviews of this literature are provided by Seibold, Cantrill, and Meyers (1986) and Wheeless, Barraclough, and Stewart (1983). Some research has investigated both what strategies people use and if those strategies work (Levine & Boster, 2001). Unfortunately few conclusions can be drawn from compliance-gaining research. To date, methodological debates (e.g., Boster, Stiff, & Reynolds, 1985; Burleson et al., 1986; Wiseman & Schenck-Hamlin, 1981) have been a dominant feature of this literature.

Research Methods in the Study of Persuasion

As with any research, the design, procedure, and analysis of persuasion studies are dictated by the questions one poses and the hypotheses one tests. Perhaps the most basic methodological issue to be addressed is whether an experimental or a nonexperimental design will be used. As we noted earlier, a great deal of persuasion research seeks to identify specific source, message, or receiver factors which enhance or inhibit persuasive effectiveness. This focus on the identification of specific causal variables in persuasion makes experimental research particularly useful. While there are exceptions, classic studies of both source and message effects on persuasion and attitude change have relied heavily on experimental methods (e.g., Aronson et al., 1963; Hovland & Weiss, 1951).

Experimental Research

Why the reliance on experimental methods? Experimental designs allow the researcher the *control* necessary to precisely specify and manipulate the source or message characteristics he or she is interested in comparing. Suppose a researcher interested in the persuasive effects of fear appeals develops hypotheses suggesting that the claimed likelihood of occurrence of some frightening event will be related to compliance with the message. The researcher might then construct a prototype persuasive message which suggests this frightening event will occur unless the receiver complies with some requested behavior. By using this message as a template, and varying only the probability of occurrence of the frightening event, the researcher creates experimental messages which differ *only* in the characteristic of interest.

The experimenter manipulates or controls levels of the independent variable, possibly including a "control" group or groups that do not receive any manipulation. Research participants are then randomly assigned to experimental conditions. Random assignment ensures that "any" participant might be assigned to "any" experimental or control condition; it helps ensure that any results are effects of the variables of interest and not things brought to the study by the participant. After exposure to the experimental messages, measurements of compliance (the dependant variable) are made and compared across different experimental "conditions."

Taken together, the consistency of procedures across experimental conditions, the random assignment of participants to conditions, and the strict control of the stimuli (in this case the variations of the persuasive message) help ensure the internal validity of the experiment (*internal validity* refers to whether a stimulus—manipulation of the independent variable—had a known effect in the study being conducted). To the researcher conducting experimental research in persuasion, the most important and fundamental question is, "Were the observed differences in the dependant variables due to variations in the manipulated independent variables?" In the example above, "Were variations in compliance due to variations in the claimed likelihood of occurrence of the frightening event?" A well designed and executed experiment allows us to answer "yes" to these questions with a high degree of confidence. The experiment allows us to study the causal relationships between variables, but does so in often very unnatural settings (i.e., the laboratory). As such, it may suffer from problems of *external validity*, a question of the extent to which the results can be generalized to other settings and populations.

Nonexperimental Research

While research on the effects of source and message variables lends itself to the manipulation inherent in experimental studies, the question of how receiver characteristics are related to persuasion is often examined via *nonexperimental* investigations. Although receiver characteristics (gender, sex role, intelligence, age, aggressiveness, or other individual difference variables) generally cannot be manipulated or randomly assigned in nonexperimental studies, they can be measured. Thus, the most basic approach to the study of these receiver variables has been to measure the characteristic of interest in a collection of people who are then exposed to some type of persuasive stimulus. Responses to the message are then compared. For example, we expose women and men (or older and younger, cognitively simply and cognitively complex participants) to the same persuasive message and compare their responses. Differences in responses are attributed to differences on the previously identified and measured independent variable.

Clearly, the internal validity of research of this type is more suspect than that of a true experiment. In an experiment, we take steps, including randomization and random assignment, to insure that our experimental groups differ *only* as a result of planned exposure to the persuasive message (or other independent variable under the experimenter's control). Thus, differences in the outcome measures are attributable to differences in the manipulated independent variable. In an investigation of receiver variables, we begin with groups we know are *already* different on at least one characteristic and then expose them to the same persuasive stimulus. Differences apparent in outcome variables are attributed to the preexisting differences in the measured receiver variable. For example, if men and women are exposed to the same persuasive message and evidence different degrees of attitude change, the researcher might attribute those differential responses to the measured independent variable of gender. However, reasonable alternative explanations for the results might be that men and women differed on some factor in addition to biological sex (sex role or interest or knowledge in the topic, for example) which might be the true explanation of the differences in attitude change.

Quasi-Experimental Research

Many persuasion studies have both manipulated and measured independent variables. These types of studies are referred to as *quasi-experimental* designs. Quasi-experimental designs have actively manipulated experimental variables, but rather than using random assignment, also rely on comparisons made across groups created via at least one measured independent variable as in nonexperimental research discussed earlier (Cook & Campbell, 1979). Although quasi-experimental research has been used in many areas of persuasion, many studies on personality and persuasibility provide clear examples of quasi-experimental designs (see, for example, several studies reported in Hovland & Janis, 1959). The sample persuasion study we discuss later in this chapter is an example of a quasi-experiment.

Attitude Measurement

Another important decision in conducting research in persuasion is the nature of the dependent variable. The majority of persuasion research in the past has used self-reports of attitudes as the dependent variable. Without a doubt one reason for the popularity of self-report measures is the apparent ease of administration. Theoretical questions about the nature of attitudes and the related issues of their valid and reliable measurement have generated a number of different approaches and techniques of attitude measurement. Probably the most common techniques of self-report measurement of attitudes involve the use of semantic–differential scales, developed by Osgood, Suci, and Tannenbaum (1957). The semantic–differential scale consists of a series of items bounded by "bipolar" terms, usually separated by seven equal spaces that participants use to evaluate an attitude or belief statement. One advantage of the semantic differential is that the same scales can be used to measure attitudes toward a variety of different topics. Since the different attitudes are measured similarly, direct comparisons are possible.

Another reason for the popularity of self-report measures of attitudes is the assumption (either explicitly or implicitly) that cognitive variables, including those generally considered to be components of attitudes, serve as "causes" or antecedents of subsequent behaviors. Although the nature of the attitude–behavior relationship was proven controversial (see Kim & Hunter, 1993, for a review), assuming that cognitive or affective restructuring precedes behavioral change has provided at least an implicit justification for the use of self-report measures of attitudes as the dependent variables in persuasion studies.

Responding to findings of frequent weak relationships between attitudes and subsequent behavior, Fishbein and associates (e.g., Fishbein & Ajzen, 1975) utilized measures of behavioral intentions. As a part of this approach to measurement, participants are asked how they *intend* to behave in situations relevant to the attitude being measured. Not surprisingly the measurement of behavioral intentions increases correspondence between self-reports of attitude and subsequent behavior.

A number of affective indicators of attitudes have also been utilized. A sampling of these approaches includes galvanic skin response (GSR), pupillary response, and facial electromyographic activity (Himmelfarb, 1993).

Another alternative is to simply measure the overt behavior itself without resorting to measures of attitude (or relying on this observation of behavior as an indicator of related attitudes). This is not always as simple as it might seem. Problems include isolating the behavior or set of behaviors of interest, selecting which behavior or behavioral array is theoretically most relevant, and operationalizing the behavioral observations.

Ultimately, the dependent variables and their operationalizations must reflect the theoretic or pragmatic interests of the researcher. What would be the most appropriate variable in, for example, a study of political persuasion? The conspicuously simple answer is voting behavior. In many cases this might also be the correct answer. However, depending on the interest and theoretic rationale of the researcher, affect toward the candidates, knowledge and beliefs about the candidates, or voting intentions might be as or more appropriate dependent variables. Even in research guided primarily by pragmatic concerns, such as that being conducted on behalf of a political candidate, attitudes, beliefs, or behavioral intentions might be the most appropriate measures of interest.

A Sample Study of Argumentativeness and Resistance to Persuasion

Research on resistance to persuasion has primarily focused on two distinct domains. First, some researchers have examined the effects of messages intended to instill resistance. Much of this research is based upon McGuire's inoculation construct (Papageorgis & McGuire, 1961). In the inoculation paradigm, participants are exposed to a message which both motivates them to counterargue future persuasive attacks and provides refutational content to assist them in this process.

Recent applications of inoculation in resistance to political attack messages (Pfau, Kenski et al., 1990) and smoking initiation among adolescents (Pfau, Van Bockern et al., 1992) have documented the effectiveness of this technique.

Second, other researchers examined characteristics of message receivers which make them more susceptible or resistant to persuasive appeals. For example, research has explored the effects of gender (e.g., Eagly, 1983), self-esteem (e.g., Rhodes & Wood, 1992), and propensity to counterargue (e.g., Stacks & Burgoon, 1981) on persuasibility. This research suggests that some individuals may be naturally more resistant to persuasion than others.

One individual difference that should have implications for resistance to persuasion is argumentativeness. Drawing upon the work of Infante and his colleagues on argumentativeness (e.g., Infante, 1981; Infante & Rancer, 1982) and the cognitive response approach to persuasion (e.g., Greenwald, 1968; Petty, Ostrom, & Brock, 1981), it is reasonable to advance argumentativeness as an important recipient factor influencing persuasion. Kazoleas (1993) found that highly argumentative individuals were more difficult to persuade, but Levine and Badger (1993) found that high argumentatives were more easily persuaded.

Explicating Argumentativeness

The proposed sample study looks at persuasibility as a function of an individual's level of argumentativeness and his or her initial agreement with a message. It is argued that the conflicting results obtained in previous research might be a result of argumentativeness by message agreement interaction. To explain why this should be the case, the cognitive response approach to persuasion, argumentativeness, and two recent studies must be discussed.

The cognitive response approach to persuasion is predicated on the view that the persuasive effect of an externally produced message is attributable to the thoughts generated by exposure to the message (Petty & Cacioppo, 1981). That is, recipient thoughts or cognitive responses "mediate" and explain message effectiveness. To the extent that a message generates promessage thoughts on the part of the receiver, the receiver will be swayed to the position advocated by the message. If, on the other hand, a message generates unfavorable thoughts (i.e., is counterargued), then less persuasion will result. Extensive counterarguing can result in attitude change opposite to message recommendations (i.e., a boomerang effect). From this perspective, any variable that systematically affects the nature of cognitive responses should systematically affect persuasion. *Argumentativeness* should be one such variable (Kazoleas, 1993; Levine & Badger, 1993).

Argumentativeness is a personality trait that reflects an individual's inherent tendency to approach or avoid arguments. *Argumentativeness* is conceptualized as a generally stable trait which predisposes the individual in communication situations to advocate positions on controversial issues and to attack the positions other people take on these issues (Infante & Rancer, 1982).

High trait argumentatives are thought to differ from their less argumentative counterparts in several ways. For example, arguing is associated with more learning, less egocentric thinking, more accurate social perspective-taking, more creativity, and better problem solving and decision making (Johnson & Johnson, 1979). Better arguing skills are also directly related to leadership skills (Schultz, 1982).

Another way high and low argumentatives differ is in how they process messages. High trait argumentatives, by definition, tend to refute others' ideas (Infante & Rancer, 1982). The refutation of others' arguments has both cognitive and behavioral elements. In order to effectively dispute another's position on an issue, one must first identify weakness in the other's argument and generate counterpoints. Such refutational thoughts are labeled counterarguments in the persuasion literature (Petty & Cacioppo, 1981).

Two recent studies hypothesized that due to high argumentatives' proclivity toward counterargumentation, highly argumentative individuals should be more difficult to persuade than their less argumentative counterparts (Kazoleas, 1993; Levine & Badger, 1993). Kazoleas's results were consistent with this hypothesis, but Levine and Badger found the opposite. Highly argumentative subjects in the Levine and Badger study showed significantly more attitude change than their less argumentative cohorts.

Important differences in the messages used in these two studies may explain these conflicting results. Kazoleas (1993) exposed participants to three persuasive advertisements. These messages encouraged moderation in drinking, opposing the clean air act, and avoiding exposure to the sun. Levine and Badger's (1993) study used persuasive speeches given in public speaking classes. The topics of the speeches were chosen by participants' classmates.

Suppose that highly argumentative individuals generate more cognitive responses, but, counter to Kazoleas's (1993) and Levine and Badger's (1993) reasoning, do not always generate more negative ones. Specifically, although such individuals should generate more counterarguments when faced with an objectionable message, they may generate more promessage thoughts when faced with an acceptable message. Such reasoning may explain the conflicting findings. Highly argumentative individuals may be more or less resistant to persuasion depending on a certain set of conditions.

Unfortunately, neither Kazoleas's (1993) nor Levine and Badger's (1993) designs allowed for a direct test of this reasoning. The information that is available, however, seems consistent with this speculation. In the Kazoleas study, the mean attitude scores suggest few subjects favored the positions advocated. Also, the largest effects were found for the topic (anticlean air act) with which the subjects least agreed. That is, the more the subjects disagreed with the message, the more resistant were the argumentative subjects.

In the Levine and Badger (1993) study, sources were allowed to select their own topics, and they seemed to pick topics they favored. Examination of initial favorability scores showed that most of these subjects favored most topics. Thus, participants in the Levine and Badger study may have heard only proattitudinal persuasive presentations.

Thus, there is reason to expect that the relationship between argumentativeness and resistance to persuasion is moderated by initial agreement with the message. Based on this reasoning, one might propose that the predicted effect of argumentativeness instilling resistance to persuasion is valid for positions that targets would not readily endorse. Alternatively, one might predict an effect like that obtained in the Levine and Badger (1993) study for proattitudinal messages. Argumentativeness should lead to less resistance to proattitudinal messages. This reasoning allows us to posit that:

H_1: Initial agreement with a persuasive message will moderate the effects of argumentativeness on resistance to persuasion such that:

H_{1a}: For counterattitudinal messages, low-trait argumentatives will report more attitude change in the direction of the message recommendations than high-trait argumentativeness, but

H_{1b}: For proattitudinal messages, high-trait argumentatives will report more attitude change in the direction of the message recommendations than low-trait argumentatives.

Method

In order to test our hypothesis, we would need to expose high- and low-argumentative subjects to pro- and counterattitudinal messages. This would produce four experimental conditions. Comparing the degree of attitude change in the different conditions would allow for a test of our hypothesis that initial agreement moderates resistance to persuasion and our subhypotheses of specific effects.

Participants

Participants in this study would be selected on the basis of a pretest. This pretest would assess their argumentativeness, as well as their opinions on a variety of potentially controversial issues.

Pretest

At the beginning of the semester, each participant would be asked to complete a questionnaire containing the 20-item Argumentativeness Scale (Infante & Rancer, 1982) and an opinion survey. By comparing their responses to the argumentativeness scale with the group median, each participant would be classified into one of two equal-size groups: high in argumentativeness or low in argumentativeness.

The opinion survey would contain a variety of topics, and three sets of items for each topic. These sets of items would assess the participants' positions on each topic, knowledge of the topics, and views of the topics' importance. The first set of items would be a measure of initial attitudes. The latter two sets of items, intended as measures of prior knowledge and issue involvement, respectively, would be included for control purposes.

For the experiment, the topic with the most variance in initial attitude (i.e., most controversial) would be utilized. Participants who were neutral on the topic would be excluded from the study. For the purpose of illustration, suppose we chose the topic of legal abortion. Some participants would be pro-life, whereas others would be pro-choice. Since we are interested in pro- and counterattitudinal messages, participants who were neutral or undecided would be excluded from the study.

Procedure and Measurement

Selected participants (either high or low in argumentativeness, who were either pro-choice or pro-life) would be randomly assigned to experimental conditions in which they would listen to a speech that would be either pro-choice or pro-life in nature. This procedure would create both pro-attitudinal messages (pro-choice participants listening to pro-choice messages, and pro-life participants listening to pro-life messages) and counterattitudinal messages (pro-choice participants listening to pro-life messages, and pro-life participants listening to pro-choice messages). Since participants are either high or low in argumentativeness, this creates four quasi-experimental conditions: High argumentatives exposed to a pro-attitudinal message, high argumentatives exposed to a counterattitudinal messages; low argumentatives exposed to a pro-attitudinal message, and low argumentatives exposed to a counter-attitudinal message.

Immediately following the persuasive speech, experimental participants would complete the opinion survey a second time. The responses to the initial attitude items would be subtracted from the post-speech attitude measures for the topic. This would serve as the dependent measure.

Results

The data would be analyzed via 2×2 analysis of variance with argumentativeness (high and low) and message–attitude agreement (proattitudinal and counterattitudinal) as the independent variables, and attitude change as the dependent variable. If the hypothesized interaction was found, the data would be consistent with our hypothesis.

Research Methods Revisited

The design used in this hypothetical experiment is an example of a quasi-experimental design. It has one measured independent variable (argumentativeness). Assignment to the high and low trait argumentativeness conditions is clearly not random. Assignment decisions would be made on the basis of responses to the measured variable of trait argumentativeness. Further, categorizing a continuous variable like argumentativeness is less than ideal for statistical reasons. Our other independent variable, proattitudinal versus counterattitudinal messages is manipulated, but we have to recognize that the manipulation is based indirectly on measures of prior agreement and disagreement.

Now consider the validity of our hypothetical study. Earlier in this chapter we noted how characteristics of design influence on the internal validity of persuasion research. An additional concern might be the generalizability of the findings (external validity). For example, our study uses only one experimental topic (legalized abortion) and one message for each message–agreement condition. This raises concerns about the degree to which the results can be generalized to other topics or to other messages on the same topic (Jackson & Jacobs, 1983). This is especially problematic if the abortion topic is being used, since people are so polarized on the issue.

Another concern is the way in which the experimental conditions are created. The pro-attitudinal condition is comprised of both pro-life participants (listening to a pro-life message) and pro-choice participants (listening to a pro-choice message). By collapsing these two groups into one experimental condition, we have implicitly assumed the two subgroups are equivalent. Whether this is the case is actually an empirical question. If the subgroups are not significantly different on the dependent measure, our decision to combine them is defensible. Otherwise, an alternative analysis to diagnose the nature and effects of nonequivalence would be appropriate.

Rather than presenting a perfect hypothetical study, one which the experimenter has complete control and unlimited resources, we have tried to present a doable study which exemplifies some of the issues, problems and even pitfalls often experienced by persuasion researchers. Our study certainly would not provide an unequivocal and complete answer to the problem. It should, however, contribute to our knowledge on how argumentativeness is related to resistance to persuasion

Summary

In much the same way, this chapter as a whole offers only a superficial and incomplete overview of persuasion research. We hope, however, it provides some important information on what we know about persuasion and how persuasion research is conducted. We note by way of concluding that persuasion is a type of social influence that can take many forms. Those forms often dictate the types of methodological decisions made. Persuasion research is also guided by a number of theoretical perspectives, each offering a different methodological perspective to its study.

Note

1. Much of the commentary on design issues in this chapter draws heavily from the work of Donald Campbell and his associates (Campbell & Stanley, 1966; Cook & Campbell, 1979).

References

Ajzen, I., & Fishbein, M. (2000). Attitudes and the attitude behavior relation: Reasoned and automatic processes. In W. Stroebe & M. Hewstone (Eds.), *European review of social psychology* (pp. 1–33). Chichester, UK: Wiley.

Ajzen, I., & Fishbein, M. (2005). The influence of attitudes on behavior. In D. Albarracín, B. T. Johnson, & M. P. Zanna (Eds.), *The handbook of attitudes* (pp. 173–221). Mahwah, NJ: Erlbaum.

Armitage, C. J., & Conner, M. (2001). Efficacy of the theory of planned behaviour: A meta-analytic review. *British Journal of Social Psychology 40*, 471–499.

Aronson, E., Turner, J. A., & Carlsmith, J. M. (1963). Communicator credibility and communication discrepancy as determinants of opinion change. *Journal of Abnormal and Social Psychology, 67*, 177–181.

Bem, D. J. (1967). Self-perception: An alternative interpretation of cognitive dissonance phenomena. *Psychological Review, 74*, 183–200.

Berlo, D. K., Lemert, J. B., & Mertz, R. J. (1969). Dimensions for evaluating the acceptability of message sources. *Public Opinion Quarterly, 33*, 563–576.

Bornstein, R. F. (1989). Exposure and affect: Overview and meta-analysis of research. *Psychological Bulletin, 106*, 265–289.

Boster, F. J., & Levine, T. R. (1988). Individual differences and compliance-gaining message selection: The effects of verbal aggressiveness, argumentativeness, dogmatism, and negativism. *Communication Research Reports, 5*, 114–119.

Boster, F. J., & Mongeau, P. (1984). Fear-arousing persuasive messages. In R. N. Bostrom (Ed.), *Communication yearbook* (Vol. 8, pp. 330–375). Beverly Hills, CA: Sage.

Boster, F. J., Stiff, J. B., & Reynolds, R. A. (1985). Do persons respond differently to inductively-derived and deductively-derived lists of compliance-gaining message strategies? A reply to Wiseman and Schenck-Hamlin. *Western Journal of Speech Communication, 49*, 177–187.

Burger, J. M. (1986). Increasing compliance by improving the deal: The that's-not-all technique. *Journal of Personality and Social Psychology, 51,* 277–283.

Burgoon, M., Jones, S. B., & Stewart, D. (1975). Toward a message-centered theory of persuasion: Three empirical investigations of language intensity. *Human Communication Research, 7,* 240–256.

Burleson, B. R., Wilson, S. R., Waltman, M. S., Goering, E. M., Ely, T. K., & Whaley, R. B. (1986). Item desirability effects in compliance-gaining research: Seven studies documenting artifacts in the strategy selection procedure. *Human Communication Research, 14,* 129–486.

Campbell, D. T., & Stanley, J. C. (1966). *Experimental and quasi-experimental designs for research.* Chicago: Rand McNally.

Cantor, J. R., Alfonso, H., & Zillmann, D. (1976). The persuasive effectiveness of the peer appeal and a communicator's first-hand experience. *Communication Research, 3,* 293–310.

Chaiken, S. (1979). Communicator physical attractiveness and persuasion. *Journal of Personality and Social Psychology, 37,* 1387–1397.

Chaiken, S. (1987). The heuristic model of persuasion. In M. P. Zanna, J. M. Olson, & C. P Herman (Eds.), *Social influence: The Ontario symposium* (Vol. 5, pp. 3–40). Hillsdale, NJ: Erlbaum.

Cho, H., & Boster, F. J. (2005). Development and validation of value-, outcome-, and impression-relevant involvement scales. *Communication Research, 32,* 235–264.

Cialdini, R. B. (1993). *Influence: Science and practice.* Glenview, IL: Scott, Foreman.

Cialdini, R. B., Cacioppo, J. T., Bassett, R., & Miller, J. A. (1978). Low-ball procedure for producing compliance: Commitment then cost. *Journal of Personality and Social Psychology, 36,* 463–476.

Cialdini, R. B., Vincent, J. E., Lewis, S. K., Catalan, J., Wheeler, D., & Darby, B. L. (1975). Reciprocal concessions procedure for inducing compliance: The door-in-the-face technique. *Journal of Personality and Social Psychology, 31,* 206–215.

Cody, M. J., McLaughlin, M. L., & Jordan, W. J. (1980). A multidimensional scaling of three sets of compliance-gaining strategies. *Communication Quarterly, 28,* 34–46.

Cook, R., & Sheeran, P. (2004). Moderation of cognition-intention and cognition-behavior relations: A meta-analysis of properties of variables from the theory of planned behavior. *British Journal of Social Psychology, 43,* 159–186.

Cook, T. D., & Campbell, D. T. (1979). *Quasi-experimentation: Design and analysis issues for field settings.* Boston, MA: Houghton Mifflin.

Crano, W. D., & Prislin, R. (2006). Attitudes and persuasion. *Annual Review of Psychology, 57,* 345–374.

Dillard, J. P., & Burgoon, M. (1985). Situational influences on the selection of compliance-gaining messages: Two tests of the predictive utility of the Cody-McLaughlin typology. *Communication Monographs, 52,* 289–318.

Dillard, J. P., & Nabi, R. L. (2006). The persuasive influence of emotion in cancer prevention and detection messages. *Journal of Communication, 56,* S123–S139.

Eagly, A. H. (1983). Gender and social influence. *American Psychologist, 34,* 971–981.

Eagly, A. H., & Chaiken, S. (1993). *The psychology of attitudes.* Fort Worth, TX: Harcourt Brace Jovanovich.

Fazio, R. H., Zanna, M. P., & Cooper, J. (1977). Dissonance and self-perception: An integrative view of each theory's proper domain of application. *Journal of Experimental Social Psychology, 13,* 464–479.

Festinger, L. (1957). *A theory of cognitive dissonance.* Evanston, IL: Row, Peterson.

Fishbein, M., & Ajzen, I. (1975). *Belief, attitude, intention, and behavior: An introduction to theory and research.* Reading, MA: Addison-Wesley.

Freedman, J. L., & Fraser, S. C. (1966). Compliance without pressure: The foot-in-the-door technique. *Journal of Personality and Social Psychology, 4,* 195–203.

French, J. R., & Raven, B. (1959). The bases of social power. In D. Cartwright (Ed.), *Studies in social power* (pp. 150–167). Ann Arbor, MI: University of Michigan Press.

Granberg, D. (1982). Social judgment theory. In M. Burgoon (Ed.), *Communication yearbook* (Vol. 6, pp. 304–329). Beverly Hills, CA: Sage.

Greenwald, A. G. (1968). Cognitive learning, cognitive response to persuasion, and attitude change. In A. G. Greenwald, T. C. Brock, & T. M. Ostrom (Eds.), *Psychological foundations of attitudes* (pp. 147–170). New York: Academic Press.

Heider, F. (1946). Attitudes and cognitive organization. *Journal of Psychology, 21*, 107–112.

Himmelfarb, S. (1993). The measurement of attitudes, in A. H. Eagly & S. Chaiken, *The psychology of attitudes* (pp. 23–87). Fort Worth, TX: Harcourt Brace Jovanovich.

Hovland, C. I., & Janis, I. L. (Eds.). (1959). *Personality and persuasibility.* New Haven, CT: Yale University Press.

Hovland, C. I., & Weiss, W. (1951). The influence of source credibility on communication effectiveness. *Public Opinion Quarterly, 15*, 635–650.

Infante, D. A. (1981). Trait argumentativeness as a predictor of communicative behavior in situations requiring argument. *Central States Speech Journal, 32*, 265–272.

Infante, D. A. (1985). Inducing women to be argumentative: Source credibility effects. *Journal of Applied Communication Research, 13*, 33–44.

Infante, D. A., & Rancer, A. S. (1982). A conceptualization and measure of argumentativeness. *Journal of Personality Assessment, 46*, 72–80.

Jackson, S., & Jacobs, S. (1983) Generalizing about messages: Suggestions for the design and analysis of expeiments. *Human Communication Research, 9*, 169–181.

Johnson, B. T., & Eagly, A. H. (1989). Effects of involvement on persuasion: A meta-analysis. *Psychological Bulletin, 106*, 290–314.

Johnson, D. W., & Johnson, R. T. (1979). Conflict in the classroom: Controversy and learning. *Review of Educational Research, 49*, 51–70.

Joule, R. V. & Azdia, T. (2003). Cognitive dissonance, double forced compliance, and commitment. *European Journal of Social Psychology, 33*, 565–571.

Kazoleas, D. (1993). The impact of argumentativeness on resistance to persuasion. *Human Communication Research, 20*, 118–137.

Kearney, P., Plax, T. G., Richmond, V. P., & McCroskey, J. C. (1985). Power in the classroom III: Teacher communication techniques and messages. *Communication Education, 34*, 19–28.

Kim, M. S., & Hunter, J. E. (1993). Attitude-behavior relations: A meta-analysis of attitudinal relevance and topic. *Journal of Communication, 43*, 101–142.

LaPiere, M. A. (1934). Attitudes vs. actions. *Social Forces, 13*, 230–237.

Leary, M. R. (2007). Motivational and emotional aspects of the self. *Annual Review of Psychology, 58*, 317–344.

Leary, M. R., & Kowalski, R. M. (1990). Impression management: A literature review and two component model. *Psychological Bulletin, 107*, 34–48.

Lehman, B. J., & Crano, W. D. (2002). The pervasive effects of vested interest on attitude-criterion consistency in political judgment. *Journal of Experimental Psychology, 38*, 101–112.

Levine, T. R., & Badger, E. E. (1993). Argumentativeness and resistance to persuasion. *Communication Reports, 6*, 71–77.

Levine, T. R., & Boster, F. J. (2001). The effects of power and message variables on compliance. *Communication Monographs, 68*, 28–48.

Marwell, G. M., & Schmitt, D. R. (1967). Dimensions of compliance-gaining behavior: An empirical analysis. *Sociometry, 30*, 350–328.

McCroskey, J. C., & Young, T. J. (1981). Ethos and credibility: The construct and its measurement after three decades. *Central States Speech Journal, 32*, 24–34.

Milgram, S. (1974). *Obedience to authority.* New York: Harper.

Miller, G. R., Boster, F. J., Roloff, M. E., & Seibold, D. R. (1977). Compliance-gaining message strategies: A typology and some findings concerning the effects of situational differences. *Communication Monographs, 44*, 37–51.

Miller, G. R., & Burgoon, M. (1973). *New techniques of persuasion.* New York: Harper & Row.

Miller, G. R., Burgoon, M., & Burgoon, J. K. (1984). The functions of human communication in changing attitudes and gaining compliance. In C. C. Arnold & J. W. Bowers (Eds.), *Handbook of rhetorical and communication theory* (pp. 400–474). Boston: Allyn & Bacon.

Miller, M. D. (1982). Friendship, power, and the language of compliance-gaining. *Journal of Language and Social Psychology, 1*, 111–121.

Miller, M. D., & Burgoon, M. (1979). The relationship between violations of expectations and the induction of resistance to persuasion. *Human Communication Research, 5,* 301–313.

O'Keefe, D. J. (1999). How to handle opposing arguments in persuasive messages: A meta-analytic review of the effects of one-sided and two-sided messages. *Communication Yearbook, 22,* 209–249.

Osgood, C. E., Suci, G. J., & Tannenbaum, P. H. (1957). *The measurement of meaning.* Urbana: University of Illinois Press.

Papageorgis, D., & McGuire, W. J. (1961). The generality of immunity to persuasion produced by pre-exposure to weakened counterarguments. *Journal of Abnormal and Social Psychology, 62,* 475–481.

Park, H. S., Levine, T. R., Kingsley, C. Y., Orfgen, T., & Foregger, S. (2007). The effects of argument quality and involvement type on attitude formation and change: A test of dual process and social judgment predictions. *Human Communication Research, 33,* 81–102.

Petty, R. E., & Cacioppo, J. T. (1981). *Attitudes and persuasion: Classic and contemporary approaches.* Dubuque, IA: William C. Brown.

Petty, R. E., & Cacioppo, J. T. (1986). The elaboration likelihood model of persuasion. In L. Berkowitz (Ed.), *Advances in experimental social psychology* (Vol. 19, pp. 123–205). San Diego, CA: Academic Press.

Petty, R. E., Ostrom, T. M., & Brock, T. C. (1981). *Cognitive responses in persuasion.* Hillsdale, NJ: Erlbaum.

Petty, R. E., Ostrom, T. M., & Brock, T. C. (1981). Historical foundations of the cognitive response approach to attitudes and persuasion. In R. E. Petty, T. M. Ostrom, & T. C. Brock (Eds.), *Cognitive responses in persuasion* (pp. 5–29). Hillsdale, NJ: Erlbaum.

Pfau, M., Kenski, H. C, Nitz, M., & Sorenson, J. (1990). Efficacy of inoculation strategies in promoting resistance to political attack messages: Application to direct mail. *Communication Monographs, 57,* 25–43.

Pfau, M., Van Bockern, S., & Kang, J. G. (1992). Use of inoculation to promote resistance to smoking initiation among adolescents. *Communication Monographs, 59,* 213–230.

Ragan, D. T. (1971). Effects of a favor and liking on compliance. *Journal of Experimental Social Psychology, 7,* 627–639.

Reinard, J. C. (1988). The empirical study of the persuasive effects of evidence: The status after fifty years of research. *Human Communication Research, 15,* 3–59.

Reynolds, R. A., & Burgoon, M. (1983). Belief processing, reasoning, and evidence. In R. N. Bostrom (Ed.), *Communication yearbook* (Vol. 7, pp 83–104). Beverly Hills, CA: Sage.

Rhodes, N., & Wood, W. (1992). Self-esteem and intelligence affect influenceability: The mediating role of message reception. *Psychological Bulletin, 111,* 156–171.

Schmitt, D. R. (1964). The invocation of moral obligation. *Sociometry, 27,* 299–310.

Schultz, B. (1982). Argumentativeness: Its effect in group decision-making and its role in leadership perception. *Communication Quarterly, 30,* 368–375.

Seibold, D. R., Cantrill, J. G., & Meyers, R. A. (1986). Communication and interpersonal influence. In M. L. Knapp & G. R. Miller (Eds.), *Handbook of interpersonal communication* (pp. 551–614). Beverly Hills, CA: Sage.

Sheeran, P. (2002). Intention-behavior relations: A conceptual and empirical review. *European Review of Social Psychology, 12,* 1–36.

Sherif, C. W., Sherif, M., & Nebergall, R. E. (1965). *Attitude and attitude change: The social judgment-involvement approach.* Philadelphia, PA: W. B. Saunders.

Staats, A. W., & Staats, C. K. (1958). Attitudes established by classical conditioning. *Journal of Abnormal and Social Psychology, 57,* 31–40.

Stacks, D. W., & Burgoon, J. K. (1981). The role of nonverbal behaviors as distractors in resistance to persuasion in interpersonal contexts. *Central States Speech Journal, 32,* 61–73.

Stiff, J. B. (1986). Cognitive processing of persuasive message cues: A meta-analytic review of the effects of supporting information on attitudes. *Communication Monographs, 53,* 75–89.

Tesser, A. (1978). Self-generated attitude change. In L. Berkowitz (Ed.), *Advances in experimental social psychology, 11,* 289–338.

Tversky, A., & Kahneman, D. (1974). Judgment under uncertainty: Heuristics and biases. *Science, 185,* 1124–1131.

Weinstein, E. A., & Deutchberger, P. (1963). Some dimensions of altercasting. *Sociometry, 26*, 454–466.

Wheeless, L. R., Barraclough, R., & Stewart, R. (1983). Compliance-gaining and power in persuasion. In R. N. Bostrum (Ed.), *Communication yearbook* (Vol. 7, pp. 105–143). Beverly Hills, CA: Sage.

Wicker, A. W. (1969). Attitude versus actions: The relationship of verbal and overt behavioral responses to attitude objects. *Journal of Social Issues, 25*, 41–78.

Wiseman, R. L., & Schenck-Hamlin, W. (1981). A multidimensional scaling validation of an inductively-derived set of compliance-gaining strategies. *Communication Monographs, 48*, 251–270.

Witte, K. (1992). Putting the fear back into fear appeals: The extended parallel process model. *Communication Monographs, 59*, 329–349.

Woodside, A. G., & Davenport, J. W., Jr. (1974). The effect of salesman similarity and expertise on consumer purchasing behavior. *Journal of Marketing Research, 11*, 198–202.

Zajonc, R. B. (1968). Attitudinal effects of mere exposure. *Journal of Personality and Social Psychology Monographs, 9* (No. 2, Part 2).

Suggested Readings

Festinger, L. (1957). *A theory of cognitive dissonance.* Stanford, CA: Stanford University Press.

Freedman, J. L., & Fraser, S. C. (1966). Compliance without pressure: The foot-in-the-door technique. *Journal of Personality and Social Psychology, 4*, 195–202.

McCroskey, J. C., & Young, T. J. (1981). Ethos and credibility: The construct and its measurement after three decades. *Central States Speech Journal, 32*, 24–34.

Milgram, S. (1963). Behavioral study of obedience. *Journal of Abnormal and Social Psychology, 67*, 371–378.

Pfau, M., Kenski, H. C., Nitz, M., & Sorenson, J. (1990). Efficacy of inoculation strategies in promoting resistance to political attack messages: Application to direct mail. *Communication Monographs, 57*, 25–43.

18

INTERPERSONAL COMMUNICATION

Charles R. Berger

Interpersonal communication concerns the study of social interaction between people. Interpersonal communication theory and research seeks to illuminate how individuals use verbal discourse and nonverbal actions, as well as written discourse, to achieve a variety of instrumental and communication goals such as informing, persuading and providing emotional support to others. Interpersonal communication traditionally has been conceived of as a process that occurs between people encountering each other face-to-face. Increasingly, social interaction is being accomplished through the use of such communication technologies as computers and mobile telephones, thus adding another dimension to this area of communication inquiry. However, technologically mediated social interaction is hardly new, having been possible since land-line telephone technology came into widespread use during the early decades of the 20th century. This older form of mediated interpersonal communication has been examined by communication researchers (Hopper, 1992).

Alternative Perspectives on Interpersonal Communication

An early and pervasive approach to defining interpersonal communication simply asserted that it is face-to-face communication between two people (King, 1979; Smith & Williamson, 1977). By contrast, face-to-face interaction involving from three to some relatively small number of people was defined as small group communication. Although this numerical distinction between interpersonal and small-group communication held sway for some time, Miller and Steinberg (1975) and Berger and Bradac (1982) questioned its utility. These researchers argued that in contrast to the number of individuals involved in an interaction, a more useful attribute for defining interpersonal communication is the kinds of knowledge people employ to make predictions about each other during their interactions.

Miller and Steinberg (1975) labeled social interactions based primarily on knowledge of cultural conventions noninterpersonal communication, since interactions depending upon the use of such conventions fail to individuate people. In these interactions, people are interchangeable members of ostensibly homogenous cultural or ethnic collectives and do not have unique, individual identities. Further, they proposed that social interaction based on what they called "sociological-level" information concerning individuals' demographic attributes such as sex, age, and socio-economic status also failed to provide a basis for interpersonal communication, although such information might provide somewhat more detail about individuals than cultural-level knowledge. Miller and Steinberg argued that interpersonal communication occurs when knowledge of individuals' beliefs, attitudes, and personalities, or what they termed "psychological-level" information, is used by cointerlocutors to make predictions about each others' beliefs, attitudes, and potential actions. When social interaction is based primarily on psychological-level information, messages are tailored to people as unique individuals rather than as members of apparently homogeneous cultural or sociological groupings. Miller and Steinberg recognized that in a large majority of social interactions, all three levels of knowledge are consulted; however, the increasing prominence of psychological-level knowledge in the prediction-making process was posited to be the sine qua non of interpersonal communication.

Cappella (1987) objected to this levels-of-knowledge approach to conceptualizing interpersonal communication on the grounds that people participating in the impersonal, role-defined relationships that Miller and Steinberg (1975) labeled "non-interpersonal relationships" still employ communication to carry out their roles. He observed that many impersonal interactions are nevertheless important in people's everyday lives, for example, transactions occurring in commercial or educational contexts. As an alternative to the knowledge-based approach to defining interpersonal communication, Cappella (1987) proposed that interpersonal communication occurs when an individual's behaviors affect the probability of another's subsequent behaviors with respect to the other's baseline rate of the behavior. When such behavioral influences are mutual, that is, when people alter each other's behaviors such that they deviate from their individual baselines, the preconditions for interpersonal communication have been met.

These two approaches to defining interpersonal communication are not necessarily incompatible. If the mutual influence postulate is granted, it is still possible to ask whether variations in message content (verbal and nonverbal) that are exchanged between people influence their psychological states and actions. Mutual influence may occur when an individual asks a store clerk for a pack of chewing gum or when the same individual requests a paramour's hand in marriage; however, the relationship consequences of these mutually influencing exchanges are radically different. Consequently, it is reasonable to assume that interpersonal communication rests on a foundation of mutual influence, and, further, the degree to which the mutually influencing messages exchanged are personal or impersonal is both constitutive and diagnostic of the type of relationship people have with each other (Bell, Buerkel-Rothfuss, & Gore, 1987; Bell & Healey, 1992). One implication of this perspective is that the concepts of interpersonal communication and interpersonal relationship are distinct. Interpersonal communication affects interpersonal relationships, and relationship states act to shape the communicative activity of those experiencing them.

Historical Antecedents of Interpersonal Communication Inquiry

The study of interpersonal communication developed during the years following World War II and grew out of two distinct areas of social-psychological research that appeared during and after the war (Delia, 1987). The more dominant area of the two concerned the role communication plays in the exercise of persuasion and social influence, while the other area, known as group dynamics, focused on social interaction within small groups. Group dynamics sought to illuminate how group interaction processes influence conformity to group norms, group cohesion, the exercise of social power, and group decision making (Cartwright & Zander, 1968). Although some group-dynamics-inspired interpersonal communication research appeared in this early period, during the 1960s most interpersonal communication research concerned the role that various source, message, channel and receiver factors play in changing audience members' attitudes and behavior; although studies of speech anxiety and communication apprehension also appeared in the interpersonal communication literature of that era.

For the most part, the vast majority of the communication and persuasion research appearing during this period did not examine social influence during the give-and-take of ongoing social interaction. Rather, experimental studies that systematically varied source and message factors were used to investigate the effects of persuasive messages on recipients' attitudes and opinions. Experimental studies of attitude change, inspired by the Yale group's communication and persuasion research program (Hovland & Janis, 1959; Hovland, Janis, & Kelley, 1953; Hovland & Rosenberg, 1960; Sherif & Hovland, 1961) and by balance (Heider, 1958; Newcomb, 1953), congruity (Osgood & Tannenbaum, 1955), dissonance (Brehm & Cohen, 1962; Festinger, 1957, 1964), reactance (Brehm, 1966), and social judgment theories (Sherif & Hovland, 1961; Sherif, Sherif, & Nebergall, 1965) dominated the interpersonal communication literature of that time. As elegant as this experimental approach to the study of persuasion was, unfortunately it did not encourage researchers to investigate reciprocal influence processes in face-to-face interaction (Berger & Burgoon, 1995; Miller, 1987). During face-to-face encounters, social influence is not a one-way street; individuals who enter such encounters with the goal of persuading their cointer-locutors may instead encounter resistance or find themselves being influenced by their partners.

Beginning in the late 1960s and early 1970s, the scope of interpersonal communication research expanded well beyond the narrow confines of the experimentally oriented, communication and persuasion paradigm to include the role social interaction plays in the development, maintenance, and deterioration of personal relationships. Much of this work was inspired by social penetration theory (Altman & Taylor, 1973) and filter theory (Duck, 1973). At the same time, relationships between interpersonal communication and interpersonal attraction began to become a focal point of study, much of this research being motivated by Byrne's studies of inter-personal attraction (Byrne, 1971) and Newcomb's (1961) earlier studies of the acquaintance process. At the same time, interpersonal communication researchers became interested in the study of self-disclosure (Jourard, 1964, 1971), an area that continues to be a research focus (Petronio, 2000, 2002). This period was also marked by a significant increase in attention to the study of nonverbal communication (Knapp, 1972; Mehrabian, 1971), and during the latter part of the 1970s, interpersonal communication research began to reflect increasing concern for under-standing the cognitive structures and processes that underlie social interaction with respect to both message production and message comprehension and interpretation (Delia, 1977; Hewes & Planalp, 1987). Deceptive communication was another research focus that emerged during this period (Knapp & Comadena, 1979; Knapp, Hart, & Dennis, 1974). In the ensuing decades, each of these research traditions has continued to attract considerable research attention.

During the 1970s, communication researchers in general and the interpersonal communication researchers in particular expressed considerable frustration over the lack of original theories expressly developed to explain various interpersonal communication phenomena. As a consequence, beginning in this decade, interpersonal communication scholars engaged in debates concerning alternative meta-theoretical perspectives from which to develop communication theory (Benson & Pearce, 1977). Since that time, interpersonal communication researchers have proposed a variety of theories concerned with explaining such phenomena as relationship development, nonverbal communication, message production, interaction adaptation, and deceptive communication.

As the theoretical and research trends set in motion in the 1970s continued to play out during the 1980s, interpersonal communication researchers became increasingly interested in illuminating the communication strategies individuals use to achieve a wide variety of goals (Daly & Wiemann, 1994). This outpouring of strategic communication research was partially set in motion by an inquiry concerned with the conditions under which individuals deploy different strategies to achieve compliance goals (Miller, Boster, Roloff, & Seibold, 1977); an inquiry based on Marwell and Schmidt's (1967) earlier research. This initial work was quickly followed by a spate of compliance-gaining studies (Boster, 1995; Cody, Canary, & Smith, 1994); moreover, during this period the purview of the strategic communication enterprise became rapidly more catholic by expanding the number of different goals studied to include acquiring information, making requests, comforting others, resisting compliance-gaining attempts, and seeking affinity (Daly & Wiemann, 1994). In conjunction with this focus on strategic social interaction, some interpersonal communication researchers developed theories and models of message production, for the purpose of explaining how such strategic interaction takes place (Berger, 1995, 1997a; Greene, 1984, 1997; Wilson, 1990, 1995). This theory development work continued through the 1990s and into the new millennium.

The interpersonal communication domain can be divided into at least six unique but related areas of study, each representing a relatively coherent body of theory and research. These six areas are concerned with (1) uncertainty; (2) interpersonal adaptation; (3) message production; (4) relationship development; (5) deceptive communication; and (6) mediated social interaction. In addition to these theoretically articulated domains, interpersonal communication researchers have addressed such specific topic areas as interpersonal conflict, bargaining, and negotiation and emotion; some of these topics will be addressed as each of the six research areas is considered below.

Uncertainty in Interpersonal Communication

Although individuals enter social interactions with funds of cultural, sociological, and psychological knowledge regarding their interaction partners (Miller & Steinberg, 1975), they cannot be completely certain of their conversational partners' current emotional states, beliefs, attitudes, and future actions, even when their interaction partners are familiar and perhaps even well known to them (Berger, 1997b). That is, it is impossible to predict accurately all of these internal states and potential future actions at any given point in time. Consequently, when individuals engage in social interaction they do so under conditions of more or less uncertainty, but uncertainty is never completely absent. Moreover, because individuals and social relationships are dynamic, and sometimes highly so, relative certainty at one point in time may be replaced by substantial uncertainty at another. Individuals who are now apparently "well known" may later become "strangers."

In addition, because individuals harbor uncertainties about cointerlocutors, they must, by necessity, have uncertainties about how they should act toward their partners; consequently, individuals experience uncertainty with respect both to themselves and others. These uncertainties are maximal when strangers meet, but uncertainties can also arise in close relationships of long duration (Planalp & Honeycutt, 1985; Planalp, Rutherford, & Honeycutt, 1988). Uncertainty Reduction Theory (URT) (Berger & Calabrese, 1975; Berger & Gudykunst, 1991) proposes that individuals must reduce their uncertainties to some degree in order to be able to fashion verbal discourse and actions that will allow them to achieve their interaction goals. The theory's propositions describe relationships between verbal and nonverbal communication and information seeking, self-disclosure and interpersonal attraction.

Berger (1979) identified three general classes of strategies for reducing uncertainty. Passive strategies do not entail social interaction between parties; rather, they involve the unobtrusive observation of others for the purpose of acquiring information about them. Active strategies also do not involve face-to-face social interaction between information seekers and their targets. Acquiring information from third parties about a target person falls into this category. Finally, interactive strategies such as asking questions, disclosing information about one's self and relaxing the target may be used to acquire information when interaction occurs. These strategies vary with respect to their efficiency and social appropriateness. For example, acquiring personal information from another by asking questions might be an efficient strategy but it could become socially inappropriate if too many questions or excessively personal questions were to be asked. Conversely, relaxing the target person might be perceived to be highly appropriate socially but, at the same time, might be relatively inefficient for acquiring specific pieces of information from the target. A person who is more comfortable might say more than one who is less so but still not reveal the desired information. Studies have also examined the strategies individuals use to resist revealing information about themselves to highly inquisitive cointerlocutors (Berger & Kellermann, 1994). URT has been found to have some purchase in explaining social interaction in intercultural (Gudykunst, 1995, 2005) and organizational (Kramer, 2004) communication contexts.

Social actors may not only harbor uncertainties about themselves and others as individuals, they may also experience uncertainty with respect to their relationship with each other or relational uncertainty (Knobloch, 2005, 2006; Knobloch, & Carpenter-Theune, 2004; Knobloch & Solomon, 2002, 2005). The relational turbulence model posits that changes in intimacy within romantic relationships potentiate relational uncertainty, defined as questions or doubts about the nature of involvement in a relationship (Solomon & Knobloch, 2004). Relational uncertainty tends to polarize emotional, cognitive, and communicative reactions to various relationship events; however, reducing uncertainty and managing such events may promote intimacy between relationship partners.

Some researchers have argued that individuals may not necessarily be motivated to reduce their uncertainty when they anticipate experiencing negative outcomes by so doing (Afifi & Weiner, 2004; Babrow, 1992, 2001; Brashers, 2001). For example, individuals who have their blood tested for HIV because they suspect that they may be HIV positive may chose not to obtain their test results; presumably because they are fearful of an HIV positive outcome. They may elect to maintain their uncertainty in order to avoid hearing bad news. Similarly, married individuals who suspect their spouses are cheating on them may avoid reducing their uncertainty in this regard because of projected negative consequences that might accrue from such knowledge. According to this perspective, then, uncertainty is something to be managed rather than necessarily reduced. Although there are situations in which some people might avoid reducing their uncertainty, the degree to which these avoidance maneuvers portend optimal adaptation to the environment is open to question. In the long run, ignorance may not necessarily be bliss (Berger, 2005a).

Interpersonal Adaptation

Students of social interaction have long recognized that when individuals converse, they show strong proclivities to reciprocate each other's verbal and nonverbal behaviors. The norm of reciprocity, which states that in the conduct of social intercourse people are obligated to help and not harm those who help them, provides a potential explanation for the ubiquity of reciprocal social interaction (Gouldner, 1960). However, behavioral reciprocity has been observed between very young infants and their caregivers, suggesting a biological basis for such behavior (Burgoon, Stern, & Dillman, 1995). Evidence for the operation of the norm of reciprocity was found in early studies of self-disclosure and was labeled the "dyadic effect" (Cozby, 1973; Jourard, 1964, 1971). When individuals disclose information about themselves at a particular intimacy level, their cointerlocutors are likely to disclose information about themselves at a similar intimacy level. Moreover, as individuals increase or decrease the intimacy level of their self-disclosures, cointerlocutors tend to follow suit (Cozby, 1973). It is not that individuals reciprocate the same information about themselves; rather, individuals tend to match the intimacy level of their disclosures. In addition to reciprocity at the level of message content, early studies demonstrated reciprocity of nonverbal behaviors in interview situations. As interviewers purposively increased or decreased their speech rate or the number of pauses in their speech, interviewees were observed to respond by adjusting their speech or pause rate to match those of the interviewers (Matarazzo, Wiens, & Saslow, 1965).

Although there are pronounced tendencies for reciprocity in social interaction, there are conditions under which interacting individuals will show compensation in response to each other's behaviors. Compensation occurs when a behavior displayed by one person is responded to with an "opposite" behavior from another. For example, a smile by one person might be responded to by another's frown or an attempt to begin a conversation by moving closer to an individual might be met with eye-gaze aversion, potentially signaling an unwillingness to converse. In the smile–frown case, compensation occurs within the same nonverbal communication channel, facial expressions; in the second case, the compensatory behavior is expressed in a channel different from the initiating behavior.

A number of alternative theories have been devised to illuminate the conditions under which reciprocity and compensation are likely to occur during social interactions, especially with respect to nonverbal behaviors. Although Expectancy Violations Theory (Burgoon, 1993), Arousal Labeling Theory (Patterson, 1983), Discrepancy-Arousal Theory (Cappella & Greene, 1982, 1984), and Cognitive Valence Theory (Andersen & Guerrero, 1998a, 1998b) differ in terms of their explanations for reciprocity/compensation, they share the assumptions that (1) individuals have expectations for each other's nonverbal behaviors and (2) when the expectations for nonverbal behavior are violated, individuals tend to experience arousal. For instance, when people who try to converse at inappropriately close conversational distances or stare at conversational partners for inordinate lengths of time, they are likely to create arousal in their cointerlocutors. Arousal Labeling and Discrepancy Arousal theories suggest that when the experience of this arousal is pleasant, reciprocity is likely to occur; however, when this arousal is experienced negatively, compensation is likely to follow. Research comparing these theories has been inconclusive and has prompted the development of Interaction Adaptation Theory (IAT) (Burgoon et al., 1995). This theory argues that when an individual's interaction position matches a cointerlocutor's behavior, reciprocity or matching is likely to occur, but when an individual's interaction position is discrepant from the other's behavior, compensation is likely to occur. Interaction position is determined by the individual's basic drives and needs, their cognitive expectations concerning social norms and behavior and their goals and preferences. Although IAT proposes a potentially more comprehensive explanation of interaction adaptation than do the other theories, its scope may be ambitious to the point that it is difficult to evaluate.

While not invoking arousal-based explanations, Speech Accommodation Theory (Giles & Powesland, 1975) argues that individuals will become more similar with respect to their dialects and accents or converge to the extent that they desire to experience solidarity in their relationships. By contrast, individuals will show dialectical and accent divergence when they wish to assert a unique identity. These speech adjustments may be accomplished consciously, however, many times they occur outside of the conscious awareness of those involved in interactions. The notions of convergence and divergence are roughly similar to the concepts of reciprocity and compensation, respectively. This theory, which later morphed into Communication Accommodation Theory, extended this analytic framework to speech parameters beyond dialect and accent (Giles, Coupland, & Coupland, 1991; Giles, Mulac, Bradac, & Johnson, 1987; Shepard, Giles, & Le Poire, 2001).

Message Production

The notion that language is a tool or an instrument for attaining everyday goals has enjoyed long acceptance among students of language and communication (Clark, 1994; Wittgenstein, 1953). Given the noncontroversial nature of this proposition, it is but a small step to contend that social interaction, like language, is a tool or an instrument for goal achievement (Berger 2003; Dillard, Anderson, & Knobloch, 2002; Wilson & Sabee, 2003). Consistent with this proposition, beginning in the 1970s and continuing through the 1990s, constructivist researchers (Delia, O'Keefe,

& O'Keefe, 1982) endeavored to determine the characteristics of messages deemed to be effective for achieving a variety of goals, most of them concerned with persuasion (Clark & Delia, 1977; Delia, Kline, & Burleson, 1979); although, a parallel line of research concerned with the provision of emotional support developed within this tradition (Burleson, 2003). A robust finding from this line of research is that when given the task of devising messages to achieve such goals, individuals with high levels of cognitive complexity tend to generate messages showing greater evidence of social perspective taking than do their less cognitively complex counterparts (Applegate, 1990). Within this research perspective, cognitive complexity is indexed by the number of psychological constructs individuals typically use to construe other persons (cognitive differentiation) and the degree to which the constructs they use are abstract (construct abstractness). Greater numbers of highly abstract constructs contribute to higher cognitive complexity levels. Because highly differentiated individuals' messages take into account their cointerlocutors' goals, emotional states, and potential responses to their messages, their messages are, as a result, potentially more effective than the less socio-centric messages generated by their less cognitively complex counterparts.

Beginning in the 1980s, a more comprehensive and abstract message production theory labeled Action Assembly Theory (Greene, 1984, 1997) was developed to explain how individuals produce actions and discourse, and during the same period theories featuring such knowledge structures as scripts, plans, and Memory Organization Packets (MOPS) were devised (Berger, 1995, 1997a; Kellermann, 1995). In the case of these latter theories, sometimes referred to as Goal-Plan-Action (GPA) theories (Dillard, Anderson, & Knobloch, 2002), scripts, plans, and MOPS are conceived of as hierarchically organized knowledge structures representing action sequences aimed at bringing about goal attainment. Once goals and knowledge structures are activated, the knowledge structures guide actions toward goal achievement. Knowledge structures vary with respect to their abstractness and level of detail, and they can be made more complex by including contingencies that anticipate points at which projected actions in them might fail. Individuals who plan ahead during conversations, anticipate their cointerlocutor's future conversational moves, and develop plan contingencies to meet these future actions are more likely to attain their social interaction goals than are individuals who do not engage in such planning activity while they converse (Waldron, 1997). However, online planning must be flexible enough to deal with uncertainties that surround message production during social interactions (Berger, 1997b).

A potential shortcoming of GPA theories is that they do not provide a detailed account of how goals arise in the first place; that is, they begin with the assumption that social actors have a goal or goals to pursue. However, there are at least two examples of attempts to formulate and test theoretical explanations for how goals arise during social interaction (Meyer, 1997; Wilson, 1990, 1995; Wilson & Sabee, 2003). Because much of everyday social interaction is aimed at satisfying recurring goals, much of everyday conversational interaction is routine (Coulmas, 1981; Wray & Perkins, 2000). Moreover, efforts to routinize service interactions are common in commercial contexts (Ford, 1999; Leidner, 1993). Nonetheless, important questions can be asked about the conditions under which specific goals are activated and the consequences that follow from the disruption of these routines once they are undertaken. Interference with the completion of these routines should provoke annoyance and other negative emotions because it prevents the efficient achievement of recurring goals (Srull & Wyer, 1986); however, there may be circumstances under which the disruption of social interaction routines provides relief from boredom or from an undesirable situation such as a routine conflict with another person.

People sometimes imagine social interactions with others. These imagined interactions may occur before an encounter, as when employees imagine what they might say to their bosses, but imagined interactions can also take place after a particular encounter has ended. Under certain conditions, imagining what one might say to another person before an interaction with them takes place can reduce the amount of apprehension that the person who has imagined the interaction shows during the actual encounter. Moreover, imagining interactions may help those who imagine them cope with negative emotions they have experienced in their relationship with the person or persons with whom they imagine conversing (Honeycutt, 2003). However, imagining interactions before they take place may have the effect of encouraging individuals to commit themselves prematurely to a particular plan for the impending interaction and, as a result, render them less inclined to recognize potential problems that arise during the actual conversation and consider contingent actions that might be undertaken to deal with these problems (Berger, 1997a, 1997b).

Relationship Development

The idea that interpersonal communication plays a critical role in the development, maintenance, and deterioration of social and personal relationships is one that has gained widespread acceptance during the past 40 years. Although a great bulk of research attention has been paid to the development of romantic relationships, probably because college students, who are frequently used as research participants, are likely to be involved in such relationships, researchers have also investigated communication between friends, spouses, and family members.

A central question researchers have sought to answer is why some relationships become closer over time while others grow distant and perhaps end. Social exchange theories have frequently been invoked to explain why relationship growth and deterioration occur (Roloff, 1981, 1987; Roloff & Campion, 1985; Thibaut & Kelley, 1959). In general, these theories suggest that individuals experience both rewards and costs for being in relationships, and individuals not only assess their own rewards and costs, they also estimate their partners' levels of rewards and costs. Rewards may be material (wealth) or emotional (emotional support) and costs may be similarly material (lack of money) or emotional (undesirable personality). Each individual puts these reward and cost estimates into ratio form (rewards/costs) and compares the two ratios (self: rewards/costs versus partner: rewards/costs). Individuals will feel equity in their relationship to the degree that the reward/cost ratios match; however, if the self's ratio is less favorable than the partner's, the individual will feel inequity and thus dissatisfaction with the relationship. Dissatisfaction arising from felt inequity is sometimes expressed verbally when people say, "I am putting more into this relationship than I am getting out of it." In general, these theories suggest that favorable relative reward/cost ratios fuel relationship growth, whereas unfavorable ratios are associated with relationship deterioration. It is not the absolute levels of rewards and costs that determine equity but the degree to which the two ratios match.

Some have argued that social exchange theories and other relationship development perspectives make the processes of relationship development and deterioration appear to be much more continuous and linear than they actually are. These researchers contend that the development of relationships is fraught with dialectical tensions that pull individuals in opposite directions simultaneously (Baxter & Montgomery, 1996; Montgomery & Baxter, 1998). For example, individuals may at once desire both novelty and predictability with respect to their partners' behaviors, and because the tension between these polarities shifts over time, relationships are in a constant state of flux. Other dialectics such as openness-closeness and autonomy-connection may interact with each other through time. Given the dialectical nature of personal relationships and their dynamic interplay, proponents of this dialectical perspective contend that complete merger of relationship partners is not possible.

Although social exchange theories and the relational dialectics perspective provide explanations for the growth and deterioration of relationships, they do not centrally address the effects of messages exchanged between people. That is, in the case of social exchange theories, individuals' judgments about relative rewards and costs are presumed to be residues of verbal and nonverbal interactions; similarly, the dialectical contradictions that individuals retrospectively report experiencing in their relationships ostensibly arise from communicative exchanges with relationship partners; however, actual message exchanges between partners are generally not examined within this research tradition. However, although not necessarily strongly motivated by theory, there has been considerable research interest in interpersonal conflict in general and marital conflict in particular, much of it based on direct observations of partners engaged in social interaction (Roloff & Soule, 2002). Within the domain of marital interaction, studies have found that couples who display a demand–withdraw pattern of message exchanges when interacting with each other, such that one person makes a demand of the other and the other person responds by withdrawing, report lower levels of relational satisfaction than do couples who acknowledge and respond to each other's demands in a conciliatory way (Gottman & Levenson, 1988; Gottman, Murray, Swanson, Tyson, & Swanson, 2002). The degree to which spouses reciprocate negative affect, or cross-complain, has also been found to potentiate reduced marital satisfaction (Gottman et al., 2002). Because the communication of emotion plays a vital role in many different types of relationships, there is increasing interest in how the regulation of emotions and emotional communication affect relationship development (Metts & Planalp, 2002; Planalp, 1998, 1999, 2003).

Deceptive Communication

Many interpersonal communication researchers subscribe to the view that deception is an integral part of social interaction (Goffman, 1959; G. R. Miller & Stiff, 1993; W. I. Miller, 2003). So-called "white lies" are commonplace in everyday social commerce. Some have gone so far as to argue that deception is an important lubricant that enables the smooth operation of the social interaction machine. Many times these lies are told to help cointerlocutors save face when potentially embarrassing circumstances arise in social situations (Brown & Levinson, 1978, 1987). For example, dinner guests might tell a host that the food they have just consumed was "wonderful" when, in fact, it was utterly horrible. Deception by commission occurs when proffered information is at variance with the "true" state of affairs, as in the previous examples; however, deception may also occur by omission; that is, individuals may intentionally withhold critical information so that others will draw erroneous inferences, as when a used car salesperson fails to reveal known mechanical defects present in a car to a prospective buyer. The customer is left to infer that the car is mechanically reliable.

Although interpersonal communication researchers have expended considerable research effort examining deceptive communication since the 1970s (Knapp & Comadena, 1979; Knapp et al., 1974), there are relatively few theories of deceptive social interaction. One of these, Information Manipulation Theory (McCornack, 1992), asserts that when individuals engage in deceptive communication, they may covertly flout one or more of Grice's (1989) four conversational maxims: quality, quantity, manner, and relevance. However, deception may also occur when verbal messages adhere to the four maxims but are delivered with nonverbal accompaniments that make them ambiguous, for example, sarcasm. Unfortunately, serious questions have been raised about the degree to which Information Manipulation Theory is falsifiable (Jacobs, Dawson, & Brashers, 1996). Interpersonal Deception Theory represents another attempt to explain the interaction between individuals' intentional attempts to deceive others and the degree to which those being deceived can detect the deceitful behavior (Buller & Burgoon, 1996). Although this theory presents 18 propositions, critics have observed that the propositions are not formulated in such a way that they address a central "why" question (DePaulo, Ainsfield, & Bell, 1996). Others have contended that some of the propositions are vague and nonfalsifiable (Levine & McCornack, 1996; McCornack, 1997).

There are at least two enduring questions concerning deceptive communication that have attracted considerable research attention. One of these questions concerns the degree to which engaging in deception alters nonverbal behaviors; that is, do truth tellers' nonverbal behaviors differ systematically from those of individuals who are telling lies? The research germane to this question has focused on nonverbal behaviors because it is generally assumed that when people engage in deceptive communication, they can carefully monitor what they are saying but cannot necessarily control their nonverbal behaviors in ways that will make them appear to be telling the truth (Ekman & Friesen, 1969). In general, research findings suggest that no one nonverbal behavior, for example, eye gaze aversion, excessive leg movements, fast or slow speech rate, or changes in body posture can be used as a universal indicator of deceptive communication across all individuals (O'Sullivan, 2005; Vrig & Mann, 2005). That is, there appears to be no nonverbal indicator of deception equivalent to Pinocchio's fabled nose. However, some specific behaviors, for example, changes in leg and foot movements and the size of pupils and the degree to which one exhibits verbal and vocal immediacy and genuine smiles may differentiate some truth tellers from some liars in some situations (DePaulo, Lindsay, Malone, Muhlenbruck, Charlton, & Cooper, 2003).

Another enduring question investigated by deception researchers is the degree to which individuals are skilled at detecting deception as they interact with others. In this case research has generally shown that most individuals are not very adept at deception detection, even those whose professions frequently require them to ascertain whether people are lying or telling the truth; for example, judges, counselors, and law enforcement personnel (Buller & Burgoon, 1996; Vrig & Mann, 2005). One explanation for the apparent inability of most individuals to detect deception is the pervasiveness of the "truth bias." The truth bias arises from the fact that in the conduct of everyday social interaction, individuals must routinely assume that their conversational partners are telling the truth, as suggested by Grice's (1989) quality maxim. Consequently, because individuals generally assume others are telling the truth, it is difficult for them to detect deceit when it is being perpetrated. Failure to attend to potentially diagnostic cues and the use of various heuristics have also been proffered as explanations for low rates of deception detection accuracy; however, even though a the vast majority of people are poor deception detectors, approximately 1/1,000 people are deception detection "wizards" who are found in a wide array of occupations (O'Sullivan, 2005). These "wizards" achieve better than chance levels of deception detection accuracy.

Mediated Social Interaction

Increasingly, social interaction is being accomplished through such communication technologies as computers with e-mail and chat room capabilities and mobile telephones with text messaging and other communication features. Teleconferencing has become a commonplace in business communication. As the use of these technologies has become progressively more widespread, there has been a concomitant increase in research aimed at understanding their potential individual and social effects. However, as indicated earlier, technologically mediated social interaction is hardly a new phenomenon, having been possible on a wide scale since the advent of the land-line telephone.

In the wake of the introduction of such mass media as film, radio, and television, research was undertaken to investigate the potential deleterious effects of the then-new medium on those exposed to it. The voluminous Payne Fund studies of the late 1920s and early 1930s attempted to identify several potential negative impacts of film on youth (Charters, 1933), and not long after

269

the widespread diffusion of television, similar research endeavors were undertaken (Schramm, Lyle, & Parker, 1961). More recently, such concerns have surfaced with respect to Internet use. Internet addiction (Griffiths, 1998) and increased social isolation and loneliness with increasing Internet use (Kraut, Lundmark et al., 1998) are among the purported toxic effects associated with Internet involvement; although, evidence for the latter association is both scant and equivocal (Kraut, Kiesler et al., 2002). An inherent difficulty in examining such effects is establishing directions of causal influence. Do people with "addictive personalities" find Internet use to be another activity to which to become addicted, or does heavy use of the Internet induce addictive behavior? Do high levels of Internet use induce people to feel socially isolated and lonely, or do people who are already socially isolated and lonely gravitate to the Internet to help them alleviate these unpleasant feelings? Yet another and perhaps more realistic possibility in each of these cases is that both causal directions interact with each other in a complex, reciprocal fashion.

Some researchers have observed that when individuals engage in anonymous Computer Mediated Communication (CMC), as they might in an Internet chat room or on e-mail, they are more likely to act in ways that they would not if they were interacting with others face-to-face (FtF) or if their identities were known to others in the CMC context. Researchers have postulated both positive and negative possibilities in this regard. On the positive side, anonymous individuals communicating with others by CMC might assume new identities, personalities, or both that could help them cope with personal problems (Turkle, 1995). For example, highly introverted and shy people who wish to overcome their social inhibitions might "try on" a highly extraverted and outgoing persona while engaging in CMC. The effect of this experimentation might be to move such individuals in the desired direction of becoming less shy and introverted in their FtF interactions. However, on the negative side, others have noted that this same cloak of anonymity may serve to embolden individuals to insult and attack others or to "flame" them, behaviors they would not normally display in most FtF interactions or in CMC if their identities were known to their cointerlocutors (Siegel, Dubrovsky, Kiesler, & McGuire, 1983).

Just as the advent of television prompted both considerable speculation and research aimed at comparing the medium's potential effects, especially with respect to its visual channel, with those of older media such as radio, so too the appearance of CMC has precipitated considerable research aimed at determining how CMC and FtF interaction differ with respect to various outcomes associated with their use (Walther & Parks, 2002). Because text-based CMC, as currently used in electronic mail (e-mail), news groups, and chat rooms, filters out many nonverbal cues typically available to people engaged in FtF interactions, it is presumed that communication via text-based CMC is more task focused than is FtF communication. Moreover, while relatively cue-deprived, text-based CMC venues may be quite useful for initially encountering and screening potential friends and romantic partners, they apparently do not afford sufficient information for developing most close relationships. Individuals who initially meet in the text-based CMC world usually elect to communicate with each other through other channels, for example, telephone and FtF encounters (Walther & Parks, 2002). These alternative communication channels afford their users potentially more rich and comprehensive samples of each other's behavior. Although the ability to send pictures and live video in the CMC context may overcome some of this cue loss in the visual realm, such nonverbal communication channels as touch, pheromones, body temperature and smell, that are at once both highly significant in most close romantic relationships and currently difficult or impossible to instantiate in CMC, probably necessitates FtF interaction for developing close relationships. In any case, for a variety of reasons a majority of relationships initially formed online fail to migrate successfully to off-line relationships (Baker, 2002).

Because text-based CMC may serve to filter out personal information that might be used to understand people as individuals rather than as group members, some researchers have suggested that when groups use CMC to communicate with each other, the lack of individuating informa-tion about group members may foster stronger in-group identity. Increased in-group loyalty may serve to "de-individuate" people to the point that they are willing to stereotype out-group mem-bers and behave negatively toward them. Although research has supported this possibility (Post-mes, Spears, Lea, & Reicher, 2000), some have observed that these findings are limited to the domain of group-based CMC and may not apply in situations in which people are using CMC to interact with others on an individual basis (Walther & Parks, 2002). Beyond the CMC realm, under the aegis of Human Computer Interaction (HCI), considerable research evidence has been adduced to support the idea that people tend to treat computers and other communication tech-nologies as if they are human agents, even when users know that they are interacting with a machine (Reeves & Nass, 1996). Apparently, technology users cannot help imputing human-like qualities to the communication technologies they encounter in their everyday lives.

Given the rapid rate at which new communication technologies that enable mediated social interaction between people are being made widely available to the public, understanding how the use of these technologies affect communication in these modes represents an opportunity to further understanding of FtF interaction processes. At the present time, FtF interaction is held as a kind of gold standard against which to compare mediated social interaction. However, prolonged use of communication technologies to enable mediated social interaction may alter the fundamental nature of FtF interaction; that is, communication conventions associated with CMC may insinuate themselves into FtF interaction over time (Berger, 2005b). This possibility represents a challenge to interpersonal communication researchers.

Other Research Areas

The six areas just considered do not exhaust the entire domain of interpersonal communication inquiry. In addition to these theoretically defined areas are specific concepts in which interper-sonal communication researchers have had an enduring interest. Some of these concepts are briefly considered below.

Everyday experience suggests that some individuals are consistently better able than others to achieve their goals during their social interactions. Some people appear to be able to induce oth-ers to like them while others seem to be very effective at comforting those in distress. The skills associated with success in these and other social interaction domains can be subsumed under the notion of communication competence. Much has been written about the communication com-petence concept, but there remains considerable ambiguity concerning its meaning; moreover, there has yet to be a theory that elaborates the concept (Spitzburg & Cupach, 2002). Some have suggested that communication competence might profitably be viewed as a theoretical term or domain of study rather than a single theoretical construct (Wilson & Sabee, 2003).

There appears to be some agreement that communication competence refers to the degree to which individuals are able to reach their goals (effectiveness) and the extent to which goal achievement is accomplished in an appropriate manner (social appropriateness) (Parks, 1994). In addition, some have suggested that efficiency may be another component of competence; that is, how quickly individuals are able to achieve their goals (Berger, 2003). Another point of convergence is that communication competence is not a generalized skill but is specific to dif-ferent kinds of communication goals and situations (Wilson & Sabee, 2003). The domain speci-ficity of communication skills is clearly demonstrated in the vast array of chapters in a volume devoted to the topic (Greene & Burleson, 2003). This work's chapters ranged from nonverbal communication (Burgoon & Bacue, 2003), message production (Berger, 2003), and reception skills (Wyer & Adaval, 2003), to emotional support (Burleson, 2003), persuasion (Dillard & Marshall, 2003), negotiation (Roloff, Putnam, & Anastasiou, 2003), informing (Rowan, 2003), and arguing (Hample, 2003) skills. Thus, an individual might be very effective at offering social support and comfort to others but at the same time might be relatively ineffective at gaining compliance from them. Although most interpersonal communication researchers acknowledge that communication competence is goal and situation specific, as yet there is no typology of goals and situations that enables us to determine specific skill sets that are associated with various classes of goals and situations.

As noted previously, much of everyday social interaction is organized around recurring goals that arise in the course of everyday living. The routines associated with everyday family and work interactions and with daily transactions in business and commerce encourage the development of communication routines in order to reach these recurring goals effectively and efficiently. If people had to plan consciously how to reach each of these recurring goals every day, the pace of social life would slow to a crawl. Instead, communication is routinized and can be enacted automatically when the occasion arises. Routinization of language use is pervasive; it has been estimated that up to 70% of adult language is formulaic (Altenberg, 1990; Sinclair, 1991). The notion of communication routines may be related to communication competence. Competent communicators may be those who, in a given situation, have rapid access to communication routines that generally eventuate in goal achievement. Of course, the relationship between the availability and accessibility of communication routines and communication competence rests on the assumption that the routines accessed are both effective and socially appropriate. A given situation may be nonroutine and require conscious planning effort; thus, the discerning communicator must be able to differentiate between those social situations that are routine and those that are not. This requirement for astute social discernment suggests that competent communicative action involves more than the production of effective messages. Relatively accurate perception of others' current circumstances, moods, and emotional states is a vital prerequisite to competent social conduct.

With few exceptions, the individual has been the point of departure for much of the theory and research presented in this chapter. Some have argued that this individually focused, psychological perspective on interpersonal communication must be augmented by a purview that takes into account the fact that individuals are embedded in a variety of social networks. The extensiveness and nature of these social networks has been shown to be consequential to the development and maintenance of specific personal relationships as well as health and well-being (Parks, 2007). Social network members may or may not provide support to particular relationships, thus affecting their outcomes, as when parents or relatives or both support or oppose the impending marriage of a child (Parks & Adelman, 1983). Clearly, the explanation of a large number of phenomena subsumed under the aegis of interpersonal communication requires that these social network influences be taken into account. After all, it is these social network ties that represent at least part of the "inter" in interpersonal communication.

Summary

Given the real possibility of future reductions in physical mobility due to increasingly expensive and scarce energy sources, people may be forced to initiate and maintain their distant social relationships through mediated communication channels (Stafford, 2005). Continuing research will be necessary to understand how technologically mediated social interaction differs from FtF interaction and how mediated interaction systems can be designed to be better approximations to FtF interaction. At the same time, physical mobility constraints may potentiate increases in the amount of time those who are already physically proximate and available to each other spend together. Increasing the frequency and intensity of FtF interactions among those readily available for interaction may serve to increase the degree to which individuals experience positive relational outcomes or exacerbate extant problems and reducing relational satisfaction. This latter possibility suggests the importance of continuing efforts to unravel the fundamental processes that enable social interaction.

References

Afifi, W. A., & Weiner, J. L. (2004). Toward a theory of motivated information management. *Communication Theory, 14*(2), 167–190.

Altenberg, B. (1990). Speech as linear composition. In G. Caie, K. Haastrup, A. L. Jakobsen, J. Nielsen, Sevaldsen et al. (Eds.), *Proceedings from the Fourth Nordic Conference for English Studies* (Vol. 1, pp. 133–143). Copenhagen, Denmark: Department of English, University of Copenhagen.

Altman, I., & Taylor, D. A. (1973). *Social penetration: The development of interpersonal relationships*. New York: Holt, Rinehart, & Winston.

Andersen, P. A., & Guerrero, L. K. (1998a). The bright side of relational communication: Interpersonal warmth as a social emotion. In P. A. Andersen & L. K. Guerrero (Eds.), *Handbook of communication and emotion: Research, theory, applications and contexts* (pp. 303–329). New York: Academic Press.

Andersen, P. A., & Guerrero, L. K. (1998b). Principles of communication and emotion in social interaction. In P. A. Andersen & L. K. Guerrero (Eds.), *Handbook of communication and emotion: Research, theory, applications and contexts* (pp. 49–96). New York: Academic Press.

Applegate, J. L. (1990). Constructs and communication: A pragmatic integration. In G. Neimeyer & R. Neimeyer (Eds.), *Advances in personal construct psychology* (Vol. 1, pp. 203–230). Greenwich, CT: JAL.

Babrow, A. S. (1992). Communication and problematic integration: Understanding diverging probability and value, ambiguity, ambivalence, and impossibility. *Communication Theory, 2*(2), 95–130.

Babrow, A. S. (2001). Uncertainty, value, communication, and problematic integration. *Journal of Communication, 51*, 553–573.

Baker, A. (2002). What makes an online relationship successful? Clues from couples who met in cyberspace. *CyberPsychology and Behavior, 5*, 363–375.

Baxter, L. A., & Montgomery, B. M. (1996). *Relating: Dialogues and dialectics*. New York: Guilford.

Bell, R. A., Buerkel-Rothfuss, N. L., & Gore, K. E. (1987). "Did you bring the yarmulke for the Cabbage Patch Kid?" The idiomatic communication of young lovers. *Human Communication Research, 14*, 47–67.

Bell, R. A., & Healy, J. G. (1992). Idiomatic communication and interpersonal solidarity in friends' relational cultures. *Human Communication Research, 18*, 307–335.

Benson, T. W., & Pearce, W. B. (Eds.). (1977). Alternative theoretical bases for the study of human communication: A symposium. *Communication Quarterly, 25*, 3–73.

Berger, C. R. (1979). Beyond initial interaction: Uncertainty, understanding and the development of interpersonal relationships. In H. Giles & R. St. Clair (Eds.), *Language and social psychology* (pp. 122–144). Oxford: Blackwell.

Berger, C. R. (1995). A plan-based approach to strategic communication. In D. E. Hewes (Ed.), *The cognitive bases of interpersonal communication* (pp. 141–179). Hillsdale, NJ: Erlbaum.

Berger, C. R. (1997a). *Planning strategic interaction: Attaining goals through communicative action*. Mahwah, NJ: Erlbaum.

Berger, C. R. (1997b). Producing messages under uncertainty. In J. Greene (Ed.), *Message production: Advances in communication theory* (pp. 221–244). Mahwah, NJ: Erlbaum.

Berger, C. R. (2003). Message production skill in social interaction. In J. O. Greene & B. R. Burleson (Eds.), *Handbook of communication and social interaction skills* (pp. 257–289). Mahwah, NJ: Erlbaum.

Berger, C. R. (2005a). Interpersonal communication: Theoretical perspectives, future prospects. *Journal of Communication, 55*, 415–447.

Berger, C. R. (2005b). Effects of interactive technology involvement on face-to-face interaction: Benign enablement or insidious insinuation? *Asian Communication Research, 2*, 5–22.

Berger, C. R., & Bradac, J. J. (1982). *Language and social knowledge: Uncertainty in interpersonal relations*. London: Edward Arnold.

Berger, C. R., & Burgoon, M. (1995). Preface. In C. R. Berger & M. Burgoon (Eds.), *Communication and social influence processes* (pp. ix–xii). East Lansing, MI: Michigan State University Press.

Berger, C. R., & Calabrese, R. J. (1975). Some explorations in initial interaction and beyond: Toward a developmental theory of interpersonal communication. *Human Communication Research, 1,* 99–112.

Berger, C. R., & Gudykunst, W. B. (1991). Uncertainty and communication. In B. Dervin & M. Voight (Eds.), *Progress in communication sciences* (pp. 21–66). Norwood, NJ: Ablex.

Berger, C. R., & Kellermann K. (1994). Acquiring social information. In J. A. Daly & J. M. Wiemann (Eds.), *Strategic interpersonal communication* (pp. 1–31). Hillsdale, NJ: Erlbaum.

Boster, F. J. (1995). Commentary on compliance-gaining message behavior research. In C. R. Berger & M. Burgoon (Eds.), *Communication and social influence processes* (pp. 91–113). East Lansing, MI: Michigan State University Press.

Brashers, D. E. (2001). Communication and uncertainty management. *Journal of Communication, 51*(3), 477–497.

Brehm, J. (1966). *A theory of psychological reactance.* New York: Academic Press.

Brehm, J., & Cohen, A. R. (1962). *Explorations in cognitive dissonance.* New York: Wiley.

Brown, P., & Levinson, S. (1978). Universals in language use: Politeness phenomena. In E. Goody (Ed.), *Questions and politeness* (pp. 56–289). Cambridge, UK: Cambridge University Press.

Brown, P., & Levinson, S. (1987). *Politeness: Some universals in language use.* Cambridge, UK: Cambridge University Press.

Buller, D. B., & Burgoon, J. K. (1996). Interpersonal deception theory. *Communication Theory, 6,* 203–242.

Burgoon, J. K. (1993). Interpersonal expectations, expectancy violations, and emotional communication. *Journal of Language and Social Psychology, 12,* 13–21.

Burgoon, J. K., & Bacue, A. E. (2003). Nonverbal communication skills. In J. O. Greene & B. R. Burleson (Eds.), *Handbook of communication and social interaction skills* (pp. 179–219). Mahwah, NJ: Erlbaum.

Burgoon, J. K., Stern, L. A., & Dillman, L. (1995). *Interpersonal adaptation: Dyadic interaction patterns.* New York: Cambridge University Press.

Burleson, B. R. (2003). Emotional support skills. In J. O. Greene & B. R. Burleson (Eds.), *Handbook of communication and social interaction skills* (pp. 551–594). Mahwah, NJ: Erlbaum.

Byrne, D. (1971). *The attraction paradigm.* New York: Academic Press.

Cappella, J. N. (1987). Interpersonal communication: Definitions and fundamental questions. In C. R. Berger & S. H. Chaffee (Eds.), *Handbook of communication science* (pp. 184–238). Newbury Park, CA: Sage.

Cappella, J. N., & Greene, J. O. (1982). A discrepancy-arousal explanation of mutual influence in expressive behavior for adult and infant–adult interaction. *Communication Monographs, 49,* 89–114.

Cappella, J. N., & Greene, J. O. (1984). The effects of distance and individual differences in arousability on nonverbal involvement: A test of discrepancy-arousal theory. *Journal of Nonverbal Behavior, 8,* 259–286.

Cartwright, D., & Zander, A. (1968). *Group dynamics: Theory and practice* (3rd ed.). New York: Harper Row.

Charters, W. W. (1933). *Motion pictures and youth: A summary.* New York: Macmillan.

Clark, H. H. (1994). Discourse in production. In M. A. Gernsbacher (Ed.), *Handbook of psycholinguistics* (pp. 985–1021). San Diego, CA: Academic Press.

Clark, R. A., & Delia, J. G. (1977). Cognitive complexity, social perspective-taking, and persuasion skills in second- to ninth-grade children. *Human Communication Research, 3,* 128–134.

Cody, M. J., Canary, D. J., & Smith, S. W. (1994). Compliance-gaining goals: An inductive analysis of actors' and goal types, strategies, and successes. In J. A. Daly & J. M. Wiemann (Eds.), *Strategic interpersonal communication* (pp. 33–90). Hillsdale, NJ: Erlbaum.

Coulmas, F. (1981). Introduction: Conversational routine. In P. Coulmas (Ed.), *Conversational routines: Explorations in standardized communication situations and prepatterned speech* (pp. 1–17). Hague, Netherlands: Mouton.

Cozby, P. C. (1973). Self-disclosure: A literature review. *Psychological Bulletin, 79,* 73–91.

Daly, J. A., & Wiemann, J. M. (Eds.). (1994). *Strategic interpersonal communication*. Hillsdale, NJ: Erlbaum.

Delia, J. G. (1977). Constructivism and the study of human communication. *Quarterly Journal of Speech, 63*, 66–83.

Delia, J. G. (1987). Communication research: A history. In C. R. Berger & S. H. Chaffee (Eds.), *Handbook of communication science* (pp. 20–98). Beverly Hills, CA: Sage.

Delia, J. G., Kline, S. L., & Burleson, B. R. (1979). The development of persuasive communication strategies in kindergartners through twelfth-graders. *Communication Monographs, 46*, 241–225.

Delia, J. G, O'Keefe, B. J., & O'Keefe, D. J. (1982). The constructivist approach to communication. In F. E. X. Dance (Ed.), *Human communication theory: Comparative essays* (pp. 147–191). New York: Harper & Row.

DePaulo, B. M., Ainsfield, M. E., & Bell, K. L. (1996). Theories about deception and paradigms for studying it: A critical appraisal of Buller and Burgoon's interpersonal deception theory and research. *Communication Theory, 6*, 297–310.

DePaulo, B. M., Lindsay, J. J. Malone, B. E., Muhlenbruck, L. Charlton, K., & Cooper, H. (2003). Cues to deception. *Psychological Bulletin, 129*, 74–118.

Dillard, J. P., Anderson, J. W., & Knobloch, L. K. (2002). Interpersonal influence. In M. L. Knapp & J. A. Daly (Eds.), *Handbook of interpersonal communication* (3rd ed., pp. 425–474). Thousand Oaks, CA: Sage.

Dillard, J. P., & Marshall, L. J. (2003). Persuasion as a social skill. In J. O. Greene & B. R. Burleson (Eds.), *Handbook of communication and social interaction skills* (pp. 479–513). Mahwah, NJ: Erlbaum.

Duck, S. W. (1973). *Personal relationships and personal constructs: A study of friendship formation*. New York: Wiley.

Ekman, P., & Friesen, W. V. (1969). Nonverbal leakage cues to deception. *Psychiatry, 32*, 88–105.

Festinger, L. (1957). *A theory of cognitive dissonance*. Stanford, CA: Stanford University Press.

Festinger, L. (1964). *Conflict, decision, and dissonance*. Stanford, CA: Stanford University Press.

Ford, W. S. Z. (1999). Communication and customer service. In M. E. Roloff (Ed.), *Communication yearbook*, (Vol. 22, pp. 341–375). Thousand Oaks, CA: Sage.

Giles, H., Coupland, N., & Coupland, J. (1991). Accommodation theory: Communication, contexts and consequences. In H. Giles, N. Coupland, & J. Coupland (Eds.), *Context of accommodation: Developments in applied linguistics* (pp. 1–68). Cambridge, UK: Cambridge University Press.

Giles, H., Mulac, A., Bradac, J. J., & Johnson, P. (1987). Speech accommodation theory: The next decade. In M. McLaughlin (Ed.), *Communication yearbook*, (Vol. 11, pp. 13–48). Newbury Park, CA: Sage.

Giles, H., & Powesland, P. (1975). *Speech style and social evaluation*. London: Academic Press.

Goffman, E. (1959). *The presentation of self in everyday life*. Garden City, NY: Doubleday.

Gottman, J. M., & Levenson, R. W. (1988). The social psychophysiology of marriage. In P. Noller & M. A. Fitzpatrick (Eds.), *Perspectives on marital interaction* (pp. 182–200). Clevedon, UK: Multilingual Matters.

Gottman, J. M., Murray, J. D., Swanson, C. C., Tyson, R., & Swanson, K. R. (2002). *The mathematics of marriage: Dynamic nonlinear models*. Cambridge, MA: MIT Press.

Gouldner, A. W. (1960). The norm of reciprocity: A preliminary statement. *American Sociological Review, 25*, 161–178.

Greene, J. O. (1984). A cognitive approach to human communication: An action assembly theory. *Communication Monographs, 51*, 289–306.

Greene, J. O. (1997). A second generation action assembly theory. In J. O. Greene (Ed.), *Message production: Advances in communication theory* (pp. 151–170). Mahwah, NJ: Erlbaum.

Greene, J. O., & Burleson, B. R. (Eds.). (2003). *Handbook of communication and social interaction skills*. Mahwah, NJ: Erlbaum.

Grice, H. P. (1989). *Studies in the ways of words*. Cambridge, MA: Harvard University Press.

Griffiths, M. (1998). Internet addiction: Does it really exist? In J. Gakenbach (Ed.), *Psychology and the Internet: Intrapersonal, interpersonal, and transpersonal implications* (pp. 61–75). London: Academic Press.

Gudykunst, W. B. (1995). Anxiety/uncertainty management (AUM) theory. In R. L. Wiseman (Ed.), *Intercultural communication theory* (pp. 8–58). Thousand Oaks, CA: Sage.

Gudykunst, W. B. (2005). An anxiety/uncertainty management (AUM) theory of effective communication. In W. B. Gudykunst (Ed.), *Theorizing about intercultural communication* (pp. 281–322). Thousand Oaks, CA: Sage.

Hample, D. (2003). Arguing skill. In J. O. Greene & B. R. Burleson (Eds.), *Handbook of communication and social interaction skills* (pp. 439–477). Mahwah, NJ: Erlbaum.

Heider, F. (1958). *The psychology of interpersonal relations.* New York: Wiley.

Hewes, D. E., & Planalp, S. (1987). The individual's place in communication science, In C. R. Berger & S. H. Chaffee (Eds.), *Handbook of communication science* (pp. 146–183). Newbury Park, CA: Sage.

Honeycutt, J. M. (2003). *Imagined interactions: Daydreaming about communication.* Cresskill, NJ: Hampton.

Hopper, R. (1992). *Telephone communication.* Bloomington, IN: Indiana University Press.

Hovland, C. I., & Janis, I. L. (1959). *Personality and persuasibility.* New Haven, CT: Yale University Press.

Hovland, C. I., Janis, I. L., & Kelley, H. H. (1953). *Communication and persuasion: Psychological studies of opinion change.* New Haven, CT: Yale University Press.

Hovland, C. I., & Rosenberg, M. J. (1960). *Attitude organization and change: An analysis of consistency among attitude components.* New Haven, CT: Yale University Press.

Jacobs, S., Dawson, E. J., & Brashers, D. (1996). Information manipulation theory: A replication and assessment. *Communication Monographs, 63,* 70–82.

Jourard, S. M. (1964). *The transparent self: Self-disclosure and well-being.* Princeton, NJ: Van Nostrand.

Jourard, S. M. (1971). *Self-disclosure: An experimental analysis of the transparent self.* New York: Wiley-Interscience.

Kellermann, K. (1995). The conversation MOP: A model of patterned and pliable behavior. In D. E. Hewes (Ed.), *The cognitive bases of interpersonal communication* (pp. 181–221). Hillsdale, NJ: Erlbaum.

King, R. G. (1979). *Fundamentals of human communication.* New York: Macmillan.

Knapp, M. L. (1972). *Nonverbal communication in human interaction.* New York: Holt, Rinehart, & Winston.

Knapp, M. L., & Comadena, M. E. (1979). Telling it like it isn't: A review of theory and research on deceptive communication. *Human Communication Research, 5,* 270–285.

Knapp, M. L, Hart, R. R., & Dennis, H. S. (1974). An exploration of deception as a communication construct. *Human Communication Research, 7,* 15–29.

Knobloch, L. K. (2005). Evaluating a contextual model of responses to relational uncertainty increasing events: The role of intimacy, appraisals, and emotions. *Human Communication Research, 31*(1), 60–101.

Knobloch, L. K. (2006). Relational uncertainty and message production within courtship: Features of date request messages. *Human Communication Research, 32,* 244–273.

Knobloch, L. K., & Carpenter-Theune, K. E. (2004). Topic avoidance in developing romantic relationships: Associations with intimacy and relational uncertainty. *Communication Research, 31,* 173–205.

Knobloch, L. K., & Solomon, D. H. (2002). Information seeking beyond initial interaction: Negotiating relational uncertainty within close relationships. *Human Communication Research, 28,* 243–257.

Knobloch, L. K., & Solomon, D. H. (2005). Relational uncertainty and relational information processing: Questions without answers? *Communication Research, 32,* 349–388.

Kramer, M. W. (2004). *Managing uncertainty in organizational communication.* Mahwah, NJ: Erlbaum.

Kraut, R., Kiesler, S., Boneva, B., Cummings, J., Helgeson, V., & Crawford, A. (2002). Internet paradox revisited. *Journal of Social Issues, 58,* 49–74.

Kraut, R., Lundmark, V., Patterson, M., Kiesler, S. Mukopadhyay, T., & Scherlis, W. (1998). Internet paradox: A social technology that reduces social involvement and psychological well-being? *American Psychologist, 53,* 1017–1031.

Leidner, R. (1993). *Fast food, fast talk: Service work and the routinization of everyday life.* Berkeley: University of California Press.

Levine, T. R., & McCornack, S. A. (1996). Can BAE explain the probing effect? *Human Communication Research, 22,* 604–613.

Marwell, G., & Schmidt, D. R. (1967). Dimensions of compliance-gaining behavior: An empirical analysis. *Sociometry, 30,* 350–364.

Matarazzo, J. D., Wiens, A. N., & Saslow, G. (1965). Studies in interview speech behavior. In L. Krasner & L. P. Ullmann (Eds.), *Research in behavior modification: New developments and implications* (pp. 179–210). New York: Holt, Rinehart & Winston.

McCornack, S. A. (1992). Information manipulation theory. *Communication Monographs, 59,* 1–16.

McCornack, S. A. (1997). The generation of deceptive messages: Laying the groundwork for a viable theory of interpersonal deception. In J. O. Greene (Ed.), *Message production: Advances in communication theory* (pp. 91–126). Mahwah, NJ: Erlbaum.

Mehrabian, A. (1971). *Silent messages.* Belmont, CA: Wadsworth.

Metts, S., & Planalp, S. (2002). Emotional communication. In M. L. Knapp & J. A. Daly (Eds.), *Handbook of interpersonal communication* (3rd ed., pp. 339–373). Thousand Oaks, CA: Sage.

Meyer, J. R. (1997). Cognitive influences on the ability to address interaction goals. In J. O. Greene (Ed.), *Message production: Advances in communication theory* (pp. 71–90). Mahwah, NJ: Erlbaum.

Miller, G. R. (1987). Persuasion. In C. R. Berger & S. H. Chaffee (Eds.), *Handbook of communication science* (pp. 446–483). Newbury Park, CA: Sage.

Miller, G. R., & Steinberg, M. (1975). *Between people: A new analysis of interpersonal communication.* Chicago: Science Research Associates.

Miller, G. R., & Stiff, J. B. (1993). *Deceptive communication.* Newbury Park, CA: Sage.

Miller, G. R., Boster, F. J., Roloff, M. E., & Seibold, D. R. (1977). Compliance-gaining message strategies: A typology and some findings concerning effects of situational differences. *Communication Monographs, 44,* 37–51.

Miller, W. I. (2003). *Faking it.* Cambridge, UK: Cambridge University Press.

Montgomery, B. M., & Baxter, L. A. (Eds.). (1998). *Dialectical approaches to the study of relationships.* Mahwah, NJ: Lawrence Erlbaum.

Newcomb, T. M. (1953). An approach to the study of communicative acts. *Psychological Review, 60,* 393–404.

Newcomb, T. M. (1961). *The acquaintance process.* New York: Holt, Rinehart, & Winston.

Osgood, C. E., & Tannenbaum, P. H. (1955). The principle of congruity in the prediction of attitude change. *Psychological Review, 62,* 42–55.

O'Sullivan, M. (2005). Emotional intelligence and deception detection: Why most people can't "read" others, but a few can. In R. E. Riggio & R. S. Feldman (Eds.), *Applications of nonverbal communication* (pp. 215–253). Mahwah, NJ: Erlbaum.

Parks, M. R. (1994). Communicative competence and interpersonal control. In M. L. Knapp & G. R. Miller (Eds.), *Handbook of interpersonal communication* (2nd ed., pp. 589–618). Thousand Oaks, CA: Sage.

Parks, M. R. (2007). *Personal relationships and personal networks.* Mahwah, NJ: Erlbaum.

Parks, M. R., & Adelman, M. B. (1983). Communication networks and the development of romantic relationships: An expansion of uncertainty reduction theory. *Human Communication Research, 10,* 55–79.

Patterson, M. L. (1983). *Nonverbal behavior: A functional perspective.* New York: Springer-Verlag.

Petronio, S. (Ed.). (2000). *Balancing the secrets of private disclosures.* Mahwah, NJ: Erlbaum.

Petronio, S. (2002). *Boundaries of privacy: Dialectics of disclosure.* Albany: State University of New York Press.

Planalp, S. (1998). Communicating emotion in everyday life: Cues, channels, and processes. In P. A. Andersen & L. K. Guerrero (Eds.), *Handbook of communication and emotion* (pp. 29–48). New York: Academic Press.

Planalp, S. (1999). *Communicating emotions: Social, moral, and cultural processes.* New York: Cambridge University Press.

Planalp, S. (2003). The unacknowledged role of emotion in theories of close relationships: How do theories feel? *Communication Theory, 13,* 78–99.

Planalp, S., & Honeycutt, J. (1985). Events that increase uncertainty in relationships. *Human Communication Research, 11,* 593–604.

Planalp, S., Rutherford, D. K., & Honeycutt, J. M. (1988). Events that increase uncertainty in personal relationships II: Replication and extension. *Human Communication Research, 14*(4), 516–547.

Postmes, T., Spears, R., Lea, M., & Reicher, S. D. (Eds.). (2000). *SIDE issues centre stage: Recent developments in studies of deindividuation of groups.* Amsterdam: Royal Netherlands Academy of Arts and Sciences.

Reeves, B., & Nass, C. I. (1996). The media equation: How people treat computers, television and new media like real people and places. New York: Cambridge University Press.

Roloff, M. E. (1981). Interpersonal communication: The social exchange approach. Beverly Hills, CA: Sage.

Roloff, M. E. (1987). Communication and reciprocity within intimate relationships. In M. E. Roloff & G. R. Miller (Eds.), Interpersonal processes: New directions in communication research (pp. 11–38). Beverly Hills, CA: Sage.

Rololff, M. E., & Campion, D. B. (1985). Conversational profit–seeking: Interaction as social exchange. In L. Street & J. N. Cappella (Eds.), Sequence and pattern in communication behavior (pp. 161–189). London: Edward Arnold.

Roloff, M. E., Putnam, L. L, & Anastasiou, L. (2003). Negotiation skills. In J. O. Greene & B. R. Burleson (Eds.), Handbook of communication and social interaction skills (pp. 801–833). Mahwah, NJ: Erlbaum.

Roloff, M. E., & Soule, K. P. (2002). Interpersonal conflict: A review. In M. L. Knapp & J. A. Daly (Eds.), Handbook of interpersonal communication (3rd ed., pp. 475–528). Thousand Oaks, CA: Sage.

Rowan, K. E. (2003). Informing and explaining skills: Theory and research on informative communication. In J. O. Greene & B. R. Burleson (Eds.), Handbook of communication and social interaction skills (pp. 403–438). Mahwah, NJ: Erlbaum.

Schramm, W. L., Lyle, J., & Parker, E. B. (1961). Television in the lives of our children. Stanford, CA: Stanford University Press.

Shepard, C. A. Giles, H., & Le Poire, B. A. (2001). Communication accommodation theory. In W. Robinson & H. Giles (Eds.), The new handbook of language and social psychology (pp. 33–56). Chichester, UK: Wiley

Sherif, C. W., Sherif, M., & Nebergall, R. E. (1965). Attitude and attitude change: The social judgment-involvement approach. Philadelphia, PA: Saunders.

Sherif, M., & Hovland, C. I. (1961). Social judgment: Assimilation and contrast effects in attitude change. New Haven, CT: Yale University Press.

Siegel, J., Dubrovsky, V., Kiesler, S., & McGuire, T. (1983). Group processes in computer-mediated communication. Organizational Behavior and Human Decision Processes, 37, 694–710.

Sinclair, J. (1991). Corpus, concordance, collocation. Oxford, UK: Oxford University Press.

Smith, D. R., & Williamson, L. K. (1977). Interpersonal communication: Roles, rules, strategies and games. Dubuque, IA: W. C. Brown.

Solomon, D. H., & Knobloch, L. K. (2004). A model of relational turbulence: The role of intimacy, relational uncertainty, and interference from partners in appraisals of irritations. Journal of Social and Personal Relationships, 21, 795–816.

Spitzberg, B. H., & Cupach, W. R. (2002). Interpersonal skills. In M. L. Knapp & J. A. Daly (Eds.), Handbook of interpersonal communication (3rd ed., pp. 564–611). Thousand Oaks, CA: Sage.

Srull, T. K., & Wyer, R. S. (1986). The role of chronic and temporary goals in social information processing. In R. Sorrentino & E. T. Higgins (Eds.), Handbook of motivation and cognition (pp. 503–549). New York: Guilford.

Stafford, L. (2005). Maintaining long-distance and cross-residential relationships. Mahwah, NJ: Erlbaum

Thibaut, J., & Kelley, H. H. (1959). The social psychology of groups. New York: Wiley.

Turkle, S. (1995). Life on the screen: Identity in the age of the Internet. New York: Touchstone.

Vrig, A., & Mann, S. (2005). Police use of nonverbal behavior as indicators of deception. In R. E. Riggio & R. S. Feldman (Eds.), Applications of nonverbal communication (pp. 63–94). Mahwah, NJ: Erlbaum.

Waldron, V. R. (1997). Toward a theory of interactive conversational planning. In J. O. Greene (Ed.), Message production: Advances in communication theory (pp. 195–220). Mahwah, NJ: Erlbaum,

Walther, J. B., & Parks, M. R. (2002). Cues filtered out, cues filtered in: Computer-mediated communication and relationships. In M. L. Knapp & J. A. Daly (Eds.), Handbook of interpersonal communication (3rd ed., pp. 529–563). Thousand Oaks, CA: Sage.

Wilson, S. R. (1990). Development and test of a cognitive rules model of interaction goals. Communication Monographs, 57, 81–103.

Wilson, S. R. (1995). Elaborating the cognitive rules model of interaction goals: The problem of accounting for individual differences in goal formation. In B. R. Burleson (Ed.), Communication yearbook (Vol. 18, pp. 3–25). Thousand Oaks, CA: Sage.

Wilson, S. R., & Sabee, C. M. (2003). Explicating communicative competence as a theoretical term. In J. O. Greene & B. R. Burleson (Eds.), *Handbook of communication and social interaction skills* (pp. 3–50). Mahwah, NJ: Erlbaum.

Wittgenstein, L. (1953). *Philosophical investigations.* Oxford, UK: Blackwell.

Wray, A., & Perkins, M. K. (2000). The functions of formulaic language: An integrated model. *Language and Communication, 20,* 1–28.

Wyer, R. S., Jr., & Adaval, R. (2003). Message reception skills in social communication. In J. O. Greene & B. R. Burleson (Eds.), *Handbook of communication and social interaction skills* (pp. 291–355). Mahwah, NJ: Erlbaum.

Suggested Readings

Greene, J. O., & Burleson, B. R. (Eds.). (2003). *Handbook of communication and social interaction skills.* Mahwah, NJ: Erlbaum.

Knapp, M. L., & Daly, J. A. (Eds.). (2002). *Handbook of interpersonal communication* (3rd ed.). Thousand Oaks, CA: Sage.

Parks, M. R. (2007). *Personal relationships and personal networks.* Mahwah, NJ: Erlbaum.

Planalp, S. (1999). *Communicating emotions: Social, moral, and cultural processes.* New York: Cambridge University Press.

Stafford, L. (2005). *Maintaining long-distance and cross-residential relationships.* Mahwah, NJ: Erlbaum.

19

MODELING CULTURES

Toward Grounded Paradigms in Organizations and Mass Culture

Mark Y. Hickson III, Jean Bodon, and Theresa Bodon

Culture, Hoebel (1966) has illustrated, as proscribed by Kroeber and Kluckhohn (1952) as "a product; is historical; is selective; is learned; is based on symbols; and is an abstraction from behavior and the products of behavior" (p. 32). But the nurture view of culture is that culture is how and when and why we engage in certain behaviors. Culture may be described as a value system that we derive from fellow human beings, which includes values about religion, intellect, social behavior, economics, political behavior, and aesthetics.[1]

Within the discipline of communication, culture has become much more pervasive in the past four decades. Much of our concern has developed from something called *cultural relativism*. This notion indicates that people who live in different places have different values. The "politically correct" position on cultural relativism is that the values in any one culture are no better nor worse than those in any other. It is important to note, too, that students of culture, especially anthropologists, have studied culture over the years with an eye toward differences.

Of course it would be foolish to enter a culture and write a report that the inhabitants eat and sleep or learn and talk. However, the constant reporting of differences, sometimes significant and sometimes insignificant, has caused us to focus on differences. Thus, we have the study of *intercultural* communication. Often the assumption is that we should naturally have more difficulty interacting with those of a different culture. The study of culture in communication, though, is not limited to interpersonal interaction across cultures. Culture has become a mainstay in the language and thought of those who study organizational communication. In the film, *Office Space*, the producers created an environment (a culture) where most of us would not want to work. We will begin by discussing the history of the study of culture from two perspectives.

Historical Perspectives

Culture as a concept, and its relationship to communication has a long history, and there has been a fervent revival of interest led by those who use such concepts as intercultural, cross-cultural, and multicultural study. Some writers trace the original research on culture to Herodotus in the 5th century BC and certainly to Tacitus in Western culture and Fa-hsien in the East. Noted anthropologist E. Adamson Hoebel (1966), however, disagreed, claiming that the early Greeks were interested only in the ideal political structure and social organization of other peoples. Hoebel did credit Tacitus with writing a tract on Germany—referring to it as "an early ethnography."

The Anthropological Track

For anthropologists, ethnography and the study of other cultures began with the French Jesuit Joseph-François Fafitau, who worked among the Iroquois and Hurons of western New York state in the 18th century (Hoebel, 1966). Another example of early research is Arthur Young, who published accounts of agricultural practices in Great Britain between 1771 and 1793 (Wax, 1971), forerunners of agri-communication studies and organizational communication studies in the United States. Some of those studies created models for what is called the diffusion of innovation (Rogers, 1995). Of course innovation works were not only to determine what the agriculture was but also to "modernize" it.

These early anthropologists were also early pioneers in what was to become two tracks of theory and research formulated from two different directions. One, the anthropological track, which came foremost from the London School of Economics, was led by Bronislaw Malinowski (Powdermaker, 1966), whose views were espoused by British and American anthropologists, including Hortense Powdermaker and Ruth Benedict (Fletcher, 1971). Malinowski, who had received a PhD in physics and mathematics from the University of Cracow, noted that there was "no such thing as 'theory-free' knowledge" (Fletcher, 1971, p. 689). He felt that social science was a basis for "social engineering," clearing the way for anthropologists to argue that social science is a way to ensure that history never repeats itself.

With Malinowski we find an option for the historicist tenets haunting anthropological evolutionism. Malinowski's (1944) method requires that segments of a cultural whole not be displaced, for they are part of institutional contexts that grant their sense. Malinowski wrote that a subject matter must be created, and a methodology must be based on that subject matter. For him, everything was a matter of getting to generalizations, a goal, however, that could only be achieved through comparative studies of a rather narrow focus. His cultural "units of analysis" for study were *institutions*. In his functional theory, the analysis of institutions included studying the institution's charter—its purpose, its rules or norms, the material apparatus (capital), its activities, and its functions.

In Malinowski's radical empiricism nothing is more imminent than culture. Culture takes a context-bound form, and a culture is "only intelligible when it is placed within its context of situation" (Malinowski, 1923, p. 306). It was Ruth Benedict, Malinowski's student, who developed the prototype cultural configuration study in her *Patterns of Culture* (Benedict, 1959). The American prototype is found in Powdermaker's (1966) study of blacks in Indianola, Mississippi.

The German-Sociological Track

The other track is one used by German professors of economics and philosophers to better understand their underprivileged class. In 1890, Paul Göhre, "a student of theology, undertook what may have been the first systematic attempt at participant observation" (Wax, 1971, p. 27). Göhre pretended to be a factory apprentice, each night recording his observations. After reading some of Göhre's publications, German sociologist Max Weber collaborated with Göhre on a study of agricultural workers.

The German influence continued in the United States. Early in his career, University of Chicago philosopher William I. Thomas was strongly influenced by William Wundt's Völkerpsychologie. Although he never met Wundt, social philosopher George Herbert Mead also was influenced by Wundt, when Mead studied at the University of Leipzig (Miller, 1973, p. 88). Thus, both the philosophy and sociology departments at Chicago were to pursue study from the German track (Rogers, 1994, pp. 139–142). Later, with Florian Znaniecki, Thomas completed the first major piece of ethnography in sociology entitled, *The Polish Peasant in Europe and America* (Coser, 1977).

Impact on Communication Theory and Research

Although both tracks have similar theoretical and methodological approaches, one will rarely find a single sociological fieldworker quoting the works of an anthropological ethnographer or vice versa. The impact of each on the field of communication, however, has been monumental. Even so, one rarely finds cross-pollination. The sociological approach has been utilized primarily by communication researchers studying organizations, such as Linda Putnam, Michael Pacanowsky, Stanley Deetz, and H. Lloyd Goodall. The anthropological approach has been used by nonverbal communication researchers such as Edward T. Hall and Ray Birdwhistell.

With this background, it is important for us to discuss terminology. Hoebel (1966) defined *culture* as "the integrated system of learned behavior patterns that are characteristic of members of a society and which are not the result of biological inheritance" (p. 5). Farb (1978) wrote:

> Although social scientists disagree about the exact definition of culture (one descriptive inventory totaled 164 items), they do agree about its general character. Culture is human-made; it includes ideas, values, and codes known to all members of the group; it is transmitted from generation to generation. Culture represents a new stage in evolution: the ability to acquire, store, and exchange information and then to pass it on to the next generation, so that it will not have to be relearned from scratch. An individual human being thereby accumulates vastly more information than could be acquired by experience alone. (pp. 11, 14)

From this, there should be little question on the importance of communication to culture. For the anthropologically oriented communication researcher, the conceptualization of culture to interact through symbols is fundamental.

Limitations on Studying Cultural Models

No one would suggest that French culture and American culture are the same. We may say that *cultures vary geographically*. We should note, too, that *cultures vary from time to time*. Some of the changes are evolutionary and others are revolutionary. *Cultures also vary in complexity*. A family-owned grocery store may have only three or four employees, and the "rules" about how to behave are often transmitted over long periods of time, in some cases beginning when some of the employees are children. That culture is substantially less complex than a major corporation, where most employees have never even met the CEO and where some have never been to the headquarters' city.

Cultures Vary Geographically

In his study of the behavior of commuter bus riders in Washington, DC, Hickson (1977) found that there was a certain alienation involving the participants. However, the same types of behavior may or may not be apparent in bus riders of other parts of the country. Because the subject area was composed of many transient riders, their commitment to the area and their work there was less than one might find in other parts of the country, regardless of the size of the city. Larger or smaller cities may even contain greater differences from the original subject pool.

Cultures Vary with Time

If we take the concept of neighborhoods we can see both changes in process. It was common in the United States in the 1950s for homes to have a front porch. The front porch was a place to sit in a rocking chair and for families to talk with one another. Many neighborhoods had sidewalks so that when friends walked by, they tended to strike up conversations with the families relaxing on the front porch.

Two revolutionary events took place which changed that culture. The popularity of the television created entertainment *inside* the home. For many, especially members of the "new" generation of the 1950s, the entertainment inside was preferred to the entertainment outside. More and more families saw the television as the "social" center rather than the porch. In addition, centralized heating and air conditioning became popular. These innovations made the comfort of the inside of the house preferable to the outside of the home.

In general, people in neighborhoods began spending significantly more time in the home. The exchange of "community" information took place more often by telephone than in person. American society became more industrialized and urbanized. More and more neighbors began moving away. Neighborhoods, especially in urban areas, became transitory.

The revolutionary changes of air conditioning and the television brought about evolutionary changes in the design of homes. Front porches were eliminated altogether or they were replaced by back decks. The evolutionary change has created a family that is substantially more isolated from its neighbors (in face-to-face communication). Home design was also changed in that the living room has been virtually eliminated. In the 1950s, the living room was a relatively formal room where business could be discussed or where neighbors could be invited into the home. Of course, with close friends, the family typically migrated to the kitchen. The den, or family room, was created with the television as the centerpiece.

For the most part, though, the television also created a more passive culture. Television is not an interactive medium. Thus, family members sit in front of the television and "take in" another culture, not that of their neighborhood. Except for eating together (or separately) there is little social interaction in front of the television.

The 1980s brought us the personal computer. It became easier to "bring work home." Individuals saw opportunities for higher productivity. In addition, computer games provided a new source of entertainment. Individuals could play games with other family members or they could play alone. Intergenerational communication weakened; adults did not know how or did not wish to participate in these games. Children isolated themselves wherever the PC was located.

With the innovation of the Internet, further changes took place. Now once again, families could interact with their neighbors or friends or colleagues or strangers through e-mails and Instant Messaging. What was regained was the technological equivalent of the porch with the disadvantage that the nonverbal communication inherent in face-to-face communication was absent. The smiley face cartoon hardly replaces a human smile.

Cultures Vary in Complexity

Anthropologist Benedict (1959) investigated the Pueblo of New Mexico. While there was substantial complexity and diversity in ceremonial activity, the lack of technological know-how provided a kind of simplicity. The same can be said of the Mississippi society that was investigated by Powdermaker (1966). Observations of media use by Americans might vary significantly even today. While we know that a large number of people utilize personal computers and the Internet, the differences among those who live in urban areas and those who live in rural areas is probably substantial. Individuals who work in many blue-collar jobs are less likely to use computer technology at work than are those who are employed in white-collar positions. Technology necessarily makes a culture more complex because each technology creates a culture within itself. In a sense technology creates classes and develops its own coding system. In addition, complexity varies in terms of human interaction. For example, in a country, family-owned store interaction is fairly simple. Typically, the family owns the store and there are few employees who are not family members. The individuals have "grown up" knowing what to say to their fellow workers. In addition, game-playing and bureaucracy would hardly work. However, General Electric or Time-Warner may have a quite complex bureaucratic culture, perhaps even including rules about who can and who cannot talk to each other, what they can say, and when they can say it.

As we expand to media cultures, complexity becomes even greater. When a public figure makes a comment "on the air," the potential reactions and responses may come from a variety of sub-cultures that are part of the general media culture are widespread. A religious comment, for example, may have quite different repercussions for the populations of Utah or Alabama than they might receive from New York or Massachusetts.

For all of the reasons we have stated, we provide two quite different examples of modeling cultures. One is the micro-study, which generally involves a much smaller group of people, in which many of the inhabitants may interact face-to-face. The types of research methods may vary, but are usually qualitative in nature. The methods include, but are not limited to, participant-observation, unstructured interviews, and content analyses (Hickson, 2003). The second is macro-study. In the macro-study, researchers must investigate larger units that do not have face-to-face interaction with the subjects. Often quantitative measures are more appropriate.

A Study of Troublemaking in an Academic Environment

The university environment is both highly complex and simple. The complexity develops because such institutions raise considerable amounts of money, and they spend this money primarily for teaching and research. In general the salaries of the faculty members are relatively low for the years of education that they have. For that reason, one might say that ego is the medium of exchange. As with any other organization or institution, though, the university attempts to maintain what system theorists refer to as balance or *homeostasis* (Hickson, 1971, 1983). A study was undertaken on that medium of exchange because it involves a certain group of persons we shall refer to as "troublemakers." As a research question, one might ask "what may disrupt homeostasis in an academic environment?" While one could study a particular social type, the troublemaker, for example (see Roebuck & Hickson, 2006), in this study, the organizational culture perspective of troublemaking as planned action is investigated. In this context, the question becomes how can troublemaking as an activity occur and how can it change the culture of the organization (Hickson & Stacks, 1998)?

This study is not one of a kind. In fact, Westhues (2005) has described one type of troublemaking that he has referred to as workplace mobbing. Tracy, Alberts, and Rivera (2007) have described another type that they call bullying. *Bullying* is undertaken by persons of authority. Tracy et al. have indicated that bullying is beyond abuse in that it is persistent and virtually impossible to defend (Hoel & Cooper, 2001). *Mobbing* may be directed by a superior, but may also be undertaken by colleagues or subordinates. The latter is largely created by a group mentality not dissimilar from the "broken window syndrome," well known in the circles of nonverbal communication. The literal version takes place by virtue of the idea that once a building is abandoned its appearance and structure remain intact so long as there is no broken window. Once one window is broken, rock throwers feel less intimidated in breaking additional windows. In mobbing, several members of the deviant group engage in recruitment of other members. Their behavior is directed toward intimidation, exclusion, and isolation, nitpicking both orally and in writing, with the ultimate goal of academic terror and occupational assassination.

In developing a theoretical, ideal-type model, a review of literature is undertaken. Gould and Kolb (1964) have described an ideal-type as neither ideal in an ethical sense, not a common denominator, and not even a statistical average (pp. 311–313). Instead it is to make sense of the relationships that occur within a system. The procedures for hiring faculty members and granting tenure in an institution are similar across schools. Subjects must have a higher education, beyond the bachelor's degree, and in most cases, must include a doctorate. University administrators assume that such candidates can work in a university environment, in part because they have been doing so for a number of years as students. As a result of their education, the ideal-type model would indicate that faculty members should know the chain-of-command of a university, at least in a general sense. They should know that teaching and research as well as service are required for a period of time, usually six years, in a probationary status. After that time, a faculty member applies for tenure, and our research has indicated that in most cases (in the communication discipline) tenure is awarded to them. The environment is a little difficult because persons in a department, chairs (or heads) and faculty, are also considered colleagues. Universities are described as *collegial* environments. During the tenure process, though, for a short period of time, the faculty member and the chair are partially colleagues and partially adversaries. For many, the period of deliberations regarding one's tenure is traumatic. Some avoid it altogether by moving from one university to another, perhaps eventually gaining tenure that way.

Moo U[2]

While undertaking such a study as this one, names of individuals may be coded. This is not always the case, depending on each study. Because Hickson (1971, 1974, 2007) was given complete access and all organization members were notified in advance, actual names were incorporated. In this study, however, we have created a fictitious university and fictitious names of faculty members. At Moo U, Julie was hired as a faculty member. She had completed graduate school more than six years earlier. She had taught at another school but had no desire to stay there. On its face, Julie appeared to be similar to other faculty members who had academic experience. She taught classes, met with students, served on committees, and attended faculty meetings. The difference between Julie and others was in her perception of power. Most new faculty members, at least in the beginning, perceive of themselves as low on the organizational chart. While Julie may have perceived that in a general way, her personality and inability to distinguish power did not allow her to act in any subordinate manner.

Other faculty members at Moo acted in accordance with the standards of the institution. A few were dissatisfied that not everything went their way, but their perception was that acting in a deviant manner would bring them no gain. One senior faculty member, Brutus, was a senior full professor who had been disheartened by a number of events that had taken place in the past. Brutus appeared to be "waiting for the right time" to engage in deviant behavior to mob the chair. Brutus is given his name because as Westhues (2005, p. 20) writes: "The target is not set upon by enemies or strangers but by people [with] whose lives his or her own life has been closely intertwined." The goal in mobbing is the social elimination of the target. Both Westhues (2005) and Zimbardo (2007) have indicated that such deviant behaviors as mobbing tend to be more attributable to the situation than the personal character flaws of the actors.

Before Julie's tenure process began, an onlooker could assess the fact that the adversarial component of the relationship between Julie and the chair was potentially related to the dissatisfaction of Brutus. At the time, the two troublemakers may or may not have known how much they held in common. As Zimbardo suggests, though, they would discover their similarities once the situation was right.

Participant Observation

When observing an organizational environment, it is important to consider typicalities and atypicalities. *Typicalities* may be described as "acting as usual," behaving in a "normal" sense. The *atypicality* is related to those situations where behavior is unusual (Schutz, 1963). In determining typical behavior, we looked at proxemics, the study of space. In the department, typical behavior each workday was for faculty members to enter the faculty lounge between 8:00 and 10:00 in the morning. Virtually all faculty members did this, although some of their stays were for shorter time frames than were others. Most drank coffee. Some poured a cup of coffee, stayed a few minutes, and left. Julie rarely showed up from the day she was hired. Julie's behavior and that of others we refer to as *team avoidance*. Brutus, on the other hand, was a regular in the lounge. The discussions included politics on campus, research projects, family stories, film criticisms, and other topics. Though there were disagreements from time to time, most were content connected.

Additionally, the pattern was for faculty to have open doors to their offices. At various times a few would close their doors or partially close their doors. Usually a knock would allow for others to enter. Brutus, however, had a habit of closing *and locking* his door. Should one infer a cause for such behavior, they are varied. For example, one might want to do so if there were intimate conversations of a personal nature taking place or if there were intimate behavior occurring. A third possibility, though, is that individuals who have a low morale and are considering conspiracy might lock their doors. While one might consider also that one might lock the door because he or she was concentrating highly on some work, that possibility is quite low. Merely closing the door would probably suffice. We will refer to this phenomenon as the *locked door syndrome*. Again the team avoidance and locked door syndrome appear to be disconnected. While the two behaviors may appear different in some respects, both are indicative of a self-imposed alienation and isolation.

As in game theory, the stakes and the behaviors become intensified as time goes on. With each memo, meeting, complaint, and grievance the stakes become higher for all parties. When additional members receive recruitment offers from the deviants, they either accept or reject them.

In this case, it is difficult to assign the leadership of the mob to either Julie or Brutus, for they have different intents, of sorts. Both want their chair out of the picture, but Julie is trying to gain tenure at all costs and Brutus wants the chair's position for himself. Under ordinary circumstances, Julie is more likely to achieve her goal. The reason is that upper-level administrators are less likely to promote Brutus, whom they now realize is a troublemaker. Many upper-level administrators fear the troublemaker although they do not respect him. Perhaps one reason for this is that they know if the mobsters can attack one level of administrator there is nothing stopping them from moving to the next level.

To this point, the chair had *never* had one complaint directed against him. He had held the position for almost two decades. There had been no grievances and not even a student grade complaint taken to the next level. Given today's methods of transmitting much information through e-mails, memoranda, and letters, the written form (called "texts") are easily available, recordable, and salvageable (Webb, Campbell, Schwartz, & Secrest, 1970). *Critical incidents* were recorded through these texts which could later be content analyzed. In a content analysis, the researcher attempts to "make sense" out of what may not have been an easy situation to analyze as it occurred.

Critical Incident Number One

The department's policy was to request external reviews of a candidate's files in the early fall. Four external reviewers (from other universities) were selected from a list of names provided by the candidate, other faculty members, and the chair. Procedures in this case were followed just the same as others over the past two decades. Julie's departmental mentor (Mentor) suggested that Julie send two vitae with her files. One of them would list her lifetime work and the other her work at Moo U. Upon hearing this news, instead of discussing it with the chair, she decided to meet with the associate provost. [There was nothing in the formal chain-of-command that would suggest this course of action. The chair had not made this suggestion; there wasn't anything in the faculty policies and procedures document to indicate it would be necessary. The mentor was merely trying to create a clear and easily read portfolio, which he himself had done a few years earlier.] Julie met with the associate provost whose advice was that two vitae were not necessary.

The Problem of Chain-of-Command versus an Open-Door Policy

At first glance, an observer might feel that the associate provost was merely trying to "advise" the candidate. However, there is a perception of the candidate that an associate provost might have additional "pull" over the other administrators, especially the chair and the dean. Julie returned from the meeting with the associate provost and notified the chair of her intent not to include two vitae. The chair indicated that this was no problem since he had not made such a request in the first place. However, an e-mail letter from Julie to the associate provost indicated more than this:

> I include this e-mail here to point out the fact that I did not intend to circumvent proper channels by carrying a *complaint* to you directly. I simply noted from a tenure instruction sheet that my dossier would end up on your desk, and I decided to go to the final point of the trail in order to short-cut confusion. It was not until our meeting that I was convinced that there are deeper issues than meet the eye. After speaking with you, a long history of difficulties seems impossible to ignore, for I have attempted to work for some time within very difficult confines. [Italics added]

The e-mail indicates that Julie had indeed intended to violate the chain-of-command by immediately going to "the final point of the trail." In addition, Julie provided excuses for her future behavior because of the "very difficult confines." Of course, she had been asked to provide reasons for her circumvention of authority and this was it. Interestingly, the letter to the associate provost was dated 12 days *after* Julie had received a letter *she had solicited* from a *former* faculty member who had been denied tenure 15 years earlier. That candidate had never filed a grievance in those 15 years. In her letter though, the previous faculty member asserted that it was a "hostile work environment" that caused her not to get tenure. Interestingly, she had only two published articles at the time, and her current vita (on her current department's website) supports that fact. One might infer that the "long history" that Julie supposedly learned about from the associate provost was in fact a history contrived by Julie. Julie's e-mail to the provost, though, is worded in such a way as to reduce or eliminate any responsibility on Julie's part. At this juncture, though, Julie agreed to communicate with the dean in the future.

Upon receiving a copy of Julie's e-mail, the dean wrote to the associate provost:

There is a troubling aspect to this e-mail, however, and that is [Julie's] insistence that the quantity and quality of her (and others') work are not major factors in tenure consideration. The department has never not given [sic] credit where credit is due in the areas of research/creative activity, service, and teaching. Evidence of this is the final vote of the faculty in [Julie's] tenure/promotion consideration. To suggest that the department does otherwise is false and does a disservice to her own credentials.

The dean's e-mail supported the department and had the potential of "slapping" Julie's hands, except for the fact that Julie did not receive a copy of the e-mail.

Critical Incident Number Two

The e-mail to the associate provost was sent on the very day of the departmental tenure meeting. In fact, the e-mail was sent approximately four hours *after* the meeting. At the meeting, Brutus conducted a very authoritarian affair. Anyone who made a negative comment was asked to "shut up." Others, who had hardly even read the vita, were allowed to make comments as often and as long as they wished. The final vote was 4–1 in favor of Julie. It can be inferred, then, that at this time Julie wanted to "paint over" the meeting she had had with the associate provost.

Critical Incident Number Three

The chair met with Brutus three days following the departmental tenure meeting. Brutus said that his letter for Julie's tenure would include a number of procedural violations by the chair, although he was not explicit about what they were at the time. The chair suggested two different letters, one about Julie's tenure and another about the procedures, but Brutus was adamant. He said, "I don't want to get sued!" As he was leaving the room, Brutus said to the chair, "Aren't you about ready to give this up [the chairmanship] anyway?" This statement was intended to notify the chair that Brutus had queued up for the position himself.

Ultimately, Brutus had drafted four different letters for Julie's promotion. The first letter was four pages. Only one-half page was about Julie's qualifications for tenure and promotion to associate professor. By this time, of course the chair was well aware of the fact that Brutus and Julie were troublemakers. He had discussed them with the university attorney and the dean. Both verbally supported the chair, but neither took any action. The dean was in a particularly precarious position because he had overruled several college-level committees over the past few years and had publicly indicated that he would not do so again anytime soon.

The chair was unaware of the extent of the deviants' plans though. As indicated by Westhues (2005) they generated a barrage of e-mails, memoranda, and letters filing grievances about issues ranging from what time each would teach classes two semesters hence to refusing to meet with the chair. The paperwork contained more than 150 pages over a six-month period. While the chair forwarded these e-mails to the dean, no action was taken.

The chair recommended that Julie not receive tenure on two primary bases. First, the research work did not meet the standards. Although there was some creative work, most of it was neither regional nor national in scope. There were no publications, despite the fact that Julie had received a grant to write a book two years earlier. Second was the issue of collegiality—or its opposite—in the form of being a troublemaker. That word, "troublemaker," was first used by the legal counsel referring to Julie and was not included in the chair's letter.

Critical Incident Number Four

Following the tenure meeting for Julie, it was obvious that she and Brutus had teamed up. Brutus began his campaign to eliminate the chair from office or better yet to have him terminated altogether. Brutus seized a graduate student who had been in the chair's class the previous semester, and they conspired to have her complain about her grade. The chair went over her paper with her and she left his office. Less than 10 minutes later, the chair walked to Brutus's office about another matter. The graduate student, Tina, stormed out when Brutus unlocked the door. The brief conversation went this way. The chair said, "If you are going to use graduate students in this little game of yours, I am not playing." To which Brutus responded: "Do you want to fight? If you want to fight, I'll fight!" But Brutus continued trying to get graduate students involved in a faculty dispute. In his class, he gave them a copy of the upcoming schedule for summer and told them the graduate program was in trouble—that it may be terminated.

A group of graduate students signed a petition about a number of "grievances" which was sent to another faculty member, not to the chair, not to the dean, not to the graduate school. The faculty member notified the chair, and the chair said he would meet with all of the graduate students. Strangely, the only one who would meet with the chair was the one who had the grade complaint. In the meeting, her statements and concerns were a duplicate of statements previously made by Brutus.

In the meantime, Brutus attempted to recruit another colleague, telling him how unfairly they both had been treated by the chair. The first one (an onlooker) refused to file any charges against the chair, but never shared any information about the pending mutiny with the chair either. A second one agreed to write a letter to the dean complaining about a salary increase three years earlier.

The troublemakers decided, at some juncture, that academia would call foul play anything that hinted of financial error, sexual discrimination, sexual harassment, and potentially any other minor policy or procedural error. Over a period of six months, they tried all of them.

The troublemaking situation ended after eight months. The chair stepped down. Although this was a victory for the troublemakers, there were other defeats. Julie was turned down by the college-level committee. The dean turned her down. The provost, under some pressure from whatever source, decided to give her three more years because she had come up early. Eventually she was promoted with yet another threat of legal action. Brutus may have been the biggest loser. He was not going to be chair now, or *ever*. He became one of very few faculty members with a file in the provost's office larger than a tenure/promotion portfolio. Two other actors, the associate provost and the Vice President for Student Affairs "stepped down" and "retired."

Troublemaking was studied using participant observation methods (Bogdan & Taylor, 1975; Bryun, 1966; Douglas, 1970; Lindlof & Taylor, 2002; McCall & Simmons, 1969) as well as unstructured interviews and content analysis of documents. In trying to establish a theory based on the disruption of homeostasis rather than its maintenance, a researcher must find information in what is called *conflict* theory. For the most part, there is little of this in the communication literature.

We went back to the work of Alinsky (1969; Hickson, 1976; Sanders, 1970). Saul Alinsky was a professional community organizer and self-proclaimed radical who was quite popular in the 1960s, during the civil rights, women's liberation, and anti-war movements. Sanders (1970) indicated that Alinsky felt the obligation to establish a "moral basis" for his actions. A moral basis in this case is based upon visualizing one's self as 100 percent right. The administration may be considered an authoritarian, dictatorial entity. The constant barrage of e-mails, memoranda, letters, and grievances is seen by the outsider as "whistle blowing" activity rather than troublemaking.

Brutus, in fact, told one faculty member that he thought he would be rewarded, not castigated. In Alinsky's era, the establishment regularly overreacted by pushing power against the rebels. In today's world, the establishment, mostly fearing lawsuits, caters to the troublemaking—thinking that one more concession will end the problem. Understandably, one more concession merely leads to another concession. Ultimately, the homeostasis is overturned and the organization remains in chaos, lacking leadership, direction, and balance.

A micro-study such as this is *not generalizable*. However, the new, grounded model provides insights for similar situations in the future. For example, those in authority need to be able to separate issues of the "open door" policy from those that are obvious attempts to circumvent authority. Julie knew, or should have known, that the associate provost was not a player in the tenure process. With that knowledge, Julie knew though that the associate provost communicated regularly with the provost and the preempting of the process could have positive repercussions in the decision making.

Three years later, the faculty lounge virtually no longer exists. Certainly no one arrives early to have conversations with colleagues. The department is split nearly evenly on "sides" of the issue arising out of the tenure decision. Amazingly, productivity (research and teaching) has hardly changed. It was the culture that was destroyed, not the work. Julie is now an associate professor who continues to present problems for the department and the university. Those who closed and locked their doors before the tenure decision continue to close and lock their doors.

Analysis of the Micro-Study

There are a number of theory and research issues that must be considered in using qualitative methods to study organizational cultures. First, as we have mentioned, any study of this kind is not capable of being generalized. A substantial number of studies may provide some movement in that direction. Second, as Schwartz and Jacobs (1979) have indicated, there are times when such methods are of somewhat of a "hunt-and-peck" variety. That is, an event during the study may trigger the researcher's going in an entirely different direction, in terms of theory or method. In the troublemaking case, the beginning of the barrage of e-mails stimulated a move in a different direction from where the participant observation was going. Thus, new or additional methods (content analysis in this case) may enter the picture at any point in the process. Third, the events must have actually occurred. The interpretation of events may vary, but the events themselves had to have actually happened. For example, Denzin (1983) has written:

> Interpretive interaction takes as its fundamental subject matter the everyday life world, as that world is taken for granted and made problematic by self-reflective, interacting individuals. The study and imputation of meaning, motive, intention, emotion, and feeling, as these mental and interactive states are experienced and organized by inter-acting individuals, are of central concern to the interpretivist. (p. 129)

The role of the participant observer may vary. For example, when studying southern blue-collar workers, Roebuck and Hickson (2006) only identified themselves as professors when they were asked about their work by those being observed (see also Hickson, Roebuck, & Murty, 1990). In Hickson's (1977) study of commuter bus riders, the researcher's occupation was never divulged nor was his role as observer. In Hickson's (1971) study of anti-poverty workers, though, there was complete disclosure. Before undertaking such studies, one should review the Institutional Research Board's guidelines (see Lindlof & Taylor, 2002).

While the troublemaking study is important to the culture that it changed, its ramifications are somewhat limited. There are other situations, though, that help create or maintain cultural values that influence people all over the world. In this case, we present two ideal types and illustrate how the power dynamics between them works.

Culture and Media

Arjun Appadurai's definition of modern globalization is that cultures are created through "imagined" landscapes mobilized by nostalgic media (1998, pp. 33–37). Anderson and Appadurai, are reminiscent of McLuhan's famous "media bytes" claiming that "we are looking toward the future through a rear view mirror," "walking backward into the future," or "doing today's job with yesterday's tools" (McLuhan & Fiore, 1967). Indeed, culture is above all a desire to be attached to the past. This imagined culture is unified through the structure of nostalgic feelings constructed by the media. For instance, in the early 21st century, most presidential political debates are formatted according to the first televised presidential debate between Kennedy and Nixon. The content of these debates is also nearly identical in regard to the questioning and the responses of the candidates. The events of such presidential debates appear to be more important than their content. McLuhan's claim that "the medium is the message," becomes in that particular case a truism in modern culture.

Furthermore, as in academia the "ego is the medium of exchange," in mass communication the medium of exchange is numbers. Indeed, box office receipts, ratings, circulation, platinum records, top 10 or number of hits, are numerical ratings used to determine the *cultural preferences* of certain groups according to viewership, readership, or listenership. Why do we have these numbers? Certainly to attempt to create a taxonomic system of human preferences that facilitates the making of a mass audience equal to the size of the earth's population. The creation of the perfect mass audience is an attempt to create a *monoculture* where people share the same values and behaviors. This monoculture is often referred to from abroad as the "Americanization." The impact of the American mass media system is evident in every aspect and in particular with the Internet. In 1887, Ludwik Zamenhof developed Esperanto, a universal language for all to share, a language of hope for globalization. Although, the language died because of the rise of nationalistic sentiments, which inevitably resulted in vast turmoil of the 20th century, the need for an international language prevails. Today, the language of preference for the Internet is English, the language of preference for globalization.

Modern globalization's central theme is encompassed by nation-states and taxonomic control over cultural differences. That is, nation-states utilize the media as the medium for visual representation of culture and technology as a tool toward communicating to the masses. Furthermore, the goal of the media and politics is to create a universal sentiment among all groups of the world. Nation-states attempt to achieve this sentiment of "sameness" by supporting a persuasive cultural media, which reifies their political ideals, a method of seducing minor groups with "imagery" and fantasy.

Appadurai (1998), defines five categories of "scapes" that encompass global culture: ethnoscape, mediascape, technoscape, financescape, and ideoscape. The suffix "scapes" represents the multiperspective views and interpretations of ethnography, media, technology, finance, and ideology.

The cultural assimilation mobilized by immigration, refugees, exiles, and guest workers, called the ethnoscapes, represents human migrations across the continents in search for satisfaction of individual needs. These human groups appear to affect politics and appear to be cultural attractors to multi-nationalist enterprises. That is, are these immigrants affecting politics? Are they affecting culture? Or are they affected by the encompassing politics and cultures of their original homeland? According to Appadurai (1998), modern migrations are similar to those of old world migrations, people are influenced by the economy and politics of their homeland. The ramifications of these human migrations are the creation of a culture of "new" nomads.

Prior to the 1960s, the organization of Western society was based on the colonialist system. A few Western European countries that exploited and administered other countries with less management capabilities, ruled the world. As the media system developed throughout the world since the late 1950s, the culture of these countries started to emancipate. However, as the people were emancipating, they were rejecting their own cultural background and were adopting the culture of their former colonialists. This resulted in migration, refugees, and exiles, which created a new form of nomadic living. This new culture of nomads encompasses similar attributes as that of the indigenous herders in Iran whose subsistence depended on migration according to the seasons, or the Native American nomadic tribes whose subsistence was dependent on the migratory patterns of the bison. Furthermore, the "modern" nomadism is influenced primarily by the patterns of free enterprise and marketing. This nomadic culture migrates according to what opportunities are offered for jobs and greater economic affluence. The media and the Internet are used as maps that lead the nomads toward their discovery of better sources of economic survival. This new societal trend is no longer based on sedentary lifestyles whereby people invest in long-term economic independence. Rather, people depend on a lifestyle that is based on finances; money is efficiently liquidated as opposed to investments, which provide profit far in the future.

Appadurai (1998) has described the advancement of technology as technoscapes. These technoscapes have dramatically evolved since the industrial revolution. One hundred years ago society relied on horses as their foremost body of transportation. As technology advanced in respect to transportation, trains, to automobiles, to planes, the mode of life and culture swayed toward a less sedentary lifestyle. Advancement in technology created instantaneous communication systems such as the telegraph in the 19th century along with improved printing methods. These innovations created efficient methods of sharing information between nations, which provided a web of human connections. The technological evolution influenced public thinking, which in turn revolutionized culture and politics. Furthermore, the advancement of computers facilitated the assimilation of instantaneous information and one of its ramifications led to the forming of multi-national enterprises. These marketing enterprises could now create more effective financial systems that would benefit financiers and change the face of culture around the world.

Entrepreneurship and private enterprise investing in technologies and media are representative of Appadurai's (1998) financescapes. The primary goal of multi-nationalist enterprise is similar to that of the colonialist ideal. Colonialists seized land and people, and exploited the resources of other nations that were not industrialized. In this sense, multi-nationalism incorporates the same reasoning in that the multi-national corporations finance domestic and small businesses at an interest rate, which is to the profitable advantage of the enterprise. The difference is that a small business can climb the ladder and create its own enterprise. Hence, once small businesses exploit other smaller businesses the cycle continues. Furthermore, the multinational banking systems created a system in which banks could transfer "imaginary" currency from one national bank to another, from one regional bank to another, then the "imaginary" number is transferred to local businesses and residences in the form of loans. With this multinationalist enterprises have created a "minor" culture of human groups categorized according to their "imaginary" credit.

Cultural values are assimilated using media or mediascapes. The financers and investors of the communication lines determine the message of the media. The lines of communication are blurred between reality and fiction as an element of seduction.

Since the 1950s, there has been a debate about cultural diversity versus homogenization of the world, according to "American popular culture," which has emerged politically and economically. Chiefs of this debate have been Daniel Toscan du Plantier (France) and Jack Valenti (United States) both representing their own respective motion picture industries.

Daniel Toscan du Plantier wrote,

the law of supply and demand is not enough to guarantee diversity; the means of representing a country's identity cannot be left to a third party; defense of pluralism is a form of defending freedom of speech; creative works are not just a commodity like any other; each population has the right to develop its distinctive culture; creative freedom must be plural and pluralist. (quoted in Frau-Meigs, 2004, p. 7)

Jack Valenti, responded,

Cultural exception is an elitist and backward looking approach; protectionism is a contravention of freedom of expression and consumption; State implication in culture does not foster talent and harms artistic expression; the "cultural exception" favors the development of an artists-in-the-unemployment-line mentality; it constitutes a block on competition and a perversion of the market. (quoted in Frau-Meigs, 2004, p. 7)

This debate, which was lost by Daniel Toscan du Plantier, is fundamental in that the goal of any mass media system is to access as many people as possible. This task cannot be attained with the concept of pluralism. Indeed, culture in essence unifies rather than separates. The demand for pluralism is a demand for mini-cultures defined by Valenti as "cultural exception." A cultural exception is indeed contradictory as "culture" is an integration of values and beliefs rather than a separation.

As an example, two chief movements emerged during the civil rights period in the United States: Martin Luther King's movement and Malcolm X's movement. King's movement was an integration within the "white Anglo-American" system, a view acceptable through the eyes of the nostalgic mass media system. Malcolm's movement was pluralist in that he wanted the freedom of the black people not to be defined by a third party. Malcolm's revolution failed because it was trying to create a "culture of exception."

Appadurai (1998) defines ideoscapes as political ideologies of nation-states and counter-ideologies. Media are the tools for assimilation of information and worldviews.

The "art" of persuasion is nothing less than mass mediated attempts to create an assimilation of one ideology to the mass population. The question is therefore, what is that common mass mediated ideology? Is a message created by the United Nations or is it created by the U.S. mass media system? Or, is the ideology based on the needs of the people around the world? Or is the ideology the new American "the manifest destiny"? The strength of the United States is that it dictates mass media trends on the global level. The American media system has created a monoculture that unifies most of the world.

The first *international medium* was the silent motion picture. Indeed, it was international because its language was only cinematographic and nonverbal and had no limitations in its viewership. In 1927, with the advent of sound, motion pictures lost their global impact and became national. However, contrary to other countries, the American studios reacted on an international rather than a national level. The American studios created stories with universal themes rather than cultural ones: they created stories with themes such as love, violence, and slapstick comedy. These new studio films were often musicals which allowed international audiences to enjoy the film rather than understand it. The Hollywood pictures have continued to work within that frame: sex, violence, humor, and death. The same phenomenon occurred in music with the first radio broadcast. As other countries developed ballads with complicated texts, the American music industry was mostly nonverbal and purely musical, the Jazz Era. The Rock-n-Roll Era followed that same route and allowed everyone around the world to understand some English words such as "She loves you, yea yea yea" or "Only you." The 20th century marked the end of pluralism in its language diversity as well as its cultural revolution.

The use of the American [English] language is only a by-product of this global revolution. The foundation of this revolution is mostly visual and aural. Prior to the turn of the last century, ethnic diversity was recognizable more by the local costumes that people were wearing than by their race or origins. From region to region people once wore different styles of clothing. With motion pictures, this changed very quickly and by the twenties, a "Westernized look" began to affect the pluralism of our societies. This "Western look" or this "Western behavior" made its way to music and is now widespread. Rap music has become a cultural commonality across cultures. The "Media American behavior" is erasing cultures that are centuries old.

What is the "Axis of Evil?" The "Axis of Evil," seems to be any culture that wants to keep or protect its identity against the "American Manifest Destiny." Similar to the spread of Christianity through the Bible against the barbaric society of the time, the American culture is now spread through the new mass media system. The Iraq war and wars of the 20th century, have been chiefly wars to impose a monoculture. The monoculture at the time of this writing seems to be the "Americanization" of the world.

Case Study

In 1992, Daniel Toscan du Plantier wanted to make a film in the United States. He was told that the state of Florida would match portions of the film budget to encourage international investments in the emerging Florida motion picture industry. Toscan du Plantier found a script that showed pluralism both in its story and in its investment. French super-star Thierry Lhermite was the first on board, which automatically brought French investors. The $10 million budget was at 75% complete. Toscan du Plantier entered into an Italian co-production. Actor Maurizio Nichetti brought another 15%. The budget was now $1 million short. American actors Rod Steiger and Molly Ringwald were cast to obtain the money from the state of Florida. The state of Florida responded that all the matching funds were not in place, and that it should be in place within two to five years, and that the funds would be competitive. Toscan du Plantier decided to forgo the so called "Florida funds" and completed the remainder of the budget from various French federal loan agencies. The budget was also cut down to arrive at the $9 million mark.

Thus, all of the money was funded in French francs and Italian lira. Yet most of the money was spent in the United States. Pre-production started in July 1993. Pre-production starts when the first salaries are being disbursed. The post-production was to end in March 1994. The shooting period was from October 20th to December 5th. During the periods of pre-production through post-production, the European currencies devaluated approximately 10%; another $1 million was lost.

On June 20th, 1994, *Variety* reported that the film was over budget by $200,000. Why did *Variety* (Evans, 1994) write a full page article about the film when by Hollywood standards, $200,000 in red production ink doesn't garner so much as a mention over drinks at Spago? The article was merely an attempt by Valenti and others who wanted to put the French film industry and its chief in the "unemployment-line."

The film was not distributed in the United States because no company wanted to get involved in this public relations war between Daniel Toscan du Plantar and Jack Valenti. Valenti knew very well that the film could not recover the $10 million in Europe alone.

Appadurai's (1998) theory of scapes (as an ideal type) illustrates mass globalization as a cultural phenomenon revolutionized by the control of political ideology and American mass media. The other aspects of scapes such as ethnoscapes, technoscapes, financescapes are simply the apparatuses used by the encompassing "Americanization" of worldviews. This is not to say that ethnicity will be diminished by American empowerment; rather, a backlash of new "ethnicities" and cultures will develop—in terms of retaliation and violence, the minority groups are not in the forefront. Yet it is the nations that have blurred reality to deceive the masses. The counter-ideologies are depicted through American media as the violent cultures, yet the structure of their feelings are embedded in the ideologies of the Western world.

From Ideal Models to Empirical Models

The models thus presented are based on theoretical understanding, a method which Weber referred to as an "ideal type" (cf. Gould & Kolb, 1964). The task at hand is, then, for the researcher to generate a grounded model (Glasser & Strauss, 1967)—one based on some form of empirical data. A grounded model is generated for future researchers to utilize as an "ideal type" theoretical paradigm.

Once the ideal type is known, the researcher must collect *capta*. Lanigan (1992) wrote:

> Fortunately, the return to the human science paradigm is refocusing attention on the performance and practice of persons communicating at the intrapersonal, interpersonal, group, and cultural levels of context for affective and cognitive meaning along with the traditional cognitive meaning orientation. The human scientist is "taking reality" (capta) as the valid source of evidence in research, rather than falling victim to the "Postmodern condition" of positivism in which the assumption of a "given reality" (data) indexes the subsequent representations of judgement ("making it operational"). (p. 2)

By using such information, the totality of *experience of otherness* becomes the basic element of substance. *Capta* are combined elements of the experiencer, the experiencing, and the experienced. Thus, the interpreter realizes that these elements must be constructed, constructing, and deconstructing, all at the same time. The experience is both an immediate and a reflecting process.

In this context, microlevel *capta* are used for constructing themes, which are, in turn, abstracted and explicated. Hickson (1977) found that among bus riders, these themes changed as a result of external forces (an energy crisis). *Capta* then must be collected over changing conditions to develop a wider sense of cultural thematic. In the genesis of what we call an "empirically derived model" of communication within a particular culture, the *capta* should be visualized as mobile, floating, and tentative to develop a more generalized macro-model of otherness.

By using the ideal type, theoretical model with its empirically derived paradigm, the researcher compares and contrasts a deductively constructed model and an inductively constructed paradigm. It is where these models intersect and overlap that we created a grounded model. Such a grounded model becomes a theoretical model for the next phase of the investigation. The ultimate goal for the communication researcher is to determine the consistency of social epoxy of the investigated group. At the same time, the researcher must determine his or her own biases, especially in regard to the making of assumptions taken from one's own culture.

As mentioned, characterization cannot be made solely based on numerical averaging, for such a construct is itself culturally biased. The essential types of questions that must be asked when studying culture include: "What are the basic, underlying assumptions unique to this culture?" "In what ways are these assumptions similar or different from other cultures?" "What are the culture's notions of otherness?" "What are the culture's notions of communication (as social epoxy)?" "What subcultures affect the integration-diversity of the culture?" "Is there really a culture?" Obviously, such questions must be further broken down to formulate microlevel questions and issues.

Grounded models may be utilized by the same researcher at a later date or utilized by another researcher for retesting. In this case, the researcher goes through the same cyclical process for developing a new grounded model.

Conclusion

The two studies presented in this chapter illustrate a number of dichotomies inherent in studying cultures. The first is a micro-study and the second is a macro-study. The second illustrates how an ideal type developed from "scapes" can be applied to a film industry, absorbed in making its template the only template available. The first case illustrates how beginning with an ideal type that assumes homeostasis in the workplace can be transformed quickly by a minority. In the organizational example, one must find another theory to replace the original, conservative model. Both qualitative and quantitative methods may be used in generating ideal types. Both methods may be used in gathering empirical data.

Notes

1. Much of the body of this chapter is based on the chapter in the previous edition of this book. See Neiva and Hickson (1992).
2. Moo U is not the name of the place where this case took place. Indeed, it was not even an agricultural institution, but the name is used for many schools across the country, hence the name. The names of individuals have been changed for obvious reasons.

References

Alinsky, S. D. (1969). *Reveille for radicals*. New York: Vintage.

Anderson, B. (1991). *Imagined communities*. London: Verso.

Appadurai, A. (1998). *Modernity at large*. Minneapolis: University of Minnesota Press.

Benedict, R. (1959). *Patterns of culture*. Boston: Mentor.

Bogdan, R., & Taylor, S. J. (1975). *Introduction to qualitative research methods: A phenomenological approach to the social sciences*. New York: Wiley.

Bruyn, S. T. (1966). *The human perspective in sociology: The methodology of participant observation*. Englewood Cliffs, NJ: Prentice-Hall.

Coser, L. A. (1977). *Masters of sociological thought: Ideas in historical and social context* (2nd ed.). New York: Harcourt Brace Jovanovich.

Denzin, N. K. (1983). Interpretive interactionism. In G. Morgan (Ed.), *Beyond method: Strategies for social research* (pp. 129–146). Beverly Hills, CA: Sage.

Douglas, J. D., (Ed.). (1970). *Understanding everyday life: Toward the reconstruction of sociological knowledge*. Chicago: Aldine.

Evans, G. (1994, June 20–26). Sundays sour to Sarasotans. *Variety*, pp. 9, 16.

Farb, P. (1978). *Humankind*. Boston: Houghton Mifflin.

Fletcher, R. (1971). *The making of sociology: A study of sociological theory* (Vol. 2). New York: Scribner's.

Frau-Meigs, D. (2004). *Globalization, audiovisual industry, and cultural diversity* (Vol. 14). Barcelona: Quadems.

Glasser, B. G., & Strauss A. L. (1967). *The discovery of grounded theory: Strategies for qualitative research*. New York: Aldine/Atherton.

Gould, J., & Kolb, W. L. (Eds.). (1964). *A dictionary of the social sciences*. New York: Free Press.

Hickson, M., III. (1971). *A systems analysis of the communication adaptation in a community action agency*. Doctoral dissertation. Southern Illinois University, Carbondale.

Hickson, M., III. (1974). Participant-observation techniques in organizational communication research. *Journal of Business Communication, 11*, 37–42, 54.

Hickson, M., III. (1976). Saul Alinsky: American Marxian strategist? In M. Hickson, III & F. E. Jandt (Eds.), *Marxian perspectives on human communication* (pp. 36–41). Rochester, NY: PSI.

Hickson, M., III. (1977). Communication in natural settings: Research tool for undergraduates. *Communication Quarterly, 25,* 23–28.

Hickson, M., III. (1983). Ethnomethodology: The promise of applied communication research? *Southern Speech Communication Journal, 48,* 182–195.

Hickson, M., III. (2003). Qualitative methodology. In J. E. Hocking, D. W. Stacks, & S. T. McDermott, *Communication research* (3rd ed., pp. 193–215). Boston: Allyn & Bacon.

Hickson, M., III. (2007). Finding a place in the Southern States Communication Association: A phenomenological auto-ethnography of "Where is Waldo?" *Southern Communication Journal, 72,* 71–81.

Hickson, M., III, & Jennings, R. W. (1993). Compatible theory and applied research: Systems theory and triangulation. In S. L. Herndon & G. L. Kreps, (Eds.), *Qualitative research: Applications in organizational communication* (pp. 140–157). Creskill, NJ: Hampton.

Hickson, M., III, Roebuck, J. B., & Murty, K. S. (1990). Creative triangulation: Toward a methodology for studying social types. In N. K. Denzin (Ed.), *Studies in symbolic interaction* (Vol. 11, pp. 103–127). Greenwich, CT: JAI Press.

Hickson, M., III, & Stacks, D. W. (1998). *Organizational communication in the personal context: From interview to retirement.* Boston: Allyn & Bacon.

Hoebel, E. A. (1966). *Anthropology: The study of man* (3rd ed.). New York: McGraw-Hill.

Hoel, H., & Cooper, C. L. (2001). Origins of bullying: Theoretical frameworks for explaining workplace bullying. In N. Tehrani (Ed.), *Building a culture of respect: Managing bullying at work* (pp. 1–20). London: Taylor & Francis.

Kroeber, A. L., & Kluckhohn, C. (1952). *Culture: A critical review of concepts and definitions* (Anthropological Papers, No. 47). Peabody Museum.

Lanigan, R. L. (1992). *The human science of communicology: A phenomenology of discourse in Foucault and Merleau-Ponty.* Pittsburgh, PA: Duquesne University Press.

Lindlof, T. R., & Taylor, B. C. (2002). *Qualitative communication research methods* (2nd ed.). Thousand Oaks, CA: Sage.

Malinowski, B. (1923). The problem of meaning in primitive languages. In C. K. Ogden & I. A. Richards (Eds.), *The meaning of meaning* (pp. 296–336). New York: Harcourt, Brace.

Malinowski. B. (1944). *A scientific theory of culture and other essays.* New York: Oxford University Press.

McCall, G. J., & Simmons, J. L. (Eds.). (1969). *Issues in participant observation: A text and reader.* Reading, MA: Addison-Wesley.

McLuhan, M., & Fiore, Q. (1967). *The medium is the massage: An inventory of effects.* New York: Bantam.

Miller, D. L. (1973). *George Herbert Mead: Self, language, and the world.* Austin: University of Texas Press.

Powdermaker, H. (1966). *Stranger and friend: The way of an anthropologist.* New York: Norton.

Roebuck, J. B., & Hickson, M., III. (2006). The *southern redneck: A phenomenological class study.* New York: Praeger.

Rogers, E. M. (1994). *A history of communication study: A biographical approach.* New York: Free Press.

Rogers, E. M. (1995). *Diffusion of innovations* (4th ed.). New York: Free Press.

Sanders, M. K. (1970). *The professional radical: Conversations with Saul Alinsky.* New York: Harper & Row.

Schutz, A. (1963). Common-sense and scientific interpretation of human action. In M. Natanson (Ed.), *Philosophy of the social sciences* (pp. 302–346). New York: Random House.

Schwartz, H., & Jacobs, J. (1979). *Qualitative sociology: A method to the madness.* New York: Free Press.

Tracy, S. J., Alberts, J. K., & Rivera, K. D. (2007, January 31). *How to bust the office bully: Eight tactics for explaining workplace abuse to decision-makers.* Tempe, AZ: Arizona State University.

Wax, R. H. (1971). *Doing fieldwork: Warnings and advice.* Chicago: The University of Chicago Press.

Webb, E. J., Campbell, D. T., Schwartz, R. D., & Sechrest, L. (1970). *Unobtrusive measures: Nonreactive research in the social sciences.* Chicago: Rand McNally.

Westhues, K. (2005). The *envy of excellence: Administrative mobbing of high-achieving professors.* Lewiston, Canada: Edwin Mellen.

White, L. A. (1968). Culturology. *International Encyclopedia of the Social Sciences, 3,* 547–550.

Zimbardo, P. (2007). *The Lucifer effect: Understanding how good people turn evil*. New York: Random House.

Suggested Readings

Garfinkel, H. (1967). *Studies in ethnomethodology*. Englewood Cliffs, NJ: Prentice-Hall.

Glaser, B. G., & Strauss, A. L. (1967). *The discovery of grounded theory: Strategies for qualitative research*. Chicago: Aldine Atherton.

Goffman, E. (1971). *Relations in public*: Microstudies of the public order. New York: Harper Colophon.

Morgan, G. (Ed.). (1983). *Beyond method: Strategies for social research*. Beverly Hills, CA: Sage.

Webb, E. J., Campbell, D. T., Schwartz, R. D., & Sechrest. (1970). *Unobtrusive measures: Nonreactive research in the social sciences*. Chicago: Rand McNally.

20

INTERCULTURAL COMMUNICATION

Thomas M. Steinfatt and Diane M. Millette

The study of intercultural communication is important in any society or culture. This is especially true in the United States, which has made *intercultural openness* a central feature of its cultural persona. The United States is currently experiencing the greatest period of immigration in its history. Although the late 19th and early 20th centuries witnessed a greater *proportional* population increase due to immigration, the actual *number* of legal immigrants entering the United States since 1980 was greater per decade than in any previous time in history. When illegal immigration is factored in, the current period of immigration is unsurpassed in American history, yielding a nation whose cultural heritage is changing, and, as a corollary, its communication is changing as well.

Communication

Following Langer (1942), we believe that communication in its most fundamental form is intrapersonal. Communication begins as an attempt by human beings to come to know their environment through symbols. This occurs through a gradual recognition by the child that symbols, objects, and ideas, and internal mental representations of them, can be related to each other in a meaningful fashion. To paraphrase Langer, children first use communication to bring objects into their minds, not into their hands. Once children learn that this is possible, then symbol-object-mind relationships are possible. Only after such relationships are learned can communication evolve to a social stage where people recognize that others also make similar symbol-object-mind inferences, and that these related networks of inferences can be used to interact with others. At the social stage, communication can be used for social tasks, such as making requests or transmitting cultural information. In all stages of human development, communication involves the assignment of meaning by the individual to external stimuli, including symbolically encoded messages from other persons. Communication is inherently a meaning assignment process within the individual. Since meaning is assigned to messages based on the beliefs, attitudes, and values of the individual, and since persons from different cultures often have different beliefs, attitudes, and values, the normal human misunderstandings which occur in same-culture interactions are often magnified by the wider differences in cultural assumptions and belief systems inherent in cross-cultural interactions.

Culture

The diversity of the concept "culture" is illustrated by Kluckhohn's (1949) 12 meanings for the term, from the way of life of a people, their social legacy, pooled learning, way of thinking, feeling, and believing, through their mechanism for normative regulation of behavior and techniques for adjusting to the environment and other people, to theories about the way these people behave. Citing Max Weber as inspiration, Geertz (1973, p. 5) holds that "man is an animal suspended in webs of significance he himself has spun, I take culture to be those webs, and the analysis of it to be therefore not an experimental science in search of law but an interpretative one in search of meaning."

We conceive of culture in its broadest sense as the accumulated knowledge and beliefs of specific portions of humanity. Thus defined, the fundamental nature of culture is phenomenological: culture exists fundamentally in the hearts and minds of people. Cultural artifacts such as paintings, sculpture, machinery, and construction projects are products of the knowledge and beliefs that constitute culture. While cultural artifacts provide clues to culture, culture itself can be passed on to other persons and future generations only through communication. No study of culture's artifacts, no matter how deep or extensive, can describe, explain, predict, or even transmit culture from one person or generation to another without communication about cultural meaning. Intercultural communication involves communication between people from different cultures, leading to several questions: What constitutes a "different" culture? Do intercultural differences necessarily involve different languages? Different ways of thinking? Different worldviews? Different beliefs, attitudes, and values?

Intercultural Communication

While there is little disagreement that communication between a Karen hill tribesman in northern Thailand and an American college student involves intercultural differences, we might ask if communication between any two persons with different attitudes, beliefs, and values also involves intercultural differences. For example, while the value system espoused by a given corporation is commonly referred to as corporate culture, does that mean that communication between workers at IBM and Microsoft necessarily involves intercultural differences? Perhaps. Between someone at IBM and a farm worker? Possibly. To study such interactions from an intercultural perspective might raise different questions and produce different answers from those found in a more standard organizational communication analysis. But rather than attempt to give final answers, we prefer to discuss the central thrust of intercultural communication, as opposed to attempting to delineate intercultural communication's absolute boundaries.

Thus, we regard the study of intercultural communication as the study of communication between people with different mind-sets and ways of looking at and perceiving the world that go beyond the differences normally found among people who regard themselves as culturally similar. Since communication occurs through cognitive processing, we might ask whether Eastern and Western ways of thinking are different. Does such a notion imply different cognitive structures or communication processes, or, can the observations which lead people to infer a different way of thinking be explained simply through different content in beliefs, attitudes, and values within the cultures? Though commonly applied to communication between persons who are each embedded in a different cultural group, intercultural communication also has heuristic utility when applied to the examination of two persons, ostensibly from the same culture, gender, age, ethnic group, and socioeconomic status, whose assumptions about the nature of the world and ways of relating to it are sufficiently divergent to produce the forms of misunderstanding commonly found in intercultural analysis. *The central thrust of intercultural communication is in the analysis of meaning assignment in interactions between persons whose attitudes, beliefs, and values differ due to a corresponding difference in their cultural or co-cultural backgrounds.* These attitudes, beliefs, and values represent, in part, the individual's theories of what others in the same culture believe, as well as how this differentiates persons of that culture from persons of other cultures.

Four Major Areas Of Intercultural Communication Study

The term *Intercultural Communication* has both a broad and a narrower referent. The broad sense is that of an encompassing term for four major areas of intercultural communication defined by their intent: I. *Cross-cultural Communication;* II. *International Communication;* III. *Development Communication;* and intercultural communication's narrower referent, IV. *Intercultural Communication proper.* These areas are not fixed and independent. Studies in each area often have relevance to studies in others, and some research traditions, linguistic relativity, for example, might be classified in several different areas. We will spend more time discussing some areas than others.

Cross-Cultural Communication

Borrowing terminology from descriptive linguistics, Pike (1966) developed his *etic* and *emic* distinction from *phonetic* and *phonemic.* He observed that phonetics studies sound and symbol production as observed by others outside the person being studied, while phonemics examines meaning, which is inside the person. Thus *emic* approaches look at a single culture, often from the perspective of a person thinking, communicating, and behaving within that culture—so their idiosyncrasies as cultures may be determined. This is the approach of ethnology and cross-cultural communication. And *etic* approaches to intercultural communication examine cultures from the outside—so their commonalities may be determined. The *etic* approach is that of intercultural communication proper.

Cross-cultural communication concerns the comparison of communication across two or more specific cultures or ethnicities, such as Japanese communication styles compared with U.S. communication styles, or African-American, Hispanic, and Anglo styles within the United States. Studies of linguistic relativity and of ethnography are also forms of cross-cultural communication so defined. Scholars concerned with multicultural education and cultural diversity are often interested in both cross-cultural communication and intercultural communication proper. Many works on cross-cultural communication are heavily weighted in the comparison, focusing on one presumably unfamiliar culture almost to the exclusion of the culture presumed to be familiar. In such cases the cross-cultural study becomes more a uni-cultural study.

Communication Across Cultures and Ethnicities

The single cross-cultural interaction which has generated the most in-depth, book-length communication research concerning intercultural communication with its members is Japanese-American communication. Barnlund (1989), Goldman (1990, 1994), Gudykunst (1993), Gudykunst and Nishida (1994), and Sato (1992) each discuss Japanese-American communication from different perspectives. Goldman (1990) and Sato (1992) focus on Japanese communicating with Americans, while Barnlund (1989), Goldman (1994), and Gudykunst and Nishida (1994) are oriented toward the American perspective in interacting with Japanese. Gudykunst (1993) contrasts the study of communication in Japan with that in the United States, and Stewart and Bennett (1991) discuss the cultural patterns of Americans.

Kim (1986) summarizes research on interethnic communication to the mid-1980s. Hecht, Jackson, and Ribeau (2003) provide an example of research on ethnic styles, delineating African-American communication patterns as contrasted with other common U.S. forms. Other views representative of a multicultural and cultural diversity approach to intercultural communication are provided in Andersen and Collins (1992) and Gonzalez, Houston, and Chen (1994). Central to these essays are concerns with the concepts of racism, sexism, prejudice, self-concept, and power differences which enter into interethnic interactions.

Gannon (2004) provides an introduction to the study of various cultures in his book *Understanding Global Cultures,* which is popular within the business community for persons whose work takes them to unfamiliar cultures. Gannon employs cultural metaphors to help those unfamiliar with a given culture attain a notion of the dominant mind-set found in that country or culture. Whether such dominant unified mind-sets exist, and whether the use of such metaphors actually assists in cross-cultural communication or simply provides comfort to prospective travelers, has not been sufficiently studied.

Linguistic Relativity

Another cross-cultural area is the study of linguistic relativity, which can be traced to Aristotle's speculations on whether doing philosophy while using Greek as a symbol system would make the knowledge discovered different if, say, Latin were the symbol system (Steinfatt,1989). Aristotle's answer was that the language in use would not make a substantial difference in the final result—that any thought could be expressed equally well in any language.

This view held sway until the late 19th century, when Cassirer (1953) suggested that the language used to conduct philosophical analyses could influence the resultant knowledge. Cassirer's work was not widely accepted in philosophy, but a young Yale anthropologist, Edward Sapir, began to write and lecture on topics in linguistic anthropology in the late 1800s. Sapir (1921) suggested that thought was potentially relative to language. Prior to 1920 Benjamin Lee Whorf, an undergraduate student in engineering at MIT who was working his way through college as an inspector for an insurance company, began to study Hopi and Mayan cultures. In the 1920s he lectured extensively on his thesis, developed independently of Sapir's ideas, that the language of thought influences its content. Though not Sapir's student at this point, he had heard of Sapir and attended one of Sapir's lectures at Yale late in that decade, eventually joining Sapir's graduate program in anthropology as a student. From this simple meeting was born what has come to be called the *Sapir–Whorf hypothesis,* that language structures thought. Mandell (1931) presents an early view of linguistic relativity; reviews of experimental research may be found in Gibson and McGarvy (1937), Woodworth (1938), Heidbreder (1948), Johnson (1950), Humphrey (1951), (1951), Diebold (1965), and Steinfatt (1988, 1989). Lee's (1996) *The Whorf Theory Complex: A Critical Reconstruction,* provides an excellent discussion of Whorf's intercultural work.

Sapir (1921), Whorf (1956), and Cassirer (1953) are perhaps the best known advocates of the notion that language influences thought. They treated linguistic relativity as an interlanguage phenomenon, a process attributable to differences between languages. Sapir and Whorf's thesis involves both "linguistic determinism" and "linguistic relativity." Linguistic determinism holds that language shapes thought, but allows that people who speak different languages could still have the same thoughts and think in similar ways. For example, a counterfactual conditional (e.g., "I would take you if I were going that way but I'm not so I can't") is very difficult to express in Chinese. But while the language makes such thoughts difficult to express, linguistic determinism suggests that such thoughts could occur in Chinese, although they would be difficult. Linguistic relativity, a more radical version of linguistic determinism, holds that different languages actually shape thought differently (Glucksberg & Danks, 1975). Linguistic relativity would argue that speakers of Chinese would have great difficulty thinking in counterfactual conditional terms and that thought processes in Chinese would have to follow the structure of the language.

As initially proposed, the *Weltanschauung*—world *view*—thesis of linguistic relativity was very general and thus almost impossible to test. Greenberg (1956), Lenneberg and Roberts (1956), Henle (1958), Fishman (1960), Osgood and Sebeok (1965), and Slobin (1979) all have suggested different ways of organizing the hypothesis. Steinfatt (1989) proposed that three groups of independent variables—phonological, syntactical, and semantic—are possible causative sets in linguistic relativity as the basis for any proposed differences in thought. At least one variable from at least one of these sets must influence at least one dependent measure in one of three variable sets—the logic of thought itself, the structure of cognition and worldview, or perception and areas of cognition—in order for a linguistic relativity effect to be claimed. Beyond looking at differences between natural languages as a source of linguistic relativity effects, Steinfatt (1989) also suggested that substantial phonological, syntactical, or semantic differences in any natural language would have to be regarded as a potential source of linguistic relativity effects. Thus, dialects such as Black-American English, compound bilingualism, aphasics relearning a language, and the deaf, should provide examples of linguistic relativity effects if such effects actually occur. Linguistic relativity should not be limited to the natural language differences proposed by Whorf (1956) and others. Additionally, Steinfatt (1989) suggested that knowledge of the methods by which language is acquired should provide insight into whether linguistic relativity effects are likely to exist.

Traditional Ethnography

The traditional referent of ethnography is the branch of anthropology dealing with the scientific description of specific human cultures, both the fieldwork and the writing that it engenders. Barfield (2001) defines ethnography as systematic description of a single existing culture that can be observed in the present. In Malinowski's (1922) classic definition, ethnography is the endeavor of describing a culture, "to grasp the native's point of view, his relation to life, to realize *his* vision of *his* world" (1922, p. 25). Kaplan (1964, p. 31) refers to this as the "act meaning," as opposed to the "action meaning" that is taken as data by many social scientists. This apprehension of the act meaning was usually accomplished through personal immersion in the object culture involving a lengthy process of participation, participant observation, and interview, often by a single observer, producing highly detailed and descriptive notes that became the raw data for later analysis. The observation process and note creation were the fundamental method, and were seen as largely devoid of theory, though they were often guided by notions of kinship systems and other important areas and classifications. No specific characteristics of culture were to be defined *a priori,* and the researcher was to ignore all preconceived notions of the culture to be studied. The important characteristics, relationships, and patterns would emerge naturally during the research, so that notes had to be very detailed as the observer would not know what would later emerge as important. This form of ethnography became a well-established method for the study of human cultures in the late 19th and early 20th centuries.

Aside from potential concerns with ethnography regarding validity and reliability—since *one* person from an *outside* culture was to assign meaning producing a single known reality— traditional cultures so described were often viewed in isolation from each other and from the world. The methods of traditional ethnography were also vulnerable to political attack since they were associated from the outset with imperialism and the colonial subordination of non-Western peoples by European powers. The observations of ethnographers necessarily occur within the form of ethnocentricity of the times, and most ethnographers believed it was possible for a single "scientific observer" to create detailed interpretations of other cultures from a detached point of view (Vidich & Lyman, 1994). Little consideration was given to the observer's role as observer, nor to the possible impact of an observer on the research, particularly as an outsider from a ruling power. Nor was consideration given to the need for a diverse set of views from multiple observers, with multiple voices speaking from within the community to be studied, who might be heard differently by different observers.

By the early 1960s these criticisms of the traditional ethnographic method were regularly taught as such in U.S. graduate programs in anthropology. This occurred in most programs, but not in all of them. By the 1970s Geertz's (1973) emphasis on "thick description," influenced by Ryle's (1968) discussion of the meaning of a wink, suggests that the descriptions within ethnography must consider the context of the behaviors described, to the point that the description of the behavior makes the behavior in its context meaningful to an outsider. Thin description results from the outside observation of behaviors with little interpretation, and thick description includes the interpretation of the behavior from the point of view of the cultural actor. Beginning with his 1960s work on Javanese religion, Geertz (1960, 1973, 1983, 1988) was one of ethnography's principal proponents. Wolcott (1994) provides a clear description of the use of ethnography in multiple settings, where researchers are especially interested in studying the ways in which people embedded in a culture make decisions. Gladwin (1989) discusses the use of "decision trees" in this process.

The Variance Within is of the Same Order as the Variance Between

Certainly a note of caution is in order whenever a given culture is being described. When discussing a culture and defining its important communication features, abstraction involves searching for what is central within the culture and ignoring the peripheral. Yet central to any culture is cultural variation often involving the peripheral. When we apply intercultural communication to specific situations as communication between, say, Vietnamese and American cultures, or Black and White cultures within American society, this conceptualization implies a certain unity of culture for Vietnamese, Americans, Whites, and Blacks. The assumption often is that people within a culture are relatively similar and the major differences are to be found between those of one culture and those of another. Naturally, nothing is further from the truth. To employ a statistical analogy from the analysis of variance, we may say that the variation within a given culture is normally of the same order of magnitude as the variation between cultures. There is often as much variation in a given culture between its social classes as there is between that culture and any other culture. In fact, ethnic variations within a given culture can easily be greater than the average variation between that culture and another. Learning how a particular cultural group thinks and communicates does not guarantee that such findings will hold for a specific member of a cultural group, especially when the cultural interaction situation is factored in. At a minimum, if the social class and ethnicity of the specific individuals involved is not considered, knowledge of the culture alone is often of little use in predicting interactional outcomes, though this is not always the case (e.g., Jones, 1979).

Postmodernism

The methods of ethnography came under further attack by postmodernism in the 1980s and beyond, an attack that in large part simply echoed the known criticisms of ethnography, emphasizing some criticisms over others, and attempting to fuse them into a postmodern critique. In general, this attempt was neither coherent and well thought out, nor worth exploring further. The most distinguishing and consistent new features of postmodernist attacks were the invention of a non-existent "modernism," allowing postmodernism's straw man attack on it, and the apparent inability of many of its major proponents to write competently in their native language. Its proponents consider this a strong point.

The New Ethnography

Although ethnography has long been a principal method of social and cultural anthropology, its use has rapidly increased as a method in social psychology and communication over the past decade (Vidich & Lyman, 1994). Ellis and Bochner (1996) provide multiple examples of ways of composing the new ethnography. Most of this ethnography as currently practiced appears to be a literary form, as in novels, short stories, and literary criticism, with standards of evidence and interpretation similar to the personal opinion and experience standards of those genres. We can learn a great deal from such forms, as in Richard Wright's classics such as *Black Boy*, *Uncle Tom's Children*, and *Native Son*. One problem is that not all writers of ethnography are as observant, accurate, and skillful writers as Wright, and that many such writers believe in obtuse rather than illuminating writing forms, possibly an influence of postmodernism. "It takes skill and effort to introspect in a way that is scientifically useful" (Kaplan, 1964, p. 141).

Traditional ethnography involved an outside observer of a culture, partially on the theory that the observer would not be blinded to the culture by being embedded in it. A fish would be the last one to notice that the environment surrounding it was wet. The new ethnography often employs a culturally embedded observer, which introduces both the fish problem, and in the case of auto-ethnography, the problem that the material to be observed is available first hand, only to that single participant. Additionally, that observer is usually employed as the only interpreter as well as the only observer. Such writings can be very helpful and illuminating of intercultural issues, and can also be descriptions that lead nowhere. We are often good judges of some of our motivations and internal states, particularly physical ones such as hunger and pain, and emotional ones such as whether or not our feelings are hurt. We may be less accurate as judges of how others see us, or of why we may have engaged in a particular communicative behavior. Individual outside observers sometimes know us better than we know ourselves. And multiple outside observers are likely to give better predictions in this regard than individual observers. The question then becomes the extent to which the new ethnography can provide more than the feeling that we now understand something better than we did before. The new ethnology will ultimately be judged not for this quality, but for what it adds to the value of studies that employ it, including its heuristic value. If ultimately we cannot describe, explain, predict, or understand the phenomenon under study in some more insightful or more useful way by using the new ethnology, then it will inevitably fade in the face of a better way of doing that.

Criticisms of Social Science Methods

The increase in the use of new ethnographic methods in intercultural communication is based in part on several criticisms of social science methodology. Specifically, proponents of ethnographic analysis usually hold *first*, that the structure required by social science in the research process emanates from the researcher's cultural assumptions, which limits the chances of finding much which does not fit these preconceived assumptions. A *second* criticism holds that generalizations from controlled to natural settings (i.e., experimental to field) are suspect. *Third*, ethnographic analysis holds that interviews must be combined with observations to understand cultural perspectives. *Fourth*, it suggests that quantification necessarily selects some aspects of what is being studied and ignores others, thus reifying and unduly increasing the importance of the selected, while ignoring the unselected. And, *fifth*, ethnographic analysis holds that quantitative analysis ignores the role of human interaction and human choice in a mechanistic analysis based only on the variables selected by the researcher. Many of these criticisms assume that social science methodology equates to quantification. Rather, the goal of social science is the ability to predict the outcome of unknown events using an explanation based on accurate description. Social science equates understanding with prediction. Ethnography equates understanding with thick description.

Criticisms of Ethnographic Methods

The rather obvious response by social science to the five criticisms is *first*, there is no reason to assume that a researcher's cultural assumptions are any less ethnocentric because the researcher chooses single-person observation and written descriptions rather than social science methods. *Second*, generalizations from writing about single person observations as in ethnography are even more suspect than controlled generalizations. *Third*, observations without social science methods will be at least as poor representations of cultural perspectives since the sampling of perspectives will be haphazard at best without those social science methods. Interviews likely should be combined with observations to understand cultural perspectives, and doing that is a good way of combining the strengths of social science and of ethnography. *Fourth*, ethnographic methods necessarily select some aspects of what is being studied and ignore others, thus reifying and unduly increasing the importance of the selected, while ignoring the unselected. And *fifth*, ethnographic analysis ignores the role of human interaction and human choice in a literary analysis based only on the observations selected by the researcher. In other words, *the problems of research are equally applicable to social science methods and to ethnographic ones.*

Hammersley (1992) discusses some of these problems and possibilities with the ethnographic approach. Perhaps the most telling criticism is that ethnography depends on realism, the doctrine that there is a reality out there to study, and on constructivism, the notion that individuals construct their own social reality. Some social scientists make these same assumptions, while others do not. Ethnographers suggest that they study observed and constructed reality through observation and interaction and then report what they have learned. The problem is that the story produced by such an approach is constructed from personal observations and interactions, a construction just as subject to the ethnographer's culture and biases as any social science account, and probably much more so. Not only do each of the five criticisms aimed at social science analysis by ethnography apply as a critique of ethnographic analysis, but some ethnographers deny that such criticisms are applicable to ethnology, thus putting ethnography close to a position of nonfalsifiability (Popper, 1968). An analysis which cannot be falsified or criticized, where there is nothing that could occur that if it did occur would invalidate the method, cannot be taken as a serious scholarly analysis. Alasuutari (1995) provides a strong introduction to the use of qualitative methods in intercultural communication and with cultural studies in general.

The Qualitative/Quantitative Distinction

While traditionally viewed as a method of social science, the new ethnography is often discussed as a "qualitative" method, to be distinguished from "quantitative" methods, which are then equated with social science. We believe that the qualitative versus quantitative research distinction is inauthentic, in that it involves multiple continuums rather than a single dichotomy. Yet it is a distinction that appears to have permeated the field. One appropriate continuum is good research versus bad research. Every known research method has examples of good, average, and bad research. Good research uses methods that are driven by the questions being asked, and by the purpose of asking these questions. If the method has the potential to answer these research questions in some useful way that can be reasonably defended by those who employ it, against reasonable attacks, then it is on the path toward good research. Some questions are inherently more quantitative: how many, how much, which is a larger effect, etc. Others are inherently more qualitative: what is the nature of the philosophic differences that exist among cultures that appear to affect intercultural communication? But intercultural communication questions of any importance demand a mix of qualitative and quantitative methods. Ethnography and the more quantitative social science methods both provide certain kinds of insights into intercultural analysis. Students of intercultural communication should learn both, as well as the strengths and weaknesses of each, and should not waste time defending any one method as the only possible approach to a problem. Some intercultural analyses have profitably combined the use of ethnographic methods with social science research. Steinfatt (2002), within a largely "quantitative" analysis, uses ethnographic reports to illustrate and illuminate ideal types representing several large subgroups of female sex workers in Thailand, and employs comparisons of Christianity and Buddhism to discuss the moral rationales for working.

Labeling a study as "quantitative" should not be used as an excuse for failing to provide the thick description needed to understand the meaning, importance, and potential application of the research. Similarly, labeling a study as qualitative or ethnographic should not be used as an excuse for entering quantitative results that would not be accepted as scholarly if they appeared in an article labeled "quantitative." For example, the statement, "According to a 1994 broadcast of *48 hours*, roughly 94% of all mentally retarded people are thought to be victims of sexual abuse," appears in a book of essays represented as blurring the boundaries between social science and the humanities (Ronai, 1996, p. 111). One hopes that this example is not what is meant by blurring these boundaries. In that essay, no reference citation is offered beyond the quotation itself, nor is there a definition of terms, nor a notion of who might be the *source* of the thoughts about sexual abuse: it is left unstated whether this was thought by others who are mentally retarded, or thought by clinical psychologists, or by psychiatrists, or by authors of a competent study of the subject, or simply by someone's wild guess. Standards for scholarly writing should receive equal application across methods.

International Communication

International Communication is the study of both (1) mass mediated communication between countries, often but not always with significantly different cultural worldviews (e.g., media imperialism), and (2) interpersonal communication, mediated or face-to-face, between persons representing different governments—one country's government's view as communicated to another country's government—and the factors, whether intercultural, cross-cultural, mediated, or political that influence both the construction and interpretation of such message exchanges.

Studies of international mass mediated communication include, for example, the pioneering work of Sydney Head (1956, 1961, 1974, 1985) on comparative international broadcasting, as well as studies such as McPhail's (2006) work on global communication. Communication in international relations includes diplomatic messages and exchanges; diplomatic posturing; ciphers and code-breaking; assigning meaning to when, where, how, from whom, and through what chain of sources and channels an official or unofficial message is received in determining its authenticity, significance, initial intent, and ultimate purpose.

Development Communication

Development Communication studies organized efforts that use communication to create social and economic improvements, as seen by the introducing culture, often but not always in developing countries. The initial phase of development communication began during the cold war. It involved organized media and interpersonal communication efforts to create social and economic improvements, usually in developing countries and sponsored by developed countries.

Initially based on the cold war theories of W. W. Rostow (1952, Rostow & Levin, 1953), together with Lerner and Schramm's (1967) belief in the apparent success of U.S. World War II heavily funded propaganda methods, development communication was initially designed to increase consumption, and thus capitalism, in developing nations in order to foster Western capitalist beliefs and keep them safe from communism (Rostow & Hatch, 1955). Heavy funding of development communication efforts from first world governments, combined with direct governmental foreign economic and military aid and World Bank funding of top-down economic development to less developed nations, consistently failed to achieve its goals. Proponents of these failed efforts saw the problems in fostering development as based within the developing nations, having little or nothing to do with international relationships. All development was seen as Westernization, conducted largely through trickle-down economics, which in turn was seen as a necessary prerequisite to a stable economy and a stable world.

Kennedy's Peace Corps began a reversal of this model in the 1960s that reached maturity in the 1970s and beyond, featuring people-to-people bubble-up programs, and a far greater consideration in its training programs and implementation of the culture, language, beliefs, attitudes, and traditions of developing nations and peoples, and a recognition of their general mistrust of "propaganda" efforts by the West. At the same time, Rogers's (1962) compilation of and theorizing about the communication processes involved in the diffusion of innovations during development was one of the first books to integrate intercultural communication considerations with development efforts. It summarized and codified most of the prior research on diffusion from research traditions as diverse as mass communication, education, and rural sociology, into a blueprint for introducing cultural change. Rogers and Shoemaker (1971) updated Rogers's initial conceptualization, and Fischer (1974) and Frey (1974) presented related aspects of the problem. Interpersonal-intercultural communication replaced the over-reliance on television of the earlier model, and the use of radio and community newspapers in the new endeavors often proved more effective than television. The entertainment-education model (Singhal & Rogers, 2004) proved particularly effective when used with radio soap operas. Television succeeded in development communication as an educational tool primarily when development programs on TV were viewed in small groups with a local opinion leader present to introduce them, who then turned off the TV after the viewing period to lead discussions of what the TV content meant.

Diffusion research centers on effective methods of introducing new ways of doing things, and of spreading awareness and adoption of the new concept throughout the culture. While innovations diffuse naturally from cross-cultural interactions, the central question of diffusion and development research concerns identifying manipulable predictor variables which affect the rates of adoption and discontinuance of an innovation. Characteristics of "innovators" and "early adopters," which lead to opinion leadership, are studied and contrasted with those of "later adopters" and "laggards." Diffusion studies examine the characteristics of the innovation itself, its compatibility with local cultural norms, the role of change agents, types of decision making, and consequences of the decision to adopt.

The majority of the consequences are often unintended, unanticipated, and not infrequently negative. Such consequences lead to the consideration of the ethics for deciding when to intervene in another culture. Ethical systems range from the rampant ethnocentrism of colonialism to the hands-off position of extreme multiculturalists. The concern with ethics is related to the more general problem of the ethics of foreign policy. What are the characteristics of a situation which justify intervention? Who should be allowed to make such a decision? Does the receiving culture have the right of refusal? Does the source culture have a similar right? Neither extreme position is tenable because no culture nor cultural practice is an island unto itself. Nazi culture led to the Holocaust; the world should have intervened sooner and more forcibly. The same might be said of Soviet culture under Stalinism and Cambodian culture under Pol Pot. But some intervention decisions that seem obvious to Western morality in areas such as prostitution, female genital mutilation, the oppression of women, and the control of disease, can lead to cultural upheaval and untold human hardship as a result. The Chinese and other Asian nations argue, for instance, that human rights are an invention of Western culture and simply a further extension of discredited colonialist practices.

What ethical system can be proposed that is not based in the moral norms of one culture over another? The traditional answer of Western philosophy is to dismiss any notion of ethical relativity (e.g., Hatch, 1983), for without set moral standards any action can be justified. Is it possible to devise a multicultural morality that allows us to distinguish the legitimate moral claims of any culture from those that are specious? Yet, if an ethical system does not take into account the fundamental conceptions and world view of all cultures in which it is to be applied, what claim can it make to being a legitimate universal absolute morality?

Intercultural Communication Proper

Intercultural Communication in the narrower sense is that of Gudykunst's (1987) reference to *intercultural communication proper*, the study of generalizations about intercultural communication independent of any specific culture or ethnicity. This is also Pike's (1966) *etic* approach, examining multiple cultures from the outside to determine their commonalities. It includes studies of how humans react to any different culture and its peoples, beliefs, and ways of acting and thinking. In this process it considers theories of intercultural competence, ways of obtaining such competence, and measurements of individuals concerning this competence. Also in this process, it may be the case that nomothetic generalizations may profitably exist hand in hand with idiosyncratic theories of specific cultures and of co-cultural groups within each culture. The combination of both types of knowledge approaches will be needed in practical settings where such laws are to be applied. While knowledge of a culture requires additional knowledge of social class and ethnicity of the specific individuals involved in order to predict and understand an interaction, intercultural communication principals alone are insufficient for dealing with many practical problems in communication between two specific cultures. Just as Hall's (1959) State Department students complained that a knowledge of Navajo culture was of little help to an administrator about to join the diplomatic corps in Paris, specific cultural, ethnicity, and social class knowledge, together with knowledge of intercultural communication principals, is needed in order to make informed practical decisions in real situations.

Foundations

Among the earliest writings on intercultural communication proper may be Durkheim's (1897) classic study of suicide among immigrants. Durkheim used his concept of *anomie*, the feeling of rootlessness, of having no culture, of not belonging to either the old country or to the new, to explain high suicide rates across immigrant populations of the time. By the 1920s, Park and Burgess (1924) and their Chicago School colleagues studied European immigrants' integration into American culture, recognizing the initial social processes of accommodation and assimilation (Rogers, 1994).

The social science approach to the study of communication in general was pioneered by scholars such as Lazarsfeld (1944), Lasswell (1948), Hovland, Janis, and Kelley (1953), and Schramm (1954), partially in response to the Hutchins Commission report (Commission of Freedom of the Press, 1947) which sought, among other goals, to identify variables that predict communication outcomes across multiple cross-cultural interactions. Schramm, who had worked as Educational Director of the U.S. Office of War Information during World War II, received a number of grants from the U.S. government following the war to work on anticommunist communication campaigns (Glander, 1996). These grants led both to the founding of communication research institutes and communication programs at Illinois, Stanford, Hawaii, and Iowa, and to the early funding of these programs and their students. The approach favored by Schramm and the government was one providing a well-grounded empirical and verifiable approach to government goals, seeking theories of intercultural communication by developing an abstract calculus of relationships between and among variables that are observable and measurable. Prior to the late 1950s, the studies of culture shock appearing in *Practical Anthropology,* and of prejudice and ethnic relations scattered throughout scholarly journals in sociology, psychology, and anthropology, formed the basis for early intercultural communication research. Schatzman and Strauss (1955) provide one of the early studies of intracultural communication.

Beginnings

The history of intercultural communication as an area is often ascribed to the 1959 publication of Edward T. Hall's *The Silent Language* (Condon, 1981; Dodd, 1982; Gudykunst, 1985b; Klopf, 1987; Samovar & Porter, 1972; Singer, 1987), in which Hall introduced the term "intercultural communication." Alternately, Leeds-Hurwitz (1990), Rogers (1994), and Rogers and Steinfatt (1999) credit the term and the beginning of intercultural communication research to the decade following World War II in Hall's work training American diplomats through the U.S. Foreign Service Institute. This work produced *The Silent Language* as a handbook for intercultural training. Many current intercultural training areas are derived from Hall's work such as those in cultural diversity, cultural sensitivity, and in student exchange and study abroad programs (Kohls, 1984; Mestenhauser, Marty, & Steglitz, 1988). Brislin and Yoshida (1994) discuss methods of assessment and evaluation of intercultural communication training programs. Applications of intercultural communication research useful in various training programs also may be found in Brislin (1990).

Hall's work also led to a major body of social science oriented communication scholarship. He refocused the study of culture as it was practiced by post-World War II anthropology in a number of ways (see Leeds-Hurwitz, 1990). One of these was a shift from anthropology's emphasis on monadic and dyadic studies of a single culture, or a comparison of two cultures—cross-cultural communication—into intercultural communication proper. Hall's concept of intercultural communication as patterned, learned, and capable of being analyzed across cultures in general, was compatible with the social science notions then taking form in mass and interpersonal communication. His emphasis on generalizations fit with American social science, seeking nomothetic lawlike generalizations, and shunning idiosyncratic knowledge characteristic of *an* individual or *a* culture.

Further, Hall's focus on training at the Foreign Service Institute created the practical need for a generalized training program useful for all American diplomats regardless of their culture of destination. Specific cultures and their features were deemphasized not because their differences were irrelevant, but because of practical considerations about packaging the information to groups of trainees about to embark to various different locations and cultures. Thus Hall concentrated on the features of culture that affected the interpersonal interactions his trainees would encounter: tone of voice, gestures, and conceptions of time and space, largely ignoring those features not directly relevant to intercultural interactions. This decision established him as one of the founders of intercultural communication, and relegated him to secondary status within the field of anthropology. While much of the current research in *intercultural communication proper* is quantitative in nature, this orientation is not derived from Hall. As an anthropologist, Hall was both qualitative and applied; his focus was on training. Rather, attention to quantitative methods has come from communication researchers' quantitative training, many of them having become interested in expanding the study of interpersonal communication into intercultural areas. Leeds-Hurwitz (1990) provides an extended analysis of the role of these factors. The publication of *The Silent Language* (1959), was followed by Hall's *The Hidden Dimension* (1966), and Smith's collection of articles in *Communication and Culture* (1966).

Teaching Intercultural Communication

By 1965, Michigan State University's Department of Communication was offering a course titled "Intercultural Communication" taught by Hideya Kumata. Several years later a similar course was offered at the University of Pittsburg. In July 1972, John Condon and Mitsuko Saito organized the Summer Conference on Intercultural Communication held at International Christian University. The conference attracted scholars from multiple disciplines with over 50 contributors and an attendance of over 2,000. One of the contributors, William S. Howell, established the doctoral program in intercultural communication at the University of Minnesota, the source of many of today's leading scholars in the field of intercultural communication.

Early Texts

In 1972, Condon and Yousef (1974) might have produced the first book written with the title of intercultural communication, but publishers were generally uninterested in publication until 1974 because there was no market for intercultural texts at the time (Kelly, 1999), and thus Condon and Yousef were second to Harms's (1973) *Intercultural Communication*. These books focused the attention of many students on the study of intercultural communication. Increasing interest in intercultural communication led to the beginning of the *International and Intercultural Communication Annual* in the mid-1970s, where much of the social science oriented research may be found. Asante, Newmark, and Blake (1979) and Asante and Gudykunst (1989) provide a number of summary articles. Theories of intercultural communication are summarized in Gudykunst (1983a), Kim (1988b), and Kim and Gudykunst (1988).

Extensive Research Programs

One of the more influential lines of research was established by Gudykunst and his colleagues who focused on three general areas applied to intercultural communication: uncertainty reduction processes, relationship issues, and communication effectiveness. In 1980, Gudykunst and Halsall generated a series of axioms and propositions synthesizing diverse research findings in various disciplines applicable to intercultural relationships. Gudykunst (1983b), reviewing the concept of *stranger*, derived a descriptive typology of stranger–host relationships that included newly arrived, newcomer, sojourner, stranger, immigrants, intruder, middle-man minority, and the marginal person. Related research focused on ethnic identity and close friendship communication patterns (Ting-Toomey, 1981), perceived similarity and social penetration (Gudykunst, 1985a), patterns of discourse (Sudweeks, Gudykunst, Ting-Toomey, & Nishida, 1990), insider and outsider perspectives (Gudykunst & Nishida, 1986b; Ting-Toomey, 1985), and self-consciousness and self-monitoring (Gudykunst, Yang, & Nishida, 1985).

Two influential articles (Gudykunst, 1988; Gudykunst, Chua, & Gray, 1987) are central in the examination of cultural influence on communication in interpersonal relationships. Early research tested Berger and Calabrese's (1975) uncertainty reduction theory by exploring similarities and differences in initial intracultural and intercultural encounters (Gudykunst, 1983c, 1985c; Gudykunst et al., 1987; Gudykunst & Nishida, 1984). Extension of the original model explored boundary conditions (Gudykunst, 1985a), attribution confidence in high- and low-context cultures (Gudykunst & Nishida, 1986a), influence of language (Gudykunst, Nishida, Koike,

& Shiino, 1986), social identity (Gudykunst & Hammer, 1988), group membership (Gudykunst, Nishida, & Schmidt, 1989), and anxiety reduction (Gao & Gudykunst, 1990).

Intercultural Competence

Dimensions of intercultural communication effectiveness have been investigated that tested sojourners' cultural perspectives (Gudykunst, Wiseman, & Hammer, 1977), participation in workshops (Gudykunst, 1979), decision-making style (Stewart, Gudykunst, Ting-Toomey, & Nishida, 1986), and ethnocentrism (Hall & Gudykunst, 1989). Kim (1988a) offered a broad-based perspective that synthesized various disciplinary viewpoints of adaptation including anthropology, communication, psychology, sociology, and sociolinguistics. Regardless of a sojourner's motivation for being in a new culture, all people share common adaptation experiences. Accordingly, as strangers they must cope with high levels of uncertainty and unfamiliarity based on their ambivalent status in the host community. Labels such as acculturation, adjustment, assimilation, and integration emphasize different aspects of the adaptation experience. Adaptation theory assumes that individuals can and do adapt to this new, unfamiliar culture. Consequently, the focus is on how adaptation is accomplished from a General Systems perspective that regards individuals and their host environment as codeterminants engaged in communication activities. Adaptation theory proposes assumptions, axioms, and theorems that increase understanding of, and ability to make predictions of, cross-cultural adaptation.

Studies of intercultural sensitivity and competence may be found in the work of Bennett and Hammer (e.g., Bennett, 1986, 1993; Bennett & Bennett, 2004a, 2004b) on their developmental model of intercultural sensitivity (DMIS), and on measuring intercultural sensitivity through the intercultural development inventory (IDI; Hammer, 1998; Hammer, Bennett, & Wiseman, 2003). This grounded theory approach derives a theory of intercultural development (DMIS) based on observing persons' responses to cultural difference, and the organization of the observations into presumed stages of increasing sensitivity to cultural difference. Six such stages are proposed, three *ethnocentric* and centrally based in the observer's culture: Denial of cultural difference, defense against cultural difference, and minimization of cultural difference. And three are *ethnorelative,* wherein the observer's culture of origin is experienced in the context of other cultures: acceptance of other cultures, adaptation to other cultures, and integration within another culture or cultures with the ability to move readily between cultures. The extent of movement between these six stages for an individual may be measured by Hammer and Bennett's IDI, representing the first five of the six DMIS stages. The IDI consists of 60 paper and pencil items drawn from interview statements. The items are designed to measure cognitive structure indicative of a given DMIS stage. This research represents an extensive group of studies using observation, theorizing, and measurement based on those observations, with the resulting theory and measuring instrument tested and verified by multiple methods. The DIMS and resulting IDI represent an impressive line of research, well founded and useful. Discussions of cultural competence may also be found in Leigh (1998), and in Hampden-Turner (1995).

Ethical Issues

A difficult problem with any research on intercultural competence, particularly but not exclusively in its application outside of the Western world, is how to confront ethical issues in the three ethnorelative stages. While a motorbike speeding down the street to market in Phnom Penh with two dozen live chickens wired to it by their feet may be compared by a person well into the ethnorelative stages with similar animal abuse conditions in a Western slaughterhouse or chicken coop, this may not hold true for attitudes toward cultural treatment of power, status, and sex. A major remaining question in intercultural communication is how to recognize the difference during the acquisition of successive ethnorelative stages in accepting cultural practices that the observing culture finds ethically abhorrent. For example, human trafficking, forced or even voluntary brothel work, FGM, the ritual animal sacrifices of Santeria, dog fighting, cock fighting, or the position of the old cleaning woman who is allowed as much of her pay to sleep under an outside stairwell with the rats and insects. Are these cultural or ethical issues? Clearly these examples involve both ethical and cultural issues, but the extent of emphasis on "culture" compared to that on "ethical" in the decisions made by the observer will result in quite different outcomes. One can and should, for example, point out the folly of applying Western norms to Eastern institutions and vice versa, yet there are major consequences for people and animals involved when the applications are or are not made. Is this the business of intercultural communication? It has to be, yet there are no simple answers to what makes the decision rule in these and similar instances one oriented by culture or by ethics. Whose culture is to rule, and whose ethics, and on what basis?

Doing Intercultural Research

How one studies intercultural communication depends on why it is being studied. Some scholars seek to build a theory of intercultural communication based on research grounded in the social sciences. Others seek to understand how people interpret behaviors and how the behaviors come to have meaning within a given culture. Governments and organizations are often concerned with introducing change into a particular culture to reduce a perceived evil, such as disease, lack of education, or the existence of human trafficking. People who must work in multicultural or cross-cultural settings, or who train others to do so, are concerned with providing practical advice for improving intercultural communication and easing the way of the trainee in the unfamiliar cultural setting. Others are concerned with the conflicts and misunderstandings which occur in cross-cultural and multicultural interactions. They seek to reduce prejudice and ethnocentrism and to promote peace and tranquility. Theory construction, cultural meaning, cultural change, practical advice to the sojourner, the reduction of prejudice and conflict between ethnic groups—these different goals of intercultural communication research lead to different research questions and different methods for answering them. No single method is always most appropriate in an intercultural setting. Method is always dependent upon the question being asked. Intercultural research is also complicated by the potential for violation of cultural norms, and by the "Heisenberg effect" of potentially changing the object of study through the means used to study it.

A Sample Study

Intercultural communication does not occur in a vacuum. It occurs in real situations with real people who have goals, desires, and much to gain or lose from the way a series of interconnected human interactions progresses. The nomothetic laws generated by research are ultimately useful if they can be applied to specific social interactions within specific cultural or cross-cultural settings. If they cannot be applied in practice, some may still remain useful heuristically, giving us diverse ways of conceptualizing intercultural communication and suggesting new studies and ways of relating to unlike others. When neither occurs, they remain just so much academic esoterica gathering dust on library shelves and computer hard drives.

One of the more interesting areas of intercultural communication is the struggle within immigrant families between parents and children, especially when an apparently socially liberal society such as the United States is the culture of entry. An inherent conflict exists between the role expectations for children in the old country and those in America. As one example, families in the Sunni Muslim community in Miami often experience conflict between parents and children. Parents complain of lack of respect, lack of obedience, willful disregard for and even ignorance of Muslim law, the Sharia, by their children. These are not the ways of the old country, and the parents are genuinely frightened of the unknown and the physical and moral dangers posed by the larger society.

Elements of the Problem

But the children have teenage friends in junior high or high school who can go unescorted to the mall. This is seen by immigrant parents as both a dangerous temptation inviting immoral activity and far too much freedom to ones so young, especially girls. The children want to go to the mall, to have fun, to be American. Such insolence can lead to punishments that would be regarded as physical abuse by American standards, and certainly by social workers. This introduces the threat of social or even governmental interference into the family's life. The parents may resort to real, verifiable threats to send their children back to the old country if they do not obey.

Male dominance introduces an added problem of husband–wife conflict, which would be accepted as normal in the old country. Some women see the need for control of the children in the old ways, in the face of the dangers posed by the existence of violence and street crime in American society, and also perceive the freedom and potential power granted by this freedom which is offered to both themselves and their children. But this freedom cannot be realized for the woman within the confines of a traditional marriage. The only way to achieve true freedom would be for the woman to leave her husband. But this would mean rejection by her extended family, which she cannot tolerate. She exists only within the nexus of the family. To let the children have their freedom while denying the same to herself seems intolerable. She may decide to sacrifice herself and side with the children allowing them some measure of freedom while denying freedom to herself. But usually she will decide to side with her husband. Once she does, she is more motivated to keep the children within the fold of the family and the old ways: If they stray, the blame will fall on her. She may then lose everything she has in terms of status in the family and in relationship to her husband, in addition to losing her children. She may even suffer the social death sentence of divorce because she could not keep the family together, a sentence which she has sought to avoid at all costs. The cultural norms that would resolve these problems in the old country are not applicable in the United States for both cultural and legal reasons.

A useful study might examine methods of managing such family conflicts in a way that keeps the family together, continues the Muslim beliefs and behaviors, yet allows small and gradual increases in freedom to all the participants and a gradual integration into the surrounding cultural nexus. Such a study would require integrating elements of ethnography, social science research methods, and, ultimately, of the diffusion of innovations, in order to be put into practice. In any applied setting, little advice is likely to be acted on which does not conform to the norms and belief systems of the participants. Rogers (1995) lists the criteria for likelihood of adoption of cross-cultural recommendations. The applied researcher in intercultural communication would be well advised to keep these recommendations in mind. The challenge is to determine a message strategy which both achieves goals and operates within the existing belief system under study.

Preliminary Considerations

A number of factors need to be considered in order to conduct the study. First, who is the client? If the study is applied, someone is paying for it, and for a reason. Second, what is the reason?

What is the problem as the client sees it? Failure to understand the reasons and reasoning behind the drive for an applied study can be a major source of problems in conducting, completing, and reporting the results of the study.

Third, is the problem, as seen by the client, a reasonable problem which can be studied in a useful manner? How will other groups involved in the problem perceive the purpose of the research and the research enterprise itself? Will there be persons or groups that are attempting to block the research or failing to cooperate with it? What can be done to phrase or rephrase the purpose and the sponsorship of the research and the way and by whom the participants are approached such that all or most parties involved can perceive ownership of the project and the results? How can this project be conceived in such a way that its results could be acted on in a manner which will help both the client and all other groups involved to achieve their goals in some manner? If questions such as these are not addressed prior to the start of data gathering the likelihood of success of the project will be reduced considerably. The project will be worth its cost only if the people and groups involved have some reasonable probability of acting on its recommendations. This point must be explained to and impressed upon the client prior to agreeing to conduct the study. Unless everyone benefits, the client will not benefit, for the results will probably not be implemented.

Fourth, is there a way that theory-driven questions could be integrated into the study without detracting from it? Applied intercultural research can often be a vehicle for testing portions of intercultural communication theories.

Fifth, what needs to be known in order to conduct the study and to achieve usable results, and, what do we already know? Answering these questions corresponds roughly to the literature review phase of typical academic research. In addition to conducting bibliographic searches for a literature review, a "walking around and looking and talking with people" phase is needed. If this pilot review of the people and situations to be studied is not conducted for at least a short time with a few people prior to the project, then at the end of the project the researchers are likely to find they have conducted a pilot review but with a large group of subjects and at considerable expense. The bibliographic review itself should include, but not be limited to, a search of the bibliographic databases available on the Internet. Both applied and theoretical research efforts need to be informed by past research. This information then needs to be sorted for applicability to the research problem. The research can then be designed and conducted.

Addressing the Issues

Assume that the client is the local Muslim Community Association. Assume further that the problem is phrased as one of how to keep families intact, with the children remaining faithful believers in Islam. The problem is translated to read that the level of overt conflict (Steinfatt & Miller, 1974) in the families needs to be reduced. The perceptions of the parents, the children, and the community at large need to be addressed. The researchers may need to attend local community functions, to talk with the people involved, and to talk privately with the children in addition to talking privately with the parents and elders. They will need to display the proper deference to the proper people, and dress, talk, and behave as though they understood the basic norms of the community. For example, men in the research group may need to eat first, with the men in the community in the dining area, while the women wait and eat later, with the community women in the kitchen. Attempts to force American norms onto the group from the start will indicate a lack of understanding and disrespect. Why should these people listen to the researchers about cultural issues if the researchers are so culturally insensitive?

If the researchers are perceived by any of the groups as either on the "side" of one group, or as aloof and distant, the effort will likely fail. Focus groups conducted as a part of the socializing after an evening community meeting can be especially helpful in this regard. Locating children who have actually left their families and the religion, to learn their perspectives, can also be quite helpful. Questionnaires and procedures giving the appearance of academic research may be more trouble than they are worth in applied efforts. Often the appearance of listening, combined with actual sensitive listening and note taking, can be far more revealing and effective than information produced through questionnaires, though it is usually difficult to convince editorial reviewers of this if later publication is desired. Interviews and focus groups with members of a Muslim group which is geographically removed from the group of interest may provide additional insights and information. But different groups can often have strikingly different problems and no firm conclusions should be drawn from work with these additional Muslim groups. If privacy can be maintained, asking members of a Muslim group which is geographically distant about conclusions and proposed solutions prior to presenting them to the client group may produce useful insights. Use of the IDI with each of the main parties might be considered as a way of measuring progress toward openness to cultural solutions, though repeated measurement with the instrument may introduce questions from the participants as well as additional measurement considerations.

One model useful in most such intercultural conflicts is based on getting the groups to sub-scribe to the norms of respect for the other's status position and views, and respectful accep-tance of the other's right to exist and to differ to an extent, within a predefined context. While everyone will usually agree with respect, and some will agree with acceptance, producing actual respect and actual acceptance through message strategies designed to reduce the conflict and tai-lored to each of the constituent groups is often the ultimate goal. The strategies themselves may be based on applications of theory according to the results of the focus groups and interviews. The message strategies must be acceptable, workable, and must meet the goals of the client and the other groups involved. Any workable message strategy set will usually have a minimum of two levels. The first level will be the initial strategy, and the second, an analysis of the various fallback positions depending on the response of the other to the initial communication attempt. Small-scale training of innovators might be part of the initial research proposal. Larger scale training proposals need to wait for the acceptance of the proposed solutions by the client and other groups involved. But without larger scale training, diffusion of the proposed solutions will be both less likely to occur and much slower in implementation.

References

Alasuutari, P. (1995). *Researching culture: Qualitative method and cultural studies*. Thousand Oaks, CA: Sage.

Andersen, M. L., & Collins, P H. (1992). *Race, class, and gender*. Belmont, CA: Wadsworth.

Asante, M. K., & Gudykunst, W. B. (Eds.). (1989). *The handbook of international and intercultural commu-nication*. Thousand Oaks, CA: Sage.

Asante, M. K., Newmark, E., & Blake, C. A. (Eds.). (1979). *The handbook of intercultural communication*. Thousand Oaks, CA: Sage.

Barfield, T. (Ed.). (2001). *The dictionary of anthropology*. London: Blackwell.

Barnlund, D. C. (1989). *Communicative styles of Japanese and Americans*. Belmont, CA: Wadsworth.

Bennett, M. J. (1986). A developmental approach to training for intercultural sensitivity. *International Journal of Intercultural Relations, 10*(2), 179–95.

Bennett, M. J. (1993). Towards ethnorelativism: A developmental model of intercultural sensitivity. In M. Paige (Ed.), *Education for the intercultural experience*. Yarmouth, ME: Intercultural Press.

Bennett, J. M., & Bennett, M. J. (2004a). *Developing intercultural competence: A reader*. Portland, OR: Intercultural Communication Institute.

Bennett, J. M., & Bennett, M. J. (2004b). Developing intercultural sensitivity: An integrative approach to global and domestic diversity. In D. Landis, J. M. Bennett, & M. J. Bennett (Eds.), *Handbook of intercultural training* (3rd ed., pp. 147–165). Thousand Oaks, CA: Sage.

Berger, C., & Calabrese, R. (1975). Some explorations in initial interactions and beyond: Toward a developmental theory of interpersonal communication. *Human Communication Research, 1,* 99–112.

Brislin, R. (1990). *Applied cross-cultural psychology.* Thousand Oaks, CA: Sage.

Brislin, R., & Yoshida, T (1994). *Intercultural communication training: An introduction.* Thousand Oaks, CA: Sage.

Cassirer, E. (1953). *The philosophy of symbolic forms: Vol. 1. Language* (R. Manheim, Trans.). New Haven, CT: Yale University Press.

Commission of Freedom of the Press. (1947). A *Free and responsible press: A general report on mass communications* (The Hutchins Commission report). Chicago: University of Chicago Press.

Condon, J. (1981). Values and ethics in communication across cultures: Some notes on the North American case. *Communication, 6,* 255–265.

Condon, J., & Yousef, F. S. (1974). *An introduction to intercultural communication.* Indianapolis, Bobbs-Merrill.

Diebold, A. R. (1965). A survey of psycholinguistic research, 1954–1964. In C. E. Osgood & T. A. Sebeok (Eds.), *Psycholinguistics* (pp. 205–291). Bloomington: Indiana University Press.

Dodd, C. H. (1982). *Dynamics of intercultural communication.* Dubuque, IA: William C. Brown.

Durkheim, E. (1897). *Le suicide; étude de sociologie [Suicide: A study in sociology].* Paris: F. Alcan.

Ellis, C., & Bochner, A. P. (1996). *Composing ethnography: Alternative forms of qualitative writing.* Walnut Creek, CA: AltaMira Press.

Fischer, J. L. (1974). Communication in primitive systems. In I. de Sola Pool, W. Schramm, F. W. Frey, N. Maccoby, & E. B. Parker (Eds.), *Handbook of communication* (pp. 313–336). Chicago: Rand McNally.

Fishman, J. A. (1960). A systematization of the Whorfian hypothesis. *Behavioral Science, 5,* 323–339.

Frey, E. W. (1974). Communication and development. In I. de Sola Pool, W. Schramm, E. W. Frey, N. Maccoby, & E. B. Parker (Eds.), *Handbook of communication* (pp. 337–461). Chicago: Rand McNally.

Gannon, M. J. (2004). *Understanding global cultures: Metaphorical journeys through 28 nations* (3rd ed.). Thousand Oaks, CA: Sage.

Gao, G., & Gudykunst, W. B. (1990). Uncertainty, anxiety, and adaptation. *International Journal of Intercultural Relations, 14,* 301–317.

Geertz, C. (1960). *The religion of Java.* Chicago/London: University of Chicago Press

Geertz, C. (1973). *The interpretation of cultures.* New York: Basic Books.

Geertz, C. (1983). *Local knowledge: Further essays in interpretive anthropology.* New York: Basic Books.

Geertz, C. (1988). *Works and lives: The anthropologist as author.* Stanford, CA: Stanford University Press.

Gibson, E. J., & McGarvy, H. R. (1937). Experimental studies of thought and reasoning. *Psychological Bulletin, 34,* 327–350.

Gladwin, C. H. (1989). *Ethnographic decision tree modeling.* Thousand Oaks, CA: Sage.

Glander, T. (1996). Wilbur Schramm and the Founding of Communication Studies. *Educational Theory, 46*(3), 373–391.

Glucksberg, S., & Danks, J. H. (1975). *Experimental psycholinguistics.* Hillsdale, NJ: Erlbaum.

Goldman, A. (1990). *For Japanese only: Intercultural communication with Americans.* Tokyo: Japan Times.

Goldman, A. (1994). *Doing business with the Japanese: A guide to successful communication, management, and diplomacy.* Albany, NY: State University of New York Press.

Gonzalez, A., Houston, M., & Chen, V. (1994). *Our voices: Essays in culture, ethnicity, and communication.* Los Angeles: Roxbury.

Greenberg, J. H. (1956). Concerning inferences from linguistic to nonlinguistic data. In H. Hoijer (Ed.), *Language in culture* (pp. 3–19). Chicago: University of Chicago Press.

Gudykunst, W. B. (1979). The effects of an intercultural communication workshop on cross-cultural attitudes and interaction. *Communication Education, 28,* 179–187.

Gudykunst, W. B. (1983a). Intercultural communication theory. In *International and intercultural communication annual.* Thousand Oaks, CA: Sage.

Gudykunst, W. B. (1983b). Toward a typology of stranger–host relationships. *International Journal of Intercultural Relations, 7*, 401–413.

Gudykunst, W. B. (1983c). Uncertainty reduction and predictability of behavior in low- and high-context cultures. *Communication Quarterly, 33*, 270–283.

Gudykunst, W. B. (1985a). The influence of cultural similarity, type of relationship, and self-monitoring on uncertainty reduction processes. *Communication Monographs, 52*, 203–217.

Gudykunst, W. B. (1985b). Intercultural communication: Current status and proposed directions. In B. Dervin & M. J. Voigt (Eds.), *Progress in communication sciences* (Vol. 6, pp. 1–46). Norwood, NJ: Ablex.

Gudykunst, W B. (1985c). A model of uncertainty reduction in intercultural encounters. *Journal of Language and Social Psychology, 4*, 79–98.

Gudykunst, W. B. (1987). Cross-cultural comparisons. In C. R. Berger & S. H. Chaffee (Eds.), *Handbook of communication science* (pp. 847–889). Thousand Oaks, CA: Sage.

Gudykunst, W. B. (1988). Culture and the development of interpersonal relationships. In J. Anderson (Ed.), *Communication yearbook* (Vol. 12, pp. 315–354). Thousand Oaks, CA: Sage.

Gudykunst, W. B. (Ed.). (1993). *Communicating in Japan and in the United States*. Albany, NY: State University of New York Press.

Gudykunst, W. B., Chua, E., & Gray, A. (1987). Cultural dissimilarities and uncertainty reduction processes. In M. McLaughlin (Ed.), *Communication yearbook* (Vol. 10, pp. 456–569). Thousand Oaks, CA: Sage.

Gudykunst, W. B., & Hammer, M. (1988). The influence of social identity and intimacy of interethnic relationships on uncertainty reduction processes. *Human Communication Research, 14*, 569–601.

Gudykunst, W. B., & Nishida, T (1984). Individual and cultural influences on uncertainty reduction. *Communication Monographs, 51*, 23–36.

Gudykunst, W. B., & Nishida, T (1986a). Attributional confidence in low- and high-context cultures. *Human Communication Research, 12*, 525–549.

Gudykunst, W. B., & Nishida, T. (1986b). The influence of cultural variability on perceptions of communication behavior associated with relationship terms. *Human Communication Research, 13*, 147–166.

Gudykunst, W. B., & Nishida, T (1994). *Bridging Japanese/North American differences*. Thousand Oaks, CA: Sage.

Gudykunst, W. B., Nishida, T., Koike, H., & Shiino, N. (1986). The influence of language on uncertainty reduction: An exploratory study of Japanese-Japanese and Japanese-North American interactions. In M. McLaughlin (Ed.), *Communication yearbook* (Vol. 9, pp. 555–575). Thousand Oaks, CA: Sage.

Gudykunst, W. B., Nishida, T., & Schmidt, K. (1989). Cultural, relational, and personality influences on uncertainty reduction processes. *Western Journal of Speech Communication, 53*, 12–29.

Gudykunst, W. B., Wiseman, R., & Hammer, M. (1977). Determinants of a sojourner's attitudinal satisfaction. In B. Ruben (Ed.), *Communication yearbook* (Vol. 1, pp. 415–425). New Brunswick, NJ: Transaction.

Gudykunst, W. B., Yang, S. M., & Nishida, T. (1985). A cross-cultural test of uncertainty reduction theory: Comparisons of acquaintance, friends; and dating relationships in Japan, Korea, and the United States. *Human Communication Research, 11*, 407–454.

Hall, E. T. (1959). *The silent language*. Garden City, NY: Doubleday.

Hall, E. T. (1966). *The hidden dimension*, Garden City, NY: Doubleday.

Hall, P. H., & Gudykunst, W. B. (1989). The relationship of perceived ethnocentrism in corporate cultures to the selection, training, and success of international employees. *International Journal of Intercultural Relations, 13*, 183–201.

Hammer, M. R. (1998). A measure of intercultural sensitivity: The Intercultural Development Inventory. In S. Fowler & M. Fowler (Eds.), *The intercultural sourcebook* (Vol. 2). Yarmouth ME: Intercultural Press.

Hammer, M. R., Bennett, M. J., & Wiseman, R. (2003). Measuring intercultural sensitivity: The Intercultural Development Inventory. In R. M. Paige (Guest Ed.), *Intercultural development* [Special issue]. *International Journal of Intercultural Relations, 27*(4), 421–443.

Hammersley, M. (1992). *What's wrong with ethnography?* New York: Routledge.

Hampden-Turner, C. (1995). *Stages in the development of intercultural sensitivity and the theory of dilemma reconciliation: Milton J. Bennett and Charles Hampden-Turner's approaches contrasted and combined.* Cambridge, UK: Cambridge University, The Judge Institute of Management Studies.

Harms, L. S. (1973). *Intercultural communication.* New York: Harper & Row.

Hatch, E. (1983). *Culture and morality: The relativity of values in anthropology.* New York: Columbia University Press.

Head, S. W. (1956). *Broadcasting in America: A survey of television and radio.* Boston: Houghton Mifflin.

Head, S. W. (1961). *A field experiment in the summertime use of open circuit television instruction to bridge the gap between high school and college.* Coral Gables, FL: University of Miami.

Head, S. W. (1974). *Broadcasting in Africa: A continental survey of radio and television.* Philadelphia: Temple University Press.

Head, S. W. (1985). *World broadcasting systems: A comparative analysis.* Belmont, CA: Wadsworth.

Hecht, M. L., Jackson, R. L., II, & Ribeau, S. A. (2003). *African American communication: Exploring identity and cultural interpretation* (2nd ed.). Mahwah, NJ: Erlbaum.

Heidbreder, E. (1948). Studying human thinking. In T. G. Andrews (Ed.), *Methods of psychology* (pp. 96–123). New York: Wiley.

Henle, P. (1958). Language, thought, and culture. In P. Henle (Ed.), *Language and culture* (pp. 1–24). Ann Arbor: University of Michigan Press.

Hovland, C. I., Janis, I. L., & Kelley, H. H. (1953). *Communications and persuasion: Psychological studies in opinion change,* New Haven, CT: Yale University Press.

Humphrey, G. (1951). *Thinking: An introduction to its experimental psychology.* New York: Wiley.

Johnson, D. M. (1950). Problem solving and symbolic processes. *Annual Review of Psychology, 1,* 297–310.

Jones, S. E. (1979). Integrating etic and emic approaches in the study of intercultural communication. In M. K. Asante, E. Newmark, & C. A. Blake (Eds.), *The handbook of intercultural communication* (pp. 57–74). Thousand Oaks, CA: Sage.

Kaplan, A. (1964). *The conduct of inquiry.* San Francisco: Chandler.

Kelly, W. (1999). Jack Condon's intellectual journey. *The Edge. The E-Journal of Intercultural Relations, 2*(1). http://www.interculturalrelations.com/v2i1Winter1999/w99kellycondon1.htm

Kim, Y. Y. (1986). *Interethnic communication current research.* Thousand Oaks, CA: Sage.

Kim, Y. Y (1988a). *Communication and cross-cultural adaptation.* Philadelphia: Multilingual Matters.

Kim, Y. Y. (1988b). On theorizing intercultural communication. In Y. Y. Kim & W. B. Gudykunst (Eds.), *International and intercultural communication annual* (Vol. 12, pp. 11–21). Thousand Oaks, CA: Sage.

Kim, Y. Y., & Gudykunst, W B. (1988). Theories in intercultural communication: *International and intercultural communication annual* (Vol. 12). Thousand Oaks, CA: Sage.

Klopf, D. W. (1987). *Intercultural encounters: The fundamentals of intercultural communication.* Englewood, NJ: Morton.

Kluckhohn, C. (1949). *Mirror for man: The relation of anthropology to modern life.* New York: Whittlesey House.

Kohls, R. L. (1984). *Survival kit for living overseas.* Yarmouth, ME: Intercultural Press.

Langer, S. K. (1942). *Philosophy in a new key.* Cambridge, MA: Harvard University Press.

Lasswell, H. (1948). The structure and function of communication in society. In L. Bryson (Ed.), *The communication of ideas* (pp. 7–51). New York: Harper.

Lazarsfeld, P. F. (1944). *The people's choice: How the voter makes up his mind in a presidential campaign.* New York: Duell, Sloan & Pearce.

Lee, P. (1996). *The Whorf theory complex: A critical reconstruction.* Philadelphia: J. Benjamins.

Leeds-Hurwitz, W. (1990). Notes in the history of intercultural communication: The Foreign Service Institute and the mandate for intercultural training. *Quarterly Journal of Speech, 76,* 262–281.

Leigh, J.W. (1998). *Communicating for cultural competence.* Boston: Allyn & Bacon.

Lenneberg, E., & Roberts, J. M. (1956). *The language of experience.* Bloomington: Indiana University Publication in Anthropology & Linguistics.

Lerner, D., & Schramm, W. (Eds.). (1967). *Communication and change in the developing countries.* Honolulu, Hawaii: East-West Center Press.

Malinowski, B. (1922). *Argonauts of the Western Pacific: An account of native enterprise and adventure in the archipelagoes of Melanesian New Guinea.* London: Routledge & Kegan Paul.

Mandell, S. (1931). The relation of language to thought. *Quarterly Journal of Speech, 17,* 522–531.

McPhail, T. (2006). *Global communication: Theories, stakeholders and trends* (2nd ed.). Malden, MA: Blackwell.

Mestenhauser, J. A., Marty, G., & Steglitz, I. (Eds.). (1988). *Culture, learning, and the disciplines: Theory and practice in cross-cultural orientation.* Washington, D.C.: National Association of Foreign Student Affairs.

Osgood, C. E., & Sebeok, T A. (1965). *Psycholinguistics.* Bloomington: Indiana University Press.

Park, R. E., & Burgess, E. W. (1924). *Introduction to the science of sociology.* Chicago: University of Chicago Press.

Pike, K. L. (1966). Etic and emic standpoints for the description of behavior. In A. G. Smith (Ed.), *Communication and culture* (pp. 152–163). New York: Holt, Rinehart & Winston.

Popper, K. R. (1968). *The logic of scientific discovery* (3rd ed.). London: Hutchinson.

Rogers, E. M. (1962). *The diffusion of innovations.* New York: Free Press.

Rogers, E. M. (1995). *Diffusion of innovations* (4th ed.). New York: Free Press.

Rogers, E. M. (1994). *A history of communication study: A biographical approach.* New York: Free Press.

Rogers, E. M., & Shoemaker, F. F. (1971). *Communication of innovations: A cross-cultural approach* (2nd ed.). New York: Free Press.

Rogers, E. M., & Steinfatt, T. M. (1999). *Intercultural communication.* Prospect Heights, IL: Waveland Press.

Ronai, C. R. (1996). My mother is mentally retarded. In C. Ellis & A. P. Bochner (Eds.), *Composing ethnography: Alternative forms of qualitative writing* (pp. 109–131). Walnut Creek, CA: AltaMira Press.

Rostow, W. W. (1952). *The process of economic growth.* New York: Norton.

Rostow, W. W., & Hatch, R. W. (1955). *An American policy in Asia.* Cambridge: MIT Technology Press.

Rostow, W. W., & Levin, A. (1953). *The dynamics of Soviet society.* New York: Norton.

Ryle, G. (1968). *The thinking of thoughts: What is "Le Penseur" doing?* (University Lectures, no.18). University of Saskatchewan. http://lucy.ukc.ac.uk/CSACSIA/Vol14/Papers/ryle_1.html

Samovar, L. A., & Porter, R. E. (1972, 1994). *Intercultural communication: A reader.* Belmont, CA: Wadsworth.

Sapir, E. (1921). *Language: An introduction to the study of speech.* New York: Harcourt, Brace, & World.

Sato, A. (1992). *Understanding Japanese communication.* Tokyo: Japan Times.

Schatzman, L., & Strauss, A. (1955). Social class and modes of communication. *American Journal of Sociology, 60,* 329–338.

Schramm, Wilbur L. (1954). *The process and effects of mass communication.* Urbana: University of Illinois Press.

Singer, M. R. (1987). *Intercultural communication: A perceptual approach.* Englewood Cliffs, NJ: Prentice-Hall.

Singhal, A., & Rogers, E. M. (2004). The status of entertainment-education worldwide. In A. Singhal, M. J. Cody, E. M. Rogers, & M. Sabido (Eds.), *Entertainment-education and social change* (pp. 3–20). Mahwah, NJ: Erlbaum

Slobin, D. T (1979). *Psycholinguistics.* Glenview, IL: Scott Foresman.

Smith, A. G. (Ed.). (1966). *Communication and culture.* New York: Holt.

Steinfatt, T. M. (1988, November). *Language and intercultural differences: Linguistic relativity.* "Top Three" paper, Intercultural Communication Division, Speech Communication Association, New Orleans, LA.

Steinfatt, T. M. (1989). Linguistic relativity: Toward a broader view. In S. Ting-Toomey & F. Korzenny (Eds.), *International and intercultural communication annual: Vol. 13. Language, communication and culture* (pp. 35–75). Thousand Oaks, CA: Sage.

Steinfatt, T. M. (2002). *Working at the bar: Sex work and health communication in Thailand.* Westport, CT: Greenwood.

Steinfatt, T., & Miller, G. R. (1974). Communication in game theoretic models of conflict. In G. R. Miller & H. W Simons (Eds.), *Perspectives on communication in social conflict* (pp. 14–75). Englewood Cliffs, NJ: Prentice-Hall.

Stewart, E. C., & Bennett, M. J. (1991). *American cultural patterns: A cross-cultural perspective*. Yarmouth, ME: Intercultural.

Stewart, L. P., Gudykunst, W. B., Ting-Toomey, S., & Nishida, T. (1986). The effects of decision-making style on openness and satisfaction within Japanese organizations. *Communication Monographs, 53*, 236–251.

Sudweeks, S., Gudykunst, W. B., Ting-Toomey, S., & Nishida, T. (1990). Developmental themes in Japanese-North American interpersonal relationships. *International Journal of Intercultural Relations, 14*, 207–233.

Ting-Toomey, S. (1981). Ethnic identity and close friendship in Chinese-American college students [Suppl.]. *International Journal of Intercultural Relations, 27*, S383–S406.

Ting-Toomey, S. (1985). Toward a theory of conflict and culture. In W. Gudykunst, L. Stewart, & S. Ting-Toomey (Eds.), *Communication, culture, and organizational processes* (pp. 71–86). Thousand Oaks, CA: Sage.

Vidich, A. J., & Lyman, S. M. (1994). Qualitative methods: Their history in sociology and anthropology. In N. K. Denzin & Y. S. Lincoln (Eds.), *Handbook of qualitative research* (pp. 23–59). Thousand Oaks, CA: Sage.

Vinacke, W. E. (1951). The investigation of concept formation. *Psychological Bulletin, 48*, 1–31.

Whorf, B. L. (1956). *Language, thought, and reality*. Cambridge, MA: MIT Press.

Wolcott, H. F. (1994). *Transforming qualitative data*. Thousand Oaks, CA: Sage.

Woodworth, R. S. (1938). *Experimental psychology*. New York: Holt.

Suggested Readings

Bennett, J. M., & Bennett, M. J. (2004a). *Developing intercultural competence: A reader*. Portland, OR: Intercultural Communication Institute.

Bennett, J. M., & Bennett, M. J. (2004b). Developing intercultural sensitivity: An integrative approach to global and domestic diversity. In D. Landis, J. M. Bennett, & M. J. Bennett (Eds.), *Handbook of intercultural training* (3rd ed., pp. 147–165). Thousand Oaks, CA: Sage.

Gudykunst, W. B. (1988). Culture and the development of interpersonal relationships. In J. Anderson (Ed.), *Communication yearbook* (Vol. 12, pp. 315–354). Thousand Oaks, CA: Sage.

Gudykunst, W. B., Chua, E., & Gray, A. (1987). Cultural dissimilarities and uncertainty reduction processes. In M. McLaughlin (Ed.), *Communication yearbook* (Vol. 10, pp. 456–569). Thousand Oaks, CA: Sage.

Hall, E. T. (1959). *The silent language*. Garden City, NY: Doubleday.

Hammer, M. R. (1998). A measure of intercultural sensitivity: The Intercultural Development Inventory. In S. Fowler & M. Fowler (Eds.), *The intercultural sourcebook* (Vol. 2). Yarmouth ME: Intercultural Press.

Hammer, M. R., Bennett, M. J., & Wiseman, R. (2003). Measuring intercultural sensitivity: The Intercultural Development Inventory. In R. M. Paige (Guest Ed.), *Intercultural Development* [Special issue] *International Journal of Intercultural Relations, 27*(4), 421–443.

Kim, Y. Y., & Gudykunst, W. B. (1988). *Theories in intercultural communication: International and intercultural communication annual* (Vol. 12). Thousand Oaks, CA: Sage.

Lee, P. (1996). *The Whorf theory complex: A critical reconstruction*. Philadelphia: J. Benjamins.

Leeds-Hurwitz, W. (1990). Notes in the history of intercultural communication: The Foreign Service Institute and the mandate for intercultural training. *Quarterly Journal of Speech, 76*, 262–281.

Pike, K. L. (1966). Etic and emic standpoints for the description of behavior. In A. G. Smith (Ed.), *Communication and culture* (pp. 152–163). New York: Holt, Rinehart & Winston.

Rogers, E. M. (1995). *Diffusion of innovations* (4th ed.). New York: Free Press.

Rogers, E. M., & Steinfatt, T. M. (1999). *Intercultural communication*. Prospect Heights, IL: Waveland Press.

Steinfatt, T. M. (1989). Linguistic relativity: Toward a broader view. In S. Ting-Toomey & F. Korzenny (Eds.), *International and intercultural communication annual: Vol. 13 Language, communication and culture* (pp. 35–75). Thousand Oaks, CA: Sage..

Steinfatt, T. M. (2002). *Working at the bar: Sex work and health communication in Thailand.* Westport, CT: Greenwood.

Whorf, B. L. (1956). *Language, thought, and reality.* Cambridge, MA: MIT Press.

21

INTRAPERSONAL COMMUNICATION AND IMAGINED INTERACTIONS

James M. Honeycutt, Christopher M. Mapp, Khaled A. Knasser, and Joyceia M. Banner

Before an interview for an internship position, a student imagines the conversation she is to have with the interviewer. She considers questions he may pose and prepares appropriate answers accordingly. In a different setting, a teenager may repeat a conversation he held with a classmate he admires, hoping to decode a love hint or find a concealed message. Such examples, which occur across cultures on a daily basis, testify to the pervasiveness of a communication phenomenon we refer to as intrapersonal communication.

In this chapter, we examine the following fundamental questions: "How can intrapersonal communication be operationalized into discrete variables that are manipulated and measured?" "How is intrapersonal communication linked with interpersonal communication and outcomes?" We briefly review some conceptualizations of intrapersonal communication followed by a discussion of the construct of imagined interactions. Imagined interactions have been used to operationalize the study of intrapersonal communication in terms of cognition and message processing. The importance of physiological correlates of intrapersonal communication variables is discussed as a method for reflecting process. Finally, a study is proposed exploring the association between physiological variables and imagined interaction variables among intimate couples.

Conceptualization of Intrapersonal Communication

Intrapersonal communication occurs inside each communicator (Stacks & Sellers, 1989). It takes different forms such as self-talk, inner speech, imagined interaction, daydreaming, listening, and emotional awareness, to name a few. Intrapersonal communication is considered as the foundation for all communication and a key source for understanding ourselves and our environment (Barker & Edwards, 1980). In differentiating levels of communication, intrapersonal communication is the most individualistic while mass communication is the most collectivistic. Depending on the number of communicators, interpersonal communication may have a number of intermediary positions on the individual–collectivistic continuum. Indeed, the distinction is between the Latin prefix "intra," which means "within," while the Latin prefix "inter" means "between." Hence, intrapersonal communication requires only one individual while interpersonal communication involves two or more people.

Many conversations, speech, decision making, planning, or conflict are mentally processed before they are communicated outwardly. Indeed, communication competence is often attributed to communicators who can articulate their own positions well. Hence, people often spend more time thinking about how they are going to communicate their positions as opposed to thinking about the viewpoints of others. Indeed, socioegocentrism argues that individuals pay more attention to their own monologues (Piaget, 1955) in order to state their own messages well while spending less time actively listening to others. Hewes (1986) provides eloquent examples of egocentric speech at cocktail parties. Persons tend to follow the basic conventions of dialogue including turn-taking and the use of trite acknowledgments of another person's statements ("Ya'll, you're right"). Yet, the meaningful dialogue of a normal conversation is missing because collective monologues are used. Diminished cognitive capacity prevents people from integrating both halves of a conversation and they rely on their own half in order to demonstrate at a minimum, that they can articulate their own point of view well. Hence, intrapersonal communication is clearly operating as individuals attend to their own thoughts and messages.

The processing of messages happens either deliberately with the individual actively reflecting on an issue (Smith, 1982), or unintentionally with thoughts popping up for no intended reason. Many scholars agree that intrapersonal communication is an inner, private communication process—in other words that the communicator is internally exchanging messages both as the sender and the receiver (Cunningham, 1989; Vocate, 1994). Yet, research in intrapersonal communication processes is vast. For example, researchers study the mind, functions of the brain, introspection, self-concept, cognition, and voicing (Heisel & Beatty, 2006; Honeycutt, 2003; LeDoux, 2003; Hamilton, 1996). Indeed, the study of intrapersonal communication has blossomed and given rise to specialized areas of research.

Cunningham (1989) distinguishes, however, between intrapersonal communication, where message exchange occurs inside a person's mind, and cognitive processing, which is basically the act of processing information. Stacks and Sellers (1989), on the other hand, include cognitive processing in the definition of intrapersonal communication when they break down the process into three areas: (1) the mental process (interpretation of self, others and environment); (2) the physical state (physiological aspects such as the impact of hormones); and (3) the biological–psychological system (relationship between the two areas).

To investigate the processes taking place in the three different areas, Stacks and Sellers (1994) propose two strategies for research. The first is observational and includes diaries, interviews, and paper and pencil measures (surveys). The second strategy is psychophysiological and involves physiological analyses (such as measuring heart rates, galvanic skin response, and respiration), measures of brain activity using the electroencephalogram (EEG) and dichotic listening. We have used both strategies in measuring intrapersonal communication. In terms of the mental process of interpreting the self and others, we briefly discuss the role of listening as part of intrapersonal communication.

Listening

Listening and hearing are two entirely separate functions of human communication. Although the two are sometimes confused, hearing strictly involves the physiological mechanisms and processes by which the ears receive and transmit sound as information to the brain. While hearing and listening often work in tandem, they are not necessarily dependent on each other, primarily because listening is an active process of comprehension that demands the listener to be cognitively alert (Witkin, 1993). Simply hearing sounds does not require one to screen or use a process of message selection. According to Barker (1971), listening requires actively focusing on specific sounds with a purpose, whereas hearing requires only passive reception of sounds. In a study by Werner (1975), people were found to spend about 55 percent of their time listening.

Listening can be divided into two main stages: signal processing and literal processing. The first, signal processing, is a mostly automatic process in which listeners analyze sounds for understanding (Anderson, 1990). The second stage, literal processing, determines the meaning or message behind the sounds. Listeners do this through two main strategies, forecasting and focusing.

Listeners do not just listen patiently for speakers to complete their meanings verbally (Marslen-Wilson & Tyler, 1980). Instead, listeners predict or forecast, sometimes erroneously, what the speaker will say next. According to Ellis and Beattie (1986), how well a listener can interpret a speaker's message depends largely on the speaker's ability to link together related concepts upon which the listener can focus. If hearing is the physiological part of the auditory process, then attending is the psychological aspect that describes the process of message selection whereby we screen sounds and filter for those needs and desires we most want met (Smeltzer & Watson, 1984).

Schemata are cognitive structures, rather like mental templates or "frames," that represent a person's knowledge about objects, people, or situations. They are derived from memory and prior experience. They simplify reality, setting up expectations about what is *probable* in relation to particular conversations. People use schemata to organize current knowledge and provide a framework for future understanding. Examples of schemata include rubrics, social roles, stereotypes, scripts, worldviews, archetypes, and prototypes. Through the use of schemata, many everyday situations do not require effortful thought; instead mindless or automatic thought is all that is required (Langer, 1997; Lee, 2005). People can quickly organize new perceptions into schemata and act effectively without effort. For example, many people have a schema for accelerating onto a highway through an entrance ramp and can apply it to new highways that they have never driven on.

New or novel situations may require the creation of scripts. Yet, we tend to assimilate information into preexisting categories because it requires less cognitive effort (Honeycutt, 1993; Mandler, 1984). Additionally, when hearing new information (e.g., listening to a lecture on physiological measures of arousal), people who hear information that activates a personal schema will listen to and recall more accurately and vividly that information as opposed to information that does not fit an existing schema (Edwards & McDonald, 1993).

After literal processing takes place, listeners usually reflect on what has been said, and if manifested as conflict in the form of imagined interactions, it can lead to a concept called "mulling." Mulling, the mental reliving of an argument, occurs when individuals replay conversations in their mind. Individuals often have retroactive imagined interactions in which they replay conversations. This use of retroactive imagined interactions allows individuals to revisit past episodes over and over and can also allow listeners to revisit the conflict online (during the course of a conversation) with the added benefit of reformulated points and counterpoints (Honeycutt, 1991, 1995).

It is important to note that when listeners, busy decoding messages from the speaker, wait to take their turn to talk, many do not simply sit in rapt attention at every word. Instead, their minds may wander, either formulating points of their own, engaging in self-talk, or day-dreaming and fantasizing. Indeed, this is a listening skill mentioned by Nichols (1987) in his classic article on skills for listening.

Listeners are advised to capitalize on thought speed. Most people encode messages more slowly than they decode them. Nichols states that we have about 400 words of thinking time to spare during every minute of speech. He wonders what people with excess thinking time do while someone is speaking. Many people become distracted because we are impatient with the slow progress of speaker encoding. Hence, thoughts may be diverted off the topic to other thoughts while periodically darting back to the speaker. Nichols advises listeners to speculate about what may be said next as well as to mentally summarize what the speaker has been saying. Hence, he is advising listeners to have imagined interactions with the speaker. Indeed, this advice reflects a proactive imagined interaction in which the listener is imagining what could be said (Honeycutt, 2003). Yet, some persons start to prepare counterarguments in advance of what is said while getting "lost" in the conversation. The speaker may have moved on to other points even though the listener may be mentally constructing arguments in response to earlier claims. When capitalizing on thought speed while listening, we can rehearse what we want to say. Indeed, research has revealed that this can help people reduce communication anxiety and increase speech fluency (Allen & Honeycutt, 1997). Imagined interactions and their functions are discussed next.

Imagined Interactions: A Construct for Operationalizing Intrapersonal Communication

Imagined interactions (IIs) are a type of social cognition and mental imagery grounded in symbolic interactionism and script theory in which individuals imagine conversations with significant others for a variety of purposes (Honeycutt, 2003; Honeycutt & Ford, 2003). The II construct has provided a beneficial mechanism for operationalizing the study of intrapersonal communication because the communication is internal and involves dialogues as well as emotional affect (individuals may feel a variety of emotions depending on what they are imagining). Often, individuals experience positive, negative, or mixed emotions (Zagacki, Honeycutt, & Edwards, 1992).

IIs are a type of daydreaming that have definitive characteristics and serve a number of functions including rehearsal, self-understanding, relational maintenance, managing conflict, catharsis, and compensation. For example, the conflict management functions explain how conflict is difficult to manage in everyday life such that it is hard to "forgive and forget." IIs are different from internal monologues and private speech. Internal monologues are self-talk in which an individual talks to him- or herself in both speaking and listening roles (Honeycutt & Ford, 2001). It is speech directed toward the self from the self. Private speech is where an individual speaks aloud to him- or herself. Roloff and Ifert (1998) discuss how private speech may occur in isolation as well as in the presence of others.

There are six functions of IIs. IIs serve to maintain relationships as intrusive thinking, which occurs when the partner is thought about outside of his or her physical presence. A second function of IIs is rehearsing and planning messages. Individuals report how they prepare for important encounters and even think of various messages depending on the response of the interaction partner. The third function is self-understanding. IIs allow people to clarify their own thoughts and promote understanding of their own views. The catharsis function allows people to release feelings and vent feelings of frustration or joy. The fifth function is compensation as IIs may be used to compensate for the lack of actual conversations. These functions are not independent of each other. Some of them may occur simultaneously. For example, compensating for the lack of real interaction in a long-distance relationship may be used to keep the relationship alive as well as rehearsing what will be said at the next telephone conversation.

The final function is conflict management. Individuals relive old arguments while simultaneously imagining statements for ensuing encounters. Conflict is kept alive within our minds as people relive old arguments in our minds. For example, we interviewed a famous actor from the Star Trek show who still recalls old arguments from her ex-husband that occurred over 30 years ago because the arguments were memorable and affected her self-concept. Individuals may be more likely to recall arguments rather than positive encounters because of the negativity bias. According to the negativity bias, negative impressions are remembered more than positive ones (Ito, Larsen, Smith, & Cacioppo, 1998). For example, if we give you three compliments and a criticism, the criticism is more likely to be recalled because it may provide more information that challenges your self-concept.

People ruminate about arguments and in some cases, become obsessed with them. Research has revealed that vengeful people ruminate on the perceived injustice that they have received and seek revenge (McCullough, Bellah, Kilpatrick, & Johnson, 2001). Rumination is associated with having retro and proactive IIs as interaction scenes are replayed, rehearsed, or both (Honeycutt, in press). Furthermore, self-focused rumination occurs when people repetitively focus on themselves and on the cause and implications of negative feelings (Lyubomirsky, Tucker, Caldwell, & Berg, 1999).

Rumination is an example of the negative consequences of IIs. Conflict is kept alive in terms of conversational memory as individuals reflect on prior arguments. In fact, conflict is associated with negative valence as well as self-dominant IIs in which individuals report more verbal imagery compared to visual imagery such as imagining the scene of the II or nonverbal elements (Zagacki, Edwards, & Honeycutt, 1992). When verbal imagery is used, more emphasis is concentrated on the content of the message itself, while visual imagery is associated with pictorial images. Hence, imagined conflict tends to be associated with more emphasis on the message (Zagacki et al., 1992).

The conflict management function has resulted in an axiomatic theory explaining why conflict is enduring, may be constructive or destructive, and can erupt anytime in interpersonal relationships (Honeycutt 2003, 2004, in press; Honeycutt & Cantrill, 2001). The theory contains 3 axioms and 9 theorems. In terms of its axioms, the theory assumes that an interpersonal relationship is maintained and developed through thinking and dwelling on a relationship partner outside of actual conversations and that managing conflict begins at the intrapersonal level of communication in terms of IIs. Communication is a critical foundation of interpersonal relationships such that the communication is the relationship and that a major theme of interpersonal relationships is conflict management (e.g., cooperation-competition). One of the theorems is concerned with physiology, which is discussed next.

Physiology

Theorem 6 of II conflict-management theory states that recurring conflict is a function of brain, neurotransmitter activity in which neurons are stimulated (Honeycutt, 2004). Communication theorists indicate the importance of neurobiological factors in determining traits such as communication apprehension and verbal aggression (Beatty, Heisel, Hall, Levine, & LaFrance, 2002). Hence, there is some support that there is a biological link to conflict, particularly verbal aggression. If certain communicative characteristics can be linked to biological determinants, then it seems logical that likelihood to engage in conflict could be linked to such factors as well (cf., Beatty & McCroskey, 1998). Hence, the physiology of intrapersonal communication is addressed in terms of managing ongoing conflict with intimates, rivals, work associates, or family members. This is based on the premise that emotions are experienced (negative, positive, mixed). Indeed, numerous studies reveal that people have a wide range of emotions when imagining conversations (Honeycutt, 2003).

Communication is filled with emotion and arousing (Guerrero & Andersen, 1988). Endorphins and adrenalin may be released depending on the situation. For example, thinking about conversations that are likely to be filled with arguments affects the autonomic nervous system (Honeycutt, in press). Interpersonal conflict often makes people vigilant and alert in order to be alert to surroundings. Physiological arousal accompanies changes in emotions (Andersen, Guerrero, & Trost, 1998; Schacter & Singer, 1962).

The autonomic nervous system regulates involuntary body functions, including those of the heart and intestine. It controls blood flow, digestion, and temperature regulation. The autonomic nervous system has two divisions: the sympathetic nervous system (SNS) accelerates heart rate, constricts blood vessels, and raises blood pressure; the parasympathetic nervous system slows heart rate, increases intestinal and gland activity, and relaxes sphincter muscles. The sympathetic nervous system is a fight/flight system that expends energy while the parasympathetic system conserves energy. Both systems influence blood pressure. The sympathetic reduces motility of the stomach and intestines while the parasympathetic increases motility. Most of the organs and glands are controlled by the autonomic nervous system and have the dual regulation of excitement or arousal and calm.

Our ancestors' physiology evolved to deal rapidly with physical threats such as fighting a rival for food or fleeing from predators (Sapolsky, 2005). In contemporary society, the SNS becomes activated when faced with a psychological or social threat. For example, you may be faced with a dilemma when your partner asks you what you think about his or her new wardrobe (which you dislike) and you want to be polite.

Lying and deception are also associated with arousal; hence, the use of galvanic skin response. Once activated, the SNS releases epinephrine, norepinephrine, and cortisol into the bloodstream. Correspondingly, there is increased respiration, blood pressure, heartbeat, and muscle tension. Research reveals that deceivers demonstrate greater sympathetic activation than unaroused truth tellers (deTurck & Miller, 1985).

The second part of the autonomic nervous system is the parasympathetic nervous system (PNS). The parasympathetic division functions with actions that do not require immediate reaction. The PNS does essentially the opposite of the SNS: it decreases heart rate, increases digestion, and so on. Hence the relaxation response turns SNS arousal *off* by turning *on* the PNS. So, in essence, you don't really control the relaxation response; instead, you do the things that result in the PNS taking control.

Aside from temperature and perspiration changes, skin plays a role in communication because humans are highly social animals. Various emotions such as anger or embarrassment may be reflected in changes of skin color. To say that communication involves one organ system or one nervous system would be in error; messaging involves every cell of the human being.

Physiological arousal involves the autonomic nervous system in a state of adrenalin release and includes pulse (heartbeats per minute), *interbeat intervals* (IBI), and somatic activity measured in terms of a wrist monitor (Honeycutt, in press). *Somatic activity* tracks wrist and hand movements used while gesturing. It reflects kinetic energy release and tension release through motion. IBI is a measure of the time in milliseconds between adjacent heartbeats. High IBI rates are related to increased levels of adrenalin, anxiety, and arousal (Porges, 1985). The lower the IBI value, the shorter the cardiac beat which reflects a faster heart rate. Under normal conditions, the heart's rate is under control of the parasympathetic nervous system. Generally, resting heart rates for men are 70 and 80 for women according to the American Heart Association. Heart rates above 105 are high, and above the effects of exercise (Rowell, 1986). We always take a baseline measure of heart rate before engaging in experimental stimuli. We use the baseline measure and age as a covariate in analyzing subsequent mean differences.

The measurement of heart rate variables is important in physiological research. The electromagnetic signal that the heart sends to the brain and every other cell as well is the most powerful signal in the body (Hughes, Patterson, & Terrell, 2005). Moreover, Childre and Martin (1999) demonstrate how the heart helps people respond to environmental and contextual cues through the production of mood-enhancing hormones. Damasio (2003) shows that people cannot make decisions without processing emotional information that incorporates beliefs about how positive and negative the situation is. These judgments reflect the synthesis of both heart and brain functions weaving together cognition and emotion in a joint, intertwined fabric.

Yet, the measurement of heart rate must be cautious. Behnke (1989) cautions researchers to be cautious about definitional issues. For example, should heart rate be averaged over the entire experiment or should averages be computed for various meaningful events? How these averages are computed and should the operational definition of physiological arousal correct for effects of other physiological responses such as respiration, sweating, or brain cortical activity? As noted earlier, we factor our baseline heart rates and instead use a running average of arithmetic means utilizing one-minute time windows.

There is a classic critique of physiological arousal by Lacey (1967) in which he demonstrated that laboratory experiments often invoke anxiety-producing stimuli resulting in higher intercorrelations. He notes that there is evidence for both association and no association across physiological measures. Yet, these intercorrelations are lower when positive stimuli are involved. Disassociation occurs under mild, neutral, or positive conditions while associations are stronger under negative conditions. Therefore, we have participants report on both positive and negative topics of interaction and report independent correlations between each of the physiological measures and outcome variables including various functions of IIs. For example, blood pressure and heart rate do not always rise together. If blood pressure increases sharply, then there are stretch receptors in the arch of the heart's aorta that join the carotid sinus which are connected to cranial nerves in the lower brain stem. These nerves act to inhibit cortical activity in the brain and lower heart rate.

Sample Study

A criticism of communication research is that components of communication are often studied in isolation from another. Yet, any theory or explanation of communication ultimately, must deal with three components: input-throughput-output. Many communication studies deal with two components; input-output, because the actual process of communication is ignored (Honeycutt, in press).

Input reflects preexisting attitudes, beliefs, experiences, or personality that is brought into a conversation. This is often measured through self-report surveys or inventories. Throughput has commonly been referred to as "process" and represents the actual behaviors and messages (verbal and nonverbal) that are transmitted. Interactions may be monitored and coded in order to determine a variety of communication strategies (statements or messages) that are used. Yet, it is common for hypothetical scenarios to be used in surveys rather than observing behavior. The fact of the matter is that behavioral observation is costly because of the time required to observe communicators as well as code the behaviors. Coders have to be trained and intercoder reliability established in order to establish that the coding scheme is valid. The time cost to observe 100 subjects may be very expensive, while 100 surveys can be administered in minutes as well as electronically coded very quickly if online HTML protocol programs are used. The data can be automatically downloaded to a spreadsheet program for statistical analyses. Finally, output, also referred to as outcome, reflects any arbitrary variable that the researcher may be interested in such as attraction, satisfaction, postinteraction attitudes, desires, emotional ratings, impressions, and so forth. Outcomes tend to be measured through simple survey instruments. As noted above, numerous studies are simple input-output studies in which surveys and hypothetical scenarios are used in lieu of actual coding of verbal and nonverbal behaviors, which are costly and time-consuming.

IIs are primarily input and output. Indeed, a proactive II represents expectations about what may happen during a conversation. They reside within the individual while ignoring actual communication processes. However, it is possible to link IIs with throughput which is done in our sample study. IIs can be induced in people and then the actual conversation can be monitored. Furthermore, we can obtain continuous physiological data while the subjects are doing the experiment.

Rationale

People easily engage in conversations with others on a daily basis across a variety of topics; however, when there is conflict, it is difficult to initiate the conversation. A confrontation episode is initiated when one participant signals the other participant that his or her behavior has violated (or is violating) a rule or expectation for appropriate conduct within the relationship or situation. Unfortunately, conflict is often associated with negative affect in interpersonal relationships; therefore the response to negative affect in a relationship may prompt an individual to avoid the conflict instead of communicating about the problem. These conclusions are similar to Gottman's (1994) studies of negative affect and reciprocity. The negative affect reciprocity model states that if one partner is negative (for example, angry), the spouse is much more likely to be negative than he or she would be. The negative affect is met with a negative response which produces a cycle of negative affect which can then escalate. Negative affect reciprocity becomes like an absorbing state that once it is entered into, it is difficult to exit. Indeed, some studies show gender differences in which men are poorer at self-soothing themselves compared to women. Once aroused, women take less time to return to a basal resting state in terms of blood pressure and heart rate variability (Gottman, 1994). Indeed, some studies reveal that brooding and ruminating about grievances may be worse for men than women. The rumination clearly reflects intrapersonal communication as individuals replay prior arguments (Honeycutt, 2003; McCullough, Bono, & Root, 2007).

A study by Sapolsky, Stocking, and Zillman (1977) describes how men and women participants were provoked to anger by their partners using hypothetical scenarios. They were given the opportunity to immediately respond after provocation or after a 6-minute wait. Waiting reduced arousal in women, but not in men. Gottman (1994) surmises that males may be worse at self-soothing than females and be more socialized to ruminate for the purpose of revenge. Thus, it is been hypothesized that men withdraw from sensitive discussions in personal relationships in order to prevent possible arousal (e.g., Gottman, 1994; Gottman & Levenson, 1988; Tannen, 2002). Still, other studies have reached conflicting conclusions. For example, Kiecolt-Glaser et al. (1996) suggest that in regards to marriage, wives are more reactive and that this explains the finding that wives exhibit poorer health than husbands in distressed marriages. Because their studies differ in methods and samples, a direct comparison of Gottman and Kiecolt-Glaser's gender findings is beyond the scope of our study.

In laboratory settings, women typically will start up a conversation about negative topics (Gottman, Coan, Carrerre, & Swanson, 1998). We also believe this is true in imagined interaction as prior research reveals sex differences with women reporting more imagined interactions than men as well as more specificity and details (Edwards, Honeycutt, & Zagacki, 1989; Honeycutt, 2003). Start-up is defined as the escalation of conflict from one partner's neutral affect to the other partner's negative affect. Gottman and Levenson (1988) proposed that the woman's likelihood to start up negative conversations is based on a biological difference between the sexes. Their hypothesis was that men are in some ways more reactive to stress than women. Gottman (1994) proposed that emotionally, males are flooded by lower levels of negative affect than are females. Because of the aversive nature of physiological arousal, men may attempt to avoid negative affect in close relationships because it is more physiologically punishing for them than for women. Since it is harder for men to physiologically soothe their own responses to negative affect, men avoid negative start-ups by avoiding conflict altogether. In addition, research by Gottman and Levenson (1988), proposed that negative affect pervades unhappy marriages in which men withdraw emotionally, and women do not. Therefore, the happiness of the marriage may depend on the wife's ability to bring up a conflict with as little negative affect as possible (soft start-up).

Hypotheses

Borrowing from Gottman's (1994) work, we hypothesize the following in linking intrapersonal and interpersonal communication processes:

H_1: In intimate, heterosexual relationships, women soften their start-up by not escalating from neutral to negative affect.

H_2: When given a choice, men will choose to talk about a topic with positive affect rather than negative affect.

H_3: There will be physiological correlates of imagined interaction and actual conversation.

Participants

Students are recruited from various undergraduate courses at the Louisiana State University using snowball sampling in which they can receive extra credit points. Students are encouraged to bring a close, intimate partner to our physiological lab popularly known as the "Relation Station Matchbox" or to recruit someone from their social network who would like to see a picture of their heart-rate graph after they have done the experiment. They are required to have been in a committed romantic relationship for a period of time no less than six months.

Procedure and Instrumentation

The couples come to our interaction laboratory. Upon entering the lab, they are connected to portable, unobtrusive physiological monitors that measure heartbeats per minute, interbeat interval, and wrist activity. They wear a comfortable, elastic, chest belt underneath the sternum and a wrist cuff. We let them decide which wrist to place the cuff on. Research on gesturing indicates little difference in gesturing between hands when participants were asked to describe how to illustrate how a mechanical device works with the aid of a predrawn diagram, regardless of whether the individual is left or right handed (Eisenstein & Davis, 2007). After three minutes, the meter signals the end of the baseline measurement time period. These readings are used as covariates in subsequent analyses controlling for baseline measures.

Next, the partners are separated: one partner imagines discussing a pleasing topic while the other imagines discussing a displeasing topic. We alternately assign men and women the pleasing/displeasing topic role. This allows us to measure agenda initiation when they are reunited to see whose topic is discussed first and if the males defer discussing the displeasing topic when they are in that condition.

Both partners complete the Survey of Imagined Interaction (SSI) (Honeycutt, 2003; in press) as well as demographic information about age, relational duration, and happiness. The following dimensions of IIs are measured: rehearsal, discrepancy, catharsis, conflict management, relational management. After completing the SII, they complete a form that lists 27 topics and they are asked to rate how satisfied they are with the topic (Honeycutt, 1989). Sample topics include social life, job satisfaction, how they argue, how they communicate, chemical dependency, and how decisions are made. After indicating the degree of satisfaction for each topic, they are asked to circle the topic(s) that they are most displeased with or the ones that they are most pleased with. Then, they are asked to take up to five minutes and role play by speaking out loud and having a conversation with their partner about the topic that is most displeasing or pleasing. The individual is to imagine what he or she would say in terms of counterarguments or reactions to what the partner is saying. After doing this, the physiological meter is signaled to indicate the end of the time period for the induced II.

The partners are reunited in our lab. Then they are instructed to discuss their respective topics for up to five minutes. An important instruction is for them to decide which topic is initially discussed. These instructions allow for the measurement of agenda initiation. After five minutes, a third signaling to the physiological meter is done after the actual conversation in order to test heart-rate differences between the induced II and actual conversation time periods. Following this signaling, the experimental session ends with each partner completing some postinteraction surveys using 7-point Likert-type items in which they rate their own and their partner's start-up as well as how satisfied they were with the preceding communication (Hecht, 1978).

Partner Evaluations of Soft versus Harsh Start-Up

Each partner is asked to give a series of 20 ratings on how harsh start-up was a problem in the actual conversation. Sample items include: My partner was very critical of me discussing his or her topic. My partner raised issues in an insulting manner. I felt picked on by my partner. My partner was unnerving and unsettling when bringing up the issue. These items are modified from Gottman and Silver's (1999) harsh start-up questionnaire and will be factor analyzed to determine the underlying dimensions. Reliable factors will be used in subsequent data analyses.

Data Analysis

The analysis uses a 2 (male/female) × 2 (pleasing/displeasing topic) factorial design with the initial heartbeats per minute and interbeat intervals specified as baseline covariates. A multivariate analysis of covariance can be used with the following dependent variables: heartbeats per minute, interbeat intervals, wrist activity, and ratings of start-up. Additional analyses can use the II indices and ratings of relationship happiness. It is possible to treat the physiological variables as repeated measures contrasting physiological changes in the induced II condition and in the actual conversation.

Summary

Interest in intrapersonal communication has grown rapidly over the years. In this regard, the National Communication Association has a special division called "Communication and Social Cognition" that began as a commission in 1986. Despite a variety of definitions, there appears to be agreement that intrapersonal communication is the study of information and cognitive processing. Hence, studies involve both psychological and physiological perspectives. The brain, along with the rest of the nervous system, serves as the processing conduit for messages. Indeed, the electromagnetic signals of the heart that are sent to the brain are the strongest in the human body. Hence, heart-rate variability has proven to be a robust measure of physiological arousal given its conduit to the brain.

The study of imagined interaction has a long history and has proven to be a good construct for the measurement of intrapersonal communication. IIs serve a variety of functions and can be measured as a personality trait as well as in specific contexts in which individuals imagine conversations with others and then the actual conversation can be measured as well as assessing a variety of postinteraction outcomes including communication satisfaction.

The sample study is offered as a way to continue the exciting study of intrapersonal communication that links the major components of communication: input (preexisting beliefs, attitudes, personality traits brought into the encounter), throughput (the actual communication encounter), and output (postinteraction assessment of ratings of the communication).

References

Allen, T. H., & Honeycutt, J. M. (1997). Planning, imagined interaction, and the nonverbal display of anxiety. *Communication Research, 24,* 64–82.

Andersen, P. A., Guerrero, L. K., & Trost, M. R. (1998). Communication and emotion: Basic concepts and approaches. In P. A. Andersen & L. K. Guerrero (Eds.), *Handbook of communication and emotions* (pp. 5–29).San Diego, CA: Academic Press.

Anderson, J. (1990). *Cognitive psychology and its implications.* New York: Freeman.

Barker, L. (1971). *Listening behavior.* Englewood Cliffs, NJ: Prentice-Hall.

Barker, L. L., & Edwards, R. (1980). *Intrapersonal communication.* Dubuque, IA: Gorsuch Scarisbrick.

Beatty, M. J., Heisel, D. A., Hall, A. E., Levine, T. R., & LaFrance, B. H. (2002). What can we learn from the study of twins about genetic and environmental influences on interpersonal affiliation, aggressiveness, and social anxiety? A meta-analytic study. *Communication Monographs, 69,* 1–18.

Beatty, M. J., & McCroskey, J. C. (1998). Interpersonal communication as temperamental expression: A communibiological paradigm. In J. C. McCroskey, J. A. Daly, M. M. Martin, & M. J. Beatty (Eds.), *Communication and personality: Trait perspectives* (pp. 41–68). Cresskill, NJ: Hampton.

Behnke, R. W. (1989). Issues of measurement, instrumentation, and analysis of physiological variables. In C. V. Roberts & K. W. Watson (Eds.), *Intrapersonal communication: Original essays* (pp. 203–216). New Orleans, LA: SPECTRA/ Gorsuch-Scarisbrick.

Childre, D. L., & Martin, H. (1999). *The heartmath solution.* San Francisco, CA: Harper.

Cunningham, S. B. (1989). Defining intrapersonal communication. In C. V. Roberts, K. W. Watson, & L. L. Barker (Eds.), *Intrapersonal communication processes* (pp. 82–94). New Orleans, LA: SPECTRA/ Gorsuch-Scarisbrick.

Damasio, A. (2003). *Looking for Spinoza.* Orlando, FL: Harcourt.

deTurck, M. A., & Miller, G. R. (1985). Deception and arousal: Isolating the behavioral correlates of deception. *Human Communication Research, 12,* 181–201.

Edwards, R., Honeycutt, J. M., & Zagacki, K. S. (1989). Gender differences in imagined interactions. *Sex Roles, 21,* 259–268.

Edwards, R., & McDonald, J. (1993). Schema theory and listening: In A. Wolvin & C. Coakley (Eds.), *Perspectives on listening* (pp. 60–77). Norwood, NJ: Ablex.

Eisenstein, J., & Davis, R. (2007, February 8). Natural gesture in descriptive monologues. Retrieved February 8, 2007, from http://rationale.csail.mit.edu/publications/Eisenstein2003 Natural.pdf.

Ellis, A., & Beattie, G. (1986). *The psychology of language & communication.* London: Weidenfeld & Nicolson.

Gottman, J. M. (1994). *What predicts divorce?* Mahwah, NJ: Erlbaum.

Gottman, J. M., Coan, J., Carrere, S., & Swanson, C. (1998). Predicting marital happiness and stability from newlywed interactions. *Journal of Marriage and the Family, 60,* 5–22.

Gottman, J. M., & Levenson, R. W. (1988). The social psychophysiology of marriage. In P. Noller & M. A. Fitzpatrick (Eds.), *Perspectives on marital interaction* (pp. 182–200). Clevedon, UK: Multilingual Matters.

Gottman, J. M., & Silver, N. (1999). *The seven principles for making marriage work.* New York: Crown.

Hamilton, M. A. (1996). Verbal auditory hallucination and the invention of alter-ego mental constructs. In J. Aitken & L. J. Shedletsky (Eds.), *Intrapersonal communication processes* (pp. 151–158). Annandale, VA: Speech Communication Association.

Hecht, M. (1978). The conceptualization and measurement of interpersonal communication satisfaction. *Human Communication Research, 4,* 253–264.

Heisel, A. D., & Beatty, M. J. (2006). Are cognitive representations of friends' request refusals implemented in the orbitofrontal and dorsolateral prefrontal cortices? A cognitive neuroscience approach to "theory of mind" in relationships. *Journal of Social and Personal Relationships, 23,* 249–265.

Hewes, D. E. (1986). A socio-egocentric model of group decision-making. In R. Y. Hirokawa & M. S. Poole (Eds.), *Communication and group decision-making* (pp. 265–292). Newbury Park, CA: Sage.

Honeycutt, J. M. (1989a). Satisfaction with marital issues and topics scale. In J. Touliatos, B. F. Perlmutter, & M. A. Straus (Eds.), *Handbook of family measurement techniques.* Newbury Park, CA: Sage.

Honeycutt, J. M. (1989b). Satisfaction with marital issues and topics scale. In J. Touliatos, B. F. Perlmutter, & M. A. Straus (Eds.) *Handbook of Family Measurement Technique* (p. 92). Newbury Park, CA: Sage.

Honeycutt, J. M. (1991). Imagined interactions, imagery and mindfulness/mindfulness. In R. Kunzendorf (Ed.), *Mental imagery* (pp.121–128). New York: Plenum.

Honeycutt, J. M. (1993). Components and functions of communication during initial interaction with extrapolations to beyond. In S. Deetz (Ed.), *Communication yearbook* (Vol. 16, pp. 461–491). Newbury Park, CA: Sage.

Honeycutt, J. M. (1995). Imagined interactions, recurrent conflict and thoughts about personal relationships: A memory structure approach. In J. E. Aitken & L. J. Shedletsky (Eds.), *Intrapersonal communication processes* (pp.138–150). Plymouth, MI: Speech Communication Association and Midnight Oil Multimedia.

Honeycutt, J. M. (2003). *Imagined interaction: Daydreaming about communication.* Cresskill, NJ: Hampton.

Honeycutt, J. M. (2004). Imagined interaction conflict-linkage theory: Explaining the persistence and resolution of interpersonal conflict in everyday life. *Imagination, Cognition, and Personality, 23,* 3–25.

Honeycutt, J. M. (in press). Physiology and imagined interactions. In J. M. Honeycutt (Ed.), *Imagine that: Studies in imagined interaction.* Cresskill, NJ: Hampton.

Honeycutt, J. M., & Cantrill, J. G. (2001). *Cognition, communication, and romantic relationships.* Mahwah, NJ: Erlbaum.

Honeycutt, J. M., & Ford, S. G. (2001). Mental imagery and intrapersonal communication: A review of research on Imagined Interactions (IIs) and current developments. In W. B. Gudykunst (Ed.), *Communication yearbook* (Vol. 25, pp. 315–345). Mahwah, NJ: Erlbaum.

Hughes, M., Patterson, B., & Terrell, J. B. (2005). *Emotional intelligence in action.* San Francisco: Pfeiffer.

Ito, T. A., Larsen, J. T., Smith, N. K., & Cacioppo, J. T. (1998). Negative information weighs more heavily on the brain: The negativity bias in evaluative categorizations. *Journal of Personality and Social Psychology, 75,* 887–900.

Kiecolt-Glaser, J. K., Newton, T., Cacioppo, J. T., MacCallum, R. C., Glaser, R., & Malarkey, W. B. (1996). Marital conflict and endocrine function: Are men really more physiologically affected than women. *Journal of Consulting and Clinical Psychology, 64,* 324–332.

Lacey, J. L. (1967). Somatic response patterning and stress: Some revisions of activation theory. In M. H. Appley & R. Trumbull (Eds.), *Psychological stress: Issues in research* (pp. 14–37). New York: Appleton-Century-Crofts.

Langer, E. (1997). *The power of mindful learning.* Reading, MA: Addison-Wesley.

LeDoux, J. E. (2003). *Synaptic self: How our brains became who we are.* New York: Penguin Putnam.

Lee, E. J. (2005). When placebic information differs from real information. *Communication Research, 32,* 615–645.

Lyubomirsky, S., Tucker, K. L., Caldwell, N. D., & Berg, K. (1999). Why ruminators are poor problem solvers: Clues from the phenomenology of dysphoric rumination. *Journal of Personality and Social Psychology, 77,* 1041–1060.

Mandler, J. M. (1984). *Stories, scripts, and scenes: Aspects of schema theory.* Mahwah, NJ: Erlbaum.

Marslen-Wilson, W., & Tyler, L. K. (1980). The temporal structure of spoken language understanding. *Cognition, 8,* 1–71.

McCullough, M. E., Bellah, C. G., Kilpatrick, S. D., Johnson, J. L. (2001). Vengefulness: Relationships with forgiveness, rumination, well-being, and the Big Five. *Personality and Social Psychology Bulletin, 27,* 601–610.

McCullough, M. E., Bono, G., & Root, L. M. (2007). Rumination, emotion, and forgiveness: Three longitudinal studies. *Journal of Personality and Social Psychology, 92,* 490–505.

Nichols, R. O. (1987). Listening is a 10-part skill. *Nation's Business, 75,* 40.

Piaget, J. (1955). *The language and thought of the child.* New York: Meridian Books.

Porges, S. W. (1985). Spontaneous oscillations in heart rate: Potential index of stress. In P. G. Moberg (Ed.), *Animal stress* (pp. 97–111). Bethesda, MD: The American Physiological Society.

Roloff, M. E., & Ifert, D. E. (1998). Exploring the role of private speech, imagined interaction, and serial interaction in mutual influence. In M. T. Palmer & G. A. Barnett (Eds.), *Progress in communication sciences* (Vol. 14, pp. 113–133). Stanford, CT: Ablex.

Rowell, L. (1986). *Human circulation: Regulation during physical stress.* New York: Oxford.

Sapolsky, B. S., Stocking, S. H., & Zillman, D. (1977). Immediate vs. delayed retaliation in male and female adults. *Psychological Reports, 40,* 197–198.

Sapolsky, R. M. (2005). The influence of social hierarchy on primate health. *Science, 308,* 648–652.

Schacter, S., & Singer. J. L. (1962). Cognitive, social and physiological determinants of emotional state. *Psychological Review, 69,* 379–399.

Smeltzer, L. R., & Watson, K.W. (1984). Listening: An empirical comparison of discussion length and level of incentive. *Central States Speech Journal, 35,* 166–170.

Smith, M. J. (1982). *Persuasion and human action: A review and critique of social influence theories.* Belmont, CA: Wadsworth.

Stacks, D. W., & Sellers, D. E. (1989). Understanding intrapersonal communication: Neurological processing implications. In C. V. Roberts, K. W. Watson, & L. L. Barker (Eds.), *Intrapersonal communication processes: Original essays* (pp. 243–267). New Orleans, LA: SPECTRA/Gorsuch-Scarisbrick.

Stacks, D. W., & Sellers, D. E. (1994). Research: Expanding our knowledge of intrapersonal communication processes. In D. Vocate (Ed.), *Intrapersonal communication: Different voices, different minds* (pp. 101–120). Hillsdale, NJ: Erlbaum.

Tannen, D. (2002). *I only say this because I love you.* New York: Ballantine.

Vocate, D. R. (1994). Self-talk and inner speech: Understanding the uniquely human aspect of intrapersonal communication. In D. Vocate (Ed.), *Intrapersonal communication: Different voices, different minds* (pp. 3–32). Hillsdale, NJ: Erlbaum.

Werner, E. K. (1975). *A study of communication time.* Unpublished master's thesis, University of Maryland, College Park.

Witkin, B. R. (1993). Human information processing. In A. D. Wolvin & C. G. Coakley (Eds.), *Perspectives on listening* (pp. 23–59). Norwood, NJ: Ablex.

Zagacki, K. S., Edwards, R., & Honeycutt, J. M. (1992). The role of mental imagery and emotion in imagined interaction. *Communication Quarterly, 40,* 56–68.

Suggested Readings

Barth, F. D. (1997). *Daydreaming: Unlocking the creative power of your mind.* New York: Penguin.

Honeycutt, J. M. (2001). *Imagined interactions: Daydreaming about communication.* Cresskill, NJ: Hampton.

Honeycutt, J. M. (in press). Physiology and imagined interactions. In J. M. Honeycutt (Ed.), *Imagine that: Studies in imagined interaction.* Cresskill, NJ: Hampton.

22

NONVERBAL COMMUNICATION

Amy S. Ebesu Hubbard and Judee K. Burgoon

As the King and his suite neared Akasaka, the palace of the Emperor, a bugle announced their arrival. The Emperor Meiji of Japan stood alone in a room adjacent to the entrance of the palace. He was dressed in European military uniform and the crest of his coat was decorated with orders. As [King] Kalakaua left the carriage and entered the palace, he stepped up to the Emperor alone and extended his arm to shake hands. For the first time in Japanese history an Emperor exchanged handshakes with a foreign sovereign. (Ogawa, 1973, p. 91)

Instead of the traditional bow, this momentous meeting between two monarchs in 1881 began with a simple handshake, which served as a precursor to friendly international relations between Japan and Hawaii. More recently, the offering or withholding of a handshake between Middle Eastern leaders, reflected in this seemingly inconsequential greeting ritual, the status of peace negotiations.

So, too, are the warp and weave of daily interactions fashioned from a thousand and often presumably insignificant nonverbal gestures. A gaze broken too soon, a forced smile, a flat voice, an unreturned phone call, a conversation conducted across the barrier of an executive desk—together, such nonverbal strands form the fabric of our communicative world, defining our interpersonal relationships, declaring our personal identities, revealing our emotions, governing the flow of our social encounters, and reinforcing our attempts to influence others. Understanding human communication requires understanding the multiple nonverbal codes by which it is transacted and the communicative functions those codes accomplish.

Theorizing about Nonverbal Communication

By nonverbal communication we mean behaviors that are typically sent with intent, are used with regularity among members of a social community, are typically interpreted as intentional, and have consensually recognizable interpretations (Burgoon, Guerrero, & Floyd, in press; Burgoon & Hoobler, 2002). This message orientation approach to communication requires attending to the meanings associated with nonverbal behaviors and focusing on meanings that are tied to communication functions within a given speech community.

Theorizing about nonverbal communication has been complicated not only by its multimodal and multifunctional nature, but also because our knowledge emanates from disparate disciplines with differing assumptions and methodologies. This makes efforts to synthesize theories and principles from all these different sources a challenge. For example, ethologists, who are interested in nonverbal communication as a basis for comparing humans to other species, approach nonverbal displays as biologically grounded signals with evolutionary survival value. Their methods require meticulous observations of nonverbal behaviors in their natural environs. Anthropologists, who see nonverbal behavior as manifestations of culture, are interested in how nonverbal rituals and norms reveal something about human society. They may rely on informants—members of a given culture—to clarify the nonverbal rules, norms, and sanctions in a given culture, or they may rely on ethnographic observations. Psychologists may examine nonverbal cues for what they reveal about intrapsychic processes such as arousal, personality, or cognition formation and processing. Among the methods used are experimental manipulations of conditions that elicit nonverbal cues or manipulations of the cues themselves. Sociologists may examine nonverbal patterns as manifestations of social hierarchies or as means toward achieving group influence and may combine observational and experimental procedures with survey methodologies. Scholars studying families, social ills, psychiatric problems, medical interactions, legal proceedings, intercultural and international relations, political image-making, and mediated versus nonmediated channels, among others, bring additional distinctive perspectives and methods to the study of nonverbal communication. Feminist scholars may address the extent to which nonverbal behaviors are tightly linked to gender and gender inequities. Computer vision experts may seek understanding of the structures and functions of nonverbal behavior to aid automated detection of human action from video. Out of all these perspectives have emerged numerous theories and models of human communication.

Obviously, no single chapter can begin to do justice to this cornucopia of nonverbal literature. We will therefore focus our attention here on a single communication function—relational communication and relationship management—and the theorizing and methods attending it. Readers interested in more broad-based reviews of nonverbal theories are directed to Burgoon and Hoobler (2002), Knapp and Hall (2006), and Manusov and Patterson (2006). Readers interested in more broad-based reviews of nonverbal measures, coding, and methodologies are directed to collections by Harrigan, Rosenthal, and Scherer (2005) and Manusov (2005).

Relational Communication and Relationship Management

Aside from emotional expression, perhaps no area has been so closely aligned with nonverbal communication as relational communication. The term *relational communication* refers *to the messages* people *exchange that define the nature of their interpersonal relationship;* more specifically, how two people feel about one another, about their relationship, or about themselves within the context of the relationship. Relational communication undergirds all interpersonal relationships. As the coinage by which people "transact" their relationships, it purchases relational trajectories of greater or lesser intimacy, trust, interdependence, commitment, and satisfaction.

Studying relational communication requires acknowledging several important features of this major communicative function. First, relational communication takes a participant perspective. This means that people's evaluations and self-images are tied to reactions to and influenced by feedback from particular others. Second, relational communication is directed toward a specific target and not toward a generalized audience. Third, relational communication spotlights the interaction between two people, where the central unit of analysis is the *dyad*. Finally, relational communication concentrates on the meanings ascribed to the behaviors of others, rather than on the behaviors that cause certain outcomes.

Beginning with Watzlawick, Beavin, and Jackson's (1967) classic work, *Pragmatics of Human Communication*, relational communication has often been treated as synonymous with nonverbal communication. According to Watzlawick et al., all communication entails two levels, the *content* or report level (the ostensive topic of conversation) and the *relational* or command level (the definition of the interpersonal relationship which serves as a metacommunication about how to interpret the content level). In reality, not all nonverbal communication is relational, nor is all relational communication nonverbal (Bavelas, 1990), but it is evident that there is a strong division of labor such that much relational "business" is handled by the nonverbal codes while the occasioned discourse is being managed by the verbal code.

Relational Communication Dimensions

Traditional approaches to relational communication originally proposed two or three dimensions—such as control, dominance, intimacy, or inclusion—that underlie all relationships (e.g., Mehrabian, 1981). For example, *control* refers to the process of interdependence and regulation of the relationship definition and direction. *Intimacy* refers to the process of reciprocal self-confirmation and the affective tone of a relationship.

Although an important starting point for analyzing relationships and relational messages, early perspectives underestimated the variety and richness of message themes that are present in interpersonal encounters. After reviewing ethological, anthropological, psychiatric, sociological, psychological, linguistic, and communication literature, Burgoon and Hale (1984) proposed that the *topoi* or themes of relational communication be expanded to twelve nonorthogonal dimensions. They included a superordinate theme of *intimacy* comprised of subthemes of affection-hostility, intensity of involvement (often equated with immediacy), inclusion-exclusion (elsewhere labeled as affiliation, empathy, rapport, or receptivity), trust, and depth-superficiality (elsewhere described as familiarity or degree of acquaintance). Additional themes they proposed were *dominance* (which equates with relational control), *emotional arousal* (often equated with activation), *composure* (often labeled as relaxation or nervousness), *similarity-dissimilarity, formality-informality,* and *task versus social orientation*. Subsequent empirical investigations (e.g., Burgoon, 1991; Burgoon & Hale, 1987; Le Poire & Burgoon, 1994) indicated that these dimensions could be combined into fewer, interrelated message clusters. These clusters offer a convenient way to organize empirical findings regarding which behaviors convey relational meanings (for summaries, see Burgoon & Hoobler, 2002; Coker & Burgoon, 1987; Hendrick & Hendrick, 1992; Le Poire & Burgoon, 1994). Subsequently, Dillard, Solomon, and Palmer (1999) argued for distinguishing relational judgments by levels of abstraction, both of which are meaningful for theorizing and research. They proposed that the more abstract level is captured by the concepts of affiliation and dominance and that Burgoon and Hale's (1984) topoi capture the lower level of abstraction, particularly for affiliation.

Intimacy

Intimacy appears to be experienced largely through nonverbal behaviors (Register & Henley, 1992). Intimacy behaviors include the use of touch to more private body regions, softer voices, postural openness, motor mimicry and mirroring (i.e., exhibiting the same behavior as another), wearing similar apparel and "identification symbols" (i.e., tie-signs), punctuality, monochronic use of time, and sharing territories and possessions. In large part, the experience of intimacy is closely tied to the expression of nonverbal involvement, which itself is composed of five dimensions: (1) *immediacy* (e.g., proximity, direct body orientation, forward lean, postural openness, gaze, and touch that signal approach and inclusion); (2) *expressiveness* (e.g., facial, gestural, postural, and vocal displays of animation and activity); (3) *altercentrism* (e.g., kinesic and auditory cues that signal one is attentive to and oriented toward the other rather than self); (4) *conversational management* (e.g., self-synchrony, fluency, coordinated movement, interactional synchrony, and short response latencies that create a well-paced, smooth interaction); and (5) *social composure* (e.g., postural and vocal cues of relaxation or fewer adaptor behaviors) (Cappella, 1994; Coker & Burgoon, 1987; Patterson, 1983).

It is important to note that the meaning of individual behaviors may be ambiguous because isolated behaviors often have multiple relational interpretations. However, appropriate interpretations are more readily apparent when combinations and patterns of behaviors are viewed. For example, when involvement is combined with positive affect (e.g., smiling, nodding, vocal pleasantness, and relaxed laughter), it creates a message of greater attraction, liking, trust, affiliation, depth, similarity, and rapport. When involvement is accompanied by negative affect, it conveys a strong signal of hostility. On the other hand, the combination of noninvolvement and nonimmediacy cues connotes detachment or privacy.

Arousal and Composure

Research has found that emotional arousal and lack of composure are created through a variety of kinesic, vocalic, and proxemic cues. For instance, composure and relaxation are communicated by behaviors such as asymmetrical limb positions, less body tonus and tension, close proximity, smiling, greater kinesic expressiveness, and faster tempo. More research needs to examine whether or not both messages of composure and noncomposure can be intentionally manipulated by people.

Dominance

Dominance can be expressed through a number of principles (Burgoon & Dunbar, 2005; Dunbar & Burgoon, 2005a, 2005b). One general principle to which we respond innately is physical potency. Potency can be conveyed nonverbally through indicators of threat such as threat stares; messages of size and strength, such as speaking with a deep-pitched voice, standing with arms akimbo, or surrounding oneself with a large entourage; and indicators of expressivity, such as using expansive gestures, animated facial expressions, and vocal variety. Another principle is resource control. Dominant individuals may occupy central locations; possess larger, more private, and more luxuriously appointed spaces; have greater access to other people's belongings, time, and territories; precede others when entering a territory or starting a conversation; and have the prerogative to engage in one-way intimacies such as touching another. A third general principle is interaction control. Dominant individuals may control who talks to whom and when; can set the pace of conversation through their speaking and gesturing tempo; can interrupt others and express their anger or irritation vocally and facially; can create a more formal and detached interaction by adopting indirect body orientation, backward lean, less frequent but more direct eye gaze; or can create a more informal interaction through greater postural relaxation and asymmetry. From this list, it is clear that the expressiveness dimension of involvement is also associated with dominance. Submissiveness is created by indications of weakness, lethargy, inexpressivity, lack of privileged access to resources, and avoidance of conversational control. It includes behaviors such as diminutive postures, breaking of eye contact, and gestures such as the head tilt and open palms that convey obeisance, for example. Submission is also conveyed by meeting rather than violating expectations for nonverbal behavior. A major controversy in the nonverbal literature has been whether dominance-subordination is gender-linked. The bulk of evidence suggests that although there are some parallels between power, status, and dominance displays and male–female displays, such that women display many low-power behavior patterns, power differences do not fully account for differences in male and female nonverbal displays (Hall, 2006).

Formality and Task versus Social Orientation

Formality, which is highly related to a task orientation, is conveyed through decreased vocal expressiveness, increased resonance and precise articulation, postural tension or erectness, and greater distance. Additionally, the use of cues such as response latency, gaze, loudness, fluency, posture, gestures, and seating position are inferred as relating to task competence and confidence (Ridgeway, Berger, & Smith, 1985). For example, a person expecting to exercise leadership typically sits at the head of a table, and individuals seated at the head of a table become more participative and influential.

Relationship Management

The preceding section identified numerous nonverbal messages associated with particular relational message themes expressed in a given interchange. One can also take a more macroscopic approach to relational communication by considering its role in longitudinal relationship development. Some research and theorizing has taken this approach, examining how nonverbal cues function in the initiation, maintenance, and dissolution of interpersonal relationships. Scholars have long recognized that nonverbal behaviors serve as good indicators of the state of the relationship and can facilitate or hinder the development of intimacy. Nonverbal cues and measures may capture the relationship state such as satisfaction, intimacy, and commitment.

Several exemplars illustrate how research has addressed relationship management from a nonverbal communication perspective. Detailed analyses of courtship stages and rituals have distinguished courtship cues from flirting behaviors and have revealed that different nonverbal behaviors are connected with each courtship stage (e.g., Givens, 1983; Simpson, Gangestad, & Biek, 1993). Work on relationship stages and types has identified variations in nonverbal intimacy, involvement, pleasantness, play, privacy, and emotional expressivity across such diverse relationships as acquaintance, friend, romantic, superior-subordinate, parent-child, and doctor-patient (Baxter, 1992; Guerrero & Andersen, 1991; Koerner & Fitzpatrick, 2002; Le Poire, Shepard, & Duggan, 1999; Planalp & Benson, 1992; Wagner & Smith, 1991). Other research on relationship phases has developed typologies of strategies and tactics, composed of verbal and nonverbal behaviors, used during relational escalation, maintenance, and deescalation (e.g., Cupach & Metts, 1986; Shea & Pearson, 1986; Tolhuizen, 1989). Studies of marital conflict have uncovered nonverbal profiles accompanying different conflict strategies and have shown that conflicts often take the form of reciprocal escalating spirals of nonverbal hostility with nonverbal expressions of affect playing a deciding factor in whether or not conflicts are resolved (e.g., Gottman, 1994; Newton & Burgoon, 1990; Sillars, Coletti, Parry, & Rogers, 1982). Work on relational satisfaction has identified which conflict resolution strategies and relational message themes influence satisfaction in physician–patient and marital relationships (e.g., Kelley & Burgoon, 1991; Rusbult, Verette, Whitney, Slovik, & Lipkus, 1991). Research that compares satisfied and dissatisfied couples indicates that dissatisfied couples are prone to misinterpret each other's nonverbal signals; that people in less satisfying relationships decode their partners' negative behaviors as more intentional, stable, and controllable and their partners' positive behaviors as external, unstable, and specific, whereas people in more satisfying relationships decode negative cues neutrally and positive cues as internal, stable, and global (Manusov, 1990; Noller & Ruzzene, 1991). One important conclusion is that nonverbal behaviors play a significant role in the life of a relationship by revealing its level of intimacy and closeness, distinguishing different stages or types of relationships, and affecting relational trajectories and outcomes.

Research Methods in Studying Nonverbal Relational Communication

Our discussion of the findings in the area of nonverbal relational communication naturally brings us to consider the methods used to conduct nonverbal research on relational communication and relationship management. The methods selected affect the validity and generalizability of the conclusions that can be drawn.

A basic decision point is whether to employ an experimental or nonexperimental design and attendant measurement strategies. This is dictated by the questions and issues at stake. Often, relational communication issues require a longitudinal focus and the need to access highly private information. In such cases, researchers may incorporate nonexperimental diary and account methods. But such methodologies are fraught with the difficulties attending the use of self-report methods. For instance, respondents may be unable to provide information regarding microlevel nonverbal behaviors. It is unreasonable to expect that people are able to report all of their nonverbal behaviors (i.e., kinesics, vocalic, physical appearance, proxemic, artifactual, chronemic, and haptic cues) or that nonverbal communication occurs at a high level of awareness. Jones's (1991) examination of the problem of validity in questionnaire studies using Jourard's tactile body-accessibility scale is illustrative. It revealed that people's recall of touch behaviors was heavily influenced by expectations about which touches should have occurred; it did not match the amount of touch. This suggests that researchers must find other ways, besides exclusive reliance on self-report data, to investigate specific nonverbal behaviors, and they must have alternate means to record nonverbal behaviors without solely relying on actual participants as the primary informants.

However, if researchers are interested in the general nonverbal encoding and decoding abilities of people (e.g., to investigate what messages people intend to send, what messages people receive, and what messages people think were intentionally sent), then questionnaire measures may be a useful method of assessment. Researchers can use a number of standardized scales which have been developed to test these nonverbal skills. These scales range from self-report questionnaires to videotape tests. A variety of measures can be found in Harrigan, Rosenthal, and Scherer's (2005) *The New Handbook of Methods in Nonverbal Behavior Research* and Manusov's (2005) *The Sourcebook of Nonverbal Measures: Going Beyond Words.*

More often than not, research on nonverbal behavior entails direct observation and coding of behavior. This may occur in nonexperimental or experimental settings. In the former case, one might ask couples to interact naturally about some topic or even to recreate a previous discussion. The kinds of interaction patterns that are exhibited are then observed and coded or rated (e.g., Burman, Margolin, & John, 1993; Gottman, 1996). In the latter case, some interactants might experimentally alter some behaviors—perhaps becoming uninvolved and detached—to see the effects on partner behavior or interpretations or on observer interpretations (e.g., Guerrero & Burgoon, 1996). Or couples might be placed under different experimental conditions, such as conducting a joint task and discussing personal fears, and their behavior patterns compared across partners and conditions (e.g., Newton & Burgoon, 1990). Although nonverbal behaviors may be observed live or "online," researchers interested in nonverbal cues often analyze a permanent record of the interaction. Nonverbal studies typically use audiotapes, videotapes, or digital recordings, depending on the specific research questions, and the ease and availability of using particular recording devices. Once they are recorded, nonverbal behaviors are frequently coded by outside observers. This is in line with a message orientation approach. In addition, in the case of relational communication, participants may also report their perceptions. One consequence of conducting nonverbal research in this manner is the additional expenses—in time and money—associated with equipment costs, hiring coders, training coders, and altering the digital recordings, videotapes, or audiotapes to aid in coding (e.g., content-filtering procedures). Another consequence is that interpretation of the nonverbal data may become more difficult as various perspectives are taken into account. In the case where both participants and outside observers judge the nonverbal behaviors recorded, there may be striking differences in their ratings. For example, various research programs comparing participant and trained observer perspectives showed that observers and participants share some commonalities in perceptions but also some notable discrepancies (e.g., Burgoon & Newton, 1991; Floyd & Markman, 1983; Rusbult et al., 1991).

A final important consideration when conducting nonverbal research is the unit of analysis. Will it consist of nonverbal measurement of single and concrete behaviors, where observation is usually event-based or time-based using small time intervals (micro level) or nonverbal measurement of larger and more abstract behaviors, where observation is usually time-based using larger time intervals or event-based using larger events (macro level)? Burgoon and Baesler (1991) suggested that nonverbal researchers should: (1) assess the representational validity between the level of measurement and the nonverbal phenomena of conceptual interest, such that the unit of measurement is socially meaningful; (2) compare the reliability using different levels of measurement; (3) consider the concurrent validity between the micro and macro measures; and (4) measure the predictive power using micro and macro measurements when determining the appropriate measurement strategy for particular research questions.

A Sample Experiment

To illustrate how nonverbal relational research might be conducted, we turn now to a sample experiment in a specific area of relational communication and management: the nonverbal aspects of relational conflict. As context, most of the research for the past 25 years has focused on the impact of the negative or positive affective tone of communication during interpersonal conflict and whether or not people engage in or avoid conflict interactions (Sillars & Weisberg, 1987). In general, work on affect during conflict revealed that couples who are unhappy or dissatisfied are more verbally and nonverbally negative during their conflict interactions (Gottman, 1979; Pike & Sillars, 1985). In regard to engagement, research results are less consistent. For example, sometimes satisfied couples confront conflict issues and other times they avoid discussing conflicts (Rusbult, Drigotas, & Verette, 1994; Ting-Toomey, 1983). Fitzpatrick (1988) suggested that the choice to engage in conflict interactions or avoid discussion of conflicts may be a function of a couple's marital type, which is based on the couple's relationship definitions. For example, couples labeled as a "traditional" marital type tended to avoid conflict whereas couples labeled as an "independent" marital type were more assertive and tended to engage in conflict.

A nonverbal study providing a useful extension of these lines of research would be to examine *both* positive–negative behaviors and engaging–avoidant behaviors during conflict interaction and how the combination of these two classes of behavior impact relationship satisfaction. In this sample study, we will consider positive–negative behaviors as those cues which exhibit positive–negative affect such as vocal pleasantness, smiling, nodding, and relaxed laughter and engaging–avoiding behaviors as cues indicative of involvement-noninvolvement. We might pose the following research question: "What are the effects of positive affect and involvement during a conflict interaction on relationship satisfaction?" We might also want to investigate couples who interact in ways that are counter to their relationship definition. We might expect that couples who believe in engaging in conflict directly and speaking one's mind would be less communicatively satisfied if they used an avoidant or noninvolved style of interaction. Similarly, we might expect that couples who tend to avoid conflicts might be less communicatively satisfied if they are confronted with a partner who engages in conflict and demonstrates high levels of involvement. Thus, we also might pose the following research question: "Are traditional marital types who engage in more involvement during conflict less communicatively satisfied than traditionals who engage in less involvement?" Likewise, "Are independent marital types who engage in less involvement during conflict less communicatively satisfied than independents who engage in more involvement?"

To investigate these questions in our sample experiment, we need to consider several things. The sample: Who will be in our sample, what criteria will we use to select participants, and how will we classify people into the traditional and independent marital types? Procedures: What will be our general procedures for conducting this study and what will be the procedure for eliciting conflict between participants? How will we record the conflict interaction? What nonverbal behaviors will be coded and who will code the nonverbal data? What measures will be used to assess relationship satisfaction and communication satisfaction? What will be the instructions for the manipulation (e.g., what instructions will be given for being more or less involved)? How will we determine whether or not participants followed the instructions? How will we analyze the data?

Specifically, we could recruit marital couples who have been married for more than two years and have never sought marital counseling or therapy to participate in this research experiment. Participants might be asked to interact in a comfortable setting that approximates a living room environment (or even their own living room). They might complete the Kansas Marital Satisfaction Scale (Schumm, Nichols, Schectman, & Grigsby, 1983) to assess the level of relationship satisfaction and the Relational Dimensions Instrument to classify couples as traditional or independent (Fitzpatrick, 1988). Couples who are classified into other marital types beyond the two types used in this investigation would be excluded from the analyses. After completing the Relational Dimensions Instrument, the couples could individually list topics of their conflicts and rate those conflicts on a scale of major to minor importance and high salience to low salience to the relationship. Comparisons of these two lists of conflict topics should yield a single topic of moderate importance and salience to both partners. Couples then might be asked to reenact the most recent conflict on that topic and to provide background information, such as when and where the conflict took place. Couples could be separated so that one member of each couple might be given instructions and training on how to behave during the interaction (either using an involving or noninvolving style).

Once reunited, couples might engage in the reenactment of the conflict while being videotaped. Following the conflict interaction, couples could be separated to assess their level of communication satisfaction using an interpersonal communication satisfaction measure (Hecht, 1978). Couples could then review their videotapes and rate their own and their partner's nonverbal behaviors (i.e., the level of involvement and the positive-negative affect cues following consideration of micro and macro measurement issues). Two trained outside observers could also rate the same nonverbal behaviors for both partners. The outsider observers' assessment of involvement would determine whether or not participants followed instructions. Statistical analyses would address the correspondence between partners' behaviors and the links among behavior-patterns, couple type, couple satisfaction, and communication satisfaction.

Conclusion

Understanding nonverbal communication entails recognition that research and theorizing in this field is based on a diverse foundation of interests. In this chapter, we sampled the vast array of approaches and methods for studying nonverbal communication to better appreciate the richness and complexity of research in this area. We gave special attention to the communicative function of relational communication, demonstrating how nonverbal scholars have sought to understand relationships through people's nonverbal behavior. In addition, we examined important decision points for those interested in research methods used in the study of nonverbal communication. Finally, we discussed a specific sample experiment to demonstrate how one might conduct a study on the nonverbal aspects of relational conflicts.

Other areas likely to attract increasing research attention are significant nonverbal events in relationships that affect the direction of a relationship's development, infrequent nonverbal events, and expected but omitted nonverbal cues as relational statements. For instance, the first time you and a potential romantic partner hold hands may signal an escalation in the relationship, or the one time that you yell and slam your fist into the wall during a conflict may signal a downward trend in your relationship. The absence of a goodbye kiss may be more telling to a spouse about the intimacy of the marriage than any other cue present. Nonverbal behaviors that are rarely performed or intermittent behaviors are likely to receive more attention as researchers try to find ways of capturing or observing them. Also, descriptions of the frequency and duration of specific relational cues, their sequences and cycles over time, the interrelatedness among cues, and changes in relational meaning depending on their placement in the relational trajectory are choice areas of investigation. The previous overemphasis on single cue and static analyses will surely give way to analyzing the interplay among multiple cues, longitudinal patterns, and the impact of those patterns on relational outcomes such as commitment and satisfaction.

As we explore these areas of study, we must recognize that answers to our questions may come from a diverse set of literatures and a variety of scholarly fields. Integration of research and theorizing on nonverbal communication can only aid in our search to better understand our nonverbal communication. Nonverbal researchers have only begun to tap this rich area of study as they strive to fully depict the role of nonverbal communication in the process of relationship communication and management.

References

Bavelas, J. B. (1990). Behaving and communicating: A reply to Motley. *Western Journal of Speech Communication, 54*, 593–602.

Baxter, L. A. (1992). Forms and functions of intimate play in personal relationships. *Human Communication Research, 18*, 336–363.

Burgoon, J. K. (1991). Relational message interpretations of touch, conversational distance, and posture. *Journal of Nonverbal Behavior, 15*, 233–259.

Burgoon, J. K., & Baesler, E. J. (1991). Choosing between micro and macro nonverbal measurement: Application to selected vocalic and kinesic indices. *Journal of Nonverbal Behavior, 15*, 57–78.

Burgoon, J. K., & Dunbar, N. E. (2005). Nonverbal expressions of dominance and power in human relationships. In V. Manusov & M. L. Patterson (Eds.), *The Sage handbook of nonverbal communication* (pp. 279–298). Thousand Oaks, CA: Sage.

Burgoon, J. K., Guerrero, L. G., & Floyd, K (in press). *Nonverbal communication*. Boston: Allyn & Bacon.

Burgoon, J. K., & Hale, J. L. (1984). The fundamental topoi of relational communication. *Communication Monographs, 51*, 193–214.

Burgoon, J. K., & Hale, J. L. (1987). Validation and measurement of the fundamental themes of relational communication. *Communication Monographs, 54*, 19–41.

Burgoon, J. K., & Hoobler, G. D. (2002). Nonverbal signals. In M. L. Knapp & G. R. Miller (Eds.), *Handbook of interpersonal communication* (3nd ed., pp. 240–299). Thousand Oaks, CA: Sage.

Burgoon, J. K., & Newton, D. A. (1991). Applying a social meaning model to relational messages of conversational involvement: Comparing participant and observer perspectives. *Southern Communication Journal, 56*, 96–113.

Burman, B., Margolin, G., & John, R. S. (1993). America's angriest home videos: Behavioral contingencies observed in home reenactments of marital conflict. *Journal of Consulting and Clinical Psychology, 61*, 28–39.

Cappella, J. N. (1994). The management of conversational interaction in adults and infants. In M. L. Knapp & G. R. Miller (Eds.), *Handbook of interpersonal communication* (2nd ed., pp. 380–418). Thousand Oaks, CA: Sage.

Coker, D. A., & Burgoon, J. K. (1987). The nature of conversational involvement and nonverbal encoding patterns. *Human Communication Research, 13,* 463–494.

Cupach, W. R., & Metts, S. (1986). Accounts of relational dissolution. *Communication Monographs, 53,* 311–334.

Dillard, J. P., Solomon, D. H., & Palmer, M. T. (1999). Structuring the concept of relational communication. *Communication Monographs, 66,* 49–65.

Dunbar, N. E., & Burgoon, J. K. (2005a). Nonverbal measurement of dominance. In V. Manusov (Ed.), *The sourcebook of nonverbal measures: Going beyond words* (pp. 361–374). Hillsdale, NJ: Erlbaum.

Dunbar, N. E., & Burgoon, J. K. (2005b). Perceptions of power and interactional dominance in interpersonal relationships. *Journal of Social and Personal Relationships, 22,* 207–233

Fitzpatrick, M. A. (1988). *Between husbands and wives: Communication in marriage.* Newbury Park, CA: Sage.

Floyd, F. J., & Markman, H. J. (1983). Observational biases in spouse observation: Toward a cognitive/behavioral model of marriage. *Journal of Consulting and Clinical Psychology, 51,* 450–457.

Givens, D. B. (1983). *Love signals.* New York: Crown.

Gottman, J. M. (1979). *Marital interaction: Experimental investigations.* New York: Academic Press.

Gottman, J. M. (1994). *What predicts divorce? The relationship between marital processes and marital outcomes.* Mahwah, NJ: Erlbaum.

Gottman, J. M. (1996). *What predicts divorce? The measures.* Mahwah, NJ: Erlbaum.

Guerrero, L. K., & Andersen, P. A. (1991). The waxing and waning of relational intimacy: Touch as a function of relational stage, gender, and touch avoidance. *Journal of Social and Personal Relationships, 8,* 147–165.

Guerrero, L. K., & Burgoon, J. K. (1996). Attachment styles and reactions to nonverbal involvement change in romantic dyads: Patterns of reciprocity and compensation. *Human Communication Research, 22,* 335–370.

Hall, J. A. (2006). Nonverbal behavior, status, and gender: How do we understand their relations? *Psychology of Women Quarterly, 30,* 384–391.

Harrigan, J. A., Rosenthal, R., & Scherer, K. R. (Eds.). (2005). *The new handbook of methods in nonverbal behavior research.* New York: Oxford University Press.

Hecht, M. L. (1978). The conceptualization and measurement of interpersonal communication satisfaction. *Human Communication Research, 4,* 253–264.

Hendrick, S., & Hendrick, C. (1992). *Liking, loving, & relating* (2nd ed.). Pacific Grove, CA: Brooks/Cole.

Jones, S. E. (1991). Problems of validity in questionnaire studies of nonverbal behavior: Jourard's Tactile Body-Accessibility Scale. *Southern Communication Journal, 56,* 83–95.

Jourard, S. M. (1966). An exploratory study of body-accessibility. *British Journal of Social and Clinical Psychology, 5,* 221–231.

Kelley, D. L., & Burgoon, J. K. (1991). Understanding marital satisfaction and couple type as functions of relational expectations. *Human Communication Research, 18,* 40–69.

Knapp, M. L., & Hall, J. A. (2006). *Nonverbal communication in human interaction* (6th ed.). Toronto, Canada: Thomson Wadsworth.

Koerner, A. F., & Fitzpatrick, M. A. (2002). Nonverbal communication and marital adjustment and satisfaction: The role of decoding relationship relevant and relationship irrelevant affect. *Communication Monographs, 69,* 33–51.

Le Poire, B., & Burgoon, J. K. (1994). Two contrasting explanations of involvement violations: Expectancy violations theory versus discrepancy arousal theory. *Human Communication Research, 20,* 560–591.

Le Poire, B. A., Shepard, C., & Duggan, A. (1999). Nonverbal involvement, expressiveness, and pleasantness as predicted by parental and partner attachment style. *Communication Monographs, 66,* 293–311.

Manusov, V. (1990). An application of attribution principles to nonverbal behaviors in romantic dyads. *Communication Monographs, 57,* 104–118.

Manusov, V. (Ed.). (2005). *The sourcebook of nonverbal measures: Going beyond words*. Mahwah, NJ: Erlbaum.

Manusov, V., & Patterson, M. L. (Eds.). (2006). *The Sage handbook of nonverbal communication*. Thousand Oaks, CA: Sage.

Mehrabian, A. (1981). *Silent messages*. Belmont, CA: Wadsworth.

Newton, D. A., & Burgoon, J. K. (1990). Nonverbal conflict behaviors: Functions, strategies, and tactics. In D. D. Cahn (Ed.), *Intimates in conflict* (pp. 77–104). Hillsdale, NJ: Erlbaum.

Noller, P., & Ruzzene, M. (1991). Communication in marriage: The influence of affect and cognition. In G. J. Fletcher & F. D. Fincham (Eds.), *Cognition in close relationships* (pp. 203–233). Hillsdale, NJ: Erlbaum.

Ogawa, D. M. (1973). *Jan ken po: The world of Hawaii's Japanese Americans*. Honolulu: University of Hawaii Press.

Patterson, M. L. (1983). *Nonverbal behavior: A functional perspective*. New York: Springer Verlag.

Pike, G. R., & Sillars, A. L. (1985). Reciprocity of marital communication. *Journal of Social and Personal Relationships, 2*, 303–324.

Planalp, S., & Benson, A. (1992). Friends' and acquaintances' conversations I: Perceived differences. *Journal of Social and Personal Relationships, 9*, 483–506.

Register, L. M., & Henley, T. B. (1992). The phenomenology of intimacy. *Journal of Social and Personal Relationships, 9*, 467–481.

Ridgeway, C. L., Berger, J., & Smith, L. (1985). Nonverbal cues and status: An expectation states approach. *American Journal of Sociology, 90*, 955–978.

Riggio, R. E. (1986). Assessment of basic social skills. *Journal of Personality and Social Psychology, 51*, 649–660.

Rusbult, C. E., Drigotas, S. M., & Verette, J. (1994). The investment model: An interdependence analysis of commitment processes and relationship maintenance phenomena. In D. J. Canary & L. Stafford (Eds.), *Communication and relational maintenance* (pp. 115–139). San Diego, CA: Academic Press.

Rusbult, C. E., Verette, J., Whitney, G. A., Slovik, L. F., & Lipkus, I. (1991). Accommodation processes in close relationships: Theory and preliminary empirical evidence. *Journal of Personality and Social Psychology, 60*, 53–78.

Schumm, W. R., Nichols, C. W., Schectman, & Grigsby, C. C. (1983). Characteristics of responses to the Kansas Marital Satisfaction Scale by a sample of 84 married mothers. *Psychological Reports, 53*, 567–572.

Shea, B. C., & Pearson, J. C. (1986). The effects of relationship type, partner intent, and gender on the selection of relationship maintenance strategies. *Communication Monographs, 53*, 352–364.

Sillars, A. L., Coletti, S. F., Parry, D., & Rogers, M. A. (1982). Coding verbal conflict tactics: Nonverbal and perceptual correlates of the "avoidance-distributive-integrative" distinction. *Human Communication Research, 9*, 83–95.

Sillars, A. L., & Weisberg, J. (1987). Conflict as a social skill. In M. E. Roloff & G. R. Miller (Eds.), *Interpersonal processes: New directions in communication research* (pp. 140–171). Newbury Park, CA: Sage.

Simpson, J. A., Gangestad, S. W., & Biek, M. (1993). *Journal of Experimental Social Psychology, 29*, 434–461.

Ting-Toomey, S. (1983). An analysis of verbal communication patterns in high and low marital adjustment groups. *Human Communication Research, 9*, 306–319.

Tolhuizen, J. H. (1989). Communication strategies for intensifying dating relationships: Identification, use and structure. *Journal of Social and Personal Relationships, 6*, 413–434.

Trimboli, A., & Walker, M. (1993). The CAST test of nonverbal sensitivity. *Journal of Language and Social Psychology, 12*, 49–65.

Wagner, H. L., & Smith, J. (1991). Facial expression in the presence of friends and strangers. *Journal of Nonverbal Behavior, 15*, 201–214.

Watzlawick, P., Beavin, J. H., & Jackson, D. D. (1967). *Pragmatics of human communication: A study of interactional patterns, pathologies, and paradoxes*. New York: Norton.

Zuckerman, M., & Larrance, D. T. (1979). Individual differences in perceived encoding and decoding abilities. In R. Rosenthal (Ed.), *Skill in nonverbal communication: Individual differences* (pp. 171–203). Cambridge, MA: Oelgeschlager, Gunn, & Hain.

Suggested Readings

Birdwhistell, R. (1970). *Kinesics and context*. Philadelphia: University of Pennsylvania Press.

Burgoon, J. K., & Hoobler, G. D. (2002). Nonverbal signals. In M. L. Knapp & G. R. Miller (Eds.), *Handbook of interpersonal communication* (3rd ed., pp. 240–299). Thousand Oaks, CA: Sage.

Manusov, V. (Ed.). (2005). *The sourcebook of nonverbal measures: Going beyond words*. Mahwah, NJ: Erlbaum.

Manusov, V., & Patterson, M. L. (Eds.) (2006). *The Sage handbook of nonverbal communication*. Thousand Oaks, CA: Sage.

Mehrabian, A. (1971). *Silent messages*. Belmont, CA: Wadsworth.

Zebrowitz, L. A. (1998). *Reading faces*. Cumnor Hill, UK: Westview Press.

23

SMALL GROUP COMMUNICATION

Joseph A. Bonito, Gwen M. Wittenbaum, and Randy Y. Hirokawa[1]

The study of small group communication focuses on the exchange of messages among three or more mutually interacting individuals.[2] The origins of this research subfield are amorphous and traverse many cognate disciplines (Gouran, 1999). Early interest in small group communication emerged from the pioneering work of sociologists like Kurt Lewin (1947, 1951) and Robert Freed Bales (1950), as well as psychologists like Raymond Cattell (1948, 1951a, 1951b). Lewin's work on group dynamics, for example, paved the way for decades of small group communication research that focused on the influence of group participation and interaction on member's attitudes and behaviors (Hirokawa et al., 1996a). Bales' development of the method of interaction analysis provided small group communication researchers with a reliable and systematic tool for empirically studying communication processes in small group settings (Gouran, 1999). Cattell's work on group synergy called to our attention the need for small group communication scholars to focus not only on the task dimensions of group communication, but also on the social aspects of it, in understanding productivity and performance of groups (Salazar, 1995).

This chapter provides a general overview of small group communication research as it emerged and developed in the field of communication. As such, it is not an exhaustive review of all group communication research.

In the Beginning

Within the field of communication, the study of small group communication first emerged as a topic of research in the 1950s. The first published study of group *communication* is credited to Edwin Black (1955), who examined interaction sequences in decision-making discussions to determine the causes of breakdowns in group deliberation. Other early works included Crowell, Katcher, and Miyamoto's (1955) investigation of the relationship between group members' confidence in their communication skills as it affected their performance in group discussions; Barnlund's (1955) research on the effects of leadership training on group participation in decision-making groups; and Scheidel, Crowell, and Shepherd's (1958) study of the effects of group members' personality characteristics on their group discussion behaviors.

It was not until the 1960s that study of group communication began to appear regularly in communication journals. Group communication research in the 1960s was largely concerned with identifying the content and structural characteristics of group communication, as well as identifying the most effective manner of engaging in group discussion (Gouran, 1999). Research by Pyron and Sharp (1963), Pyron (1964), and Sharp and Milliken (1964) examined the effectiveness of a group discussion agenda based on Dewey's (1910) method of "reflective thinking." In 1964, Thomas Scheidel and Laura Crowell published a study of idea development in group discussions. Their investigation utilized the innovative interaction analysis method proposed by Bales

(1950) to analyze the role of communication in idea development in group deliberation. This was followed by research examining feedback sequences (Scheidel & Crowell, 1964), communicative traits of leaders (Geier, 1967), and thematic development of ideas in group discussion (Berg, 1967).

Emergent Lines of Research

The study of small group communication began to hit its full stride in the 1970s. Between 1970 and 1978 alone, a total of 114 studies dealing with groups were published in communication journals (Cragan & Wright, 1980). That number increased by an additional 89 articles by 1990 (Cragan & Wright, 1990). Five basic questions guided small group communication research between 1970 and 1990s:

1. Is group communication characterized by recognizable and predictable patterns of interaction?
2. Are certain discussion methods better than others?
3. Is group communication associated with group outcomes like consensus and group satisfaction?
4. Is group communication associated with effective group performance?
5. Is group communication associated with group leadership?

Group Interaction Structure

One major line of research emerging in the 1970s examined the interactional and developmental structure of group communication. Researchers focusing on the interactional structure of group communication sought to determine whether group discussion is characterized by discernible structure (or patterns) of communication acts and, if so, how those structures become patterned over time (Baird, 1974; Fisher & Hawes, 1971; Gouran & Baird, 1972; Saine & Bock, 1973; Saine, Schulman, & Emerson, 1974). In general, these various investigations found that the utterances of group members tend to follow each other in predictable patterns such that it is often possible to anticipate what a group member will say if we know what another has said previously.

In contrast, investigations of the developmental structure of group communication were concerned with understanding whether group communication displays qualitatively different "phases" or stages of group interaction during which certain types of communication behaviors appear more or less frequently than other phases of interaction. Fisher (1970), for instance, studied the developmental nature of group discussion leading to consensus group decisions. His research provided evidence suggesting that decision-making groups go through a four-phase process in reaching consensus. He labeled these stages orientation, conflict, emergence, and reinforcement. In the orientation phase, utterances asking for, and providing, clarification were at their peak; in the conflict phase, evaluative comments and comments expressing disagreements tended to dominate the discussion; in the emergence phase, disagreements dropped off dramatically and comments providing support for particular ideas increased in frequency; and in the reinforcement phase, comments providing support and reinforcement of ideas dominated the discussion. Other researchers (Cheseboro, Cragan, & McCullough, 1973; Ellis & Fisher, 1975; Mabry, 1975a, 1975b) utilized different sets of communication variables to investigate the developmental nature of group interaction. The findings of these descriptive studies formed the corpus of a theoretical model of group interaction development referred to as the "unitary sequence model" (Poole, 1981). In essence, this model posited that all groups display the same phases (or stages) of discussion development as they move toward completion of their task.

In the early 1980s, Poole and his colleagues provided empirical evidence challenging the unitary sequence model's notion that all groups move through the same phases of development in the same sequential order (Poole, 1981, 1983; Poole & Roth, 1989a, 1989b). To the contrary, Poole's research revealed that groups will not necessarily proceed through the same phases of development in the same sequential order, because each group responds to existing contingencies and exigencies in unique ways. On the basis of their research, Poole and his colleagues (Poole, 1983; Poole & Doelger, 1986; Poole & Roth, 1989a, 1989b) described the group process as consisting of a complex set of group communication activities characterized by "extreme variability of phases and phase sequences" (Poole, 1983, p. 325). Poole and his colleagues (Poole & Doelger, 1986; Poole & Roth, 1989b) subsequently outlined the features of the developmental theory of group interaction that posited that task characteristics (e.g., novelty, goal clarity, time requirements) and group structural characteristics (e.g., conflict history, group size) influence the development of the decision in three ways: (1) the nature of the "path" (i.e., sequence of decision activities) that a group employs in reaching a decision; (2) the complexity of the path that the group employs in reaching a decision; and (3) the degree of disorganization during group interaction.

Group Discussion Methods

A second major line of research beginning in the 1970s centered on the study of effective group discussion methods. Among the discussion techniques examined were brainstorming (Jablin, Seibold, & Sorenson, 1977; Jablin, Sorenson, & Seibold, 1978; Philipsen, Mulac, & Dietrich, 1979), Delphi method (Delbecq, Van de Ven, & Gustafson, 1975), PERT (Applbaum & Anatol, 1971; Phillips, 1966), reflective thinking (Bayless, 1967; Brilhart & Jochem, 1964; Larson, 1969), and T-groups (Larson & Gratz, 1970). The central concern of these studies was to identify the most effective discussion procedures.

The findings of these studies, bolstered by the results of more recent investigations (Burleson, Levine, & Samter, 1984; Comadena, 1984; Hiltz, Johnson, & Turoff, 1986; Hirokawa, 1985; Jablin, 1981; Jarboe, 1988), suggest strongly that the discussion procedures used by a group in problem solving or decision making are not necessarily a determinant to effective group performance. Hirokawa (1985), for example, compared four different discussion formats (reflective thinking, single question, ideal solution, and free discussion) and found no difference among them in terms of their association with high-quality decisions. Similarly, Jarboe (1988) compared the reflective thinking format to the nominal group technique to determine which better facilitated group decision making. She found that the nominal group technique led to a greater number of ideas than the reflective thinking procedure, but that the two procedures did not differ in terms of the uniqueness or quality of the ideas it produced. Hiltz et al. (1986) compared computerized conferences and face-to-face discussion procedures. They found that both discussion formats produced equally good decisions, although group members found it more difficult to reach consensus in a computerized conference.

Group Communication and Group Outcomes

Another important line of research in the 1970s examined the relationship between communication variables and group decision-making outcomes. Gouran (1969) focused on the relationship between communication characteristics and a group's ability to reach consensus (unanimous agreement). He found that the communication variable most closely related to consensus decision making is orientation. That is, groups that reached consensus, as contrasted with those that did not, made more statements that attempted to clarify and familiarize members with the group task, goals, procedures, and the like. Gouran's findings stimulated a series of investigation focusing on the relationship between orientation and group consensus (e.g., Kline, 1972; Kline & Hullinger, 1973; Knutson, 1972; Knutson & Holdridge, 1975; Knutson & Kowitz, 1977).

Group consensus research continued to receive attention in the 1980s. DeStephen (1983), for example, found that there were communication characteristics which differentiated high and low consensus groups. She, along with Hirokawa (DeStephen & Hirokawa, 1988), also developed an instrument to measure the degree of consensus in decision-making groups. Further, Canary, Brossman, and Seibold (1987) found that groups arriving at consensus tended to use a greater percentage of convergent arguments than groups that did not arrive at consensus. Beatty (1989), meanwhile, examined the effect of group members' "decision rule orientation" on consensus formation. He found that groups composed of members with similar criteria for making a decision among a set of alternatives (similar decision rule orientation), arrived at consensus decisions with greater frequency than groups whose members were dissimilar in their selection criteria.

Group Communication and Group Performance

The 1970s also brought the emergence of research focusing on the relationship between group communication and group performance. Leathers (1972) found that groups characterized by high quality communication also tended to make high quality decisions. That is, groups experiencing good feedback (e.g., high quality, positive, task-oriented when necessary and maintenance-oriented when necessary) also tended to make good decisions. This line of research continued and increased in the 1980s with the development and testing of the functional perspective of communication and group decision-making effectiveness (Gouran & Hirokawa, 1983; Hirokawa & Scheerhorn, 1983). This theory posited that communication influences group performance by affecting the satisfaction of a group's particular task requirements. These "functional requisites" include assessment of the problematic situation, identification of goals, identification of viable choices, and evaluation of choices (Gouran & Hirokawa, 1983; Hirokawa & McLeod, 1993). Central to the functional perspective is the notion that communication can function to promote or inhibit the effective facilitation of the four requisite functions (Gouran & Hirokawa, 1986).

On the basis of this theory, Hirokawa (1983) developed an interaction coding system that focused on the task-relevant group communication; that is, communication that attends to the functional requisites of the task in question. Using this new system, Hirokawa found that groups which displayed utterances that fulfilled the functional requisites of a group's task tended to arrive at higher quality decisions than those that did not (Hirokawa, 1988). Further, as suggested earlier, the order in which the requisites were fulfilled did not appear to make a difference, nor did the particular format used by the group in fulfilling those requisites appear to matter (Burleson et al., 1984). Rather, what appeared to make the greatest difference for group performance was the number of functional requisites satisfied by a group during the course of its deliberation (Hirokawa, 1985). In short, in the 1980s, the functional perspective dominated research focusing on the relationship between group communication and group decision-making performance.

Communication and Group Leadership Research

Finally, the 1970s marked the emergence of research focused on the communicative aspects of group leadership. A number of studies focused on the communication characteristics of emergent group leaders. Investigations that exemplify this research interest included those by Geier (1967), which focused on the communicative traits of emergent group leader communication traits; Morris and Hackman (1969), which focused on the relationship between talkativeness and leader emergence; Schultz (1982), which focused on the effects of argumentativeness on emergent group leadership; and Smith and Powell (1988), which focused on the relationship between humor and leadership emergence. Other researchers sought to obtain a clearer understanding of the effects of different communication styles of group leadership on various socioemotional and task outputs in groups (Downs & Pickett, 1977; Rosenfeld & Fowler, 1976; Rosenfeld & Plax, 1975; Sargent & Miller, 1971; Wood, 1977; Yerby, 1975).

Contemporary Research

Research directions that emerged in the 1970s, and reached their peak in the 1980s, continued into the 1990s. At the same time, important developments beginning in the 1990s infused renewed energy and excitement in the study of small group communication. Around 1997, group communication scholars acquired enough support to form their own division in the National Communication Association (NCA). This division serves as an important source of identity and community for group communication scholars, allowing its members to discuss research at the annual NCA convention and recognize top work in the field. Also during this period, group communication scholars began to forge new connections with scholars who study groups in other disciplines, such as psychology and information systems (see Wittenbaum, Keyton, & Weingart, 2006). These connections are reflected in the research trends that have emerged since the mid-1990s.

With few exceptions, group communication research since 1996 falls into four main areas: (1) performance, (2) participation, (3) bona fide groups, and (4) technology. *Performance* research is concerned with predicting group outcomes, such as decisions, from knowing relevant features of the group (e.g., its task and members) and communication between members. *Participation* research focuses on understanding the frequency, content, and patterning of communication in groups. Research in the *bona fide group* perspective examines ongoing, natural groups that are interdependent with their context. The newest trend in group communication research, *technology*, focuses on the influence of and processes within communication technologies and the Internet. These areas reflect not only distinct research trends, but also particular theoretical perspectives and methodological tendencies. We will review these four research areas, demonstrating the main theoretical and empirical themes within each.

Performance

Group communication scholars have long been interested in understanding how communication impacts performance on group decision-making and problem-solving tasks. Much of the work in the performance area comes from a functional perspective where the quality of a group's output is a function of inputs (e.g., group size, leader style) and communication processes (Gouran & Hirokawa, 1983; Wittenbaum et al., 2004). Salazar (1995) proposed that group outputs are the function of interactions between inputs and communication processes. In his ambiguity model, he argued that communication processes and performance are more strongly related under conditions of high rather than low ambiguity, where features of the group's situation (task, diversity of information, and preference) interact with individual differences between members to impact the level of ambiguity. Given its long tradition of study, it should not be surprising that work designed to understand the relation between group communication and performance has continued and grown in recent years. A few studies continued classic lines of work on group polarization (Henningsen & Henningsen, 2004), and groupthink (Henningsen, Henningsen, Eden, & Cruz, 2006). But by far, the recent work in this area examines processes that are new to the study of group communication: information sharing, remembering, and resource sharing. What is not new, however, are the methods used to understand group performance. Nearly all of the research in this area is experimental and conducted using ad hoc student groups in a laboratory.

Information Sharing

Since the mid-1990s, group communication research has exploded with interest in information processing in groups. Much of this work was inspired by psychological research on information sharing in decision-making groups, originally conducted by Stasser and Titus (1985, 1987) but later replicated and extended by scholars across many fields (see Wittenbaum, Hollingshead, & Botero, 2004 for a review). Stasser and Titus originally expected that unique and novel arguments would be particularly persuasive in decision-making groups as predicted by persuasive arguments theory (see Stasser & Titus, 2003). Instead, they found that *unshared* information, which is uniquely known by a single group member, was less likely to appear in group discussions and impact group decisions compared to *shared* information that all members knew (Gigone & Hastie, 1993). This *collective information sharing bias* would not be a problem if it were not for the fact that it can impair group decision quality when thorough pooling of unshared information is essential for determining the best decision alternative—a condition called a *hidden profile*. Much of the research since Stasser and Titus's (1985) original study has sought to understand the conditions that increase the likelihood of groups discussing unshared information and thus making a better decision.

It should not be surprising why this line of work caught on in the field of communication. It fits a functional perspective well, examining how various input factors influence the communication of shared and unshared information during group discussion to impact the group output or decision quality. The hidden profile task, which involves giving all group members shared information that supports an inferior decision alternative and each group member unshared information that supports the optimal decision alternative, makes it easy to examine the relation between quality of communication and group decision. In the past decade, group communication scholars have published at least ten research articles using a hidden profile task to examine information exchange in decision making in groups (Cruz, Boster, & Rodriguez, 1997; Cruz, Henningsen, & Smith, 1999; Cruz, Henningsen, & Williams, 2000; Henningsen & Henningsen, 2003; Henningsen, Henningsen, Jakobsen, & Borton, 2004; Hollingshead, 1996; Reimer, Kuendig, Hoffrage, Park, & Hinsz, 2007; Savadori, Van Swol, & Sniezek, 2001; Van Swol & Ludutsky, 2007; Van Swol, Savadori, & Sniezek, 2003). From these works, we have learned that information exchange and group decisions suffer when members choose one decision alternative rather than rank them all (Hollingshead, 1996a,b), when the group leader tries to influence the group to select his or her poor quality preference (Cruz, Henningsen, & Smith, 1999), and when members emphasize shared information through repetition (Van Swol, Savadori, & Sniezek, 2003). Composing groups of equal status members (Hollingshead, 1996) and being able to compare each decision alternative on common dimensions (Reimer et al., 2007) improves members' performance on a hidden profile task.

Although the hidden profile task provides an interesting group decision making case, over-reliance on this task can be problematic. Wittenbaum et al. (2004) argued that the hidden profile paradigm carries with it assumptions that may not reflect the processes in natural decision-making groups, namely that members are cooperative communicators and unshared information is more important than shared information. To the contrary, members may hold competitive goals, motivating them to withhold unshared information from fellow group members or communicate it in goal-congruent ways (Wittenbaum, Hollingshead, & Bowman, 2003).

Interesting information sharing processes may be seen in decision-making groups that do not work on a hidden profile. For example, Wittenbaum (1998, 2000) showed that the bias toward shared information holds for high rather than low status members when deciding between equally attractive decision alternatives. When information is given to members so that they can communicate either shared or unshared information, those who communicate shared information are judged as more task capable (Wittenbaum, Hubbell, & Zuckerman, 1999). This mutual enhancement effect may occur because communicated shared information is judged as more important than communicated unshared information (Van Swol & Ludutsky, 2007). Shared information is not always favored, however. Sometimes, one group member (i.e., the judge) makes the decision for the group upon hearing information and advice from "advisors." In such a Judge-Advisor System (JAS), judges solicit more information from the advisor who knows a lot of unshared information compared to the advisor who knows a lot of shared information. In a JAS, judges probably associate the role of advisor with communicating novel information, which is why they may favor such advisors. Although assessing group decision quality was not paramount in these studies, they highlight the value of examining information sharing processes under various group decision making conditions.

Remembering

Several information sharing studies have examined group members' retrieval of shared and unshared information using a free recall or recognition task. This focus on remembering represents another new direction for group communication research. Research shows that group members recall shared information better than unshared information (Reimer et al., 2007; Savadori et al., 2001), an effect that replicates even when just considering information that supports the optimal decision alternative (Henningsen et al., 2006). And, the unshared information of high status members is better recognized than that of low status members (Wittenbaum, 2000). These studies highlight the added challenge of getting decision-making groups to use unshared information: members are less likely to recall it, particularly when mentioned by members with low regard.

Group memory was highlighted in a colloquy published in a 2003 issue of *Human Communication Research*. Remembering often occurs collaboratively in small groups—a phenomenon examined by Pavitt (2003). He lamented that group members do not reap the potential benefits of collective remembering, and, instead, they fall short of the recall performance of those remembering alone—a problem exacerbated by a large group size. Group discussion has the potential to help members recall more collectively than alone, but process losses during discussion (e.g., difficulty coordinating or reduced motivation) prevent this from happening. One potential criticism of Pavitt's work was that he did not examine communication processes directly, linking only inputs (e.g., group size) with outputs (recall performance) (Wittenbaum, 2003). Likewise, Hollingshead and Brandon (2003) argued that examining how encoding, storage, and retrieval of information occur via communication in transactive memory systems can demonstrate the central role of communication processes in producing collective recall output that exceeds the potential output of individual members. When communication has been examined in group memory research, it tends to be operationalized in overly simplistic ways (Propp, 2003). The recent interest of group communication scholars in collective memory shows great promise in uncovering ways that communication processes help or hinder the encoding, storage, and retrieval of information.

Resource Sharing

Finally, a new line of work examines communication processes in the context of resource dilemmas and highlights the potential contributions that group communication scholars can make to understanding pressing social problems. Social dilemma research provides an analogue to the "tragedy of the commons"—the tendency for group members to act selfishly by hoarding a scarce resource, depleting it for others and eventually for themselves in the long run (Komorita & Parks, 1994). Despite years of research on the topic by scholars in psychology, economics, and environmental sciences, Pavitt and colleagues were the first to link it with communication processes (Pavitt, McFeeters, Towey, & Zingerman, 2005; Pavitt, Zingerman, Towey, & McFeeters, 2006). In these experiments, students played a game in small groups where they consumed a resource that replenished itself at a higher or lower rate. Results showed that groups with a higher replenishment rate performed better (harvested more of the resource) and contributed more maintenance and procedural comments during group discussion compared to groups with a lower replenishment rate. This research nicely fits the input-process-output framework of the functional perspective, showing that a higher replenishment rate facilitates communication that is conducive to cooperation, which helped groups to harvest more of the resource. As the depletion of clean water and oil become more widespread problems on Earth, it will be important for communication scholars to aid the understanding of how people share resources in groups.

Participation

One of the first sustained lines of theory and research on small group communication was on participation. Bales, Strodtbeck, Mill, and Roseborough (1951) and Stephan and Mishler (1952) were among the first to document the problem and outline some of its characteristics. It has proved to be an important problem because it is not uncommon for participation to influence discussion and outcomes, and it is also an attractive problem because it lends itself to sophisticated statistical modeling techniques (for reviews see Bonito & Hollingshead, 1997; Stasser & Vaughan, 1996).

The scope of participation research depends, in part, on one's conceptualization of the problem. The narrow view is that the phenomenon consists of just the number of behaviors, irrespective of variation in content, substance, or function. This is bolstered by research that reveals the amount of participation predicts influence on group outcomes, with some qualifications (Bottger, 1984; Sorrentino & Boutillier, 1975). The broad view, and the one adopted here, is that participation is an umbrella term for studies that (1) categorize contributions in theoretically relevant ways; (2) look for patterns in such contributions; or (3) model the conditions under which contributions are produced during discussion. In general, the evaluation of group outcomes and its relation to participation is of secondary importance, if at all (cf. Gouran, 1990). Thus, the broad view includes areas such as argumentation, coherence and relevance, and deliberation.

There are three theoretical issues that drive participation research from a communication perspective. First is a concern with the nature of participation itself. This is important, because, as Wilson (2002) noted, the typology one uses to describe contributions is inextricably bound to the explanations for the process of participation. A second theoretical objective is to explain the co-occurrence of different types of contributions. Co-occurrence can be defined in many ways, including simple correlation (within and across groups) to lag-sequential analyses (e.g., Jackson & Poole, 2003). A third theoretical problem is to explain the influence of exogenous (to discussion) factors on participation. Here researchers run into an important issue. Some research assumes (often implicitly) a "mediated" view, which characterizes communication as a conduit through which individual differences are made manifest (Hirokawa, Erbert, & Hurst, 1996). Communication features do not otherwise figure in the process of participation. Others assume a "constitutive" view in which the process of participation itself creates opportunities for participation that individual differences or contextual features cannot predict. The truth is that participation is a function of both mediation and constitutive processes, but issues are not often framed that way.

Bonito's Participation Model

Bonito's (2007) local model of participation adopts a constitutive role for the process of participation. The model has three components. First, participants make judgments regarding the relative abilities of their colleagues to contribute usefully to discussion. Members perceived as more able are provided with and take more speaking turns than those who are judged as less able. Second, substantive participation occurs only if members possess active (i.e., available in short term memory) relevant information at certain points during the discussion. Third, discussion influences both the activation of information and the development of participator judgments. Findings from this line of work indicate support for the model. Information resources are associated with participation (Bonito, 2001, 2003a) but there is some evidence that colleagues' information resources also influence one's participation (Bonito & Lambert, 2005). Participator judgments are related to interaction (Bonito, 2003b; Bonito, DeCamp, Coffman, & Fleming, 2006) such that the more one participates substantively the more favorably colleagues perceive him or her. Finally, participation is an interdependent phenomenon such that one's participation is affected by other members' behavior and cognitions, including the extent to which information is shared (Bonito, 2001), the degree to which members share expectations regarding the purpose of discussion (Bonito, 2004), and satisfaction with discussion (Bonito, 2000). Criticisms of this work include a fairly rudimentary typology of participation types and vague or ill-specified features of temporal change of participator judgments within discussions.

Argument in Small Groups

The study of argument is central to the communication discipline, and several scholars, most notably Meyers, Seibold, and their associates, have examined the occurrence and patterning of argument in small groups (for a review, see Seibold & Meyers, 2007). Coding schemes for argument have been in development for some time (Meyers & Brashers, 1998a), with scholars focusing on the quality and type of arguments produced during discussion. The work is often framed within a structuration account of group processes, with arguments assumed to be the function of the intersection of micro (e.g., individual abilities in arguing) and macro (e.g., interaction patterns) processes. Fundamentally, interaction is viewed as constitutive to both the production of argument as well as its effects.

Meyers and Brashers (1998b) explicated a process model of argument in which disagreement generates argument within groups, and that different argument types, especially their distribution within groups, is associated with group outcomes. In general, studies of argument have evaluated distributions of argument types across members and within context. For example, Meyers, Brashers, and Hanner (2000) noted that majorities and minorities (in terms of the number of persons advocating a particular solution) differed in the number and type of arguments produced during discussion. For example, "winning" majorities produced more arguables (e.g., assertions and elaborations), disagreements, and delimiters (e.g., framing and securing common ground) than did losing majorities. In addition, losing minorities contributed more disagreement than did winning minorities. Finally, across all subgroups, winning teams produced more convergence statements than did losing teams. Sex differences also influence the distribution of arguments to some degree, as women are more likely to state agreement and provide propositions than is expected given their overall contributions, whereas men provided fewer of those comments (Meyers, Brashers, Winston, & Grob, 1997). However, men issued more challenges and asked more context-framing questions, given the number of their overall contributions, than did women.

Coherence

Several group communication scholars have addressed Hewes's (1996) challenge to look for coherence in terms of the connections among contributions to discussion that are unambiguously a function of interaction processes rather than preexisting individual differences or contextual constraints. Two types of coherence, *local* and *global*, characterize group discussion (Pavitt & Johnson, 1999). Local refers to connections among contiguous contributions whereas global describes coherence over larger stretches of the interaction. Pavitt and Johnson (1999) investigated features of local coherence in their study of proposal sequencing during problem solving discussion. They found that proposals were sequenced contiguously; any given proposal was likely to be followed by a comment relevant to that proposal. Pavitt and Johnson (Pavitt & Johnson, 2001, 2002) also evaluated more global aspects of coherence, including spirals (in which a proposal made early in discussion is evaluated later), finding that groups vary in the extent to which spiraling occurs. In addition, spiraling is less common in groups with a linear process orientation than those with a "reach-testing" (i.e., interested in trying a new idea then dropping them in favor of others) one. In an ambitious study, Corman and Kuhn (2005) asked participants to rate the coherence of computer-generated egocentric discussion transcripts (i.e., ones in which the sequence of contributions were randomly assembled by a computer) and actual group discussions. (Participants were asked to evaluate two transcripts, and were told in advance that the transcript might be from actual discussions or computer-generated.) Unexpectedly, participants were unable to distinguish between the two types of transcripts. Additional analyses revealed that the ability to distinguish among transcripts was aided (or made worse) by focusing on such attributes as clarity, reasoning, or depth. Thus, although participants in general could not tell computer-generated from actual discussion, there are cases when, using the appropriate evaluation orientation, such distinctions could reliably be made.

Deliberation

Research on deliberation has focused on jury groups, but it is not limited to those groups. Instead, deliberation refers to face-to-face discussions involving political or policy issues; the decisions have the potential to affect many people, not just group members (Burkhalter, Gastil, & Kelshaw 2002). Theoretical accounts are found in Burkhalter, Gastil, and Kelshaw, and Sunwolf and Seibold (1998), the central focus of which is understanding the conditions under which people contribute to deliberative discussions. Moy and Gastil (2006) tested a model in which network size, network heterogeneity, and media exposure predicted willingness to deliberate. Results varied across the two samples, one of which consisted of well-educated, politically aware participants, and the other a group of adult literacy students. One consistency in the findings was the network effect—the more persons with whom one discusses political events influences the extent to which he or she is willing to engage in deliberation. Gastil, Burkhalter, and Black (2007) asked if juries deliberate, and, if so, what are the antecedents to deliberation. Self-reports from actual jurors indicated that juries do indeed deliberate, and the vast majority indicated that they had ample opportunities to express themselves. Antecedents, including political knowledge, partisanship, and political self-confidence were associated with features of deliberation. However, uneven distribution with juries of some of these antecedents (e.g., political knowledge) seemed to inhibit, or at least reduce, levels of deliberation. Finally, Sager and Gastil (2002) noted that agreeableness (from the so-called Big 5 personality factors inventory) was correlated with perceived confirming interaction (i.e., the extent to which one feels confirmed or validated by other group members), and that confirming interaction was associated with perceptions of democratic decision making. Although not tested, the implication is that confirming interaction moderates member agreeableness with perceived democratic deliberations.

Bona Fide Groups

Scholars have long been interested in the communication practices of existing or "real world" groups. There are two reasons for this. First is a general dissatisfaction with the limitations of zero-history or experimental groups. Although laboratory studies provide useful information regarding input, process, and output characteristics of small groups, such groups are divorced from, or are rarely forced to encounter, exigencies that most real world groups encounter. Second, existing groups provide research contexts that are either unanticipated by the researcher or impossible to recreate validly in the laboratory. For example, Sigman (1984) detailed how members of a nursing home admissions board were responsible for certain types of information (e.g., knowing the number of available beds) and the conditions under which leaders structured discussion such that relevant information was contributed as needed. Laboratory groups rarely work on tasks with such important implications for the group, the organization, and the environment (i.e., those who are admitted and those who are not).

Much of that context-based research prior to the 1990s was theoretically fragmented, with no real unifying theme or perspective that allowed for comparisons of communicative behavior across contexts. The *bona fide perspective* (Putnam & Stohl, 1990) is a recent attempt to provide unity by making context a central feature of theory and research. A central feature of the bona fide perspective is to characterize "a group as a social system linked to its context, shaped by fluid boundaries, and altering its environment" (Putnam & Stohl, 1996, p. 148). There are two main assumptions (Frey, 2003b). The first is the notion that boundaries are permeable and fluid. A boundary is typically thought of in one of several ways, for example, as a physical space that delineates the group from other entities (e.g., a meeting room), a set of member characteristics that separate the group from others (e.g., faculty members), or a job or set of responsibilities that differentiate the group from other groups (e.g., a faculty search committee). These features are certainly important and at least function to provide the group with a "nominal" basis for starting and maintaining their collective work. The bona fide perspective, however, assumes a social constructionist approach to boundaries such that whatever defines a group is brought about by or is a function of a group's interactions, both internal and external (Stohl & Putnam, 2003). The second element of the bona fide perspective is interdependence with immediate context. Features of group processes, as well as outcomes, affect and are affected by a group's working environment. This includes, but is not limited to, historical context, anticipated outcomes, economics, location, and technological resources and support (Frey, 2003b). Intergroup communication is an integral component, as perceived support at a variety of levels depends on the extent to which the group successfully interacts with other groups with an interest in the outcome.

As one might imagine, given the scope of the bona fide perspective, there is no one "correct" set of methods and analyses; research is not "methodologically determinant" (Stohl & Putnam, 2003, p. 401). Thus, one finds many different types of investigations, including ethnographies, participant observations, textual analyses, and field and laboratory experiments. As Stohl and Putnam noted, the type of method is inconsequential as long as the starting point for the research questions involves interdependence between the group and its contexts. An advantage to this approach is a description of group processes of unparalleled depth and breadth, whereas disadvantages include comparability of results across studies and, in some cases, the inability to generalize to a larger population of groups and group members.

Researchers working from the bona fide perspective have examined groups in a wide variety of natural settings. The bulk of the work is collected in the edited volume by Frey (2003a), although a fair number of studies have appeared in peer-reviewed journals. Not surprisingly, the research might be usefully grouped into themes based on the extent to which studies investigate issues related to membership or interaction with immediate contexts. Some studies examine both boundaries and interaction with context, the notable case being Lammers and Krikorian (1997) who not only endeavored to apply virtually every aspect of the bona fide perspective extant in the contemporary literature to surgical teams, but added several constructs to the mix. Most studies have been more modest in their reach, examining a few issues in some detail.

Two recent examples of research from the bona fide perspective are Kramer's (2005) examination of a fund raising group (that raised funds by soliciting sponsorships for a charity marathon), and Sunwolf and Leets's (2004) study of adolescent and child peer groups. Kramer (a member of the group at the time of the study) used ethnographic methods to document, among other things, the role of communication in the formation of the group, as well as its relationship to external contexts. In terms of group formation, members used communication to develop both a sense of joint activities (although not every member participated in each activity) and a group identity. Members engaged external contexts in order to solicit sponsorships, and people external to the group provided valuable support to members while they (members) trained for the marathon. The findings, Kramer argued, are important for understanding how volunteer groups form and work together. Sunwolf and Leets used surveys and interviews to examine how children form groups, with emphasis on the development of boundaries. Children use a variety of communication methods, including ignoring, disqualifying, insulting, and blaming, to prevent outsiders from joining. In addition, the authors evaluated "rejection stress," the negative emotional impact of being denied access to groups. They argue that such experiences likely have consequences for attitudes toward working in more traditional groups.

Technology

With the advent of communication technologies and the Internet, group members no longer need to be co-present in space and time to collaborate and socialize. These technological advancements have opened up a new area of investigation for group communication scholars. Without a doubt, the newest explosion of research has examined groups whose members use computer-mediated communication (CMC). The initial research in this area, not surprisingly, compared the differences in process and performance between groups whose members communicate face-to-face (FTF) versus those who communicate via computer (e.g., see Baltes, Dickson, Sherman, Bauer, & LaGanke, 2002 for a review of work in group decision making). FTF and CMC groups often differ in member anonymity (awareness of one another's identities), familiarity with the communication medium, degree of synchrony of communication, and social collocation. These differences highlight a major theme in group technology research: understanding the effects of member identification. We will address this theme in addition to issues of stability of effects over time, status equalization, and online communities.

Most of the group technology work has centered on issues of group member identity and the processing of social information about the self and fellow members. The most prevalent theory in this area, the Social Identity Model of Deindividuation Effects (SIDE) predicts that the anonymity of CMC heightens social identity and leads to a loss of individual identity of the self (i.e., deindividuation) (Reicher, Spears, & Postmes, 1995). Because CMC often does not permit the communication of social cues that would be salient in FTF settings (e.g., attractiveness, sex, race), members are less likely to think of themselves in terms of their individuating characteristics. Instead, membership in the CMC group takes precedence over one's individual identity, which leads members to conform to in-group norms more readily (Postmes, Spears, & Lea, 1998) and increasingly over the course of interaction (Postmes, Spears, & Lea, 2000). However, conformity to group norms is reduced when personal dimensions of the self are made salient (Lee, 2004). Not all forms of anonymity were created equally, as Scott (1999) showed with groups using Group Decision Support Systems (GDSS). In his research, discursive anonymity (whether member messages were preceded by the member's name or not) influenced identification and communication outcomes more than physical anonymity (whether members were physically co-present or not).

One thing to keep in mind is that deindividuation effects in CMC groups may attenuate over time. Once members become familiar with the new communication medium, differences between CMC and FTF groups tend to dissipate (Hollingshead, 2001). Walther (1992) made a similar claim in his Social Information Processing Theory (SIPT), arguing that members of CMC groups will exchange social information to get to know one another personally, but it just takes more time than in FTF groups. Most of the SIDE research examines identification in short-lived groups, so its predictions for deindividuation may not hold over time in CMC groups.

Because cues indicating member status are less salient in CMC groups, some have argued that participation should be more equal across members in CMC than in FTF groups (DeSanctis & Gallupe, 1987). Despite some effects to the contrary (e.g., Peña, Walther, & Hancock, 2007), a meta-analysis of 44 different experiments showed that CMC groups demonstrated greater equality of participation and member influence and lower member dominance compared to those meeting FTF (Raines, 2005). Admittedly, there are probably several factors that moderate this status equalizing effect (Hollingshead, 2001). Nevertheless, the desire for fair and equal participation among members is apparent, especially among female members of mixed-sex groups who probably realize their potential low status vis-à-vis men (Flanagin, Tiyaamornwong, O'Connor, & Seibold, 2002). Such women may exploit the anonymity benefits of CMC by misrepresenting their sex to fellow members (Flanagin et al., 2002). Dissatisfaction with the group process is seen more generally, however, for both sexes working in CMC groups as participation rates become more unequal across members (Flanagin, Park, & Seibold, 2004).

Research on technology and groups can be characterized as using a wide variety of research methods. Although much of the research (particularly that in the SIDE tradition) uses experimental designs with student participants, many of the studies examine groups that interact over several weeks in the field rather than in a laboratory hour (e.g., Contractor, Seibold, & Heller, 1996; Flanagin, Park, & Seibold, 2004). In this regard, research on CMC groups reflects the processes of natural groups more than research in the group performance tradition. Increasingly, scholars are bringing more of a bona fide groups' perspective to the study of online groups. As an example, Matei and Ball-Rokeach (2005) described how WELL (Whole Earth Lectronic Link) navigated the ideological tensions experienced by being one of the first virtual communities by analyzing the discourse in their postings regarding being a virtual community. Research on technology and groups will likely continue to thrive with the use of experiments and surveys, content and discourse analysis, and laboratory and field methods. Because this research area has exploded so quickly, it can be criticized, however, for lacking theoretical integration and unity (Hollingshead, 2001). Future efforts may address this problem.

Sample Study

It is impossible to describe a sample study that touches all of the possible research questions suggested by our review of the group communication literature. It seems reasonable, however, to limit our discussion to quantitative social science research because (1) it is our area of methodological expertise, and (2) the majority of the work reviewed here is of that type. Rather than focus on just one area of the typical input-process-output model of group communication, we provide general guidelines regarding all three areas.

Input

Inputs are features of the group that are exogenous to discussion and precede or are antecedents of group interaction. Typically, but not always, the researcher manipulates inputs along theoretically important lines hoping that such manipulations have predicted effects on processes, outputs, or on both. As noted, an important research question concerns the conditions under which information is mentioned during discussion. This often entails that the researcher distributes the information to groups (usually of the zero-history, laboratory kind) such that some is shared and the rest unique (assuming a hidden profile design). Doing so often creates a set of initial solution preferences that are incorrect or at least suboptimal. (And this assumes the task has a correct or optimal answer, and that the researcher has identified in advance which information is important for correctly solving the problem.) The researcher will often manipulate other inputs (e.g., status of role of participants, communication channel) that he or she thinks will influence information sharing in groups. Other researchers have taken a different approach by using judgmental tasks (i.e., ones without correct answers) and measuring information units generated by participants (e.g., Bonito, 2001). Researchers must also identify the nature and measurement of the criterion variables, including characteristics of discussion, affective or perceptual issues (e.g., satisfaction), or nature of group outcomes, where appropriate.

Process

Researchers interested in process generally conceptualize and measure features of discussion, and are generally interested in the relation among discussion features. There is no correct way to categorize messages but one might, if not careful, generate inappropriate typologies (O'Keefe, 2003); one's choices depend on the research question of interest and, to some extent, on the properties of observed communication practices. Thus, for example, a scheme that is sensitive to variations in group argument is unlikely to be of much use for examining idea generation or information exchange. This type of research often occurs without manipulation of input variables, and often without concern for any inputs at all. Process research is reliant on recording and transcribing group interactions. Transcriptions must be reliably unitized (divided into smaller units that are of analytical interest) and then reliably coded, typically not by the researchers (because of the possibility of bias) but by "naïve" (to the study's purpose and hypotheses, if any) research assistants. Analysis of process data is often complex because of the interdependent (or nonindependent) nature of the data—it is often the case that one's contributions to discussion are influenced by those of others. Bonito (2001, 2006), for example, used multilevel models to analyze process; such models "nest" individuals within groups, and that allows for evaluation of (among other things) the extent to which behaviors are correlated within groups.

Outcomes

Group research is replete with a host of outcomes at a variety of levels of analysis (for a review, see Bonito & Hollingshead, 1997). In some cases, the outcomes are categorical in nature and determined by the researcher before the fact, as when groups are asked to choose from among three "candidates" for a hypothetical faculty position (Larson, Foster-Fishman, & Keys, 1994). Or they consist of range of choices that reflect an ordinal level of measurement, as in the case of the choice dilemma often used in studies of argumentation (e.g., Meyers & Brashers, 1998a). In other cases, outcomes take the form of self-reports that, for example, indicate affective reactions to discussion (e.g., satisfaction) or toward one's colleagues (e.g., credibility, perceptions of competence or ability). These outcomes are often evaluated against features of process (e.g., if the use of certain types of argument predicts a group's choice) or certain types of inputs, for example if distributions of information are related to perceptions of one's colleagues (Wittenbaum et al., 1999).

Summary

This chapter provides an overview of group communication research, including the central issues and questions that drive it. First and foremost is understanding the characteristics of the group communication process, including (1) the quality of messages produced during discussion; (2) their relation to other messages; and (3) the extent to which messages of certain types are reliably patterned during discussion. In addition, researchers have focused on antecedents to discussion and discussion outcomes at various levels of analysis (e.g., group outcomes, individual cognitions and attitudes). Recent theoretical development, as well as a wider set of analytical choices (e.g., multilevel modeling) will provide researchers with an exciting array of new questions to ask regarding the character of small group communication. An important issue yet to be fully addressed includes the extent to which group outcomes reflect communication-based processes, antecedents (e.g., initial preferences, social comparison), or some combination of the two. The following set of recommended readings will alert the reader to such issues, as well as other questions and issues relevant to research on group communication processes.

Notes

1. Portions of this chapter are excerpted from an earlier version of this chapter written by Randy Y. Hirokawa, Abran J. Salazar, Larry Erbert, and Richard J. Ice.
2. The number of people involved for their communication to count as "small group communication" is rather arbitrary. Most definitions identify small group communication as involving between 3 and 12 individuals.

References

Applbaum, R. L., & Anatol, K. (1971). PERT: A tool for communication research planning. *Journal of Communication, 21,* 368–380.

Baird, J. E., Jr. (1974). A comparison of distributional and sequential structure in cooperative and competitive group discussion. *Speech Monographs, 41,* 226–232.

Bales, R. F. (1950). *Interaction process analysis: A method for the study of small groups.* Cambridge, MA: Addison-Wesley.

Bales, R. F., Strodtbeck, F. L., Mills, T. M., & Roseborough, M. E. (1951). Channels of communication in small groups. *American Sociological Review, 16,* 461–468.

Baltes, B. B., Dickson, M. W., Sherman, M. P., Bauer, C. C., & LaGanke, J. (2002). Computer-mediated communication and group decision making: A meta-analysis. *Organizational Behavior and Human Decision Processes, 87*(1), 156–179.

Barnlund, D. C. (1955). Experiments in leadership training for decision-making discussion groups. *Speech Monographs, 22,* 1–14.

Bayless, O. (1967). An alternate pattern for problem-solving discussion. *Journal of Communication, 17,*188–198.

Beatty, M. J. (1989). Group members' decision rule orientations and consensus. *Human Communication Research, 16,* 279–296.

Berg, D. M. (1967). A descriptive analysis of the distribution and duration of themes discussed by small groups. *Speech Monographs, 34,* 172–175.

Black, E. B. (1955). A consideration of the rhetorical causes of breakdown in discussion. *Speech Monographs, 22,* 15–19.

Bonito, J. A. (2000). The effect of contributing substantively on perceptions of participation. *Small Group Research, 31*(5), 528–553.

Bonito, J. A. (2001). An information-processing approach to participation in small groups. *Communication Research, 28*(3), 275–303.

Bonito, J. A. (2003a). Information processing and exchange in mediated groups: Interdependence and interaction. *Human Communication Research, 29*(4), 533–559.

Bonito, J. A. (2003b). A social relations analysis of participation in small groups. *Communication Monographs, 70*(2), 83–97.

Bonito, J. A. (2004). Shared cognition and participation in small groups: Similarity of member prototypes. *Communication Research, 31,* 704–730.

Bonito, J. A. (2006). A longitudinal social relations analysis of participation in small groups. *Human Communication Research, 32*(3), 302–321.

Bonito, J. A. (2007). A local model of information sharing in small groups. *Communication Theory, 17*(3), 252–280.

Bonito, J. A., DeCamp, M. H., Coffman, M., & Fleming, S. (2006). Participation, information, and control in small groups: An actor-partner interdependence model. *Group Dynamics: Theory, Research, and Practice, 10*(1), 16–28.

Bonito, J. A., & Hollingshead, A. B. (1997). Participation in small groups. In B. R. Burleson (Ed.), *Communication yearbook* (Vol. 20, pp. 227–261). Newbury Park, CA: Sage.

Bonito, J. A., & Lambert, B. L. (2005). Information similarity as a moderator of the effect of gender on participation in small groups: A multilevel analysis. *Small Group Research, 36*(2), 139–165.

Bottger, P. C. (1984). Expertise and air time as bases of actual and perceived influence in problem-solving groups. *Journal of Applied Psychology, 69*(2), 214–221.

Brilhart, J. K., & Jochem, L. M. (1964). Effects of different patterns on outcomes of problem-solving discussion. *Journal of Applied Psychology, 48,* 175–79.

Burkhalter, S., Gastil, J., & Kelshaw, T. (2002). A conceptual definition and theoretical model of public deliberation in small face-to-face groups. *Communication Theory, 12*(4), 398–422.

Burleson, B. R., Levine, B. J., & Samter, W. (1984). Decision-making procedure and decision quality. Human *Communication Research, 10,* 557–574.

Canary, D. J., Brossman, B. G., & Seibold, D. R. (1987). Argument structures in decision-making groups. *Southern States Communication Journal, 53,* 18–37.

Cattell, R. B. (1948). Concepts and methods in the measurement of group syntality. *Psychological Monographs, 55,* 48–63.

Cattell, R. B. (1951a). Determining syntality dimension as a basis for morale and leadership measurement. In H. Guetzkow (Ed.), *Groups, leadership, and men* (pp. 16–27). Pittsburgh, PA: Carnegie Press.

Cattell, R. B. (1951b). New concepts for measuring leadership in terms of group syntality. *Human Relations, 4,* 161–184.

Cheseboro. J. W., Cragan, J. E., & McCullough, P. (1973). The small group techniques of the radical revolutionary: A synthetic study of consciousness-raising. *Communication Monographs, 40,* 136–146.

Comadena, M. E. (1984). Brainstorming groups: Ambiguity tolerance, communication apprehension, task attraction, and individual productivity. *Small Group Behavior, 15,* 251–254.

Contractor, N. S., Seibold, D. R., & Heller, M. A. (1996). Interactional influence in the structuring of media use in groups: Influence in members' perceptions of group decision support system use. *Human Communication Research, 22*(4), 451–481.

Corman, S. R., & Kuhn, T. (2005). The detectability of socio-egocentric group speech: A quasi-turing test. *Communication Monographs, 72*(2), 117–143.

Cragan, J. F., & Wright, D. W. (1980). Small group communication of the 1970s: A synthesis and critique of the field. *Central States Speech Journal, 31*,197–213.

Cragan, J. F., & Wright, D. W. (1990). Small group communication of the 1980s: A synthesis and critique of the field. *Communication Studies, 41,* 212–236.

Crowell, L., Katcher, A., & Miyamoto, S. F. (1955). Self-concepts of communication skill and performance in small group discussions. *Speech Monographs, 22,* 20–27.

Cruz, M. G., Boster, F. J., & Rodriguez, J. I. (1997). The impact of group size and proportion of shared information on the exchange and integration of information in groups. *Communication Research, 24*(3), 291–313.

Cruz, M. G., Henningsen, D. D., & Smith, B. A. (1999). The impact of directive leadership on group information sampling, decisions and perceptions of the leader. *Communication Research, 26*(3), 349–369.

Cruz, M. G., Henningsen, D. D., & Williams, M. L. M. (2000). The presence of norms in the absence of groups? the impact of normative influence under hidden-profile conditions. *Human Communication Research, 26*(1), 104–124.

Delbecq, A. L., Van de Ven, A. H., & Gustafson, D. H. (1975). *Group techniques for program planning: A guide to nominal group and delphi process.* Glenview, IL: Scott, Foresman.

DeSanctis, G., & Gallupe, R. B. (1987). A foundation for the study of group decision support systems. *Management Science, 33*(5), 589–609.

DeStephen, R. S. (1983). High and low consensus groups: A content and relational interaction analysis. *Small Group Behavior, 14,* 143–162.

DeStephen, R. S., & Hirokawa, R. Y. (1988). Small group consensus: Stability of group support of the decision, task process, and group relationship. *Small Group Behavior, 19,* 227–239.

Dewey, J. (1910). *How we think.* Boston: D. C. Heath.

Downs C. W., & Pickett, T. (1977). Analysis of the effects of nine leadership-group compatibility contingencies upon productivity and member satisfaction. *Communication Monographs, 44,* 220–230.

Ellis. D. G., & Fisher, B. A. (1975). Phases of conflict in small group development: A Markov analysis. *Human Communication Research, 1,* 195–212.

Fisher, B. A. (1970). Decision emergence: Phases in group decision-making. *Speech Monographs, 37,* 53–66.

Fisher, B. A., & Hawes, L. (1971). An interact system model: Generating a grounded theory of small groups. *Quarterly Journal of Speech, 57,* 444–453.

Flanagin, A. J., Park, H. S., & Seibold, D. R. (2004). Group performance and collaborative technology: A longitudinal and multilevel analysis of information quality, contribution equity, and members' satisfaction in computer-mediated groups. *Communication Monographs, 71*(3), 352–372.

Flanagin, A. J., Tiyaamornwong, V., O'Connor, J., & Seibold, D. R. (2002). Computer-mediated group work: The interaction of member sex and anonymity. *Communication Research, 29*(1), 66–93.

Frey, L. R. (Ed.). (2003a). *Group communication in context: Studies of bona fide groups* (2nd ed.). Mahwah, NJ: Erlbaum.

Frey, L. R. (2003b). Group communication in context: Studying bona fide groups. In L. R. Frey (Ed.), *Group communication in context: Studies of bona fide groups* (2nd ed., pp. 1–20). Mahwah, NJ: Erlbaum.

Gastil, J., Burkhalter, S., & Black, L. W. (2007). Do juries deliberate? A study of deliberation, individual difference, and group member satisfaction at a municipal courthouse. *Small Group Research, 38*(3), 337–359.

Geier, J. G. (1967). A trait approach to the study of leadership in small groups. *Journal of Communication, 17,* 316–323.

Gigone, D., & Hastie, R. (1993). The common knowledge effect: Information sharing and group judgment. *Journal of Personality & Social Psychology, 65*(5), 959–974.

Gouran, D. S. (1969). Variables related to consensus in group discussion of questions of policy. *Speech Monographs, 36,* 387–391.

Gouran, D. S. (1990). Exploiting the predictive potential of structuration theory. In J. A. Anderson (Ed.), *Communication yearbook* (Vol. 13, pp. 313–322). Newbury Park, CA: Sage.

Gouran, D. S. (1999). Communication in groups: The emergence and evolution of a field of study. In L. R. Frey, D. S. Gouran, & M. S. Poole (Eds.), *The handbook of group communication theory and research* (pp. 3–36). Thousand Oaks, CA; Sage.

Gouran, D. S., & Baird, J. E., Jr. (1972). An analysis of distributional and sequential structure in problem-solving and informal group discussions. *Speech Monographs, 39,* 18–22.

Gouran, D. S., & Hirokawa, R. Y. (1983). The role of communication in decision-making groups: A functional perspective. In M. S. Mander (Ed.), *Communications in transition* (pp. 168–185). New York: Praeger.

Gouran, D. S., & Hirokawa, R. Y. (1986). Counteractive functions of communication in effective group decision-making. In R. Y. Hirokawa & M. S. Poole. (Eds.), *Communication and group decision making* (pp. 81–90). Beverly Hills, CA: Sage.

Henningsen, D. D., & Henningsen, M. L. M. (2003). Examining social influence in information-sharing contexts. *Small Group Research, 34*(4), 391–412.

Henningsen, D. D., & Henningsen, M. L. M. (2004). The effect of individual difference variables on information sharing in decision-making groups. *Human Communication Research, 30*(4), 540–555.

Henningsen, D. D., Henningsen, M. L. M., Eden, J., & Cruz, M. G. (2006). Examining the symptoms of groupthink and retrospective sensemaking. *Small Group Research, 37*(1), 36–64.

Henningsen, D. D., Henningsen, M. L. M., Jakobsen, L., & Borton, I. (2004). It's good to be leader: The influence of randomly and systematically selected leaders on decision-making groups. *Group Dynamics: Theory, Research, and Practice, 8*(1), 62–76.

Hewes, D. E. (1996). Small group communication may not influence decision making: An amplification of socio-egocentric theory. In R. Y. Hirokawa & M. S. Poole (Eds.), *Communication and group decision making* (2nd ed., pp. 179–212). Thousand Oaks, CA: Sage.

Hiltz, S. R., Johnson, K., & Turoff, M. (1986). Experiments in group decision-making: Communication process and outcome in face-to-face versus computerized conferences. *Human Communication Research, 13,* 225–252.

Hirokawa, R. Y. (1983). Group communication and problem-solving effectiveness: An investigation of procedural functions. *Western Journal of Speech Communication, 47,* 59–74.

Hirokawa, R. Y. (1985). Discussion procedures and decision performance. Human Communication Research, 12, 203–224.

Hirokawa, R. Y., & Scheerhorn, D. R. (1986). Communication and Faulty Group Decision-Making. In R. Y. Hirokawa & M. S. Poole (Eds.), *Communication and group decision-making* (pp. 63–80). Beverly Hills, CA: Sage.

Hirokawa, R. Y., & McLeod, P. L. (1993, November). *Communication, decision development, and decision quality in small groups: An integration of two approaches.* Paper presented at the annual meeting of the Speech Communication Association, Miami Beach.

Hirokawa, R. Y., Erbert, L., & Hurst, A. (1996a). Communication and group decision-making effectiveness. In R. Y. Hirokawa & M. S. Poole (Eds.), *Communication and group decision making* (pp. 269–300). Thousand Oaks, CA: Sage.

Hollingshead, A. B. (1996a). Information suppression and status persistence in group decision making: The effects of communication media. *Human Communication Research, 23*(2), 193–219.

Hollingshead, A. B. (1996b). The rank-order effect in group decision making. *Organizational Behavior & Human Decision Processes, 68*(3), 181–193.

Hollingshead, A. B. (2001). Communication technologies, the internet, and group research. In M. A. Hogg & R. S. Tindale (Eds.), *Blackwell handbook of social psychology: Group processes* (pp. 557–573). Malden, MA: Blackwell.

Hollingshead, A. B., & Brandon, D. P. (2003). Potential benefits of communication in transactive memory systems. *Human Communication Research, 29*(4), 607–615.

Jablin, F. M. (1981). Cultivating imagination: Factors that enhance and inhibit creativity in brainstorming groups. *Human Communication Research, 7,* 245–258.

Jablin, F. M., Seibold. D. R., & Sorenson, R. (1977). Potential inhibitory effects of group participation on brainstorming performance. *Central States Speech Journal, 28,* 113–121.

Jablin, F. M., Sorenson, R., & Seibold, D. R. (1978). Interpersonal perception and group brainstorming performance. *Communication Quarterly, 26*, 36–44.

Jackson, M. H., & Poole, M. S. (2003). Idea-generation in naturally occurring contexts: Complex appropriation of a simple group procedure. *Human Communication Research, 29*(4), 560–591.

Jarboe, S. (1988). A comparison of input-output, process-output, and input-process-output models of small group problem-solving effectiveness. *Communication Monographs, 55*, 121–142.

Kline, J. A. (1972). Orientation and group consensus. *Central States Speech Journal, 23*, 44–47.

Kline, J. A., & Hullinger, J. L. (1973). Redundancy, self-orientation, and group consensus. *Speech Monographs, 40*, 72–74.

Knutson, T. J. (1972). An experimental study of the effects of orientation behavior on small group consensus. *Speech Monographs, 39*, 159–165.

Knutson, T. J., & Holdridge, W. E. (1975). Orientation behavior, leadership, and consensus: A possible functional relationship. *Speech Monographs, 42*, 107–114.

Knutson, T. J., & Kowitz, A. C. (1977). Effects of information type and level of orientation on consensus achievement in substantive and affective small-group conflict. *Central States Speech Journal, 28*, 54–63.

Komorita, S. S., & Parks, C. D. (1994). *Social dilemmas*. Madison, WI: Brown & Benchmark.

Kramer, M. W. (2005). Communication in a fund-raising marathon group. *Journal of Communication, 55*(2), 257–276.

Lammers, J. C., & Krikorian, D. H. (1997). Theoretical extension and operationalization of the bona fide group construct with an application to surgical teams. *Journal of Applied Communication Research, 25*, 17–38.

Larson, C. E. (1969). Forms of analysis and small group problem-solving. *Speech Monographs, 36*, 452–455.

Larson, J. R., Foster-Fishman, P. G., & Keys, C. B. (1994). Discussion of shared and unshared information in decision-making groups. *Journal of Personality and Social Psychology, 67*(3), 446–461.

Larson, C. E., & Gratz, R. D. (1970). Problem-solving discussion training and T-group training: An experimental comparison. *Speech Teacher, 19*, 54–57.

Leathers, D. G. (1972). Quality of group communication as a determinant of group product. *Speech Monographs, 39*, 166–173.

Lee, E. (2004). Effects of visual representation on social influence in computer-mediated communication: Experimental tests of the social identity model of deindividuation effects. *Human Communication Research, 30*(2), 234–259.

Lewin, K. (1947). Frontiers in group dynamics. *Human Relations, 1*, 5–41.

Lewin, K. (1951). *Field theory in social science: Selected theoretical papers* (D. Cartwright, Ed.). New York: Harper & Row.

Mabry, E. A. (1975a). Exploratory analysis of a developmental model for task-oriented small groups. *Human Communication Research, 2*, 66–74.

Mabry, E. A. (1975b). An instrument for assessing content themes in group interaction. *Communication Monographs, 42*, 291–297.

Matei, S. A., & Ball-Rokeach, S. (2005). Watts, the 1965 Los Angeles riots, and the communicative construction of the fear epicenter of Los Angeles. *Communication Monographs, 72*(3), 301–323.

Meyers, R. A., & Brashers, D. E. (1998a). Argument in group decision making: Explicating a process model and investigating the argument-outcome link. *Communication Monographs, 65*(4), 261–281.

Meyers, R. A., & Brashers, D. E. (1998b). Argument in group decision making: Explicating a process model and investigating the argument-outcome link. *Communication Monographs, 65*(4), 261–281.

Meyers, R. A., Brashers, D. E., & Hanner, J. (2000). Majority-minority influence: Identifying argumentative patterns and predicting argument-outcome links. *Journal of Communication, 50*(4), 3–30.

Meyers, R. A., Brashers, D. E., Winston, L., & Grob, L. (1997). Sex differences and group argument: A theoretical. *Communication Studies, 48*(1), 19.

Morris, C. G., & Hackman, J. R. (1969). Behavioral correlates of perceived leadership. *Journal of Personality and Social Psychology, 13*, 350–361.

Moy, P., & Gastil, J. (2006). Predicting deliberative conversation: The impact of discussion networks, media use, and political cognitions. *Political Communication, 23*(4), 443–460.

O'Keefe, D. J. (2003). Message properties, mediating states, and manipulation checks: Claims, evidence, and data analysis in experimental persuasive message effects research. *Communication Theory, 13*(3), 251–274.

Pavitt, C. (2003). Colloquy: Do interacting groups perform better than aggregates of individuals? Why we have to be reductionists about group memory. *Human Communication Research, 29*(4), 592.

Pavitt, C., & Johnson, K. K. (1999). An examination of the coherence of group discussions. *Communication Research, 26*(3), 303–321.

Pavitt, C., & Johnson, K. K. (2001). The association between group procedural MOPs and group discussion procedure. *Small Group Research, 32*(5), 595–624.

Pavitt, C., & Johnson, K. K. (2002). Scheidel and Crowell revisited: A descriptive study of group proposal sequencing. *Communication Monographs, 69*(1), 19–32.

Pavitt, C., McFeeters, C., Towey, E., & Zingerman, V. (2005). Communication during resource dilemmas: 1. Effects of different replenishment rates. *Communication Monographs, 72*(3), 345–363.

Pavitt, C., Zingerman, V., Towey, E., & McFeeters, C. (2006). Group communication during resource dilemmas: 2. Effects of harvest limit and reward asymmetry. *Communication Research, 33*(1), 64–91.

Peña, J., Walther, J. B., & Hancock, J. T. (2007). Effects of geographic distribution on dominance perceptions in computer-mediated groups. *Communication Research, 34*(3), 313–331.

Philipsen, G., Mulac, A., & Dietrich, D. (1979). The effects of social interaction on group idea generation. *Communication Monographs, 46*, 119–125.

Phillips, G. M. (1966). *Communication and the small group.* Indianapolis: Bobbs-Merrill.

Poole, M. S. (1981). Decision development in small groups I: A comparison of two models. *Communication Monographs, 48*, 1–24.

Poole, M. S. (1983). Decision development in small groups III: A multiple sequence model of group decision development. *Communication Monographs, 50*, 321–341.

Poole, M. S., & Doelger, J. A. (1986). Developmental processes in group decision-making. In R. Y. Hirokawa & M. S. Poole (Eds.), *Communication and group decision making* (pp. 35–61). Beverly Hills, CA: Sage.

Poole, M. S., & Roth, J. (1989a). Decision development in small groups IV: A typology of group decision paths. *Human Communication Research, 15*, 323–356.

Poole. M. S., & Roth, J. (1989b). Decision development in small groups V: Test of a contingency model. *Human Communication Research, 15*, 549–589.

Postmes, T., Spears, R., & Lea, M. (1998). Breaching or building social boundaries? SIDE-effects of computer-mediated communication. *Communication Research, 25*(6), 689–715.

Postmes, T., Spears, R., & Lea, M. (2000). The formation of group norms in computer-mediated communication. *Communication Research, 26*(3), 341–371.

Propp, K. M. (2003). In search of the assembly bonus effect: Continued exploration of communication's role in group memory. *Human Communication Research, 29*(4), 600–606.

Putnam, L. L., & Stohl, C. (1990). Bona fide groups: A reconceptualization of groups in context. *Communication Studies, 41*, 248–265.

Putnam, L. L., & Stohl, C. (1996). In Hirokawa R. Y. & Poole M. S. (Eds.), *Bona fide groups: An alternative perspective for communication and small group decision making.* Thousand Oaks, CA: Sage.

Pyron, H. C. (1964). An experimental study of the role of reflective thinking in business and professional conferences and discussions. *Speech Monographs, 31*, 157–161.

Pyron, H. C., & Sharp, H., Jr. (1963). A quantitative study of reflective thinking and performance in problem-solving discussion. *Journal of Communication, 13*, 46–53.

Raines, S. (2005). Leveling the organizational playing field—virtually: A meta-analysis of experimental research assessing the impact of group support system use on member influence behaviors. *Communication Research, 32*, 193–234.

Reicher, S., Spears, R., & Postmes, T. (1995). A social identity model of deindividuation phenomena. *European Review of Social Psychology, 6*, 161–198.

Reimer, T., Kuendig, S., Hoffrage, U., Park, E., & Hinsz, V. (2007). Effects of the information environment on group discussions and decisions in the hidden-profile paradigm. *Communication Monographs, 74*(1), 1–28.

Rosenfeld, L. B., & Fowler, G. D. (1976). Personality, sex and leadership style. *Communication Monographs*, 43, 320–324.

Rosenfeld, L. B., & Plax, T. G. (1975). Personality determinants of autocratic and democratic leadership. *Speech Monographs*, 42, 203–208.

Sager, K. L., & Gastil, J. (2002). Exploring the psychological foundations of democratic group deliberation: Personality factors, confirming interaction, and democratic decision making. *Communication Research Reports*, 19(1), 56–65.

Saine, T. J., & Bock, D. G. (1973). A comparison of the distributional and sequential structures of interaction in high and low consensus groups. *Central States Speech Journal*, 24, 125–130.

Saine, T. J., Schulman, L. S., & Emerson, L. C. (1974). The effects of group size on the structure of interaction in problem-solving groups. *Southern Speech Communication Journal*, 39, 333–345.

Salazar, A. J. (1995). Understanding the synergistic effects of communication in small groups: Making the most out of group members' abilities. *Small Group Research*, 26, 169–199.

Sargent, J. F., & Miller, G. R. (1971). Some differences in certain communication behaviors of autocratic and democratic leaders. *Journal of Communication*, 21, 233–252.

Savadori, L., Van Swol, L. M., & Sniezek, J. A. (2001). Information sampling and confidence within groups and judge advisor systems. *Communication Research*, 28(6), 737–771.

Scheidel, T. M., & Crowell, L. (1964). Idea development in small discussion groups. *Quarterly Journal of Speech*, 50, 140–145.

Scheidel, T. M., Crowell, L., & Shepherd, J. R. (1958). Personality and discussion behavior: A study of possible relationships. *Speech Monographs*, 25, 261–267.

Schultz. B. (1982). Argumenativeness: Its effect in group decision-making and its role in leadership perception. *Communication Quarterly*, 30, 368–475.

Scott, C. R. (1999). Communication technology and group communication. In L. R. Frey, D. Gouran, & M. S. Poole (Eds.), *Handbook of group communication and research* (pp. 432–472). Thousand Oaks, CA: Sage.

Seibold, D. R., & Meyers, R. A. (2007). Group argument: A structuration perspective and research program. *Small Group Research*, 38(3), 312–336.

Sharp, H., Jr., & Milliken, J. (1964). The reflective thinking ability and the product of problem-solving discussion. *Speech Monographs*, 31, 124–127.

Sigman, S. J. (1984). Talk and interaction strategy in a task-oriented group. *Small Group Research*, 15(1), 33–51.

Smith, C. M., & Powell, L. (1988). The use of disparaging humor by group leaders. *Southern Speech Communication Journal*, 53, 279–292.

Sorrentino, R. M., & Boutillier, R. G. (1975). The effect of quantity and quality of verbal interaction on ratings of leadership ability. *Journal of Experimental Social Psychology*, 11(5), 403–411.

Stasser, G., & Titus, W. (1985). Pooling of unshared information in group decision making: Biased information sampling during discussion. *Journal of Personality and Social Psychology*, 48(6), 1467–1478.

Stasser, G., & Titus, W. (1987). Effects of information load and percentage of shared information on the dissemination of unshared information during group discussion. *Journal of Personality and Social Psychology*, 53, 81–93.

Stasser, G., & Titus, W. (2003). Hidden profiles: A brief history. *Psychological Inquiry*, 14(3), 304–313.

Stasser, G., & Vaughan, S. I. (1996). Models of participation during face-to-face unstructured discussion. In E. H. Witte & J. H. Davis (Eds.), *Understanding group behavior* (pp. 165–192). Mahwah, NJ: Erlbaum.

Stephan, F. F., & Mishler, E. G. (1952). The distribution of participation in small groups: An exponential approximation. *American Sociological Review*, 17, 598–608.

Stohl, C., & Putnam, L. L. (2003). Communication in bona fide groups: A retrospective and prospective account. In L. R. Frey (Ed.), *Group communication in context: Studies of bona fide groups* (2nd ed., pp. 399–414). Mahwah, NJ: Erlbaum.

Sunwolf, & Leets, L. (2004). Being left out: Rejecting outsiders and communicating group boundaries in childhood and adolescent peer groups. *Journal of Applied Communication Research*, 32(3), 195–223.

Sunwolf, & Seibold, D. R. (1998). Jurors' intuitive rules for deliberation: A structurational approach to communication in jury decision making. *Communication Monographs*, 65(4), 282–307.

Van Swol, L. M., & Ludutsky, C. L. (2007). Tell me something I don't know. *Communication Research, 34*(3), 297–312.

Van Swol, L. M., Savadori, L., & Sniezek, J. A. (2003). Factors that may affect the difficulty of uncovering hidden profiles. *Group Processes & Intergroup Relations, 6*(3), 285–304.

Walther, J. B. (1992). Interpersonal effects in computer-mediated interaction: A relational perspective. *Communication Research, 19*(1), 52–90.

Wilson, S. R. (2002). *Seeking and resisting compliance: Why people say what they do when trying to influence others.* Thousand Oaks, CA: Sage.

Wittenbaum, G. M. (1998). Information sampling in decision-making groups: The impact of members' task-relevant status. *Small Group Research, 29*(1), 57–84.

Wittenbaum, G. M. (2000). The bias toward discussing shared information: Why are high- status group members immune? *Communication Research, 27*(3), 379–400.

Wittenbaum, G. M. (2003). Putting communication into the study of group memory. *Human Communication Research, 29*(4), 616.

Wittenbaum, G. M., Bowman, J. M., & Hollingshead, A. B. (2003, November). *Strategic information sharing in mixed-motive decision-making groups.* Paper presented at the annual meeting of the National Communication Association, Miami Beach, FL.

Wittenbaum, G. M., Hollingshead, A. B., & Botero, I. C. (2004). From cooperative to motivated information sharing in groups: Moving beyond the hidden profile paradigm. *Communication Monographs, 71*(3), 286–310.

Wittenbaum, G. M., Hollingshead, A. B., Paulus, P. B., Hirokawa, R. Y., Ancona, D. G., Peterson, R. S., et al. (2004). The functional perspective as a lens for understanding groups. *Small Group Research, 35*(1), 17–43.

Wittenbaum, G. M., Hubbell, A. P., & Zuckerman, C. (1999). Mutual enhancement: Toward an understanding of the collective preference for shared information. *Journal of Personality and Social Psychology, 77*(5), 967–978.

Wittenbaum, G. M., Keyton, J., & Weingart, L. R. (2006). A new era for group research: The formation of INGRoup. *Small Group Research, 37*, 1–7.

Wood, J. T. (1977). Leading in purposive discussions: A study of adaptive behavior. *Communication Monographs, 44*, 152–165.

Yerby, J. (1975). Attitude, task and sex composition as variables affecting female leadership in small problem-solving groups. *Speech Monographs, 42*, 160–168.

Suggested Readings

Hewes, D. E. (1996). Small group communication may not influence decision making: An amplification of socio-egocentric theory. In R. Y. Hirokawa & M. S. Poole (Eds.), *Communication and group decision making* (2nd ed., pp. 179–212). Thousand Oaks, CA: Sage.

Pavitt, C. (1993). Does communication matter in social influence during small group discussion? Five positions. *Communication Studies, 44*, 216–227.

Poole, M. S., & Hollingshead, A. B. (2005). *Theories of small groups: Interdisciplinary perspectives.* Thousand Oaks, CA: Sage.

Poole, M. S., Keyton, J., & Frey, L. R. (1999). Group communication methodology. In L. R. Frey (Ed.), *The handbook of group communication theory and research* (pp. 93–112). Thousand Oaks, CA: Sage.

Seibold, D. R., & Meyers, R. A. (2007). Group argument: A structuration perspective and research program. *Small Group Research, 38*, 312–336.

Wittenbaum, G. M., Hollingshead, A. B., & Botero, I. C. (2004). From cooperative to motivated information sharing in groups: Moving beyond the hidden profile paradigm. *Communication Monographs, 71*, 286–310.

24

WATCH YOUR NEIGHBOR WATCHING YOU
Applying Concertive Control in Changing Organizational Environments

Phillip K. Tompkins, Yvonne J. Montoya, and Carey B. Candrian

People have studied and discussed communication processes within dominant organizations since antiquity. Because of rapid social and organizational change, however, great pressure has been placed on organizational communication researchers to continually develop useful concepts and studies to match the complex interactions of contemporary workplaces. From the time of its formal introduction in the 1950s, the area of organizational communication has "borrowed" heavily from numerous academic disciplines (e.g., industrial psychology, social psychology, organizational behavior, administrative science, contemporary rhetorical theory, sociology, anthropology, linguistics, political science, and the philosophy of science; Putnam & Cheney, 1985; Redding & Tompkins, 1988). Moreover, scholars from a variety of disciplines conduct research on organizational communication. Consequently, literature abounds on historical, theoretical, and methodological issues. Rather than providing a thorough overview of relevant literature, this chapter instead briefly discusses selected theoretical/conceptual frameworks and related research perspectives and examples relevant to organizational communication.

Theoretical Frameworks and Research Activities

Among several writers who review theoretical and methodological developments in organizational communication, Redding and Tompkins (1988) offered a two-dimensional schema of dominant approaches to theory and research. First, they outlined three phases or frames of reference (formulary-prescriptive, empirical-prescriptive, and applied-scientific) for conducting scholarly work between 1900 and 1970, noting that, to a certain extent, each perspective persists. Second, they outlined three orientations (modernist, naturalist, and critical) to organizational communication studies.

During the *formulary-prescriptive* phase (1900–1940s), publications offered formulas, rules, or guidelines about how to be an effective communicator (written as well as oral). Major themes included a focus on one-way communication, a concern for successful communication, and an underlying assumption that managers were the most important employees.

In the second phase, the *empirical prescriptive* (1950s), researchers were concerned with helping managers or supervisors develop expertise in speaking, listening, and writing. During this phase, researchers became a bit more sophisticated by gathering in-depth information, often using case study methods.

Although prescription remained important during the third phase (*applied-scientific,* 1948–1970s), investigators presented themselves as neutral and objective. They employed traditional scientific methods associated with logical positivism and hypotheticodeductive designs (e.g., experiments, quasi-experiments, content-analytic studies, network analysis, and readability studies). Popular research topics included superior-subordinate relationships and organizational communication climate.

The second part of Redding and Tompkins' schema outlined three orientations to organizational communication studies: modernist, naturalistic, and critical. Other organizational communication articles and edited volumes have also provided in depth explanations of the various orientations and/or paradigms (Deetz, 2001; May & Mumby, 2005). Therefore, rather than provide another overview of these areas, this piece will address the implications of including feminist and multicultural perspectives.

Buzzanell (1994) describes feminist organizational communication theorizing as:

> the moral commitment to investigate the subordinated, to focus on gendered interactions in ordinary lives, and to explore the standpoints of women who have been rendered invisible by their absence in theory and research. This theorizing acknowledges its assumptional basis and biases, to create change in the values and interaction patterns that characterize organizational life. (p. 340)

Feminist work also utilizes reflexive, multivoiced texts that focus on the experiences of oppressed people and includes narration in the form of essays, stories, and experimental writing (Denzin & Lincoln, 2005). Allen (1998) notes that "When we privilege the knowledge of the oppressed or outsiders, we reveal aspects of the social order that previously have not been exposed" (p. 646). Additionally, more recent feminist work has taken a postmodern perspective that has been successful in its effort to capture the dynamics of the active co-construction of gender and organization as well as gendered organizing as it unfolds around questions of discourse, identity, and power (Martin, Knopoff, & Beckman, 1998; Townsley & Geist, 2000; Trethewey, 1997).

One influential perspective in capturing the dynamics of the active co-construction of gender and organization has been Ashcraft and Mumby's (2004) *feminist communicology*. In their book, they identify four prevalent ways of seeing or framing feminist organizational communication theory with the hope that overlooked patterns and relations of power will emerge, providing an opportunity to create alternative forms of feminist thinking. Influenced by the linguistic turn and postmodern approaches to language and meaning, Ashcraft and Mumby turn to discourse to elaborate relations between and of gender and organization. They argue for a feminist communicology that dislocates mainstream notions of what collective forms of organizing might look like by centering gender in the organizing discursive process. In doing so, the aim is to challenge the common view of gender in order to "rework the conversation" of gender in public and private lives. Also central to their perspective is how gender literally shapes and is shaped by interaction. This is a useful starting point from which to "rework gender" and the question of agency to form a ground for new choices in our public and private lives that embraces a feminist goal of social change.

Research is being done using a feminist lens, but "organizational communication scholarship rarely and inadequately attends to racial issues" (Ashcraft & Allen, 2003, p. 6). Although there have been future calls for work which focus on race, based on a survey of scholars in the organizational field, Cox (1990) argues that "white Americans generally do not consider racio-ethnicity a topic of universal importance" instead they view it as an issue relevant to minority group members (p. 7). As Parker (2003) notes, instead of focusing on race, gender, and class as interdependent processes, most research has focused on unraced constructions of gender. Not delineating among or exploring race, class, gender, and other characteristics as separate, as well as intertwined variables can be problematic. For example, when race is presumed to be neutral, racial privilege can be taken for granted (McIntosh, 1988); diversity can be constructed as an asset to be managed for competitive advantage, rather than considering individual members of the organization (Kirby & Harter, 2001); and without exploration of gender, class, and race as separate entities, it will be difficult to identify the everyday communicative practices that contribute to subordination and oppression in the U.S. labor market (Parker, 2003).

Despite the fact that racial privilege and differences in experience can be taken for granted, race is prevalent in personal lives and in the work place. Allen (1995) contends that race-ethnicity is salient because it is usually physically observable, its roots lie in affirmative action/equal employment opportunity programs, it references the fastest rising groups to enter the workplace, and because most diversity initiatives center around people of color and women (p. 144). Moreover, when race is examined as a separate variable, similarities with other workers have been found, but there are also important differences in their experiences.

Barnett, Del Campo, Del Campo, and Steiner (2003) found that Mexican-American couples with lower levels of acculturation to mainstream U.S. society assessed their families as more cohesive, and reported higher levels of job satisfaction, compared with Mexican-Americans who were highly acculturated. Family cohesion and job satisfaction were positively linked to work–family balance. Unfortunately hourly earnings are lower for low-skilled workers associated with downward assimilation and there is an upward trend in earnings among high-skilled Mexicans associated with Anglo-conformity (Valdez, 2006). Although conformity does allow for higher wages and better opportunities, it does not erase inequities in the workplace. Research has shown that first generation Mexican men are able to close earnings gaps with U.S. born Mexican-Americans, but they are not able to close the gap with non-Hispanic whites (Allensworth, 1997). Therefore, despite the fact that better family cohesion and job satisfaction help families balance work–life struggles, nonconformity to Anglo standards and race/ethnicity can negatively impact earnings.

In other studies, results showed that both race and gender were significantly related to how workers experience uncertainty, information seeking, and learning (Teboul, 1999), as well as promotion potential (Landau, 1995). These factors can impact employees' earnings, tenure with the organization, and job satisfaction. Other variables associated with race/ethnicity also impact employees' experiences. Ethnic labels such as Mexican, Hispanic, Chicano, Spanish, and so on allow people to present their own ethnic selves, and discourse from and about these individuals can invoke themes such as hard work (Aoki, 2000); employees with Spanish surnames are often expected to speak Spanish regardless of their country of origin or whether they were ever taught to speak Spanish (Montoya, 2006); value orientations related to activity and time, integration with kin, and trust can be significantly different for Anglo Americans versus Mexican Americans (Chandler, 1979); African-American women faculty members may be asked to give lectures about race and gender, attend lunches or dinners with minority job applicants, and mentor students of color, which add to their workload (Allen, 2000); and it is difficult for African-American women to find mentors who are from similar ethnic backgrounds, which impacts their career development process (Parker, 2003). These examples illustrate ways in which employees' work experiences are impacted by race, gender, social class, as well as other variables.

In order to better understand these factors, organizational scholars need to do research that encompasses a multitude of employees and careers, as well as work that highlights the ways in which everyday micropractices, as well as overarching organizational structures impact the workplace. If researchers do not interrogate the ways in which race, class, and gender impact workers' identities and how these factors affect the ways in which employees control themselves and others, or allow themselves to be controlled, we will alienate employees and theories will primarily remain relevant to one subgroup.

Considering the goals of feminist and race perspectives, like Redding and Tompkins (1988), we too believe that "*all forms of inquiry* are vital to continued progress in the study of organizational communication" (p. 27) and therefore want to address the limited organizational studies involving multiple ethnicities.

Organizational Communication: A Definition and Brief History

Organizational communication research is itself a rich communicative process. But what exactly is organizational communication? Tompkins (1984) defined *organizational communication* as "the study of sending and receiving messages that create and maintain a system of consciously coordinated activities or forces of two or more persons" (pp. 662–663). While such a definition is certainly viable in its attempt to reveal the dynamic and interactive processes by which communication constitutes organizations, it limits, however, communication's significant discursive organizing processes that coordinate and enact behaviors for particular people in particular ways. As such, Deetz (2001) reminds us that ultimately the question, "What is organizational communication" is misleading. A more interesting question is, "what do we see or what are we able to do if we think of organizational communication in one way versus another" (p. 4)?

Thus, throughout this chapter we will approach organizational communication through a distant lens that shows how organizational discourses bring subjects such as identity, knowledge, and power relations into existence and how they are manifested in organizational practices (Ashcraft & Mumby, 2003; McPhee & Zaug, 2000). Furthermore, this perspective illustrates the multiple and diverse ways in which people discursively construct, contest, and understand organizing process inherent in forms of communication that generate, and are generated by, organizational practices (Axley, 1984; Taylor, Cooren, Giroux, & Robichaud, 1996). Communication scholars studying organizations through an organizational discursive approach are interested in the social constructionist effects of language and meaning in organizational settings (Fairhurst & Putnam, 2004). As Mumby and Clair (1997) noted,

> Organizations exist only in so far as their members create them through discourse. This is not to claim that organizations are 'nothing but' discourse, but rather that discourse is the principle means by which organization members create coherent social reality that frames their sense of who they are. (p. 181)

Additionally, a dialogic approach to organizations allows organizational communication researchers to examine the messy moment-to-moment manner in which people and institutions construct coherent, complete meanings out of essentially partial, incomplete, hidden, and fragmented points of discursive struggle (Alvesson & Deetz, 2000). As a result, studying organizations from a discursive organizational communicative perspective allows organizational communication researchers to examine different levels and sites of discursive practices as "moments," that act as powerful ordering forces in organizations.

Although organizational communication officially commenced as a specialized area of speech communication in the early 1950s (Putnam & Cheney, 1985), Tompkins (1997) marked the late 1920s as the preparatory stage of the field, when universities first began offering courses on business and professional speaking to train men and women to communicate effectively in the workplace. Thus, the area's conceptual foundation derives primarily from three sources: (1) a traditional rhetorical theory (the study of formal, structured public discourse, with an emphasis on persuasion); (2) human relations "models" of informal, interpersonal interaction; and (3) early versions of "management–organization 'prototheories'" (Redding & Tompkins, 1988).

Since the area's inception, organizational communication researchers worked to understand the means whereby an individual or organization could achieve *effectiveness* (Redding & Tompkins, 1988). However, the area is evolving from an emphasis on managerial concerns to an interest in everyday interactions among organizational actors. Furthermore, it has expanded its initial focus on trying to solve applied, pragmatic problems to include in-depth examinations of the complexities of social collectivities (e.g., organizational culture, identification, power, and control). Accordingly, as discussed next, researchers have applied a variety of theoretical frameworks and methodologies to address a multiplicity of research questions, specifically, surrounding issues of control, culture, and identification in the workplace.

Theoretical Framework and Literature Review

Although there was an attempt to develop an approach we might call "how-to-do communication in order to manage workers" dating back to the 1920s, it was not until the late 1930s that Chester Barnard (1938) provided an analytic framework to the whole organization-qua-communication system. The field of Speech was content to give courses and write books about "business and professional speaking" until the doctoral emphasis on "organizational communication" was developed by W. Charles Redding at Purdue University in the late 1950s. As this subdivision of the field gained status as a division in the professional associations, members began to call for theory development *within* the field—rather than adopting existing theories in, say, sociology and business administration.

In response to this felt need, Tompkins and Cheney (1983, 1985) introduced a systematic theoretical approach to communication as *control* in organizations—giving it an unmistakably rhetorical aura, consistent with the traditions of the field.[1] Control was seen to be a three-step process that is clearly communicative in nature, made up of (1) ordering and directing; (2) monitoring workers' responses; and (3) rewarding the behavior consistent with the orders, and correcting those that were inconsistent with the desired outcome. Although Tompkins and Cheney (1985) drew on a historical sketch of control in U.S. organizations, they added a fourth basic form and used the rhetorical theory of identification to amplify it and bring it up to date. We shall introduce their theory by turning to the historical framework of control developed by Edwards (1981).

Edwards (1981) demonstrated that owner-managers have moved over time from obtrusive control (bullying or "in your face") to unobtrusive control in three stages: (1) "Simple Control," in which management openly exercised power over workers by face-to-face communication; in the beginning it was the owner, but as organizations grew in size the limitations of the span of control—the maximum number one boss could manage—required the owner to appoint foremen and other supervisors to control the workers. (2) "Technical Control," in which the machinery and equipment determine the pace of the work. The first assembly line is thought to have been a slaughterhouse in which workers, at fixed stations, chopped off cuts and pieces meat from large carcasses to sell at markets. Henry Ford, of course, made the assembly line famous for its efficient production of automobiles. His system of technical control allowed him to reduce significantly the number of supervisors required to direct, monitor, and correct the workers. (3) "Bureaucratic Control" was a natural alternative to simple control as organizations got bigger and bigger. Max Weber (1958) called this the rational-legal method of authority or control in that people were controlled by the rules and regulations they were required to enforce in making all decisions. This made the control of the trained and salaried worker much more impersonal than simple control.

Over time, each method of control in American organizations produced resistance against it. Foremen used their power of hiring and firing to exploit workers, by insisting on bribes and demanding sexual favors from female workers. Mary Parker Follett (1941) had found in her studies in Great Britain that workers made grievances about the manner or method of giving orders, claiming there was an art to giving orders without alienating workers. Workers who were bullied and abused by supervisors became open to attempts to organize them into unions, an outcome managers sought to avoid then as now (e.g., WalMart). Owners and managers began to search for new methods. Thus, technical control was introduced. The assembly line, however, turned workers into robots, or as they used to say, mere cogs in the machines. A fast pace could be dangerous and exhausting as well as mind-numbing in producing boredom as efficiently and effectively as automobiles (e.g., see Hamper, 1986). Workers staged sit-down strikes in which they refused to work. But by taking possession of the assembly line and their tools they prevented other workers from taking their place. Bureaucratic control also generated resistance: The very impersonality that made the human supervisor less obtrusive also turned the bureaucrats into bloodless computers. They began to make the organizations ineffective by *making the rules more important than the goals of the organization.*

When Tompkins and Cheney began work on the postbureaucratic theory that has become known as "Concertive Control," the ambiance of the period promoted teamwork. The time was right for such a theory but they did not have a term for it. Working at the dining room table in the Tompkins' home in West Lafayette, Indiana, they asked Elaine Tompkins, also on the faculty in the Communication Department at Purdue University, who was in the kitchen, "What should we call a theory in which people who are highly identified with their organization engage in face-to-face, intensive oral communication to make decisions by drawing conclusions from preferred premises?" Without hesitating she coined a word, *concertive*, meaning symbolic action in *concert.* Over the years scholars stopped treating it as a neologism by putting quotation marks around it, but the computer program we are using still underlines it in red.

In the 1985 essay Tompkins and Cheney integrated Kenneth Burke's New Rhetoric of Identification with that of Aristotle's Old Rhetoric. The proofs of classical rhetoric—*pathos, logos, ethos*—are still employed in organizational discourse. For example, Herbert Simon's definition of organizational decision making, that is, drawing conclusions from premises, is not inconsistent with one in the *logos* of the Old Rhetoric. Aristotle's concept of the enthymeme or rhetorical syllogism, for example, operates when persuaders draw on premises in the mind of the listener to help them reach the desired conclusion. Tompkins and Cheney referred to this as Enthymeme 1; Enthymeme 2 is the method used in concertive control. The organization socializes its members with a set of preferred decision premises, factual and value. As the situation arises, the group or even an individual can apply the preferred premises and draw the organizationally preferred decision. High levels of identification make the process all the more powerful in exercising control, control of decision making. The more an individual identifies with an organization, the more likely she is to internalize its premises. The more the premises are appealing to the worker, the more she is likely to identify with the organization.

Indeed, Tompkins and Cheney defined organizational identification as the extent to which an employee, when faced with a decision to be made, chooses "the alternative that best promotes the perceived interests of that organization" (Tompkins & Cheney, 1985, p. 194). As mentioned above, the theory of identification was modified from the New Rhetoric of Kenneth Burke (1937, 1969, 1973). These ideas were integrated with the provocative chapter on Organizational Identification in Herbert Simon's (1976) *Administrative Behavior.* At the heart of concertive control lies the communication and inculcation of shared values, objectives, and decision premises. Tompkins and Cheney (1985) argued that the trend is away from obtrusive control…to the unobtrusive control of workers by shared premises…from negative sanctions that instill fear to the positive incentives of security, identification, and common mission; from personal, localized, and capricious control to the nonpersonal, pervasive and predictable. (p. 185)

Identification prompts organizational actors to attend to particular organizationally sanctioned values, facts, and goals, first by influencing which problems and alternatives they see. Assigning responsibility for tasks affects the very *perception* of problems and solutions. The explanation: "The organizational member is limited at the outset to alternatives tied to his/her identifications; other options will simply not come into view, and therefore will not be considered" (Tompkins & Cheney, 1985, p. 194). Moreover, identification directs organizational actors' choices to particular alternatives. To measure an individual's level of identification with an organization, Cheney (1982) developed the Organizational Identification Questionnaire (OIQ), a 30-item instrument containing such items as: "I have warm feelings toward Organization X."

As the first edition of this book and chapter pointed out in 1996, the literature at that time contained numerous research articles and essays about concertive control or organizational identification (e.g., Barker, 1993; Barker & Cheney, 1994; Barker & Tompkins, 1994; Bullis & Tompkins, 1989; Cheney, 1983a, 1983b; Cox, 1983; Kelley & Busemeyer, 1992; Pribble, 1990; Sewell & Wilkinson, 1992; Tompkins & Cheney, 1983; and the first study of organizational identification, Tompkins, Fisher, Infante, & Tompkins, 1975). For instance, Tompkins and Cheney (1983) adapted account analysis—the study of excuses and justifications—and used it with the OIQ in a study of decision making within the Department of Communication at Purdue University. This led them to a reformulation of Simon's definition of organization presented above. This study also provided glimpses of the process of identifying, both the *coming to* and the *resisting of* the organization's attempts to foster identification.

Cox (1983) modified the OIQ to create a Black Identification Questionnaire. He found that white staff members at a mainly white university had higher organizational identification scores than blacks. Blacks who identified most highly with their organization also tended to score highest on black identification scores. In short, blacks who identified highly with their organization were not "Uncle Toms." To the contrary, they also tended to identify with their black "brothers and sisters" within and without the organization. This finding also indicated that there are individual differences in regard to the potential for identifying with one's race or organization.

An analysis of house organs revealed several strategies aimed at increasing organizational identification among employees (Cheney, 1983a). The most common strategy was *common ground*, or pointing out shared interests between the organization and the individual employee. In a separate study Pribble (1990) evaluated the ethical dimension of a Fortune 500 company's formal (videotaped) orientation program, finding that the organization attempted to evoke organizational identification by again, demonstrating shared values and the family metaphor. Bullis and Tompkins (1989) analyzed interview data to discover decision premises, linked to level of identification, among rangers in the U.S. Forest Service. They also found that a shift away from concertive control to more obtrusive control resulted in decreased organizational identification among Forest Service employees. Identification is, of course, highly related to morale. Older members of the organization expressed regret over the changes and nostalgia for the "good old days."

A major study of concertive control was conducted by James R. Barker. As a graduate student working with Tompkins and Cheney at the University of Colorado at Boulder, he was well aware of their theory and the existing body of research. He began working in the early 1990s as an ethnographer, or close observer, at an electronics manufacturing firm that was consciously moving from traditional, bureaucratic control processes to self-directed work teams—that is, concertive control. Barker (1993) found that the new approach made the organization much more effective and efficient. It also corroborated the prediction of Tompkins and Cheney (1985) that moving from traditional to concertive processes would *increase the total amount of control in the system*. To paraphrase a worker's comment to Barker, it used to be that we could relax when the boss left the work area, but now *everyone is a boss*. The workers got incentives that encouraged them to increase productivity; they monitored each other, and pointedly scolded their colleagues for tardiness or absences. Barker's article in the *Administrative Science Quarterly* won a prize from the Academy of Management. This gave the theory of concertive control and organizational identification wider exposure to specialists in sociology, management, business administration, and other disciplines concerned with human organization. Barker later presented his study in book form: *The Discipline of Teamwork: Participation and Concertive Control* (1999).

A follow-up study (Barker & Tompkins, 1994) in the same manufacturing firm employed the OIQ. Workers were asked to complete two forms of the questionnaire; the first measured their identification with the total organization, the second with their specific teams. It was hypothesized that they would identify more highly with their teams than with the organization. Employees who had worked longer in the teams tended to identify with them more highly than with the larger body, whereas newcomers were not so highly identifying (Barker & Tompkins, 1994). As important as these studies were, the reader must not assume that the self-directed work teams had absolute freedom to do as they pleased. Although they made decisions as a group, as teams, they were still subject to organizational control. Despite the removal of a layer of supervision, the organization still maintained tight control by dictating the premises—including incentives and quotas—of their individual and group decisions.

We now turn to several significant papers related to concertive control and organizational identification that have been produced since the first edition (1996) of this volume. While the first edition was in press a significant paper was published in the journal *Communication Theory* (Papa, Auwal, & Singhal, 1995). The title of the article is "Dialectic of Control and Emancipation in Organizing for Social Change: A Multitheoretic Study of the Grameen Bank in Bangladesh." The abstract of the paper is reproduced here:

> In recent years, the Grameen (rural) Bank of Bangladesh gained international fame for successfully organizing grassroots microenterprises for productive self-employment and social change. The Grameen Bank provides collateral-free loans and various social services for the poor, charging 20% interest on capital loans and yet maintaining a 99% loan recovery rate. Many of the bank's 1.9 million members, of whom 94% are women, attribute their present well-being to its ameliorative qualities. Using multiple theories (coorientation, concertive control, and critical feminist theories), we analyze the Grameen Bank's programs to explicate the dialectic between control and emancipation in organizing for social change. By examining the Grameen Bank's organizational process from multiple perspectives, we draw insights about theory and praxis in organizing for social change. (p. 189)

The authors employed concertive control as a theoretical approach to the Bank study because the members who get the loans, the poorest of the poor, are assigned to groups of five in which they monitor and control each other's behavior. They pressure each other to repay the loans because failure to do so could jeopardize the credit opportunities for other members. In addition, bank workers who monitor the small groups also employ concertive control. Acting collectively, they pressure each other to maintain the miraculous loan recovery rate of 99%. This goal was generated not by upper management, but by the bank workers as a group.

It must be stressed that women generally experience discrimination in Bangladeshi society;

access by these women to bank loans and to the equality and teamwork of concertive control is truly a transformational experience for them. The loans and advice lift them out of dire poverty and the group experience helps emancipate them. Women who are financially independent have a greater level of equality which offers better chances of being treated with respect, having ideas taken seriously, and provides an avenue for others to recognize their formerly taken-for-granted perspectives. Perhaps this type of organizational control can achieve a similar effect with subordinated groups in the United States and in other countries.

In the concluding section of the research report on the Grameen Bank, the authors say this about the

> concertive control system operative among the members. This control system is clearest in terms of socially constructed norms regarding loan repayment. Members pressure one another to repay loans because failure to do so can jeopardize the loans of other center members. Also, our survey interviews indicated that some members identified so strongly with the bank that they may lack objectivity in determining which aspects of the bank's programs are in their best interest. (p. 217)

Thus, one can lose objectivity in a high state of organizational identification, again illustrating the dialectic of control and emancipation.

The idea of the Grameen Bank was conceived by Muhammad Yunus when he returned to Bangladesh with a doctorate from Vanderbilt University in the United States. The great success of this project was recognized when Dr. Yunus received the Nobel Peace Prize for 2006. Students of communication should pay close attention to this 1995 study by Papa, Auwal, and Singhal, the better to appreciate the power of concertive control in emancipating the poorest of the poor.

In 1997 the theory of concertive control was extended to the problem of electronic performance monitoring (Alder & Tompkins, 1997). In an analytic piece that integrates concertive control and organizational justice, eight propositions are introduced. We reproduce three of them:

> Proposition 6: Higher levels of organizational identification and performance will result when employee input is solicited prior to the implementation of electronic monitoring systems than when monitoring systems are implemented without employee input. (p. 275)

> Proposition 7: Unobtrusive, concertive systems of control based on effective communication and the inculcation of decision premises will result in higher levels of organizational identification than will obtrusive systems of control. (p. 278)

> Proposition 8: To the extent that organizations use data obtained from electronic performance monitoring concertively by emphasizing open, two-way communication and supportive feedback, members will respond favorably to the monitoring and increased organizational identification will result. (p. 283)

The final paragraph of this study cites the Bullis and Tompkins (1989) study as demonstrating that because concertive control is

> simultaneously unobtrusive and a source of high morale, the use of electronic monitoring in this manner may result in decreased employee stress, heightened satisfaction, and improved morale. Finally, because perceived organizational justice leads to increased

effort on the part of organization members...this approach can also be expected to improve an organization's productivity. (Alder & Tompkins, 1997, p. 284)

A year later an important article by Sewell (1998), an expert outside the communication field, demonstrated how concertive control works with technical surveillance to create a system of heightened control.

Recall that Edwards (1981) showed that each of the first three forms of control—simple, technical, and bureaucratic—developed resistance from the people being controlled, the workers. Would concertive control develop resistance as well? A publication by Larson and Tompkins (2005) attempted to answer this question: "Ambivalence and Resistance: A Study of Management in a Concertive Control System." The organization, called JAR, is an important aerospace contractor in the Rocky Mountain West. The 2,500 employees design and manufacture satellites for the government and commercial aerospace customers. It is a matrix organization with standing functional units, such as engineering, and project or program offices as well.

Most of the employees are engineers and other professionals, people with high mobility. They are attracted to JAR because it uses an unobtrusive, normative control system—concertive control. The engineers are collectively powerful; most of the top managers were engineers who got promoted. The company had a reputation for their ability to solve complex technical problems and build high-quality hardware. In the 1990s, however, one of its biggest customers, National Aeronautics and Space Administration (NASA), adopted a new and different culture and a new mantra: "Faster, Better, Cheaper." To quote Larson and Tompkins,

> JAR, like NASA in its unmanned space program, was attempting to change from being a "high-reliability organization" that valued primarily technical excellence to one that focused more on profit, efficiency and best value. In the late 1990s, JAR managers began an aggressive campaign to change the company value system to focus on cost/schedule rather than technical excellence. (For a detailed discussion of these three values or 'topoi' see Tompkins, 1993). (Larson & Tompkins, 2005, p. 6)

During the course of the research project, the engineers who used concertive control resisted the efforts of management to raise profit and lower quality. "As JAR managers attempted to implement a significant change to the concertive system, *they subtly undermined their own change efforts*" (Larson & Tompkins, 2005, p. 11, emphasis in original). Many of the managers still identified strongly with the old value premise of high reliability. They experienced ambivalence about the logical reasons for adapting to what the customer wanted because of their pride in the past. Their discourse became ambiguous, calling for change while praising their history. "Finally, despite pushing for change, some managers expressed hope that the environment of the past would someday return" (Larson & Tompkins, 2005, p. 13). They began to hope that NASA would change, would abandon Faster, Better, Cheaper for high reliability and quality. We reproduce the final paragraph of the article (Larson & Tompkins, 2005):

> In this study, we explored how challenges to the identities of managers arose as a result of changes in a concertive value system in one high-tech organization. This study suggests that managers may subtly support employee resistance through communicated ambivalence and that concertive systems of control might not only be an "iron cage" (Weber, 1958) for employees, but also for managers. Finally, this case should not be read as a failure of management, but rather a reflection of the material, discursive, and identity struggles which both management and employees must negotiate. While tempted

simply to explain the ambivalence many managers experience when confronted with changes in value premises. Close empirical studies that take into account managers as well as employees are needed to further understand how control and resistance are enacted and balanced in organizational practice. (pp. 17–18)

There is a footnote, number three to be exact, in the Larson and Tompkins paper that notes the ironic, circular coincidence linking the study of an aerospace contractor and the second author's original studies (Tompkins, 1977, 1978) of NASA during the Apollo or Moon Project. It was during that time that Tompkins first saw teamwork in action, saw concertive control being exercised, and that *reliability* or *quality* was the number one decision premise. During those early studies Tompkins observed the highest levels of organizational identification; indeed, he experienced it himself, discovering how he moved from the individual pronoun "I" to the collective "we" and "us" in referring to NASA in thought and conversations with others. He went to the Moon and returned safely to Earth—albeit metaphorically. (For accounts of different dynamics in control-resistance and organizational culture, see his subsequent studies of the *Challenger* and *Columbia* space shuttle disasters; Tompkins 1993, 2005.) NASA in its days of glory served as the inspiration for the concertive control-organizational identification theory, which in turn has become a benchmark by which to measure contemporary organizations, including a NASA contractor and NASA itself.

While NASA was once the inspiration for the concertive control-organizational identification theory, as discussed earlier, other organizations such as banks and technological organizations are also benefiting from implementation of the theory. As workplaces change in order to respond to the demands for family friendly policies and employers deal with a changing workforce (e.g. single mothers; partially retired Baby Boomers; ethnic minorities; and Generation Y employees), concertive control may become even more prevalent within a multitude of organizations.

Hypothetical Research Project

From an early interest in helping managers become effective to contemporary concerns of empowering and emancipating workers, organizational communication scholars have studied control and decision making in organizations. The hypothetical problem initially proposed in the original chapter addresses these enduring issues by applying one of only a few theoretical frameworks which arise from organizational communication. In revising this chapter, we felt the need to revisit these enduring issues through a feminist perspective to problematize the suggested methods and approach.

The project proposed in the original chapter was intended to describe, interpret, and document control practices and attitudes among work team members in a manufacturing company which was implementing diversity initiatives by hiring more females and members of ethnic minority groups. Developed from modernist, naturalistic, and critical perspectives a few of the questions the previous research project sought to answer include:

1. According to their own reports or accounts, what decision premises do team members use to accomplish work-related tasks?
2. According to their own reports, how do members of a work team learn decision premises?
3. Do team members report or exhibit varying preferences for decision premises according to individual differences (e.g., gender, race or ethnicity, age, tenure within the organization)?
4. What decision premises are advocated by management?
5. How does management attempt to inculcate decision premises?

6. (a) Does a relationship exist between organizational actors' identification with the organization and the extent to which they are most likely to use decision strategies preferred by management? (b) Does a relationship exist between team members' identification with their team and the extent to which they are most likely to use decision premises and strategies preferred by management? (c) Do relationships assessed in 6a and 6b vary across time?
7. Does a relationship exist between control and organizational identification?

Methodology

To answer these questions, a team of three researchers conducted a longitudinal (one year), triangulated research project, using a sample of five work teams (each team consists of 10–12 employees) from various manufacturing plants. In order to defer from selecting a convenient or snowball sample, which can often be comprised of one race, age group, social class, or education level, the researchers took specific steps to ensure a more representative sample. Researchers determined the number of employees needed to conduct the study and purposely recruited from five ethnic categories: African-American/black, Asian-American, Caucasian, Latino, and Native American. Researchers were able to recruit a sufficient number of participants from each category by cold calling local organizations that cater to these groups, contacting key leaders in the various communities and asking for referrals and advertising mediums, and ads were run in local newspapers and community newsletters with an ethnic readership. Researchers were also cognizant of issues related to employees' attitudes toward the topic of race/ethnicity, interviewer effects, and intragroup differences which have been noted as important aspects to consider when conducting research (Allen, 1995).

Once the participants were selected researchers were able to employ a variety of qualitative techniques including: participant-observation, interviews, taped meetings, and document analysis. For instance, during one-on-one semistructured interviews, organizational actors were asked to tell stories about decision-making experiences and to account for their own decision-making behaviors. Transcripts of audio- and videotaped meetings were analyzed to assess reflexive comments related to decision-making processes (see Geist & Chandler, 1984; Harre & Secord, 1972).

Researchers also applied a variety of research analytical methods, including: inductive interpretation of interview transcripts (e.g., the constant comparative method, in which data are sorted into categories and labeled), and statistical analysis of quantitative data (e.g., the OIQ, the control graph questionnaire, demographic information). But in revisiting the proposed study, there are several limitations and implications that are exposed and awakened if viewed through a feminist lens.

Implications

As outlined, the original proposed project signifies several implications and limitations for advancing the study of organizational communication. First and foremost, feminist theory argues that it is nearly impossible to study and theorize adequately about organizational power and control without addressing its gendered character.

The proposed study did, however, respond to a recurring call to provide motion pictures rather than "snapshots" of organizational life. Furthermore, it answered a general need to conduct research that helps to solve human interaction problems or dilemmas (e.g., DeWine & Daniels, 1993), and two related concerns: first, to explore decision-making behaviors in *actual organizations* (e.g., O'Reilly, Chatman, & Anderson, 1987), and second, to focus on *connectedness* and collaborative interaction among organizational actors (Stohl, 1995). Aside from the benefits, we propose a set of questions to engage new ways of thinking, acting, and organizing from which we rework the limitations and implications of the original research project.

1. Deconstructing the decision premises that team members used to accomplish work-related tasks, how does communication continuously create, solidify, and alter gendered selves and organizational forms?
2. How do societal discourses arrange gender and work through team members' decision premises?
3. Do team members report or exhibit varying preferences for decision premises according to individual differences (e.g., gender, race or ethnicity, age, class, sexuality, tenure within the organization)? And how does power and control slip in as various discourses circulate and entwine, and those with greater institutional support tend to "look" and "feel" more persuasive than others (Ashcraft & Mumby, 2004)?
4. How do larger societal narratives direct the formation of choices about identities and organizational forms?
5. Where do decision premises advocated by management come from? And how do premises become representations that promote particular identities that people draw upon or resist?
6. What forms of inducement does management "recruit" members with in order to inculcate decision premises? Furthermore, how does one discourse get articulated with another at a given historical moment and how do these identities open and close possibilities for agency?
7. (a) Does a relationship exist between organizational actors' identification with the organization and the extent to which they are most likely to use decision strategies preferred by management? (b) Does a relationship exist between team members' identification with their team and the extent to which they are most likely to use decision premises and strategies preferred by management? (c) Do relationships assessed in 7a and 7b vary across time and is there room for difference and creativity?
8. Does a relationship of dependency exist between control and organizational identification? How can a deconstruction method of team members' narratives expose and awaken different discourses that promote different premises there were potentially glossed over or suppressed through identification?

As outlined earlier in this chapter, feminist and multicultural perspectives matter. Such thoughts offer significant insight into organizing discourses and the coconstruction of work, knowledge, and gender. These perspectives offer insight in part by de- and reconstructing individuals' practice as the mode of explanation, understanding, and emancipation of dominant ways of thinking and being. Furthermore, in engaging in such methods as Derrida's deconstruction (e.g., 1976, 1978) for example, researchers will be able to retrace how the rhetorical and linguistic forms used to signify knowledge work under the assumption that they represent a referent which is external to language.

Summary

As researchers continue to study the ways in which organizations and organizational stakeholders operate within various structures, it is important to deconstruct or problematize different modalities of power and control that are capable of producing a netlike organization of practices and discourses that society ends up calling knowledge. This type of knowledge is part and parcel of members acting in concert. We encourage multiple perspectives to be enacted in organizational communication studies in order to explore the active coconstruction of race/ethnicity, gender, and organization, as well as their implications for theory, practice, and the feminist goal of social change. Perhaps journal editors and tenure review committees could incorporate the diversity of the study participants into their considerations. By foregrounding issues of identity, power, discourse, and gender, the ensuing understanding should prove vital to analysis, critique, and possible micro emancipation within and beyond gender, race/ethnicity, work, and organizational studies.

Note

1. For a more systematic study of the connection between rhetorical theory and the theory of organization and management, see Tompkins (1987).

References

Alder, S., & Tompkins, P. (1997). Electronic performance monitoring: An organizational justice and concertive control perspective. *Management Communication Quarterly, 10,* 259–288.

Allen, B. J. (1995). "Diversity" and organizational communication. *Journal of Applied Communication Research, 23,* 143–155.

Allen, B. J. (1998). Black womanhood and feminist standpoints. *Management Communication Quarterly, 11,* 644–655.

Allen, B. J. (2000). "Learning the ropes": A Black feminist standpoint analysis. In P. Buzzanell (Ed.), *Rethinking organizational and managerial communication from feminist perspectives* (pp. 177–208). Thousand Oaks, CA: Sage.

Allensworth, E. M. (1997). Earnings mobility of first and "1.5" generation Mexican-origin women and men: A comparison with U.S.-born Mexican Americans and Non-Hispanic Whites. *International Migration Review, 31,* 386–410.

Alvesson, M., & Deetz, S. (2000). *Doing critical management research.* London: Sage.

Aoki, E. (2000). Mexican American ethnicity in Biola, CA: An ethnographic account of hard work, family, and religion. *The Howard Journal of Communications, 11,* 207–227.

Ashcraft, K. L., & Allen, B. J. (2003). The racial foundation of organizational communication. *Communication Theory, 13,* 5–38.

Ashcraft, K. L., & Mumby, D. K. (2004). *Reworking gender: A feminist communicology of organization.* Thousand Oaks, CA: Sage.

Axley, S. (1984). Managerial communication in terms of the conduit metaphor. *Academy of Management Review, 9,* 428–437.

Barker, J. (1993). Tightening the iron cage: Concertive control in self-managing teams. *Administrative Science Quarterly, 38,* 408–437.

Barker, J. R. (1999). *The discipline of teamwork: Participation and concertive control.* Thousand Oaks, CA: Sage.

Barker, J. R., & Cheney, G. (1994). The concept and the practices of discipline in contemporary organizational life. *Communication Monographs, 61,* 19–43.

Barker, J., & Tompkins, P. (1994). Identification in the self-managing organization: Characteristics of target and tenure. *Human Communication Research, 21,* 223–243.

Barnard, C. (1938). *The functions of the executive.* Cambridge, MA: Harvard University Press.

Barnett, K. A., Del Campo, R. L., Del Campo, D. S., & Steiner, R. L. (2003). Work and family balance among dual-earner working-class Mexican-Americans: Implications for therapists. *Contemporary Family Therapy, 25,* 353–366.

Bullis, C., & Tompkins, P. (1989). The forest ranger revisited: A study of control practices and identification, *Communication Monographs, 56,* 287–306.

Burke, K. (1937). *Attitudes toward history.* New York: New Republic.

Burke, K. (1969). *A rhetoric of motives.* Berkeley, CA: University of California Press.

Burke, K. (1973). The rhetorical situation. In L. Thayer (Ed.), *Communication: Ethical and moral issues* (pp. 263–275). London: Gordon & Breach.

Buzzanell, P. M. (1994). Gaining a voice: Feminist organizational communication theorizing. *Management Communication Quarterly, 7,* 339–383.

Chandler, C. (1979). Traditionalism in a modern setting: A comparison of Anglo- and Mexican-American value orientations. *Journal of the Society for Applied Anthropology, 82,* 153–159.

Cheney, G. (1982). *Organizational identification as process and product: A field study.* Unpublished master's thesis, Purdue University, West Lafayette, IN.

Cheney, G. (1983a). On the various and changing meanings of organizational membership: A field study of organizational identification. *Communication Monographs, 50,* 342–363.

Cheney, G. (1983b). The rhetoric of identification and the study of organizational communication. *Quarterly Journal of Speech, 69,* 143–158.

Cox, M. (1983). *The effectiveness of black identification and organizational identification on communication supportiveness.* Unpublished doctoral dissertation, Purdue University, West Lafayette, IN.

Cox, T. R. (1990). Problems with research by organizational scholars on issues of race and ethnicity. *The Journal of Applied Behavioral Science, 26,* 5–23.

Deetz, S. (2001). Conceptual Foundations. In F. M. Jablin & L. L. Putnam (Eds.), *The new handbook of organization studies: Advances in theory, research, and methods* (pp. 3–46). Thousand Oaks, CA: Sage.

Denzin, N. K., & Lincoln, Y. S. (2005). The discipline and practice of qualitative research. In N. K. Denzin & Y. S. Lincoln (Eds.), *The Sage handbook of qualitative research* (3rd ed., pp. 1–32). Thousand Oaks, CA: Sage.

Derrida, J. (1976). *Speech and phenomenon.* Evanston: Northwestern University Press.

Derrida, J. (1978). *Spurs.* Chicago: University of Chicago Press.

DeWine, S., & Daniels, T. (1993). Beyond the snapshot: Setting a research agenda in organizational communication. In S. Deetz (Ed.), *Communication yearbook* (Vol. 16, pp. 331–346). Newbury Park, CA: Sage.

Edwards, R. (1981). The social relations of production at the point of production. In M. Zey Ferrel & M. Aiken (Eds.), *Complex organizations: Critical perspectives* (pp. 156–182). Glenview, IL: Scott, Foresman.

Fairhurst, G. T., & Putnam, L. L. (2004). Organizations as discursive constructions. *Communication Theory, 14,* 5–26.

Follett, M. P. (1941). Constructive conflict. In H. C. Metcalf & L. Urwick (Eds.), *Dynamic administration: The collected papers of Mary Parker Follett* (pp. 30–49). New York: Harper & Brothers.

Geist, P., & Chandler, T. (1984). Account analysis of influence in group decision making. *Communication Monographs, 51,* 67–78.

Hamper, B. (1986). *Rivethead: Tales from the assembly line.* New York: Warner.

Harre, R., & Secord, P. F. (1972). *The explanation of social behavior.* Totawa, NJ: Littlefield, Adams.

Kelley, L., & Busemeyer, S. (1992). *Unobtrusive control in organizations: A barrier to social change.* Paper presented at the Eastern Communication Association Convention, Portland, ME.

Kirby, E. L., & Harter, L. M. (2001). Discourses of diversity and the quality of work life. *Management Communication Quarterly, 15,* 121–127.

Landau, J. (1995). The relationship of race and gender to managers' ratings of promotion potential. *Journal of Organizational Behavior, 16,* 391–400.

Larson, G., & Tompkins, P. (2005). Ambivalence and resistance: A study of management in a concertive control system. *Communication Monographs, 72,* 1–21.

Martin, J., Knopoff, K., & Beckman, C. (1998). An alternative to bureaucratic impersonality and emotional labor: Bounded emotionality at The Body Shop. *Administrative Science Quarterly, 43,* 429–469.

May, S., & Mumby, D. K. (2005). *Engaging organizational communication theory research: Multiple perspectives.* Thousand Oaks, CA: Sage.

McIntosh, P. (1988). *White privilege and male privilege: A personal account of coming to see correspondences through work in women's studies* (Working Paper No. 189). Wellesley, MA: Center for Research on Women, Wellesley College.

McPhee, R. D., & Zaug, P. (2000). The communicative constitution of organizations: A framework for explanation. *The Electronic Journal of Communication, 10.* Retrieved January 15, 2007, from http://www. cios.org/getfile%5CMcPhee_V10n1200.

Montoya, Y. J. (2006, November). *Chicana, Hispanic, Latina socialization into management positions.* Paper presented at the annual meeting of the National Communication Association Convention, San Antonio, TX.

Mumby, D. K., & Clair, R. P. (1997). Organizational Discourse. In T. A. van Dijk (Ed.), *Discourse studies: Vol. 2. Discourse as social interaction* (pp. 181–205). London: Sage.

O'Reilly, C. A., Chatman, J. A., & Anderson, J. C. (1987). Message flow and decision making. In F. M. Jablin, L. L. Putnam, K. H. Roberts, & L. W. Porter (Eds.), *Handbook of organizational communication: An interdisciplinary perspective* (pp. 600–623). Newbury Park, CA: Sage.

Papa, M., Auwal, M., & Singhal, A., (1995). Dialectic of control and emancipation in organizing for social change: A multitheoretical study of the Grameen Bank in Bangladesh. *Communication Theory, 5,* 189–223.

Parker, P. S. (2003). Control, resistance, and empowerment in raced, gendered, and classed work contexts: The case of African American women. *Communication Yearbook, 27,* 257–291.

Pribble, P. (1990). Making an ethical commitment: A rhetorical case of organizational socialization. *Communication Quarterly, 38,* 255–267.

Putnam, L. L., & Cheney, G. (1985). Organizational communication: Historical development and future directions. In T. W. Benson (Ed.), *Speech communication in the 20th century.* (pp. 130–156). Carbondale: Southern Illinois University Press.

Redding, W. C., & Tompkins, P. (1988). Organizational communication—Past and present tenses. In G. Goldhaber & G. Barnett (Eds.), *Handbook of organizational communication* (pp. 5–33). Norwood, NJ: Ablex.

Sewell, G. (1998). The discipline of teams: The control of team-based industrial work through electronic and peer surveillance. *Administrative Science Quarterly, 43,* 397–428.

Sewell, G., & Wilkinson, B. (1992). Someone to watch over me: Surveillance, discipline and the just-in-time labour process. *Sociology, 26,* 271–289.

Simon, H. (1976). *Administrative behavior.* New York: Free Press.

Stohl, C. (1995). *Organizational communication: Connectedness in action.* Thousand Oaks, CA: Sage.

Taylor, J. R., Cooren, F., Giroux, N., & Robichaud, D. (1996). The communicational basis of organization: Between the conversation and the text. *Communication Theory, 6,* 1–39.

Teboul, J. C. B. (1999). Racial/ethnic "Encounter" in the workplace: Uncertainty, information-seeking, and learning patterns among racial/ethnic majority and minority new hires. *The Howard Journal of Communications, 10,* 97–121.

Tompkins, P. (1977). Management qua communication in rocket research and development. *Communication Monographs, 44,* 1–26.

Tompkins, P. (1978). Organizational metamorphosis in space research and development. *Communication Monographs, 45,* 110–118.

Tompkins, P. (1993). *Organizational communication imperatives: Lessons of the space program.* Los Angeles: Roxbury.

Tompkins, P. (2005). *Apollo, Challenger, Columbia: The decline of the space program.* Los Angeles: Roxbury.

Tompkins, P., & Cheney, G., (1983). Account analysis of organizations: Decision making and identification. In L. Putnam & M. Pacanowsky (Eds.), *Communication and organization: An interpretative approach* (pp. 123–146). Beverly Hills, CA: Sage.

Tompkins, P., & Cheney, G. (1985). Communication and unobtrusive control in contemporary organizations. In R. D. McPhee & P. K. Tompkins (Eds.), *Organizational communication: Traditional themes and new directions* (pp. 179–209). Newbury Park, CA: Sage.

Tompkins, P., Fisher, J., Infante, D., & Tompkins, E. (1975). Kenneth Burke and the inherent characteristics of formal organizations. A field study. *Speech Monographs, 42,* 135–142.

Tompkins, P. K. (1984). Functions of communication in organizations. In C. Arnold & J. W. Bowers (Eds.), *Handbook of rhetorical and communication theory* (pp. 659–719). New York: Allyn & Bacon.

Tompkins, P. K. (1987). The future of organizational communication: An outline of postmodernism. *Bulletin of the Association for Communication Administration, 61,* 136–142.

Tompkins, P. K. (1997). How to think and talk about organizational communication. In P. Y. Byers (Ed.), *Organizational communication: Theory and behavior* (pp. 361–373). Boston, MA: Allyn & Bacon.

Townsley, N. C., & Geist, P. (2000). The discursive enactment of hegemony: Sexual harassment in academic organizing. *Western Journal of Communication, 64*, 190–217.

Trethewey, A. (1997). Resistance, identity, and empowerment: A postmodern feminist analysis of clients in a human service organization. *Communication Monographs, 64*, 281–301.

Valdez, Z. (2006). Segmented assimilation among Mexicans in the southwest. *The Sociological Quarterly, 47*, 397–424.

Weber, M. (1958). *The Protestant ethic and the spirit of capitalism* (T. Parsons, Trans.). New York: Charles Scribner.

Suggested Readings

Ashcraft, K. L., & Allen, B. J. (2003). The racial foundation of organizational communication. *Communication Theory, 13*, 5–38.

Ashcraft, K. L., & Mumby, D. K. (2004). *Reworking gender: A feminist communicology of organization.* Thousand Oaks, CA: Sage.

Barker, J. (1993). Tightening the iron cage: Concertive control in self-managing teams. *Administrative Science Quarterly, 38*, 408–437.

Deetz, S. (2001). Conceptual foundations. In F. M. Jablin & L. L. Putnam (Eds.), *The new handbook of organization studies: Advances in theory, research, and methods* (pp. 3–46). Thousand Oaks, CA: Sage.

Larson, G., & Tompkins, P. (2005). Ambivalence and resistance: A study of management in a concertive control system. *Communication Monographs, 72*, 1–21.

Papa, M., Auwal, M., & Singhal, A., (1995). Dialectic of control and emancipation in organizing for social change: A multitheoretical study of the Grameen Bank in Bangladesh. *Communication Theory, 5*, 189–223.

Redding, W. C., & Tompkins, P. (1988). Organizational communication-past and present tenses. In G. Goldhaber & G. Barnett (Eds.), *Handbook of organizational communication* (pp. 5–33). Norwood, NJ: Ablex.

Tompkins, P. K. (1996). How to think and talk about organizational communication. In P. Byers (Ed.), *Organizational communication: Theory and behavior.* Boston, MA: Allyn & Bacon.

Tompkins, P., & Cheney, G., (1983). Account analysis of organizations: Decision making and identification. In L. Putnam & M. Pacanowsky (Eds.), *Communication and organization: An interpretative approach* (pp. 123–146). Beverly Hills, CA: Sage.

Tompkins, P., & Cheney, G. (1985). Communication and unobtrusive control in contemporary organizations. In R. D. McPhee & P. K. Tompkins (Eds.), *Organizational communication: Traditional themes and new directions* (pp. 179–209). Newbury Park, CA: Sage.

Part IV

INTEGRATED APPROACHES
TO COMMUNICATION

25

INTERNET COMMUNICATION

Marcus Messner and Bruce Garrison

Since the World Wide Web made the Internet accessible for mass audiences in the early and mid-1990s, it has taken its place as the fourth type of mass medium besides print, television, and radio by matching penetration rates and audience sizes. Today, the Internet is omnipresent in people's lives. According to the Pew Internet and American Life Project, 73 percent of adults in the United States used the Internet in 2006, an increase from 66 percent only a year earlier. In the age groups of the 18- to 29-year-olds and 30- to 49-year-olds, the Internet penetration rate is well over 80 percent at this point. Already in the age group of 12- to 17-year-olds, 87 percent are Internet users (Madden, 2006). This development stresses the current and future importance of the medium. It is further enhanced by the increasing and widespread international adoption of high-speed and wireless Internet connections, which allow users to not only work faster, but also to access their online applications from anywhere. While 42 percent of adults in the United States had a high-speed connection at home, 34 percent of the users entered the Internet through a wireless connection in 2006 (Horrigan, 2006a, 2007). Many of the online activities have become routine tasks for the users. More than 40 percent of American Internet users utilize search engines on a daily basis and more than 50 percent send e-mails (Rainie & Shermak, 2005).

Most commonly, the Internet has developed into a mass medium for news and information. Online news has been growing ever since the first news organizations offered their services online in the early 1980s. In the last decade, Internet usage has drastically increased during major news events and, thereby, the Internet has become a part of the 24-hour news cycle first established by cable news. During the 2006 Congressional mid-term elections, 13 percent of all adults in the United States used the Internet on an average daily basis to retrieve political information (Horrigan, 2006b). While overall media ownership has concentrated on a few internationally operating corporations, new Internet news formats such as blogs with interactive, multilinked features have increased the overall news flow and enjoy high popularity especially with younger Internet users (Bucy, Gantz, & Wang, 2007; Klopfenstein, 2002). Burnett and Marshall (2003) pointed out that these new formats enable Internet users to retrieve information that has previously not been disseminated by the traditional media.

The emergence of the Internet as a mass medium has caused widespread interest in academia and has produced a constantly growing body of research. Tomasello (2001) was one of the first researchers to analyze the state of Internet research and found that between 1994 and 1999 only 4 percent of the articles published in leading communication journals focused on the Internet. However, Kim and Weaver (2002) found in an analysis of journal articles that the number of Internet-related studies increased from 2.3 percent in 1996 to 8.4 percent in 1999. In addition, Cho and Khang (2006) found in an analysis of 15 communication journals between 1994 and 2003 that 13.3 percent of the articles studied the Internet and its applications. Their study also revealed that only 14.5 percent of the Internet studies were theory-driven and concluded that Internet research "has not yet achieved an equivalent level of theoretical rigorousness" (p. 158) as other areas in communication research. Many studies were of an exploratory nature.

Internet research has not yet developed a distinct theory or theoretical base that would explain or predict certain online phenomena and behavior, but rather applies existing theories, many of which are discussed in other chapters of this book. This chapter, therefore, traces the most significant advancement of existing theories through the study of mass communication on the Internet, which includes changes in gatekeeping theory, intermedia agenda-setting, the concept of credibility, as well as the uses and gratifications model. In addition, the Internet specific concepts of interactivity and hyperlinking will be discussed.

Besides studying the diffusion of the Internet, researchers have especially focused on the gatekeeping and agenda setting dimensions of the Internet and its distinct news formats. Recent research has challenged the foundations of gatekeeping theory developed by White (1950), which established the central role of traditional news media editors in the news flow (Williams & Delli Carpini, 2000, 2004). This circumstance has also led a variety of researchers to analyze the credibility of online information.

The emergence of distinct Internet formats, such as the collaborative formats of blogs and wikis, which are generally referred to under the concept of the Web 2.0, has also led to a new focus in agenda-setting research, which was originally applied to mass communication by McCombs and Shaw (1972) in their much-cited Chapel Hill study. The new direction of agenda-setting research increasingly focuses on the impact of Internet sources and their intermedia influence on the traditional media agenda (Bucy, Gantz, & Wang, 2007; McCombs, 2005). Furthermore, social networking and uses and gratifications have been emergent fields of Internet research in recent years. The interactive nature of the Internet has led researchers to focus on the constantly emerging online social networks and their impact on communication (Barnett & Sung, 2005; Flew, 2005; McMillan, 2006). The concept of hyperlinking has established a new means to measure popularity of information and levels of influence (Tremayne, 2004). In addition, the application of the model of uses and gratifications, based on the assumption by Katz, Blumler, and Gurevitch (1974) that the news audience is active and that media compete with other sources to fulfill audience need gratifications, has also produced a growing body of Internet research that has contributed to explaining the Internet phenomenon in its initial stages (Bucy, Gantz, & Wang, 2007).

Cho and Khang (2006) view the application of these existing theories as the preceding step to the development of distinct theories that explain the Internet and its effects: "We not only need to apply more existing concepts and theories to comprehend general Internet phenomena, but should also strive to develop new concepts and theories for understanding new aspects of the Internet that might not be completely explained by the existing knowledge structure" (p. 158). This chapter, therefore, will help to lay the basis for much-needed Internet theory development.

Gatekeeping Challenges

The impact of the Internet is most profound in how it has changed the overall media environment and the channels through which news is disseminated. While gatekeeping research studied how information is filtered for publication, starting with White's (1950) "Mr. Gates," and had long established the central position of traditional media journalists in the news flow, the emergence of the Internet and its distinct formats has posed a challenge to the traditional news cycle. Even in the most advanced gatekeeping model by Shoemaker (1991), which accounted for individual, organizational, and social influences, the media gatekeepers made the ultimate decision on the news flow. There was no competition for the gatekeepers' media outlets. This started to change when the Internet became a mass medium in the mid-1990s and diversified the media environment. While at first, new media research focused on the changes caused by the Internet within the traditional media, it has gradually changed its focus towards the changes of the entire media environment. Through the diversification of news channels with newly developed Internet formats, the central gatekeeping position of the traditional news media editor has been challenged.

Singer (1997) was one of the first mass communication scholars to examine the changing gatekeeping roles within the traditional media and to conclude that the role of the editor had to be modified in the online environment. Based on interviews with reporters and editors of the printed and the online versions of newspapers, Singer found that traditional journalists still viewed themselves as the central gatekeepers in the news flow in 1995. The editors did not view the selection process itself as their most important task, but the protection of news quality.

However, only a few years later, Singer (2001) found gatekeeping modifications in news selection through a content analysis of print and online versions of newspapers. While at that point in time, the majority of the content was still duplicated from the printed versions, the study showed an increasing local focus in the online content. Singer concluded that the only way for newspapers to compete in the global news environment of the Internet was to stress the local news expertise online. However, in the early stages of traditional news media moving online, only little original information was produced for these websites (Matheson, 2004). While the format was changing, journalism was not. Even the adoption of the popular blog formats by traditional news outlets preserved the role of the journalistic gatekeeper. New media applications by major news outlets, thereby, mostly remained traditional media at the time.

In surveys of newspaper editors involved in the coverage of the 2000 and 2004 presidential elections, nevertheless, Singer (2003a, 2006) found that their gatekeeping roles were further evolving. The 2000 election exemplified that newspapers were starting to use their online versions to break news faster and report it in more detail as space restraints were abandoned online. In the 2004 election, however, the emphasis of the gatekeepers shifted toward using online news content to engage Internet users. While most editors were still focusing their central gatekeeping task on delivering credible information, they began to acknowledge the necessity to reconceptualize their gatekeeping roles to include newly developed, distinct formats of the Internet. Chats, forums, and blogs became important tools exclusively available online. User-generated content, which was not provided by journalists but by readers, became a much more important element. Singer (2006) concluded that an "evolution in online journalists' thinking" (p. 275) was occurring.

A survey of print and online newspaper journalists by Cassidy (2005) also stressed the development of different interpretations of gatekeeping roles. While print journalists perceived their traditional roles as interpreters and investigators most important, online journalists stressed the quick news delivery as their main concern. The online coverage of the Iraq War also showed that the websites of some newspapers moved beyond duplicating content of the printed versions. Dimitrova and Neznanski (2006) found in a content analysis of U.S. and international newspaper websites that multimedia content gained increasing importance in the online war coverage. Hoffman (2006), however, found that "online newspapers provide content that simply reinforces print content" (p. 69).

In addition to the modification of the gatekeeping roles within the traditional media, a significant challenge to the central gatekeeping position of journalists has occurred with the emergence of distinct online formats, most predominantly through blogs. Most scholars refer to the Clinton-Lewinsky scandal in 1998 as the first incident involving an online news outlet circumventing the traditional media gatekeepers. In their analysis of the scandal, Williams and Delli

Carpini (2000, 2004) concluded that the authoritative gatekeeping role of traditional media had broken down when a national magazine halted a story on the president's affair with an intern and a blog decided to report the story and subsequently forced the traditional media, including the magazine to follow. The researchers concluded that traditional journalists had lost their central gatekeeping position, being unable to control or shape news events. This new media environment allowed individuals previously barred by gatekeepers to influence public discourse. Thereby online journalism evolved into another type of mass media, besides print, radio, and television.

As Kahn and Kellner (2004) pointed out, citizens equipped with laptops were now able to provide alternative news coverage and commentary. The resignation of U.S. Senate Majority Leader Trent Lott in 2002 over racist remarks, largely ignored by traditional media at first but propelled into public outrage by bloggers, demonstrated how significant the challenge to gatekeeping had become. Later, in the 2004 presidential election, weblogs reported exit poll results while the traditional media had decided to shield its readers from possibly unreliable facts based on problems in the previous election (Messner & Terilli, 2007).

Singer (2003b) pointed out that the rise of alternative news formats such as blogs blurred the line between professional and non-professional journalists. While the traditional gatekeeper sorted and limited the news flow in order to maintain quality, the challenge of this position increased the quantity of the information available to the public while at the same time decreasing the overall quality. Any person now had the ability to circumvent the traditional gatekeepers, shape the flow of news, and influence public discourse (Poor, 2006).

The war in Iraq has exemplified this new gatekeeping environment like no other news event over the course of several years. Wall (2005) analyzed blogs throughout the initial phase of the war in 2003 and found that in contrast to the neutral and detached tone of traditional media journalists bloggers are involved in their stories with a personalized and opinionated tone. While traditional news stories are aimed at giving the most complete and objective picture of an event, blog entries are fragmented, evolve over time, and are supplemented by reader comments. While Wall (2006) did not find a broadening of the discussion on the war as bloggers' opinions were linked to the pro-war and anti-war sentiments in society overall, the researcher concluded that bloggers became "secondary war correspondents" (p. 122), critical of the traditional news media reporting. Deuze (2003) notes that this opportunity to provide alternative information on news events "challenges perceptions of the roles and functions of journalism as a whole" (p. 216). Kovach and Rosenstiel (2001) concluded that journalists do not determine the news flow anymore, but they help by sorting it for their audience.

The challenges to journalism gatekeepers, however, are not distinct in the new media environment. Alternative formats enabled by the Internet also challenge gatekeepers in other areas of information distribution. The collaborative wiki format for instance, mostly known through the development of the online encyclopedia Wikipedia, has challenged the elitist model of encyclopedia worldwide. Before Wikipedia was developed in 2001, Nobel and Pulitzer Prize winners among other experts acted as gatekeepers who defined encyclopedia entries. Today, as DiStaso, Messner, and Stacks (2007) pointed out, any individual can participate in the definition process using the wiki format.

Gaining Credibility

The challenge of the traditional gatekeepers is intensified by the high credibility of online information in general, despite the continuing proliferation of hoaxes and rumors on the Internet. While traditional media journalists have long questioned the credibility of alternative online sources (Ruggerio & Winch, 2004), online news sites have already overtaken print and broadcast sources in popularity and are steadily increasing their audiences.

In one of the first studies measuring the credibility of online information and comparing it to traditional media sources before and after the 1996 presidential election, Johnson and Kaye (1998) found that Internet users viewed political information online as more credible than in the traditional media counterparts. Nevertheless, in this survey, all media were ranked low on credibility. In a follow-up study, Johnson and Kaye (2000) confirmed that reliance on online media also influences their credibility ranking. The more often someone uses a medium, the higher will that individual rank the credibility of the medium. Thereby, the results of the study linked the credibility of online information to its growing popularity.

In the late 1990s, Internet users already viewed the credibility of general online information as being equal to that of television, magazines, and radio. A survey by Flanagin and Metzger (2000) found that only newspapers still had a credibility advantage over online information. The results were surprising because the researchers themselves viewed information on the Internet at the time as deriving from "the least critical medium" (p. 529). The Internet users surveyed, nevertheless, only rarely verified information found online with traditional media. The researchers excluded a direct transfer of traditional media credibility to online media, because newspapers ranked higher than their online counterparts.

By the 2000 presidential election, online information had gained significant credibility with Internet users in the four years since the 1996 campaign (Johnson & Kaye, 2002). Bucy (2003) found in an experiment in 2001 that students viewed television and online news as more credible than adults did. In addition, alternative Internet formats such as blogs were also gaining credibility. In a 2003 survey of blog readers, Johnson and Kaye (2004) found that blogs were ranked as more credible than traditional sources. While weblogs were rated as highly credible, traditional media information was rated as moderately credible. Only 3.5 percent of the respondents rated blogs as not credible. This high credibility rating was mainly based on the notion that blogs provide more depth and better analysis than other media outlets. The fact that blogs were not viewed as fair by the respondents but were still ranked credible constitutes another challenge to journalistic standards of fairness and objectivity. Abdulla, Garrison, Salwen, Driscoll, and Casey (2005) also found that online news in general is viewed as more biased than other media. Their survey, however, also established the higher credibility of online information over newspapers and television.

In their survey on the effects of audience participation on the perception of journalism, Lowrey and Anderson (2005) found that the definition of news is broadening. Two-thirds of the respondents used non-traditional news sources online to gather information. More than a quarter also personalized the news retrieved from the Internet. In addition, Choi, Watt, and Lynch (2006) analyzed the perceptions on credibility in regard to online information on the war in Iraq. They found that war opponents, who were in the minority in 2003, viewed online information as highly credible based on the greater diversity of information and the perception of less alignment with a pro-government position in comparison to traditional news media. Supporters of the war and people with neutral viewpoints gave online information lower credibility ratings. In conclusion, the researchers asked what balancing means in news reporting "when people can access a virtually limitless number of news sources."

Media Agenda Setters

Williams and Delli Carpini (2004), who had concluded that traditional media gatekeeping had broken down in the aftermath of the Clinton–Lewinsky scandal, were also the first scholars to claim the same for mass media agenda-setting. The researchers argued that traditional media journalists had not only lost their central gatekeeping position, but also their central position as agenda setters. "Traditional journalists are now one among many agenda setters and issue framers

within the media…the new media environment with its multiple points of access and more continuous news cycle has increased the opportunities for less mainstream individuals and groups to
influence public discourse" (p. 1225). While the news sites of the traditional media generally have
similar editorial policies as their counterparts, independently developed Internet formats such
as blogs are mostly responsible for the changes in gatekeeping and agenda setting. However, the
readership of blogs has not reached levels that would allow conclusions on their effects on public
opinion. Thirty-nine percent of Internet users in the United States read blogs in 2006 (Lenhart &
Fox, 2006). Hargrove and Stempel (2007) came to the conclusion that blogs have not developed
into a major source of news for the general public and are more of a media phenomenon.

Consequently, most research has focused on the intermedia agenda-setting effects of Internet formats. McCombs (2005) described the importance of research on the agenda-setting role
of Internet formats as follows: "Blogs are part of the journalism landscape, but who sets whose
agenda under what circumstances remains an open question. Intermedia agenda setting at both
the first and second levels is likely to remain high on the journalism research agenda for a very
long time" (p. 549).

The intermedia dimension of agenda-setting research developed in the late 1980s, most notably by Atwater, Fico, and Pizante (1987), Rogers and Dearing (1988), and Danielian and Reese
(1989). In recent years this intermedia concept, which studies how the media influence themselves, has been applied to Internet-related research by a variety of scholars. Roberts, Wanta, and
Dzwo (2002) were among the first scholars to analyze the effects of the traditional news media
agenda on discussions on electronic bulletin boards during the 1996 presidential election. They
found that *The New York Times*, The Associated Press, *Reuters*, *Time*, and *CNN* all had agenda-
setting effects on the discussions, but also found that the impact of *The New York Times* was
most significant, confirming previous findings that established the special influence of certain
elite media. This approach was extended by Lee, Lancendorfer, and Lee (2005), who looked at
intermedia agenda-setting effects in both directions. During the 2000 general election in South
Korea, they documented agenda-setting effects of newspapers' agendas on the opinions posted
on bulletin boards. They also established that discussions on bulletin boards had an influence on
the newspapers' agenda. They concluded that traditional journalists use the Internet to gather
a variety of opinions on issues and that the Internet has the power to shape public opinion
by affecting the agendas of other media. This constituted a shift in Internet-related research
towards a focus on the effects of the Internet rather than the effects of traditional media on
online formats.

The growing influence of Internet-generated information on the traditional news media has
led several scholars to analyze intermedia agenda-setting effects of Internet formats in political
elections (Bichard, 2006; Davis, 2005; Verser & Wicks, 2006). Ku, Kaid, and Pfau (2003) found
a strong influence of website campaigns on the traditional news agenda and public opinion.
They studied the intermedia agenda-setting effects between the campaign websites and *The
New York Times*, *The Washington Post*, ABC, CBS, and NBC in the 2000 presidential election
and concluded that "Internet-based communication has established powerful new links between
politicians and voters and created great impact on the information flow of the traditional news
media" (p. 544).

With the emergence of blogs as a new influential Internet format during the last five years,
most intermedia agenda-setting research has focused on the impact of these online journals on
the traditional media agenda. Tremayne (2007) pointed out that this influence of blogs is greatest when they influence news events as a collective by creating a buzz. Lowrey (2006) also found
that blogs derive their influence on the traditional media from a focus on partisan expression and
stories that are based on alternative, non-elite sources and thereby become sources themselves.
However, as Drezner and Farrell (2004) stressed, while the blogosphere is growing rapidly, only

few blogs have agenda-setting power on the traditional media. Filter blogs serve as "focal points" (p. 35) that bring attention to less renowned blogs. The researchers also found that traditional media journalists tend to concentrate on the same filter weblogs. Through these filter blogs, it becomes easier and less time consuming for journalists to survey the blogosphere on a daily basis and select them as sources for stories.

Research on the agenda-setting power of blogs has mainly focused on the creation of buzz within the blogosphere, the increasing blogging during certain news events. Cornfield, Carson, Kalis, and Simon (2005) traced the buzz on filter blogs during the 2004 presidential campaign and compared it with the buzz in the traditional media, campaign statements, and Internet forums. They found that blogs had difficulties to influence other media when there was no advancement of the stories, such as results of an investigation. Overall, their study concluded that "blogger power, the capacity of blog operators to make buzz and influence decision makers, is circumstantial" (p. 2). However, they also found that bloggers served as guides for the traditional media to the discourse on the Internet. Schiffer (2006) also found in his analysis of blog buzz about the Downing Street Memo controversy during the 2004 presidential election that the issue was transferred into the traditional media, but was only covered there for a short time. The researcher concluded that activists have a better chance to influencing traditional media by targeting media agenda setters, e.g. politicians, rather than the traditional media themselves. However, hyperlinking within the blogosphere is the factor that makes blog buzz accessible to the traditional media. This has also led political campaigns to adopt the blog format for their information distribution purposes (Bichard, 2006; Trammell, Williams, Postelnicu, & Landreville, 2006; Williams, Trammell, Postelnicu, Landreville, & Martin, 2005).

Overall, the coverage of blogs in the traditional media has changed from a focus "on the sexy or 'hot' aspects of new media technology" (Perlmutter & McDaniel, 2005, p. 60) to the use of weblogs as sources in the reporting. Through the inherent agenda-setting power of news sources, blogs gain influence over the traditional media agenda. While Perlmutter and McDaniel (2005) found a sharp increase in mentioning of blogs in the traditional media between 1998 and 2005, Messner and DiStaso (2008) also analyzed the use of blogs as sources in *The New York Times* and *The Washington Post* from 2000 to 2005 and found steady increase of the overall number of articles. They found that the reporting on the weblog phenomenon did not increase as much as the use of weblogs as sources and the simple mentioning of weblogs in the articles. At the same time, however, blogs were also found to use traditional media 43 percent of the time as sources in the posts. Scott (2007) had similar findings with 49.5 percent of sources in blogs as traditional media in the 2004 presidential election.

While Lim (2006) found support for the notion of intermedia agenda-setting between online media and traditional media in South Korea, other scholars have also noted that it would be an oversimplification to state that online news sources set the agenda of the traditional media. Song (2007) studied the impact of online news services in South Korea on the traditional media reporting and argued that intermedia agenda-setting cannot only be studied by counting news stories and issues over time to build correlations, but that an in-depth analysis of the decision making process is necessary to fully understand the interaction of new and old media. This suggested approach would combine the gatekeeping and agenda-setting dimensions of the new media phenomenon.

Hyperlinking Networks

As mentioned above, the Internet is capable of creating a buzz, or intensive public discussion, on certain issues that consequently has the potential of influencing the traditional media agenda. The main characteristic that allows the creation of a buzz and that distinguishes Internet news formats from traditional media formats are interactivity and networking capabilities. Flew (2005) defined interactivity as a system "where each pattern of use leads the user down a distinctive 'pathway'" (p. 13). Hyperlinks make it possible to connect news websites with other websites and contribute to the creation of Internet networks. As the dominant search engine Google bases the rankings of its search results on the principles of interactivity, hyperlinking, and networking, success on the Internet is measured by the number of hyperlinks to a certain website. Therefore, "understanding interactivity is central to developing theory and research about new media," according to McMillan (2006, p. 205).

Tremayne (2004) was one of the first mass communication scholars to apply network theory to research on Internet news formats and has advanced this still developing research track the furthest to date. A content analysis of ten traditional news media websites between 1997 and 2001 found that the number of links associated with individual news stories increased sharply over time. The researcher concluded that the increase of hyperlinks will have a significant influence on the future of journalism: "If television news favors good pictures to hold an audience, we might expect Web editors to use links strategically to keep readers on their site" (p. 250). In addition, as hyperlinks allow editors to provide more context for the news stories, the news coverage on the Internet overall may become more driven by event reporting rather than contextual analysis.

Harp and Tremayne (2006) also applied network theory to the emerging blogosphere and detected through a discourse analysis that an inequality exists in the hyperlinking patterns of the blogosphere, which disadvantages female bloggers. While overall the blogosphere enables almost anybody to enter the public sphere, hyperlinking patterns give greater audience and thereby more power to certain websites and prevent others from gaining attention. As the scholars pointed out, ignored groups can increase their popularity on the Internet by creating their own hyperlinking network.

Further research into hyperlinking patterns of blogs drew the focus on the central opinion leaders within the blogosphere. Tremayne, Zheng, Lee, and Jeong (2006) identified several key blogs out of a sample of 70 blogs in the war blogosphere that connected the opposing sides, conservatives and liberals, in the discourse on the war in Iraq. The researchers concluded that blogs in a public limited to one issue—like the war—tend to link to blogs that support their viewpoints, but that there is space within the blogosphere for open discussion by utilizing these central blogs through hyperlinking. Trammell and Keshelashvili (2005) also examined 209 popular blogs and found that they reveal more about themselves and manage their impressions in their Internet presence than less popular blogs.

While the Internet and blogs in particular have certainly contributed to a more diverse media environment, the evolving research on online networks has shown that a hierarchy is developing within the new Internet formats. Thereby, some websites will gain more influence over the discourse on a certain issue than others. This is a concept similar to the structure of the traditional media. For this reason, Haas (2005) argued that the central filter blogs take on a role within the blogosphere similar to the one that elite media like *The New York Times, The Washington Post*, and the television networks play within the traditional media. Overall, however, research involving the concepts of interactivity and hyperlinking and their influence on the news flow is only emergent at this point. With the growing impact of Internet news formats and the transformation of the traditional media towards converged online news outlets, more research and scholarly attention will be necessary to explain this evolving phenomenon.

Revitalizing Uses and Gratifications

The increasing Internet penetration rate and the increasingly popular use of websites as sources of news has revitalized research utilizing the uses and gratifications model developed by Katz,

Blumler, and Gurevitch (1974). Kaye and Johnson (2004) called it a "renaissance in the uses and gratifications tradition as scholars are increasingly interested in going beyond discovering who uses the Internet to examine why they use this new medium" (p. 197). The model has been criticized by mass communication scholars for being "too descriptive and insufficiently theoretical, and for relying too heavily on audiences for reporting their true motivations for media use" (Bucy, Gantz, &Wang, 2007, p. 150). However, an increasing number of scholars have employed the model for the study of Internet use (Flanagin & Metzger, 2001; LaRose & Eastin, 2004; Lin, 1999; Ogan & Cagiltay, 2006). Ruggerio (2000) even argued that the future development of mass communication theory inevitably must include a uses and gratifications dimension as it "has always provided a cutting-edge theoretical approach in the initial stages of each new mass communications medium: newspaper, radio and television, and now the Internet" (p. 3). Nevertheless, the researcher added that the traditional uses and gratifications approach must incorporate the concepts of interactivity and hypertextuality as well as demassification and asynchroneity to account for a greater media selection menu and the breakdown of a set time scheme under which news was delivered in the past, which gives the audience greater ability to choose its media use.

While only few studies have analyzed uses and gratifications aspects of the online news and information environment to date, an increasing number of studies has explored the adoption and use patterns on the Internet in general. Charney and Greenberg (2002) found eight gratifications dimensions related to Internet use in a 1996 survey: keeping informed, diversion/entertainment, peer identity, good feelings, communications, sights and sounds, career, and coolness. Nevertheless, the researchers pointed out that the gratification of keeping informed was so dominant "that it encompasses virtually all of the apparent uses" (p. 400). In two subsequent surveys during the 1996 and 2000 presidential elections, Kaye and Johnson (2002, 2004) found that online political information was primarily used for guidance, meaning that those interested in politics rely on the Internet for political information. In their second survey in 2000, the researchers also examined the motivations for using message boards and electronic mailing lists and found that guidance was a weaker indicator for use and entertainment/social utility, information seeking, and convenience were stronger indicators. Overall, the researchers found that convenience became a weaker motivator for Internet use, which they interpreted to be a result of maturing and more skilled users seeking specific information online.

In addition to studying motivations for Internet use, several scholars have conducted uses and gratifications research with a focus on how audiences differentiate in their use between online and traditional news formats. Tewksbury and Althaus (2000) explored in an experiment how the greater selection opportunities for online newspaper users impact the knowledge acquisition and found that online users of *The New York Times* read fewer international, national and political stories and were less likely to recall public affairs events. The researchers suggested that additional content online diverts readers' attention away from public affairs stories and that differences in the online layout reduce importance cues and have an effect on which stories are noticed and read by the readers. They warned that "with this increased opportunity to personalize the flow of news, fewer people may be exposed to politically important stories. As a consequence, online news providers may inadvertently develop a readership that is more poorly informed than traditional newspaper readers" (p. 459). The findings of Lin, Salwen, and Abdulla (2005), however, partially contradicted this assumption. Their survey showed that the information scanning gratification was stronger for online use than for traditional media use and they concluded that the Internet was the best tool for newspapers to compete with cable news networks in the 24-hour news cycle: "If newspapers are able to attract more users to their Web sites, they may be able to help stabilize existing users and readers" (p. 234). This was underlined by the findings of Dimmick, Chen, and Li (2004), who found that the Internet has a "competitive displacement effect on traditional news media in the daily news domain" (p. 19). Their survey showed that 33.7 percent of the broadcast television viewers and 28 percent of newspaper readers used these media less often after they started using the Internet for news. The researchers concluded that the new medium provides more contemporary solutions to gratify audiences' needs and thereby competes with the traditional media.

Methodologies

Internet-related studies have employed a variety of research methodologies, generally those that are common practice in communication and mass communication research. Nevertheless, Internet-related research still differs in its overall distribution of the applied methodologies from the broader discipline. While the communication field in general has a greater emphasis on quantitative than qualitative methods, this emerging field of research has had a greater emphasis on qualitative methods to date. Kim and Weaver (2002) found that between 1996 and 1999 only 26.7 percent of journal articles on Internet-related research used quantitative methods. Cho and Khang (2006) stated that between 1994 and 2003 the most used methods in communication research articles related to the Internet were critiques and essays (30.8 percent), surveys (19.3 percent), and content analyses (16 percent). They found experiments to have a stronger presence in advertising and marketing related research than in communication research overall. However, they also found a more evenly distributed use of quantitative and qualitative methods, with over 46 percent of Internet-related communication journal articles using quantitative methods.

Interestingly, the researchers also detected a methodological difference between leading communication journals and Internet-specific journals. The dominant method in the leading journals was survey (29.4 percent), while critiques and essays (39.6 percent) dominated the methodologies in the Internet-specific journals. This, on one hand, underlines the more rigorous review process of the leading journals, but on the other hand also stresses the need for exploratory research in an emerging field of mass communication research. Researchers report that 71.5 percent of the Internet-related research in communication journals was exploratory, 24.1 percent descriptive and only 4.3 percent explanatory. Overall, only 14.5 percent of all Internet-related journal articles used a theoretical framework, while 27.2 percent generated hypotheses. However, the researchers found an increase of theory-driven research when comparing the time frames of 1994 to 1998 (8.7 percent) and 1999 to 2003 (16.3 percent). Cho and Khang (2006) concluded "that Internet-related research is becoming more theoretically sound," but that "more explanatory research studies are needed" (p. 158).

Critiques and Essays

Many of the early studies on Internet-related communication took exploratory approaches through media critiques and essayist analysis that attempted to modify existing theories. Ruggerio (2000) for instance used a critical analysis of the historical development of the uses and gratifications model to justify its application in Internet research. From the application of uses and gratifications in the 1950s and the development of the model in the 1970s, the scholar developed theoretical modifications that allow researchers to apply the model to the contemporary media environment. Williams and Carpini (2000) also used a historical–critical approach to outline the changes to the gatekeeping environment in the late 1990s. They described media incidents, in which the traditional media gatekeepers were circumvented by new Internet formats. In a subsequent study, Williams and Delli Carpini (2004) extended their theoretical modification to agenda-setting theory, by closely examining media incidents, in which Internet formats influenced the traditional media news agenda. While these exploratory approaches were mostly dominant in the development stage of the Internet, they are still valued today within the discipline as new Internet formats continue to develop. Haas (2005), for instance, wrote an essay in which the development of blogs and their increasing influence are analyzed, also contributing to the developing model of intermedia agenda-setting within the blogosphere.

Surveys

An increasing number of research studies has used survey methodologies to describe and explain Internet communication. Johnson and Kaye (2002) used a Web-based survey technique to explore the credibility of online and traditional media. They used a convenience sample of politically interested Internet users, as a central registry of Internet users is not available. Before and after the 1996 presidential election, the survey was promoted for a total of one month on newsgroups, mailing lists as well as chat rooms and several websites also helped to promote participation through hyperlinks. This resulted in 442 responses. Johnson and Kaye (2004) used a similar technique when they analyzed the credibility of blogs. They used a Web-based survey that was posted online for one month in 2003 and established links from 131 blogs as well as bulletin boards and mailing lists to sample blog readers. Again, since a random sample of blog users is impossible to generate, they used a convenience sample, which resulted in 3,747 responses. Response rates cannot be assessed with these techniques. However, other researchers are still relying on the more traditional mail and telephone surveys, which generally allow the researcher to gain more control over sampling and responses than Web-based surveys. Abdulla et al. (2005) conducted a national telephone survey to assess online news credibility. They drew a probability sample from all states and completed 536 interviews, which constituted a response rate of 41 percent. Other researchers also use electronic mail to distribute surveys. In a study to analyze the gatekeeping role of online newspaper editors in 2004, Singer (2006) sampled the largest newspaper in each state and other daily newspapers with circulations over 250,000 and identified the news editors. Depending on the speed of responses, a total of one to four e-mails were sent to 77 editors. This resulted in 43 responses, a rate of 61 percent.

Content Analyses

Similar to the increase in survey research, quantitative content analyses are more frequently used in Internet-related studies in recent years. Especially when measuring the influence of new media formats on the traditional media, researchers rely on content analyses instruments to measure the degree of influence. Ku, Kaid, and Pfau (2003) studied the impact of campaign websites on traditional media during the 2000 presidential campaign. They sampled content from the *New York Times* and the *Washington Post* as well as the television networks ABC, CBS, and NBC and the news releases from the candidates' websites during three constructed weeks. In addition they drew secondary data from public opinion polls. The researchers developed rank orders of issues for the media, campaign and public agendas and used cross-lagged comparisons to determine correlations between the agendas. Lim (2006) used a similar approach when exploring intermedia agenda-setting effects among online news media in South Korea. However, as in most intermedia analysis, the researcher only conducted content analyses. A content sample was drawn from an online news agency and two online newspapers in two constructed weeks. The researcher also developed issue agendas from the sample content and analyzed correlations through cross-lagged comparisons to establish causal relationships between variables in different time periods. Content analysis is also utilized in studies that explore networks on the Internet. Trammell and

Keshelashvili (2005) identified 209 single-authored blogs from a popularity ranking based on hyperlinks and examined their content on impression management tactics and self-presentation. Tremayne (2004), on the other hand, sampled ten traditional media websites and examined their hyperlinks over a five-year period.

Experiments

Experimental studies, which allow researchers to identify causal relationships, are still rare in research on the Internet as a news medium. This also explains the low rate of explanatory research to date. Tewksbury and Althaus (2000) conducted one of the few experiments to study differences in knowledge acquisition among readers of online and print versions of the *New York Times*. The researchers sampled student volunteers into three groups, one of them a control group, another one exposed to the online version of the newspaper, and the third exposed to the print version for five consecutive days. The posttest of the experiment tested the participants on how much knowledge they had acquired and revealed differences between reading the online or printed versions of the newspaper. Bucy (2003) also used an experimental design to analyze the synergy effects between on-air and online network news. Students and older adults were sampled into eight groups, which were exposed to television news online, online news online, television and online news, and no exposure and then completed media credibility questionnaires.

Future Research

While the field of Internet communication has already developed a broad body of research, the field in general is still emerging as a research discipline at this point. Research has explored the issues and uses of the Internet as a mass medium, but has only recently started to analyze the effects of Internet communication. More empirical research is needed to explain Internet phenomena and their consequences for society. This includes more frequent applications of existing theories, which also have to be further modified to suit this new media environment, as well as the development of Internet specific models and theories. Future research approaches should include the following five characteristics:

Collaborative Information

The concept of Web 2.0 so far has only been explored through research on the blogosphere. Only a few researchers have turned their attention to the wiki concept, which has become influential with Internet users through the growing popularity of the online encyclopedia Wikipedia, which changes the way information is generated. In addition, online portals such as YouTube, Facebook, MySpace, and Flickr have not been explored at all, but are likely to cause even greater changes to the overall media environment.

New Gatekeepers

Elitist gatekeepers are likely to be replaced by collective information gathering models. While blogs have already posed a challenge to traditional media gatekeepers, multimedia search portals such as Google will only intensify these challenges. The search rankings of Google and other search engines are most likely to determine which information is accessed by Internet users. As Google interlinks more news content of traditional and online media outlets, its strengthening gatekeeping position within the news flow needs much more scholarly attention.

Hyperlinking as Agenda Setting

Some researchers have focused their research on the concepts of interactivity and hyperlinking, but much more empirical research is needed to explore the gatekeeping and agenda-setting dimensions of hyperlinking on the Internet. Hyperlinking, on the one hand, can be used as a new way of gatekeeping, while on the other hand it can also be utilized as an intermedia agenda-setting device. Future research should engage with the question of which medium links to which medium, and with what effect.

Intermedia Sourcing

Some research has indicated that traditional media and online media increasingly use each other as sources in their reporting and editorializing. Research should explore whether Internet formats are used by the traditional media as a way to explore online buzz and opinion. In addition, research is needed to analyze under which conditions one medium becomes a source for the other.

Mainstreaming Internet Formats

Traditional media organizations are increasingly adopting the newly developed Internet formats such as blogs. Research should not only analyze the adoption rates, but also the evolution of these initially alternative formats into mainstream media applications.

Summary

While still evolving as a scholarly field, there is no doubt that research on Internet communication will continue to grow and become more dominant within the overall communication field as the media environment converges further and the lines between broadcasting, print, and online are slowly disappearing. While the study of the effects of Internet communication should be the main priority of the current research agenda, scholars should also turn more of their attention to much needed Internet-specific model and theory development.

References

Abdulla, R. A., Garrison, B., Salwen, M. B., Driscoll, P. D., & Casey, D. (2005). Online news credibility. In M. B. Salwen, B. Garrison, & P. D. Driscoll (Eds.), *Online news and the public* (pp. 147–163). Mahwah, NJ: Erlbaum.

Atwater, T., Fico, F., & Pizante, G. (1987). Reporting on the state legislature: A case study of inter-media agenda-setting. *Newspaper Research Journal, 8*(2), 53–61.

Barnett, G. A., & Sung, E. (2005). Culture and structure of the international hyperlink network. *Journal of Computer-Mediated Communication, 11*(1), article 11. Retrieved June 5, 2007, from http://jcmc.indiana.edu/vol11/issue1/barnett.html

Bichard, S. L. (2006). Building blogs: A multi-dimensional analysis of the distribution of frames on the 2004 presidential candidate web sites. *Journalism & Mass Communication Quarterly, 83*(2), 329–345.

Bucy, E. P. (2003). Media credibility reconsidered: Synergy effects between on-air and online news. *Journalism & Mass Communication Quarterly, 80*(2), 247–264.

Bucy, E. P., Gantz, W., & Wang, Z. (2007). *Media technology and the 24-hour news cycle.* In C. A. Lin & D. J. Atkin (Eds.), *Communication technology and social change: Theory and implications.* (pp. 143–166). Mahwah, NJ: Erlbaum.

Burnett, R., & Marshall, P. D. (2003). *Web theory: An introduction.* London: Routledge.

Cassidy, W. P. (2005). Web-only online sites more likely to post editorial policies than are daily paper sites. *Newspaper Research Journal, 26*(1), 53–58.

Charney, T., & Greenberg, B. S. (2002). Uses and gratifications of the Internet. In C. A. Lin & D. J. Atkin (Eds.), *Communication technology and society: Audience adoption and uses* (pp. 379–407). Cresskill, NJ: Hampton Press.

Cho, C. H., & Khang, H. K. (2006). The state of Internet-related research in communications, marketing, and advertising: 1994–2003. *Journal of Advertising, 35*(3), 143–163.

Choi, J. H., Watt, J. H., & Lynch, M. (2006). Perceptions of news credibility about the war in Iraq. Why war opponents perceived the internet as the most credible medium. *Journal of Computer-Mediated Communication, 12*(1), article 11. Retrieved June 5, 2007, from http://jcmc.indiana.edu/vol12/issue1/choi.html

Cornfield, M., Carson, J., Kalis, A., & Simon, E. (2005). Buzz, blogs, and beyond: The Internet and the national discourse in the fall of 2004. *Pew Internet & American Life Project.* Retrieved February 15, 2006, from http://www.pewinternet.org

Danielian, L. H., & Reese, S. D. (1989). A closer look at intermedia influences on agenda setting: The cocaine issue of 1986. In P. Shoemaker (Ed.), *Communication campaigns about drugs: Government, media and the public* (pp. 47–66). Hillsdale, NJ: Erlbaum.

Davis, S. (2005). Presidential campaigns fine-tune online strategies. *Journalism Studies, 6*(2), 241–244.

Deuze, M. (2003). The web and its journalisms: Considering the consequences of different types of news media online. *New Media & Society, 5*(2), 203–230.

Dimitrova, D. V., & Neznanski, M. (2006). Online journalism and the war in cyberspace: A comparison between U.S. and international newspapers. *Journal of Computer-Mediated Communication, 12*(1), article 11. Retrieved June 5, 2007, from http://jcmc.indiana.edu/vol12/issue1/dimitrova.html

Dimmick, J., Chen, Y., & Li, Z. (2004). Competition between the Internet and traditional news media: The gratification-opportunities niche dimension. *The Journal of Media Economics, 17*(1), 19–33.

DiStaso, M. W., Messner, M., & Stacks, D. W. (2007). The wiki factor: A study of reputation management. In S. C. Duhé (Ed.), *New media & public relations* (pp. 121–133). New York: Peter Lang.

Drezner, D. W., & Farrell, H. (2004). Web of influence. *Foreign Policy, 145*, 32–40.

Flanagin, A. J., & Metzger, M. J. (2000). Perceptions of internet information credibility. *Journalism & Mass Communication Quarterly, 77*(3), 515–540.

Flanagin, A. J., & Metzger, M. J. (2001). Internet use in the contemporary media environment. *Human Communication Research, 27*(1), 153–181.

Flew, T. (2005). *New media: An introduction.* Victoria, Australia: Oxford University Press.

Haas, T. (2005). From "public journalism" to the "public's journalism"? Rhetoric and reality in the discourse on weblogs. *Journalism Studies, 6*(3), 387–396.

Hargrove, T., & Stempel, G. H., III. (2007). Use of blogs as a source of news presents little threat to mainline news media. *Newspaper Research Journal, 28*(1), 99–102.

Harp, D., & Tremayne, M. (2006). The gendered blogosphere: Examining inequality using network and feminist theory. *Journalism & Mass Communication Quarterly, 83*(2), 247–264.

Hoffman, L. H. (2006). Is internet content different after all? A content analysis of mobilizing information in online and print newspapers. *Journalism & Mass Communication Quarterly, 83*(1), 58–67.

Horrigan, J. B. (2006a). Home broadband adoption 2006. *Pew Internet & American Life Project.* Retrieved April 5, 2007, from http://www.pewinternet.org

Horrigan, J. B. (2006b). Politics online. *Pew Internet & American Life Project.* Retrieved April 5, 2007, from http://www.pewinternet.org

Horrigan, J. B. (2007). Wireless Internet access. *Pew Internet & American Life Project.* Retrieved April 5, 2007,from http://www.pewinternet.org

Johnson, T. J., & Kaye, B. K. (1998). Cruising is believing? Comparing Internet and traditional sources on media credibility measures. *Journalism & Mass Communication Quarterly, 75*(2), 325–340.

Johnson, T. J., & Kaye, B. K. (2000). Using is believing: The influence of reliance on the credibility of online political information among politically interested internet users. *Journalism & Mass Communication Quarterly, 77*(4), 865–879.

Johnson, T. J., & Kaye, B. K. (2002). Webelievability: A path model examining how convenience and reliance predict online credibility. *Journalism & Mass Communication Quarterly, 79*(3), 619–642.

Johnson, T. J., & Kaye, B. K. (2004). Wag the blog: How reliance on traditional media and the internet influence credibility perceptions of weblogs among blog users. *Journalism & Mass Communication Quarterly, 81*(3), 622–642.

Kahn, R., & Kellner, D. (2004). New media and internet activism: From the "Battle of Seattle" to blogging. *New Media & Society, 6*(1), 87–95.

Katz, E., Blumler, J. G., & Gurevitch, M. (1974). *The uses of mass communications: Current perspectives on gratifications research.* Beverly Hills, CA: Sage.

Kaye, B. K., & Johnson, T. J. (2002). Online and in the know: Uses and gratifications of the web for political information. *Journal of Broadcasting & Electronic Media, 46*(1), 54–71.

Kaye, B. K., & Johnson, T. J. (2004). A web for all reasons: Uses and gratifications of Internet components for political information. *Telematics and Informatics, 21*, 197–223.

Kim, S. T., & Weaver, D. (2002). Communication research about the Internet: A thematic meta-analysis. *New Media & Society, 4*(4), 518–538.

Klopfenstein, B. (2002). *The Internet and web as communication media.* In C. A. Lin & D. J. Atkin (Eds.), *Communication technology and society: Audience adoption and uses* (pp. 353–378). Cresskill, NJ: Hampton Press.

Kovach, B., & Rosenstiel, T. (2001). *The elements of journalism.* New York: Three Rivers Press.

Ku, G., Kaid, L. L., & Pfau, M. (2003). The impact of web site campaigning on traditional news media and public information processing. *Journalism & Mass Communication Quarterly, 80*(3), 528–547.

LaRose, R., & Eastin, M. S. (2004). A social cognitive theory of Internet uses and gratifications: Toward a new model of media attendance. *Journal of Broadcasting & Electronic Media, 48*(3), 358–377.

Lee, B., Lancendorfer, K. M., & Lee, K. J. (2005). Agenda-setting and the Internet: The intermedia influence of Internet bulletin boards on newspaper coverage of the 2000 general election in South Korea. *Asian Journal of Communication, 15*(1), 57–71.

Lenhart, A., & Fox, S. (2006). Bloggers: A portrait of the internet's new storytellers. *Pew Internet & American Life Project.* Retrieved November 24, 2006, from http://www.pewinternet.org.

Lim, J. (2006). A cross-lagged analysis of agenda setting among online news media. *Journalism & Mass Communication Quarterly, 83*(2), 298–312.

Lin, C. (1999). Online-service adoption likelihood. *Journal of Advertising Research. 39*(2), 79–89.

Lin, C., & Salwen, M. B., & Abdulla, R. A. (2005). *Uses and gratifications of online and offline news: New wine in an old bottle.* In M. B. Salwen, B. Garrison, & P. D. Driscoll (Eds.), *Online news and the public* (pp. 221–236). Mahwah, NJ: Erlbaum.

Lowrey, W. (2006). Mapping the journalism-blogging relationship. *Journalism, 7*(4), 477–500.

Lowrey, W., & Anderson (2005). The journalists behind the curtain: Participatory functions of the internet and their impact on perceptions of the work of journalism. *Journal of Computer-Mediated Communication, 12*(1), article 11. Retrieved June 5, 2007, from http://jcmc.indiana.edu/vol10/issue3/lowrey.html

Madden, M. (2006). Internet penetration and impact. *Pew Internet & American Life Project.* Retrieved April, 5, 2007, from http://www.pewinternet.org

Matheson, D. (2004). Weblogs and the epistemology of the news: Some trends in online journalism. *New Media & Society, 6*(4), 443–468.

McCombs, M. (2005). A look at agenda-setting: Past, present and future. *Journalism Studies, 6*(4), 543–557.

McCombs, M., & Shaw, D. (1972). The agenda-setting function of the media. *Public Opinion Quarterly, 36*, 176–187.

McMillan, S. J. (2006). Exploring models of interactivity from multiple research traditions: Users, documents and systems. In L. A. Lievrouw & S. Livingstone (Eds.), *The handbook of new media* (pp. 162–182). London: Sage.

Messner, M., & DiStaso, M. W. (2008). The source cycle: How traditional media and weblogs use each other as sources. *Journalism Studies, 9*(3), 447–463.

Messner, M., & Terilli, S. (2007). Gates wide open: The impact of weblogs on the gatekeeping role of the traditional media in the 2004 presidential election. *Florida Communication Journal, 35*(1), 1–14.

Ogan, C. L., & Cagiltay, K. (2006). Confession, revelation and storytelling: Patterns of use on a popular Turkish website. *New Media & Society, 8*(5), 801–823.

Perlmutter, D. P., & McDaniel, M. (2005). The ascent of blogging. *Nieman Reports, 59*(3), 60–64.

Poor, N. (2006). Playing internet curveball with traditional media gatekeepers: Pitcher Curt Schilling and Boston Red Sox fans. *Convergence, 12*(1), 41–53.

Rainie, L., & Shermak, J. (2005). Search engine use. *Pew Internet & American Life Project.* Retrieved April 5, 2007, from http://www.pewinternet.org

Roberts, M., Wanta, W., & Dzwo, T.-H. (2002). Agenda setting and issue salience online. *Communication Research, 29*(4), 452–465.

Rogers, E. M., & Dearing, J. W. (1988). Agenda-setting research: Where has it been, where is it going? *Communication Yearbook, 11,* 555–594.

Ruggerio, T. E. (2000). Uses and gratifications theory in the 21st century. *Mass Communication & Society, 3*(1), 3–37.

Ruggiero, T. E., & Winch, S. P. (2004). The media downing of Pierre Salinger: Journalistic mistrust of the internet as a news sources. *Journal of Computer-Mediated Communication, 10*(2), article 8 Retrieved June 5, 2007, from http://jcmc.indiana.edu/vol10/issue2/ruggiero.html

Schiffer, A. J. (2006). Blogswarms and press norms: News coverage of the Downing Street Memo controversy. *Journalism & Mass Communication Quarterly, 83*(3), 494–510.

Scott, D. T. (2007). Pundits in muckrakers' clothing: Political blogs and the 2004 U.S. presidential election. In M. Tremayne (Ed.), *Blogging, citizenship, and the future of media* (pp. 39–57). New York: Routledge.

Shoemaker, P. J. (1991). *Gatekeeping.* Newbury Park, CA: Sage.

Singer, J. B. (1997). Still guarding the gate? The newspaper journalist's role in an on-line world. *Convergence, 3*(1), 72–89.

Singer, J. B. (2001). The metro wide web: Changes in newspapers' gatekeeping role online. *Journalism & Mass Communication Quarterly, 78*(1), 65–80.

Singer, J. B. (2003a). Campaign contributions: Online newspaper coverage of election 2000. *Journalism & Mass Communication Quarterly, 80*(1), 39–56.

Singer, J. B. (2003b). Who are these guys? The online challenge to the notion of journalistic professionalism. *Journalism, 4*(2), 139–163.

Singer, J. B. (2006). Stepping back from the gate: Online newspaper editors and the co-production of content in campaign 2004. *Journalism & Mass Communication Quarterly, 83*(2), 265–280.

Song, Y. (2007). Internet news media and issue development: A case study on the roles of independent online news services as agenda-builders for anti-US protests in South Korea. *New Media & Society, 9*(1), 71–92.

Tewksbury, D., & Althaus, S. L. (2000). Differences in knowledge acquisition among readers of the paper and online versions of a national newspaper. *Journalism & Mass Communication Quarterly, 77*(3), 457–479.

Tomasello, T. K. (2001). The status of Internet-based research in five leading communication journals, 1994–1999. *Journalism & Mass Communication Quarterly, 78*(4), 659–674.

Trammell, K. D., & Keshelashvili, A. (2005). Examining the new influencers: A self-presentation study of A-list blogs. *Journalism & Mass Communication Quarterly, 82*(4), 968–982.

Trammell, K. D., Williams, A. P., Postelnicu, M., & Landreville, K. D. (2006). Evolution of online campaigning: Increasing interactivity in candidate web sites and blogs through text and technical features. *Mass Communication & Society, 9*(1), 21–44.

Tremayne, M. (2004). The web of context: Applying network theory to the use of hyperlinks in journalism on the web. *Journalism & Mass Communication Quarterly, 81*(2), 237–253.

Tremayne, M. (2007). *Blogging, citizenship and the future of media.* New York: Routledge.

Tremayne, M., Zheng, N., Lee, J. K., Jeong, J. (2006). Issue politics on the Web: Applying network theory to the war blogosphere. *Journal of Computer-Mediated Communication, 12*(1), article 15. Retrieved June 5, 2007, from http://jcmc.indiana.edu/vol12/issue1/tremayne.html

Verser, R., & Wicks, R. H. (2006). Managing voter impressions: The use of images on presidential candidate web sites during the 2000 campaign. *Journal of Communication, 56,* 178–197.

Wall, M. (2005). Blogs of war. *Journalism, 6*(2), 153–172.

Wall, M. (2006). Blogging Gulf War II. *Journalism Studies, 7*(1), 111–126.

White, D. M. (1950). The "gate keeper": A case study in the selection of news. *Journalism Quarterly, 27*, 383–390.

Williams, A. P., Trammell, K. D., Postelnicu, M., Landreville, K. D., & Martin, J. D. (2005). Blogging and hyperlinking: Use of the Web to enhance viability during the 2004 US campaign. *Journalism Studies, 6*(2), 177–186.

Williams, B. A., & Delli Carpini, M. X. (2000). Unchained reaction: The collapse of media gatekeeping and the Clinton-Lewinsky scandal. *Journalism, 1*(1), 61–85.

Williams, B. A., & Delli Carpini, M. X. (2004). Monica and Bill all the time and everywhere: the collapse of gatekeeping and agenda setting in the new media environment. *The American Behavioral Scientist, 47*(9), 1208–1230.

Suggested Readings

Burnett, R., & Marshall, P. D. (2003). *Web theory: An introduction*. London: Routledge.

Duhé, S. C. (2007). *New media and public relations*. New York: Peter Lang.

Johnson, T. J., & Kaye, B. K. (2004). Wag the blog: How reliance on traditional media and the internet influence credibility perceptions of weblogs among blog users. *Journalism & Mass Communication Quarterly, 81*(3), 622–642.

Lin, C. A., & Atkin, D. J. (2007). *Communication technology and social change: Theory and implications*. Mahwah, NJ: Erlbaum.

Salwen, M. B., Garrison, B., & Driscoll, P. D. (2005). *Online news and the public*. Mahwah, NJ: Erlbaum.

Singer, J. B. (2006). Stepping back from the gate: Online newspaper editors and the co-production of content in campaign 2004. *Journalism & Mass Communication Quarterly, 83*(2), 265–280.

Tewksbury, D., & Althaus, S. L. (2000). Differences in knowledge acquisition among readers of the paper and online versions of a national newspaper. *Journalism & Mass Communication Quarterly, 77*(3), 457–479.

Tremayne, M. (2007). *Blogging, citizenship and the future of media*. New York: Routledge.

Williams, B. A., & Delli Carpini, M. X. (2004). Monica and Bill all the time and everywhere: The collapse of gatekeeping and agenda setting in the new media environment. *The American Behavioral Scientist, 47*(9), 1208–1230.

26

ORGANIZATIONAL LEGITIMACY
Lessons Learned from Financial Scandals

Marcia W. DiStaso and Terri A. Scandura

In recent years it has been nearly impossible to open the newspaper or turn on the news without learning about another corporate scandal. Enron, WorldCom, Tyco, and HealthSouth are just some of the major U.S. and multinational corporations whose corporate and accounting practices have made the news. As a frontrunner in this new corporate landscape, Enron has forever altered public trust in corporate morality (Sethi, 2002). In the words of the American Institute of Certified Public Accountants (2003):

> The media frenzy on Enron seemed to come from nowhere. Suddenly, every major daily and broadcast news program was talking about Enron…. The result has been…a severe blow to the public's confidence in the capital markets…. Many employees lost their life savings and tens of thousands of investors lost billions. (¶1–3)

Corporate scandals have not only threatened the reputation of the involved firms but also provoked critical doubt in the legitimacy of corporations in general. A persistent problem organizations face is their standing and relationship with a variety of stakeholders. Ethics, accountability, and corporate responsibility are now expected by the public, investors, and the government.

As a result of the scandals, governmental and regulatory agencies have responded to failing investor confidence by mandating new regulations with stricter reporting rules. In 2002, President Bush signed the Sarbanes-Oxley Act that was designed to "demonstrate to investors a commitment to fairness and integrity in corporate America" by deterring corporate misconduct and restoring investor confidence (Shelby, 2003, ¶3). To accomplish this, the Act requires company executives to certify the accuracy and legitimacy of corporate financial statements, or face the possibility of punitive and criminal action.

Corporate responses to these scandals are varied, given the recent nature of these events and governmental responses. Of course corporations are implementing the necessary actions to comply with financial laws, but how they are working to restore confidence is unclear. The research and scholarly literature provides a variety of theoretical foundations to view the emergence of these current issues, including resource dependency, issue management, stakeholder theory, and legitimacy (DeBlasio, 2007).

With the emergence of corporate legitimacy now as a critical organizational challenge, this chapter focuses on identifying what organizational legitimacy is, why it is important, how legitimacy crisis occurs, and what organizations can do to gain, maintain, or restore legitimacy. Legitimacy lessons learned from financial scandals are offered as a new theoretical lens for examining organizational response in a legitimacy crisis.

Organizational Legitimacy

The corporate desire for public legitimation has not always existed. In fact, before this century, corporations had very little accountability to the consumer public, legally or otherwise (Boyd, 2000). Historically, organizations existed for profit and there was little attention to stakeholders other than shareholders.

Corporate legitimacy deals with the appropriate role of corporations in society. Suchman (1995) defined organizational legitimacy as a "generalized perception or assumption that the actions of an entity are desirable, proper, or appropriate within some socially constructed system of norms, values, beliefs, and definitions" (p. 574). An organization is thus considered legitimate if its stakeholders or publics perceive it to be responsible and useful; it is not defined solely by what is legal or illegal (Epstein, 1972). In other words, an organization is considered to be legitimate within a particular stakeholder group if it complies with that group's norms and values. Legitimacy typically refers to evaluations of the organization's output, consequences, procedures, techniques, structures, and leaders.

Stillman (1974) asked, "Who decides legitimacy" (p. 36)? Legitimacy cannot be established in isolation; instead, as Allen and Caillouet (1994) wrote, legitimacy decisions are based on messages in "the public arena" (p. 56). Therefore, the media plays an important role in filtering and presenting information which may or may not cue an organization's legitimacy to its various stakeholders.

Pfeffer and Salancik (1978) believed that legitimacy involved the value or worth of an organization in the larger social system, but they confined this by stating that it is "always controlled by those outside the organization" (pp. 193–194). In this conception, then, external publics alone determine legitimacy—what about internal publics? Elsbach and Sutton (1992) clarified this point when they argued that organizations can secure legitimacy when stakeholders both internal (i.e., organizational members) and external publics (i.e., customers, clients, suppliers, shareholders) support an organization's goals and activities. Without continued support, the organization's existence may be jeopardized. Massive sell-offs of stock during a crisis of legitimacy, for example, may exacerbate the decline of an organization.

Because legitimacy is a "perception" or an "assumption" by the organization's stakeholders, it largely depends on organizations adopting appropriate practices and by conforming to widespread understandings of what is considered "proper, adequate, rational, and necessary" (Meyer & Rowan, 1977, p. 340). Based upon institutional theory, an organization acquires legitimacy through managing the expectations of outsiders as well as insiders through rites and rituals (symbols). Aspects of organizational structure are employed to rationalize the organization to stakeholders and external constituents. To accomplish this, organizations follow formal, systematic, and consistent procedures, to achieve both greater results and to legitimize their actions (Meyer & Rowan, 1977).

Legitimation is a process that results from the interaction of organizations (actually organizational decision makers; executives) and their environments. Actors representing both the organization and the environment are involved in the legitimation process. In this process the organization's legitimacy is continuously tested, evaluated, and redefined by the environment while the organization itself attempts to make sense of the legitimacy requirements by observing, learning, interpreting, and even influencing the requirements (Kostova & Zaheer, 1999).

Strategic versus Institutional Approaches

Suchman (1995) noted a bifurcation in the literature about legitimacy containing strategic and institutional approaches. From the strategic perspective, management makes decisions that are designed to enhance a particular aspect of organizational legitimacy. This approach has an emphasis on legitimacy as an action that can be controlled by management. As a strategic approach, legitimacy is a concept that helps explain the tactics organizations use to convince the publics that they are useful, responsible, and deserve support (Hearit, 1995). In this view, legitimacy is an operational resource that can be extracted and used in pursuit of organizational goals.

The institutional approach suggests that organizational legitimacy is shaped by more than simply the perceptions of the environment and the actions of an organization. Instead, it is based on three factors: (1) the characteristics of the environment; (2) the organization's actions and characteristics; and (3) the legitimation process by which the environment builds its perceptions of the organization (Kostova & Zaheer, 1999).

The distinction between the strategic and institutional approaches is a matter of perspective with strategic theorists positioning organizational management as looking "out" and institutional theorists adopting the viewpoint of society looking "in" (Suchman, 1995). This is an important distinction because when scholars adopt one view they are essentially overlooking the opposing view. In reality, organizations most likely operate within both strategic operational challenges and institutional constitutive pressures, and considering this duality permits a more comprehensive approach to understanding organizational legitimacy. There is a reflexive relationship between strategy and the environment in which the organization's decision makers respond to environmental events and stakeholders then respond to those actions (Thompson, 1967).

Three Types of Organizational Legitimacy

In addition to the strategic and institutional split, there are further divisions in legitimacy research. Specifically, three broad types of legitimacy are identified: pragmatic legitimacy, moral legitimacy (also called normative legitimacy), and cognitive legitimacy (Suchman, 1995).

Pragmatic Legitimacy

Pragmatic legitimacy results from the calculations of self-interested individuals, who are part of the organization's key audience; for example, their primary stakeholders (Suchman, 1995). These individuals will deem the organization legitimate as long as they perceive that they will benefit from the organization's activities—through dividends or cost reduction. In other words, the organization's audiences scrutinize its behavior in order to determine the consequences for themselves and thus decide on their actions toward the organization. For example, a corporation's shareholders receive dividend payments and their decision to continue to support the organization through stock ownership reflects their evaluation of its legitimacy. Thus, legitimacy is likely to be given to those organizations that "have our best interests at heart," that "share our values," or that are "honest" "trustworthy," "decent," and "wise" (Suchman, 1995, p. 578).

An organization must influence individuals' calculations and persuade key stakeholders—as well as the wider public—of the usefulness of its output, procedures, structures, and leadership behavior (Ashforth & Gibbs, 1990). This can be accomplished in various ways, such as providing direct benefits to constituents, by creating informative messages to stakeholders, by inviting stakeholders to participate in corporate decision making, or by strategic manipulation of perceptions (e.g., through symbolic management or instrumental public relations) (Palazzo & Scherer, 2006). For example, on February 9, 2007, the *New York Times* reported that the founder and chief executive of JetBlue Airways, David Neeleman was "humiliated and mortified" by a huge breakdown in the airline's operations that left passengers stranded on planes for hours:

David G. Neeleman said in a telephone interview yesterday that his company's management was not strong enough. And he said the current crisis, which has led to about 1,000 canceled flights in five days, was the result of a shoestring communications system that left pilots and flight attendants in the dark, and an undersize reservation system. (Bailey, 2007, ¶1)

Moral Legitimacy

Moral (or normative) legitimacy questions moral and ethical norms. Unlike pragmatic legitimacy, where actions are evaluated based on benefits to the individual, normative legitimacy is granted because the action or behavior is the "right thing to do" (Suchman, 1995, p. 579).

Suchman describes the moral legitimacy of organizations as the result of "explicit public discussion" and in his view, corporations can win moral legitimacy only through their deliberative participation in these discussions (Suchman, 1995, p. 585). Rather than manipulating and persuading opponents, the challenge is to convince others through reasonable and informative arguments (Palazzo & Scherer, 2006). As indicated in the example of JetBlue above, the challenge for the CEO is to convince the public that the organization will provide benefits to those injured by the problems caused by the management team at JetBlue.

Cognitive Legitimacy

Cognitive legitimacy considers the comprehensibility or the "taken-for-grantedness" of the organization's behavior (Zyglidopoulos, 2003). Comprehensibility refers to the organization meeting plausible explanations and conducting business in a predictable and meaningful manner. Reaching a "taken-for-granted" status is the most powerful source of legitimacy, but it is difficult to obtain because it operates mainly at the subconscious level of stakeholders (Suchman, 1995). If a manipulation attempt is uncovered, cognitive legitimacy can collapse because behaviors are perceived as unacceptable (Ashforth & Gibbs, 1990). Therefore, in many cases cognitive legitimacy can be minimally managed but only indirectly (Suchman, 1995). To explain this, DeBlasio (2007) provides the example of a restaurant serving meat. The processing of the meat into an edible meal in the restaurant is understandable, but if unsanitary processing or animal cruelty were discovered, cognitive legitimacy would be threatened. This is because once the previously taken for granted acts of sanitary operation or humaneness are questioned, legitimacy is affected.

Importance of Organizational Legitimacy

Overall, an organization is perceived as legitimate, if it pursues "socially acceptable goals in a socially acceptable manner" (Ashforth & Gibbs, 1990, p. 177). Organizational scholars have focused on such a role of corporations in society with research on topics such as "corporate social responsibility" (CSR), "corporate citizenship," "corporate sustainability," "business ethics," and "stakeholder theory" (Palazzo & Scherer, 2006). Legitimacy and reputation are also closely linked in the literature. This is because there are many similarities between legitimacy and reputation.

First, they both result from stakeholder evaluations of an organization (Fombrun & Shanley, 1990). Next, the concepts have been linked to similar antecedent conditions, such as organizational size, charitable giving, strategic alliances, and regulatory compliance (Fombrun & Shanley, 1990). Finally, an important consequence of legitimacy and reputation is the improved ability to acquire resources (Suchman, 1995).

Although legitimacy and reputation have many similarities, a comparison of the definitions provides important distinctions between the two. With legitimacy, stakeholders evaluate an organization based on their perceptions or assumptions regarding congruence between their values, norms, and beliefs and those of the organization. Essentially, legitimacy is a perception of appropriate organizational activity (Suchman, 1995).

Reputation on the other hand is "the overall estimation in which a particular company is held by its various constituents" (Fombrun, 1996, p. 37). Thus, central to reputation is a comparison of organizations (Deephouse & Carter, 2005). Organizational reputation is essentially a type of feedback, received by an organization from its stakeholders. For any two organizations, the likelihood is that one will have a better reputation than the other (Deephouse & Carter, 2005).

Research has shown that legitimacy serves as a prerequisite to reputation—that organizational reputation is a socially constructed outcome of an organization's legitimization process (Zyglidopoulos, 2003). By achieving legitimacy, an organization can then move towards attaining a high reputation as a level of excellence.

Legitimacy focuses on the "acceptability" of an organization's values and actions and reputation focuses on the "favorability" of organizations as compared to their competitors and peers (Zyglidopoulos, 2003, p. 75). Before an organization's actions can be considered favorable, the organization must first adhere to the norms of social acceptability, indicating that legitimacy must come first. Furthermore, according to Hamilton (2006), a loss of legitimacy will taint an organization's reputation.

When an organization is perceived to be legitimate, it will be easier to attract economic resources and gain the social and political support necessary for its continued successful operation (Ogden & Clarke, 2005). This is because a legitimate organization is perceived not only as more worthy, but also as "more meaningful, more predictable, and more trustworthy" (Suchman, 1995, p. 571). Even the threat of a loss in legitimacy can harm the flow of necessary resources (Arthaud-Day, Certo, Dalton, & Dalton, 2006). External groups are likely to distance themselves from organizations suffering legitimacy losses to avoid the risk of "negative contagion," and ultimately, taking with them the financial, social, and intellectual capital that the damaged organization needs to recover and survive (Suchman, 1995, p. 597).

Past research indicates that if a company's actions deviate from expectations, it can have its legitimacy questioned and challenged, and, in an extreme case, it can be judged illegitimate (Pfeffer & Salancik, 1978). As Deephouse and Carter (2005) noted, "Organizations that deviate from normal behavior violate cultural or legal expectations and theories of organizing. They are subject to legitimacy challenges and may be deemed unacceptable by stakeholders" (p. 333). Reputation on the other hand has been viewed as less dire. According to Deephouse and Carter (2005), having a lower reputation than another organization does not threaten continued existence as long as the organization's legitimacy remains unchallenged.

Challenges of Legitimacy

Admittedly, no organization can completely satisfy all stakeholders and no management action can serve as *the* legitimizing action. However, there are leadership activities that can make a substantial difference in the extent to which organizational activities are perceived as desirable, proper, and appropriate (Suchman, 1995). Like most organizational processes, legitimacy management relies heavily on communication. Specifically, this includes communication between the organization and its various stakeholders.

The multiplicity of legitimacy dynamics provides considerable latitude for management action. Legitimacy is associated not only with good leadership but also with effective leadership. Responsible leaders attend to the perspectives and values of stakeholders, seeking to represent their interests in organizational decisions. This is best accomplished through the use of various communications through multiple channels.

In the absence of communication, stakeholder's values remain unclear, confused, and equivocal. Little consensus develops about which values are dominant in a particular context, and the probabilities of making an ethically suspect judgment and inviting criticism are significantly enhanced (Ashforth & Gibbs, 1990).

Because of the numerous advantages of being viewed as legitimate, many organizational leaders have become concerned about the impact that their actions and communication can have (Hall, 1992). Companies have many ways in which they can attempt to manage stakeholder perceptions such as press releases, advertising, press conferences, letters to shareholders, annual reports, and interviews with business publications (Fombrun, 1996). Overall, the intensity and mix of legitimation practices are likely to vary according to whether management is attempting to gain, maintain, or restore the organization's legitimacy.

Gaining Legitimacy

The process of gaining legitimacy (also called extending legitimacy) occurs when an organization is first being established or when it is entering into new activities or using new structures or processes (Ashforth & Gibbs, 1990). New organizations are always vulnerable to what has been called the "liabilities of newness" (Aldrich & Fiol, 1994). This is because new organizations, by definition, lack the familiarity and credibility required to be viewed as legitimate. In other words, most organizations do not start with a blank slate.

A new organization's stakeholders will find it difficult to weigh risk/reward trade-offs without clear guidelines for assessing performance. This is especially true for new organizations in new industries where leaders have the difficult task of convincing stakeholders to follow their directives without tangible evidence that such actions will pay off. In established companies, however, leaders can simply cite past performance as a justification for particular actions. No such appeal is available to leaders in new companies and industries (Aldrich & Fiol, 1994).

Therefore, on what basis should stakeholders trust the organization and deem it legitimate? According to Suchman (1995), gaining legitimacy should be handled proactively by conforming to societal expectations, selecting supportive stakeholders, and creating new ideas of what is legitimate behavior.

By conforming to societal expectations, management can either offer symbolic assurances such as relying on its reputation in related activities or on the reputation of its key personnel or actually produce concrete meritorious outcomes (Suchman, 1995). An even more proactive approach would be to select supportive stakeholders through market research. The goal of this is to identify and attract stakeholders who value what the organization has to offer (Ashforth & Gibbs, 1990). This is often conducted through the use of informative public relations campaigns. An organization could also create new ideas of what is legitimate behavior through the use of persuasion in communications such as advertising. If the organization is able to create a legitimate image of itself, it must work hard to maintain that image.

Maintaining Legitimacy

Attempts to maintain legitimacy occur when an organization has attained a status in support of its ongoing activity. Maintaining legitimacy is often depicted as an easier position to be in for management than gaining or repairing legitimacy (Ashforth & Gibbs, 1990; Suchman, 1995). Three things in particular make the maintenance of legitimacy problematic: stakeholder heterogeneity, stability versus rigidity, and structural inertia (Suchman, 1995).

First, stakeholder heterogeneity refers to the fact that a firm's stakeholder groups are varied and changing, and continued satisfaction of these various stakeholders is therefore challenging. Second, stability versus rigidity refers to the combination of actions and reactions between the organization and its stakeholders. As changes occur in an organization's stakeholder groups, an organization's responsiveness may lead to changes that can ultimately result in an imbalance with other stakeholder groups. Such instabilities can lead to the legitimation projects attracting unwanted attention, for example, advertising aimed at gaining clients in the gay, lesbian, and transsexual community may cause boycotts from religious communities.

To meet these challenges, organizational leaders must be proactive and anticipate stakeholder demands and environmental developments that can cause the organization's legitimacy to be questioned. This can be accomplished by management serving as boundary spanners continually scanning the environment to stay abreast of possible changes. In addition to protecting for unforeseen challenges, management should also protect past accomplishments that brought about legitimacy. This includes maintaining a "business-as-usual" state through the use of consistent and predictable communication and activities that meet stakeholder needs while reducing uncertainties and exemplifying responsibility (Suchman, 1995, p. 596). Another legitimacy maintenance strategy is to stockpile goodwill and support. The idea behind this is that an organization should work to build relationships with stakeholders based on trust so if they do deviate from the norm they can do so without loosing legitimacy (Jones, Jones, & Little, 2000).

Restoring Legitimacy

Restoring legitimacy (also called repairing or defending legitimacy) is much like gaining legitimacy, except that restoring legitimacy is usually reactive rather than proactive. Restoring legitimacy happens when the organization is faced with a legitimacy crisis in which their actions have somehow been deemed inappropriate and illegitimate by stakeholders (Suchman, 1995). An illegitimate status demands that the organization respond, or else organizational failure could result (Hamilton, 2006).

Large and complex organizations are answerable to many constituents with frequently conflicting expectations and perceptions, and an example of how this can lead to a legitimacy crisis is a transnational organization. They are faced with legitimacy concerns that arise out of their operations across national boarders, because not only are they accountable to the stakeholders in the country of their headquarters, they are also subject to varying expectations regarding the social norms and methods of operation in different parts of the world. The legitimacy of organizations comes under scrutiny when there is perceived inconsistencies between the way companies do business and the changing goals and priorities of people in the various societies (Warren, 1999). An organization would be declared legitimate if the way it does business is consistent with the norms of the society it does business in, and therefore, an organization may be granted legitimacy in one country but not another.

Ultimately, as a result of a legitimacy crisis organizational management face the task of repairing legitimacy. This is somewhat similar to the acts of creating legitimacy; however, legitimacy repair is usually reactive rather than proactive (Suchman, 1995). Somehow stakeholders have deemed the organization's actions illegitimate. An illegitimate status demands that organizational management respond, or else organizational failure could result (Hamilton, 2006).

Legitimacy Lessons Learned From Financial Scandals

Corporate fraud in the United States has affected market values, decimated private 401(k) accounts, destroyed workers' incomes, devalued public pension funds, and devastated investor confidence; all the while casting a shadow over the integrity and legitimacy of corporate America. Tyco, WorldCom, Global Crossing, Adelphia, ImClone, Xerox, and others joined Enron's fraudulent accounting ranks in 2002. HealthSouth became a member of that notorious group a year later. In addition, numerous lesser-known companies have also engaged in a host of improper and illegal accounting activities. Through a better understanding of these financial scandals, one can gain insight into how some companies can bounce back from a legitimacy crisis and others cannot.

Financial Scandal Background

Over the past few years, the nature of financial legitimacy crises has varied widely. However, there are two main types of fraud that can be a basis for securities violations: material misrepresentations or omissions and insider trading (Kloss, Adler, & Stone, 2006). The seemingly endless legal cases include accounting cover-ups, protection of company stock through the inflation of earnings, the defrauding of investors through misleading advice, and actions that directly benefit the personal wealth and ego of top executives such as spending company money on personal property or lavish parties.

Not only have companies been the focus of intense media coverage, but the corporate executives involved in these scandals have also become household names in many cases; consider Ken Lay, the founder and past CEO of Enron, and Bernard Ebbers, the former CEO of WorldCom. Overall awareness of corporate wrongdoings has increased in the past few years.

Ultimately, many people have been affected by the recent corporate financial scandals. As we saw with Enron and WorldCom, many long-time employees lost their jobs and their retirement pensions. Shareholders have also been hit hard in the aftermath of corporate scandals. Going back to peak valuations, shareholders saw a loss of market capitalization of some $66 billion in the case of Enron and $177 billion in the case of WorldCom (Savage & Chung, 2005). Plus, it has not just been the wealthy investors and institutions that have suffered by the market reactions to fraud—today, nearly half of all adult Americans participate in the stock market (Guynn, 2005).

It is important to identify not only what happened, but also how it happened. Most scholars believe that companies engaged in actions that have led to financial scandals did so to gain or maintain legitimacy in the face of mounting market pressures (Arthaud-Day et al., 2006). Others have tied the fraud back to CEO pay packages that include stock options (Erickson, Hanlon, & Maydew, 2006). In other words, CEOs have incentives to see the market price of the corporate stock increase; because when it does increase, so does their compensation. In either scenario, there are enormous incentives to move the share price up, and as the scandals have shown, this is often accomplished by any means possible. Specifically, when executives were unable to meet their targets they began to make use of misleading financial reporting, which helped to hide their actual performance. In some cases, businesses that reported clear and accurate numbers were actually at a competitive disadvantage. The term "creative accounting" became a popular euphemism for non-standard accounting practices involving novel ways of characterizing income, assets, and liabilities (Guynn, 2005, p. 388).

The Sarbanes-Oxley Act of 2002 officially marked a changing of the tide with respect to governmental and regulatory attitudes. It was designed to improve investor confidence and prevent corporate scandals by making CEOs and CFOs of public companies legally accountable for the veracity and integrity of their financial statements (Goodman, 2004). Then, in 2003, the SEC Regulation G established rules limiting the use of "creative accounting" or accounting done by means other than by following generally accepted accounting principles (GAAP) (Bowen, Davis, & Matsumoto, 2005). These governmental actions were implemented with the goal of ensuring ethical behavior and subsequently improved organizational legitimacy.

Legitimacy Explained

According to Boyd (2000), companies must clearly establish their legitimacy because they "explicitly operate to profit financially from their publics" (p. 345). This can be a difficult task given that the 2006 Edelman Trust Barometer found that 51% of the American public did not trust corporate institutions to "do what is right" (Edelman, 2006, p. 5).

Gaining Legitimacy

Given the current legitimacy crisis status of corporate America, new start-up companies are faced with a difficult challenge of gaining legitimacy. These companies will benefit from establishing relationships with stakeholders and should follow SEC guidelines for financial reporting. Start-up companies must gain legitimacy to attract investors in many cases. They must also present themselves to the public and consumers as viable business entities. Therefore, establishing legitimacy is a necessary condition for launching a new business. Once legitimacy is gained, new start-ups and established corporations must maintain that legitimacy over time.

Maintaining Legitimacy

Companies that have remained scandal-free can learn a great deal from the companies that have been caught. It is critical that they ensure that their corporate actions are appropriate. Jennings (2004) identified the seven common traits of ethical collapse over the last 20 years. These include (1) pressure to maintain performance; (2) fear and silence preventing employees from coming forward when they have concerns; (3) a disparity in age between senior managers and employees; (4) a weak executive board; (5) conflicts of interest between the board and management; (6) a strong culture of innovation; and (7) a culture of social irresponsibility. Companies should be aware of their actions at all levels and identify possible areas of concern by starting with this list. It is prudent to have procedures in place to maintain legitimacy rather than have to face the potential costs of losing it. However, most organizations are vulnerable in some way to possible legitimacy issues and their leaders may be faced with having to restore it.

Restoring Legitimacy

There are a number of ways that an organization's legitimacy may be questioned by stakeholders. As we have noted earlier, some of the most prominent examples have involved financial wrongdoing. Once a company has been accused of committing a financial misdeed it must work to rebuild its legitimacy. Not all companies are able to withstand such scandals. Unlike Enron and WorldCom, which sought bankruptcy after their financial misdeeds became public, HealthSouth avoided bankruptcy. The company's process of avoiding bankruptcy also served as efforts to repair its legitimacy. Before explaining how this was possible, a quick review of the HealthSouth scandal is necessary.

On March 19, 2003 the SEC filed civil fraud charges against HealthSouth and Richard Scruchy, the founder/CEO. One week later the CFO plead guilty to doctoring company financial statements. The following week Scruchy and HealthSouth auditors were fired. Overall, HealthSouth was accused of overstating earnings by $2.6 billion, and 19 HealthSouth employees, including all five former CFOs, pleaded guilty to criminal charges (Timeline, 2004).

Following this, HealthSouth pursued what Suchman (1995) termed "building a firewall" by restructuring, offering normalizing accounts, and not panicking. In August of 2003, HealthSouth hired Jay Grinney, a "widely respected hospital executive" from HCA. This provided a symbolic assurance because Grinney's previous experience could help to reestablish legitimacy. Leadership must play a key role in the process of regaining legitimacy.

When legitimacy is challenged, organizations offer normalizing accounts in an attempt to separate the legitimacy-threatening act from the company through denial, excuses, justifications, and explanations (Suchman, 1995). Grinney issued explanations:

> The facts speak for themselves. A massive fraud was committed; 19 individuals have pled guilty. My job is to pick up the pieces and put them together in a way that brings shareholder value, maintains the quality of this institution and allows us to grow. (quoted in Freudenheim, 2005, p. 1)

Grinney also appeared to follow the third strategy for repairing legitimacy; that of not panicking. This allowed him to change the corporate culture to be more focused and to quickly set out to provide the corrected audited financial reports thereby finally giving investors and analysts HealthSouth's performance figures. He also worked to settle the SEC allegations and worked with attorneys on the class-action suit on behalf of shareholders. Another area of focus for Ginney was restoring morale among employees. Although approximately 10% of the employees left after the fraud was publicized, some doctors were persuaded to return (Freudenheim, 2005). While HealthSouth's mission statement from before the SEC charges is not available, its current mission statement includes a dimension for integrity:

> We consider trust and integrity to be essential in all our relationships. We are committed to operating our business honestly, with financial integrity, and in adherence with all federal, state and local regulatory obligations affecting the operation of our business. (p. C1)

Has HealthSouth regained legitimacy from the 2003 financial scandal? If legitimacy could be determined by stock price alone the answer would be yes, the company share prices had risen from a low in the pennies to $20.29 on Friday, April 20, 2007. However, it is not that easy. HealthSouth is ranked 637 on *Fortune's* list of largest companies, but size is also not necessarily a guarantee of legitimacy. Legitimacy can only be determined by the stakeholders and therefore, further research into impressions of stakeholders would be required to truly determine, but it appears that the company has come a long way since March 2003.

Conclusion

The matter of organizational legitimacy has received increased awareness due to media coverage of corporate financial scandals. The literature on organizational legitimacy provides new ways of viewing the actions of leaders as they attempt to gain, maintain, and perhaps restore legitimacy in a crisis. Some organizations do not survive a financial scandal and, therefore, legitimacy is now considered essential to the long-term viability of a corporation. However, knowledge of stakeholder reactions might result in an organization emerging from a financial scandal, as in the example of HealthSouth. After the recent financial scandals, the landscape for organizational legitimacy has been forever changed. Legislation has been enacted such as the Sarbanes-Oxley Act as we have noted. However, increased awareness of the potential for wrongdoing has likely resulted in organizations taking a proactive approach toward organizational actions. The integrity of leaders in corporations has now become a necessary condition for continued support from stakeholders.

References

Aldrich, H. E., & Fiol, C. M. (1994). Fools rush in? The institutional context of industry creation. *Academy of Management Review, 19*(4), 654–670.

Allen, M. W., & Caillouet, R. H. (1994). Legitimation endeavors: Impression management strategies used by an organization in crisis. *Communication Monographs, 61,* 44–62.

American Institute of Certified Public Accountants. (2003). *A bird's eye view of the Enron debacle.* Retrieved March 26, 2007, from http://thecaq.aicpa.org/Resources/

Arthaud-Day, M. L., Certo, S. T., Dalton, C. M., & Dalton, D. R. (2006). A changing of the guard: Executive and director turnover following corporate financial restatements. *Academy of Management Journal, 49*(6), 1119–1136.

Ashforth, B. E., & Gibbs, B. W. (1990). The double-edge of organizational legitimation. *Organization Science, 1,* 177–194.

Bailey, J. (2007, February 19). Chief "mortified" by JetBlue crisis. *The New York Times,* p. A1.

Bowen, R. M., Davis, A. K., & Matsumoto, D. A. (2005). Emphasis on pro forma versus GAAP earnings in quarterly press releases: Determinants, SEC intervention and market reactions. *The Accounting Review, 80*(4), 1011–1038.

Boyd, J. (2000). Actional legitimacy: No crisis necessary. *Journal of Public Relations Research, 12*(4), 341–353.

DeBlasio, G. G. (2007). Coffee as a medium for ethical, social, and political messages: Organizational legitimacy and communication. *Journal of Business Ethics, 72,* 47–59.

Deephouse, D. L., & Carter, S. M. (2005). An examination of differences between organizational legitimacy and organizational reputation. *Journal of Management Studies, 42*(2), 329–360.

Edelman Trust Barometer. (2006). Retrieved April 21, 2007, from http://www.edelman.com/trust/2007/prior/2006/FullSupplement_final.pdf

Elsbach, K. D., & Sutton, R. I. (1992). Acquiring organizational legitimacy through illegitimate actions: A marriage of institutional and impression management theories. *Academy of Management Journal, 35*(4), 699–738.

Epstein, E. M. (1972). The historical enigma of corporate legitimacy. *California Law Review, 60,* 1701–1717.

Erickson, M., Hanlon, M., & Maydew, E. L. (2006). Is there a link between executive compensation and accounting fraud? *Journal of Accounting Research, 44*(1), 113–143.

Fombrun, C. J. (1996). *Reputation: Realizing value from the corporate image.* Boston, MA: Harvard Business School Press.

Fombrun, C., & Shanley, M. (1990). What's in a name? Reputation building and corporate strategy. *Academy of Management Journal, 33*(2), 233–258.

Freudenheim, M. (2005, January, 27). Vital signs return to HealthSouth. *The New York Times,* p. C1.

Goodman, G. (2004). *Sarbanes-Oxley: Are we there yet?* Retrieved April 22, 2007, from http://www.sarbanes-oxley.com/

Guynn, J. (2005). Ethical challenges in a market economy. *Vital Speeches of the Day, 71*(13), 386–390.

Hall, R. (1992). The strategic analysis of intangible resources. *Strategic Management Journal, 13,* 135–44.

Hamilton, E. A. (2006). An exploration of the relationship between loss of legitimacy and the sudden death of organizations. *Group & Organization Management, 31*(3), 327–358.

Hearit, K. M. (1995). Mistakes were made: Organizations, apologia and crises of social legitimacy. *Communication Studies, 46,* 1–17.

Jennings, M. M. (2004). Preventing organizational ethical collapse, *The Journal of Government Financial Management, 53*(1), 12–19.

Jones, G. H., Jones, B. H., & Little, P. (2000). Reputation as reservoir: Buffering against loss in times of economic crisis. *Corporate Reputation Review, 3*(1), 21–29.

Kloss, B., Adler, J., & Stone, M. (2006). Securities fraud. *The American Criminal Law Review, 43*(2), 921–989.

Kostova, T., & Zaheer, S. (1999). Organizational legitimacy under conditions of complexity: The case of the multinational enterprise. *Academy of Management Review, 24*(1), 64–81.

Meyer, J., & Rowan, B. (1977). Institutionalized organizations: Formal structure as myth and ceremony. *American Journal of Sociology, 83*(2), 340–363.

Ogden, S., & Clarke, J. (2005). Customer disclosures, impression management and the construction of legitimacy. *Accounting, Auditing & Accountability Journal, 18*(3), 313–345.

Palazzo, G., & Scherer, A. G. (2006). Corporate legitimacy as deliberation: A communicative framework. *Journal of Business Ethics, 66,* 71–88.

Pfeffer, J., & Salancik, G. R. (1978). *The external control of organizations: A resource dependence perspective.* New York: Harper & Row.

Savage, J., & Chung, C. S. (2005). Trends in corporate fraud enforcement: A clam during the storm? *Business Crimes Bulletin, 13*(2), 1–3.

Sethi, S. P. (2002). Standards for corporate conduct in the international arena: Challenges and opportunities for multinational corporations. *Business and Society Review, 107,* 20–40.

Shelby, R. (2003, September 9). *The implementation of the Sarbanes-Oxley Act and restoring investor confidence.* Retrieved March 26, 2007, from http://banking.senate.gov/

Stillman, P. G. (1974). The concept of legitimacy. *Polity, 7,* 32–56.

Suchman, M. C. (1995). Managing legitimacy: Strategic and institutional approaches. *Academy of Management Review, 20*(3), 571–610.

Thompson, J. D. (1967). *Organizations in action.* New York: McGraw-Hill.

Timeline of accounting scandal at HealthSouth. (2004, September 30). *The Washington Post.* Retrieved April 22, 2007, from http://www.washingtonpost.com/wp-dyn/articles/A24671-2003Oct14.html

Warren, R. C. (1999). Company legitimacy in the new millennium. *Business Ethics: A European Review, 8*(4), 214–224.

Zyglidopoulos, S. C. (2003). The issue life-cycle: Implications for reputation for social performance and organizational legitimacy. *Corporate Reputation Review, 6*(1), 70–81.

Suggested Readings

Ashforth, B. E., & Gibbs, B. W. (1990). The double-edge of organizational legitimation. *Organization Science, 1,* 177–194.

DeBlasio, G. G. (2007). Coffee as a medium for ethical, social, and political messages: Organizational legitimacy and communication. *Journal of Business Ethics, 72,* 47–59.

Deephouse, D. L., & Carter, S. M. (2005). An examination of differences between organizational legitimacy and organizational reputation. *Journal of Management Studies, 42*(2), 329–360.

Hamilton, E. A. (2006). An exploration of the relationship between loss of legitimacy and the sudden death of organizations. *Group & Organization Management, 31*(3), 327–358.

Suchman, M. C. (1995). Managing legitimacy: Strategic and institutional approaches. *Academy of Management Review, 20*(3), 571–610.

27

DIFFUSION OF INNOVATIONS

Everett M. Rogers, Arvind Singhal, and Margaret M. Quinlan

What Is Diffusion?

When the World Health Organization launched a worldwide campaign to eradicate smallpox, it was engaged in diffusion. When Apple launched iPod, it was diffusing a new product. When Bob Dylan wrote "The Times They Are A-Changin'," he was describing diffusion (Dearing & Meyer, 2006). When professional dancers—both standing up and sitting down (in wheelchairs)—perform on stage, as do the artistes of the Dancing Wheels dance company in Cleveland, they are diffusing a new image of what constitutes (dis)ability.[1]

Diffusion is the process by which an innovation is communicated through certain channels over time among the members of a social system (Rogers, 2003). An *innovation* is an idea, practice, or object perceived as new by an individual or other unit of adoption. The diffusion process typically involves both mass media and interpersonal communication channels. And, in today's world, information technologies such as the Internet and cell phones—which combine aspects of mass media and interpersonal channels, represent formidable tools of diffusion (Morris & Ogan, 1996). Consider the following experience of co-author Singhal in the Philippines.

In May 2006, as Singhal strolled down Epifanio de los Santas Avenue (known as "Edsa") in Manila, Philippines, a Filipina colleague noted that "Edsa was the street where the government of President Estrada was brought down by cell phones."[2] Grasping the puzzled expression on Singhal's face, she elaborated: "Some five years ago, a text message appeared on my cell phone. It said 'Go 2EDSA.'" Within a few hours, Edsa was teeming with tens of thousands of Filipinos who had received the same message. They were demonstrating against the corrupt Estrada regime. Within a few days, the crowd swelled to over a million. Estrada was toppled.

Upon returning to the United States, author Singhal's Internet search revealed that in January 2001, the impeachment trial against President Estrada was halted by senators who supported him. Within minutes, using cell phones, the opposition leaders broadcast a text message "Go 2EDSA. Wear blck" to folks on their telephone lists. The recipients, in turn, forwarded the message to others. The rapid (almost instant) diffusion of a text message led the military to withdraw support; the government fell without a single shot being fired.

After reading the story on the Internet, Singhal forwarded it by e-mail to the 28 undergraduate students enrolled in his *Communication and Information Diffusion* class at Ohio University, asking them to share it with interested family and friends. Many did. So here we see how an innocuous interpersonal exchange on a street in Manila—about the consequential spread of an SMS message—was itself diffused from a single source (the instructor of a course) to many recipients and, in turn, to others in multiple cascading diffusion waves.

This chapter analyzes the research tradition of the diffusion of innovations, focusing on the origins of the diffusion paradigm, its methodological tenets, and its influence on communication research. We identify the distinctive aspects of diffusion research, detail the seminal Iowa hybrid seed corn study, explain the strengths and limitations of the dominant paradigm that guided diffusion study for several decades, and look into the future of diffusion practice and research. We end our chapter by discussing the positive deviance approach which, we believe, provides an alternative ("inside-out") way of thinking about diffusing innovations, and one that capitalizes on peoples' indigenous wisdom.

Distinctive Aspects of Diffusion Research

Several distinctive aspects of the diffusion of innovations set it off from other specialized fields of communication study.

1. The study of the diffusion of innovations began during World War II, prior to the establishment of communication study in university schools and departments (Rogers, 2003). So diffusion research was well underway as a research activity before communication scholars entered this research front.

2. Although most observers agree that the diffusion of innovations is fundamentally a communication process, communication scholars constitute only one of the dozen research traditions presently advancing the diffusion field (along with geography, education, marketing, public health, rural sociology, agricultural economics, general economics, political science, and others). Other communication research areas such as persuasion and attitude change and mass communication effects also began prior to the institutionalization of communication study in university units (Rogers, 1962, 1983, 1995, 2003; Singhal & Dearing, 2006).

3. Diffusion research is also distinctive in that the communication messages of study are perceived as *new* by the individual receivers. This novelty necessarily means that an individual experiences a high degree of uncertainty in seeking information about, and deciding to adopt and implement an innovation. In the sense of the newness of the message content, the diffusion of innovations is unlike any other communication study except the diffusion of news. Diffusion of news, however, studies the spread of news events, concentrating mainly on such matters as how we become aware of news. In contrast, research on the diffusion of innovations centers not only on awareness-knowledge, but also on attitude change, decision making, and implementation of the innovation. The new ideas investigated by scholars of the diffusion of innovations are mainly technological innovations, so the behavior studied is quite different from that investigated in news diffusion studies. Obviously, however, both communication research areas involve a similar diffusion process, and both have been informed by the other (Rogers, 2003).

4. Diffusion research considers time as a variable to a much greater degree than do other fields of communication study. Time is involved in diffusion in (a) the *innovation-decision process,* the mental process through which an individual passes from first knowledge of a new idea, to adoption and confirmation of the innovation; (b) *innovativeness,* the degree to which an individual is relatively earlier in adopting new ideas than other members of a system; and (c) an innovation's *rate of adoption,* the relative speed with which an innovation is adopted by members of a system (Rogers, 2003).

5. The diffusion of innovations field emphasizes interpersonal communication networks more than any other type of communication research. From the first diffusion studies conducted about 60 years ago, the nature of diffusion was found to be essentially a social process involving interpersonal communication among similar individuals (Rogers & Kincaid, 1981; Rosen, 2002; Valente, 1995, 2006). A person evaluates a new idea and decides whether or not to adopt it on the basis of discussions with peers who have already adopted or rejected the innovation. The main function of mass media communication in the diffusion process is to create awareness—knowledge about the innovation. Study of the diffusion of innovations involves both mass communication and interpersonal communication, and thus spans the dichotomy that otherwise

divides communication into two subdisciplines. These dichotomies blur further when diffusion occurs through the Internet, cell phones, and Blackberry devices.

Background of Diffusion Research

The study of the diffusion of innovations in its present-day form can be traced from the theories and observations of Gabriel Tarde, a French sociologist and legal scholar (Rogers, 2003). Tarde originated such key diffusion concepts as opinion leadership, the S-curve of diffusion, and the role of socioeconomic status in interpersonal diffusion, although he did not use such concepts by these names. Such theoretical ideas were set forth by Tarde (1903) in his book, *The Laws of Imitation*.

The intellectual leads suggested by Tarde were soon followed up by anthropologists, who began investigating the role of technological innovations in bringing about cultural change. Illustrative of these anthropological studies was Clark Wissler's (1923) analysis of the diffusion of the horse among the Plains Indians. As in other anthropological works, the emphasis was on the consequences of innovation. For example, Wissler (1923) showed that adding horses to their culture led the Plains Indians, who had lived in peaceful coexistence, into a state of almost continual warfare with neighboring tribes.

The basic research paradigm for the diffusion of innovations can be traced to Bryce Ryan and Neal C. Gross's classic 1943 study of the diffusion of hybrid seed corn among Iowa farmers. This investigation was grounded in previously conducted anthropological diffusion work, which Ryan had studied while earning his doctoral degree at Harvard University, prior to becoming a faculty member in rural sociology at Iowa State University, where Gross was a graduate student. We discuss the hybrid corn study in detail later in this chapter.

During the 1950s many diffusion studies were conducted, particularly by rural sociologists at land-grant universities in the Midwestern United States. They were directly influenced by the Ryan and Gross investigation. As soon as communication study began to be institutionalized, this new breed of scholars became especially interested in the diffusion of news events, particularly through an influential study by Paul J. Deutschmann and Wayne A. Danielson (1960).

Communication Research on Diffusion

Deutschmann, a former newspaper reporter and editor, earned his doctorate in communication at Stanford University, gaining competence in quantitative methods, communication theory, and social psychology. He became a friend and research collaborator with Danielson, his fellow doctoral student at Stanford, and an individual with a similar background of professional newspaper experience.

Ev Rogers met Danielson in 1959 at the newly established Department of Communication at Michigan State University, where Deutschmann showed him the S-shaped diffusion curves for the spread of the news events that he was then studying. Compared to the diffusion curves for the agricultural innovations that Rogers was investigating, the news events spread much more rapidly. As Deutschmann stated at the time, this was "damn fast diffusion" (personal communication). Thanks to Deutschmann and Danielson's (1960) article on the diffusion of news events, this research topic became popular among communication scholars. Work on this topic has ebbed considerably, although spectacular news events—such as 9/11 or the 2003 space shuttle Columbia disaster—continue to attract scholars (Rogers & Seidel, 2002; Singhal, Rogers, & Mahajan, 1999).

In the early 1960s, Deutschmann moved to San José, Costa Rica, and collaborated with Dr. Orlando Fals Borda, a sociologist at the National University of Colombia in Bogotá, who had been studying diffusion patterns in the Colombian village of Saució, a small Andean community of 71 farm households. Deutschmann and Fals Borda's (1962) diffusion study in Saució represented one of the first diffusion investigations in a developing nation. Soon there would be several hundred such diffusion studies, many conducted by communication scholars. The six agricultural innovations of study in Saució (such as chemical fertilizer, a new potato variety, and a pesticide) had been introduced in previous years by Fals Borda, who acted as an agricultural *change agent*—or one who introduced innovations to the public. The familiar S-shaped curve characterized the rate of adoption for each of these innovations in the Colombian village (Deutschmann & Fals Borda, 1962).

Deutschmann's study with Fals Borda in Colombia stimulated interest among communication scholars in the diffusion of technological innovations. He attracted doctoral students to Michigan State University who were interested in diffusion research. When Deutschmann's life was cut short in 1962, Everett Rogers was hired as his replacement at Michigan State University to continue diffusion research in developing nations. The number of diffusion studies completed by communication scholars has expanded rapidly since 1960. By mid-2007, an estimated 600 diffusion publications by communication scholars were available out of the cache of 6,000 diffusion studies,[3] more than any other diffusion research tradition after rural sociology and marketing. Unlike rural sociologists, who are mainly concerned with agricultural innovations, or education diffusion scholars, who are interested in new educational innovations (for example, modern math or the multicultural curriculum), communication scholars investigate a wide range of different types of technological innovations. Communication scholars are interested in diffusion as a communication *process*, independent of the type of innovations that are diffused.

The Iowa Hybrid Seed Corn Study

When Ryan arrived in Ames, Iowa, in 1938, he was intrigued with the scholarly question of noneconomic influences on economic behavior. This issue had become important to him during his doctoral studies in the Department of Sociology at Harvard University, where Robert K. Merton, a young faculty member who had recently completed his own dissertation research on the sociology of science, was Ryan's doctoral advisor. The Harvard doctoral program in sociology was relatively new, and somewhat interdisciplinary in nature. Students earning degrees in sociology were encouraged to take courses in economics, anthropology, and in social psychology. Professor Talcott Parsons, the intellectual leader of Harvard sociology, had been trained in economics in Europe and helped introduce the theories of Vilfredo Pareto to American sociology. This interdisciplinary intellectual background was good preparation for Ryan, the individual who, more than any other, was to formulate the paradigm for research on the diffusion of innovations.

Iowa State University was an agricultural college, and so Ryan decided to investigate the diffusion of hybrid seed corn. This innovation was a profoundly important new idea for Iowa farmers, leading to increased corn yields of about 20 percent per acre. Ryan received funding for his proposed study of the diffusion of hybrid seed from the Iowa Agricultural Experiment Station, Iowa State University's research and development organization, which had played an important role in developing hybrid seed. This important innovation had spread widely to Iowa farmers in previous years, but Iowa State administrators were concerned that such an obviously advantageous agricultural technology had required so many years (about a dozen) for widespread use. This type of frustration on the part of officials who cannot understand why a seemingly advantageous innovation is not adopted more immediately explains why many diffusion studies continue to be sponsored.

Ryan collaborated with several economics professors at Iowa State University in designing the hybrid corn study, and his familiarity with anthropological research also affected the study's design. However, Ryan proposed the seed corn study mainly as a survey relying on questionnaire-generated data, rather than using the ethnographic approaches of the previous anthropological research.

A newly arrived master's student at Iowa State, Neal C. Gross, was assigned as Ryan's research assistant. Ryan told Gross that if he would personally interview the several hundred farmers in the two Iowa communities of study, he could use the data for his master's thesis. Gross, who came from an urban background, was unfamiliar with the ways of Iowa farmers. Someone told Gross that farmers began work early in the morning, so he appeared at the farmstead of his first respondent at 4 a.m.[4]

The choice of hybrid seed corn as the innovation of study in the Ryan and Gross investigation was to cast a long intellectual shadow over future generations of diffusion scholarship. Hybrid seed was an overwhelmingly beneficial innovation, boosting corn yields considerably. Given the sponsorship of the hybrid corn study, it is understandable that Ryan and Gross tended to assume that Iowa farmers ought to adopt the innovation, and that the rate of adoption should have been more rapid. This proinnovation bias still characterizes most diffusion studies today. Ryan and Gross (1943) indicated their surprise that the diffusion of hybrid corn required 12 years to reach widespread diffusion, and that the average farmer needed seven years to progress from initial awareness of the innovation to full-scale adoption (indicated by planting all of the corn acreage on his farm in hybrid seed).

Stated another way, the hybrid corn study demonstrated just how difficult it was for most individuals to adopt an innovation. Hybrid corn had to be purchased from a seed corn company, at a price per bushel not trivial to Iowa farmers in the Depression years. Further, adopting the innovation meant that Iowa farmers no longer selected the more beautiful-appearing ears of corn for use as seed the following year. So the adoption of hybrid corn meant the unadoption of a previously existing practice, the visual selection of open-pollinated seed. Hybrid corn was one of the first of the new wave of scientifically based farm innovations that were to radically change the nature of Midwestern agriculture in the ensuing decades. In 1939, Iowa farmers were not accustomed to agricultural innovations that were later to flow from the land-grant universities like Iowa State and the U.S. Department of Agriculture.

Iowa State University was the perfect place for founding the paradigm for diffusion research in yet another sense: Ames was the principal point of importation for the introduction of statistical methods in America. These techniques for quantitative data analysis began among agricultural statisticians such as Sir Ronald Fisher and Karl Pearson in England. They were created to test hypotheses about the effects of fertilizers, new crop varieties, and livestock rations. Such statistical methods as analysis of variance and regression came to the United States in the early 1930s when Sir Ronald visited Iowa State University, where he helped establish the Statistical Laboratory. George Snedecor, leader of the Iowa State program in statistics, named the F statistic (for determining the significance of analyses of variance and regression) after Fisher. Snedecor popularized statistical methods for agricultural research in his book, *Statistical Methods* (1931). Iowa State's Statistical Laboratory went on to develop the area sampling methods widely used in survey research. Professors in the Department of Statistics, such as Paul G. Homemeyer, Ray J. Jessen, and Snedecor, served as informal consultants to Ryan in planning the hybrid corn study, and this pioneering diffusion investigation was designed as a highly quantitative analysis, utilizing statistical methods to test hypotheses. As noted earlier, this was a marked departure from anthropological ethnographic diffusion research.

In the late 1930s sociological research in the United States was moving toward quantification, away from the qualitative methods that had been pioneered by the Chicago School in the 1915 to 1935 era (Rogers, 2003). Sociologists thought that to become scientific was to pattern themselves after the biological and physical sciences, at least in their research methods. This move to quantification implied the use of individuals as units of response and as units of analysis, so that statistical methods, borrowed from agricultural–biological research, could be utilized in sociological studies.

Ryan and Gross's hybrid corn diffusion research expressed this sociological search for scientific respectability in its choice of methods. Data were gathered by personal interviews with all of the farmers in the two Iowa communities of Jefferson and Grand Junction (by coincidence, these communities were located within 30 miles of where Rogers grew up on a farm). Each farmer was regarded by the two rural sociologists as a decision-making unit for the adoption of hybrid corn.

The focus on individual farmers led to the greatest shortcoming of the hybrid corn investigation. Sociometric questions to measure the interpersonal network links among the Iowa farmers of study were not asked. This mistake is all the more puzzling given that diffusion is essentially a social process. While the mass media often create awareness-knowledge of an innovation, interpersonal communication with peers is necessary to persuade most individuals to adopt a new idea (Rogers & Kincaid, 1981).

Ryan and Gross gathered data from a complete census of the farmers in Jefferson and Grand Junction, Iowa, an ideal sampling design for measuring network links and thus for determining peer influences on farmers' decisions to adopt the innovation. The farmer-respondents were asked about the sources and channels from which they first learned about hybrid corn (commercial seed dealers and salespeople were mentioned as most important) versus the sources and channels that convinced them to adopt (other farmers like neighbors and friends were reported as most important). So Ryan and Gross established the importance of social networks in diffusion, but failed to investigate them in an appropriate way.

Applying the Diffusion Model in San Francisco's STOP AIDS Program

In the early days of the AIDS epidemic in San Francisco, in 1981 and 1982, considerable disagreement existed within the gay and bisexual community about how to cope with HIV/AIDS. By 1992, an astounding 48 percent of them in this city were HIV-positive. Some outspoken individuals questioned whether sexual behavior spread HIV (they suspected that straight society was using the AIDS threat to close the San Francisco bathhouses, in order to limit the sexual freedom of gay men). Eventually, gay organizations pulled together to combat the epidemic through the STOP AIDS program, founded by gay San Franciscans. It was based on social psychologist Kurt Lewin's small group communication theory and on diffusion of innovations theory (Rogers, 2003).

Focus group interviews were initially conducted by STOP AIDS in order to assess how much gay men already knew about the epidemic, and what they wanted to know (Singhal & Rogers, 2003). This formative research was carried out in order to design an effective intervention. Gradually, the STOP AIDS founders realized that the focus group interviews were having a strong educational effect on the participants, as the group members exchanged useful information about HIV prevention. Men were recruited on Castro and other streets in gay neighborhoods to attend the small group meetings that were held in homes and apartments. STOP AIDS employed a cadre of outreach workers to organize and lead these meetings.

STOP AIDS "relied heavily on diffusion theory, which suggests that only those early adopters, who make up a relatively small segment of the population, need to initiate a new behavior for it to spread throughout the population" (Wohlfeiler, 1998, p. 231). A well-respected individual who was HIV-positive led each small group of a dozen or so gay and bisexual men. The means of transmission of the virus were explained, and individuals were urged to use condoms and/or to seek monogamous partnerships. Questions were asked and the answers were discussed by the group. At the conclusion of the meeting, each member was asked to make a commitment to safer sex, and to volunteer to organize and lead future small-group meetings of other gay men (such commitment, witnessed by other members of a group, is part of the Lewinian social psychology of individual behavior change).[5]

From 1985 to 1987, STOP AIDS reached 30,000 men through its various outreach activities, with 7,000 of these individuals participating in the small-group meetings that launched the diffusion process in the gay community. A media campaign was aimed at the gay population of San Francisco to raise awareness-knowledge about HIV/AIDS. The number of new HIV infections dropped from 8,000 annually in the earliest years of the epidemic, to only 650 by the mid-1980s. Then attendance at the small-group meetings fell off, and it became difficult for STOP AIDS to recruit fresh volunteers. The critical mass of early adopters of safer sex in the gay community had been reached, and the idea of safer sex would continue to spread spontaneously thereafter. STOP AIDS declared victory in 1987, and closed down its local operations. In 1990, however, STOP AIDS swung back into action in San Francisco in order to carry the safer sex message to new cohorts of younger gay men who were migrating to the city (Rogers, 2004).

San Francisco was one of the first cities in the world in which prevention programs caused a major decrease in the rate of new HIV infections. Unfortunately, by the late 1980s, about half of the gay and bisexual men in San Francisco were infected and were on their way to AIDS-related deaths. Nevertheless, further infection was greatly slowed.

Why was STOP AIDS so successful in bringing about this massive sexual behavior change? This intervention (1) was highly targeted to a specific population of high-risk individuals; (2) it was founded and implemented by respected leaders of the target community, rather than by "outside" professional organizers and educators; (3) it depended mainly on volunteer leaders, which kept costs low; and (4) the intervention was based on two theories of behavior change communication: Lewin's theory of small group communication and individual commitment, and Rogers' diffusion of innovations theory (2003). These theories provided a basis for the communication strategies utilized in the STOP AIDS intervention in San Francisco, and subsequently in other parts of the world (Singhal & Rogers, 2003; Svenkerud, Singhal, & Papa, 1998).[6]

The Dominant Paradigm for the Diffusion of Innovations

One can still detect the intellectual influence of the hybrid corn study on diffusion research, 64 years and some 6,000 publications later. More than any other diffusion investigation, the Ryan and Gross study formed the paradigm for later diffusion research. What were the essential elements of this diffusion paradigm?

1. The main dependent variable was innovativeness, defined as the degree to which an individual or other unit is relatively earlier to adopt than are others. For convenience in understanding diffusion research results, the continuous variable of innovativeness is often divided into adopter categories, such as innovators, early adopters, early majority, late majority, and laggards (Rogers, 1983). Ryan and Gross (1943) were the first to use adopter categories in their analysis (although they did not use these five categories by name).

2. When the cumulative number of farmers adopting hybrid corn was plotted over time, the distribution formed an S-shaped curve. When plotted on a frequency basis, the number of adopters over time formed a normal, bell-shaped curve (which later scholars utilized to divide the variable of innovativeness into the five adopter categories in a standard way).

3. The Iowa farmers' sources and channels of communication were found to differ at various stages in the innovation–decision process with the mass media more important at the awareness–knowledge stage and with interpersonal communication, especially from peers, more important at the persuasion stage. The notion of stages in the individual's innovation–decision process has been widely utilized by later diffusion scholars (Rogers, 1983).

The importance of the hybrid corn study in forming the paradigm for work on the diffusion of innovations is illustrated by Diane Crane's (1972) analysis of the invisible college of rural sociology diffusion researchers: 18 of the 30 most important scholarly innovations in the field were reported in the Ryan and Gross (1943) study. Each intellectual innovation consisted of the first time that either a dependent or an independent variable was used in an empirical study of diffusion. Thus, the methods of study, as well as what to look for in diffusion investigations, were established by Ryan and Gross.

Because of World War II, the diffusion paradigm created by Ryan and Gross did not spread immediately among rural sociologists. A decade-long delay, until the mid-1950s, resulted from Gross's serving in the Navy while Ryan worked for a United Nations agency (he did not return to the faculty at Iowa State University after World War II). Two other Iowa State rural sociologists, George M. Beal and Joe M. Bohlen, popularized the diffusion paradigm, starting in 1954, and soon this approach to studying the diffusion of agricultural innovations was taken up by a widening circle of rural sociologists, especially at land-grant universities in the Midwestern states. By 1960, some 405 diffusion publications had appeared, with the largest number authored by rural sociologists. However, this diffusion research tradition soon ran out of intellectual gas, and thereafter fewer and fewer diffusion studies were conducted by rural sociologists.

Spread of the Diffusion Paradigm

Meanwhile, the diffusion approach infected the other social sciences, and spread to other fields such as marketing, industrial engineering, and education. The key event in this wider acceptance was James S. Coleman, Elihu Katz, and Herbert Menzel's 1966 study of the diffusion of tetracycline, a new medical drug, among physicians. This investigation began when the director of marketing at the Pfizer drug company approached the three sociologists, then at Columbia University's Bureau of Applied Social Research, with a request to determine the effectiveness of Pfizer's tetracycline advertising in medical journals. This rather humdrum marketing question was converted into a particularly influential diffusion study by Coleman et al. (1966).

They collected data via personal interviews with virtually all of the medical doctors in four small communities in Illinois. Prescription data were also collected from pharmacies, so they knew the date when each doctor first prescribed the new drug. This represented an important methodological improvement—observed actual adoption—over the usual diffusion investigation, which depended upon respondent accuracy in recalling the date at which an innovation was adopted. Further, Coleman et al. asked sociometric questions to determine the interpersonal network links among their sample. Interestingly, they were not aware of Ryan and Gross's hybrid seed corn study until after they had completed their data-gathering.

The rate of adoption of tetracycline followed an S-shaped curve, as had the rate of adoption for hybrid corn, although only 17 months elapsed before most doctors had adopted (compared to 12 years for the Iowa farmers adopting hybrid seed). The most innovative medical doctors were cosmopolite, making numerous out-of-town trips to medical specialty meetings. Similarly, the farmer-innovators in the hybrid corn study made numerous tripsto Des Moines, the largest city in Iowa, located about 90 miles away. As with the Iowa farmers, mass media channels (such as articles in medical journals) were most important in creating awareness-knowledge, while interpersonal communication channels with peers were most important in persuading a doctor to try the medical innovation.

By far the most unique intellectual contribution of the medical drug study was the evidence that it provided of diffusion as a social process. For instance, Coleman et al. (1966) found that doctors who were linked in more interpersonal networks adopted the innovation more rapidly than did more isolated doctors. Even though tetracycline had been scientifically evaluated in numerous clinical trials, which were reported to the medical doctors of study in medical journals, and even though Pfizer salespeople gave them free samples, they evaluated the innovation mainly through the personal experiences of their fellow doctors. An early adopting doctor might tell his office partner, a social friend, or a golfing partner, "Look doctor, I prescribed tetracycline to several patients of mine last week and it acted like a miracle drug. Perhaps you should try it." Thus, the meaning of the medical innovation was socially constructed through interpersonal communication among peers. Since the Coleman et al. (1966) medical drug study, many other diffusion researches (i.e., Anwal & Singhal, 1992; Rogers & Kincaid, 1981) have gathered network data to better understand the social influences on individual's innovation-decisions.

The Bureau of Applied Social Research at Columbia University was a particularly prestigious center for social science research at the time of the drug study, and Coleman and Katz were soon to become much-admired scholars. The diffusion paradigm spread rapidly and was utilized by other sociologists. Publication of a general textbook about diffusion (Rogers, 1962) helped widen paradigm application in such fields as geography, economics, psychology, political science, and, as related previously, communication.

Research Methods for Studying Diffusion

Most diffusion researchers have followed the methodological path set forth by Ryan and Gross in the hybrid corn study. Data are mainly gathered by personal or telephone interviews from respondents who are asked to retrospect about their time of adoption, the sources or channels of communication that they used in the innovation–decision process, to report their network links with others, and other variables such as their personal and social characteristics. The individual is usually the unit of analysis, although in recent years a number of studies have been conducted in which an organization is the unit of analysis (Wildemuth, 1992; Zaltman, Duncan, & Holbek, 1973). Inadequate scholarly attention has been given to the consequences of technological innovations (only anthropologists have investigated such consequences in any significant way).

Alternative methods of data gathering have been little utilized, even as a means to supplement the predominant approach of survey data gathering and quantitative methodologies of data analysis. One wonders why ethnographic methods like in-depth interviews and observation have not been utilized more widely, especially in the organizational innovation studies—many of which are conducted by organizational communication scholars and by students of organizational behavior, both of whom increasingly utilize ethnographic methods. The dominant style of diffusion investigations is thus the quantitative analysis of data gathered by survey interview methods from large samples. The overall effect of these dominant research methods has been to emphasize an understanding of the diffusion process as the product of individual decisions and actions. Interpersonal influences on individuals in the diffusion process have been underemphasized because of the research methods used. Perhaps the approach to studying diffusion formulated by Ryan and Gross has become overly stereotyped.

However, in recent years, several communication scholars have investigated the critical mass and individual thresholds in the diffusion process, especially for the spread and adoption of interactive innovations such as electronic mail or fax in an organization or in some other system (Kramer, 1993; Markus, 1987). At a certain point in the diffusion process for any innovation, the

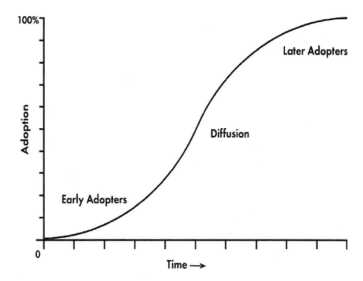

Figure 27.1 The diffusion S-curve. Reprinted from *Diffusion of Innovations* (4th ed., p. 11) by E. M. Rogers, 1995, New York: Free Press. Copyright 1995 by E. M. Rogers. Reprinted with permission of the author.

rate of adoption begins to suddenly increase at an inordinate rate. This take-off in the rate of adoption creates the S-curve of diffusion (see Figure 27.1).

However, for innovations that are essentially a means of interactive communication, such as the new communication technologies of fax and e-mail, a critical mass occurs when the diffusion process becomes self-sustaining. After the critical mass point, individuals in a system perceive that "everybody else" has adopted the interactive innovation. With each successive adopter of an interactive innovation, the new idea becomes more valuable not only for each future adopter, but also for each previous adopter.

For example, consider the first adopter of the telephone in the United States about 120 years ago. This innovation had zero utility to the first adopter. But when a second adoption occurred, the innovation became more valuable to both parties. And so it went until gradually there were so many adopters that an individual could assume that anyone he or she might wish to call would also have a telephone. Note that the first adopters of the telephone had a very low threshold of resistance to the innovation (they adopted when there was little actual benefit for doing so). Valente (1995) reanalyzed the Coleman et al. data in light of such concepts as the critical mass and individual thresholds, which he helped formulate and sharpen theoretically. Perhaps Allen (1983) said it all when he described the diffusion process for an interactive innovation as one in which "everyone is watching while being watched" (p. 270).

Future Directions: Inside-Out Diffusion

Perhaps one might wonder why diffusion research has persevered for so many years, and why the number of diffusion publications continues to grow. Few other areas of communication research have such a lengthy history and represent such a tremendous scholarly outpouring. We suggest that the popularity of diffusion research is due to its practical importance and its applied nature. The agricultural officials at Iowa State University in the late 1930s who sponsored the hybrid corn study have contemporary counterparts in other organizations who are equally frustrated

The Internet: A Spectacular Innovation

The Internet has spread more rapidly than any technological innovation in the history of mankind, removing the physical, spatial distance in who talks to whom about a new idea (Rogers, 2003).

The origins of the Internet trace to the Cold War era. Because the U.S. Pentagon feared a nuclear attack from the Soviet Union, computer scientists designed and implemented ARPANET, the predecessor of the Internet, without a central headquarters. Each networked computer passes along a message to another computer in the direction of the message's destination (indicated by its address) by means of a wired or wireless connection with no predetermined or prescribed route. Thus an e-mail message on an Internet server from Hanoi, Vietnam to San Francisco may travel through any one of millions of possible routes (Singhal & Rogers, 2001).

This computer network, ARPANET, designed for national defense purposes, evolved into the Internet by the late 1980s, when the number of users in the United States, and then in other countries, began to explode. Compared to other communication channels like postal mail or long distance telephone calls, communication via the Internet is quicker, cheaper, and more reliable. A very rapid rate of adoption of the Internet, including the World Wide Web, occurred during the 1990s, in large part because of the prior adoption of personal computers through which the Internet was accessed. Many observers consider the Internet one of the great transformational technologies (ranking with the steam engine, railroads, electricity, etc.) that at first challenged, and then fundamentally changed, the way that people learn, play, create, communicate, and work.

By September, 2007, the Internet had 1.24 billion worldwide users—that is, about 19 percent of the world's population. The United States and Canada account for about 18 percent of all users, down from 62 percent in 1998, as the Internet continues to make rapid inroads in countries of Asia, Africa, and Latin America.[7] This massive adoption of the Internet in developing countries is largely fueled by the establishment of cyber cafes, telecenters, and public access facilities; that is, to be an Internet user one no longer needs to own a personal computer.

Among millions of applications, the Internet spawned the era of e-business (electronic business), which consists mainly of e-marketing and e-commerce. *E-marketing* is the use of the Internet to market one's products or services; *e-commerce* is commercial transactions between two parties on the Internet. Almost $10 trillion of commercial transactions had occurred on the Internet by 2007.

The growth of the Internet has boosted interest in the study of diffusion, especially the study of communication networks. Unlike in the pre-Internet era when communication networks were ephemeral and difficult to capture, the Internet keeps an electronic record of human message exchanged. So, the proliferation of the Internet has also made possible a better understanding of how communication networks work in the spread of an innovation.

as to why their innovations are not adopted more rapidly; thus, diffusion studies continue to flourish.

The classical diffusion paradigm has been criticized for reifying expert-driven, top-down approaches to address problems and thus, by default, overlooking, and rejecting local solutions (Papa, Singhal, & Papa, 2006; Singhal & Dearing, 2006). Diffusion of innovation experts now increasingly (and humbly) acknowledge the value of local expertise and indigenous wisdom in finding culturally appropriate solutions to community problems. One such inside-out approach to innovation diffusion is exemplified by the positive deviance approach.

Positive deviance (PD) is an approach to social change that enables communities to discover the wisdom they already have, and then to act on it (Pascale & Sternin, 2005; Sternin & Choo, 2000). PD initially gained recognition in the work of Tufts University nutrition professor Marian Zeitlen in the 1980s, when she began focusing on why some children in poor communities were better nourished than others (Zeitlin, Ghassemi, & Mansour, 1990). Zeitlin's work privileged an assets-based approach, identifying what's going right in a community in order to amplify it, as opposed to focusing on what's going wrong in a community and fixing it.

Jerry Sternin, a visiting scholar at Tufts University, and his wife Monique built on Zeitlin's ideas to organize various PD-centered social change interventions around the world. They institutionalized PD as an organizing for social change approach by showing how it could be operationalized in a community-setting (Papa, Singhal, & Papa, 2006).

In 1991, the Sternins faced what seemed like an insurmountable challenge in Vietnam. As Director of Save the Children in Vietnam, Jerry was asked by government officials to create an effective, large-scale program to combat child malnutrition and to show results within six months. More than 65 percent of all children living in Vietnamese villages were malnourished at the time. The Vietnamese government realized that the results achieved by traditional supplemental feeding programs were rarely maintained after the programs ended. The Sternins had to come up with an approach that enabled the community to take control of their nutritional status. And quickly!

Building on Zeitlin's ideas of PD, the Sternins helped in seeking out poor families that had managed to avoid malnutrition without access to any special resources. These families were the positive deviants. They were "positive" because they were doing things right, and "deviants" because they engaged in behaviors that most others did not. The Sternins helped the community to discover that mothers in the PD families collected tiny shrimps and crabs from paddy fields, and added those with sweet potato greens to their children's meals. These foods were accessible to everyone, but most community members believed they were inappropriate for young children (Sternin & Choo, 2000). Also, these PD mothers were feeding their children three to four times a day, rather than the customary twice a day.

The Sternins helped the community members create a program that allowed them to emulate the positive deviants in their midst. Mothers, whose children were malnourished, were asked to forage for shrimps, crabs, and sweet potato greens, and in the company of other mothers were taught to cook new recipes that their children ate right there. Within weeks, mothers could see their children becoming healthier. After the pilot project, which lasted two years, malnutrition had decreased by an amazing 85 percent in the communities where the PD approach was implemented. Over the next several years, the PD intervention became a nationwide program in Vietnam, helping over 2.2 million people, including over 500,000 children improve their nutritional status (Sternin & Choo, 2000; Sternin, Sternin, & Marsh, 1999).

Positive deviance questions the role of outside expertise, believing that the wisdom to solve the problem lies inside. Social change experts, usually, make a living discerning the deficits in a community, prioritizing the problems, and then trying to implement outside solutions to change them. In the PD approach, the role of experts is to find positive deviants, identify the uncommon but effective things that positive deviants do, and then to make them visible and actionable (Pascale, Millemann, & Gioja, 2000). PD is led by internal change agents who present the social proof to their peers. In PD, the role of the expert is mainly to facilitate a process that can help amplify this wisdom locally. In so doing, solutions and benefits can be sustained, since the solution resides locally.

The PD approach emphasizes hands-on learning and actionable behaviors.[8] As Jerry Sternin notes: "It is easier to act your way into a new way of thinking than to think your way into a new way of acting" (quoted in Sparks, 2004). So, the PD approach turns the well-known KAP (knowledge, attitude, practice) framework on its head. As opposed to subscribing to a framework that says increased knowledge changes attitudes, and attitudinal changes change practice; PD believes in changing practice. PD believes that people change when that change is distilled from concrete action steps.

Evaluations of PD initiatives show that PD works because the community owns the problem, as well as its solutions (Sternin, 2003). Positive deviance is now being used to address such diverse issues as childhood anemia, the eradication of female genital mutilation, curbing the trafficking of girls, increasing school retention rates, and promoting higher levels of condom use among commercial sex workers (Sternin, 2003).

The positive deviance approach to innovation diffusion is located at the intersection of theory, method, and praxis. Theoretically, it privileges local knowledge. Methodologically, PD does not treat deviance as an anomaly. In contrast to traditional diffusion approaches that favor "regression to the mean," PD valorizes outliers. PD's praxis is humane. It believes in inside-out social change with the help of outside expertise and facilitation.

When author Singhal visited Jerry and Monique Sternin in their Cambridge home in January 2005, they were making preparations to travel to Davos, Switzerland to conduct a Positive Deviance workshop at the World Economic Forum. When Singhal noted that PD was "going places," Jerry winked and responded: "Yes, the world could do better with more deviance."

Conclusion

Diffusion of innovations research promises to enhance our understanding of how social change occurs, a fundamental issue for all scholars of society. What is the role of technology in bringing about social change? One way to find out is through diffusion research, a microlevel type of study of the macrolevel issue of social change. Scholarly interest in new communication technologies by communication students has given a special boost to interest in diffusion research in recent years. There is no reason to expect that the scholarly popularity of diffusion research by communication (and other) scholars will decrease in the foreseeable future. Innovations continue to be generated and studied.[9]

However, we do not need more-of-the-same diffusion research (Meyer, 2004). The overwhelming focus on the individual as the unit of adoption needs to be broadened to the levels of organizations and communities-of-practice. More scholarly attention needs to paid to the consequences of technological innovations. Alternative methods of data gathering including ethnography, in-depth interviews, and participant observation should supplement the predominant quantitative methodologies of data collection and analysis.

Also, diffusion of innovations practice needs to increasingly acknowledge and value the role of indigenous wisdom and solutions. Indeed innovations that are generated locally are not just more likely to be culturally appropriate, but also more likely to be owned by the potential adopters. When adopters are externally persuaded to buy into the vision of an outside expert, they tend to demonstrate inertia and resistance, much like the Iowa farmers who for years resisted the adoption of hybrid seed corn.

Everett M. Rogers and Diffusion of Innovations

This chapter is dedicated to our senior co-author Everett M. Rogers, a prolific scholar of communication and social change and a wonderful human being, who passed away in Albuquerque, NM in October 2004. Best known for his book, *Diffusion of Innovations* (published in the fifth edition in 2003), Ev Rogers' life—all 73 years—represented a curious engagement with the topic of innovation diffusion.

The story begins on the family Pinehurst Farm in Carroll, Iowa, where Ev Rogers was born on March 6, 1931.[10] The Great Depression was raging, and life on Pinehurst Farm was tough for everyone, especially for young Ev, who was responsible for carrying out such daily chores as milking cows, feeding chickens, and cleaning the barn. Ev credited that daily hard work ethic, learned early on an Iowa farm, for his illustrious scholarly career, complete with 36 books, over 300 peer-reviewed essays, and countless research reports.

Who would now believe that Ev almost never went to college? He would have stayed home and farmed if it were not for Pep Martens, a high school teacher, who packed a bunch of promising seniors in his car and drove them to Ames, Iowa, the home of Iowa State University. It was Ev's first visit to Ames, located 60 miles from the family farm. Ev liked Ames, and decided to pursue a degree in agriculture.

Iowa State in those years had a great intellectual tradition in agriculture and in rural sociology. Numerous agricultural innovations were generated by scientists at Iowa State. Rural sociologists—including Bryce Ryan and George Beal, Ev's doctoral advisor—were conducting pioneering studies on the diffusion of these innovations—like the high-yielding hybrid seed corn, chemical fertilizers, and weed sprays. Questions were being asked about why some farmers adopted these innovations, and some did not. These questions intrigued Ev.

At the farm, Ev remembers that his father loved electro-mechanical farm innovations; but was resistant to biological–chemical innovations such as the new hybrid seed corn, even though it yielded 20 percent more crop, and was resistant to drought. However, during the Iowa drought of 1936, while the hybrid seed corn stood tall on the neighbors' farm; the crop on the Rogers' farm wilted. Ev's father was finally convinced. It took him eight years to make up his mind.

These questions about innovation diffusion, including the strong resistances, and how they could be overcome, formed the core of Ev's graduate work at Iowa State University in the mid-1950s. Ev's doctoral dissertation sought to analyze the diffusion of the 2-4-D weed spray (and a cluster of other agricultural innovations) in Collins, Iowa, a community close to Pinehurst Farm. In the review of literature chapter, Ev reviewed the existing studies of the diffusion of all kinds of innovations—agricultural innovations, educational innovations, medical innovations, and marketing innovations. He found several similarities in these studies. For instance, innovations tend to diffuse following an S-Curve of adoption.

In 1962, Ev published this review of literature chapter, greatly expanded, enhanced, and refined, as the *Diffusion of Innovations* book. He argued that diffusion was a general process, not bound by the type of innovation studied, by who the adopters were, or by place or culture. By reviewing diffusion studies across a range of disciplines, he concluded that the diffusion process displayed patterns and regularities, across a range of conditions, innovations, and cultures (Rogers, 2004).

The book provided a comprehensive theory of how innovations diffused, or spread, in a social system. The book's appeal was global (Hornik, 2004). Its timing was uncanny. National governments of newly independent countries of Asia, Africa, and Latin America were wrestling with how to diffuse agricultural, health, and family planning innovations in their newly independent countries (Barker, 2004; Bertrand, 2004; Haider & Kreps, 2004; Murphy, 2004). Here was a theory that was useful. During the 1960s and 1970s, for every copy of *Diffusion of Innovations* that was purchased in the U.S., Ev estimated that four were being purchased in countries of Asia, Africa, and Latin America.

When the first edition of *Diffusion of Innovations* was published, Ev was 31 years old. But he had also become a world-renowned academic figure. As per the Social Science Citation Index, *Diffusion of Innovations* is the second most cited book in the social sciences.

Not bad for an Iowa farm boy who almost did not go to college!

Notes

1. Founded in 1980, Dancing Wheels has performed, taught, and inspired children and adults of all (dis) abilities. In the United States, the company presents more than 100 performances reaching audiences of 125,000 each year. Co-author Quinlan performed with Dancing Wheels in June 2007. Retrieved June 18, 2008, from http://www.gggreg.com/DW/pages/company.htm
2. This case is discussed in detail in Singhal and Quinlan (in press).
3. No other field of behavior science research represents more effort by more scholars in more disciplines in more nations (Rogers, 2003).
4. Gross averaged 14 personal interviews per day during the summer of 1939, an enviable record for survey research by today's standards.
5. Kurt Lewin was a German-born scholar who migrated to the United States in the 1930s in order to escape Hitler's fascism. Lewin fathered the modern field of social psychology.
6. Another behavior change theory, which was implicitly involved in the STOP AIDS program's use of opinion leaders, was Albert Bandura's (1986, 1997) social learning/social modeling/social cognitive theory. DiFrancisco and others (1999) found that a national sample of 77 HIV prevention programs in the United States reported that Bandura's theory was the most widely used theoretical basis.
7. See http://www.internetworldstats.com/stats.htm (Retrieved November 15, 2007).
8. A positive deviance inquiry focuses on eliminating those client behaviors from the strategy mix that are true but useless (TBU). TBU is a sieve through which a facilitator passes the uncommon qualities of positive deviants to ensure that the identified practices can be practiced by everyone.
9. However, as Dearing (2004) and Dearing and Meyer (2006) argue, there is a strong tendency to "reward the new at the expense of the proven." Usually, heavy investment is made in generating "best practices" or innovations, and scant resources are then set aside to diffuse it.
10. This boxed case draws upon Singhal and Dearing (2006).

References

Allen, D. (1983). New telecommunication services: Network externalities and critical mass. *Telecommunications Policy, 12,* 257–271.

Bandura, A. (1986). *Social foundations of thought and action: A social cognitive theory.* Englewood Cliffs, NJ: Prentice-Hall.

Bandura, A. (1997). *Self-efficacy: The exercise of control.* New York: Freeman.

Barker, K. (2004). Diffusion of innovations: A world. *Journal of Health Communication, 9*(1), 131–137.

Bertrand, J. T. (2004). Diffusion of innovations and HIV/AIDS. *Journal of Health Communication, 9*(1), 113–121.

Coleman, J. S., Katz, E., & Menzel, H. (1966). *Medical innovation: Diffusion of a medical drug among doctors.* Indianapolis: Bobbs-Merrill.

Crane, D. (1972). *Invisible colleges.* Chicago: University of Chicago Press.

Dearing, J. W., & Meyer, G. (2006). Revisiting diffusion theory. In A. Singhal & J. W. Dearing (Eds.), *Communication of innovations: A journey with Ev Rogers* (pp. 29–60). Thousand Oaks, CA: Sage.

Deutschmann, P. J., & Danielson, W. A. (1960). Diffusion of knowledge of the major news story. *Journalism Quarterly, 37,* 345–355.

Deutschmann, P. J., & Fals Borda, O. (1962). *Communication and adoption patterns in an Andean village.* San José, Costa Rica: Programa Interamericano de Informacíon Popular.

DiFrancisco, W., Kelly, J. A, Otto-Salaj, L.,. McAuliffe, T. L. Somlai, A. M., Hackl, K., et al. (1999). Factors influencing attitudes within AIDS service organizations toward the use of research-based HIV prevention interventions. *AIDS Education and Prevention, 12*(1),72–86.

Haider, M., & Kreps, G. L. (2004). Forty years of diffusion of innovations: Utility and value in public health. *Journal of Health Communication, 9*(1), 3–11.

Hornik, R. (2004). Some reflections on diffusion theory and the role of Everett Rogers. *Journal of Health Communication, 9,* 143–148.

Kramer, R. (1993). The policies of information: A study of the French Minitel system. In J. R. Schement & B. D. Ruben (Eds.), *Between communication and information* (pp. 453–586). New Brunswick, NJ: Transaction.

Markus, M. L. (1987). Toward a "critical mass" theory of intensive media: Universal access, interdependence, and diffusion. *Communication Research, 14,* 491–511.

Meyer, G. (2004). Diffusion methodology: Time to innovate? *Journal of Health Communication, 9*(1), 59–69.

Morris, M., & Ogan, C. (1996). The Internet as mass medium. Journal of Communication, 45(1), 39–50.

Murphy, E. (2004). Diffusion of innovations: Family planning in developing countries. *Journal of Health Communication, 9*(1), 123–129.

Papa, M. J., Singhal, A., & Papa, W. H. (2006). *Organizing for social change: A dialectic journey of theory and praxis.* Thousand Oaks, CA: Sage.

Pascale, R. T., & Sternin, J. (2005). Your company's secret change agents. *Harvard Business Review,* May, 1–11.

Pascale, R. T., Millemann, M., & Gioja (2000). *Surfing the edge of chaos: The laws of nature and the new laws of business.* New York: Crown.

Rogers, E. M. (1962). *Diffusion of innovations* (1st ed.). New York: Free Press.

Rogers, E. M. (1983). *Diffusion of innovations* (3rd ed.). New York: Free Press.

Rogers, E. M. (1994). *A history of communication study: A biographical approach.* New York: Free Press.

Rogers, E. M. (1995). *Diffusion of innovations* (4th ed.). New York: Free Press.

Rogers, E. M. (2003). *Diffusion of innovations* (5th ed.). New York: Free Press.

Rogers, E. M. (2004). A prospective and retrospective look at diffusion model. *Journal of Health Communication, 9*(1), 13–19.

Rogers, E. M., & Kincaid, D. L. (1981). *Communication networks: A new paradigm for research.* New York: Free Press.

Rogers, E. M., & Seidel, N. (2002). Diffusion of news of the terrorist attacks of September 11, 2001. *Prometheus, 20*(3), 209–219.

Rosen, E. (2002). The anatomy of buzz: How to create word of mouth marketing. New York: Currency.

Ryan, B., & Gross, N. C. (1943). The diffusion of hybrid seed corn in two Iowa communities. *Rural Sociology, 8,* 15–24.

Singhal, A., & Dearing, J. W. (Eds.) (2006). *Communication of innovations: A journey with Ev Rogers.* Thousand Oaks, CA: Sage.

Singhal, A., & Quinlan, M. M. (in press). *Diffusion of innovations and political communication. Encyclopedia of political communication.* Thousand Oaks, CA: Sage.

Singhal, A., & Rogers, E. M. (2001). *India's communication revolution: From bullock carts to cyber marts.* Thousand Oaks, CA: Sage.

Singhal, A., & Rogers, E. M. (2003). *Combating AIDS: Communication strategies in action.* Thousand Oaks, CA: Sage.

Singhal, A., Rogers, E. M., & Mahajan, M. (1999). The Gods are drinking milk! Word-of-mouth diffusion of a major news event in India. *Asian Journal of Communication, 9*(1), 86–107.

Snedecor, G. (1931). *Statistical methods.* Ames: Iowa State University Press.

Sparks, D. (2004). From hunger aid to school reform: An interview with Jerry Sternin. *Journal of Staff Development, 25*(1), 12–21.

Sternin, J. (2003). Practice positive deviance for extraordinary social and organizational change. In D. Ulrich, M. Goldsmith, L. Carter, J. Bolt, & N. Smallwood (Eds.), *The change champion's field guide* (pp. 20–37). New York: Best Practice.

Sternin, J., & Choo, R. (2000). The power of positive deviancy. *Harvard Business Review,* January-February, 2–3.

Sternin, M., Sternin, J., & Marsh, D. (1999). Scaling up poverty alleviation and nutrition program in Vietnam. In T. Marchione (Ed.), *Scaling up, scaling down* (pp. 97–117). Gordon & Breach.

Svenkerud, P. J., Singhal, A., & Papa, M. J. (1998). Diffusion of innovations theory and effective targeting of HIV/AIDS programmes in Thailand. *Asian Journal of Communication, 8*(1), 1–30.

Tarde, G. (1903). *The laws of imitation* (E. C. Parsons, Trans.). New York: Holt.

Valente, T. W. (1995). *Network models of the diffusion of innovations.* Cresskill, NJ: Hampton Press.

Valente, T. W. (2006). Communication network analysis and the diffusion of innovations. In A. Singhal & J. W. Dearing (Eds.), *Communication of innovations: A journey with Ev Rogers* (pp. 61–82). Thousand Oaks, CA: Sage.

Wissler, C. (1923). *Man and culture.* New York: Thomas Y. Crowell.

Wildemuth, B. M. (1992). An empirically grounded model of the adoption of intellectual technologies. *Journal of the American Society for Information Sciences, 43,* 210–224.

Wohlfeiler, D. (1998). Community organizing and community building among gay and bisexual men: The STOP AIDS Project. In M. Minkler (Ed.), *Community organizing and community building for health* (pp. 230–243). New Brunswick, NJ: Rutgers University Press,.

Zaltman, G., Duncan, R., & Holbek, J. (1973). *Innovations and organizations.* New York: Wiley.

Zeitlin, M., Ghassemi, H., & Mansour, M. (1990). *Positive deviance in child nutrition.* New York: UN University Press.

Suggested Readings

Coleman, J. S., Katz, E., & Menzel, H. (1966). *Medical innovation: Diffusion of a medical drug among doctors.* Indianapolis, Bobbs-Merrill.

Rogers, E. M. (2003). *Diffusion of innovations* (5th ed.). New York: Free Press.

Ryan, B., & Gross, N. C. (1943). The diffusion of hybrid seed corn in two Iowa communities. *Rural Sociology, 8,* 15–24.

Singhal, A., & Dearing, J. W. (2006). *Communication of innovations: A journey with Ev Rogers.* Thousand Oaks, CA: Sage.

28

CREDIBILITY

Charles C. Self

Credibility is one of the oldest communication concepts. It is also one of intense recent interest. Both communication scholars and professional communicators have tried to understand why people find some communications to be more credible than others. Credibility has been studied by students of both interpersonal communication and mass communication and it has been of interest by those examining online and new media. Most people intuitively sense that they can judge some communications to be more credible than others.

The concept originated with the ancient Greeks and it has been the focus of continuing study ever since. The development of mass communication in the 20th century intensified interest in credibility—especially in its mediated forms. Recent developments in new technology and online media have generated a new outpouring of interest in how individuals judge online messages to be credible. The literature on credibility is plentiful, contradictory, and confused. It taps into core theories of rhetoric, persuasion, interpersonal communication, mass communication, and now interactive communication. The concept is based in fundamental differences in presupposition made by conflicting concepts of communication itself. The complexity has been intensified by the ambiguity of sources of information in online media. Thus, at the opening of the 21st century, credibility scholars appear to be shifting the theoretical center of the concept away from source credibility toward a new grounding in community, collaboration, and interactivity by active recipients assumed to be judging credibility within personal or communal contexts of motivation, goals, and projects.

The Concept

Credibility has been defined as believability, trust, perceived reliability, and dozens of other concepts and combinations of them (Burgoon, Burgoon, & Wilkinson, 1981; Greenberg & Roloff, 1974; Metzger, Flanagin, Eyal, & McCann, 2003; Shaw, 1976, 1973). Recent research has also focused on online "credibility markers" (Walther, Wang, & Loh, 2004; Wathen & Burkell, 2001), technological "cues" to signal recipient "heuristics" for judging credibility (Sundar, 2007) or collaborative "social endorsements" that signal credibility (Flanagin & Metzger, 2008). In the past, credibility has been defined in terms of the credulity of those trusting; the characteristics of those presenting—the individual, organization, or medium; the information or message offered; and the circumstances under which the message is being perceived. It also has been defined in terms of the recipient of the message, the characteristics of the social setting within which the communication takes place, and the underlying perceived dimensions of communication. The new, mediated interactive environments, particularly of online media, have led to an emphasis upon situated judgments of credibility (Metzger et al., 2003).

Beginning with Aristotle, communication scholars have explored the role of source credibility in persuasive messages. It was not until the mid-20th century, however, that communication scholars began the scientific study of credibility—intrinsically tied to interpersonal and persuasion research. The development of online communication, open source technology, and other interactive media forms at the turn of the 21st century created yet another shift, this one toward active, collaborative judgments of credibility within the context of interactive readings of communication messages with ambiguous, or what Sundar calls "murky" message sourcing (Sundar, 2007; Sundar & Nass, 2001). The focus of this chapter moves from rhetorical, interpersonal, and persuasive communication to mass communication and to interactive mediated communication. It will examine the impact of the new interactive media technologies on the core ideas of credibility and how collaborative media use is shifting notions of credibility from source manipulation toward user actions to extend or withhold credibility for messages.

Late 20th century research was centered on studies of news report credibility and mass media. These studies produced conflicting findings (Whitney, 1985), driven by institutional interests within news organizations, by critics with a variety of political and social agendas (Dennis, 1986; Whitney, 1986), and by researchers representing a range of theoretical orientations (Delia, 1976; Salmon, 1986; Stamm & Dube, 1994). These approaches used polling data, discourse data, and case study data (Self, 1988a). On the other hand, more recent 21st century research has focused on the impact of technology, interactivity, and collaboration in face of messages that often mask information sources within multiple layers of organizational and technological structures (see especially Metzger et al., 2003; Sundar & Nass, 2000; Wathen & Burkell, 2001).

A great deal of work has yet to be done to sort out the meaning of the construct. As such, it offers an excellent case study of the relationships among pretheoretical assumption, theory building, methodological approach, and research programs. This review will begin with a brief historical overview of the origins, approaches, and related research.

Historical Development

The idea that some sources of information are more reliable than others is as old as discussions of rhetoric itself. Plato's famous description of the dialogue on rhetoric between Socrates and Phaedrus grapples with the issue. Socrates and Phaedrus discuss the rhetorical skills taught by various sophist teachers.

Socrates describes the skills advocated by the Sophists and used by their orators: "only the probabilities should be told either in accusation or defense, and that always in speaking, the orator should keep probability in view, and say good-bye to truth. And the observance of this principle throughout a speech furnishes the whole art" (Plato, 1952, p. 137). Socrates counters with his own view of true rhetoric: "the probability of which [the sophist] speaks was engendered in the minds of the many by the likeness of the truth,…he who knew the truth would always know best how to discover the resemblances of the truth" (p. 138). He objects to the notion that one should be driven by shaping the message to fit the predisposition of the audience, "unless a man estimates the various characters of his hearers and is able to divide all things into classes and to comprehend them under single ideas, he will never be a skillful rhetorician even within the limits of human power" (p. 138). The ontological assumption was that the better the speaker understood universal ideals of truth, the greater trust that individual would evoke in the audience, which would recognize the resemblances to truth offered by the speaker. According to Plato, credibility was engendered by the knowledge of truth.

If Plato delineated one pole of the concept of credibility of the source, Aristotle represented the other: "Rhetoric may be defined as the faculty of observing in any given case the available means of persuasion" (Aristotle, 1952, p. 595). He couched the concept of credibility within a group of characteristics he referred to as the *ethos* of the communicator—the communicator's ability to inspire confidence and belief in what was being said. This group of characteristics was among three major modes of persuasion and was responsible for evoking trust among the hearers of a message.

> Persuasion is achieved by the speaker's personal character when the speech is so spoken as to make us think him credible. We believe good men more fully and more readily than others: this is true generally whatever the question is, and absolutely true where exact certainty is impossible and opinions are divided. This kind of persuasion, like the others, should be achieved by what the speaker says, not by what people think of his character before he begins to speak. It is not true, as some writers assume in their treatises on rhetoric, that the personal goodness revealed by the speaker contributes nothing to his power of persuasion; on the contrary, his character may almost be called the most effective means of persuasion he possesses. (p. 595)

Three ideas behind source credibility are revealed in this debate. First, sources are credible because the audience perceives that the message is "rightness" or true. Second, sources are credible because they rightly know how to reveal themselves to particular audiences. And, third, sources are perceived to be credible because the character of the audience makes it credulous.

The concept of credibility reaches back to this great debate among the idealists and the realists over the nature of truth and rhetoric. Persuasion and credibility have been discussed in most of the theories of communication since Aristotle. These theories varied in how they deal with the issue but usually centered on source, message, or audience characteristics. The issue has been whether an audience's trust is won as a consequence of the knowledge of truth and, thus, the strength of the argument; the empirical observation of audience characteristics and the communicator's ability to match delivery and message to audience needs; or the situation of the audience members themselves—their credulity or persuasibility.

Early Empirical Research

Systematic *empirical* research in the modern sense came only in the 20th century. Initially, this research was centered in what Harold Lasswell referred to as *administrative research* in the mass media. This research was driven by concern about the power of propaganda (Lasswell, Lerner, & Speier, 1980) and by the need for the new broadcast media managers to demonstrate the power of their media. The desire to attract advertising dollars to radio from newspapers produced a series of studies through polling organizations, some inspired by Lasswell himself (c.f., Smith, 1969, especially pp. 42–89). The crucial ones included Roper, Gallup, National Opinion Research Center, and the Survey Research Center at the University of Michigan (Cantril, 1951). They attempted to determine which mass communication medium was "trusted" most for information and news.

The studies began in the 1930s and have continued since.[1] The assumption of this research was that the medium itself was seen to be the source and was trusted or not. Grounded in what has been called the hypodermic-needle model of communication (see Lemert, 1981, and chapter 5, this volume, for a discussion of the approach's shortcomings), the research assumed that media had high levels of credibility among audiences to change attitudes, and that the crucial issue was which of the media were attended to most by audiences. Over time, the reliance on a medium was shown to be a major predictor credibility (see, for example, Bucy, 2003; Johnson & Kaye, 2000, 2002; Rimmer & Weaver, 1987; Wanta & Hu, 1994).

Initially, researchers found that newspapers were the most trusted source of information for news. In the late 1930s, they found that radio had become the most trusted source. In the early 1950s, television assumed the role of most trusted source of information (Erskine, 1970–1971). These studies could not determine what caused one medium to be more trusted than another. For the most part, respondents were simply asked which source they trusted most on which issues. By the early part of the 21st century, online media had been found to be the most trusted source in some studies, although results were mixed and depended heavily upon how the study was conducted (Flanagin & Metzger, 2001; Johnson & Kaye, 2002; Pew Research Center, 2000, 2006; Sundar & Nass, 2001).

Source Credibility Studies

It was, however, the need to develop support for the war effort in the 1940s that produced the first truly paradigmatic study of research examining why audiences believe a message from one communicator and not another.

Psychologist Carl Hovland and associates worked for the War Department in World War II and continued their experimental research at Yale University after the war. They studied how to persuade soldiers through wartime messages. Hovland and colleagues developed a message-learning approach based on what Hovland (1951) called "a strong predilection for stimulus-response learning-theory formulations and…an attempt is made to see how far the general principles of behavior theory can be extended into this field.… Attitudes are viewed as internalized anticipatory approach or avoidance tendencies toward objects, persons, or symbols" (p. 427). He thus accepted the source-message-channel-receiver (SMCR) model of communication advocated by a number of theorists interested in attitude change research in the second half of the 20th century (Rogers, 1994).

Hovland and colleagues defined *credibility* as "trustworthiness" and "expertise" (Hovland, Janis, & Kelley, 1953; Hovland & Weiss, 1951–1952), studying the credibility of mass communication messages by examining how individuals received such messages from "high credibility" sources. In order to measure the change in attitude evoked by a given message, Hovland controlled all variables but one in the communication chain from source to destination. This concept echoed Aristotle's argument that persuasion was based upon fitting the message to audience needs in the linear model of speaker-message-hearer.

Hovland and colleagues presented positive and negative messages from high credibility and low credibility sources to audiences and measured learning of information and changes in opinion. This study was followed up by measuring information retention by the same participants four months later. Hovland found that high credibility sources changed attitudes more than low credibility sources, but that information was learned about equally well from both source types. An unanticipated *sleeper effect* was found in the follow-up four months later (Hovland, Lumsdaine, & Sheffield, 1949; Hovland & Weiss, 1951–1952).

Hovland and colleagues drew a distinction among source credibility, message variables, and audience credulity in persuasion. They produced the first systematic knowledge about media credibility.

Variations on Three Themes

Following the work of Hovland and colleagues, a broad interest in the credibility of media sources of information developed. That research centered on the three possible reasons messages are credible: source characteristics (institutional media, individual speakers, organizations as sources), message characteristics, and audience characteristics and credulity.

Source Characteristics

Because credibility theories have applied value for mass media organizations (i.e., selling newspapers, increasing ratings), mass communication researchers have devoted inordinate attention to *media* credibility; speech or human communication researchers have also spent considerable time examining the impact of *source* credibility (i.e., speaker, organization). Interest in media or source characteristics is seen in studies such as Shaw (1967), who found that increased reliance upon news sent by telegraph brought a sharp decline in stories judged to be "biased" about presidential campaigns in the 1880s. Baxter and Bittner (1974) found that among high school and college students of the "television generation," television was more credible than other media, overriding previous findings of differences for sex and educational level. Brownlow (1992) found that baby-faced female speakers induced more agreement with their position when trust was questioned and mature-faced female speakers induced more attitude change when expertise was questioned.

Source characteristic research attempts to identify which information sources were believed or which characteristics of these sources lead to greater believability. A more recent approach has been to develop *dimensions* of characteristics that were thought to be related to credibility. These studies used statistical techniques such as factor analysis or measurement techniques such as Q-Sort.[2] For example, McCroskey and colleagues (McCroskey, 1966; McCroskey & Jensen, 1975) employed three different instruments to measure credibility. One (McCroskey, 1966) employed a 42-item battery of statements with five-point answer sets in Likert-type format (*strongly agree, agree, neutral, disagree, strongly disagree*). The second employed 12 bipolar adjective semantic differential statements (McCroskey, 1966). Both revealed two dimensions of credibility: authoritativeness and character. The third used a 25 bipolar adjective semantic differential to measure source credibility (McCroskey & Jensen, 1975). They found the same two dimensions plus three more: sociability, composure, and extroversion. Sample items from each measure are presented in Table 28.1.

Table 28.1   Sample Credibility Scales

Sample Likert-Type Scale Items[a]

Authoritativeness Scales
I respect this speaker's opinion on the topic.
This speaker is not of very high intelligence.
I have little confidence in this speaker.
This speaker lacks information on the topic.
Character Scales
I deplore this speaker's background.
This speaker is basically honest.
This speaker is a reputable person.
The character of this speaker is good.

Semantic Differential Scale Adjective Pairs

Authoritativeness	Character
Reliable-Unreliable	Honest-Dishonest
Informed-Uninformed	Friendly-Unfriendly
Qualified-Unqualified	Pleasant-Unpleasant
Intelligent-Unintelligent	Unselfish-Selfish
Valuable-Worthless	Nice-Awful
Expert-Inexpert	Virtuous-Sinful

Note. [a]Responses: *strongly agree, agree, neutral, disagree, strongly disagree.*

One of the most frequently used operational definitions for *media source credibility* comes out of the long series of Roper studies of differences in credibility of the news media (Roper, 1985). Those studies asked simply: "If you got conflicting or different reports of the same news story from radio, television, the magazines and the newspapers, which of the four versions would you be most inclined to believe—the one on radio or television or magazines or newspapers?" This question and others asked by Roper were aimed at discovering the *relative credibility* of different news media.

Carter and Greenberg (1965), skeptical of the Roper questions, believed them to be biased against newspapers. They altered the wording of two Roper questions and found that for general dependency, newspapers were indeed rated more credible. However, for belief when conflicting stories were reported, they found that even more of their respondents chose television over newspapers than had been reported by Roper.

Berlo, Lemert, and Mertz (1969) asked respondents to rate credibility across widely different types of sources. They identified three credibility factors or dimensions—safety, qualification, and dynamism. When media sources have been explored, similar results were obtained. Singletary (1976), for instance, generated 403 adjectives, which described credible mass media sources. He asked 181 students to rate how consistent the words were with their understanding of the term *credibility*. His analysis yielded 41 different dimensions for mass media credibility, which he collapsed into 16 credibility categories and conducted a detailed analysis of six: knowledgeability, attraction, trustworthiness, articulation, hostility, and stability. Lee (1978) reported different dimensions of credibility for television and newspapers reporting national and international or state and local news. Whereas television was consistently seen as more credible, levels of credibility varied along the 45 scales of bipolar adjectives for both newspapers and television, according to what types of stories were being reported. Factor analysis revealed different dimensions of credibility for each condition. Only the dimension, *intimacy*, surfaced for all conditions.

Another set of measures came out of the 1985 American Society of Newspaper Editors' study of credibility. Gaziano and McGrath (1986), asked 875 respondents to rate 16 bipolar semantic differential items. Their results yielded three factors, one of which was generated from 12 of the items that grouped together and that they labeled "credibility." The other two factors were labeled "social concerns" and "patriotic." The 12 credibility items were: *is fair or unfair; is biased or unbiased; tells the whole story or doesn't tell the whole story; is accurate or inaccurate; invades or respects people's privacy; does or does not watch after readers'/viewers' interests; is or is not concerned about the community's well-being; does or does not separate fact and opinion; can or cannot be trusted; is concerned about the public interest or is concerned about making profits; is factual or opinionated; has well-trained or poorly trained reporters.* The other four were: *cares or does not care what audience thinks; sensationalizes or does not sensationalize; is moral or immoral; is patriotic or unpatriotic.*) Respondent ratings for each of the 12 credibility factor items were then used to create an "index" of credibility.

Several attempts to validate or modify the Gaziano and McGrath scale were attempted. For example, Meyer (1988) produced two dimensions from the Gaziano-McGrath scales—one narrowly defined as *credibility* (believability), the other more broadly drawn to represent *affiliation with the community.* A further validation attempt was made by West (1994), who found the Meyer credibility scale to "validly and reliably measure credibility per se" (p. 164). He reported that the community affiliation scale was insufficiently reliable and that the Gaziano-McGrath scale appeared to measure more than one underlying credibility dimension.

Wanzenried and Powell (1993) employed the Leathers Personal Credibility Scale (Leathers, 1992), which posits three dimensions of credibility (competence, trustworthiness, and dynamism). Each dimension containing four sets of bipolar adjectives was used to measure the credibility of presidential candidates (see also Wanzenried, Smith-Howell, & Powell, 1992; Powell & Wanzenried, 1992).

These studies have attempted to elaborate on the basic concept of source characteristics associated with credibility. Instead of positing one or two characteristics, they attempted to identify underlying dimensions of perceived character that would promote confidence in these sources.

Message Characteristics

Interest in message characteristics is seen in studies such as Anderson and Clevenger (1963), who suggested in their review of experimental research from 1921 to 1961 that message impact is related to source credibility. McCroskey (1969), in a series of experiments empirically testing the relationship of evidence and source credibility to persuasiveness in public speaking situations, found that the credibility of evidence (high or low) used in a message alone did not persuade. When source credibility (high or low) was added as an intervening variable, however, persuasion occurred, but only when a source was *not* highly credible. Thus, we know that message credibility is important and more so when a source is not seen as highly credible. In a media credibility study, Slattery and Tiedge (1992) examined the effects on credibility of labeling staged video in television news stories and found that "labeling news video as staged is not in itself enough to bring about a change in the evaluation of news story credibility...[and] raise[s] the possibility that repeated use of labels identifying video as a dramatization or re-creation may raise questions about...authenticity" (p. 284).

Graber (1987) and Robinson (1987) conducted studies of the way respondents processed messages about presidential candidates in the 1984 election. Graber studied cues or spin in television pictures and Robinson examined cues or spin based on television's words or "what the journalists said about the candidates [sic] qualities as a leader" (p. 147). Graber found that television had more impact when character traits rather than issues were illustrated with pictures. Robinson found that televised words had little impact on public opinion regarding political candidates (in this case, presidential).

One of the more promising lines of message research has been studies of *familiarity*. Boehm (1994) examined the effect on perceived validity of repeating statements several times to increase familiarity. He concluded that familiarity is the basis of judged validity. Further evidence about familiarity was found by Begg, Anas, and Farinacci (1992) who cued respondents about whether a source's messages were truthful. In a series of experiments, respondents heard statements from familiar sources and unfamiliar sources. In the early phases of the experiments, they were told which sources would be lying. The respondents then rated statements as either true or false in later experiments. Begg et al., found that familiarity increased the credibility of even false statements, even when respondents remembered that the statements were being made by a source that was lying.[3]

More recently, Fico, Richardson, and Edwards (2004) have studied the effects of balanced and imbalanced story structure on perceived story bias and news organization credibility. They found that participants perceived imbalanced stories as biased and evaluated newspapers apparently responsible for balanced stories as more credible. Imbalanced story structure directly led to negative evaluation of the credibility of the newspaper publishing the imbalanced story. Similarly, Maier (2005), in a study of 4,800 news sources, found that newspaper credibility, as perceived by news sources, significantly declined in relation to frequency and severity of errors and affected source willingness to cooperate with the press. Subjective errors were considered to be the most egregious.

Audience Characteristics

Interest in audience characteristics is seen in studies such as Becker, Cobbey, and Sobowale (1978), Greenberg (1966), and Lewis (1981). These studies attempted to trace the relationship between audience demographics and perceived media credibility. Others (Westley & Severin, 1964) attempted to develop an ideal type of audience likely to assign high credibility to a newspaper based upon demographic characteristics. Al-Makaty, Boyd, and Van Tubergen (1994) used Q-Methodology to discover types of Saudi men who found different media credible during the Gulf War. Wanta and Hu (1994) attempted to link uses and gratifications research (see chapter 10, this volume) with agenda setting (see chapter 7, this volume) to examine "how people use the news media, rather than how media affect people" (p. 91). To accomplish this, Wanta and Hu tested Meyer's (1988) credibility scales (believability and community affiliation) as predictors of media reliance, exposure, and, ultimately, agenda setting effects. The objective was to find out if audience perceptions of credibility predict media agenda setting effects. They found that credibility (defined as believability and community affiliation) leads to reliance on a medium and reliance leads to exposure. Exposure, in its turn, leads to agenda setting effects. In something of a surprise, they also found that perceived affiliation of the media also produces a statistically significant path coefficient with agenda-setting effects.

Applied Research

Credibility research represents one of those unusual areas of scholarly research that also has attracted a great deal of attention among communication industry owners and managers. Perhaps the reason for this interest has been the changing relationship of the mass media and their publics. In the 1960s, the role and place of news media came under scrutiny, along with a popular reexamination of many social institutions.

Lionel Trilling (1965) attributed this skepticism toward public institutions to a broad displacement of the "public" outside its social institutions. He suggested that it began with intellectuals in the 1930s and had a major impact among college students and the broader public in the 1960s, leading to a redefinition of communication's role in society—to give journalists an independent and authentic voice distinct from that of their organizations (Learner, 1992; Wolfe, 1972).

The skepticism of media grew during the Vietnam War era. A series of high profile reports blamed media coverage in part for social problems of the time. The Kerner Commission Report (National Advisory Commission on Civil Disorders, 1968), for example, concluded that the way the media handled coverage of the 1967 Detroit riots might have contributed to the violence.

In 1971, the Nixon administration applied for and received a temporary restraining order blocking publication of the *Pentagon Papers,* claiming that national security would be endangered. Final clearance for publication was eventually granted by the U.S. Supreme Court. The prolonged series of revelations associated with Watergate, and subsequent Congressional hearings into illegal actions by Nixon Administration officials, were accompanied by bitter disputes about whether the revelations were damaging to the government. Increased investigative journalism led to a counter-attack on media reports by officials in both political parties.[4] A series of media scandals were revealed during the 1970s including the finding by *The Washington Post* that one of its reporters, Janet Cooke, had fabricated information for a drug story that won a Pulitzer Prize (National News Council, 1981). In the 1980s, well-organized attempts by the Reagan administration to manipulate the press also called into question the media's role in reporting public affairs (Hertsgaard, 1988).

These polarizing trends continued with bitter partisan wrangling over the impeachment of Bill Clinton following the Monica Lewinski scandal. The role of the media in covering the scandal became a focal point for partisans on all sides (Busby, 2001). This was followed by a series of media scandals, starting with the revelation that *New York Times* reporter Jayson Blair had plagiarized and fabricated elements of his stories. Then came the Iraq War and charges that the press had failed to serve its watchdog role in the lead up to the war or that it had shown disloyalty during time of war, depending upon partisan perspective (Katovsky & Carlson, 2003).

Media Credibility

A series of popular books and articles in news magazines about the credibility of the news media appeared in the late 1970s and early 1980s (e.g., Goldstein, 1985). Goldstein's book described the effects of political power struggles and a clash of ideas about the role communication should play in society, and described a "news credibility problem" for the mass media. This literature cited public opinion polls (Tillson, 1984), changing circulation and audience patterns, libel judgments (Hunsaker, 1979; Libel Defense Resource Center, 1985), and reader complaints (Griffith, 1983; Henry, 1983; Sanoff, 1981) in their arguments.

The publications created a debate among journalists in the late 1970s and led to a series of credibility studies, this time centered on the credibility of the news media *themselves*. The five most important of these studies were sponsored by The American Society of Newspaper Editors (ASNE; 1985), the Associated Press Managing Editors Association (APNE; 1985), the Gannett Center for Media Studies (Whitney, 1985), The Times-Mirror Company (Times-Mirror, 1986, 1987a, 1987b), and the *Los Angeles Times* media poll (Lewis, n.d.). Several other organizations also published studies about this time (i.e., APME, 1984; American Press Institute [API], 1984).

Gaziano and McGrath (1986), who handled the ASNE study, employed focus groups and polling techniques. The Times-Mirror Company and Gallup conducted focus group studies, following up with polling data. The Times-Mirror completed a series of survey studies. The Gannett Center did an extensive reanalysis of historical credibility studies, including polling data. The *Los Angeles Times* conducted a national poll. The Associated Press managing editors examined discourse data among editors.

Gaziano (1988) summarized the findings from all these studies. She said they generally agreed that: media bias is a public concern; there are frequent complaints about bad news, overdramatization, and sensationalism; media favoritism is an issue; media are out of touch with average citizens and treat ordinary people unfavorably; the public supports coverage of government and public officials; media have higher confidence ratings than other social institutions; and media critics are both the best and least educated, the most and least knowledgeable, the highest and lowest income, and the most and least heavy users of media. She said that journalists are overwhelmingly believed, that people like getting news, and that they think the watchdog role is important.

On the other hand, the studies found that three-fourths of adults have some problem with the media's credibility in general; one-sixth express frustrations with reporter treatment of victims, issues, or social institutions; and media sources, newspapers and television have similar credibility ratings.

In a separate study for ASNE in 1991, researcher Robert O. Wyatt observed that findings revealed a new right—"the right not to be offended" (Wyatt, Neft, & Badger, 1991, p. 21). This finding was consistent with Rodney Smolla's study of the growth in numbers of libel suits. He argued that people now believe that whatever offends them personally should be restricted or prohibited; they believe they have a legal right to protect themselves from offense (Smolla, 1986).

The Times-Mirror study, carried out by the Gallup Organization, suggested that, if credibility is defined as believability, then there is no credibility crisis for the nation's news media, that the public appreciates the press more than it approves of its performance, and that critics are more critical than supporters are supportive.

Shortcomings of Applied Studies

These studies have not been without criticism. Journalists pointed out contradictory findings in polling data even before these studies were undertaken (Greenberg & Roloff, 1974; McCombs & Washington, 1983; Tillson, 1984; Whitney, 1984). Others pointed out "contradictory findings" in the studies themselves ("Inconsistency of Surveys," 1985; Meyer, 1985; Rimmer & Weaver, 1987). The chairman of the APME credibility committee argued that credibility is best understood as a measure of whether the public believes *in* the press rather than whether it *believes* the press (Southerland, 1985).

Academic researchers have challenged data interpretations and questioned the methods employed. Meyer (1985), for example, challenged the interpretation of the data. He argued that it could be interpreted as demonstrating *high* levels of credibility (see also Rimmer & Weaver, 1987). Meyer (1988) also challenged the scaling technique in the ASNE study. He demonstrated a response set pattern generated by the structure of positive and negative scales, generating different factors (dimensions of credibility) by simply altering the positive/negative structure.

This raises fundamental conceptual questions about credibility research. The professionally sponsored research depended on hypotheses based upon the limited effects model. The studies assumed that source or message characteristics could be revealed through polling techniques. These studies asked respondents to rate media credibility and specific media characteristics. The ASNE study factor analyzed scaled responses to operationalizations of source (news media) characteristics.

In short, credibility dimensions had not yet proved stable when the scales measuring them were expanded or altered. Furthermore, evidence points to mediating constructs at work within audiences (e.g., constructions, involvement, familiarity, and cognitive processing).

Measurement was also a problem. The ASNE study used 16 statement scales, 12 of which clustered on a *credibility* dimension. Their factor loadings were used to create a credibility score. Research has shown that expanding or changing the scales alters the numbers and types of factors. A study of credibility literature and professionally sponsored studies identified more than 100 such scalable items (Self, 1988a). The introduction of any additional items would likely alter the ASNE credibility index. Mediating constructs also remained a problem. This study implies that cognitive schema or templates change individual responses in unpredictable ways, depending upon how the questions concerning credibility are asked and the degree (intensity and direction) of involvement in the issue.

The Challenge of Interaction

Two challenges have shifted credibility research in recent years: one theoretical and one technological. The theoretical challenge has focused on the active perceptions (or cognitive mediations) and involvement (or familiarity) of recipients of communication messages. This represents a long line of thought that echoes back at least to the congruence (Osgood & Tannenbaum, 1954) and cognitive dissonance (Festinger, 1957) theories of the 1950s and that has moved forward through structural and systems theories, critical theory, semiotic and language theories, discourse analysis, poststructuralism, and other theories that have destabilized the idea that the recipients of messages are passive and manipulated through strong effects. Credibility, in this context, involves a variety of cognitive mediations posited by approaches such as the *constructivism* advocated by

Delia and associates (Delia, 1976), the *social judgment-involvement approach* (Salmon, 1986), and the *cognitive processing approach* advocated by Stocking and Gross (1989).

Delia (1976) argued that a constructivist viewpoint sees credibility as consisting of "situational constructs." Salmon (1986) pointed out that the social judgment-involvement approach deals with highly involving attitudes regarded as components of self-concept or ego. Stocking and Gross (1989) argued that because journalists themselves see some sources as more credible than others, they engage in categorization processes that create cognitive biases. These category "filters" bias the cognitive processes by which stories are selected and facts reported.

As early as 1965, Sargent reported essential differences in how personal news sources (i.e., other people) were perceived compared to impersonal news sources. When she presented news stories variously attributed to individuals and organizations, she found significant differences in credibility evaluations by respondents rating story credibility for individuals and organizations. Newhagen and Nass (1989) argued that research requiring cross-media comparisons means that respondents employ different levels of analysis—that people compare judgments about the credibility of individuals to judgments about the credibility of organizations. They found evidence supporting this view in the 1985 American Society of Newspaper Editors' study. This research calls into question the validity of much of the cross-media comparative research.

Albert C. Gunther (1988, 1992), following on the work of social judgment theorists (Sherif & Hovland, 1961; Sherif, Sherif, & Nebergall, 1965), conceived that credibility was *relational*. He argued that "involvement" helps explain "a connection between an individual's personal involvement with issues or groups and distrust of media" (Gunther, 1992, p. 150; see also Johnson & Eagly, 1989; Salmon, 1986). Gunther suggested that "a person's involvement in situations, issues, or groups will show the greatest explanatory power" (p. 152). He offered four propositions underlying this approach:

- Media credibility is a receiver assessment, not a source characteristic.
- Audience demographics, proposed as predictors of trust in media, have little theoretical basis and little empirical support.
- Situational factors often outweigh a more general skeptical disposition as predictors of credibility judgments.
- Group involvement will stimulate biased processing, affecting evaluations of messages and sources.

Stamm and Dube (1994) joined Gunther in his critique of studies that define credibility as "a trait possessed by a source or a message; as inherent to the source or message.... The receiver's relationship to the content of the source's message must also be taken into account as something that makes a difference in credibility attributed to a source" (p. 105). They explored "other components" of attitude and their relationship to credibility.[5]

This interest in credibility as a judgment of a recipient also reflects the influence of postmodern critiques of linearity, and structural and poststructural observations about the emergent, situated quality of meaning structures and their impact on credibility (Babcock & Whitehouse, 2005; Proctor, Papasolomou-Doukakis & Proctor, 2001).

Most recently, this shift has been manifest in new approaches to credibility. Flanagin & Metzger (2008) argue that credibility is based in "group and social engagement" that provides endorsements to bestow credibility upon online sources. They suggest that "endorsed credibility in the digital media environment compensates for the relative anonymity of tools like the web.... The means of sharing these assessments can take many forms resulting in several variants of credibility, most notably *conferred, tabulated, reputed,* and *emergent* credibility" (p. 7). They add that digital media "have in many ways shifted the burden of information evaluation from professional gatekeepers to individual information consumers" (p. 9).

More evidence of the invested quality of credibility evaluations is found in a study by Choi, Watt, and Lynch, 2006, who examined cross-media credibility perception of news coverage of the Iraq War. In a survey of 481 online users, they found opponents of the war perceived the Internet as less aligned with a progovernment position and as more credible than did neutrals or supporters of the war. "For the minority partisan group, the diversity of information and views on the war was the main reason for the perception of high credibility of the Internet as a news channel," they wrote. "...As suggested in this study, whenever a salient issue creates a highly partisan split between supporters and opponents, news credibility is both a subjective perception by audiences and a function of their cognitive processing mechanisms, rather than simply an innate quality of news stories or sources themselves" (p. 223).

This concept of endorsed credibility shares some assumptions with more technological approaches to establishing credibility, called trust metrics, within computer networks developed by information systems theorists (e.g., Ziegler & Lausen, 2005). These propagation models "compute quantitative *estimates* of how much trust an agent *a* should accord to its peer *b*, taking into account trust ratings from other persons on the network" (p. 338).

A further step in the direction of an active recipient theory is implied in the work of Shaym Sundar (2008a), who describes the impact of digital "affordances" or technological innovations that offer new opportunities for interactions with digital media. He argues that these affordances cue "heuristics," or mental shortcuts, by which recipients judge the relative credibility of sources available on the Internet. He suggests (Sundar, 2008b) that this process shifts "agency" in creating credibility by empowering the individual self to become the source in the communication process. "When the system allows the self to serve as the source of messages, the communication becomes truly interpersonal," he says (p. 10). He points out that the self, as the active agent in navigating among possible messages, is empowered to generate the pattern that defines the communication message. The self chooses from among the affordances those cues that are meaningful, or heuristic, for its own purposes. He adds, "...the ability to imbue sourcing to users is an artifact of recent technological developments in the area of customization. In particular, it is a direct consequence of interactivity afforded by the interface" (p. 13).

Approaches such as these have established limits to the perceived influence of traditional message sources. For example, Druckman (2001) has argued that "contrary to many portrayals, elites face systematic constraints to using frames to influence and manipulate public opinion" (p. 1042). He conducted an experiment that found that "framing effects may occur, not because elites seek to manipulate citizens, but rather because citizens delegate to credible elites for guidance. In so doing, they choose which frames to follow in a systematic and sensible way" (p. 1052). He adds "that both framing and media priming work largely through deliberative processes where people seek guidance from sources they believe to be credible" (p. 1053). Similarly, Miller and Krosnick (2000) found that

> trust plays a central role in regulating media effects...trust and knowledge appear to moderate agenda setting in much the same way that they moderate priming. This reinforces the notion that agenda setting results partly from a choice by some individuals to make inferences of national problem importance based upon the content of news media coverage. (p. 306)

What has given these theoretical observations about an active recipient some urgency for credibility research has been the arrival of the Internet. A number of online credibility researchers have pointed out that meaning in the online environment emerges from the active construction of source patterns by online users. Online sources often are layered, collaborative, and communal (Metzger et al., 2002). At best they are "murky" and often they are anonymous (Sundar, 2008a). In such an environment, resorting to an Aristotelian notion of source ethos seems less useful than examining the "heuristics," collaborations, and "project motivations" driving the recipient to select the pattern of sources and source cues best suited to his or her purposes.

One area of interest to online researchers has been the impact that reliance on media has had on online credibility. Johnson and Kaye (1998, 2000, 2002, 2004) have conducted a series of studies of this issue. In 1998, they found that among Internet users, online sources were judged more credible than traditional sources. In 2000, they found that reliance on both traditional and online media was the strongest predictor of the credibility of online sources. In 2002, they reported that a greater percentage of respondents judged online media credible in 2000 than in the 1996 presidential campaign. The also found that reliance on traditional media was the best predictor of online credibility. In 2004, they found that among blog users, blogs were judged to be highly credible—more credible than traditional media sources—although respondents rated them higher for depth of information than they did for fairness. The data showed that when users found media in general and online sources in particular, useful—that is, they relied upon them—they also judged them to be credible.

Spiro Kiousis (2001) reported that in data from a cross-sectional study of residents of Austin, Texas, "a marginal association was noted between media use and public perceptions of credibility across all 3 media channels" (newspaper, television, and online news) (p. 381) (see, also, Rimmer & Weaver, 1987). He suggested that "…people may orient themselves to media content that is analogous across media channels, triggering parallel opinions of credibility" (pp. 397–398). "Survey participants seemed to perceive all of the media channels in the same direction, indicating that people probably have an overall perception of news credibility that only slightly fluctuates across media," he wrote (p. 396).

Bucy (2003) also reported a usage effect. In an experimental study of undergraduate students in the weeks immediately following the September 11 terrorist attacks, he found that

> when adults were placed in the telewebbing condition with exposure to both TV and Net news, evaluations of Net news credibility jumped to their highest levels….For students, telewebbing caused perceptions of TV and Net news credibility to increase in relation to the control group, but dip slightly or show no difference compared to other forms of media exposure….similar to the association of media reliance with high credibility evaluations revealed by surveys, audiences seem to regard media they have just used more favorably than media to which they are not exposed. (pp. 257–258)

Another area of concern for online credibility researchers has been identifying technological markers that serve as cues for credibility among users. As indicated above, Sundar (2008b) has suggested that such markers cue heuristic judgments by online users. Walther et al. (2004) factor analyzed results of an intercept survey of 111 individuals who were given Web page mockups and asked to complete a questionnaire about health care information. Using elaboration likelihood theory, they found that domain site cues interact with advertising cues: "…credibility perceptions may not be invariant or stable, but rather are sensitive to topic and context," they wrote (p. 2). Similarly, Wathen and Burkell (2001) have suggested that users pass through three levels to judge credibility: the first deals with surface characteristics of a site (with questions such as: Does this site look professional?); the second deals with the message (source expertise, competence, and credentials); the third deals with the user's cognitive state (Does it match previous knowledge? How badly do I need the information?). They suggest that layering by the recipient renders a judgment about credibility.

Pollach (2005) uses content, linguistic, and discourse analysis to examine "About Us" sections of corporate websites for cues to credibility. She suggests that companies enhance their web sites by permitting "users to make choices about the content they want to be exposed to...." (p. 299). "With high-involvement audiences...the quality of the information matters and they will hardly be convinced by self-congratulatory statements with little information value," she writes (p. 298).

Greer (2003) examined source credibility and advertising cues in a study of college students. She found that "the evaluation of the story credibility was more closely tied to source cues rather than the advertising cues because participants paid so little attention to the ads" (p. 24). However, she added that "Participants who said they were heavy Internet users rated the story as more credible than light Internet users" (p. 25).

Rains (2007) examined the impact of anonymity on perceptions of source credibility online. Drawing from adaptive structuration theory in a study of computer mediated meetings in which participants were permitted to provide anonymous comments, he found that "The anonymous confederate reportedly was less trustworthy, less persuasive, and had less goodwill toward the group," although "anonymity did not differentially affect members' satisfaction with either decisions or perceptions of decision quality" (p. 117).

Gentzkow and Shapiro (2006) created a model of media bias in which firms slant their reports toward the prior beliefs of their customers in order to build a reputation for quality. They suggest that bias "arises as a natural consequence of a firm's desire to build a reputation for accuracy and in spite of the fact that eliminating bias could make all agents in the economy better off" (p. 310). They found that the model predicts that bias will be less severe when consumers receive independent evidence on the true state of the world and that competition between independently owned news outlets can reduce bias.

These studies of source cues in the online environment find that recipients are actively involved in weighing online credibility cues against other cues, against communal assessments, and against the usefulness of communications for individual purposes and projects.

Further Study

This critique points to the significant potential for new research regarding mass media credibility. Credibility remains an undertheorized concept. Many researchers have made assumptions about powerful effects and measured the impact of source characteristics, medium characteristics, and message characteristics assumed to manipulate recipient response. This was evident in the linear assumptions about stimulus and response in the original Hovland studies. It continued to drive more complex dimensional analyses of the many late 20th century studies. However, those studies also revealed wide differences of opinion between journalists and the public about the news media's role and the task of the news report, and the perceived task of the news report was shown to predict which medium people choose for news (Self, 1988c).

Social judgment-involvement theory, constructivism, and cognitive processing theories all suggest that audiences make judgments about media credibility based on schemas or templates from prior experience with the issues and events reported. The literature suggests that journalists, too, make judgments on the basis of such schema (Stocking & Gross, 1989). Issue involvement and partisanship have been shown to influence credibility judgments (Arpan & Raney, 2003; Choi, Watt, & Lynch, 2006; Gunther & Chia, 2001). The literature suggests that public ideas about the task of the news report may itself be changing (Burgoon, Burgoon, & Atkin, 1982; Clark 1979). When concepts of the task of the news report change, they change what the news media are thought to do for their readers. Successful news organizations, however, are slower to adopt new ideas about the task of news than are their customers (Schudson, 1978).

Theories of the social construction of reality exemplified by Tuchman (1978) indicate that professional training and professional associations routinize (provide schema for) the journalist's thinking and behaviors just as surely as social involvement provides templates for ego involvement and cognitive processing by readers or viewers. Weaver and Wilhoit (1986) reported a high degree of professionalism among contemporary journalists when compared to the degree of professionalism in the past.

At the opening of the 21st century new research into the "murky" sourcing on the Internet has reinvigorated observations about how active communities and individuals searching online sites seem to be in structuring credibility when sources are anonymous or so heavily layered that they mask the origins of messages. In such circumstances, recipients choose the cues that are meaningful within the context of their own activities.

This suggests that research into the role of communities, context, and individual goals in information seeking need significantly more study. Such research can help clarify the nature of recipient activity in imputing credibility and can help develop a more stable definition of credibility itself.

Conclusion

This chapter has reviewed how changing concepts of communication change theories and research about a fundamental construct—credibility. The Greek philosophers Plato and Aristotle laid out the fundamental questions. They suggested that credibility might emanate from a confident knowledge of the truth or grow from a communicator's ability to read the needs of the audience.

Modern communication researchers began the systematic empirical study of the issue using a strong-effects model. They have examined source and media characteristics, message characteristics and the familiarity of the message, and audience demographics and credulity.

As the research has proceeded, it has become clear that credibility is an exceedingly complex construct. Researchers have identified many dimensions of source characteristics. They have found that not only manipulating messages changes their credibility, but repeating those messages or offering them to involved recipients alters the messages' believability. They discovered that the audience hearing or viewing a message is active in shaping meaning based upon communal or individual needs and experience.

The interest of politicians and media managers in credibility has driven large-scale media industry studies of credibility. Research suggests that media credibility research needs to take into account the involvement of media users if it is to make sense of public perceptions of media credibility.

The development of the Internet and other interactive media forms has shifted the focus of credibility research. Layered, anonymous, and "murky" sourcing has encouraged research on social and collaborative endorsement cues, technological markers and heuristic strategies to signal credible information. Individual purposes, projects, and motivation have been shown to influence evaluations of credibility. Cultural and textual theories have yet to be brought to bear on the problem. Much needs to be done to create a coherent theoretical foundation and stable definition for this familiar and yet strangely illusive concept called credibility. It should provide many more opportunities for fruitful study.

Notes

1. For a linear overview of the nature of these early findings about credibility, see Erskine (1970–1971).
2. Factor analysis is a *statistical technique* that seeks to identify dimensions or factors of scales that "group together" in "semantic space" whereby scale items or statements are created by a researcher and then

given to respondents and then analyzed for their dimensionality. Q-Methodology (e.g., Q-Sort) is a *measurement technique* that takes a large number of potential scale items and asks respondents to sort them into piles (usually 11). The items are then analyzed and a scale is created using items from all or most groups. For more information on each, see Kerlinger (1986). Factor analysis has been conducted in media studies of source credibility. See, for example, Salwen (1987, 1992) and Mosier and Ahlgren (1981).

3. For more on this line of research, see Bacon (1979), Begg, Armour, and Kerr (1985), and Pratkanis, Greenwald, Leippe, and Baumgardner (1988).

4. For more on the relational approach, see Vallone, Ross, and Lepper (1985) on perceptions of media bias among partisans on Mideast issues, or Perloff (1989) on the "Third Person Effect." Chaffee (1982) has also argued that credibility is situational or relational.

5. For a sampling of this argument, see Sigal (1973), Porter (1976), and Demac (1988).

REFERENCES

Al-Makaty, S. S., Boyd, D. A., & Van Turbergen, G. N. (1994). Source credibility during the Gulf War: A Q-study of rural and urban Saudi Arabian citizens. *Journalism Quarterly, 71,* 55–63.

American Press Institute. (1984). *The public perception of newspapers: Examining credibility.* Reston, VA: Author.

American Society of Newspaper Editors. (1985). *Newspaper credibility: Building reader trust.* Washington D.C.: Author.

American Society of Newspaper Editors. (1986). *Newspaper credibility: 206 practical approaches to heighten reader trust.* Washington, D.C.: Author.

Anderson, K. & Clevenger, T. (1963). A summary of experimental research in ethos. *Speech Monographs, 30,* 77.

Aristotle. (1952). *The works of Aristotle II—Rhetoric* (W. Rhys Robers, Trans.). Chicago: Encyclopedia Britannica.

Arpan, L., & Raney, A. (2003). An experimental investigation of news source and the hostile media effect. *Journalism and Mass Communication Quarterly, 80*(2), 265–281.

Associated Press Managing Editors Association. (1984). *Credibility.* Miami: Author.

Associated Press Managing Editors Association. (1985). *Journalists and readers: Bridging the credibility gap.* San Francisco: Author.

Babcock, W.,. & Whitehouse, V. (2005). Celebrity as a postmodern phenomenon, ethical crisis for democracy, and media nightmare. *Journal of Mass Media Ethics, 20*(2&3), 176–191.

Bacon, F. T. (1979). Credibility of repeated statements: Memory for trivia. *Journal of Experimental Psychology, 5,* 241–252.

Baxter, L. A., & Bittner, J. R. (1974). High school and college perceptions of media credibility. *Journalism Quarterly, 57,* 517–520.

Becker, L. B., Cobbey, R. E., & Sobowale, I. (1978). Public support for the press. *Journalism Quarterly, 55,* 421–430.

Begg, I. M., Anas, A., & Farinacci, S. (1992). Dissociation of processes in belief: Source recollection, statement familiarity, and the illusion of truth. *Journal of Experimental Psychology, 121,* 446–458.

Begg, I., Armour, V., & Kerr, T. (1985). On believing what we remember. *Canadian Journal of Behavioural Science, 17,* 199–214.

Berlo, D. K., Lemert, J. B., & Mertz, R. J. (1969). Dimensions for evaluating the acceptability of message sources. *Public Opinion Quarterly, 33,* 563–576.

Boehm, L. E. (1994). The validity effect: A search for mediating variables. *Personality and Social Psychology Bulletin, 20,* 285–293.

Brownlow, S. (1992). Seeing is believing: Facial appearance, credibility, and attitude change. *Journal of Nonverbal Behavior, 16,* 101–115.

Bucy, E. P. (2003). Media credibility reconsidered: Synergy effects between on-air and online news, *Journalism and Mass Communication Quarterly, 80*(2), 247–264.

Burgoon, J. K., Burgoon, M., & Atkin, C. K. (1982, May). *What is news? Who decides? And how? A preliminary report*. Washington, D.C.: American Society of Newspaper Editors.

Burgoon, M., Burgoon, J., & Wilkinson, M. (1981). Newspaper image and evaluation. *Journalism Quarterly, 58*, 411–419, 433.

Busby, R. (2001). *Defending the American presidency: Clinton and the Lewinski scandal*. New York: Palgrave.

Cantril, H. (1951). *Public opinion, 1935–1946*. Princeton, NJ: Princeton University Press.

Carter, R. F., & Greenberg, B. S. (1965). Newspapers or television: Which do you believe? *Journalism Quarterly, 42*, 29–34.

Chaffee, S. H. (1982). Mass media and interpersonal channels: Competitive, convergent, or complementary? In G. Gumpert & R. Cathcart (Eds.), *Inter/media: Interpersonal communication in a media world* (pp. 57–77). New York: Oxford University Press.

Choi, J., Watt, J. H., & Lynch, M. (2006). Perceptions of news credibility about the war in Iraq: Why war opponents perceived the Internet as the most credible medium. *Journal of Computer-Mediated Communication, 12*, 209–229.

Clark, R. (1979). *Changing needs of changing readers*. Charlotte, NC: American Society of Newspaper Editors.

Delia, J. G. (1976). A constructivist analysis of the concept of credibility. *Quarterly Journal of Speech, 62*, 361–375.

Demac, D. A. (1988) *Liberty denied: The current rise of censorship in America*. New York: PEN American Center.

Dennis, E. (1986, March 28). *The politics of media credibility*. Lecture delivered at Journalism Ethics Institute, Washington and Lee University, Lexington, VA.

Druckman, J. N. (2001). On the limits of framing effects: Who can frame? *Journal of Politics, 63*(4), 1041–1067.

Erskine, H. G. (1970–1971). The polls: Opinion of the news media. *Public Opinion Quarterly, 34*, 630–634.

Festinger, L. (1957). *A theory of cognitive dissonance*. Evanston, IL: Row Peterson.

Fico, F.., Richardson, J. D., & Edwards, S. M. (2004). Influence of story structure on perceived story bias and news organization credibility. *Mass Communication & Society, 7*(3), 301–318.

Flanagin, A., & Metzger, M. (2001, January). Internet use in the contemporary media environment, *Human Communication Research, 27*, 153–181.

Flanagin, A. J., & Metzger, M. J. (2008). Digital media and youth: Unparalleled opportunity and unprecedented responsibility. In M. Metzger & A. Flanagin (Eds.), *Digital media, youth, and credibility* (pp. 5–27). Cambridge, MA: MIT Press.

Gaziano, C. (1988). How credible is the credibility crisis? *Journalism Quarterly, 65*, 267–278.

Gaziano, C., & McGrath, K. (1986). Measuring the concept of credibility. *Journalism Quarterly, 63*, 451–462.

Gentzkow, M., & Shapiro, J. M. (2006). Media bias and reputation, *The Journal of Political Economy, 114*(2), 280–316.

Goldstein, T. (1985). *The news at any cost: How journalists compromise their ethics to shape the news*. New York: Simon & Schuster.

Graber, D. (1987). Kind pictures and harsh words. In K. L. Schlozman (Ed.), *Elections in America* (pp. 115–141). Boston: Allen & Unwin.

Greenberg, B. S. (1966). Media use and believability: Some multiple correlates. *Journalism Quarterly, 43*, 665–670, 737.

Greenberg, B. S., & Roloff, M. E. (1974). Mass media credibility: Research results and critical issues. *ANPA News Research Bulletin, 6,*, 20–29.

Greer, J. D. (2003). Evaluating the credibility of online information: A test of source and advertising influence, *Mass Communication & Society, 6*(1), 11–28.

Griffith, T. (1983, May 9). Why readers mistrust newspapers. *Time*, p. 94.

Gunther, A. C. (1988). Attitude extremity and trust in media. *Journalism Quarterly, 65*, 279–287.

Gunther, A. C. (1992). Biased press or biased public? Attitudes toward media coverage of social groups. *Public Opinion Quarterly, 56*, 147–167.

Gunther, A. C., & Chia, S. (2001). Predicting pluralistic ignorance: The hostile media percept and its consequences. *Journalism and Mass Communication Quarterly, 78*(4), 688–701.

Henry, W. A., III. (1983, December 12). Journalism under fire. *Time, 115,* 76–93.

Hertsgaard, M. (1988). *On bended knee: Press relations with Reagan.* New York: Farrar, Straus, Giroux.

Hovland, C. I. (1951). Changes in attitude through communication. *Journal of Abnormal and Social Psychology, 46,* 424–437.

Hovland, C. I., Janis, I. L., & Kelley, H. H. (1953). *Communication and persuasion.* New Haven, CT: Yale University Press.

Hovland, C. I., Lumsdaine, A. A., & Sheffield, F. D. (1949). *Experiments on mass communication.* Princeton, NJ: Princeton University Press.

Hovland, C. I., & Weiss, W. (1951–1952). The influence of source credibility on communication effectiveness. *Public Opinion Quarterly, 15,* 635–650.

Hunsaker, D. (1979). Freedom and responsibility in First Amendment theory: Defamation law and media credibility. *The Quarterly Journal of Speech, 65,* 23–35.

"Inconsistency of surveys." (1985, November 30). *Editor and Publisher,* 118.

Johnson, B. T., & Eagly, A. H. (1989). Effects of involvement on persuasion: A meta analysis. *Psychological Bulletin, 106,* 290–314.

Johnson, T. J., & Kaye, B. K. (1998, Summer). Cruising is believing? Comparing Internet and traditional sources on media credibility measures. *Journalism and Mass Communication Quarterly, 75* (2), 325–340.

Johnson, T. J., & Kaye, B. K. (2000). Using is believing: The influence of reliance on the credibility of online political information among politically interested Internet users. *Journalism and Mass Communication Quarterly, 77*(4), 865–879.

Johnson, T. J., & Kaye, B. K. (2002, Autumn). Webelievability: A path model examining how convenience and reliance predict online credibility. *Journalism and Mass Communication Quarterly, 79*(4), 619–642.

Johnson, T. J., & Kaye, B. K. (2004, Autumn). Wag the blog: How reliance on traditional media and the Internet influence credibility perceptions of weblogs among blog users, *Journalism and Mass Communication Quarterly, 81*(3) , 622–642.

Katovsky, B., & Carlson, T. (2003). *Embedded: The media at war in Iraq.* Guilford, CT: Lyons Press.

Kerlinger, F. N. (1986). *Foundations of behavioral research* (3rd ed.). New York: Holt, Rinehart, & Winston.

Kiousis, S. (2001). Public trust or mistrust? Perceptions of media credibility in the information age. *Mass Communication & Society, 4*(4), 381–403.

Lasswell, H. D., Lerner, D., & Speier, H. (1980). *Propaganda and communication in world history: Vol. 2. Emergence of public opinion in the west.* Honolulu: University Press of Hawaii.

Leamer, L. (1972). *The paper revolutionaries.* New York: Simon & Schuster.

Leathers, D. G. (1992). *Successful nonverbal communications: Principles and applications.* New York: Macmillan.

Lee, R. S. H. (1978). Credibility of newspaper and television news. *Journalism Quarterly, 55,* 282–287.

Lewis, I. A. (1981). *The media: Los Angeles Times Poll no. 46.* Los Angeles: Times-Mirror.

Lewis, I. A. (Director). (n. d.). *Los Angeles Times Poll no. 94.* Los Angeles: Times-Mirror.

Libel Defense Resource Center. (1985, June 30). *LDRC Bulletin, 14.*

Maier, S. R. (2005). Accuracy matters: A cross-market assessment of newspaper error and credibility," *Journalism and Mass Communication Quarterly, 82*(3), 533–551.

McCombs, M. E., & Washington, L. (1983, February). Opinion surveys offer conflicting clues as to how public views press. *Presstime,* 4–9.

McCroskey, J. C. (1966). Scales for the measurement of ethos, *Speech Monographs, 33,* 65–72.

McCroskey, J. C. (1969). A survey of experimental research on the effects of evidence in persuasive communication. *Speech Monographs, 55,* 169–176.

McCroskey, J. C, & Jensen, T. A. (1975). Image of mass media news sources. *Journal of Broadcasting, 19,* 169–180.

Metzger, M. J., Flanagin, A. J., Eyal, K., Lemus, D. R., & McCann, R. M. (2003). Credibility for the 21st century: Integrating perspectives on source, message, and media credibility in the contemporary media environment. In P. J. Kalfleisch (Ed.), *Communication yearbook* (Vol. 27, pp. 293–335). Mahwah, NJ: Erlbaum.

Meyer, P. (1985, July). There's encouraging news about newspapers' credibility, and it's in a surprising location, *Presstime*, 26–27.

Meyer, P. (1988). Defining and measuring credibility of newspapers: Developing an index. *Journalism Quarterly, 65,* 567–574.

Miller, J. M., & Krosnick, J. A. (2000). News media impact on the ingredients of presidential evaluations: Politically knowledgeable citizens are guided by a trusted source. *American Journal of Political Science, 44*(2), 295–309.

Mosier, N. R., & Ahlgren, A. (1981). Credibility of precision journalism. *Journalism Quarterly, 58,* 375–381, 518.

National Advisory Commission on Civil Disorders. (1968). *Report.* New York: Bantam.

National News Council. (1981). *After "Jimmy's World:" Tightening up in editing.* New York: Author.

Newhagen, J., & Nass, C. (1989). Differential criteria for evaluating credibility of newspaper and television news. *Journalism Quarterly, 66,* 277–284.

Osgood, C. E., & Tannenbaum, P. (1954). Attitude change and the principle of congruity. In W. Schramm (Ed.), *Process and effects of mass communication* (pp. 251–260). Urbana: University of Illinois Press.

Perloff, R. M. (1989). Ego-involvement and the third person effect of televised news coverage. *Communication Research, 16,* 236–262.

Pew Research Center. (2000). Internet sapping broadcast news audience: Investors now go online for quotes, advice. Retrieved from http://www.people-press.org/reports. June 11.

Pew Research Center. (June 11, 2006). Online papers modestly boost newspaper readership: Maturing Internet news audience broader than deep. Retrieved June 18, 2008, from http://www.people-press.org/reports

Plato. (1952). *The dialogues of Plato—Phaedrus* (B. Jowett, Trans.). Chicago: Encyclopedia Britannica.

Pollach, I. (2005). Corporate self-presentation on the WWW: Strategies for enhancing usability, credibility and utility. *Corporate Communications, 10*(4), 285–301.

Porter, W. E. (1976) *Assault on the media: The Nixon years.* Ann Arbor: University of Michigan Press.

Powell, F. C., & Wanzenried, J. W. (1992). An empirical test of the Leathers Personal Credibility Scale: Panel responses to the Clinton candidacy. *Perceptual and Motor Skills. 75,* 1255–1261.

Pratkanis, A. R., Greenwald, A., Leippe, M. R., & Baumgardner, M. H. (1988). In search of reliable persuasion effects: The sleeper effect is dead. Long live the sleeper effect. *Journal of Personality & Social Psychology, 54,* 203–218.

Proctor, S., Papasolomou-Doukakis, I., & Proctor, T. (2002). What are television advertisements really trying to tell us? A postmodern perspective, *Journal of Consumer Behaviour, 1*(3), 246–255.

Rains, S. (2007). The impact of anonymity on perceptions of source credibility and influence in computer-mediated group communication: A test of two competing hypotheses. *Communication Research, 34*(1), 100–125.

Rimmer, T., & Weaver, D. (1987). Different questions, different answers? Media use and media credibility. *Journalism Quarterly, 64,* 28–36, 44.

Robinson, M. J. (1987). News media myths and realities: What network news did and didn't do in the 1984 general campaign. In K. L. Schlozman (Ed.), *Elections in America* (pp. 143–170). Boston: Allen & Unwin.

Rogers, E. M. (1994). *A history of communication study.* New York: Free Press.

Roper, B. (1985) *Public attitudes toward television and other media in a time of change.* New York: Television Information Office.

Salmon, C. T. (1986). Perspectives on involvement in consumer and communication research. In B. Dervin & M. Voigt (Eds.), *Progress in communication sciences* (Vol. 7, pp. 243–268). Reading, MA: Ablex.

Salwen, M. B. (1987). Credibility of newspaper opinion polls: Source, source intent and precision. *Journalism Quarterly, 64,* 813–819.

Salwen, M. B. (1992). The influence of source intent: Credibility of a news media health story. *World Communication, 21,* 63–68.

Sanoff, A. P. (1981, June 29). Uneasy press sets out to refurbish its image. *U.S. News and World Report, 91,* 71–72.

Sargent, L. (1965). The dimension of source credibility of television. *Journalism Quarterly, 42,* 35–42.

Schudson, M. (1978). *Discovering the news: A social history of American newspapers*. New York: Basic Books.

Self, C. C. (1988a). *An examination of themes and recommendations about the "news credibility issue*. Paper presented at the regional meeting of the newspaper division of The Association for Education in Journalism and Mass Communication, Tuscaloosa, AL.

Self, C. C. (1988b). A study of news credibility and task perception among journalists in the United States and England. *International Communication Bulletin, 23,* 16–24.

Self, C. C. (1988c). Task of news report as a predictor of choice of medium. *Journalism Quarterly, 65,* 119–125.

Shaw, D. L. (1967). News bias and the telegraph: A study of historical change. *Journalism Quarterly, 44,* 3–12.

Shaw, E. (1973). Media credibility: Taking the measure of the measure. *Journalism Quarterly, 50,* 306–311.

Shaw, E. F. (1976). The popular meaning of media credibility. *ANPA News Research Bulletin, 3,* 1–17.

Sherif, C. W., Sherif, M., & Nebergall, R. E. (1965). *Attitude and attitude change: The social judgment-involvement approach*. Philadelphia: W. B. Saunders.

Sherif, M., & Hovland, C. I. (1961). *Social judgment*. New Haven, CT: Yale University Press.

Sigal, L. V. (1973). *Reporters and officials: The organization and politics of new smoking*. Lexington, MA: D.C. Heath.

Singletary, M. (1976). Components of the credibility of a favorable news source. *Journalism Quarterly, 53,* 316–319.

Slattery, K., & Tiedge, J. T. (1992). The effect of labeling staged video on the credibility of TV news stories. *Journal of Broadcasting & Electronic Media, 36,* 279–286.

Smith, B. L. (1969). The mystifying intellectual history of Harold D. Lasswell. In A. A. Rogow (Ed.), *Politics, personality, and social science in the twentieth century: Essays in honor of Harold D. Lasswell* (pp. 41–105). Chicago: University of Chicago Press.

Smolla, R. A. (1986). *Suing the press*. New York: Oxford University Press.

Southerland, B. (1985, December 5). *Lecture to students in seminar on news credibility*. University of Missouri, Columbia.

Stamm, K., & Dube, R. (1994). The relationship of attitudinal components to trust in media. *Communication Research, 21,* 105–123.

Stephenson, W. (1953). *The study of behavior*. Chicago: University of Chicago Press.

Stocking, S. H., & Gross, P. H. (1989). *How do journalists think? A proposal for the study of cognitive bias in newsmaking*. Indianapolis: ERIC Clearinghouse on Reading and Communication Skills.

Sundar, S. S. (2008a). The MAIN model: A heuristic approach to understanding technology effects on credibility. In M. Metzger & A. Flanagin (Eds.), *Digital media, youth, and credibility* (pp. 72–100). Cambridge, MA: MIT Press.

Sundar, S. S. (2008b). Self as source: Agency and customization in interactive media. In E. Konijn, S. Utz, M. Tanis, & S. Barnes (Eds.), *Mediated interpersonal communication* (pp. 58–74). Mahwah, NJ: Erlbaum.

Sundar, S. S., & Nass, C. (2000). Source orientation in human-computer interaction: Programmer, networker, or independent social actor? *Communication Research, 27*(6), 683–703.

Sundar, S. S., & Nass, C. (2001). Conceptualizing sources in online news. *Journal of Communication, 51*(1), 52–72.

Tillson, J. B. (1984). We're suffering declining confidence in all institutions. *Credibility* (pp. 31–32). Miami: Associated Press Managing Editors Association.

Times-Mirror Company. (1986). *The people and the press (Part I)*. Los Angeles: Author.

Times-Mirror Company. (1987a). *We're interested in what you think. A sampling of a year's letters to the chairman of Times-Mirror (Part II)*. Los Angeles: Author.

Times-Mirror Company. (1987b). *The people and the press (Part III)*. Los Angeles: Author.

Trilling, L. (1965). *Beyond culture: Essays on literature and learning*. New York: Harcourt, Brace, Jovanovich.

Tuchman, G. (1978). *Making news*. New York: The Free Press.

Vallone, R. P., Ross, L., & Lepper, M. R. (1985). The hostile media phenomenon: Biased perceptions and perceptions of media bias in coverage of the Beirut massacre. *Journal of Personality and Social Psychology, 49*, 577–585.

Walther, J. B., Wang, S., & Loh, T. (2004). The effect of top-level domains and advertisements on health web-site credibility. *Journal of Medical Internet Research 6*(3), e24. Retrieved June 18, 2008, from http://www.jmir.org/2004/3/e24/

Wanta, W., & Hu, Y. (1994). The effects of credibility, reliance, and exposure on media agenda-setting: A path analysis model. *Journalism Quarterly, 71*, 90–98.

Wanzenried, J. W., & Powell, F. C. (1993). Source credibility and dimensional stability: A test of the Leathers Personal Credibility Scale using perceptions of three presidential candidates. *Perceptual and Motor Skills, 77*, 403–406.

Wanzenried, J. W., Smith-Howell, D., & Powell, F. C. (1992). Source credibility and presidential campaigns: Governor Clinton and the allegation of marital infidelity. *Psychological Reports, 70*, 992–994.

Wathen, C. N., & Burkell, J. (2001). Believe it or not: Factors influencing credibility on the Web. *Journal of the American Society for Information Science and Technology, 53*(2), 134–144.

Weaver, D. H., & Wilhoit, G. C. (1986). *The American journalist*. Bloomington, IN: Indiana University Press.

West, M. D. (1994). Validating a scale for the measurement of credibility: A covariance structure modeling approach. *Journalism Quarterly, 71*, 158–168.

Westley, B. H., & Severin, W. J. (1964). Some correlates of media credibility. *Journalism Quarterly, 41*, 325–335.

Whitney, D. C. (1984, May). *Attitudes toward the news media: Three publics*. Paper presented to the American Association for Public Opinion Research, Lake Lawn Lodge, Delavan, WI.

Whitney, D. C. (1985). *The media and the people: Americans' experience with the news media: A fifty-year review*. New York: Columbia University, Gannett Center for Media Studies.

Whitney, D. C. (1986, April 8). *The news media and the public trust: The rise and fall of a public issue*. Remarks presented for the McGovern Distinguished Lecture in Journalism, University of Texas at Austin.

Wolfe, T. (1972). *The new nonfiction*. New York: Harper & Row.

Wyatt, R. O., Neft, D., & Badger, D. P. (1991). *Free expression and the American public: A survey commemorating the 200th anniversary of the First Amendment*. Washington, D.C.: American Society of Newspaper Editors.

Ziegler, C.-N., & Lausen, G. (2005). Propagation models for trust and distrust in social networks. *Information Systems Frontiers, 7*(4/5), 337–348.

Suggested Readings

American Society of Newspaper Editors. (1985). *Newspaper credibility: Building reader trust*. Washington, D.C.: Author.

Erskine, H. G. (1970–1971). The polls: Opinion of the news media. *Public Opinion Quarterly, 34*, 630–634.

Flanagin, A. J., & Metzger, M. J. (2008). Digital media and youth: Unparalleled opportunity and unprecedented responsibility. In M. Metzger & A. Flanagin (Eds.), *Digital media, youth, and credibility* (pp. 5–27). Cambridge, MA: MIT Press.

Gunther, A. C. (1992). Biased press or biased public? Attitudes toward media coverage of social groups. *Public Opinion Quarterly, 56*, 147–167

Hovland, C. I., & Weiss, W. (1951–1952). The influence of source credibility on communication effectiveness. *Public Opinion Quarterly, 15*, 635–650.

McCroskey, J. C., & Jenson, T. A. (1975). Image of mass media news sources. *Journal of Broadcasting, 19*, 169–180.

Metzger, M. J., Flanagin, A. J., Eyal, K., Lemus, D. R., & McCann, R. M. (2003). Credibility for the 21st century: Integrating perspectives on source, message, and media credibility in the contemporary media environment. In P. J. Kalfleisch (Ed.), *Communication yearbook* (Vol. 27, pp. 293–335). Mahwah, NJ: Erlbaum.

Meyer, P. (1988). Defining and measuring credibility of newspapers: Developing an index. *Journalism Quarterly, 65,* 567–574.

Powell, F. C., & Wanzenried, J. W. (1992). An empirical test of the Leathers Personal Credibility Scale: Panel responses to the Clinton candidacy. *Perceptual and Motor Skills, 75,* 1255–1261.

Roper, B. (1985). *Public attitudes toward television and other media in a time of change.* New York: Television Information Office.

Salmon, C. T. (1986). Perspectives on involvement in consumer and communication research. In B. Dervin & M. Voigt (Eds.), *Progress in communication sciences* (pp. 243–268). Norwood, NJ: Ablex.

Sundar, S. S. (2008a). The MAIN model: A heuristic approach to understanding technology effects on credibility. In M. Metzger & A. Flanagin (Eds.), *Digital media, youth, and credibility* (pp. 72–100). Cambridge, MA: MIT Press.

Sundar, S. S. (2008b). Self as source: Agency and customization in interactive media. In E. Konijn, S. Utz, M. Tanis, & S. Barnes (Eds.), *Mediated interpersonal communication* (pp. 58–74). Mahwah, NJ: Erlbaum.

Times-Mirror. (1986). *The people and the press* (Part I). Los Angeles: *Times-Mirror.*

Times-Mirror. (1987a). *We're interested in what you think* (Part II). Los Angeles: Times-Mirror.

Times-Mirror. (1987b). *The people and the press* (Part III). Los Angeles: Times-Mirror.

Whitney, D. C. (1985). *The media and the people: Americans' experience with the news media: A fifty-year review.* Gannett Center for Media Studies. New York: Columbia University.

29

POLITICAL COMMUNICATION

Lynda Lee Kaid

Political communication traces its roots to the earliest formal studies of communication. Classical studies from the time of Plato and Aristotle were interested in communication as it affected the political and legal institutions of the day. As a modern field of study, political communication, while incorporating this earlier focus, is an interdisciplinary field embracing concepts from communication, political science, journalism, sociology, psychology, history, and others. Unlike many of the traditional areas of study, political communication reflects communication theory, concern, and research from both mass and human approaches to communication.

Although propaganda studies (Doob, 1950) and early empirical voting behavior studies by sociologists (Berelson, Lazarsfeld, & McPhee, 1954; Lazarsfeld, Berelson, & Gaudet, 1944) can be labeled political communication studies, Nimmo and Sanders (1981) suggest in their seminal *Handbook of Political Communication* that political communication emerged as a distinctly cross-disciplinary field in the 1950s. Many definitions of *political communication* have been advanced, but none has gained universal acceptance. Perhaps the best is the simplest—Chaffee's (1975) offering that political communication is the "role of communication in the political process" (p. 15).

Background and Dimensions of the Discipline

From an emerging concern in the 1950s, through the next decade, political communication evolved slowly. In the early 1970s, however, political communication as a discipline marked several milestones. University courses began to focus on political communication, publications were initiated,[1] and professional recognition quickly followed. Of particular significance was the 1973 founding of the International Communication Association's Political Communication Division. For nearly two decades, this organization served as the major scholarly division devoted to political communication. Later, the American Political Science Association and the National Communication Association also established political communication sections.

During the 1970s and early 1980s, several important books, articles, and resource materials were published, providing researchers with the important background and conceptual information necessary to understand the roots and development of political communication. For instance, Dan Nimmo's *The Political Persuaders* (1970) was an important early text and research resource. The first five volumes of the International Communication Association's *Communication Yearbook* series contained useful bibliographic essays that helped define the area and guide researchers (Jackson-Beeck & Kraus, 1980; Larson & Wiegele, 1979; Mansfield & Weaver, 1982; Nimmo, 1977; Sanders & Kaid, 1978) and were supplemented by subsequent overviews (Johnston, 1990; Kaid & Sanders, 1985).

Bibliographic resources focusing on campaign communication were available in two volumes that provided multidisciplinary citations (Kaid, Sanders, & Hirsch, 1974; Kaid & Wadsworth,

1984). The earliest mainstream resource book was the *Handbook of Political Communication*. Permeating all of these background materials was a preoccupation with political communication from a political campaign or public opinion influence perspective, a viewpoint broadened somewhat by Swanson and Nimmo (1990) in *New Directions in Political Communication*. The most comprehensive current work in the field is represented in the *Handbook of Political Communication Research* (Kaid, 2004) and the *Encyclopedia of Political Communication* (Kaid & Holtz-Bacha, 2008).

In keeping with both the mainstream approaches to political communication and the broadening of the area in new directions, this chapter outlines the dominant approaches and theories that constitute political communication. It then addresses specific topics that have been the recent focus of particular research interest. In each case an effort is made to describe the primary research methods used to pursue each approach and topic.

Approaches, Theories, and Perspectives

Four basic perspectives guide most political communication research: (1) rhetorical, critical, and interpretive approaches (see chapters 15 and 16, this volume); (2) effects research (see chapter 4, this volume); (3) agenda-setting theory (see chapter 7, this volume); and (4) framing perspectives (see chapter 10, this volume). Each shares background theory and research methods with other research traditions.

Rhetorical, Critical, and Interpretive Approaches

Political communication research in the rhetorical (see chapter 16, this volume), critical, and interpretive vein focuses primarily on the source and message aspects of the political communication process. Researchers seek common themes in political messages, analyze the underlying motives of speakers, ferret out strategies and techniques of communication devices, analyze language characteristics and styles, and suggest ways of interpreting language and message variables. The classical roots of the rhetorical/critical approach are well explained by Bruce Gronbeck (2004). Critical theory analysts also fit into this category, although they concentrate more on underlying sociological, structural, and ideological aspects of messages and sources, rather than on individual analysis (Swanson & Nimmo, 1990). The work of European theorist Juergen Habermas (1989) in explaining the significance of communication in the public sphere also fits this perspective.

Many researchers approaching political communication this way concentrate on a particular political message or series of messages. For instance, a mainstay of speech and rhetoric scholars for many years was the analysis of specific political speeches. The political speeches of great orators such as William Jennings Bryan (Sloan, 1965) and Winston Churchill (Underhill, 1966) made good subjects for analysis, as did later performances by John F. Kennedy, Martin Luther King, and the "great communicator," Ronald Reagan. Some of these analyses have been recently organized under the rubric of genre studies, grouping together the analyses of different types of political speeches into categories or genres. For instance, rhetoricians studied a speaking genre called the *apologia* in which the speaker attempts to apologize for some wrongdoing. Edward Kennedy's Chappaquiddick speech is an oft-cited example of this genre. Other researchers follow a simple descriptive or historical path, providing important background and factual information on a particular communication message(s).

It would be misleading to suggest that all such analyses share a common theoretical perspective; many different rhetorical and analytical underpinnings are at play. Such research, however, does share an interpretive philosophy and a humanistic, nonbehavioral approach. It is important to note that most current political communication studies in the rhetorical and interpretive mode have been concerned with modern communication messages, particularly those carried by the mass media. Such studies also proceed from a variety of perspectives.

A particularly interesting category is dramatistic analysis. Generally rooted in Kenneth Burke's analysis of the pentad, analysts interpret political events and messages in terms of dramatistic elements. The work of Nimmo and Combs (1983, 1990), in which they argue that many aspects of politics are experienced as mediated political reality, emanates from this perspective.

Another popular interpretive perspective example is fantasy-theme analysis, advocated by Bormann (1972, 1973) as the way political messages take on meaning and "chain-out" among media audiences. Narrative analysis (Bennett & Edelman, 1985; Fisher, 1985) is another important example of this type of political communication research.

The research methods used to study political communication from the rhetorical and critical perspective are generally qualitative. Some combine basic historical and factual reporting with descriptive and interpretive analysis. Researchers who use these methods are generally trained in rhetorical criticism or in the tenets of a particular approach, such as dramatistic analysis, which is then applied to the particular message(s) or political event(s) under examination. In some cases a quantitative methodology (e.g., content analysis) provides more conclusive and reliable evidence for descriptive findings. Particularly useful is the work of Roderick Hart (1984) who has developed a method of analyzing the verbal style of presidential speaking, demonstrating how the dimensions of activity, certainty, realism, optimism, and communality are represented in presidential communication.

Effects Research

While it is possible to argue that rhetorical and interpretive researchers are implicitly interested in the effects of messages, they offer no evidence beyond their own interpretations that such effects extend to wider publics. Research in the effects paradigm usually offers some type of behavioral or attitudinal evidence for the results attributed to messages. The modern dominance of social science and the behavioral research paradigm in communication should have made effects research important to political communication researchers. Whereas such interests underpinned early voting research, direct effects research was eschewed by many researchers because of a pervasive belief in the "minimal" or "limited effects" model that dominated intellectual thought during the 1960s and early 1970s (Klapper, 1960). Although Klapper's limited effects perspective was itself based on limited evidence, his findings about mass communication effects were widely extended and adopted. By the mid-1970s, however, researchers were discounting the minimal effects model and reasserting the usefulness of direct effects research (Chisman, 1976; Kaid & Sanders, 1978; Kraus & Davis, 1976).

Examples of direct effects political communication research have been more apparent in the last three decades. A leading contributor to this perspective has been research on the effects of political advertising (Kaid, 1981, 2004; Kaid & Holtz-Bacha, 2006). Research on the short- and long-term effects of political media messages on the formation of candidate images has also been important. Other types of direct effects research looked for more longitudinal effects of media and messages by focusing on political socialization (Atkin, 1975; Connell, 1987), the spiral of silence effect (Noelle-Neumann, 1974, 1977, 1984; Noelle-Neumann & Peterson, 2004; see also chapter 11, this volume), or media exposure or attention (Reese & Miller, 1981). Modern effects researchers, however, are not simply blind repeaters of the mistakes of early "hypodermic needle" or "bullet theory" proponents; contemporary effects research acknowledges multiple causes and effects. They readily accept the notion that a given channel or message effect may be related to many intervening variables of source, situation, and receiver.

Another perspective on effects research is exemplified by the uses and gratifications approach. The contemporary uses and gratifications perspective received its major thrust and testing in the British political campaign settings of the 1960s (Blumler & McQuail, 1969). Although the intellectual roots of this model can be traced back decades earlier (McLeod & Becker, 1981), Blumler and his colleagues developed a method for identifying the reasons why audiences watched or avoided campaign programs on television. Early and subsequent research focused on an active audience. Unlike the passive audience myth of early direct effects research, uses and gratifications research posits that audience members have expectations about communication they receive, resulting in gratifications that are sought and received—or avoided (see Katz, Blumler, & Gurevitch, 1973, and chapter 10, this volume, for more on uses and gratifications).

In political communication, these ideas have been applied to suggest that different types of communication messages perform different types of functions for voters. For instance, voters might expect to use news media (Mendelsohn & O'Keefe, 1976) to serve a surveillance function (to keep up with what is happening in the campaign, to get to know more about the issues or candidates) or they might attend a campaign rally to participate in the campaign's excitement (Sanders & Kaid, 1981).

Effects researchers employ a variety of methods to seek answers to political communication outcomes. The most common methods are probably experiments and surveys. With experimental methods researchers can identify specific variable effects. For instance, Robinson (1976) was able to use experimental methods to establish that viewing the television documentary *The Selling of the Pentagon* affected viewer beliefs about the military system and, in combination with survey research results, was able to suggest that television viewing might create "political malaise." Mitchell McKinney and his colleagues have also used multiple methodological approaches (surveys, experiments, and focus groups) to demonstrate the effects of presidential debates (Kaid, McKinney, & Tedesco, 2000; McKinney, 2005; McKinney, Dudash, & Hodgkinson, 2003). Surveys and polls taken after televised presidential debates have been used to provide evidence not only of "who won and who lost," but also about the types of effects such debates might have on viewer attitudes and beliefs about issues and candidate images.

Agenda-Setting

Agenda-setting research might be considered a subcomponent of effects research, advocating a cognitive effect of the media. However, because it has been such an influential approach in political and mass communication research, it is considered separately. Agenda-setting research posits the notion, based on Cohen's (1963) assertion, that the media do not tell us what to *think*, but what to *think about*.

McCombs and Shaw (1972) first tested the agenda-setting principle during the 1968 presidential campaign and provided evidence that the agenda of issues communicated by the media became the agenda of issues salient to voters. This research and the subsequent efforts inspired by it (Protess & McCombs, 1991; Weaver, McCombs, & Shaw, 2004) rejuvenated media effects research, establishing that the media did, indeed, have significant effects and that it was possible to identify those effects and the contingent conditions related to them (McCombs, 1976; Weaver, 1987; see chapter 7, this volume for more details).

Agenda-setting is a good example of a research approach that combines different methodologies. Agenda-setting researchers typically use content analysis to measure the issue content of media messages (i.e., media issue agenda) and survey research to measure public issue agendas (i.e., the public issue agenda). These two agendas are then statistically correlated to reveal the level of association between the media issue agenda and the public issue agenda.

Framing

Framing theory is concerned with how the media present information to an audience and how the selection of one method or content of presentation over another affects how an audience perceives a person, event, or issue. Several conceptualizations of framing have been offered by scholars. Tankard, Handerson, Silberman, Bliss, and Ghanem (1991) have called a frame the "central organizing idea for news content that supplies context and suggests what the issue is using selection, emphasis, exclusion, and elaboration" (p. 3). Gamson and Modigliani (1987) refer to a frame as "the central organizing idea or story line that provides meaning to an unfolding strip of events." (p. 143). Entman (1993) suggests that "to frame is to select some aspects of a perceived reality and make them more salient in a communicating text" (p. 52).

Thus, when the media decide to discuss some elements of a story and leave other aspects unremarked, the media are determining how the audience will interpret the event or person upon which the story focuses. For instance, if a reporter discusses a new weather warning system in terms of its high price and extensive resource requirements, the audience is likely to interpret the story in this economic sense, rather than focusing on the potential of the warning device to save lives. Framing can mean many different things, but researchers have developed a list of "generic frames" that seem to be repeated in many news situations. These include a (1) conflict frame; (2) human interest frame; (3) economic consequences frame; (4) morality frame; and (5) responsibility frame (Semetko & Valkenburg, 2000). A frame can also be analyzed in terms of its valence, whether it presents an idea in a positive or negative construction (DeVreese & Boomgaarden, 2003). Other researchers distinguish between episodic frames which focus on specific events or happenings and thematic frames which relate to broader, contextual circumstances (Iyengar & Simon, 1993) and between substantive frames which provide extensive depth and detailed information and ambiguous frames which are vague and lacking in specificity (Williams & Kaid, 2006).

Agenda-setting researchers have suggested that framing can be thought of as "second-level agenda-setting" (Weaver, McCombs, & Shaw, 2004) in that framing is merely a discussion of the various attributes of issues or persons. However, Scheufele (1999) argues convincingly that framing has more to do with perceived importance invested in an idea by framing, rather than its salience or accessibility as determined by agenda-setting. Scheufele also makes a strong case for considering audience frames as well as media frames.

Methodologically, framing research is still a developing area. Most commonly, framing research begins with a content analysis that identifies recurring or generic frames in media presentations. Experimental studies have also been used to test the effects on audiences of different types of frames presented in the media.

Selected Topics in Political Communication

The discussion of major theoretical thrusts offers a hint of the topics that characterize political communication. Because political communication is broad and interdisciplinary, it is not possible to provide a comprehensive analysis or listing of topics. The areas discussed illustrate mainstream lines of research and methodologies.

Media Coverage of Political Campaigns and Events

How the mass media cover political campaigns and major political events is a dominant line of political communication inquiry and has been approached from many different perspectives. The overarching questions being asked here include: How are the media covering campaigns and events? What are the characteristics of such coverage? Is the coverage biased in any way? How does this coverage affect public perceptions of politics?

The first three questions are media content questions. They are generally answered by content analysis. Thus, researchers have investigated how the news media have covered political campaigns, concluding that for both newspapers and television the coverage is more focused on "horserace" journalism, concentrating on images over substantive issues (Graber, 1976, 2005; Farnsworth & Lichter, 2006; Patterson, 1993; Patterson & McClure, 1976). Other studies concern questions pertaining to media bias in coverage (i.e., do the media exhibit favoritism in their selection and presentation of political candidates, issues, or events?). Here the results have been mixed and less certain: some researchers found political bias, while others find coverage differences more attributable to the structural characteristics of the media (Farnsworth & Lichter, 2006; Frank, 1973; Hofstetter, 1976).

The most prevalent criticism of this research vein has been that the categories used to analyze content do not fully tap the message content conveyed by newspaper and television stories about campaigns. Early criticisms were particularly valid in pointing to the lack of attention to nonverbal messages and the visual aspects of television coverage. Although efforts have been made to address these concerns, content analyses of media coverage still suffer from these problems.

Media coverage is one area of political communication where researchers have clearly stepped past the voter or campaign paradigm. Many researchers have examined media coverage of noncampaign political events and public affairs happenings (Paletz & Entman, 1981), and even crisis events and coverage of policy issues. For example, Nimmo and Combs's analyses of crisis events and their detailing of mediated politics apply a dramatic perspective to many noncampaign political events (Nimmo & Combs, 1983, 1985, 1990). Other researchers have considered the role of press coverage of the president in noncampaign times (Foote, 1990) and of Congress and the Supreme Court (see Johnston, 1990, for a review of additional media coverage areas, including cartoons and editorials, coverage of opinion polls, and international news flow). A number of media coverage studies have focused on how the media convey the Iraq war and terrorism (Aday, Cluverius, & Livingston, 2005; Bucy, 2003; Norris, Kern, & Just, 2003).

While the overwhelming amount of research on news coverage has been devoted to analyses of content and its characteristics, and are thus primarily descriptive or interpretive in nature, some researchers employed survey and experimental methods to tie media coverage to public perceptions. Agenda-setting research is perhaps the best known example of the combination of media content analyses with public opinion surveys, establishing a crucial link between what the media cover and what people judge to be important. Chaffee, Zhao, and Leshner (1994) offered a helpful review of research linking media exposure to public campaign knowledge levels. A large body of research (primarily survey research) concerns the relationship between media use/ exposure/attention/dependency and political attitudes, knowledge levels, evaluations of political leaders, and levels of political cynicism/efficacy/alienation. Iyengar, Peters, and Kinder (1982) demonstrated experimentally that television news can have an impact on political beliefs. Kaid, Downs, and Ragan (1990) used experimental methods to show that the 1988 encounter between President George Bush and Dan Rather on the *CBS Evening News* affected viewer images of both the politician and the news commentator. Neuman, Just, and Crigler (1992) employed a combination of experimental, survey, content analysis, and in-depth interview methods to examine media effects on political knowledge.

Political Debates

Because political debating with its expected interchange of competing ideas is often seen as the epitome of the democratic process, it has been popular with political communication researchers.

While early rhetorical scholars analyzed the historic Lincoln–Douglas debates, modern research-ers have concentrated on debates carried via electronic media. Since the first presidential debates in 1960 between Kennedy and Nixon, such encounters have fascinated political communication researchers. Sidney Kraus's *The Great Debates* (1962) remains a classic collection in political communication. It was not until the Federal Communication Commission reinterpreted the Equal Time Provision, however, that debates began to proliferate in the American political sys-tem.[2] In 1960 Congress voted to suspend the Equal Time Provision to allow the Kennedy–Nixon debates. Before the 1976 election, the FCC interpreted the Equal Time Provision to allow the media to cover debates as bona fide news events, thereby eliminating the need to open debates to every legally qualified candidate for the presidency.

Presidential debates are now organized and sponsored by the nonpartisan Commission on Presidential Debates. Researchers examine political debates from multiple angles, including analyses of rhetorical arguments and styles, presentations of specific issues, candidate images conveyed, and effects on voter learning, image evaluations, and voting decisions. Researchers have also now considered the effects of different formats, such as the Town Hall Format where citizens, instead of journalists, ask the questions.

Good surveys of the research on political debates have followed the 1960 (Katz & Feldman, 1962) and 1976 (Sears & Chaffee, 1979) debates, and McKinney and Carlin (2004) have provided a comprehensive survey of research from a variety of viewpoints. Media coverage of debates has been approached from many methodological standpoints, most commonly rhetorical analysis, content analysis, focus groups, experiments, and survey research.

Political Advertising

No area of political communication has achieved more prominence in recent years than the study of political advertising. Researchers in political communication recognize that political advertising, particularly on television, is the major form of communication between candidates and voters, constituting the overwhelming majority of campaign budgets in high-level races. Early research provided evidence that television ads were effective in overcoming selective expo-sure, influenced candidate images, conveyed issue information, had more effect on voter knowl-edge levels than did television news, and sometimes influenced voting behavior (Kaid, 1981).

A proliferation of content analysis studies in the 1980s and early 1990s demonstrated that political advertising more often contained issue information than image information (Joslyn, 1980; Kaid & Johnston, 1991) and that there were identifiable video styles for candidate advertis-ing (Kaid & Johnston, 2001). Several researchers provided important historical and descriptive analyses of political advertising (Diamond & Bates, 1984; Jamieson, 1996; West, 2005). Par-ticularly useful is the series of descriptive and analytical accounts of presidential advertising by Patrick Devlin (1973–1974, 1977, 1981, 1987, 1989, 1993, 1997, 2001, 2005).

Great strides have also been made in identifying experimentally specific effects from political television ads. Political television advertising research often more closely follows effects theories than do other avenues of political communication research. Thus, political advertising research-ers have demonstrated the superiority of some types of ads over others (i.e., positive vs. negative ads, image vs. issue ads) and explicated the conditions under which televised ads may be success-ful in influencing candidate images, voter issue awareness, or vote likelihood (e.g., Biocca, 1991; Kaid, 1997, 2001, 2002; Kaid, Nimmo, & Sanders, 1986; Kaid & Sanders, 1978). Survey research has been less successful in obtaining definitive effects from political advertising exposure or attention (Chaffee et al., 1994).

Negative advertising is an increasingly salient topic in political advertising research. Content analysis has demonstrated that negative advertising comprised about one third of presidential ads between 1968 and 1988 (Kaid & Johnston, 1991) but reached new levels in 1992 when Clinton's rate of negative advertising reached the highest level ever in a presidential campaign—69 percent of Clinton ads were negative (Kaid, 1994). Negative advertising has received descriptive coverage as a genre by Johnston-Cartee and Copeland (1991) who outlined different types and strategies of negative advertising. Impressive experimental work spearheaded by Garramone also demonstrated that negative ads, although sometimes backfiring, can decrease an opponent's image evaluation, be offset by rebuttal ads, and are particularly effective when sponsored by a third party or independent group (Garramone, 1984, 1985; Roddy & Garramone, 1988). The increased use of negative political ads has also renewed interest in political advertising ethics and in the uses of technology to create potentially misleading and distorted ads (Kaid, 1991, 1993).

Relatively new to political advertising research are combined studies of media coverage and political advertising effects. As television advertising's campaign dominance has grown, news media have realized that they must cover the ads "as news" to capture the major streams of campaign dialogue. Consequently, the newspaper and television media have engaged in "ad watches" in which the news media attempt to analyze, interpret, and evaluate campaign advertising. Television news coverage of political ads has become an important aspect of political advertising (West, 2005), increasing dramatically between 1972 and 1988 (Kaid, Gobetz, Garner, Leland, & Scott, 1993). Such ad watches are now receiving attention from experimental researchers who have shown that the ad watches may affect how voters react to particular ads and candidates (Cappella & Jamieson, 1994; McKinnon & Kaid, 1999; Pfau & Louden, 1994).

Political Rhetoric

Like news coverage, debates, and political advertising, studies of political speaking and language research generally revolve around either message analysis or effects analysis. Rhetorical critics often analyze the content of particular speakers or speeches (or public utterances in any form through any channel). They might examine collections of speeches on particular topics. For instance, Richard Nixon's resignation speech or Clinton's inaugural address might be analyzed, or speeches by a number of political leaders on civil rights issues or health care could be grouped together for analysis. Generally, this research utilizes rhetorical, critical, or interpretive perspectives, and a qualitative approach. However, some researchers have made interesting contributions by applying more quantitative or combinations of quantitative and qualitative methodologies. An outstanding example is the work of Roderick Hart, who developed a computerized content analysis system (DICTION) and applied it to presidential speeches beginning with Truman (Hart, 1984). Hart's research explicated the "verbal style" of the presidency. Analyses of political language and its implications take on other forms. Conversation analysis looked at political messages, and Murray Edelman's (1964, 1988) analyses of symbolic language in politics are landmarks.

Researchers concerned with measuring the effects of political speaking often conduct experimental or survey studies to determine whether a particular speech or set of speeches affect public opinion or actions. For instance, polling organizations often conduct surveys after a major presidential speech to see how it affected the president's approval ratings. Such studies may combine effects concerns with other theoretical perspectives, as did Sanders and Kaid (1981) who employed a field experiment to measure changes in candidate image resulting from speeches of presidential primary candidates (effects) and how audiences used the candidate appearances to fulfill needs such as surveillance, vote guidance, and excitement (uses and gratifications).

New Research Directions and Methodologies

Political communication has grown dramatically in the past few decades. The theoretical perspectives and selected topics represent some of the major areas of inquiry that characterize the field. Many other topics are evolving. Great strides are being made in political communication study concerning interpersonal communication, group decision making within political institutions, media and political ethics, pragmatic politics, and gender issues.

One of the most significant new directions in political communication is interest in cross-cultural research. Gurevitch and Blumler (1990), in calling for more such research, remarked that "the practices and ideologies of the American political communication industry are taking hold worldwide" (p. 311). Researchers have heeded the call and begun to broaden their perspectives, looking at the transference of political models and theories across political systems. For instance, agenda-setting has been applied to elections in Britain (Semetko, Blumler, Gurevitch, & Weaver, 1991) and Germany (Schoenbach & Semetko, 1992). A research team of French and American scholars applied multiple theoretical and methodological perspectives to compare the 1988 French and American presidential campaigns (Kaid, Gerstlé, & Sanders, 1991). Comparisons have been made of political advertising content similarities in France, Germany, the United States, Italy, Israel, and Britain (Kaid & Holtz-Bacha, 1995, 2006). Hardt (1988) has called for recognition of cultural and critical theory concerns in such work. The evolution of new democratic systems in Eastern and Central Europe has made this even more important.

Other important new directions are encompassed by studies of the role of the Internet in political communication. The sweeping changes in campaign and government communication spurred by the Web have increased citizen access to information and provided new ways for the audience to interact directly with political candidates and leaders (Foot & Schneider, 2006; Oates, Owen, & Gibson, 2006; Williams & Tedesco, 2006). Researchers are studying how blogging, podcasting, YouTube, FaceBook, and many other new technologies are affecting political campaigns and the political process (Trammell, Williams, Postelnicu, & Landreville, 2006; Tremayne, 2006).

As new directions of political communication research develop, research methods and techniques are maturing and diversifying. Certainly traditional methodological approaches such as rhetorical/interpretive analysis, content analysis, survey research, and experimental methods remain the mainstays of political communication research. However, new technologies are being applied: Computer and video technology and the Internet have made it possible to conduct experimental tests in which audience responses to political messages are measured every second, keyed to exact points in video message content; sophisticated focus group techniques have been developed for political message analysis; interactive media techniques are proliferating; and physiological measures are being applied in innovative ways.

There can be no doubt that communication, in all its forms and channels, plays a major role in how democratic systems are formed, in how they govern, and in how their publics respond. Political communication theory and research must therefore retain a preeminent place in communication study.

Sample Political Communication Research Project

With interest in political advertising—particularly negative political advertising—at the forefront of political communication today, an interesting research project might measure the comparative effectiveness of negative and positive ads across different channels of communication (print, radio, television, and Internet media). A theoretical argument could be developed from the literature on effects of positive and negative ads (Biocca, 1991) and on channel variables

Table 29.1   2 × 4 Factorial Design

| | Advertisement Type | |
Medium	Positive	Negative
Print		
Radio		
Television		
Internet		

(Cohen, 1976; Kaid, 2002; Kaid & Postelnicu, 2005; McKinnon, Tedesco, & Kaid, 1993), resulting in a possible hypothesis that negative ads are more effective on television, and positive ads are more effective on the Internet. An experimental study could be designed using a 2 × 4 factorial design depicted in Table 29.1.

Stimulus materials could be prepared in the form of political ads with similar content but altered to be positive or negative and to be presented via the print, radio, Internet, or television media. This would result in eight political spots to serve as the stimulus materials for the experiment: negative spot in print, negative spot on radio, negative spot on television, negative spot on the Internet, positive spot in print, positive spot on radio, positive spot on television, and positive spot on the Internet. Each could be produced either by adapting spots from real political campaigns, or the researcher could create the spots using realistic production techniques in a television studio or with computer-aided video technology. In either case, the candidate would be the same in each spot.

The researcher would then develop measurement techniques for the study, perhaps a series of measures to assess audience reactions to or recall of the candidate in the spots to determine if issue or image information is learned or has an effect on vote likelihood. With the stimulus materials prepared and the measurement device or questionnaire constructed, the researcher would then need to recruit participants for the experiment. Once a participant pool has been identified, the researcher would randomly assign participants to each of the eight cells in the experiment. Each cell would watch the spot appropriate for that cell and fill out the questionnaire developed to measure reactions.

Following data gathering, the researcher would analyze the data to determine if the hypotheses were supported. Two-way analysis of variance would be an appropriate technique here, allowing the researcher to determine if there are main effects (for medium and for ad type) and if there are interaction effects between medium and ad type. Depending on the outcome of the research project, the researcher might be able to advance the current level of knowledge about the effects of medium variables as well as positive and negative ads.

Summary

Political communication is an interdisciplinary field of study that has grown substantially in the past few decades. The major theories and approaches to the subdiscipline of political communication include rhetorical/critical/interpretive work, effects research, agenda-setting theories, and uses and gratifications approaches. Among the most important topics currently considered by political communication researchers are media coverage of political campaigns and events, political debates, political advertising, and political rhetoric. Political communication researchers look at these topics from a wide variety of perspectives, ranging from qualitative methods that are critical and interpretive to quantitative methods such as content analysis, experimental design, and survey research.

Notes

1. Of particular interest was *Political Communication Review,* sponsored by the Political Communication Division of the International Communication Association from 1975 through 1991. In 1993, this publication was incorporated, along with *Political Communication and Persuasion,* into a new journal, *Political Communication,* co-sponsored by the political communication divisions of the International Communication Association and the American Political Science Association.
2. Starting in 1976, there has been some form of presidential debate(s) in each presidential election. These televised spectacles are common in presidential primaries and in primary and general election campaigns at virtually every election level—even in local races.

References

Aday, S., Cluverius, J., & Livingston, S. (2005). As goes the statue, so goes the war: The emergence of the victory frame in television coverage of the Iraq war. *Journal of Broadcasting & Electronic Media, 49*(3), 314–331.

Atkin, C. (1975). Communication and political socialization. *Political Communication Review, 1,* 2–6

Bennett, W. L., & Edelman, M. (1985). Toward a new political narrative. *Journal of Communication, 55,* 156–171.

Berelson, B. R., Lazarsfeld, P. F., & McPhee, W. N. (1954). *Voting.* Chicago: University of Chicago Press.

Biocca, F., (Ed.). (1991). *Television and political advertising* (Vols. 1–2). Hillsdale, NJ: Erlbaum.

Blumler, J. G., & McQuail, D. (1969). *Television in politics.* Chicago: University of Chicago Press.

Bormann, E. G. (1972). Fantasy and rhetorical vision: The rhetorical criticism of social reality. *Quarterly Journal of Speech, 58,* 396–407.

Bormann, E. G. (1973). The Eagleton affair: A fantasy theme analysis. *Quarterly Journal of Speech, 59,* 143–159.

Bucy, E. P. (2003). Emotion, presidential communication, and traumatic news: Processing the World Trade Center attacks. *The Harvard International Journal of Press/Politics, 8*(4), 76–96.

Cappella, J. N., & Jamieson, K. H. (1994). Broadcast adwatch effects: A field experiment. *Communication Research, 21,* 342–365.

Chaffee, S. (Ed.). (1975). *Political communication.* Beverly Hills, CA: Sage.

Chaffee, S. H., Zhao, X., & Leshner, G. (1994). Political knowledge and the campaign media in 1992. *Communication Research, 21,* 305–324.

Chisman, F. P. (1976). *Attitude psychology and the study of public opinion.* University Park, PA: Pennsylvania University Press.

Cohen, A. (1976). Radio vs. TV: The effect of the medium. *Journal of Communication, 26,* 29–35.

Cohen, B. (1963). *The press and foreign policy.* Princeton, NJ: Princeton University Press.

Connell, R. W. (1987). Why the political socialization paradigm failed and what should replace it. *International Political Science Review, 8,* 215–223.

Devlin, L. P. (1973–1974). Contrasts in presidential campaign commercials of 1972. *Journal of Broadcasting, 18,* 17–26.

Devlin, L. P. (1977). Contrasts in presidential campaign commercials of 1976. *Central States Speech Journal, 28,* 238–249.

Devlin, L. P. (1981). Reagan's and Carter's ad men review the 1980 television campaigns. *Communication Quarterly, 30,* 3–12.

Devlin, L. P. (1987). Contrasts in presidential campaign commercials of 1984. *Political Communication Review, 12,* 25–55.

Devlin, L. P. (1989). Contrasts in presidential campaign commercials of 1988. *American Behavioral Scientist, 32,* 384–414.

Devlin, L. P. (1993). Contrasts in presidential campaign commercials of 1992. *American Behavioral Scientist, 37,* 272–290.

Devlin, L. P. (1997). Contrasts in presidential campaign commercials of 1996. *American Behavioral Scientist, 40,* 1058–1084.

Devlin, L. P. (2001), Contrasts in presidential campaign commercials of 2000. *American Behavioral Scientist, 44,* 2338–2369.

Devlin, L. P. (2005). Contrasts in presidential campaign commercials of 2004. *American Behavioral Scientist, 49*(2), 279–313.

Diamond, E., & Bates, S. (1988). *The spot* (Rev. ed). Cambridge, MA: MIT Press.

Doob, L. W. (1950). Goebbels' principles of propaganda. *Public Opinion Quarterly, 14,* 419–442.

Edelman, M. (1964). *Symbolic uses of politics.* Urbana: University of Illinois Press.

Edelman, M. (1988). *Constructing the political spectacle.* Chicago: University of Chicago Press.

Entman, R. M. (1993). Framing: Toward a clarification of a fractured paradigm. *Journal of Communication, 43*(4), 51–58.

Farnsworth, S., & Lichter, S.R. (2006). *The nightly news nightmare: Television coverage of U.S. presidential elections, 1988–2004* (2nd ed.). Lanham, MD: Rowman & Littlefield.

Fisher, W. R. (1985). The narrative paradigm: In the beginning. *Journal of Communication, 35,* 74–89.

Foot, K, A., & Schneider, S. (2006). *Web campaigning.* Cambridge, MA: MIT Press.

Foote, J. S. (1990). *Television access and political power.* New York: Praeger.

Frank, R. S. (1973). *Message dimensions of television news.* Lexington, MA: Lexington Books.

Gamson, W. A., & Modigliana, A, (1987). The changing culture of affirmative action. In R. A. Braumgart (Ed.), *Research in political sociology* (Vol. 3, pp. 137–177). Greenwich, CT: JAL.

Garramone, G. M. (1984). Voter responses to negative political ads. *Journalism Quarterly, 61,* 250–259.

Garramone, G. M. (1985). Effects of negative political advertising: The roles of sponsor and rebuttal. *Journal of Broadcasting & Electronic Media, 29,* 147–159.

Graber, D. (1976). Press and television as opinion resources in presidential campaigns. *Public Opinion Quarterly, 40,* 285–303.

Graber, D. A. (2005). *Mass media and American politics* (7th ed.). Washington, D.C.: Congressional Quarterly Press.

Gronbeck, B. E. (2004). Rhetoric and politics. In L. L. Kaid (Ed.), *The handbook of political communication research* (pp. 135–154). Mahwah, NJ: Lawrence Erlbaum.

Gurevitch, M., & Blumler, J. G. (1990). Comparative research: The extending frontier. In D. Swanson & D. Nimmo (Eds.), *New directions in political communication* (pp. 305–325). Newbury Park, CA: Sage.

Habermas, J. (1989). *The structural transformation of the public sphere* (T. McCarthy, Trans.). Cambridge, MA: MIT Press.

Hardt, H. (1988). Comparative media research: The world according to America. *Critical Studies in Mass Communication, 5,* 129–146.

Hart, R. P. (1984). *Verbal style and the presidency: A computer-based analysis.* New York: Academic Press.

Hofstetter, C. R. (1976). *Bias in the news.* Columbus: Ohio State University Press.

Iyengar, S., Peters, M. D., & Kinder, D. R. (1982). Experimental demonstrations of the "not-so-minimal" consequences of television news programs. *American Political Science* Review, *76,* 848–858.

Iyengar, S., & Simon, A. (1993). News coverage of the Gulf crisis and public opinion. *Communication Research, 20,* 365–383.

Jackson-Beeck, M., & Kraus, S. (1980). Political communication theory and research: An overview 1978–1979. In D. Nimmo (Ed.), *Communication yearbook* (Vol. 4, pp. 449–465). New Brunswick, NJ: Transaction.

Jamieson, K. H. (1996). *Packaging the presidency* (3rd ed.). New York: Oxford University Press.

Johnson-Cartee, K. S., & Copeland, G. A. (1991). *Negative advertising: Coming of age.* Hillsdale, NJ: Erlbaum.

Johnston, A. (1990). Trends in political communication: A selective review of research in the 1980s. In D.

L. Swanson & D. Nimmo (Eds.), *New directions in political communication* (pp. 329–362). Newbury Park, CA: Sage.

Joslyn, R. A. (1980). The content of political spot ads. *Journalism Quarterly, 57,* 92–98.

Kaid, L. L. (1981). Political advertising. In D. Nimmo & K. R. Sanders (Eds.), *Handbook of political communication* (pp. 249–271). Beverly Hills, CA: Sage.

Kaid, L. L. (1991). Ethical dimensions of political advertising. In R. Denton (Ed.), *Ethical dimensions of political communication* (pp. 145–169). New York: Praeger.

Kaid, L. L. (1993, May). *Ethics in televised political advertising: Guidelines for evaluation of technological distortions.* Paper presented at the International Communication Association Convention, Washington, D.C.

Kaid, L. L. (1994). Political advertising in the 1992 campaign. In R. E. Denton (Ed.), *The 1992 presidential campaign: A communication perspective* (pp. 111–127). Westport, CT: Praeger.

Kaid, L. L. (1997). Effects of the television spots on images of Dole and Clinton. *American Behavioral Scientist, 40,* 1085–1094.

Kaid, L. L. (2001). Technodistortions and effects of the 2000 political advertising. *American Behavioral Scientist, 44,* 2370–2378.

Kaid, L. L. (2002, Spring). Political advertising and information seeking: Comparing the exposure via traditional and Internet media channels. *Journal of Advertising, 31,* 27–35.

Kaid, L. L. (Ed.). (2004). *Handbook of political communication research.* Mahwah, NJ: Erlbaum.

Kaid, L. L., Downs, V. C., & Ragan S. (1990). Political argumentation and violations of audience expectations: An analysis of the Bush–Rather encounter. *Journal of Broadcasting & Electronic Media, 34,* 1–15.

Kaid, L. L., Gerstlé, J., & Sanders, K. R. (Eds.). (1991). *Mediated politics in two cultures.* New York: Praeger.

Kaid, L. L., Gobetz, R., Garner, J., Leland, C. M., & Scott, D. (1993). Television news and presidential campaigns: The legitimization of televised political advertising. *Social Science Quarterly, 74,* 274–285.

Kaid, L. L., & Holtz-Bacha, C. (Eds.). (1995). *Political advertising in Western democracies.* Newbury Park, CA: Sage.

Kaid, L. L., & Holtz-Bacha, C. (Eds.). (2006). *The Sage handbook of political advertising.* Thousand Oaks, CA: Sage.

Kaid, L. L., & Holtz-Bacha, C. (Eds.). (2008). *The encyclopedia of political communication.* Thousand Oaks, CA: Sage.

Kaid, L. L., & Johnston, A. (1991). Negative versus positive television advertising in U.S. presidential campaigns. *Journal of Communication, 41,* 53–64.

Kaid, L. L., & Johnston, A. (2001). *Videostyle in presidential campaigns: Style and content of televised political advertising.* Westport, CT: Praeger/Greenwood.

Kaid, L. L., McKinney, M. S., & Tedesco, J. C. (2000). *Civic dialogue in the 1996 presidential campaign: Candidate, media, and public voices.* Cresskill, NJ: Hampton Press.

Kaid, L. L., Nimmo, D., & Sanders, K. R. (1986). *New perspectives on political advertising.* Carbondale: Southern Illinois University Press.

Kaid, L. L., & Postelnicu, M. (2005). Political advertising in the 2004 election: Comparison of traditional television and Internet messages. *American Behavioral Scientist, 49*(2), 265–278.

Kaid, L. L., & Sanders, K. R. (1978). Political television commercials: An experimental study of type and length. *Communication Research, 5,* 57–70.

Kaid, L. L., & Sanders, K. R. (1985). Survey of political communication theory and research. In K. R. Sanders, L. L. Kaid, & D. Nimmo (Eds.), *Political communication yearbook 1984* (pp. 283–308). Carbondale: Southern Illinois University Press.

Kaid, L. L., Sanders, K. R., & Hirsch, R. O. (1974). *Political campaign communication: A bibliography and guide to the literature.* Metuchen, NJ: Scarecrow Press.

Kaid, L. L., & Wadsworth, A. (1984). *Political campaign communication: A bibliography and guide to the Literature 1972–82.* Metuchen, NJ: Scarecrow Press.

Katz, E., Blumler, J. G., & Gurevitch, M. (1973). Uses and gratifications research. *Public Opinion Quarterly, 37,* 509–523.

Katz, E., & Feldman, J. (1962). The debates in light of research: A survey of surveys. In S. Kraus (Ed.), *The great debates* (pp. 173–223). Bloomington, IN: Indiana University Press.

Klapper, J. (1960). *The effects of mass communication.* Glencoe, IL: Free Press.

Kraus, S. (Ed.). (1962). *The great debates.* Bloomington: Indiana University Press.

Kraus, S., & Davis, D. K. (1976). *The effects of mass communication on political behavior.* University Park, PA: Pennsylvania University Press.

Larson, C. U., & Wiegele, T. C. (1979). Political communication theory and research: An overview. In D. Nimmo (Ed.), *Communication yearbook* (Vol. 3, pp. 457–473). New Brunswick, NJ: Transaction Books.

Lazarsfeld, P. F., Berelson, B. R., & Gaudet, H. (1944). *The people's choice.* New York: Duell, Sloan & Pearce.

Mansfield, M. W., & Weaver, R. A. (1982). Political communication theory and research: An overview. In M. Burgoon (Ed.), *Communication yearbook* (Vol. 5, pp. 605–625). New Brunswick, NJ: Transaction.

McCombs, M. E. (1976). Agenda setting research: A bibliographic essay. *Political Communication Review, 1,* 1–7.

McCombs, M. E., & Shaw, D. L. (1972). The agenda-setting function of the mass media. *Public Opinion Quarterly, 36,* 176–87.

McKinney, M. S. (2005). Engaging citizens through presidential debates: Does the format matter? In M. S. McKinney, L. L. Kaid, D. G. Bystrom, & D. B. Carlin (Eds.), *Communicating politics: Engaging the public in democratic life* (pp. 209–221). New York: Peter Lang.

McKinney, M. S., & Carlin, D. B. (2004). Political campaign debates. In L. L. Kaid (Ed.), *Handbook of political communication research* (pp. 203–234). Mahwah, NJ: Erlbaum.

McKinney, M. S., Dudash, E. A., & Hodgkinson, G. (2003). Viewer reactions to the 2000 presidential debates: Learning issue and image information. In L. L. Kaid, J. C. Tedesco, D. G. Bystrom, & M. M. McKinney (Eds.), *The millennium election: Communication in the 2000 campaign* (pp. 43–58). Lanham, MD: Rowman & Littlefield.

McKinnon, L. M., & Kaid, L. L. (1999, August). Advertising effects: An experimental study of adwatch effects on voter evaluations of candidates and their ads. *Journal of Applied Communication Research, 27,* 217–236.

McKinnon, L. M., Tedesco, J. C, & Kaid, L. L. (1993). The effects of presidential debates: Channel and commentary comparisons. *Argumentation and Advocacy, 30,* 1–14.

McLeod, J. M., & Becker, L. B. (1981). The uses and gratifications approach. In D. Nimmo & K. R. Sanders (Eds.), *Handbook of political communication* (pp. 67–99). Beverly Hills, CA: Sage.

Mendelsohn, H., & O'Keefe, G. J. (1976). *The people choose a president.* New York: Praeger.

Neuman, W. R., Just, M. R., & Crigler, A. M. (1992). *Common knowledge: News and the construction of political meaning.* Chicago: University of Chicago Press.

Nimmo, D. (1970). *The political persuaders.* Englewood Cliffs, NJ: Prentice-Hall.

Nimmo, D. (1977). Political communication theory and research: An overview. In B. Ruben (Ed.), *Communication yearbook* (Vol. 1, pp. 441–452). New Brunswick, NJ: Transaction.

Nimmo, D., & Combs, J. E. (1983). *Mediated political realities.* New York: Longman.

Nimmo, D., & Combs, J. E. (1985). *Nightly horrors.* Knoxville: University of Tennessee Press.

Nimmo, D., & Combs, J. E. (1990). *Mediated political realities* (2nd ed.). New York: Longman.

Nimmo, D., & Sanders, K. R. (Eds.). (1981). *Handbook of political communication.* Beverly Hills, CA: Sage.

Noelle-Neumann, E. (1974). The spiral of silence. *Journal of Communication, 24,* 43–51.

Noelle-Neumann, E. (1977). Turbulences in the climate of opinion: Methodological applications of the spiral of silence theory. *Public Opinion Quarterly, 41,* 113–158.

Noelle-Neumann, E. (1984). *The spiral of silence: Our social skin.* Chicago: University of Chicago Press.

Noelle-Neumann, E., & Peterson, T. (2004). The spiral of silence and the social nature of man. In L. L. Kaid (Ed.), *Handbook of political communication research* (pp. 339–356). Mahwah, NJ: Erlbaum.

Norris, P., Kern, M., & Just, M. (Eds.) (2003). *Framing terrorism: The news media, the government, and the public.* New York: Routledge.

Oates, S., Owen, D., & Gibson, R. K. (Eds.). (2006). *The Internet and politics: Citizens, voters and activists.* New York: Routledge.

Paletz, D. L., & Entman, R. M. (1981). *Media-power-politics.* New York: Free Press.

Patterson, T., & McClure, R. (1976). *The unseeing eye.* New York: Putnam.

Patterson, T. E. (1993). *Out of order*. New York: Knopf.

Pfau, M., & Louden, A. (1994). Effectiveness of adwatch formats in deflecting political attack ads. *Communication Research, 21*, 325–341.

Protess, D. L., & McCombs, M. (Eds.). (1991). *Agenda setting: Readings on media, opinion, and policy-making*. Hillsdale, NJ: Erlbaum.

Reese, S. D., & Miller, M. M. (1981). Political attitude holding and structure: The effects of newspaper and television news. *Communication Research, 8*, 167–188.

Robinson, M. J. (1976). Public affairs television and the growth of political malaise: The case of the "Selling of the Pentagon." *American Political Science Review, 70*, 409–432.

Roddy, B., & Garramone, G. M. (1988). Appeals and strategies of negative political advertising. *Journal of Broadcasting & Electronic Media, 32*, 415–427.

Sanders, K. R., & Kaid, L. L. (1978). Political communication theory and research: An overview 1976–1977. In B. Ruben (Ed.), *Communication yearbook* (Vol. 2, pp. 375–389). New Brunswick, NJ: Transaction.

Sanders, K. R., & Kaid, L. L. (1981). Political rallies. *Central States Speech Journal, 32*, 1–11.

Scheufele, D. A. (1999). Framing as a theory of media effects. *Journal of Communication, 49*(4), 103–22.

Schoenbach, K., & Semetko, H. A. (1992). Agenda-setting, agenda reinforcing or agenda-deflating? A study of the 1990 German national election. *Journalism Quarterly, 69*, 837–846.

Sears, D. O., & Chaffee, S. H. (1979). The uses and effects of the 1976 debates: An overview of empirical studies. In S. Kraus (Ed.), *The great debates: Carter vs. Ford* (pp. 223–261). Bloomington: Indiana University Press.

Semetko, H. A., Blumler, J. G., Gurevitch, M., & Weaver, D. H. (1991). *The formation of campaign agendas: A comparative analysis of party and media roles in recent American and British elections*. Hillsdale, NJ: Erlbaum.

Semetko, H. A., & Valkenburg, P. M. (2000). Framing European politics: A content analysis of press and television news. *Journal of Communication, 50*(2), 93–109.

Sloan, J. H. (1965). "I have kept the faith": William Jennings Bryan and the Democratic National Convention of 1904. *Southern Speech Communication Journal, 31*, 114–123.

Swanson, D. L., & Nimmo, D. (Eds.). (1990). *New directions in political communication*. Newbury Park, CA: Sage.

Tankard, J. W., Handerson, L., Silberman, J., Bliss, K., & Ghanem, S. (1991). *Media frames: Approaches to conceptualization and measurement*. Paper presented at the Association for Education in Journalism and Mass Communication Annual Convention, Boston, MA.

Trammell, K. D., Williams, A. P., Postelnicu, M., & Landreville, K. D. (2006). Evolution of online campaigning: Increasing interactivity in candidate web sites and blogs through text and technical features. *Mass Communication and Society, 9*(1), 21–44.

Tremayne, M. (Ed.). (2006). *Blogging, citizenship and the future of media*. New York: Routledge.

Underhill, W. R. (1966). Fulton's finest hour. *Quarterly Journal of Speech, 52*, 155–163.

Vreese, C. de, & Boomgaarden, H. (2003). Valenced news frames and public support for the EU. *Communications, 28*, 361–381.

Weaver, D. (1987). Media agenda-setting and elections: Assumptions and implications. In D. Paletz (Ed.), *Political communication research* (pp. 176–193). Norwood, NJ: Ablex.

Weaver, D. H., McCombs, M., & Shaw, D. L. (2004). Agenda-setting research: Issues, attributes, and influences. In L. L. Kaid (Ed.), *Handbook of political communication research* (pp. 257–282). Mahwah, NJ: Erlbaum.

West, D. (2005). *Air wars* (4th ed.). Washington, D.C.: Congressional Quarterly Press.

Williams, A. P., & Kaid, L. L. (2006). Media framing of the European Parliamentary elections: A view from the United States. In M. Maier & J. Tenscher (Eds.), *Campaigning in Europe—Campaigning for Europe: Political parties, Campaigns, mass media and the European Parliament elections 2004* (pp. 295–304). London: LIT.

Williams, A. P., & Tedesco, J. C. (Eds.). (2006). *The Internet election: Perspectives on the Web in campaign 2004*. Lanham, MD: Rowman & Littlefield.

Suggested Readings

Kaid, L. L. (Ed.). (2004). *The handbook of political communication research*. Mahwah, NJ: Erlbaum.

Kaid, L. L., & Holtz-Bacha, C. (Eds.). (2008). *The encyclopedia of political communication*. Thousand Oaks, CA: Sage.

Mancini, P., & Hallin, D. C. (2004). *Comparing media systems: Three models of media and politics*. Cambridge, UK: Cambridge University Press.

McCombs, M. E., & Shaw, D. L. (1972). The agenda-setting function of the mass media. *Public Opinion Quarterly, 36,* 176–87.

Nimmo, D., & Combs, J. E. (1990). *Mediated political realities* (2nd ed.). New York: Longman.

Patterson, T. E. (1993). *Out of order*. New York: Knopf.

Williams, A. P., & Tedesco, J. C. (Eds.). (2006). *The Internet election: Perspectives on the Web in campaign 2004*. Lanham, MD: Rowman & Littlefield.

30

PUBLIC RELATIONS AND INTEGRATED COMMUNICATION

Doug Newsom

Public relations is a discipline that must incorporate theory and research to be useful in solving practical problems. Although the origins of public relations demonstrate efforts to do so, public relations theories and research to test them have exploded, more than emerged, in the 21st century.

To be effective in affecting opinions and behaviors, public relations practice needs a toolkit of various communication tactics that include publicity, publications (electronic and paper), advertising, special events, and other promotions that attract attention. The interactivity of publics with these tactics provides feedback making it possible to adjust policies, projects, and presentations to accomplish better understanding.

In a technological communication environment that dissolves boundaries so all messages are available instantly around the world, it is ever more imperative for all messages to be consonant. Speaking in one voice— consistency in message—challenges both theory and research. A misstep can result in misunderstandings with the potential to create a global crisis.

Background for Merging Messages

Early in the development of public relations, in order to use communication tools effectively, practitioners applied and adapted theory from both sociology and psychology (Newsom, Turk, & Kruckeberg, 2007, p. 118). Discovering how well these applications worked evolved later when technology, primarily the computer, made it easier to apply various research methods, borrowed again from sociology and psychology disciplines as well as from math and the natural sciences.

Public relations is a social science, and was declared so in the 1920s by public relations pioneer Edward L. Bernays (Bernays, 1923, p. 110, p. 121; 1928, p. 27; 1969, p. vi; 1986, p. 65; Moyers, 1982; Newsom et al., 2007, p. 118).

Bernays's personal background, plus his experience on the Committee on Public Information (Newsom et al., 2007, note 56, p. 359), may have contributed to his understanding of how to use various communication tactics to achieve results. That committee's effort to gain support from the American public to enter World War I combined, or integrated, advertising and public relations, as these disciplines were practiced then. When public support was needed for the next world war, the communication task was divided. The new structure was made up of two committees: the War Advertising Council and the Office of War Information, which became the U.S. Information Agency until it was disbanded in 1999. The split between what was seen as information and what was advertising formalized what was occurring in practice, and the two areas remained apart until the 1970s.

However, the logic of having an organization speak with one voice was a consideration in the 1950s with the collaboration of Harold Burson, founder of a public relations firm in New York (subsequently Burson-Marsteller), and William (Bill) Marsteller, founder of Marsteller, Inc., an advertising firm in Chicago. The idea was to encourage the clients of one firm to also use the other so campaigns and message statements could be consistent. That concept didn't work as well as anticipated, but economics in the 1970s and 1980s set in motion the purchase of public relations firms by advertising agencies, thus facilitating structural integration (Newsom et al., 2007, p. 60).

Social events of the late 1950s and 1960s in some ways created a need to put more theory and research into public relations practice and focused public attention on discrepancies in message statements. Public upheavals from social movements such as civil rights, consumerism, environmentalism, and women's rights dramatically changed the nature of public relations (Newsom et al., 2007, pp. 37–41).

Public relations got the attention of chief executive officers faced with hostile publics influencing public opinion so negatively that sounder-based public relations efforts were needed. Many public relations practitioners in the companies and in outside agencies that many companies used lacked the theoretical background and research expertise to be effective. Furthermore, more sophisticated media, especially television, exposed conflicting messages to broader audiences. Marketing messages especially were publicly challenged by contrasting their claims with messages intended for other publics. The conflict specifically affected employees and other insiders.

Without theoretical underpinnings, solid research, and some coordination of message strategy, the conflicting voices from employee relations, media publicity, advertising, and marketing limited appropriate action. Furthermore, technology was accelerating the movement of messages in all venues (Newsom et al., 2007, p. 60).

Public relations' first "toe-in-the-water" was a PR/marketing mix that became prominent during the 1960s and 1970s in the external relations of nonprofit organizations, especially hospitals and museums, neither of which had previously bothered much with either public relations or marketing. The change occurred when a competitive economy forced hospitals to explain rising costs. Museums that hosted traveling mega-exhibits were trying to broaden their constituency as well as expand both their collections and their buildings. This change also involved the newly deregulated airlines and financial institutions that were on their way to becoming financial supermarkets. A good example for museums was the well-packaged and promoted "Treasures of Tutankhamen," in the 1970s, an exhibit of Egyptian art sponsored by a consortium of six museums and overseen by the Metropolitan Museum of Art in New York (Newsom & Scott, 1985, pp. 378–381). By the late 1980s it had become apparent that the best blend of PR and marketing occurred when both tactics were in the mind of the person in charge (Newsom et al., 1989, p. 327).

It was not until December 1993 that the advertising division and the public relations division of the Association for Education in Journalism and Mass Communication published the results of a two-year study by a task force of working professionals in advertising and public relations and academics, recommending integrated curricula to prepare students for a more unified practice (Duncan, Caywood, & Newsom, 1993).

To illustrate the need for changing how students were being prepared for the field, this task force set forward eleven observations of the economic climate for advertising and public relations:

1) increasing audience fragmentation; 2) mergers and acquisitions of communication agencies and functions; 3) increasing media fragmentation and the growing number

of alternative media; 4) changing cost of traditional media; 5) increasing overlap of stakeholders; 6) increasing number of commodity products giving consumers an array of choices; 7) decreasing credibility of persuasive messages, or, perhaps, increasing skepticism of audiences; 8) increasing sophistication of communication technology with its consequences; 9) increasing power of retailers to control product manufacture, including creation of their own brands; 10) increasing ability of clients buying advertising and public relations services to plan and manage their own communication plans; 11) increasing pressure on bottom lines from top management and conflict with accountability. (Duncan et al., 1993, appendix A)

Although the integration of advertising and public relations was not as appealing to public relations practitioners as it was to those in advertising, other factors focused attention on the issues raised, particularly changes in the news media.

Less challenged than the concept of integrating the disciplines was the task force's recommended undergraduate core curricula for integrated communication: (1) strong emphasis on liberal arts; (2) training in verbal, written, and visual communications; (3) a solid understanding of business and organizational behavior; (4) an understanding and respect for other communication disciplines and specialties; and (5) mastery of basic research skills.

Plans and Problems

The concept seemed workable, but the plan ran into difficulties at both the professional and academic levels. At the professional level, the economics of advertising and public relations businesses are different. Whereas public relations charges for professional services on a fee as well as an hourly basis, similar to other fields such as law and psychological counseling, advertising billings are based on media placements that agencies buy for the client and present the media with finished products. A more subtle difference is that public relations clients tend to buy counsel and direction as well as implementation. Public relations practitioners, seeing their role as communication counselors, are reluctant "order takers" from clients. On the other hand, advertising agencies are more accustomed to designing and planning to the will and direction of the client. Reconciling these different approaches was more of an issue initially than later as Integrated Marketing Communications (IMC) began to stress relationship building, which requires more counsel.

Structure for integration created difficulty for both professionals and academics. Both were heavily invested in people with skills in one area or the other. Commercial organizations tend to embrace change quicker than academic institutions, so universities were slower to change curricula than companies were to change their approaches.

Few universities in the 1990s had truly integrated advertising/public relations teaching units, although many had advertising/public relations tracks, with some core courses; but students then chose one track as a major.[1] At most schools in the 1990s, either subject could be chosen as a major so it was not a truly integrated sequence. That remains the case in the early 21st century, but many public relations units offer courses in integrated communication. Northwestern was the first university to change the name of its graduate public relations unit to integrated marketing communication, under the guidance of Dr. Clarke Caywood, one of the task force members. The same year that the task force's report was published, 1993, Dr. Tom Duncan, founded the Integrated Marketing Communication graduate program at the University of Colorado, taken over in 2002 by the Daniels College of Business at the University of Denver. Another task force member, Dr. Doug Newsom and her colleague at Texas Christian University (TCU), Dr. Jack Raskopf, had developed an advertising/public relations sequence there in the 1970s because both had experienced having to combine the two in their professional careers before they began teaching.

In the nonprofit world, changes have come slowly too. TCU's public relations director, Larry Lauer, an early proponent of the concept, has lectured on integrated marketing communication at meetings of other academic institutional public relations directors. Lauer's title at TCU, vice chancellor for marketing and communication, expresses the shift toward an integrated approach. In Lauer's first book on the topic (1997) he noted:

> Often as a matter of practical consequence, the activities of public relations, marketing communications, advertising, special events, and promotions are done by separate people at different times. While coordination may be attempted, the true synergy potential of a completely integrated approach is never achieved....
>
> Integrated communication simply is a holistic approach to organizational communication. (pp. 10–11)

Change began picking up pace in the corporate world. In 1993, about a third of 243 marketing executives of consumer, industrial, and service companies who responded to a telephone survey were spending about 20 percent of their annual marketing budgets on public relations. In 1997, it was estimated at 70 percent (Harris, 1997, p. 91).

Solutions

The key to integration is corporate structure, as Duncan and Moriarty (1997) noted. For the strategy to work, the organization has to be internally integrated in order "to do cross-functional planning and monitoring, create core competencies in those responsible for managing IM programs, and set up and use integrated data bases to ensure universal customer information and create a learning organization" (p. xvi). Supporting that concept as a model for nonprofit organizations, Lauer's 10 steps for successful integration start with an internal educational process that establishes a way of thinking about how the organization is represented, especially to opinion leaders. The next step is clarification of mission so everyone in the organization is "on the same page." Other steps involve finding a champion of the integration concept in the CEO's office, identifying market segments and opinion leaders in each, using an audit to measure consistency of identity and message, monitoring with research tools the shifting within and among market segments, setting priorities, establishing action teams, focusing on the branding of the institution, and building in feedback for evaluation (Lauer 2002, pp. 196–197).

Sometimes the process is difficult to maintain within an organization, essential though it may be. Another aspect of achieving successful integration is finding and working with an integrated communication agency, Duncan and Moriarty (1997) state. The idea is described in chapter 5, "Develop Strategic Consistency," where the one voice strategy is said to be "...analogous to a choir singing in unison; however, multiple voices singing in harmony are much more engaging and enjoyable" (p. 81).

The need for speaking with one voice also is supported by findings in a significant public relations document, *Excellence in Public Relations Management* edited by James E. Grunig and published in 1992 by the International Association of Business Communicators (IABC), which funded the research project. In a 1991 IABC project report from initial data analysis, the major characteristics of an excellent public relations department were listed, and among these is the observation that all public relations voices within in an institution need to be unified so that the institutional voice "is an integrated one, rather than being split among functions that may include community relations, government affairs, internal communications, and media relations."

Marketing was not included in the communication mix. The comment was that public relations is "separate from marketing (although in efforts such as product promotion they may function in a complementary fashion)." Added is the explanation that "Public relations addresses all of an organization's strategic publics, rather than focusing on the customer or client public" (L. A. Grunig, 1996, pp. 470–471).[2] Due to that difference, public relations proponents of any inclusion of advertising or promotions or institutional identification prefer the term, "integrated communication" (Duncan, Caywood, Newsom, 1993, pp. 9–10, 24–25; Newsom & Carrell, 1992).

Areas of Commonality

The differences between public relations and marketing remain in place, although both now refer to publics as "stakeholders" because the idea is that many individuals and groups may have a "stake" in the organization's policies and actions.

Compare these two definitions.

> **IMC Definition**: A management concept that is designed to make all aspects of marketing communication such as advertising, sales promotion, public relations, and direct marketing work together as a unified force, rather than permitting each to work in isolation. (http://marketing.about.com/cs/glossaryofterms/1/)

> **Public Relations Definition**: Public relations involves responsibility and responsiveness in policy and information to the best interests of the organization and its publics. (Newsom et al., 1989, p. 2)

The *American Heritage Dictionary* (2006) offers these definitions of public relations:

1. (used with a sing. verb) The art or science of establishing and promoting a favorable relationship with the public.
2. (*used with a pl. verb*) The methods and activities employed to establish and promote a favorable relationship with the public.
3. (*used with a sing. or pl. verb*) The degree of success obtained in achieving a favorable relationship with the public.

In practice, public relations practitioners are concerned about recognition and reputation, much the same way as both are embraced by the term "branding," used by IMC. Promotions and special events where attendance is open generally use advertising, even when these are handled by a public relations firm or an internal public relations department. Campaigns that may originate from a public relations source also generally employ advertising. If the organization itself or the client happens to be a nonprofit organization, public service announcements (PSAs), essentially nonpaid for advertising given by media, are used. Since PSAs, print and broadcast, depend upon the discretion of the media, efforts are made to get ads sponsored by commercial supporting organizations. If there is a budget, ads are simply purchased outright. So, the campaign may appear similar to one from an IMC group.

Types of advertising typically handled by public relations people are (1) public policy ads, often prepared from position papers; (2) positioning or image advertising that emphasizes either or all of the organization's mission, vision, and values; (3) feature ads that read like editorial copy, but are marked, as required by law, as paid advertising; (4) public service ads/commercials; (5) special event ads, posters, and flyers; and (6) special sections for publications (Newsom & Haynes, 2008, chapter 13).

Model 30.1

This symmetrical feedback model goes beyond communication to behavior.

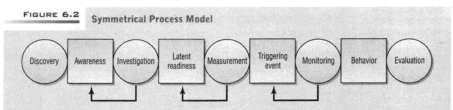

FIGURE 6.2 **Symmetrical Process Model**

Discovery — Awareness — Investigation — Latent readiness — Measurement — Triggering event — Monitoring — Behavior — Evaluation

The symmetrical behavioral model involves five steps (represented as circles in the above schematic diagram): first, *gauging* existing levels of awareness and discovering conditions under which publics are likely to respond positively to an effort to create, enhance or increase awareness of some desired behavioral goal; second, *investigating* responses to the attempt to create, raise or sustain awareness, to determine any problems with the desired behavior goal that may already be apparent and should cause goal modification (or even abandonment) with respect to one or more publics; third, *measuring* latent readiness to act, so that the action's direction can be anticipated, depending on certain conditions; fourth, *monitoring* responses to the triggering event, to anticipate the level of resulting behavior, and interceding with action or communication or both if the behavior seems likely to be undesirable; fifth, *evaluating* behavior to determine why that particular action was taken, whether it is likely to be sustained and (if it is desired) what is needed to sustain it. Each of these five stages builds in the opportunity for publics to communicate their desires, needs and concerns so that goals can be adjusted or at least a mutual understanding can be negotiated.

Source: Reprinted with permission of *pr reporter*, Exeter, N.H., 33(30) (July 30, 1990), p. 1.

The five steps in this model are represented by circles, each of which gives a public the opportunity to respond so goals can be adjusted, or some mutual understanding arrived at. The first step, **discovery**, gauges existing levels of awareness and discovers conditions under which publics are likely to respond positively. The second step is **investigation** of responses of various publics in an attempt to create, raise, or sustain awareness and to determine any problems that might result in modifying goals or even abandoning some publics. The third step, **measurement**, involves evaluating the latent readiness to act so action can be anticipated along with the conditions under which it may be expected. The fourth step is to **monitor** responses so the level and direction of action can be anticipated and some intercession be planned if the action is undesirable or some reenforement if the action is going in a positive direction. The fifth step, **evaluation,** involves evaluating the behavior to see what action was taken by which publics and how it can be sustained, if positive, or counteracted, if negative.

Source: This model was created by the late Patrick Jackson and published in *pr reporter, 33*(30), Exeter, N.H., July 30, 1990. The model appears also in Doug Newsom, Judy VanSlyke Turk, and Dean Kruckeberg (2007), *This is PR*, 9th ed., p. 22; and in Doug Newsom and Jim Haynes (2008), *Public relations writing form and style*, 8th ed. Used by permission.

When a strategist is trying to change behavior, all the tools in the toolbox that can be used should be used. Both public relations and integrated communication rely on behavior models from communication theory to effect change. One model that works for both, because it allows for serious consideration of feedback from stakeholders, was developed in 1990 by the late Patrick Jackson, a former president of the Public Relations Society of America (PRSA).

The effectiveness of messages in achieving results, thus, draws on four disciplines: marketing, psychology, communication, and sociology, as explicated by David Therelsen and Christina L. Fiebich.

Making such models work effectively and efficiently in an environment of communication cacophony is the challenge not only in maintaining consistency of an organization's message but assuring that these get to all stakeholders. For consistency to be strategic, Duncan and Moriarty say these all must have an origin in corporate core values and mission because in execution these communication messages will vary, with each stakeholder group accenting its vested interest (Duncan & Moriarty, 1997, p. 70).

Model 30.2   Communication Effectiveness Model

		In order to be effective, a message must be:					
Field	*Discipline*	*Received*	*Attended to*	*Understood*	*Believed*	*Remembered*	*Acted on*
Marketing	Demographics	1	3	9	13		
	Psychographic	2	4		14		
Psychology	Persuasion				15		21
	Information processing		5			18	22
Communication	Linguistics			10			
	Writing		6	11		19	
	Design		7	12		20	
Social Sciences	Sociology				16		
	Anthropology				17		
	Economics		8			23	

Just to get a message from here to there, from sender to receiver, requires a reasonable command of the social sciences, communication, psychology, marketing—and subdivisions of each. To be successful, a message must be *received* by the intended individual or audience. It must be the audience's *attention*. It must be *understood*. It must be *believed*. It must be *remembered*. And ultimately, in some fashion, it must be *acted upon*. Failure to accomplish any of these tasks means the entire message fails. It fails because it does not accomplish the purpose for which it was created.

Source: David Therelsen, Christina L. Fiebich, "Message to Desired Action," *Journal of Communication Management*, Vol. 5, No. 4, May 2001. Used by permission.

The IMC model is similar to a public relations model that roots all campaigns in the organization's mission statement and values, demonstrated by the corporate culture. Speaking with one voice makes it possible to form and keep positive relationships that result in an understanding of organizational values manifest in its reputation (Newsom et al., 2007, p. 202).

Model 30.3   Consistency Hierarchy (pyramid format)

Source: Tom Duncan & Sandra Moriarty (1997). Developing strategic consistency. In *Driving Brand Value*, p. 71. Used by permission.

The challenge to all organizations that attempt to speak with one voice is to coordinate the various messages to stakeholders because these will overlap and compete with messages from outside sources and some internal ones, from employees, for example. The impact of some of the uncontrolled, unplanned messages, especially from sources credible to different stakeholders, is often greater than the controlled messages (Duncan & Moriarty, 1997, p. 76).

Persuasion as an Ongoing Issue In PR/IMC Tensions

One of the arguments used by public relations people—academics and practitioners—who do not want to embrace the idea of integration in their work is the idea that "marketing" is "selling." While it is true that marketing usually is identified with products or services, it can be identified with ideas as well. The root of the argument is not so much "selling" as it is persuasion. The existence of persuasion in public relations practice with or without integration, and what has changed, is described this way (Newsom & Haynes, 2008):

> Persuasion is implicit, if not explicit, every time a person tries to communicate with another. It is just that public relations is widely known for trying to persuade publics to a particular point of view.
>
> Persuasion is explicitly part of the public relations fabric. If it is done ethically and legally, it logically is no more objectionable than most other human activities. Persuasive efforts now may seem more focused than in the past. That's because more and more companies are taking an *integrated* approach to planning and implementation. Integration simply means that a single communication strategy undergirds all messages from an organization. It is intended to give them unity and consistency. (p. 37)

The literature labels this approach variously as *integrated marketing communications, marketing communication,* or simply *integrated communication.* We prefer integrated communication because it seems to encompass a range of activities not often central to the selling emphasis of marketing. The term used is not important, but it is important to recognize that public relations efforts by many companies now seem to have a sharper focus than in the past. That tends to sensitize people to the persuasive role of public relations.

This integrated approach affects every public relations writer in at least two ways. First, writers will be expected to adapt any message to any medium. That certainly is not a new development, but an integrated communication philosophy will make it far more common than in the recent past. Second, writers who can think about persuasion at the strategic level will be at a premium. It is clear that a writer who knows *how* will always have a job. But the writer who knows *why* will always be the boss.

The Persuasion Cycle and Decisions About Communication Tactics

Persuasion is a key element in gaining acceptance from stakeholders for an idea, product, or service. Information alone has considerable competition with multiple voices in an array of channels. Simply gaining attention is difficult enough, although there is no question that credibility depends on behavior (policies, products, services, style, and actions, including the spoken word). The cycle of persuasion has six sequential steps (McGuire, 1973, p. 221). Presenting happens first and the person for whom the message is intended has to be able, physically, to receive the message and then has to be mentally receptive to it. If the message is ignored, though, the process stops there. The second step in the cycle is attending—the message has to capture the attention of the intended receiver. Comprehending is the third step because the receiver has to be able to understand it, so the symbols—art and language—must be suitable for the intended recipient. Fourth, the recipient has to agree with the message, which is called yielding. The next step is retaining the message, a reason that messages are repeated often in the same and/or different formats. Finally, the sixth step is acting, when the recipient takes observable action intended by the message. Acting meaning the results must be evident in a measurable way.

The tactics chosen for a campaign generally vary in their emphases depending upon where the idea, service or product is in its life cycle. When the presentation involves something new, the campaign generally is heavy on advertising and promotion. To get the word out in a controlled way to be sure the message is delivered is generally the most costly campaign because it is introducing something new or at least something that most stakeholders don't know about. The number of audiences and the different media needed to reach them can be expensive. The sheer cost of presentation has sent some communicators to the Internet to broaden the scope of free messages. If the campaign is a sustaining one to keep mind and market share among stakeholders, the messages are more targeted to specific receivers. The tactics in a campaign of that sort are more likely to have a heavy public relations component. When the effort is designed to increase the number of adopters or to change the composition of stakeholders, there is more likely to be a blending and balancing of all persuasive components.

PR Emphasis

The decision about where the emphasis should be placed usually is determined by the goal of the campaign.

Case Illustration

The nonprofit Institute for Healthcare Improvements (IHI) is dedicated to saving lives by reducing the number of hospital deaths from avoidable medical errors. The low-profile Cambridge, Massachusetts-based Institute set a high goal with its 100,000 Lives Campaign. The number came from the total of lives lost each year in the United States due to hospital mistakes. The 18-month campaign designed and implemented for IHI by Goodman Media International (GMI) involved choosing hospital sites and being sure credible healthcare spokespeople in each were trained to deliver the message. Once the hospitals were chosen, media at each site were identified. About halfway through the campaign, GMI organized a bus tour, literally taking its show on the road from coast to coast. The tour created hospital visits, media events, interviews with professional health providers, and generated extensive publicity in print and broadcast outlets such as NPR, BBC, *The Wall Street Journal*, and more than 60 trade publications. That created awareness, but more substantially, the tour resulted in enlisting the participation of 3,100 hospitals. The campaign claimed more than its 100,000 goal: 122,300 lives saved (*PR Week*, 2007, p. 13).

Ad Emphasis

When promotion is driving the campaign, especially in the case of a product with a problem or some issue such as unusual application or use, the emphasis generally results in using advertising as the principal force in the campaign.

Case Illustration

The Kiwifruit in China. The sweet green fruit with the black seeds, known as a kiwi generally is associated with New Zealand, but China's locally grown kiwi is cheaper in that country than the premium fruit from New Zealand so ZESPRI Kiwifruit International asked GolinHarris China for help. While the China-grown fruit is 10 times cheaper, it didn't have a substantial market share over the New Zealand product. ZESPRI wanted a 200 percent increase in sales for their China product. The GolinHarris strategy was to separate the country into submarkets and create a positioning approach for each. In Beijing the kiwi was given a new Chinese name and in stylish Shanghai it was introduced with a fashion event, including models wearing kiwi headdresses. A new kiwi dessert was developed with a local chain of stores and in four months the campaign had passed its goal, claiming sales revenue increases of 360 percent. The target audience recognition of ZESPRI kiwifruit increased from 10 percent to 56.2 percent (International Public Relations Association, 2007).

Blend and Balance

Often, especially in a global campaign, the best solution combines tools and tactics. Especially is this true when dealing with international media and when a website is a crucial tool.

Case Illustration

The Dove Campaign was created to overcome growing criticism worldwide, especially from women's groups and health experts over the thinness of models used in fashion shows and the unrealistically perfect presentation of women in advertising, on magazine covers, and on television. The image of thin perfection as the ideal for women had resulted in both emotional and physical damage, the latter through dangerous dieting and other eating disorders, often on the part of girls as young as 8 years old.

With its major market being women, Dove soap and Edelman launched a worldwide campaign to use real women as models—women with different sizes and shapes—all "normal" in their appearances. Called the "Dove Campaign for Real Beauty," publicity about the new approach of using models in advertising generated global attention, especially a place on the Dove website that showed the transformation of a model from her "natural" state to the way she would appear in advertising. Some of that attention came from women e-mailing others the scenario. The result was getting international media coverage of a soap brand through media personalities talking about the initiative, health professionals, parents, teachers, and religious leaders writing about it, and solid research that backed the mission of the campaign.

Through its global research study, Dove found that only 2 percent of the world's women described themselves as "beautiful." Dove's mission for the campaign was to make more women everywhere in the world feel more beautiful and to improve the lives of female children, at least one million of them, through building self-esteem.

The campaign used controversial images and stirred up both positive and negative comment, which it was open about sharing. It directly attacked stereotypes of female beauty while creating a place for Dove as the advocate for female self-acceptance and self-esteem and staking out its position as the expert on real beauty. An important part of the campaign was continually presenting Dove's images of beauty and actively participating in the global discourse that the campaign generated. Consumers praised Dove publicly on the website and privately in interpersonal discussions praised Dove for calling attention to the issue of a damaging stereotype (Kuntz, 2006).

How Integration Adds Value

The addition of public relations tools and tactics to the marketing mix helps prepare the way for an initiative, gives depth, and extends the messages, according to Tom Harris, APR.[3] Specifically,

Harris says that marketers understand now the need to speak with one voice to consumers of products and services and to the various segmented publics that can influence decisions (Harris, 1997, pp. 94–95). Strategic use of public relations in integrated programs adds 10 significant assets: (1) To build marketplace excitement before advertising breaks; (2) to drive the communications program when there is no advertising; (3) to make advertising news where there is no product news; (4) to bring advertising to life; (5) to extend promotion programs; (6) to build personal relationships with consumers; (7) to influence the influentials; (8) to communicate new product benefits; (9) to demonstrate a company's social responsibility and build consumer trust; (10) to defend products at risk and give consumers permission to buy.

The persuasion cycle suggests how important presentation and attention are in starting the cycle and how significant retention of the message is to action. Beyond that, the integrity of the product or service and the credibility of the institution offering the message are best accomplished through public relations. Harris also calls attention to building consumer trust and demonstrating corporate social responsibility.

How Failure to Integrate Causes Problems

Two cases that got the wrong kind of publicity are good examples of missteps that can occur when there is a failure to include public relations in a marketing effort. Both examples reinforce public relations practitioners' negative attitudes toward marketing. Actually, the cases demonstrate the urgent need to include public relations in planning, execution, and evaluation, rather than "damage control."

The first case involves a Dr Pepper promotional idea that ran into trouble in Boston's historic graveyard where many notables such as Samuel Adams, John Hancock, Paul Revere, Benjamin Franklin, and his family are buried. Dr Pepper staged a hunt, involving 23 U.S. and Canadian cities, with a North American jackpot of $1 million. In Boston the hunt was for a valuable coin in a leather pouch. The clue "by the name of a patriot at rest in Philly" indicated the 347-year-old Granary Burying Ground in Boston. Alarmed that treasure seekers would damage the cemetery, the Boston Park Department closed the cemetery. Dr Pepper learned about the closing from the *Boston Globe*.

Dr Pepper's corporate owner, Cadbury Schweppes PLC, canceled the entire promotion. In doing so, Greg Artkop, Cadbury spokesmen, confirmed that the coin was inside that Boston park, but said the company did not want to desecrate the cemetery. The coin was left there. Dr Pepper substituted a $10,000 award in a random drawing for Boston-area contestants registered on their website. Contestants were notified by e-mail.

Dr Pepper said in canceling the promotion that the $1 million prize was actually in Houston, not Boston.

None of the other 22 cities in the United States and Canada had complained, Artkop said, but Boston told Dr Pepper that the city's lawyers would follow up with Cadbury Schweppes. Boston park officials expressed dismay that a major corporation would authorize a stunt at such an historic site. The city's park officials said some compensation might be demanded to cover the costs of paying extra police to protect the site (Mishra & Ellement, 2007).

Boston also was the site of another marketing gimmick that ran into trouble. That event was Turner Broadcasting's stunt to promote Adult Swim's Aqua Teen Hunger Force, a Cartoon Network show. The stunt, developed and executed by Interference, a New York guerilla-marketing firm, involved installing briefcases with blinking lights on highways and bridges in 10 U.S. cities. When Boston residents reported seeing what they considered suspicious packages, the city closed highways and bridges. The two Boston men who installed the promotional pieces were arrested and faced criminal charges.

Turner hired outside legal and PR counsel and posted an apology on the Adult Swim's Website. Turner Senior Vice President Shirley Powell said, "We're a very responsible company.... We're committed to doing the right thing here" (Iacono, 2007b, p. 1; Mishra & Ellement, 2007). The marketing firm also apologized. Compensation to law enforcement agencies and local government totaled $2 million.

Measurement Issues

Attempts to show how much publicity actually adds to any campaign has been a constant, and troublesome, "measurement issue." Sometimes called the "multiplier effect," or "ad value equivalency," the notion that publicity, being mediated by editors and presented as news, has a measurable value to compare with paid advertising at some specific ratio has been around since the 1940s. The ratio was sometimes said to be 7 to 1 or 5 to 1 inches for publicity over advertising. The concept was that the information in publicity treated as news carried some sort of third-party endorsement. Some publicists used to measure the inches of their successful placements and multiply that by the publication's advertising rate.

Only during the 1990s, when more accountability for public relations came to the forefront, did serious testing of the concept start, although public relations researchers had discounted the notion for decades. Some tests showed that people might recall information about a product, service, event, or such, but not recall whether the information retained came from an ad or a news story generated by successful publicity placement. The notion of some validity for "third party endorsement" doesn't occur. PR scholar Glen Cameron's research indicated some delayed memory of a message from publicity but not enough to be significant. Kirk Hallahan's research found that even when people knew an ad was trying to sell them something, they preferred to get their information from the ad if the topic was particularly important to them (Cameron, 1994; Hallahan, 1996; Hallahan, 1999).

Still the debate continues. Ad value equivalency (AVE) remains a controversial subject in measurement (Iacono, 2007a, p. 13). Ketchum uses a model developed by Chris Atkins, vice-president of communications at Standard & Poor's. This model uses a special algorithm that considers the placement medium's reach, type, and prominence of the story and position in scoring each story. The data goes to VMS's PRTrak where value is calculated based on word count. The ad rate established is conservative, Atkins says, not necessarily what the real cost was to the advertiser because rates change and contract rates may differ. Atkins says AVE should not be misapplied and that Standard and Poor's uses the figures only in planning. The question is what exactly does that AVE figure calculated this way explain? Angela Jeffery, vice president of editorial research at VMS, says the validity is in media cost data. What VMS research shows is more accurate than story counts and audience impressions. Not much argument with that, but the question is what really happened as a result of the publicity? Katie Paine, president of K.D. Paine & Partners, emphasized this by noting that what matters is audience behavior driven from audience response to the publicity.

The World Health Organization's HIV-AIDS Effort: A Case Study in a Need for and Attempts at Integration

A long and intensive global campaign, probably the largest ever launched, is the World Health Organization's (WHO) HIV-AIDS effort. As might be expected, the campaign has encountered many problems. One easily identified problem involves extraordinary communication barriers due to regional languages and dialects beyond more widely used languages. Another, also easily identified, is the difference in government regulations regionally as well as across borders. Tied to government differences is the contrast in media and media systems.

Some media are entirely controlled by the government and all others must follow government regulations, even in very free, democratic countries. When governments are not secular, but religious, the faith, in all of its variety of practice, rules. Some of the issues may be matters of interpretation of faith and some may be simply cultural taboos. The HIV-AIDS campaign becomes an issue for social conservatives in any culture because their position is that any education about sexual practices encourages promiscuity.

To cope with all of these issues, WHO provides basic educational materials to health authorities in various countries so the information can be adapted for local use. As a result, many of those health and health information providers have turned for assistance with the campaign to professionals in public relations, advertising, and marketing.

The basic problem, then, is infrastructure. The issue is global and the same facts need global dissemination through campaigns tailored for publics in different ethnic and cultural groups around the world in such a way as to generate compliance.

A number of solutions to shore up infrastructure are being used. One is the use of global firms with the ability to handle a campaign locally, but coordinate with their associates in other parts of the world. Another is to gather groups of media representatives and public relations counselors for workshops and seminars, such as one held in Vanuatu for the Pacific Region in 1997. Some countries and regions are extremely active, but others are lagging.

The WHO effort was launched December 1, 2003, World AIDS Day as a crisis campaign with the idea of completing by 2005 the availability of antiretroviral drug treatment to 3 million people at 5,000 sites in less-developed countries by 2006. WHO named the campaign the "3 by 5 Initiative." About 15,000 health care workers were trained to deliver and monitor the therapy at the different sites. Six months into the campaign the goal of reaching 100,000 was not met, not even by half. Only 40,000 were enrolled in the therapies.

It's understandable that the campaign would get off to a slow start, given all of the complexities. One advantage was being able to combine all of the AIDS therapies into one pill that is only one third the cost of treatment in developed countries. Although most of the infected people live in sub-Saharan Africa, AIDS is increasing in Eastern Europe, Russia, China, Vietnam, Indonesia, and other parts of Asia. More than half of those infected are women, not only because they are physically the most vulnerable but also due to cultural problems of power and gender-based violence (Newsom et al., 2007, pp. 314, 337).

The WHO educational effort began long before the launch of the 2003 treatment campaign. The HIV-AIDS problem caught the attention of communication scholars, who have attempted to figure out how behavior changes can be achieved through messages that must be acted on by individuals involved in this highly personal issue. Using various theories from social psychology, three scholars proposed an analytical framework as a guide to policies to change behavior (Melkote, Muppidi, & Goswami, 2000). Significantly, the author-scholars concluded that information is not enough to change behaviors, and messages must address risk factors and how those risk factors are perceived.

> …[M]erely giving people facts/knowledge of AIDS may not always lead to risk reduction behaviors…. Therefore, for effective intervention strategies, there is a need to identify perceptions of risk and also examine factors that predict risk. Once the determinants of risk are identified, communication and educational strategies may be specifically directed toward changing the mental images that give rise to perceptions of risk…. An effective strategy for HIV/AIDS prevention will require long-term and sustained

strategies that should also address the social, cultural, economic, and political facts that influence the spread of AIDS. (Melkote et al., 2000 pp. 24–25)

The WHO campaign has attempted to address this issue and has gone beyond that to realize the pragmatic approach to a campaign, physically making the therapies available. The question remains, as it does with any campaign, are the resources there to accomplish that?

The clinics may not be accessible to as many people as the goals of the campaigns identify. A campaign in India conducted during the period 1988 to 1990 to encourage women to get their children inoculated for many common childhood diseases involved putting health care clinics in larger villages. The questions raised were: "How are the women going to get there, find someone to leave their other children with, have others do their work and then get home with an unhappy child?" For most of the women in rural India at that time it meant a whole day, one probably spent walking, carrying or walking along with a reluctant and then hurt, unhappy child, and, finally, tending to neglected tasks when they got home. India is much more developed now, but like many parts of the world, there still are small villages where the effort is too onerous and the risk not perceived as being worth the effort.

The HIV/AIDS campaign is worth studying because it is a global effort, and a serious one since the consequences leave many orphans, some also infected. This causes a large generational population gap and creates a dearth of laborers to contribute to the global economy. The campaign challenges the use and application of research, adaptation of theories from many fields, and the integration of many different message strategies.

Conclusions

As a management strategy, integration is becoming more accepted by public relations because of some realities of working in a high-tech world. The global marketplace has fragmented channels of communication and segmented audiences so that building and retaining relationships is more challenging, and the personalization of messages more significant. With global competition, branding—instant identification and recognition of a company—is more imperative.

The need for understanding a public relations partnership is also putting pressure on marketing, as suggested by this *Wall Street Journal* headline: "A New Force in Advertising—Protest By Email." The article is about images in an ad by a privately owned Italian fashion house that caused so much of an international uproar, all registered by e-mail, that the ad was dropped. The comments of one fashion publication's editor pinpointed the problem: "…[T]he explosion of Internet, email and blogs means 'every complaint gets magnified and gets spread much more quickly. They can make a lot more noise than before, even if it isn't the prevailing view'" (Passariello, Johnson, & Vranica, 2007, pp. B1–2).

This new avenue for crisis development is not restricted to advertising, but afflicts public relations as well, integrated or not. The question of how prepared public relations professionals are to cope was raised by two U.S. practitioners in a segment of their article about the future of public relations practice called "Digital Fear and Denial" (Cody & Vaughn, 2007).

> Many PR firms don't have their own blogs or podcasts. Many PR firms don't counsel clients on ways to integrate digital into a larger, integrated campaign. In addition, an alarming number of corporate PR professionals have ceded control of their organization's digital work to advertising or interactive peers. (pp. 7, 10–11)

The answer, the authors say, is fear, fear of loss of control and also fear of engaging in open, honest dialogues with consumers.

The problem is that developing and maintaining an ongoing, personal relationship with all publics is not in the future. It is now.

Notes

1. *Where Shall I Go to Study Advertising and Public Relations* (1993, 29th edition) lists 23 combined advertising/public relations programs, but at most of the schools either subject could be chosen as a major so it was not a truly integrated sequence.

2. Larissa A. Grunigs's statements, which she attributes to the 1991 IABC report on research findings include a summary of 12 general principles for excellence in public relations departments. The list does not appear as such in the *Excellence* book itself. "The excellent public relations department practices (1) a judicious mix of asymmetrical and symmetrical models of public relations; (2) is managed strategically; (3) enjoys a direct reporting relationship to senior management; (4) is headed by a practitioner in the managerial, (5) rather than technical role; requires expert practitioners, those who know how to manage the department strategically and symmetrically; (6) embraces a symmetrical world view or schema for public relations; (7) is separate from marketing (although in efforts such as product promotion, they may function in a complementary fashion); (8) is an integrated one, rather than being split among functions that may include communication relations, government affairs, internal communication and media relations; (9) provides equal opportunities for men and women; (10) has the support of top management; (11) operates in an organizational culture that is more participative than authoritarian; (12) exists in an environment more characterized by dynamism and even hostility than by stability (pp. 470–471; numbering added for clarity).

3. Thomas L. Harris was formerly president, vice chairman, and named partner of Golin/Harris International. Now he is managing partner of Thomas L. Harris & Company, a public relations consultancy that serves corporations and public relations firms.

References

Bernays, E. L. (1923). *Crystallizing public opinion*. New York: Boni & Liveright.

Bernays, E. L. (1928). *Propaganda*. New York: Horace Liveright.

Bernays, E. L. (1945). *Public relations*. Boston, MA: Bellman.

Bernays, E. L. (1961). *Crystallizing public opinion.*, revised and edited by author. New York: Liveright.

Bernays, E L. (1969). *The engineering of consent*. Norman, OK: University of Oklahoma Press.

Bernays, E. L. (1986). *The later years: Public relations insights, 1956–1986*. Rhinebeck, NY: H&M.

Cameron, G. T. (1994). Does publicity outperform advertising? An experimental test of the third-party endorsement. *Journal of Public Relations Research, 6,,* pp. 185–297.

Cody, S., & Vaughn, R. (2007, Winter). The future. *The Strategist,*

Duncan, T., Caywood, C., & Newsom, D. (1993). *Preparing advertising and public relations students for the communication industry in the 21st century: A report of the task force on integrated communications*. Columbia, SC: Association for Education in Journalism and Mass Communication.

Duncan, T., & Moriarty, S. (1997). *Driving brand value: Using integrated marketing to manage profitable stakeholder relationships*. New York: McGraw-Hill.

Grunig, L. A. (1996). Public relations. In M. B. Salwen & D. W. Stacks (Eds.), An integrated approach to communication theory and research (chapter 29). Mahwah, NJ: Erlbaum.

Hallahan, K. (1996). Product publicity: An orphan of marketing research. In E. Thorson & J. Moore (Eds.), *Integrated communication: The search for synergy in communication voices* (pp. 305–330). Mahwah, NJ: Erlbaum.

Hallahan, K. (1999). No, Virginia, it's not true what they say about publicity's implied third party endorsement effect. *Public Relations Review, 25,* 331–350.

Harris, T. L (1997). Integrated marketing public relations. In C. L. Caywood (Ed.), *The handbook of strategic public relations and integrated communications* (pp. 90–105). New York: McGraw-Hill.

Iacono, E. (2007a, March 19). Measuring the value of AVEs. *PR Week*.

Iacono, E. (2007b, February 5). Turner enlists PR aid as publicity stunt goes awry. *PR Week*,

International Public Relations Association (IPRA). (2007). IPRA Golden World Awards for Excellence 2006. Surrey, UK.

Kuntz, C. (2006, November 1–2). Presentation at the International Public Relations Association's Annual PR Summit, London.

Lauer, L. (1997). *Communication power: Energizing your nonprofit organization.* Gaithersburg, MD: Aspen.

Lauer, L. (2002). *Competing for students, money and reputation: Marketing the academy in the 21st century.* New York: Council for Advancement and Support of Education.

McGuire, W. J. (1973). Persuasion, resistance and attitude change. In I. de Sola Pool et al. (Eds.), *Handbook of communication* (pp. 216–252). Chicago: Rand McNally.

Melkote, S. R., Muppidi, S. R., & Goswami, D. (2000). Social and economic factors in an integrated behavioral and society approach to communication in HIV/AIDS [Supplement]. *Journal of Health Communication, 5,* 17–27.

Mishra, R., & Ellement, J. R. (2007). Marketing treasure hunt trips in historic graveyard. Retrieved March 23, 2007, from http://www.boston.com/news/local/articles/2007.

Moyers, B. (1982a). *A walk through the 20th century.* [Television broadcast]. Washington, D.C.: The Corporation for Entertainment and Learning/Bill Moyers.

Moyers, B. (1982b). *The image makers* [Television broadcast]. Washington, D.C.: The Corporation for Entertainment and Learning/Bill Moyers.

Newsom, D., & Carroll, T. (1992). *Tower of Babel: A descriptive report about attitudes toward the idea of integrated communication programs.* Paper presented at the AEJMC Conference, Montreal.

Newsom, D., & Haynes, J. (2008), *Public relations writing: Form and style.* Belmont, CA: Thomson.

Newsom, D., & Scott, A. (1985). *This is PR: The realities of public relations.* Belmont, CA: Wadsworth.

Newsom, D., Scott, A., & Turk, J. (1989). *This is PR: The realities of public relations.* Belmont, CA: Wadsworth.

Newsom, D., Turk, J., & Kruckeberg, D. (2007). *This is PR: The realities of public relations.* Belmont, CA: Wadsworth/Thomson.

Passariello, C., Johnson, K., & Vranica, S. (2007, March 22). *The Wall Street Journal,* pp. B1–2.

PR Week.(2007, March 12). PR Week awards, healthcare campaign of the year 2007. *PR Week.*

Therkelsen, D., & Fiebich, C. (2001). Message to desired action. *Journal of Communication Management* 6, 4.

Suggested Readings

IMC Articles

Low, G. S. (2000, January-February). Correlates of integrated marketing communications. *Journal of Advertising Research, ,40,* 27–39. Article identifies factors important to degree of integration.

Swain, W. N. (2003, Spring). An exploratory assessment of the IMC paradigm: Where are we, and where do we go from here? *IMC, 9,* 3–11. University of Colorado. Discussion of status of the discipline and difficulties of measurement.

Books

Duncan, T., & Moriarty, S. (1997). *Driving brand value: Using integrated marketing to manage profitable stakeholder relationships.* New York: McGraw-Hill. Chapter 5, "Develop Strategic Consistency" stresses speaking with one voice.

Lauer, L. (1997). *Communication power: Energizing your nonprofit organization.* Gaithersburg, MD: Aspen. Emphasizes importance of coordination and continuity in nonprofit messages to improve identity.

Newsom, D. (2007). *Bridging the gaps in global communication.* Oxford: Blackwell. See chap. 12.

Newsom, D., & Haynes, J. (2008). *Public relations writing: Form and style.* Belmont, CA: Wadsworth. Book treats organizational messages of all types and stresses consonance of message for an organization's credibility.

31

HEALTH COMMUNICATION

Charles Atkin and Kami Silk

Health communication has grown into an increasingly significant specialty at the forefront of research and instruction in the field of communication. This area of study formally originated in the mid-1970s when members of an International Communication Association (ICA) interest group adopted the label "health communication," although the interdisciplinary marriage between health and communication was "certainly a common-law relationship" long before that (Finnegan, 1989, p. 9). This specialization has developed rapidly in response to growing pragmatic and policy interests, particularly in federal public health agencies and among private sector health care providers. Pressing needs to address problems such as smoking, substance abuse, obesity, poor nutritional habits, and AIDS have given a strong impetus (and expanded funding) to the systematic study of health communication processes and effects, as the area provides a ripe context for testing and advancing communication theory.

The area's popularity and legitimacy are evinced by rising membership in health communication divisions in both ICA and the National Communication Association, the wide readership of two major journals (*Health Communication* and *Journal of Health Communication*), the publication of the *Handbook of Health Communication* (Thompson, Dorsey, Miller, & Parrott, 2003), and the explosion of health communication curricula across the country, including a health emphasis in 28 communication doctoral programs. *Healthy People 2010*, a government document that sets goals to improve the nation's health, now includes objectives specific to health communication (U.S. Department of Health and Human Services, 2000).

Health communication research often focuses on the development of effective health messages, the dissemination of health-related information through broadcast, print, and electronic media, and the role of interpersonal relationships in individual health communication, particularly provider–patient communication and the effects of social support on health and illness. The common thread weaving these diverse areas together is the emphasis on "health" as the desired outcome of communication. Whether investigating the effects on patient satisfaction of patient-centered communication behaviors exhibited by physicians, or the examination of public health campaign effectiveness on individuals engaging in safer sex, the ultimate goal has been to identify effective communication strategies for improving society's overall health.

History

Although communication scholars have been applying their expertise to health promotion and disease prevention only in recent decades, there have been sporadic efforts to use communication to improve public health for almost three centuries. According to Paisley (2001), the history of American communication campaigns has several notable examples involving health-related problems. The earliest case occurred in 1721, when religious and political leader Cotton Mather utilized pamphlets and speeches to successfully promote inoculation during Boston's serious smallpox epidemic.

Nineteenth century social and health problems associated with alcohol misuse resulted in the mobilization of a major movement lead by the Women's Christian Temperance Union. With a deft combination of grassroots organizing, legislative testimony, mass communication via newspapers and emerging magazines, and occasional confrontational incidents, charismatic leaders were able to promote anti-alcohol reforms at both the societal and individual level. Although the prohibitionists achieved little direct impact in persuading drinkers to give up their "vice," the temperance movement eventually produced the ultimate form of environmental engineering: a constitutional amendment banning the production and distribution of alcoholic beverages. As with many attempts to change unhealthy but pleasurable lifestyles, the effort unraveled when many drinkers evaded the law and public opinion shifted.

Early in the 1900s, "muckraker" reformers targeted a number of health-related problems, such as impure food and inadequate health care for the poor. The print media disseminated alarming stories that raised these issues higher on the public agenda, and eventually government agencies were created to address these public health problems.

Theory and research played a minimal role in early efforts, which occurred prior to the ascendance of social science methodology and the articulation of communication principles. Campaign leaders and allied journalists relied on intuition and conventional wisdom to formulate strategies and advocate solutions. It was not until the mid-20th century that researchers began working in an uneasy tandem with strategists and creative personnel to advance sophisticated campaign design and implementation. The relationship has evolved into a partnership with a higher degree of cooperation and mutual appreciation, particularly at the formative stage of campaign development. A critical turning point for the systematization of the health and communication relationship followed World War II, when the private medical sector and the public health sector began focusing on the behavioral aspects of health. As epidemiologists discovered connections between chronic diseases and culturally reinforced and induced behaviors, professionals and the public alike turned to the issues of prevention, particularly to identify strategies to effectively disseminate health-related information to the public. Critical communication processes such as persuasion and information dissemination were seen as playing a central role in an individual's health.

The prevalence of health campaigning steadily increased over last half of the 20th century. Very few campaigns were disseminated via media channels in the 1950s. The major campaign topic of the 1960s was smoking, with extensive news media publicity in the mid-60s and a major national PSA campaign on television later in the decade. In the 1970s to early 80s, heart disease campaigns were tested in several locales. Substantial national campaigns increased during the 1980s, emphasizing drunken driving, safety belts, drugs, and AIDS. Due to diminishing free media placements, the 1990s were characterized by paid messages about drugs, smoking, AIDS, and alcohol.

Neal (1962) was among the first to acknowledge the equally important role interpersonal communication played when he identified the communication between practitioners and patients as vital to study in the health field. The study of doctor–patient relationships emerged out of dissatisfaction among patients with the communication, or "bedside manner," of their health care providers. Korsch and her colleagues were among the first to identify the effects of various communicative behaviors exhibited by physicians during the medical encounter on outcomes such as patient satisfaction and compliance (Korsch, Gozzi, & Francis, 1968). Their landmark findings of the importance of physician expression of positive affect, respect, friendliness, and empathy have stood the test of time in both academic and practitioner circles (Korsch, 1989; Roter, 1977). As the study of the health and communication relationship in both public and private domains has matured, so too has the use of more sophisticated research methodology and theory development.

Classic Case

The leading cause of premature death in Western society is heart disease, and a significant portion of this health problem is due to lifestyle factors such as smoking, lack of exercise, high-fat diet, and chronic stress. Because these risk factors are partially preventable, communication researchers became interested in strategies for influencing the community environment and individual decisions that contribute to heart disease. The preeminent research program investigating this problem has been Stanford University's Three Community Study (TCS) and Five City Project (FCP). Combining expertise from the medical school and communication department, the Stanford program began in the early 1970s with a simple experimental design comparing media vs. interpersonal interventions, a sophisticated theoretical conceptualization of processes to change knowledge, attitudes, and practices, and elaborate applied implementation in the communities.

It has become the most influential and frequently cited health campaign in history; indeed, it is recognized by Rogers (1994) as the most significant turning point in the development of health communication. At the behavioral level, the campaigns sought to reduce intake of saturated fat, cholesterol, salt, and excessive calories; to eliminate tobacco use; to increase physical activity; and to promote blood pressure checks and adherence to hypertension control medication.

The original TCS combined various theoretical perspectives such as social learning, innovation diffusion, learning hierarchies, inoculation, social comparison, and reasoned action, the investigators created a Communication-Behavior Change model (Farquhar, Maccoby, & Solomon, 1984). The key audience of middle-age males was targeted with a heavy flow of messages, which included TV and radio spots, newspaper columns, cookbooks, booklets, and bus cards that were developed through formative evaluation. The summative evaluation research featured a quasi-experimental design in three comparable sites: a media-only community, a second community where the same basic media campaign was supplemented by face-to-face communication, and a no-intervention control community. The results showed that knowledge-gain impact occurred to a similar degree in both intervention communities, but that actual behavioral change was greater in the media-plus-interpersonal treatment site after the first year of the campaign. The key outcome measure was a heart disease risk score composed of plasma cholesterol, systolic blood pressure, and relative weight. After a second year of message dissemination, the sample in the media-only town caught up with those experiencing the more intensive intervention. The subsequent Five City Project sought to increase the exportability of the campaign by reducing the scope of the externally introduced intervention; the Stanford team relied more heavily on local community mobilization to sustain the campaign. A similar quasi-experimental design was used to isolate the effects of the communication effort over a far longer period, and more bottom-line outcomes such as morbidity and mortality were added to the study; significant reductions were demonstrated in treatment communities (Farquhar et al., 1990).

Theory Development

Communication as a discipline has been criticized for its limited and unsystematic theory development, particularly in the applied areas such as health communication. According to Berger (1991), communication phenomena occurring within health and other applied contexts are so distinctive that they may merit their own context-specific theories; Sharf (1993) observes that "applied research can be complementary rather than antithetical to theory generation" (p. 39).

For example, Rice and Atkin (1989) note: "While health campaigns are typically viewed as merely applied communication research, the most effective campaigns carefully review and apply relevant theories; further, campaign results can be used to extend and improve theories about media effects and social change" (p. 9).

Health communication scholars have drawn upon a wide range of theoretical perspectives from communication, social psychology, public health, and anthropology. A popular persuasion framework for guiding campaign efforts is McGuire's (2001) input-output model and classification of psychological theories. Communication variables such as source credibility and message organization constitute the laundry list of input factors, while the 12 output response steps proceed from exposure to post-behavioral consolidation. McGuire also discusses variants to the straightforward communication/persuasion model, including the peripheral route posited in the elaboration likelihood model (Petty & Cacioppo, 1986) and reversal of certain sequences proposed in dissonance and self-perception theories. Several theories and frameworks have been particularly popular among health communication researchers and practitioners. Social learning theory (Bandura, 1986) directs attention to the importance of modeling healthy behaviors and rewarding consequences. Bandura also emphasizes self-efficacy of performance as a key factor in the success of health persuasion. The theory of reasoned action (Ajzen & Fishbein, 1980) focuses on the combination of the individual's belief expectancies about outcomes related to health practices and evaluation of those outcomes; it also accentuates the role of social norms in behavioral intentions. Subsequent variations were introduced by Ajzen (2002) in his influential theory of planned behavior, which specifies key health behavior predictors such as perceived behavioral control and subjective norms.

From the public health discipline, similar theoretical perspectives have made significant contributions to the understanding of the persuasion process. According to the Health Belief Model advanced by Janz and Becker (1984) and Strecher and Rosenstock (1997), major components of health behavior are perceived susceptibility and severity along with benefits and barriers. Protection Motivation Theory includes similar elements encompassing threat and efficacy (Rogers & Prentice-Dunn, 1997). Prochaska and Velicer (1997) developed the Transtheoretical Model that features stages of change in the precaution adoption process.

A complementary framework is social marketing (Kotler, Roberto, & Lee, 2002), which is based on the fundamental principle of exchange theory. Social marketing applies practical techniques from commercial marketing such as packaging and positioning the health practice as an attractive product, minimizing the monetary (and social, psychological, and effort) costs, skillfully segmenting the audience according to demographic and risk profiles, and strategically mixing personal and media channels for promoting the product. The diffusion of innovation concepts articulated by Rogers (1983) has also helped guide strategies of health campaign designers. Most recently, techniques of media advocacy have been refined and applied in health campaign contexts (Wallack, Dorfman, Jernigan, & Themba, 1994). Finally, scholars interested in the interpersonal aspects of health communication are embracing a broader range of theoretical approaches. For example, Sharf (1993) points to the merits of narrative theory to examine the discourse between health care providers and patients. Lupton (1994) calls for the adoption of a more critical approach that allows for recognition and explicit examination of the inherent power differential and asymmetry of knowledge between health care providers and patients.

Features of Mediated and Interpersonal Channels

Health information can be communicated through almost all of the remarkably diverse array of channels available in the modern communication system. The still-central medium of television disseminates messages in varied forms, such as public service announcements (PSAs), hard news items, feature stories, paid spots, talk show discussions, full-length educational programs, and entertainment program plot inserts. The Internet has rapidly become a central mode of health communication, particularly the featuring of information-rich website pages, interactive messages, and experience-sharing blogs utilized by motivated health information seekers. For example, screening questionnaires on websites can assess each individual's readiness stage, knowledge levels, and current beliefs, and then direct them to narrowly targeted customized messages that are precisely designed to address their needs and predispositions.

The other key mass media are radio (e.g., announcer commentary, PSAs), and newspapers and magazines (e.g., news, features, advice columns, editorials, ads). In addition, pamphlets and direct mail materials are distributed to individuals, slide shows and videos are shown to groups, and posters and billboards are seen by passersby. Among newer technologies, entertaining interactive formats such as games are particularly well suited as vehicles for health information aimed at youthful audience segments.

Finally, interpersonal communication takes the form of interactions between patients and health care providers, contacts by health organization workers and volunteers, and informal discussions and support-giving among family members and friends.

In assessing each option for channeling health messages, myriad advantages and disadvantages can be taken into consideration along basic communicative dimensions such as *reach* (proportion of community exposed to the message); *specialization* (targetability for reaching specific subgroups); *intrusiveness* (capability for overcoming selectivity and commanding attention); *safeness* (minimizing risk of boomerang or irritation); *participation* (active receiver involvement while processing stimuli); *meaning modalities* (array of senses employed in conveying meaning); *personalization* (human relational nature of source-receiver interaction); *decodability* (mental effort required for processing stimulus); *depth* (channel capacity for conveying detailed and complex content); *credibility* (believability of material conveyed); *agenda-setting* (potency of channel for raising salience priority of issues); *accessibility* (ease of placing messages in channel); *economy* (low cost for producing and disseminating stimuli); *efficiency* (simplicity of arranging for production and dissemination). There are substantial differences among channels on these dimensions, which can be illustrated by comparisons among three leading forms of health information communication: *interpersonal* communication is superior for specialization, intrusiveness, participation, modalities, credibility, and safeness; *PSAs* have greater reach, intrusiveness, decodability, and agenda potency; *websites* are advantageous on specialization, safeness, participation, depth, accessibility, economy, and efficiency. Thus, there are distinct roles for various channels and modes; the optimum mix depends on the nature of the health topic, the target audience characteristics, and the communication objectives.

Research Methods

Health communication researchers typically borrow standard methodological techniques from the mainstream social sciences rather than develop new methods. Despite a general acceptance and valuing of both quantitative and qualitative methodologies, the preponderance of health communication research to date has relied on quantitative approaches. The distinctive feature of health communication research is the way that certain methods have been applied to investigations. In particular, evaluation research approaches have been given greater emphasis in health-related studies than other domains of communication research. This section will describe the basic elements of health campaign evaluation methods, and then briefly illustrate the application of other techniques such as experiments and doctor–patient interaction analysis.

Formative and Summative Evaluation

Evaluation research seeks to answer practical questions about audiences via collection of background information prior to message production and the measurement of effectiveness after dissemination. *Formative research* occurs both before campaigns are designed and during the development of messages. At the preproduction phase, Atkin and Freimuth (2001) describe how evaluation data are useful in identifying target audience characteristics and predispositions, specifying the crucial intermediate response variables and behavioral outcomes, ascertaining channel exposure patterns, and determining receptivity to potential message components. The primary research techniques are focus group discussions and formal surveys conducted with audience members.

For example, survey interviews with representative samples are typically used to segment the population along a number of dimensions defined in terms of demographic and psychographic characteristics, social role position, behavioral risk profile, beliefs and attitudes, and communication patterns. Ratings on a checklist of potential sources and arguments might also be measured. By contrast, focus group moderators elicit qualitative information to guide the development and refinement of message themes and appeals; the participants' in-depth comments yield insights into audience predispositions and provide feedback about substantive and stylistic message ideas that are under consideration.

The second phase of formative evaluation research focuses on message pretesting. Investigators solicit audience reactions to preliminary versions of message executions to determine which alternatives are most promising. This may involve either focus group comments following exposure to message components and rough executions, or systematic paper-and-pencil (or physiological) measures with larger samples of individuals. The purpose is to ascertain the amount of attention, extent of comprehension, degree of personal relevance, and level of persuasiveness. Strong and weak points are also identified, along with suggestions for improvements.

Federal health agencies created the "Health Message Testing Service," a standardized system to pretest radio and television spots (U.S. Department of Health and Human Services, 2003). It employed the "theater testing" approach, where groups are exposed to test messages realistically embedded in entertainment programming. Researchers measure evaluation of message qualities as well as recall, comprehension, and learning,

Summative research encompasses an array of techniques that are designed to ascertain the campaign outcomes. This form of post-campaign evaluation is widely practiced in the health domain because of the pragmatic results-oriented goals of health campaigns and the need for accountability. Summative research measures size and characteristics of the audience reached, the influence of the campaign on attitudes and health behavior. Investigators also seek to isolate causal pathways and to determine if any lack of effect is attributable to theory failure or program failure. Flay and Cook (1989) describe three summative evaluation models employed. The superficial "advertising" model sensitively measures the early stages of audience response such as exposure, recall, and subjectively perceived effectiveness; sample surveys are most often used for this type of research. Second, the "impact-monitoring" model typically examines overt behavioral or aggregate societal outcomes, usually via secondary analyses of archival data. Finally, the "experimental" model focuses on large-scale tests of causal influences via controlled manipulation of treatments, typically at the community level; additional comparisons may be made between individuals with higher versus lower exposure to messages within experimental communities.

Other Interpersonal and Mass Communication Methods

Content analysis is one of the most widely used techniques in mass communication. Although systematic measurement of health-related message features does not permit inferences about the impact of the content, it does provide a basis for predicting likely effects as well as exploring the motives of media gatekeepers. For example, researchers track media health portrayals such as smoking, drinking, or breast cancer in news, entertainment, and advertising and then they may relate the content to health outcomes, media policies, or external pressures.

Laboratory experiments are frequently conducted to examine the impact of health messages. The most basic design is a simple after-only comparison between experimental and control groups that are exposed or not exposed to a particular health PSA, program, or news item. More sophisticated designs have been used to compare content manipulations featuring two or three versions of the same message (e.g., high versus medium versus low fear, or celebrity versus ordinary source), or factorial designs (e.g., level of fear by type of source).

Time series analyses have been computed with archival data collected on a regular basis. For example, researchers may track fluctuations of health related products or practices and relate these trends to variations in the frequency or nature of messages disseminated over a period of months or years.

Relatively few research studies have employed the true field experiment featuring a manipulated set of messages disseminated to randomly assigned treatment groups under naturalistic conditions; the high cost and difficulty of controlling dissemination seldom permits the application of this elaborate but rigorous technique.

In the interpersonal domain of health communication, the vast majority of studies have relied on interaction analysis to systematically examine doctor–patient interaction. Korsch and her colleagues were the first to adapt Bales's (1950) "Interaction Process Analysis" scheme to categorize both physicians' and patients' statements (Korsch et al., 1968). Numerous other coding schemes have subsequently been developed relying on Bales's scheme as a foundation, most notably Roter's "Modified Interaction Process Analysis" (Roter, 1977). This has produced a plethora of studies that provide a numerical accounting of types of utterances present during typical medical encounters. Despite their descriptive utility and continued existence, such studies have faced criticism for their limited ability to definitively describe the complex process of physician–patient interaction (i.e., Wasserman & Inui, 1983).

Research Findings and Applications

Given the inherent applied nature of health communication, researchers are interested in discovering which approaches work the best to provide useful advice to practitioners. Those practicing on the front lines, such as doctors, health agency officials, and PSA campaign designers need to know what to say and how to say it. Communication skills training programs and the campaign design contexts are two key areas for practical applications of communication research.

Communication Skills

With respect to interpersonal health communication, the most fundamental application rests in the development and implementation of training programs for health care providers (HCPs) (e.g., physicians, nurses, public health professionals), as well as patients to improve the effectiveness of their interactions. Due to the diverse ethnic and racial composition of patient populations, increasing the cultural competence of HCPs has been a primary focus of training programs. In 1999, the Accreditation Council for Graduate Medical Education (ACGME) included interpersonal and communication skills in the six areas of general competencies for medical students. In response to the new communication competencies required for medical residents to become certified, medical schools have made communication training classes a required part of their curricula. Interdisciplinary teams across the country have designed, and now deliver and evaluate communication skills training programs, incorporating many of the early fundamental findings of researchers such as Korsch and her colleagues.

Outside of the United States, programs like the *Cascade Communication Skills Teaching Project*, have been developed and implemented to deliver evidence-based communication skills training to general practitioners (GPs) in the East Anglia Deanery (Draper, Silverman, Hibble, Berrington, & Kurtz, 2002). GPs can continue their own professional development as well as train other GPs. The implications of these programs suggest that fundamental communication skills are teachable, and that these communicative behaviors significantly affect the relationship that develops between HCPs and patients. Additionally, both nonverbal and verbal communication behaviors have been found to lead to improved patient outcomes, such as greater patient satisfaction, recall, adherence, symptom resolution, and overall quality of health (Beck, Dautridge, & Sloane, 2002). Along with the strong focus on HCP training, improving patient communication skills has also been a priority, with many hospitals and public health programs offering training and educational materials to patients. For example, *The Infant Feeding Study* (TIFS), a curriculum developed for low-income mothers to delay the introduction of solid foods into infants' diets, devoted one of its seven lessons to training mothers on how to communicate with HCPs (Horodynski, Olson, Brophy-Herb, Silk, & Shurer, in press). The clear emphasis on improving communication skills across multiple populations demonstrates the important role that effective communication plays in patient health outcomes.

Campaign Research Applications

There are numerous practical implications of the plethora of public health campaigns research. The central questions examined in the theoretically-based lab experiments and in the more applied pretesting research involve the relative effectiveness of health message appeals. For example, researchers are seeking to determine whether the public will be more effectively motivated by positive versus negative messages: promises of wellness or safety versus threats of illness or death. They are also examining which dimensions of persuasive incentives are most influential: physical health versus economic (e.g., saving money. losing a job) versus psychological (e.g., achievement, anxiety. regret, self-esteem) versus cognitive (consistency, ignorance, rationality) versus moral (e.g., propriety, guilt, fairness) versus social (e.g., acceptance, embarrassment, altruism, deviance). Furthermore, research is useful in isolating the most effective types of sources, evidence, organization of material, channels, and styles of presentation.

At a more macro level, summative evaluation research provides answers to questions about the overall impact of large-scale campaigns. Although it is difficult to isolate the relative contribution of various components of lengthy multi-faceted efforts to disseminate health information (e.g., community-wide heart disease prevention campaign or national AIDS program), investigators attempt to ascertain the extent to which these comprehensive campaigns influence the knowledge, attitudes, and behaviors of the public. The following sections describe some of the key concepts that have been investigated, present some principles that have been developed, and summarize the overall impact of health communication campaigns.

Guidelines for Designing Effective Health Messages

Based on the array of theoretical perspectives advanced by the academic community and the increasing body of lessons learned by practitioners, a basic set of principles for devising communication strategies has emerged in recent years (Salmon & Atkin, 2003). The listing below provides a useful summary of some key conclusions from the research literature, beginning with substantive material in message development and proceeding to mechanical and stylistic presentational factors.

Selection of Incentive Appeals

Messages should feature persuasive reasons for adopting the recommended behavior. In health campaigns, there has been an over-reliance on fear appeals that threaten physical harm; these should be supplemented with positive arguments and with economic, social, or psychological incentives (e.g., rather than focusing on overdose death, anti-drug messages should engender concerns about corporate drug-testing or portray a drug-free lifestyle as normal, healthy, and satisfying). It is preferable to use multiple rather than single appeals, within a typical length message, and particularly across a series of messages in a campaign.

Evidence

In conveying an incentive appeal, it is usually more effective to provide dramatized case examples rather than statistical documentation supporting claims made in the message (e.g., the tragedy of a car crash victim or the triumph of a person who has successfully quit smoking). In processing health information, audiences tend to be more responsive to depictions of other people's experiences rather than complex and often unimpressive facts and figures.

One-Sided versus Two-Sided Message Content

A two-sided strategy that refutes, downplays, or concedes disadvantages of the target response is generally more influential. This strategy is superior when the drawbacks are familiar and the audience is resistant to change, as is the case with many health topics.

Source Featured in Message

The source is the manifest messenger appearing in messages. Eight types of source presenters are used in health messages: celebrity (e.g., famous athlete, entertainer); public official (government leader, agency director); expert specialist (doctor, researcher); organization leader (hospital administrator, corporate executive); professional performer (standard spokesperson, attractive model, actor); average person (blue-collar male, middle-class female); specially experienced person (victim, survivor, successful role model); and unique character (animated, anthropomorphic, costumed). The effectiveness of each type depends on topic and audience; the relative contribution of source credibility (expertise and trustworthiness), similarity, and likeability vary according to the situation, so selection of the messengers should be guided by formative evaluation research.

Realism and Personalization

Messages should depict situations and models that enable audiences to connect the material to own experiences; increasing perceived relevance is particularly important in reaching those who do not feel that health messages apply to them.

Attractiveness and Vividness

Entertaining styles generally enhance message impact; cleverness is an effective feature, but humor produces diverse responses and must be used carefully. Messages should use lively language, striking statements, fascinating facts, and vibrant visuals (and alluring alliteration).

Impact of Health Campaigns

Several hundred health campaigns have been evaluated and reported in the research literature over the past three decades. A review by Atkin and Schiller (2002) summarizes the key findings for all major media-based campaigns from 1990 to 2002. Snyder (2001) performed a meta-analysis of the degree of behavioral impact across a subset of 48 media health campaigns (measuring responses of almost 170,000 participants), typically comparing treatment communities with control communities or exposed vs. non-exposed audiences. On the average, behavior change occurs among approximately 7% to 10% more of the people in the campaign sites than those in control communities.

The effects are stronger for adoption of a new behavior (average 12% adopting practices such as exercise, condom use, dental care) than cessation of current habits (average 5% ceasing practices such as smoking, binge drinking, risky sex). Campaigns promoting health services achieved modest impact (average 7% for using services such as cancer screening or hypertension treatment). Across all of these campaigns, the level of exposure to media messages averages about 40% of the target audiences. The size of effects is much greater in communities where higher exposure is achieved.

In assessing health campaign effects, the key determinants are the degree of audience receptivity, the quality and quantity of messages, the dissemination channels, and the larger communication environment. Audiences are more readily influenced on certain topics and target responses (e.g., the designated driver to prevent drunk driving), while they are resistant in other cases (e.g., reducing binge drinking). Some segments of the audience are much more receptive than others (e.g., casual versus hard core drug users, or children versus teenagers).

Quantitative potency of campaign stimuli is necessary but not sufficient for success. Both the total volume of messages and the prominence of message placement are crucial. Multiplicity of channels, appeals, and executions increases impact, providing there is some uniformity of elements across the various messages in a campaign.

Qualitative potency factors are also important, particularly the incentive appeals featured in the persuasive strategy. Incentives are needed to change attitudes and motivate action; both promises of rewards to be gained or threats of punishment are effective. Credibility plays a significant role in convincing people that the arguments are valid through the use of evidence and credible source presenters. Relevance is another quality that is essential in actively involving the audience and demonstrating how the target response and incentives are pertinent to their own situation. Attractive styles of presentation help attract audience attention, especially when subject matter is dull or distant topics and when quantity is limited.

Media channel effectiveness varies, depending on the target audience and the type of message. Televised PSA spots and newscast/newspaper publicity tend to be most influential, but other channels are effective in certain situations. Interpersonal communication usually augments the impact of media messages, especially via normative and personal influences on attitudes and practices.

The effects of health campaigns are often undermined by counter-messages such as commercial advertising that glamorizes alcohol and tobacco, or entertainment programming that portrays the pleasures of sex or cocaine use. Occasionally, a consonant message environment will increase impact by reinforcing the campaign messages (e.g., ads for low-fat foods, entertainment depicting the designated driver, or news stories about AIDS deaths).

In conclusion, the overall magnitude of behavioral effects is modest in most campaigns; while a few health campaigns have achieved substantial impact, others have been notably weak. This may be partly due to the difficulty in accounting for effects that occur over lengthy periods of time (e.g., cumulative level of media exposure and developmental issues), which decreases the likelihood of definitively detecting existing effects (Hornik, 2002). It is important to note that the most successful campaigns (e.g., drugs, drunk driving, and smoking) involve receptive sub-audiences, employ compelling rewards and punishments, and high quantities of message dissemination over a sustained period of time. Ineffective campaigns (e.g., cancer, safe sex, and responsible drinking) tend to suffer from widespread audience resistance resulting from large immediate sacrifices relative to distant benefits; poor presentation of incentives; low prominence of message placement; lack of relevant message content; unattractive stylistic quality; and counteracting media environment.

Future Directions

On the positive side, the health communication field can be currently characterized by a rapidly expanding research literature and increasingly sophisticated conceptual frameworks. However, researchers have a long way to go in advancing both theoretical knowledge and practical applications (Atkin & Arkin, 1990).

One area of interest that resonates for health communication is health literacy, defined as "the degree to which individuals have the capacity to obtain, process, and understand basic health information and services needed to make appropriate health decisions" (U.S. Department of Health & Human Services, 2000). While there is great interest in improving the health literacy of individuals, measurement of health literacy as a construct needs further refinement as current measurement is limited to word recognition tests, reading ability, spelling, fill-in-the-blank, and some arithmetic questions (Davis, Michielutte, Askov, Williams, & Weiss, 1998), which are typically only partially reflective of the conceptual definition of health literacy. A related dimension of health literacy deserving further study is numeracy, particularly as it pertains to the effective presentation of statistical evidence to the lay public and its role in patient decision making and compliance. With the overwhelming amount of health information available to individuals via the Internet and other media sources, it is essential that researchers determine how best to communicate statistical information to large sub-groups lacking numeracy skills.

In many ways, health communication serves as an excellent umbrella to merge researchers across disciplines with community advocates and the lay public at large. When one considers that significant behavior change is a complex process that requires a readiness to change among a target audience, theoretically driven campaigns and interventions, and environmental support, it is critical for multiple stakeholders to participate in the process. The breast cancer and environment research centers (BCERC), provide one example of a transdisciplinary model where researchers from biology, epidemiology, and communication backgrounds have partnered with breast cancer advocates to investigate environmental links to cancer (Breast Cancer and Environment Research Centers, 2007). Ultimately, the project will develop health messages designed to inform the lay public about the state of the evidence for breast cancer prevention using communication theory and principles. Alternative models for conducting research and implementing campaigns are becoming increasingly necessary if complex problems are to be addressed, and communication researchers can serve as the integrating glue for large scale projects.

Perhaps the biggest criticism facing researchers engaged primarily in interpersonal health communication work is that the majority of studies have been conducted in a formal health care or medical setting; most investigations have been restricted to the relationship between physician and patient. When one considers the array of health care workers with whom patients interact (e.g., radiologists, lab technicians, receptionists, etc.), the paucity of interpersonal communication research outside of the physician–patient interaction is revealed. Researchers should also systematically examine health-related interactions between family members, friends, peers, and co-workers, because Americans spend the majority of their time talking about health-related issues and learning health-related information in non-medical settings (e.g., at home, work). Rootman and Hershfield (1994) call on health communication researchers to expand their scope of investigation to recognize the critical role such settings play in the arena of health communication. Research should examine more closely the extent to which health-related communication activities are occurring in health care settings versus social or work-related settings. Moreover, investigators should extend this examination to encompass the ultimate effects of these context-specific health communication messages on individual behavior.

Health communication researchers should continue in their efforts to identify effective mass and interpersonal communication strategies for motivating individuals to engage in desirable health behaviors. In particular, researchers should be encouraged to isolate potentially unique strategies necessary to motivate individuals that have been disenfranchised in society (e.g., the homeless, people living in poverty, people of color, members of the gay and lesbian communities). Media-oriented scholars and practitioners should widen their focus beyond the personal level to encompass strategies designed to change societal-level environmental conditions within which individuals make health decisions. Wallack et al. (1993) pioneered the "media advocacy" approach for using mass communication to apply pressure for changes in policies that will promote public health goals. Finally, the intersection between technology and health has only begun to be investigated with telehealth applications in health care, health information seeking and provision on the Internet, and health education gaming opportunities.

In conclusion, despite health communication's applied focus and warnings voiced concerning the uniqueness of the context rather than phenomena, health communication researchers should generate theories about the nature and process of health communication. Only through such consideration and reflection will health communication scholars understand the inextricable link between communication and health.

Suggested Readings

A large number of monographs, textbooks, and readers have been published on the subject of health communication, primarily by scholars in the areas of mass communication, interpersonal communication, social psychology, and public health. This section briefly identifies the basic content of 19 key books published since 1990: Atkin and Wallack (1990) examine the intersection of mass communication and public health; Backer, Rogers, and Sopory (1992) provide guidelines for designing health campaigns; Backer and Rogers (1993) describe organizational aspects and case studies of campaign implementation; Crano and Burgoon (2002) assemble a series of theoretical perspectives and research activities focusing of the role of the media in drug abuse prevention; Edgar, Noar, and Freimuth (2007) focus on public and private communication about HIV/AIDS in the United States and other countries; Hornik (2002) assembles 16 major studies using various methods to investigate health communication programs in many nations; Kotler et al. (2002) discuss social marketing approaches to health; Kreuter, Farrell, Olevitch, and Brennan (1999) describe how media technologies enable production of tailored health messages; Maibach and Parrott (1995) address theoretical and practical approaches to health message design; Ray (2005) covers a wide variety of practical case studies in health care, family, and societal settings; Rice and Atkin (2001) feature many health-related chapters in a general communication campaign book; Rice and Katz (2000) analyze changes in health care, information seeking, and support resulting from the Internet technologies; Singhal, Cody, Rogers, and Sabido (2004) trace the history and review international cases of the expanding practice of entertainment-education to promote health. Thompson, Dorsey, Miller, and Parrott (2003) present a comprehensive handbook with sections on patient–provider interaction, the mass media, and community and organizational issues; Tones and Green (2004) present an international perspective on the complexities of health promotion strategies; Salmon (1989) examines the balance between social values and social change in information campaigns; Wallack et al. (1993) focus on the media advocacy approach to health promotion; Witte, Meyer, and Martell (2001) provide a detailed blueprint for constructing effective health messages. In addition, there is an elaborate manual presenting useful guidance on the design of health programs published by the federal government (U.S. Department of Health and Human Services, 2003).

References

Accreditation Council for Graduate Medical Education. (1999). *ACGME outcome project*. Retrieved September 2007, from http://www.acgme.org/Outcome/

Ajzen, I. (2002). Perceived behavioral control, self-efficacy, locus of control, and the theory of planned behavior. *Journal of Applied Social Psychology, 32*, 665–683.

Ajzen, I., & Fishbein, M. (1980). *Understanding attitudes and predicting social behavior*. Englewood Cliffs, NJ: Prentice-Hall.

Atkin, C., & Arkin, E. (1990). Issues and initiatives in communicating health information to the public. In C. Atkin & L. Wallack (Eds.), *Mass communication and public health: Complexities and conflicts* (pp. 5–32). Newbury Park, CA: Sage.

Atkin, C., & Freimuth, V. (2001). Formative evaluation research in campaign design. In R. Rice & C. Atkin (Eds.), *Public communication campaigns* (pp. 125–145). Thousand Oaks, CA: Sage.

Atkin, C., & Schiller, L. (2002). The impact of public service advertising. In L. Schiller & T. Hoff (Eds.), *Public service advertising in a new media age* (pp. 21–30). Menlo Park, CA: Kaiser Family Foundation.

Atkin, C., & Wallack, L. (Eds.). (1990). *Mass communication and public health: Complexities and conflicts*. Newbury Park, CA: Sage.

Backer, T., & Rogers, E. (1993). *Organizational aspects of health communication campaigns: What works?* Newbury Park, CA: Sage.

Backer, T., Rogers, E., & Sopory, P. (1992). *Designing health communication campaigns: What works?* Newbury Park, CA: Sage.

Bales, R. (1950). *Interaction analysis process*. Cambridge, MA: Addison-Wesley Press.

Bandura, A. (1986). *Social foundations of thought and action: A social cognitive theory*. Englewood Cliffs, NJ: Prentice-Hall.

Beck, R. S. Daughtridge, R., & Sloane, P. D. (2002). Physician–patient interaction in the primary care office: A systematic review. *Journal of the American Board of Family Medicine, 15*(1), 25–38.

Berger, C. (1991). Communication theories and other curios. *Communication Monographs, 58*, 101–113.

Breast Cancer and Environment Research Centers. (2007). Retrieved September 5, 2007, from http://www.bcerc.org.

Crano, W., & Burgoon, M. (Eds.). (2002), *Mass media and drug prevention: Classic and contemporary theories and research*. Mahwah, NJ: Erlbaum.

Davis, T. C., Michielutte, R., Askov, E. N., Williams, M. V., & Weiss, B. D. (1998). Practical assessment of adult literacy in health care. *Health Education & Behavior, 25*(5), 613–624.

Draper, J., Silverman, J., Hibble, A., Berrington, R. M., & Kurtz, S. M. (2002). The East Anglia Deanery communication skills teaching project. *Medical Teacher, 24*(3), 294–298.

Edgar, T., Noar, S., & Freimuth, V. (2007). *Communication perspectives on HIV/AIDS for the 21st century.* Mahwah, NJ: Erlbaum.

Farquhar, J., Fortmann. S., Flora, J., Taylor, C., Haskell, W., & Williams, P. (1990). Effects of community-wide education on cardiovascular disease risk factors: Stanford Five-City Project. *Journal of the American Medical Association, 264,* 359–365.

Farquhar, J., Maccoby, N., & Solomon, D. (1984). Community applications of behavioral medicine. In E. Gentry (Ed.), *Handbook of behavioral medicine* (pp. 437–478). New York: Guilford.

Finnegan, J. (1989). Health and communication: Medical and public health influences on the research agenda. In E. Ray & L. Donohew (Eds.), *Communication and health: Systems and applications* (pp. 9–24). Hillsdale, NJ: Erlbaum.

Flay, B., & Cook. T. (1989). Three models for summative evaluation of prevention campaigns with a mass media component. In R. Rice & C. Atkin (Eds.), *Public communication campaigns* (pp. 175–196). Newbury Park, CA: SAGE.

Hornik, R. (2002). *Public health communication: Evidence for behavior change.* Mahwah, NJ: Erlbaum.

Horodynski, M., Olson, B., Brophy-Herb, H., Silk, K., & Shirer, K. (in press). The Infant Feeding Series (TIFS) Curriculum. *Journal of Nutrition Education and Behavior.*

Janz, N. K., & Becker, M. H. (1984). The health belief model: A decade later. *Health Education Quarterly, 11,* 1–47.

Korsch, B. (1989). Studying health communication: An agenda for the future. *Health Communication, 1,* 5–9.

Korsch, B., Gozzi, E., & Francis, V. (1968). Gaps in doctor–patient communication: Doctor–patient interaction and patient satisfaction. *Pediatrics, 42,* 855–871.

Kotler, P., Roberto N., & Lee, N. (2002). *Social marketing: Improving the quality of life.* Thousand Oaks, CA: Sage.

Kreuter, M., Farrell, D., Olevitch, L., & Brennan, L. (1999). *Tailoring health messages.* Mahwah, NJ: Erlbaum.

Lupton, L. D. (1994). Toward the development of critical health communication praxis. *Health Communication, 6,* 55–67.

Maibach, E., & Parrott. R. (1995). *Designing health messages: Approaches from communication theory and public health practice.* Newbury Park, CA: Sage.

McGuire, W. (2001). Input and output variables currently promising for constructing persuasive communications. In R. Rice & C. Atkin (Eds.), *Public communication campaigns* (pp. 22–48). Thousand Oaks, CA: SAGE.

Neal, H. (1962). *Better communication for better health.* New York: Columbia University Press.

Paisley, W. (2001). Public communication campaigns: The American experience. In R. Rice & C. Atkin (Eds.), *Public communication campaigns* (pp. 3–21). Thousand Oaks, CA: Sage.

Petty, R., & Cacioppo, J. (1986). *Communication and persuasion: Central and peripheral routes to attitude change.* New York: Springer-Verlag.

Prochaska, J., & Velicer, W. (1997). The transtheoretical model of health behavior change. *American Journal of Health Promotion, 12,* 38–48.

Ray, E. B. (2005). *Health communication in practice: A case study approach.* Mahwah, NJ: Erlbaum.

Rice, R., & Atkin, C. (Eds.). (2001). *Public communication campaigns.* Newbury Park, CA: Sage.

Rice, R., & Katz, J. (2000). *The internet and health communication.* Thousand Oaks, CA: Sage.

Rogers, E. (1983). *Diffusion of innovations* (3rd ed.). New York: Free Press.

Rogers, E. (1994). The field of health communication today. *American Behavioral Scientist, 38,* 208–214.

Rogers, R. W., & Prentice-Dunn, S. (1997). Protection motivation theory. In D. Gochman (Ed.), *Handbook of health behavior research* (pp. 113–132). New York: Plenum.

Rootman. I., & Hershfield, L. (1994). Health communication research: Broadening the scope. *Health Communication, 6,* 69–72.

Roter, D. (1977). Patient participation in the patient–provider interaction. *Health Education Monographs, 5,* 281–315.

Salmon, C. (1989). *Information campaigns: Balancing social values and social change.* Newbury Park, CA: Sage.

Salmon, C., & Atkin, C. (2003). Media campaigns for health promotion. In T. Thompson, A. Dorsey, K. Miller, & R. Parrott (Eds.), *Handbook of health communication.* Mahwah, NJ: Erlbaum.

Sharf, B. (1993). Reading the vital signs: Research in health care communication. *Communication Monographs, 60,* 35–41.

Singhal, A., Cody, M., Rogers, E., & Sabido, M. (2004). *Entertainment-education and social change: History, research, and practice.* Mahwah, NJ: Erlbaum.

Snyder, L. (2001). How effective are media health campaigns? In R. Rice & C. Atkin (Eds.), *Public communication campaigns.* Newbury Park, CA: Sage.

Strecher, V. J., & Rosenstock, I. M. (1997). The health belief model. In K. Glanz, F. M. Lewis, & B. K. Rimer (Eds.), *Health behavior and health education: Theory, research, and practice.* San Francisco: Jossey-Bass.

Thompson, T., Dorsey, A., Miller, K., & Parrott, R. (Eds.). (2003), *Handbook of health communication.* Mahwah, NJ: Erlbaum.

Tones, K., & Green, G. (2004). *Health promotion: Planning and strategies.* London: Sage.

U.S. Department of Health and Human Services. (2000). *Healthy people 2010.* Washington, D.C.: U.S. Government Printing Office.

U.S. Department of Health and Human Services. (2003). *Making health communication programs work.* Bethesda. MD: Office of Cancer Communications, National Cancer Institute.

Wallack, L., Dorfman, L., Jernigan, D., & Themba, M. (1993). *Media advocacy and public health.* Newbury Park, CA: Sage.

Wasserman, R., & Inui, T. (1983). Systematic analysis of clinician–patient interactions: A critique of recent approaches with suggestions for future research. *Medical Care, 21,* 279–293.

Witte, K., Meyer, G., & Martell, D. (2001). *Effective health risk messages.* Thousand Oaks, CA: Sage.

32

FEMINIST THEORY AND RESEARCH

Katharine Sarikakis, Ramona R. Rush, Autumn Grubb-Swetnam,
and Christina Lane

The *focus* of this chapter is the ways in which communication theory and method can provide a richer, more complex and enlightening canvas of the human condition, when they draw their attention *from the abstract to the specific*, and when they integrate the *politics of ethical commitment* to the communities they study. These two principles refer to the feminist approach to theory and research. The *thesis* of this chapter is that the integration of (mainstream) theory and research in communications may have large parts of the scholarship missing, distorted or even silenced—and that it is our ethical and moral social responsibility as intellectual workers and leaders to acknowledge that this may be the case. In a metaphorical sense, the *call* of this chapter is for the "greening" of communication—the integration of theory and research as if "others," mattered.[1] The *difficulty* in this chapter is to provide within one section a representative sample of what feminist thought and research offer to communication studies.

Feminist enquiry is complex, comprehensive and fluid: it is as much about formulating and researching questions of fact as it is about exploring those of values and policy, thereby covering the conceptual and methodological ground of communication research and theory as Salwen and Stacks describe it in the first chapter of this book ("Integrating Theory and Research: Starting with Questions"). The challenge for communication scholars is twofold: firstly to re-enter research questions and methodologies into the process of studying communication/s, meaning re-starting from the basic question of "how social investigation should be approached" (Ramazanoglu with Holland, 2006, p. 11) in communication so that it can redress the gaps in knowledge deriving from gender imbalances. To achieve that, our ways of knowing and enquiring knowledge ought to be re-examined, reflected upon and revisited. Secondly, the challenge is to re-frame, re-phrase and re-design our approaches, which consist of theoretical as well as method oriented knowledge, to understanding the ontology of communications, in other words to radically expand our intellectual horizon so as to tune in to women's and gendered constructed experiences.

"Mainstream" theories and research have assumed the universality of particular (male-centered[2]) experience and used it as the yardstick of un-biased research. The "greening" (see Griswold & Swenson, 1991) of communications, which recognizes and actively seeks to learn about the lived experience of non-privileged social categories will come about if communication students are *aware* that feminist scholarship is often conspicuous by its absence in curricula, in informal conversations, and in mainstream research papers and journals. Therefore the overarching question for communication scholars should be "How do we know what we know?" This question refers not only to the theory and method of communication but also to the very study of communication institutions, processes, meanings and actors who, in one way or another, impart and construct forms of meanings, cultures and therefore knowledge.

A Beginner's Guide to Feminisms: Definitional Distinctions, Blurrings

"Feminist thought resists categorization, especially categorization based on 'fathers'' labels" writes Tong (1998) in her book *Feminist Thought*. Yet the history of feminist thought has provided its own labels (liberal, radical, Marxist-socialist. etc.), which, however, "signal to the broader public that feminism is not a monolithic ideology, that all feminists do not think alike, and that, like all time-honored modes of thinking, feminist thought has a past as well as a present and a future" (Tong, 1998, p.1). Sheryl Bowen and Nancy Wyatt (1993) suggested that there is no precise definition of *feminism* or *feminist* because by nature these concepts resist definitive statements (p. 2). Bowen and Wyatt noted that there are a number of statements that might ease the understanding, such as: feminism is concerned with women's lives; theories about humans; the nature of knowledge; the way in which knowledge is generated and legitimated; the "canon" of traditional knowledge; and process and connection (pp. 2–6).

Feminist theory and research as a scholarship field is nearly beyond a summary chapter like this because women speak with many voices. However, it is possible to discuss feminism and do feminist research and theory-building because there are common, distinctive elements in the politics of doing research and scholarship that are shared by feminists. Karen Warren (1993) used the "boundaries of a quilt or collage" to describe what she calls *boundary conditions* of a feminist ethic. Warren writes that the boundaries "delimit the territory of the piece without dictating what the interior, the design, the actual pattern of the piece looks like. Because the actual design of the quilt emerges from the multiplicity of voices of women in a cross-cultural context, the design will change over time. It is not something static" (p. 331).

The feminist theory perspectives frequently used—the quilt designs we now often recognize— are briefly summarized here. For example, *liberal feminist theory* (e.g., Friedan, 1974; Rossi, 1970; Wollstonecraft, 1792/1975) is developed out of liberal political philosophy, arguing that through legal and political avenues of the mainstream, women can change laws and politics and therefore achieve gender justice. Although liberal thought is also multifaceted, a central theme underlying much of its historical development is that of the attention to personhood and agency. Liberal feminists focus on the centrality of an ideal state that respects all its citizens, thereby granting and protecting equal rights and equal opportunities for women and men. Here, the point is not to change but reform existing norms and systems so as to include women. *Marxist-socialist feminists* (e.g. Gimenez, 2005; Holmstrom, 1982; Jaggar, 1983; Malos, 1980; Young, 1980) focus on class division as the major factor in women's oppression, paying attention to the intersections between women's work and women's self-perception. Structural conditions and macro level processes that exploit one's labor are based on the gendered division of labor and are combined with gender oppression to constitute the basis of patriarchal capitalism. Marxist-socialist thought recognizes women's agency as laborers, activists and political agents of change, albeit within conditions not of their own making. For Marxist-feminist thought the focus is on the overhauling of capitalism and patriarchy as systems inherently exploitative and the change towards a different society. *Radical feminists* (e.g., Daly, 1973; Frye, 1983; Hoagland, 1988) describe women's oppression as being grounded in reproduction, mothering, gender, and sexuality. They call for women to absent themselves emotionally and sexually from men so they may realize their full and whole selves as women. *Psychoanalytic feminists* (e.g., Belenky, Clinchy, Goldberger, & Tarule, 1986; Chodorow, 1978; Gilligan, 1993) theorize that women's nature is not biologically determined, but socially constructed. Women's oppression is based on childhood experiences where masculinities and femininities are constructed and communicated, leading to the ways of thinking about oneself. Gender (or cultural) feminists stress that values traditionally associated with women (gentleness, modesty, supportiveness, empathy) are morally better values than those associated with men (Ton, 1998, p. 131). These lines of thought emphasize the internal ways of thinking:

for psychoanalytic feminism women must fight not only for their rights as citizens but also to free themselves from the "father within" and allow the space to think for themselves (Tong, 1998, p. 171). *Cultural feminists* (e.g., Faderman, 1981; Gilligan, 1982) propose women should provide ways of being, thinking, and speaking that allow for openness, diversity, and difference. In addition, *postmodernist theory* has moved feminist debates significantly forward in recent decades. *Postmodern feminists* (e.g., Bonner, Goodman, Allen, Jones, & King, 1992; Butler, 1990; Radway, 1984) focus on questions of meaning and identity, contending that these categories are fluid rather than fixed, and proposing that men and women may perform characteristics of either gender, or even slide between gender identities. Claiming that reality can never be fully known, they challenge universal notions of History (with a capital H) or Theory (with a capital T). As Tong observes: "although postmodern feminists' refusal to develop one overarching explanation and solution for women's oppression poses major problems for feminist theory, this refusal also adds needed fuel to the feminist fuel of plurality, multiplicity, and difference" (1998, p. 193). Related to postmodern feminism, a *Cyborg feminist perspective* has emerged as a way of theorizing women's relationship to science and technology. Specifically conceived by Donna Haraway, cyborg feminism has produced a major intervention in communication scholarship because it appropriates "androcentric" language to expose both bodies and science as socially constructed. Valuing hybridity, as she searches for ways to negotiate the difficulties posed by feminist research and women's political differences, Haraway declares: "Perhaps, ironically, we can learn from our fusions with animals and machines how not to be man, the embodiment of Western logos" (1991, p. 173).

Postmodern feminists "take their intellectual cue from existentialist Simone de Beauvoir" (Tong, 1998, p. 194) as they focus on women's "otherness" with their attention to the symbolic order of society and its internalization; and Jacques Derrida's deconstructionism that challenges "dualistic" thinking, speaking, and writing, and the artificial separation of body and mind, reason and emotion, self and other—as well as those between science and art or psychology and biology (Tong, 1998, p. 195).

Contributions by women of color (e.g., Anzaldua, 1990; Hill-Collins, 1990; hooks, 1984) have been influential, as they argue the condition of otherness enables woman to stand back and criticize the norms, values, and practices that the dominant culture seeks to impose on everyone. One such framework is *African Feminism* (sometimes called *Womanism*) (Kolawole, 1997; Oyewumi, 2003), which foregrounds the diasporic experiences of women of African descent, finding links transnationally between Africa, the United States, the Caribbean, and Latin America. African and African-American women often find that they have more in common with men from their communities than with white American, Anglo, or European women and they sometimes organize around diasporic issues that would otherwise be overlooked, such as forced marriage, female circumcision, or neo-colonialism (Guy-Sheftall, 2006, p. 26).[3] bell hooks (1994) spoke directly to this point:

> Visions of solidarity between women became more complex. Suddenly, neither the experiences of materially privileged groups of white females nor the category of "woman" (often used to refer to white women's experiences) could be evoked without some contestation, without white supremacy looming as the political ground of such assertions. These changes strengthened the power of feminist thought and feminist movement politically. (p. 42)

In the search to "integrate viewpoints, improve inclusivity, and promote solidarity" is *ecofeminism*: "Ecofeminists claim that environmental issues are feminist issues because it is women and children who are the first to suffer the consequences of injustice and environmental destruction"

(Gaard & Gruen, 1993, p. 11). Gaard and Gruen also note that "ecofeminists believe that the current global crises are the result of the mutually reinforcing ideologies of racism, sexism, classism, imperialism, naturism, and speciesism" (p. 25). Ecofeminist theory is theory in process, built on community-based knowing and valuing; the strength of this knowledge is dependent on the inclusivity, flexibility and reflexivity of the community in which it is generated. Further, ecofeminist theory grows out of dialogue and focuses on reaching consensus (pp. 32–33). Karen Warren (1993) wrote that

> Ecofeminists insist that the sort of logic of domination used to justify the domination of humans by gender, racial or ethnic, or class status is also used to justify the domination of nature. Because eliminating a logic of domination is part of a feminist critique— whether a critique of patriarchy, white supremacist culture, or imperialism—ecofeminists insist that naturism [discrimination against nature and other living organisms] is properly viewed as an integral part of any feminist solidarity movement to end sexist oppression and the logic of domination which conceptually grounds it. (pp. 325–326)

The historical development of the feminist movement is also expressed and identified in "waves" which have prioritized specific social demands in different socioeconomic historical periods. If, in simple terms, the first wave has demanded a civic, legal entity for women as proprietors and voters, with the suffragette movement, the second wave, working with and from the civil rights movement, has focused on expanding the agenda of legal recognition into women's equality in work, pay, welfare, control over one's body and access to child care and abortion, eradication of violence against women and generally extend full human rights for women (Dicker & Piepmeier, 2003, p. 9). Some cultural critics (Walker, 1992) observe that there was a major tidal shift when more voices by women of color and global women began to be incorporated. The Third Wave highlights differences between and among women, often making visible the positive aspects of woman as "other." For example, with increasing globalization, women around the world have looked for ways to come together across national borders, mobilizing the category "woman" n order to fight for such common goals as human right, poverty or illiteracy, while remaining loyal to locally specific (or national) struggles. This framework, emerging out of international feminist movements, is often called global feminisms (Mohanty, 2003; Rupp, 2000; Smith, 2000), invoking the plural form to signal that these activists constantly strive for multiplicity of perspectives. Naomi Zack (2005.) proposes a relational feminism that transcends differences among feminists without negating them and which moves beyond intersectionality of race, class and gender, as a theory for Third Wave feminism. Some claim that we are living the Fourth Wave, a mixture of spirituality and political activism. The boundaries of these Waves appear to be more generational than philosophical and although it is difficult to categorize feminist thought in neat sets of principles and values, it is possible to draw from this the universal aim to explore and expose the truth about women's condition in the world—and of course, change it! Moreover, as Linden asserts while exploring the dynamics of Lesbian feminism, it is also a matter of how dominant features of perceiving feminisms operate, for example in relation to girlpower, "strong women," radical feminism etc, not only of what the main characteristics of feminist thought and activism might be, but also its representation and assigned value (Linden 2008).

This brief overview of the plurality of feminist theoretical frameworks demonstrates the complexity and sophistication of feminist thought, but also its flexibility and responsiveness to the real world of lived, material or other, experience. Readers will of course make up their own minds as to the most suitable analytical approach explored here, but it is important to recognize and respect the enormous contribution that each approach makes to our understanding of the human condition.

Feminist Communication Theories and Research

Although numerous works by feminist scholars who draw upon all of these frameworks have documented and analyzed women's communication concerns, Rakow and Wackwitz (2004) assert that it was only after the second half of the 1980s that feminist theory was brought to the communication studies field in a significant way (p. 5). Yet like them, other authors, too, observe that the impact of feminist scholarship on the field is disappointing (Rush, Oukrop, & Creedon, 2004; Sarikakis & Shade, 2008); the compartmentalization and artificial separation of sub-disciplines/sub-fields and sub-groups, with their methodological and ontological tensions and rivalries does not enhance a project of intellectual multi-vocality such as feminist theory and research. Feminist communication theory and research draws from multiple fields of study, from technology and science studies to policy, cultural studies and linguistics, sociology and political sciences. Feminist communication theory and research have sought to address the macro and micro levels of communication through the study of processes, institutions, politics and actions as they impact upon and are shaped by women's agency. Yet mainstream scholarship has difficulty in accepting the non-conformist approach of multi-perspectival research and theory that does not privilege "objectivity" or "anonymity" (the "superior" values of scientific research whereby "data" is dislocated and decontextualised from the subject/s studied).

> Feminist claims are "unthinkable" within the domain assumptions of established social science not only because they forthrightly assert that the discourses of science are manmade, but also because they ascribe to the far more radical claims that the epistemologies and the theories of knowledge that produced these discourses are systematically skewed by both Eurocentric and masculinist interpretative and textual practices. (Jansen, 2002, p. 30)

In Rush et al. (2005) we learn that from 1989 to 1999, *Journalism & Mass Communication Educator* and *Journalism & Mass Communication Quarterly* have published articles that deal with gender/women and/or utilize feminist methodology an average of 4.5 percent of their total articles in 10 years. Studying entries for "women's/gender studies" in *Communication Abstracts* from 1983 to 1992, Kathryn Cirksena (1996) found a relatively small percentage increase over the 10-year period. Cirksena wrote that:

> while some renditions of the development of communication studies in these years would attribute undue influence to feminist critiques and reworkings and others would hope to claim that feminist ideas have received increasingly wide discussion and use, the volume of work found in this analysis does not suggest that either is occurring. The pervasiveness of feminist re/formations of communication is not a claim that can be supported by this data.

Thus, even when feminist theory and research is conceived, researched, written, and published, getting it into the traditional academic curriculum through mainstream scholarship journals and books remains an obstacle. The traditional members of faculties and editorial boards of scholarly publications are conspicuous by their *presence*. As Dale Spender (1983) wrote, "while both sexes may have been making theories for as far back as we can trace, only one sex is seen as the theorists, one sex has its theories accepted as legitimate, only one sex owns the realm of theory" (p. 1). The view a decade later is hardly any different (Rakow & Wackwitz, 2004; Rush et al., 2004; Rush, Oukrop, & Sarikakis, 2005).

For researchers of women's issues in communication in the early 1970s, there was little preserved or shared information about the role and status of women in society, and few theories or methods to guide research. Women's theories had been around for a long time but were destroyed, silenced, distorted, or co-opted. When Rush (1972, with Oukrop & Ernst) formulated the initial study about the role and status of women in journalism education, for example, she borrowed and used as a guide a questionnaire developed by women sociologists, not knowing how to ask questions about inequality and discrimination. In the mid-1980s when Rush and coeditor, Donna Allen, the founder of *Media Report to Women* and the Women's Institute for Freedom of the Press, were trying to bring together written voices for *Communications at the Crossroads: The Gender Gap Connection* (1989), feminist theories were in their formative stages, especially in communication. In the early 1990s, a female reviewer pointed to a need for more feminist theory in *Crossroads*. This statement indicates the tremendous progress made from those initial descriptive studies and beginning publications about women's issues in the late 1960s and early 1970s to the 1990s, when feminist theories and research were abundant enough to notice that they were largely conspicuous by their absence.

Theories of feminism and feminist research have provided communication scholars with insights into the ways in which the scientific model has figuratively and literally paled in comparison with other frameworks which indicate sexist, racist, homophobic, and classist social projects (Harding, 1991). Through nearly four decades of current feminist scholarship, we have learned that women's communication, along with minorities of both gender, have been "othered" or silenced in mainstream research. Gender theories and feminist research in communication have helped to reveal that we must be mindful in future research of actively refusing to continue the silencing, drawing out instead and making visible those who have been silenced, revealing their voices in social and historical contexts.

Lana Rakow (1986) argues that in the early stages of integrating feminism and communication, two major research foci predominated: sex differences and gender studies. Leslie Steeves (1988) delineated three approaches to feminist scholarship in speech, media, and literary studies in the United States: liberal, radical, and socialist. She explained that each branch of feminism makes different assumptions about the role of the media and the function of communication in society.[4]

Kathryn Carter and Carole Spitzack (1989) examined *problematics* of feminism and social science, *theoretics* of feminism and communication studies, and *methods* for studying women's communications. Their introductory comments about the difficulties faced by feminist scholars are as important reading now as they were in 1989.

Kathryn Cirksena and Lisa Cuklanz (1992) examined five feminist frameworks for communication studies—liberal feminism (reason and emotion), socialist-feminism (public and private), radical feminism (nature and culture), psychoanalytic feminism (subject and object), and cultural feminism (mind and body). They also looked at feminist critiques of communication research methods, as well as discussing whether the set of oppositional dualisms which are the central organizing principle for much of Western thought is necessary. They noted that

> First, [feminist critiques] elucidate the constructed nature of knowledge, seeking to elaborate the ways in which knowledge depends on factors such as habit, language use, perspective, and personal experience. Second, feminist work argues that what has traditionally been considered the personal or private constitute valid areas for scholarship. Third, they point out and discuss perspective, both within text and audiences, and among scholars themselves. Feminist work in the humanities has most recently focused on the contingent nature of knowledge. (p. 40)

Bowen and Wyatt's 1993 book[5] explored the role of feminist scholarship in interpersonal, small-group, organizational, mass communication, and intercultural communications as well as theatre studies and rhetorical criticism. Many of the feminist critiques in Bowen and Wyatt about traditional research groupings are briefly summarized in Rakow (1992):

> In media studies, feminist scholars have moved past initial work on women's images in content and women's employment in industries to more complex questions that make it impossible to separate study of the media from all other communication contexts. (p. 12)

Important and oft-used and -cited contributions to women in the mass media are included in Pam Creedon's (1989, 1993) work on the topic. One of the "mothers of mass communication" is Margaret Gallagher's international account of *Unequal Opportunities: The Case of Women and the Media* (1981) providing some of the first reflections towards the global and internationally observed condition of women and their relation to the media. Liesbet van Zoonen (1994) contemplated using the typical liberal, radical, socialist feminism classifications in *Feminist Media Studies*, but was dissuaded because of the many *-isms* or standpoints emanating from current feminist literature. Instead, she begins by outlining her position on feminism (including gender and power) and cultural studies followed by identification of feminist themes in communication studies, such as stereotypes and socialization, pornography, and ideology. Van Zoonen goes on to examine key questions posed by a gendered approach within communication and cultural studies, including theories of transmission, representation, construction and discourse; structures of media organization and production; interpreting media representation through content analysis and semiotics; contradictions of the gendered image as spectacle; new approaches to understanding the audience and the politics of media reception; the potential of feminist and interpretative research strategies.

In concluding van Zoonen noted that:

> It would be my assertion when assessing the relevance of (studying) media and popular culture for feminist concerns, that one should distinguish at least between the different struggles feminism is involved in. As a social movement it has the double edge of being an interest group lobbying and struggling for social and legal changes beneficial to women and of challenging cultural preoccupations and routines concerning femininity and gender. Undeniably, both struggles are political and inform each other, nevertheless, they are of a different kind resulting in different interactions with the media and different requirements of media performance. (pp. 151–152)

In 2004 Rakow and Wackwitz identified three main themes of feminist communication theory: difference, voice and representation. Difference refers to the ways in which political, symbolic and other systems establish oppressive relationships between "racial" and ethnic groups, sexualities, economic classes and political orientations. Feminist communication theory addresses the differences among and between women problematizing their contexts, consequences and possibilities for common action (pp. 8–9). The theme of voice refers to the possibility of women's access to communicative fora, the conditions and obstacles to them being heard and the systems and processes through which women are being silenced (p. 9). Representation refers to the consequences of women's misrepresentation in popular culture and the media, processes of exclusion and the imposition of boundaries such as class, age, etc. The authors argue that Feminist Communication Theory theorizes *gender*; *communication*; and *social change* (p. 5).

This underlying "solidarity with the oppressed," which calls for an ethics of social justice and change intertwined in research and theory building, evident in the conceptualization of feminist communication scholars described above is Jansen's (2002) central action oriented argument in her analysis of "commitment" of critical scholarship (p 11). For Jansen, critical feminism and critical social theory share many of such commitments. In her book *Critical Communication Theory* Jansen approaches communication as a process in democratic opinion formation (the limits of deliberative democracy), a set of technologies from information to artificial intelligence, a discursive "battlezone" and a material context of domination, from war to sports and the news paradox. Her theorization rests on the understanding that in individual terms and as a totality, these processes are parts of social and cultural processes, socializations, actions and constructs. The inherently gendered character of these processes rests in the absence as well as presence of gender.

In an attempt to showcase and further feminist scholarship that deals with the global, international and transnational aspects of contemporary communications, Sarikakis and Shade (2008) in their anthology *Feminist Interventions in International Communication* approach the relationship of women and media in the following four dimensions: they identify international policy regimes and explore the ways in which international/supranational structures of decision making serve to maintain the status quo of gendered discrimination, violence and expediency. For example, the current structural controls of mobile technologies are explored as gatekeeping mechanisms impacting upon women's access to technologies (Crow & Sawchuk, 2008); the need for gender sensitive communication policies is discussed by Prasad (2008); the ways in which cultural policy—which includes communication policy—uses the idea of women for specific treaties, but does not benefit women, are analyzed by Beale (2008), while the limitations of current pornography regulation are explored from the perspective of the socialization of porn and the conditions of labor for porn workers (Sarikakis & Zaukhat, 2008). Second, the book turns its attention to the mediation of meanings as mediations of power relations in the global mediasphere through the contributions of authors who look into the expressions of violence and sexualization in the Western (Jiwani, 2008) and Arab world (Al-Mahadin, 2008), but also through the promises and limitations of new technologies in mediating liberatory meanings and subvert power relations as in the cases of HIV/AIDS (Made, 2008), online media (Rodgers, 2008) and the millennium development goals (Van Leuven, Giffard, & Cunningham, 2008). The third locus of the anthology's attention is that of labor. The authors (McLaughlin, 2008; Mosco, McKercher, & Stevens, 2008; Shade & Porter, 2008) address the multifaceted and hidden dimensions of the making of international communications. The fourth dimension explored in the book is that of the global/local effect. Contributions in this area include those from authors locating their analyses in the ways in which globalization impacts upon local relationships of women and the media; by exploring feminist presses (Murray, 2008); the impact of globalization on women's access to and representation in the media in the former Eastern European countries (Marinescu, 2008); local/national responses to the globalized porn trade (Griffiths, 2008); and efforts to develop and utilize gender evaluation methodologies for telecentres in developing countries (Bure, 2008). The book identifies as core cross-sectional elements in a feminist analysis of inter/transnational and global communication the need to revisit the field of international communications with a feminist lens, the need to address questions of structural constraints in accessing, changing, controlling the media, dichotomies such as public/private, and the potential and actuality of communication technologies for democratization.

More than a decade ago Cirksena (1996) wrote that overview critiques of communication from a feminist perspective that attempt to define a feminist paradigm converge on the following five points: (1) communication studies should foreground and make explicit the inequitable power dimensions of gender relations in all human communication; (2) communication studies should "put women at the center" of research; (3) scholarship should not attempt to abstract gender from other aspects of identity, especially, but not be limited to identity based on race and class; (4) it should be "action-oriented"—part of the research should be linked to improving the status of women; and, (5) the "researched" (those people at the center of the investigation) should have some input into the framing of the issues and the research process.

Rush (1996) attempted a boundary-spanning approach of a normative character, with the following "10 Tenets of Deeper Communications" to transform theory and research:

1. A theory and its research will be ecologically based, inclusive and, thus, diverse.
2. A theory and its research will go beyond dualistic thinking and action.
3. A theory and its research must basically be concerned about human spirituality and sexuality—sometimes interchangeably, often interactively.
4. A theory and its research will be healing and liberatory.
5. A theory will employ realistic frameworks and will not be disregarded or discounted if it supports social action research.
6. A theory and its research will assess the traditional mass media, in their current corporate state, as demographic investigators and reporters of "who we are."
7. The alternative media will be included in a theory and its research as scenario servers for the strategic role they assume.
8. A theory and its research will emphasize peace, equality, and justice as dynamic growth forces through peace education and the processes of conflict resolution, especially mediation.
9. Envisionary media are possible when theory and research include both destructive and constructive roles and functions of communications.
10. A theory and its research will have a global civil society worldview with concern and respect for the integration of, through proactive and interactive communication and information with, its citizenry.

Rakow and Wackwitz (2004) identify the properties of feminist communication theory as "political, polyvocal and transformative" (p. 6). For them, feminist communication theory is explanatory ("It speaks of and to experience," p. 6); political (and "because it is political it is personal," p. 6); polyvocal (is "generated by multiple voices and experiences, with sometimes conflicting interpretations of reality," p. 6); transformative ("contributes to intellectual and spiritual growth by providing different perspectives through which to conceptualize experiences and the structures of society," p. 6). As it is obvious, feminist communication theory is charged not only with the intellectual task of research and analysis (which, however, obeys an enhanced sense of responsibility towards research subjects and for self-reflection) but also with that of transformation; therefore with the task of social responsibility to speak truth to the power.

Research: Recycled, New, and an Example

Reinharz (1992) identified 10 tenets of feminist research:

1. Feminism is a perspective, not a research method.
2. Feminists use a multiplicity of research methods.
3. Feminist research involves an ongoing criticism of nonfeminist scholarship.
4. Feminist research is guided by feminist theory.
5. Feminist research may be transdisciplinary.
6. Feminist research aims to create social change.
7. Feminist research strives to represent human diversity.
8. Feminist research frequently includes the researcher as a research subject and tool.
9. Feminist research frequently attempts to develop special relations with the people studied (in interactive research).
10. Feminist research frequently defines a special relation with the reader. (p. 240)

It should be clear that feminist theory and research, like other forms of inquiry, is as varied as those studying it. Shulamit Reinharz (1992) displays a whole range of feminist methods in social research, including traditional methods of research such as survey, experimental, and case studies, as well as original feminist research methods. Feminist research methods are often "feminist-enhanced" in that, as Reinharz noted, the "use of the term 'original' does not signify a method never considered or used prior to the instance discussed here. Rather, it reflects the researcher's effort to create a new approach that met her feminist criteria" (p. 215). Such new methods included consciousness-raising, creating group diaries, drama, genealogy and network tracing, the non-authoritative research voice or multiple-person stream-of-consciousness narrative, conversation, using intuition or writing associatively, identification, studying unplanned personal experience, structured conceptualization, photography or the talking-pictures techniques, speaking freely into a tape recorder or answering long, essay-type questionnaires.

Reinharz wrote that most feminist researchers who develop original methods do not argue that these methods necessarily meet the norms of science (p. 238). Perhaps it should be noted here and sprinkled generously throughout this chapter, however, that finding or creating methods suited to feminist ideology is no different in principle than creating conventional science methods to suit a positivist ideology (Wood, 1994).

In "Some Final Thoughts" about original feminist research methods, as the chapter is titled, Reinharz wrote:

> Not all feminist social research is innovative with regard to method. In fact, some feminist scholars regard methodological innovation as counterproductive because only studies conducted according to "rigorous" scientific procedures will convince the skeptics. For those who do not share this concern, however, feminism typically leads to the study of new topics that require or allow new forms of study. For these people, the feminist spirit is one of breaking free, including breaking free of methodological traditions.
>
> One of the many ways the women's movement has benefited women is in freeing up our creativity in the realm of research. And one of the ways feminist researchers, in turn, have benefited the societies in which we live is by the spirit of innovation. Although I have listed several types of "original" research and writing, there is room for many more. *As feminists gain greater control of publishing opportunities and academic positions, we will undoubtedly see evidence of more of these.* (italics added; 1992, pp. 238–239)

In her dissertation, Autumn Grubb-Swetnam's interpretation of women's use of fashion and beauty magazines (1994) serves as a communication research example. Surprisingly or sadly her remarks but also the material she collected and studied are relevant and present today nearly 15 years later. In her introduction, she wrote:

> As women, we stand in grocery store lines where magazines beckon us with promises of "thin thighs in thirty days," "meals in a minute," "supermom sagas," and "make your man melt tonight." As we sweat and grunt at the spa, lithe feminine bodies in slick magazine spreads look on. As we sit waiting in doctors' and dentists' offices, these mass-mediated messages entice us to pick them up, promising the secrets to feminine happiness. In middle-and upper-class adolescent female bedrooms and mothers' kitchens, living rooms or sewing rooms, these magazines lie about the place, accessories to the well-decorated home. In school libraries and in female dorm rooms, these magazines become interspersed among academic textbooks and journals. (p. 1)

She noted that the purpose of her research was to apply a feminist interpretive approach to studying women's use of mass communication and popular culture. Explication of magazine use was limited to Euro-American and African-American heterosexuals, lesbians, and bisexuals to provide insights into understanding how race, class, gender, and sexuality are experienced by women when they negotiate and interpret mass-mediated images. The second part of her purpose involved *praxis*: to provide understanding about women's use and interpretation of mass mediated images "so that we may be mindful of our media choices" (p. 2).

To ground her research initially, Grubb-Swetnam chronicled the historical evolution of women's magazines in American culture and discussed nuances of the editorial content in women's magazines. In another chapter, she delineated feminist cultural studies approaches to examining women's use of the media, evolution and types of standpoint epistemologies, and research questions pertinent to the study.

In the method chapter, Grubb-Swetnam explained that her reliance on the standpoint of women was a methodological choice. She described the general characteristics of the sample, the interview locations and structure, her assumptions approaching the data, and the process of data analysis. Grubb-Swetnam discussed problems she encountered in the elicitation of working class, poor, African-American and lesbian perspectives. Further, she paid particular attention to how traditional methods of data collection limit and restrain the researcher attempting to document women's voices—the other in relation to White, middle-class heterosexual women.

The analysis section of the dissertation provides the reader with information about the individual women that participated in the study, the ways they used magazines, how they defined and described the magazines, and their general criticisms of magazines. She also discussed the women's talk about their bodies in relation to magazine use, and the perspective of the outsider-within as it relates to magazine use.

The magazines in the study included *Cosmopolitan*, *Ladies' Home Journal*, *Red-book*, *Good Housekeeping*, *Elle*, *Mademoiselle*, *Family Circle*, *Woman's Day*, *Upscale*, *Deneuve*, *Vogue*, *Essence*, *Glamour*, *McCall's*, *Self*, and *Working Mother*.

Feminist *Praxis* in Research

This section explains how feminist theory and *praxis* (practical application) is integrated into the research process. Earlier, we noted specific themes that exist in feminist research, as defined by Reinharz. Five of those themes are addressed in this section.

Theme 1: Feminist Research Strives To Represent Human Diversity

Typically, traditional sample techniques have been shown to generate a majority of Euro-American, middle-class respondents (Cannon, Higginbotham, & Leung, 1991). This claim is supported in mass communication research generated in the 1970s when academicians studied commercial television's attempts at ascertainment information. These studies found that, typically, White middle-class males were the majority of ascertainment respondents, revealing that researchers do not often gather a diverse population in their sample due to sampling techniques. The techniques did not assure that diverse communities would be accessed, because they were not socially ordered—nor did they utilize the same social structures—as White, middle-class communities (e.g., Heller, 1977; Leroy & Ungurait, 1975; Walker & Rudelius, 1976).

To decrease this tendency, snowball sampling technique (a sampling technique in which respondents are asked to identify other respondents) was used to increase sample diversity. Andrea Press (1991) defended the technique as effective in building samples when respondents are needed from particular social groups. The study on women's magazine use required both

African- and Euro-American women of heterosexual, lesbian, and bisexual standpoints as well as from a variety of economic classes. The snowball sampling technique collected diverse voices in the data. To generate the core group of female respondents, electronic mail discussion lists were used. The women who responded were then asked to inform their friends, families, and co-workers about the research. If the women they told seemed interested in participating in the research, they were given a phone number for contact. The snowball sampling that occurred with the core group of women (through word of mouth) secured the majority of African-American respondents, lesbian respondents, and working-class respondents. Because of this sample, the analyses reflected the varied—and sometimes contradictory ways—women use, interpret, and negotiate media messages aimed at them. The diverse sample provided data that made visible the complex ways in which women consume and make sense of media messages.

Theme 2: Feminist Research Includes the Researcher as a Person
Theme 3: Feminist Research Frequently Attempts to Develop Special Relations with the People Studied

Themes 2 and 3 are incorporated in the discussion of how they were integrated into the research. This section will provide specific examples of how Grubb-Swetnam intertwined themes 2 and 3 into the research process and in writing.

In-depth interviews generated data about the women's lived experience with women's magazines. During these in-depth interviews, stories that were similar to those told by respondents were shared when appropriate by Grubb-Swetnam. Because the questions were open-ended, respondents sometimes seemed unsure about question meanings. At those times, a personal story was provided as an example response to the question. Jenny Nelson (1989) supported this interviewing technique:

> In my own research, I have discovered that disclosure on my part can open the entire interview situation to more explicit descriptions on the part of my co-researchers. When I tell a story, this can help to elicit a story from the other person. The stories may not be similar (in fact, they often express variations), and my input provides the respondent with a comfortable format by which she can relate her story. (p. 228)

Nelson believed that this interviewing technique minimizes the "perceived authority of the interviewer, and promotes an intersubjective, conversation style to the situation" (p. 228).

Another way Grubb-Swetnam integrated herself into the research process and writing was to illuminate clearly for the respondents and the reader the researcher's personal experiences and knowledge about women's magazines. In the methods chapter, the section titled "Approaching the Data," for example, Grubb-Swetnam wrote:

> In order to interpret the data, it is important the reader be aware of three assumptions I make. First, I make the assumption that a variety of interpretive (Lindlof, 1988) or epistemological communities exist within the sample. Approaching the data with this assumption allows me to be sensitive to the similarities and differences in women's magazine use. It also affords me the opportunity to explicate the variety of interpretive communities.
>
> Another assumption I hold is that race, class, gender, and sexuality are not simply individual differences but function as sites of experiencing and generating oppression, as well as pleasure, resistance, and creativity. I also believe that these facets of the self interact with one another in an organic fashion, driven by the particular context of each woman's life. With this assumption I approach the data for indications of women's

magazine use that explicate these sites of oppression, as well as reveal women's enjoyment, resistance and creativity in magazine use.

A third assumption I use when approaching the data is that I have used women's magazines in the past and am familiar with their contents. This will assist me when analyzing data to understand the terminologies the women use to describe particular types of stories, articles, advice columns, or advertisements. These statements about the assumptions I hold when approaching the data are meant to help the reader understand my standpoint in this research. (pp. 78–79)

Grubb-Swetnam also acknowledged her presence in the research process within the analysis section. She did this to help readers make sense of what the women were saying about their magazine use, as well as validate their experiences with magazines. For example, in one of the analysis chapters, after providing the reader with several respondent quotations about negotiating mediated images of femininity that described internal struggle, she wrote:

I am intimately familiar with Libby's struggle with the mediated images of appropriate femininity. In 1992, I wrote in my journal about my negotiation and struggle between self and mediated cultural norms. A portion of this journal entry was: I have come to realize in myself that I could not and did not begin to generate (let alone hear) my original thought and voice until I accepted my natural, wild beauty. Until I quit putting chemicals on my hair and face; until I quit cinching my waist and chest into confining, uncomfortable clothing; until I quit hating myself as an imperfect commodity; until I explored that pain and gently laid it down I could not hear and know and believe in my original thought and voice. I could not breathe in whole breaths; could not see the background for the blinding, neon foreground; and could not move in freedom and grace as long as I accepted the commodity model for myself. Now that I know this, I must constantly recreate this knowing of self-acceptance that struggles against some unseen ideological circle that is maintained in our cultural systems. (pp. 167–168)

This conscious effort to maintain a connection to the reader and respondents by the researcher is one way Themes 2 and 3 were incorporated as feminist praxis in research.

Theme 4: Feminist Research is Guided by Feminist Theory

Generally, feminist theorists study, describe, and analyze issues impacting women's lives. This underlying assumption of the worth of women's lived experiences does not tend to be shared in traditional research goals. Specifically, Grubb-Swetnam's dissertation drew from feminist standpoint theorists such as Patricia Hill-Collins (1990), Gloria Anzaldua (1990), bell hooks (1984), and Liz Stanley and Sue Wise (1993).[6] Standpoint theorists discuss the position of individuals in society who must function both in the mainstream and the margins. Explicating and analyzing the political and social positions marginalized individuals must juggle help to illuminate how a society acts out race, class, gender, and sexuality as social relations.

Feminist cultural and media audience theorists provided a second framework for the dissertation. At the time of writing, for example, Angela McRobbie (e.g., 1991) and Janice Radway (1984) provided a theoretical understanding of women as active, complex media users.

Theme 5: Feminist Research May Be Transdisciplinary

The feminist theorists who grounded and guided Grubb-Swetnam's study represent a variety of disciplines: Patricia Hill-Collins, sociology; Gloria Anzuldua and bell hooks, English and literature disciplines; Stanley and Wise, philosophy; Angela McRobbie, media and cultural studies; and Janice Radway, literary criticism. Investigating their theoretical writings, we find their work also represents a transdisciplinary approach that includes Marxism, psychology, semiotics and theology. This transdisciplinary approach allows for new opportunities in communication research. Rakow (1992) posits a cross-discipline approach evident in feminist theories offers an ability to ask new research questions. Additionally, she argued:

> Feminist scholarship is essential because it will help transcend the traditional, theoretical boundaries between domains of communication research such as socio-linguistics, speech communication, interpersonal, organizational, and mass communication which are currently informed by incompatible theories and methods. (p. 24)

Summary

In summary, the examples provided in this section have made visible the ways in which feminist praxis in the research process calls for an open acknowledgment of the positioning of the researcher as a person engaged in the research process. Second, these examples made visible how feminist praxis in research strives to break down barriers of authority between the researcher and respondents, and attempts to incorporate ways for the respondents to be co-researchers. Moreover, the examples provided in this section have made visible how feminist praxis strives to reveal humanity in all its complex diversity.

We hope that this chapter conveys successfully, despite its limitations, the underlying priorities and principles for feminist communication theory and research and makes visible that in this case, perhaps more than any other approach, *integration* of theory and research is of paramount importance. Not only are theoretical and analytical frameworks integrated with the methods and methodology employed by feminist researchers but also researchers themselves are "integrated" in the research process by self-reflecting on their praxis—and therefore dispelling the myth of "objectivity" or "neutrality," which in most cases perpetuate the status quo, thereby already taking a position. Subjects are integrated in the research process as active participants, whom academic research seeks to serve.

Feminist communication theory and research have left no stone unturned in their pursuit of explanation and transformation in our field. Nevertheless, given the new imperatives deriving from the intensified processes of globalization, human mobility and technological and economic integration, large scale, comparative, as well as ethnographic research is needed to explore in a longitudinal manner the experiences of women across different socioeconomic contexts. International in design and global in scope feminist projects are needed in order to address the shifts in decision making powers on the globe, women's changing experiences of material and symbolic worlds, and the connection of macro level analysis to the micro level exploration of globalization's consequences.

Notes

1. The initial title of the first version of this chapter in 1996 was: "The 'Greening' of Communication: The Integration of Theory and Research as if 'Others,' including Women, Mattered." E. F. Schumacher's (1973) classic contribution is acknowledged by paraphrasing the subtitle from *Small is Beautiful: Economics as if People Mattered.* New York: Harper & Row.
2. The categories of "woman" and "man" are understood as socially constructed. We follow Ramazanoglu and Holland's approach to "social research on gendered lives" (Ramazanoglu with Holland, 2006, p. 5).

3. It should not escape the reader's attention that this chapter primarily reflects the work of White women, complete with attitudes, biases, and class and racial blindness forced by "White privilege."

4. See Bowen and Wyatt (1993) for a distillation of Steeves's work.

5. Bowen and Wyatt edited a volume about feminist approaches that was envisioned as supplementary reading for any course in speech communication where "very few courses...incorporate either feminist readings or feminist principle or practices" (p. ix). They noted that:

> Feminism advocates interdisciplinary study by breaking down artificial barriers between areas of scholarship. We had to decide whether to live up to our principles by spanning boundaries and creating new areas for communication study based on feminist perspectives or whether we should limit ourselves in this initial effort to the critique of traditional areas of study within the relatively amorphous discipline called speech communication. Meeting as a group of authors, we decided that our primary goal was to reach the widest possible audience that could be achieved most easily by working within familiar areas of scholarship, providing critiques and correctives to the traditional scholarship that has historically excluded women's and minority concerns and perspectives. By detailing the distortions within traditional areas of our discipline, we could position ourselves to argue for new definitions and new connections among the disparate areas of our discipline. (p. vii)

6. In this chapter we make use of "old" but classic texts in feminist research. The plethora of feminist writing is such that we can only use a small section in order to illustrate the underlying ethics, philosophy and praxis of feminist communication research.

References

Al Mahadin, S. (2008). From religious fundamentalism to pornography? The female body as text in Arabic song videos. In K. Sarikakis & L. R. Shade, *Feminist interventions in international communication: Minding the gap* (pp. 146–160). Lanham, MD: Rowman & Littlefield.

Anzaldua, G. (1990). La consciencia de la mestiza [The conscience of the Mestiza]: Towards a new consciousness. In G. Anzaldua (Ed.), *Making face, making soul: Creative and critical perspectives of feminists of color* (pp. 377–389). San Francisco: Aunt Lute Books.

Beale, A. (2008). The expediency of women. In K. Sarikakis & L. R. Shade (Eds.), *Feminist interventions in international communication: Minding the gap* (pp. 59–73). Lanham, MD: Rowman & Littlefield.

Belenky, M. F., Clinchy, B. M., Goldberger, N. R., & Tarule, J. M. (1986). *Women's ways of knowing: The development of self, voice and mind.* New York: Basic Books.

Bonner, F., Goodman, L., Allen, R., Jones, L., & King, C. (Eds.). (1992). *Imagining women: Cultural representations and gender.* Cambridge, UK: Polity Press/Open University.

Bowen, S., & Wyatt, N. (Eds.). (1993). *Transforming visions: Feminist critiques in communication studies.* Cresskill, NJ: Hampton Press.

Bure, C. (2008). Grounding gender evaluation methodology (GEM) for relecentres: The experiences of Ecuador and the Philippines. In K. Sarikakis & L, Regan Shade (Eds.), *Feminist interventions in international communication.* Lanham, MD Rowman & Littlefield.

Butler, J. (1990). *Gender trouble.* New York: Routkedge.

Cannon, L. W., Higginbotham, E., & Leung, M. (1991). Race and class bias in qualitative research on women. In M. M. Fonow & J. A. Cook (Eds.), *Beyond methodology: Feminist scholarship as lived experience* (pp. 107–118). Bloomington: Indiana University Press.

Carter, K., & Spitzack C. (1989). *Doing research on women's communication: Perspectives on theory and method.* Norwood, NJ: Ablex.

Chodorow, N. (1978). *The politics of mothering.* Berkeley: University of California Press.

Cirksena, K. (1996). Resistance and circulation of feminist paradigms in communication studies. In D. Allen, R. R. Rush, & S. J. Kaufman (Eds.), *Women transforming communication* (pp. 153–160). Thousand Oaks, CA: Sage.

Cirksena, K., & Cuklanz, L. (1992). Male is to female as _____ is to _____: A guided tour of five feminist frameworks for communication studies. In L. Rakow (Ed.), *Women making meaning: New feminist directions in communications* (pp. 18–44). New York: Routledge.

Creedon, P. J. (Ed.). (1989). *Women in mass communication: Challenging gender values*. Newbury Park, CA: Sage.

Creedon, P. J. (Ed.). (1993). *Women in mass communication*. Newbury Park, CA: Sage.

Crow, B., & Sawchuk, K. (2008). The spectral politics of mobile communication technologies: Gender, infrastructure and international policy. In K. Sarikakis & L. R. Shade (Eds.), *Feminist interventions in international communication: Minding the gap* (pp. 90–105). Lanham, MD: Rowman & Littlefield.

Daly, M. (1973). *Beyond God the father: Toward a philosophy of women's liberation*. Boston, MA: Beacon Press.

Dicker, R., & Piepmeier, A. (2003). *Catching a wave: Reclaiming feminism for the 21st century*. Boston: Northeastern University Press

Faderman, L. (1981). *Surpassing the love of men*. New York: Morrow.

Friedan, B. (1974). *The feminine mystique*. New York: Dell.

Frye, M. (1983). *The politics of reality: Essays in feminist theory*. Freedom, CA: The Crossing Press.

Gaard, G., & Gruen, L. (1993). Ecofeminism: Toward global justice and planetary health. Feminism and ecology issue. *Society and Nature: The International Journal of Political Ecology, 2,* 1–35.

Gallagher, M. (1981). *Unequal opportunities: The case of women and the media*. Paris: UNESCO.

Gilligan, C. (1982). *In a different voice: Psychological theory and women's development*. Cambridge, MA: Harvard University Press.

Gilligan, C. (1993). *Meeting at the crossroads*. Cambridge, MA: Harvard University Press.

Gimenez, M. E. (2005). Capitalism and the oppression of women: Marx revisited. *Science and Society, 69*(1), 11–32.

Griffiths, M. (2008). GodZone? NZ's classification of explicit material in an era of global fundamentalism. In K. Sarikakis & L, Regan Shade (Eds.), *Feminist interventions in international communication*. Lanham, MD Rowman & Littlefield.

Griswold, W. F., & Swenson, J. D. (1991). The greening of the mass media: On the ethics of reporting environmental issues. In G. Bortynk (Ed.), *Earth ethics report* (pp. 313–319). Seminole, FL: The Journal of Earth Ethics Research Group.

Grubb-Swetnam, A. (1994). *Women's use, negotiation and interpretation of women's service, fashion and beauty magazines: Generating gynergetic tales through standpoint epistemology*. Unpublished doctoral dissertation, University of Kentucky, Lexington.

Guy-Sheftall, B. (2006). African feminisms: The struggle continues. In C. Berkin, J. L. Pinch, & C. S. Appel (Eds.), *Exploring women's studies: Looking forward, looking back* (pp. 25–37). Upper Saddle River, NJ: Pearson Prentice-Hall.

Haraway, D. J. (1991). *Simians, cyborgs, and women: The reinvention of nature*. New York: Routledge.

Harding, S. (1991). *Whose science? Whose knowledge?* Ithaca, NY: Cornell University Press.

Heller, M. A. (1977). Problems in ascertainment procedures. *Journal of Broadcasting, 21,* 427–433.

Henderson, H. (1989). Eco-feminism and eco-communication: Toward the feminization of economics. In R. Rush & D. Allen (Eds.), *Communications at the crossroads: The gender gap connection* (pp. 289–304), Norwood, NJ: Ablex.

Hill-Collins, P. (1990). *Black feminist thought: Knowledge, consciousness, and the politics of empowerment*. New York: Routledge.

Hoagland, S. (1988). *Lesbian ethics: Toward new value*. Palo Alto, CA: Institute of Lesbian Studies.

Holmstrom, N. (1982). Women's work, the family and capitalism. *Science and Society, 42,* 186–211.

hooks, b. (1984). *Feminist theory: From margin to center*. Boston, MA: South End Press.

hooks, b. (1994, January). Sisters of the yam: Feminist opportunism. Z *Magazine,* 42–44.

Jaggar, A. (1983). *Feminist politics and human nature*. Totowa, NJ: Rowman & Littlefield.

Jansen, S. C. (2002), *Critical communication theory: Power, media, gender and technology*. Lanham, MD: Rowman & Littlefield.

Jiwani, Y. (2008). Mediations of domination: Gendered violence within and across borders. In K. Sarikakis & L. R. Shade (Eds.), *Feminist interventions in international communication: Minding the gap* (pp. 129–145). Lanham, MD: Rowman & Littlefield.

Kolawole, M. (1997). *Womanism and African consciousness*. Trenton, NJ: African World Press.

Leroy, D. L., & Ungurait, D. F. (1975). Ascertainment surveys: Problem perception and voluntary station contact. *Journal of Broadcasting, 19,* 23–30.

Linden, M. (2008). Radical to raunch: Articulating and anticipating contemporary lesbian feminism, an analysis of Levy's female chauvinist pigs: Women and the rise of raunch culture. Retrieved from http://igitur-archive.library.uu.nl/student-theses/2008-0429-200701/Linden/- CWSCP/Thesis.doc

Made, P. (2008). Deadly synergies: Gender inequality, HIV/AIDS and the media. In K. Sarikakis & L. R. Shade (Eds.), *Feminist interventions in international communication: Minding the gap* (pp. 176–187). Lanham, MD: Rowman & Littlefield.

Malos, E. (Ed.). (1980). *The politics of housework.* London: Allison & Busby.

Marinescu, V. (2008). Communication and women in Eastern Europe: Challenges in reshaping the democratic sphere. In K. Sarikakis & L. R. Shade (Eds.), *Feminist interventions in international communication: Minding the gap.* Lanham, MD: Rowman & Littlefield.

McLaughlin, L. (2008). Women, information, work and the corporatisation of development. In K. Sarikakis & L. R. Shade (Eds.), *Feminist interventions in international communication: Minding the gap* (pp. 224–240). Lanham, MD: Rowman & Littlefield.

McRobbie, A. (1991). *Feminism and youth culture.* Boston: Unwin Hyman.

Mohanty, C. T. (2003). *Feminism without borders: Decolonizing theory, practicing solidarity.* Durham, NC: Duke University Press.

Mosco V., McKercher, C., & Stevens, A. (2008). Convergences: Elements of a feminist political economy of labor and communication. In K. Sarikakis & L. R. Shade (Eds.), *Feminist interventions in international communication: Minding the gap* (pp. 207–223). Lanham, MD: Rowman &Littlefield.

Murray, S. (2008). Feminist print cultures in the digital era. In K. Sarikakis & L. R. Shade (Eds.), *Feminist interventions in international communication: Minding the gap.* (pp. 259–275). Lanham, MD: Rowman & Littlefield.

Nelson, J. (1989). Phenomenology of feminist methodology: Explicating interviews. In K. Carter & C. Spitzack (Eds.), *Doing research on women's communication: Perspectives on theory and method* (pp. 221–241). Norwood, NJ: Ablex.

Oyewumi, O. (Ed.). (2003). *African women and feminism: Reflecting on the politics of sisterhood.* Trenton, NJ: African World Press.

Prasad, K. (2008). Gender sensitive communication policies for women's development: Issues and challenges. In K. Sarikakis & L, Regan Shade (Eds.), *Feminist interventions in international communication.* Lanham, MD Rowman & Littlefield.

Press, A. (1991). *Women watching television: Gender, class and generation in the American television experience.* Philadelphia: University of Pennsylvania Press.

Radway, J. (1984). *Reading the romance: Women, patriarchy and popular literature.* Chapel Hill: University of North Carolina Press.

Rakow, L. F. (1992). *Women making meaning: New feminist directions in communication.* New York: Routledge.

Rakow, L. F. (1986). Rethinking gender research in communication. *Journal of Communication, 36,* 11–26.

Rakow, L. F., & Wackwitz, L. A. (2004). *Feminist communication theory: Selections in context.* Thousand Oaks, CA: Sage

Ramazanoglu. C., with Holland, J. (2006). *Feminist methodology challenges and choices* Thousand Oaks, CA: Sage

Reinharz, S. (1992). *Feminist methods in social research.* New York: Oxford University Press.

Rodgers J, (2008). Online news: Setting new agendas? In K. Sarikakis & L. R. Shade (Eds.), *Feminist interventions in international communication: Minding the gap* (pp. 188–204). Lanham, MD: Rowman & Littlefield.

Rossi, A. S. (Ed.). (1970). *Essays on sex equality: John Stuart Mill & Harriet Taylor Mill.* Chicago: University of Chicago Press.

Rupp, L. (1997). *Worlds of women: The making of an international women's movement.* Princeton, NJ: Princeton University Press.

Rush, R. R. (1989, May). *Global eco-communications: Assessing the communication and information environment*. Paper presented to the International Communication Association, San Francisco.

Rush, R. R. (1992, August). *Global eco-communications: Grounding and re/finding the concepts*. Paper presented to the International Association for Mass Communication Research, Guaruja, Brazil.

Rush, R. R. (1996). Ten tenets of deep communications: Transforming communication theory and research. In D. Allen, R. R. Rush, & S. J. Kaufman (Eds.), *Women transforming communications* (pp. 3–18). Thousand Oaks, CA: Sage.

Rush, R., & Allen, D. (Eds.). (1989). *Communications at the crossroads: The gender gap connection*. Norwood, NJ: Ablex.

Rush, R. R., Oukrop, C. E., & Creedon, P. J. (Eds.). (2004). *Seeking equity for women in journalism and mass communication education: A 30-year update*. Mahwah, NJ: Erlbaum.

Rush, R., R., Oukrop, C, E., & Ernst, S. W. (1972). *(More than you ever wanted to know) about women and journalism education*. Paper presented at the annual meeting of the Association for Education in Journalism, Southern Illinois University, Carbondale, IL.

Rush, R. R., Oukrop, C. E., & Sarikakis, K. (2005). A global hypothesis for women in journalism and mass communications: The ration of recurrent and reinforced residuum. *International Communication Gazette, 67,* 239–253

Rush, R. R., Oukrop, C., Sarikakis, K., Daufin, E. K., Andsager, J., & Wooten, B. (2005). Junior scholars in search for equity for women and minorities. *Journalism & Communication Monographs, 6*(4), 151–121.,

Sarikakis, K., & Shade, L. R. (Eds.).(2008). *Feminist interventions in international communication: Minding the gap*. Lanham, MD: Rowman & Littlefield.

Sarikakis K., & Zaukhat, Z. (2008). The global structures and cultures of pornography: The global brothel. In K. Sarikakis & L, Regan Shade (Eds.), *Feminist interventions in international communication*. Lanham, MD Rowman & Littlefield.

Schumacher, E. F. (1973). *Small is beautiful: Economics as if people mattered*. New York: Harper & Row.

Shade, L., & Porter, N. (2008). Empire and sweatshop girlhoods: The two faces of the global culture industry. In K. Sarikakis & L, Regan Shade (Eds.), *Feminist interventions in international communication*. Lanham, MD Rowman & Littlefield.

Smith, B. (Ed.). (2000). *Global feminisms since 1945*. London: Routledge.

Spender, D. (Ed.). (1983). *Feminist theorists: Three centuries of key women thinkers*. New York: Pantheon Books.

Stanley, L., & Wise, S. (1993). *Breaking out again: Feminist ontology and epistemology* (2nd ed.). London: Routledge.

Steeves, H. L. (1988, Spring). What distinguishes feminist scholarship in communication studies. *Women's Studies in Communication, 11,* 12–17.

Tong, R. P. (1998). *Feminist thought* (2nd ed.). Boulder CO: Westview.

Van Leuven, N., Giffard, C. A., Cunningham, S., & Newton, D. (2008). Female faces in the millennium development goals: Reflections in the mirrors of media. In K. Sarikakis & L. R. Shade (Eds.), *Feminist interventions in international communication: Minding the gap*. Lanham, MD: Rowman & Littlefield.

van Zoonen, L. (1994). *Feminist media studies*. Thousand Oaks, CA: Sage.

Walker, O. C., & Rudelius, W. (1976). Ascertaining programming needs of "voiceless" community groups. *Journal of Broadcasting, 20,* 89–99.

Walker, R. (1992, January/February). Becoming the third wave. *Ms. Magazine.,* 39–41.

Warren, K. J. (1993). The power and the promise of ecological feminism. In M. E. Zimmerman, J. B. Callicott, G. Sessions, K. J. Warren, & J. Clark (Eds.), *Environmental philosophy: From animal rights to radical ecology* (pp. 320–341). Englewood Cliffs, NJ: Prentice-Hall.

Wollstonecraft, M. (1975). *A vindication of the rights of women*. In C. H. Poston (Ed.), New York: Norton. (Original work published 1792)

Wood, J. T. (1994). *Gendered lives: Communication, gender, and culture*. Belmont, CA: Wadsworth.

Young, I. (1980). Socialist feminism and the limits of dual systems theory. *Socialist Review, 10,* 173–182.

Zack, N. (2005). *Inclusive feminism: A thrid wave theory of women's commonality*. Lanham, MD: Rowman & Littlefield.

Selected Bibliography

Allen, D. (n.d.). *Media without democracy and what to do about it.* (Available from Women's Institute for Freedom of the Press, 3306 Ross Place, NW, Washington, D.C. 20008)

Bannerji, H., Carty, L., Dehli, K., Heald, S., & McKenna, K. (1992). *Unsettling relations: The university as a site of feminist struggles.* Boston, MA: South End Press.

Beasley, M., & Gibbons, S. (1993). *Taking their place: A documentary history of women and journalism.* Washington, D.C.: American University Press.

Boulding, E. (1976). *The underside of history: A view of women through time.* Boulder, CO: Westview.

Bunch, C. (1987). *Passionate politics: Feminist theory in action.* New York: St. Martin's Press.

Carlsson, U. (Ed.). (1994). Women and the media [special issue]. *The Nordicom Review of Nordic Mass Communication Research, 1*

Creedon, P. J. (Ed.) (1994). *Women, media, and sport: Challenging gender values.* Newbury Park, CA: Sage.

DuBois, E. C., Kelly, G. P., Kennedy, E. L., Korsmeyer, C. W., & Robinson, L. S. (1987). *Feminist scholarship: Kindling in the groves of academe.* Chicago: University of Illinois Press.

Einerson, M. J. (1994). *Female pre-adolescent interpretations of popular music experience: An interpersonal perspective.* Unpublished doctoral dissertation, Lexington, University of Kentucky.

French, M. (1992). *The war against women.* New York: Ballantine Books.

Gallagher, M. (1989). A feminist paradigm for communication research. In B. Dervin, L. Grossberg, B. J. O'Keefe, & E. Wartella (Eds.), *Rethinking communication* (pp. 75–87). Newbury Park, CA: Sage.

Grossberg, L., Nelson, C., & Treichler, P. (Eds.). (1991). *Cultural studies.* New York: Routledge.

Griffin, G. B. (1992). *Calling: Essays on teaching in the mother tongue.* Pasadena, CA: Trilogy Books.

Henderson, H. (1969, Spring). Access to the media: A problem in democracy. *Columbia Journalism Review,* 5–8.

Henderson, H. (1991). *Paradigms in progress: Life beyond economics.* Indianapolis, IN: Knowledge Systems.

hooks, b. (1992, July/August). Out of the academy and into the streets. *Ms. Magazine,* 80–82.

Kramarae, C., & Spender, D. (1992). *The knowledge explosion: Generations of feminist scholarship.* New York: Teachers College Press.

Miedzian, M. (1991). *Boys will be boys: Breaking the link between masculinity and violence.* New York: Doubleday.

Rush, R.R. (1989a). Communications at the crossroads: The gender gap connection. In R. Rush & D. Allen (Eds.), *Communications at the crossroads: The gender gap connection* (pp. 3–19). Norwood, NJ: Ablex.

Rush, R. R. (1989b). From silent scream to silent scheme: The role of women in international communication. In G. Osborne & M. Madrigal (Eds.), *International communication: In whose interest?* (pp. 388–397). Canberra, Australia: University of Canberra, Centre for Communication and Information Research.

Rush, R. R. (1993). Being all that we can be: Harassment, barriers prevent progress. *Journalism Educator, 48,* 71–79.

Rush, R. R., Buck, E., & Ogan, C. (1982, July–September). Women and the communications revolution: Can we get there from here? *Chasqui* (publication of the Centro Internacional de Estudios Superiores de la Comunicacion para America Latina [CIESPAL], Quito, Ecuador).

Rush, R. R., Oukrop, C. E., & Creedon, P. J. (2004). (Eds.). *Seeking equity for women in journalism and mass communication education: A 30-year update.* Mahwah, NJ: Erlbaum.

Schumacher, E. F. (1973). *Small is beautiful: Economics as if people mattered.* New York: Harper & Row.

Steeves, H. L. (1987). Feminist theories and media studies. *Critical Studies in Mass Communication, 4,* 95–135.

Steinem, G. (1992). *Revolution from within: A book of self-esteem.* Boston, MA: Little, Brown.

Steinem, G. (1994). *Moving beyond words.* New York: Simon & Schuster.

Stuart, M. (1989). Social change through human exchange: Listening moves people than telling. In R. Rush & D. Allen (Eds.), *Communications at the crossroads: The gender gap connection* (pp. 177–192). Norwood, NJ: Ablex.

Tuchman, G., Daniels, A., & Benet, J. (1978). *Hearth and home: Images of women in the mass media.* New York: Oxford University Press.

Women's Action Coalition. (1993). *The facts about women.* New York: The New Press.

33

COMMUNICATION ETHICS

Donald K. Wright

Although the study of ethics has been a significant part of social science scholarship for centuries and of communication study for many decades, it is a huge understatement to say the importance of ethics in communication has increased dramatically during the first years of the current century.

There are many reasons for this, including, but not necessarily limited to, serious ethical questions that concern communication scholars and practitioners. Some of these questions center upon the tactics journalists use to get information as the news business has become increasingly competitive in today's era of the non-stop, 24/7 news cycle complete with 24-hour news channels coupled with newspaper and broadcast station websites, not to mention bloggers and others who disseminate information through what have become known as consumer generated information channels. There has been some focus on public relations as this aspect of communication has advanced from merely helping organizations to say things, to providing guidance and counsel regarding what these organizations should do and how they should do it. Advertising, organizational communication and other aspects of the field also have faced their own stream of new ethical questions and concerns.

Philip Meyer (1987), who enjoyed two distinguished professional careers in the communication field—first as a newspaper reporter with *The Miami Herald* and then as a journalism professor at the University of North Carolina-Chapel Hill—called communication ethics "a slippery topic," and likened the assignment of defining ethical behavior to the task of defining art (p. vii).

Ethics—in all aspects of communication study and practice—has attracted a good deal of attention over the past few decades. Many who work in various aspects of communication are bombarded regularly with diverse ethical cues, and too few of these communications practitioners really have developed frameworks for making ethical judgments. This chapter explores the concept of ethics from several perspectives, aiming at a *broad* understanding of the pragmatic, the conceptual, and the practical implications of *communication* ethics across disciplinary areas.

The Desire to Be Ethical

The desire for ethical behavior depends entirely upon the actions of individuals and the assumption that these people wish to act responsibly. Goodpaster and Matthews (1989) addressed three important concerns in terms of the ethical *responsibility* of individuals: someone is to blame, something has to be done, and some kind of trustworthiness can be expected.

The first of these affects an individual's action and whether he or she was responsible for the action. The second exists in circumstances in which individuals are responsible for others: lawyers to clients, physicians to patients; or, in the communication context, journalists to their readers, public relations professionals to their organizations, and the public, and so on. The third meaning of ethical responsibility focuses on the individual's moral reasoning and the intellectual and emotional processes connected to it. Thus, ethical responsibility rests on the decisions people make regarding who is responsible for acting responsibly. These decisions are influenced by a variety of factors, most of which are often beyond the individual's understanding at the time (the individual is unprepared to deal with them for a variety of reasons, including lack of training in ethical reasoning), deal with a relationship with another person, or other persons, or communication environmental factors. However looked at, communication ethics boils down to making—or not making—a decision.

Ethics and Decision Making

The topic of ethics has attracted a good deal of attention throughout the communication community over the past few decades. Although those working in journalism, advertising, broadcasting, public relations, organizational communication, corporate communications, and communication education are bombarded with many diverse ethical cues, too few really have developed frameworks for making ethical judgments.

Ethics is the division of philosophy that deals with questions of moral behavior. Making ethical decisions in the communication environment is easy when the facts are clear and the choices are black and white. It's a different story when ambiguity clouds the situation along with incomplete information, multiple points of view, and conflicting responsibilities. In such situations, ethical decisions depend on both the decision-making process and on the decision makers—their experience, intelligence, and integrity.

Much of the applied communication and ethics literature centers on the role of the decision maker in ethical behavior. Although communication professionals do not always make decisions, their counsel quite frequently enters that decision-making process. There are circumstances where the decision-making role rests firmly within the communication function. An important aspect of many communication jobs is trying to help management make decisions.

In this process, the ethical question might be whether or not to say something as much as it might be whether or not to do something. Unfortunately, for some it is easy: to say nothing and later blame the unethical results on somebody else's decision. Dick Rosenberg (1991), Chairman of the Bank of America, told an audience of corporate communication professionals that, "We don't shoot people for bringing us bad news; we shoot them for delivering it too late." This view suggests that communications managers who can head off serious problems before they blow up in the company's face, surface in a newspaper's columns, or ruin an individual's reputation are two steps ahead of the game.

George (2007) encourages people to have an "internal compass that guides you successfully through life" (p. xxiii). He says individuals should establish personal ethical boundaries that could become "moral compasses (that) will kick in when you reach your limits and tell you it is time to pull back, even if the personal sacrifices may be significant" (p. 101). George claims that's what Enron executives Kenneth Lay and Jeffrey Skilling lacked during the crisis that destroyed their company. According to George, a good way to understand individual ethical boundaries is to apply what he calls "the *New York Times* test."

> Before proceeding with any action, ask yourself, "How would I feel if this entire situation, including transcripts of our discussions was printed on the first page of the New York Times?" If your answers are negative, then it is time to rethink your actions; if they are positive, you should feel comfortable proceeding, even if others criticize your actions later. (p. 101)

Outside of individual responsibility, people must assume that they work for somebody who wants to be told the truth. Further, that truth should be respected. Some system of ethics must serve as a cornerstone for any civilized society. Communication cannot be effective without being ethical and socially responsible.

Unfortunately, the people who make the decisions in American business do not always possess responsible moral judgments. Harvard business school professor Kenneth R. Andrews (1989) contends that ethical decisions require three qualities that can be identified and developed by individuals. These are:

1. Competence to recognize ethical issues and to think through the consequences of alternative resolutions.
2. Self-confidence to seek out different points of view and then to decide what is right at a given place and time, in a particular set of relationships and circumstances.
3. "Tough-mindedness," which is the willingness to make decisions when all that needs to be known cannot be known and when the questions that press for answers have no established and incontrovertible solutions. (p. 2)

Some Basic Questions

Most people understand the clear-cut differences in moral choice. They can recognize and decide what is good or evil, right or wrong, honest or dishonest. There is, however, a faulty assumption held by many in our society that communication practitioners can be unethical—as long as they resolve conflicting claims in their own hearts and minds. There are people who often resort to certain rationalizations that appear to justify questionable behavior.

Although ethical decisions are often hard enough to make, there is much more to communication ethics than struggling with the short-range decisions on a case-by-case basis. Ethical communication begins with individuals' capacity for socially constructing a long-range moral realism.

One way or another, most people break some law at least once every day. Those who fall into that category rationalize away some of their illegal (and morally wrong) behavior. The speed limit is 55 miles-per-hour but a person drives at 62 ("everyone's doing it; it would be unsafe to do otherwise"). People jaywalk ("no traffic, why walk to the corner and then back?"). Healthy people sometimes park their cars in places reserved for handicapped drivers. Merely breaking the law, however, is not necessarily equivalent to acting unethically; sometimes adhering to the law can be unethical, as examples of Martin Luther King, Jr. and Mahatma Gandhi illustrate.

Communication scholars often see ethically perplexing situations where deciding who is ethical and who is not might depend more upon individual or organizational beliefs than anything else. Paul (1994) pointed out that although the fast-food industry frequently gets called unethical for producing food that is high in fat and cholesterol and encourages obesity, nobody forces people to eat the products of the fast-food restaurant industry. In recent years, retailers have been accused of being unethical for encouraging the concept of "vanity sizing," which involves changing labels "extra large" sized clothes to "large" or "medium" so customers will ignore the reality they are gaining weight. As the *New York Times* (2007) pointed out, when controversial nationally syndicated radio "shock-jock" Don Imus was fired for making racially and sexually insulting remarks, some questioned why the exact same words Imus used on the radio are allowed to be broadcast daily as part of the genre known as rap music. Poniewozik (2007) said although "it was clear he [Imus] crossed a line. What's unclear is. Where's the line and who can cross it?" (p. 32). Carr (2007) addressed the Imus situation this way, pointing out that remarks such as Imus made were much less damaging years ago before new technologies were a factor in the ethics of communication:

Mr. Imus is an old school radio guy caught in a very modern media paradigm. When he started 30 years ago, if he made the same kind of remark, it would have floated off into the ether—the Federal Communications Commission, if it received complaints, might have taken notice, but few others.

But radio is now visible—Mr. Imus's show was simulcast on MSNBC, and more to the point, it is downloadable. By Friday, reporters and advocates could click up the remark on the Media Matters for America website, and later YouTube, and see a vicious racial insult that delighted him visibly as it rolled off his tongue. The ether now has a memory.

Time heals, time forgets, but Mr. Imus was seeking to shore up his career immediately. Mr. Imus never caught a breath because he was in the middle of a 24-hour news cycle that kept him in the crosshairs. It is the kind of media ceremony that generally ends in a human sacrifice. (2007, pp. C1, C5)

Defining the Concept of Ethics

As noted earlier, *ethics* is the branch of philosophy that deals with questions of moral behavior. It is similar to a set of principles or a code of moral conduct (Fink, 1988). The study of ethics can provide the tools for making difficult moral choices. Students of communication do not need to know as much about how to make ethical decisions as they need to possess the knowledge and ability to defend critical judgments on some rational basis. Perhaps more than anything else, they need to recognize ethical problems when they arise.

It is inevitable that conflicts among competing values will emerge in this process. The study of ethics and moral reasoning cannot necessarily resolve such conflicts, but they can provide the tools to make it easier to live with difficult ethical choices. And, cutting through the rhetoric, most—if not all—know when we are ethical and when we are not.

According to ethics scholar Richard Johannesen (1983), ethical situations are multifaceted. They usually arise when a *moral agent* (the one making the ethical decision) commits an *act* (either verbal or nonverbal) within a specific *context* with a particular *motive* directed at an *audience*. Johannesen argues that *each* factor must be taken into account before passing judgment on the outcome of any moral scenario.

As a formal field of inquiry, ethics can be further divided into three related subareas (Callahan, 1988). *Meta-ethics* attempts to assign meanings to the abstract language of moral philosophy. *Normative ethics* provides the foundation for decision making through the development of general rules and principles of moral conduct. *Applied ethics* is concerned with using these theoretical norms to solve real-world ethical problems. Each provides ethics scholars with areas from which to construct ethical frameworks at varying levels of the decision-making process, from the language used in rationalizing an ethical decision to applying an ethical framework in real-world situations.

Why This Concern about Ethics?

Why this concern about communication ethics? One popular answer suggests that Americans have become morally adrift without traditional anchors. We have compromised our individual ethics so frequently that it sometimes becomes just as easy to compromise our professional ethics.

Followers of Sigmund Freud suggest that the development of moral character and habits of moral thought essentially are complete in early childhood. This Freudian view meets considerable resistance, particularly from Lawrence Kohlberg (1981) and his followers who believe that moral development undergoes significant structural changes well into adulthood.

Despite some huge differences between these two theses, there is strong agreement that moral development is *learned* behavior. The following scenario, filled with communication examples, forces us to think about that:

> A man and a woman take their two children, whose ages are 6 and 13, to a movie. The neighbors think they're great parents. En route to the theatre the man breaks the speed limit, drives through one stoplight after it has turned from green to amber and fails to come to a complete stop at two separate stop signs. He also fails to signal while making turns and changing lanes. Just before purchasing the movie tickets, the woman tells the 13-year-old to claim he is 12, so the parents can pay the less expensive children's ticket rate. After the movie the family eats in a buffet restaurant. The parents ask the 6-year-old to claim she is 5 so they can pay less. What message do these children learn from these examples?
>
> Does it matter that the man was speeding? Does it matter that there was no other traffic at the intersections where he did not completely stop at the stop signs?
>
> A week later the 13-year-old is arrested for shoplifting at a local mall. The parents, and the neighbors, wonder why.

Many of these decisions present us with difficulty. Some ethical decisions are simple. Others are more complex. If you support abortion you are a killer of babies; if you oppose abortion you do not respect the rights of women. To attempt to justify a principle morally, belief, attitude, policy, or action is to seek good reasons in support of it. *Good* reasons are reasons you are willing to commend to others rather than simply accept privately.

A large portion of our concern about ethics comes from a realization that possessing a system of ethics is not merely a *sufficient* condition for social intercourse, but is a *necessary* requirement. Ethics is the foundation of advanced civilization, a cornerstone that provides some stability to society's moral expectations. In the communication business it is essential that we enter into agreements with others. As such, we must be able to trust one another to keep those agreements—even if to do so is not always in our best self-interest.

Ethics not only has to be the cornerstone of effective practice of organizational communication, it also must be the cornerstone of any civilization where virtues such as truth, honesty, and integrity are to prevail. A system of ethics is essential for:

1. building trust and cooperation among individuals in society;
2. serving as a moral gatekeeper in apprising society of the relative importance of certain moral values;
3. acting as a moral arbitrator in resolving conflicting claims based on individual self interests; and
4. clarifying for society the competing values and principles inherent in emerging and novel moral dilemmas.

Can Ethics Be Taught?

There are two schools of thought on the question of whether ethics can be taught. One school claims it is a waste of time to study ethics because moral character and habits of moral thought are fully developed even before children begin formal education. Advocates of this position (e.g.,

Freud, 1923/1961; Simon, 1971) pointed out that knowledge about ethical principles does not always produce moral behavior. These skeptics also believe that the process of moral development is completed in most people before they are 6 years old. They do not believe the teaching of ethics in public schools is needed, much less at colleges and universities.

The other school of thought views ethics as a subject like history, sociology, chemistry or mathematics. Advocates (e.g., Florman, 1978; Jaska & Pritchard, 1994; Toffler, 1986) argue that ethics has its own sets of standards and rules as well as distinctive methods of problem solving.

The study of ethics comes with its own unique set of problems. More than most academic subjects, ethical viewpoints are shaped and molded through a variety of different aspects of society. A person's individual ethical beliefs are the product of many factors, including family, religion, economic status, environment, age, gender, race, and so forth.

One of the strongest arguments in favor of studying ethics comes from scholars who believe in the process of moral reasoning (e.g., Kohlberg, 1981). These scholars believe ethics involves much more than memorizing a list of ethical principles and view ethics instruction as an important component in moral conduct because it provides information and perspectives that people need to make ethical judgments.

Ethical decisions are not made in a vacuum. Day (1991) pointed out that these decisions involve a variety of considerations which can be grouped into three categories: (1) the situational definition; (2) an analysis of the situation; and (3) the ethical judgment. Advocates of moral reasoning view it as a structured, systematic approach to ethical decision making. It also provides an intellectual means of defending ethical judgments against criticisms. The Hastings Center (1980), a pioneer in ethics education, recommended these five steps be followed in preparing people to be effective in the process of moral reasoning: stimulating the moral imagination, recognizing ethical issues, developing analytical skills, eliciting a sense of moral obligation and personal responsibility, and tolerating disagreement.

Ethical Theories

The study of ethics is certainly not new. In his history of philosophy, Anders Wedberg (1982) traces ethical theories to antiquity, to the ancient Greeks. From these early beginnings can be traced the modern moral questions that contemporary communication researchers and theorists now study.

Classical Ethical Theory

The study of ethics began in ancient Greece with Socrates (c. 470–399 BC), who claimed virtue could be identified and practiced. Plato (c. 428–348 BC), who was his disciple, advocated moral conduct, even in situations when responsible behavior might run counter to societal norms. Plato's student, Aristotle (384–322 BC), argued that moral virtue often required tough choices.

Development of the Judeo-Christian ethic brought forward the concept of "love thy neighbor as thyself," which introduced the importance of a love for God and all other people. In the 18th century, Immanuel Kant (1724–1804), a German philosopher, introduced the *categorical imperative* which was a duty-based moral philosophy. Kant (1785/1982) believed in the duty to tell the truth even if it resulted in harm to others. Partially in response to Kant came the progressive relativism school of thought that believes what is right or good for one is not necessarily right or good for another, even under similar circumstances.

Classical ethical theory views ethical obligation in two different ways. *Teleological ethics* underscores the consequences of an act or decision, whereas *deontological ethics* emphasizes the nature of an act or decision.

The teleological approach deals with two basic approaches, *ethical egoism* and *utilitarianism*. Egoists make decisions based on what result is best for them, whereas utilitarianism attempts to foster whatever is best for the entire society. The tradition of egoism dates to Epicurus (c. 342–271 BC), who advocated people should do those things that would lead to their own satisfaction (Albert, Denise, & Peterfreund, 1980). Writings of more contemporary egoism theorists, such as Ayn Rand (1964), are much more a blend of reason and justification of self-interest. Jeremy Bentham (1748–1832) is noted as the founder of utilitarianism, a philosophy that endeavors to provide "the greatest happiness for the greatest number" (Christians, Rotzoll, & Fackler, 1987, pp. 12–13). Bentham's "hedonistic calculus" was designed to serve as a manual to direct his followers in taking appropriate actions. Now seen as old-fashioned, the calculus has given way to the broad overview of Bentham's philosophy. The more modern versions of utilitarianism focus on either acts or rules. *Act utilitarianism* places little value in precepts, claiming rules such as "thou shalt not kill," "never lie," and so forth, only provide rough directions for moral and ethical experiences. *Rule utilitarianism*, in contrast, is more concerned with what rule or action, when followed, will maximize the greatest good rather than with what rule or action will result in the greatest good result (Boyce & Jensen, 1978).

In examining the nature of the act in determining the lightness of an action, deontologists believe there are acts that are moral or immoral by their very nature, regardless of consequences or outcome. Immanuel Kant generally is considered the forefather of deontological ethics. He is especially known as the seminal thinker in *pure rule deontology*, by which people follow a rationally derived duty to tell the truth. Another branch of this thinking, known as *pure act deontology*, asserts that because no two circumstances are alike the nature of acts and decisions constantly change (Kant, 1785/1982). As such, act deontologists reject reason as a means to calculate moral conduct and are influenced more by the urgency of the moment and their innate ethical sense. Some deontologists consider not only the nature of an act in determining its lightness, but also its consequences. These people are known as *mixed deontologists* (Lambeth, 1986).

As ethical theory and research developed in the traditional areas of scholarship—philosophy, the classics, and so forth—*moral rules* came to represent the fuel that powered the ethical system. They provided guideposts for resolving ethical dilemmas and posed moral duties on individuals. In fulfilling moral duties people took into account all parties, including themselves, who may be touched by our ethical decisions.

Moral Reasoning Theories

Four criteria form the basis of any system of ethics. These are shared values, wisdom, justice, and freedom. First of all, an ethical system must have shared values. Before ethical judgments can be made, society must reach agreement on its standards of moral conduct. Second, these standards should be based on reason and experience. They should seek to harmonize people's rights and interests with their obligations to their fellow citizens. Third, a system of ethics should seek justice. There should be no double standard of treatment unless there is an overriding and morally defensible reason to discriminate. Finally, an ethical system should be based on freedom of choice. Moral agents must be free to render ethical judgments without coercion. Only in this way will the individual's ethical level of consciousness be raised.

In the cosmopolitan sense of the terms, ethics and moral values outline the ideals and standards people should live by. However, as those who study ethics quickly realize, no set of principles exists that will solve all ethical dilemmas. Much of the literature involved with communication ethics views ethics with a focus on what too many people refer to as *degrees* of *rightness* and *wrongness*. While ethics certainly deals with truth, fairness, and honesty, in the United States at least, the legal environment has the clear-cut mandate to be concerned with right and wrong.

Differences between *Law* and *Ethics*

The central core of what ethics and morality are all about deals with differences between what is *good* or *bad*. Laws focus on questions of what is *right* or *wrong*. Although it is possible for a law to be bad, something ethically good always should be right. Societies make and change laws, but ethical principles, theoretically at least, remain constant over time.

For example, for decades in the United States certain laws prevented African-Americans and women from voting. Many considered these laws to be bad because they violated a greater good. And, of course, eventually these laws were changed. Although societies can enact these laws, they are not ethical. Most laws, however, are consistent with ethical philosophy. Few would challenge laws that protect members of a society against those who murder, rape, or commit armed robbery. However, laws frequently are challenged by members of society who do not believe the ordinances are good.

Various Sets of Loyalties

The morally and ethically responsible person gives each set of loyalties its share of attention before rendering an ethical determination. For most of us the following categories must be examined: duty to ourselves, duty to one's organization or firm, duty to professional colleagues, and duty to society.

These loyalty sets provide interesting questions for professional communicators. Some newspaper journalists might believe their first duty is to their readers, advertising people could think their first loyalty to clients, public relations professionals might think their first loyalty is to client stockholders. An ethical issue could present itself for communicators if actions that might be moral for one public are unethical for another.

The issue of loyalty and ethics frequently surfaces in the area of religion, especially among fundamentalists. Muslim fundamentalists planned and carried out the horrible terrorist attacks of September 11, 2001 while apparently believing they were performing actions approved by a supreme being. Christian fundamentalists have been accused of bridging unethical territory when they urge believers to rally against what others perceive as the human rights of women seeking abortions and homosexuals seeking a world devoid of prejudice based upon sexual preference.

Issues Involving Communication Ethics Research

Most research involving ethics and responsibility in communication and related disciplines is concerned with problems of justice and duties—that is, *good, truth,* and *right*—and with stages of moral judgments and duties. Frankena (1963) claimed the academic study of ethics involves three kinds of normative or moral judgments. These include:

> judgments of moral obligation or deontic judgments, which say a certain action is right or obligatory; judgments of morally good or aretaic judgments, which say that certain people, motives, or character traits are morally good, virtuous; and judgments of nonmoral value in which we evaluate not so much actions and persons but all sorts of other things including experiences, paintings, forms of government, and what not. (p. 147)

The study of ethics in contemporary communication public relations research and practice generally reflects some interpretation or judging of value systems and is representative of much contemporary research. As Wilcox, Ault, and Agee (1986) described it, "a person determines what is right or wrong, fair or unfair, just or unjust. It is expressed through moral behavior in specific situations" (p. 108).

Early work involving communication ethics usually considered the basic human need to function in honest and ethical ways. A good number of these articles also combined ethics and professionalism while some concerned themselves with accreditation and licensing. Writings of Appley (1948), Bateman (1957), Bernays (1979, 1980), and Harlow (1951, 1969) justify this claim. Bateman was one of the first to encourage communication practice to develop a philosophic structure to serve as the source of its ethics. The early works of Carr-Saunders and Wilson (1993) and Flexner (1930) suggest that professions be "guided by altruism." Greenwood (1966) and Liberman (1956) were among the first to mention a code of ethics as part of the criteria which must be satisfied for an "occupation" to be a "profession."

A Divergence of Communications Viewpoints

Ethics in communication can be confusing, especially when scholars and practitioners do not always agree with their colleagues in other segments of the discipline.

Print and broadcast journalists, for example, frequently differ from people who work in public relations. These disagreements can be over simple matters such as whether or not journalists are ethical if they accept free food and beverages at press conferences. They also can entail more complex and serious controversy. For example, some journalists actually believe that anything that happens in public relations is unethical and would deny organizations the right to seek counsel on matters related to public opinion. Izard (1984–1985) reported that many journalists believe some forms of deception are permissible "if the situation demands it and circumstances are right" (p. 8). Some public relations people, on the other hand, point out that the media's agendas often hurt society, even though they might sell publications and attract broadcasting audiences.

Disagreements of this nature were common during the Watergate scandals in the early 1970s. Although journalists praised the work of *Washington Post* reporters Bob Woodward and Carl Bernstein in exposing the misdeeds of big government, many public relations experts questioned the ethics that appeared to permit these journalists to practice deception while seeking information. In academic research, for instance, the ethical perceptions journalists and public relations professionals have for similar situations been found to differ (Ryan & Martinson, 1984).

Codes of Ethics

Any discussion about communication ethics would not be complete without devoting some time to issues such as licensing, accreditation, and codes of ethics. In some ways, ethical research involving these topics has raised more issues than it has resolved. Rarely, if ever, is the total agreement regarding topics such as licensing, accreditation, and codes of ethics.

In all likelihood American communication professionals never will become licensed by the government. One reason for this might be found in the First Amendment. Print and broadcast journalists as well as those who work in public relations, advertising, and organizational communication, hold strong beliefs suggesting free and open communication for all is more important than the restrictions some would face through licensing in any of these areas.

Codes of ethics are fairly commonplace throughout the communication industry. Most communication professional organizations have ethical codes. The most noted of these codes are those of the Society of Professional Journalists, the Public Relations Society of America, the International Public Relations Association, and the International Association of Business

Communicators. Such codes represent industry self-regulation in the absence of government restrictions and are controversial to say the least (Bernays, 1979, 1980).

Although many have praised the merits of communication codes of ethics, critics point out these codes usually are unenforceable. They also are dismissed by many as being merely cosmetic (Merrill & O'Dell, 1983). Still, supporters claim the field is better with them than without them. Just as the voluntary nature of codes of ethics makes most of them unenforceable, professional accreditation programs have not made ethical codes any more accountable, and this situation is unlikely to change in Western society.

The fact that there are no legal restrictions on the practice of communication—as there are in law or medicine—poses dilemmas for the communication industry that must be resolved. The problem is that any person—qualified or not—who wants to work in journalism, public relations, broadcasting, advertising, or any other aspect of communication in most Western nations, can do so. Violations of conduct codes have kept a small minority out of some professional organizations, but codes cannot prevent them from working in the field.

Codes of ethics in communication have some strengths and can be valuable, but their voluntary nature—that is, their inability to be enforced—breeds inherent problems. Most codes of ethics for communication-related associations are filled with meaningless rhetoric, do not accomplish much, and are not taken seriously by most of the people who work in organizational communication. These codes might be able to make ethical behavior less likely because of awareness. With or without professional codes of conduct, most who practice communication will choose to be ethical because they behave ethically themselves and want others to respect them. In light of the voluntary nature of these codes, most communicators are ethical because they want to be, not because they have to be. Some claimed that enforcement of these codes often is infrequent and uneven (e.g., Cutlip, Center, & Broom, 1985). Others pointed out that many communications professionals do not belong to professional associations and note the inability of these organizations to prohibit these nonmember practitioners from violating these codes, even if the organization belongs to or adheres to a professional code of conduct (Grunig & Hunt, 1984).

Is Ethics an Individual Issue?

Our own studies of communicators in a number of contexts—including corporate communications, public relations, broadcasting and journalism—suggest that ethics is an individual issue, claiming it is up to individual practitioners to decide whether or not to be ethical regardless of professional ethical codes (Wright, 1976, 1979, 1982, 1985).

Although not dealing directly with the wide variety of occupational duties in public relations practice—including the four Grunig (1976) models of practice and the Broom-Dozier (Broom & Dozier, 1986) assessment of different practitioner roles—a major assumption of this doctrine of the individual implies press agents could be as ethical as the two-way symmetrical communicators if they had such a desire (see chapter 29). It also would contend that communication managers are not necessarily more ethical than communication technicians. We have suggested many times that public relations and communication never will be any more ethical than the level of basic morality of the people who are in public relations. This is to agree with those who claim the occupational or professional ethics of a person cannot be separated from that individual's personal ethics. Indeed one major sign of ethical and moral maturity, in Kohlberg's (1981) opinion, is the ability to make ethical judgments and formulate moral principles on our own rather than our ability to conform to moral judgments of people around us. Scholars have supported this argument for centuries. Socrates, Plato, and Aristotle all stressed the importance of individual moral convictions in their writings about ethics.

Ethics in Group Decision Making

Most ethical choices center around decision making. Although some decision-making situations in organizational communication involve the individual, most include task-oriented small groups of employees.

Modern-day organizations consider sensitivity to ethical behavior to be a strong leadership attribute. Although management groups are not always able to comprehend the ethical and moral value interpretations of all their decisions, groups try to avoid making unethical decisions. Dennis Gouran (1991) suggested five ideas that help encourage more ethical group decisions:

1. show proper concern for all affected by the group's decision;
2. explore the discussion stage of decision making as responsibly as possible;
3. avoid misrepresenting any position or misusing any information;
4. do not say or do anything that could diminish any group member's sense of self-worth; and,
5. make certain all group members respect each other. (pp. 166–167, 222)

Herbert E. Gulley (1968) provided another set of guidelines for ethical communication in small-group settings. These suggest:

1. communicators have the responsibility for defending the policy decisions of groups in whose deliberations they have participated;
2. communicators must be well informed and accurate;
3. communicators should actively encourage the comments of others and explore all viewpoints;
4. communicators should openly reveal their own biases and identify their sources of information;
5. communicators should neither lie, deceive, fabricate evidence, falsify facts, nor invent information or sources;
6. communicators should not attempt to manipulate group discussions unfairly so that selfish motives are served at the expense of the group; and,
7. communicators should avoid the use of tactics such as name calling, emotionally "loaded" language, guilt-by-association, hasty generalizations, shifting definitions, and oversimplified either-or alternatives. (pp. 334–366)

Examining Communication Ethics Research

The contemporary study of ethics in communication research and practice is fairly young and generally reflects some interpretation or judging. Opinions about ethics and moral values in all aspects of communication vary widely. Some of the early research, particularly in journalism, attempted to determine what was right and what was wrong, fair or unfair, just or unjust. Other research approached the study of ethics through moral behavior in specific situations, much of which also considered the basic human need to function in honest and ethical ways.

Most of the research concerning ethics and communication employs a wide variety of quantitative and qualitative methodologies, traceable to three separate and unique areas: journalism and broadcasting, public relations, and speech communication. These studies include survey research, personal interviews, focus groups, experimental, and critical methods.

Journalism and *broadcasting studies* involving ethics have existed for nearly half a century. The Hutchins Commission report on freedom of the press in 1947 criticized print journalism for its lack of social responsibility (Hocking, 1947). Journalism ethics also concerns the First

Amendment, business aspects of the mass media, invasion of privacy, the relationship between reporters and a wide variety of news sources, pornography and allegedly morally offensive material, and a variety of case study reports dealing with examples in many of these topical areas.

Most of these ethical topics are discussed thoroughly in four of the foremost books on the topic of journalism ethics. Rivers and Mathews (1988) provided a fairly thorough clarification of ethical issues combined with specific and practical suggestions for solutions. Their work included journalistic virtues, objectivity, basic news gathering, standards for news reporters, press councils, and media codes of ethics. The book also addresses sexism, investigative reporting, privacy, photojournalism, and freedom of the press. Christians, Flacker, and Rotzoll (1995) devoted several editions of a book that used commentaries and cases taken from actual media experiences to encourage journalists and other media practitioners to think analytically and to improve ethical awareness.

Lambeth (1986) concentrated on outlining the principles journalists should consider in making ethical judgments. His work also attempts to provide direction on to whom, or what, journalists owe professional loyalty—themselves, the public, an employer, or colleagues. Hulteng (1985) used the case study approach to illustrate the problems media practitioners face in making practical applications of ethical principles and moral standards. Meyer's research (1987) involved a large survey of editors, publishers, and reporters and documents ethical confusion in American journalism during the Watergate and Pentagon Papers controversy. Swain (1978) explored how newspaper reporters handle the delicate questions of ethics that arise repeatedly in their pressured daily routines.

Public Relations ethics research studies began in the 1950s with articles that encouraged public relations to develop a philosophic structure to serve as the source of its ethics. Since then, a number of empirical studies examined various aspects of the public relations process including ethical questions concerning individual practice, dealings with the news media, and the overall improvement of professional working standards.

Ferre and Willihnganz (1991) reported that nearly 300 books or articles had been published on the subject of public relations ethics since 1922, which, since public relations considers itself to be the conscience of corporations and society, is a very low number indeed. Unlike other areas of communication, in which many books were written, Ferre and Willihnganz noted that most of the ethics articles that concern public relations are short essays. The majority also are positive articles, claiming, for the most part, that public relations people believe in honesty, integrity, and in telling the truth.

Public relations ethics receive some coverage, albeit minor, in some of the books concerned mainly with ethics in journalism and mass communication (Christians et al., 1995, pp. 225–262; Day, 1991, pp. 71–75, 89–90, 131, 148–158, 171–174, 273–275, 313–315). Of the many journal articles, Ryan and Martinson's (1984) comparison of differences between journalists and public relations professionals stands alone, as does Kruckeberg's (1989) research on codes of ethics, Pearson's (1989) work on the theory of public relations ethics, and some of Wright's articles involving communicator analysis studies of individual public relations practitioners (Wright, 1979, 1982, 1985, 1989).

Speech Communication ethics research has been conducted from political, human nature, dialogical, and situational perspectives. The literature in this area also lists studies regarding ethics and various aspects of oral communication skills—public speaking, interpersonal, and small-group communication.

Much of the speech communication studies involving ethics explore ethical implications of a wide variety of human communication experiences, both oral and written. One of the most prolific scholars in this area is Richard L. Johannesen, whose work also attempts to provide direction to participants in the communication process and to encourage individuals to develop their own working approach to assessing communication ethics (e.g., Johannesen, 1983). Other leading research in this area includes Nilsen's (1974) efforts to provide a general orientation by which to guide communication conduct, Barnlund's (1962) insistence that all human communication theory must include moral standards specifications, and Miller's (1969) perceptions about ethical implications between communicators and audiences.

Practical Applications of Communication Ethics Research

This section examines two practical applications of communication ethics research. One involves journalism; the other corporate communications. Both of these studies could be adapted to other aspects of communication research.

Sample Journalism Ethics Study

The journalism study involves the moral values of journalists that would be measured via a mail questionnaire sent to a large, random national sample of members of the Society of Professional Journalists.

Assuming a 40 percent return rate for studies of this nature, obtaining 350 usable responses would necessitate an initial mailing of no fewer than 875 questionnaires. If funding was available, 1,000 questionnaires would be mailed. Questionnaires, accompanied by a cover letter from a noted journalist encouraging participation in the study, and a self-addressed and stamped return envelope would be mailed to randomly selected participants. Any questionnaire of this nature would need to be extremely user-friendly and probably no longer than three or four pages to enhance the return rate.

In addition to a small number of basic demographic questions, the questionnaire would concentrate on three areas: perceived moral values of subjects themselves; perceived moral values of subjects' peers; and, subjects' job satisfaction. Questions could be arrived from any number of indices and previous research questions measuring these items. Data analysis would compare and contrast scores registered in each of these three areas. If additional funding could be acquired the researcher might wish to test results through five or six focus groups of journalists in various parts of the nation.

Sample Corporation Communication Ethics Study

The corporate communications study is concerned with the impact on corporate public relations professionals of organizational codes of ethics, sometimes known as *corporate vision, values,* or *beliefs statements.* The sample would consist of senior-level corporate public relations executives; the most likely sources for the sample's population would be the directories of the Public Relations Seminar or the Arthur W. Page Society, both populated by senior-level public relations professionals.

Data gathering would consist of two parts. First, the researcher would identify several organizations that have corporate ethical codes, value statements, or similar codes. Ideally these would be Fortune 100 companies and should yield no fewer than five and no more than ten organizations. Public relations practitioners in these organizations would be surveyed in an attempt to measure the perceived impact these organizational behavior codes have on professional behavior in their specific organizations.

Second, public relations executives from other organizations would be surveyed to determine how they perceived the impact of these behavior codes. This external study also would attempt to gather information concerning the impact, if any, on corporate communications and public relations behavior caused through codes of ethics of professional societies such as the Public Relations Society of America and the International Public Relations Association.

Data analysis would test for differences between the perceived effectiveness of various aspects of these codes of ethics.

Conclusion

All in all, those who work in various professional aspects of the field of communication have made considerable progress in the direction of more ethical behavior. The field has come a long way, but it still has a long way to go.

When it comes to the bottom line, the final arbiter in separating right from wrong or good from evil in communication is the decision maker. And the authenticity of any decision depends on a universal form of morality. The higher good is purity of motive rather than the good or harm of outcome. The central value in the unwritten contract people make with society is fairness or decision making guided by principles anyone and everyone would agree with.

References

Albert, E. M., Denise, T. C., & Peterfreund, S. (1980). *Great traditions in ethics*. New York: Van Nostrand.

Andrews, K. R. (Ed.). (1989). *Ethics in practice: Managing the moral corporation*. Boston: Harvard Business School Press.

Appley, L. A. (1948). The obligations of a new profession. *Public Relations Journal, 4*, 4–9.

Barnlund, D. C. (1962). Toward a meaning-centered philosophy of communication. *Journal of Communication, 12*, 198.

Bateman, J. C. (1957). The path to professionalism. *Public Relations Journal, 13*, 6–8, 19.

Bernays, E. L. (1979). The case for licensing and registration for public relations. *Public Relations Quarterly, 24*, 26–28.

Bernays, E. L. (1980). Gaining professional status for public relations. *Public Relations Quarterly, 25*, 20.

Boyce, W. D., & Jensen, L. C. (1978). *Moral reasoning*. Lincoln: University of Nebraska Press.

Broom, G. M., & Dozier, D. M. (1986). Advancement for public relations role models. *Public Relations Review, 12*, 37–56.

Callahan, J. C. (Ed.). (1988). *Ethical issues in professional life*. New York: Oxford University Press.

Carr, D. (2007). Flying solo past the point of no return. *New York Times* (April 13), C1 & C5.

Carr-Saunders, A. M., & Wilson, P. A. (1933). *The professions*. Oxford: Clarendon Press.

Christians, C. G., Fackler, M., & Rotzoll, K. B. (1995). *Media ethics: Cases and moral reasoning* (4th ed.). White Plains, NY: Longman.

Christians, C. G., Rotzoll, K. B., & Fackler, M. (1987). *Media ethics: Cases and moral reasoning* (2nd ed.). White Plains, NY: Longman.

Cutlip, S. M., Center, A. H., & Broom, G. M. (1985). *Effective public relations* (6th ed.). Englewood Cliffs, NJ: Prentice-Hall.

Day, L. A. (1991). *Ethics in media communications: Cases and controversies*. Belmont, CA: Wadsworth.

Ferre, J. P., & Willihnganz, S. C. (1991). *Public relations and ethics: A bibliography*. Boston, MA: Hall.

Fink, C. C. (1988). *Media ethics: In the newsroom and beyond*. New York: McGraw-Hill.

Flexner, A. (1930). *Universities: American, English, German*. Oxford: Oxford University Press.

Florman, S. (1978, October). Moral blueprints. *Harpers*, 31.

Frankena, W. K. (1963). *Ethics*. Englewood Cliffs, NJ: Prentice-Hall.

Freud, S. (1961). *Civilization and its discontents* (J. Strachey, Ed. & Trans.). New York: Norton. (Original work published 1923)

George, B. (2007). *True north: Discover your authentic leadership*. San Francisco: Jossey-Bass.

Goodpaster, K. E., & Matthews, J. B., Jr. (1989). Can a corporation have a conscience? In K. R. Andrews (Ed.), *Ethics in practice: Managing the moral corporation* (pp. 155–167). Boston: Harvard Business School Press.

Gouran, D. (1991). *Making decisions in groups.* Glenville, IL: Scott Foresman.

Greenwood, E. (1966). The elements of professionalism. In H. M. Vollmer & D. L. Mills (Eds.), *Professionalization* (pp. 9–19). Englewood Cliffs, NJ: Prentice-Hall.

Grunig, J. E. (1976). Organizations and public relations: Testing a communication theory. *Journalism Monographs, 46,* 1–59..

Grunig, J. E., & Hunt, T. (1984). *Managing public relations.* New York: Holt, Rinehart & Winston.

Gulley, H. E. (1968). *Discussion, conference, and group process* (2nd ed.). New York: Holt, Rinehart & Winston.

Harlow, R. F. (1951). A plain lesson we should heed. *Public Relations Journal, 5,* 7–10.

Harlow, R. F. (1969). Is public relations a profession? *Public Relations Quarterly, 14,* 37.

Hastings Center. (1980). *The teaching of ethics in higher education.* Hastings-on-Hudson, NY: Author.

Hocking, W. E. (1947). *Freedom of the press: A framework of principle* (Report from the Commission on Freedom of the Press). Chicago: University of Chicago Press.

Hulteng, J. L. (1985). *The messenger's motives: Ethical problems of the news media* (2nd ed.). Englewood Cliffs, NJ: Prentice-Hall.

Izard, R. S. (1984–1985). *Deception: Some cases rate approval if other methods don't work* (Journalism Ethics Report). Chicago: Society of Professional Journalists.

Jaska, J. A., & Pritchard, M. S. (1994). *Communication ethics: Methods of analysis* (2nd ed.). Belmont, CA: Wadsworth.

Johannesen, R. L. (1983). *Ethics in human communication* (2nd ed.). Prospect Heights, IL: Waveland Press.

Kant, I. (1982). The good will and the categorical imperative. In T. L. Beauchamp (Ed.), *Philosophical ethics: An introduction to moral philosophy* (pp. 3–17). New York: McGraw-Hill. (Original work published 1785)

Kohlberg, L. (1981). *Essays on moral development: Vol. 1. The philosophy of moral development: Moral stages and the idea of justice.* New York: Harper & Row.

Kruckeberg, D. (1989, Summer). The need for an international code of ethics. *Public Relations Review,* 6–18.

Lambeth, E. B. (1986). *Committed journalism: An ethic for the profession.* Bloomington, IN: Indiana University Press.

Liberman, M. (1956). *Education as a profession.* Englewood Cliffs, NJ: Prentice-Hall.

Merrill, J. C., & O'Dell, S. J. (1983). *Philosophy and journalism.* White Plains, NY: Longman.

Meyer, P. (1987). *Ethical journalism.* New York: Longman.

Miller, G. R. (1969). Contributions of communication research to the study of speech. In A. H. Monroe & D. Ehniger (Eds.), *Principles and types of speech communication* (6th brief ed., p. 355). Glenview, IL: Scott, Foresman.

Nilsen, T. R. (1974). *Ethics of speech communication* (2nd ed.). Indianapolis: Bobbs-Merrill.

New York Times. (2007). The light goes out for Don Imus: CBS radio joins MSNBC in cutting ties to broadcaster. (April 13), p. C1, C5.

Paul, R. N. (1994). Status and outlook of the chain-restaurant industry. *Cornell Hotel & Restaurant Administration Quarterly, 35*(3), 23–27.

Pearson, R. (1989, September 20). Remarks to the San Francisco Academy, San Francisco, CA.

Poniewozik, J. (2007, April 23). Who can say what? *Time,* 32–37.

Rand, A. (1964). *The virtue of selfishness.* New York: New American Library/Signet Books.

Rivers, W. L., & Mathews, C. (1988). *Ethics for the media.* Englewood Cliffs, NJ: Prentice-Hall.

Rosenberg, R. (1991, September 20). *Remarks to the San Francisco Academy.* San Francisco, CA.

Ryan, M., & Martinson, D. L. (1984). Ethical values, the flow of journalistic information, and public relations persons. *Journalism Quarterly, 61,* 27–34.

Simon, S. (1971). Value-clarification vs. indoctrination. *Social Education, 35,* 902.

Swain, B. M. (1978). *Reporters' ethics.* Ames: Iowa University Press.

Toffler, B. (1986). *Tough choices: Managers talk ethics.* New York: Wiley.

Wedberg, A. (1982). *A history of philosophy: Antiquity and the middle ages* (Vol. 1). Oxford: Clarendon Press.

Wilcox, D. L., Ault, P. H., & Agee, W. K. (1986). *Public relations strategies and tactics.* New York: Harper & Row.

Wright, D. K. (1976). Social responsibility in public relations: A multi-step theory. *Public Relations Review, 2,* 24–36.

Wright, D. K. (1979). Professionalism and social responsibility in public relations. *Public Relations Review, 5,* 20–33.

Wright, D. K. (1982). The philosophy of ethical development in public relations. *IPRA Review, 9,* 18–25.

Wright, D. K. (1985). Individual ethics determine public relations practice. *Public Relations Journal, 41,* 38–39.

Wright, D. K. (1989, Summer). Examining ethical and moral values of public relations people. *Public Relations Review,* 19–33.

Part V

FUTURE OF THEORY AND RESEARCH
IN COMMUNICATION

COMMUNICATION THEORY AND RESEARCH
The Quest for Increased Credibility in the Social Sciences

Tony Atwater

From its humble beginnings in the early 20th century to the first decade of the 21st century, the formal study of communication has matured as a social science. However, there is progress yet to be made in establishing the field's empirical credibility among its peers in such academic fields as sociology, anthropology, and political science. Only in recent decades have recognized research programs sponsored by the Ford and Fulbright foundations, among others, recognized the academic legitimacy of communication. Part of the field's lack of empirical credibility and standing as a social science is related to its youth compared to older, more established disciplines. However, youth does not tell the whole story in the field's continuing pursuit of intellectual and scholarly credibility.

Challenges on the Road to Pedagogical Credibility

Earlier chapters in this volume have addressed the value of integrating theoretical propositions with empirical research methods. Another area in which additional integration is called for is in the theoretical frames of mass communication and human communication. The need for increased synthesis and fusion between the two areas represents a handicap to the field's theoretical symmetry and empirical credibility. As the 21st century progresses, communication is at an important historical crossroads in developing theoretical and methodological linkages between mass and human communication. Recent advances in electronic and digital communication technologies mandate such linkages.

The communication field also faces the challenge of successfully developing synergy and synthesis among its most accepted and popular theoretical frames such as agenda-setting, dissonance theory, cultivation theory, and other research domains. The late 20th century saw a host of theoretical frameworks emerge with little attention to how they relate to or build upon existing communication theories and paradigms. More often, new communication theoretical frameworks are linked with those older and more established social sciences. This is not, altogether, an undesirable practice. It is important that communication theory demonstrates theoretical compatibility with the other social sciences. However, the time has come for communication scholarship to take a bold step forward in recognizing its own autonomy as a social scientific enterprise, to actively examine how new theoretical frameworks relate to established ones in the field.

Early in its history, communication scholarship borrowed heavily from sociology, social psychology, and political science (among others) in building its theoretical frameworks. This was understandable given the interdisciplinary nature of the field and its youthfulness among the social sciences. As we move forward into the 21st century, communication scholarship should set for itself the goal of conceiving more theoretical frameworks that other social sciences will borrow. In the early 21st century we are seeing some, albeit limited, evidence of this practice. One of the most important signs of the field's increased empirical credibility will be the frequency with which scholars in other social science disciplines cite and employ our theoretical frameworks.

Preaching to an Academic Choir

It is ironic that a discipline devoted to analyzing human perceptions, attitudes, and communication behaviors does a poor job of communicating its own relevance and utility to the public at large. The quest for credibility as a field in the 21st century will require that communication scholars become more active in educating the general public—and specific constituencies—about the importance and relevance of communication theory and research. The nature of the communication field is such that its findings and theoretical propositions have broad social, political, and economic implications. We are a field that can hardly afford to be satisfied with preaching to our own academic choir. The choir needs to take to the road and find new ways of demonstrating the relevance of communication to many different constituencies, both private and public.

The quest for credibility inherently involves articulation of the field's validity and salience both in and outside of the academy. More progress is needed in educating publics outside of the academy about how communication theory and research relates to everyday human experience, professional contexts, and shaping public policy. One of the critical risks faced by communication is that commercial and technological currents of the latter 20th century and the first half of the 21st century will define and redefine the field to external publics with limited input from the academy. This risk should provide an incentive for communication scholars to take a lead role in telling the world what communication science is, and how it is addressing the new challenges of the present century.

How do we get beyond preaching to the choir in the quest for empirical credibility? Because of its broad and pervasive relevance, the communication field carries an additional disciplinary responsibility to make its issues and theoretical tenets comprehensible to the lay public. One way of addressing this responsibility is by publishing journals that impart significant findings and theories in language that nonacademic communities can understand and appreciate. In the professional context, for example, communication research findings and theories could be made more comprehensible for communication professionals such as journalists, advertisers, public relations personnel, as well as our own professional communication educators at the secondary, junior and community college, and college levels. Here our research institutions need to provide leadership in making communication theory and research accessible and available to others.

Additional national foundations and centers that support and promote communication research outside of colleges and universities can further advance the visibility of communication as a viable and respected social science. Institutions such as the Annenberg Foundation and the Poynter Institute have paved the way for future national support structures which enhance the visibility and political standing of the communication field. The establishment of numerous additional centers which prioritize communication research and interpret it to varied publics will play a key role in promoting the field's credibility into the 21st century.

Third, communication scholars must become more active in the political discourse and policy debates that relate to communication research findings, theories, and agendas. While some academicians are wary of tainting empirical research by examining timely policy questions, others have chosen to use empirical research to help clarify, if not reframe, debates involving public policy. Raging policy debates involving such issues as personal privacy on the information highway, media violence, and concentration of media ownership, as well as communication analysis of political campaigns, and business and technical communication provide opportunities for communication theory and research to assert their salience, and utility intellectual validity. Consequently, communication scholars should continue to identify policy matters where communication expertise is called for and be ready to respond with studies based on sound theory and methodological procedures. The field addressed public policy more in the latter 20th century than in the earlier decades. This trend needs to continue and grow. To enhance the credibility of the field, a more intentional and strategic role is called for in contributing to the development of public policy in the information, media, and communication arenas.

Meeting the Credibility Challenge

Whereas stronger pedagogical credibility can be achieved by educating external publics about communication theory and research, an internal challenge must be met on college and university campuses. The 1990s may be remembered as the decade when academic departments received a wake-up call as to their centrality to the academic mission in institutions of higher education. Although communication departments were not the only units targeted for consolidation and reallocation of resources, the message was clear. As an academic discipline, communication can and must do a better job of communicating its intellectual significance and establishing its role as a valued academic citizen inside today's university. To accomplish these objectives, we need to take full advantage of our genuinely interdisciplinary character to forge both instructional and scholarly alliances with appropriate units and disciplines throughout the university.

Like most other social sciences, communication continually faces the risk that its theoretical and research agendas will be driven by topical issues of the day as related by the media. However, the communication field faces an additional challenge: commercial and technological trends in the professional sphere also guide our research agenda. Consequently, topical issues and events that become the focus of research can detract from a much-needed larger empirical view of relevant phenomena and dynamics warranting examination and theoretical testing. A trend in communication theory has been to extrapolate from and refine existing theoretical frameworks. While such undertakings are needed and represent legitimate research endeavors, more attention is due to developing and introducing new theoretical frameworks. To do so requires innovation, hard work, and courage. More and newer theories contribute to a discipline's vitality and credibility. Even when a flawed theoretical framework is introduced, it can become the germ for the evolution of later valid theories. Therefore, the communication field should exercise the courage and assume the risks of identifying and presenting new ideologies and theoretical frameworks, if the field is to enjoy increased credibility in future years.

Although the communication field seldom enjoys the controlled research environments of the natural and physical sciences, communication has ready-made laboratories in many different social and cultural settings. Communication theory and research have been enriched by systematic inquiries in both the human and mass communication areas. In the study of mass communication, we have seen how the research agenda has focused on both media consumer issues, media organizational issues, and media practitioner issues. Media theory and research in or during the 1960s was heavily devoted to the media consumer. In the 1980s and 1990s, more attention was devoted to exploring the dynamics and processes relative to how media fare is produced and framed, providing for the study of media sociology.

For a field that entertains both basic and applied research interests, communication has much to do in generating theoretical frameworks which link both areas of inquiry. Further, there is considerable opportunity for developing new theoretical frameworks in the applied research arena. Often in the academic world, applied research is viewed as second-rate scholarship because it is atheoretical. This perspective is unfortunate; applied research offers an opportunity for the academy to demonstrate the relevance of its research to non-academic communities. Some applied communication research would benefit significantly from theoretical treatment. Further, active theory-building in the area of applied communication research seems long overdue. This arena appears to be a venue that could be better exploited in promoting the scholarly credibility and visibility of the communication field. The communication academy may need to rethink its evaluation of the merit of applied research when it successfully integrates appropriate theoretical frameworks.

In the early 21st century, the communication field has continued to cultivate a growing international academic community. The contributions of international scholars to communication theory and research have been noteworthy, and the future outlook appears bright for continued internationalization of the field. However, agendas for expanding such internationalization are needed to confirm to the world academy that communication is an autonomous social science with a promising intellectual future. Worldwide, as in the United States, the communication field is waging a continuing battle to be recognized as an individual academic discipline, as opposed to an appendage to one or more of the traditional social sciences.

Beyond making a statement to the world academic community, the field has much more to accomplish in broadening its theoretical and research interests across different national cultures, doctrines, and ideologies. While noticeably more published communication studies have involved international subjects, there is a demonstrated need for more comparative studies that assess communication behavior and issues across multiple cultures and longitudinally. Such research needs to become a high priority on the communication research agenda of tomorrow as the global village becomes a reality. International and intercultural communication studies offer excellent opportunities to test the universality of communication theory and research.

Future Trends in Media Theory and Research

As a maturing social science, communication has faced many challenges alluded to earlier in the chapter. It is a field that initially borrowed heavily from the theoretical pastures of the older, established social sciences, as well as the humanities. This early practice has served as a two-edged sword, offering some intellectual credibility in one instance, but connoting theoretical dependence and a subdisciplinary status in another instance. Over the decades of the 1970s and 1980s, and into the 1990s, the field has emerged as an autonomous academic discipline by virtue of its growing body of empirical research and its curricular contributions at many colleges and universities. Still, as a field we have some distance to go in gaining unqualified acceptance of our disciplinary autonomy within the academic community, as well as by some external publics. Additionally, the field's academic credibility continues to be variously impacted by trends and behaviors of professional communication industries. These conditions suggest that now is not the time for complacency in projecting a strong academic identity. Instead, communication scholars and administrators must seize the initiative in articulating their intellectual worth as an autonomous academic discipline.

Further, because more sophisticated research tools are being spawned due to digital technology, it can be expected that communication theory and research will entertain a higher level of precision and validity. Advances in research technology will afford greater use of controlled and field experimentation in exploring communication issues. Fiber optics-based technologies also will contribute to more precision in the most highly utilized data gathering method in communication, the survey. Increased use of cellular technologies to record studied communication behaviors will likely become a more common research tool in coming decades. Consequently, increased precision in testing theoretical propositions will be the result. Such developments further enhance the generalizability of communication studies providing the public at large a new and more applied vision of communication theory and research. This bodes well for promoting the field's empirical credibility.

Another future trend relates to an increased emphasis in research on the processes, roles, and relationships within an organizational context. In the 1960s and 1970s, much attention was devoted to the individual and to groups as captive recipients and consumers in the communication process. However, communication studies in the 1990s and into the 21st century have begun to focus more on the dynamics that affect communication relationships and the production of communication products within organizations. Communication behavior with two-way interactive communication technologies will continue to be the focus of many empirical studies. Additionally, future studies are likely to analyze how different constituent groups respond to communications and media fare with a precision not possible in earlier decades.

Theoretical precision and research validity are likely to benefit by more extensive utilization of multivariate statistical methods. As data gathering techniques become easier and statistical software more powerful and user friendly, communication research is likely to examine more variables than in the past and routinely will provide options for controlling extraneous variables. Consequently, research in the future will be cleaner, more powerful, and more rigorous in testing theoretical propositions.

To date, much communication research, especially in mass communication, has been satisfied with basing its propositions on relationships between and among theoretically linked variables. Communication scholarship has aggressively sought to identify causal relationships to predict effects in communication behavior. Limitations in identifying and controlling extraneous variables and in conducting experimental studies have posed obstacles for reporting causality. The advances foreseen in research technology are likely to remove such obstacles, providing for more robust tests of potential causal relationships in the communication process. However, promising results will still warrant that findings be replicated before a causal relationship is confirmed.

In the mass communication area, future research trends will be exciting, if not altogether predictable. Many observers foresee a media environment in which mass communication as we have known it no longer exists. These observers envision a future of interpersonally mediated communications facilitated by the information super highway and fiber optics technology. However, media history suggests that modern media seldom, if ever, replace older existing media. Consequently, our future media environment likely will include both mass and interpersonally mediated communications media. Likewise, media research will entertain both kinds of media, their related issues, and consumption patterns. Future media research likely will address itself to examining a set or portfolio of media behaviors shaped by the media technologies available to most consumers. Comparative analyses of interpersonally mediated communication behavior versus mass communication behavior (by demographic profile) should prove interesting.

A challenge for communication theorists will be to not allow the commercial and technological trends of the early 21st century to dictate the communication theoretical agenda. Theorists must be able to step back to gain a broader view of what new communication needs and problems are emerging. They must see phenomena and dynamics in the communication experience that elude commercial interests but that are vital to a better understanding of human behavior and relationships in the advanced information age. Concomitantly, individual citizens and external publics will be looking for ways to interpret and understand a new communication environment governed by a new set of communication dynamics. Such a scenario provides an awesome challenge and opportunity for the communication academy to demonstrate its inherent intellectual and practical worth.

35

THE FUTURE OF COMMUNICATION THEORY AND RESEARCH

Hartmut B. Mokros and Gustav W. Friedrich

Our contribution to this book engages the same challenge—commentary on "the future of communication theory and research"—requested of Friedrich for his contribution to the 1996, first edition of this book. His comments identified two problematic features of communication's disciplinary climate, whose consequences he examined in relation to the discipline's approach to doctoral education, namely the preparation of its future professoriate. The discipline's traditional partitioning of its subject matter into two fields of study, and distinction in approach to theory and research in the study of each was the first of these problematic features. Referred to as the mass–human communication bifurcation by Stacks and Salwen, the book's editors, they also recognized the bifurcation as problematic. It contributed to the creation and perpetuation of a climate of difference and polarization among communication's members, even though the bifurcation oft times proved arbitrary in relation to theory and research. Nevertheless, then available communication theory and research textbooks focused on either mass or human communication but not an integration of both approaches. The 1996 publication of *An Integrated Approach to Communication Theory and Research*, the first edition of this book, introduced an alternative approach, one that offered an integration of mass and human communication approaches to theory and research.

For Friedrich, the bifurcation of theory-research, namely the separation of communication's subject matter from the conduct of communication research in the design and delivery of the doctoral curriculum, was a second problematic feature of the discipline. Its consequence was evident in the middling levels of research sophistication among communication's doctorates. Coupled with resort to either mass or human communication as primary identifications and affiliations among the discipline's membership, this second bifurcation contributed to a view of communication as not yet a mature, distinct, and coherent scholarly discipline.

Communication as Discipline

Communication recently achieved a remarkable milestone in its history, accomplished through its invited participation in the 2006 to 2007 National Research Council (NRC) study of doctoral programs. The NRC restricted its invitations to those disciplines that produced at least 500 doctorates during the prior five years. Conducted roughly every decade, the NRC survey of doctoral programs provides an important source of comparative information for university administrators, funding agencies, benefactors, and would-be students. The 2006 to 2007 NRC study is the first to include doctoral programs in communication in its survey. Communication's legitimacy and singularity as a discipline of scholarship in relation to other disciplines is thereby recognized.

While such recognition acknowledges the productivity of communication's doctoral programs, the achieved requisite level of productivity could not have been reached without shared commitment to lobbying efforts on behalf of a unified discipline of communication. Communication's participation in the NRC study is certainly suggestive of a more integrated discipline than was the case in 1996. The divisive potential of the mass–human communication bifurcation would thus seem less of a problem than it was perceived to be at the time the first edition of this book was published.

For purposes of the study, the NRC taxonomy positions each discipline within one of the four familiar divisions of scholarship: Physical Sciences, Mathematics, and Engineering; Life Sciences; Arts and Humanities; and Social and Behavioral Sciences. Communication's position locates it as one of ten disciplines included within the Social and Behavioral Sciences, with Agricultural and Resource Economics, Anthropology, Economics, Geography, Linguistics, Political Science, Public Affairs, Public Policy and Public Administration, Psychology, and Sociology as sister disciplines.

In addition to its location within one of these four divisions, the NRC taxonomy identified a set of subfields for each discipline, these subfields in a sense defining the internal or constituent identity of each discipline. The study restricted program reports of their faculty's scholarly specialization to the set subfields identified for that program's discipline. For communication, the set of scholarly specialization includes 13 subfields. In alphabetical order, communication's subfields are: (1) Broadcast and Video Studies, (2) Communication Technology and New Media, (3) Critical and Cultural Studies, (4) Gender, Race, Sexuality, and Ethnicity in Communication, (5) Health Communication, (6) International and Intercultural Communication, (7) Interpersonal and Small Group Communication, (8) Journalism Studies, (9) Mass Communication, (10) Organizational Communication, (11) Public Relations and Advertising, (12) Social Influence and Political Communication, and finally (13) Speech and Rhetorical Studies. Nine of these 13 subfields have compound titles that combine two, and in one case four, titles of research areas into a single subfield. When the individual research areas combined within these nine compound subfields are each taken into account, the subfields include 24 research areas all together.

Communication Profiles Compared

When viewed as a set, the 24 areas of research listed as terms within the titles of the 13 subfields provide a form of data that makes possible the rendering of a profile of the discipline's constituent identity. Similarly, the terms included among the chapter titles of this book provide a comparative profile of the identity of communication, as is then also true of the terms in the chapter titles of the 1996 first edition of this book. Working with the assumption that these purported profiles do indeed offer a view of the discipline's identity, we now direct our commentary on *the future of communication* to the comparison of the subfield profile with that offered by the terms in the chapter titles of the 1996 book. We assume in doing so that our empirical exercise will yield both reasonable and meaningful evidence to allow our commentary to focus specifically on observable shifts from 1996 to the present in communication's constituent identity.

Our comparison is restricted to 28 of the chapters of the 1996 book, those that focus on specific areas of research. Thereby excluded are its two concluding commentary chapters and four introductory overview chapters on theory and research. Twenty of the 28 chapters considered were grouped within separate sections of mass communication approaches and human communication approaches, each containing ten chapters. The other eight chapters were included in a third section titled integrated approaches to communication. The editors' choice of section titles for grouping the majority of the chapters contributed to the book rather prominently, and curiously, reproduced the mass–human communication bifurcation, the very problem that the book's development was meant to counteract. The persuasive sway of the bifurcation on the editors' organizational choices is rather remarkable in light of the experienced arbitrariness they describe in their efforts to assign individual chapters to one or the other section.

New Research Areas

Of the 13 NRC subfields, five have no match to terms in chapter titles. Four of these subfields bear compound titles, with a total of 11 areas of research represented among the five. The five include (1) Broadcast and Video Studies, (2) Communication Technology and New Media, (3) Critical and Cultural Studies, (4) Gender, Race, Sexuality, and Ethnicity in Communication, and (5) Journalism Studies.

Kept Research Areas

The remaining eight NRC subfield titles include terms that either fully or partially match terms in the titles of one or more book chapters, including 11 chapters altogether. Three subfield–chapter pairs fully match terms in their titles: (5) Health Communication, (9) Mass Communication, and (10) Organizational Communication. The terms in the titles of three compound subfields each combine terms from the titles of two separate chapters: (6) International and Intercultural Communication, (7) Interpersonal and Small Group Communication, and (11) Public Relations and Advertising. The last two subfields include partial term matches with the (12) Social Influence and Political Communication subfield a match with the "Political Communication" chapter and the (13) Speech and Rhetorical Studies subfield a match with the "The Rhetorician's Quest" chapter (with Social Influence and Speech Studies newly added areas).

Lost Research Areas

With only 11 chapter titles either a full or a partial match to titles of subfields, the majority of research areas identified by the book's 28 chapters are not visible in the 2007 NRC-profile of communication's internal identity. The 17 unrepresented chapters include 7 of 10 chapter titles grouped within the mass communication approaches section of the book (i.e., "Media Gatekeeping," "The Agenda Setting Role," "Knowledge Gap Research," "Violence and Sex in Media," "Cultivation Analysis," "Uses and Gratifications," and "Spiral of Silence"). Five additional chapters without match to subfield titles were grouped within the human approaches section: chapters on "Persuasion," "Modeling Cultures," "Intrapersonal Communication," and "Nonverbal Communication;" and the overview chapter for this section (i.e. "Human Communication Theory and Research"). The final five chapters without match to subfields were all grouped within the integrated communication section (i.e., "Multichannel Leadership," "Diffusion of Innovation," "Credibility," "Communication Ethics," and "Feminist Approaches to Communication").

Comparison Summarized

Our comparison of subfield and chapter titles yielded 52 named research areas, with 41 of these unique. Seventeen of these unique areas were restricted to the 1996 profile, 11 areas were common to both the 1996 and 2007 profile, and 13 were new to the 2007 profile of communication's constituent identity. The majority of areas in both 1996 and 2007 are unique to that time, with less than 30% of all areas represented in both profiles of the discipline.

Communication's Bifurcations

The mass–human communication bifurcation served as the impetus for the 1996 book. It defined the organization of the book's contents, with 20 of the book's 28 chapters (71%) grouped within higher order sections, 10 representative of mass, and another 10 representative of human communication approaches. The integrated approach introduced by the book is thus dependent on and defined by this bifurcation

The Mass–Human Communication Bifurcation Update

The construction of an integrated approach is accomplished through the inclusion of both mass approaches and human approaches within the same volume. It is also accomplished through the inclusion of chapters within an integrative approaches section, whose chapters discuss research areas whose interests involve the application of both mass and human approaches. The profile of communication's constituent identity gleaned from the areas of research included in the 1996 book is dominated by the mass–human communication bifurcation despite the perceived problems the bifurcation was said to perpetuate.

The 2007 NRC taxonomic profile of communication is in sharp contrast. The mass–human communication bifurcation is absent from the 2007 profile of communication. While no longer a visible organizer of communication's areas of research, areas representative of each approach are nevertheless included in the 2007 profile. However, latent manifestation of the mass–human communication bifurcation as a structural organizer is not discernible. Although the NRC taxonomy does include hierarchical clustering of research areas, these occur within its individual subfields rather than across them. Thus, the 13 subfields each stand alone, as representatives of distinct areas of research specialization equally interdependent in relation to communication, the discipline.

Mass communication is but one subfield among 13. Two subfields combine areas grouped into separate sections in 1996. The first, International and Intercultural Communication, combines areas representing mass and human communication approaches, while the second, Public Relations and Advertising, combines an integrated approach to communication with a mass communication approach. This combining, into a single subfield, of research areas that in 1996 were representative of differing approaches further illustrates the seeming irrelevance of the mass–human communication bifurcation in 2007. If anything, the 2007 subfields are, in comparison to the rather conservative integrative approach presented in 1996, suggestive of a radical, pluralistic integration of communication's interests.

The profile of communication's interests in 2007 supports the sense that the 1996 book allocated disproportionate conceptual space to mass communication approaches in comparison to human communication approaches. As reported, 11 research areas appear both in 1996 and 2007. Of the 10 representative areas of mass communication in 1996, three appear once more in 2007. In comparison, 5 of the 10 human communication approaches and 3 of 8 integrated approaches appear once more in 2007. Thus, among the 3 types of approaches organized into separate sections of the 1996 book, mass communication approaches are proportionately least represented among research areas also included in 2007.

The "[X] Communication" Area Title Format

While the mass–human communication bifurcation seems to have little if any bearing on the 2007 organization of areas, the specific areas that appear both in 1996 and 2007 have a sense of order about them. Eight of the 11 areas that appear both years share a common name or title format that distinguishes them from the three other areas. The common format places "Communication" as the final, delimiting term of either a two- or three-term title. The organizational force of the format highlights a levels, codes, and contexts conceptualization of communication's disciplinary research agenda (cf., Berger & Chafee, 1987).

Health, Intercultural, International, Interpersonal, Mass, Organizational, Political, and Small Group (to each add *Communication*) are the eight areas that appear in both 1996 and 2007. Although three 1996 areas that share the same title format (i.e., Human Communication, Intrapersonal Communication, and Nonverbal Communication) do not reappear in 2007, the majority of areas with titles of this type (73%) do. In contrast, only 18% (3 of 17) of the areas whose titles differ from this format reappear in 2007. Thus, across all 1996 area titles, those that conform to the "[X] Communication" format are significantly more often represented in 2007 than is true of titles not formatted this way (Chi-Square = 8.45, df = 1, p < .005).

The "[[[X], Y] ... n] Studies" Area Title Format

None of the titles of the five subfields, whose areas are unique to 2007, with 11 research areas among them, conform to the "[X] Communication" title format. Although "Communication" does appear as the final term for one of these five subfields (Gender, Race, Sexuality, and Ethnicity in Communication), its format differs by virtue of the inclusion of the prepositional "in" immediately before "Communication." Interestingly, four of the 2007 subfields share a patterned titling format not employed in 1996. Rather than "Communication," the term "Studies" is the final, delimiting term of this title format. Three of the five subfields whose areas are unique to 2007 follow this format (i.e., Broadcast and Video Studies, Critical and Cultural Studies, and Journalism Studies) with Speech and Rhetorical Studies the fourth. The inclusion of "studies" is quite easily "felt" as plausible, if not perceived as implicit within the titles of the other two subfields (viz. Communication Technology and New Media [*Studies*]/Gender, Race, Sexuality and Ethnicity [*Studies*] in Communication [*Studies*]). The activity of research rather than the phenomenon, whether level, code, or context, is the meaningful conceptual sense that this title format arouses.

Bifurcation Anew

The introduction of "[[[X], Y] ... n] Studies" formatted titles joined with the re-presented "[X] Communication" formatted titles among the 2007 subfields calls attention to an identity distinction within the discipline already evident in 1996 (e.g., "Feminist Approaches to Communication"). One might perhaps argue that the absence of "Studies" as a final, delimiting term for the Communication Technology and New Media subfield as meant to avoid the inference that a Critical and Cultural Studies perspective defined its research agenda. The Critical and Cultural Studies perspective is inseparable from the Gender, Race, Sexuality, and Ethnicity in Communication subfield. Its influence helps make sense of the rise of Broadcast and Video Studies and Journalism Studies as fields of scholarship that historically have been associated with professional practice and skill-based production of mass communications, not scholarship of mass communication.

From self-evident organizer of one prominent area of research, mass communication is now understood narrowly, as an area of research that primarily studies the psychological effects of media content through traditional social scientific methods. While not included among subfield terms, Media Studies, Critical and Cultural Studies its next of kin, has fostered the "erasure" of mass communication, quite literally so in the renaming of departments (e.g., from Journalism and Mass Communication, to Journalism and Media Studies).

Media Studies and the NRC "Studies" formatted subfields share greater scholarly affinity with cultural studies perspectives developed within the Arts and Humanities and thereby challenge communication's NRC divisional placement within the Social and Behavioral Sciences. Scholarly practices emphasize theorizing not theory. Theorizing locates the subject as positioned within discourse by virtue of the organizational incline of power towards administrative, capitalist, Eurocentric, gendered, and modernist worldviews. Texts are read as tokens of discursive types within which the subject is theorized as a situated cultural, social, and psychological being, constituted through the distinctions these worldviews empower.

Our discussion has until now failed to mention the absence of human communication as an identifiable subfield. The absence would not in the least surprise a former colleague who asked, "What other kind is there?" when told Human Communication was to be the initial name assigned Rutgers University's Department of Communication when founded in 1971. And yet, the absence of human communication from the NRC taxonomy is not logically self-evident. The taxonomic organization of communication could quite reasonably include "Human Communication" as a subdisciplinary division had the rich ethological tradition of "Animal Communication" developed within anthropology, biology, and psychology been integrated into the discipline. Affinities with the Life Sciences would then, along with the Arts and Humanities, broaden the challenge of communication's logical placement as a discipline within the Social and Behavioral Sciences. To push our point further, the employment of computational and robotic technologies, increasingly as assistants and collaborators in everyday activities, suggests "Machine Communication" as reasonably a third subdisciplinary division of communication's logical interests. Affinities between this third subdiscipline of communication with the Physical Sciences, Mathematics, and Engineering would further broaden the challenge of communication's placement within the NRC taxonomy. Taxonomies clearly have their limitations when a discipline forges its development in relationship to the problematic aspects of its interests.

The Theory–Research Bifurcation Revisited

As we noted at the outset, Friedrich (1996) regarded the theory–research bifurcation as equally problematic to the mass–human bifurcation. Both bifurcations were embedded within and thereby perpetuated by the discipline's reductionistic design and delivery of doctoral education through coursework. Historical connections and common interests between and across areas were largely absent from the curriculum with research expertise, gained through experience, added onto the curriculum rather than integrated within it.

Distinctions between quantitative/qualitative research methods, scientific/humanistic traditions, and theory/theorizing offer productive sites of dialogue, argument, and debate about communication theory and research in doctoral education. However, when dialogue, argument, and debate are avoided or separated from the history of ideas that saw their development, and divorced from the doing of research, polarized identifications emerge instead. When these distinctions are treated as topics within reductionistic coursework, the scholarship of students begins to fuse distinctions and blur boundaries of notable significance to theory and research. Thus, the operationalization of discursive power seems quite sensible to some. The research questions of others harbor an implicitly held, inductive, variable analytic methodological framework (e.g., tests of individual difference or of association for specific communication factors or message characteristics) despite overt claims of an interpretive grounded theory approach to the recovery of discursive meanings. Interviews are claimed to yield rich data (in comparison to quantitative self-report measures by implication) without concern about the interview process as a contributor to the shaping of the data and without recognition that perhaps what is not talked about might at times offer at least some and on occasion considerable interpretive relevance in comparison to that which is talked about. Remarks in conclusion point out generalizability as a limitation of research reported even though the literature within which the research was developed fails to warrant generalizability as a relevant criterion of its scholarly objectives.

Although the theory–research bifurcation continues to proffer concerns for communication's disciplinary maturity, the discipline's participation in the NRC study is indeed significant. For it points to a shared sense of disciplinary commitment to communication as subject matter, rather than to identifications with traditions that fail to see their commonality of interest. To be sure, that its taxonomy includes (Advertising) and excludes (Language and Social Interaction) as subfields is hard to figure. Nevertheless, the profile of communication as defined by the NRC taxonomy, when compared to its 1996 profile, reflects the work of a discipline capable of moving past a highly meaningful, yet unproductive bifurcation, a vestige of its historical emergence quite distinct from its scholarly calling to communication as its problem.

References

Berger, C. R., & Chafee, S. H. (Eds.). (1987). *Handbook of communication science.* Beverly Hills, CA: Sage.

Friedrich, G. W. (1996). The future of communication theory and research: Human communication. In M. B. Salwen & D. W. Stacks (Eds.), *An integrated approach to communication theory and research* (pp. 547–550). Mahwah, NJ: Erlbaum.

Salwen, M. B., & Stacks, D. W. (Eds.). (1996). *An integrated approach to communication theory and research.* Mahwah, NJ: Erlbaum.

Suggested Readings

Craig, R. T. (1999). Communication theory as a field. *Communication Theory, 9,* 119–161.

Deetz, S. A. (1994). Future of the discipline: The challenges, the research, and the social contribution. In S. A. Deetz (Ed.), *Communication yearbook* (Vol. 17, pp. 565–600). Thousand Oaks, CA: Sage.

Delia, J, (1987). Communication research: A history. In C. Berger & S. Chafee (Eds.), *Handbook of communication science* (pp. 20–98). Beverly Hills, CA: Sage.

Peters, J. D. (1999). *Speaking into the air: A history of the idea of communication.* Chicago: University of Chicago Press.

CONTRIBUTORS

James A. Anderson (Ph.D., University of Iowa): Anderson is Professor of Communication and Director of the Center for Communication and Community at the University of Utah. He is the author/co-author/editor of 16 books including *Communication Theory* (Guilford, 1996), *The Organizational Self and Ethical Conduct* (Thomson, 2001), and *Media Violence and Aggression* (Sage, 2008). His 100-plus chapters, articles, and research monographs are in the areas of family studies, cultural studies, media literacy, organizational studies, communicative ethics, methodology, and epistemology.

Charles Atkin (Ph.D., University of Wisconsin): Atkin is chair of the Department of Communication at Michigan State University. He has published six books and 150 journal articles and chapters dealing with media effects on health, political, and social behavior. The Decade of Behavior consortium recognized his work with the 2006 Award for Applied Social Science Research.

Tony Atwater (Ph.D., Michigan State University): Atwater is president of Indiana University of Pennsylvania. He previously served as provost and vice president for Academic Affairs at Youngstown State University in Ohio. In this capacity, he oversaw academic programs, academic policy, and academic assessment, while providing leadership and strategic direction to approximately 750 faculty members serving six academic colleges, the School of Graduate Studies and Research, and the Library. He is the recipient of three graduate certificates in higher education administration from the Harvard Graduate School of Education.

Joyceia M. Banner (Ph.D., Louisiana State University): Banner is a Assistant Professor of Management and Organizational Communication St. Edwards University. She is currently analyzing communication in family businesses and intergenerational conflict as well as the interface between private and public life in these businesses.

Vanessa B. Beasley (Ph.D., University of Texas): Beasley is Associate Professor of Communication Studies at Vanderbilt University. She is the author of *You, the People: American National Identity in Presidential Rhetoric* and editor of *Who Belongs in America: Presidents, Rhetoric and Immigration.*

Michael J. Beatty (Ph.D., Ohio State University): Beatty is Professor of Communication and Social Interaction and Vice Dean for Graduate Studies and Research at the University of Miami, School of Communication.

Charles R. Berger (Ph.D. Michigan State University): Berger is Professor of Communication at the University of California, Davis. His research interests include message production and the processing of threatening messages. He is Past President of the International Communication Association and former editor of *Human Communication Research* and former co-editor of *Communication Research.*

Jean Bodon (Ph.D., Florida State University): Boton is Professor of Communication Studies at the University of Alabama at Birmingham, Birmingham, AL.

Theresa Bodon (M.A.E., University of Alabama at Birmingham): Boton is a Social Sciences Teacher, Tarrant High School, Birmingham, AL.

Joseph A. Bonito (Ph.D., University of Illinois at Urbana-Champaign): Bonito is an Associate Professor of Communication at the University of Arizona. His research interests include participation and decision making in small group discussion.

Jennings Bryant (Ph.D., Indiana University): Bryant is CIS Distinguished Research Professor, holder of the Reagan Chair of Broadcasting, and Associate Dean for Graduate Studies in the College of Communication and Information Sciences at the University of Alabama. His research interests are in entertainment theory, media effects, mass communication theory, and media, children, and family.

Judee K. Burgoon (Ed.D., West Virginia University): Burgoon is Professor of Communication, Family Studies and Human Development, and site director for the Center for Identification Technology Research at the University of Arizona. Among her many honors, Dr. Burgoon was awarded the National Communication Association's Distinguished Scholar Award for a lifetime of scholarly achievement.

Carey B. Candrian: Candrian is a doctoral student in the Department of Communication at the University of Colorado at Boulder. She earned her master's degree in organizational communication from the University of Colorado in 2007. She is interested in the intersection of organizational and health communication, including topics such as power and control, theories of change, and the co-construction of narratives of resistance in healthcare.

Steven H. Chaffee (Ph.D., Stanford University): Chaffee (1936–2001) was Janet M. Peck Professor of International Communication at Stanford University, Stanford, CA.

J. David Cisneros: Cisneros is a Ph.D. candidate in Speech Communication at the University of Georgia. He is interested in ethnicity, race, and rhetorics of immigration and citizenship. His work is forthcoming in *Rhetoric & Public Affairs.* He received the Robert G. Gunderson award from the National Communication Association.

R. Glenn Cummins (Ph.D., University of Alabama): Cummins is Assistant Professor in the Department of Electronic Media and Communications in the College of Mass Communications at Texas Tech University. His research interests include entertainment theory and media effects, and he has examined numerous areas of media content including sports media, music videos, reality television, and horror films.

Marcia W. DiStaso (Ph.D., University of Miami): DiStaso is an Assistant Professor of Public Relations in the College of Communications at Pennsylvania State University. She is an executive board member for the financial communications division of the Public Relations Society of America. Her research focuses on investor relations.

Gustav W. Friedrich (PhD, University of Kansas): Friedrich is Professor II and former Dean in the School of Communication, Information and Library Studies at Rutgers, The State University of New Jersey (1998-present). Before coming to Rutgers, he was a tenured faculty member at Purdue University, the University of Nebraska-Lincoln, and the University of Oklahoma. He is a former president of the National Communication Association and the Central States Communication Association. His research interests are in communication theory and in instructional and applied communication.

Bruce Garrison (Ph.D., Southern Illinois University): Garrison is Professor of Journalism at the University of Miami School of Communication.

Cecilie Gaziano (Ph.D., University of Minnesota): Gaziano owns a consulting business, Research Solutions, Inc., in Minneapolis, MN. She holds master's and doctoral degrees in mass communication from the University of Minnesota. She has authored or co-authored several chapters in edited books and published numerous articles in *Journalism & Mass Communication Quarterly, Public Opinion Quarterly, Communication Research, Newspaper Research Journal, Mass Communication & Society, Journal of Health Communication, Mass Comm Review, Critical Studies in Mass Communications, Journalism Monographs*, and other social science and medical journals.

Emanuel Gaziano (M.A. University of Chicago and Ph.D. student Indiana University): Gaziano is a computer science consultant in Minneapolis, NV. He has two co-authored chapters in edited books with Cecilie Gaziano, published in the *American Journal of Sociology*, and wrote a chapter with Andrew Abbott in G. A. Fine (Ed.), *A Second Chicago School? The Development of a Postwar American Sociology*, University of Chicago Press.

Carroll J. Glynn (Ph.D., University of Wisconsin): Glynn is the Director of the School of Communication at Ohio State University. Her area of research is the study of public opinion and social issues. She also investigates how opinion expression becomes "normative." Dr. Glynn has published in a variety of journals including *Public Opinion Quarterly, Communication Research*, and *Journal of Communication* as well as two editions of her book, *Public Opinion*.

Bradley S. Greenberg (Ph.D., University of Wisconsin): Greenberg is University Distinguished Professor Emeritus of Communication, Telecommunication, Information Studies & Media at Michigan State University. His research interests center on the social influences of the mass media, with particular emphasis on content, news flow in crises, and media effects on young people.

Autumn Grubb-Swetnam (Ph.D., University of Kentucky): Grubb-Swetnam is Associate Professor of Teaching and Learning at Georgia College & State University. She teaches graduate courses and trains postsecondary educators in the knowledge, skills, and values of implementing technology and learner-centered assessment into teaching and learning processes.

Mark Y. Hickson, III (Ph. D., Southern Illinois University): Hickson is Professor of Communication Studies at the University of Alabama at Birmingham, Birmingham, AL.

Randy Y. Hirokawa (Ph.D., University of Washington): Hirokawa is currently Dean of Arts and Sciences at the University of Hawaii at Hilo. He is known widely for his work in the area of small-group communication and decision-making effectiveness. His publications include three edited books, 36 refereed journal articles, and 24 book chapters.

James M. Honeycutt (Ph.D., University of Illinois): Honeycutt is Professor of Communication Studies at the Louisiana State University and director of the Matchbox Interaction Laboratory. He is the author/coauthor of books and articles dealing with intrapersonal communication and relational processes. Currently, he is investigating the physiology of imagined interactions in conflict resolution among couples.

Amy S. Ebesu Hubbard (Ph.D., University of Arizona): Hubbard is Associate Professor of Speech at the University of Hawai'i at Manoa. Dr. Hubbard's research and teaching focuses on nonverbal communication and interpersonal relationships. She also conducts communication training seminars to various community groups and organizations.

Yun Jin (M.A., University of Missouri-Columbia): Jin is currently working as a PR professional at Dell Inc., managing relationships with IT industry analysts and influencers. A native Chinese, Yun Jin had a B.A. in journalism from Fudan University, Shanghai and was a news reporter at the *Xin Min Evening News*, Shanghai.

Lynda Lee Kaid (Ph.D., Southern Illinois University): Kaid is Professor of Telecommunication at the University of Florida. A Fulbright Scholar, she has also done work on political television in several Western European countries. She is the author/editor of more than 25 books, including *The Handbook of Political Communication Research, The Sage Handbook of Political Advertising, Videostyle in Presidential Campaigns, Civic Dialogue in the 1996 Campaign, New Perspectives on Political Advertising, Mediated Politics in Two Cultures,* and *Political Advertising in Western Democracies*. She has received over $1.8 million in external grant funds for her research efforts, including support from the U. S. Department of Commerce, the U.S. Department of Education, the National Endowment for the Humanities, the Election Assistance Commission, and the National Science Foundation.

Khaled A. Knasser: Knasser is a doctoral student in communication studies at the Louisiana State University. He is currently studying the communication of emotions and imagined interactions in arranged marriage cases, where individuals develop their relationships at the behest of cultural and family norms.

Christina Lane (Ph.D., University of Texas at Austin): Lane is Assistant Professor of Film at the University of Miami, School of Communication. She is the author of *Feminist Hollywood: From Born in Flames to Point Break* (2000) and has published articles in *Cinema Journal* and the *Journal of Popular Film and TV*. She has also served as coordinating editor of *The Velvet Light Trap*.

Timothy R. Levine (Ph.D., Michigan State University): Levine is a Professor of Communication at Michigan State University. His research interests include deception, interpersonal communication, personal relationships, persuasion and social influence, intercultural communication, communication traits, and measurement validation. Levine has published more than 70 journal articles including approximately 30 articles in *Communication Monographs* and *Human Communication Research*.

Christopher M. Mapp: Mapp is a doctoral student in communication studies at the Louisiana State University and recent co-author of articles about imagined interaction facilitating in coping after disasters. He is currently studying musical effects on cognitive processing including imagined interactions and deception.

Kristen L. McCauliff: McCauliff is a doctoral candidate in the Speech Communication department at the University of Georgia. She is a teaching assistant in the women's studies department. She is interested in citizenship and feminism.

Maxwell McCombs (Ph.D., Stanford University): McCombs holds the Jesse H. Jones Centennial Chair at the University of Texas at Austin, has received an honorary doctorate from the University of Antwerp, the Paul Deutschmann Award of the Association for Education in Journalism and Mass Communication and with Donald Shaw the Murray Edelman Award of the American Political Science Association.

James C. McCroskey (Ed.D., Pennsylvania State University): McCroskey is Scholar in Residence in the Department of Communication Studies at the University of Alabama at Birmingham, Birmingham, AL.

Marcus Messner (ABD, University of Miami): Messner is Assistant Professor of Mass Communications at Virginia Commonwealth University, Richmond, VA.

Michael D. Miller (Ph.D., University of Florida): Miller is Professor and Chair of Communication, Media and Theatre at Henderson State University. He previously taught at the University of Hawaii and Michigan State University. His research interests include persuasion and social influence, intercultural communication and related areas. He has published in communication, psychology, and writing journals.

Diane M. Millette (Ed.D., West Virginia University): Millette is Associate Professor and Director of Communication and Social Interaction of the University of Miami's School of Communication. Areas of specialization are intercultural and instructional communication. She has co-authored two books and several articles.

Hartmut B. Mokros (Ph.D., University of Chicago): Mokros is Professor and Senior Associate Dean in the School of Communication, Information and Library Studies at Rutgers, the State University of New Jersey (1988-present). Before coming to Rutgers, he was an assistant professor of psychiatry, psychology, and behavioral sciences and director of research in child psychiatry at Rush University in Chicago. His research interests are in communication theory, language and social interaction, childhood psychopathology, and research methods.

Yvonne J. Montoya: Montoya is a doctoral student in the Hugh Downs School of Human Communication, and a communication and marketing specialist for the Office of the Vice President for Education Partnerships at Arizona State University (ASU). She was a research associate for the Project for Wellness and Work Life at ASU and holds a bachelor's degree in communication and a master's in organizational management. Her areas of study include organizational socialization and retention; work/life wellness; and Latinos in organizations.

Michael Morgan (Ph.D., University of Pennsylvania): Morgan is Professor of Communication at the University of Massachusetts Amherst. His teaching and research interests include cultivation analysis, media effects, and communication policy and technology. He has authored or co-authored over 75 national and international studies on television and its effects.

Doug Newsom (Ph.D., University of Texas at Austin): Newsom is Professor and Director of the Ad/PR graduate program of the Schieffer School of Journalism at Texas Christian University She is a public relations practitioner and served for 24 years on the board of directors of a publicly held company. Newsom holds the APR, is an elected Fellow PRSA, is the author of one textbook, *Bridging Gaps in Global Communication*, and the senior co-author of three others: *Media Writing* (with the late James Wollert); *This Is PR* (with Judy VanSlyke Turk and Dean Kruckeberg), and *Public Relations Writing: Form and Style* (with Jim Haynes). She is co-editor of a book of women's colloquium papers, *Silent Voices* (with the late Bob Carrell). Her book, *Bridging Gaps in Global Communication*, was published in 2008. A Fulbright lecturer in India in 1988 and Singapore in 1998–1999, she also has conducted public relations workshops in Singapore (1988), South Africa (1992), Bulgaria (1993), Hungary (1994 and 1995), Romania (1994), Poland (1995), Vanuatu (1997), and Latvia (1998).

Zizi Papacharissi (Ph.D., University of Texas at Austin): Papacharissi is Professor and Head of the Department of Communication at the University of Illinois-Chicago. Her research interests include social and political uses and consequences of new(er) media.

Margaret M. Quinlan: Quinlan is a doctoral student at Ohio University whose scholarly interests lie in the intersections between health and organizational communication. Drawing on narrative and feminist sensibilities, her work focuses on a range of social justice issues including disability-rights, gender inequities, and other marginalized populations including the elderly.

Virginia P. Richmond (Ph.D., University of Nebraska): Richmond is Professor and Chair of the Department of Communication Studies at the University of Alabama at Birmingham.

Shelly Rodgers (Ph.D., University of Missouri): Rodgers is Associate Professor of Strategic Communication at the Missouri School of Journalism. She teaches in the areas of strategic communication and health communication with expertise in Internet health advertising, marketing, and communication. Rodgers is nationally ranked as the most productive Internet advertising scholar in the United States and is among the top 10 most cited Internet advertising researchers in the country. Rodgers's research examines the effects of interactive communications on audience processing with emphasis on how to use the Internet to promote healthy behaviors. Research areas include cancer communication and smoking cessation/prevention and tobacco control. Her research on interactive advertising has appeared in numerous journals including the *Journal of Advertising, Journal of Communication, Journal of Advertising Research, Journal of Interactive Advertising, Marketing Research, Social Marketing Research* and *Journal of Health Communication.*

Everett M. Rogers (Ph.D., Iowa State University): Rogers (1931–2004) was Distinguished Professor Emeritus in the Department of Communication and Journalism, University of New Mexico. He was author of some 35 books, including the *Diffusion of Innovations* (2003, 5th edition), one of the most cited books in the social sciences.

Ramona R. Rush (Ph.D., University of Wisconsin): Rush is Dean/Professor Emerita of Communications at the University of Kentucky. Her publications include *Women Transforming Communications* (Sage, 1996), *Communications at the Crossroads: The Gender Gap Connection* (Ablex, 1989), and *Seeking Equity for Women in Journalism and Mass Communication Education: A_30-Year Update* (LEA, 2004). She currently is writing her memoirs in Lexington, Kentucky, and working as a Master Conservationist at her tree farm, Ecowoods, in Menifee County, Kentucky.

Charles T. Salmon (Ph.D., University of Minnesota): Salmon is Dean of the College of Communication Arts and Sciences and the Ellis N. Brandt Professor of Public Relations at Michigan State University. A former Fulbright scholar and UNICEF consultant, he works at the intersection of public opinion, public information, and public health.

Michael B. Salwen (Ph.D., Michigan State University): Salwen (1954–2007) was Professor of Journalism at the University of Miami, School of Communication.

Katharine Sarikakis (Ph.D., Glasgow Caledonian University): Sarikakis is Director of the Centre for International Communications Research at the Institute of Communications Studies, University of Leeds, UK. Her work includes *Feminist Interventions in International Communication* (Rowman & Littlefield; ed. with L Shade, 2008) *Media Policy and Globalization* (Edinburgh University Press/Palgrave co-authored with P Chakravartty, 2006) *Powers in Media Policy* (Peter Lang, 2004). She is the Chair of the Communication Law and Policy of the European Communication Research and Education Association and an Honorary Fellow at Hainan University, China.

Terri A. Scandura (Ph.D., University of Cincinnati): Scandura is Dean of the University of Miami Graduate School, and Professor of Management. Her teaching and research has focused on organizational behavior, leadership, mentoring, team building, and coaching techniques. She is an associate editor of the *Journal of Management, Group & Organization Management,* and the *Journal of International Business Studies.*

Charles C. Self (Ph.D., University of Iowa): Self is Director of the University of Oklahoma Gaylord College Institute for Research and Training. He is President of the Association for Education in Journalism and Mass Communication.

Pamela J. Shoemaker (Ph.D. University of Wisconsin-Madison): Shoemaker is the John Ben Snow Professor at the S.I. Newhouse School of Public Communications at Syracuse University. She was previously director of the School of Journalism at The Ohio State University, and on the Journalism faculty at The University of Texas-Austin. She is co-author of *Mediating the Message* and *News Around the World.*

Nancy Signorielli (Ph.D., University of Pennsylvania): Signorielli is Professor of Communication at the University of Delaware. She has conducted research on media images and cultivation analysis for the past 35 years, publishing extensively on gender role images, television violence and health-related images on television. Her books include *Violence in the Media: A Reference Handbook* (ABC: Clio, 2005).

Kami Silk (Ph.D., University of Georgia): Silk is Associate Professor of Communication at Michigan State University. Her research interests focus on influencing health behavior through the development of effective health messages for the lay public and diverse audiences that are sensitive to health literacy issues.

Arvind Singhal (Ph.D., University of South California): Singhal is Samuel Shirley and Edna Holt Marston Endowed Professor of Communication, University of Texas, El Paso. His teaching and research interests lie in the areas of diffusion of innovations, organizing and communicating for social change, and the entertainment-education communication strategy. He is author or editor of eight books including *Communication of Innovations: A Journey with Everett M. Rogers* (2006); *Organizing for Social Change* (2006); *Entertainment-Education Worldwide: History, Research, and Practice* (2004); and *Combating AIDS: Communication Strategies in Action* (2003).

Don W. Stacks (Ph.D., University of Florida): Stacks is Professor of Public Relations and Director of the Public Relations program University of Miami School of Communication. He is a board member of the Institute for Public Relation and the International Public Relations Association.

Thomas M. Steinfatt (Ph.D., Michigan State University): Steinfatt is Professor of Communication and Social Interaction at the University of Miami, School of Communication. He is a Fulbright Senior Scholar; he specializes in health, political, and intercultural communication and statistical methodology. His work in human trafficking has been funded by USAID, and was honored by the United Nations Interagency Project on Human Trafficking with the First Prize in its 2007 international competition.

Robert L. Stevenson (Ph.D., University of Washington): Stevenson (1941–2006) was Professor of Journalism at the University of North Carolina at Chapel Hill, NC.

Esther Thorson (Ph.D., University of Minnesota): Thorson is Acting Dean of the School of Journalism at the University of Missouri-Columbia, and Director of Research for the Reynolds

Journalism Institute. Along with professors Steve Lacy and Murali Mantrala she has developed econometric models that link newspaper budget management with revenue/profit patterns. Dr. Thorson has published extensively on the news industry, advertising, news effects, and health communication. Her scholarly work has won many research and writing awards and she has advised more than 35 doctoral dissertations. Her newest book, co-edited with David Schumann is *Internet Advertising: Theory and Research* (Lawrence Erlbaum, 2007). She applies research, both hers and that of her colleagues, in newsrooms and advertising agencies across the United States and abroad. She serves on an extensive list of journal editorial boards. Thorson has two central management goals, first to integrate theory and practice in graduate journalism and persuasion education, and second to bring scholarly research to bear on the news industry.

Phillip K. Tompkins (Ph.D., Purdue University): Tompkins is Professor Emeritus of Communication and Comparative Literature, University of Colorado at Boulder. He was in the first generation of graduate students to earn a doctorate (1962) in organizational communication at Purdue University. Because of their similar philosophy of organization, NASA's Marshall Space Flight Center (MSFC) recruited him in 1967 and 1968 to serve as a Summer Faculty Consultant in Organizational Communication. He is well-known for his theories of organizational identification and "concertive" control which were inspired by his observations and research program at MSFC. A Fellow and Past President of the International Communication Association, Tompkins also served in a number of positions in the National Communication Association; he is the author of many articles and books, the most recent of which is *Apollo, Challenger, Columbia: The Decline of the Space Program* (Roxbury, 2005). He has been a Friday volunteer for the past seven years at the St. Francis Center, a homeless shelter in Denver. His next book has as its working title: *Toward Ending Homelessness in Denver: Charity vs. Justice.*

Sebastián Valenzuela: Valenzuela is currently a doctoral student at the School of Journalism, University of Texas at Austin. His research focuses mainly on political communication, both in the United States and in Latin America. He is particularly interested in media effects on voting behavior, civic engagement and agenda-setting theory.

Tim P. Vos (Ph.D. Syracuse University): Vos is Assistant Professor of Journalism Studies at the University of Missouri-Columbia. He is co-author of the forthcoming book, *Gatekeeping Theory*, author of book chapters on gatekeeping and media history, and author of conference papers on media sociology, media policy, political communication, and media history.

Gwen M. Wittenbaum (Ph.D., Miami University): Wittenbaum received her doctoral training in social psychology and is Associate Professor of Communication at Michigan State University. Her research examines cognitive and motivational processes in small groups. Recent research has examined strategic information sharing in decision-making groups and social ostracism.

Donald K. Wright (Ph.D., University of Minnesota): Wright is Professor of Public Relations in the College of Communication at Boston University and a former print and broadcast journalist and public relations practitioner. He is a past president of the International Public Relations Association (IPRA) and long-time member of the Boards of Trustees of the Arthur W. Page Society and the Institute for Public Relations.

INDEX

A

Abstract concept, 7, 223
  relationship to theory, 13
Academic speech departments, 226
Accountability, organizational legitimacy, 407
Action assembly theory, 266
Active recipient theory, credibility, 446
Addressability, Internet advertising, 204
Administrative research, 171
Advertainment advertising, 199
Advertising
  attention, 201
  classic theoretical approaches, updates, 200–203
  concepts, 199–203
  content analysis, 80–81
  defined, 199
  emotion, 201–202
  hierarchy of effects, 200
  involvement, 201
  means-end theories, 201
  media gatekeeping, 80
  memory, 202–203
  psychologically-based theories, 201–203
  pull *vs.* push model, 199
  research methodology, 77–82
  social science theories, 198–211
  taxonomy, 199
Affinity, uses and gratifications, 141
Affordances, credibility, 446
African Feminism, 506
Agenda setting
  blogs, 394–395
  framing
    compared, 96–97
    knowledge activation, 96
  hyperlinking, 401
  Internet communication, for mass media, 393–395
  model, 65
  news media, 90–102
    attribute agenda setting effects, 94–96
    behavioral consequences, 100
    causality, 92
    Chapel Hill study, 90–92
    constraints, 93–94
    content analysis, 91
    external sources, 97–99
    first level, 94–95
    media priming effects, 99–100
    most important problem, 91
    need for orientation, 93
    new research arenas, 101–102
    origins of idea, 90–92
    panel studies, 92
    presidential agenda, 97–98
    process, 92–94
    research methodology, 100–101
    second level, 94–95
    timeframe, 93
    who sets media agenda, 97–99
  opinions, 99–100
  policy, 98
  political communication, 460
Aggression, *see also* Violence
  media violence, 185–186
  video games, 186
Agriculture, Iowa Hybrid Seed Corn Study, 421–423, 424
AIDS, 423–424, 484–486, 490
American culture, mass media, 292–294
Americanization, 291
Analysis unit, *see* Unit of analysis
Anthropologists, culture, 281
Argument, small group communication, 356–357
Argumentativeness
  explicating, 251–253
  persuasion, 251–255
Aristotle, 234, 528
  credibility, 436–437
  Rhetoric, 224–225
Arousal
  communication, 328

Arousal (*continued*)
  relational communication, 339
Attention, advertising, 201
Attitude
  behavior, relationship, 245
  definitional issues, 245
  measurement, 250–251
Audience characteristics, credibility, 442
Authority, 32
Autonomic nervous system, 327–328

B
Behavior
  attitude, relationship, 245
  definitional issues, 245
Behavioral science, 63, 64–65
Belief, definitional issues, 245
Bivariate analysis, 25–26
Black Identification Questionnaire, 376
Blogs
  agenda setting, 394–395
  uses and gratifications, 145–146
Bonito's participation model, small group
    communication, 356
Broadcast media, 127
Broken window syndrome, 284–285
Bullying, 284–291
Burke, Kenneth, 236–237

C
Campaign communication, *see* Political
    communication
Capta
  defined, 295
  ideal type, 295
Causality, 8, *14*, 15
Cell phones, Philippine government brought
    down by, 418
Chain-of-command, 287–288
Channels, defined, 77
Chicago School of Sociology, 63
Cigarette smoking, social control, 158
Civil rights, 293
Class, rhetorical theory, 238
Codes of ethics, 531–532
Coding, 40
Cognitive legitimacy, organizational legitimacy,
    409
Cognitive theories, 183–184
Coherence, small group communication, 357
Collaborative information, Internet
    communication, 400
Colonialism, 308
Colonialist system, 292
Common sense, 3, 5–6, 31
Communication, *see also* Specific type
  across cultures and ethnicities, 301–302
  American Rhetorical Study, 225–226

arousal, 328
bifurcations, 549, 550–552
characterized, 4, 299
contemporary applied and academic,
    229–230
culture, 227
definitions, 4
  definitional matrix, 169–170
as discipline, 546–547
emotion, 327–328
heart rate, 328
history, 223, 224–226
information, relationship, 5
mass *vs.* human communication, 549
parasympathetic nervous system, 328
process, 4–5
profiles compared, 547–548
relational tradition, 227–229
  transitioning to, 227–228
rhetorical tradition, 224–227
  perspectives, 226–227
skin, 328
as strategic tool, 226–227
study classifications, 223–224
unscientific sources of knowledge about,
    30–33
Communication competence, 271–272
Communication effectiveness model, *479*
Communication research, *see* Research
Communication theory, culture, 282
Community, knowledge gap, 124
Compensation, interpersonal communication,
    264–265
Composure, relational communication, 339
Computer-mediated communication, 270–271
  small group communication, 359–360
Concept explication, 14, 16–22
  derived terms, 19–20
  observation, 19
  preliminary definition, 18–19
  preliminary identification, 17–18
  primitive terms, 19–20
  reliability, 20–21
  time relationship, 22
  validity, 20
Concertive control
  organizational environments, 370–383
    Black Identification Questionnaire, 376
    communication as control in
      organizations, 374
    gender, 377–378
    Grameen Bank, 377–378
    literature review, 374–382
    method of control, 374–375
    organizational identification, 375–382
    Organizational Identification
      Questionnaire, 376, 377
    organization goals, 375

postbureaucratic theory, 374, 375
race, 376
research activities, 370–373
research project proposal, 380–382
theoretical frameworks, 370–373,
374–382
poverty, 377–379
resistance, 379–380
Conflict, physiology, 327–329
Conflict management, physiology, 327–329
Conflict theory, 289
Conformity, spiral of silence, 160
Consistency hierarchy, *479*
Consistency theories, persuasion, 247
Consonance, 160
Constructivism, credibility, 444–445
Construct validation, 26
Consumer-generated advertising, 199
Content analysis, 53, 189
advertisers, 80–81
health communication, 495
vs. critical analysis, 53
Contingency, rhetorical theory, 233
Conversational interview, qualitatitive research,
50–51
Corporate legitimacy, *see* Organizational
legitimacy
Corporate responsibility campaigns, Internet
advertising, 209–211
effects of fit, 210–211
online message context, 209–211
Covariance analysis, 35
Credibility, 435–449
active recipient theory, 446
affordances, 446
applied research, 442–443
shortcomings, 444
Aristotle, 436–437
audience characteristics, 442
communication research, 541–545
communicating relevance, 542–543
pedagogical credibility challenges,
541–542
concept, 435–436
historical development, 436–437
constructivism, 444–445
defined, 435–436, 438, 445
early empirical research, 437–438
endorsed, 445–446
interactivity, 444–448
Internet communication, 392–393
mass media, 436
message characteristics, 441
message sources, 446
Plato, 436–437
relational, 445
social sciences, 541–545
communicating relevance, 542–543

pedagogical credibility challenges,
541–542
Socrates, 436
Sophists, 436
source characteristics, *439*, 439–441
source credibility, 438
themes, 438–442
Critical research
Frankfurt School researchers, 170–171
international communication, 170–171
Cross-cultural communication, 9, 301
Cross-national communication, 9
Cultivation analysis, 106–118
background, 107–108
basics, 109–110
characterized, 106–107
criticisms, 113
General Social Survey, 115
procedures, 113–116
scope, 107–108
television, 106–118
choice, 110–111
cultivation variations, 112
diversity, 110–111
industry's programming practices, 111
mainstreaming, 112–113, 116
new delivery systems, 111
resonance, 112
secondary analysis, 114–116
selectivity, 110–111
trends, 116–117
violence, 111, 112
Cultural context, 128
Cultural differences, nation-states' taxonomic
control, 291
Cultural feminists, 505–506
Cultural Indicators Project, 106, 107
Cultural norms, television, 109
Cultural preferences, 291
Cultural relativism, 280
Culture
anthropologists, 281
basic, underlying assumptions, 295
communication, 227
communication theory, 282
complexity variations, 283–284
concept, 299–300
defined, 280, 300
as desire to be attached to the past, 291
ethnography, 281
geographical variation, 282
German-sociological track, 281–282
historical perspectives, 280–282
limitations on studying cultural models,
282–284
London School of Economics, 281
media, 291–295
study of troublemaking in academia, 284–291

Culture (*continued*)
   terminology, 282
   variation over time, 283
   Western culture, 280–282
Cumulative change model of social structure, 123
Curiosity, 33
Cybernetic model of information delivery systems, 126

D

Data collection, Internet advertising, 204
Deceptive communication, interpersonal communication, 268–269
Decision making
   ethical issues, 524–525
      decision qualities, 525–526
      ethics defined, 526
      reasons for concern, 526–528
   small group communication, 350–351, 352–353
Deduction, 5–6, 32–33
Definition questions, 6, 7
Deliberation, small group communication, 357–358
Derived terms, concept explication, 19–20
Descriptive statistics, 25
Desensitization, 183
Design error, 36
Development communication, 307–309
   defined, 307
Dialectics, 224
Difference, feminist communication theory, 510
Diffusion, defined, 418
Diffusion of innovations, 418–432
   diffusion S-curve, 426–427, *427*
   dominant paradigm, 424–426
      spread, 425–426
   future directions, 427–430
   inside-out diffusion, 427–430
   Internet, 428
   Iowa Hybrid Seed Corn Study, 421–423, 424
   positive deviance, 429–430
   research, 419–420
      background, 420
      communication research, 420–421
      distinctive aspects, 419–420
      methods, 426–427
   STOP AIDS Program, 423–424
Diffusion research, 308
Discrepancy, persuasion, 246
Disinhibition, 183, 188
Dissertation process, 3
   purpose, 3
Dissonance theory, persuasion, 247
Diversity, feminist research, 514–515
Dominance, relational communication, 339

Dominant paradigm, Third World, 174
Domination, 506–507
   rhetorical theory, 238
Dramatistic analysis, political communication, 459
DVDs, 111

E

Eastern Communication Association, 225
Eastern societies, 227
Ecofeminists, 506–507
Effects research, political communication, 459–460
Ego, as medium of exchange, 291
Electronic word-of-mouth, 206
Emotion
   advertising, 201–202
   communication, 327–328
Empirical definition, 24
   rules of inclusion and exclusion, 24
Empirical study, 24–26
Empirical theory, 14, *14*
Empiricism, 6
Enron, 406, 413
Entertainment, multinational corporate production, 176
Epistemological assumptions, 30
Ethical issues, 523–536
   can ethics be taught?, 527–528
   codes of ethics, 531–532
   communication ethics research, 530–536
      practical applications, 535–536
      sample corporation communication ethics study, 535–536
      sample journalism ethics study, 535
   decision making, 524–525
      decision qualities, 525–526
      ethics defined, 526
      reasons for concern, 526–528
   desire for ethical behavior, 523–526
   divergence of communications viewpoints, 531
   diverse loyalties, 530
   ethical theories, 528–529
      classical ethical theory, 528–529
      moral reasoning theories, 529
   ethics and law distinguished, 530
   group decision making, 533
   importance, 523
   as individual issue, 532
   intercultural communication, 308–309, 312–313
   qualitative research, 53–55
   research, 53–55
   science, 53–55
Ethnography
   culture, 281
   intercultural communication, 304

criticisms of ethnographic methods, 306
new ethnography, 304–305
qualitative/quantitative distinction,
306–307
postmodernism, 304
Ethnoscapes, 292
Ethos, 224–225
Evaluation research, health communication,
494
Excitation transfer, 184
Expectancy-value models, uses and
gratifications, 142
Experience of otherness, 295
Experiential advertising, 199
Experimental control, 36
Experimental research, media gatekeeping, 82
Exposure, Internet advertising, 205

F
Face-to-face communication, in small groups,
359–360
Family interaction, gender, 16–17
Federal Republic of Germany, public opinion,
156–157, 160
Feminist communication theory
difference, 510
international communication, 508–512
properties, 512
representation, 510
voice, 510
Feminist communicology, 371–372
Feminist research, 512–517
diversity, 514–515
feminist theory, relationship, 516
feminist theory and *praxis* integrated,
514–517
includes researcher as person, 515–516
mass communication, 513–514
popular culture, 513–514
special relations with people studied,
515–516
tenets, 512
transdisciplinary, 516–517
vs. mainstream theories and research, 504
Feminist theory, 504–517
feminist research, relationship, 516
historical development, 507
perspectives, 505
race, 506
rhetorical theory, 238–239
vs. mainstream theories and research, 504
Field experiments, 191
Field theory
defined, 77
media gatekeeping, 78, 79, 82–83
Financescapes, 292
Financial scandals, 406, 412–415
background, 413

organizational legitimacy
gaining legitimacy, 414
lessons learned, 412–415
maintaining legitimacy, 414
restoring legitimacy, 414–415
Fluoridation, 131, *131*
Force
characteristics, 84–85
defined, 84
media gatekeeping, 84–87
Forced exposure, Internet advertising, 208
Formality, relational communication, 339–340
Formative research, health communication,
494
Framing
agenda setting
compared, 96–97
knowledge activation, 96
definition, 96
political communication, 461
Frankfurt school researchers, critical research,
170–171
Fright reactions, 185

G
Gatekeeping, 75–87
advertisers, 80
changes in gatekeeping research, 82–83
characteristics of individual journalists,
82–83
concept origin, 75–77, *77*
defined, 75, *77*
early studies, 77–80
experimental research, 82
field theory, 78, 79, 82–83
force, 84–87
impartial rules, *78*, 78–79
Internet communication, 390–392
new gatekeepers, 400
interviews, 81
levels, 78–80
models, 77–80
observation, 81–82
personal decisions, 78, 79
social institutions, 80
study proposal on influences, 84–87
surveys, 81
Gates, defined, 77
Gender, 377–378
family interaction, 16–17
gender role stereotyping, television, 114
rhetorical theory, 238–239
Gender feminists, 505–506
Generalizability, 5–6
General Social Survey
cultivation analysis, 115
Mean World Syndrome, 115
German-sociological track, culture, 281–282

Globalization, definition, 291
Goal-Plan-Action theories, 266
Grameen Bank, 377–378
Greek philosophy, rhetorical theory, 233–234
Grounded model, ideal type, 295
Group communication, *see also* Small group communication
Group decision making, ethical issues, 533
Group discussion methods, small group communication, 350
Group interaction structure, small group communication, 349–350
Group leadership, small group communication, 351–352
Group memory, small group communication, 354
Group performance, small group communication, 351

H
Handshakes, 336
Health communication, 489–501
  campaign research applications, 496
  communication skills, 495–496
  content analysis, 495
  designing effective health messages, 497–498
  evaluation research, 494
  evidence, 497
  formative research, 494
  future directions, 499–500
  growth, 489
  health campaign impact, 498–499
  Health Message Testing Service, 494
  history, 489–491
  incentive appeals selection, 497
  interpersonal communication, 490–491
    features, 492–493
  laboratory experiments, 495
  mediated communication, features, 492–493
  message pretesting, 494
  one-sided *vs.* two-sided message content, 497
  personalization, 497–498
  realism, 497–498
  research findings and applications, 495–498
  research methods, 493–495
  source, 497
  summative research, 494
  theory development, 491–493
  time series analyses, 495
Health Message Testing Service, health communication, 494
HealthSouth, 414–415
Hearing, characterized, 324–326
Heart disease, interpersonal communication, classic case, 491
Heart rate, communication, 328
Hermeneutic empiricism, *see* Qualitative research

Hierarchy of effects, advertising, 200
Hitler, Adolf, 237
HIV, 423–424, 484–486, 490
Human Computer Interaction, 271
Humanism, 6
Hyperlinking
  agenda setting, 401
  Internet communication, 395–396
Hypodermic-needle theory, 62
Hypotheses, *14,* 14–15
Hypothesis-testing research, 14–15
Hypothetico-deductive logic, 5–6

I
Ideal type, 295
  capta, 295
  grounded model, 295
Ideology, rhetorical theory, 238–240
Ideoscapes, 291–292
  defined, 293
Image event, 241
Images
  rhetorical theory, 240–241
  texts, differentiated, 240–241
Imagetext, 241
Imagined interactions, intrapersonal communication, 323–332
  input-throughput-output, 329–332
  operationalizing construct, 326–327
  sample study, 329–332
Imitation, 183
Impartial rules, media gatekeeping, *78,* 78–79
Inductive process, 5–6
Information
  characterized, 4
  communication, relationship, 5
  knowledge, distinguished, 123–124
Information Manipulation Theory, 268–269
Information sharing, small group communication, 353–354
Information sources, 30–33
Innovation, *see* Diffusion of innovations
Input, small group communication, 361
Inside-out diffusion, 427–430
Institutional process analysis, 106
Integrated communication, public relations, 473–487
  areas of commonality, 477–480
  background for merging messages, 473–475
  communication effectiveness model, *479*
  communication tactics, 480–482
  concept, 473–475
  consistency hierarchy, *479*
  corporate structure, 475–477
  how failure to integrate causes problems, 483–484
  how integration adds value, 482–483

Integrated Marketing Communications, 475,
479
integration, 475–477
measurement, 484
persuasion as ongoing issue, 480–482
problems, 475–476
solutions, 475–477
symmetrical feedback model, *478*
World Health Organization's HIV-AIDS
effort, 484–486
Integrated Marketing Communications, 475,
479
Interactivity
credibility, 444–448
Internet advertising, 203, 208
Intercultural communication, 299–316, *see also*
Specific type
defined, 300
early texts, 311
ethical issues, 312–313
ethical systems, 308–309
ethnography, 304
criticisms of ethnographic methods, 306
new ethnography, 304–305
qualitative/quantitative distinction,
306–307
traditional ethnography, 303–304
history, 310–311
intercultural communication proper,
309–313
characterized, 309
foundations, 309–310
history, 310–311
intercultural competence, 312
linguistic relativity, 302–303
postmodernism, 304
research, 313–316
sample study, 313–316
research programs, 311–312
social science methodology, 305
study areas, 301–304
universities, teaching intercultural
communication, 311
variance within *vs.* variance between, 304
Intercultural competence, intercultural
communication, 312
International Association for Mass
Communication Research, 176
International communication, 169–178, 307
critical research, 170–171
defined, 307
definitional matrix, 169–170
feminist communication theory, 508–512
issues, 173–177
methods, 170–173
national development, 173–174
news flow, Anglo-American dominance of,
175–176

research *vs.* polemic, 171–173
social change, 173–174
studying foreign images, 176–177
Western dominance, 175
International Communication Association,
227, 228
International medium, 293
Internet advertising, 203–204
addressability, 204
advertising-related factors, 206–208
applications, 209–211
concepts, 199–203
consumer-related managerial approaches,
205–206
consumer-related psychological approaches,
205
context-related factors, 209
corporate responsibility campaigns, 209–211
effects of fit, 210–211
online message context, 209–211
data collection, 204
defined, 203–204
design-related factors, 207
exposure, 205
forced exposure, 208
individual differences, 206
individual goals and motivations, 205
information richness, 204
interactivity, 203, 208
message-related factors, 207
multi-media presentation, 204
organizing framework, 204–209
prior experience, attitudes and skills, 206
product-related factors, 208–209
reciprocal and simultaneous
communication, 203–204
targeting, 204
traditional advertising differences, 203–204
types, 206–207
user control, 203–204
user involvement, 205
Internet communication, 389–401
agenda setting, for mass media, 393–395
collaborative information, 400
content analyses, 399–400
credibility, 392–393
critiques, 398–399
diffusion of innovations, 428
essays, 398–399
experiments, 400
formats, 390
future research, 400–401
gatekeeping, 390–392
new gatekeepers, 400
hyperlinking networks, 395–396
intermedia sourcing, 401
mainstreaming, 401
methodologies, 398–400

Internet communication (*continued*)
  research, 389–390
  sexually explicit content, 187–188
  surveys, 399
  usage, 389
  uses and gratifications model, 396–398
Interpersonal adaptation
  interpersonal communication, 264–265
  social interaction, 264–265
Interpersonal communication, 228–230,
    260–272
  alternative perspectives, 260–261
  compensation, 264–265
  deceptive communication, 268–269
  health communication, 490–491
    features, 492–493
  heart disease, classic case, 491
  historical study, 261–263
  interpersonal adaptation, 264–265
  interpersonal relationship, 261
  levels-of-knowledge approach, 260–261
  message production, 265–267
  relationship development, 267–268
    relational dialectics perspective, 267–268
    social exchange theories, 267
  research areas, 271
  spiral of silence, 155–156
  uncertainty, 263–264
Interpretive turn, *see* Qualitative research
Interviews
  media gatekeeping, 81
  qualitatitive research, 50–51
Intimacy, relational communication, 338–339
Intrapersonal communication
  conceptualization, 323–324
  imagined interactions, 323–332
    input-throughput-output, 329–332
    operationalizing construct, 326–327
    sample study, 329–332
Intuition, 30–31
  defined, 30
  factors, 31
Involvement, advertising, 201
Iowa Hybrid Seed Corn Study
  agriculture, 421–423, 424
  diffusion of innovations, 421–423, 424

J
Journalism education, 64

K
Knowledge
  awareness *vs.* depth, 130
  definition, 123
  information, distinguished, 123–124
  measurement, 123
  operational definitions, 131, *131*
  theoretical definitions, 131, *131*

Knowledge activation, 96
Knowledge gap, 122–132
  as atomic naturalism, 126–127
  community, 124
  deficit interpretation, 126
  as individual voluntarism, 125–126
  research, 127–131, *132*
    analysis level, 129
    broadcast media, 127
    cultural context, 128
    factors reinforcing gaps, 128
    fluoridation, 131, *131*
    focus on families, 128
    how theory translates into research, *129*,
      129–130, *130*
    interest, 128
    motivation, 128
    print media, 127
    research design, 129
    research report, 129
    trends, 132
  sense-making approach, 126–127
  situation, 125
  as societal naturalism, 122–124
  socioeconomic status, 123, 129
  structurally functional, 124
  symbolic interaction, 125
  systemic social relationships, 123

L
Laboratory experiments, 190
  health communication, 495
Language intensity, persuasion, 246
Leadership, small group communication,
    351–352
Leathers Personal Credibility Scale, 440–441
Liberal feminist theory, 505
Limited-effects model, 65–66
Linguistic relativity, intercultural
    communication, 302–303
Listening
  characterized, 324–326
  literal processing, 324–325
  signal processing, 324–325
  stages, 324–325
Literature review, 4–5, 22–24
  meaning analysis, 23
  operational contingencies, 23–24
  synthesis, 24
Local model of participation, small group
    communication, 356
Locked door syndrome, 286
Locus of control, uses and gratifications,
    140–141
Logic, 32–33
Logical positivism, 6
Logos, 224–225
London School of Economics, culture, 281

Longitudinal studies, 191

M

Magnitude of effects, 37–38
Mainstreaming, 112–113, 116
   Internet communication, 401
Marxist-socialist feminists, 505
Mass communication, *see also* Mass media
   academic emergence, 64–65
   age of models, 65–67
   empirical tradition, 63
   feminist research, 513–514
   methodological development, 62–63
   model of models, 67–72, *68, 72*
      processes of dissemination, 70
      processes of reception, 70–71
      process of creation, 69
      process of selection, 68
   multifarious nature, 61
   process model, *78*
   profit motive, 10
   qualitative research, 65
   quantitative methods, 65
   raison d'étre, 10
   spiral of silence, 154
   theoretical development, 62
Mass culture, grounded paradigms, 280–296
Mass media
   agenda setting, Internet, 393–395
   American culture, 292–294
   credibility, 436
   economic goals, 10
   spiral of silence, 154
Matched design, 35
Means-end theories, advertising, 201
Mean World Syndrome, General Social Survey, 115
Measurement error, 36
Media, *see also* Specific type
   credibility, 443–444
      new research, 448–449
   culture, 291–295
   multinational corporate production, 176
   political campaign/event coverage, 461–462
   sex, 186–193
      aggression, 189
      content analyses, 189
      definitions, 187
      effects, 187–189
      field experiments, 191
      laboratory experiments, 190
      longitudinal studies, 191
      meta-analysis, 191
      psychophysiological studies, 190
      research methods, 189–193
      sample study, 192–193
      surveys, 191
   social interaction, 269–271

source credibility, 440
spiral of silence, 157–158
uses and consequences, *see* Uses and gratifications
violence, 181–186, 189–193
   behavioral theories, 182–183
   catharsis, 182–183
   cognitive theories, 183–184
   content analyses, 189
   cultivation, 184
   desensitization, 183
   disinhibition, 183
   effects, 185–186
   emotional theories, 184–185
   entertainment or communications medium, 181
   excitation transfer, 184
   field experiments, 191
   fright reactions, 185
   imitation, 183
   laboratory experiments, 190
   longitudinal studies, 191
   meta-analysis, 191
   priming, 184
   psychophysiological studies, 190
   reasons for featuring, 182
   research methods, 189–193
   sample study, 192–193
   surveys, 191
   third-person effect, 184
Media dependency, uses and gratifications, 142
Mediascapes, 292
Mediated communication, health communication, features, 492–493
Memory, advertising, 202–203
Memory, small group communication, 354
Message characteristics, credibility, 441
Message pretesting, health communication, 494
Message production, interpersonal communication, 265–267
Messages, processing, 324
Message sidedness, persuasion, 246
Message sources, credibility, 446
Message system analysis, 106
Meta-analysis, 191
Methodological individualism, 41–42
Metric empiricism, 42
   characteristics explanation, 42
Metrics, spiral of silence, 162–163
Mexican-Americans, organizational communication, 372
Minority status, spiral of silence, actual *vs.* perceived, 163
Mobbing, 284–291
Models
   characterized, 65–66
   usefulness, 66

Modern nomadism, 292
Monoculture, 291
Moral legitimacy, organizational legitimacy, 409
Moral reasoning theories, 529
Motives, uses and gratifications, 140–141
Muckraker reformers, 490
Mulling, 325
Multi-attribute theory, advertising, 200–201
Multi-media presentation, Internet advertising, 204
Multinational corporate production, media, 176

N
National Communication Association, 225
National development
    international communication, 173–174
    social change, 173–174
National Society for the Study of Communication, 227, 228
Nation-states, cultural media, 291
Naturalistic inquiry, *see* Qualitative research
Negative advertising, 463–464
News, multinational corporate production, 176
News flow, international, Anglo-American dominance, 175–176
News media, agenda setting, 90–102
    attribute agenda setting effects, 94–96
    behavioral consequences, 100
    causality, 92
    Chapel Hill study, 90–92
    constraints, 93–94
    content analysis, 91
    external sources, 97–99
    first level, 94–95
    how agenda setting works, 92–94
    media priming effects, 99–100
    most important problem, 91
    need for orientation, 93
    new research arenas, 101–102
    origins of idea, 90–92
    panel studies, 92
    presidential agenda, 97–98
    research methodology, 100–101
    second level, 94–95
    timeframe, 93
    who sets media agenda, 97–99
New World Information and Communication Order, 174, 175, 176, 177
Noelle-Neumann, Elisabeth, 153–163, 165
Noninterpersonal communication, 260, 261
Nonverbal communication, 336–344
    relational communication, 337–340
    relationship management, 337–340
    research methods, 340–342
    sample experiment, 342–343
    theorizing about, 336–337
Nutrition, television, 114

O
Observation, 5–6
    concept explication, 19
    media gatekeeping, 81–82
Open-door policy, 287–288
Operational definitions, 7, *14,* 14–15, 34
Opinions, agenda setting, 99–100
Organizational communication
    definition, 373–374
    feminist theorizing, 371
    history, 373–374
    Mexican-Americans, 372
    race, 372
Organizational environments, concertive control, 370–383
    Black Identification Questionnaire, 376
    communication as control in organizations, 374
    gender, 377–378
    Grameen Bank, 377–378
    literature review, 374–382
    method of control, 374–375
    organizational identification, 375–382
    organization goals, 375
    postbureaucratic theory, 374, 375
    race, 376
    research activities, 370–373
    research project proposal, 380–382
    theoretical frameworks, 370–373, 374–382
Organizational identification, 375–382
Organizational Identification Questionnaire, 376, 377
Organizational legitimacy, 406–415
    accountability, 407
    challenges, 410–412
    characterized, 407
    cognitive legitimacy, 409
    financial scandals
        gaining legitimacy, 414
        lessons learned, 412–415
        maintaining legitimacy, 414
        restoring legitimacy, 414–415
    gaining, 411
    importance, 409–410
    maintaining, 411–412
    moral legitimacy, 409
    pragmatic legitimacy, 408–409
    restoring, 412
    strategic *vs.* institutional approaches, 407–408
    types, 408–409
Organizations, grounded paradigms, 280–296
Orientation, 93
Outcomes, small group communication, 361–362

P
Parallel propositions, *14,* 14–15

Parasympathetic nervous system, communication, 328
Participant observation, 286
　qualitatitive research, 45–50
Participation, small group communication, 355–356
Pathos, 224–225
Permission advertising, 199
Personal decisions, media gatekeeping, 78, 79
Personal experience, 31–32
Personalization, health communication, 497–498
Persuasion, 245–255
　argumentativeness, 251–255
　consistency theories, 247
　definitional issues, 245
　discrepancy, 246
　dissonance theory, 247
　experimental research, 249
　factors affecting, 246–247
　language intensity, 246
　message generation, 248
　message selection, 248
　message sidedness, 246
　nonexperimental research, 249–250
　prevention of message acceptance, 246
　public relations, 480–482
　quasi-experimental research, 250
　recipient characteristics, 246–247
　refutational message strategies, 246
　research methods, 248–251, 254–255
　research types, 245
　resistance, 250–251251–255
　self-presentation, 247
　social judgment theory, 247
　source credibility, 246
　source effects, 246
　theories, 247–248
　theory of planned behavior, 248
Philippines, cell phones bring government down, 418
Plato, 233–234, 528
　credibility, 436–437
Polemic, 171–173
Policy issues, 6–7, 9–10
　agenda setting, 98
Political communication, 457–467
　agenda setting, 460
　background, 457–458
　critical approaches, 458–459
　dramatistic analysis, 459
　effects research, 459–460
　framing, 461
　interpretive approaches, 458–459
　media coverage of campaigns and events, 461–462
　methodologies, 465
　political advertising, 463–464

　negative advertising, 463–464
　political debates, 462–463
　research
　　dimensions, 457–458
　　new directions, 465
　　rhetorical approaches, 458–459
　　sample research project, 465–466, *466*
Political debates, political communication, 462–463
Political rhetoric, 464
Popper, Karl, 170–171
Popular culture, feminist research, 513–514
Pornography, *see also* Sex
　defined, 187
　sex crimes, 188
Positive deviance
　diffusion of innovations, 429–430
　social change, 429–430
Positivism, 170–171
Postmodern feminists, 506
Postmodernism
　ethnography, 304
　intercultural communication, 304
Poverty, concertive control, 377–379
Power, 37
　rhetorical theory, 238
Pragmatic legitimacy, organizational legitimacy, 408–409
Preliminary definition, concept explication, 18–19
Preliminary identification, concept explication, 17–18
Priming, 184
Primitive terms, concept explication, 19–20
Printing press, 61
Print media, 127
Problem-solving, small group communication, 350–351, 352–353
Process, small group communication, 361
Prohibition, 490
Propaganda, theory, 62
Propaganda analysis, 63
Propaganda war, first, 61
Psychoanalytic feminists, 505
Psychological violence, 182
Psychophysiological studies, 190
Public address, 235–236
Public opinion, *see also* Spiral of silence
　conceptualization, 153
　defined, 153
　Federal Republic of Germany, 156–157, 160
　process, 153
　social control, relationship, 153–165
　spiral of silence
　　dynamic version, 155–156
　　static version, 155
Public relations
　definitions, 477

Public relations (*continued*)
  influence on news agenda, 98–99
  integrated communication, 473–487
    areas of commonality, 477–480
    background for merging messages,
      473–475
    communication effectiveness model, *479*
    communication tactics, 480–482
    concept, 473–475
    consistency hierarchy, *479*
    corporate structure, 475–477
    how failure to integrate causes problems,
      483–484
    how integration adds value, 482–483
    Integrated Marketing Communications,
      475, 479
    integration, 475–477
    measurement, 484
    persuasion as ongoing issue, 480–482
    problems, 475–476
    solutions, 475–477
    symmetrical feedback model, *478*
    World Health Organization's HIV-AIDS
      effort, 484–486
  media relations, 85
  television news, study proposal on
    influences, 84–87

Q
Qualitative research, 40–55
  acceptance of agency, 44
  action signs, 44
  centrality of communication, 44
  characteristics explanation, 42
  characterized, 40
  conduct of, 45–53
  conversational interview, 50–51
  emphasis on historic performances, 44
  ethical issues, 53–55
  focus on relationships, 44
  functions, 40
  interview, 50–51
  mass communication, 65
  multiple domains of experience, 43
  paradigmatic, 41–44
  participant observation, 45–50
  philosophical assumptions, 41–43
  place of the critical in, 53
  referential analysis, 51
  subjectivity of analysis, 44
  textual analysis, 52–53
  theory, 43–44
Quantitative methods, 30–38
  conceptualizing, 33–34
  data analysis, 36–38
  mass communication, 65
  operationalizing, 34–35
  thinking quantitatively in scientific

    perspective, 33–38
Questions of definition, 7
Questions of fact, 6
Questions of policy, 6–7, 9–10
Questions of value, 6, 8–9
Questions of variable relations, 6, 8

R
Race, 376
  feminist theory, 506
  organizational communication, 372
  rhetorical theory, 239–240
Radical feminists, 505
Randomization, 35–36
Rationalism, 32–33
Realism, health communication, 497–498
Reciprocity, social interaction, 264–265
Referential analysis, qualitatitive research, 51
Relational communication
  arousal, 339
  composure, 339
  dimensions, 338–340
  dominance, 339
  formality, 339–340
  intimacy, 338–339
  nonverbal communication, 337–340
  relationship management, 337–340
  research methods, 340–342
  sample experiment, 342–343
  social orientation, 339–340
  task, 339–340
Relational conflict, nonverbal aspects, 342–343
Relational dialectics perspective, 267–268
Relationship advertising, 199
Relationship development, interpersonal
    communication, 267–268
  relational dialectics perspective, 267–268
  social exchange theories, 267
Relationship management
  nonverbal communication, 337–340
  relational communication, 337–340
Reliability, 34–35
  concept explication, 20–21
Reportative definitions, 7
Representation, feminist communication
    theory, 510
Research, *see also* Specific type
  characterized, 171–173
  comparison summarized, 548
  consistent results, 13–15
  credibility, 541–545
    communicating relevance, 542–543
    pedagogical credibility challenges,
      541–542
  defined, 3
  ethical issues, 53–55
  future trends, 544–545
  good questions, 10–11

kept research areas, 548
knowledge gap, 127–131, *132*
  analysis level, 129
  broadcast media, 127
  cultural context, 128
  factors reinforcing gaps, 128
  fluoridation, 131, *131*
  focus on families, 128
  how theory translates into research, *129,*
    129–130, *130*
  interest, 128
  motivation, 128
  print media, 127
  research design, 129
  research report, 129
  trends, 132
knowledge of previous explorers, 4
lost research areas, 548
new research areas, 548
process, 5–11
questions, 5–11
skills, 3–4
study areas, 547
theory, integrating, 3–11
[[[X], Y] ... *n]* Studies area title format, 550
[X] Communication area title format,
  549–550
Resonance, 112
Resource sharing, small group communication,
  354–355
Rhetoric, 224–227, 229–230
  defined, 224
Rhetoric, Aristotle, 224–225
Rhetorical theory
  class, 238
  constitutive approaches, 236–238
  contingency, 233
  defined, 232
  different theoretical senses, 232
  domination, 238
  feminist criticism, 238–239
  gender, 238–239
  goals, 232, 234–235
  Greek philosophy, 233–234
  ideological approaches, 238–240
  images, 240–241
  instrumental approaches to rhetoric,
    235–236
  power, 238
  race, 239–240
  research trajectories, 234–235
  symbolic approaches, 236–238
  themes, 233–235
  unit of analysis, 234–235
  uses, 234–235
  value of rhetoric, 233–234
  video, 240–241
  visual turn, 240–241

image event, 241
imagetext, 241

S
Sampling error, 36
Sapir–Whorf hypothesis, 302
Sarbanes-Oxley Act, 406, 413
Scapes, 292
Schemata, 325
Schramm, Wilbur, 63–64
Science
  ethical issues, 53–55
  place of the critical in, 53
  value-free, 53
Scientific method, 33
  conceptualizing, 33–34
  data analysis, 36–38
  designing test, 35–36
  executing test, 35–36
  operationalizing, 34–35
  thinking quantitatively in scientific
    perspective, 33–38
Scripts, 325
Self-presentation, persuasion, 247
Sense-making approach, knowledge gap,
  126–127
Sex
  Internet, sexually explicit content, 187–188
  media, 186–193
    aggression, 189
    content analyses, 189
    definitions, 187
    effects, 187–189
    field experiments, 191
    laboratory experiments, 190
    longitudinal studies, 191
    meta-analysis, 191
    psychophysiological studies, 190
    research methods, 189–193
    sample study, 192–193
    surveys, 191
  sex crimes and pornography, 188
Situation, knowledge gap, 125
Skin, communication, 328
Small group communication, 348–362
  argument, 356–357
  bona fide groups, 358–359
  Bonito's participation model, 356
  coherence, 357
  computer-mediated communication,
    359–360
  contemporary research, 352–362
  decision making, 350–351, 352–353
  deliberation, 357–358
  early research, 348–352
  face-to-face communication, 359–360
  group discussion methods, 350
  group interaction structure, 349–350

Small group communication (*continued*)
  group leadership, 351–352
  group memory, 354
  group performance, 351
  information sharing, 353–354
  input, 361
  leadership, 351–352
  local model of participation, 356
  outcomes, 361–362
  participation, 355–356
  problem-solving, 350–351, 352–353
  process, 361
  remembering, 354
  resource sharing, 354–355
  sample study, 360–362
  technology, 359–360
Social change
  international communication, 173–174
  national development, 173–174
  positive deviance, 429–430
Social control
  cigarette smoking, 158
  public opinion, relationship, 153–165
Social exchange theories, 267
Social interaction
  imagining, 266–267
  interpersonal adaptation, 264–265
  media, 269–271
  mediated, 269–271
  reciprocity, 264–265
Social judgment theory, persuasion, 247
Social learning theory, violence, 183
Socially constructed realities, 41–43
Social orientation, relational communication, 339–340
Social sciences
  credibility, 541–545
    communicating relevance, 542–543
    pedagogical credibility challenges, 541–542
  methodology
    criticisms, 305
    intercultural communication, 305
Social–scientific movement, 228
Socioeconomic status, 25–26
  knowledge gap, 123, 129
Socrates, 528
  credibility, 436
Sophists, 224, 234
  credibility, 436
Source
  health communication, 497
  persuasion, 246
  source accuracy, 80
  source credibility, 438
    characteristics, *439*, 439–441
Speech tradition, 226
Spiral of silence, 153–165

classic study design, 161–164
conceptualization issues, 158–161
conformity, 160
contemporary applications, 157–158
crossing international boundaries, 155
historical origins, 156–157
individual in social setting, 155
interpersonal communication, 155–156
issue differences, 161
mass communication, 154
mass media, 154
media, 157–158
methodological considerations, 161–164
metrics, 162–163
minority status, actual *vs.* perceived, 163
model, 154–156
public opinion
  dynamic version, 155–156
  static version, 155
survey research, 163–164
theoretical origins, 156–157
Stanford University
  Five City Project, 491
  Three Community Study, 491
Statistical analysis, 63
Statistical significance, 37–38
Stipulative definitions, 7
STOP AIDS Program, diffusion of innovations, 423–424
Storytelling, 107
  television, 107
Summative research, health communication, 494
Survey research, 163–164, 191
  media gatekeeping, 81
Symbolic interaction
  defined, 125
  knowledge gap, 125
Symmetrical feedback model, *478*

T
Targeting, Internet advertising, 204
Task, relational communication, 339–340
Team avoidance, 286
Technology, small group communication, 359–360
Technoscapes, 292
Television
  cultivation analysis, 106–118
    choice, 110–111
    cultivation variations, 112
    diversity, 110–111
    industry's programming practices, 111
    mainstreaming, 112–113, 116
    new delivery systems, 111
    resonance, 112
    secondary analysis, 114–116
    selectivity, 110–111

trends, 116–117
violence, 111, 112
cultural norms, 109
gender role stereotyping, 114
nutrition, 114
public relations influence on news study
    proposal, 84–87
socially constructed reality, 109
storytelling, 107
usage characterized, 108–109
violence, 111, 112, 181–186, 189–193
Tenacity, 31
Texts, images, differentiated, 240–241
Textual analysis, qualitatitive research, 52–53
Theory
    abstract ideas, relationship, 13
    defined, 3, 232
    meanings, 13
    as predictable findings, 13–15
    research, integrating, 3–11
    schematic view of theorizing, 13, *14*
    thinking about, 13–28
    uses, 4
Theory of planned behavior, persuasion, 248
Third-person effect, 184
Third World, dominant paradigm, 174
Thought speed, 325–326
Time relationship, concept explication, 22
Time series analyses, health communication, 495
TiVo, 111
Toscan du Plantier, Daniel, 292–294
Tradition, 31
Type I error, 37
Type II error, 37

U
Uncertainty, interpersonal communication,
    263–264
UNESCO, General Conference in Nairobi in
    1976, 176–177
United States, immigration, 299
Unit of analysis
    concept explication, 21–22
    rhetorical theory, 234–235
Univariate analysis, 25
Universities
    cultural study, 284–291
    teaching intercultural communication, 311
Unwillingness to communicate, uses and
    gratifications, 141
User-generated content, 199, 206
Uses and gratifications model, 137–146
    affinity, 141
    analysis framework, 139–142
    assumptions, 139
    blogging, 145–146
    consequences or effects of media use,
        141–142

contemporary studies, 143–144
criticisms, 138–139
defined, 137
expectancy-value models, 142
historical origins, 137–139
Internet communication, 396–398
locus of control, 140–141
media dependency, 142
motives, 140–141
psychological antecedents, 140–142
social antecedents, 140–142
theoretical and conceptual adjustments,
    138–139
trends, 144–145
unwillingness to communicate, 141
uses, 137

V
Valenti, Jack, 292–294
Validity, 34–35
    concept explication, 20
Value questions, 6, 8–9
Variable relations questions, 6, 8
    uses, 8
Variables, 6
Variance, 36–37
VCRs, 111
Video, rhetorical theory, 240–241
Video games
    aggression, 186
    violence, 15–16, 181–186, 186, 189–193
Video news release, 84–87
Vienna school researchers, 170–171
Violence, 112
    defined, 181–182
    media, 181–186, 189–193
        behavioral theories, 182–183
        catharsis, 182–183
        cognitive theories, 183–184
        content analyses, 189
        cultivation, 184
        desensitization, 183
        disinhibition, 183
        effects, 185–186
        emotional theories, 184–185
        entertainment or communications
            medium, 181
        excitation transfer, 184
        field experiments, 191
        fright reactions, 185
        imitation, 183
        laboratory experiments, 190
        longitudinal studies, 191
        meta-analysis, 191
        priming, 184
        psychophysiological studies, 190
        reasons for featuring, 182
        research methods, 189–193

Violence (*continued*)
    sample study, 192–193
    surveys, 191
    third-person effect, 184
  social learning theory, 183
  television, 181–186, 189–193
  video games, 15–16, 181–186, 186, 189–193
Visual turn, rhetorical theory, 240–241
  image event, 241
  imagetext, 241
Voice, feminist communication theory, 510

W
Weltanschauung thesis of linguistic relativity,
    302–303
Western culture, 226–227, 280–282
Western dominance, international
    communication, 175
Workplace mobbing, 284–291
WorldCom, 413
World Health Organization, HIV-AIDS effort,
    484–486

eBooks – at www.eBookstore.tandf.co.uk

A library at your fingertips!

eBooks are electronic versions of printed books. You can store them on your PC/laptop or browse them online.

They have advantages for anyone needing rapid access to a wide variety of published, copyright information.

eBooks can help your research by enabling you to bookmark chapters, annotate text and use instant searches to find specific words or phrases. Several eBook files would fit on even a small laptop or PDA.

NEW: Save money by eSubscribing: cheap, online access to any eBook for as long as you need it.

Annual subscription packages

We now offer special low-cost bulk subscriptions to packages of eBooks in certain subject areas. These are available to libraries or to individuals.

For more information please contact webmaster.ebooks@tandf.co.uk

We're continually developing the eBook concept, so keep up to date by visiting the website.

www.eBookstore.tandf.co.uk